the latest 'hot' topics

The Organization of Long-Term Care *p. 348*
A Variety of Approaches to Finding the Dream Job *p. 448*
Female Athletes Say "Show Me the Money" *p. 525*
The Dragon Lady of TruServ *p. 571*
The Language of Diversity *p. 594*

The Business of Ethics

When Good CEOs Go Bad *p. 15*
Enron's In-Your-Face Culture *p. 87*
No Guarantee of Good Behavior *p. 114*
"Our Work, Our Tradition" *p. 148*
The Decision-making Responsibility of Corporate Boards *p. 216*
Ethical E-mailing *p. 327*
How to Organize an Ethical Bank *p. 359*
Is BP "Beyond Petroleum"? *p. 406*
An Ethical Stand-off for Unions and Corporations *p. 462*
No Longer "The Sweetest Place on Earth" *p. 491*
"Us Versus Them" at United Airlines *p. 532*
"Mamas, Don't Let Your Babies Grow up to Be CEOs" *p. 573*

Concept Checks

New to this edition, each major section concludes with two questions tied to concepts just learned. The first question tests recall of a basic fact, definition, or concept. The second is more thought provoking and/or analytical in nature.

Building Effective Skills Exercises

Each chapter concludes with three useful skill-development exercises, at least one of which is tied to the Internet. These exercises give insights into how managers approach various situations.

Building Effective Communication/Interpersonal Skills
Building Effective Diagnostic/Decision-Making Skills
Building Effective Conceptual Skills
Building Effective Technical Skills
Building Effective Time-Management Skills

Chapter Closing Cases

Each chapter concludes with a detailed case study, discussing a real-world management situation.

management

management

8th edition

Ricky W. Griffin

Texas A & M University

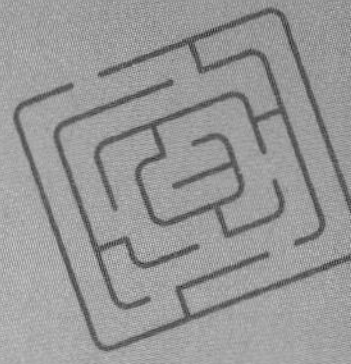

Houghton Mifflin Company

Boston New York

For Glenda—The anchor of my life and the center of my universe.

V.P., Editor-in-Chief: George Hoffman
Technology Manager/Development Editor: Damaris Curran
Associate Sponsoring Editor: Joanne Dauksewicz
Senior Project Editor: Cecilia Molinari
Editorial Assistants: Celeste Ng, Sean McGann
Senior Production/Design Coordinator: Carol Merrigan
Senior Manufacturing Coordinator: Marie Barnes
Senior Marketing Manager: Steve Mikels

Cover image: © Fernando Bueno/Getty Images.

Twenty-two end of chapter exercises on the following pages were prepared by Margaret Hill and are reprinted here with her permission: 31–32, 32–33, 65–66, 66–67, 101–102, 169, 197, 231, 268, 268–269, 296–297, 334, 429–430, 468–469, 505, 506, 543, 543–544, 578, 611–612, 640–642, 643

Photo credits may be found on page 769.

Printed in the U.S.A.

Library of Congress Control Number: 2003109909

ISBN: 0-618-35459x

4 5 6 7 8 9 – DOW – 08 07 06 05

brief contents

part one **An Introduction to Management** **2**

CHAPTER 1 Managing and the Manager's Job *4*
CHAPTER 2 Traditional and Contemporary Issues and Challenges *38*

part two **The Environmental Context of Management** **70**

CHAPTER 3 The Environment and Culture of Organizations *72*
CHAPTER 4 The Ethical and Social Environment *106*
CHAPTER 5 The Global Environment *140*
CHAPTER 6 The Multicultural Environment *174*

part three **Planning and Decision Making** **202**

CHAPTER 7 Basic Elements of Planning and Decision Making *204*
CHAPTER 8 Managing Strategy and Strategic Planning *236*
CHAPTER 9 Managing Decision Making and Problem Solving *274*
CHAPTER 10 Managing New Venture Formation and Entrepreneurship *302*

part four **The Organizing Process** **338**

CHAPTER 11 Basic Elements of Organizing *340*
CHAPTER 12 Managing Organization Design *372*
CHAPTER 13 Managing Organization Change and Innovation *402*
CHAPTER 14 Managing Human Resources in Organizations *436*

part five **The Leading Process** **474**

CHAPTER 15 Basic Elements of Individual Behavior in Organizations *476*
CHAPTER 16 Managing Employee Motivation and Performance *510*
CHAPTER 17 Managing Leadership and Influence Processes *548*
CHAPTER 18 Managing Interpersonal Relations and Communication *584*
CHAPTER 19 Managing Work Groups and Teams *616*

part six **The Controlling Process** **648**

CHAPTER 20 Basic Elements of Control *650*
CHAPTER 21 Managing Operations, Quality, and Productivity *684*
CHAPTER 22 Managing Information and Information Technology *716*

contents

Preface *xxi*

part one
An Introduction to Management **2**

1 Managing and the Manager's Job **4**

An Introduction to Management *6*
The Management Process *9*
Planning and Decision Making: Determining Courses of Action *10*
Organizing: Coordinating Activities and Resources *10*
Leading: Motivating and Managing People *12*
Controlling: Monitoring and Evaluating Activities *12*
Kinds of Managers *13*
Managing at Different Levels of the Organization *13*
Top Managers 13 ▪ Middle Managers 14 ▪ First-Line Managers 15
Managing in Different Areas of the Organization *16*
Marketing Managers 16 ▪ Financial Managers 16 ▪ Operations Managers 16 ▪ Human Resource Managers 16 ▪ Administrative Managers 16 ▪ Other Kinds of Managers 16
Basic Managerial Roles and Skills *18*
Managerial Roles *18*
Interpersonal Roles 18 ▪ Informational Roles 18 ▪ Decisional Roles 18
Managerial Skills *20*
Technical Skills 20 ▪ Interpersonal Skills 21 ▪ Conceptual Skills 21 ▪ Diagnostic Skills 21 ▪ Communication Skills 21 ▪ Decision-Making Skills 21 ▪ Time-Management Skills 22
The Nature of Managerial Work *22*
The Science and the Art of Management *23*
The Science of Management 23 ▪ The Art of Management 23
Becoming a Manager *23*
The Role of Education 23 ▪ The Role of Experience 24
The Scope of Management *25*
Managing in Profit-Seeking Organizations 25 ▪ Managing in Not-for-Profit Organizations 26
The New Workplace *27*
Summary of Key Points *30*
Discussion Questions *30*
Building Effective Time-Management Skills *31*
Building Effective Interpersonal and Communication Skills *32*
Building Effective Conceptual Skills *33*
Chapter Closing Case: Southwest Still Flies High *35*
The World of Management: Want a MacBrioche with that MacEspresso? 11
The Business of Ethics: When Good CEOs Go Bad 15
Technology Toolkit: The Low-Tech Solution to High-Tech Difficulties 17

2 Traditional and Contemporary Issues and Challenges **38**

The Role of Theory and History in Management *40*
The Importance of Theory and History *41*
Why Theory? 41 ▪ Why History? 41
Precursors to Management Theory *42*
Management in Antiquity 42 ▪ Early Management Pioneers 43
The Classical Management Perspective *43*
Scientific Management *43*
Administrative Management *45*
The Classical Management Perspective Today *46*

The Behavioral Management Perspective *47*
The Hawthorne Studies *48*
The Human Relations Movement *49*
The Emergence of Organizational Behavior *50*
The Behavioral Management Perspective Today *51*

The Quantitative Management Perspective *52*
Management Science *52*
Operations Management *53*
The Quantitative Management Perspective Today *53*

Integrating Perspectives for Managers *54*
The Systems Perspective *55*
The Contingency Perspective *56*
An Integrating Framework *56*

Contemporary Management Issues and Challenges *58*
Contemporary Applied Perspectives *59*
Contemporary Management Challenges *60*

Summary of Key Points *62*
Discussion Questions *63*
Building Effective Decision-making Skills *64*
Building Effective Communication Skills *65*
Building Effective Conceptual Skills *66*
Chapter Closing Case: Yellow Freight Is on the Move *67*

Today's Management Issues: Speeds-up Speed Up 50
Technology Toolkit: E-Business Grows Up 61

part two
The Environmental Context of Management 70

3 The Environment and Culture of Organizations 72

The Organization's Environments *74*
The External Environment *75*
The General Environment *76*
The Economic Dimension 76 ■ *The Technological Dimension 76* ■ *The Sociocultural Dimension 77* ■ *The Political-Legal Dimension 78* ■ *The International Dimension 78*
The Task Environment *79*
Competitors 79 ■ *Customers 80* ■ *Suppliers 80* ■ *Strategic Partners 81* ■ *Regulators 81*

The Internal Environment *83*
Owners *83*
Board of Directors *83*
Employees *84*
Physical Work Environment *85*

The Organization's Culture *86*
The Importance of Organization Culture *86*
Determinants of Organization Culture *86*
Managing Organization Culture *88*

Organization-Environment Relationships *89*
How Environments Affect Organizations *89*
Environmental Change and Complexity 89 ■ *Competitive Forces 90* ■ *Environmental Turbulence 92*
How Organizations Adapt to Their Environments *92*
Information Management 92 ■ *Strategic Response 93* ■ *Mergers, Acquisitions, and Alliances 93* ■ *Organization Design and Flexibility 94* ■ *Direct Influence 94*

The Environment and Organizational Effectiveness *96*
Models of Organizational Effectiveness *96*
Examples of Organizational Effectiveness *98*

Summary of Key Points *99*
Discussion Questions *99*
Building Effective Time-Management Skills *100*
Building Effective Diagnostic Skills *101*
Building Effective Communication Skills *102*
Chapter Closing Case: Lighting Up Every Nook and Cranny at GE *103*

Working with Diversity: Why Aren't Boards of Directors More Diverse? 84
The Business of Ethics: Enron's In-Your-Face Culture 87
Today's Management Issues: Do Corporations Have a Right to Freedom of Speech? 95

4 The Ethical and Social Environment 106

Individual Ethics in Organizations *108*
Managerial Ethics *109*
How an Organization Treats Its Employees 109 ■

How Employees Treat the Organization 109 ■ *How Employees and the Organization Treat Other Economic Agents 111*

Ethics in an Organizational Context *111*

Managing Ethical Behavior *113*

Emerging Ethical Issues in Organizations *117*

Ethical Leadership *117*

Ethical Issues in Corporate Governance *117*

Ethical Issues in Information Technology *118*

Social Responsibility and Organizations *120*

Areas of Social Responsibility *120*

Organizational Stakeholders 120 ■ *The Natural Environment 121* ■ *General Social Welfare 122*

Arguments For and Against Social Responsibility *122*

Arguments For Social Responsibility 122 ■ *Arguments Against Social Responsibility 123* ■ *Organizational Approaches to Social Responsibility 124* ■ *Obstructionist Stance 124* ■ *Defensive Stance 125* ■ *Accommodative Stance 125* ■ *Proactive Stance 125*

The Government and Social Responsibility *126*

How Government Influences Organizations *127*

Direct Regulation 127 ■ *Indirect Regulation 127*

How Organizations Influence Government *127*

Personal Contacts 127 ■ *Lobbying 127* ■ *Political Action Committees 128* ■ *Favors 128*

Managing Social Responsibility *128*

Formal Organizational Dimensions *129*

Legal Compliance 129 ■ *Ethical Compliance 129* ■ *Philanthropic Giving 129*

Informal Organizational Dimensions *130*

Organization Leadership and Culture 130 ■ *Whistle Blowing 130*

Evaluating Social Responsibility *130*

Summary of Key Points *132*

Discussion Questions *133*

Building Effective Diagnostic and Decision-making Skills *134*

Building Effective Interpersonal Skills *134*

Building Effective Conceptual Skills *135*

Chapter Closing Case: Cruise Ships May Pollute the Environment They Rely On *136*

The Business of Ethics: No Guarantee of Good Behavior 114

Technology Toolkit: The Most Common Password? "Password" 119

Working with Diversity: Men, Women, and Ethics 131

5 The Global Environment 140

The Nature of International Business *142*

The Meaning of International Business *143*

Trends in International Business *144*

Managing the Process of Globalization *145*

Importing and Exporting 145 ■ *Licensing 145* ■ *Strategic Alliances 146* ■ *Direct Investment 147*

Competing in a Global Market *148*

The Structure of the Global Economy *150*

Mature Market Economies and Systems *150*

High-Potential/High-Growth Economies *152*

Other Economies *153*

The Role of the GATT and the WTO *153*

General Agreement on Tariffs and Trade (GATT) 153 ■ *World Trade Organization (WTO) 154*

Environmental Challenges of International Management *154*

The Economic Environment *155*

Economic System 155 ■ *Natural Resources 155* ■ *Infrastructure 156*

The Political/Legal Environment *156*

Government Stability 156 ■ *Incentives for International Trade 157* ■ *Controls on International Trade 157* ■ *Economic Communities 158*

The Cultural Environment *159*

Values, Symbols, Beliefs, and Language 159 ■ *Individual Behaviors Across Cultures 161*

Competing in a Global Economy *164*

Globalization and Organization Size *164*

Multinational Corporations 164 ■ *Medium-Size Organizations 164* ■ *Small Organizations 164*

Management Challenges in a Global Economy *166*

Planning and Decision Making in a Global Economy 166 ■ *Organizing in a Global Economy 166* ■ *Leading in a Global Economy 166* ■ *Controlling in a Global Economy 167*

Summary of Key Points *167*

Discussion Questions *168*

Building Effective Interpersonal Skills *169*

Building Effective Technical Skills *169*

Building Effective Communication Skills *170*
Chapter Closing Case: The Final Frontier? *171*
The Business of Ethics: "Our Work, Our Tradition" 148
Working with Diversity: Cowgirl Is Still a Maverick 160

6 **The Multicultural Environment 174**

The Nature of Diversity and Multiculturalism *176*
Diversity and Multiculturalism in Organizations *177*
Trends in Diversity and Multiculturalism *177*
Dimensions of Diversity and Multiculturalism *179*
Age Distributions 179 ■ *Gender 181* ■ *Ethnicity 181* ■ *Other Dimensions of Diversity 182* ■ *Multicultural Differences 182*
Effects of Diversity and Multiculturalism in Organizations *183*
Diversity, Multiculturalism, and Competitive Advantage *184*
Diversity, Multiculturalism, and Conflict *187*
Managing Diversity and Multiculturalism in Organizations *189*
Individual Strategies *189*
Understanding 189 ■ *Empathy 189* ■ *Tolerance 190* ■ *Willingness to Communicate 190*
Organizational Approaches *190*
Organizational Policies 191 ■ *Organizational Practices 191* ■ *Diversity and Multicultural Training 192* ■ *Organization Culture 193*
Toward the Multicultural Organization *193*
Summary of Key Points *195*
Discussion Questions *196*
Building Effective Technical Skills *196*
Building Effective Time-Management Skills *197*
Building Effective Decision-making Skills *198*
Chapter Closing Case: The IKEA-ization of America, The Americanization of IKEA *198*
Today's Management Issues: On the Horizon, a Labor Shortage Looms 180
Working with Diversity: Wanted: Stay-at-Home Husband 183
Technology Toolkit: Non-Americans Online 187

part three
Planning and Decision Making 202

7 **Basic Elements of Planning and Decision Making 204**

Decision Making and the Planning Process *206*
Organizational Goals *207*
Purposes of Goals *207*
Kinds of Goals *208*
Level 208 ■ *Area 210* ■ *Time Frame 210*
Responsibilities for Setting Goals *210*
Managing Multiple Goals *211*
Organizational Planning *211*
Kinds of Organizational Plans *211*
Strategic Plans 212 ■ *Tactical Plans 212* ■ *Operational Plans 212*
Time Frames for Planning *212*
Long-Range Plans 212 ■ *Intermediate Plans 213* ■ *Short-Range Plans 213*
Responsibilities for Planning *213*
Planning Staff 213 ■ *Planning Task Force 215* ■ *Board of Directors 215* ■ *Chief Executive Officer 215* ■ *Executive Committee 215* ■ *Line Management 215*
Contingency Planning and Crisis Management *216*
Tactical Planning *218*
Developing Tactical Plans *219*
Executing Tactical Plans *220*
Operational Planning *220*
Single-Use Plans *220*
Programs 221 ■ *Projects 221*
Standing Plans *222*
Policies 222 ■ *Standard Operating Procedures 222* ■ *Rules and Regulations 222*
Managing Goal-Setting and Planning Processes *223*
Barriers to Goal Setting and Planning *224*
Inappropriate Goals 224 ■ *Improper Reward System 224* ■ *Dynamic and Complex Environment 225* ■

Reluctance to Establish Goals 225 ■ *Resistance to Change 225* ■ *Constraints 225*

Overcoming the Barriers *226*

Understand the Purposes of Goals and Planning 226 ■ *Communication and Participation 226* ■ *Consistency, Revision, and Updating 226* ■ *Effective Reward Systems 226*

Using Goals to Implement Plans *227*

The Nature and Purpose of Formal Goal Setting 227 ■ *The Formal Goal-setting Process 227* ■ *The Effectiveness of Formal Goal Setting 228*

Summary of Key Points *229*

Discussion Questions *230*

Building Effective Communication and Interpersonal Skills *231*

Building Effective Time-Management Skills *232*

Building Effective Technical Skills *232*

Chapter Closing Case: Can Ford Rev Up? *233*

Technology Toolkit: Grokking the Internet 214

The Business of Ethics: The Decision-making Responsibility of Corporate Boards 216

8 Managing Strategy and Strategic Planning 236

The Nature of Strategic Management *238*

The Components of Strategy *238*

Types of Strategic Alternatives *239*

Strategy Formulation and Implementation *239*

Using SWOT Analysis to Formulate Strategy *240*

Evaluating an Organization's Strengths *241*

Common Organizational Strengths 241 ■ *Distinctive Competencies 241* ■ *Imitation of Distinctive Competencies 242*

Evaluating an Organization's Weaknesses *243*

Evaluating an Organization's Opportunities and Threats *244*

Formulating Business-Level Strategies *244*

Porter's Generic Strategies *244*

The Miles and Snow Typology *246*

Strategies Based on the Product Life Cycle *247*

Implementing Business-Level Strategies *248*

Implementing Porter's Generic Strategies *249*

Differentiation Strategy 249 ■ *Overall Cost Leadership Strategy 250*

Implementing Miles and Snow's Strategies *250*

Prospector Strategy 250 ■ *Defender Strategy 251* ■ *Analyzer Strategy 251*

Formulating Corporate-Level Strategies *252*

Single-Product Strategy *252*

Related Diversification *252*

Bases of Relatedness 253 ■ *Advantages of Related Diversification 253*

Unrelated Diversification *254*

Implementing Corporate-Level Strategies *255*

Becoming a Diversified Firm *255*

Development of New Products 255 ■ *Replacement of Suppliers and Customers 257* ■ *Mergers and Acquisitions 257*

Managing Diversification *258*

BCG Matrix 258 ■ *GE Business Screen 259*

International and Global Strategies *260*

Developing International and Global Strategies *260*

Global Efficiencies 261 ■ *Multimarket Flexibility 261* ■ *Worldwide Learning 261*

Strategic Alternatives for International Business *263*

Summary of Key Points *265*

Discussion Questions *266*

Building Effective Decision-making Skills *267*

Building Effective Conceptual Skills *268*

Building Effective Diagnostic Skills *268*

Chapter Closing Case: Toyota Revs up U.S. Sales *270*

Working with Diversity: Journey to Diversity 242

Today's Management Issues: Acquisitions Hard to Swallow, Even Harder to Digest 256

9 Managing Decision Making and Problem Solving 274

The Nature of Decision Making *276*

Decision Making Defined *276*

Types of Decisions *277*

Decision-making Conditions *278*

Decision Making Under Certainty 278 ■

Decision Making Under Risk 278 ■ Decision Making Under Uncertainty 279

Rational Perspectives on Decision Making *280*

The Classical Model of Decision Making *281*

Steps in Rational Decision Making *281*

Recognizing and Defining the Decision Situation 281 ■ Identifying Alternatives 283 ■ Evaluating Alternatives 283 ■ Selecting an Alternative 284 ■ Implementing the Chosen Alternative 285 ■ Following up and Evaluating the Results 285

Behavioral Aspects of Decision Making *286*

The Administrative Model *286*

Political Forces in Decision Making *288*

Intuition and Escalation of Commitment *288*

Intuition 288 ■ Escalation of Commitment 289

Risk Propensity and Decision Making *290*

Ethics and Decision Making *290*

Group and Team Decision Making in Organizations *291*

Forms of Group and Team Decision Making *291*

Interacting Groups and Teams 291 ■ Delphi Groups 292 ■ Nominal Groups 292

Advantages of Group and Team Decision Making *293*

Disadvantages of Group and Team Decision Making *293*

Managing Group and Team Decision-making Processes *294*

Summary of Key Points *295*

Discussion Questions *295*

Building Effective Conceptual Skills *296*

Building Effective Decision-making Skills *297*

Building Effective Technical Skills *298*

Chapter Closing Case: Exploding the Myth of the Superhero CEO *299*

The World of Management: The Future of Multinational Energy Companies in Iraq 280

Working with Diversity: Uneasy Partners: Rappers and the Recording Industry 289

10 Managing New Venture Formation and Entrepreneurship 302

The Nature of Entrepreneurship *304*

The Role of Entrepreneurship in Society *305*

Job Creation *307*

Innovation *309*

Importance to Big Business *310*

Strategy for Entrepreneurial Organizations *310*

Choosing an Industry *310*

Services 311 ■ Retailing 313 ■ Construction 313 ■ Finance and Insurance 314 ■ Wholesaling 314 ■ Transportation 314 ■ Manufacturing 315

Emphasizing Distinctive Competencies *316*

Identifying Niches in Established Markets 316 ■ Identifying New Markets 317 ■ First-Mover Advantages 317

Writing a Business Plan *318*

Entrepreneurship and International Management *318*

Structure of Entrepreneurial Organizations *319*

Starting the New Business *319*

Buying an Existing Business 319 ■ Starting from Scratch 320

Financing the New Business *320*

Personal Resources 320 ■ Strategic Alliances 321 ■ Lenders 321 ■ Venture Capital Companies 321 ■ Small-Business Investment Companies 321 ■ SBA Financial Programs 322

Sources of Management Advice *322*

Advisory Boards 323 ■ Management Consultants 323 ■ The Small Business Administration 323 ■ Networking 324

Franchising *324*

The Performance of Entrepreneurial Organizations *326*

Trends in Small-Business Start-ups *326*

Emergence of E-Commerce 327 ■ Crossovers from Big Business 328 ■ Opportunities for Minorities and Women 328 ■ Better Survival Rates 330

Reasons for Failure *330*

Reasons for Success *331*

Summary of Key Points *332*

Discussion Questions *332*

Building Effective Diagnostic Skills *333*

Building Effective Interpersonal Skills *334*

Building Effective Conceptual Skills *335*

Chapter Closing Case: Laughing All the Way to the Bank *335*

Today's Management Issues: Is ETS Too Entrepreneurial? 306

The World of Management: Marcel Telles—Brazilian Beer Entrepreneur 312

The Business of Ethics: Ethical E-mailing 327

part four

The Organizing Process 338

11 Basic Elements of Organizing 340

The Elements of Organizing *342*

Designing Jobs *343*

Job Specialization *343*

Benefits and Limitations of Specialization *344*

Alternatives to Specialization *344*

Job Rotation 344 ■ Job Enlargement 345 ■ Job Enrichment 345 ■ Job Characteristics Approach 346 ■ Work Teams 347

Grouping Jobs: Departmentalization *347*

Rationale for Departmentalization *347*

Common Bases for Departmentalization *349*

Functional Departmentalization 349 ■ Product Departmentalization 350 ■ Customer Departmentalization 350 ■ Location Departmentalization 351 ■ Other Forms of Departmentalization 351 ■ Other Considerations 351

Establishing Reporting Relationships *352*

Chain of Command *352*

Narrow Versus Wide Spans *352*

Tall Versus Flat Organizations *354*

Determining the Appropriate Span *355*

Distributing Authority *356*

The Delegation Process *357*

Reasons for Delegation 357 ■ Parts of the Delegation Process 357 ■ Problems in Delegation 358

Decentralization and Centralization *360*

Coordinating Activities *361*

The Need for Coordination *361*

Structural Coordination Techniques *362*

The Managerial Hierarchy 362 ■ Rules and Procedures 362 ■ Liaison Roles 362 ■ Task Forces 363 ■ Integrating Departments 363

Electronic Coordination *363*

Differentiating Between Positions *364*

Differences Between Line and Staff *364*

Administrative Intensity *364*

Summary of Key Points *365*

Discussion Questions *366*

Building Effective Conceptual Skills *367*

Building Effective Diagnostic Skills *367*

Building Effective Technical Skills *368*

Chapter Closing Case: Too Much Delegation at Nissan? *369*

Working with Diversity: The Organization of Long-Term Care 348

The Business of Ethics: How to Organize an Ethical Bank 359

12 Managing Organization Design 372

The Nature of Organization Design *374*

Universal Perspectives on Organization Design *375*

Bureaucratic Model *375*

Behavioral Model *376*

Situational Influences on Organization Design *379*

Core Technology *379*

Environment *382*

Organizational Size *383*

Organizational Life Cycle *383*

Strategy and Organization Design *384*

Corporate-Level Strategy *384*

Business-Level Strategy *385*

Organizational Functions *385*

Basic Forms of Organization Design *386*

Functional (U-Form) Design *386*

Conglomerate (H-Form) Design *387*

Divisional (M-Form) Design *388*

Matrix Design *389*

Hybrid Designs *391*

Emerging Issues in Organization Design *391*

The Team Organization *392*

The Virtual Organization *392*

The Learning Organization *393*

Issues in International Organization Design *393*

Summary of Key Points *395*
Discussion Questions *395*
Building Effective Conceptual Skills *396*
Building Effective Technical Skills *397*
Building Effective Decision-making Skills *397*
Chapter Closing Case: Customers Say "Yum!" *399*
The World of Management: An American Revolution at Deutsche Bank 377
Technology Toolkit: Flexible FedEx 381

13 **Managing Organization Change and Innovation** **402**

The Nature of Organization Change *404*
Forces for Change *404*
External Forces 404 ■ Internal Forces 405
Planned Versus Reactive Change *405*
Managing Change in Organizations *407*
Steps in the Change Process *407*
The Lewin Model 407 ■ A Comprehensive Approach to Change 408
Understanding Resistance to Change *409*
Uncertainty 409 ■ Threatened Self-Interests 410 ■ Different Perceptions 410 ■ Feelings of Loss 410
Overcoming Resistance to Change *411*
Participation *411*
Education and Communication 411 ■ Facilitation 411 ■ Force-Field Analysis 411
Areas of Organization Change *412*
Changing Organization Structure and Design *413*
Changing Technology and Operations *413*
Changing People, Attitudes, and Behaviors *415*
Changing Business Processes *416*
The Need for Business Process Change 416 ■ Approaches to Business Process Change 417
Organization Development *417*
OD Assumptions 417 ■ OD Techniques 418 ■ The Effectiveness of OD 419
Organizational Innovation *420*
The Innovation Process *420*
Innovation Development 420 ■ Innovation Application 420 ■ Application Launch 421 ■ Application Growth 421 ■ Innovation Maturity 422 ■ Innovation Decline 422
Forms of Innovation *422*
Radical Versus Incremental Innovations 422 ■ Technical Versus Managerial Innovations 423 ■ Product Versus Process Innovations 423
The Failure to Innovate *424*
Lack of Resources 424 ■ Failure to Recognize Opportunities 425 ■ Resistance to Change 425
Promoting Innovation in Organizations *425*
The Reward System 425 ■ Organization Culture 426 ■ Intrapreneurship in Larger Organizations 427
Summary of Key Points *428*
Discussion Questions *428*
Building Effective Time-Management Skills *429*
Building Effective Decision-making Skills *430*
Building Effective Diagnostic Skills *431*
Chapter Closing Case: Changing Cargill *432*
The Business of Ethics: Is BP "Beyond Petroleum"? 406
The World of Management: A Reluctant Change Agent at Ericsson 408
Today's Management Issues: Do Deviants Drive Change? 426

14 **Managing Human Resources in Organizations** **436**

The Environmental Context of Human Resource Management *438*
The Strategic Importance of HRM *438*
The Legal Environment of HRM *439*
Equal Employment Opportunity 440 ■ Compensation and Benefits 440 ■ Labor Relations 441 ■ Health and Safety 441 ■ Emerging Legal Issues 443
Social Change and HRM *443*
Attracting Human Resources *444*
Human Resource Planning *444*
Job Analysis 444 ■ Forecasting Human Resource Demand and Supply 444 ■ Matching Human Resource Supply and Demand 446

Recruiting Human Resources *446*
Selecting Human Resources *447*
Application Blanks 448 ■ *Tests 449* ■ *Interviews 449* ■ *Assessment Centers 449* ■ *Other Techniques 449*
Developing Human Resources *450*
Training and Development *450*
Assessing Training Needs 451 ■ *Common Training Methods 451* ■ *Evaluation of Training 451*
Performance Appraisal *452*
Common Appraisal Methods 453 ■ *Errors in Performance Appraisal 455*
Performance Feedback *456*
Maintaining Human Resources *457*
Determining Compensation *457*
Wage-Level Decision 457 ■ *Wage Structure Decision 458* ■ *Individual Wage Decisions 458*
Determining Benefits *458*
Career Planning *459*
Managing Labor Relations *460*
How Employees Form Unions *460*
Collective Bargaining *462*
New Challenges in the Changing Workplace *463*
Managing Knowledge Workers *463*
The Nature of Knowledge Work 463 ■ *Knowledge Worker Management and Labor Markets 464*
Contingent and Temporary Workers *464*
Trends in Contingent and Temporary Employment 465 ■ *Managing Contingent and Temporary Workers 465*
Summary of Key Points *466*
Discussion Questions *467*
Building Effective Decision-making Skills *468*
Building Effective Communication Skills *468*
Building Effective Technical Skills *470*
Chapter Closing Case: The Retirement That Isn't *471*
Today's Management Issues: A Fair Day's Pay for a Fair Day's Work? 442
Working with Diversity: A Variety of Approaches to Finding the Dream Job 448
The Business of Ethics: An Ethical Stand-off for Unions and Corporations 462

part five
The Leading Process 474

15 **Basic Elements of Individual Behavior in Organizations 476**

Understanding Individuals in Organizations *478*
The Psychological Contract *478*
The Person-Job Fit *479*
The Nature of Individual Differences *481*
Personality and Individual Behavior *481*
The "Big Five" Personality Traits *483*
The Myers-Briggs Framework *484*
Other Personality Traits at Work *485*
Emotional Intelligence *487*
Attitudes and Individual Behavior *487*
Work-related Attitudes *488*
Job Satisfaction or Dissatisfaction 488 ■ *Organizational Commitment 489*
Affect and Mood in Organizations *489*
Perception and Individual Behavior *490*
Basic Perceptual Processes *490*
Selective Perception 491 ■ *Stereotyping 492*
Perception and Attribution *492*
Stress and Individual Behavior *493*
Causes and Consequences of Stress *495*
Causes of Stress 495 ■ *Consequences of Stress 496*
Managing Stress *496*
Creativity in Organizations *498*
The Creative Individual *498*
Background Experiences and Creativity 498 ■ *Personal Traits and Creativity 498* ■ *Cognitive Abilities and Creativity 499*
The Creative Process *499*
Preparation 499 ■ *Incubation 499* ■ *Insight 500* ■ *Verification 500*
Enhancing Creativity in Organizations *500*
Types of Workplace Behavior *501*
Performance Behaviors *501*

Withdrawal Behaviors *501*
Organizational Citizenship *502*
Dysfunctional Behaviors *503*

Summary of Key Points *503*

Discussion Questions *504*

Building Effective Interpersonal Skills *505*

Building Effective Conceptual Skills *506*

Building Effective Time-Management Skills *506*

Chapter Closing Case: Too Much Character Building? *507*

Today's Management Issues: Up—and Down—the Economic Roller-Coaster 480

The World of Management: American-Style Management Comes to Global-Dining 482

The Business of Ethics: No Longer "The Sweetest Place on Earth" 491

16 **Managing Employee Motivation and Performance** **510**

The Nature of Motivation *512*

The Importance of Employee Motivation in the Workplace *512*

Historical Perspectives on Motivation *513*

The Traditional Approach 513 ■ *The Human Relations Approach 513* ■ *The Human Resource Approach 514*

Content Perspectives on Motivation *514*

The Needs Hierarchy Approach *514*

Maslow's Hierarchy of Needs 515 ■ *The ERG Theory 517*

The Two-Factor Theory *517*
Individual Human Needs *519*
Implications of the Content Perspectives *520*

Process Perspectives on Motivation *520*

Expectancy Theory *520*

Effort-to-Performance Expectancy 521 ■ *Performance-to-Outcome Expectancy 521* ■ *Outcomes and Valences 521* ■ *The Porter-Lawler Extension 523*

Equity Theory *523*

Goal-setting Theory *524*

Goal Difficulty 524 ■ *Goal Specificity 524*

Implications of the Process Perspectives *526*

Reinforcement Perspectives on Motivation *527*

Kinds of Reinforcement in Organizations *527*
Providing Reinforcement in Organizations *528*
Implications of the Reinforcement Perspectives *529*

Popular Motivational Strategies *530*

Empowerment and Participation *530*

Areas of Participation 530 ■ *Techniques and Issues in Empowerment 530*

Alternative Forms of Work Arrangements *531*

Variable Work Schedules 531 ■ *Flexible Work Schedules 533* ■ *Job Sharing 533* ■ *Telecommuting 533*

Using Reward Systems to Motivate Performance *534*

Merit Reward Systems *534*
Incentive Reward Systems *535*

Incentive Pay Plans 535 ■ *Other Forms of Incentive 536*

Team and Group Incentive Reward Systems *536*

Common Team and Group Reward Systems 537 ■ *Other Types of Team and Group Rewards 537*

Executive Compensation *538*

Standard Forms of Executive Compensation 538 ■ *Special Forms of Executive Compensation 539* ■ *Criticisms of Executive Compensation 540*

New Approaches to Performance-based Rewards *540*

Summary of Key Points *541*

Discussion Questions *542*

Building Effective Interpersonal and Communication Skills *543*

Building Effective Decision-making Skills *543*

Building Effective Conceptual and Diagnostic Skills *544*

Chapter Closing Case: You've Got to Love This Job *545*

Today's Management Issues: Does It Pay to Work? 516

Working with Diversity: Female Athletes Say "Show Me the Money" 525

The Business of Ethics: "Us Versus Them" at United Airlines 532

17 Managing Leadership and Influence Processes 548

The Nature of Leadership *550*

The Meaning of Leadership *550*

Leadership and Management *551*

Leadership and Power *553*

Legitimate Power 553 ■ *Reward Power 553* ■ *Coercive Power 553* ■ *Referent Power 554* ■ *Expert Power 554* ■ *Using Power 554*

Generic Approaches to Leadership *555*

Leadership Traits *555*

Leadership Behaviors *556*

Michigan Studies 556 ■ *Ohio State Studies 557* ■ *Managerial Grid 557*

Situational Approaches to Leadership *559*

LPC Theory *560*

Favorableness of the Situation 561 ■ *Favorableness and Leader Style 561* ■ *Flexibility of Leader Style 561*

Path-Goal Theory *562*

Leader Behavior 563 ■ *Situational Factors 563*

Vroom's Decision Tree Approach *564*

Basic Premises 565 ■ *Decision-Making Styles 566* ■ *Evaluation and Implications 567*

The Leader-Member Exchange Approach *567*

Related Approaches to Leadership *568*

Substitutes for Leadership *569*

Charismatic Leadership *569*

Transformational Leadership *670*

Emerging Approaches to Leadership *571*

Strategic Leadership *571*

Cross-Cultural Leadership *572*

Ethical Leadership *572*

Political Behavior in Organizations *574*

Common Political Behaviors *574*

Impression Management *575*

Managing Political Behavior *575*

Summary of Key Points *576*

Discussion Questions *577*

Building Effective Diagnostic Skills *578*

Building Effective Decision-making Skills *579*

Building Effective Conceptual Skills *579*

Chapter Closing Case: The "New and Improved" Procter & Gamble *580*

Today's Management Issues: Should We Stop the CEO Compensation Madness? 552

Working with Diversity: The Dragon Lady of TruServ 571

The Business of Ethics: "Mamas, Don't Let Your Babies Grow up to Be CEOs" 573

18 Managing Interpersonal Relations and Communication 584

The Interpersonal Nature of Organizations *586*

Interpersonal Dynamics *587*

Outcomes of Interpersonal Behaviors *588*

Communication and the Manager's Job *588*

A Definition of Communication *589*

The Role of Communication in Management *589*

The Communication Process *590*

Forms of Communication in Organizations *592*

Interpersonal Communication *592*

Oral Communication 593 ■ *Written Communication 593* ■ *Choosing the Right Form 594*

Communication in Networks and Work Teams *594*

Organizational Communication *595*

Vertical Communication 596 ■ *Horizontal Communication 597*

Electronic Communication *597*

Formal Information Systems 597 ■ *Personal Electronic Technology 599*

Informal Communication in Organizations *600*

The Grapevine *600*

Management by Wandering Around *601*

Nonverbal Communication *602*

Managing Organizational Communication *603*

Barriers to Communication *603*

Individual Barriers 603 ■ *Organizational Barriers 605*

Improving Communication Effectiveness *606*

Individual Skills 606 ■ *Organizational Skills 608*

Summary of Key Points *609*
Discussion Questions *610*
Building Effective Technical Skills *611*
Building Effective Interpersonal Skills *611*
Building Effective Communication Skills *612*
Chapter Closing Case: Communicating the Truth about Smoking *613*
Working with Diversity: The Language of Diversity 592
The World of Management: "There's No Substitute for Being There" 598
Today's Management Issues: Heartfelt Apologies 600

19 Managing Work Groups and Teams 616

Groups and Teams in Organizations *618*
Types of Groups and Teams *619*
Functional Groups 619 ■ *Informal or Interest Groups 620* ■ *Task Groups 620*
Why People Join Groups and Teams *622*
Interpersonal Attraction 623 ■ *Group Activities 623* ■ *Group Goals 623* ■ *Need Satisfaction 623* ■ *Instrumental Benefits 623*
Stages of Group and Team Development *624*
Characteristics of Groups and Teams *625*
Role Structures *625*
Role Ambiguity 626 ■ *Role Conflict 626* ■ *Role Overload 626*
Behavioral Norms *627*
Norm Generalization 627 ■ *Norm Variation 628* ■ *Norm Conformity 628*
Cohesiveness *629*
Factors That Increase Cohesiveness 629 ■ *Factors That Reduce Cohesiveness 630* ■ *Consequences of Cohesiveness 630*
Formal and Informal Leadership *631*
Interpersonal and Intergroup Conflict *631*
The Nature of Conflict *632*
Causes of Conflict *633*
Interpersonal Conflict 633 ■ *Intergroup Conflict 634* ■ *Conflict Between Organization and Environment 635*
Managing Conflict in Organizations *636*
Stimulating Conflict *636*
Controlling Conflict *637*
Resolving and Eliminating Conflict *638*
Summary of Key Points *639*
Discussion Questions *639*
Building Effective Decision-making Skills *640*
Building Effective Conceptual Skills *642*
Building Effective Communication Skills *643*
Chapter Closing Case: No Teamwork at Disney? *644*
Technology Toolkit: The Reality of Virtual Teams 622
The World of Management: Transatlantic Teamwork at Citigroup 632

part six The Controlling Process 648

20 Basic Elements of Control 650

The Nature of Control *652*
The Purpose of Control *653*
Adapting to Environmental Change 653 ■ *Limiting the Accumulation of Error 654* ■ *Coping with Organizational Complexity 655* ■ *Minimizing Costs 655*
Types of Control *655*
Areas of Control 655 ■ *Levels of Control 656* ■ *Responsibilities for Control 656*
Steps in the Control Process *657*
Establishing Standards 657 ■ *Measuring Performance 658* ■ *Comparing Performance Against Standards 658* ■ *Considering Corrective Action 659*
Operations Control *660*
Preliminary Control *660*
Screening Control *661*
Postaction Control *661*
Financial Control *662*
Budgetary Control *663*
Types of Budgets 663 ■ *Developing Budgets 664* ■ *Strengths and Weaknesses of Budgeting 665*
Other Tools for Financial Control *666*

Financial Statements 666 ■ Ratio Analysis 666 ■ Financial Audits 667

Structural Control *668*

Bureaucratic Control *669*

Decentralized Control *669*

Strategic Control *670*

Integrating Strategy and Control *670*

International Strategic Control *671*

Managing Control in Organizations *672*

Characteristics of Effective Control *672*

Integration with Planning 672 ■ Flexiblity 673 ■ Accuracy 673 ■ Timeliness 673 ■ Objectivity 673

Resistance to Control *674*

Overcontrol 674 ■ Inappropriate Focus 674 ■ Rewards for Inefficiency 675 ■ Too Much Accountability 675

Overcoming Resistance to Control *675*

Encourage Employee Participation 676 ■ Develop Verification Procedures 676

Summary of Key Points *676*

Discussion Questions *677*

Building Effective Time-Management Skills *678*

Building Effective Decision-making and Diagnostic Skills *679*

Building Effective Technical Skills *680*

Chapter Closing Case: Wake up, "Zombies"! *681*

Today's Management Issues: "The Most Inefficient Organization in the Federal Government" 654

The World of Management: Is Vivendi "the Enron of France"? 671

21 Managing Operations, Quality, and Productivity 684

The Nature of Operations Management *686*

The Importance of Operations *687*

Manufacturing and Production Operations *687*

Service Operations *688*

The Role of Operations in Organizational Strategy *688*

Designing Operations Systems *689*

Determining Product-Service Mix *689*

Capacity Decisions *689*

Facilities Decisions *690*

Location 690 ■ Layout 690

Organizational Technologies *692*

Manufacturing Technology *692*

Automation 692 ■ Computer-assisted Manufacturing 693 ■ Robotics 694

Service Technology *695*

Implementing Operations Systems Through Supply Chain Management *696*

Operations Management as Control *696*

Purchasing Management *696*

Inventory Management *697*

Managing Total Quality *698*

The Meaning of Quality *699*

The Importance of Quality *699*

Competition 700 ■ Productivity 700 ■Costs 700

Total Quality Management *700*

Strategic Commitment 701 ■ Employee Involvement 701 ■ Technology 701 ■ Materials 701 ■ Methods 702

TQM Tools and Techniques *702*

Value-Added Analysis 702 ■ Benchmarking 702 ■ Outsourcing 703 ■ Reducing Cycle Time 704 ■ ISO 9000:2000 and ISO 14000 704 ■ Statistical Quality Control 705

Managing Productivity *705*

The Meaning of Productivity *706*

Levels of Productivity 706 ■ Forms of Productivity 706

The Importance of Productivity *707*

Productivity Trends *707*

Improving Productivity *708*

Improving Operations 708 ■ Increasing Employee Involvement 709

Summary of Key Points *710*

Discussion Questions *710*

Building Effective Communication Skills *711*

Building Effective Diagnostic Skills *712*

Building Effective Conceptual Skills *713*

Chapter Closing Case: America's (Civilian) Military *713*

Technology Toolkit: Is an Ounce of Prevention Really Worth a Pound of Cure? 703

The World of Management: Pity the Rich, Overworked Americans 708

22 Managing Information and Information Technology 716

Information and the Manager *718*

The Role of Information in the Manager's Job *719*

Characteristics of Useful Information *720*

Accurate 720 ▪ Timely 721 ▪ Complete 721 ▪ Relevant 721

Information Management as Control *722*

Building Blocks of Information Technology *723*

Types of Information Systems *725*

User Groups and System Requirements *725*

Managers at Different Levels 725 ▪ Functional Areas and Business Processes 726

Major Systems by Level *726*

Transaction-processing Systems 726 ▪ Systems for Knowledge Workers and Office Applications 727 ▪ Systems for Operations and Data Workers 727 ▪ Knowledge-Level and Office Systems 727 ▪ Management Information Systems 727 ▪ Decision Support Systems 728 ▪ Executive Support Systems 728 ▪ Artificial Intelligence and Expert Systems 729

The Internet *729*

The World Wide Web 731 ▪ Servers and Browsers 731 ▪ Directories and Search Engines 731 ▪ Intranets 732 ▪ Extranets 732

Managing Information Systems *732*

Creating Information Systems *733*

Integrating Information Systems *735*

Using Information Systems *735*

Managing Information Security *736*

Understanding Information System Limitations *736*

The Impact of Information Systems on Organizations *738*

Leaner Organizations *738*

More Flexible Operations *738*

Increased Collaboration *738*

More Flexible Work Sites *739*

Improved Management Processes *740*

Changed Employee Behaviors *740*

Summary of Key Points *741*

Discussion Questions *741*

Building Effective Technical Skills *742*

Building Effective Interpersonal Skills *743*

Building Effective Time-Management Skills *744*

Chapter Closing Case: The Right Way to Deliver Groceries *745*

The World of Management: Blockbuster Controls Its European Operations 722

Technology Toolkit: "Meet My New Partner—A Computer" 730

appendix
Tools for Planning and Decision Making 748

Forecasting *749*

Sales and Revenue Forecasting *749*

Technological Forecasting *750*

Other Types of Forecasting *750*

Forecasting Techniques *751*

Time-Series Analysis 751 ▪ Causal Modeling 751 ▪ Qualitative Forecasting Techniques 753

Other Planning Techniques *754*

Linear Programming *754*

Breakeven Analysis *756*

Simulations *758*

PERT *759*

Decision-making Tools *761*

Payoff Matrices *761*

Decision Trees *763*

Other Techniques *763*

Inventory Models 764 ▪ Queuing Models 765 ▪ Distribution Models 765 ▪ Game Theory 765 ▪ Artificial Intelligence 765

Strengths and Weaknesses of Planning Tools *766*

Weaknesses and Problems *766*

Strengths and Advantages *766*

Summary of Key Points *767*

Photo Credits *769*

Name Index *771*

Organization and Product Index *778*

Subject Index *787*

preface

Since the publication of its first edition in 1984, more than a million students have used *Management* in preparation for their careers in business. *Management* continues to be used in hundreds of universities, graduate programs, community colleges, and management development programs throughout the world today. Indeed, the last edition of the book was used in over forty countries and translated into several foreign languages.

In this edition, I have retained all the elements that have contributed to the book's success in the past while also taking a clear look toward the future—the future of business, of management, and of textbooks.

Writing a survey book poses a number of challenges. First, because it is a survey, it has to be comprehensive. Second, it has to be accurate and objective. Third, because management is a real activity, the book has to be relevant. Fourth, it has to be timely and up-to-date. And fifth, it must be as interesting and as engaging as possible. Feedback on previous editions of my text has always suggested that I have done an effective job of meeting these goals. In this edition, I think these goals have been met even more effectively.

I believe that previous users of *Management* will be pleased with how we retained the essential ingredients of a comprehensive management textbook while adding a variety of new elements and perspectives. I also believe that those new to this edition will be drawn to the solid foundations of management theory and practice combined with new and exciting material.

Improvements and Highlights in the Eighth Edition

The eighth edition of *Management* is a significant revision of the earlier work. Rather than simply adding the "hot topics" of the moment, I continue to thoroughly revise this book with the long-term view in mind. There are significant revisions of key chapters; an increased emphasis on the service sector, ethics, global management, and information technology; and an integrated organization of chapters. These changes reflect what I believe, and what reviewers and employers have confirmed, students will need to know as they enter a brand new world of management. In addition, several new pedagogical features such as "Concept Check" will also prove to be invaluable.

Integrated Coverage

Many books, including early editions of this text, set certain material off from the rest of the text in a separate section at the end of the book called "Emerging Trends,"

"Special Challenges," or something similar. New and emerging topics, and other material that don't easily fit anywhere else, are covered in that section. Unfortunately, by setting those topics apart in this way, the material often gets ignored or receives low-priority treatment.

But I decided that if this material was really worth having in the book to begin with, it needed to be fully merged with the core material. Thus, all material has been integrated throughout the text in order to provide more uniform and cohesive coverage of the entire field of management. This framework also helps to streamline the book's overall organization into six logical and symmetrical parts. Because reviewers and students responded so favorably to this approach, it has been retained in the eighth edition. Furthermore, cross-referencing strengthens the integrated coverage throughout the text.

Effective Chapter Organization

This integrated approach to management also results in very effective chapter organization. Part I introduces the field of management, while Part II focuses on the environment of management. The remaining four parts cover the basic managerial functions of planning and decision making, organizing, leading, and controlling.

New Material for a Brand New World of Management

A variety of topics are new to this edition, and coverage of other areas has been increased and/or heavily revised. In addition, new research and new examples have been integrated throughout the book. A few of the highlights are noted below.

Chapter 1: Managing and the Manager's Job The expanded managerial skills framework incorporates technical, interpersonal, conceptual, diagnostic, communication, decision-making, and time-management skills. An entirely new section also introduces and discusses critical contemporary topics that relate to the new workplace.

Chapter 2: Traditional and Contemporary Issues and Challenges An expanded discussion of contemporary applied perspectives introduces the work of Senge, Covey, Porter, Kotter, Adams, and other modern popular-press business authors. The heavily revised section on contemporary management challenges introduces today's critical management issues. The chapter also contains all new coverage of supply chain management and enterprise resource planning (ERP).

Chapter 3: The Environment of Organizations and Managers Corporate culture, covered in another chapter in the last two editions, has been moved back to this chapter for the eighth edition because reviewers and students generally agreed that it fit better with the other material here. In addition, new and expanded sections cover such critical contemporary issues as corporate governance and the continuing aftermath of the terrorist attacks of September 11, 2001. Finally, this chapter also covers the growing impact of enterprise resource planning and references the crash of the space shuttle Columbia.

Chapter 4: The Ethical and Social Environment In light of recent controversies, this chapter received special attention. It now includes new coverage of triggers for unethical behavior and a new model for assessing ethical decisions.

Chapter 5: The Global Environment The discussion of developing economies was revised, updated, and reframed in terms of high potential/high growth economies. This chapter contains completely updated data and statistics, and expanded coverage of cultural issues in international business. In addition, new material covers current issues in the European Union, the General Agreement on Tariffs and Trade (GATT), and the World Trade Organization (WTO).

Chapter 6: The Multicultural Environment All data, statistics, and trends were updated. In addition, coverage of corporate culture has been moved from this chapter to Chapter 3. This allows Chapter 6 to focus more specifically on multiculturalism and diversity, both streamlining the discussion and further highlighting its importance.

Chapter 7: Basic Elements of Planning and Decision Making This chapter includes expanded coverage of contingency planning and a new section on crisis management. In today's turbulent world, these issues have taken on even greater importance.

Chapter 8: Managing Strategy and Strategy Planning A major new section on global strategy has been added to this chapter. This section reflects the continued and growing importance of international business.

Chapter 10: Managing Entrepreneurship and New Venture Formation Coverage of entrepreneurship and international management was expanded.

Chapter 11: Basic Elements of Organizing This chapter includes a new section on how organizations are increasingly using electronic coordination techniques.

Chapter 12: Managing Organization Design Chapter 12 covers the team organization, the virtual organization, and the learning organization.

Chapter 13: Managing Change and Innovation This chapter includes new coverage of business process change and enterprise resource planning.

Chapter 14: Managing Human Resources In Organizations Coverage of change and human resource management was revamped and coverage of ADA and the management of high-skill workers was substantially revised. In addition, this chapter features new material about the concept of human capital as well as electronic recruiting and the growing importance of corporate universities.

Chapter 15: Basic Elements of Individual Behavior In Organizations This chapter includes the "big five" model of personality, as well as expanded discussions of affect and mood in organizations and individual creativity in organizations. In addition, totally new coverage of emotional intelligence, the Myers-Briggs framework, and dysfunctional work behaviors was also added.

Chapter 16: Managing Employee Motivation and Performance Coverage of the goal-setting theory of motivation has been improved. Coverage of reward systems and executive compensation was also heavily revised and expanded.

Chapter 17: Managing Leadership and Influence Processes This chapter was substantially reorganized and includes coverage of the latest version of Vroom's decision-making model. In addition, a major new section introduces and discusses the concepts of strategic leadership, cross-cultural issues in leadership, and the growing awareness of the importance of ethical leadership.

Chapter 18: Managing Interpersonal Relations and Communication Coverage of communication in teams was revised and reframed. This chapter now contains material about electronic communication and the pros and cons of e-mail.

Chapter 19: Managing Work Groups and Teams This chapter includes new coverage of virtual teams.

Chapter 20: Basic Elements of Control This chapter includes new material addressing recent accounting and auditing scandals as they relate to the control function in organizations.

Chapter 21: Managing Operations, Quality, and Productivity The organization of this chapter has been improved by first discussing operations management and then using it as a framework for introducing quality and productivity. New topics added to this chapter include supply chain management, value added analysis, ISO 9000:2000 and ISO 14000, and six sigma.

Chapter 22: Managing Information and Information Technology This chapter has been thoroughly revised, including new and expanded coverage of the Internet, corporate intranets, and instant messaging.

In addition to these content revisions and additions, all in-text examples have been carefully reviewed and most have been replaced or updated.

Features of the Book

Basic Themes

Several key themes are prominent in this edition of *Management.* One critical theme is the ethical scrutiny under which managers work today. While the book has always included substantial coverage of ethics and social responsibility, even more attention has been devoted this time to topics such as corporate governance, ethical leadership, and the proper role of auditing. Another continuing theme is the global character of the field of management, which is reinforced throughout the book by examples and cases. A third key theme, information technology, is covered in detail in Chapter 22, and is also highlighted in boxed inserts in other chapters, and is integrated into the text itself throughout the book. Still another theme is the balance of theory and practice: managers need to have a sound basis for their decisions, but the theories that provide that basis must be grounded in reality. Throughout the book I explain the theoretical frameworks that guide managerial activities, and provide illustrations and examples of how and when those theories do and do not work. A fifth theme is that management is a generic activity not confined to large businesses. I use examples and discuss management in both small and large businesses as well as in not-for-profit organizations.

A Pedagogical System That Works

The pedagogical elements built into *Management,* Eighth Edition, continue to be effective learning and teaching aids for students and instructors.

- *Learning objectives* and a *chapter outline* preview key themes at the start of every chapter, as in the previous edition. *Key terms* and concepts are highlighted in boldface type, and most terms are defined in the margin next to where they are discussed. Effective *figures, tables,* and *photographs* with their own detailed captions help bring the material to life.
- Another exciting feature is called *Concept Check.* Each major section in every chapter concludes with two questions tied back to that section. The first question tests recall of a basic fact, definition, or concept. The second is more thought provoking and analytical in nature. These questions allow students to continuously assess their mastery of the subject as they are reading and studying the material.
- Three kinds of questions at the end of every chapter are designed to test different levels of student understanding. *Questions for Review* ask students to recall specific information, *Questions for Analysis* ask students to integrate and synthesize material, and *Questions for Application* ask students to apply what they've learned to their own experiences.
- Each chapter also concludes with three useful skill-development exercises. These exercises give student insight into how they approach various management situations and how they can work to improve their management skills in the future. The exercises are derived from the overall managerial skills framework developed in Chapter 1. For this edition, many of the exercises were replaced or substantially revised.

Applications That Keep Students Engaged

To fully appreciate the role and scope of management in contemporary society, it is important to see examples and illustrations of how concepts apply in the real world. I rely heavily on fully researched examples to illustrate real-world applications. They vary in length, and all were carefully reviewed for their timeliness. To give the broadest view possible, I include examples of both traditional management roles and nontraditional roles; profit-seeking businesses and nonprofits; large corporations and small businesses; manufacturers and services; and international examples and United States examples. Other applications include:

- *Opening incidents at the beginning of every chapter.* These brief vignettes draw the student into the chapter with a real-world scenario that introduces a particular management theme. Most opening incidents are new to this edition.
- *Boxed features.* Each chapter includes three or four boxed features. These boxes are intended to briefly depart from the flow of the chapter to highlight or extend especially interesting or emerging points and issues. Altogether there are five types of featured boxes represented throughout the text:

"The Business of Ethics"
(the increasing importance of ethics in management)

"Technology Toolkit"
(new technology and its role in management)

"Today's Management Issues"
(current controversies, challenges, and dilemmas facing managers)

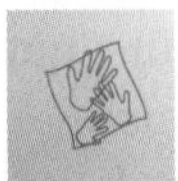
"Working with Diversity"
(the role of diversity in organizations)

"The World of Management"
(global issues in management)

- *End-of chapter cases.* Each chapter concludes with a detailed case study. Virtually all the cases in the eighth edition are new and have been especially written for this book.

An Effective Teaching and Learning Package

- *Instructor's Resource Manual* (Margaret Hill). This resource includes suggested class schedules and detailed teaching notes for every chapter. These notes include chapter summaries; learning objectives; detailed chapter lecture outlines, including opening incident summaries, highlighted key terms, teaching tips, group exercise ideas, and references to the transparencies; responses to review, analysis, and case questions; and information to help facilitate the skills-development exercises. Teaching guides to accompany the video cases are also included.

- *Test Bank* (Jill Whaley, Mount Saint Mary College). Well over 4,000 test items have been carefully and substantially revised for the eighth edition. The *Test Bank* includes true/false, multiple-choice, completion, matching, and essay questions. Each type of question is identified as a definition or fact (DEF), a concept or term relating to real-life incidences (APP), or a denotative understanding of a term or concept (COMP).
- *HMTesting.* The electronic version of the *Test Bank*, included on the ClassPrep CD, allows instructors to select, edit, and add questions, or generate randomly selected questions to produce a test master for easy duplication. Online Testing and Gradebook functions allow instructors to administer tests via their local area network or the World Wide Web, set up classes, record grades from tests or assignments, analyze grades, and compile class and individual statistics. This program can be used on both PCs and Macintosh computers.
- *Website.* This site offers valuable information for both students and instructors. For students, the site includes ACE Self-Tests, Management Skills Assessments, Ready Notes, Flashcards, Term Paper Help, Related Web Resources, Learning Objectives, Outlines, and Web Links. For instructors, PowerPoint slides, lecture outlines, and the instructor resources for Exercises in Management are available.
- *HM ClassPrep CD-ROM.* This CD-ROM for instructors, with HMTesting, contains about 250 PowerPoint slides and provides an effective presentation tool for lectures. In addition to unique content not found in the text, the slides highlight key textual material and provide interesting exercises and discussion questions.
- *Color Transparencies.* The 130 full-color transparencies illustrate every major topic in the text. The package consists of several key figures from the book as well as new materials that can be used to enrich classroom discussions. Five types of transparencies are included. *Chapter Text* transparencies reproduce key chapter figures. *Chapter Enrichment* transparencies provide images not in the text that will enhance chapter material. *Text Transition* transparencies introduce material in each of the six parts. *Supplemental Resource* transparencies provide general information that can be used when and as the instructor chooses.
- *Video Package.* An expanded, professionally developed video case collection is available with the eighth edition, and supplementary video case material can be found in the Instructor's Resource Manual. These videos explore various aspects of the management process.
- *eStudy CD-ROM.* This CD for students includes ACE Self-Tests, web links, and selected videos. Chapter objectives, outlines, summaries, and glossary terms are designed and presented to students as an interactive study guide.
- *Study Guide* (Joseph Thomas, Middle Tennessee State University). The *Study Guide* has been revised to optimize student comprehension of definitions, concepts, and relationships presented in the text. Each chapter contains an expanded chapter outline to facilitate note taking, multiple-choice and true/false questions, and targeted questions that ask students to integrate

material from lectures and the text. Annotated answers appear at the end of the *Study Guide.*

- *Exercises in Management* (Linda Morable, Dallas County Community College). This student manual provides experiential exercises for every chapter. The overall purpose of each exercise is given, along with the time required for each step, the materials needed, the procedure to be followed, and questions for discussion.
- *Blackboard and WebCT CD-ROM.* This CD-ROM, which includes chapter review materials, PowerPoint slides, web links, ACE Self-Tests, and HMTesting, allows instructors to customize content for online/distance learning courses.

I would also like to invite your feedback on this book. If you have any questions, suggestions, or issues to discuss, please feel free to contact me. The most efficient way to reach me is through e-mail. My address is rgriffin@tamu.edu.

R.W.G.

acknowledgements

I am frequently asked by my colleagues why I write textbooks, and my answer is always, "Because I enjoy it." I've never enjoyed writing a book more than this one. For me, writing a textbook is a challenging and stimulating activity that brings with it a variety of rewards. My greatest reward continues to be the feedback I get from students and instructors about how much they like this book.

I owe an enormous debt to many different people for helping me create *Management.* My colleagues at Texas A&M have helped create a wonderful academic climate. The rich and varied culture at Texas A&M makes it a pleasure to go to the office every day. My co-workers Phyllis Washburn, Linda Perry, and Debby Swick deserve special recognition for putting up with me and making me look good.

The fine team of professionals at Houghton Mifflin has also been instrumental in the success of this book. Sponsoring Editor George Hoffman, Associate Sponsoring Editor Joanne Dauksewicz, and Technology Manager/Development Editor Damaris Curran each had a major role in the development and creation of this edition of *Management.* Cecilia Molinari, Carol Merrigan, Bonnie Melton, Rich Brewer, Scott Harris, and Marcy Kagan were instrumental in the production of this edition.

Many reviewers have played a critical role in the evolution of this project. They examined my work in detail and with a critical eye. I would like to tip my hat to the following reviewers, whose imprint can be found throughout this text:

Ramon J. Aldag
University of Wisconsin

Dr. Raymond E. Alie
Western Michigan University

William P. Anthony
Florida State University

Jeanne Aurelio
Stonehill College

Jay B. Barney
Ohio State University

Richard Bartlett
Muskigum Area Technical College

John D. Bigelow
Boise State University

Allen Bluedorn
University of Missouri

Henry C. Bohleke
Tarrant County College

Marv Borglett
University of Maryland

Gunther S. Boroschek
University of Massachusetts—Harbor Campus

Gerald E. Calvasina
University of North Carolina, Charlotte

Joseph Cantrell
DeAnza College

George R. Carnahan
Northern Michigan University

Ron Cheek
University of New Orleans

Thomas G. Christoph
Clemson University

Charles W. Cole
University of Oregon

Elizabeth Cooper
University of Rhode Island

Carol Cumber
South Dakota State University

Joan Dahl
California State University, Northridge

Carol Danehower
University of Memphis

Satish Deshpande
Western Michigan University

Gregory G. Dess
University of Kentucky

Gary N. Dicer
University of Tennessee

Nicholas Dietz
State University of New York—Farmingdale

Thomas J. Dougherty
University of Missouri

Shad Dowlatshahi
University of Wisconsin—Platteville

John Drexler, Jr.
Oregon State University

Stan Elsea
Kansas State University

Douglas A. Elvers
University of South Carolina

Jim Fairbank
West Virginia University

Dan Farrell
Western Michigan University

Gerald L. Finch
Universidad Internacional del Ecuador and Universidad San Francisco de Quito

Charles Flaherty
University of Minnesota

Ari Ginsberg
New York University Graduate School of Business

Norma N. Givens
Fort Valley State University

Carl Gooding
Georgia Southern College

George J. Gore
University of Cincinnati

Jonathan Gueverra
Lesley College

Stanley D. Guzell, Jr.
Youngstown State University

John Hall
University of Florida

Mark A. Hammer
Washington State University

Barry Hand
Indiana State University

Paul Harmon
University of Utah

John Huges
Texas Tech University

J.G. Hunt
Texas Tech University

John H. Jackson
University of Wyoming

Neil W. Jacobs
University of Denver

Arthur G. Jago
University of Missouri

Madge Jenkins
Lima Technical College

Gopol Joshi
Central Missouri State University

Norman F. Kallaus
University of Iowa

Ben L. Kedia
University of Memphis

Joan Keeley
Washington State University

Thomas L. Keon
University of Central Florida

Charles C. Kitzmiller
Indian River Community College

Barbara Kovach
Rutgers University

William R. LaFollete
Ball State University

Kenneth Lawrence
New Jersey Institute of Technology

Clayton G. Lifto
Kirkwood Community College

John E. Mack
Salem State University

Myrna P. Mandell, Ph.D.
California State University, Northridge

Particia M. Manninen
North Shore Community College

Thomas Martin
University of Nebraska—Omaha

Barbara J. Marting
University of Southern Indiana

Wayne A. Meinhart
Oklahoma State University

Melvin McKnight
Northern Arizona University

Aratchige Molligoda
Drexel University

Linda L. Neider
University of Miami

Mary Lippitt Nichols
University of Minnesota

Winston Oberg
Michigan State University

Michael Olivette
Syracuse University

Eugene Owens
Western Washington University

Sheila Pechinski
University of Maine

Monique Pelletier
San Francisco State University

E. Leroy Plumlee
Western Washington University

Raymond F. Polchow
Muskigum Area Technical College

Boris Porkovich
San Francisco State University

Paul Preston
University of Texas—San Antonio

John M. Purcell
State University of New York—Farmingdale

James C. Quick
University of Texas—Arlington

Ralph Roberts
University of West Florida

Nick Sarantakas
Austin Community College

Gene Schneider
Austin Community College

H. Schollhammer
University of California—Los Angeles

Diane R. Scott
Wichita State University

Harvey Shore
University of Connecticut

Marc Siegall
California State University

Nicholas Siropolis
Cuyahoga Community College

Michael J. Stahl
University of Tennessee

Marc Street
University of Tulsa

Charlotte D. Sutton
Auburn University

Robert L. Taylor
University of Louisville

Mary Thibodeaux
University of North Texas

Joe Thomas
Middle Tennessee State University

Sean Valentine
University of Wyoming

Robert D. Van Auken
University of Oklahoma

Billy Ward
The University of West Alabama

Fred Williams
University of North Texas

James Wilson
University of Texas—Pan American

Carl P. Zeithaml
University of Virginia

I would also like to make a few personal acknowledgments. The fine work of Randy Newman, Roy Orbison, Lyle Lovett, Johnny Rivers, and the Nylons helped me make it through many late evenings and early mornings of work on the manuscript that became the book you hold in your hands. And Stephen King, Tom Clancy, James Lee Burke, Peter Straub, and Carl Barks provided me with a respite from my writings with their own.

Finally, there is the most important acknowledgement of all—my feelings for and gratitude to my family. My wife, Glenda, and our children, Dustin, Ashley, and Matt are the foundation of my professional and personal life. They help me keep work and play in perspective and give meaning to everything I do. It is with all my love that I dedicate this book to them.

R.W.G.

management

PART one

An Introduction to Management

CHAPTER 1

Managing and the Manager's Job

CHAPTER 2

Traditional and Contemporary Issues and Challenges

1

Managing and the Manager's Job

CHAPTER OUTLINE

An Introduction to Management

The Management Process
- Planning and Decision Making: Determining Courses of Action
- Organizing: Coordinating Activities and Resources
- Leading: Motivating and Managing People
- Controlling: Monitoring and Evaluating Activities

Kinds of Managers
- Managing at Different Levels of the Organization
- Managing in Different Areas of the Organization

Basic Managerial Roles and Skills
- Managerial Roles
- Managerial Skills

The Nature of Managerial Work
- The Science and the Art of Management
- Becoming a Manager
- The Scope of Management

The New Workplace

LEARNING OBJECTIVES

After studying this chapter, you should be able to:

1 ***Describe the nature of management, define management and managers, and characterize their importance to contemporary organizations.***

OPENING INCIDENT

CEO J.W. (Bill) Marriott, head of the Marriott International hotel chain, was watching television on September 11, 2001, when he saw a plane crash into the World Trade Center. Marriott knew then that his hotel at the site and the people inside it were in jeopardy. Later that day Marriott learned that the hotel was a complete loss and—much worse—that two of his managers had died evacuating guests. "It was the most difficult thing I'd experienced in 45 years of business," Marriott claims. In addition to their unthinkable human costs, the terrorist attacks had a severe dampening effect on tourism and business travel. Hotels experienced sharp declines in demand, on top of months-long decreases following the economy's worsening in 2001.

Marriott, the largest American hotel chain, with half a million rooms worldwide, was severely hurt by the drop. Marriott suffered more than most other hotel operators, such as Hilton and Starwood (which owns Sheraton and Westin), because more than half of Marriott's rooms are in high-end, urban properties. That segment of the market declined faster and more severely than any other. Marriott was also hurt by its high expenses, as it also had 60,000 new rooms under construction. On the

2 *Identify and briefly explain the four basic management functions in organizations.*

3 *Describe the kinds of managers found at different levels and in different areas of the organization.*

4 *Identify the basic managerial roles that managers may play and the skills they need in order to be successful.*

5 *Discuss the science and the art of management, describe how people become managers, and summarize the scope of management in organizations.*

6 *Characterize the new workplace that is emerging in organizations today.*

"Bulgari hotels are a daring move, I admit. . . ."

—Francesco Trapani, CEO, Bulgari

J.W. (Bill) Marriott greets employees at the new Marriott hotel in St. Louis

positive side, the firm's hotels are operated by franchisees that pay fees to Marriott International. Thus, when the economy worsens, the hotel operators bear part of the loss. However, if the operators cannot pay, the company must often make concessions.

To meet these challenges, Bill Marriott and his team have had to reinvent the way they do business. One of their first targets was the company's strict reliance on standard operating procedures (SOPs). Since its founding, Marriott has relied on hundreds of policies to keep standardization and quality high at its far-flung facilities. "This is a company that has more controls, more systems, and more procedural manuals than anyone—except the government. And they actually comply with them," says one industry veteran. The SOPs cover everything from how to knock on a guest's door to how many pens to supply in each room. Marriott is eliminating some SOPs to give local managers more flexibility in decision making, to better accommodate the needs of guests.

Marriott has distinguished itself by exemplary employee relations many times in the past, and the firm is making every effort to maintain those high standards even when times are rough. For the twelfth straight year, for instance, Marriott was recently named one of the "100 Best Companies for Working Mothers" by *Working Mother* magazine, due to its childcare arrangements, flextime, new-parent leave, and excellent promotion opportunities for women. Half of Marriott's managers are women; 20 percent of all managers came up from the ranks of hourly workers. Although the firm has had fewer funds available for employee raises in recent times, it still gave raises to top performers and managed to avoid layoffs. That meant no raises for many workers, but for most employees the opportunity to keep their job, even without a raise, is good news.

To soothe worried franchisees, Marriott has developed a website to allow hotel owners online access to details about their fees. They are also refunding fees to some owners. Cost-cutting efforts have reduced overhead expenses by 20 percent. New marketing campaigns target travelers who live in the local area and can travel by car. Innovative efforts include a joint venture with luxury jeweler Bulgari to create Bulgari-branded resorts in Milan, London, Paris, Miami, and New York. "Bulgari hotels are a daring move, I admit, but we both see good returns," says the Italian firm's CEO, Francesco Trapani.

Bill Marriott admits that the challenges of 2001 were the toughest his company has faced, but he is optimistic about the firm's future. "We only have 8 percent market share in the U.S. and less than 1 percent outside the U.S.," he says. "We see tremendous growth opportunities." The travel industry seems to be rebounding, and consumer confidence is increasing. Investors are believers in the strength of the industry, leading to hotel stock prices that grew by 16 percent in 2002, compared to a 5 percent drop for the stock index overall. Despite severe challenges, Marriott demonstrates that a well-run company and a great brand reputation can lead to success.[1]

Bill Marriott is clearly a manager. So, too, are Philip Knight (CEO of Nike), Carly Fiorina (CEO of Hewlett-Packard), Mikio Sasaki (president of Mitsubishi), Sir David Wilson (director of the British Museum), Debbie Fields (president of Mrs. Fields cookie stores), Mike Sherman (general manager of the Green Bay Packers), George W. Bush (president of the United States), John Paul II (pope of the Roman Catholic Church), and Marilyn Ferguson (owner of the Garden District Gift Shop in Bryan, Texas). As diverse as they and their organizations are, all of these managers are confronted by many of the same challenges, strive to achieve many of the same goals, and apply many of the same concepts of effective management in their work.

For better or worse, our society is strongly influenced by managers and their organizations. Most people in the United States are born in a hospital (an organization), educated by public or private schools (all organizations), and buy virtually all of their consumable products and services from businesses (organizations). And much of our behavior is influenced by various government agencies (also organizations). We define an **organization** as a group of people working together in a structured and coordinated fashion to achieve a set of goals. The goals may include profit (Starbucks Corporation), the discovery of knowledge (Iowa State University), national defense (the U.S. Army), coordination of various local charities (United Way of America), or social satisfaction (a sorority). Because organizations play such a major role in our lives, understanding how they operate and how they are managed is important.

organization A group of people working together in structured and coordinated fashion to achieve a set of goals

This book is about managers and the work they do. In Chapter 1, we examine the general nature of management, its dimensions, and its challenges. We explain the concepts of management and managers, discuss the management process, present an overview of the book, and identify various kinds of managers. We describe the different roles and skills of managers, discuss the nature of managerial work, and examine the scope of management in contemporary organizations. In Chapter 2, we describe how both the practice and the theory of management have evolved. As a unit, then, these first two chapters provide an introduction to the field by introducing both contemporary and historical perspectives on management.

An Introduction to Management

Although defining "organization" is relatively simple, the concept of "management" is a bit more elusive. It is perhaps best understood from a resource-based perspective. As we discuss more completely in Chapter 2, all organizations use four basic kinds of resources from their environment: human, financial, physical, and information. Human resources include managerial talent and labor. Financial resources are the capital used by the organization to finance both ongoing and long-term operations. Physical resources include raw materials, office and production facilities, and equipment. Information resources are usable data needed to make effective decisions. Examples of resources used in four very different kinds of organizations are shown in Table 1.1.

Managers are responsible for combining and coordinating these various resources to achieve the organization's goals. A manager at Royal Dutch/Shell Group, for example,

TABLE 1.1

Examples of Resources Used by Organizations

All organizations, regardless of whether they are large or small, profit-seeking or not-for-profit, domestic or multinational, use some combination of human, financial, physical, and information resources to achieve their goals. These resources are generally obtained from the organization's environment.

Organization	Human Resources	Financial Resources	Physical Resources	Information Resources
Shell Oil/ Royal Dutch	Drilling platform workers Corporate executives	Profits Stockholder investments	Refineries Office buildings	Sales forecasts OPEC proclamations
Iowa State University	Faculty Administrative staff	Alumni contributions Government grants	Computers Campus facilities	Research reports Government publications
New York City	Police officers Municipal employees	Tax revenue Government grants	Sanitation equipment Municipal buildings	Economic forecasts Crime statistics
Susan's Corner Grocery Store	Grocery clerks Bookkeeper	Profits Owner investment	Building Display shelving	Price lists from suppliers Newspaper ads for competitors

uses the talents of executives and drilling platform workers, profits earmarked for reinvestment, existing refineries and office facilities, and sales forecasts to make decisions regarding the amount of petroleum to be refined and distributed during the next quarter. Similarly, the mayor (manager) of New York City might use police officers, a government grant (perhaps supplemented with surplus tax revenues), existing police stations, and detailed crime statistics to launch a major crime prevention program in the city.

How do these and other managers combine and coordinate the various kinds of resources? They do so by carrying out four basic managerial functions or activities: planning and decision making, organizing, leading, and controlling. **Management**, then, as illustrated in Figure 1.1, can be defined as a set of activities (including planning and decision making, organizing, leading, and controlling) directed at an organization's resources (human, financial, physical, and information), with the aim of achieving organizational goals in an efficient and effective manner.

The last phrase in our definition is especially important because it highlights the basic purpose of management—to ensure that an organization's goals are achieved in an efficient and effective manner. By **efficient**, we mean using resources wisely and in a cost-effective way. For example, a firm like Toyota Motor Corp., which produces high-quality products at relatively low costs, is efficient. By **effective**, we mean making the right decisions and successfully implementing them. Toyota also makes cars with the styling and quality to inspire consumer interest and confidence.

Managers must juggle a variety of functions, activities, and responsibilities. Peter Morrissey, shown here on the left, owns and operates Morrissey and Co., a small New England public relations firm. While his small firm cannot afford an expensive employee fitness center, he encourages his employees to join him after lunch for a brisk walk along the Charles River in Boston each day.

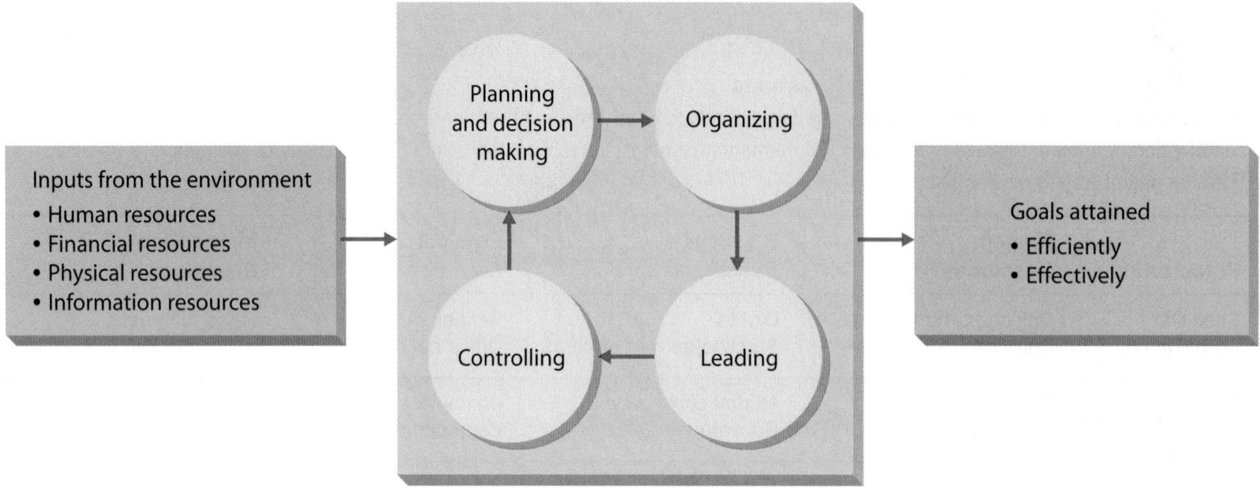

FIGURE 1.1

Management in Organizations

Basic managerial activities include planning and decision making, organizing, leading, and controlling. Managers engage in these activities to combine human, financial, physical, and information resources efficiently and effectively and to work toward achieving the goals of the organization.

management A set of activities (including planning and decision making, organizing, leading, and controlling) directed at an organization's resources (human, financial, physical, and information), with the aim of achieving organizational goals in an efficient and effective manner

efficient Using resources wisely and in a cost-effective way

effective Making the right decisions and successfully implementing them

manager Someone whose primary responsibility is to carry out the management process

A firm could very efficiently produce big-screen black-and-white televisions with few options and limited capabilities but still not succeed, because black-and-white televisions are no longer popular. A firm that produces products that no one wants is therefore not effective. In general, successful organizations are both efficient and effective.[2]

With this basic understanding of management, defining the term *manager* becomes relatively simple—a **manager** is someone whose primary responsibility is to carry out the management process. In particular, a manager is someone who plans and makes decisions, organizes, leads, and controls human, financial, physical, and information resources. Today's managers face a variety of interesting and challenging situations. The average executive works sixty hours a week, has enormous demands placed on his or her time, and faces increased complexities posed by globalization, domestic competition, government regulation, shareholder pressure, and Internet-related uncertainties. The job is complicated even more by rapid changes, unexpected disruptions, and both minor and major crises. The manager's job is unpredictable and fraught with challenges, but it is also filled with opportunities to make a difference. Good managers can propel an organization into unprecedented realms of success, whereas poor managers can devastate even the strongest of organizations.[3]

Many of the characteristics that contribute to the complexity and uncertainty of management stem from the environment in which organizations function. For example, as shown in Figure 1.1, the resources used by organizations to create products and services all come from the environment. Thus it is critical that managers understand this environment. Part Two of the text discusses the environmental context of management in detail. Chapter 3 provides a general overview and discussion of the organization's environment, and Chapters 4 through 6 address specific aspects of the environment more fully. In particular, Chapter 4 discusses the ethical and social context of management. Chapter 5 explores the global context of management. Chapter 6 describes the cultural and multicultural environment of management. After reading these chapters, you will be better prepared to study the essential activities that comprise the management process.

The Management Process

We note earlier that management involves the four basic functions of planning and decision making, organizing, leading, and controlling. Because these functions represent the framework around which this book is organized, we introduce them here and note where they are discussed more fully. Their basic definitions and interrelationships are shown in Figure 1.2. (Note that Figure 1.2 is an expanded version of the central part of Figure 1.1.)

Recall the details of the Marriott case discussed earlier. Bill Marriott must first create a clear set of goals and plans that articulate what he wants the company to become. He then creates an effective organization to help make those goals and plans reality. Marriott also pays close attention to the people who work for the company. And he keeps a close eye on how well the company is performing. Each of these activities represents one of the four basic managerial functions illustrated in the figure—setting goals is part of planning, setting up the organization is part of organizing, managing people is part of leading, and monitoring performance is part of controlling.

It is important to note, however, that the functions of management do not usually occur in a tidy, step-by-step fashion. Managers do not plan on Monday, make decisions on Tuesday, organize on Wednesday, lead on Thursday, and control on Friday. At any given time, as illustrated in the cartoon, for example, a manager is likely to be engaged in several different activities simultaneously. Indeed, from one setting to another, managerial work is as different as it is similar. The similarities that pervade most settings are the phases in the management process. Important differences include the emphasis, sequencing, and implications of each phase.[4] Thus the solid lines in Figure 1.2 indicate how, in theory, the functions of management are performed. The dotted lines, however, represent the true reality of management. In the sections that follow, we explore each of these activities.

FIGURE 1.2

The Management Process

Management involves four basic activities–planning and decision making, organizing, leading, and controlling. Although there is a basic logic for describing these activities in this sequence (as indicated by the solid arrows), most managers engage in more than one activity at a time and often move back and forth between the activities in unpredictable ways (as shown by the dotted arrows).

Planning and Decision Making: Determining Courses of Action

planning Setting an organization's goals and deciding how best to achieve them

decision making Part of the planning process that involves selecting a course of action from a set of alternatives

In its simplest form, **planning** means setting an organization's goals and deciding how best to achieve them. **Decision making**, a part of the planning process, involves selecting a course of action from a set of alternatives. Planning and decision making help maintain managerial effectiveness by serving as guides for future activities. In other words, the organization's goals and plans clearly help managers know how to allocate their time and resources. Carly Fiorina was appointed as CEO of Hewlett-Packard in 1999 and given a mandate to get the struggling firm back on track. Her first actions, in turn, included developing a new set of corporate goals refocusing the company on its core competencies and outlining a new business strategy to energize the company and integrate Internet technology throughout all its operations. More recently she masterminded the firm's merger with Compaq Computer.[5]

The World of Management discusses some of the planning and decision making that has gone into McDonald's efforts to expand its market.

Four chapters making up Part Three of this text are devoted to planning and decision making. Chapter 7 examines the basic elements of planning and decision making, including the role and importance of organizational goals. Chapter 8 looks at strategy and strategic planning, which provide overall direction and focus for the organization. Chapter 9 explores managerial decision making and problem solving in detail. Finally, Chapter 10 addresses planning and decision making as they relate to the management of new ventures and entrepreneurial activities, increasingly important parts of managerial work.

"Do you mind? I happen to be on the phone!"

Managers are constantly engaged in many different activities. The types and sequences of activities are often difficult to predict from one day to the next, however, and managers often do their work in impromptu settings or on airplanes, in taxis, over meals, or even when walking down the street. The manager shown here, for example, may be helping a colleague develop goals for the next quarter (planning), discussing a proposed company restructuring (organizing), praising a subordinate for outstanding performance (leading), or checking on last month's sales information (controlling).

Organizing: Coordinating Activities and Resources

Once a manager has set goals and developed a workable plan, the next management function is to organize people and the other resources necessary to carry out the plan. Specifically, **organizing** involves determining how activities and resources are to be grouped. One of the immediate obstacles facing Carly Fiorina at Hewlett-Packard was a rigid and bureaucratic hierarchy that promoted insular thinking and limited innovation. She swept this structure aside, creating a much more organic and flexible organization which, in turn, quickly became much more responsive and forward looking. She has now turned her attention to integrating the complex operations of Hewlett-Packard and Compaq.

Organizing is the subject of Part Four. Chapter 11 introduces the basic elements of organizing, such as job design, departmentalization, authority relationships, span

THE WORLD OF management

Want a MacBrioche with that MacEspresso?

"Our future business will be selling more than burgers and fries."

— Charlie Bell, president of McDonald's European operations*

After decades of sharply increasing sales, Americans' love affair with fast food may finally be coming to an end. The industry has seen explosive growth in domestic and international sales. Standardization has evolved, with new menu items and new methods of preparing custom food orders quickly.

McDonald's is at the forefront of this dynamic industry, with 30,000 restaurants in 121 countries. Yet in recent years, McDonald's seems to have lost its competitive edge. The company's menu is unhealthy, its stores outdated, and its customer service skills slipping. McDonald's no longer leads in technology, with rivals inventing new processing and cooking technologies. The firm's traditional markets, children and young men, are spending less on food, while markets McDonald's doesn't target, notably women and older consumers, spend more. Profits have dropped, and Starbucks has replaced McDonald's as the food industry success story.

To grow, McDonald's had to move out of the highly saturated American market and into Europe and Japan. However, consumers in many of those countries do not like McDonald's Americanized look and products. So the burger maker has had to cater to local tastes. That means serving brioche and espresso in France, salmon sandwiches in Scandinavia, and beer in Germany. A Premiere line features more expensive and upscale offerings, such as chicken served on focaccia bread with salsa.

McDonald's is also customizing the look of its stores. In France, the "Mountain" has ski chalet décor—hardwood floors, televisions, and armchairs. The "Music" features 1950s-style booths with their own CD players. Managers hope that customers attracted to the more upscale restaurants may also be willing to pay more for premium food. Charlie Bell, McDonald's European president, claims, "Our future business will be selling more than burgers and fries."

So far the new appearance and menu are paying off. U.S. sales continue their downward trend, but French sales increased after the makeover. Ken Clement, a franchisee and former McDonald's vice president, claims the changes are not necessary in America. "People are not coming to swoon over the décor," he says. "They are coming in and getting out of here. They don't give a rip what is inside." However, if the French market continues to improve, the innovations may make it to the States, where the risk and the return could be great. The change could alienate McDonald's traditional customers, or it could revitalize the firm and spark a renaissance for the entire fast food industry.

References: Grainger David, "Remaking McDonald's," *Fortune*, April 14, 2003, pp. 120–131. Amy Tsao, "For McDonald's, the Fat's in the Fire," *BusinessWeek*, October 15, 2002, www.businessweek.com on November 23, 2002; Julie Forster, "Thinking Outside the Burger Box," *BusinessWeek*, September 16, 2002, pp. 66–67; Shirley Leung, "Armchairs, TVs and Espresso—Is It McDonald's?" *Wall Street Journal*, August 30, 2002, pp. A1, A6 (*quote p. A6).

of control, and line and staff roles. Chapter 12 explains how managers fit these elements and concepts together to form an overall organization design. Organization change and innovation are the focus of Chapter 13. Finally, processes associated with managing the organization's workforce so as to most effectively carry out organizational roles and perform tasks are described in Chapter 14.

organizing Determining how activities and resources are to be grouped

Leading: Motivating and Managing People

leading The set of processes used to get members of the organization to work together to further the interests of the organization

The third basic managerial function is leading. Some people consider leading to be both the most important and the most challenging of all managerial activities. **Leading** is the set of processes used to get members of the organization to work together to further the interests of the organization. Carly Fiorina came to Hewlett-Packard with a reputation for being a trustworthy and honest manager, but also one who would make tough decisions and hard choices. Her personality blended perfectly with those of other top managers at the company, and they were soon working together as a cohesive and effective team. She also demonstrated her determination in leading the charge to acquire Compaq, over the opposition of several major investors.

Leading involves a number of different processes and activities, which are discussed in Part Five. The starting point is understanding basic individual and interpersonal processes, which we focus on in Chapter 15. Motivating employees is discussed in Chapter 16, and leadership itself and the leader's efforts to influence others are covered in Chapter 17. Managing interpersonal relations and communication is the subject of Chapter 18. Finally, managing work groups and teams, another important part of leading, is addressed in Chapter 19.

Controlling: Monitoring and Evaluating Activities

controlling Monitoring organizational progress toward goal attainment

The final phase of the management process is **controlling**, or monitoring the organization's progress toward its goals. As the organization moves toward its goals, managers must monitor progress to ensure that it is performing in such a way as to arrive at its "destination" at the appointed time. A good analogy is that of a space mission to Mars. NASA does not simply shoot a rocket in the general direction of the planet and then look again in four months to see whether the rocket hit its mark. NASA monitors the spacecraft almost continuously and makes whatever course corrections are needed to keep it on track. Controlling similarly helps ensure the effectiveness and efficiency needed for successful management. Although Carly Fiorina is off to a great start at Hewlett-Packard, the firm still has a long way to go to regain its technological leadership. Thus she has set in place numerous benchmarks that will be used to assess the firm's progress over the next few years as it evolves toward her model of strategic competitiveness. She will also be accountable to investors for the eventual profitability and competitiveness of the firm after it has fully implemented its integration of Compaq.

The control function is explored in Part Six. First, Chapter 20 explores the basic elements of the control process, including the increasing importance of strategic control. Managing operations, quality, and productivity is explored in Chapter 21. Finally, Chapter 22 addresses the management of information and information technology, still other critical areas of organizational control.

concept CHECK

What is a manager, and what are the fundamental functions that comprise the management process?

Describe examples of how the management functions might be performed in different sequences.

Kinds of Managers

Earlier in this chapter we identify as managers people from a variety of organizations. Clearly, there are many kinds of managers. One point of differentiation is among organizations, as those earlier examples imply. Another point occurs within an organization. Figure 1.3 shows how managers within an organization can be differentiated by level and area.

Managing at Different Levels of the Organization

Managers can be differentiated according to their level in the organization. Although large organizations typically have a number of **levels of management**, the most common view considers three basic levels: top, middle, and first-line managers.

levels of management The differentiation of managers into three basic categories—top, middle, and first-line

Top Managers Top managers make up the relatively small group of executives who manage the overall organization. Titles found in this group include president, vice president, and chief executive officer (CEO). Top managers create the organization's goals, overall strategy, and operating policies. They also officially represent the organization to the external environment by meeting with government officials, executives of other organizations, and so forth. Howard Schultz, CEO of Starbucks,

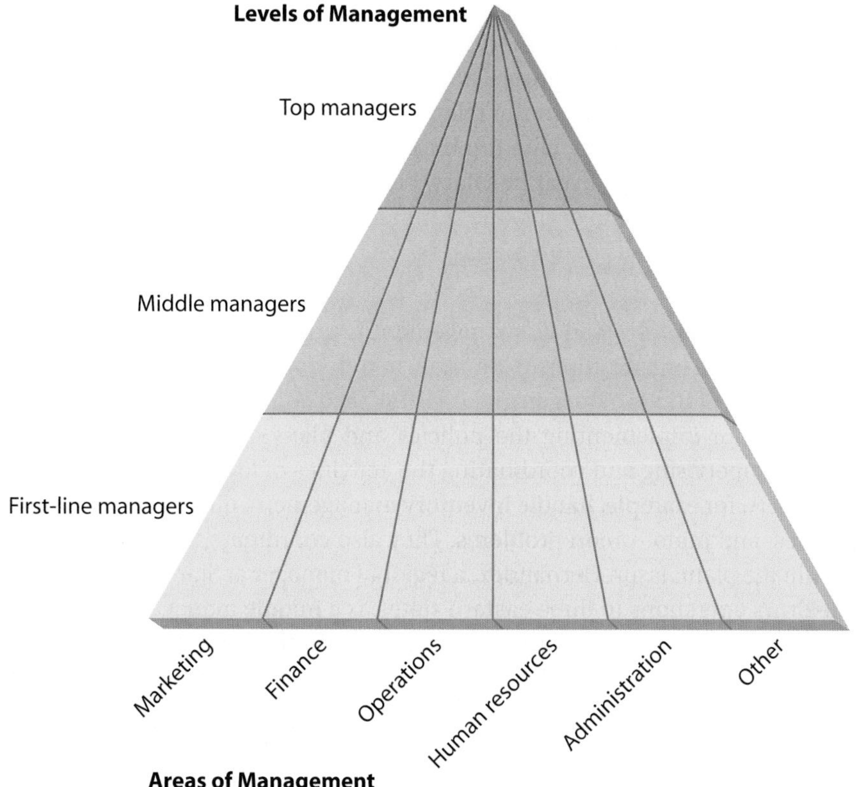

FIGURE 1.3

Kinds of Managers by Level and Area

Organizations generally have three levels of management, represented by top managers, middle managers, and first-line managers. Regardless of level, managers are also usually associated with a specific area within the organization, such as marketing, finance, operations, human resources, administration, or some other area.

Organizations rely on many different kinds of managers. Cherly Brantley, shown here on the right, is responsible for staffing all of Donald Trump's operations in Atlantic City. The Trump organization just opened a new training center for its employees in Atlantic City and Ms. Brantley is shown here inspecting the facilities with her own staff.

is a top manager, as is Deidra Wager, the firm's senior vice president for retail operations. The job of a top manager is likely to be complex and varied. Top managers make decisions about such activities as acquiring other companies, investing in research and development, entering or abandoning various markets, and building new plants and office facilities. They often work long hours and spend much of their time in meetings or on the telephone. In most cases, top managers are also very well paid. In fact, the elite top managers of very large firms sometimes make several million dollars a year in salary, bonuses, and stock.[6] Unfortunately, recent corporate scandals such as the one summarized in *The Business of Ethics* have tarnished the reputations of top managers.

Middle Managers Middle management is probably the largest group of managers in most organizations. Common middle-management titles include plant manager, operations manager, and division head. Middle managers are responsible primarily for implementing the policies and plans developed by top managers and for supervising and coordinating the activities of lower-level managers.[7] Plant managers, for example, handle inventory management, quality control, equipment failures, and minor union problems. They also coordinate the work of supervisors within the plant. Jason Hernandez, a regional manager at Starbucks responsible for the firm's operations in three eastern states, is a middle manager.

In recent years, many organizations have thinned the ranks of middle managers to lower costs and eliminate excess bureaucracy. Still, middle managers are necessary to bridge the upper and lower levels of the organization and to implement the strategies developed at the top. Although many organizations have found that they can indeed survive with fewer middle managers, those who

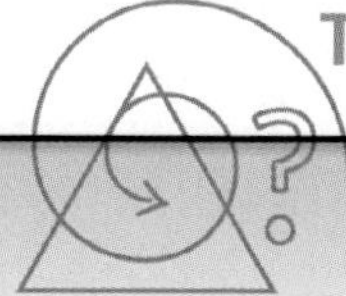

THE BUSINESS of ethics

When Good CEOs Go Bad

"Tyco really needs to go from worst to first."

– Jerry Useem, Wharton professor of management*

CEOs of large, publicly traded corporations seldom commit profound ethical violations. They are in the public and regulatory eye, are the product of years of selection and training, and must report to corporate boards. Dennis Kozlowski, CEO of Tyco until June 2002, is one of the rare CEOs who "went bad." Allegedly, Kozlowski and other top executives stole more than $170 million from Tyco. Most of the funds went to Kozlowski's outrageous expenditures: a $6,000 shower curtain; a $2,000 wastebasket; the 1934 America's Cup yacht, which cost $20 million and had a $700,000 annual maintenance budget; his wife's $2.1 million birthday party; $40 million in loans that were not repaid; and so on, and so on.

Why would Kozlowski perpetrate such a fraud? Before 1997 he ran Tyco as a model of frugality—for example, limiting his own salary voluntarily to $1 million and eliminating many of the usual executive perquisites. A glowing *Wall Street Journal* article cited his no-frills offices and lean corporate staff, and quoted Kozlowski as saying, "I like to avoid costs wherever I can in the company." Although Kozlowski was far from the highest-paid CEO, he enjoyed a good reputation and was much admired for his amazing rise from a working-class background.

And how did Tyco's oversight fail? Disclosure failures should have been detected by both the board and external auditors. Kozlowski nominated insiders to the board, reported financial results to the board himself, and paid large fees to outside directors, reducing the board's ability to make independent judgments about his performance. Tyco's board was so poor that it was named to *BusinessWeek's* "Hall of Shame." Even the government was deceived—the Securities and Exchange Commission investigated the firm in 1999 but found no evidence of wrongdoing.

With Kozlowski and his directors on the way out, new Tyco CEO Edward D. Breen has hired Jerry Useem to overhaul corporate governance. Useem, a Wharton professor and former Kozlowski fan, seems an unlikely choice, and it remains to be seen how he will handle the job of running such a troubled corporation. But Useem seems to be on the right track, saying, "Tyco really needs to go from worst to first. It really does have to transform itself."

References: Geoffrey Colvin, "Liar, Liar, Pants on Fire," *Fortune*, September 16, 2002, www.fortune.com on November 23, 2002; Louis Lavelle, "Rebuilding Trust in Tyco," *BusinessWeek*, November 25, 2002, pp. 94–96 (*quote p. 96); Nicholas Varchaver, "The Big Kozlowski," *Fortune*, November 18, 2002, pp. 123–126; "Table: Hall of Shame," *BusinessWeek*, October 7, 2002, p. 114; William C. Symonds, "Tyco: How Did They Miss a Scam So Big?" *BusinessWeek*, September 30, 2002, pp. 40–42.

remain play an even more important role in determining how successful the organization will be.

First-Line Managers First-line managers supervise and coordinate the activities of operating employees. Common titles for first-line managers are supervisor, coordinator, and office manager. Positions like these are often the first held by employees who enter management from the ranks of operating personnel. Wayne Maxwell and Jenny Wagner, managers of Starbucks coffee shops in Texas, are first-line managers. They oversee the day-to-day operations of their respective stores, hire operating employees to staff them, and handle other routine administrative duties required of them by the parent corporation. In contrast to top and middle managers, first-line managers typically spend a large proportion of their time supervising the work of subordinates.

Managing in Different Areas of the Organization

areas of management Managers can be differentiated into marketing, financial, operating, human resource, administration, and other areas

Regardless of their level, managers may work in various areas within an organization. In any given firm, for example, **areas of management** may include marketing, financial, operations, human resource, administrative, and other areas.

Marketing Managers Marketing managers work in areas related to the marketing function—getting consumers and clients to buy the organization's products or services (be they Motorola digital cell phones, Ford automobiles, *Newsweek* magazines, Associated Press news reports, flights on Southwest Airlines, or cups of latte at Starbucks). These areas include new-product development, promotion, and distribution. Given the importance of marketing for virtually all organizations, developing good managers in this area can be critical. Carly Fiorina worked in several marketing jobs as she moved up the corporate ranks.

Financial Managers Financial managers deal primarily with an organization's financial resources. They are responsible for such activities as accounting, cash management, and investments. In some businesses, such as banking and insurance, financial managers are found in especially large numbers. Stanley O'Neal, the most powerful executive at Merrill Lynch, spent much of his career in the financial side of the business.

Operations Managers Operations managers are concerned with creating and managing the systems that create an organization's products and services. Typical responsibilities of operations managers include production control, inventory control, quality control, plant layout, and site selection. Gordon Bethune, CEO of Continental Airlines, worked in many different jobs managing various aspects of operations.

Human Resource Managers Human resource managers are responsible for hiring and developing employees. They are typically involved in human resource planning, recruiting and selecting employees, training and development, designing compensation and benefit systems, formulating performance appraisal systems, and discharging low-performing and problem employees.

Administrative Managers Administrative, or general, managers are not associated with any particular management specialty. Probably the best example of an administrative management position is that of a hospital or clinic administrator. Administrative managers tend to be generalists; they have some basic familiarity with all functional areas of management rather than specialized training in any one area.[8]

Other Kinds of Managers Many organizations have specialized management positions in addition to those already described. Public relations managers, for example, deal with the public and media for firms like Philip Morris Companies and The Dow Chemical Company to protect and enhance the image of the organization. Research and development (R&D) managers coordinate the activities of scientists and engineers working on scientific projects in organizations such as Monsanto Company, NASA, and Merck & Company. Internal consultants are used in organizations such as Prudential Insurance to provide specialized expert advice to operating managers. International operations are often coordinated by specialized managers in organizations like Eli Lilly and Rockwell International. The number, nature, and importance of these specialized managers vary tremendously from one organization to another. *Technology Toolkit* discusses some interesting new kinds of management positions. As contemporary organizations continue to grow in complexity and size, the number and importance of such managers are also likely to increase.

TECHNOLOGY toolkit

The Low-Tech Solution to High-Tech Difficulties

There is no question that technological innovations—the personal computer, cell phones, the Internet—have radically changed the way companies do business. Often, however, these new technologies seem to have taken the "soul" out of commerce, causing businesspeople to spend hours a day staring at a flickering screen rather than talking to their coworkers or customers, for example. However, one consulting firm, Stone Yamashita, headed by Keith Yamashita, is changing all that.

Stone Yamashita has attracted quite a following among high-technology and other companies for its advice on how to integrate strategy, culture, and branding into one consistent, meaningful package. *Fast Company* magazine calls Keith Yamashita "the most influential consultant you've never heard of." The firm has tackled an ambitious range of projects, ranging from writing some of Carly Fiorina's speeches as she attempted to set forth a coherent Internet strategy for Hewlett-Packard, to helping the Jordan division of Nike find a way to expand its brand beyond its traditional market of young urban males.

"The experience of having a meeting . . . with them actually changes the way you approach your work."

— **Debra Dunn, senior vice president of corporate affairs, Hewlett Packard***

To handle these diverse products, Stone Yamashita has principals who were formerly graphic designers, Internet experts, attorneys, writers, business managers, and a poet. Every client receives not only a write-up of the results of meetings, but also tangible deliverables, which often include items such as the nine-volume set of bound paperbacks the firm produced for Hewlett-Packard. When Stone Yamashita was helping HP develop its e-business strategy, deliverables included a video, sales brochures, newspapers, flashcards, and a 30,000-square-foot executive briefing center.

In spite of its emphasis on high-technology firms, Stone Yamashita's methods are often distinctly low-tech. It holds brainstorming sessions, plays games, writes ideas down on storyboards, and role-plays as it helps its clients communicate and envision a shared future. "The people at Stone Yamashita don't just craft strategy, they bring it to life," says HP senior vice president Debra Dunn. "Not only do they produce tangible outputs, but the experience of having a meeting or an engagement with them actually changes the way you approach your work." Keith Yamashita sees his job another way: "What we're trying to do in our work is engineer epiphanies. We're trying to move people to a place where it makes sense to act."

References: "Annual Design Awards—The Complete List of 2001 Winners," *BusinessWeek*, June 24, 2001, www.businessweek.com on November 24, 2002; James Aley, "Mr. Fusion: Keith Yamashita," *Fortune*, October 28, 2002, www.fortune.com on November 24, 2002; Polly LaBarre, "Keith Yamashita Wants to Reinvent Your Company," *Fast Company*, November, 2002, www.fastcompany.com on November 24, 2002 (*quote); Pui-Wang Tam, "The New Pioneers Working on Technology's Cutting Edge," *Wall Street Journal*, May 13, 2002.

concept CHECK

Identify different kinds of managers by level and area of an organization.

How might the importance of different areas of management vary as a function of the firm's business?

Basic Managerial Roles and Skills

Regardless of their level or area within an organization, all managers must play certain roles and exhibit certain skills if they are to be successful. The concept of a role, in this sense, is similar to the role an actor plays in a theatrical production. A person does certain things, meets certain needs in the organization, and has certain responsibilities. In the sections that follow, we first highlight the basic roles managers play and then discuss the skills they need to be effective.

Managerial Roles

Henry Mintzberg offers a number of interesting insights into the nature of managerial roles.[9] He closely observed the day-to-day activities of a group of CEOs by literally following them around and taking notes on what they did. From his observations, Mintzberg concluded that managers play ten different roles, as summarized in Table 1.2, and that these roles fall into three basic categories: interpersonal, informational, and decisional.

TABLE 1.2

Ten Basic Managerial Roles

Research by Henry Mintzberg suggests that managers play ten basic managerial roles.

Category	Role	Sample Activities
Interpersonal	Figurehead	Attending ribbon-cutting ceremony for new plant
	Leader	Encouraging employees to improve productivity
	Liaison	Coordinating activities of two project groups
Informational	Monitor	Scanning industry reports to stay abreast of developments
	Disseminator	Sending memos outlining new organizational initiatives
	Spokesperson	Making a speech to discuss growth plans
Decisional	Entrepreneur	Developing new ideas for innovation
	Disturbance handler	Resolving conflict between two subordinates
	Resource allocator	Reviewing and revising budget requests
	Negotiator	Reaching agreement with a key supplier or labor union

interpersonal roles The roles of figurehead, leader, and liaison, which involve dealing with other people

Interpersonal Roles There are three **interpersonal roles** inherent in the manager's job. First, the manager is often asked to serve as a *figurehead*—taking visitors to dinner, attending ribbon-cutting ceremonies, and the like. These activities are typically more ceremonial and symbolic than substantive. The manager is also asked to serve as a *leader*—hiring, training, and motivating employees. A manager who formally or informally shows subordinates how to do things and how to perform under pressure is leading. Finally, managers can have a *liaison* role. This role often involves serving as a coordinator or link among people, groups, or organizations. For example, companies in the computer industry may use liaisons to keep other companies informed about their plans. This enables Microsoft, for example, to create software for interfacing with new Hewlett-Packard printers at the same time those printers are being developed. And, at the same time, managers at Hewlett-Packard can incorporate new Microsoft features into the printers they introduce.

informational roles The roles of monitor, disseminator, and spokesperson, which involve the processing of information

Informational Roles The three **informational roles** flow naturally from the interpersonal roles just discussed. The process of carrying out these roles places the manager at a strategic point to gather and disseminate information. The first informational role is that of *monitor*, one who actively seeks information that may be of value. The manager questions subordinates, is receptive to unsolicited information, and attempts to be as well informed as possible. The manager is also a *disseminator* of information, transmitting relevant information back to others in the workplace. When the roles of monitor and disseminator are viewed together, the manager emerges as a vital link in the organization's chain of communication. The third informational role focuses on external communication. The *spokesperson* formally relays information to people outside the unit or outside the organization. For example, a plant manager at Union Carbide may transmit information to top-level managers so that they will be better informed about the plant's activities. The manager may also represent the organization before a chamber of commerce or consumer group. Although the roles of spokesperson and figurehead are similar, there is one basic difference between them. When a manager acts as a figurehead, the manager's presence as a symbol of the organization is what is of interest. In the spokesperson role, however, the manager carries information and communicates it to others in a formal sense.

All managers must play certain roles and exhibit certain skills to be successful. For years Coca-Cola struggled with its operations in India. But when it finally promoted Sanjeev Gupta to head up its operations in that country he began to turn things around. His keen understanding of the local market combined with his knowledge of management roles and skills has allowed him to dramatically improve Coke's performance in India.

Decisional Roles The manager's informational roles typically lead to the **decisional roles**. The information acquired by the manager as a result of performing the informational roles has a major bearing on important decisions that he or she makes. Mintzberg identified four decisional roles. First, the manager has the role of *entrepreneur*, the voluntary initiator of change. A manager at 3M

decisional roles The roles of entrepreneur, disturbance handler, resource allocator, and negotiator, which relate primarily to making decisions

Company developed the idea for the Post-it note pad but had to "sell" it to other skeptical managers inside the company. A second decisional role is initiated not by the manager but by some other individual or group. The manager responds to her role as *disturbance handler* by handling such problems as strikes, copyright infringements, or problems in public relations or corporate image.

The third decisional role is that of *resource allocator*. As resource allocator, the manager decides how resources are distributed and with whom he or she will work most closely. For example, a manager typically allocates the funds in the unit's operating budget among the unit's members and projects. A fourth decisional role is that of *negotiator*. In this role the manager enters into negotiations with other groups or organizations as a representative of the company. For example, managers may negotiate a union contract, an agreement with a consultant, or a long-term relationship with a supplier. Negotiations may also be internal to the organization. The manager may, for instance, mediate a dispute between two subordinates or negotiate with another department for additional support.

technical skills The skills necessary to accomplish or understand the specific kind of work being done in an organization

Managerial Skills

In addition to fulfilling numerous roles, managers also need a number of specific skills if they are to succeed. The most fundamental management skills are technical, interpersonal, conceptual, diagnostic, communication, decision-making, and time-management skills.[10]

Management is an important part of any organization, regardless of its size or mission. Luke Davis combines his business acumen with technical skills as he reaches out to a wide array of different kinds of organizations and offers his services as a web site designer. Here, for instance, he is demonstrating the new web site he designed for the Tyburn Convent in London. Davis has become quite successful by focusing on diverse kinds of religious, civic, and social organizations.

Technical Skills **Technical skills** are the skills necessary to accomplish or understand the specific kind of work being done in an organization. Technical skills are especially important for first-line managers. These managers spend much of their time training subordinates and answering questions about work-related problems. They must know how to perform the tasks assigned to those they supervise if they are to be effective managers. Horst Schulze, CEO of Ritz-Carlton, got his start washing dishes and waiting tables at hotels in Germany. Over the next several years he also worked as a bellhop, a front desk clerk, and a concierge. These experiences gave him keen insight into the inner workings of a quality hotel operation, insights he has used to take Ritz-Carlton to the top of its industry.[11]

Interpersonal Skills Managers spend considerable time interacting with people both inside and outside the organization. For obvious reasons, then, the manager also needs **interpersonal skills**—the ability to communicate with, understand, and motivate both individuals and groups. As a manager climbs the organizational ladder, she must be able to get along with subordinates, peers, and those at higher levels of the organization. Because of the multitude of roles managers must fulfill, a manager must also be able to work with suppliers, customers, investors, and others outside of the organization. Although some managers have succeeded with poor interpersonal skills, a manager who has good interpersonal skills is likely to be more successful. When A. G. Lafley was recently appointed CEO of Procter & Gamble, observers were quick to praise him for his strong interpersonal skills. As one colleague put it, "A. G. has a reputation for both people skills and strategic thinking."[12]

interpersonal skills The ability to communicate with, understand, and motivate both individuals and groups

Conceptual Skills **Conceptual skills** depend on the manager's ability to think in the abstract. Managers need the mental capacity to understand the overall workings of the organization and its environment, to grasp how all the parts of the organization fit together, and to view the organization in a holistic manner. This allows them to think strategically, to see the "big picture," and to make broad-based decisions that serve the overall organization.

conceptual skills The manager's ability to think in the abstract

Diagnostic Skills Successful managers also possess **diagnostic skills**, or skills that enable a manager to visualize the most appropriate response to a situation. A physician diagnoses a patient's illness by analyzing symptoms and determining their probable cause. Similarly, a manager can diagnose and analyze a problem in the organization by studying its symptoms and then developing a solution. When the original owners of Starbucks failed to make a success of the business, Howard Schultz took over and reoriented the business away from mail order and moved it into retail coffee outlets. His diagnostic skills enabled him to understand both why the current business model was not working and how to construct a better one.

diagnostic skills The manager's ability to visualize the most appropriate response to a situation

Communication Skills **Communication skills** refer to the manager's abilities both to effectively convey ideas and information to others and to effectively receive ideas and information from others. These skills enable a manager to transmit ideas to subordinates so that they know what is expected, to coordinate work with peers and colleagues so that they work well together properly, and to keep higher-level managers informed about what is going on. In addition, they help the manager listen to what others say and to understand the real meaning behind letters, reports, and other written communication.

communication skills The manager's abilities both to effectively convey ideas and information to others and to effectively receive ideas and information from others

Decision-Making Skills Effective managers also have good decision-making skills. **Decision-making skills** refer to the manager's ability to correctly recognize and define problems and opportunities and to then select an appropriate course of action to solve problems and capitalize on opportunities. No manager makes the right decision *all* the time. However, effective managers make good decisions *most*

decision-making skills The manager's ability to correctly recognize and define problems and opportunities and to then select an appropriate course of action to solve problems and capitalize on opportunities of the time. And, when they do make a bad decision, they usually recognize their mistake quickly and then make good decisions to recover with as little cost or damage to their organization as possible.

time-management skills The manager's ability to prioritize work, to work efficiently, and to delegate appropriately

Time-Management Skills Finally, effective managers usually have good time-management skills. **Time-management skills** refer to the manager's ability to prioritize work, to work efficiently, and to delegate appropriately. As already noted, managers face many different pressures and challenges. It is too easy for a manager to get bogged down doing work that can easily be postponed or delegated to others.[13] When this happens, unfortunately, more pressing and higher-priority work may get neglected.[14] Jeff Bezos, CEO of Amazon.com, schedules all his meetings on three days a week, but insists on keeping the other two days clear so that he can pursue his own ideas and maintain the flexibility to interact with his employees informally.[15]

concept CHECK

List and define the basic managerial skills that contribute to success.	How might the various managerial skills relate to different managerial roles?

The Nature of Managerial Work

We have already noted that managerial work does not follow an orderly, systematic progression through the workweek. Indeed, the manager's job is fraught with uncertainty, change, interruption, and fragmented activities. Mintzberg's study, mentioned earlier, found that, in a typical day, CEOs were likely to spend 59 percent of their time in scheduled meetings, 22 percent doing "desk work," 10 percent in unscheduled meetings, 6 percent on the telephone, and the remaining 3 percent on tours of company facilities. (These proportions, of course, are different for managers at lower levels.) Moreover, the nature of managerial work continues to change in complex and often unpredictable ways.[16]

In addition, managers perform a wide variety of tasks. In the course of a single day, for example, a manager might have to make a decision about the design of a new product, settle a complaint between two subordinates, hire a new assistant, write a report for the boss, coordinate a joint venture with an overseas colleague, form a task force to investigate a problem, search for information on the Internet, and deal with a labor grievance. Moreover, the pace of the manager's job can be relentless. She may feel bombarded by mail, telephone calls, and people waiting to see her. Decisions may have to be made quickly and plans formulated with little time for reflection.[17] But, in many ways, these same characteristics of managerial work also contribute to its richness and meaningfulness. Making critical decisions under intense pressure, and making them well, can be a major source of intrinsic satisfaction. And managers are usually well paid for the pressures they bear.

The Science and the Art of Management

Given the complexity inherent in the manager's job, a reasonable question relates to whether management is a science or an art. In fact, effective management is a blend of both science and art. And successful executives recognize the importance of combining both the science and the art of management as they practice their craft.[18]

The Science of Management Many management problems and issues can be approached in ways that are rational, logical, objective, and systematic. Managers can gather data, facts, and objective information. They can use quantitative models and decision-making techniques to arrive at "correct" decisions. And they need to take such a scientific approach to solving problems whenever possible, especially when they are dealing with relatively routine and straightforward issues. When Starbucks considers entering a new market, its managers look closely at a wide variety of objective details as they formulate their plans. Technical, diagnostic, and decision-making skills are especially important when practicing the science of management.

The Art of Management Even though managers may try to be scientific as much as possible, they must often make decisions and solve problems on the basis of intuition, experience, instinct, and personal insights. Relying heavily on conceptual, communication, interpersonal, and time-management skills, for example, a manager may have to decide among multiple courses of action that look equally attractive. And even "objective facts" may prove to be wrong. When Starbucks was planning its first store in New York, market research clearly showed that New Yorkers preferred drip coffee to more exotic espresso-style coffees. After first installing more drip coffee makers and fewer espresso makers than in their other stores, managers had to backtrack when the New Yorkers lined up clamoring for espresso. Starbucks now introduces a standard menu and layout in all its stores, regardless of presumed market differences, and then makes necessary adjustments later. Thus managers must blend an element of intuition and personal insight with hard data and objective facts.[19]

FIGURE 1.4

Sources of Management Skills

Most managers acquire their skills as a result of education and experience. Though a few CEOs today do not hold college degrees, most students preparing for management careers earn college degrees and go on to enroll in MBA programs.

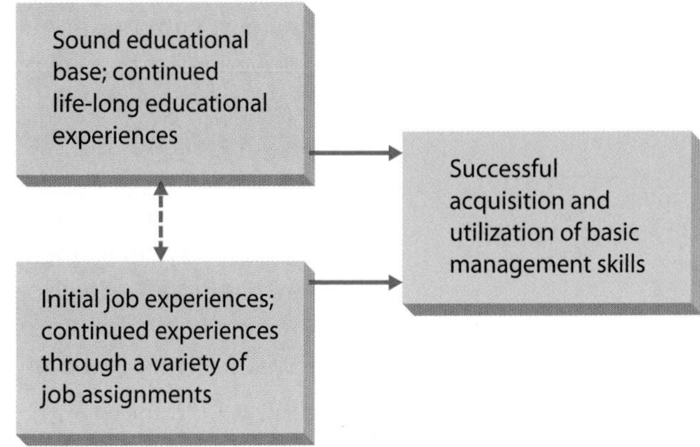

Becoming a Manager

How does one acquire the skills necessary to blend the science and art of management and to become a successful manager? Although there are as many variations as there are managers, the most common path involves a combination of education and experience.[20] Figure 1.4 illustrates how this generally happens.

The Role of Education Many of you reading this book right now are doing so because you are enrolled in a management course at a college or university. Thus you are acquiring management skills in an educational setting. When you complete the course (and this book), you will have a foundation for developing your management skills in more advanced courses. A college degree has become almost a requirement for career advancement in business, and virtually all CEOs in the United States have a college degree. MBA degrees are also common among successful executives today. More and more foreign universities, especially in Europe, are also beginning to offer academic programs in management.

Even after obtaining a degree, most prospective managers have not seen the end of their management education. Many middle and top managers periodically return to campus to participate in executive or management development programs ranging in duration from a few days to several weeks. First-line managers also take advantage of extension and continuing education programs offered by institutions of higher education. A recent innovation in extended management education is the executive MBA program offered by many top business schools, in which middle and top managers with several years of experience complete an accelerated program of study on weekends.[21] Finally, many large companies have in-house training programs for furthering managers' education. Indeed, some firms have even created what are essentially corporate universities to provide the specialized education they feel is required for their managers in order for them to remain successful. McDonald's and Shell Oil are among the leaders in this area. Regardless of the type of training, there is also a distinct trend toward online educational development for managers.[22]

The primary advantage of education as a source of management skills is that, as a student, a person can follow a well-developed program of study, becoming familiar with current research and thinking on management. And many college students can devote full-time energy and attention to learning. On the negative side, management education is often very general, to meet the needs of a wide variety of students, and specific know-how may be hard to obtain. Further, many aspects of the manager's job can be discussed in a book but cannot really be appreciated and understood until they are experienced.

The Role of Experience This book will help provide you with a solid foundation for enhancing your management skills. Even if you were to memorize every word in every management book ever written, however, you could not then step into a top-management position and be effective. The reason? Management skills must also be learned through experience. Most managers advanced to their present position from other jobs. Only by experiencing the day-to-day pressures a manager faces and by meeting a variety of managerial challenges can an individual develop insights into the real nature and character of managerial work.

For this reason, most large companies, and many smaller ones as well, have developed management training programs for their prospective managers. People are hired from college campuses, from other organizations, or from the ranks of the organization's first-line managers and operating employees. These people are systematically assigned to a variety of jobs. Over time, the individual is exposed to most, if not all, of the major aspects of the organization. In this way the manager learns by experience. The training programs at some companies, such as Procter &

Gamble, General Mills, and Shell Oil are so good that other companies try to hire people who have gone through their training.[23] Even without formal training programs, managers can achieve success as they profit from varied experiences. For example, Herb Kelleher was a practicing attorney before he took over at Southwest Airlines. Of course, natural ability, drive, and self-motivation also play roles in acquiring experience and developing management skills.

Most effective managers learn their skills through a combination of education and experience. Some type of college degree, even if it is not in business administration, usually provides a foundation for a management career. The individual then gets his or her first job and subsequently progresses through a variety of management situations. During the manager's rise in the organization, occasional education "updates," such as management development programs, may supplement on-the-job experience. And, increasingly, managers need to acquire international expertise as part of their personal development. As with general managerial skills, international expertise can also be acquired through a combination of education and experience.[24]

The Scope of Management

When most people think of managers and management, they think of profit-seeking organizations. Throughout this chapter we use people like Bill Marriott, Howard Schultz of Starbucks, and Carly Fiorina of Hewlett-Packard as examples. But we also mentioned examples from sports, religion, and other fields in which management is essential. Indeed, any group of two or more persons working together to achieve a goal and having human, material, financial, or informational resources at its disposal requires the practice of management.

Managing in Profit-Seeking Organizations Most of what we know about management comes from large profit-seeking organizations because their survival has long depended on efficiency and effectiveness. Examples of large businesses include industrial firms such as Tenneco, BP, Toyota, Xerox, Unilever, and Levi Strauss; commercial banks such as Citicorp, Fuji Bank, and Wells Fargo; insurance companies such as Prudential, State Farm, and Metropolitan Life; retailers such as Sears, Safeway, and Target; transportation companies such as Delta Air Lines and Consolidated Freightways; utilities such as Pacific Gas & Electric and Consolidated Edison of New York; communication companies such as CBS and The New York Times Company; and service organizations such as Kelly Services, KinderCare Learning Centers, and Century 21 Real Estate.

Although many people associate management primarily with large businesses, effective management is also essential for small businesses, which play an important role in the country's economy. In fact, most of this nation's businesses are small. In some respects, effective management is more important in a small business than in a large one. A large firm such as ExxonMobil or Monsanto can easily recover from losing several thousand dollars on an incorrect decision; even losses of millions of dollars would not threaten their long-term survival. But a small business may ill afford even a much smaller loss. Of course, some small businesses become big ones. Dell Computer, for example, was started by one person—Michael

Dell—in 1984. By 2003 it had become one of the largest businesses in the United States, with annual sales of over $31 billion.

In recent years, the importance of international management has increased dramatically. The list of U.S. firms doing business in other countries is staggering. ExxonMobil, for example, derives almost 75 percent of its revenues from foreign markets, and Coca-Cola derives more than 80 percent of its sales from foreign markets. Other major U.S. exporters include General Motors, General Electric, Boeing, and Caterpillar. And even numbers like Ford's are deceptive. For example, the auto maker has large subsidiaries based in many European countries whose sales are not included as foreign revenue. Moreover, a number of major firms that do business in the United States have their headquarters in other countries. Firms in this category include the Royal Dutch/Shell Group (the Netherlands), Fiat S.p.A. (Italy), Nestlé S.A. (Switzerland), and Massey Ferguson (Canada). International management is not, however, confined to profit-seeking organizations. Several international sports federations (such as Little League Baseball), branches (embassies) of the federal government, and the Roman Catholic Church are established in most countries as well. In some respects, the military was one of the first multinational organizations. International management is covered in depth in Chapter 5.

Managing in Not-for-Profit Organizations Intangible goals such as education, social services, public protection, and recreation are often the primary aim of not-for-profit organizations. Examples include United Way of America, the U.S. Postal Service, Girl Scouts of the U.S.A., the International Olympic Committee, art galleries, museums, and the Public Broadcasting System (PBS). Although these and similar organizations may not have to be profitable to attract investors, they must still employ sound management practices if they are to survive and work toward their goals.[25] And they must handle money in an efficient and effective way. If the United Way were to begin to spend large portions of its contributions on administration, contributors would lose confidence in the organization and make their charitable donations elsewhere.

The management of government organizations and agencies is often regarded as a separate specialty: public administration. Government organizations include the Federal Trade Commission (FTC), the Environmental Protection Agency (EPA), the National Science Foundation, all branches of the military, state highway departments, and federal and state prison systems. Tax dollars support government organizations, so politicians and citizens' groups are acutely sensitive to the need for efficiency and effectiveness.

Public and private schools, colleges, and universities all stand to benefit from the efficient use of resources. Taxpayer "revolts" in states such as California and Massachusetts have drastically cut back the tax money available for education, forcing administrators to make tough decisions about allocating remaining resources.

Managing health-care facilities such as clinics, hospitals, and HMOs (health maintenance organizations) is now considered a separate field of management. Here, as in other organizations, scarce resources dictate an efficient and effective approach. In recent years many universities have established health-care administration programs to train managers as specialists in this field.

Good management is also required in nontraditional settings to meet established goals. To one extent or another, management is practiced in religious organizations, terrorist groups, fraternities and sororities, organized crime, street gangs, neighborhood associations, and households. In short, as we note at the beginning of this chapter, management and managers have a profound influence on all of us.

concept CHECK

Is management an art or a science?

Identify four very different kinds of organizations and describe the role of management in their success.

The New Workplace

One of the most interesting characteristics of managerial work is the rapidly changing workplace. Indeed, this new workplace is accompanied by dramatic challenges and amazing opportunities. Among other things, workplace changes relate in part to both workforce reductions and expansion. But even more central to the idea of workplace change are such developments as workforce diversity and characteristics of new workers themselves.

The management of diversity is an important organizational challenge today. The term *diversity* refers to differences among people. Diversity may be reflected along numerous dimensions, but most managers tend to focus on age, gender, ethnicity, and physical abilities and disabilities.[26] For example, the average age of workers in the United States is gradually increasing. This is partly because of declining birthrates and partly because people are living and working longer. Many organizations are finding retirees to be excellent part-time and temporary employees. McDonald's has hired hundreds of elderly workers in recent years. Apple Computer has used many retired workers for temporary assignments and projects. By hiring retirees, the organization gets the expertise of skilled workers, and the individuals get extra income and an opportunity to continue to use their skills.

An increasing number of women have also entered the American workforce. In 1950 only about one third of American women worked outside their homes; today, almost two-thirds work part time or full time outside the home. Many occupations traditionally dominated by women—nursing, teaching, secretarial work—continue to be popular with females. But women have also moved increasingly into occupations previously dominated by males, becoming lawyers, physicians, and executives. Further, many blue-collar jobs are increasingly being sought by women; and women are increasingly moving into positions of both business ownership as entrepreneurs and senior executives in major corporations. Similarly, more and more men are also entering occupations previously dominated by women. For example, there are more male office assistants and nurses today than ever before.

The ethnic composition of the workplace is also changing. One obvious change has been the increasing number of Hispanics and African Americans entering the workplace.[27] Further, many of these individuals now hold executive positions. In addition, there has been a dramatic influx of immigrant workers in the last few years. Immigrants and refugees from Central America and Asia have entered the American workforce in record numbers.

The passage of the Americans with Disabilities Act also brought to the forefront the importance of providing equal employment opportunities for people with various disabilities. As a result, organizations are attracting qualified employees from groups that they may perhaps once have ignored. Clearly, then, along just about any dimension imaginable, the workforce is becoming more diverse. Workforce diversity enhances the effectiveness of most organizations, but it also provides special challenges for managers. We return to these issues in Chapter 6.

Aside from its demographic composition, the workforce today is changing in other ways. During the 1980s, many people entering the workforce were what came to be called "yuppies," slang for "young urban professionals." These individuals were highly motivated by career prospects, sought employment with big corporations, and were often willing to make work their highest priority. Thus they put in long hours and could be expected to remain loyal to the company, regardless of what happened.

But younger people entering the workforce in the 1990s were frequently quite different from their predecessors. Sometimes called "Generation X-ers," these workers were less devoted to long-term career prospects and less willing to adapt to a corporate mind-set that stresses conformity and uniformity. Instead, they often sought work in smaller, more entrepreneurial firms that allowed flexibility and individuality. They also placed a premium on lifestyle considerations, often putting location high on their list of priorities when selecting an employer. And, of course, new workers entering the workforce in the 2000s are likely to be different still from both their counterparts in the 1980 and those in the 1990s.

Thus managers are increasingly faced with the challenge of first creating an environment that will be attractive to today's worker. Second, managers must address the challenge of providing new and different incentives to keep people motivated and interested in their work. Finally, they must build enough flexibility into the organization to accommodate an ever-changing set of lifestyles and preferences.

Managers must also be prepared to address organization change.[28] This has always been a concern, but the rapid, constant environmental change faced by businesses today has made change management even more critical. Simply put, an organization that fails to monitor its environment and to change to keep pace with that environment is doomed to failure. But more and more managers are seeing change as an opportunity, not a cause for alarm. Indeed, some managers think that, if things get too calm in an organization and people start to become complacent, managers should shake things up to get everyone energized.

New technologies have greatly changed the way managers work. Jennifer Castagnier, for instance, is responsible for managing patient care in one unit of the Indiana Heart Hospital. She can use a bedside workstation to check a patient's medical history, monitor vital signs, order tests and medications, and issue discharge instructions. Work that once required hours of time and pages of paperwork can now be done in minutes and be handled electronically.

New technology, especially as it relates to information, also poses an increasingly important challenge for managers. Specific forms of technology, such as cellular telephones, personal digital assistants, and wireless communication networks, have made it easier than ever for managers to communicate with one another. At the same time, these innovations have increased the work pace for managers, cut into their time for thoughtful contemplation of decisions, and increased the amount of information they must process.

A final element of the new workplace we will note here is the complex array of new ways of organizing that managers can consider. Many organizations strive for greater flexibility and the ability to respond more quickly to their environment by adopting flatter structures. These flat structures are characterized by few levels of management; broad, wide spans of management; and fewer rules and regulations. The increased use of work teams also goes hand in hand with this new approach to organizing. We will examine these new ways of organizing in Chapters 12 and 19.

concept CHECK

What are the central components that characterize the new workplace?

What are some even newer issues that managers today confront?

Summary of Key Points

ACE self-test

business.college.hmco.com/students

Management is a set of activities (including planning and decision making, organizing, leading, and controlling) directed at an organization's resources (human, financial, physical, and information) with the aim of achieving organizational goals in an efficient and effective manner. A manager is someone whose primary responsibility is to carry out the management process within an organization.

The basic activities that comprise the management process are planning and decision making (determining courses of action), organizing (coordinating activities and resources), leading (motivating and managing people), and controlling (monitoring and evaluating activities). These activities are not performed on a systematic and predictable schedule.

Managers can be differentiated by level and by area. By level, we can identify top, middle, and first-line managers. Kinds of managers by area include marketing, financial, operations, human resource, administrative, and specialized managers.

Managers have ten basic roles to play: three interpersonal roles (figurehead, leader, and liaison), three informational roles (monitor, disseminator, and spokesperson), and four decisional roles (entrepreneur, disturbance handler, resource allocator, and negotiator). Effective managers also tend to have technical, interpersonal, conceptual, diagnostic, communication, decision-making, and time-management skills. The manager's job is characterized by varied, unpredictable, nonroutine, and fragmented work, often performed at a relentless pace. Managers also receive a variety of intrinsic and extrinsic rewards.

The effective practice of management requires a synthesis of science and art; that is, a blend of rational objectivity and intuitive insight. Most managers attain their skills and positions through a combination of education and experience.

Management processes are applicable in a wide variety of settings, including profit-seeking organizations (large, small, and start-up businesses and international businesses) and not-for-profit organizations (government organizations, educational organizations, health-care facilities, and nontraditional organizations).

The new workplace is characterized by workforce expansion and reduction. Diversity is also a central component, as is the new worker. Organization change is also more common, as are the effects of information technology and new ways of organizing.

Discussion Questions

Questions for Review

1. Contrast efficiency and effectiveness. Give an example of a time when an organization was effective but not efficient, efficient but not effective, both efficient and effective, and neither efficient nor effective.
2. What are the four basic activities that comprise the management process? How are they related to one another?
3. Briefly describe the ten managerial roles described by Mintzberg. Give an example of each.

4. Describe a typical manager's day. What are some of the expected consequences of this type of daily experience?

Questions for Analysis

5. Recall a recent group project or task in which you have participated. Explain how members of the group displayed each of the managerial skills.
6. The text notes that management is both a science and an art. Recall an interaction you have had with a superior (manager, teacher, group leader). In that interaction, how did the superior use science? If he or she did not use science, what could have been done to use science? In that interaction, how did the superior use art? If he or she did not use art, what could have been done to use art?
7. Using the Internet, go to the website of at least five large corporations and locate a biography of each CEO. What formal management education do these leaders have? In your opinion, what is the appropriate amount of formal education needed to be a corporate CEO? Why?

Questions for Application

8. Interview a manager from a local organization. Learn about how he or she performs each of the functions of management, the roles he or she plays, and the skills necessary to do the job.
9. Find an organization chart. You can find them in the library or by searching online. Locate top, middle, and first-line managers on the chart. What are some of the job titles held by persons at each level?
10. Watch a movie that involves an organization of some type. *Harry Potter, Training Day, Star Wars,* and *Minority Report* would all be good choices. Identify as many management activities, skills, and roles as you can.

BUILDING EFFECTIVE time-management SKILLS

business.college.hmco.com/students

Exercise Overview

Time-management skills refer to the manager's ability to prioritize work, to work efficiently, and to delegate appropriately. This exercise allows you to assess your current time-management skills and to gain suggestions for how you can improve in this area.

Exercise Background

As described in this chapter, effective managers must be prepared to switch between the four basic activities in the management process. Managers must be able to fulfill a number of different roles in their organizations, and they must employ many different managerial skills as they do so. In addition, managers' schedules are busy and full of complex, unpredictable, and brief tasks, requiring managers to "switch gears" frequently throughout a workday.

Franklin Covey, management consultant and author of *The 7 Habits of Highly Effective People*, has developed a way of prioritizing tasks. He characterizes tasks using the terms *urgent* and *critical.* "Urgent" refers to tasks that must be done right away, such as tasks that have an approaching deadline. Critical tasks are those that have a high importance; that is, tasks that will have a big impact on critical areas of one's life. Thus, according to Covey, tasks fall into one of four quadrants: urgent, critical, urgent and critical, or not urgent and not critical.

Covey claims that most people spend too much time on tasks that are urgent, when they should instead be focused on tasks that are important. He asserts that workers who concentrate on urgent tasks meet their deadlines, but they may neglect critical areas such as long-term planning, and they may also neglect the critical areas of their personal lives. Effective managers can balance the demands of the urgent tasks with an understanding of the need to spend an appropriate amount of time on those that are critical.

Exercise Task

1. Visit the website of Franklin Covey, at www.franklincovey.com. Click on the tab marked "Effectiveness Zone," then select "assessment sector." Take the Urgency Analysis Profile. This short online survey will require you to answer several questions and will take about ten minutes.
2. Look at your profile. Explore the information available there, including the assessment of your current use of time and the suggestions for how you can improve your time management.
3. Do you agree with Covey's ideas about critical and urgent tasks? Explain your answer.
4. What is one thing that you can do today to make better use of your time? Try it and see if your time management improves.

BUILDING EFFECTIVE interpersonal and communication SKILLS

Exercise Overview

Interpersonal skills refer to the manager's ability to communicate with, understand, and motivate individuals and groups, whereas communication skills require the manager to effectively convey ideas and information to others and to effectively receive ideas and information from others. This exercise allows you to practice these skills, while investigating the validity of Mintzberg's results regarding managerial roles.

Exercise Background

Many people have studied and written about the job of general management. Almost all of these theories were developed by scholars of management; few of these scholars have studied real managers in action. Thus we do not know much about what managers really do.

Henry Mintzberg decided that the best way to understand what managers do was to observe them directly. He got permission from five corporate CEOs to study their work habits. He followed them around, recording everything they did. He timed their meetings and phone calls, counted their mail, copied memos and minutes of meetings, went to lunch with them, commuted to and from work, and lived with them. From his detailed notes, he was able to piece together a picture of a general manager's working life. He reported his results in his classic management book *The Nature of Managerial Work*.

Mintzberg's managers spent four weekday evenings working at the office, entertaining for business, or at their home office. They handled a tremendous number of short tasks, resulting in a very fragmented day. The executives engaged in between 237 and 1,073 incidents each day, with an average of 650 incidents. (Even if we assume ten-hour days, this can be over 100 incidents per hour, or more than 1 incident per minute!) They were often interrupted, and they had no breaks at all during the day, working from the moment they arrived until late in the evening. Their calendars ruled their lives.

They had almost no time to notice routine information. They had, on an average day, thirty-six pieces of mail requiring their attention, had five extended phone conversations, and attended eight scheduled and even more unscheduled meetings. On average, they received ten routine reports per week, but responded to only one. They received twenty periodicals per week, but spent less than thirty minutes reading periodicals. Between 50 percent and 90 percent of their time was spent talking or listening (mostly listening) in face-to-face conversations. They were most actively involved in the most difficult and pressing problems of the firm. These problems required many different skills and abilities to resolve.

As a result of living this challenging life, we expect corporate CEOs to have little time or energy for thoughtful or detailed reflection, and to experience a great deal of stress. The evidence shows, for example, that business executives have the second highest rate of stress-related illnesses of any occupational group in the United States. Based on Mintzberg's research, successful managers must be motivated to tackle a job characterized by long hours, stress, and constant attention to difficult situations.

Exercise Task

1. Identify someone who is a manager. This could be your boss, a friend, a coworker, your roommate, parent, or relative—anyone who is supervising others and overseeing work. The work can be either paid or volunteer work.
2. If possible, arrange to shadow the manager for an hour. Go to their workplace and follow them as they perform their duties. Take notes. Specifically note how many people they communicate with and the nature of the communications, how many tasks they perform, and if they experience any interruptions. If it is not possible to shadow the manager, interview him or her instead and ask about these areas.
3. Compare your results to the results given in the Exercise Background above. What is similar and what is different?
4. How do you explain any differences you found?

BUILDING EFFECTIVE conceptual SKILLS

Exercise Overview

Conceptual skills form the manager's ability to think in the abstract. This exercise will help you extend your conceptual skills by identifying potential generalizations of management functions, roles, and skills for different kinds of organizations.

Exercise Background

This introductory chapter discusses four basic management functions, ten common managerial roles, and seven vital management skills. The chapter also stresses that management is applicable across many different kinds of organizations.

Identify one large business, one small business, one educational organization, one health-care organization, and one government organization. These might be organizations about which you have some personal knowledge or simply organizations that you recognize. Now imagine yourself in the position of a top manager in each organization.

Write the names of the five organizations across the top of a sheet of paper. List the four functions, ten roles, and seven skills down the left side of the paper. Now think of a situation, problem, or opportunity relevant to the intersection of each row and column on the paper. For example, how might a manager in a government organization engage in planning and need diagnostic skills? Similarly, how might a manager in a small business carry out the organizing function and play the role of negotiator?

Exercise Task

1. What meaningful similarities can you identify across the five columns?
2. What meaningful differences can you identify across the five columns?
3. Based on your assessment of the similarities and differences as identified in Exercise Tasks 1 and 2, how easy or difficult do you think it might be for a manager to move from one type of organization to another?

CHAPTER CLOSING case

SOUTHWEST STILL FLIES HIGH

"We aren't in the 'airline business'; we are in the 'Customer Service business,' and we just happen to fly airplanes."

– Colleen Barrett, President and COO, Southwest Airlines*

Would you like the opportunity to work for a company that just lost its charismatic founder, replacing him with the company's lawyer and the CEO's one-time secretary? Would you jump at the chance to get a job with a firm that pays one-half to two-thirds as much as its rivals and doubles the workload, then asks employees to clean up their workplace, to avoid hiring a cleaning service? Would you be thrilled to land a position in a business where there is no pension plan, just a stock ownership program, and where the stock has declined 24 percent?

As it turns out, yes, you would, if you were one of the 200,000 people who submitted resumes for just 6,000 jobs at Southwest Airlines last year. Positions with the firm are so coveted that Southwest can be more selective than Harvard.

Following the retirement in 2001 of founder and long-time CEO Herb Kelleher, long-time corporate counsel Jim Parker assumed the CEO role and secretary-turned-human-resources-manager Colleen Barrett became president and chief operating officer (COO). These two leaders have done an exemplary job of carrying on the carrier's tradition of success.

From the beginning, Southwest did not adopt the hub-and-spoke system, preferring a short-haul, point-to-point schedule instead. This keeps costs low. The carrier operates out of smaller, less expensive airports in many major markets, such as its use of Long Island's Islip rather than New York's LaGuardia or Kennedy. The company flies only one type of jet, the Boeing 737, reducing its expenses in every area from purchasing to maintenance to training. Due to these early, smart decisions, Southwest "has long-term, systematic advantages the other carriers can likely never match," says pilot and industry consultant Vaughn Cordle.

Southwest obtains its most significant advantages in human resources. Although Southwest is highly unionized, it has never experienced a labor strike. The firm's management sits down personally to negotiate every union contract. "The biggest complaint in the industry is that management doesn't listen to employees," says Southwest pilot Brad Bartholomew. "But you can't say that at Southwest. The top guy is in the room." Among the benefits that Southwest employees enjoy are extensive training, a no-layoffs policy, and generous profit sharing and stock ownership. Even though there are few profits to share just now and stock price is down, employees are optimistic that this situation will not last. At a time when other airlines are reducing wages, Southwest is giving pay hikes.

Compare Southwest's position to that of other airlines. U.S. Airways filed for Chapter 11 bankruptcy and seems likely to go out of business. United Airlines' managers claim that they, too, are headed for bankruptcy. Further, in the wake of September 11, the major carriers laid off 100,000 employees, most of whom have not been replaced. Layoffs and pay cuts have contributed to low morale, which leads to low productivity, further hurting the traditional carriers. Analysts estimate that the major carriers would need to collectively reduce expenses by $18.6 billion, about 29 percent, to match Southwest's low-cost performance. Consultant Ron Kuhlmann says, "There's no easy way to [cut costs]. The problem is that major carriers are preserving their own model rather than paying attention to what customers are willing to pay for." Consultant Michael Boyd says, "I'm very concerned over whether the airline industry can survive." "JetBlue may be the only [airline] out there that can compete head-to-head with Southwest," says Daryl Jenkins, director of the Aviation Institute.

Every airline has adopted some of Southwest's pioneering concepts, such as eliminating meals. "Stepping up to the new reality is a healthy thing," says Gordon Bethune, CEO of Continental Airlines. "Only those companies that change with it will survive." However, to stay on top, Southwest must learn to compete with firms that are imitating its strategies. And it will have to grow, yet maintain the personalized service and customer loyalty associated with small size. Barrett sums up the carrier's culture, saying, "We aren't in the 'airline business'; we are in the 'Customer Service business,' and we just happen to fly airplanes."

The prevailing, optimistic view is pithily summed up by Michael O'Leary, CEO of Ryanair, a European-based carrier following Southwest's no-frills model. Evaluating the traditional carriers, O'Leary asserts, "They're basket cases. They're incredibly high-cost, very ineffective. . . . These are stupid businesses for the amount of capital tied up in them. They never make any money. . . . I think they'll limp along from crisis to crisis. . . . [Air fares will continue to] decline for another 20, 30, 40 years." When O'Leary is asked, "What about Southwest?" he replies, "If I were Southwest, I wouldn't be worried."

Case Questions

1. Name at least two things that Southwest is doing efficiently. Name at least two things that Southwest is doing effectively. In what ways do efficiency and effectiveness support each other at Southwest? In what ways do they contradict each other?
2. Based on information in the case, describe the managerial skills that Colleen Barrett and Jim Parker use in their jobs at Southwest.
3. Neither Colleen Barrett nor Jim Parker has a formal education in management. Explain then how they can be effective managers. Would formal education help them to be better managers? Why or why not?

Case References

Amy Tsao, "Can Airlines Bring Costs Down to Earth?" *BusinessWeek*, October 23, 2002, www.businessweek.com on November 22, 2002; Amy Tsao, "Full-Service Airlines Are 'Basket Cases'," *BusinessWeek*, September 12, 2002, www.businessweek.com on November 22, 2002; Amy Tsao, "The Wrong Time to Jump on Southwest?" *BusinessWeek*, August 22, 2002, www.businessweek.com on November 22, 2002; Colleen Barrett, "The Southwest Difference," Southwest Airlines website, www.iflyswa.com on November 22, 2002 (*quote); Peter Coy, "The Airlines: Caught Between a Hub and a Hard Place," *BusinessWeek*, August 5, 2002, www.businessweek.com on November 22, 2002; Sally B. Donnelly, "One Airline's Magic," *Time*, pp. 45–47; Wendy Zellner, "It's Showtime for the Airlines," *BusinessWeek*, pp. 36–37.

Chapter Notes

1. "50 Best Companies for Minorities," *Fortune*, July 7, 2003, pp. 103–120. Alynda Wheat, "The Anatomy of a Great Workplace," *Fortune*, February 4, 2002, www.fortune.com on November 21, 2002; Christopher Palmeri, "Travel Makes a Swift Trip Back," *BusinessWeek*, May 27, 2002, p. 46; Eryn Brown, "Heartbreak Hotel?" *Fortune*, November 26, 2001, www.fortune.com on November 21, 2002; "Marriott International Named One of the 100 Best Companies for Working Mothers," Marriott website, www.marriottnewsroom.com on November 21, 2002; "Marriott Names Four to Top Positions," Marriott website, www.marriottnewsroom.com on November 21, 2002; Michelle Conlin, "Going Sideways on the Corporate Ladder," *BusinessWeek*, September 30, 2002, p. 39; Richard Heller, "Fight to Quality," *Forbes*, October 25, 2002, (quote) biz.yahoo.com on November 21, 2002.
2. Fred Luthans, "Successful vs. Effective Real Managers," *Academy of Management Executive*, May 1988, pp. 127–132. See also "The Best Performers," *The Business Week 50*, Spring 2003 Special Issue, pp. 34–42.
3. See "The Best (& Worst) Managers of the Year," *BusinessWeek*, January 13, 2003, pp. 58–92.
4. Sumantsa Ghospal and Christopher A. Bartlett, "Changing the Role of Top Management: Beyond Structure to Process," *Harvard Business Review*, January–February 1995, pp. 86–96.
5. Patricia Sellers, "These Women Rule," *Fortune*, October 25, 1999, pp. 94–96; Patricia Sellers, "True Grit," *Fortune*, October 14, 2002, pp. 101–112.
6. See "Executive Pay," *BusinessWeek*, April 15, 2002, pp. 80–100. See also Jim Collins, "The Ten Greatest CEO's of All Times," *Fortune*, July 21, 2003, pp. 54–68.
7. Rosemary Stewart, "Middle Managers: Their Jobs and Behaviors," in Jay W. Lorsch (ed.), *Handbook of Organizational Behavior* (Englewood Cliffs, N.J.: Prentice-Hall, 1987), pp. 385–391.
8. John P. Kotter, "What Effective General Managers Really Do," *Harvard Business Review*, March–April 1999, pp. 145–155.
9. Mintzberg, *The Nature of Managerial Work*.
10. See Robert L. Katz, "The Skills of an Effective Administrator," *Harvard Business Review*, September–October 1974, pp. 90–102 for a classic discussion of several of these skills.
11. "Ritz-Carlton Opens with Training Tradition," *USA Today*, June 29, 2000, p. 3B.
12. "New P&G Chief Is Tough, Praised for People Skills," *Wall Street Journal*, June 6, 2000, pp. B1, B4.

13. See "I'm Late, I'm Late, I'm Late," *USA Today*, November 26, 2002, pp. 1B, 2B.
14. For a recent discussion of the importance of time-management skills, see David Barry, Catherine Durnell Cramton, and Stephen J. Carroll, "Navigating the Garbage Can: How Agendas Help Managers Cope with Job Realities," *Academy of Management Executive*, May 1997, pp. 26–42.
15. "Taming the Out-of-Control In-Box," *Wall Street Journal*, February 4, 2000, pp. B1, B4.
16. See Michael A. Hitt, "Transformation of Management for the New Millennium," *Organizational Dynamics*, Winter 2000, pp. 7–17.
17. James H. Davis, F. David Schoorman, and Lex Donaldson, "Toward a Stewardship Theory of Management," *Academy of Management Review*, January 1997, pp. 20–47.
18. Gary Hamel and C. K. Prahalad, "Competing for the Future," *Harvard Business Review*, July–August 1994, pp. 122–128.
19. James Waldroop and Timothy Butler, "The Executive as Coach," *Harvard Business Review*, November–December 1996, pp. 111–117.
20. Walter Kiechel III, "A Manager's Career in the New Economy," *Fortune*, April 4, 1994, pp. 68–72.
21. "The Executive MBA Your Way," *BusinessWeek*, October 18, 1999, pp. 88–92.
22. "Turning B-School into E-School," *BusinessWeek*, October 18, 1999, p. 94.
23. See "Reunion at P&G University," *Wall Street Journal*, June 7, 2000, pp. B1, B4 for a discussion of Procter & Gamble's training programs.
24. For an interesting discussion of these issues see Rakesh Khurana, "The Curse of the Superstar CEO," *Harvard Business Review*, September 2002, pp. 60–70.
25. James L. Perry and Hal G. Rainey, "The Public-Private Distinction in Organization Theory: A Critique and Research Strategy," *Academy of Management Review*, April 1988, pp. 182–201; see also Ran Lachman, "Public and Private Sector Differences: CEOs' Perceptions of Their Role Environments," *Academy of Management Journal*, September 1985, pp. 671–680.
26. Patricia L. Nemetz and Sandra L. Christensen, "The Challenge of Cultural Diversity: Harnessing a Diversity of Views to Understand Multiculturalism," *Academy of Management Review*, 1996, vol. 21, no. 2, pp. 434–462; Frances J. Milliken and Luis L. Martins, "Searching for Common Threads: Understanding the Multiple Effects of Diversity in Organizational Groups," *Academy of Management Review*, 1996, vol. 21, no. 2, pp. 402–433.
27. Geoffrey Colvin, "The 50 Best Companies for Asians, Blacks, and Hispanics," *Fortune*, July 19, 1999, pp. 52–57.
28. Craig L. Pearce and Charles P. Osmond, "Metaphors for Change: The ALPS Model of Change Management," *Organizational Dynamics*, Winter 1996, pp. 23–35.

2

Traditional and Contemporary Issues and Challenges

CHAPTER OUTLINE

The Role of Theory and History in Management

The Importance of Theory and History

Precursors to Management Theory

The Classical Management Perspective

Scientific Management

Administrative Management

The Classical Management Perspective Today

The Behavioral Management Perspective

The Hawthorne Studies

The Human Relations Movement

The Emergence of Organizational Behavior

The Behavioral Management Perspective Today

The Quantitative Management Perspective

Management Science

Operations Management

The Quantitative Management Perspective Today

Integrating Perspectives for Managers

The Systems Perspective

The Contingency Perspective

An Integrating Framework

Contemporary Management Issues and Challenges

Contemporary Applied Perspectives

Contemporary Management Challenges

LEARNING OBJECTIVES

After studying this chapter, you should be able to:

1 ***Justify the importance of history and theory to management and discuss precursors to modern management theory.***

OPENING INCIDENT

Managers come and go. Management theories come and go. But some managers, eschewing the trendy advice of management gurus, insist that a focus on the fundamentals is the most important ingredient for success. One such manager is Jim Sinegal, co-founder, CEO, and president of Costco Wholesale Corporation. Sinegal has led the giant retailer for nineteen years with a single-minded focus on selling goods at the lowest possible price. *BusinessWeek* writer Nanette Byrnes says about Sinegal, "[He] defies the management ideal of the 1990s . . . [he is] not a change agent."

Even if he is not "the management ideal" or "a change agent," Sinegal is not afraid to buck conventional wisdom if it suits his low-cost strategy. One of the CEO's rules is to have low markup on Costco's products. Senior vice president John McKay remembers a time when the firm was doing a good business in Calvin Klein jeans at $29.99 and then got a better deal, allowing them to sell at $22.99. "In theory, we could have kept selling them and pocketed the seven bucks and had a great quarter," says McKay. "But we didn't. The members count on us to deliver the best deal. Jim doesn't cheat on that." Some Wall Street analysts say that the firm could raise

2	3	4	5	6
Summarize and evaluate the classical perspective on management, including scientific and administrative management, and note its relevance to contemporary managers.	***Summarize and evaluate the behavioral perspective on management, including the Hawthorne studies, human relations movement, and organizational behavior, and note its relevance to contemporary managers.***	***Summarize and evaluate the quantitative perspective on management, including management science and operations management, and note its relevance to contemporary managers.***	***Discuss the systems and contingency approaches to management and explain their potential for integrating the other areas of management.***	***Identify and describe contemporary management issues and challenges.***

"James Sinegal defies the management ideal of the 1990s."

—Nanette Byrnes, BusinessWeek writer

profits by raising prices. Bill Dreher, analyst with W.R. Hambrecht & Company, says, "We believe [it] places club member interests too far ahead of shareholder interests." Sinegal ignores the critics—he maintains a customer focus.

To cut costs, Sinegal answers his own phone. His furniture is twenty years old, and the rest of his Issaquah, Washington, headquarters is equally Spartan. He was mentioned by *BusinessWeek* as one of the top five U.S. executives whose company did the best relative to his fairly modest pay. But Sinegal is no blind slave to low prices at any cost to the organization. For example, some have suggested that Costco could cut its wages, the highest in the industry, but Sinegal disagrees. "Paying good wages is not in opposition to good productivity," he claims. "If you hire good people, give them good jobs, and pay them good wages, generally something good is going to happen." And, even though the firm is known for its bulk and low-cost items, Sinegal's strategy is to stock at least 25 percent of what he calls "treasure-hunt" items, such as Tiffany jewelry, Dom Perignon champagne, and Waterford crystal.

Thus far, Sinegal's single-minded adherence to a strategy has paid off. Costco is the only firm to successfully challenge Wal-Mart and has a larger share of the discount warehouse industry. The sales of both stores improve when a Wal-Mart opens near a Costco. When Wal-Mart recently announced a move into Canada, its stock price rose 58 cents per share, but Costco's rose 62 cents. Costco also continues to expand. The firm has 40 million members worldwide and 407 warehouses in 36 states, Canada, the United Kingdom, Mexico, Japan, Korea, and Taiwan. And there are rumors that the firm is looking for suitable locations in Europe, including Spain, Poland, and Germany.

Sinegal has been among the most successful leaders in building a highly focused corporate culture. That culture has led the company in a number of unusual directions, from its no-advertising policy, to its \$1.50 in-store daily meal special, to its frugal limit of 4,000 items per store. Every single item gets scrutinized. When Gatorade was selling 24-packs for \$16.99, Costco developed a store brand that sold for \$9.99, inspiring Gatorade to slash prices by \$2.00. When Nike refused to discount its shoes for Costco, the firm hired Nike's subcontractors to produce Costco's Court Classics brand, priced at \$13.99. Even large manufacturers give in to Costco's price pressure—Levi's 550s sell for \$21.99, less than the typical \$48.00. The company is moving into innovative areas, too, selling cruise vacations, Internet access, and online investment services.

Costco helps keep prices down by selling bulk goods in spartan facilities.

Sinegal has a passionate adherence to his values and prefers the spotlight to be on his company, not on himself. He personifies the unassuming "good" CEO, as profiled in author Jim Collins's book *Good to Great.* About exceptional CEOs Collins says, "They looked a little like tofu. They were clearly part of the meal. They seemed to be integral to the nutrition of the meal. But they did not stand out. Everything else was the spice."[1]

One lesson managers can learn from Jim Sinegal is that they need to have a keen understanding of what makes their business work. As one part of this understanding, it is critically important that all managers focus on today's competitive environment and how that environment will change tomorrow. But it is also important that they use the past as context. Managers in a wide array of different kinds of organizations can learn both effective and less effective practices and strategies by understanding what managers have done in the past. Indeed, history plays an important role in many businesses today, and more and more managers are recognizing that the lessons of the past are an important ingredient in future success.

This chapter provides an overview of traditional management thought, so that you, too, can better appreciate the importance of history in today's business world. We set the stage by establishing the historical context of management. We then discuss the three traditional management perspectives—classical, behavioral, and quantitative. Next we describe the systems and contingency perspectives as approaches that help integrate the three traditional perspectives. Finally, we introduce and discuss a variety of contemporary management issues and challenges.

The Role of Theory and History in Management

Practicing managers are increasingly seeing the value of theory and history in their work. In this section, we first explain why theory and history are important and then identify important precursors to management theory.

No one knows the origins of Stonehenge, a mysterious circle of huge stones rising from Salisbury Plain in England. But one fact that is known is that whoever built the ancient monument must have relied heavily on a variety of management tools and techniques. For example, the stones were probably cut over 300 miles away, in Wales, and transported to Salisbury Plain. This enormous feat alone would have required careful planning and coordination and the united efforts of hundreds of laborers.

The Importance of Theory and History

Some people question the value of history and theory. Their arguments are usually based on the assumptions that history has no relevance to contemporary society and that theory is abstract and of no practical use. In reality, however, both theory and history are important to all managers today.

Why Theory? A **theory** is simply a conceptual framework for organizing knowledge and providing a blueprint for action.[2] Although some theories seem abstract and irrelevant, others appear very simple and practical. Management theories, used to build organizations and guide them toward their goals, are grounded in reality.[3] Practically any organization that uses assembly lines (such as DaimlerChrysler, Black & Decker, and Fiat) is drawing on what we describe later in this chapter as "scientific management." Many organizations, including Monsanto, Texas Instruments, and Seiko, use the behavioral perspective (also introduced later) to improve employee satisfaction and motivation. And naming a large company that does not use one or more techniques from the quantitative management perspective would be difficult. For example, retailers like Kroger and Target routinely use operations management to determine how many check-out stands they need to have.

theory A conceptual framework for organizing knowledge and providing a blueprint for action

In addition, most managers develop and refine their own theories of how they should run their organization and manage the behavior of their employees. For example, Jim Sinegal believes that paying his Costco employees well but otherwise keeping prices as low as possible are the key ingredients in success for his business. This belief is based essentially on his personal theory of competition in the warehouse retailing industry.

Why History? Awareness and understanding of important historical developments are also important to contemporary managers.[4] Understanding the historical context of management provides a sense of heritage and can help managers avoid the mistakes of others. Most courses in U.S. history devote time to business and economic developments in this country, including the Industrial Revolution, the early labor movement, and the Great Depression, and to such captains of U.S. industry as Cornelius Vanderbilt (railroads), John D. Rockefeller (oil), and Andrew Carnegie (steel). The contributions of those and other industrialists left a profound imprint on contemporary culture.[5]

Many managers are also realizing that they can benefit from a greater understanding of history in general. For example, Ian M. Ross of AT&T's Bell Laboratories cites *The Second World War* by Winston Churchill as a major influence on his approach to leadership. Other books often mentioned by managers for their relevance to today's business problems include such classics as Plato's *Republic*, Homer's *Iliad*, and Machiavelli's *The Prince*.[6] And, in recent years, new business history books are directed more at women managers and the lessons they can learn from the past.[7]

Managers at Wells Fargo clearly recognize the value of history. For example, the company maintains an extensive archival library of its old banking documents and records, and even employs a full-time corporate historian. As part of their orientation and training, new managers at Wells Fargo take courses to become acquainted with the bank's history.[8] Similarly, Shell Oil, Levi Strauss, Ford, Lloyd's of London, Disney, Honda, and Unilever all maintain significant archives about their past and frequently evoke images from that past in their orientation and training programs, advertising campaigns, and other public relations activities.

Precursors to Management Theory

Even though large businesses have been around for only a few hundred years, management has been practiced for thousands of years. By examining management in antiquity and identifying some of the first management pioneers, we set the stage for a more detailed look at the emergence of management theory and practice over the last hundred years.

Management in Antiquity The practice of management can be traced back thousands of years. The Egyptians used the management functions of planning, organizing, and controlling when they constructed the pyramids. Alexander the Great employed a staff organization to coordinate activities during his military campaigns. The Roman Empire developed a well-defined organizational structure that greatly facilitated communication and control. Socrates discussed management practices and concepts in 400 B.C., Plato described job specialization in 350 B.C., and Alfarabi listed several leadership traits in A.D. 900.[9] Figure 2.1 is a simple time line showing a few of the most important management breakthroughs and practices over the last 4,000 years.

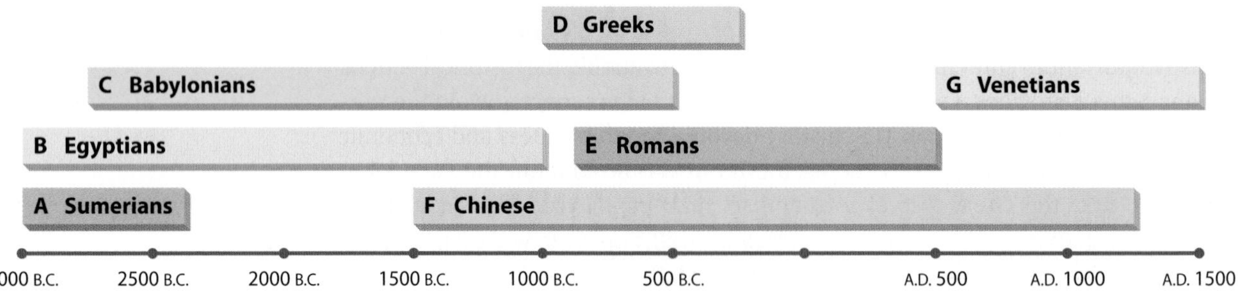

A Used written rules and regulations for governance

B Used management practices to construct pyramids

C Used extensive set of laws and policies for governance

D Used different governing systems for cities and state

E Used organized structure for communication and control

F Used extensive organization structure for government agencies and the arts

G Used organization design and planning concepts to control the seas

FIGURE 2.1

Management in Antiquity

Management has been practiced for thousands of years. For example, the ancient Babylonians used management in governing their empire, and the ancient Romans used management to facilitate communication and control throughout their far-flung territories. The Egyptians used planning and controlling techniques in the construction of their pyramids.

Early Management Pioneers In spite of this history, however, management per se was not given serious attention for several centuries. Indeed, the study of management did not begin until the nineteenth century. Robert Owen (1771–1858), a British industrialist and reformer, was one of the first managers to recognize the importance of an organization's human resources. Until his era, factory workers were generally viewed in much the same way that machinery and equipment were. A factory owner himself, Owen believed that workers deserved respect and dignity. He implemented better working conditions, a higher minimum working age for children, meals for employees, and reduced work hours. He assumed that giving more attention to workers would pay off in increased output.

Whereas Owen was interested primarily in employee welfare, Charles Babbage (1792–1871), an English mathematician, focused his attention on efficiencies of production. His primary contribution was his book *On the Economy of Machinery and Manufactures.*[10] Babbage placed great faith in the division of labor and advocated the application of mathematics to such problems as the efficient use of facilities and materials. In a sense, his work was a forerunner to both the classical and the quantitative management perspectives. Nor did he overlook the human element. He understood that a harmonious relationship between management and labor could serve to benefit both, and he favored such devices as profit-sharing plans. In many ways, Babbage was an originator of modern management theory and practice.

concept CHECK

Why are theory and history each important to managers?

Identify a key historical figure who interests you and then describe that person's contributions from a managerial or an organizational perspective.

The Classical Management Perspective

At the dawn of the twentieth century, the preliminary ideas and writings of these and other managers and theorists converged with the emergence and evolution of large-scale businesses and management practices to create interest and focus attention on how businesses should be operated. The first important ideas to emerge are now called the **classical management perspective**. This perspective actually includes two different viewpoints: scientific management and administrative management.

classical management perspective Consists of two distinct branches—scientific management and administrative management

Scientific Management

Productivity emerged as a serious business problem during the first few years of this century. Business was expanding and capital was readily available, but labor was in short supply. Hence, managers began to search for ways to use existing labor more efficiently. In response to this need, experts began to focus on ways to improve the

Frederick W. Taylor was a pioneer in the field of labor efficiency. He introduced numerous innovations in how jobs were designed and how workers were trained to perform them. These innovations resulted in higher-quality products and improved employee morale. Taylor also formulated the basic ideas of scientific management.

scientific management Concerned with improving the performance of individual workers

soldiering Employees' deliberately working at a slow pace

performance of individual workers. Their work led to the development of **scientific management**. Some of the earliest advocates of scientific management included Frederick W. Taylor (1856–1915), Frank Gilbreth (1868–1924), Lillian Gilbreth (1878–1972), Henry Gantt (1861–1919), and Harrington Emerson (1853–1931).[11] Taylor played the dominant role.

One of Taylor's first jobs was as a foreman at the Midvale Steel Company in Philadelphia. It was there that he observed what he called **soldiering**—employees' deliberately working at a pace slower than their capabilities. Taylor studied and timed each element of the steelworkers' jobs. He determined what each worker should be producing, and then he designed the most efficient way of doing each part of the overall task. Next he implemented a piecework pay system. Rather than paying all employees the same wage, he began increasing the pay of each worker who met and exceeded the target level of output set for his or her job.

After Taylor left Midvale, he worked as a consultant for several companies, including Simonds Rolling Machine Company and Bethlehem Steel. At Simonds he studied and redesigned jobs, introduced rest periods to reduce fatigue, and implemented a piecework pay system. The results were higher quality and quantity of output, and improved morale. At Bethlehem Steel, Taylor studied efficient ways of loading and unloading rail cars and applied his conclusions with equally impressive results. During these experiences, he formulated the basic ideas that he called "scientific management." Figure 2.2 illustrates the basic steps Taylor suggested. He believed that managers who followed his guidelines would improve the efficiency of their workers.[12]

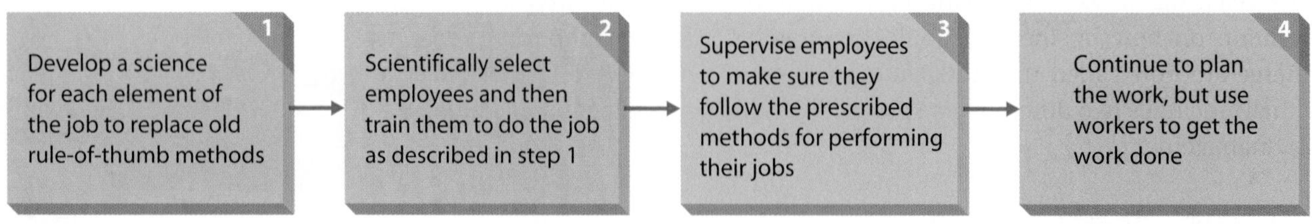

FIGURE 2.2

Steps in Scientific Management

Frederick Taylor developed this system of scientific management, which he believed would lead to a more efficient and productive workforce. Bethlehem Steel was among the first organizations to profit from scientific management and still practices some parts of it today.

Taylor's work had a major impact on U.S. industry. By applying his principles, many organizations achieved major gains in efficiency. Taylor was not without his detractors, however. Labor argued that scientific management was just a device to get more work from each employee and to reduce the total number of workers needed by a firm. There was a congressional investigation into Taylor's ideas, and evidence suggests that he falsified some of his findings.[13] Nevertheless, Taylor's work left a lasting imprint on business.[14]

Frank and Lillian Gilbreth, contemporaries of Taylor, were a husband-and-wife team of industrial engineers. One of Frank Gilbreth's most interesting contributions was to the craft of bricklaying. After studying bricklayers at work, he developed several procedures for doing the job more efficiently. For example, he specified standard materials and techniques, including the positioning of the bricklayer, the bricks, and the mortar at different levels. The results of these changes were a reduction from eighteen separate physical movements to five and an increase in output of about 200 percent. Lillian Gilbreth made equally important contributions to several different areas of work, helped shape the field of industrial psychology, and made substantive contributions to the field of personnel management. Working individually and together, the Gilbreths developed numerous techniques and strategies for eliminating inefficiency. They applied many of their ideas to their family and documented their experiences raising twelve children in the book and movie *Cheaper by the Dozen.* Of course, as illustrated in the cartoon, concerns for efficiency can be carried too far!

Harley L. Schwadron

All organizations, of course, should be concerned about efficiency and productivity. But, as this cartoon illustrates, they might sometimes go a bit too far! Although there are no organizations that are likely to go as far as this one, there are work sites today that forbid talking among employees at work, prohibit any personal telephone calls, and require employees to have permission to take a restroom break. Managers responsible for such practices would most likely argue that employees should be doing nothing but work when they are being paid and that they cannot be trusted to exercise self-control about work, so they must be tightly supervised and strictly controlled.

Henry Gantt, another contributor to scientific management, was an associate of Taylor at Midvale, Simonds, and Bethlehem Steel. Later, working alone, he developed other techniques for improving worker output. One, called the "Gantt chart," is still used today. A Gantt chart is essentially a means of scheduling work and can be generated for each worker or for a complex project as a whole. Gantt also refined Taylor's ideas about piecework pay systems.

Like Taylor, the Gilbreths, and Gantt, Harrington Emerson was also a management consultant. He made quite a stir in 1910 when he appeared before the Interstate Commerce Commission to testify about a rate increase requested by the railroads. As an expert witness, Emerson asserted that the railroads could save $1 million a day by using scientific management. He was also a strong advocate of specialized management roles in organizations, believing that job specialization was as relevant to managerial work as it was to operating jobs.

Administrative Management

Whereas scientific management deals with the jobs of individual employees, **administrative management** focuses on managing the total organization. The

administrative management
Focuses on managing the total organization

primary contributors to administrative management were Henri Fayol (1841–1925), Lyndall Urwick (1891–1983), Max Weber (1864–1920), and Chester Barnard (1886–1961).

Henri Fayol was administrative management's most articulate spokesperson. A French industrialist, Fayol was unknown to U.S. managers and scholars until his most important work, *General and Industrial Management,* was translated into English in 1930.[15] Drawing on his own managerial experience, he attempted to systematize the practice of management to provide guidance and direction to other managers. Fayol also was the first to identify the specific managerial functions of planning, organizing, leading, and controlling. He believed that these functions accurately reflect the core of the management process. Most contemporary management books (including this one) still use this framework, and practicing managers agree that these functions are a critical part of their job.

After a career as a British army officer, Lyndall Urwick became a noted management theorist and consultant. He integrated scientific management with the work of Fayol and other administrative management theorists. He also advanced modern thinking about the functions of planning, organizing, and controlling. Like Fayol, he developed a list of guidelines for improving managerial effectiveness. Urwick is noted not so much for his own contributions as for his synthesis and integration of the work of others.

Although Max Weber lived and worked at the same time as Fayol and Taylor, his contributions were not recognized until some years had passed. Weber was a German sociologist, and his most important work was not translated into English until 1947.[16] Weber's work on bureaucracy laid the foundation for contemporary organization theory, discussed in detail in Chapter 12. The concept of bureaucracy, as we discuss later, is based on a rational set of guidelines for structuring organizations in the most efficient manner.

Chester Barnard, former president of New Jersey Bell Telephone Company, made notable contributions to management in his book *The Functions of the Executive.*[17] The book proposes a major theory about the acceptance of authority. The theory suggests that subordinates weigh the legitimacy of a supervisor's directives and then decide whether to accept them. An order is accepted if the subordinate understands it, is able to comply with it, and views it as appropriate. The importance of Barnard's work is enhanced by his experience as a top manager.

The Classical Management Perspective Today

The contributions and limitations of the classical management perspective are summarized in Table 2.1. The classical perspective is the framework from which later theories evolved, and many of its insights still hold true today. For example, many of the job specialization techniques and scientific methods espoused by Taylor and his contemporaries are still reflected in the way that many industrial jobs are designed today.[18] Moreover, many contemporary organizations still use some of the bureaucratic procedures suggested by Weber. Also, these early theorists were the first to focus attention on management as a meaningful field of study. Several aspects of the classical perspective are also relevant to our later discussions of planning, organizing,

TABLE 2.1

The Classical Management Perspective

General Summary	The classical management perspective had two primary thrusts. Scientific management focused on employees within organizations and on ways to improve their productivity. Noted pioneers of scientific management were Frederick Taylor, Frank and Lillian Gilbreth, Henry Gantt, and Harrington Emerson. Administrative management focused on the total organization and on ways to make it more efficient and effective. Prominent administrative management theorists were Henri Fayol, Lyndall Urwick, Max Weber, and Chester Barnard.
Contributions	Laid the foundation for later developments in management theory. Identified important management processes, functions, and skills that are still recognized today. Focused attention on management as a valid subject of scientific inquiry.
Limitations	More appropriate for stable and simple organizations than for today's dynamic and complex organizations. Often prescribed universal procedures that are not appropriate in some settings. Even though some writers (such as Lillian Gilbreth and Chester Barnard) were concerned with the human element, many viewed employees as tools rather than resources.

and controlling. And recent advances in areas such as business-to-business (B2B) commerce also have efficiency as their primary goal.

The limitations of the classical perspective, however, should not be overlooked. These early writers dealt with stable, simple organizations; many organizations today, in contrast, are changing and complex. They also proposed universal guidelines that we now recognize do not fit every organization. A third limitation of the classical management perspective is that it slighted the role of the individual in organizations. This role was much more fully developed by advocates of the behavioral management perspective.

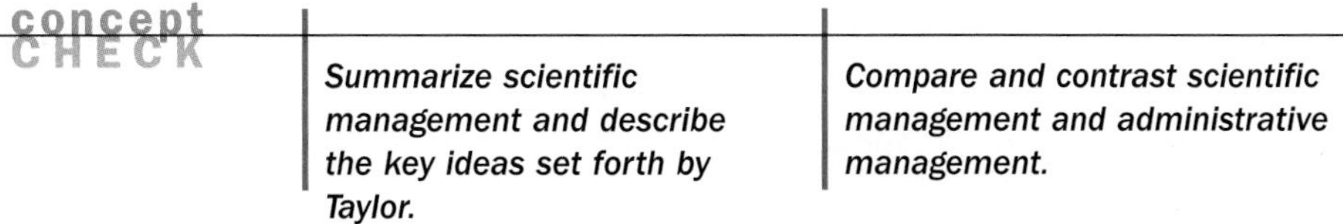

The Behavioral Management Perspective

Early advocates of the classical management perspective viewed organizations and jobs from an essentially mechanistic point of view; that is, they essentially sought to conceptualize organizations as machines and workers as cogs within those machines. Even though many early writers recognized the role of individuals, their focus tended to be on how managers could control and standardize the behavior of

behavioral management perspective Emphasizes individual attitudes and behaviors and group processes

their employees. In contrast, the **behavioral management perspective** placed much more emphasis on individual attitudes and behaviors and on group processes, and recognized the importance of behavioral processes in the workplace.

The behavioral management perspective was stimulated by a number of writers and theoretical movements. One of those movements was *industrial psychology*, the practice of applying psychological concepts to industrial settings. Hugo Munsterberg (1863–1916), a noted German psychologist, is recognized as the father of industrial psychology. He established a psychological laboratory at Harvard in 1892, and his pioneering book *Psychology and Industrial Efficiency* was translated into English in 1913.[19] Munsterberg suggested that psychologists could make valuable contributions to managers in the areas of employee selection and motivation. Industrial psychology is still a major course of study at many colleges and universities. Another early advocate of the behavioral approach to management was Mary Parker Follett (1868–1933).[20] Follett worked during the scientific management era, but quickly came to recognize the human element in the workplace. Indeed, her work clearly anticipated the behavioral management perspective, and she appreciated the need to understand the role of behavior in organizations.

The Hawthorne Studies

Although Munsterberg and Follett made major contributions to the development of the behavioral approach to management, its primary catalyst was a series of studies conducted near Chicago at Western Electric's Hawthorne plant between 1927 and 1932. The research, originally sponsored by General Electric, was conducted by Elton Mayo and his associates.[21] Mayo was a faculty member and consultant at Harvard. The first study involved manipulating illumination for one group of workers and comparing their subsequent productivity with the productivity of another group whose illumination was not changed. Surprisingly, when illumination was increased for the experimental group, productivity went up in both groups. Productivity continued to increase in both groups, even when the lighting for the experimental group was decreased. Not until the lighting was reduced to the level of moonlight did productivity begin to decline (and General Electric withdrew its sponsorship).

The Hawthorne studies were a series of early experiments that focused on behavior in the workplace. In one experiment involving this group of workers, for example, researchers monitored how productivity changed as a result of changes in working conditions. The Hawthorne studies and subsequent experiments lead scientists to the conclusion that the human element is very important in the workplace.

Another experiment established a piecework incentive pay plan for a group of nine men assembling terminal banks for telephone exchanges. Scientific management would have predicted that each man would try to maximize his pay by producing as many units as possible. Mayo and his associates, however, found that the group itself informally established an acceptable level of output for its members. Workers who overproduced were branded "rate busters," and underproducers were labeled "chiselers." To be accepted by the group, workers produced at the accepted level. As they approached this acceptable level of output, workers slacked off to avoid overproducing.

Other studies, including an interview program involving several thousand workers, led Mayo and his associates to conclude that human behavior was much more important in the workplace than had been previously believed. In the lighting experiment, for example, the results were attributed to the fact that both groups received special attention and sympathetic supervision for perhaps the first time. The incentive pay plans did not work because wage incentives were less important to the individual workers than was social acceptance in determining output. In short, individual and social processes played a major role in shaping worker attitudes and behavior.

The Human Relations Movement

human relations movement Argued that workers respond primarily to the social context of the workplace

The **human relations movement**, which grew from the Hawthorne studies and was a popular approach to management for many years, proposed that workers respond primarily to the social context of the workplace, including social conditioning, group norms, and interpersonal dynamics. A basic assumption of the human relations movement was that the manager's concern for workers would lead to increased satisfaction, which would in turn result in improved performance. Two writers who helped advance the human relations movement were Abraham Maslow (1908–1970) and Douglas McGregor (1906–1964).

In 1943 Maslow advanced a theory suggesting that people are motivated by a hierarchy of needs, including monetary incentives and social acceptance.[22] Maslow's hierarchy, perhaps the best-known human relations theory, is described in detail in Chapter 16. Meanwhile, Douglas McGregor's Theory X and Theory Y model best represents the essence of the human relations movement (see Table 2.2).[23] According to McGregor, Theory X and Theory Y reflect two extreme belief sets

TABLE 2.2

Theory X and Theory Y

Douglas McGregor developed Theory X and Theory Y. He argued that Theory X best represented the views of scientific management and Theory Y represented the human relations approach. McGregor believed that Theory Y was the best philosophy for all managers.

Theory X Assumptions	1. People do not like work and try to avoid it. 2. People do not like work, so managers have to control, direct, coerce, and threaten employees to get them to work toward organizational goals. 3. People prefer to be directed, to avoid responsibility, and to want security; they have little ambition.
Theory Y Assumptions	1. People do not naturally dislike work; work is a natural part of their lives. 2. People are internally motivated to reach objectives to which they are committed. 3. People are committed to goals to the degree that they receive personal rewards when they reach their objectives. 4. People will both seek and accept responsibility under favorable conditions. 5. People have the capacity to be innovative in solving organizational problems. 6. People are bright, but under most organizational conditions their potential is underutilized.

Source: D. McGregor and W. Bennis, *The Human Side Enterprise: 25th Anniversary Printing*, 1960, Copyright © 1960 The McGraw-Hill Companies, Inc. Reprinted with permission.

TODAY'S management ISSUES

Speed-ups Speed Up

"A lot of us are unhappy, but what are we going to do—go somewhere else?"

— A longtime Dell employee*

With a sluggish economy, a depressed technology sector, and the continuing economic fallout of September 11, U.S. companies need all the help they can get. To lower expenses, managers have turned to firing employees (also called "terminating," "downsizing," "right-sizing," or "getting the pink slip").

A quick review of recent business headlines shows a bleak picture for workers: "American Airlines Cuts 7,000 Jobs." "United Slashes 9,000 Jobs in Bid for Solvency." "IBM Laid off 15,600 in Second Quarter." All told, over 3 million U.S. workers lost their jobs in 2001 and 2002. While the economy began to show signs of improvement in late 2003, there was still considerable uncertainty about when job growth might again start to increase.

The job cuts, coupled with higher productivity and better use of automation, have made U.S. firms more efficient. But at what price? The remaining workers, who must learn new tasks and work harder in order to replace their laid-off colleagues, are prone to stress. Hamilton Beazley, a management consultant, calls such additional duties "ghost work." He describes ghost work as very challenging for employees, saying, "It can be totally demoralizing and can cripple the individual as well as the organization."

Not surprisingly, most workers are not pleased with having to pick up the slack for laid-off coworkers. Workers refer to ghost work as "speed up," because each remaining worker has to work harder, or "stretch out," because they have to put in longer hours. Land Windham, a labor spokesman, says, "*They* call it productivity," referring to management.

However, given the shaky job market today, most workers are willing to endure the stress and discouragement of ghost work. Computer maker Dell laid off 6,000 of its 40,000 workers in 2001, allowing the firm to cut PC prices and increase sales and profits. A longtime employee says, "A lot of us are unhappy, but what are we going to do—go somewhere else?" The danger for employers is that, if the job market improves, many disgruntled workers may do just that.

References: Lisa Takeguchi Cullen, "Where Did Everyone Go?" *Time*, November 18, 2002, pp. 64–66 (*quote p. 65); "Lower Paid Workers Face Job Cuts," CNN Money website, cnnmoney.com on November 23, 2002; "Pink Slip Blizzard," CBS News website, www.cbsnews.com on November 23, 2002; Yahoo! News website, http://story.news.yahoo.com on November 23, 2002.

Theory X A pessimistic and negative view of workers consistent with the views of scientific management

Theory Y A positive view of workers; it represents the assumptions that human relations advocates make

that different managers have about their workers. **Theory X** is a relatively pessimistic and negative view of workers and is consistent with the views of scientific management. **Theory Y** is more positive and represents the assumptions that human relations advocates make. In McGregor's view, Theory Y was a more appropriate philosophy for managers to adhere to. Both Maslow and McGregor notably influenced the thinking of many practicing managers.

The Emergence of Organizational Behavior

Munsterberg, Mayo, Maslow, McGregor, and others have made valuable contributions to management. Contemporary theorists, however, have noted that many assertions of the human relationists were simplistic and inadequate descriptions of work behavior. For example, the assumption that worker satisfaction leads to improved performance has been shown to have little, if any, validity. If anything, satisfaction follows good performance rather than precedes it. (These issues are addressed in Chapters 15 and 16.)

Current behavioral perspectives on management, known as **organizational behavior**, acknowledge that human behavior in organizations is much more complex than the human relationists realized. The field of organizational behavior draws from a broad, interdisciplinary base of psychology, sociology, anthropology, economics, and medicine. Organizational behavior takes a holistic view of behavior and addresses individual, group, and organization processes. These processes are major elements in contemporary management theory.[24] Important topics in this field include job satisfaction, stress, motivation, leadership, group dynamics, organizational politics, interpersonal conflict, and the structure and design of organizations.[25] A contingency orientation also characterizes the field (discussed more fully later in this chapter). Our discussions of organizing (Chapters 11–14) and leading (Chapters 15–19) are heavily influenced by organizational behavior. And, finally, managers need a solid understanding of human behavior as they address such diversity-related issues as ethnicity and religion in the workplace. Indeed, all of these topics are useful to help managers better deal with fallout from the consequences of layoffs and job cuts, as discussed in *Today's Management Issues.*

organizational behavior Contemporary field focusing on behavioral perspectives on management

The Behavioral Management Perspective Today

Table 2.3 summarizes the behavioral management perspective and lists its contributions and limitations. The primary contributions relate to ways in which this

TABLE 2.3

The Behavioral Management Perspective

General Summary	The behavioral management perspective focuses on employee behavior in an organizational context. Stimulated by the birth of industrial psychology, the human relations movement supplanted scientific management as the dominant approach to management in the 1930s and 1940s. Prominent contributors to this movement were Elton Mayo, Abraham Maslow, and Douglas McGregor. Organizational behavior, the contemporary outgrowth of the behavioral management perspective, draws from an interdisciplinary base and recognizes the complexities of human behavior in organizational settings.
Contributions	Provided important insights into motivation, group dynamics, and other interpersonal processes in organizations. Focused managerial attention on these same processes. Challenged the view that employees are tools and furthered the belief that employees are valuable resources.
Limitations	The complexity of individual behavior makes prediction of that behavior difficult. Many behavioral concepts have not yet been put to use because some managers are reluctant to adopt them. Contemporary research findings by behavioral scientists are often not communicated to practicing managers in an understandable form.

approach has changed managerial thinking. Managers are now more likely to recognize the importance of behavioral processes and to view employees as valuable resources instead of mere tools. On the other hand, organizational behavior is still relatively imprecise in its ability to predict behavior, especially the behavior of a specific individual. It is not always accepted or understood by practicing managers. Hence, the contributions of the behavioral school have yet to be fully realized.

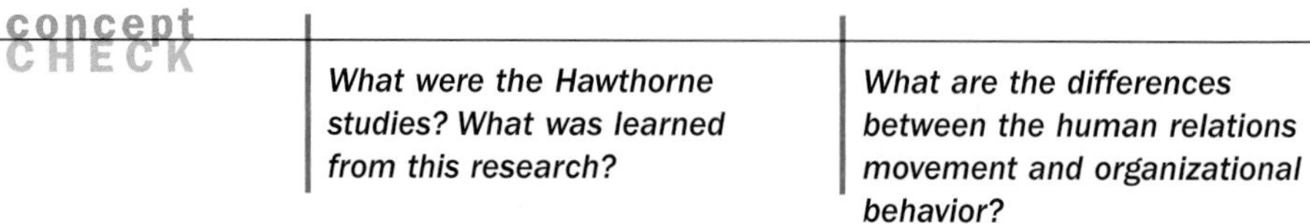

The Quantitative Management Perspective

The third major school of management thought began to emerge during World War II. During the war, government officials and scientists in England and the United States worked to help the military deploy its resources more efficiently and effectively. These groups took some of the mathematical approaches to management developed decades earlier by Taylor and Gantt and applied them to logistical problems during the war.[26] They learned that problems regarding troop, equipment, and submarine deployment, for example, could all be solved through mathematical analysis. After the war, companies such as DuPont and General Electric began to use the same techniques for deploying employees, choosing plant locations, and planning warehouses. Basically, then, this perspective is concerned with applying quantitative techniques to management. More specifically, the **quantitative management perspective** focuses on decision making, economic effectiveness, mathematical models, and the use of computers. There are two branches of the quantitative approach: management science and operations management.

quantitative management perspective Applies quantitative techniques to management

Management Science

Unfortunately, the term *management science* appears to be related to scientific management, the approach developed by Taylor and others early in this century. But the two have little in common and should not be confused. **Management science** focuses specifically on the development of mathematical models. A mathematical model is a simplified representation of a system, process, or relationship.

management science Focuses specifically on the development of mathematical models

At its most basic level, management science focuses on models, equations, and similar representations of reality. For example, managers at Detroit Edison use mathematical models to determine how best to route repair crews during blackouts. Citizens Bank of New England uses models to figure out how many tellers need to be on duty at each location at various times throughout the day. In recent years, paralleling the advent of the personal computer, management science techniques have become increasingly sophisticated. For example, automobile manufacturers DaimlerChrysler and General Motors use realistic computer simulations to study collision damage to cars. These simulations give them precise information and avoid the costs of crashing so many test cars.

Operations Management

Operations management is somewhat less mathematical and statistically sophisticated than management science and can be applied more directly to managerial situations. Indeed, we can think of **operations management** as a form of applied management science. Operations management techniques are generally concerned with helping the organization produce its products or services more efficiently and can be applied to a wide range of problems.

operations management Concerned with helping the organization more efficiently produce its products or services

For example, Rubbermaid and The Home Depot each use operations management techniques to manage their inventories. (Inventory management is concerned with specific inventory problems, such as balancing carrying costs and ordering costs, and determining the optimal order quantity.) Linear programming (which involves computing simultaneous solutions to a set of linear equations) helps United Airlines plan its flight schedules, Consolidated Freightways develop its shipping routes, and General Instrument Corporation plan what instruments to produce at various times. Other operations management techniques include queuing theory, breakeven analysis, and simulation. All of these techniques and procedures apply directly to operations, but they are also helpful in such areas as finance, marketing, and human resource management.

The Quantitative Management Perspective Today

Like the other management perspectives, the quantitative management perspective has made important contributions and has certain limitations. Both are summarized in Table 2.4. It has provided managers with an abundance of decision-making tools

TABLE 2.4

The Quantitative Management Perspective

General Summary	The quantitative management perspective focuses on applying mathematical models and processes to management situations. Management science deals specifically with the development of mathematical models to aid in decision making and problem solving. Operations management focuses more directly on the application of management science to organizations. Management information systems are developed to provide information to managers.
Contributions	Developed sophisticated quantitative techniques to assist in decision making. Application of models has increased our awareness and understanding of complex organizational processes and situations. Has been very useful in the planning and controlling processes.
Limitations	Cannot fully explain or predict the behavior of people in organizations. Mathematical sophistication may come at the expense of other important skills. Models may require unrealistic or unfounded assumptions.

and techniques and has increased understanding of overall organizational processes. It has been particularly useful in the areas of planning and controlling. Relatively new management concepts such as supply chain management and new techniques such as Enterprise Resource Planning, both discussed later in this book, also evolved from the quantitative management perspective. On the other hand, mathematical models cannot fully account for individual behaviors and attitudes. Some believe that the time needed to develop competence in quantitative techniques retards the development of other managerial skills. Finally, mathematical models typically require a set of assumptions that may not be realistic.

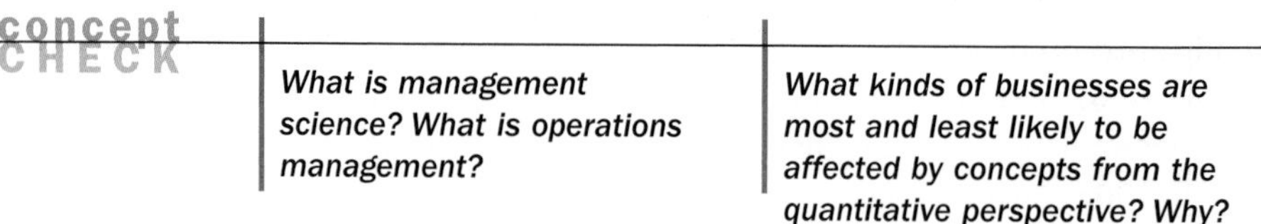

Integrating Perspectives for Managers

It is important to recognize that the classical, behavioral, and quantitative approaches to management are not necessarily contradictory or mutually exclusive. Even though each of the three perspectives makes very different assumptions and predictions, each can also complement the others. Indeed, a complete understanding of management requires an appreciation of all three perspectives. The systems and contingency perspectives can help us integrate the earlier approaches and enlarge our understanding of all three.

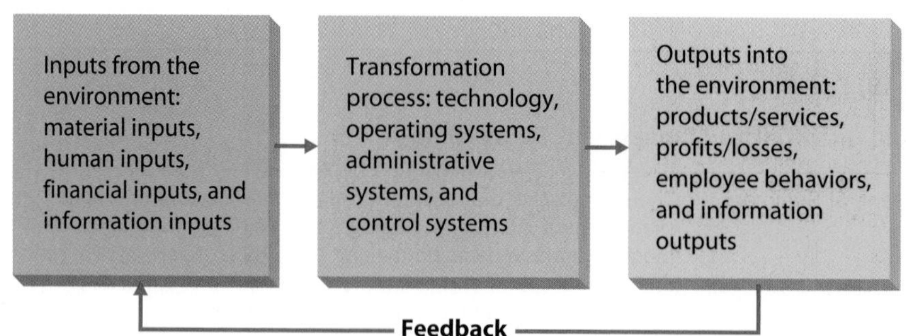

FIGURE 2.3

The Systems Perspective of Organizations

By viewing organizations as systems, managers can better understand the importance of their environment and the level of interdependence among subsystems within the organization. Managers must also understand how their decisions affect and are affected by other subsystems within the organization.

The Systems Perspective

We briefly introduce the systems perspective in Chapter 1 in our definition of management. A **system** is an interrelated set of elements functioning as a whole.[27] As shown in Figure 2.3, by viewing an organization as a system, we can identify four basic elements: inputs, transformation processes, outputs, and feedback. First, inputs are the material, human, financial, and information resources the organization gets from its environment. Next, through technological and managerial processes, inputs are transformed into outputs. Outputs include products, services, or both (tangible and intangible); profits, losses, or both (even not-for-profit organizations must operate within their budgets); employee behaviors; and information. Finally, the environment reacts to these outputs and provides feedback to the system.

system An interrelated set of elements functioning as a whole

open system A system that interacts with its environment

closed system A system that does not interact with its environment

subsystem A system within another system

synergy Two or more subsystems working together to produce more than the total of what they might produce working alone

Thinking of organizations as systems provides us with a variety of important viewpoints on organizations, such as the concepts of open systems, subsystems, synergy, and entropy. **Open systems** are systems that interact with their environment, whereas **closed systems** do not interact with their environment. Although organizations are open systems, some make the mistake of ignoring their environment and behaving as though their environment is not important.

The systems perspective also stresses the importance of **subsystems**—systems within a broader system. For example, the marketing, production, and finance functions within Mattel are systems in their own right but are also subsystems within the overall organization. Because they are interdependent, a change in one subsystem can affect other subsystems as well. If the production department at Mattel lowers the quality of the toys being made (by buying lower-quality materials, for example), the effects are felt in finance (improved cash flow in the short run owing to lower costs) and marketing (decreased sales in the long run because of customer dissatisfaction). Managers must therefore remember that, although organizational subsystems can be managed with some degree of autonomy, their interdependence should not be overlooked.

Managers who can build on potential synergy can often achieve impressive results. When Tracy Hester couldn't raise the capital to open a free-standing hair and nail salon in Durham, North Carolina, she negotiated a deal to set up shop inside the Durham Athletic Club. This arrangement provided her with a solid base of customers (about 80 percent of her customers are also gym members). And the presence of her salon also helps the gym's owners—it gives them something else to promote in their advertising and the rent Hester pays provides extra revenues.

Synergy suggests that organizational units (or subsystems) may often be more successful working together than working alone. The Walt Disney Company, for example, benefits greatly from synergy. The company's movies, theme parks, television programs, and merchandise-licensing programs all benefit one another. Children who enjoy a Disney movie like *Finding Nemo* want to go to Disney World, see the *Finding Nemo* show there, and buy stuffed toys of the film's characters.

Music from the film generates additional revenues for the firm, as do computer games and other licensing arrangements for lunchboxes, clothing, and so forth. Synergy was also the major objective in the first megamerger of 2000 between America Online and Time Warner, and more recent mergers between such firms as Hewlett-Packard and Compaq.[28] Synergy is an important concept for managers because it emphasizes the importance of working together in a cooperative and coordinated fashion.[29]

entropy A normal process leading to system decline

Finally, **entropy** is a normal process that leads to system decline. When an organization does not monitor feedback from its environment and make appropriate adjustments, it may fail. For example, witness the problems of Studebaker (an automobile manufacturer) and Kmart (a major retailer). Each of these organizations went bankrupt because it failed to revitalize itself and keep pace with changes in its environment. A primary objective of management, from a systems perspective, is to continually re-energize the organization to avoid entropy.

The Contingency Perspective

universal perspective An attempt to identify the one best way to do something

contingency perspective Suggests that appropriate managerial behavior in a given situation depends on, or is contingent on, a wide variety of elements

Another noteworthy recent addition to management thinking is the contingency perspective. The classical, behavioral, and quantitative approaches are considered **universal perspectives** because they tried to identify the "one best way" to manage organizations. The **contingency perspective**, in contrast, suggests that universal theories cannot be applied to organizations, because each organization is unique. Instead, the contingency perspective suggests that appropriate managerial behavior in a given situation depends on, or is contingent on, unique elements in that situation.[30]

Stated differently, effective managerial behavior in one situation cannot always be generalized to other situations. Recall, for example, that Frederick Taylor assumed that all workers would generate the highest possible level of output to maximize their own personal economic gain. We can imagine some people being motivated primarily by money—but we can just as easily imagine other people being motivated by the desire for leisure time, status, social acceptance, or any combination of these (as Mayo found at the Hawthorne plant). Leslie Wexner, founder and CEO of The Limited, used one managerial style when his firm was small and rapidly growing, but that style did not match as well when The Limited became a huge, mature enterprise. Thus Wexner had to alter his style at that point to better fit the changing needs of his business.

An Integrating Framework

We note earlier that the classical, behavioral, and quantitative management perspectives can be complementary and that the systems and contingency perspectives can help integrate them. Our framework for integrating the various approaches to management is shown in Figure 2.4. The initial premise of the framework is that, before attempting to apply any specific concepts or ideas from the three major perspectives, managers must recognize the interdependence of

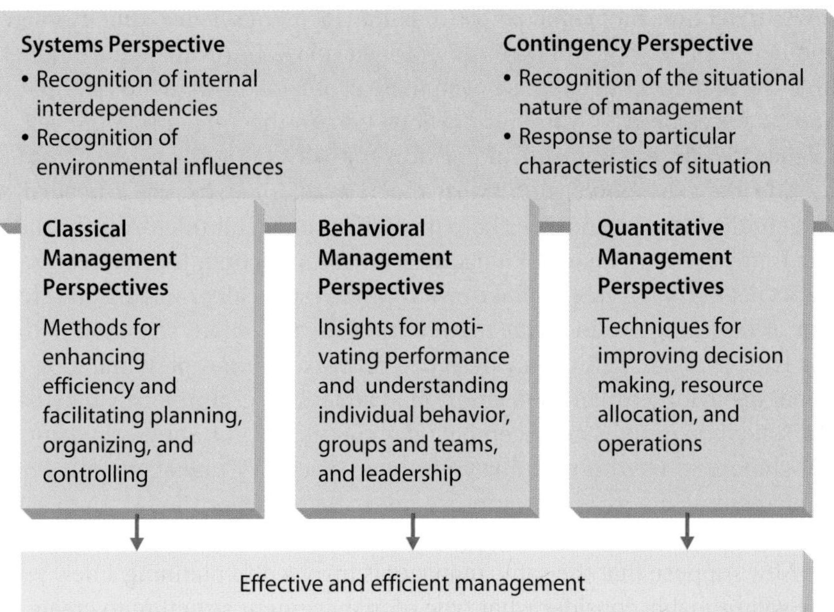

FIGURE 2.4

An Integrative Framework of Management Perspectives

Each of the major perspectives on management can be useful to modern managers. Before using any of them, however, the manager should recognize the situational context within which they operate. The systems and contingency perspectives serve to integrate the classical, behavioral, and quantitative management perspectives.

units within the organization, the effect of environmental influences, and the need to respond to the unique characteristics of each situation. The ideas of subsystem interdependencies and environmental influences are given to us by systems theory, and the situational view of management is derived from a contingency perspective.

With these ideas as basic assumptions, the manager can use valid tools, techniques, concepts, and theories of the classical, behavioral, and quantitative management perspectives. For example, managers can still use many of the basic techniques from scientific management. In many contemporary settings, the scientific study of jobs and production techniques can enhance productivity. But managers should not rely solely on these techniques, nor should they ignore the human element. The behavioral perspective is also of use to managers today. By drawing on contemporary ideas of organizational behavior, the manager can better appreciate the role of employee needs and behaviors in the workplace. Motivation, leadership, communication, and group processes are especially important. The quantitative perspective provides the manager with a set of useful tools and techniques. The development and use of management science models and the application of operations management methods can help managers increase their efficiency and effectiveness.

Consider the new distribution manager of a large wholesale firm whose job is to manage one hundred truck drivers and to coordinate standard truck routes in the most efficient fashion. This new manager, with little relevant experience, might attempt to increase productivity by employing strict work specialization and close supervision (as suggested by scientific management). But doing so may decrease employee satisfaction and morale, and increase turnover (as predicted by organizational behavior). The manager might also develop a statistical formula to use route driver time more efficiently (from management science). But this new system could disrupt existing work groups and social patterns (from organizational behavior). The manager might create even more problems by trying to impose programs and practices derived from her previous job. An incentive program welcomed by retail clerks, for example, might not work for truck drivers.

The manager should soon realize that a broader perspective is needed. Systems and contingency perspectives help provide broader solutions. Also, as the integrative framework in Figure 2.4 illustrates, applying techniques from several schools works better than trying to make one approach solve all problems. To solve a problem of declining productivity, the manager might look to scientific management (perhaps jobs are inefficiently designed or workers improperly trained), organizational behavior (worker motivation may be low, or group norms may be limiting output), or operations management (facilities may be improperly laid out, or material shortages may be resulting from poor inventory management). And, before implementing any plans for improvement, the manager should try to assess their effect on other areas of the organization.

Now suppose that the same manager is involved in planning a new warehouse. She will probably consider what type of management structure to create (classical management perspective), what kinds of leaders and work-group arrangements to develop (behavioral management perspective), and how to develop a network model for designing and operating the facility itself (quantitative perspective). As a final example, if employee turnover is too high, the manager might consider an incentive system (classical perspective), plan a motivational enhancement program (behavioral perspective), or use a mathematical model (quantitative perspective) to discover that turnover costs may actually be lower than the cost of making any changes at all.

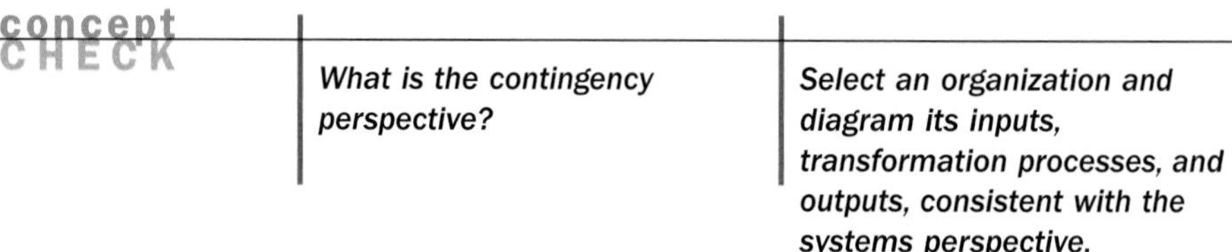

concept CHECK

What is the contingency perspective?

Select an organization and diagram its inputs, transformation processes, and outputs, consistent with the systems perspective.

Contemporary Management Issues and Challenges

Interest in management theory and practice has heightened in recent years as new issues and challenges have emerged. No new paradigm has been formulated that replaces the traditional views, but managers continue to strive toward a better understanding of how they can better compete and lead their organizations toward improved effectiveness. Figure 2.5 summarizes the historical development of the major models of management, described in the preceding sections, and puts into historical context the contemporary applied perspectives discussed in the next section.

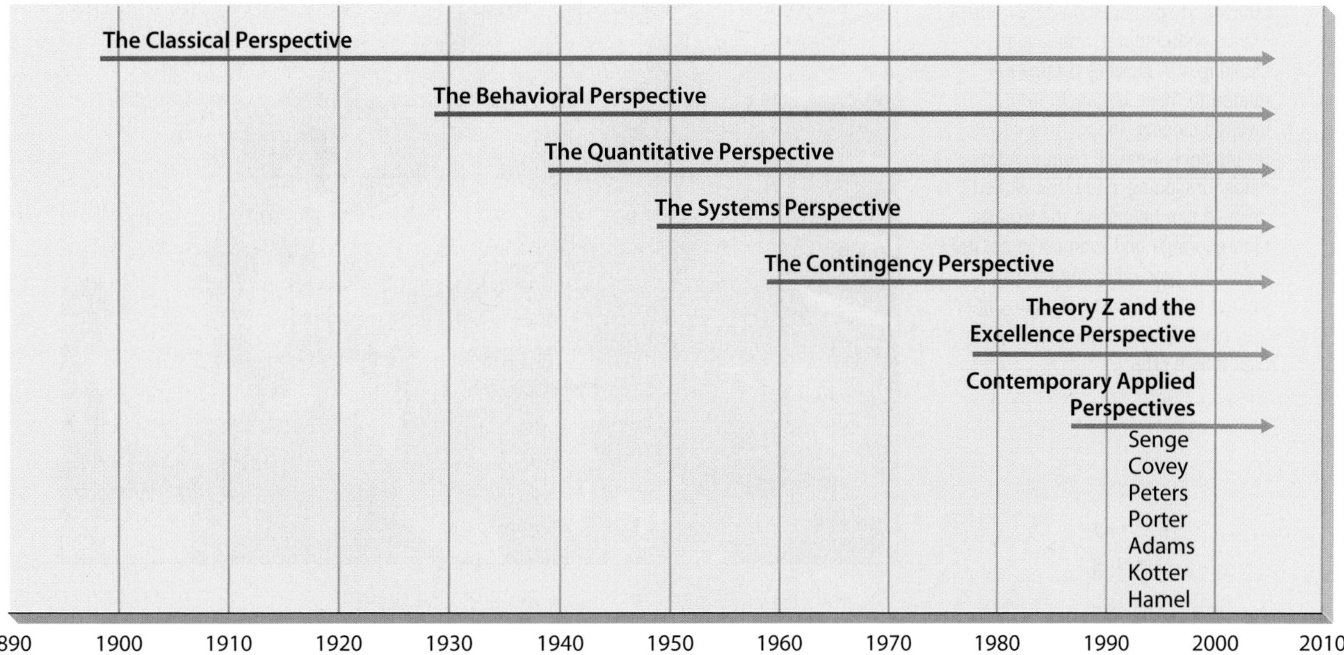

FIGURE 2.5

The Emergence of Modern Management Perspectives

Most contemporary management perspectives have emerged and evolved over the last hundred years or so. Beginning with the classical management perspective, first developed toward the end of the nineteenth century, and on through contemporary applied perspectives, managers have an array of useful techniques, methods, and approaches for solving problems and enhancing the effectiveness of their organizations. Of course, managers also need to recognize that not every idea set forth is valid, and that even those that are useful are not applicable in all settings. And new methods and approaches will continue to be developed in the future.

Contemporary Applied Perspectives

In recent years, books written for the popular press have also had a major impact on both the field of organizational behavior and the practice of management. This trend first became noticeable in the early 1980s with the success of such classics as William Ouchi's *Theory Z* and Thomas Peters's and Robert Waterman's *In Search of Excellence.* Each of these books spent time on the *New York Times* best-seller list and was required reading for any manager wanting to at least appear informed. Biographies of executives like Lee Iacocca and Donald Trump also received widespread attention. And bidding for the publishing rights to Jack Welch's memoirs, published when he retired as CEO from General Electric, exceeded $7 million.[31]

In recent years, other applied authors have had a major impact on management theory and practice. Among the most popular applied authors today are Peter Senge, Stephen Covey, Tom Peters, Jim Collins, Michael Porter, John Kotter, and Gary Hamel.[32] Their books highlight the management practices of successful firms like Shell, Ford, IBM, and others, or outline conceptual or theoretical models or frameworks to guide managers as they formulate strategy or motivate their employees. Scott Adams, creator of the popular comic strip *Dilbert,* is also immensely

Ethics and social responsibility reflect critical contemporary management challenges. A growing controversy related to these issues, in turn, involves cloning. These three calves, for instance, were all cloned. Advocates for cloning argue that cloned animals can help solve the world's food shortage and even serve as "factories" for producing certain drugs. Animal rights activists, though, argue that cloning is inhumane and has a high failure rate.

popular today. Adams is a former communications industry worker who developed his strip to illustrate some of the absurdities that occasionally afflict contemporary organizational life. The daily strip is routinely posted outside office doors, above copy machines, and beside water coolers in hundreds of offices.

Contemporary Management Challenges

Managers today also face an imposing set of challenges as they guide and direct the fortunes of their companies. Coverage of each of these is thoroughly integrated throughout this book. In addition, many of them are also highlighted or given focused coverage in one or more special ways.

One of the most critical challenges facing managers today is a stalled economy that limits growth. A second important challenge is the management of diversity, as noted in Chapter 1. Another is employee privacy. A related issue has to do with the increased capabilities that technology provides for people to work at places other than their office. The appropriate role of the Internet in business strategy is also a complex arena for managers. This topic is highlighted in *Technology Toolkit.*

Globalization is another significant contemporary challenge for managers. Managing in a global economy poses many different challenges and opportunities. For example, at a macro level, property ownership arrangements vary widely. So does the availability of natural resources and components of the infrastructure, as well as the role of government in business. But, for our purposes, a very important consideration is how behavioral processes vary widely across cultural and national boundaries. For example, values, symbols, and beliefs differ sharply among cultures. Different work norms and the role that work plays in a person's life, for example, influence patterns of both work-related behavior and attitudes toward work. They also affect the nature of supervisory relationships, decision-making styles and processes, and organizational configurations. Group and intergroup processes, responses to stress, and the nature of political behaviors also differ from culture to culture. Chapter 5 is devoted to such global issues.

Another management challenge that has taken on renewed importance is ethics and social responsibility and their relationship to corporate governance. Unfortunately, business scandals involving unethical conduct have become almost commonplace today. From a social responsibility perspective, increasing attention has been focused on pollution and business's obligation to help clean up our environment, business contributions to social causes, and so forth. The proper framework for corporate governance is often at the center of these debates and discussions. Chapter 4 covers ethics and social responsibility in more detail.

E-Business Grows Up

"The Information Revolution requires a huge process of learning and cultural change."

— Chris Freeman, professor and author*

Throughout human history, countless innovations have revolutionized society, from the development of fire, agriculture, and the wheel to such modern inventions as the steam engine and television. E-business is one of the newest technologies, coming into widespread commercial use in 1995. It is not unique, merely the latest in a chain of dramatic developments.

In the 1990s, as dot-com industries heated up, hundreds of firms flooded into the new competitive arena. Initial public offerings, an indicator of new business activity, were at an all-time high. Society's fascination with the promise of the Internet led to a sharp increase in the price of e-business stocks. However, the feverish development and investment activity were followed by an equally sharp decline, as the dot-com bubble burst in 2000. The pundits who had naively predicted that the Internet would completely transform American life in just a few short years were quick to reverse themselves, and many declared, "The Internet is dead." The truth, though, is that the rapid rise and fall of the Internet is nothing new. The same boom-bust cycle was displayed by the telegraph, railway, telephone, banking, and auto industries in their infancy.

What lies ahead for online industries? Are they "dead"? History tells us that the strongest growth in an industry begins *after* the bust, as the failure of weaker firms paves the way to success for stronger ones. This pattern has been demonstrated in countless industries and is unfolding in online industries too. Although online sales currently account for less than 2 percent of all trade, that percentage is growing steadily.

Looking ahead, with the past in mind, there are three important lessons. First, be patient while changes unfold over a long period of time, probably for decades to come. Chris Freeman, professor and author of *As Time Goes By: From the Industrial Revolutions* to the Information Revolution, agrees, saying, "It requires a huge process of learning and cultural change." Second, expect a lot of slow, difficult, and expensive work, as standards are developed, privacy and security issues are resolved, and millions of users get connected to the Internet. Third, be ready for continuing advances and even for the next technology revolution. It is on its way.

References: Robert D. Hof and Steve Hamm, "How E-Biz Rose, Fell, and Will Rise Anew," *BusinessWeek*, May 13, 2002, pp. 64–72 (*quote on p. 66); Timothy J. Mullaney, "Break out the Black Ink," *BusinessWeek*, May 13, 2002, pp. 74–76; Joan O'C. Hamilton, "Hey, We've Got History on Our Side," *BusinessWeek*, May 13, 2002, p. 78.

Quality also continues to pose an important management challenge today. Quality is an important issue for several reasons. First, more and more organizations are using quality as a basis for competition. Continental Airlines, for example, stresses its high rankings in the J.D. Power survey of customer satisfaction in its print advertising. Second, improving quality tends to increase productivity because making higher-quality products generally results in less waste and rework. Third, enhancing quality lowers costs. Whistler Corporation once found that it was using 100 of its 250 employees to repair defective radar detectors that were built incorrectly in the first place. Quality is also important because of its relationship to productivity. Quality is highlighted in Chapter 21.

Finally, the shift toward a service economy also continues to be important. Traditionally, most businesses were manufacturers—they used tangible resources like raw materials and machinery to create tangible products like automobiles and steel. In the last few decades, however, the service sector of the economy has become much more important. Indeed, services now account for well over half of the gross domestic product in the United States and play a similarly important role in many other industrialized nations as well. Service technology involves the use of both tangible resources (such as machinery) and intangible resources (such as intellectual property) to create intangible services (such as a haircut, insurance protection, or transportation between two cities). Although there are obviously many similarities between managing in a manufacturing and a service organization, there are also many fundamental differences.

concept CHECK

Besides Dilbert, what other comic strips routinely reflect contemporary organizational life?

Which contemporary management challenge interests you the most? Why?

Summary of Key Points

ACE self-test

business.college.hmco.com/students

Theories are important as organizers of knowledge and as road maps for action. Understanding the historical context and precursors of management and organizations provides a sense of heritage and can also help managers avoid repeating the mistakes of others. Evidence suggests that interest in management dates back thousands of years, but a scientific approach to management has emerged only in the last hundred years. During the first few decades of the last century, three primary perspectives on management emerged. These are called the classical perspective, the behavioral perspective, and the quantitative perspective.

The classical management perspective had two major branches: scientific management and administrative management. Scientific management was concerned with improving efficiency and work methods for individual workers. Administrative management was more concerned with how organizations themselves should be structured and arranged for efficient operations. Both branches paid little attention to the role of the worker.

The behavioral management perspective, characterized by a concern for individual and group behavior, emerged primarily as a result of the Hawthorne studies. The human relations movement recognized the importance and potential of behavioral processes in organizations but made many overly simplistic assumptions about those processes. Organizational behavior, a more realistic outgrowth of the behavioral perspective, is of interest to many contemporary managers.

The quantitative management perspective and its two components, management science and operations management, attempt to apply quantitative techniques to decision making and problem solving. These areas are also of considerable importance to contemporary managers. Their contributions have been facilitated by the tremendous increase in the use of personal computers and integrated information networks.

The three major perspectives should be viewed in a complementary, not a contradictory, light. Each has something of value to offer. The key is understanding how to use them effectively. Two relatively recent additions to management theory, the systems and contingency perspectives, appear to have great potential both as approaches to management and as frameworks for integrating the other perspectives.

A variety of popular applied perspectives influence management practice today. Important issues and challenges facing managers include employee retention, diversity, the new workforce, organization change, ethics and social responsibility, the importance of quality, and the continued shift toward a service economy.

Discussion Questions

Questions for Review

1. Briefly describe the principles of scientific management and administrative management. What assumptions are made about workers?
2. What are the differences between the contingency and the universal perspectives on management? How is the contingency perspective useful in the practice of management today?
3. Describe the systems perspective. Why is a business organization considered an open system?
4. For each of the contemporary management challenges, give at least one example, other than the examples found in the text.

Questions for Analysis

5. Young, innovative, or high-tech firms often adopt the strategy of ignoring history or attempting to do something radically new. In what ways will this strategy help them? In what ways will this strategy hinder them?
6. Can a manager use tools and techniques from several different perspectives at the same time? For example, can a manager use both classical and behavioral perspectives? Give an example of a time when a manager did this and explain how it enabled him or her to be effective.
7. Visit the website of Amazon.com. Select the tab "Books," then the tab "Bestsellers," and then click on "Business & Investing" from the categories listed down the left side of the screen. Look at Amazon's list of best-selling business books. What ideas or themes do you see in the list? Which business leaders do you see?

Questions for Application

8. Go to the library or go online and locate material about Confucius. Outline his

major ideas. Which seem to be applicable to management in the United States today?

9. Find a company that has laid off a significant number of workers in the last year. (*Hint:* Use the word *layoff* as a search term on the Internet.) Investigate that company. Why did the firm make the layoffs? In your opinion, are the layoffs likely to accomplish their intended goal? Why or why not?
10. Read about management pioneer Frederick Taylor at www.cftech.com/BrainBank/TRIVIABITS/FredWTaylor.html or another source. Describe Taylor's background and experience. How does an understanding of Taylor's early career help you to better understand his ideas about scientific management?

BUILDING EFFECTIVE decision-making SKILLS

Exercise Overview

Decision-making skills refer to a manager's ability to recognize and define problems and opportunities correctly and then to select an appropriate course of action to solve those problems and capitalize on the opportunities. This exercise will help you develop your own decision-making skills while also helping you to better understand the importance of subsystem interdependencies in organizations.

Exercise Background

Assume you are the vice president for a large manufacturing company. Your firm makes home office furniture and cabinets for home theater systems. Because of the growth in each product line, the firm has also grown substantially in recent years. At the same time, this growth has not gone unnoticed, and several competitors have entered the market in the last two years. Your CEO has instructed you to determine how to cut costs by 10 percent so that prices can be cut by the same amount. She feels that this tactic is necessary to retain your market share in the face of new competition.

You have looked closely at the situation and have decided that there are three different ways you can accomplish this cost reduction. One option is to begin buying slightly lower-grade materials, such as wood, glue, and stain. Another option is to lay off a portion of your workforce and then pressure the remaining workers to work harder. As part of this same option, employees hired in the future will be selected from a lower-skill labor pool and thus be paid a lower wage. The third option is to replace your existing equipment with newer, more efficient equipment. Although this will require a substantial up-front investment, you are certain that lower production costs can be achieved.

Exercise Task

With this background in mind, respond to the following:

1. Carefully examine each of the three alternatives under consideration. In what ways might each alternative affect other parts of the organization?
2. Which is the most costly option (in terms of impact on other parts of the organization, not absolute dollars)? Which is the least costly?
3. What are the primary obstacles that you might face regarding each of the three alternatives?
4. Can you think of other alternatives that might accomplish the cost reduction goal?

BUILDING EFFECTIVE communication SKILLS

business.college.hmco.com/students

Exercise Overview

Communication skills refer to a manager's ability to effectively receive information and ideas from others and to effectively convey information and ideas to others. This exercise will help you develop your communication skills while also helping you to understand communication challenges in the age of e-mail.

Exercise Background

Lincoln's Gettysburg Address is surely one of the most important examples of effective communication in American history. President Lincoln delivered the speech on November 19, 1863, at Gettysburg, Pennsylvania, the site of one of the bloodiest battles of the Civil War. The president and other speakers delivered speeches to dedicate Gettysburg National Cemetery, where the battle of Gettysburg had been fought from July 1 to July 3 of the same year. In that battle, nearly 50,000 men were killed or wounded, making it the most lethal engagement that the U.S. Army has ever fought. The text of Lincoln's speech follows:

> *"Fourscore and seven years ago our fathers brought forth on this continent, a new nation, conceived in Liberty, and dedicated to the proposition that all men are created equal. Now we are engaged in a great civil war, testing whether that nation or any nation so conceived and so dedicated, can long endure. We are met on a great battle-field of that war. We have come to dedicate a portion of that field as a final resting place for those who here gave their lives that that nation might live. It is altogether fitting and proper that we should do this.*
>
> *But, in a larger sense, we cannot dedicate—we cannot consecrate—we cannot hallow—this ground. The brave men, living and dead, who struggled here, have consecrated it, far above our poor power to add or detract. The world will little note, nor long remember what we say here, but it can never forget what they did here. It is for us the living, rather, to be dedicated here to the unfinished work which they who fought here have thus far so nobly advanced. It is rather for us to be here dedicated to the great task remaining before us—that from these honored dead we take increased devotion to that cause for which they gave the last full measure of devotion—that we here highly resolve that these dead shall not have died in vain—that this nation, under God, shall have a new birth of freedom—and that government of the people, by the people, for the people, shall not perish from the earth."*

Lincoln, in characteristically modest fashion, believed the speech was a failure because it was met with more than a minute of stunned silence. However, another speaker at the event, Edward Everett, wrote to Lincoln, "I should be glad, if I could flatter myself that I came as near to the central idea of the occasion, in two hours, as you did in two minutes." Yet it is obvious that Lincoln's emotional tone, his profound sentiments, and his skillful orator's blend of acknowledgment of the past and hope for the future are incomparable. The speech is considered one of the most eloquent ever delivered.

In many ways, the principles of effective communication have not changed since Lincoln's day. Yet modern devices such as presentation software (Microsoft's PowerPoint is one example) have made changes. PowerPoint provides the capability to automatically generate presentations based on data supplied by the user, which can be helpful or not, depending on the circumstances.

Exercise Task

1. For a lighthearted, yet meaningful, take on the ways in which advances in electronic communication have both helped and hindered communication today,

visit the website titled "The Gettysburg Powerpoint Presentation," at www.norvig.com/Gettysburg/index.htm. This site answers the hypothetical question "What if President Lincoln had used Microsoft PowerPoint automation tools to help him write and present his Gettysburg Address?" View the presentation, then be sure to read the information about "the making of" this site, found at the bottom of the home page.

2. After viewing the site and reading Peter Norvig's comments, can you generalize from this one example to state some principles for the effective use of presentation software and automation tools?

BUILDING EFFECTIVE conceptual SKILLS

Exercise Overview

Conceptual skills relate to a manager's ability to think in the abstract. This exercise allows you to practice your conceptual skills, while also giving you exposure to the management wisdom of another culture, conveyed in a way that is traditional in that culture.

Exercise Background

The scholarly study of management is a relatively new discipline. However, there have been managers as long as there have been organizations, and there is a great deal of management wisdom for you to discover from some very old sources.

One of these sources is Sun Tzu, a Chinese general who lived around 400 B.C. Sun Tzu rose from humble beginnings to become the most powerful general in the largest army on earth during his time. This was a remarkable accomplishment for a peasant in a feudal society, and we can only speculate that Sun Tzu must have been an extraordinary person to have achieved this. Sometime after Sun Tzu's death, probably around 200 B.C. or 200 years later, a book was written about him, called *The Art of War*. This book describes principles that are ascribed to Sun Tzu and that are supposed to have formed the basis for his remarkable success.

Sun Tzu's book provided the organizing principles for the samurai warriors who emerged in medieval Japan, and it was used by Mao Zedong and Chiang Kai-shek in their fighting during the Chinese Communist revolution. The book was introduced to Western societies in 1772 after being translated by a Jesuit monk, and Napoleon is known to have read it. Today, the work is used extensively by American military forces, as well as by many CEOs.

The book is written in an unusual style for today's tastes, and it deals exclusively with warfare, yet many contemporary treatments of the book relate Sun Tzu's principles in terms that can be useful in any competitive arena, such as war, business, or sports. Here is an example of Sun Tzu's ideas:

> *"With more careful calculations, one can win; with less, one cannot. How much less chance of victory has one who makes no calculations at all! Therefore, I say: Know the enemy and know yourself; in a hundred battles, you will never be defeated. When you are ignorant of the enemy but know yourself, your chances of winning or losing are equal. If ignorant both of your enemy and of yourself, you are sure to be defeated in every battle."*

This is clearly a description of a principle of battle, yet it can be applied just as clearly to business.

If you are interested in reading more of Sun Tzu's ideas, an excellent translation of the full text of *The Art of War* is available online at www.sonshi.com/learn.html. Other translations can be found at many other sites or in books.

Exercise Task

1. Listen as your instructor tells you stories about Sun Tzu, in the Confucian style. Discuss your interpretation of these stories with your instructor and classmates.
2. Would a Confucian teaching style be appropriate for the courses taught at your school? Why or why not?

CHAPTER CLOSING case

YELLOW FREIGHT IS ON THE MOVE

"You have to keep reinventing the company, because the market keeps changing."

– Bill Zollars, CEO, Yellow Corporation*

When Bill Zollars became the new CEO of Yellow Freight System in 1996, he headed a firm that was losing money, suffering from labor strikes, and worst of all, seemed hopelessly trapped in old-fashioned, inefficient business practices. Since the firm's founding in 1924, Yellow had grown to cover many regions of the United States and some international areas, but had failed to update its business model. Competition in the ground transportation industry was changing, starting with deregulation in 1980, which encouraged new entrants and allowed nationwide competition for the first time. This quickly led to overcapacity and fierce price wars, dropping industry profitability. Other challenges followed, including difficulties with union relations, undersupply of manual laborers and drivers, and more demands from customers.

Yellow, like its competitors, kept up "business as usual," scheduling, loading, and shipping freight the same way it always had. The result was erratic deliveries, giving Yellow little ability to control or even monitor performance. When Zollars asked employees to estimate the firm's defect rate—the number of late, incorrect, or damaged shipments—they guessed 10 or 20 percent. The real rate was 40 percent. Zollars says, "The [workers'] response was classic denial. People thought, 'We're as good as anyone else in this industry.'" The CEO recollects his early days at Yellow: "I remember one caller who said, 'I'd like to get this stuff from Chicago to Atlanta in two days,' and we said, 'We can get it there in three days.' The customer thanked us and hung up. We didn't think there was anything wrong with that. The attitude was, 'If you don't like what we do, too bad.'"

Zollars knew that the firm could benefit from technological innovations, but first he would have to change the vision and behavior of his employees. To do that, he spent eighteen months traveling to Yellow's hundreds of locations to describe his ideas in person. He found a workforce ready to hear his message. "We were a defensive company—a follower, not a leader," claims James Welch, president and COO. "We were yearning for leadership. This company was ready to change."

One of Zollars's most important changes was to refocus workers on satisfying the needs of customers. With that goal in mind, Yellow has provided additional services, such as less-than-truckload, regional, and expedited deliveries. It has moved further into cross-border and international shipping. Yellow has also expanded into more services, offering transportation-management consulting services and providing computers and training for customers. Zollars instituted a customer satisfaction survey that questioned 10,000 randomly selected customers in the first round and followed up with monthly assessments of 600 customers. Focus on customers led to some breakthrough rethinking of every aspect of the business, from technology to operations to sales.

Another initiative was the dramatic expansion of Yellow's use of information technology. Lynn

Caddell, chief information officer, formerly of America West Airlines, finds the trucking industry far more challenging. "We're moving a product from one place to another, but there's a lot more complexity to it. Each of my 'passengers' is a different size and weight and needs a different amount of space. And they don't simply go from airport to airport. They go to hundreds of zip codes and addresses. Many of them need to arrive at their final destination at a specific time. Coordinating all of that is a huge challenge."

To cope with the complexity in its business, Yellow's technological innovations include a wide range of applications, such as a website for customers to track their deliveries, a sophisticated model for predicting transportation needs, and training for every dock worker and driver in the use of a hand-held computer. One system provides centralized control of every delivery and driver, with a map displaying red lights whenever a shipment is in danger of being late. Even the definition of quality has changed at Yellow. The firm always assumed that customers wanted their deliveries made as quickly as possible, but after surveying thousands of clients, it discovered that reliable and undamaged deliveries were more important.

Today, Yellow's defect rate is down to 5 percent, and although the volume of shipments is down, the firm's profitability is up, showing its improved efficiency. The company seems to have successfully met challenges related to labor, quality, service, and customer focus. Perhaps the most positive sign is this: Zollars is emphasizing the need for continuous improvement. For those employees who believe that the changes they just made were the last step in the process, Zollars says, "I don't think that you're ever done. You have to keep reinventing the company, because the market keeps changing. If you don't, you end up coasting."

Case Questions

1. Which of the contemporary management challenges is Yellow Freight facing?
2. Choose one of the challenges you listed in the answer to question 1 above. What additional challenges do you think Yellow Freight will face in that area in the future?
3. What are some of the benefits that Yellow Freight can expect to gain if it copes with the challenges it is facing? What are some of the negative consequences if it does not cope well?

Case References

"America's Most Admired Companies: 2002 All-Stars," *Fortune*, March 4, 2002, www.fortune.com on November 17, 2002; "Case Studies: Yellow Freight System," XcelleNet website, www.xcellenet.com on November 17, 2002; Chuck Salter, "On the Road Again," *Fast Company*, January 2002, pp. 50–58 (*quote p. 58); "The 2002 Fortune 500," *Fortune*, April 15, 2002, www.fortune.com on November 17, 2002; "Yellow: Burning Up the Roadway?" *BusinessWeek*, September 8, 2003, p. 83.

Chapter Notes

1. "Fastest Growing Online Brokerage to Take Costco Partnership National in Q1 '03," *Business Wire*, hoovnews.hoovers.com on November 24, 2002; "Investors Overview: Historical Highlights," Costco website, www.costco.com on November 24, 2002; Nanette Byrnes, "James Sinegal, Costco," *BusinessWeek*, September 23, 2002, pp. 82–82; Nanette Byrnes, "The Good CEO," *BusinessWeek*, September 23, 2002, pp. 80–81; "Pay for Performance: Both Ends of the Scale," *BusinessWeek*, April 16, 2001, www.businessweek.com on November 24, 2002; "Report: Costco Eyeing European Expansion Sites," *Puget Sound Business Journal*, November 20, 2002, seattle.bizjournals.com on November 24, 2002; Richard Bloom, "Round 2: Wal-Mart v. Costco," *The Globe and Mail* (Toronto), November 22, 2002, www.theglobeandmail.com on November 24, 2002; "Wholesale Retailer Costco's Boss Gets Cheap Thrills Offering, Finding Bargains," *The News Tribune* (Tacoma, Washington), November 22, 2002, hoovnews.hoovers.com on November 24, 2002.
2. Terence Mitchell and Lawrence James, "Building Better Theory: Time and the Specification of When Things Happen," *Academy of Management Review*, 2001, vol. 26, no. 4, pp. 530–547.
3. Peter F. Drucker, "The Theory of the Business," *Harvard Business Review*, September–October 1994, pp. 95–104.
4. "Why Business History?" *Audacity*, Fall 1992, pp. 7–15. See also Alan L. Wilkins and Nigel J. Bristow, "For Successful Organization Culture, Honor Your Past," *Academy of Management Executive*, August 1987, pp. 221–227.
5. Daniel Wren, *The Evolution of Management Theory*, 4th ed. (New York: Wiley, 1994); Page Smith, *The Rise of Industrial America* (New York: McGraw-Hill, 1984).
6. Martha I. Finney, "Books That Changed Careers," *HRMagazine*, June 1997, pp. 141–145.

7. See Harriet Rubin, *The Princessa: Machiavelli for Women* (New York: Doubleday/Currency, 1997). See also Nanette Fondas, "Feminization Unveiled: Management Qualities in Contemporary Writings," *Academy of Management Review*, January 1997, pp. 257–282.
8. Alan M. Kantrow (ed.), "Why History Matters to Managers," *Harvard Business Review*, January–February 1986, pp. 81–88.
9. Wren, *The Evolution of Management Theory.*
10. Charles Babbage, *On the Economy of Machinery and Manufactures* (London: Charles Knight, 1832).
11. Wren, *The Evolution of Management Theory.*
12. Frederick W. Taylor, *Principles of Scientific Management* (New York: Harper and Brothers, 1911).
13. Charles D. Wrege and Amedeo G. Perroni, "Taylor's Pig-Tale: A Historical Analysis of Frederick W. Taylor's Pig-Iron Experiment," *Academy of Management Journal*, March 1974, pp. 6–27; Charles D. Wrege and Ann Marie Stoka, "Cooke Creates a Classic: The Story Behind Taylor's Principles of Scientific Management," *Academy of Management Review*, October 1978, pp. 736–749.
14. Robert Kanigel, *The One Best Way* (New York: Viking, 1997); Oliver E. Allen, "'This Great Mental Revolution'," *Audacity*, Summer 1996, pp. 52–61; Jill Hough and Margaret White, "Using Stories to Create Change: The Object Lesson of Frederick Taylor's'Pig-Tale'," *Journal of Management*, 2001, vol. 27, pp. 585–601.
15. Henri Fayol, *General and Industrial Management*, trans. J. A. Coubrough (Geneva: International Management Institute, 1930).
16. Max Weber, *Theory of Social and Economic Organizations*, trans. T. Parsons (New York: Free Press, 1947); Richard M. Weis, "Weber on Bureaucracy: Management Consultant or Political Theorist?" *Academy of Management Review*, April 1983, pp. 242–248.
17. Chester Barnard, *The Functions of the Executive* (Cambridge, Mass.: Harvard University Press, 1938).
18. "The Line Starts Here," *Wall Street Journal*, January 11, 1999, pp. R1, R25.
19. Hugo Munsterberg, *Psychology and Industrial Efficiency* (Boston: Houghton Mifflin, 1913).
20. Wren, *The Evolution of Management Theory*, pp. 255–264.
21. Elton Mayo, *The Human Problems of an Industrial Civilization* (New York: Macmillan, 1933); Fritz J. Roethlisberger and William J. Dickson, *Management and the Worker* (Cambridge, Mass.: Harvard University Press, 1939).
22. Abraham Maslow, "A Theory of Human Motivation," *Psychological Review*, July 1943, pp. 370–396.
23. Douglas McGregor, *The Human Side of Enterprise* (New York: McGraw-Hill, 1960).
24. Sara L. Rynes and Christine Quinn Trank, "Behavioral Science in the Business School Curriculum: Teaching in a Changing Institutional Environment," *Academy of Management Review*, 1999, vol. 24, no. 4, pp. 808–824.
25. See Gregory Moorhead and Ricky W. Griffin, *Organizational Behavior*, 7th ed. (Boston: Houghton Mifflin, 2004), for a recent review of current developments in the field of organizational behavior.
26. Wren, *The Evolution of Management Thought*, Chapter 21.
27. For more information on systems theory in general, see Ludwig von Bertalanffy, C. G. Hempel, R. E. Bass, and H. Jonas, "General Systems Theory: A New Approach to Unity of Science," I–VI *Human Biology*, vol. 23, 1951, pp. 302–361. For systems theory as applied to organizations, see Fremont E. Kast and James E. Rosenzweig, "General Systems Theory: Applications for Organizations and Management," *Academy of Management Journal*, December 1972, pp. 447–465. For a recent update, see Donde P. Ashmos and George P. Huber, "The Systems Paradigm in Organization Theory: Correcting the Record and Suggesting the Future," *Academy of Management Review*, October 1987, pp. 607–621.
28. "Morning After," *Forbes*, February 7, 2000, pp. 54–56.
29. Kathleen M. Eisenhardt and D. Charles Galunic, "Coevolving—At Last, a Way to Make Synergies Work," *Harvard Business Review*, January–February 2000, pp. 91–103.
30. Fremont E. Kast and James E. Rosenzweig, *Contingency Views of Organization and Management* (Chicago: Science Research Associates, 1973).
31. "Welch Memoirs Fetch $7.1M," *USA Today*, July 14, 2000, p. 1B.
32. "The Business Week Best-Seller List," *BusinessWeek*, November 4, 2002, p. 26.

PART two

THE ENVIRONMENTAL CONTEXT OF MANAGEMENT

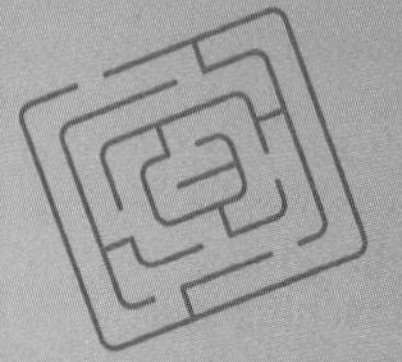

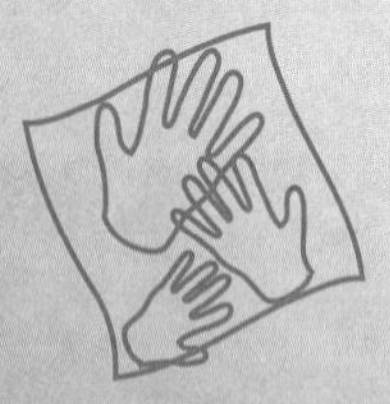

CHAPTER 3

The Environment and Culture of Organizations

CHAPTER 4

The Ethical and Social Environment

CHAPTER 5

The Global Environment

CHAPTER 6

The Multicultural Environment

の動き
22.04
+238.28

3 The Environment and Culture of Organizations

CHAPTER OUTLINE

The Organization's Environments

The External Environment
- The General Environment
- The Task Environment

The Internal Environment
- Owners
- Board of Directors
- Employees
- Physical Work Environment

The Organization's Culture
- The Importance of Organization Culture
- Determinants of Organization Culture
- Managing Organization Culture

Organization-Environment Relationships
- How Environments Affect Organizations
- How Organizations Adapt to Their Environments

The Environment and Organizational Effectiveness
- Models of Organizational Effectiveness
- Examples of Organizational Effectiveness

LEARNING OBJECTIVES

After studying this chapter, you should be able to:

1 ***Discuss the nature of the organizational environment and identify the environments of interest to most organizations.***

OPENING INCIDENT

When Starbucks opened a new store near It's A Grind, a Long Beach–based independent coffeehouse, locals feared that the giant retailer would put their neighborhood favorite out of business. Natives of San Diego turned out to protest a Starbucks' opening so close to their locally owned coffeehouses. But owners and customers are finding out something surprising about Starbucks stores—sales increase for all coffeehouses wherever the international chain has an outlet.

At first glance, the customers' qualms appear to be correct. After all, it only makes sense that a huge multinational firm like Starbucks would enjoy advantages in pricing, new-product development, and other areas that would tend to give it an advantage. Using size as a competitive weapon has been a common tactic for decades, used by firms ranging from Standard Oil, Sears, and General Motors to the most contemporary example—Wal-Mart. "A big company like Starbucks can come in and lose money for two years until they wipe everybody else out," editorializes the *Indianapolis Star*, reporting the closing of a local coffeehouse. "It's the old Wal-Mart thing."

Fear of the power of Starbucks has even caused owners to take some

2	3	4	5	6
Describe the components of the general and task environments and discuss their impact on organizations.	***Identify the components of the internal environment and discuss their impact on organizations.***	***Discuss the importance and determinants of an organization's culture and how the culture can be managed.***	***Identify and describe how the environment affects organizations and how organizations adapt to their environment.***	***Describe the basic models of organizational effectiveness and provide contemporary examples of highly effective firms.***

"Starbucks helped our business, but I don't want to give them any credit for it."

—Jon Cates, co-owner of the Broadway Cafe in Kansas City

extraordinary measures to reduce the possibility of head-to-head competition. One owner, Courtney Bates of Kansas City's City Market Coffee Company, required her landlord to sign a clause preventing rental to any other coffeehouse. Another owner was approached by Starbucks about a possible buyout but was too suspicious of the firm to share any store information with it. "I don't think they really wanted to buy it. They just wanted a peek inside my business," claims Jeff Schmidt, owner of LatteLand in Kansas City. One thousand customers in Kansas City signed a petition asking the city to ban Starbucks. Katerina Carson, owner of Katerina's in Chicago, sums up this view when she says tersely, "Starbucks is a corporate monster."

But the statistics just do not support the assertion that Starbucks is eliminating competition and slashing profits in the coffeehouse industry. In fact, while Starbucks outlets in the United States have grown from 1,000 in 1997 to just over 3,000 today, independents have increased from 7,000 to 10,000 over that same period. And, while the total number of coffeehouses has grown from 8,000 to 13,000 since 1997, sales have more than doubled, which demonstrates that sales volume per store is increasing.

Indeed, many coffeehouse owners are forced to admit that, in spite of their fears, their sales increased when a Starbucks located a new store in their vicinity. Jon Cates, co-owner of the Broadway Cafe in Kansas City, says, "Starbucks helped our business, but I don't want to give them any credit for it." Some owners have gone further, embracing the entrance of the chain into local markets. "Competition is good," says Norma Slaman, owner of Newbreak Coffee in San Diego, who saw sales rise 15 percent after Starbucks' arrival. Some chains have even adopted the strategy of following Starbucks into a neighborhood. Doug Zell located his Intelligentsia Coffee Roasters store near not just one, but two, Starbucks locations in Chicago. "It's been double-digit growth every year," says Zell.

Starbucks is increasing competitive pressure on independent coffeehouses, yet the independents are prospering right along with their giant competitor. This might be because the independents are so fearful of Starbucks that they implement improvements even before the chain arrives. It's A Grind fixed up stores, improving customer service and staff training, too, when a Starbucks opened nearby, and found that sales have been rising 10 percent or more annually since then. Other independents have been prompted to ban smoking or roast their own beans, two significant aspects of Starbucks' operations. Focus on local activities and preferences is another way for independents to compete successfully, through poetry readings, live jazz, works by local artists, and regional food choices.

Starbucks is rapidly expanding into new markets everywhere—including China!

It seems that Starbucks has not merely increased rivalry, but also shifted industry dynamics in areas such as customers and new entrants. Although Starbucks and the independent coffeehouses are more profitable than ever, it appears that, for now, the customers are the big winners in this evolving industry.[1]

The world operates in what frequently appears to be mysterious ways. Sometimes competition hurts, but sometimes it helps. When Starbucks opens a new store, its closest competitors often benefit. Ford and General Motors compete with each other for consumer dollars but work together to promote the interests of the U.S. auto industry. And CEOs face growing pressure to curb their salaries but grow their businesses. Clearly, the environmental context of business today is changing in unprecedented ways.

As we note in Chapter 1, managers must have a deep understanding and appreciation of the environment in which they and their organizations function. Without this understanding they are like rudderless ships—moving along but with no way of maneuvering or changing direction. This chapter is the first of four devoted to the environmental context of management. After introducing the nature of the organization's environment, we describe first the general and then the task environment in detail. We then discuss key parts of the internal environment of an organization. We then address organization-environment relationships and, finally, how these relationships determine the effectiveness of the organization.

The Organization's Environments

To illustrate the importance of the environment to an organization, consider the analogy of a swimmer crossing a wide stream. The swimmer must assess the current, obstacles, and distance before setting out. If these elements are properly evaluated, the swimmer will arrive at the expected point on the far bank of the stream. But if they are not properly understood, the swimmer might end up too far upstream or downstream. The organization is like a swimmer, and the environment is like the stream. Thus, just as the swimmer needs to understand conditions in the water, the organization must understand the basic elements of its environment in order to properly maneuver among them.[2] More specifically, a key element in the effective management of an organization is determining the ideal alignment between the environment and the organization and then working to achieve and maintain that alignment. In order to do so, however, the manager must first thoroughly understand the nature of the organization's environments.[3]

external environment Everything outside an organization's boundaries that might affect it

internal environment The conditions and forces within an organization

The **external environment** is everything outside an organization's boundaries that might affect it. As shown in Figure 3.1, there are actually two separate external environments: the general environment and the task environment. An organization's **internal environment** consists of conditions and forces within the organization. Of course, not all parts of these environments are equally important for all organizations. A small, two-person partnership does not have a board of directors, for example, whereas a large public corporation is required by law to have one. A private university with a large endowment (like Harvard) may be less concerned about general economic conditions than might a state university (like the University of Missouri), which is dependent on state funding from tax revenues. Still, organizations need to fully understand which environmental forces are important and how the importance of others might increase.

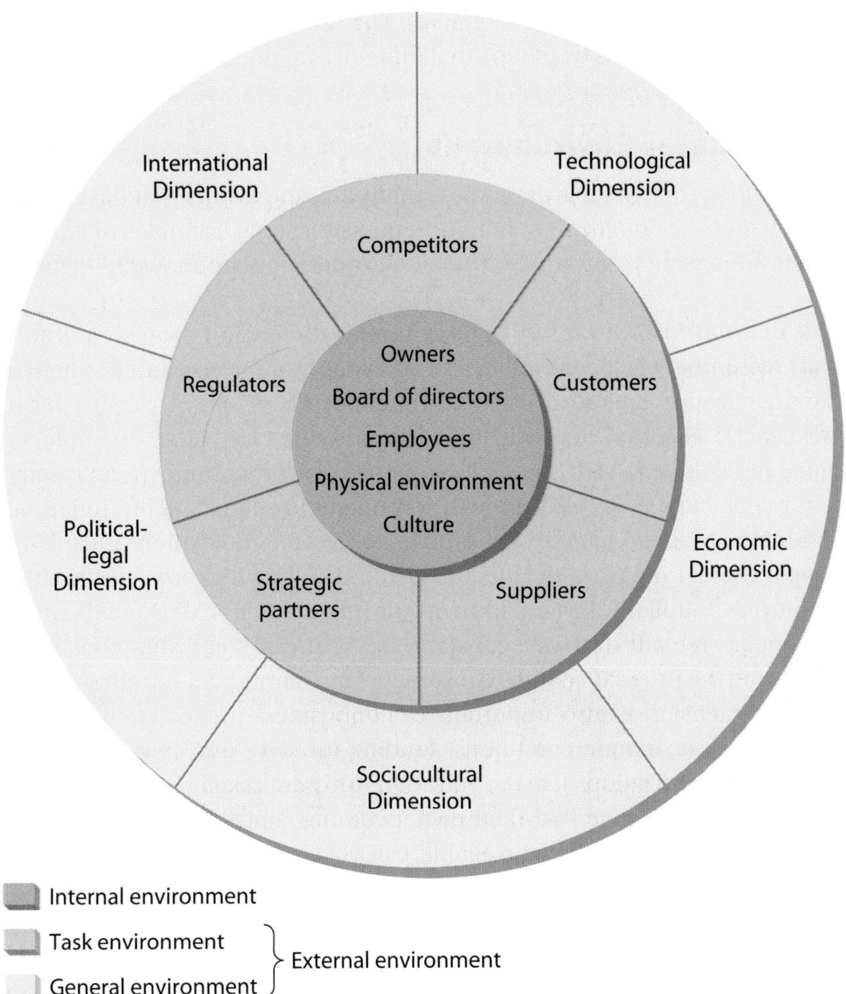

FIGURE 3.1

The Organization and Its Environments

Organizations have both an external and an internal environment. The external environment consists of two layers: the general environment and the task environment.

concept CHECK

Define "environment" as it relates to organizations.

How easily differentiated are an organization's external and internal environments?

The External Environment

As just noted, an organization's external environment consists of two parts. The **general environment** of an organization is the set of broad dimensions and forces in its surroundings that create its overall context. These dimensions and forces are not necessarily associated with other specific organizations. The general environment of most organizations has economic, technological, sociocultural, political-legal, and international dimensions. The other significant external environment for

general environment The set of broad dimensions and forces in an organization's surroundings that create its overall context

task environment Specific organizations or groups that influence an organization

an organization is its task environment. The **task environment** consists of specific external organizations or groups that influence an organization.

The General Environment

Each of these dimensions embodies conditions and events that have the potential to influence the organization in important ways. Some examples to illustrate these dimensions as they relate to McDonald's Corporation are shown in Figure 3.2.

economic dimension The overall health and vitality of the economic system in which the organization operates

The Economic Dimension The **economic dimension** of an organization's general environment is the overall health and vitality of the economic system in which the organization operates.[4] Particularly important economic factors for business are general economic growth, inflation, interest rates, and unemployment. As noted in Figure 3.2, McDonald's U.S. operation is functioning in an economy currently characterized by weak growth, low unemployment, and low inflation.[5] These conditions produce paradoxical problems. Low unemployment means that more people can eat out, but McDonald's also has to pay higher wages to attract new employees.[6] Similarly, low inflation means that the prices McDonald's must pay for its supplies remain relatively constant, but it also is somewhat constrained from increasing the prices it charges consumers for a hamburger or milkshake. The economic dimension is also important to nonbusiness organizations. For example, during weak economic conditions, funding for state universities may drop, and charitable organizations like the Salvation Army are asked to provide greater assistance at the same time that their own incoming contributions dwindle. Similarly, hospitals are affected by the availability of government grants and the number of low-income patients they must treat free of charge.

The Technological Dimension The **technological dimension** of the general environment refers to the methods available for converting resources into products or services. Although technology is applied within the organization, the forms and availability of that technology come from the general environment. Computer-assisted manufacturing and design techniques, for example, allow Boeing to simulate the more than three miles of hydraulic tubing that run through a 777 aircraft. The results include decreased warehouse needs, higher-quality tube fittings, fewer employees, and major time savings. Although some people associate technology with manufacturing firms, it is also relevant in the service sector. For example, just as an automobile follows a predetermined path along an assembly line as it is built, a hamburger at McDonald's follows a predefined path as the meat is cooked, the burger assembled, and the finished product wrapped and

The techological dimension of the general environment continues to evolve at breakneck speed. The pace of change and complexity involving computers and information technology is especially pronounced. Take this marketplace in Kampala, Uganda, for example. Buyers and sellers of fruits and vegetables have gathered here for centuries. But the presence of an Internet Service Provider is a new feature at the market, and one that has the potential to revolutionize how the citizens of Africa live, work, and interact with the rest of the world.

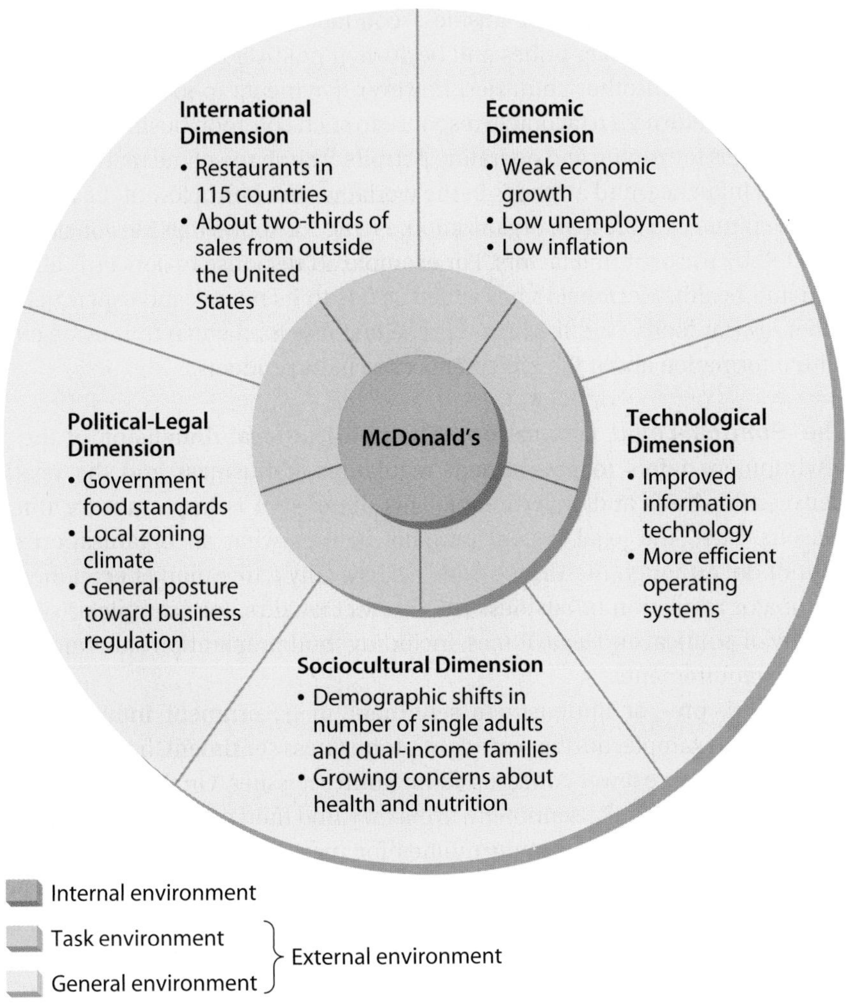

FIGURE 3.2

McDonald's General Environment

The general environment of an organization consists of economic, technological, sociocultural, political-legal, and international dimensions. This figure clearly illustrates how these dimensions are relevant to managers at McDonald's.

bagged for a customer. The rapid infusion of the Internet into all areas of business is also a reflection of the technological dimension. Another recent advancement is the rapid growth of integrated business software systems.

technological dimension The methods available for converting resources into products or services

The Sociocultural Dimension The **sociocultural dimension** of the general environment includes the customs, mores, values, and demographic characteristics of the society in which the organization functions. Sociocultural processes are important because they determine the products, services, and standards of conduct that the society is likely to value. In some countries, for example, consumers are willing to pay premium prices for designer clothes, whereas the same clothes have virtually no market in other countries. Consumer tastes also change over time. Preferences for color, style, taste, and so forth change from season to season, for example. Drinking hard liquor and smoking cigarettes are less common in the United States today than they were just a few years ago. And sociocultural factors influence how workers in a society feel about their jobs and organizations.

sociocultural dimension The customs, mores, values, and demographic characteristics of the society in which the organization functions

Appropriate standards of business conduct also vary across cultures. In the United States, accepting bribes and bestowing political favors in return are considered unethical. In other countries, however, payments to local politicians may be expected in return for a favorable response to such common business transactions as applications for zoning and operating permits. The shape of the market, the ethics of political influence, and attitudes in the workforce are only a few of the many ways in which culture can affect an organization. Figure 3.2 shows that McDonald's is clearly affected by sociocultural factors. For example, in response to concerns about nutrition and health, McDonald's has added salads to its menus and experimented with other low-fat foods. And the firm was the first fast-food chain to provide customers with information about the ingredients used in its products.

political-legal dimension The government regulation of business and the relationship between business and government

The Political-Legal Dimension The **political-legal dimension** of the general environment refers to government regulation of business and the relationship between business and government. This dimension is important for three basic reasons. First, the legal system partially defines what an organization can and cannot do. Although the United States is basically a free market economy, there is still major regulation of business activity. McDonald's, for example, is subject to a variety of political and legal forces, including food preparation standards and local zoning requirements.

Second, pro- or antibusiness sentiment in government influences business activity. For example, during periods of probusiness sentiment, firms find it easier to compete and have fewer concerns about antitrust issues. On the other hand, during a period of antibusiness sentiment, firms may find their competitive strategies more restricted and have fewer opportunities for mergers and acquisitions because of antitrust concerns. Among the most recent examples of the effects of the political-legal dimension were legal constraints imposed on Microsoft in 2000, President George W. Bush's legal mandate to end a West Coast port labor dispute in 2002, and the investigation of Martha Stewart for possible insider stock trading in 2003.

Finally, political stability has ramifications for planning. No business wants to set up shop in another country unless trade relationships with that country are relatively well defined and stable. Hence, U.S. firms are more likely to do business with England, Mexico, and Canada than with Haiti and Afghanistan. Similar issues are relevant to assessments of local and state governments. A new mayor or governor can affect many organizations, especially small firms that do business in only one location and are susceptible to deed and zoning restrictions, property and school taxes, and the like.

international dimension The extent to which an organization is involved in or affected by business in other countries

The International Dimension Yet another component of the general environment for many organizations is the **international dimension**, or the extent to which an organization is involved in or affected by businesses in other countries.[7] As we discuss more fully in Chapter 5, multinational firms such as General Electric, Boeing, Nestlé, Sony, Siemens, and Hyundai clearly affect and are affected by international conditions and markets. For example, as noted in Figure 3.2, McDonald's operates restaurants in 115 countries and derives about two-thirds of its total sales from outside the United States. Even firms that do business in only one country may face foreign competition at home, and they may use materials or production equipment imported from abroad. The international dimension also has implications for not-for-profit organizations. For example, the Peace Corps sends representatives to underdeveloped countries. As a result of advances in transportation and information technology in the past century, almost no part of the world is cut off from the rest. As a result, virtually every organization is affected by the international dimension of its general environment.

The Task Environment

competitor An organization that competes with other organizations for resources

Because the impact of the general environment is often vague, imprecise, and long term, most organizations tend to focus their attention on their task environment. This environment includes competitors, customers, suppliers, strategic partners, and regulators. Although the task environment is also quite complex, it provides useful information more readily than does the general environment, because the manager can identify environmental factors of specific interest to the organization, rather than having to deal with the more abstract dimensions of the general environment.[8] Figure 3.3 depicts the task environment of McDonald's.

FIGURE 3.3

McDonald's Task Environment

An organization's task environment includes its competitors, customers, suppliers, strategic partners, and regulators. This figure clearly highlights how managers at McDonald's can use this framework to identify and understand their key constituents.

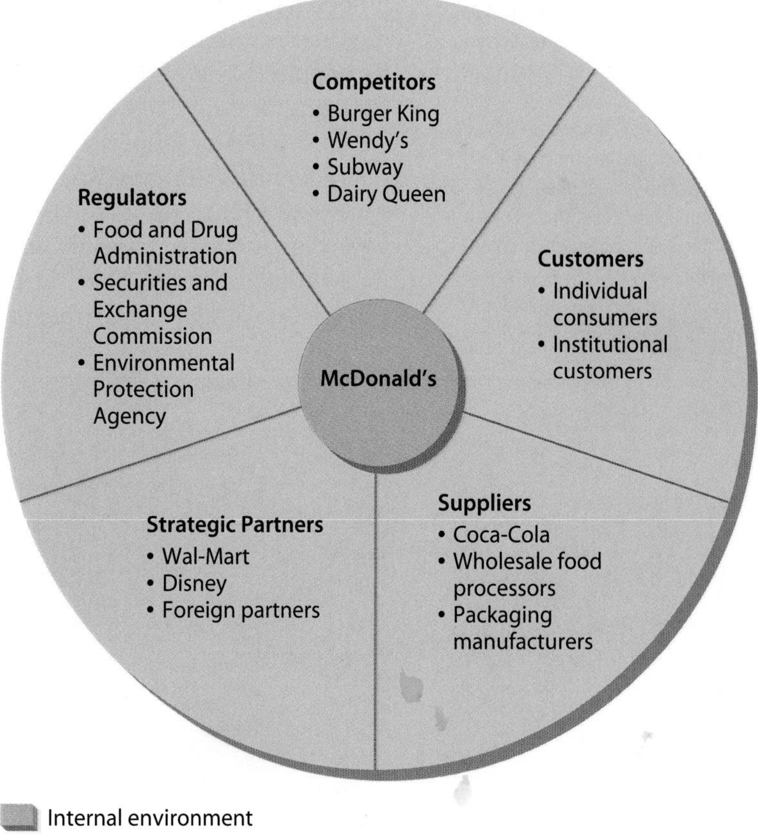

Competitors An organization's **competitors** are other organizations that compete with it for resources. The most obvious resources that competitors vie for are customer dollars. Reebok, Adidas, and Nike are competitors, as are Albertson's, Safeway, and Kroger. McDonald's competes with other fast-food operations, such as Burger King, Wendy's, Subway, and Dairy Queen. But competition also occurs between substitute products. Thus Ford competes with Yamaha (motorcycles) and Schwinn (bicycles) for your transportation dollars; and Walt Disney World, Club Med, and Carnival Cruise Lines compete for your vacation dollars. Nor is competition limited to business firms. Universities compete with trade schools, the military, other universities, and the external labor market to attract good students; and art galleries compete with each other to attract the best exhibits.

Organizations may also compete for different kinds of resources besides consumer dollars. For example, two totally unrelated organizations might compete to acquire a loan from a bank that has only limited funds to lend. Two retailers might compete for the right to purchase a prime piece of real estate in a growing community. In a large city, the police and fire departments might compete for the same tax dollars. And businesses also compete for quality labor, technological breakthroughs and patents, and scarce raw materials.

customer Whoever pays money to acquire an organization's products or services

Customers A second dimension of the task environment is **customers**, or whoever pays money to acquire an organization's products or services. Most of McDonald's customers are individuals who walk into a restaurant to buy food. But customers need not be individuals. Schools, hospitals, government agencies, wholesalers, retailers, and manufacturers are just a few of the many kinds of organizations that may be major customers of other organizations. Some institutional customers, such as schools, prisons, and hospitals, also buy food in bulk from restaurants like McDonald's.

Dealing with customers has become increasingly complex in recent years. New products and services, new methods of marketing, and more discriminating customers have all added uncertainty to how businesses relate to their customers, as has lower brand loyalty. A few years ago, McDonald's introduced a new sandwich called the Arch Deluxe, intended to appeal to adult customers. Unfortunately, the product failed because most adult customers preferred existing menu choices like the Quarter Pounder. Similarly, the discount giant Target has recently lost some of its popularity with customers because its product mix has not kept pace with changing tastes and trends.[9]

Companies face especially critical differences among customers as they expand internationally. McDonald's sells beer in its German restaurants, for example, and wine in its French restaurants. Customers in those countries see those particular beverages as normal parts of a meal, much as customers in the United States routinely drink water, tea, or soft drinks with their meals. The firm has even opened restaurants with no beef on the menu! Those restaurants are in India, where beef is not a popular menu option. Instead, the local McDonald's in that country use lamb in their sandwiches.

Suppliers are an integral part of an organization's task environment. Hewlett-Packard, for instance, buys keyboards from suppliers in Asia. When it recently ramped up production for a major new product line, it had to call on its suppliers to get their own production going more quickly than had been expected. And because they all responded, HP was able to meet its earlier launch dates for its new product line.

Suppliers **Suppliers** are organizations that provide resources for other organizations. McDonald's buys soft drink products from Coca-Cola; individually packaged servings of ketchup from Heinz; ingredients from wholesale food processors; and napkins, sacks, and wrappers from packaging manufacturers. Common wisdom in the United States used to be that a business should try to avoid depending exclusively on particular suppliers. A firm that buys all of a certain resource from one supplier may be crippled if the supplier goes out of business or is faced with a strike. This practice can also help maintain a competitive relationship among suppliers, keeping costs down. But firms eager to emulate successful Japanese firms have recently tried to change their approach. Japanese firms have a history of building major ties with only one or two major suppliers. This enables them to work together better for their mutual benefit and makes the supplier more responsive to the customer's needs.

supplier An organization that provides resources for other organizations

Honda picked Donnelly Corporation to make all the mirrors for its U.S.-manufactured cars. Honda chose Donnelly because it learned enough about the firm to know that it did high-quality work and that its corporate culture and values were consistent with those endorsed by Honda. Recognizing the value of Honda as a customer, Donnelly built an entirely new plant to make the mirrors. And all this was accomplished with only a handshake. Motorola goes even further, providing its principal suppliers with access to its own renowned quality training program and evaluating the performance of each supplier as a way of helping that firm boost its own quality.

strategic partners (strategic allies) An organization working together with one or more other organizations in a joint venture or similar arrangement

Strategic Partners Another dimension of the task environment is **strategic partners** (also called **strategic allies**)—two or more companies that work together in joint ventures or other partnerships.[10] As shown in Figure 3.3, McDonald's has several strategic partners. For example, it has one arrangement with Wal-Mart whereby small McDonald's restaurants are built in many Wal-Mart stores. The firm also has a long-term deal with Disney: McDonald's will promote Disney movies in its stores, and Disney will build McDonald's restaurants or kiosks in its theme parks. And many of the firm's foreign stores are built in collaboration with local investors. Strategic partnerships help companies get from other companies the expertise they lack. They also help spread risk and open new market opportunities. Indeed, most strategic partnerships are actually among international firms. For example, Ford has strategic partnerships with Volkswagen (sharing a distribution and service center in South America) and Nissan (building minivans in the United States).

regulator A unit that has the potential to control, legislate, or otherwise influence the organization's policies and practices

regulatory agency An agency created by the government to regulate business activities

interest group A group organized by its members to attempt to influence business

Regulators **Regulators** are elements of the task environment that have the potential to control, legislate, or otherwise influence an organization's policies and practices. There are two important kinds of regulators. The first, **regulatory agencies**, are created by the government to protect the public from certain business practices or to protect organizations from one another. The second, **interest groups**, are organized by their members to attempt to influence organizations.

Powerful federal regulatory agencies include the Environmental Protection Agency (EPA), the Securities and Exchange Commission (SEC), the Food and Drug Administration (FDA), and the Equal Employment Opportunity Commission (EEOC). Many of these agencies play important roles in protecting the rights of individuals. The FDA, for example, helps ensure that the food we eat is free from contaminants and thus is an important regulator for McDonald's. At the same time, many managers complain that there is too much government regulation. Most large companies must dedicate thousands of labor hours and hundreds of thousands of dollars a year to complying with government regulations. To complicate the lives of managers even more, different regulatory agencies sometimes provide inconsistent—even contradictory—mandates.

Copyright Danny Shanahan

The regulatory environment of business imposes numerous constraints on organizations. Laws regarding employment practices have become particularly complicated in recent years. For example, a firm that uses discriminatory practices can be sued for not hiring someone or for firing a current employee. But the firm can also be penalized if it should reject or fire someone but fails to do so! Not surprisingly, then, many employment decisions today are routinely reviewed by attorneys. And the opinions of these attorneys often determine whether or not someone will be hired or fired.

For example, several years ago the *Exxon Valdez* tanker ran aground, spilling 11 million gallons of crude oil off the coast of Alaska. The EPA forced ExxonMobil to cover the costs of the ensuing cleanup. Because an investigation suggested that the ship's captain was drunk at the time, the EPA also mandated that ExxonMobil impose stricter hiring standards for employees in high-risk jobs. To comply with this mandate, ExxonMobil adopted a policy of not assigning anyone with a history of alcohol or substance abuse to certain jobs like tanker captain. However, another regulatory agency, the EEOC, then sued ExxonMobil on the grounds that restricting people who have been rehabilitated from alcohol abuse from any job violates their rights under the Americans with Disabilities Act. ExxonMobil was thus forced to change its policy, but was then again criticized by the EPA. The cartoon provides another take on this type of issue.

The regulatory environment in other countries, however, is even more stringent. When U.S. retailer Wal-Mart wants to open a new store, its regulatory requirements are actually quite low, and the procedures it must follow are clearly spelled out. In a sense, within reason and general basic ground rules, the firm can open a store just about anywhere it wants and operate it in just about any manner it wants. But conditions in Germany are quite different. That country's largest retailer, Allkauf, tried for over fifteen years to open a store in one town—on land that it already owned. But the city government did not allow it because it feared that local competitors would suffer. And, by German law, Allkauf's existing stores can be open only 68.5 hours a week; they must close no later than 6:30 P.M. on weekdays and 2:00 P.M. on Saturday, and must remain closed on Sunday. They can hold large sales only twice a year and can never discount food items.

The other basic form of regulator is the interest group. Prominent interest groups include the National Organization for Women (NOW), Mothers Against Drunk Drivers (MADD), the National Rifle Association (NRA), the League of Women Voters, the Sierra Club, Ralph Nader's Center for the Study of Responsive Law, Consumers Union, and industry self-regulation groups like the Council of Better Business Bureaus. Although interest groups lack the official power of government agencies, they can exert considerable influence by using the media to call attention to their positions. MADD, for example, puts considerable pressure on alcoholic-beverage producers (to put warning labels on their products), automobile companies (to make it more difficult for intoxicated people to start their cars), local governments (to stiffen drinking ordinances), and bars and restaurants (to refuse to sell alcohol to people who are drinking too much).

concept CHECK

List the dimensions of the general and the task environments of a business.	*Identify linkages between dimensions of the general environment and dimensions of the task environment.*

The Internal Environment

As we show earlier in Figure 3.1, organizations also have an internal environment that consists of their owners, board of directors, employees, physical work environment, and culture.

Owners

The **owners** of a business are, of course, the people who have legal property rights to that business. Owners can be a single individual who establishes and runs a small business, partners who jointly own the business, individual investors who buy stock in a corporation, or other organizations. McDonald's has 700 million shares of stock, each of which represents one unit of ownership in the firm. The family of McDonald's founder Ray Kroc stills owns a large block of this stock, as do several large institutional investors. In addition, there are thousands of individuals who own just a few shares each. McDonald's, in turn, owns other businesses. For example, it owns several large regional bakeries that supply its restaurants with buns. Each of these is incorporated as a separate legal entity and managed as a wholly owned subsidiary by the parent company. McDonald's has also recently bought partial ownership of Chipolte Mexican Grill and Donatos Pizza chain.

owner Whoever can claim property rights to an organization

Board of Directors

A corporate **board of directors** is a governing body elected by the stockholders and charged with overseeing the general management of the firm to ensure that it is being run in a way that best serves the stockholders' interests. Some boards are relatively passive. They perform a general oversight function but seldom get actively involved in how the company is really being run. But this trend is changing, as more and more boards are carefully scrutinizing the firms they oversee and exerting more influence over how they are being managed. This trend has in part been spurred by numerous recent business scandals. In some cases, board members have been accused of wrongdoing. In other cases, boards have been found negligent for failing to monitor the actions of firm executives.[11] At issue is the concept of corporate governance—who is responsible for governing the actions of a business. *Working with Diversity* discusses an alarming lack of diversity on corporate boards of directors.

board of directors Governing body elected by a corporation's stockholders and charged with overseeing the general management of the firm to ensure that it is being run in a way that best serves the stockholders' interests

WORKING WITH diversity

Why Aren't Boards of Directors More Diverse?

"... the depth of talent is there. So why aren't we being called?"

– Carl Brooks, head of the Executive Leadership Council*

Although the U.S. workforce today is increasingly diverse, corporate boards of directors are dominated by white males. White men make up 43 percent of workers but 82 percent of board members of Fortune 1000 corporations. Other groups are underrepresented–white women are 36 percent of workers but just 11 percent of directors. African Americans make up 11 percent and 3 percent, respectively, whereas Latinos account for 10 percent and 2 percent, respectively. Reducing diversity further, many minorities serve on more than one board. For example, there are 388 board seats filled by African Americans, but only 186 individuals hold those seats.

Some point to a lack of qualified minority candidates, but with more minorities in management roles, this is less true than it used to be. Carl Brooks, head of the Executive Leadership Council, a networking group for high-level African-American managers, says, "For a long time, the argument was there wasn't enough talent. But the depth of talent is there. So why aren't we being called?" Howard University President H. Patrick Swygert, who serves on several boards, says that he is often approached about adding another company to his memberships. "I try to direct headhunters and CEOs to other qualified candidates. In 2002, it's simply unacceptable and very dated for anyone to say they can't find qualified candidates."

James Kristie, editor of *Directors & Boards* magazine, proposes a lack of exposure to other top executives, saying, "It's like being invited into a secret club." Others are more blunt in their assessments of discrimination. "Frankly, there are a number of minorities I thought would be on boards by now," says Roger Raber, head of a directors' trade group. Susan Schultz, author of *The Board Book*, says, "There is still a fear of diversity. It's natural to surround ourselves with people just like us. Anything different requires a proactive leap of faith."

Still, there is hope that the diversity of boards will continue to increase, as American firms better appreciate the advantages of diversity. Dr. Westina Matthews Shatteen, first vice president at Merrill Lynch, sums up the importance of diversity, saying, "It's important for board members to present themselves as agents of change, so that corporations will follow more inclusive practices and embrace the changing faces of the global market."

References: Gary Strauss, "Civilian Labor Force and Participation Rates with Projections: 1970 to 2008," *Statistical Abstract of the United States:* 2000, U.S. Census Bureau, p. 403; "Good Old Boys' Network Still Rules Corporate Boards," *USA Today*, November 1, 2002, pp. 1A–B (*quote p. 1A); "Operation: Boardroom Diversity," *KIP Business Report*, March 8, 2002, www.kipbusinessreport.com on November 18, 2002.

Employees

An organization's employees are also a major element of its internal environment. Of particular interest to managers today is the changing nature of the workforce, as it becomes increasingly more diverse in terms of gender, ethnicity, age, and other dimensions. Workers are also calling for more job ownership—either partial ownership in the company or at least more say in how they perform their jobs.[12] Another trend in many firms is increased reliance on temporary workers—individuals hired for short periods of time with no expectation of permanent employment. Employers often prefer to use "temps" because they provide greater flexibility, earn lower wages, and often do not participate in benefits programs. But these managers also have to deal with what often amounts to a two-class workforce and with a growing number of employees who have no loyalty to the organization where they work, because they may be working for a different one tomorrow.[13]

The permanent employees of many organizations are organized into labor unions, representing yet another layer of complexity for managers. The National Labor Relations Act of 1935 requires organizations to recognize and bargain with a union if that union has been legally established by the organization's employees. Presently, around 23 percent of the U.S. labor force is represented by unions. Some large firms, such as Ford, Exxon, and General Motors, have several different unions. Even when an organization's labor force is not unionized, its managers do not ignore unions. For example, Honda of America, Wal-Mart, and Delta Air Lines all actively work to avoid unionization. And, even though people think primarily of blue-collar workers as union members, many white-collar workers, such as government employees and teachers, are also represented by unions.

Physical Work Environment

A final part of the internal environment is the actual physical environment of the organization and the work that people do. Some firms have their facilities in downtown skyscrapers, usually spread across several floors. Others locate in suburban or rural settings and may have facilities more closely resembling a college campus. Some facilities have long halls lined with traditional offices. Others have modular cubicles with partial walls and no doors. The top hundred managers at Mars, makers of Snickers and Milky Way, all work in a single vast room. Two copresidents are located in the very center of the room, while others are arrayed in concentric circles around them. Increasingly, newer facilities have an even more open arrangement, where people work in large rooms, moving among different tables to interact with different people on different projects. Freestanding computer workstations are available for those who need them, and a few small rooms might be off to the side for private business.[14]

The physical work environment is an important consideration for many businesses. This construction supervisor is overseeing work at the new Academy Awards Center in Los Angeles. Because of the nature of his physical work environment, he relies on wireless communication equipment to keep in contact with different work crews. As construction progresses, his methods for communicating will also change.

concept CHECK

Identify the main parts of an organization's internal environment.	What is corporate governance, and how is it related to the environment of business?

The Organization's Culture

organization culture The set of values, beliefs, behaviors, customs, and attitudes that helps the members of the organization understand what it stands for, how it does things, and what it considers important

An especially important part of the internal environment of an organization is its culture. **Organization culture** is the set of values, beliefs, behaviors, customs, and attitudes that helps the members of the organization understand what it stands for, how it does things, and what it considers important.[15] Culture is an amorphous concept that defies objective measurement or observation. Nevertheless, because it is the foundation of the organization's internal environment, it plays a major role in shaping managerial behavior.

The Importance of Organization Culture

Executives at Ford Motor Company recently decided to move the firm's Lincoln Mercury division from Detroit to southern California. Interestingly, though, this move had little to do with costs or any of the other reasons most business relocations occur. Instead, they wanted to move Lincoln Mercury out from the corporate shadow of its dominating, larger corporate cousin, Ford itself. For years, Lincoln Mercury managers had complained that their business was always given short shrift and that most of Detroit's attention was focused on Ford. And, at least partially as a result, Mercury products all tended to look like clones of Ford products, and the division consistently failed to meet its goals or live up to its expectations. Finally, the company decided that the only way to turn the division around was to give it its own identity. And where better to start than by moving the whole operation—lock, stock, and barrel—to car-centric southern California, where its managers could be freer to hire new creative talent and start carving out a new and unique business niche for themselves.[16] In short, they wanted to create a new culture. But, as discussed in *The Business of Ethics*, a strong culture can be bad as well as good!

Culture determines the "feel" of the organization. The stereotypic image of Microsoft, for example, is a workplace where people dress very casually and work very long hours. In contrast, the image of Bank of America for some observers is a formal setting with rigid work rules and people dressed in conservative business attire. And Texas Instruments likes to talk about its "shirtsleeve" culture, in which ties are avoided and few managers ever wear jackets. Southwest Airlines maintains a culture that stresses fun and excitement.

Of course, the same culture is not necessarily found throughout an entire organization. For example, the sales and marketing department may have a culture quite different from that of the operations and manufacturing department. Regardless of its nature, however, culture is a powerful force in organizations, one that can shape the firm's overall effectiveness and long-term success. Companies that can develop and maintain a strong culture, such as Hewlett-Packard and Procter & Gamble, tend to be more effective than companies that have trouble developing and maintaining a strong culture, such as Kmart.[17]

Determinants of Organization Culture

Where does an organization's culture come from? Typically, it develops and blossoms over a long period of time. Its starting point is often the organization's founder.

THE BUSINESS of ethics

Enron's In-Your-Face Culture

"It was completely hands-off management."

— A former Enron manager*

Corporate culture profoundly affects the behavior of employees. Unfortunately, in Enron's case, the firm's in-your-face culture encouraged some employees to lie and steal. Enron executives are now claiming that they were completely unaware of any illegal activity. That assertion is a bit unbelievable, given that one of the alleged ringleaders, Ken Lay, has a Ph.D. in economics and another, Jeffrey Skilling, has a Harvard M.B.A. and was a consultant at prestigious McKinsey & Company.

But, just to help them out, here are some signs that Enron's culture may have been headed for trouble:

1. Andrew Fastow, chief financial officer, had an office display that named "Communication" as a corporate value. Underneath, the small print explained, "When Enron says it's going to rip your face off, it will rip your face off."
2. Employees unwound together after work—in a strip bar. "[Enron's] guys were known for spending big money and letting you know they worked there," says Brittany Lucas, an exotic dancer. The accounting department reminded employees not to use company credit cards at that type of place, but instead to charge personal cards and then apply for reimbursement.
3. One division put pressure on the other divisions to buy products and services supplied by the family members of top executives. "It was beyond encouraged," claims a divisional financial chief.
4. The firm was supposed to be negotiating impartially with an independent supplier, but the supplier was represented by a firm employee. Other firms bidding on those contracts were not informed of the relationship.

Enron engaged in every one of these outrageous practices, not just occasionally, but as a matter of routine. It is no wonder, then, that executives are convicted or awaiting trial on charges of fraud, illegal securities transactions, lying to Congress under oath, money laundering, and other felonies. Was every Enron employee dishonest or unethical? Of course not. But top managers created a corporate climate where such behavior was tolerated or even rewarded.

"The environment was ripe for abuse. Nobody at corporate was asking the right questions," says a former Enron manager. "It was completely hands-off management. A situation like that requires tight controls. Instead, it was a runaway train."

References: Anita Raghavan, Kathryn Kranhold and Alexei Barrionuevo, "How Enron Bosses Created a Culture of Pushing Limits," *Wall Street Journal*, August 26, 2002, pp. A1, A7; John A. Byrne, "At Enron, the Environment Was Ripe for Abuse," *BusinessWeek*, February 25, 2002, pp. 118–120 (*quote p. 119); Wendy Zellner, "Jeff Skilling: Enron's Mystery Man," *BusinessWeek*, February 11, 2002, pp. 38–40.

For example, James Cash Penney believed in treating employees and customers with respect and dignity. Employees at J.C. Penney are still called "associates" rather than "employees" (to reflect partnership), and customer satisfaction is of paramount importance. The impact of Sam Walton, Ross Perot, and Walt Disney is still felt in the organizations they founded.[18] As an organization grows, its culture is modified, shaped, and refined by symbols, stories, heroes, slogans, and ceremonies. For example, an important value at Hewlett-Packard is the avoidance of bank debt. A popular story still told at the company involves a new project that was being considered for several years. All objective criteria indicated that HP should borrow money from a bank to finance it, yet Bill Hewlett and David Packard rejected it out of hand simply because "HP avoids bank debt." This story, involving two corporate heroes and based on a slogan, dictates corporate culture today. And many decisions at Walt Disney Company today are still framed by asking, "What would Walt have done?"

Corporate success and shared experiences also shape culture. For example, Hallmark Cards has a strong culture derived from its years of success in the greeting card industry. Employees speak of "the Hallmark family" and care deeply about the company; many of them have worked at the company for years. At Kmart, in contrast, the culture is quite weak, the management team changes rapidly, and few people sense any direction or purpose in the company. The differences in culture at Hallmark and Kmart are in part attributable to past successes and shared experiences.

Managing Organization Culture

How can managers deal with culture, given its clear importance but intangible nature? Essentially, the manager must understand the current culture and then decide if it should be maintained or changed. By understanding the organization's current culture, managers can take appropriate actions. At Hewlett-Packard, the values represented by "the HP way" still exist, guiding and directing most important activities undertaken by the firm. Indeed, the firm's CEO, Carly Fiorina, launched her tenure at the firm with a series of television commercials focusing on the firm's Silicon Valley roots and the garage where it started. Culture can also be maintained by rewarding and promoting people whose behaviors are consistent with the existing culture and by articulating the culture through slogans, ceremonies, and so forth.

But managers must walk a fine line between maintaining a culture that still works effectively and changing a culture that has become dysfunctional. For example, many of the firms already noted, as well as numerous others, take pride in perpetuating their culture. Shell Oil, for example, has an elaborate display in the lobby of its Houston headquarters that tells the story of the firm's past. But other companies may face situations in which their culture is no longer a strength. For example, some critics feel that General Motors' culture places too much emphasis on product development and internal competition among divisions, and not enough on marketing and competition with other firms.

Culture problems sometimes arise from mergers or the growth of rival factions within an organization. For example, Wells Fargo, which relies heavily on flashy technology and automated banking services, acquired another large bank, First Interstate, which had focused more attention on personal services and customer satisfaction. Blending the two disparate organization cultures was difficult for the firm, as managers argued over how best to serve customers and operate the new enterprise.[19]

To change culture, managers must have a clear idea of what they want to create. When Continental Airlines "reinvented" itself a few years ago, employees were taken outside the corporate headquarters in Houston to watch the firm's old policies and procedures manuals set afire. The firm's new strategic direction is known throughout Continental as the "Go Forward" plan, intentionally named to avoid reminding people about the firm's troubled past and instead to focus on the future.

One major way to shape culture is by bringing outsiders into important managerial positions. The choice of a new CEO from outside the organization is often a clear signal that things will be changing. Indeed, a new CEO was the catalyst for the changes at Continental. Adopting new slogans, telling new stories, staging new ceremonies, and breaking with tradition can also alter culture. Culture can also be changed by methods discussed in Chapter 13.[20]

concept CHECK	*What is organization culture?*	*Does your college or university have a culture? How would you describe it to someone?*

Organization-Environment Relationships

Our discussion to this point identifies and describes the various dimensions of organizational environments. Because organizations are open systems, they interact with these various dimensions in many different ways. Hence, we will now examine those interactions. First we discuss how environments affect organizations, and then we note a number of ways in which organizations adapt to their environments.

How Environments Affect Organizations

Three basic perspectives can be used to describe how environments affect organizations: environmental change and complexity, competitive forces, and environmental turbulence.[21]

Environmental Change and Complexity James D. Thompson was one of the first people to recognize the importance of the organization's environment.[22] Thompson suggested that the environment can be described along two dimensions: its degree of change and its degree of homogeneity. The degree of change is the extent to which the environment is relatively stable or relatively dynamic. The degree of homogeneity is the extent to which the environment is relatively simple (few elements, little segmentation) or relatively complex (many elements, much segmentation). These two dimensions interact to determine the level of uncertainty faced by the organization.

Environmental change and complexity personify the world of management. Following the overthrow of the Taliban in Afghanistan, much of the country's infrastructure needed to be rebuilt. A German construction company rebuilding a major highway found these Afghan women to be ready and eager to work. Under the previous regime they were not allowed to work. At the same time, though, the Germans still had to train them and provide accomodations for their religious beliefs.

uncertainty Unpredictability created by environmental change and complexity

Uncertainty, in turn, is a driving force that influences many organizational decisions. Figure 3.4 illustrates a simple view of the four levels of uncertainty defined by different degrees of homogeneity and change.

The least environmental uncertainty is faced by organizations with stable and simple environments. Although no environment is totally without uncertainty, some entrenched franchised food operations (such as Subway and Taco Bell) and many container manufacturers (like Ball Corporation and Federal Paper Board) have relatively low levels of uncertainty to contend with. Subway, for example, focuses on a certain segment of the consumer market, produces a limited product line, has a constant source of suppliers, and faces relatively consistent competition.

Organizations with dynamic but simple environments generally face a moderate degree of uncertainty. Examples of organizations functioning in such environments include clothing manufacturers (targeting a certain kind of clothing buyer but sensitive to fashion-induced changes) and compact disk (CD) producers (catering to certain kinds of music buyers but alert to changing tastes in music). Levi Strauss faces relatively few competitors (Wrangler and Lee), has few suppliers and few regulators, and uses limited distribution channels. This relatively simple task environment, however, also changes quite rapidly as competitors adjust prices and styles, consumer tastes change, and new fabrics become available.

Another combination of factors is one of stability and complexity. Again, a moderate amount of uncertainty results. Ford, DaimlerChrysler, and General Motors face these basic conditions. Overall, they must interact with myriad suppliers, regulators, consumer groups, and competitors. Change, however, occurs quite slowly in the automobile industry. Despite many stylistic changes, cars of today still have four wheels, a steering wheel, an internal combustion engine, a glass windshield, and many of the other basic features that have characterized cars for decades.

Finally, very dynamic and complex environmental conditions yield a high degree of uncertainty. The environment has a large number of elements, and the nature of those elements is constantly changing. Intel, Compaq, IBM, Sony, and other firms in the electronics field face these conditions because of the rapid rate of technological innovation and change in consumer markets that characterize their industry, their suppliers, and their competitors. Internet-based firms like eBay and Amazon.com face similarly high levels of uncertainty.

FIGURE 3.4

Environmental Change, Complexity, and Uncertainty

The degree of homogeneity and the degree of change combine to create uncertainty for organizations. For example, a simple and stable environment creates the least uncertainty, and a complex and dynamic environment creates the most uncertainty.

Source: From J.D. Thompson, *Organizations in Action*, 1967. Copyright © 1967 The McGraw-Hill Companies, Inc. Reprinted with permission.

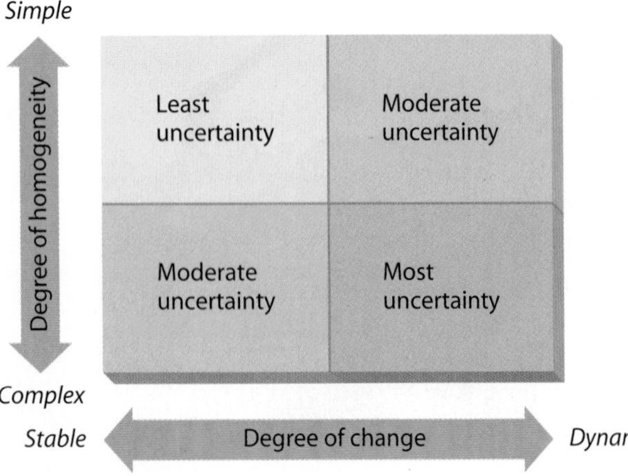

Competitive Forces Although Thompson's general classifications are useful and provide some basic insights into organization-environment interactions, in many ways they lack the precision and specificity needed by managers who must deal with their environments on a day-to-day basis. Michael E. Porter, a Harvard professor and expert in strategic management, has proposed a more refined way to assess environments. In particular, he suggests that managers view the environments of their organization in terms of **five competitive forces**: the threat of new entrants, competitive rivalry, the threat of substitute products, the power of buyers, and the power of suppliers.[23]

five competitive forces The threat of new entrants, competitive rivalry, the threat of substitute products, the power of buyers, and the power of suppliers

The threat of new entrants is the extent to which new competitors can easily enter a market or market segment. It takes a relatively small amount of capital to open a dry-cleaning service or a pizza parlor, but it takes a tremendous investment in plant, equipment, and distribution systems to enter the automobile business. Thus the threat of new entrants is fairly high for a local hamburger restaurant but fairly low for Ford and Toyota. The advent of the Internet has reduced the costs and other barriers of entry in many market segments, however, so the threat of new entrants has increased for many firms in recent years.

Competitive rivalry is the nature of the competitive relationship between dominant firms in the industry. In the soft-drink industry, Coca-Cola and PepsiCo often engage in intense price wars, comparative advertising, and new-product introductions. Other firms that have intense rivalries include American Express and Visa, and Fuji and Kodak. And U.S. auto companies continually try to outmaneuver one another with warranty improvements and rebates. Xerox also faces extreme competition from a variety of firms.[24] Local car-washing establishments, in contrast, seldom engage in such practices.

The threat of substitute products is the extent to which alternative products or services may supplant or diminish the need for existing products or services. The electronic calculator eliminated the need for slide rules. The advent of personal computers, in turn, reduced the demand for calculators as well as for typewriters and large mainframe computers. NutraSweet is a viable substitute product threatening the sugar industry. And DVD players may render VCRs obsolete in the next few years.

The power of buyers is the extent to which buyers of the products or services in an industry have the ability to influence the suppliers. For example, a Boeing 777 has relatively few potential buyers. Only companies such as Delta, Northwest, and KLM Royal Dutch Airlines can purchase them. Hence, these buyers have considerable influence over the price they are willing to pay, the delivery date for the order, and so forth. On the other hand, some DaimlerChrysler dealerships charged premium prices for the company's PT Cruiser when it was first introduced. They could do this because, if the first buyer would not pay the price, two more customers who would were waiting in line. In this case, buyers had virtually no power.

The power of suppliers is the extent to which suppliers have the ability to influence potential buyers. The local electric company is the only source of electricity in your community. Subject to local or state regulation (or both), it can therefore charge what it wants for its product, provide service at its convenience, and so forth. Likewise, even though Boeing has few potential customers, those same customers have only two suppliers that can sell them a 300-passenger jet (Boeing and Airbus, a European firm). So Boeing, too, has power. Indeed, the firm recently exercised its power by entering into long-term, sole-supplier agreements with three major U.S. airlines.[25] On the other hand, a small vegetable wholesaler has little power in selling to restaurants because, if they do not like the produce, they can easily find an alternative supplier.

Environmental Turbulence Although always subject to unexpected changes and upheavals, the five competitive forces can nevertheless be studied and assessed systematically, and plans developed for dealing with them. At the same time, though, organizations face the possibility of environmental change or turbulence, occasionally with no warning at all. The most common form of organizational turbulence is a crisis of some sort.

The terrorist attacks on September 11, 2001, are, of course, the most obvious illustration of environmental turbulence. Beyond the human and social costs, these events profoundly affected myriad businesses ranging from airlines, to New York's entertainment industry, to those firms with operations in the World Trade Center itself.[26] Another notable example of crisis was the crash of the space shuttle Columbia in 2003, which seemed likely to paralyze the U.S. space program for years. Another type of crisis that has captured the attention of managers in recent years is workplace violence—situations in which disgruntled workers or former workers assault other employees, often resulting in injury and sometimes in death. Finally, yet another kind of crisis that can affect business today is the rapid spread of computer viruses, such as the so-called love bug that shut down businesses around the world in early 2000.

Such crises affect organizations in different ways, and many organizations have developed crisis plans and teams.[27] When a Delta Air Lines plane crashed at the Dallas–Fort Worth airport a few years ago, fire-fighting equipment was at the scene in minutes. Only a few flights were delayed, and none had to be canceled. Similarly, a grocery store in Boston once received a threat that someone had poisoned cans of its Campbell's tomato juice. Within six hours, a crisis team from Campbell Soup Company removed two truckloads of juice from all eighty-four stores in the grocery chain. Still, far too few companies in the United States have a plan for dealing with major crises.

How Organizations Adapt to Their Environments

Given the myriad issues, problems, and opportunities in an organization's environments, how should the organization adapt? Obviously, each organization must assess its own unique situation and then adapt according to the wisdom of its senior management. Figure 3.5 illustrates the six basic mechanisms through which organizations adapt to their environments. One of these, social responsibility, is given special consideration in Chapter 4.

Information Management One way organizations adapt to their environments is through information management. Information management is especially important when forming an initial understanding of the environments and when monitoring the environments for signs of change. One technique for managing information is relying on boundary spanners. A *boundary spanner* is an employee, such as a sales representative or a purchasing agent, who spends much of his or her time in contact with others outside the organization. Such people are in a good position to learn what other organizations are doing. All effective managers engage in *environmental scanning*, the process of actively monitoring the environments through activities such as observation and reading. Within the organization, most

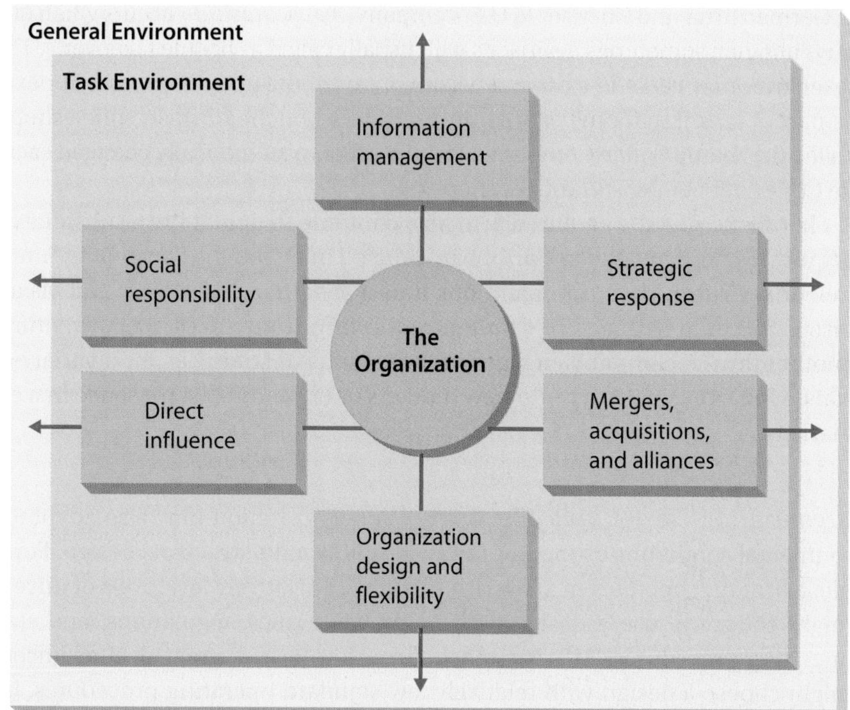

FIGURE 3.5

How Organizations Adapt to Their Environments

Organizations attempt to adapt to their environments. The most common methods are information management; strategic response; mergers, acquisitions, and alliances; organization design and flexibility; direct influence; and social responsibility.

firms have also established computer-based *information systems* to gather and organize relevant information for managers and to assist in summarizing that information in the form most pertinent to each manager's needs (information systems are covered more fully in Chapter 22). Enterprise Resource Planning techniques are also useful methods for improving information management.

Strategic Response Another way that an organization adapts to its environments is through a strategic response. Options include maintaining the status quo (for example, if its management believes that it is doing very well with its current approach), altering strategy a bit, or adopting an entirely new strategy. If the market that a company currently serves is growing rapidly, the firm might decide to invest even more heavily in products and services for that market. Likewise, if a market is shrinking or does not provide reasonable possibilities for growth, the company may decide to cut back. For example, during the late 1990s managers at Starbucks realized that the firm's growth opportunities in the United States were slowing simply because there already were so many Starbucks shops. Accordingly, they devised a new plan to expand aggressively into international markets, thus providing an avenue for continued rapid growth.

Mergers, Acquisitions, and Alliances A related strategic approach that some organizations use to adapt to their environments involves mergers, acquisitions, and alliances. A *merger* occurs when two or more firms combine to form a new firm. For example, DaimlerChrysler was created as a result of a merger between Daimler-Benz (a German firm) and Chrysler (a U.S. company). An *acquisition* occurs when one firm buys another, sometimes against its will (usually called a "hostile takeover"). The firm taken over may cease to exist and becomes part of the other company. For example, as part of its international expansion, Starbucks bought a British coffee shop chain called the Seattle Coffee Company. Starbucks then systematically changed each Seattle Coffee outlet into a Starbucks shop.

In other cases, the acquired firm may continue to operate as a subsidiary of the acquiring company. Royal Caribbean Cruise Lines bought controlling interest in Celebrity Cruise Lines but maintains it as a separate cruise line. And, as already discussed, in a *partnership* or *alliance* the firm undertakes a new venture with another firm. A company engages in these kinds of strategies for a variety of reasons, such as easing entry into new markets or expanding its presence in a current market.

Organization Design and Flexibility An organization may also adapt to environmental conditions by incorporating flexibility in its structural design. For example, a firm that operates in an environment with relatively low levels of uncertainty might choose to use a design with many basic rules, regulations, and standard operating procedures. Alternatively, a firm that faces a great deal of uncertainty might choose a design with relatively few standard operating procedures, instead allowing managers considerable discretion and flexibility with decisions. The former type, sometimes called a "mechanistic organization design," is characterized by formal and rigid rules and relationships. The latter, sometimes called an "organic design," is considerably more flexible and permits the organization to respond quickly to environmental change. We learn much more about these and related issues in Chapter 12.

Direct Influence Organizations are not necessarily helpless in the face of their environments. Indeed, many organizations are able to directly influence their environments in many different ways. For example, firms can influence their suppliers by signing long-term contracts with fixed prices as a hedge against inflation. Or a firm might become its own supplier. Sears, for example, owns some of the firms that produce the goods it sells, and Campbell Soup Company makes its own soup cans. Similarly, almost any major activity in which a firm engages affects its competitors. When Mitsubishi lowers the prices of its DVD players, Sony may be forced to follow suit. Organizations also influence their customers by creating new uses for a product, finding entirely new customers, taking customers away from competitors, and convincing customers that they need something new. Automobile manufacturers use this last strategy in their advertising to convince people that they need a new car every two or three years.

Organizations influence their regulators through lobbying and bargaining. Lobbying involves sending a company or industry representative to Washington in an effort to influence relevant agencies, groups, and committees. For example, the U.S. Chamber of Commerce lobby, the nation's largest business lobby, has an annual budget of more than $100 million. The automobile companies have been successful on several occasions in bargaining with the EPA to extend deadlines for compliance with pollution control and mileage standards. Continental Airlines routinely criticizes what it considers an antiquated air traffic control system in an effort to get the U.S. government to upgrade its technology and systems. As discussed in *Today's Management Issues*, though, there is some controversy over how far a business can go in trying to influence its environments.

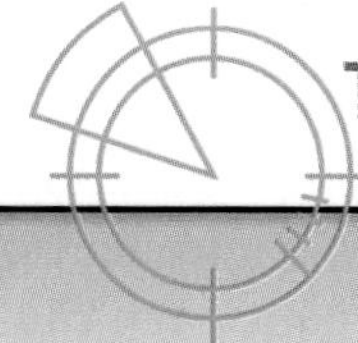

TODAY'S management ISSUES

Do Corporations Have a Right to Freedom of Speech?

"As much as it pains me to say it, I am not in favor of stifling the speech of the loud and obnoxious and terminally exploitative Nike Corporation."

— Bob Herbert, New York Times columnist*

The First Amendment to the U.S. Constitution says, in part, "Congress shall make no law . . . abridging the freedom of speech. . . . " Does that protection extend to corporations? While the ultimate answer hasn't been determined, recent events suggest that it may not. Consider the interesting case of *Nike vs. Kasky.*

Nike manufactures its products under contract from independent operators, mainly in Pacific Rim countries. There have long been allegations and some evidence of child labor, unsafe working conditions, and violations of local regulations. Nike strenuously denies the charges and claims that the contractors themselves are responsible for conditions in the factories. In response, many claim that it is ultimately Nike that has a responsibility to the workers.

A *New York Times* columnist, Bob Herbert, accused Nike of shirking that responsibility saying, "Nike executives . . . are not bothered by the cries of the oppressed. Each cry is a signal that their investment is paying off." Nike responded to this and other criticism with public statements, news releases, and a letter to the *Times* asserting that the accusations were untrue. But then a California activist, Marc Kasky, sued Nike, claiming that the firm's communication was actually advertising and that it violated consumer protection laws against deceptive advertising.

Kasky won the case and the California Supreme Court upheld the verdict. After the United States Supreme Court refused to hear Nike's appeal, the firm settled its dispute by making a $1.5 million donation to a labor rights group. So for now, at least, companies must remain cautious in what they say, but it is likely only a matter of time before a similar case does end up before the high court.

What's at stake is a company's right to free speech. In 1942, the U.S. Supreme Court ruled that commercial speech was actually not protected by the First Amendment. This allowed the government to regulate advertisements, so that, for example, a product that claimed to be "effective," "organic," or "made in the U.S.A.," had to live up to the claim. On the one hand, consumers are protected from fraud and lies. On the other hand, however, individuals can accuse Nike yet the firm cannot respond in its own defense. First Amendment scholar Walter Dellinger claims, "This case is not about the right to lie . . . But truly free speech can't tolerate the risk of substantial penalties for misstatement or an erroneous judgment."

Other manufacturers are unwilling to publicly support Nike's approach for fear of inviting scrutiny of their own practices. But *Times* columnist Bob Herbert, who is decidedly *not* a Nike fan, finds himself siding with the firm. "As much as it pains me to say it," Herbert wrote, "I am not in favor of stifling the speech of the loud and obnoxious and terminally exploitative Nike Corporation."

References: Bob Herbert, "In America: Nike's Pyramid Scheme," *New York Times*, June 10, 1996 (*quote); "Marc Kasky, Plaintiff and Appellant, vs. Nike, Inc., et. al., Defendants and Respondents," California First Amendment Coalition website, www.cfac.org on November 24, 2002; Roger Parloff, "Can We Talk?" *Fortune*, September 2, 2002, pp. 102–110; "A Blow to Free Speech," *USA Today*, September 15, 2003, p. 13A.

concept CHECK

How do environments affect organizations? How do organizations affect their environments?

What are some recent high-profile mergers? Why do you think they occurred?

The Environment and Organizational Effectiveness

Earlier in this chapter we note the vital importance of maintaining proper alignment between the organization and its environments. The various mechanisms through which environments and organizations influence one another can cause this alignment to shift, however, and even the best-managed organizations sometimes slip from their preferred environmental position. But well-managed companies recognize when this happens and take corrective action to get back on track. Recall that we say in Chapter 1 that effectiveness involves doing the right things. Given the interactions between organizations and their environments, it follows that effectiveness is related ultimately to how well an organization understands, reacts to, and influences its environments.[28]

Models of Organizational Effectiveness

Unfortunately, there is no consensus on how to measure effectiveness. For example, an organization can make itself look extremely effective in the short term by ignoring research and development (R&D), buying cheap materials, ignoring quality control, and skimping on wages. Over time, though, the firm will no doubt falter. On the other hand, taking action consistent with a longer view, such as making appropriate investments in R&D, may displease investors who have a short-term outlook. Little wonder, then, that there are many different models of organizational effectiveness.

The *systems resource approach* to organizational effectiveness focuses on the extent to which the organization can acquire the resources it needs.[29] A firm that can get raw materials during a shortage is effective from this perspective. The *internal processes approach* deals with the internal mechanisms of the organization and focuses on minimizing strain, integrating individuals and the organization, and conducting smooth and efficient operations.[30] An organization that focuses primarily on maintaining employee satisfaction and morale and on being efficient subscribes to this view. *The goal approach* focuses on the degree to which an organization reaches its goals.[31] When a firm establishes a goal of increasing sales by 10 percent and then achieves that increase, the goal approach maintains that the organization is effective. Finally, the *strategic constituencies approach* focuses on the groups that have a stake in the organization.[32] In this view, effectiveness is the extent to which the organization satisfies the demands and expectations of all these groups.

Although these four basic models of effectiveness are not necessarily contradictory, they do focus on different things. The systems resource approach focuses on inputs, the internal processes approach focuses on transformation processes, the

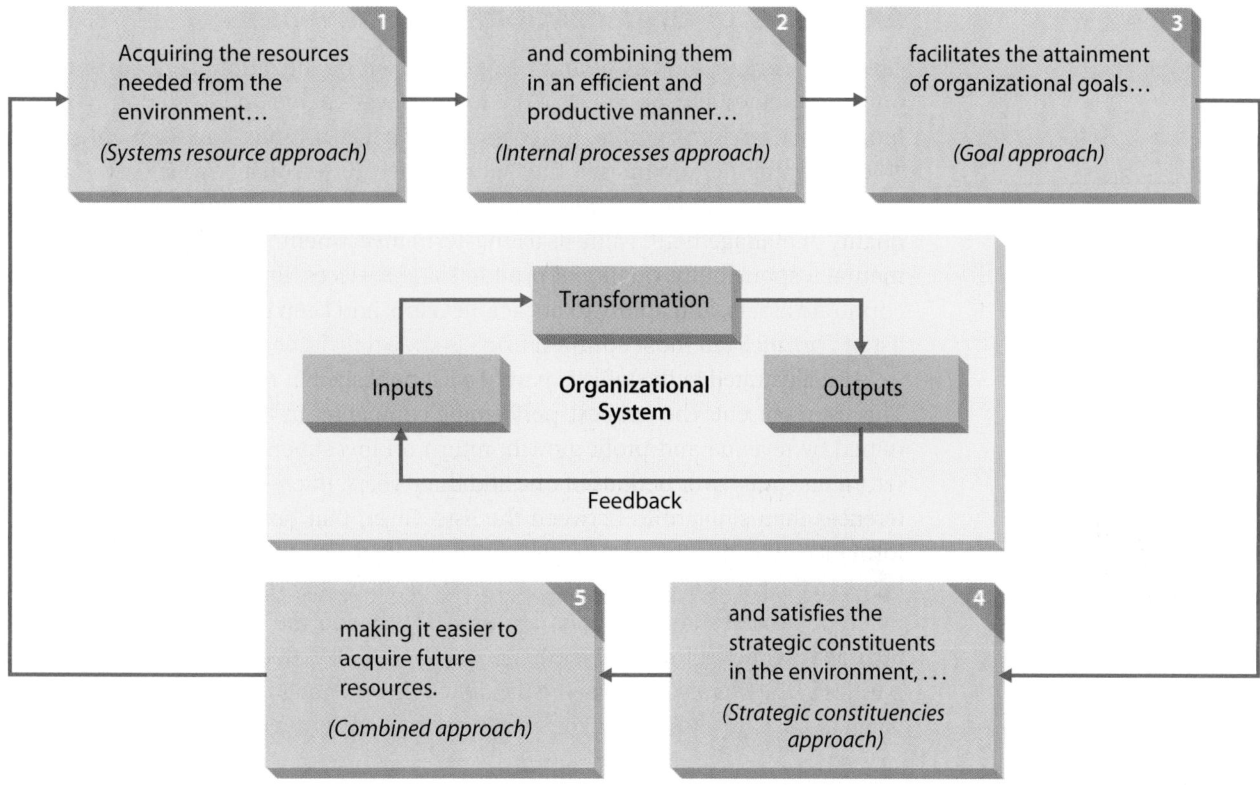

FIGURE 3.6

A Model of Organizational Effectiveness

The systems resource, internal processes, goal, and strategic constituencies each focuses on a different aspect of organizational effectiveness. Thus they can be combined to create an overall integrative perspective on effectiveness.

goal approach focuses on outputs, and the strategic constituencies approach focuses on feedback. Thus, rather than adopting a single approach, one can best understand organizational effectiveness through an integrated perspective like that illustrated in Figure 3.6. At the core of this unifying model is the organizational system, with its inputs, transformations, outputs, and feedback. Surrounding this core are the four basic approaches to effectiveness as well as a combined approach, which incorporates each of the other four. The basic argument is essentially that an organization must satisfy the requirements imposed on it by each of the effectiveness perspectives.

Achieving organizational effectiveness is not an easy task. The key to doing so is understanding the environment in which the organization functions. With this understanding as a foundation, managers can then chart the "correct" path for the organization as it positions itself in that environment. If managers can identify where they want the organization to be relative to other parts of their environment, and how to best get there, they stand a good chance of achieving effectiveness. On the other hand, if they pick the wrong target to aim for, or if they go about achieving their goals in the wrong way, they are less likely to be effective.

Examples of Organizational Effectiveness

Given the various models of and perspectives on organizational effectiveness, it is not surprising that even the experts do not always agree on which companies are most effective. For example, for years *Fortune* has compiled an annual list of the "Most Admired" companies in the United States. Based on a large survey of leading executives, the rankings presumably reflect the organizations' innovativeness, quality of management, value as a long-term investment, community and environmental responsibility, quality of products and services, financial soundness, use of corporate assets, and ability to attract, develop, and keep talented people. The 2003 list of *Fortune's* ten most admired firms is shown in Table 3.1.

Also illustrated in the table is part of a list published in *BusinessWeek*, also in 2003. This list represents the ten best-performing companies in the United States as determined by revenue and profit growth, return on investment, net profit margins, and return on equity over periods of one and three years. Interestingly, there are more differences than similarities between the lists. Given that both "admiration" and "performance" would seem to be highly related to effectiveness, a stronger correspondence between the two lists might have been expected. It is important to note, of course, that different variables and methods are used to develop the two lists, and every firm included on one list but not the other is still a very well managed company. But the disparities in the lists also underscore the difficulties and judgment calls that are involved when trying to really evaluate the effectiveness of any given company or organization.

concept CHECK

What are the four basic models of organizational effectiveness?

What local businesses do you especially admire? Why?

TABLE 3.1

Examples of Admired and High-Performing Firms

***Fortune's* Most Admired Companies (2003)**	***BusinessWeek's* Best Performing Companies (2003)**
1. Wal-Mart	1. Forest Laboratories
2. Southwest Airlines	2. Wellpoint Health Networks
3. Berkshire Hathaway	3. United Health Group
4. Dell Computer	4. Johnson & Johnson
5. General Electric	5. Progressive
6. Johnson & Johnson	6. Amerisourcebergen
7. Microsoft	7. Lowe's
8. FedEx	8. Pfizer
9. Starbucks	9. Dell Computer
10. Procter & Gamble	10. St. Jude Medical

Source: "America's Most Admired Companies," *Fortune*, March 3, 2003, p. 81; "The Business Week 50," *BusinessWeek (special issue)*, Spring, 2003, p. 61.

Summary of Key Points

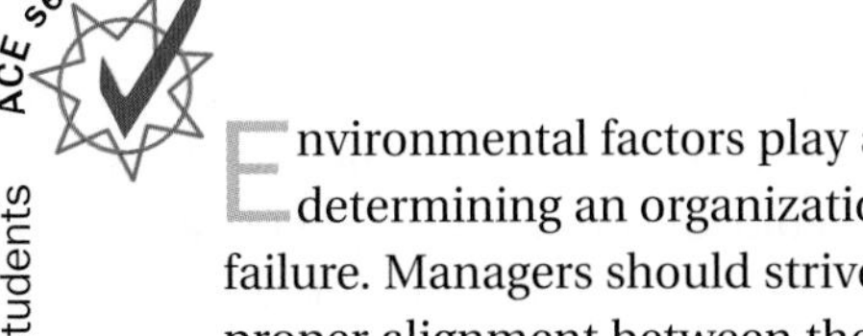

business.college.hmco.com/students

Environmental factors play a major role in determining an organization's success or failure. Managers should strive to maintain the proper alignment between their organization and its environments. All organizations have both external and internal environments.

The external environment is composed of general and task environment layers. The general environment is composed of the nonspecific elements of the organization's surroundings that might affect its activities. It consists of five dimensions: economic, technological, sociocultural, political-legal, and international. The effects of these dimensions on the organization are broad and gradual. The task environment consists of specific dimensions of the organization's surroundings that are very likely to influence the organization. It also consists of five elements: competitors, customers, suppliers, strategic partners, and regulators. Because these dimensions are associated with specific organizations in the environment, their effects are likely to be more direct and immediate.

The internal environment consists of the organization's owners, board of directors, employees, physical environment, and culture. Owners are those who have claims on the property rights of the organization. The board of directors, elected by stockholders, is responsible for overseeing a firm's top managers. Individual employees and the labor unions they sometimes join are other important parts of the internal environment. The physical environment, yet another part of the internal environment, varies greatly across organizations.

Organization culture is the set of values, beliefs, behaviors, customs, and attitudes that helps the members of the organization understand what it stands for, how it does things, and what it considers important. Organization culture is an important environmental concern for managers. Managers must understand that culture is an important determinant of how well their organization will perform. Culture can be determined and managed in a number of different ways.

Organizations and their environments affect each other in several ways. Environmental influences on the organization can occur through uncertainty, competitive forces, and turbulence. Organizations, in turn, use information management; strategic response; mergers, acquisitions, and alliances; organization design and flexibility; direct influence; and social responsibility to adapt to their environments.

One important indicator of how well an organization deals with its environments is its level of effectiveness. Organizational effectiveness requires that the organization do a good job of acquiring resources, managing them properly, achieving its goals, and satisfying its constituencies. Because of the complexities associated with meeting these requirements, however, experts may disagree as to the effectiveness of any given organization at any given point in time.

Discussion Questions

Questions for Review

1. Consider the three environments of a firm. Which of the environments has the most direct and immediate impact on the firm? Which of the environments has a more diffuse and delayed impact? Explain.
2. Describe the organization's general environment. For each dimension, give at least one

specific example, other than the examples mentioned in your text.

3. What are the major forces that affect organization-environment relationships? Describe those factors.
4. Describe the four approaches to organizational effectiveness. Give a specific example of something that a company should measure in order to evaluate its effectiveness under each approach.

Questions for Analysis

5. Elements from the general environment affect all organizations, but they may not affect all organizations in the same way. Choose an industry and discuss the impact of at least two different elements from the general environment on firms in that industry. Are all firms affected equally? Explain.
6. Which of the firm's environments is most readily changed by the firm? Which of the firm's environments is least amenable to change by the firm? How does this influence the actions that firms take?

Questions for Application

7. Go to Hoover's Online at www.hoovers.com. Enter a company name in the Search boxes, then go to the company's "Capsule." Here you can learn who the firm's top competitors are. Were you surprised by the list? How do you think Hoover's determines the list?
8. Go to the library or get online and research a company. Characterize its level of effectiveness according to each of the four basic models. Share your results with the class.
9. Interview a manager from a local organization about his or her organization's internal environment, including owners, directors, employees, the physical work environment, and the organization culture. How do these various elements interact?
10. Consider an organization with which you are familiar. Outline its environments in detail. Then provide specific examples to illustrate how each dimension affects your organization.

BUILDING EFFECTIVE time-management SKILLS

Exercise Overview

Time-management skills refer to the manager's ability to prioritize work, to work efficiently, and to delegate appropriately. This exercise will provide you with an opportunity to relate time-management issues to environmental pressures and opportunities.

Exercise Background

As discussed in this chapter, managers and organizations must be sensitive to a variety of environment dimensions and forces reflected in the general, task, and internal environments. The general environment consists of the economic, technological, sociocultural, political-legal, and international dimensions. The task environment includes competitors, customers, suppliers, strategic partners, and regulators. The internal environment consists of owners, board of directors, employees, physical work environment, and organization culture.

One key problem faced by managers is that time is a finite resource. There are only so many hours in a day and only so many tasks that can be accomplished in a given period of time. Thus managers must constantly make choices about how they spend their time. Clearly, they should try to use their time wisely and direct it at the more important challenges and opportunities they face. Spending time on a trivial issue while neglecting an important one is a mistake.

Time-management experts often suggest that managers begin each day by listing what they need to accomplish that day. After the list is compiled, the manager is then advised to sort these daily tasks into three groups: those that must be addressed that day, those that should be addressed that day but could be postponed if necessary, and those that can easily be postponed. The manager is then advised to perform the tasks in order of priority.

Exercise Task

With the background information above as context, do the following:

1. Write across the top of a sheet of paper the three priority levels noted above.
2. Write down the left side of the same sheet of paper the various elements and dimensions of the task and internal environments of business.
3. At the intersection of each row and column, think of an appropriate example that a manager might face; that is, think of a higher-priority, moderate-priority, and lower-priority situation involving a customer.
4. Form a small group with two or three classmates and share the examples you have developed. Focus on whether or not there is agreement about the prioritization of each example.

BUILDING EFFECTIVE diagnostic SKILLS

business.college.hmco.com/students

Exercise Overview

Diagnostic skills enable a manager to visualize the most appropriate response to a situation. This exercise helps you develop your diagnostic skills through an investigation of corporate influences on politics.

Exercise Background

Businesses are very interested in the political system of their country, because legislation and the political climate of the country—for example, conservative or progressive—can have a significant impact on various aspects of their operations. To some extent, businesses are at the mercy of the political and legal systems; that is, they must adapt to and comply with the requirements that political institutions place on them. However, American businesses are also very powerful and influential in their efforts to shape the political system to meet the corporation's needs.

Large and profitable firms in particular command the resources that can give them a great deal of political clout. (For example, if Wal-Mart were a city and its employees were citizens, it would be the sixth largest city in the United States—bigger than San Diego and almost as big as number five, Philadelphia.) One source of that power is their ability to fund political campaigns and to tie that funding to issues, through the use of lobbying and direct contributions. Although federal laws prohibit corporations from giving large sums directly to political figures, political action committees, which contribute pooled money, are legal. Also, corporations may raise pooled contributions from their employees and give them as a combined amount.

Federal law also requires that all contributions be publicly disclosed. The information is available from the Federal Election Commission, and several print and online sources publish the information. One of these is the Center for Responsive Politics, a nonpartisan, nonprofit research group based in Washington, D.C., which tracks money in politics and its effect on elections and public policy.

Exercise Task

1. Visit the website of the Center for Responsive Politics, at www.opensecrets.org. At its home page, type your zip code into the "Who's My Rep?" box. You will then see information related to your senators and your representative.
2. Based on what you see at the website, who are the top contributors to your legislators? Consider the top organizations, the top industries, and the top issues.
3. Choose one of the organizations you see in the list. Find that organization's website and explore. Can you find any connection between your legislator and the contributor? In other words, why do you think that organization contributed? (*Hint:* The answer may be related to the important industries or issues in your area, or it may be related to the legislator's committee assignments. You can see current committee assignments by reading the individual's "Summary Data.")

BUILDING EFFECTIVE communication SKILLS

Exercise Overview

Communication skills refer to a manager's ability to effectively receive information and ideas from others and to effectively convey information and ideas to others. This exercise will help you develop your communication skills while also helping you to understand the importance of knowing the customer segments in an organization's task environment.

Exercise Background

Assume that you are a newly hired middle manager in the marketing department of a large food manufacturer. You have just completed your formal study of management and are excited about the opportunity to apply some of those theories to the real-life problems of your firm. One problem in particular intrigues you. Your boss, the marketing vice president, developed a consumer survey to solicit feedback about products from customers. The feedback varies considerably, ranging from a 2 to a 5 on a scale of 1 to 5, which gives your firm no helpful data. In addition, sales of your company's products have been slowly but steadily declining over time, and the marketing department is under some pressure from upper management to determine why.

You have an idea that the survey is not an accurate reflection of consumer preferences, so you make a suggestion to your boss: "Why don't we gather some information about our customers, in order to understand their needs better? For example, our products are purchased by individual consumers, schools, restaurants, and other organizations. Maybe each type of consumer wants something different from our product." Your boss's response is to stare at you, perplexed, and say, "No. We're not changing anything about the survey." When you ask, "Why?" the boss responds that the product has been a best-seller for years, that "good quality is good quality," and thus that all customers must want the same thing. He then says, "I'll spare you the embarrassment of failure by refusing your request."

Exercise Task

1. With this background in mind, compose a written proposal for your boss, outlining your position. Be sure to emphasize your fundamental concern—that the marketing department needs to better understand the needs of each customer segment in order to provide products that meet those needs. Consider ways to persuade your boss to change his mind. (*Hint:* Telling him bluntly that he is wrong is unlikely to be effective.)
2. Based on what you wrote in response to Exercise Task 1 above, do you think your boss will change his mind? If yes, what persuaded him to change his mind? If no, what other actions could you take to attempt to have your ideas adopted by the firm?

CHAPTER CLOSING case

LIGHTING UP EVERY NOOK AND CRANNY AT GE

"People are looking for cleaner stories. Some of them will ask if there's more to come."

— John Inch, analyst, Merrill Lynch*

This story starts with the good news. In 2002 General Electric (GE) was selected for the number-one spot on *Fortune's* list of "America's Most Admired Companies" for the fifth straight year in a row. The bad news comes in the second chapter. Profits declined more than 50 percent from 2000 to 2002, and highly admired CEO Jack Welch retired in 2001 after twenty years of leadership. At the time of the award, observers were losing confidence in the conglomerate that was until recently the most valuable company on earth.

Welch led GE to a profitability that consistently grew by at least 10 percent annually, beating analysts' expectations for earnings in all but one of the forty quarters from 1991 to 2001. (In that missed quarter, profits were only 1 cent below expectations.) The company's profitability was higher than 90 percent of the Fortune 1000. High, consistent, steadily rising profitability made GE the favorite of investors and analysts.

However, after recent corporate accounting scandals, companies were pressured to be "transparent"; that is, to clearly show where money came from and where it was spent. Most firms have some "gray" areas that, while legal, are not very transparent, but GE seems to have more than most. GE's performance history suddenly looked *too* good.

The next few chapters of our story underscore a variety of investor concerns. Just the complexity of the firm, which provides products as diverse as light bulbs, refrigerators, jet engines, power plants, the ABC television network, and credit cards, is overwhelming, even for experienced corporate observers. One analyst says, "You really have no idea what the quality of those earnings are." The numerous, isolated divisions of GE also allow the firm to switch funds between units whenever needed, increasing confusion over earnings. Another example of complexity is GE's use of off-the-books entities, which were favored by Enron and thus have a questionable reputation. GE sells reinsurance, a product that, with a little manipulation, can mask true earnings. GE Capital, GE's financing business, has $117 billion worth of high-interest, high-risk commercial loans outstanding and, unlike a bank, is not required to maintain reserves to cover potential losses. GE itself is heavily in debt in order to finance a glut of acquisitions.

In the most tawdry chapter of the story, after much-admired CEO Welch retired, the press uncovered details of his retirement package. When the public learned that Welch's compensation included items such as exclusive use of a jet, an $80,000-per-month apartment in New York, a car and chauffeur, several servants, and more, they were outraged. These were in addition to

Welch's retirement pay of over $2 million per year, the millions he made selling GE stock, and the $7 million advance he was paid by Warner Books for his autobiography. The squeaky-clean reputation of this legendary leader was tarnished. Suddenly, Welch did not seem very different from any other "celebrity CEO."

Although the company and its famous leader were both damaged, this was not the end of the story for GE. In response to public concern, the company has undertaken a number of initiatives to improve performance and satisfy investor concerns. Jeff Immelt, the new CEO, has announced a reorganization that will sell off some of the firm's low-performing units to free up resources for badly needed innovations in other areas. Units that Immelt is rumored to be considering for sale include GE's home appliances and lighting divisions. The decision to divest its lighting unit will be a difficult one for the firm, because the company, founded by Thomas Edison in 1890, had its origin as a manufacturer of light bulbs.

Immelt has also restructured the board of directors and implemented new accounting procedures to make the company's financial results more transparent and to increase stockholder control of the firm. GE's new policies are being used as an ideal for other firms to strive toward. Other improvements include giving more information to investors and soliciting their feedback through over two hundred meetings each year. Immelt says, "I am very interested in what people who own the stock think." He goes on to conclude, "It's our goal to get out there and tell our story, and we think that the more clearly people understand it, the more they're going to like us." Paradoxically, the more information GE discloses, the more investors may demand. Analyst John Inch of Merrill Lynch says, "People are looking for cleaner stories. Some of them will ask if there's more to come." The next chapter in the ongoing story will show whether Immelt and GE can satisfy investors' concerns while also focusing more attention on developing products that can effectively compete in the marketplace.

Case Questions

1. In your opinion, does the general environment of GE present more opportunities for the firm or more threats at this time? Why?
2. What are some actions that GE could take or has taken to make favorable changes in its environment? What are some actions that GE could take or has taken to change the firm in order to respond more effectively to its environments?
3. Based on information in the case, under which of the models presented in the text is GE an effective organization? Under which models is GE ineffective? Explain your answers.

Case References

Diane Brady, "GE Capital, in Four Easy Pieces," *BusinessWeek*, August 2, 2002, www.businessweek.com on November 19, 2002; Diane Brady, "What's Pulling GE Down," *BusinessWeek*, July 9, 2002 (*quote), www.businessweek.com on November 19, 2002; Justin Fox, "What's So Great About GE?" *Fortune*, March 4, 2002, www.fortune.com on November 19, 2002; Melanie Warner, "Can GE Light up the Market Again?" *Fortune*, November 11, 2002, pp. 108–117.

Chapter Notes

1. Cora Daniels, "Mr. Coffee," *Fortune*, April 14, 2003, pp.139–143; Chester Dawson, "Online Extra: Q&A with Starbucks' Howard Schultz," *BusinessWeek*, September 9, 2002, www.businessweek.com on November 18, 2002; Christina W. Passariello, "The Java Joint That's Swallowing France," *BusinessWeek*, September 11, 2002, www.businessweek.com on November 18, 2002; Kevin Helliker and Shirley Leung, "Despite the Jitters, Most Coffeehouses Survive Starbucks," *Wall Street Journal*, September 24, 2002, pp. A1, A11 (*quote p. A1); Stanley Holmes, "Planet Starbucks," *BusinessWeek*, September 9, 2002, pp. 100–110; "Not a Johnny-Come-Latte," *USA Today*, September 9, 2003, p. 3B.
2. Arie de Geus, *The Living Company—Habits for Surviving in a Turbulent Business Environment* (Boston: Harvard Business School Press, 1997). See also John G. Sifonis and Beverly Goldberg, *Corporation on a Tightrope* (New York: Oxford University Press, 1996), for an interesting discussion of how organizations must navigate through the environment.
3. Eric D. Beinhocker, "Robust Adaptive Strategies," *Sloan Management Review*, Spring 1999, pp. 95–105.

4. See Jay B. Barney and William G. Ouchi (eds.), *Organizational Economics* (San Francisco: Jossey-Bass, 1986), for a detailed analysis of linkages between economics and organizations.
5. "How Prosperity Is Reshaping the American Economy," *BusinessWeek*, February 14, 2000, pp. 100–110.
6. See "Firms Brace for a Worker Shortage," *Time*, May 6, 2002, p. 44.
7. See Ricky Griffin and Michael Pustay, *International Business: A Managerial Perspective*, 4th ed. (Upper Saddle River, NJ: Prentice Hall, 2005), for an overview.
8. For example, see Susanne G. Scott and Vicki R. Lane, "A Stakeholder Approach to Organizational Identity," *Academy of Management Review*, 2000, vol. 25, no. 1, pp. 43–62.
9. "Target: The Cool Factor Fizzles," *BusinessWeek*, February 24, 2003, pp. 42–43.
10. Richard N. Osborn and John Hagedoorn, "The Institutionalization and Evolutionary Dynamics of Interorganizational Alliances and Networks," *Academy of Management Journal*, April 1997, pp. 261–278. See also "More Companies Cut Risk by Collaborating with Their 'Enemies'," *Wall Street Journal*, January 31, 2000, pp. A1, A10.
11. "The Best & Worst Boards," *BusinessWeek*, October 7, 2002, pp. 104–114. See also Amy Hillman and Thomas Dalziel, "Boards of Directors and Firm Performance: Integrating Agency and Resource Dependence Perspectives," *Academy of Management Review*, 2003, Vol. 23, No. 3, pp. 383–396.
12. "The Wild New Workforce," *BusinessWeek*, December 6, 1999, pp. 38–44.
13. "Temporary Workers Getting Short Shrift," *USA Today*, April 11, 1997, pp. 1B, 2B.
14. "Curves Ahead," *Wall Street Journal*, March 10, 1999, pp. B1, B10.
15. Terrence E. Deal and Allan A. Kennedy, *Corporate Cultures: The Rights and Rituals of Corporate Life* (Reading, Mass.: Addison-Wesley, 1982).
16. Sue Zesinger, "Ford's Hip Transplant," *Fortune*, May 10, 1999, pp. 82–92.
17. Jay B. Barney, "Organizational Culture: Can It Be a Source of Sustained Competitive Advantage?" *Academy of Management Review*, July 1986, pp. 656–665.
18. For example, see Carol J. Loomis, "Sam Would Be Proud," *Fortune*, April 17, 2000, pp. 131–144.
19. "Why Wells Fargo Is Circling the Wagons," *Wall Street Journal*, June 9, 1997, pp. 92–93.
20. See Tomothy Galpin, "Connecting Culture to Organizational Change," *HRMagazine*, March 1996, pp. 84–94.
21. For a recent review, see Allen C. Bluedorn, "Pilgrim's Progress: Trends and Convergence in Research on Organizational Size and Environments," *Journal of Management*, vol. 19, no. 2, 1993, pp. 163–191.
22. James D. Thompson, *Organizations in Action* (New York: McGraw-Hill, 1967).
23. Michael E. Porter, *Competitive Strategy: Techniques for Analyzing Industries and Competitors* (New York: Free Press, 1980). See also Joel A.C. Baum and Helaine J. Korn, "Competitive Dynamics of Interfirm Rivalry," *Academy of Management Journal*, April 1996, pp. 255–291.
24. See "Xerox Faces Mounting Challenge to Copier Business," *Wall Street Journal*, December 17, 1999, p. B4.
25. "Plane Maker May Not Seek More 'Sole Supplier' Deals," *USA Today*, June 26, 1997, p. 3B.
26. "Starting Over," *Fortune*, January 21, 2002, pp. 50–68.
27. Bala Chakravarthy, "A New Strategy Framework for Coping with Turbulence," *Sloan Management Review*, Winter 1997, pp. 69–82.
28. Gareth Jones, *Organizational Theory and Design*, 3rd ed. (Upper Saddle River, NJ: Prentice Hall, 2001).
29. E. Yuchtman and S. Seashore, "A Systems Resource Approach to Organizational Effectiveness," *American Sociological Review*, vol. 32, 1967, pp. 891–903.
30. B. S. Georgopoules and A. S. Tannenbaum, "The Study of Organizational Effectiveness," *American Sociological Review*, vol. 22, 1957, pp. 534–540.
31. Jones, *Organizational Theory and Design.*
32. Anthony A. Atkinson, John H. Waterhouse, and Robert B. Wells, "A Stakeholder Approach to Strategic Performance Measurement," *Sloan Management Review*, Spring 1997, pp. 25–37.

4

The Ethical and Social Environment

CHAPTER OUTLINE

Individual Ethics in Organizations
- Managerial Ethics
- Ethics in an Organizational Context
- Managing Ethical Behavior

Emerging Ethical Issues in Organizations
- Ethical Leadership
- Ethical Issues in Corporate Governance
- Ethical Issues in Information Technology

Social Responsibility and Organizations
- Areas of Social Responsibility
- Arguments For and Against Social Responsibility

The Government and Social Responsibility
- How Government Influences Organizations
- How Organizations Influence Government

Managing Social Responsibility
- Formal Organizational Dimensions
- Informal Organizational Dimensions
- Evaluating Social Responsibility

LEARNING OBJECTIVES

After studying this chapter, you should be able to:

1 ***Discuss managerial ethics, three areas of special ethical concern for managers, and how organizations manage ethical behavior.***

OPENING INCIDENT

Just try to name all of the CEOs with highly publicized ethical problems in recent years—the list could fill this page. The roll call would have to begin with Kenneth Lay and Jeffrey Skilling at Enron, perpetrators of the largest corporate fraud ever; former Tyco CEO Dennis Kozlowski; former WorldCom CEO Bernard Ebbers; former Sunbeam CEO Al Dunlap (the man *Fortune* calls "The Destroyer"); and former Adelphia CEO John Rigas, all of whom led their firm into bankruptcy after allegations of financial hanky-panky. Together, investors lost billions on these firms, over 100,000 workers lost their jobs, and resultant declines in the U.S. stock market adversely affected the entire global economy.

By comparison, the accusations against other CEOs seem mild, ranging from failure to disclose financial information, to illegal activity such as bribes or harassment, to merely being overpaid. Citigroup's Sanford Weill, Disney's Michael Eisner, and even much-admired Jack Welch, General Electric's former CEO, have made headlines that shocked readers and stunned investors. Fortunately, these CEOs are not the whole story—they are simply the part of the story that gets the most attention in the media. There are hundreds of

2

Identify and summarize several emerging ethical issues in organizations today.

3

Discuss the concept of social responsibility, specify to whom or what an organization might be considered responsible, and describe four types of organizational approaches to social responsibility.

4

Explain the relationship between the government and organizations regarding social responsibility.

5

Describe some of the activities organizations may engage in to manage social responsibility.

"It takes a lifetime to build a reputation, and only a short time to lose it all."

—Joseph Neubauer, Aramark CEO

Today's headlines might suggest that most CEOs belong in handcuffs. But in reality, of course, most are honest and strive to do the right things.

"good" CEOs out there—men and women who are competent, professional, diligent, and ethical.

Aramark CEO Joseph Neubauer is one example. His global outsourcing firm, with businesses such as office cleaning and food services, was just days away from completing a $100 million acquisition when Neubauer saw the company's detailed financial records for the first time—and did not like what he saw. His company walked away from the deal, giving up the millions that were already spent. Neubauer did not think twice. He says, "It takes a lifetime to build a reputation, and only a short time to lose it all. We chose to eat the loss on the time and the money because we couldn't live with their business practices." Stockholders and coworkers knew they could count on Neubauer to do the right thing, because he had done it before. When corporate raiders staged a hostile takeover run at Aramark in the 1980s, they offered Neubauer 5 percent of the company for himself and 5 for his friends if he would support their bid. Neubauer refused and took out a second mortgage on his home to help finance his own management-led buyout, sharing ownership with seventy other executives.

Similarly, Costco CEO James Sinegal shows his fairness through myriad interactions with customers and employees. Sinegal has a strict policy of keeping markups on retail prices to 14 percent or less. He also pays employees more than does any other discount retailer—cashiers with four years of experience can earn more than $40,000. He could raise profits by charging more for products or paying less for labor, but Sinegal insists, "Paying good wages is not in opposition to good productivity. If you hire good people, give them good jobs, and pay them good wages, generally something good is going to happen." Harold Messmer, CEO of staffing firm Robert Half International, believes in growing his business by expansion from within, rather than through acquisition. "I do think some firms make acquisitions to keep the revenues and earnings machines going," says the former merger and acquisition attorney. "I've never approved of that."

These CEOs are quite different in their backgrounds, hailing from all parts of the United States, with educations ranging from college dropout to Harvard M.B.A. Yet they and their ethical peers have much in common. This new breed of leader is keenly focused on the needs of stakeholders. They see their firm as more important than themselves. They seek stability, harmony, and fairness. They are known for being likable, in a profession that attracts many overblown egos. They are modest, admitting that they do not know everything. Gap CEO Paul Pressler says, "My first 100 days [as CEO] are all about listening and learning." Good CEOs are just as horrified as the rest of us by the trouble caused by their less-than-ethical colleagues. "[We] can't do a lot about the things going on at the Tycos and the Enrons of the world," says Jim Kilts, CEO of Gillette. "One thing we have to do is reinforce the importance of doing the right things the right way."[1]

Businesses everywhere need to earn profits in order to remain in existence. But there are disparate views on how a firm can legitimately pursue and should then use those profits. Some companies aggressively seek to maximize their profits, grow at any cost, and focus on nothing but what is best for the company. Others, like some of those mentioned above, take a much different approach to business and actively work for the betterment of society, even when it means less profit for the owners. Most businesses, however, adopt a position somewhere between these extremes. Decisions about which of these approaches to take are, in turn, affected by managerial ethics and social responsibility.

This chapter explores the basic issues of ethics and social responsibility in detail. We first look at individual ethics and their organizational context and then note several emerging ethical issues in organizations today. Next, we expand our discussion to the more general subject of social responsibility. After we explore the relationships between businesses and the government regarding socially responsible behavior, we examine the activities organizations sometimes undertake to be more socially responsible.

Individual Ethics in Organizations

ethics An individual's personal beliefs about whether a behavior, action, or decision is right or wrong

ethical behavior Behavior that conforms to generally accepted social norms

unethical behavior Behavior that does not conform to generally accepted social norms

We define **ethics** as an individual's personal beliefs about whether a behavior, action, or decision is right or wrong.[2] Note that we define ethics in the context of the individual—people have ethics; organizations do not. Likewise, what constitutes ethical behavior varies from one person to another. For example, one person who finds a twenty-dollar bill on the floor of an empty room believes that it is okay to keep it, whereas another feels compelled to turn it in to the lost-and-found department. Further, although **ethical behavior** is in the eye of the beholder, it usually refers to behavior that conforms to generally accepted social norms. **Unethical behavior**, then, is behavior that does not conform to generally accepted social norms.

A society generally adopts formal laws that reflect the prevailing ethical standards—the social norms—of its citizens. For example, because most people consider theft to be unethical, laws have been passed to make such behaviors illegal and to prescribe ways of punishing those who do steal. But, although laws attempt to be clear and unambiguous, their application and interpretation still lead to ethical ambiguities. For example, virtually everyone would agree that forcing employees to work excessive hours, especially for no extra compensation, is unethical. Accordingly, laws have been established to define work and pay standards. But applying the law to organizational settings can still result in ambiguous situations, which can be interpreted in different ways.

An individual's ethics are determined by a combination of factors. People start to form ethical standards as children, in response to their perceptions of their parents' and other adults' behaviors and in response to the behaviors they are allowed to choose. As children grow and enter school, they are also influenced by peers with whom they interact every day. Dozens of important individual events shape people's lives and contribute to their ethical beliefs and behavior as they grow into adulthood. Values and morals also contribute to ethical standards, as do religious beliefs. People who place financial gain and personal advancement at the top of their list of priorities, for example, will adopt personal codes of ethics that promote the pursuit of wealth. Thus they may be ruthless in efforts to gain these rewards, regardless of the costs to others. In contrast, people who clearly establish their family and friends as their top priority will adopt different ethical standards.

The Container Store is consistently ranked as one of the best companies to work for in the United States. One key factor in this recognition is the manner in which management treats the firm's employees. For example, the company allows all employees to have access to all its financial information. The company also provides extensive training for its employees and works to insure that its compensation and benefits packages are the best in the industry. And all employees from top management on down are treated as equals.

Managerial Ethics

Managerial ethics are the standards of behavior that guide individual managers in their work.[3] Although ethics can affect managerial work in any number of ways, three areas of special concern for managers are shown in Figure 4.1.

managerial ethics Standards of behavior that guide individual managers in their work

How an Organization Treats Its Employees One important area of managerial ethics is the treatment of employees by the organization. This area includes areas such as hiring and firing, wages and working conditions, and employee privacy and respect. For example, both ethical and legal guidelines suggest that hiring and firing decisions should be based solely on an individual's ability to perform the job. A manager who discriminates against African-Americans in hiring is exhibiting both unethical and illegal behavior. But consider the case of a manager who does not discriminate in general, but occasionally hires a close friend or relative when other applicants might be just as qualified. Although these hiring decisions may not be illegal, they may be objectionable on ethical grounds.

Wages and working conditions, although tightly regulated, are also areas for potential controversy. For example, a manager paying an employee less than he deserves, simply because the manager knows the employee cannot afford to quit or risk losing his job by complaining, might be considered unethical. Finally, most observers would also agree that an organization is obligated to protect the privacy of its employees. A manager's spreading a rumor that an employee has AIDS or is having an affair with a coworker is generally seen as an unethical breach of privacy. Likewise, the manner in which an organization responds to and addresses issues associated with sexual harassment involves employee privacy and related rights.

How Employees Treat the Organization Numerous ethical issues stem from how employees treat the organization, especially in regard to conflicts of interest, secrecy and confidentiality, and honesty. A conflict of interest occurs when a

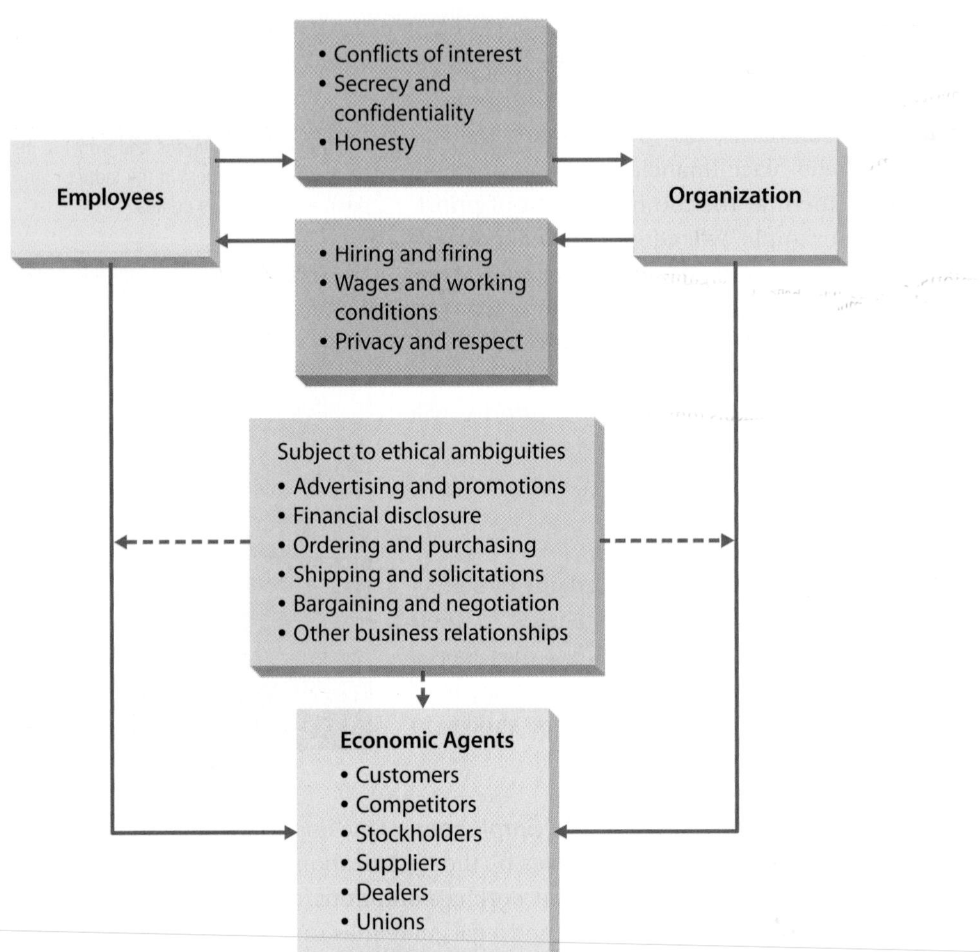

FIGURE 4.1

Managerial Ethics

The three basic areas of concern for managerial ethics are the relationships of the firm to the employee, the employee to the firm, and the firm to other economic agents. Managers need to approach each set of relationships from an ethical and moral perspective.

decision potentially benefits the individual to the possible detriment of the organization. To guard against such practices, most companies have policies that forbid their buyers from accepting gifts from suppliers. Divulging company secrets is also clearly unethical. Employees who work for businesses in highly competitive industries—electronics, software, and fashion apparel, for example—might be tempted to sell information about company plans to competitors. A third area of concern is honesty in general. Relatively common problems in this area include such activities as using a business telephone to make personal long distance calls, surfing the Internet at work, stealing supplies, and padding expense accounts.

In recent years, new issues regarding such behaviors as personal Internet use at work have also become more pervasive. Another disturbing trend is that more workers are calling in sick simply to get extra time off. In one recent survey, for instance, between 2001 and 2002 the number of workers who reported taking more time off for personal needs increased by 21 percent. And, in that same study, 20 percent of those surveyed indicated that they try to take more vacation days than they are entitled to.[4]

Although most employees are inherently honest, organizations must nevertheless be vigilant to avoid problems from such behaviors.

How Employees and the Organization Treat Other Economic Agents Managerial ethics also come into play in the relationship between the firm and its employees with other economic agents. As listed previously in Figure 4.1, the primary agents of interest include customers, competitors, stockholders, suppliers, dealers, and unions. The behaviors between the organization and these agents that may be subject to ethical ambiguity include advertising and promotions, financial disclosures, ordering and purchasing, shipping and solicitations, bargaining and negotiation, and other business relationships.

For example, businesses in the pharmaceuticals industry have been under growing fire because of the rapid escalation of the prices they charge for many of their drugs. These firms counter that they need to invest more heavily in research and development programs to develop new drugs and that higher prices are needed to cover these costs. The key in situations like this, then, is to find the right balance between reasonable pricing and price gouging. And, as in so many other questions involving ethics, there are significant differences of opinion.[5] Another area of concern in recent years involves financial reporting by various e-commerce firms. Because of the complexities inherent in valuing the assets and revenues of these firms, some of them have been very aggressive in presenting their financial position in a highly positive light. And, in at least a few cases, some firms have substantially overstated their earnings projections to entice more investment. Moreover, some of today's accounting scandals in traditional firms have stemmed from similarly questionable practices.[6]

Additional complexities faced by many firms today are the variations in ethical business practices in different countries. In some countries, bribes and side payments are a normal and customary part of doing business. However, U.S. laws forbid these practices, even if a firm's rivals from other countries are paying them. For example, a U.S. power-generating company once lost a $320 million contract in the Middle East because government officials demanded a $3 bribe. A Japanese firm paid the bribe and won the contract. Enron once had a big project in India cancelled because newly elected officials demanded bribes. Although these kinds of cases are illegal under U.S. law, other situations are more ambiguous. In China, for example, local journalists expect their cab fare to be paid if they are to cover a business-sponsored news conference. In Indonesia, the normal time for a foreigner to get a driver's license is over a year, but it can be "expedited" for an extra $100. And, in Romania, building inspectors routinely expect a "tip" for a favorable review.[7]

Ethics in an Organizational Context

Of course, although ethics are an individual phenomenon, ethical or unethical actions by particular managers do not occur in a vacuum. Indeed, they most often occur in an organizational context that is conducive to them. Actions of peer managers and top managers, as well as the organization's culture, all contribute to the ethical context of the organization.[8]

The starting point in understanding the ethical context of management is, of course, the individual's own ethical standards. Some people, for example, would risk personal embarrassment or lose their job before they would do something unethical. Other people are much more easily swayed by the unethical behavior they see around them and other situational factors, and they may even be willing to commit major crimes to further their own career or for financial gain. Organizational practices may strongly influence the ethical standards of employees. Some organizations openly permit unethical business practices as long as they are in the firm's best interests.

If managers become aware of unethical practices and allow them to continue, they have contributed to an organization culture that says such activity is permitted. For example, Hypercom Corporation, a Phoenix company that makes card-swiping machines for retailers, has come under fire because of the actions and alleged wrongdoing of a senior marketing executive named Jairo Gonzalez. Gonzalez was accused of rape by his former secretary (she was paid a $100,000 settlement by the firm), and three other women accused him of sexual harassment. He also set up his own outside business—run by his father—to charge Hypercom for handling overseas shipping. Gonzalez got a job for his girlfriend at a video production firm used by Hypercom in Miami; when she moved to Phoenix, the firm switched its account to the video production firm she joined there. But the firm's CEO, George Wallner, defended his decision to retain Gonzalez because of the huge revenues Gonzalez generated. In Wallner's words, "He [is] bringing in $70 million a year. Do you fire your number one rock star because he's difficult?" And, regarding the payment to Gonzalez's former secretary, Wallner asserted, "On a moral level this is confusing. But if you think of only the business decision, it was dead right." Perhaps it is not surprising, then, that another Hypercom manager married a temp and then got her a job at the firm, or that Wallner and his brother borrowed $4.5 million from the firm, some of it interest free.[9]

The organization's environment also contributes to the context for ethical behavior. In a highly competitive or regulated industry, for example, a manager may feel more pressure to achieve high performance. When managers feel pressure to

Managers should strive to be ethical in all their dealings with their employees. Sometimes the pressures and stresses they experience cause them to apply those same pressures and stresses to employees, often in inappropriate ways. For example, as illustrated here, managers sometimes go too far in their efforts to entice employees to work harder or to spend more time on the job. The result can be disgruntled employees and low morale.

Reprinted with Special Permission of King Features Syndicate

meet goals or lower costs, they may explore a variety of alternatives to help achieve these ends. And, in some cases, the alternative they choose may be unethical or even illegal. The cartoon illustrates one way this can happen—if a manager feels pressure to get more work done, she or he may apply similar pressure on others to work extra hours, stay later in the evening, and so forth.

Managing Ethical Behavior

Spurred partially by increased awareness of ethical scandals in business and partially by a sense of enhanced corporate consciousness about the importance of ethical and unethical behaviors, many organizations have reemphasized ethical behavior on the part of employees. This emphasis takes many forms, but any effort to enhance ethical behavior must begin with top management. It is top managers, for example, who establish the organization's culture and define what will and will not be acceptable behavior. Some companies have also started offering employees training in how to cope with ethical dilemmas. At Boeing, for example, line managers lead training sessions for other employees, and the company also has an ethics committee that reports directly to the board of directors. The training sessions involve discussions of different ethical dilemmas that employees might face and how managers might handle those dilemmas. Chemical Bank and Xerox also have ethics training programs for their managers.

Organizations are also going to greater lengths to formalize their ethical standards. Some, such as General Mills and Johnson & Johnson, have prepared guidelines that detail how employees are to treat suppliers, customers, competitors, and other constituents. Others, such as Whirlpool, Texas Instruments, and Hewlett-Packard, have developed formal **code of ethics**—written statements of the values and ethical standards that guide the firms' actions. Of course, firms must adhere to such codes if they are to be of value. In one now-infamous case, Enron's board of directors voted to set aside the firm's code of ethics in order to implement a business plan that was in violation of that code.[10]

code of ethics A formal, written statement of the values and ethical standards that guide a firm's actions

And, of course, no code, guideline, or training program can truly make up for the quality of an individual's personal judgment about what is right behavior and what is wrong behavior in a particular situation. Such devices may prescribe what people should do, but they often fail to help people understand and live with the consequences of their choices. Making ethical choices may lead to very unpleasant outcomes—firing, rejection by colleagues, and the forfeiture of monetary gain, to name a few. Thus managers must be prepared to confront their own conscience and weigh the options available when making difficult ethical decisions. These issues are explored more fully in *The Business of Ethics.*

Unfortunately, what distinguishes ethical from unethical behavior is often subjective and subject to differences of opinion. So how does one go about deciding whether or not a particular action or decision is ethical? Traditionally, experts have suggested a three-step model for applying ethical judgments to situations that may arise during the course of business activities. These steps are (1) gather the relevant factual information, (2) determine the most appropriate moral values, and (3) make

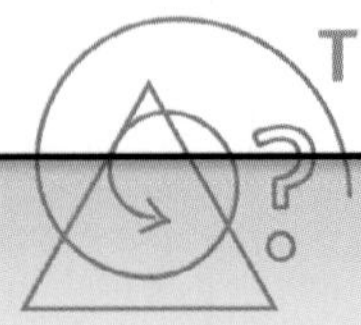

THE BUSINESS OF ethics

No Guarantee of Good Behavior

"If [managers] didn't get a sense of right and wrong from their families or their faith, it's unlikely a business school professor can instill one."

– Robert Prentice, professor, University of Texas*

Corporate scandals like those at WorldCom and ImClone have firms struggling to find some way of preventing such problems among their employees. One approach is to create a new top-level management position for a corporate ethics officer. The Ethics Officer Association recently added 100 new members, showing that this role is becoming more widespread. Ethics officers craft a simple and easy-to-use code of ethics, help develop policy, and support whistle blowing. Another option that is growing in popularity is online, interactive ethics training for employees.

However, because federal law lightens violators' sentences when the company has a training program, critics assert that companies are doing just enough to get by. Barbara Ley Toffler, a professor at Columbia University, says that companies are just paying lip service, stating "[Under the guidelines], you don't have to understand what is going on in an organization or correct anything." Critics also claim that most ethical violators are aware of their actions, so ethical training will not help. "Ethical failures are usually not the result of people not knowing the law or regulations," says Toffler. In addition, companies can easily avoid compliance with policies, as when Enron's board of directors repeatedly waived its own ethical code of conduct.

Perhaps ethical problems should be treated earlier, before managers leave college. Harvard, the alma mater of former Enron CEO Jeffrey Skilling, has begun assessing M.B.A. applicants for integrity. Harvard and other universities teach ethics courses to undergraduate business majors. However, the courses vary widely, and their effectiveness is unclear. In fact, one syllabus states, "The Ethics Project does not guarantee that all Wharton graduates will behave ethically. . . . The intellectual understanding of ethical obligations may not be sufficient to ensure ethical behavior."

Robert Prentice, a professor of business law at the University of Texas, feels that students need more than ethics training. "Research shows that it is very difficult to teach ethical values to undergraduates. . . . If they didn't get a sense of right and wrong from their families or their faith, it's unlikely a business school professor can instill one." Prentice believes that more exposure to business law would help. He says, "[The scandals] occurred, at least in part, because their participants had an insufficient knowledge of, appreciation for and yes, fear of the law."

References: "A Sampling of Lesson Plans in Business Ethics at Nation's Business Schools," *Austin American-Statesman* (Austin, Texas), August 25, 2002, p. H4; Lynnley Browning, "Weeding out the Bad Apples (Before They Get to Harvard)," *New York Times*, September 8, 2002, p. BU2; Richard B. Schmitt, "Companies Add Ethics Training; Will It Work?" *Wall Street Journal*, November 4, 2002, pp. B1, B4; Robert Prentice, "Students of Business Must Learn to Fear the Law," *New York Times*, August 23, 2002 (*quote).

an ethical judgment based on the rightness or wrongness of the proposed activity or policy.

But this analysis is seldom as simple as these steps might imply. For instance, what if the facts are not clear-cut? What if there are no agreed-upon moral values? Nevertheless, a judgment and a decision must be made. Experts point out that, otherwise, trust is impossible, and trust, they add, is indispensable to any business transaction. Thus, in order to more completely assess the ethics of a particular behavior, a more complex perspective is necessary. To illustrate this perspective, consider a common dilemma faced by managers, involving their expense account.[11]

Companies routinely provide their managers with an account to cover their work-related expenses when they are traveling on company business or entertaining clients for business purposes. Common examples of such expenses include hotel bills, meals, rental cars or taxis, and so forth. But employees, of course, are expected to claim only expenses that are accurate and work related. For example, if a manager takes a client out to dinner while in another city on business and spends $100 for dinner, submitting a receipt for that dinner to be reimbursed for $100 is clearly accurate and appropriate. Suppose, however, that the manager then has a $100 dinner the next night in that same city with a good friend for purely social purposes. Submitting that receipt for full reimbursement would be unethical. A few managers, however, might rationalize that it would be okay to submit a receipt for dinner with a friend. They might argue, for example, that they are underpaid, so this is just a way for them to increase their income.

Other principles that come into play in a case like this include various ethical norms. Four such norms involve utility, rights, justice, and caring. By utility, we mean whether a particular act optimizes what is best for its constituencies. By rights, we mean whether the act respects the rights of the individuals involved. By justice, we mean whether the act is consistent with what most people would see as fair. And, by caring, we mean whether the act is consistent with people's responsibilities to one another. Figure 4.2 illustrates a model that incorporates these ethical norms.

Now, reconsider the case of the inflated expense account. Although the utility norm would acknowledge that the manager benefits from padding an expense account, others, such as coworkers and owners, would not. Similarly, most experts would agree that such an action does not respect the rights of others. Moreover, it is clearly unfair and compromises responsibilities to others. Thus this particular act would appear to be clearly unethical. However, the figure also provides mechanisms for considering unique circumstances that might fit only in certain limited situations. For example, suppose the manager loses the receipt for the legitimate dinner but has the receipt for the same amount for the social dinner. Some people would now argue that it is okay to submit the social dinner receipt because the manager is only doing so to get what he or she is entitled to. Others, however, would still argue that submitting the social receipt is wrong under any circumstances. The point, simply, is that changes in the situation can make things more or less clear-cut.

concept CHECK

What are the three basic areas of managerial ethics?

Identify an ethical situation you have experienced or observed and analyze it in terms of the framework presented in Figure 4.2.

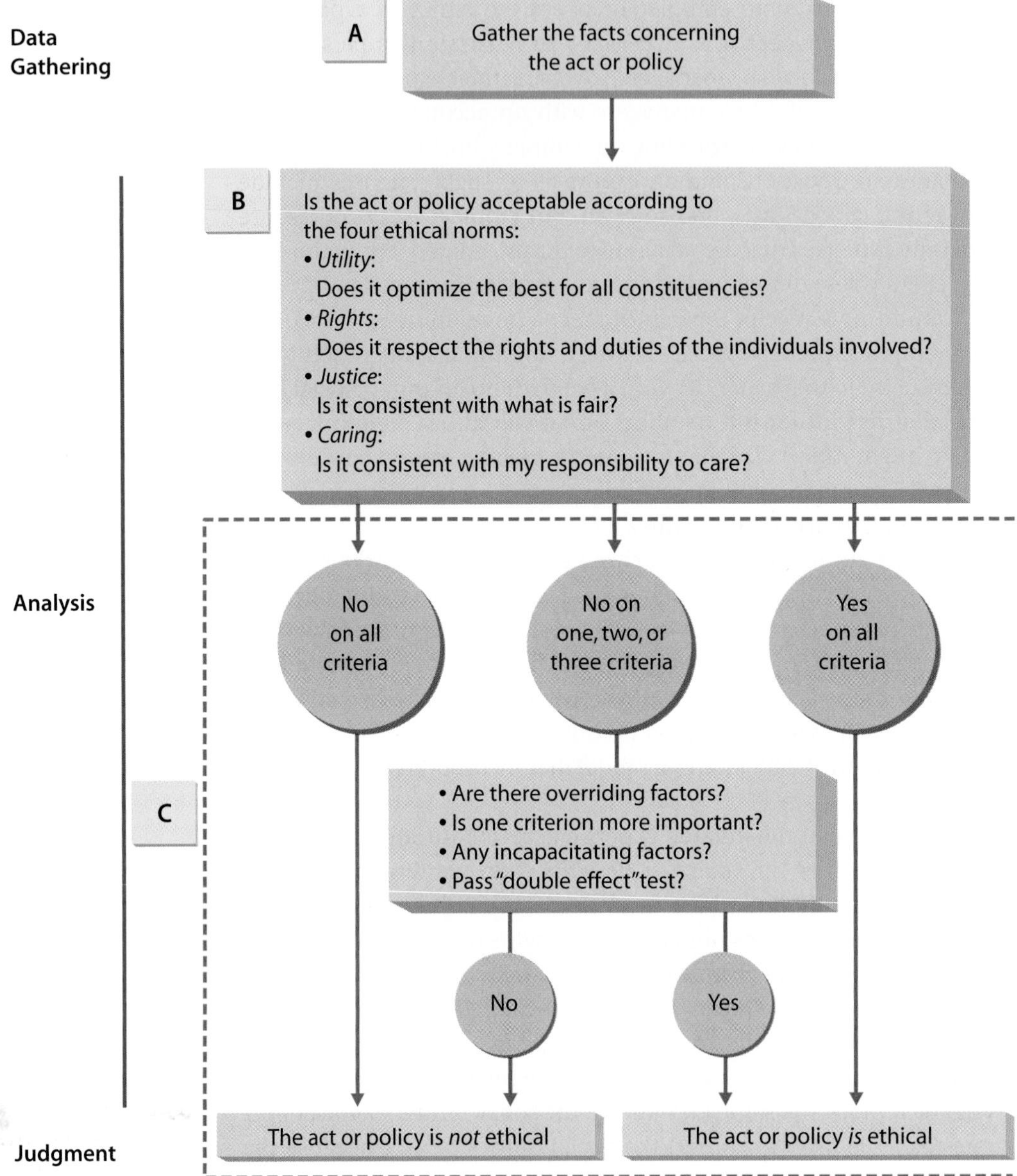

FIGURE 4.2

A Guide for Ethical Decision Making

Managers should attempt to apply ethical judgment to the decisions they make. For example, this useful framework for guiding ethical decision making suggests that managers apply a set of four criteria based on utility, rights, justice, and caring when assessing decision options. The resulting analysis allows a manager to make a clear assessment of whether or not a decision or policy is ethical.

Source: Adapted from Gerald F. Cavanagh, Dennis J. Moberg, and Manuel Velasquez, "Making Business Ethics Practical," *Business Ethics Quarterly* (July 1995); and Manuel Velasquez, Gerald F. Cavanagh, and Dennis Moberg, "Organizational Statesmenship and Dirty Politics," *Organizational Dynamics* (Autumn, 1983), p. 84. Copyright 1983, with permission from Elsevier Science. Reprinted from Gerald F. Cavanagh, *American Business Values*, 4th Edition (Upper Saddle River, N.J.: Prentice-Hall, 1998). Reprinted by permission of Prentice-Hall, Inc.

Emerging Ethical Issues in Organizations

Ethical scandals have become almost commonplace in today's world. Ranging from business to sports to politics to the entertainment industry, these scandals have rocked stakeholder confidence and called into question the moral integrity of our society. But, at the same time, it is important to remember that most women and men today conduct themselves and their affairs with nothing but the highest ethical standards. Hence, as we summarize several emerging ethical issues in organizations, it is important to remember that one cannot judge everyone by the transgressions of a few.

Ethical Leadership

This chapter's opening incident highlights several key examples that illustrate precisely the point made above: For every unethical senior manager, there are many highly ethical ones. But the actions of such high-profile deposed executives as Dennis Kozlowski (Tyco), Kenneth Lay (Enron), and Bernard Ebbers (WorldCom) have substantially increased the scrutiny directed at all executives. As a direct result, executives everywhere are being expected to exhibit nothing but the strongest ethical conduct. This leadership, in turn, is expected to help set the tone for the rest of the organization and to help establish both norms and a culture that reinforce the importance of ethical behavior.[12]

The basic premise behind ethical leadership is that, because leaders serve as role models for others, their every action is subject to scrutiny. If a senior executive exercises questionable judgment, this sends a signal to others that such actions are acceptable. This signal may, in turn, be remembered by others when they face similar situations. As a result, CEOs like Aramark's Joseph Neubauer and Costco's James Sinegal are now being held up as the standard against which others are being measured. The basic premise is that CEOs must set their company's moral tone by being honest and straightforward and by taking responsibility for any shortcomings that are identified. And, to support this view, in 2002 Congress passed the **Sarbanes-Oxley Act**, requiring CEOs and CFOs to personally vouch for the truthfulness and fairness of their firm's financial disclosures. The law also imposes tough new measures to deter and punish corporate and accounting fraud and corruption.

Sarbanes-Oxley Act of 2002
Requires CEOs and CFOs to personally vouch for the truthfulness and fairness of their firm's financial disclosures and imposes tough new measures to deter and punish corporate and accounting fraud and corruption.

Ethical Issues in Corporate Governance

A related area of emerging concern relates to ethical issues in corporate governance. As discussed in Chapter 3, the board of directors of a public corporation is expected to ensure that the business is being properly managed and that the decisions made by its senior management are in the best interests of shareholders and other stakeholders. But, in far too many cases, the recent ethical scandals alluded to above have actually started with a breakdown in the corporate governance structure. For instance, WorldCom's board approved a personal loan to the firm's CEO, Bernard Ebbers, for $366 million, when there was little evidence that he could repay it. Likewise, Tyco's board approved a $20 million bonus for one of its own members for helping with the acquisition of another firm.

But boards of directors are also increasingly being criticized even when they are not directly implicated in wrongdoing. The biggest complaint here often relates to board independence. Disney, for instance, has faced this problem. Several key members of the firm's board of directors are from companies that do business with Disney, and others are longtime friends of Disney CEO Michael Eisner. The concern, then, is that Eisner may be given more autonomy than might otherwise be warranted because of his various relationships with board members. Although board members need to have some familiarity with both the firm and its industry in order to function effectively, they also need to have sufficient independence to carry out their oversight function.[13]

Ethical Issues in Information Technology

A final set of issues that has emerged in recent times involves information technology. Among the specific questions in this area are individual rights to privacy and the potential abuse of information technology by individuals. Indeed, online privacy has become a hot topic, as companies sort out the ethical and management issues. DoubleClick, an online advertising network, is one of the firms at the eye of the privacy storm. The company has collected data on the habits of millions of Web surfers, recording which sites they visit and which ads they click on. DoubleClick insists the profiles are anonymous and are used to better match surfers with appropriate ads. However, after the company announced a plan to add names and addresses to its database, it was forced to back down because of public concerns over invasion of online privacy.

DoubleClick is not the only firm gathering personal data about people's Internet activities. People who register at Yahoo! are asked to list date of birth, among other details. Amazon.com, eBay, and other sites also ask for personal information. As Internet usage increases, however, surveys show that people are troubled by the amount of information being collected and who gets to see it.

One way management can address these concerns is to post a privacy policy on the website. The policy should explain exactly what data the company collects and who gets to see the data. It should also allow people a choice about having their information shared with others and indicate how people can opt out of data collection. Disney, IBM, and other companies support this position by refusing to advertise on websites that have no posted privacy policies.

In addition, companies can offer Web surfers the opportunity to review and correct information that has been collected, especially medical and financial data. In the offline world, consumers are legally allowed to inspect credit and medical records. In the online world, this kind of access can be costly and cumbersome, because data are often spread across several computer systems. Despite the technical difficulties, government agencies are already working on Internet privacy guidelines, which means that companies will need internal guidelines, training, and leadership to ensure compliance. *Technology Toolkit* presents another contemporary perspective on ethical issues and information technology.

TECHNOLOGY toolkit

The Most Common Password? "Password"

"... who knows how long this would have gone on?"

– Farzad Dibachi, CEO of software maker Niku Corporation*

If you use the Internet, you probably have one or more accounts with a password, a bank account or two, credit cards, travel sites, e-mail, school, and work accounts. Altogether, there are probably a lot of data that you do not want people to know and a lot of harm that could be done to you by unauthorized access. Now, consider how much more vulnerable are corporations, which must be concerned about employee privacy, trade secrets, confidential memos, and strategic plans. Recently there have been several high-profile cases of hackers' gaining access to corporate information, many involving the cracking of passwords.

In one case, Niku Corporation's rival, Business Engine, is accused of sneaking into Niku's network 6,000 times over many months through the fraudulent use of legitimate passwords. Business Engine stole product plans and customer lists, and then used that information to steal Niku customers. The hacking was discovered accidentally, because one of Niku's clients, who was also contacted by Business Engine, happens to be the brother-in-law of a Niku executive. Farzad Dibachi, Niku CEO, says, "It was sheer coincidence. Otherwise, who knows how long this would have gone on?"

Passwords are a weak spot in many information systems. Users help hackers by writing their passwords down—taped under a keyboard is the number-one location. Another not-too-bright idea is the use of familiar names, birth dates, and other easily obtainable information. For example, one survey found that over 70 percent of users in federal agencies had a password that was a variant of "Redskins," the Washington, D.C., professional football team. Corporations have a very tough time preventing these common errors among their employees.

Technology, too, has eased the way for password crackers. Today, the speed of personal computers is so fast that millions of passwords can be attempted in just seconds. With a sophisticated hacking algorithm, a fast personal computer can attempt 1 million English-language words in just half a second. (The twenty-volume *Oxford English Dictionary* has just 500,000 words.) For 20 million words, it takes just ten seconds.

There are software programs, such as Password Tracker, that allow a firm to record all passwords and other account information. But do not rely on software to solve this problem—there is also a similar-appearing product, named Gator, that transmits account information directly to a corporate database, an example of "spyware."

References: Jim Kerstetter, "You're Only as Good as Your Password," *BusinessWeek*, September 2, 2002, pp. 78–80 (*quote p. 80); Richard Lowe, "Passwords," Internet Tips website, www.internet-tips.net on December 6, 2002; Todd Pukanecz and Doug Edmonds, "Stealing and Cracking Passwords," Virginia Polytechnic Institute website, http://mmdev.ag.vt.edu/security on December 6, 2002.

concept CHECK

What are three emerging ethical issues in business today?

In what ways are information privacy and information technology relevant to you?

Social Responsibility and Organizations

As we have seen, ethics relate to individuals and their decisions and behaviors. Organizations themselves do not have ethics, but do relate to their environment in ways that often involve ethical dilemmas and decisions. These situations are generally referred to within the context of the organization's social responsibility. Specifically, **social responsibility** is the set of obligations an organization has to protect and enhance the societal context in which it functions.

social responsibility The set of obligations an organization has to protect and enhance the societal context in which it functions

Areas of Social Responsibility

organizational stakeholder Person or organization who is directly affected by the practices of an organization and has a stake in its performance

Organizations may exercise social responsibility toward their stakeholders, toward the natural environment, and toward general social welfare. Some organizations acknowledge their responsibilities in all three areas and strive diligently to meet each of them, whereas others emphasize only one or two areas of social responsibility. And a few acknowledge no social responsibility at all.

FIGURE 4.3

Organizational Stakeholders

All organizations have a variety of stakeholders who are directly affected by the organization and who have a stake in its performance. These are people and organizations to whom an organization should be responsible.

Organizational Stakeholders In Chapter 3 we describe the task environment as comprising those elements in an organization's external environment that directly affect the organization in one or more ways. Another way to describe these same elements is from the perspective of **organizational stakeholders**, or those people and organizations who are directly affected by the practices of an organization and have a stake in its performance.[14] Major stakeholders are depicted in Figure 4.3.

Most companies that strive to be responsible to their stakeholders concentrate first and foremost on three main groups: customers, employees, and investors. They then select other stakeholders that are particularly relevant or important to the organization and attempt to address their needs and expectations as well.

Organizations that are responsible to their customers strive to treat them fairly and honestly. They also seek to charge fair prices, to honor warranties, to meet delivery commitments, and to stand behind the quality of the products they sell. Companies that have established excellent reputations in this area include L.L.Bean, Lands' End, Dell Computer, and Johnson & Johnson.

Organizations that are socially responsible in their dealings with employees treat their workers fairly, make them a part of the team, and respect their dignity and basic human needs. Organizations such as 3M Company, Hoescht AG, SAS Institute, and Southwest Airlines have all established strong reputations in this area. In addition, they go to great lengths to find, hire, train, and promote qualified minorities.

To maintain a socially responsible stance toward investors, managers should follow proper accounting procedures, provide appropriate information to shareholders about the financial performance of the firm, and manage the organization to protect shareholder rights and investments. Moreover, they should be accurate and candid in their assessment of future growth and profitability, and avoid even the appearance of improprieties involving such sensitive areas as insider trading, stock price manipulation, and the withholding of financial data.

Respect for the natural environment is a key part of social responsibility. Vandana Shiva runs an organization called Navdanya (Nine Seeds). Her organization helps teach farmers in India how to produce hardy native varieties of crops that can be grown organically with natural fertilizer and no artifical chemicals.

The Natural Environment A second critical area of social responsibility relates to the natural environment.[15] Not long ago, many organizations indiscriminately dumped sewage, waste products from production, and trash into streams and rivers, into the air, and on vacant land. When Shell Oil first explored the Amazon River Basin for potential drilling sites in the late 1980s, its crews ripped down trees and left a trail of garbage in their wake. Now, however, many laws regulate the disposal of waste materials. In many instances, companies themselves have become more socially responsible in their release of pollutants and general treatment of the environment. For example, when Shell launched its most recent exploratory expedition into another area of the Amazon Basin, the group included a biologist to oversee environmental protection and an anthropologist to help the team interact more effectively with native tribes.[16]

Still, much remains to be done. Companies need to develop economically feasible ways to avoid contributing to acid rain, global warming, and depletion of the ozone layer, and to develop alternative methods of handling sewage, hazardous wastes, and ordinary garbage.[17] Procter & Gamble, for example, is an industry leader in using recycled materials for containers. Hyatt Corporation established a new company to help recycle waste products from its hotels. Monsanto is launching an entire new product line aimed at improving the environment with genetically engineered crops.[18] Ford has also announced its intention to create a new brand to develop and market low-pollution and electrically powered vehicles.[19] The Internet is also seen as having the potential to play an important role in resource conservation, as many e-commerce businesses and transactions are reducing both energy costs and pollution.[20]

Maintaining the delicate balance between economic development and environmental protection seems to be a never-ending battle. These workers are fighting to clean up a beach threatened by an oil spill before too much damage is done. An oil barge leaked about 14,000 gallons of oil into Buzzards Bay near Cape Cod before the leak could be plugged. And as always seems to be the case, litigation as to who will pay the costs of the clean-up will most likely take years to settle.

Companies also need to develop safety policies that cut down on accidents with potentially disastrous environmental results. When one of Ashland Oil's storage tanks ruptured several years ago, spilling more than 500,000 gallons of diesel fuel into Pennsylvania's Monongahela River, the company moved quickly to clean up the spill but was still indicted for violating U.S. environmental laws.[21] After the Exxon oil tanker *Valdez* spilled millions of gallons of oil off the coast of Alaska, the firm adopted new and more stringent procedures to keep another disaster from happening.

General Social Welfare Some people believe that, in addition to treating constituents and the environment responsibly, business organizations also should promote the general welfare of society. Examples include making contributions to charities, philanthropic organizations, and not-for-profit foundations and associations; supporting museums, symphonies, and public radio and television; and taking a role in improving public health and education. Some people also believe that organizations should act even more broadly to correct the political inequities that exist in the world. For example, these observers would argue that businesses should not conduct operations in countries with a record of human rights violations. Thus they stand in opposition to companies' doing business in China and Vietnam.

Arguments For and Against Social Responsibility

On the surface, there seems to be little disagreement about the need for organizations to be socially responsible. In truth, though, those who oppose broad interpretations of social responsibility use several convincing arguments.[22] Some of the more salient arguments on both sides of this contemporary debate are summarized in Figure 4.4 and further explained in the following sections.

Arguments For Social Responsibility People who argue in favor of social responsibility claim that, because organizations create many of the problems that need to be addressed, such as air and water pollution and resource depletion, they should play a major role in solving them. They also argue that, because corporations are legally defined entities with most of the same privileges as private citizens, businesses should not try to avoid their obligations as citizens. Advocates of social responsibility point out that, whereas governmental organizations have stretched their budgets to the limit, many large businesses often have surplus revenues that could be used to help solve social problems. For example, IBM routinely donates surplus computers to schools, and many restaurants give leftover food to homeless shelters.

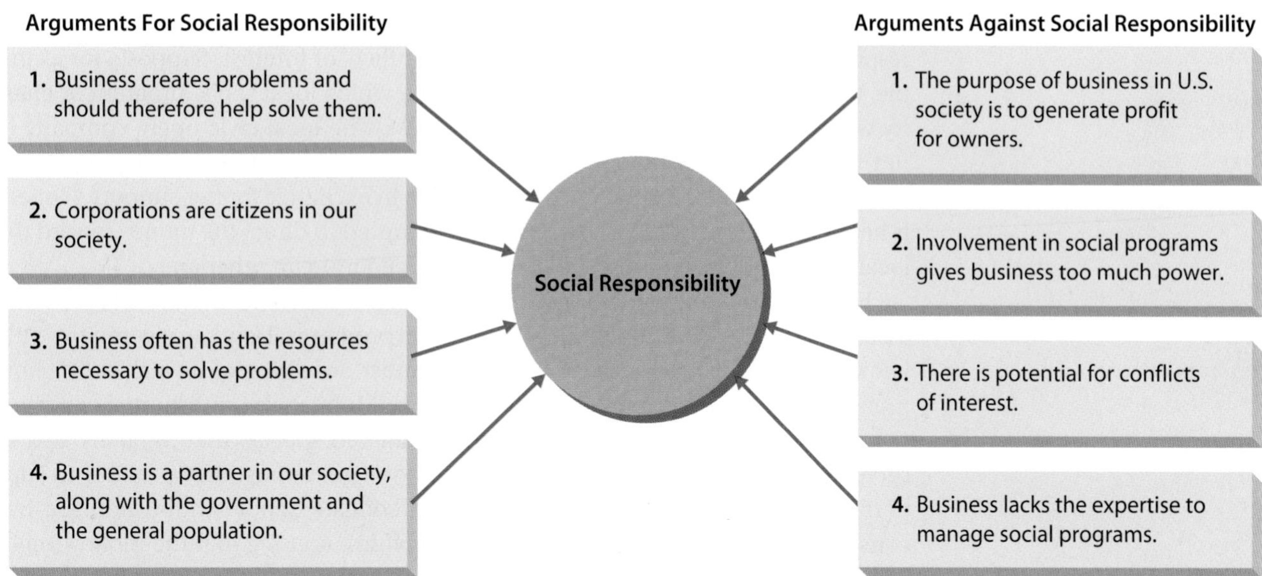

FIGURE 4.4

Arguments For and Against Social Responsibility

While many people want everyone to see social responsibility as a desirable aim, there are in fact several strong arguments that can be used both for and against social responsibility. Hence, organizations and their managers should carefully assess their own values, beliefs, and priorities when deciding which stance and approach to take regarding social responsibility.

Although each of the arguments just summarized is a distinct justification for socially responsible behaviors on the part of organizations, another more general reason for social responsibility is profit itself. For example, organizations that make clear and visible contributions to society can achieve an enhanced reputation and garner greater market share for their products. Although claims of socially responsible activities can haunt a company if they are exaggerated or untrue, they can also work to the benefit of both the organization and society if the advertised benefits are true and accurate.

Arguments Against Social Responsibility Some people, however, including the famous economist Milton Friedman, argue that widening the interpretation of social responsibility will undermine the U.S. economy by detracting from the basic mission of business: to earn profits for owners. For example, money that Chevron or General Electric contributes to social causes or charities is money that could otherwise be distributed to owners as a dividend. A few years ago, shareholders of Ben & Jerry's Homemade Holdings expressed outrage when the firm refused to accept a lucrative exporting deal to Japan simply because the Japanese distributor did not have a strong social agenda.[23]

Another objection to deepening the social responsibility of businesses points out that corporations already wield enormous power and that their activity in social programs gives them even more power. Still another argument against social responsibility focuses on the potential for conflicts of interest. Suppose, for example, that one manager is in charge of deciding which local social program or charity will receive a large grant from her business. The local civic opera company (a not-for-profit organization that relies on contributions for its existence) might offer her front-row tickets for the upcoming season in exchange for her support. If opera is her favorite form of music, she might be tempted to direct the money toward the local company, when it might actually be needed more in other areas.[24]

Finally, critics argue that organizations lack the expertise to understand how to assess and make decisions about worthy social programs. How can a company truly know, they ask, which cause or program is most deserving of its support or how money might best be spent? For example, ExxonMobil makes substantial contributions to help save the Bengal tiger, an endangered species that happens also to serve as the firm's corporate symbol. ExxonMobil gives most of the money to support breeding programs in zoos and to help educate people about the tiger. But conservationists criticize the firm and its activities, arguing that the money might be better spent instead on eliminating poaching, the illegal trade of tiger fur, and the destruction of the tiger's natural habitat.[25]

Organizational Approaches to Social Responsibility As we have seen, some people advocate a larger social role for organizations, and others argue that the role is already too large. Not surprisingly, organizations themselves adopt a wide range of positions on social responsibility. As Figure 4.5 illustrates, the four stances that an organization can take concerning its obligations to society fall along a continuum ranging from the lowest to the highest degree of socially responsible practices.

Obstructionist Stance The few organizations that take what might be called an **obstructionist stance** to social responsibility usually do as little as possible to solve social or environmental problems. When they cross the ethical or legal line that separates acceptable from unacceptable practices, their typical response is to deny or avoid accepting responsibility for their actions. For example, a few years ago a senior executive of Astra USA, a subsidiary of a Swedish pharmaceutical firm, was charged with sexual harassment and misusing corporate assets. When these problems were first reported, officials at both the U.S. company and its Swedish parent company denied any wrongdoing without even conducting an inquiry. They only acknowledged the problem when the executive was indicted and found guilty. More recently, both Enron and its auditor, Arthur Andersen, appear to have taken this approach, based on the numerous denials from officials at

obstructionist stance An approach to social responsibility in which firms do as little as possible to solve social or environmental problems

FIGURE 4.5

Approaches to Social Responsibility

Organizations can adopt a variety of approaches to social responsibility. For example, a firm that never considers the consequences of its decisions and tries to hide its transgressions is taking an obstructionist stance. At the other extreme, a firm that actively seeks to identify areas where it can help society is pursuing a proactive stance toward social responsibility.

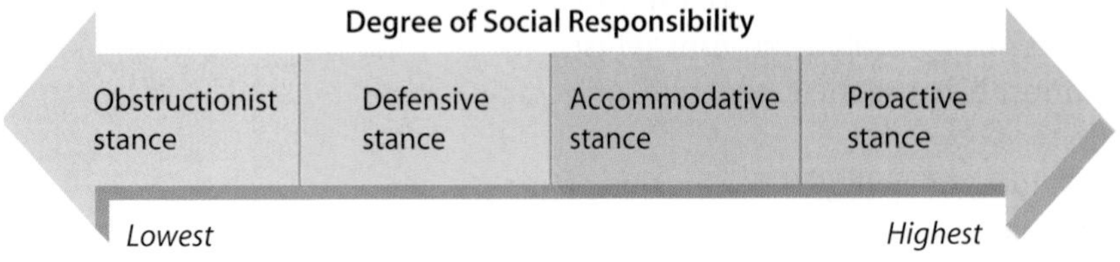

both firms regarding various charges of wrongdoing, as well as their intentional destruction of important legal and financial documents.

Defensive Stance One step removed from the obstructionist stance is the **defensive stance**, whereby the organization does everything that is required of it legally, but nothing more. This approach is most consistent with the arguments used against social responsibility. Managers in organizations that take a defensive stance insist that their job is to generate profits. For example, such a firm would install pollution control equipment dictated by law, but would not install higher-quality but slightly more expensive equipment even though it might limit pollution further. Tobacco companies like Philip Morris take this position in their marketing efforts. In the United States, they are legally required to include warnings to smokers on their products and to limit their advertising to prescribed media. Domestically they follow these rules to the letter of the law but use stronger marketing methods in countries that have no such rules. In many African countries, for example, cigarettes are heavily promoted, contain higher levels of tar and nicotine than those sold in the United States, and carry few or no health warning labels.[26] Firms that take this position are also unlikely to cover up wrongdoing, and will generally admit their mistakes and take appropriate corrective actions.

defensive stance A social responsibility stance in which an organization does everything that is required of it legally, but nothing more

Accommodative Stance A firm that adopts an **accommodative stance** meets its legal and ethical obligations but will also go beyond these obligations in selected cases. Such firms voluntarily agree to participate in social programs, but solicitors have to convince the organization that the programs are worthy of its support. Both ExxonMobil and IBM, for example, will match contributions made by their employees to selected charitable causes. And many organizations will respond to requests for donations to Little League, Girl Scouts, youth soccer programs, and so forth. The point, though, is that someone has to knock on the door and ask—the organizations do not proactively seek such avenues for contributing.

accommodative stance A social responsibility stance in which an organization meets its legal and ethical obligations but will also go beyond these obligations in selected cases

Proactive Stance The highest degree of social responsibility that a firm can exhibit is the **proactive stance**. Firms that adopt this approach take to heart the arguments in favor of social responsibility. They view themselves as citizens in a society and proactively seek opportunities to contribute. An excellent example of a proactive stance is the Ronald McDonald House program undertaken by McDonald's. These houses, located close to major medical centers, can be used by families for minimal cost while their sick children are receiving medical treatment nearby. Sears offers fellowships that support promising young performers while they develop their talents. Target stopped selling guns in its stores, and Toys "R" Us stopped selling realistic toy guns, both due to concerns about escalating violence. These and related activities and programs exceed the accommodative stance—they indicate a sincere and potent commitment to improving the general social welfare in this country and thus represent a proactive stance to social responsibility.

proactive stance A social responsibility stance in which an organization views itself as a citizen in a society and proactively seeks opportunities to contribute

Remember that these categories are not discrete but merely define stages along a continuum of approaches. Organizations do not always fit neatly into one category.

The Ronald McDonald House program has been widely applauded, for example, but McDonald's also came under fire a few years ago for allegedly misleading consumers about the nutritional value of its food products. And, even though both Enron and Arthur Andersen took an obstructionist stance in the cases cited above, many individual employees and managers at both firms no doubt made substantial contributions to society in a number of different ways.

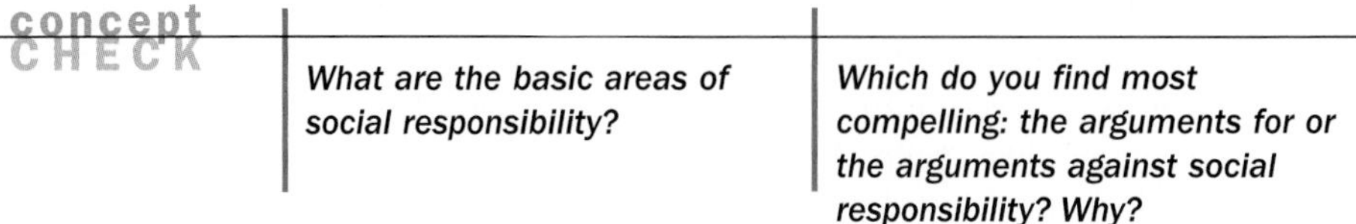

The Government and Social Responsibility

An especially important element of social responsibility is the relationship between business and government. For example, in planned economies the government heavily regulates business activities, ostensibly to ensure that business supports some overarching set of social ideals. And even in market economies there is still considerable government control of business, much of it again directed at making sure that social interests are not damaged by business interests. On the other side of the coin, business also attempts to influence the government. Such influence attempts are usually undertaken in an effort to offset or reverse government restrictions. As Figure 4.6 shows, organizations and the government use several methods in their attempts to influence each other.

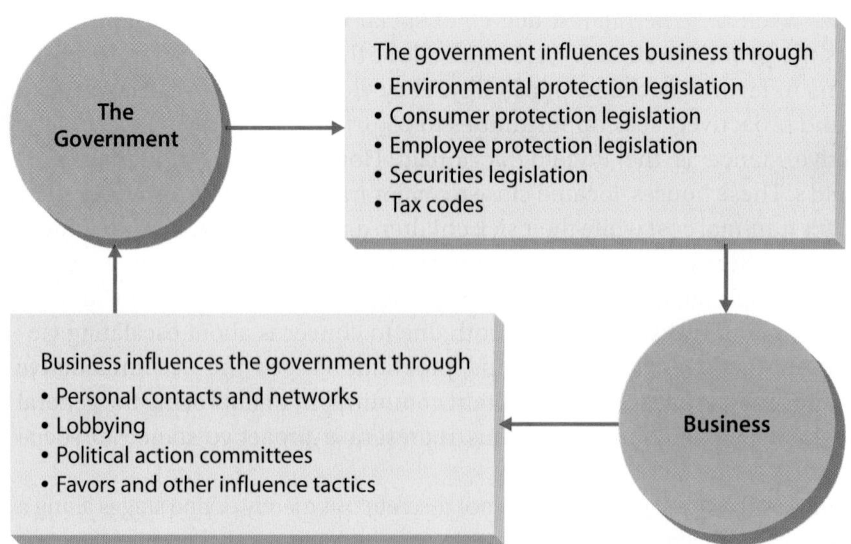

FIGURE 4.6

How Business and the Government Influence Each Other

Business and the government influence each other in a variety of ways. Government influence can be direct or indirect. Business influence relies on personal contacts, lobbying, political action committees (PACs), and favors. Federal Express, for example, has a very active PAC.

How Government Influences Organizations

The government attempts to shape social responsibility practices through both direct and indirect channels. Direct influence most frequently is manifested through regulation, whereas indirect influence can take a number of forms, most notably taxation policies.

Direct Regulation The government most often directly influences organizations through **regulation**, or the establishment of laws and rules that dictate what organizations can and cannot do. As noted earlier in the chapter, this regulation usually evolves from societal beliefs about what businesses should or should not be allowed to do. To implement legislation, the government generally creates special agencies to monitor and control certain aspects of business activity. For example, the Environmental Protection Agency handles environmental issues; the Federal Trade Commission and the Food and Drug Administration focus on consumer-related concerns; the Equal Employee Opportunity Commission, the National Labor Relations Board, and the Department of Labor help protect employees; and the Securities and Exchange Commission handles investor-related issues. These agencies have the power to levy fines or bring charges against organizations that violate regulations.

regulation Government's attempts to influence business by establishing laws and rules that dictate what businesses can and cannot do

Indirect Regulation Other forms of regulation are indirect. For example, the government can indirectly influence the social responsibility of organizations through its tax codes. In effect, the government can influence how organizations spend their social responsibility dollars by providing greater or lesser tax incentives. For instance, suppose that the government wanted organizations to spend more on training the hard-core unemployed. Congress could then pass laws that provided tax incentives to companies that opened new training facilities. As a result, more businesses would probably do so. Of course, some critics argue that regulation is already excessive. They maintain that a free market system would eventually accomplish the same goals as regulation, with lower costs to both organizations and the government.

How Organizations Influence Government

As we mention in Chapter 3, organizations can influence their environment in many different ways. In particular, businesses have four main methods of addressing governmental pressures for more social responsibility.

Personal Contacts Because many corporate executives and political leaders travel in the same social circles, personal contacts and networks offer one method of influence. A business executive, for example, may be able to contact a politician directly and present his or her case regarding a piece of legislation being considered.

Lobbying **Lobbying**, or the use of persons or groups to formally represent an organization or group of organizations before political bodies, is also an effective way to influence the government. The National Rifle Association (NRA), for example, has a staff of lobbyists in Washington, with a substantial annual budget. These lobbyists work to represent the NRA's position on gun control and to potentially influence

lobbying The use of persons or groups to formally represent a company or group of companies before political bodies to influence the government members of Congress when they vote on legislation that affects the firearms industry and the rights of gun owners.

political action committee (PAC) An organization created to solicit and distribute money to political candidates

Political Action Committees Companies themselves cannot legally make direct donations to political campaigns, so they influence the government through political action committees. **Political action committees (PACs)** are special organizations created to solicit money and then distribute it to political candidates. Employees of a firm may be encouraged to make donations to a particular PAC because managers know that it will support candidates with political views similar to their own. PACs, in turn, make the contributions themselves, usually to a broad slate of state and national candidates. For example, Federal Express's PAC is called Fed Expac. Fed Expac makes regular contributions to the campaign funds of political candidates who are most likely to work in the firm's best interests.

Favors Finally, organizations sometimes rely on favors and other influence tactics to gain support. Although these favors may be legal, they are still subject to criticism. A few years back, for example, two influential members of a House committee attending a fund-raising function in Miami were needed in Washington to finish work on a piece of legislation that Federal Express wanted passed. The law being drafted would allow the company and its competitors to give their employees standby seats on airlines as a tax-free benefit. As a favor, Federal Express provided one of its corporate jets to fly the committee members back to Washington. Federal Express was eventually reimbursed for its expenses, so its assistance was not illegal, but some people argue that such actions are dangerous because of how they might be perceived.

concept CHECK

Identify the specific ways in which the government and organizations influence each other.

Do you think current levels of government regulation of business are excessive? Why or why not?

Managing Social Responsibility

The demands for social responsibility placed on contemporary organizations by an increasingly sophisticated and educated public are probably stronger than ever. As we have seen, there are pitfalls for managers who fail to adhere to high ethical standards and for companies that try to circumvent their legal obligations. Organizations therefore need to fashion an approach to social responsibility in the same way that they develop any other business strategy. In other words, they should view social responsibility as a major challenge that requires careful planning, decision making, consideration, and evaluation. They may accomplish this through both formal and informal dimensions of managing social responsibility.

Formal Organizational Dimensions

Some dimensions of managing social responsibility are a formal and planned activity on the part of the organization. Formal organizational dimensions that can help manage social responsibility are legal compliance, ethical compliance, and philanthropic giving.

Legal Compliance **Legal compliance** is the extent to which the organization conforms to local, state, federal, and international laws. The task of managing legal compliance is generally assigned to the appropriate functional managers. For example, the organization's top human resource executive is responsible for ensuring compliance with regulations concerning hiring, pay, and workplace safety and health. Likewise, the top finance executive generally oversees compliance with securities and banking regulations. The organization's legal department is also likely to contribute to this effort by providing general oversight and answering queries from managers about the appropriate interpretation of laws and regulations. Unfortunately, though, legal compliance may not be enough—in some cases, for instance, perfectly legal accounting practices have still resulted in deception and other problems.[27]

legal compliance The extent to which an organization complies with local, state, federal, and international laws

Ethical Compliance **Ethical compliance** is the extent to which the members of the organization follow basic ethical (and legal) standards of behavior. We note earlier that organizations have increased their efforts in this area—providing training in ethics and developing guidelines and codes of conduct, for example. These activities serve as vehicles for enhancing ethical compliance. Many organizations also establish formal ethics committees, which may be asked to review proposals for new projects, help evaluate new hiring strategies, or assess a new environmental protection plan. They might also serve as a peer review panel to evaluate alleged ethical misconduct by an employee.[28]

ethical compliance The extent to which an organization and its members follow basic ethical standards of behavior

Philanthropic Giving Finally, **philanthropic giving** is the awarding of funds or gifts to charities or other worthy causes. Dayton Hudson Corporation routinely gives 5 percent of its taxable income to charity and social programs. Giving across national boundaries is also becoming more common. For example, Alcoa gave $112,000 to a small town in Brazil to build a sewage treatment plant. And Japanese firms like Sony and Mitsubishi make contributions to a number of social programs in the United States. However, in the current climate of cutbacks, many corporations have also had to limit their charitable gifts over the past several years as they continue to trim their own budgets.[29] And many firms that continue to make contributions are increasingly targeting them to programs or areas where the firm will get something in return. For example, firms today are more likely to give money to job training programs than to the arts than was the case just a few years ago. The logic is that they get more direct payoff from the former type of contribution—in this instance, a better-trained workforce from which to hire new employees.[30]

philanthropic giving Awarding funds or gifts to charities or other worthy causes

Informal Organizational Dimensions

In addition to these formal dimensions for managing social responsibility, there are also informal ones. Leadership, organization culture, and how the organization responds to whistle blowers all help shape and define people's perceptions of the organization's stance on social responsibility.

Organization Leadership and Culture Leadership practices and organization culture can go a long way toward defining the social responsibility stance an organization and its members will adopt.[31] As described earlier, for example, ethical leadership often sets the tone for the entire organization. For example, Johnson & Johnson executives for years provided a consistent message to employees that customers, employees, communities where the company did business, and shareholders were all important—and primarily in that order. Thus, when packages of poisoned Tylenol showed up on store shelves in the 1980s, Johnson & Johnson employees did not need to wait for orders from headquarters to know what to do: They immediately pulled all the packages from shelves before any other customers could buy them.[32] By contrast, the message sent to Hypercom employees by the actions of their top managers communicated much less regard for social responsibility.

whistle blowing The disclosing by an employee of illegal or unethical conduct on the part of others within the organization

Whistle Blowing **Whistle blowing** is the disclosure by an employee of illegal or unethical conduct on the part of others within the organization.[33] How an organization responds to this practice often indicates its stance on social responsibility. Whistle blowers may have to proceed through a number of channels to be heard, and they may even get fired for their efforts.[34] Many organizations, however, welcome their contributions. A person who observes questionable behavior typically first reports the incident to his or her boss. If nothing is done, the whistle blower may then inform higher-level managers or an ethics committee, if one exists. Eventually, the person may have to go to a regulatory agency or even the media to be heard. For example, Charles W. Robinson, Jr., worked as a director of a SmithKline lab in San Antonio. One day he noticed a suspicious billing pattern that the firm was using to collect lab fees from Medicare: The bills were considerably higher than the firm's normal charges for those same tests. He pointed out the problem to higher-level managers, but his concerns were ignored. He subsequently took his findings to the U.S. government, which sued SmithKline and eventually reached a settlement of $325 million.[35] *Working with Diversity* discusses some other interesting ideas regarding whistle blowers.

Evaluating Social Responsibility

Any organization that is serious about social responsibility must ensure that its efforts are producing the desired benefits. Essentially this requires applying the concept of control to social responsibility. Many organizations now require current and new employees to read their guidelines or code of ethics and then sign a statement agreeing to abide by it. An organization should also evaluate how it responds to instances of questionable legal or ethical conduct. Does it follow up immediately? Does it punish those involved? Or does it use delay and cover-up tactics? Answers to these questions can help an organization form a picture of its approach to social responsibility.

WORKING WITH diversity

Men, Women, and Ethics

"As the President, Congress, the SEC, and thousands of companies respond to the trust crisis, let's not forget who revealed quite a bit of it."

— Geoffrey Colvin, editorial director, Fortune*

Accountants Cynthia Cooper of WorldCom and Sherron Watkins of Enron survived the recent scandals with reputations intact. In fact, they wrote the audit documents that uncovered the two enormous frauds. Is it just a coincidence that the primary whistle blowers happened to be female?

Perhaps not. Dr. Jennifer Kreie of New Mexico State University and Dr. Tim Cronan of the University of Arkansas found that women were more likely than men to make ethical decisions. The researchers presented situation descriptions to business students and asked them to make ethical choices. One scenario told about a person who received a mail order that included something not ordered or paid for, and then kept the extra item. Some 45 percent of men found this acceptable, compared to 33 percent of women. In addition, 63 percent of men, versus 45 percent of women, said that they would probably do the same. The gender gap was the same for every scenario.

Kreie and Cronan also found differences in their subjects' ethical reasoning processes. Men considered their personal values and legality in reaching their decisions. Women considered these and in addition thought about what others would do and the company's response. Perhaps a broader context helped women make ethical choices.

Dr. Carol Gilligan of Harvard theorizes that men tend to be interested in justice and rules, and to act ethically by refraining from violating anyone's rights. Women, on the other hand, are interested in caring and relationships, and they act ethically by fulfilling needs. Under Gilligan's theory, whistle blowers Cooper and Watkins felt concern for their firms, not a need to punish rule breakers. This seems to be borne out in a line from Watkins's memo: "None of that will protect Enron if these transactions are ever disclosed in the bright light of day."

Writing in *Fortune*, editor Geoffrey Colvin speculates that Cooper and Watkins acted as they did because, as women, they were not part of the existing power structure. "Or," Colvin says, "maybe my theory is nonsense. Maybe Sherron Watkins and Cynthia Cooper are just two courageous people. The important thing is, as the President, Congress, the SEC, and thousands of companies respond to the trust crisis, let's not forget who revealed quite a bit of it."

References: "Persons of the Year," *Time*, January 6, 2003, pp. 30–50; Carol Gilligan, *In a Different Voice: Psychological Theory and Women's Development* (Cambridge, Mass.: Harvard University Press, 1982); Geoffrey Colvin, "Wonder Women of Whistleblowing," *Fortune*, August 12, 2002, www.fortune.com on November 24, 2002 (*quote); Jennifer Kreie and Tim P. Cronan, "Making Ethical Decisions: What Would You Do? Can Companies Influence the Decision?" *Communication of the ACM* (Association for Computing Machinery), December 2000, vol. 23, no. 12, pp. 66–71; "Two Ethical Styles: The Debate About Gender," The Center for Ethics and Business, Loyola Marymount University website, ethicsandbusiness.org on December 6, 2002.

More formally, an organization may sometimes actually evaluate the effectiveness of its social responsibility efforts. For example, when BP Amoco established a job-training program in Chicago, it allocated additional funds to evaluate how well the program was meeting its goals. Additionally, some organizations occasionally conduct corporate social audits. A **corporate social audit** is a formal and thorough analysis of the effectiveness of a firm's social performance. The audit is usually conducted by a task force of high-level managers from within the firm. It requires that the organization clearly define all of its social goals, analyze the resources it devotes

corporate social audit A formal and thorough analysis of the effectiveness of a firm's social performance to each goal, determine how well it is achieving the various goals, and make recommendations about which areas need additional attention. Recent estimates suggest that around 45 percent of the world's largest 250 firms and 36 of the largest 100 U.S. firms now issue annual reports summarizing their efforts in the areas of environmental and social responsibility; these percentages are expected to continue to increase in the years ahead.[36]

concept CHECK

What formal and informal organizational dimensions can be used to manage social responsibility?

What are the advantages and disadvantages of requiring organizations to perform annual social audits?

Summary of Key Points

business.college.hmco.com/students

Ethics are an individual's personal beliefs about what constitutes right and wrong behavior. Important areas of ethical concern for managers are how the organization treats its employees, how employees treat the organization, and how the organization and its employees treat other economic agents. The ethical context of organizations consists of each manager's individual ethics and messages sent by organizational practices. Organizations use leadership, culture, training, codes, and guidelines to help them manage ethical behavior.

In recent years a variety of new ethical issues have begun to emerge. One of these is ethical leadership and its key role in shaping ethical norms and the culture of the organization. Another involves corporate governance and focuses on the need for the board of directors to maintain appropriate oversight of senior management. And, third, ethical issues in information technology relate to issues such as individual privacy and the potential abuse of an organization's information technology resources by individuals.

Social responsibility is the set of obligations an organization has to protect and enhance the society in which it functions. Organizations may be considered responsible to their stakeholders, to the natural environment, and to the general social welfare. Even so, organizations present strong arguments both for and against social responsibility. The approach an organization adopts toward social responsibility falls along a continuum of lesser to greater commitment: the obstructionist stance, the defensive stance, the accommodative stance, and the proactive stance.

Government influences organizations through regulation, which is the establishment of laws and rules that dictate what businesses can and cannot do in prescribed areas. Organizations, in turn, rely on personal contacts, lobbying, political action committees, and favors to influence the government.

Organizations use three types of activities to formally manage social responsibility: legal compliance, ethical compliance, and philanthropic giving. Leadership, culture, and allowing for whistle blowing are informal means of managing social responsibility. Organizations should evaluate the effectiveness of their socially responsible practices as they would any other strategy.

Discussion Questions

Questions for Review

1. Define ethical and unethical behavior. Give three specific examples of ethical behavior and three specific examples of unethical behavior.
2. Summarize the basic stances that an organization can take regarding social responsibility.
3. Who are the important stakeholders of your college or university? What does each stakeholder group get from the school? What does each give to the school?
4. Describe the formal and informal dimensions of social responsibility.

Questions for Analysis

5. What is the relationship between the law and ethical behavior? Can illegal behavior possibly be ethical?
6. Where do organizational ethics come from? Describe the contributions made by the organization's founder, managers, and workers, as well as laws and social norms. Which do you think is most influential? Why?
7. There are many worthy causes or programs that deserve support from socially responsible companies. In your opinion, which types of causes or programs are the most deserving? Explain your reasoning.

Questions for Application

8. Since 2000 a number of corporate scandals have been brought to light. Many organizations have responded by, for example, appointing a chief ethics officer, beginning an ethics training program for workers, writing a formal code of ethics, or setting up a hotline for whistle blowers. In your opinion, are these measures likely to increase organizational ethics in the long run? If so, why? If not, what would be effective in improving organizational ethics?
9. Review the arguments for and against social responsibility. On a scale of 1 to 10, rate the validity and importance of each point. Use these ratings to develop a position regarding how socially responsible an organization should be. Now compare your ratings and position with those of two of your classmates. Discuss your respective positions, focusing primarily on disagreements.
10. Give three specific examples of a way in which the government has influenced an organization. Then give three specific examples of a way in which an organization has influenced the government. Do you think the government's actions were ethical? Were the company's actions ethical? Why or why not?

BUILDING EFFECTIVE diagnostic and decision-making SKILLS

business.college.hmco.com/students

Exercise Overview

Diagnostic skills are the skills that enable a manager to visualize the most appropriate response to a situation. Effective diagnosis of a situation then provides a foundation for effective decision making. Decision-making skills refer to the manager's ability to recognize and define problems and opportunities correctly and then to select an appropriate course of action to solve problems and capitalize on opportunities. This exercise will help you develop your diagnostic and decision-making skills by applying them to an ethical business dilemma.

Exercise Background

As businesses, industries, societies, and technologies become more complex, ethical dilemmas become more puzzling. Consider the ethical dilemmas inherent in the online publication of music. The advent of fast Internet connections, the desire of many businesses to bypass intermediaries, and changing societal definitions of "theft" have all contributed to the difficult situation for the industry today. Use the Internet to investigate up-to-date information about online music publishing and then answer the following questions.

Exercise Task

1. Consider each of the stakeholders in the online music publishing industry—recording artists, recording companies, online file-sharing companies such as Napster, and consumers. From the point of view of each party, what are the ethical problems within the online music industry today?
2. What would be the "best" outcome for each of the parties?
3. Is there any way to satisfy the needs of all the stakeholders? If yes, tell how this can be accomplished. If no, tell why a mutually beneficial solution will not be possible.
4. What impact did your personal ethics have on your answer to question 3?

BUILDING EFFECTIVE interpersonal SKILLS

Exercise Overview

Interpersonal skills refer to the ability to communicate with, understand, and motivate individuals and groups. Interpersonal skills may be especially important in a situation in which ethics and social responsibility issues are involved. This exercise will help you better relate interpersonal skills to ethical situations.

Exercise Background

Assume that you are a department manager in a large retail store. Your work group recently had a problem with sexual harassment. Specifically, one of your female employees reported to you that a male employee was telling off-color jokes and making mildly suggestive comments. When you asked him about the charges, he did not deny them but instead attributed them to a misunderstanding.

He was subsequently suspended with pay until the situation was investigated. The human resource manager who interviewed both parties, as well as other employees, concluded that the male employee should not be fired but should instead be placed on six months probation. During this period, any further substantiated charges against him will result in immediate dismissal.

The basis for this decision included the following: (1) The male had worked in the store for over ten years, had a good performance record, and has had no earlier problems; (2) the female indicated that she did not believe that he was directly targeting her for harassment but instead was guilty of general insensitivity; and (3) the female did not think that his actions were sufficiently blatant as to warrant dismissal but simply wanted him to stop those behaviors.

Tomorrow will be his first day back at work. You are a bit worried about tensions in the group when he returns. You intend to meet with the female today and with the male tomorrow morning and attempt to minimize this tension.

Exercise Task

With the background information above as context, do the following:

1. Write general notes about what you will say to the male.
2. Write general notes about what you will say to the female.
3. What are the ethical issues in this situation?
4. If you have the option of having them work closely together or keeping them separated, which would you do? Why?

BUILDING EFFECTIVE conceptual SKILLS

Exercise Overview

Conceptual skills form the manager's ability to think in the abstract. This exercise provides practice in analyzing corporate ethics and social responsibility, both in theory and in practice in a real organization, and asks you to understand the relationship between the theory and the practice.

Exercise Background

Enron has been in the news recently because of ethical problems. Among the concerns are Enron's lack of disclosure of accurate financial results to investors and its overly close relationship with its auditor, Arthur Andersen, which allowed the lack of disclosure to go undetected for some time. Enron also engaged in many questionable business transactions, enriched its top managers from the stock purchases made by lower-level employees, and ignored the concerns of more than one whistle blower.

However, Enron had a very complete, sixty-four-page code of ethics. The values expressed in the firm's code are apparent from these quotes from it: "We want to be proud of Enron and to know that it enjoys a reputation for fairness and honesty and that it is respected." [Foreword by former CEO Kenneth Lay, now under indictment] "Enron's Values: (1) Respect—We treat others as we would like to be treated ourselves. We do not tolerate abusive or disrespectful treatment. Ruthlessness, callousness, and arrogance don't belong here. (2) Integrity—We work with customers and prospects openly, honestly and sincerely. When we say we will do something, we will do it; when we say we cannot or will not do something, then we don't do it. (3) Communication—We have an obligation to communicate. Here, we take the time to talk with one another . . . and to listen. We believe that information is meant to move and that information moves people. (4) Excellence—We are satisfied with nothing less than the very best in everything we do. We will continue to raise the bar for everyone. The great fun here will be for all of us to discover just how good we can really be."

If you are interested in seeing the entire Enron Code of Ethics, visit the website of The Smoking Gun, a clearing-house for government documents and materials from court cases, owned by Court TV, at www.thesmokinggun.com/enron/enron.pdf. If you need more information about Enron, just enter the firm's name as a search term on any Internet search engine.

Exercise Task

1. For each of the principles or values listed in Enron's code of ethics, give an example of behavior at Enron that did *not* support that value.
2. What are some reasons that a firm's code of ethics might be so poorly upheld?
3. What are some actions that companies can take to increase the probability that their managers and employees will behave in accordance with the firm's values?

CHAPTER CLOSING case

> *"This [case] is like the Enron of the seas."*
>
> – William Amlong, attorney*

Cruise Ships May Pollute the Environment They Rely On

Over 8 million passengers take an ocean voyage each year, cruising many areas of the world's oceans in search of pristine beaches and clear tropical waters. Although tourists and the giant ships that carry them are usually welcome for the revenues that they bring, the ships also bring something less desirable—pollution.

A modern cruise ship carries an average of 2,000 passengers and 1,000 crew members, who generate a lot of waste. On a typical day, a ship will produce 7 tons of solid garbage, which is incinerated and then dumped; 15 gallons of highly toxic chemical waste; 30,000 gallons of sewage; 7,000 gallons of bilge water containing oil; and 225,000 gallons of gray water from sinks and laundries. Cruise ships also pick up ballast water whenever and wherever it is needed and then discharge it later, releasing creatures and pollution from other parts of the world. Multiply this problem by 167 ships worldwide, cruising 50 weeks per year, and the scope of the damage is staggering.

Environmental groups see the top pollution-related problem as death of marine life, including extinction. Foreign creatures bring parasites and diseases, and in some cases, replace native species entirely. Bacteria that are harmless to humans kill coral that provides food and a habitat for many species. Oil and toxic chemicals, even in minute quantities, are deadly to wildlife. Turtles swallow plastic bags, thinking they are jellyfish, and starve; and seals and birds drown after becoming entangled in the plastic rings that hold beverage cans.

Other problems include habitat destruction or disease that affects U.S. industries, costing $137 billion each year. For example, cholera, picked up in ships' ballast water off the coast of Peru, caused a devastating loss to fishermen and shrimpers in the Gulf of Mexico in the 1990s, when infected catches had to be destroyed. Heavy-metal poisoning of fish is rising, and there is concern that the poisons are passing up the food chain from microscopic creatures to fish, and ultimately to humans. Phosphorus, found in detergents, causes an overgrowth of algae, which then consume all the available oxygen in the water, making it incapable of supporting any flora or fauna. One such "dead zone" occurs each summer in the Gulf of Mexico, at the mouth of the Mississippi River. The area, caused by pollution and warm water, is about the size of Massachusetts—8,000 square miles of lifelessness.

Lack of regulation is the biggest obstacle to solving the problem. By international law, countries may regulate oceans for three miles off their shores. International treaties provide some regulation up to twenty-five miles offshore. Beyond the twenty-five-mile point, however, ships are allowed free rein. Also, each country's laws and enforcement policies vary considerably, and even when laws are strict, enforcement may be limited. The U.S. Coast Guard enforces regulations off the American coast, but they are spread thinly. Only about 1 percent of the Coast Guard's annual budget is spent on environmental oversight.

Over the last decade, as enforcement has tightened, ten cruise lines have collectively paid $48.5 million in fines related to illegal dumping. In the largest settlement to date, Royal Caribbean paid $27 million for making illegal alterations to facilities, falsifying records, lying to the Coast Guard, and deliberately destroying evidence. The fine may seem high, but it covers thirty different charges and ten years of violations, and seems small compared to the firm's 2001 profits of almost $1 billion. Observers agree that Royal Caribbean's fine was less than what the firm would have paid to dispose of the waste properly over a decade. In addition, a lawsuit is pending regarding the firing of a whistle blower, the firm's former vice president for safety and environment. "This [case] is like the Enron of the seas," says attorney

William Amlong, who represents the whistle blower.

Many feel that the fines have not been steep enough. In 2002 Norwegian Cruise Lines paid just $1 million for falsifying records in a case that included "some of the worst [violations] we've ever seen," according to Rick Langlois, an EPA investigator. Langlois and others are outspoken against the cruise lines' profiteering from an environment that they are destroying, but the critics note that the companies will not stop as long as the profits continue. Technology exists to make the waste safe, but industry experts estimate that dumping can save a firm millions of dollars annually. From that perspective, Norwegian's actions were just a "brilliant business decision," says Langlois.

Case Questions

1. Should cruise lines be required to use expensive waste treatment systems, such as installing facilities aboard the ships or storing waste until reaching a port? Justify your answer using the arguments for and against social responsibility.
2. Which of the four approaches to social responsibility do the cruise lines seem to be taking? Tell why you chose that answer.
3. In your opinion, is the cruise lines' approach to social responsibility the most effective response? If yes, explain why. If no, tell what the cruise lines should do to increase the effectiveness of their response.

Case References

Bill McAllister, "Alaska Still out Front on Environmental Monitoring," *The Juneau Empire* (Juneau, Alaska), May 29, 2002, juneauempire.com on December 7, 2002; "Cruise Ships in Florida," Oceana website, www.oceana.org on December 7, 2002; Marilyn Adams, "Former Carnival Exec Says He Was Fired for Helping Federal Inquiry," *USA Today*, November 8–10, 2002, p. 2A (*quote); Marilyn Adams, "Cruise-Ship Dumping Poisons Seas, Frustrates U.S. Enforcers," *USA Today*, November 8–10, 2002, pp. 1–2A; Michael Connor, "Norwegian Cruise Line Pleads Guilty in Pollution Case," Reuters, at www.planetark.org on December 7, 2002; "What Is a Dead Zone?" Oceana website, www.oceana.org on December 7, 2002.

Chapter Notes

1. Jim Collins, "The 10 Greatest CEOs of All Time," *Fortune,* July 21, 2003, pp. 54–68; Jerry Useem, "CEOs Under Fire," *Fortune,* November 18, 2002, www.fortune.com on December 2, 2002; Nanette Byrnes, "The Good CEO," *BusinessWeek,* September 23, 2002, pp. 80–88 (*quote p. 80); Patricia Sellers, "The New Breed," *Fortune,* November 18, 2002, www.fortune.com on December 2, 2002.
2. See Norman Barry, *Business Ethics* (West Lafayette, Indiana: Purdue University Press, 1999).
3. Thomas Donaldson and Thomas W. Dunfee, "Toward a Unified Conception of Business Ethics: An Integrative Social Contracts Theory," *Academy of Management Review,* vol. 19, no. 2, 1994, pp. 252–284.
4. "Faced with Less Time off, Workers Take More," *USA Today,* October 29, 2002, p. 1A.
5. "Drug Companies Face Assault on Prices," *Wall Street Journal,* May 11, 2000, pp. B1, B4.
6. Jeremy Kahn, "Presto Chango! Sales Are Huge," *Fortune,* March 20, 2000, pp. 90–96; "More Firms Falsify Revenue to Boost Stocks," *USA Today,* March 29, 2000, p. 1B.
7. "How U.S. Concerns Compete in Countries Where Bribes Flourish," *Wall Street Journal,* September 29, 1995, pp. A1, A14; Patricia Digh, "Shades of Gray in the Global Marketplace," *HRMagazine,* April 1997, pp. 90–98.
8. Patricia H. Werhane, *Moral Imagination and Management Decision Making* (New York: Oxford University Press, 1999).
9. "Bad Boys," *Forbes,* July 22, 2002, pp. 99–104.
10. William Dill, "Beyond Codes and Courses," *Selections,* Fall 2002, pp. 21–23.
11. Gerald F. Cavanagh, *American Business Values,* 2nd ed. (Upper Saddle River, N.J.: Prentice-Hall, 1998).
12. See "Restoring Trust in Corporate America," *BusinessWeek,* June 24, 2002, pp. 30–35.
13. "How to Fix Corporate Governance," *BusinessWeek,* May 6, 2002, pp. 68–78. See also Catherine Daily, Dan Dalton, and Albert Cannella, "Corporate Governance: Decades of Dialogue and Data," *Academy of Management Review,* 2003, Vol. 28, No. 3, pp. 371–382.
14. Thomas Donaldson and Lee E. Preston, "The Stakeholder Theory of the Corporation: Concepts, Evidence, and Implications," *Academy of Management Review,* 1995, vol. 20, no. 1, pp. 65–91. See also Jeffrey S. Harrison and R. Edward Freeman, "Stakeholders, Social Responsibility, and Performance: Empirical Evidence and Theoretical Perspectives," *Academy of Management Journal,* 1999, vol. 42, no. 5, pp. 479–495.
15. Aseem Prakash, *Greening the Firm* (Cambridge, U.K.: Cambridge University Press, 2000); Forest L. Reinhardt, *Down to Earth* (Cambridge, Mass.: Harvard Business School Press, 2000).
16. "Oil Companies Strive to Turn a New Leaf to Save Rain Forest," *Wall Street Journal,* July 17, 1997, pp. A1, A8.
17. See J. Alberto Aragon-Correa and Sanjay Sharma, "A Contingent Resource-Based View of Proactive Corporate Environmental Strategy," *Academy of Management Review,* 2003, vol. 28, no. 1, pp. 71–88.
18. Linda Grant, "There's Gold in Going Green," *Fortune,* April 14, 1997, pp. 116–118.
19. "Ford to Reveal Plans for Think Brand," *USA Today,* January 10, 2000, p. 1B. See also "Lean Green Machine," *Forbes,* February 3, 2003, p. 44.
20. Christine Y. Chen and Greg Lindsay, "Will Amazon(.com) Save the Amazon?" *Fortune,* March 20, 2000, pp. 224–226.
21. "Ashland Just Can't Seem to Leave Its Checkered Past Behind," *BusinessWeek,* October 31, 1988, pp. 122–126.
22. For discussions of this debate, see Jean B. McGuire, Alison Sundgren, and Thomas Schneeweis, "Corporate Social Responsibility and Firm Financial Performance," *Academy of Management Journal,* December 1988, pp. 854–872, and Margaret A. Stroup, Ralph L. Neubert, and Jerry W. Anderson, Jr., "Doing Good, Doing Better: Two Views of Social Responsibility," *Business Horizons,* March–April 1987, pp. 22–25.
23. "Is It Rainforest Crunch Time?" *BusinessWeek,* July 15, 1996, pp. 70–71; "Yo, Ben! Yo, Jerry! It's Just Ice Cream," *Fortune,* April 28, 1997, p. 374.
24. Andrew Singer, "Can a Company Be Too Ethical?" *Across the Board,* April 1993, pp. 17–22.
25. "Help or Hype from Exxon?" *BusinessWeek,* August 28, 1995, p. 36.
26. "Inside America's Most Reviled Company," *BusinessWeek,* November 29, 1999, pp. 176–192.
27. "Legal-But Lousy," *Fortune,* September 2, 2002, p. 192.
28. Lynn Sharp Paine, "Managing for Organizational Integrity," *Harvard Business Review,* March–April 1994, pp. 106–115.
29. "Battling 'Donor Dropsy'," *Wall Street Journal,* July 19, 2002, pp. B1, B4.
30. "A New Way of Giving," *Time,* July 24, 2000, pp. 48–51. See also Michael Porter and Mark Kramwe, "The Competitive Advantage of Corporate Philanthropy," *Harvard Business Review,* December 2002, pp. 57–66.
31. David M. Messick and Max H. Bazerman, "Ethical Leadership and the Psychology of Decision Making," *Sloan Management Review,* Winter 1996, pp. 9–22.
32. "Ethics in Action: Getting It Right," *Selections,* Fall 2002, pp. 24–27.

33. See Janet P. Near and Marcia P. Miceli, "Whistle-Blowing: Myth and Reality," *Journal of Management*, 1996, vol. 22, no. 3, pp. 507–526, for a recent review of the literature on whistle blowing. See also Michael Gundlach, Scott Douglas, and Mark Martinko, "The Decision to Blow the Whistle: A Social Information Processing Framework," *Academy of Management Review*, 2003, vol. 28, no.1, pp. 107–123.
34. For instance, see "The Complex Goals and Unseen Costs of Whistle-Blowing," *Wall Street Journal*, November 25, 2002, pp. A1, A10.
35. "A Whistle-Blower Rocks an Industry," *BusinessWeek*, June 24, 2002, pp. 126–130.
36. "How Green Was My Report Card?" *BusinessWeek*, September 2, 2002, p. 12.

5

The Global Environment

CHAPTER OUTLINE

The Nature of International Business
- The Meaning of International Business
- Trends in International Business
- Managing the Process of Globalization
- Competing in a Global Market

The Structure of the Global Economy
- Mature Market Economies and Systems
- High-Potential/High-Growth Economies
- Other Economies
- The Role of the GATT and the WTO

Environmental Challenges of International Management
- The Economic Environment
- The Political/Legal Environment
- The Cultural Environment

Competing in a Global Economy
- Globalization and Organization Size
- Management Challenges in a Global Economy

LEARNING OBJECTIVES

After studying this chapter, you should be able to:

1 ***Describe the nature of international business, including its meaning, recent trends, management of globalization, and competition in a global market.***

OPENING INCIDENT

The latest hot spot of international competition? The clash of titans General Motors and DaimlerChrysler, the ongoing soda wars that pit Coca-Cola and PepsiCo against each other, and the fierce struggle between Boeing and Airbus all spring to mind, but competition in the global brewing industry may be the biggest match-up yet. Indeed, the improbable but intense rivalry between Interbrew, a 636-year-old Belgian beer maker, and Heineken, a Dutch brewer just 200 years younger, is starting to heat up.

The history of the two firms is strikingly similar. Both began hundreds of years ago as small, family-owned breweries which grew to become the largest beer makers in their region. During the 1870s, both began to export their products to neighboring countries—Interbrew to Germany and France, Heineken to France and the United Kingdom. About 1930 both firms decided to bottle the beer themselves, rather than selling kegs only. This led to a rapid increase in the consumption of beer. After World War II, both brewers began to make acquisitions of small European firms to increase their strength in different countries. Growth in Europe was also accomplished through the building of breweries near every major market. In

2

Discuss the structure of the global economy and describe the GATT and the WTO.

3

Identify and discuss the environmental challenges inherent in international management.

4

Describe the basic issues involved in competing in a global economy, including organization size and the management challenges in a global economy.

"[Interbrew is] the world's local brewer."

—Website of Interbrew, Belgian brewer

Since "every bit helps" in the global beer battle, Interbrew's CEO Hugo Powell pitches in and pulls a pint.

addition, the two companies began to license foreign firms to produce their flagship brands (Heineken brand for Heineken and Stella Artois brand for Interbrew). Licensees were concentrated in African, Asian, and North and Latin American countries, many of them former European colonies. In the 1990s, Interbrew stepped up the pace of acquisition, acquiring dozens of smaller firms over the decade. Heineken grew more slowly and with fewer acquisitions, in order to keep control in the hands of the Heineken family.

The rivals now face three significant challenges related to globalization. First, when acquisitions are made, the operations, staff, and brands of the acquired companies are maintained and continue to operate semi-independently. This has several advantages: Local control eases resistance from family owners; preservation of jobs lessens government opposition to foreign ownership; and maintaining local brands guarantees stable local demand and customization for local tastes. However, as the firms have gotten larger and larger, they may now be reaching the limits of a highly decentralized organization. Stronger control by headquarters would allow each firm to achieve cost savings through increased economies of scale, as well as facilitate the spread of learning and best practices throughout all parts of the firm.

Second, Interbrew and Heineken must carefully consider the degree of customization that is really necessary to please local tastes. Interbrew today markets Stella Artois, Beck's, and Bass as its international brands, and offers sixty local brands in addition. The firm calls itself "the world's local brewer." Heineken has just one international brand but also produces eighty local brands. For every additional brand, however, the company must have different sources of inputs, different procedures, equipment, training, and so on, which drive up the costs of production. If the number of brands could be reduced, cost savings would result and knowledge could be more readily shared. The challenge will be to discover ways to eliminate products without losing customers who prefer a local brand. This problem is worsened by the recent success of microbreweries that produce very small batches of local product. Their cachet, combined with their small scope and extreme customization, allow microbreweries to charge premium prices to offset their relatively high expenses.

Third, the competitors will have to find a way to compete successfully against a very similar rival. This is the same problem that is being faced in industry after industry as globalization increases. Consolidation and standardization result in firms that are virtually identical. Any significant competitive advantages are immediately copied, causing any advantage to be short-lived. In order to forestall attacks from number-three Interbrew, second-largest Heineken will have to borrow money and acquire more small companies. Heineken must do this quickly, to ensure that the best targets are not all acquired by their competitor. However, merely "catching up" will not allow Heineken to move into the forefront. For the foreseeable future, it seems that the international beer industry will follow a well-worn path from the heady days of expansion, to the increased competitive rivalry of consolidation, to settling down for a tough and drawn-out battle, seemingly without end.[1]

Although every business is unique, the challenges and opportunities facing Heineken and Interbrew are increasingly common among today's multinational corporations. Specifically, such businesses must make critical decisions regarding how they will allocate their resources in different markets and how they will strive to gain a competitive advantage in those markets. Indeed, to be successful today, managers have to understand the global context within which they function. And this holds true regardless of whether the manager runs a Fortune 500 firm or a small independent company.

This chapter explores the global context of management. We start by describing the nature of international business. We then discuss the structure of the global market in terms of different economies and economic systems. The basic environmental challenges of management are introduced and discussed next. We then focus on issues of competition in a global economy. Finally, we conclude by characterizing the managerial functions of planning and decision making, organizing, leading, and controlling as management challenges in a global economy.

It is also important to remember, though, that it is no longer feasible to segregate a discussion of "international" management from a discussion of "domestic" management as if they were unrelated activities. Hence, although we highlight the central issues of international management in this chapter, we also integrate international issues, examples, opportunities, and challenges throughout the rest of this book. This treatment provides the most realistic possible survey and discussion of the international environment of management.

The Nature of International Business

As you prepared breakfast this morning, you may have plugged in a coffee pot manufactured in Asia and perhaps ironed a shirt or blouse made in Taiwan with an iron made in Mexico. The coffee you drank was probably made from beans grown in South America. To get to school, you may have driven a Japanese car. Even if you drive a Ford or a Chevrolet, some of its parts were engineered or manufactured abroad. Perhaps you did not drive a car to school but rode a bus (manufactured by DaimlerChrysler, a German company) or a motorcycle (manufactured by Honda, Kawasaki, Suzuki, or Yamaha—all Japanese firms).

Our daily lives are strongly influenced by businesses from around the world. But no country is unique in this respect. For instance, people drive Fords in Germany, use Dell computers in China, eat McDonald's hamburgers in France, and snack on Mars candy bars in England. They drink Pepsi and wear Levi Strauss jeans in China and South Africa. The Japanese buy Kodak film and use American Express credit cards. People around the world fly on American Airlines in planes made by Boeing. Their buildings are constructed with Caterpillar machinery, their factories are powered by General Electric engines, and they buy Chevron oil.

In truth, we have become part of a global village and have a global economy where no organization is insulated from the effects of foreign markets and competition.[2] Indeed, more and more firms are reshaping themselves for international competition and discovering new ways to exploit markets in every corner of the world. Failure to take a global perspective is one of the biggest mistakes managers can make.[3] Thus we start laying the foundation for our discussion by introducing and describing the basics of international business.

The Meaning of International Business

There are many different forms and levels of international business. Although the lines that distinguish one from another may be arbitrary, we can identify four general levels of international activity that differentiate organizations.[4] These are illustrated in Figure 5.1. A **domestic business** acquires essentially all of its resources and sells all of its products or services within a single country. Most small businesses are essentially domestic in nature; this category includes local retailers and restaurants, agricultural enterprises, and small service firms, such as dry cleaners and hair salons. However, there are very few large domestic businesses left in the world today.

domestic business A business that acquires all of its resources and sells all of its products or services within a single country

Indeed, most large firms today are either international or multinational companies. An **international business** is one that is based primarily in a single country but acquires some meaningful share of its resources or revenues (or both) from other countries. Sears fits this description. Most of its stores are in the United States, for example, and the retailer earns around 90 percent of its revenues from its U.S. operations, with the remaining 10 percent coming from Sears stores in Canada. At the same time, however, many of the products it sells, such as tools and clothing, are made abroad.[5]

international business A business that is based primarily in a single country but acquires some meaningful share of its resources or revenues (or both) from other countries

A **multinational business** has a worldwide marketplace from which it buys raw materials, borrows money, and manufactures its products and to which it subsequently sells its products. Ford Motor Company is an excellent example of a multinational company. It has design and production facilities around the world. The Ford Focus, for instance, was jointly designed by European and U.S. teams and is sold with only minor variations in dozens of foreign markets. Ford makes and sells other cars in Europe that are never seen in the United States. Ford cars are designed, produced, and sold for individual markets, wherever they are and without regard for national boundaries. Multinational businesses are often called *multinational corporations*, or *MNCs*.[6]

multinational business One that has a worldwide marketplace from which it buys raw materials, borrows money, and manufactures its products and to which it subsequently sells its products

The final form of international business is the global business. A **global business** is one that transcends national boundaries and is not committed to a single home country. Although no business has truly achieved this level of internationalization, a few are edging closer and closer. For example, Hoechst AG, a large German

global business A business that transcends national boundaries and is not committed to a single home country

FIGURE 5.1

Levels of International Business Activity

chemical company, portrays itself as a "non-national company." Similarly, Unocal Corporation is legally headquartered in California, but in its company literature, Unocal says it "no longer considers itself as a U.S. company" but is, instead, a "global energy company."[7]

Trends in International Business

To understand why and how these different levels of international business have emerged, we must look briefly to the past. Most of the industrialized countries in Europe were devastated during World War II. Many Asian countries, especially Japan, fared no better. There were few passable roads, few standing bridges, and even fewer factories dedicated to the manufacture of peacetime products. And those regions less affected by wartime destruction—Canada, Latin America, and Africa—had not yet developed the economic muscle to threaten the economic preeminence of the United States.

Businesses in war-torn countries like Germany and Japan had no choice but to rebuild from scratch. Because of this position, they essentially had to rethink every facet of their operations, including technology, production, finance, and marketing. Although it took many years for these countries to recover, they eventually did so, and their economic systems were subsequently poised for growth. During the same era, many U.S. companies grew somewhat complacent. Their customer base was growing rapidly. Increased population spurred by the baby boom and increased affluence resulting from the postwar economic boom greatly raised the average person's standard of living and expectations. The U.S. public continually wanted new and better products and services. Many U.S. companies profited greatly from this pattern, but most were also perhaps guilty of taking it for granted.

But U.S. firms are no longer isolated from global competition or the global market. A few simple numbers help tell the full story of international trade and industry. First of all, the volume of international trade increased more than 3,000 percent between 1960 and 2000. Further, although 164 of the world's largest corporations are headquartered in the United States, there are also 115 in Japan, 38 in France, 40 in Germany, and 32 in Britain.[8] Within certain industries, the preeminence of non-U.S. firms is even more striking. For example, only two each of the world's ten largest banks and ten largest electronics companies are based in the United States. Only two of the ten largest chemical companies are U.S. firms. On the other hand, U.S. firms comprise six of the eight largest aerospace companies, four of the seven largest airlines, five of the ten largest computer companies, four of the five largest diversified financial companies, and six of the ten largest retailers.[9]

U.S. firms are also finding that international operations are an increasingly important element of their sales and profits. For example, in 2002 Exxon Corporation realized 84 percent of its revenues and 65 percent of its profits abroad. For Avon, these percentages were 68 percent and 73 percent, respectively.[10] From any perspective, then, it is clear that we live in a truly global economy. Virtually all businesses today must be concerned with the competitive situations they face in lands far from home and with how companies from distant lands are competing in their homeland.

Managing the Process of Globalization

Licensing is an increasingly popular method for entering foreign markets. Franchising, a form of licensing, is especially popular these days. Pizza Hut, for example, is rapidly expanding into new markets around the world via franchising agreements with local investors and managers. The popular restaurants can now be found in over 100 different countries. St. Petersburg, Russia, is one of the more recent markets where Pizza Hut has set up shop.

Managers should also recognize that their global context dictates two related but distinct sets of challenges. One set of challenges must be confronted when an organization chooses to change its level of international involvement. For example, a firm that wants to move from being an international to a multinational business has to manage that transition.[11] The other set of challenges occurs when the organization has achieved its desired level of international involvement and must then function effectively within that environment. This section highlights the first set of challenges, and the next section introduces the second set of challenges. When an organization makes the decision to increase its level of international activity, there are several alternative strategies that can be adopted.

Importing and Exporting Importing or exporting (or both) is usually the first type of international business in which a firm gets involved. **Exporting**, or making the product in the firm's domestic marketplace and selling it in another country, can involve both merchandise and services. **Importing** is bringing a good, service, or capital into the home country from abroad. For example, automobiles (Mazda, Ford, Volkswagen, Mercedes-Benz, Ferrari) and stereo equipment (Sony, Bang & Olufsen, Sanyo) are routinely exported by their manufacturers to other countries. Likewise, many wine distributors buy products from vineyards in France, Italy, or California and import them into their own country for resale. U.S. sports brands have become one of the latest hot exports.[12]

exporting Making a product in the firm's domestic marketplace and selling it in another country

importing Bringing a good, service, or capital into the home country from abroad

An import/export operation has several advantages. For example, it is the easiest way of entering a market with a small outlay of capital. Because the products are sold "as is," there is no need to adapt the product to the local conditions, and little risk is involved. Nevertheless, there are also disadvantages. For example, imports and exports are subject to taxes, tariffs, and higher transportation expenses. Furthermore, because the products are not adapted to local conditions, they may miss the needs of a large segment of the market. Finally, some products may be restricted and thus can be neither imported nor exported.

Licensing A company may prefer to arrange for a foreign company to manufacture or market its products under a licensing agreement. Factors that may lead to this decision include excessive transportation costs, government regulations, and home production costs. **Licensing** is an arrangement whereby a firm allows another company to use its brand name, trademark, technology, patent, copyright, or other assets. In return, the licensee pays a royalty, usually based on sales. For example,

licensing An arrangement whereby one company allows another company to use its brand name, trademark, technology, patent, copyright, or other assets in exchange for a royalty based on sales

Kirin Brewery, Japan's largest producer of beer, wanted to expand its international operations but feared that the time involved in shipping it from Japan would cause the beer to lose its freshness. Thus it has entered into a number of licensing arrangements with breweries in other markets. These brewers make beer according to strict guidelines provided by the Japanese firm and then package and market it as Kirin Beer. They then pay a royalty back to Kirin for each case sold. Molson produces Kirin in Canada under such an agreement, while the Charles Wells Brewery does the same in England.[13]

Two advantages of licensing are increased profitability and extended profitability. This strategy is frequently used for entry into less-developed countries where older technology is still acceptable and, in fact, may be state of the art. A primary disadvantage of licensing is inflexibility. A firm can tie up control of its product or expertise for a long period of time. And, if the licensee does not develop the market effectively, the licensing firm can lose profits. A second disadvantage is that licensees can take the knowledge and skill to which they have been given access for a foreign market and exploit them in the licensing firm's home market. When this happens, what used to be a business partner becomes a business competitor.

strategic alliance A cooperative arrangement between two or more firms for mutual gain

joint venture A special type of strategic alliance in which the partners share in the ownership of an operation on an equity basis

Strategic Alliances In a **strategic alliance**, two or more firms jointly cooperate for mutual gain.[14] For example, Kodak and Fuji, along with three other major Japanese camera manufacturers, collaborated on the development of a new film cartridge. This collaboration allowed Kodak and Fuji to share development costs, prevented an advertising war if they had developed different cartridges, and made it easier for new cameras to be introduced at the same time as the new film cartridges. A **joint venture** is a special type of strategic alliance in which the partners actually share ownership of a new enterprise. General Mills and Nestlé formed a new company called Cereal Partners Worldwide (CPW) to produce and market cereals. General Mills supplies the technology and proven formulas, while Nestlé provides its international distribution network. The two partners share equally in ownership and profits from CPW. Strategic alliances have enjoyed a tremendous upsurge in the past few years. In most cases, each party provides a portion of the equity or the equivalent in physical plant, raw materials, cash, or other assets. The proportion of the investment then determines the percentage of ownership in the venture.[15]

Strategic alliances have both advantages and disadvantages. For example, they can allow quick entry into a market by taking advantage of the existing strengths of participants. Japanese automobile manufacturers employed this strategy to their advantage to enter the U.S. market by using the already-established distribution systems of U.S. automobile manufacturers. Strategic alliances are also an effective way to gain access to technology or raw materials. And they allow the firms to share the risk and cost of the new venture. One major disadvantage of this approach lies with the shared ownership of joint ventures. Although it reduces the risk for each participant, it also limits the control and return that each firm can enjoy.[16]

Direct Investment Another level of commitment to internationalization is direct investment. **Direct investment** occurs when a firm headquartered in one country builds or purchases operating facilities or subsidiaries in a foreign country. The foreign operations then become wholly owned subsidiaries of the firm. Ford's acquisitions of Jaguar, Volvo, and Kia, as well as British Petroleum's acquisition of Amoco, were major forms of direct investment. Similarly, Dell Computer's new factory in China is also a direct investment, as is the new Disney theme park under construction in Hong Kong. And Coca-Cola recently committed $150 million to build a new bottling and distribution network in India.[17]

direct investment When a firm headquartered in one country builds or purchases operating facilities or subsidiaries in a foreign country

A major reason many firms make direct investments is to capitalize on lower labor costs. In other words, the goal is often to transfer production to locations where labor is cheap. Japanese businesses have moved much of their production to Thailand because labor costs are much lower there than in Japan. Many U.S. firms are using maquiladoras for the same purpose. **Maquiladoras** are light assembly plants built in northern Mexico close to the U.S. border. The plants are given special tax breaks by the Mexican government, and the area is populated with workers willing to work for very low wages. More than 1,000 plants in the region employ 300,000 workers, and more are planned. The plants are owned by major corporations, primarily from the United States, Japan, South Korea, and major European industrial countries. This concentrated form of direct investment benefits the country of Mexico, the companies themselves, and workers who might otherwise be without jobs. Some critics argue, however, that the low wages paid by the maquiladoras amount to little more than slave labor.[18] A related theme is discussed in *The Business of Ethics.*

maquiladoras Light assembly plants built in northern Mexico close to the U.S. border which are given special tax breaks by the Mexican government

Like the other approaches for increasing a firm's level of internationalization, direct investment carries with it a number of benefits and liabilities. Managerial control is more complete, and profits do not have to be shared as they do in joint ventures. Purchasing an existing organization provides additional benefits in that the human resources and organizational infrastructure (administrative facilities, plants, warehouses, and so forth) are already in place. Acquisition is also a way to purchase the brand-name identification of a product. This could be particularly important if the cost of introducing a new brand is high. When Nestlé bought the U.S. firm Carnation Company several years ago, it retained the firm's brand names for all of its products sold in the United States. Likewise, when Daimler-Benz acquired Chrysler (and changed its corporate name to DaimlerChrysler), it kept all of Chrysler's product names. Notwithstanding these advantages, the company is now operating a part of itself entirely within the borders of a foreign country. The additional complexity in the decision making, the economic and political risks, and so forth may outweigh the advantages that can be obtained by international expansion.

Of course, we should also note that these approaches to internationalization are not mutually exclusive. Indeed, most large firms use all of them simultaneously. MNCs have a global orientation and worldwide approach to foreign markets and production. They search for opportunities all over the world and select the best strategy to serve each market. In some settings, they may use direct investment, in others licensing, in others strategic alliances; in still others, they might limit their

THE BUSINESS OF ethics

"Our Work, Our Tradition"

"To survive, we keep arriving at the same solution: work."

— Mexican agricultural worker Manuel Navarro*

Globalization has brought more goods and lower prices to consumers in wealthy nations. But what about those who cannot afford to consume?

In San Miguelito, Mexico, 4,500 inhabitants sew soccer balls. No machine has yet been invented that can perform the labor-intensive task. Workers can make a ball in two hours, and in return, they receive $1. The workers include children as young as eight, whose smaller hands make the sewing easier. The youngsters attend school and then put in six or more hours of sewing each evening, for an average daily wage of $3. Ruben Ramos, principal of the village school, dislikes the practice. "The problem is that the kids don't do their homework, and they don't have aspirations to do anything else or continue their education," Ramos says. "There is not one single child from this village who has gone on to become a professional or take up a craft. Not a mechanic, not a carpenter." Raymundo Rodriguez, a seventeen-year-old worker, thinks that he will never leave and neither will his children. "It is the tradition here," Rodriguez claims. Another worker, Jose Barcenas, disagrees with others' concern about child labor, saying, "A child who can go to school with a few centavos in his pocket is better off than one who is hungry."

Hundreds of miles to the south, in Simojovel, the work is amber mining, but the story is the same. The men excavate deep into unsafe tunnels, while the women and children cart and sort the debris. Although a quarter-ounce of amber can be sold to tourists for $100, the miners work for $3 per day. The women and children make half that. One miner, Genaro Bonifaz Diaz, says, "What [else] can we do? This is our work."

Mexico's labor force includes between 4 and 5 million school-age children; 1 in 5 children works, and 1 million are hired as field hands. Although child labor is illegal, the law is rarely enforced. Even President Fox's family ranch employed workers as young as twelve in its slaughterhouse. Justifications include the necessity of passing on skills and a chronic labor shortage. However, simple economic necessity is the most common cause. Agricultural worker Manuel Navarro, whose children and grandchildren down to the age of four work together on a ranch, says, "To survive, we keep arriving at the same solution: work."

References: "Sweatshops: Finally, Airing the Dirty Linen," *BusinessWeek*, June 23, 2003, pp. 100–102; Amparo Trejo, "Scandal for President-Elect Highlights Mexico's Child Labor Problem," *North County Times* (Oceanside, California), September 2, 2000, www.nctimes.com on December 8, 2002 (*quote); Dan La Botz, "Women and Children: Labor Base of Mexican, North American Economy," CorpWatch website, www.corpwatch.org on December 8, 2002; Jo Tuckman, "'Tradition' Perpetuating Poverty," *Houston Chronicle*, June 23, 2002, p. 28A; Karen Fanning, "Voices from the Field: Mexico," Scholastic website, teacher.scholastic.com on December 8, 2002; Tim Weiner, "Mexico's Amber Miners Find Risk, Not Riches," *New York Times*, December 1, 2002, p. 22.

involvement to exporting and importing. The advantages and disadvantages of each approach are summarized in Table 5.1.

Competing in a Global Market

Even when a firm is not actively seeking to increase its desired level of internationalization, its managers are still responsible for seeing that it functions effectively

TABLE 5.1

Advantages and Disadvantages of Different Approaches to Internationalization

When organizations decide to increase their level of internationalization, they can adopt several strategies. Each strategy is a matter of degree, as opposed to being a discrete and mutually exclusive category. And each has unique advantages and disadvantages that must be considered.

Approach to Internationalization	Advantages	Disadvantages
Importing or Exporting	1. Small cash outlay 2. Little risk 3. No adaptation necessary	1. Tariffs and taxes 2. High transportation costs 3. Government restrictions
Licensing	1. Increased profitability 2. Extended profitability	1. Inflexibility 2. Competition
Strategic Alliances/ Joint Ventures	1. Quick market entry 2. Access to materials and technology	Shared ownership (limits control and profits)
Direct Investment	1. Enhanced control 2. Existing infrastructure	1. Complexity 2. Greater economic and political risk 3. Greater uncertainty

within whatever level of international involvement the organization has achieved. In one sense, the job of a manager in an international business may not be that much different from the job of a manager in a domestic business. Each may be responsible for acquiring resources and materials, making products, providing services, developing human resources, advertising, or monitoring cash flow.

In another sense, however, the complexity associated with each of these activities may be much greater for managers in international firms. Rather than buying raw materials from sources in California, Texas, and Missouri, an international purchasing manager may buy materials from sources in Peru, India, and Spain. Rather than train managers for new plants in Michigan, Florida, and Oregon, the international human resources executive may be training new plant managers for facilities in China, Mexico, and Scotland. And, instead of developing a single marketing campaign for the United States, an advertising director may be working on promotional efforts in France, Brazil, and Japan.

The key question that must be addressed by any manager trying to be effective in an international market is whether to focus on globalization or on regionalism. A global thrust requires that activities be managed from an overall global perspective as part of an integrated system. Regionalism, on the other hand, involves managing within each region with less regard for the overall organization. In reality, most larger MNCs manage some activities globally (for example, finance and manufacturing are commonly addressed globally) and others locally (human resource management and advertising are frequently handled this way). We explore these approaches more fully later.

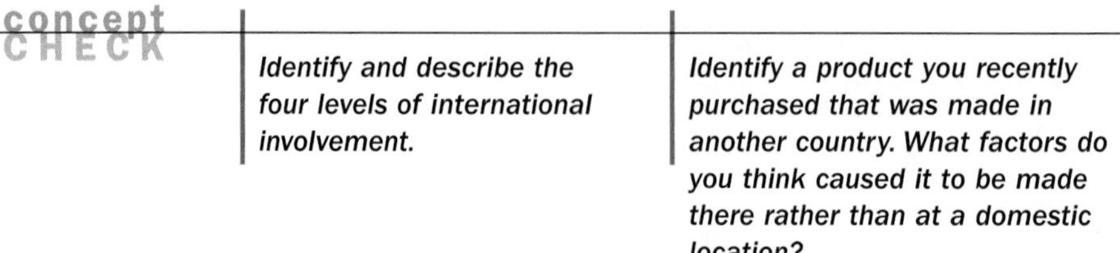

The Structure of the Global Economy

One thing that can be helpful to managers seeking to operate in a global environment is to better understand the structure of the global economy. Although each country and indeed many regions within any given country are unique, we can still note some basic similarities and differences. We describe three different elements of the global economy: mature market economies and systems, high-potential/high-growth economies, and other economies.[19]

Mature Market Economies and Systems

market economy An economy based on the private ownership of business which allows market factors such as supply and demand to determine business strategy

A **market economy** is based on the private ownership of business and allows market factors such as supply and demand to determine business strategy. Mature market economies include the United States, Japan, the United Kingdom, France, Germany, and Sweden. These countries have several things in common. For example, they tend to employ market forces in the allocation of resources. They also tend to be characterized by private ownership of property, although there is some variance along this dimension. France, for example, has a relatively high level of government ownership among the market economies.

U.S. managers have relatively few problems operating in market economies. Many of the business "rules of the game" that apply in the United States, for example, also apply in Germany or England. And consumers there often tend to buy the same kinds of products. For these reasons it is not unusual for U.S. firms seeking to expand geographically to begin operations in other market economies. Although the task of managing an international business in an industrial market economy is somewhat less complicated than operating in some other type of economy, it still poses some challenges. Perhaps foremost among them is that the markets in these economies are typically quite mature. Many industries, for example, are already dominated by large and successful companies. Thus competing in these economies poses a major challenge.

market systems Clusters of countries that engage in high levels of trade with one another

The map in Figure 5.2 highlights three relatively mature market systems. **Market systems** are clusters of countries that engage in high levels of trade with one another. One mature market system is North America. The United States, Canada, and Mexico are major trading partners with one another; more than 70 percent of

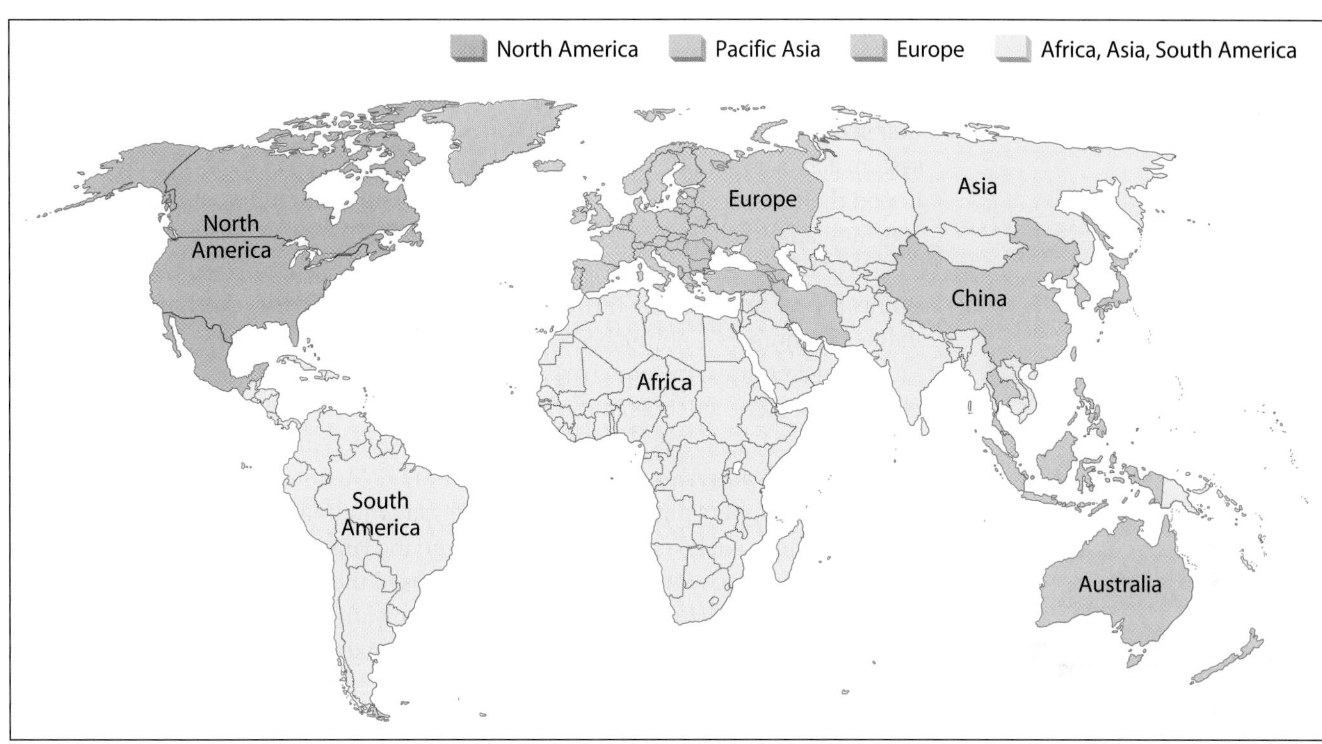

FIGURE 5.2

The Global Economy

The global economy is dominated by three relatively mature market systems. As illustrated here, these market systems consist of North America, Europe (especially those nations in the European Union), and Pacific Asia (parts of which are high-potential/high-growth economies). Other areas of Asia, as well as Africa and South America, have the potential for future growth but currently play only a relatively small role in the global economy.

Mexico's exports go to the United States, and more than 65 percent of what Mexico imports comes from the United States. During the last several years these countries have negotiated a variety of agreements to make trade even easier. The most important of these, the **North American Free Trade Agreement, or NAFTA** eliminates many of the trade barriers—quotas and tariffs, for example—that existed previously.[20]

North American Free Trade Agreement (NAFTA) An agreement between the United States, Canada, and Mexico to promote trade with one another

Another mature market system is Europe. Until recently, Europe was really two distinct economic areas. The eastern region consisted of communist countries such as Poland, Czechoslovakia, and Romania. These countries relied on government ownership of business and greatly restricted trade. In contrast, Western European countries with traditional market economies have been working together to promote international trade for decades. In particular, the **European Union** (or *EU*, as it is often called) has long been a formidable market system. The EU's origins can be traced to 1957 when Belgium, France, Luxembourg, Germany, Italy, and the Netherlands signed the Treaty of Rome to promote economic integration. Between 1973 and 1986 these countries were joined by Denmark, Ireland, the United

European Union (EU) The first and most important international market system

Kingdom, Greece, Spain, and Portugal and the group became known first as the European Committee and then the European Union. More recently, Austria, Finland, and Sweden joined the EU in 1995. For years these countries have followed a basic plan that led to the systematic elimination of most trade barriers. The new market system achieved significantly more potential when eleven of the EU members eliminated their home currencies (such as French francs and Italian lira) on January 1, 2002 and adopted a new common currency called the *euro.*

The European situation has recently grown more complex, however. Communism has collapsed in the Eastern countries, and they are trying to develop market economies. They also want greater participation in trade with the Western European countries. In some ways the emergence of the East has slowed and complicated business activities in the West. Twelve countries have applied for membership in the EU. This has led to controversy, as some current members want rapid expansion and others prefer a slower and more deliberate strategy. Sharp divisions among EU members regarding the U.S.-led war with Iraq in 2003 have also strained relations among such key nations as Spain and the United Kingdom (who supported the war) and France and Germany (who opposed the war). In the long term, however, the EU is almost certain to remain an important force in the global economy.

Pacific Asia A market system located in Southeast Asia

Yet another mature market system is **Pacific Asia**. As shown in Figure 5.2, this market system includes Japan, China, Thailand, Malaysia, Singapore, Indonesia, South Korea, Taiwan, the Philippines, and Australia. Indeed, Japan, Taiwan, Singapore, Thailand, and South Korea were major economic powerhouses until a regional currency crisis slowed their growth in the late 1990s. That crisis appears to be coming to an end, however; trade among these nations is on the rise, and talk has started about an Asian economic community much like the EU.[21]

High-Potential/High-Growth Economies

In contrast to the highly developed and mature market economies just described, other countries have what can be termed *high-potential/high-growth economies.* These economies have been relatively underdeveloped and immature and, until recently, were characterized by weak industry, weak currency, and relatively poor consumers.[22] The governments in these countries, however, have been actively working to strengthen their economies by opening their doors to foreign investment and by promoting international trade. Some of these countries have only recently adopted market economies, whereas others still use a command economy.

Even though it is technically part of Pacific Asia, the People's Republic of China is largely underdeveloped. But its market potential is enormous. For example, it is already the world's fourth largest automobile market and will likely become number three soon.[23] The transfer of control of Hong Kong from Great Britain to China in 1997 focused even more attention on the market potential in the world's most populous country.[24] India is also showing signs of becoming a major market in the future, although there is still considerable risk.[25] Vietnam has also become a potentially important market, and Brazil is becoming more important as well.[26] Likewise, Russia and the other states and republics that previously made up the

Commonwealth of Independent States are being closely watched by many companies for emerging market opportunities.[27] South Africa also holds considerable promise.

The primary challenges presented by the developing economies to those interested in conducting international business there are potential consumers' lack of wealth and an underdeveloped infrastructure. Developing economies have enormous economic potential, but much of it remains untapped. Thus international firms entering these markets often have to invest heavily in distribution systems, in training consumers how to use their products, and even in providing living facilities for their workers. They also run the risk of major policy changes that can greatly distort the value of their investments.[28]

Other Economies

There are some economic systems around the world that defy classification as either mature markets or high-potential/high-growth economies. One major area that falls outside of these categories is the oil-exporting region generally called the Middle East. The oil-exporting countries present mixed models of resource allocation, property ownership, and infrastructure development. These countries all have access to major amounts of crude oil, however, and thus are important players in the global economy.

These countries include Iran, Iraq, Kuwait, Saudi Arabia, Libya, Syria, and the United Arab Emirates. High oil prices in the last three decades have created enormous wealth in these countries. Many of them invested heavily in their infrastructures. Whole new cities were built, airports were constructed, and the population was educated. The per capita incomes of the United Arab Emirates and Qatar, for example, are among the highest in the world. Although there is great wealth in the oil-producing nations, they provide great challenges to managers. Political instability (as evidenced by the Persian Gulf War in 1991 and the U.S.-led war against Iraq in 2003) and tremendous cultural differences, for example, combine to make doing business in many parts of the Middle East both very risky and very difficult.

Other countries pose risks of a different sort to business. Politically and ethnically motivated violence, for example, still characterizes some countries. Foremost among these are Peru, El Salvador, Turkey, Colombia, and Northern Ireland. Cuba presents special challenges because it is so insulated from the outside world. With the demise of other communist regimes, some experts believe that Cuba will eventually join the ranks of the market economies. If so, its strategic location will quickly make it an important business center.

The Role of the GATT and the WTO

The global economy is also increasingly being influenced by the General Agreement on Tariffs and Trade (GATT) and the World Trade Organization (WTO).

General Agreement on Tariffs and Trade (GATT) The General Agreement on Tariffs and Trade, or GATT, was first negotiated following World War II in an effort

GATT A trade agreement intended to promote international trade by reducing trade barriers and making it easier for all nations to compete in international markets

to avoid trade wars that would benefit rich nations and harm poorer ones. Essentially, the **GATT** is a trade agreement intended to promote international trade by reducing trade barriers and making it easier for all nations to compete in international markets. The GATT was a major stimulus to international trade after it was first ratified in 1948 by 23 countries; by 1994 a total of 117 countries had signed the agreement.

One key component of the GATT was the identification of the so-called *most favored nation* (MFN) principle. This provision stipulates that if a country extends preferential treatment to any other nation that has signed the agreement, that preferential treatment must be extended to all signatories of the agreement. Members can extend such treatment to non-signatories as well, but are not required to do so.

World Trade Organization (WTO) An organization, which currently includes 140 member nations and 32 observer countries, that requires members to open their markets to international trade and follow WTO rules

World Trade Organization (WTO) The **World Trade Organization,** or WTO, came into existence on January 1, 1995. The **WTO** replaced the GATT and absorbed its mission. The WTO is headquartered in Geneva, Switzerland, and currently includes 140 member nations and 32 observer countries. Members are required to open their markets to international trade and follow WTO rules. The WTO has three basic goals:

1. To promote trade flows by encouraging nations to adopt nondiscriminatory and predictable trade policies
2. To reduce remaining trade barriers through multilateral negotiations
3. To establish impartial procedures for resolving trade disputes among its members

The World Trade Organization is certain to continue to play a major role in the evolution of the global economy. At the same time, it has also become a lightning rod for protesters and other activists who argue that the WTO focuses too narrowly on globalization issues to the detriment of human rights and the environment.

concept CHECK

What are the three major mature market systems? What are the GATT and WTO?

What impact has the U.S.-Iraq war in 2003 had on international business?

Environmental Challenges of International Management

We note earlier that managing in a global context both poses and creates additional challenges for the manager. As illustrated in Figure 5.3, three environmental challenges in particular warrant additional exploration at this point—the economic environment, the political/legal environment, and the cultural environment of international management.[29]

FIGURE 5.3

Environmental Challenges of International Management

Managers functioning in a global context must be aware of several environmental challenges. Three of the most important include economic, political/legal, and cultural challenges.

The Economic Environment

Every country is unique and creates a unique set of challenges for managers trying to do business there. However, there are three aspects of the economic environment in particular that can help managers anticipate the kinds of economic challenges they are likely to face in working abroad.

Economic System The first of these is the economic system used in the country. As we describe earlier, most countries today are moving toward a market economy. In a mature market economy, the key element for managers is freedom of choice. Consumers are free to make decisions about which products they prefer to purchase, and firms are free to decide what products and services to provide. As long as both the consumer and the firm are free to decide to be in the market, then supply and demand determine which firms and which products will be available.

A related characteristic of market economies that is relevant to managers concerns the nature of property ownership. There are two pure types—complete private ownership and complete public ownership. In systems with private ownership, individuals and organizations—not the government—own and operate the companies that conduct business. In systems with public ownership, the government directly owns the companies that manufacture and sell products. Few countries have pure systems of private ownership or pure systems of public ownership. Most countries tend toward one extreme or the other, but usually a mix of public and private ownership exists.

Natural Resources Another important aspect of the economic environment in different countries is the availability of natural resources. A very broad range of resources is available in different countries. Some countries, like Japan, have few natural resources of their own. Japan is thus forced to import all of the oil, iron ore, and other natural resources it needs to manufacture products for its domestic and overseas markets. The United States, in contrast, has enormous natural resources and is a major producer of oil, natural gas, coal, iron ore, copper, uranium, and other metals and materials that are vital to the development of a modern economy.

One natural resource that is particularly important in the modern global economy is oil. As we note earlier, a small set of countries in the Middle East, including Saudi Arabia, Iraq, Iran, and Kuwait, controls a very large percentage of the world's total known reserves of crude oil. Access to this single natural resource has given these oil-producing countries enormous clout in the international economy. One of the more controversial global issues today involving natural resources is the South American rain forest. Developers and farmers in Brazil, Peru, and other countries are clearing vast areas of rain forest, arguing that it is their land and that they can do what they want with it. Many environmentalists, however, fear the deforestation is wiping out entire species of animals and may so alter the environment as to affect weather patterns around the world.[30]

infrastructure The schools, hospitals, power plants, railroads, highways, ports, communication systems, air fields, and commercial distribution systems of a country

Infrastructure Yet another important aspect of the economic environment of relevance to international management is infrastructure. A country's **infrastructure** comprises its schools, hospitals, power plants, railroads, highways, shipping ports, communication systems, air fields, commercial distribution systems, and so forth. The United States has a highly developed infrastructure. For example, its educational system is modern, roads and bridges are well developed, and most people have access to medical care. Overall, the United States has a relatively complete infrastructure sufficient to support most forms of economic development and activity.

Some countries, on the other hand, lack a well-developed infrastructure. Some countries do not have enough electrical generating capacity to meet demand. Such countries—Kenya, for example—often schedule periods of time during which power is turned off or reduced. These planned power failures reduce power demands but can be an enormous inconvenience to business. In the extreme, when a country's infrastructure is greatly underdeveloped, firms interested in beginning businesses may have to build an entire township, including housing, schools, hospitals, and perhaps even recreational facilities, to attract a sufficient overseas workforce.

The Political/Legal Environment

A second environmental challenge facing the international manager is the political/legal environment in which he or she will do business. Four especially important aspects of the political/legal environment of international management are government stability, incentives for multinational trade, controls on international trade, and the influence of economic communities on international trade.

Government Stability Stability can be viewed in two ways—as the ability of a given government to stay in power against opposing factions in the country and as the permanence of government policies toward business. A country that is stable in both respects is preferable, because managers have a higher probability of successfully predicting how government will affect their business. Civil war in countries such as Angola has made it virtually impossible for international managers to predict what government policies are likely to be and whether the government will be able to guarantee the safety of international workers. Consequently, international firms have been very reluctant to invest in Angola.

In many countries—the United States, Great Britain, and Japan, for example—changes in government occur with very little disruption. In other countries—India, Argentina, and Greece, for example—changes are likely to be somewhat chaotic. Even if a country's government remains stable, the risk remains that the policies adopted by that government might change. In some countries, foreign businesses may be **nationalized** (taken over by the government) with little or no warning. For example, the government of Peru once nationalized Perulac, a domestic milk producer owned by Nestlé, because of a local milk shortage.

nationalized Taken over by the government

Incentives for International Trade Another facet of the political environment is incentives to attract foreign business. For example, the state of Alabama offered Mercedes-Benz huge tax breaks and other incentives to entice the German firm to select a location for a new factory in that state. In like fashion, the French government sold land to the Walt Disney Company far below its market value and agreed to build a connecting freeway in exchange for the company's agreeing to build a European theme park outside of Paris.

Such incentives can take a variety of forms. Some of the most common include reduced interest rates on loans, construction subsidies, and tax incentives. Less-developed countries tend to offer different packages of incentives. In addition to lucrative tax breaks, for example, they can also attract investors with duty-fee entry of raw materials and equipment, market protection through limitations on other importers, and the right to take profits out of the country. They may also have to correct deficiencies in their infrastructures, as noted above, to satisfy the requirements of foreign firms.

tariff A tax collected on goods shipped across national boundaries

Controls on International Trade A third element of the political environment that managers need to consider is the extent to which there are controls on international trade. In some instances, a country's government might decide that foreign competition is hurting domestic trade. To protect domestic business, such governments may enact barriers to international trade. These barriers include tariffs, quotas, export restraint agreements, and "buy national" laws.

A **tariff** is a tax collected on goods shipped across national boundaries. Tariffs can be collected by the exporting country, countries through which goods pass, and the importing country. Import tariffs, which are the most common, can be levied to protect domestic companies by increasing the cost of foreign goods. Japan charges U.S. tobacco producers a tariff on cigarettes imported into Japan as a way to keep their prices higher than the prices charged by domestic firms. Tariffs can also be levied, usually by less-developed countries, to raise money for the government.

Tariffs and quotas are common methods used to control imported products. President George Bush recently signed a bill that places a tariff of up to 30 percent on all steel products imported into the United States. As a result, the manufacturer of these steel coils, imported from France, will have to raise prices by 30 percent to earn the same profits as before. Such tariffs are intended to benefit domestic producers.

In the United States, the recently passed Byrd Amendment (named after West Virginia Senator Robert Byrd) stipulates that, if a domestic firm successfully demonstrates that a foreign company is dumping (selling for less than fair-market value) its products in the U.S. market, those products will be hit with a tariff and the proceeds given to the domestic company filing the complaint. In 2002, for instance, U.S. ball-bearing maker Torrington received $63 million under provisions of this statute.[31]

quota A limit on the number or value of goods that can be traded

Quotas are the most common form of trade restriction. A **quota** is a limit on the number or value of goods that can be traded. The quota amount is typically designed to ensure that domestic competitors will be able to maintain a certain market share. Honda is allowed to import 425,000 autos each year into the United States. This quota is one reason why Honda opened manufacturing facilities here. The quota applies to cars imported into the United States, but the company can produce as many other cars within our borders as it wants, as they are not considered imports. **Export restraint agreements** are designed to convince other governments to voluntarily limit the volume or value of goods exported to or imported from a particular country. They are, in effect, export quotas. Japanese steel producers voluntarily limit the amount of steel they send to the United States each year.

export restraint agreements Accords reached by governments in which countries voluntarily limit the volume or value of goods they export to or import from one another

economic community A set of countries that agree to markedly reduce or eliminate trade barriers among member nations (a formalized market system)

"Buy national" legislation gives preference to domestic producers through content or price restrictions. Several countries have this type of legislation. Brazil requires that Brazilian companies purchase only Brazilian-made computers. The United States requires that the Department of Defense purchase only military uniforms manufactured in the United States, even though the price of foreign uniforms would be half as much. Mexico requires that 50 percent of the parts of cars sold in Mexico be manufactured inside its own borders.

Brazil is increasingly being seen as an emerging economy that holds considerable potential. Many automobile manufacturers, for instance, have opened plants there to supply the entire South American market. This worker is helping assemble a Volkswagen at a factory in Sao Paulo.

Economic Communities Just as government policies can either increase or decrease the political risk facing international managers, trade relations between countries can either help or hinder international business. Relations dictated by quotas, tariffs, and so forth can hurt international trade. There is currently a strong movement around the world to reduce many of these barriers. This movement takes its most obvious form in international economic communities.

An international **economic community** is a set of countries that agree to markedly reduce or eliminate trade barriers among member nations. The first and in many ways still the most important of these economic communities is the European Union (EU), discussed earlier. The passage of NAFTA, as also noted earlier, represents perhaps the first step toward the formation of a North American economic community. Other important economic communities include the Latin American Integration Association (Bolivia, Brazil, Colombia, Chile, Argentina, and other South American countries) and the Caribbean Common Market (the Bahamas, Belize, Jamaica, Antigua, Barbados, and twelve other countries).

The Cultural Environment

Another environmental challenge for the international manager is the cultural environment and how it affects business. A country's culture includes all the values, symbols, beliefs, and language that guide behavior.

Values, Symbols, Beliefs, and Language Cultural values and beliefs are often unspoken; they may even be taken for granted by those who live in a particular country. Cultural factors do not necessarily cause problems for managers when the cultures of two countries are similar. Difficulties can arise, however, when there is little overlap between the home culture of a manager and the culture of the country in which business is to be conducted. For example, most U.S. managers find the culture and traditions of England relatively familiar. The people of both countries speak the same language and share strong historical roots, and there is a history of strong commerce between the two countries. Of course, as *Working with Diversity* illustrates, important differences can also be identified even between these related cultures. When U.S. managers begin operations in Japan or the People's Republic of China, however, most of those commonalities disappear.

In Japanese, the word hai (pronounced "hi") means "yes." In conversation, however, this word is used much like people in the United States use "uh-huh"; it moves a conversation along or shows the person with whom you are talking that you are paying attention. So when does hai mean "yes," and when does it mean "uh-huh"? This turns out to be a relatively difficult question to answer. If a U.S. manager asks a Japanese manager if he agrees to some trade arrangement, the Japanese manager is likely to say, "Hai"—which may mean "Yes, I agree," "Yes, I understand," or "Yes, I am listening." Many U.S. managers become frustrated in negotiations with the Japanese because they believe that the Japanese continue to raise issues that have already been settled (because the Japanese managers said, "Yes"). What many of these managers fail to recognize is that "yes" does not always mean "yes" in Japan.

Cultural differences between countries can have a direct impact on business practice. For example, the religion of Islam teaches that people should not make a living by exploiting the misfortune of others; as a result, charging interest payments is seen as immoral. This means that in Saudi Arabia there are few businesses that provide auto-wrecking services to tow stalled cars to the garage (because that would be capitalizing on misfortune), and in the Sudan banks cannot pay or charge interest. Given these cultural and religious constraints, those two businesses—automobile towing and banking—do not seem to hold great promise for international managers in those particular countries!

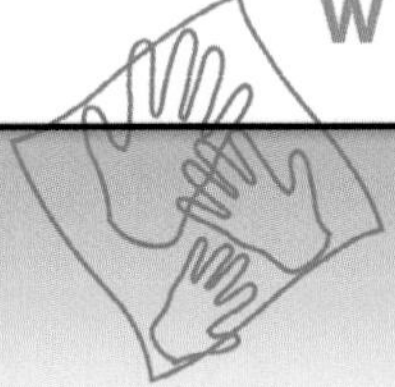

WORKING WITH diversity

Cowgirl Is Still a Maverick

"Hmm . . . Whatever happened to Marjorie Scardino? That girl who was a rodeo barrel-racing champion from Texarkana, Texas? She majored in French at Baylor University, graduating in 1969, and got a job as a dictation clerk. What's she doing today? Why, she's the CEO of a $3.6-billion-a-year company, headquartered in London, and heads *Fortune's* list of the fifty most powerful women in the world for the second year in a row."

Marjorie Scardino's amazing rise to the top of the corporate hierarchy sounds improbable, but it is perfectly true. She is the first woman and the first non-British person to hold the position of CEO at Pearson, a 150-year-old British publishing house. She is also one of the few women in the world to rise to the top of the corporate ladder purely on merit, not through an inheritance or marriage. Along the way, her unlikely career path has included law school, a stint as a reporter, shrimping off the Georgia coast, and founding a small-town newspaper with husband Albert, a Pulitzer Prize–winning reporter. She leveraged a marketing job at *The Economist* into the CEO's seat and then became chief of Pearson, half-owner of *The Economist*. Today, the company she runs is a conglomerate of British and American publishing and education businesses, ranging from the *Financial Times* and Penguin Publishing to textbook publishers such as Prentice Hall.

"[Marjorie Scardino is] a mixture of Boston bluestocking, Southern good ol' girl, and dockworker."

– Pearson employee, where Scardino is CEO*

Her distinctly American style has ruffled the feathers of some of Pearson's managers, who are Oxford and Cambridge graduates. In a culture that still values the "stiff upper lip," Scardino is "an enthusiast and an enthuser," according to Pearson board member and champion Dennis Stevenson. A coworker describes her as "a mixture of Boston bluestocking, Southern good ol' girl, and dockworker." She is known both for her bluntness—telling critics, "Oh get over yourself"—and her use of Americanisms, such as "muscle in" and "mooch." Scardino is deliberating trying to shake up the formerly stodgy company, to help it survive in an increasingly tough industry. Will wearing a baseball cap to work and asking everyone to call her "Marjorie" do the trick? So far, Pearson's performance has not improved much, but that only gives Scardino a chance to recite her favorite slogan: "You learn more from failure than you do from success."

References: Janet Guyon, "The Power 50," *Fortune*, September 27, 2002, www.fortune.com on November 24, 2002; Laura Colby, "Yankee Expansionist Builds British Empire," *Fortune*, March 16, 1998, www.fortune.com on December 8, 2002 (*quote); "Resume: Marjorie Scardino," *BusinessWeek*, January 22, 2001, www.businessweek.com on December 8, 2002; Stanley Reed, "Can Scardino Get Pearson out of This Pickle?" *BusinessWeek*, July 22, 2002, www.businessweek.com on December 8, 2002; "The Most Powerful Women in Business: International," *Fortune*, October 14, 2002, www.fortune.com on December 8, 2002.

Some cultural differences between countries can be even more subtle and yet have a major impact on business activities. For example, in the United States most managers clearly agree about the value of time. Most U.S. managers schedule their activities very tightly and then adhere to their schedules. Other cultures do not put such a premium on time. In the Middle East, managers do not like to set appointments, and they rarely keep appointments set too far into the future. U.S. managers interacting with managers from the Middle East might misinterpret the late arrival

DILBERT by Scott Adams

DILBERT Reprinted by permission of UNITED FEATURES SYNDICATE Inc.

Dealing with people from other cultures can be a rewarding experience, and it can also be a challenge. Language barriers, for example, pose major obstacles. Interestingly, some people believe that if they talk slower or louder, people who do not speak their language will somehow have a better understanding of what is being said. As illustrated in this cartoon, this flawed logic can even extend to electronic communication.

of a potential business partner as a negotiation ploy or an insult, when it is rather a simple reflection of different views of time and its value.[32]

Language itself can be an important factor. Beyond the obvious and clear barriers posed by people who speak different languages, subtle differences in meaning can also play a major role. For example, Imperial Oil of Canada markets gasoline under the brand name Esso. When the firm tried to sell its gasoline in Japan, it learned that Esso means "stalled car" in Japanese. Likewise, when Chevrolet first introduced a U.S. model called the Nova in Latin America, General Motors executives could not understand why the car sold poorly. They eventually learned, though, that, in Spanish, no va means "it doesn't go." The color green is used extensively in Moslem countries, but it signifies death in some other countries. The color associated with femininity in the United States is pink, but in many other countries yellow is the most feminine color.

Individual Behaviors Across Cultures From another perspective, there also appear to be clear differences in individual behaviors and attitudes across different cultures. For example, Geert Hofstede, a Dutch researcher, studied 116,000 people working in dozens of different countries and found several interesting differences.[33] Hofstede's initial work identified four important dimensions along which people seem to differ across cultures. More recently, he has added a fifth dimension. These dimensions are illustrated in Figure 5.4.

The first dimension identified by Hofstede is social orientation.[34] **Social orientation** is a person's beliefs about the relative importance of the individual versus groups to which that person belongs. The two extremes of social orientation are individualism and collectivism. *Individualism* is the cultural belief that the person comes first. Hofstede's research suggested that people in the United States, the United Kingdom, Australia, Canada, New Zealand, and the Netherlands tend to be relatively individualistic. *Collectivism,* the opposite of individualism, is the belief that the group comes first. Hofstede found that people from Mexico, Greece, Hong Kong, Taiwan, Peru, Singapore, Colombia, and Pakistan tend to be relatively collectivistic in their values. In countries with higher levels of individualism, many workers may prefer reward systems that link pay with the performance of individual employees. In a more collectivistic culture, such a reward system may in fact be counterproductive.

social orientation A person's beliefs about the relative importance of the individual versus groups to which that person belongs

A second important dimension is **power orientation**, the beliefs that people in a culture hold about the appropriateness of power and authority differences in hierarchies such as business organizations. Some cultures are characterized by *power respect.*

power orientation The beliefs that people in a culture hold about the appropriateness of power and authority differences in hierarchies such as business organizations

FIGURE 5.4

Individual Differences Across Cultures

Hofstede identified five fundamental differences that can be used to characterize people in different cultures. These dimensions are social orientation, power orientation, uncertainty orientation, goal orientation, and time orientation. Different levels of each dimension affect the perceptions, attitudes, values, motivations, and behaviors of people in different cultures.

Source: R. W. Griffin/M. Pustay, *International Business* 4th Ed. © 2005. Reprinted by permission of Pearson Education, Inc. Upper Saddle River, NJ 07458.

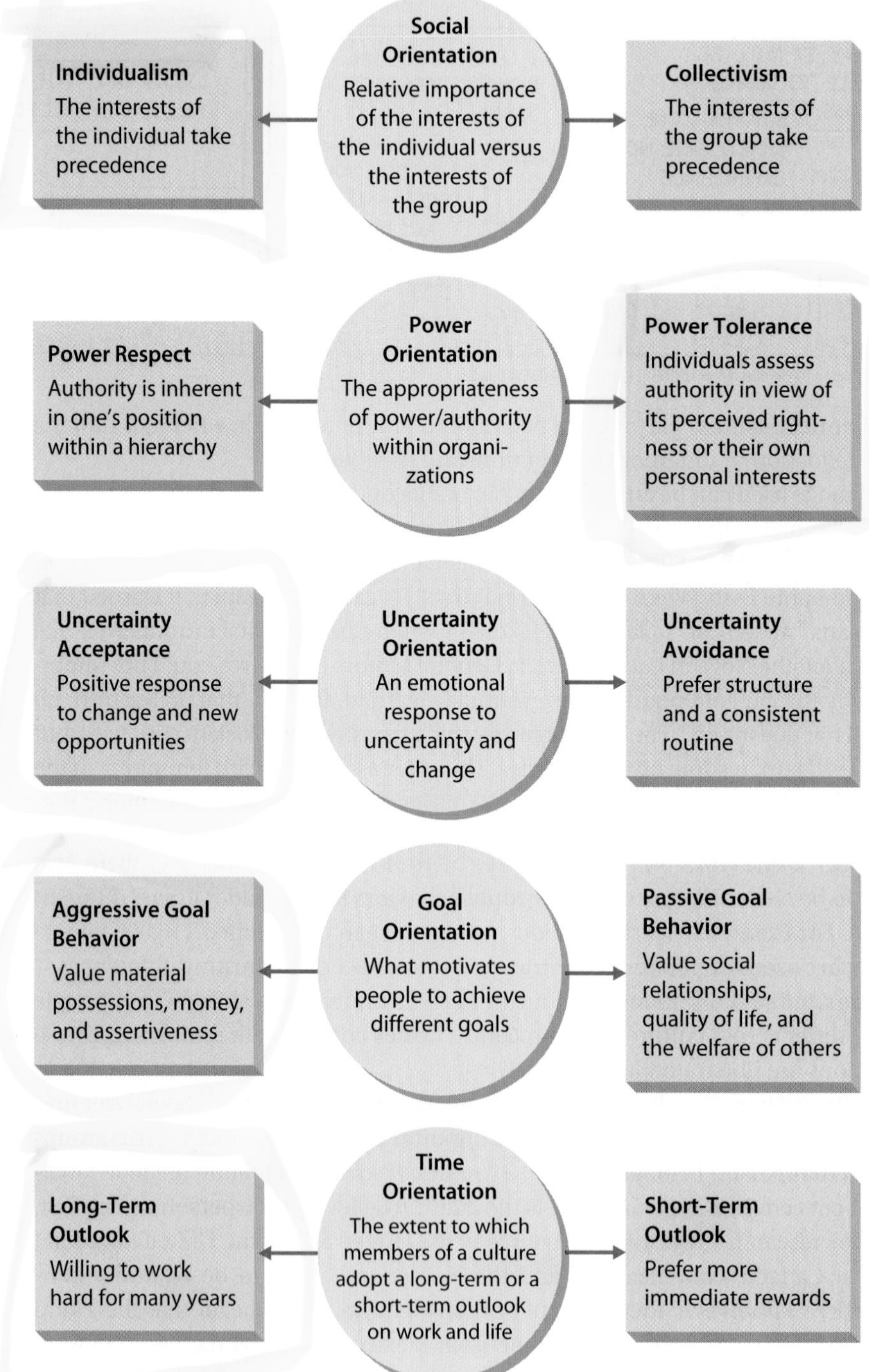

This means that people tend to accept the power and authority of their superiors simply on the basis of their position in the hierarchy and to respect their right to control that power. Hofstede found that people in France, Spain, Mexico, Japan, Brazil, Indonesia, and Singapore are relatively power accepting. In contrast, people in cultures with a *power tolerance* orientation attach much less significance to a person's position in the hierarchy. These individuals are more willing to question a decision or mandate from someone at a higher level or perhaps even refuse to accept it. Hofstede's work suggested that people in the United States, Israel, Austria, Denmark, Ireland, Norway, Germany, and New Zealand tend to be more power tolerant.

The third basic dimension of individual differences studied by Hofstede was uncertainty orientation. **Uncertainty orientation** is the feeling individuals have regarding uncertain and ambiguous situations. People in cultures with *uncertainty acceptance* are stimulated by change and thrive on new opportunities. Hofstede suggested that many people from the United States, Denmark, Sweden, Canada, Singapore, Hong Kong, and Australia are among those in this category. In contrast, people with *uncertainty avoidance* tendencies dislike and will avoid ambiguity whenever possible. Hofstede found that many people in Israel, Austria, Japan, Italy, Columbia, France, Peru, and Germany tend to avoid uncertainty whenever possible.

uncertainty orientation The feeling individuals have regarding uncertain and ambiguous situations

The fourth dimension of cultural values measured by Hofstede is goal orientation. In this context, **goal orientation** is the manner in which people are motivated to work toward different kinds of goals. One extreme on the goal orientation continuum is *aggressive goal behavior*. People who exhibit aggressive goal behaviors tend to place a high premium on material possessions, money, and assertiveness. On the other hand, people who adopt *passive goal behavior* place a higher value on social relationships, quality of life, and concern for others. According to Hofstede's research, many people in Japan tend to exhibit relatively aggressive goal behaviors, whereas many people in Germany, Mexico, Italy and the United States reflect moderately aggressive goal behaviors. People from the Netherlands and the Scandinavian countries of Norway, Sweden, Denmark, and Finland all tend to exhibit relatively passive goal behaviors.

goal orientation The manner in which people are motivated to work toward different kinds of goals

A recently identified fifth dimension is called **time orientation**.[35] Time orientation is the extent to which members of a culture adopt a long-term versus a short-term outlook on work, life, and other elements of society. Some cultures, such as Japan, Hong Kong, Taiwan, and South Korea, have a longer-term orientation. One implication of this orientation is that people from these cultures are willing to accept that they may have to work hard for many years before achieving their goals. Other cultures, like Pakistan and West Africa, are more likely to have a short-term orientation. As a result, people from these cultures may prefer jobs that provide more immediate rewards. Hofstede's work suggests that the United States and Germany tend to have an intermediate time orientation.

time orientation The extent to which members of a culture adopt a long-term versus a short-term outlook on work, life, and other elements of society

concept CHECK

What are the four elements of the political/legal environment that are most relevant to international managers?

How might cultural factors influence a computer manufacturer differently than they might influence a fashion-oriented apparel company?

Competing in a Global Economy

Competing in a global economy is both a major challenge and an opportunity for businesses today. The nature of these challenges depends on a variety of factors, including the size of the organization. In addition, international management has implications for the basic functions of planning and decision making, organizing, leading, and controlling.

Globalization and Organization Size

Although organizations of any size may compete in international markets, there are some basic differences in the challenges and opportunities faced by MNCs, medium-size organizations, and small organizations.

Multinational Corporations The large MNCs have long since made the choice to compete in a global marketplace. In general, these firms take a global perspective. They transfer capital, technology, human resources, inventory, and information from one market to another. They actively seek new expansion opportunities wherever feasible. MNCs tend to allow local managers a great deal of discretion in addressing local and regional issues. At the same time, each operation is ultimately accountable to a central authority. Managers at this central authority (headquarters, a central office) are responsible for setting the overall strategic direction for the firm, making major policy decisions, and so forth. MNCs need senior managers who understand the global economy and who are comfortable dealing with executives and government officials from a variety of cultures. Table 5.2 lists the world's largest multinational enterprises.

Medium-Size Organizations Many medium-size businesses remain primarily domestic organizations. But they still may buy and sell products made abroad and compete with businesses from other countries in their own domestic market. Increasingly, however, medium-size organizations are expanding into foreign markets as well. For example, Gold's Gym, a U.S. fitness chain, has opened a very successful facility in Moscow.[36] In contrast to MNCs, medium-size organizations doing business abroad are much more selective about the markets they enter. They also depend more on a few international specialists to help them manage their foreign operations.

Small Organizations More and more small organizations are also finding that they can benefit from the global economy. Some, for example, serve as local suppliers for MNCs. A dairy farmer who sells milk to Carnation Company, for example, is actually transacting business with Nestlé. Local parts suppliers also have been successfully selling products to the Toyota and Honda plants in the United States. Beyond serving as local suppliers, some small businesses also buy and sell products and services abroad. For example, the Collin Street Bakery, based in Corsicana, Texas, ships fruitcakes around the world. In 2003 the firm shipped over 150,000 pounds of fruitcake to Japan. Most small businesses rely on simple importing or exporting operations (or both) for their international sales. Thus only a few specialized management positions are needed. Collin Street Bakery, for example, has

TABLE 5.2

The World's Largest MNCs: Industrial Corporations

Rank, 2002	2001	Company	Country	Revenues $ (millions)	% change
1	1	Wal-Mart Stores	U.S	246,525.0	12.2
2	3	General Motors	U.S.	186,763.0	5.4
3	2	Exxon Mobil	U.S.	182,466.0	(4.8)
4	8	Royal Dutch/Shell Group	Netherlands/Britain	179,431.0	32.7
5	4	BP	Britain	178,721.0	2.6
6	5	Ford Motor	U.S.	163,871.0	0.9
7	7	DaimlerChrysler	Germany	141,421.1	3.3
8	10	Toyota Motor	Japan	131,754.2	9.1
9	9	General Electric	U.S.	131,698.0	4.6
10	12	Mitsubishi	Japan	109,386.1	3.4
11	13	Mitsui	Japan	108,630.7	7.3
12	18	Allianz	Germany	101,930.2	18.6
13	11	Citigroup	U.S.	100,789.0	(10.0)
14	15	Total	France	96,944.9	2.8
15	14	ChevronTexaco	U.S.	92,043.0	(7.7)
16	16	Nippon Telegraph & Telephone	Japan	89,644.0	—
17	20	ING Group	Netherlands	88,102.3	6.1
18	17	Itochu	Japan	85,856.4	(5.8)
19	19	International Business Machines	U.S.	83,132.0	(3.2)
20	21	Volkswagen	Germany	82,203.7	3.7
21	22	Siemens	Germany	77,205.2	(0.2)
22	23	Sumitomo	Japan	75,745.2	(1.8)
23	25	Marubeni	Japan	72,164.8	0.6
24	26	Verizon Communications	U.S.	67,625.0	0.6
25	34	American International Group	U.S.	67,482.0	8.1
26	32	Hitachi	Japan	67,228.0	5.2
27	29	U.S. Postal Service	U.S.	66,463.0	1.0
28	41	Honda Motor	Japan	65,420.4	11.1
29	35	Carrefour	France	64,978.6	4.4
30	24	Altria Group	U.S.	62,182.0	(14.8)
31	30	Axa	France	62,050.8	(5.4)
32	37	Sony	Japan	61,334.6	1.2
33	33	Nippon Life Insurance	Japan	61,174.5	(4.2)
34	45	Matsushita	Japan	60,744.3	10.5
35	38	Royal Ahold	Netherlands	59,454.6	(0.3)
36	188	ConocoPhillips	U.S.	58,384.0	141.4
37	46	Home Depot	U.S.	58,247.0	8.8
38	55	Nestlé	Switzerland	57,279.1	14.1
39	57	McKesson	U.S.	57,129.2	14.2
40	70	Hewlett-Packard	U.S.	56,588.0	25.1
41	58	Nissan Motor	Japan	56,040.8	13.1
42	51	Vivendi Universal	France	54,977.1	7.0
43	42	Boeing	U.S.	54,069.0	(7.1)
44	50	Assicurazioni Generali	Italy	53,598.9	4.3
45	52	Fannie Mae	U.S.	52,901.1	4.1
46	49	Fiat	Italy	52,612.5	1.3
47	27	Deutsche Bank	Germany	52,133.2	(22.0)
48	31	Credit Suisse	Switzerland	52,121.7	(18.8)
49	79	Munich Re Group	Germany	51,980.0	24.1
50	62	Merck	U.S.	51,790.3	8.5
51	56	Kroger	U.S.	51,759.5	3.3
52	65	Peugeot	France	51,465.7	11.2
53	61	Cardinal Health	U.S.	51,135.7	6.6
54	44	BNP Paribas	France	51,127.3	(7.1)
55	75	Deutsche Telekom	Germany	50,759.5	17.3
56	63	State Farm Insurance, Cos.	U.S.	49,653.7	6.3
57	48	Aviva	Britain	49,533.3	(5.3)
58	72	Metro	Germany	48,714.5	9.8
59	105	Samsung Electronics	South Korea	47,605.6	32.4
60	123	Vodafone	Britain	46,987.0	43.6

Source: From *Fortune*, July 21, 2003, p. 100.

one local manager who handles international activities. Mail-order activities within each country are subcontracted to local firms in each market.

Management Challenges in a Global Economy

The management functions that constitute the framework for this book—planning and decision making, organizing, leading, and controlling—are just as relevant to international managers as to domestic managers. International managers need to have a clear view of where they want their firm to be in the future; they have to organize to implement their plans; they have to motivate those who work for them; and they have to develop appropriate control mechanisms.[37]

Management challenges in a global economy require organizations to carefully assess how they will enter and compete in various foreign markets. For instance, when Samsung, a Korean firm, began exporting its electronic products to China, it relied on marketing research to determine that it needed to advertise and promote those products heavily in both Chinese and English.

Planning and Decision Making in a Global Economy To effectively plan and make decisions in a global economy, managers must have a broad-based understanding of both environmental issues and competitive issues. They need to understand local market conditions and technological factors that will affect their operations. At the corporate level, executives need a great deal of information to function effectively. Which markets are growing? Which markets are shrinking? What are our domestic and foreign competitors doing in each market? They must also make a variety of strategic decisions about their organization. For example, if a firm wishes to enter the market in France, should it buy a local firm there, build a plant, or seek a strategic alliance? Critical issues include understanding environmental circumstances, the role of goals and planning in a global organization, and how decision making affects the global organization. We note special implications for global managers as we discuss planning and decision making in Chapters 7 through 10.

Organizing in a Global Economy Managers in international businesses must also attend to a variety of organizing issues. For example, General Electric has operations scattered around the globe. The firm has made the decision to give local managers a great deal of responsibility for how they run their business. In contrast, many Japanese firms give managers of their foreign operations relatively little responsibility. As a result, those managers must frequently travel back to Japan to present problems or get decisions approved. Managers in an international business must address the basic issues of organization structure and design, managing change, and dealing with human resources. We address the special issues of organizing the international organization in Chapters 11 through 14.

Leading in a Global Economy We note earlier some of the cultural factors that affect international organizations. Individual managers must be prepared to deal with these and other factors as they interact with people from different cultural backgrounds. Supervising a group of five managers, each of whom is from a different state in the United States, is likely to be much simpler than supervising a group of five managers, each of whom is from a different culture. Managers must understand how cultural factors affect individuals, how motivational processes vary across cultures, the role of leadership in different cultures, how communication varies across cultures, and the nature of interpersonal and group processes in different cultures. In Chapters 15 through 19 we note special implications for international managers that relate to leading and interacting with others.

Controlling in a Global Economy Finally, managers in international organizations must also be concerned with control. Distances, time zone differences, and cultural factors also play a role in control. For example, in some cultures close supervision is seen as being appropriate, whereas in other cultures it is not. Likewise, executives in the United States and Japan may find it difficult to communicate vital information to one another because of the time zone differences. Basic control issues for the international manager revolve around operations management, productivity, quality, technology, and information systems. These issues are integrated throughout our discussion of control in Chapters 20 through 22.

concept CHECK

How do the four basic management functions relate to international business?

What kinds of small business might have the greatest success in international markets? What kinds might have the least success?

Summary of Key Points

business.college.hmco.com/students

International business has grown to be one of the most important features of the world's economy. Learning to operate in a global economy is an important challenge facing many managers today. Businesses can be primarily domestic, international, multinational, or global in scope. Managers need to understand both the process of internationalization and how to manage within a given level of international activity.

To compete in the global economy, managers must understand its structure. Mature market economies and systems dominate the global economy today. North America, the European Union, and Pacific Asia are especially important. High-potential/high-growth economies in Eastern Europe, Latin America, the People's Republic of China, India, and Vietnam are increasingly important to managers. The oil-exporting economies in the Middle East are also important. The GATT and the WTO play critical roles in the evolution of the global economy.

Many of the challenges of management in a global context are unique issues associated with the international environmental context. These challenges reflect the economic, political/legal, and cultural environments of international management.

Basic issues of competing in a global economy vary according to whether the organization is an MNC, a medium-size organization, or a small organization. In addition, the basic managerial functions of planning and decision making, organizing, leading, and controlling must all be addressed in international organizations.

Discussion Questions

Questions for Review

1. Describe the four basic levels of international business activity. Do you think any organization will achieve the fourth level? Why or why not?
2. For each of the four globalization strategies, describe the risks associated with that strategy and the potential returns from that strategy.
3. Describe the various types of political controls on international trade. Be sure to highlight the differences between the types.
4. Explain the relationship between organizational size and globalization. Are large firms the only ones that are global?

Questions for Analysis

5. What are the advantages and disadvantages for a U.S.-based multinational firm entering a mature market economy? What are the advantages and disadvantages for such a firm entering a high-potential/high-growth economy?
6. Choose an industry. Describe the impact that international business has had on firms in that industry. Are there any industries that might not be affected by the trend toward international business? If so, what are they? If not, why are there none?
7. You are the CEO of an up-and-coming toy company and have plans to go international soon. What steps would you take to carry out that strategy? What areas would you stress in your decision-making process? How would you organize your company?

Questions for Application

8. Use the Internet to locate information about a company that is using a global strategic alliance or global joint venture. (*Hint:* Almost any large multinational firm will be involved in these ventures, and you can find information at corporate home pages.) What do you think are the major goals for the venture? Do you expect that the firm will accomplish its goals? If so, why? If not, what stands in its way?
9. Assume that you are the CEO of Ford. What are the basic environmental challenges you face as your company continues its globalization efforts? Give some specific examples that relate to Ford.
10. Review the following chart of Hofstede's cultural dimensions. Based on the chart, tell which country you would most like to work in and why. Tell which country you would like least and why.

	Power Distance Range: 11–104	**Individualism Range: 6–91**	**Uncertainty Avoidance Range: 8–112**	**Aggressiveness Range: 5–95**
Germany	35	67	65	66
India	77	48	40	56
Israel	13	54	81	47
United Kingdom	35	89	35	66
United States	40	91	46	62

Adapted from: Geert Hofstede, *Cultures and Organizations: Software of the Mind: Intercultural Cooperation and Its Importance for Survival* (London: HarperCollins, 1994), pp. 26, 55, 84, 113.

BUILDING EFFECTIVE interpersonal SKILLS

Exercise Overview

Interpersonal skills refer to the manager's ability to communicate with, understand, and motivate individuals and groups. Managers in international organizations must understand how cultural manners and norms affect communication with people in different areas of the world. This exercise helps you evaluate your current level of cultural awareness and develop insights into areas for improvement.

Exercise Background

As firms become increasingly globalized, they look for managers with international experience or skills. Yet many American college graduates do not have strong skills in foreign languages, global history, or international cultures.

Exercise Task

Take the International Culture Quiz below. Then, based on your score, answer the question at the end. In order to make the quiz more relevant, choose your answers from one or more of the ten largest countries in the world. In order, these are China, India, the United States, Indonesia, Brazil, Pakistan, Russia, Bangladesh, Nigeria, and Japan.

The International Culture Quiz

1. Name the major religion practiced in each of the ten largest countries.
2. When greeting a business associate, in which country or countries is it proper to shake hands? to bow? to hug or kiss?
3. In which country or countries should you avoid wearing the color purple?
4. In which country or countries would smiling be considered suspicious?
5. In which country or countries are laughter and smiling often used as a way of covering up feelings of embarrassment or displeasure?
6. Which part of someone else's body should you never touch in Indonesia? in India? Which part of your own body should you never touch in China?
7. In which country or countries would a server or small-business person require that a tip be paid before the service is rendered?
8. In which country or countries would it be an insult to address someone in Spanish?
9. In which country or countries is whistling considered bad luck?
10. In which country or countries is it important to give printed business cards to all business associates?
11. In which country or countries might you be asked your family size or income on a first meeting with a new business associate?
12. In which country or countries should gum not be chewed at work?

Your instructor will provide the answers. Was your score high or low? What does your score tell you about your cultural awareness?

What do you think you could do to improve your score? Share your ideas with the class.

BUILDING EFFECTIVE technical SKILLS

business.college.hmco.com/students

Exercise Overview

Technical skills are the skills necessary to accomplish or understand the specific kind of work being done in an organization. Companies must continually analyze population and trade data in order to form reasonable international strategies. This exercise will help you develop technical skills related to finding information and then see the impact that the information can have on a firm.

Exercise Background

In 2002 the five largest countries in the world, in population, were China, India, the United States, Indonesia, and Brazil, in that order. Assume you are the manager of a large multinational firm headquartered in the United States. Use the Internet to help you answer the questions below about trade and population in each of these countries. (Estimates of future population can be found at the U.S. Census Bureau, www.census.gov/ipc/www/idbrank.html. Import/export data are also found at the U.S. Census Bureau, at www.census.gov/foreign-trade/aip/index.html#profile. From this main page, find the most recent figures. The remainder of the data can be found in the World Factbook, published by the Central Intelligence Agency, located at www.cia.gov/cia/publications/factbook/index.html.) Then consider the implications this information could have for your firm.

Exercise Task

1. List the five countries in the world that are estimated to have the largest populations in 2050. Describe how the list has changed since 2002.
2. What are the top five countries that receive exports from the United States?
3. What are the top five countries that import U.S. products?
4. What is the average life span (a measure of individual prosperity) in each of the largest countries and each of the top exporters and importers?
5. What is the gross domestic product per capita (a measure of economic health of an economy) in each of those countries, in U.S. dollars?
6. What are the implications for your firm? In other words, what do the data suggest about the desirability of various countries as trading partners today? What do the data suggest about the countries' desirability in the future?

BUILDING EFFECTIVE communication SKILLS

business.college.hmco.com/students

Exercise Overview

Communication skills refer to the manager's ability both to convey ideas and information effectively to others and to receive ideas and information effectively from others. International managers have additional communication complexities due to differences in language, time zones, and so forth. This exercise will enable you to enhance your communication skills by better understanding the impact of different time zones.

Exercise Background

Assume that you are a manager in a large multinational firm. Your office is located in San Francisco. You need to arrange a conference call with several other managers to discuss an upcoming strategic change by your firm. The other managers are located in New York, London, Rome, Moscow, Tokyo, Singapore, and Sydney.

Exercise Task

Using the information above, do the following:

1. Determine the time zone differences in each of these cities.
2. Assuming that people in each city have a "normal" workday of 8:00 A.M. to 5:00 P.M., determine the optimal time for your conference call; that is, what time can you place

the call and minimize the number of people who are inconvenienced?

3. Now assume that you need to visit each office in person. You need to spend one full day in each city. Using the Internet, review airline schedules, account for differences in time zones, and develop an efficient itinerary.

CHAPTER CLOSING case

THE FINAL FRONTIER?

"Wal-Mart is formidable, but we aren't afraid of the challenge."

– Ricardo Martin, CEO of Mexican retailer Soriana*

What frontiers are left for an enormous retailer that has become the most profitable corporation on earth? Wal-Mart is gigantic by any measure. Sales totaled $218 billion in 2001, and the discounter employed 1.3 million workers in 4,300 stores. Over 100 million customers per week visit Wal-Mart stores worldwide. In 2002 Wal-Mart topped the Fortune 500, the first time that a nonmanufacturing firm had reached that position.

With domestic sales flat and the discount market saturated, Wal-Mart is seeking expansion opportunities. It can aggressively attack specialty retailers, such as PETsMART, Albertsons, Toys "R" Us, and Best Buy. It can introduce new categories at its existing stores. "Wal-Mart's aggressive roll-out of retail gas stations could be followed closely with the company selling used cars, financial services, home improvement, and food service," says Ira Kalish, a retail consultant. The most appealing option, however, is international expansion.

Wal-Mart's international expansion began in 1991, when the firm opened a Sam's Club near Mexico City. Today, the firm's International Division operates 1,100 overseas outlets, with stores located in Argentina, Brazil, Canada, China, Germany, Korea, Mexico, Puerto Rico, and the United Kingdom. In each of these markets, acquisitions have played a more important role than internal growth. For example, in Canada, Wal-Mart purchased 122 Woolco stores to enter that market. In Germany, Wal-Mart began with an acquisition of 21 Wertkauf hypermarkets and then added 74 Interspar stores. The company's U.K.-based acquisitions have been its most ambitious to date, with the 1999 purchase of 230 ASDA stores. The firm integrates the acquired stores into its operations, changes the names, renovates the facilities, brings in store managers from the United States, and changes the product mix.

Wal-Mart is still learning how to deal effectively with differences in culture and business practices across borders. An initial difficulty was the relatively small size of most of the acquired stores, with one-third the floor space of a typical Wal-Mart. Wal-Mart's "one-stop" strategy depends, in part, on size, but European customers are turned off by the impersonal feel of very large stores. European customers also dislike greeters. "Germans are skeptical. Customers said that they don't want to be paying the salary of that guy at the door," claims Nikolai Baltruschat, a Deutsche Bank analyst. Also, Europeans typically shop more frequently but buy less at each visit than do Americans, so they do not like pushing around a large cart. Smaller carts could allow the company to cram more products into a small space, but they do not encourage large purchases.

Regulation creates yet another set of hurdles for Wal-Mart. Twenty-four-hour stores are banned in England and Germany. A German court upheld employees' rights to wear earrings and sport facial hair. When the retailer tried to forbid English employees from drinking beer during their lunch break, English labor groups threatened a lawsuit. European laws are much stricter about the sale of "loss leaders," popular products that are sold below cost in order to bring customers into the store. Negotiations with suppliers are also more heavily regulated. In Mexico, Wal-Mart's cost pressure on suppliers is under investigation, after the firm demanded deep discounts on many products.

Wal-Mart's entry into a new market "is a nightmare for a lot of retailers," says Michael P. Godliman, a retail consultant. To fight back, local retailers have imitated Wal-Mart's strategy by cutting costs and increasing variety. In order to attract more customers, firms have also added products and services geared to local tastes. Soriana supermarkets of Mexico are battling Wal-Mart with in-store mariachi concerts. "Wal-Mart is formidable, but we aren't afraid of the challenge," says Soriana CEO Ricardo Martin. Carrefour, a French retailer, is hoping to forestall Wal-Mart's entry into its country, the second-largest retail market in Europe. Carrefour is competing by adding such amenities as travel agents and shoe fitters and by banning fluorescent lighting. A recently announced merger with France's number-two retailer, Promodes, creates market power for Carrefour. "They're just relentless," says a French retail executive, referring to Carrefour. "The toughest competitor I've ever seen anywhere." Other European retailers, such as Dutch grocer Ahold, are considering preemptive mergers, too.

In 2002 Wal-Mart's results from international operations were mixed. The firm had a modest increase in sales, far less than the increase in previous years. Its gross margin on international sales was just 4.1 percent, compared to 7.1 percent for domestic stores. Yet, flush with the profits from its thousands of domestic stores, Wal-Mart will not be deterred. The international retailing industry will undoubtedly consolidate until just a few very large, cross-border retailers remain. And Wal-Mart aims to be one of them.

Case Questions

1. What are some of the advantages that Wal-Mart hopes to gain by globalization? What are some of the challenges it faces in its efforts to globalize?
2. What methods has Wal-Mart used to globalize? Are those the most appropriate methods for the firm? Why or why not?
3. There is a trend toward more international agreements between countries to reduce trade barriers, such as the formation of NAFTA, the European Community, and ASEAN (a trade organization for Southeast Asia). In your opinion, will this trend help or hurt Wal-Mart, and how?

Case References

"2002 Annual Report," "International Operations," "Wal-Mart International Operations," "Wal-Mart Stores, Inc. at a Glance," Wal-Mart website, www.walmartstores.com on December 9, 2002; Amy Tsao, "Will Wal-Mart Take over the World?" *BusinessWeek*, November 27, 2002, www.businessweek.com on December 9, 2002; Geri Smith, "War of the Superstores," *BusinessWeek*, September 23, 2002, p. 60; "The 2002 Global 500," *Fortune*, July 8, 2002, www.fortune.com on December 9, 2002.

Chapter Notes

1. "An International Brewer," Heineken website, www.heinekencorp.com on December 8, 2002; Dan Bilefsky, "How 'Peasant' Beer Became Extraordinary," *Wall Street Journal*, April 14, 2002; "Our Company," Interbrew website, www.interbrew.com on December 8, 2002 (*quote); Stephen Baker, "Freddy Heineken's Recipe May Be Scrapped," *BusinessWeek*, January 28, 2002, p. 56; "What Now for Bass Beer Brands?" BBC News, news.bbc.co.uk on December 8, 2002; "Waking Up Heineken," *BusinessWeek*, September 8, 2003, pp. 68–69.
2. See Ricky W. Griffin and Michael Pustay, *International Business*, 4th ed. (Upper Saddle River, NJ: Prentice-Hall, 2005), for an overview of international business.
3. See Thomas Begley and David Boyd, "The Need for a Global Mind-Set," *Sloan Management Review*, Winter 2003, pp. 25–36.
4. For a more complete discussion of forms of international business, see Griffin and Pustay, *International Business.*
5. *Hoover's Handbook of American Business 2003* (Austin, Texas: Hoover's Business Press, 2003), pp. 1266–1267.
6. John H. Dunning, *Multinational Enterprises and the Global Economy* (Wokingham, U.K.: Addison-Wesley, 1993); Christopher Bartlett and Sumantra Ghoshal, *Transnational Management* (Homewood, Ill.: Irwin, 1992).
7. "A Company Without a Country?" *BusinessWeek*, May 5, 1997, p. 40.

8. "The *Fortune* Global 5 Hundred—World's Largest Corporations," *Fortune*, July 21, 2003, pp. 106–119.
9. "The *Fortune* Global 5 Hundred Ranked Within Industries," *Fortune*, July 21, 2003, pp. 106–119.
10. *Hoover's Handbook of American Business 2003* (Austin, Texas: Hoover's Business Press, 2003), pp. 198–199; 574–575.
11. "Going Global—Lessons from Late Movers," *Harvard Business Review*, March–April 2000, pp. 132–142.
12. See "Spanning the Globe," *USA Today*, April 30, 2002, pp. 1C, 2C.
13. "Creating a Worldwide Yen for Japanese Beer," *Financial Times*, October 7, 1994, p. 20.
14. Kenichi Ohmae, "The Global Logic of Strategic Alliances," *Harvard Business Review*, March–April 1989, pp. 143–154.
15. Jeremy Main, "Making Global Alliances Work," *Fortune*, December 17, 1990, pp. 121–126.
16. Hans Mjoen and Stephen Tallman, "Control and Performance in International Joint Ventures," *Organization Science*, May–June 1997, pp. 257–274.
17. "Finally, Coke Gets It Right," *BusinessWeek*, February 10, 2003, p. 47.
18. "The Border," *BusinessWeek*, May 12, 1997, pp. 64–74.
19. Griffin and Pustay, *International Business*.
20. For an excellent discussion of the effects of NAFTA, see "In the Wake of Nafta, a Family Firm Sees Business Go South," *Wall Street Journal*, February 23, 1999, pp. A1, A10.
21. Griffin and Pustay, *International Business*. See also "Overseas Economies Rally, Giving the U.S. a Very Mixed Blessing," *Wall Street Journal*, August 19, 1999, pp. A1, A8.
22. Eileen P. Gunn, "Emerging Markets," *Fortune*, August 18, 1997, pp. 168–173.
23. "World's Car Makers Race to Keep up with China Boom," *Wall Street Journal*, December 13, 2002, pp. A1, A7.
24. "In Many Ways, Return of Hong Kong to China Has Already Happened," *Wall Street Journal*, June 9, 1997, pp. A1, A2; "How You Can Win in China," *BusinessWeek*, May 26, 1997, pp. 66–68.
25. "Investing in India: Not for the Fainthearted," *BusinessWeek*, August 11, 1997, pp. 46–47.
26. "Argentina Cries Foul as Choice Employers Beat a Path Next Door," *Wall Street Journal*, May 2, 2000, pp. A1, A8.
27. "GM Is Building Plants in Developing Nations to Woo New Markets," *Wall Street Journal*, August 4, 1997, pp. A1, A4.
28. For example, see "China Weighs Lifting Curbs on Foreign Firms," *Wall Street Journal*, January 1, 2000, p. A17.
29. Griffin and Pustay, *International Business*.
30. "Oil Companies Strive to Turn a New Leaf to Save Rain Forest," *Wall Street Journal*, July 17, 1997, pp. A1, A8.
31. "Host of Companies Pocket Windfalls from Tariff Law," *Wall Street Journal*, December 5, 2002, pp. A1, A14.
32. "What if There Weren't Any Clocks to Watch?" *Newsweek*, June 30, 1997, p. 14.
33. Geert Hofstede, *Culture's Consequences: International Differences in Work Related Values* (Beverly Hills, Calif.: Sage, 1980).
34. I have taken the liberty of changing the actual labels applied to each dimension for several reasons. The terms I have chosen to use are more descriptive, simpler, and more self-evident in their meaning.
35. Geert Hofstede, "The Business of International Business Is Culture," *International Business Review*, vol. 3, no. 1, 1994, pp. 1–14.
36. "Crazy for Crunchies," *Newsweek*, April 28, 1997, p. 49.
37. Stratford Sherman, "Are You as Good as the Best in the World?" *Fortune*, December 13, 1993, pp. 95–96.

6

The Multicultural Environment

CHAPTER OUTLINE

The Nature of Diversity and Multiculturalism

Diversity and Multiculturalism in Organizations

Trends in Diversity and Multiculturalism

Dimensions of Diversity and Multiculturalism

Effects of Diversity and Multiculturalism in Organizations

Diversity, Multiculturalism, and Competitive Advantage

Diversity, Multiculturalism, and Conflict

Managing Diversity and Multiculturalism in Organizations

Individual Strategies

Organizational Approaches

Toward the Multicultural Organization

LEARNING OBJECTIVES

After studying this chapter, you should be able to:

1 ***Describe the nature of diversity and multiculturalism.***

OPENING INCIDENT

The world's first microprocessor, a "computer on a chip," was built by the small Silicon Valley high-tech startup called Intel in 1971. The firm's breakthrough technology allowed the processing power of a 3,000-cubic-foot ENIAC computer (the most powerful available just a few years earlier) to be contained in a space the size of a thumbnail. That invention drove the growth of the modern-day Intel, a giant semiconductor chip maker, employing 85,000 workers in forty-five countries. The firm has been phenomenally successful, producing more than 80 percent of all semiconductor chips sold worldwide.

Today, Intel's managers are faced with the difficult task of running sales and production facilities on every continent. In its international operations, Intel must balance a number of needs simultaneously—to be efficient, to remain competitive, to share resources and learning, to consider issues of equity and fairness, and to be sensitive to local norms and laws. Each region and each country requires knowledge of different languages, customs, religions, work practices, and government regulations. For example, in some countries the firm is required to provide health

2

Identify and describe the major trends and dimensions of diversity and multiculturalism in organizations.

3

Discuss the primary effects of diversity and multiculturalism in organizations.

4

Describe individual strategies for and organizational approaches to managing diversity and multiculturalism in organizations.

5

Discuss the six characteristics of the fully multicultural organization.

"Understand your own diversity and value it."

—Gustavo de la Torre, Intel's Worldwide Diversity Initiatives Manager

Intel's diverse workforce helps it remain competitive in a rapidly changing business world.

and life insurance to all employees. In other countries, health insurance is provided by the government, and in yet other areas, choices about insurance benefits are left up to each firm.

In the United States, Intel managers are responsible for helping employees who are foreign nationals adjust to work life in America. Many of the firm's employees in the States are engineers and scientists from overseas who are here on an H-1B temporary visa. This type of visa allows them to work for a limited time in "specialty" occupations, such as engineering, mathematics, the physical sciences, medicine, education, business, law, theology, and the arts. A specialty occupation requires theoretical and practical application of a body of specialized knowledge, along with at least a bachelor's degree or its equivalent. Intel hires hundreds of employees under this program each year, mainly Indians, Chinese, and Russians.

To cope with its many different national cultures, both in overseas locations and in the United States, Intel has built an organization that seeks out, encourages, and rewards diversity. Of the 54,000 employees in the United States, 17,000, or about one-third, are ethnic minorities. The firm's website has several pages devoted to diversity and immigration issues, beginning with a statement of the firm's diversity commitment. It says, in part, "From individuals to ideas, Intel champions diversity. We believe that the wide-ranging cultures, perspectives and experiences of our workforce are key to the success of our company and our people." A former Intel employee says, "There is not as much of a problem with a stagnant 'old boys network' as at other firms." The firm's managers have worked to establish a culture of "egalitarianism and meritocracy." For workers of different ethnicities, this means that they will be judged based only on the quality of their work.

To help diverse workers understand their role at Intel and be more comfortable at work, a Multicultural Education Program trains all new employees on workplace expectations. This program benefits new college graduates and those new to the high-tech sector as much as it does the foreign-born workers. The class covers the gamut of issues, from personal hygiene and professional dress, to the need for assertiveness, to familiarization with American slang. The firm even surveys new employees to find out their needs, so that it can tailor training for them. In the past, foreign-born workers have described their discomfort with calling their boss by his or her first name, criticizing their boss, and speaking up in large meetings.

Intel works hard to ensure that every employee feels that he or she belongs to the corporation's unique culture and that each can make a valuable contribution to the firm. Yet the focus is not on forcing people to assimilate into U.S. culture. Gustavo de la Torre, Intel's Worldwide Diversity Initiatives Manager, advises new hires, "Understand your own diversity and value it. We all have bias and that's part of recognizing your own diversity."[1]

Like many other organizations in the world today, Intel faces a variety of challenges, opportunities, and issues in its quest to remain competitive in its industry. One key ingredient in the firm's continued success is its ability to attract, motivate, and retain talented employees who reflect diversity from a variety of perspectives and to meld them into a focused and dedicated workforce. Their multicultural backgrounds pose challenges for the firm but also provide enormous potential. This chapter is about diversity and multiculturalism in organizations. We begin by describing trends in diversity and multiculturalism, and identify and discuss several common dimensions of diversity. The effects of diversity and multiculturalism on organizations are then explored. We next address individual strategies for and organizational approaches to managing diversity and multiculturalism. Finally, we characterize and describe the fully multicultural organization.

The Nature of Diversity and Multiculturalism

We introduce the concept of organization culture in Chapter 3. We also note some of the basic managerial issues associated with doing business across national cultures in Chapter 5. At a much broader level, then, culture can be used to characterize the community of people who comprise an entire society. But a different set of issues involving social culture also arises within the boundaries of an organization. In other words, when the people comprising an organization represent different national cultures, their differences in values, beliefs, behaviors, customs, and attitudes pose unique opportunities and challenges for managers. These broad issues are generally referred to as **multiculturalism**.

multiculturalism The broad issues associated with differences in values, beliefs, behaviors, customs, and attitudes held by people in different cultures.

diversity Exists in a group or organization when its members differ from one another along one or more important dimensions, such as age, gender, or ethnicity

A related area of interest is diversity. **Diversity** exists in a community of people when its members differ from one another along one or more important dimensions. These differences can obviously reflect the multicultural composition of a community. In the business world, however, the term *diversity* per se is more generally used to refer to demographic differences among people within a culture—differences in gender, age, ethnicity, and so forth. Diversity is not an absolute phenomenon, of course, wherein a group or organization is or is not diverse. Instead, diversity can be conceptualized as a continuum. If everyone in the community is exactly like everyone else, there is no diversity whatsoever. If everyone is different along every imaginable dimension, total diversity exists. In reality, of course, these extremes are more hypothetical than real. Most settings are characterized by a level of diversity somewhere between these extremes. Therefore, diversity should be thought of in terms of degree or level of diversity along relevant dimensions.

Organization culture, multiculturalism, and diversity are all closely interrelated. For example, the culture of an organization will affect the levels of diversity and multiculturalism that exist within its boundaries. Intel, for example, has an open and accepting culture that promotes diversity throughout its business. And similarities and differences arising from diversity and multicultural forces will also influence the culture of an organization. In addition, social culture and diversity are interrelated. For example, the norms reflected in a social culture will partially determine how that culture values demographic differences among people of that culture.

Each of these levels of culture represents important opportunities and challenges for managers. As we will see, if managers effectively understand, appreciate, and manage diversity and multiculturalism, their organization is more likely to be effective. But, if managers ignore cultural forces or, even worse, attempt to circumvent or control them, then their organization is almost certain to experience serious problems.

concept CHECK

Define multiculturalism and diversity.	*How are multiculturalism and diversity related? How are they distinct?*

Diversity and Multiculturalism in Organizations

Beyond their strict definitions, diversity and multiculturalism essentially relate to differences among people. Therefore, because organizations today are becoming more diverse and multicultural, it is important that all managers understand the major trends and dimensions of diversity and multiculturalism.

Trends in Diversity and Multiculturalism

The most fundamental trend in diversity and multiculturalism is that virtually all organizations, simply put, are becoming more diverse and multicultural. The composition of their workforce is changing in many different ways. The basic reasons for this trend are illustrated in Figure 6.1.

One factor contributing specifically to increased diversity is changing demographics in the labor force. As more women and minorities have entered the labor force, for example, the available pool of talent from which organizations hire employees has changed in both size and composition. If talent within each segment of the labor pool is evenly distributed (for example, if the number of very talented men in the workforce as a percentage of all

Year in and year out Fannie Mae, the Washington D.C. financial services organization, comes in at or near the top of the list of best places to work for minorities. As shown here, the organization's top management team itself reflects diversity along virtually every possible dimension.

FIGURE 6.1

Reasons for Increasing Diversity and Multiculturalism

Diversity and multiculturalism are increasing in most organizations today for four basic reasons. These reasons promise to make diversity even greater in the future.

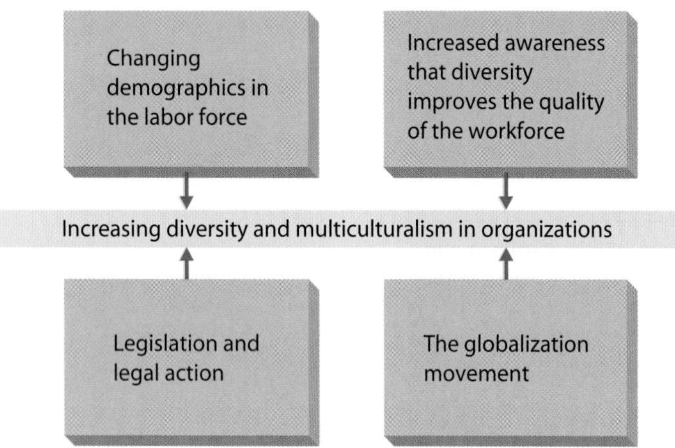

men in the workforce is the same as the number of very talented women in the labor force as a percentage of all women in the workforce), it follows logically that, over time, proportionately more women and proportionately fewer men will be hired by an organization. For example, suppose that a firm's top management team is 90 percent men and only 10 percent women. If the relevant labor pool is, say, 40 percent female, then women are clearly underrepresented in this firm. Over time, though, as men leave and are replaced by women at a percentage close to their representation in the labor pool, the composition of the top management team will gradually move closer to reflecting that labor pool.

A related factor contributing to diversity is organizations' increased awareness that they can improve the overall quality of their workforce by hiring and promoting the most talented people available. By casting a broader net in recruiting and looking beyond traditional sources for new employees, organizations are finding more broadly qualified and better-qualified employees from many different segments of society. Thus these organizations are finding that diversity can be a source of competitive advantage.[2]

Another reason for the increase in diversity is that both legislation and judicial decisions have forced organizations to hire more broadly. In earlier times, organizations in the United States were essentially free to discriminate against women, African-Americans, and other minorities. Although not all organizations consciously or openly engaged in these practices, many firms nevertheless came to be dominated by white males. But, starting with the passage of the Civil Rights Act in 1964, numerous laws have outlawed discrimination against these and most other groups. As we detail in Chapter 14, organizations must hire and promote people today solely on the basis of their qualifications.

A final factor contributing to increased multiculturalism in particular is the globalization movement. Organizations that have opened offices and related facilities in other countries have had to learn to deal with different customs, social norms, and mores. Strategic alliances and foreign ownership also contribute, as managers today are more likely to have job assignments in other countries or to work with foreign managers within their own countries. As employees and managers move from assignment to assignment across national boundaries, organizations and their subsidiaries within each country thus become more diverse and multicultural.

Increased multiculturalism and diversity can result in conflict for a variety of different reasons. A variety of factors can account for this conflict. In the example shown here, for instance, problems are almost certain! But if Santa can figure out how to effectively blend the diverse experiences and abilities of his new team, then he is likely to have even more success than before.

"I think I preferred it before he became an equal-opportunity employer."

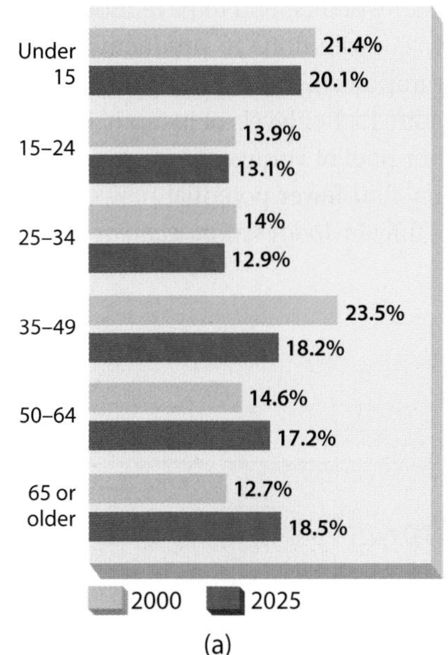

(a)

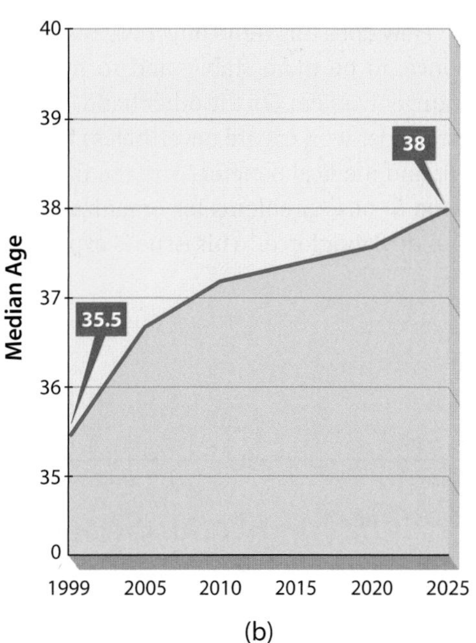

(b)

FIGURE 6.2

Age Distribution Trends in the United States

The U.S. population is gradually growing older. For example, in 1999 the median age in the United States was 35.5 years; by 2025, however, this figure will rise to 38 years. By that same year, more than one-third of the entire U.S. population will be over age 50.

Source: U.S. Census Bureau.

Dimensions of Diversity and Multiculturalism

As we indicate earlier, many different dimensions of diversity and multiculturalism can characterize an organization. In this section we discuss age, gender, ethnicity, and other dimensions of diversity.

Age Distributions One important dimension of diversity in any organization is the age distribution of its workers. The average age of the U.S. workforce is gradually increasing and will continue to do so for the next several years. Figure 6.2 presents age distributions for U.S. workers in 1999 and projected age distributions through the year 2025; over that span, the median age is expected to rise from 35.5 years to 38 years. Moreover, as shown in Figure 6.3, this trend is truly an international phenomenon, with Japan leading the way.

Several factors are contributing to this pattern. For one, the baby-boom generation (a term used to describe the unusually large number of people who were born in the twenty-year period after World War II) continues to age. Declining birth rates among the post-baby-boom generations simultaneously account for smaller percentages of new entrants into the labor force. Another factor that contributes to the aging workforce is improved health and medical care. As a result of these improvements, people are able to remain productive and active for longer periods of time. Combined with higher legal

FIGURE 6.3

Aging populations represent new challenges for industrialized countries. As the proportion of working people drops there are increased pressures on retirement funds, for example, and an aging population also means higher health care costs. As this graph illustrates, the average age in Japan, Germany, China, and the United States continues to grow. Japan, with the world's longest average lifespan, has especially significant challenges ahead.

Source: From *Wall Street Journal*, February 11, 2003. Copyright © 2003 by Dow Jones & Co., Inc. Reproduced with permission of Dow Jones & Co., Inc. via Copyright Clearance Center.

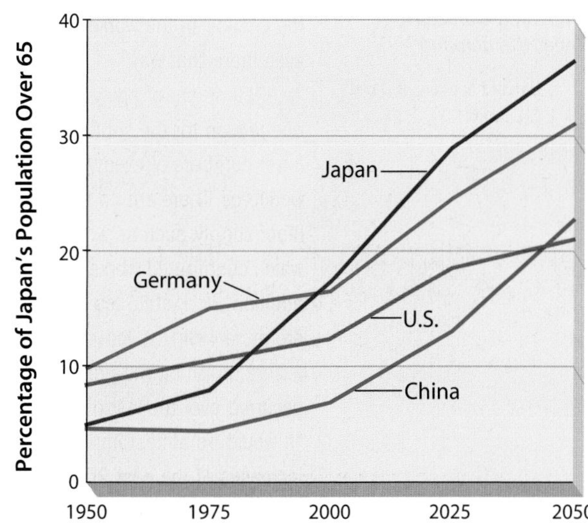

limits for mandatory retirement, more and more people are working beyond the age at which they might have retired just a few years ago.

How does this trend affect organizations? Older workers tend to have more experience, to be more stable, and to make greater contributions to productivity than younger workers. On the other hand, despite the improvements in health and medical care, older workers are nevertheless likely to require higher levels of insurance coverage and medical benefits. And the declining labor pool of younger workers will continue to pose problems for organizations as they find fewer potential new entrants into the labor force.[3] This issue is explored more fully in *Today's Management Issues.*

TODAY'S management ISSUES

On the Horizon, a Labor Shortage Looms

". . . we're not going to have enough college-educated workers to meet the demand."

— Harvard economist David T. Ellwood*

Layoffs have become common in the American economy, as businesses face slowing demand and a shrinking high-tech sector. In October 2002, 4.1 million persons in the United States were unemployed, of a workforce of 130 million.

However, James E. Oesterreicher, labor expert, says, "The U.S. faces a worker gap and a skills gap—and both are right around the corner." Even as the economy remains stalled, unemployment has held steady, at a modest 5.6 percent. Labor shortages are beginning in health care and construction. Harvard economist Dale W. Jorgenson claims, "If employers thought the '90s were the decade of the worker, the next decade will be even more that way."

Retirement of aging baby-boomers is just one reason for the shortage. Another factor is the lower numbers of twenty-somethings entering the workforce. There are no untapped pockets of labor supply, such as women or immigrants, which contributed workers during the 1990s. In addition, work attitudes have shifted, and workers are more willing to leave jobs to gain time for leisure or family. The productivity gains that occurred over the last decade may be at a limit. "It would be almost impossible to match the increases of the past 20 years," says David T. Ellwood, Harvard economist. Finally, the pool of new labor entrants, such as welfare-to-work recipients, is almost depleted.

Employers may choose to offer incentives to attract applicants, or they may concentrate on better retention of current employees. Workers can best prepare themselves for the change by seeking higher education, especially in technical or professional fields. Ellwood states, "If you believe that technological change isn't going to slow down, we're not going to have enough college-educated workers to meet the demand." Although layoffs grew in 2002, they grew much more rapidly for low-skilled workers than for professionals. John Challenger, CEO of an outplacement firm, claims, "Even when the economy is fully recovered and companies are back in expansion mode, we may not see a revival in hiring of the rank-and-file worker." The proverb "A rising tide raises all boats" may be true, but it may not raise all boats equally.

References: Aaron Bernstein, "Too Many Workers? Not for Long," *BusinessWeek*, May 20, 2002, www.businessweek.com on November 23, 2002 (*quote); "Lower Paid Workers Face Job Cuts," *CNN Money*, September 10, 2002, money.cnn.com on November 23, 2002; "Statement of U.S. Secretary of Labor Elaine L. Chao on Unemployment Numbers for October 2002," U.S. Department of Labor, November 23, 2002, www.dol.gov on November 23, 2002; "Table A-7. Reason for Unemployment," U.S. Bureau of Labor Statistics, November 1, 2002, www.bls.gov on November 23, 2002.

Gender As more and more women have entered the workforce, organizations have subsequently experienced changes in the relative proportions of male and female employees. In the United States, for example, the workforce in 1964 was 66 percent male and 34 percent female. In 1994 the relative proportions had changed to 54 percent male and 46 percent female. By 2000 the proportions were around 52 percent male and 48 percent female.

These trends aside, a major gender-related problem that many organizations face today is the so-called glass ceiling. The **glass ceiling** describes a barrier that keeps women from advancing to top-management positions in many organizations.[4] This ceiling is a real barrier that is difficult to break, but it is also so subtle as to be hard to see. Indeed, whereas women comprise over 45 percent of all managers, there are very few female CEOs among the thousand largest businesses in the United States. Similarly, the average pay of women in organizations is lower than that of men. Although the pay gap is gradually shrinking, inequalities are present nonetheless.

glass ceiling A perceived barrier that exists in some organizations that keeps women from advancing to top-management positions

Why does the glass ceiling still seem to exist? One reason may be that real obstacles to advancement for women, such as subtle discrimination, may still exist in some organizations.[5] Another is that many talented women choose to leave their job in a large organization and start their own business. Still another factor is that some women choose to suspend or slow their career progression to have children. But there are also many talented women continuing to work their way up the corporate ladder and getting closer and closer to a corporate "top spot."[6] An interesting consequence of this trend is described in *Working with Diversity*.

ethnicity The ethnic composition of a group or organization

Ethnicity A third major dimension of cultural diversity in organizations is ethnicity. **Ethnicity** refers to the ethnic composition of a group or organization. Within the United States, most organizations reflect varying degrees of ethnicity, comprising whites, African Americans, Latinos, and Asians. Figure 6.4 shows the ethnic composition of the U.S. workforce in 1999 and as projected for the year 2025 in terms of these ethnic groups.[7]

John Avila is just one of literally millions of Hispanic business owners in the United States. His Old Town Albuquerque store "Casa de Avila" has become a booming success by catering to the needs of the city's tourists.

The biggest projected changes involve whites and Latinos. In particular, the percentage of whites in the workforce is expected to drop from 72 percent to 62.4 percent. At the same time, the percentage of Latinos is expected to climb from 11.5 percent to 17.6 percent. The percentage of African Americans, Asians, and others is also expected to climb, but at lower rates. As with women, members of the African American, Latino, and Asian groups are generally underrepresented in the executive ranks of most organizations today. And their pay is similarly lower than might be expected. But, as is also the case for women, the differences are gradually disappearing as organizations fully embrace

FIGURE 6.4

Ethnicity Distribution Trends in the United States

Ethnic diversity in the United States is also increasing. For example, although 72 percent of the U.S. population was white in 1999, this will drop to 62.4 percent by 2025. Latinos will reflect the largest percentage increase, moving from 11.5 percent in 1999 to 17.6 percent of the U.S. population by 2025.

Source: U.S. Census Bureau.

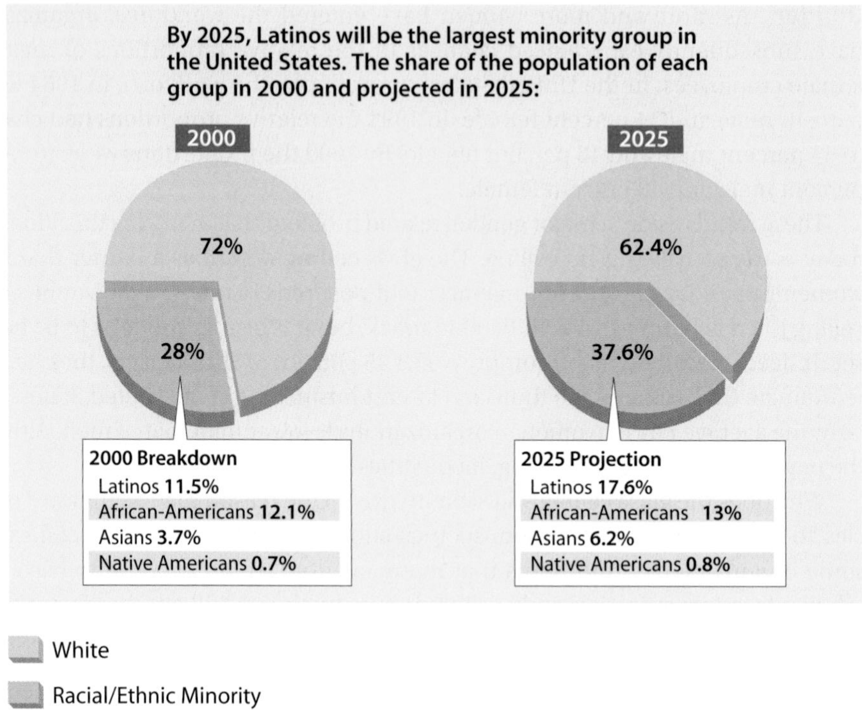

equal employment opportunity and recognize the higher overall level of talent available to them.[8]

Other Dimensions of Diversity In addition to age, gender, and ethnicity, organizations are confronting other dimensions of diversity. Handicapped and physically challenged employees are increasingly important in many organizations, especially since the recent passage of the Americans with Disabilities Act. Different religious beliefs also constitute an important dimension of diversity.[9] And single parents, dual-career couples, gays and lesbians, people with special dietary preferences (such as vegetarians), and people with different political ideologies and viewpoints also represent major dimensions of diversity in today's organizations.[10]

Multicultural Differences In addition to these various diversity-related dimensions, organizations are increasingly being characterized by multicultural differences as well. Some organizations, especially international businesses, are actively seeking to enhance the multiculturalism of their workforce. But even organizations that are more passive in this regard may still become more multicultural because of changes in the external labor market. Immigration into the United States is at its highest rate since 1910, for example. Over 5 million people from Asia, Mexico, Europe, and other parts of the world entered the United States between 1991 and 1995 alone.[11]

concept CHECK

Identify several dimensions of diversity that are most relevant to organizations.	*How might these dimensions be related to one another?*

WORKING WITH diversity

Wanted: Stay-at-Home Husband

"A precondition to having more women in positions of power is to have more sharing in the burdens of parenthood."

– Dina Dublon, chief financial officer, J.P. Morgan Chase*

The "glass ceiling" hypothesis claims that working women are the victims of gender discrimination. But only 45 percent of successful executive women mention stereotyping as a barrier to advancement, whereas 68 percent cite family responsibilities. According to these women, prejudice is not the biggest issue—what they really need is a wife. Executive women may choose not to have children—49 percent of women executives are childless, compared to 10 percent of men. But for those female managers who want to have a family, their husbands are the best caregivers for the kids. Dina Dublon, chief financial officer at J.P. Morgan Chase bank, says, "A precondition to having more women in positions of power is to have more sharing in the burdens of parenthood."

In the Stevens family, director Anne heads twenty-nine Ford manufacturing plants, while househusband Bill describes his job as "the domestic executive assistant." The situation is the same at the Lepore household, where wife Dawn is a vice chairman of Charles Schwab. Ditto for Anne Mulcahy, CEO of Xerox; Carly Fiorina, CEO of Hewlett Packard; and many, many more.

It would not be fair to categorize their spouses as "trophy husbands." Most of them were successful businessmen who chose to retire early or work part time in order to support their wife's career. Few expected to be in this situation. Terry Brennan, whose wife is a Ford executive, claims, "It's taking a while to adjust to this. I've been programmed all my life to be a provider."

Echoing a sentiment expressed by many working women, Brennan says a lack of role models makes being a full-time dad tough. "My father still doesn't know a washer from a dryer." Househusbands suffer from other all-too-familiar problems, such as the boredom and frustration of spending all day without adult companionship. On their part, the working moms admit they sometimes feel guilty and, even worse, they fear they are missing out on their children's lives.

These families feel that they are radical. However, their division of labor is in fact quite traditional, with one working partner and one stay-at-home partner. The spouses have traded places, but the fundamental challenges of raising a family while reaching career success remain the same.

References: Betsy Morris, "Trophy Husbands," *Fortune*, September 27, 2002, www.fortune.com on December 8, 2002 (*quote); Lisa Belkin, "Do Women Lack Drive? Or a Wife?" *New York Times*, October 13, 2002, p. NJ-1; Marci Alboher Nusbaum, "Creative Thinking by a Working Mom," *New York Times*, October 27, 2002, p. BU-14.

Effects of Diversity and Multiculturalism in Organizations

There is no question that organizations are becoming ever more diverse and multicultural. But how does this affect organizations? As we see, diversity and management provide both opportunities and challenges for organizations. They also play a number of important roles in organizations today.

Diversity, Multiculturalism, and Competitive Advantage

Many organizations are finding that diversity and multiculturalism can be a source of competitive advantage in the marketplace. In general, six arguments have been proposed for how they contribute to competitiveness.[12] These are illustrated in Figure 6.5.

The *cost argument* suggests that organizations that learn to manage diversity and multiculturalism generally have higher levels of productivity and lower levels of turnover and absenteeism. Those organizations that do a poor job of managing diversity and multiculturalism, on the other hand, suffer from problems of lower productivity and higher levels of turnover and absenteeism. Because each of these factors has a direct impact on costs, the former types of organizations remain more competitive than will the latter. Ortho McNeil Pharmaceutical estimates that it has saved $500,000 by lowering turnover among women and ethnic minorities.[13]

The *resource acquisition argument* suggests that organizations that manage diversity and multiculturalism effectively become known among women and minorities as good places to work. These organizations are thus better able to attract qualified employees from among these groups. Given the increased importance of these groups in the overall labor force, organizations that can attract talented employees from all segments of society are likely to be more competitive.[14] Table 6.1 lists companies that have an especially good reputation as a good place for minorities to work.

The *marketing argument* suggests that organizations with a diverse and multicultural workforce are better able to understand different market segments than are less diverse organizations. For example, a cosmetics firm like Avon, which wants to sell its products to women and African-Americans, can better understand how to create such products and effectively market them if women and African-American managers are available to provide inputs into product development, design, packaging, advertising, and so forth.[15] Similarly, both Sears and Target have profited by focusing part of their marketing efforts on building consumer awareness among Latinos.[16] *Technology Toolkit,* on page 187, illustrates another perspective on the marketing argument for diversity.

The *creativity argument* suggests that organizations with diverse and multicultural workforces are generally more creative and innovative than other organizations. If an organization is dominated by one population segment, it follows that its members will generally adhere to norms and ways of thinking that reflect that segment. Moreover, they have little insight or stimulus for new ideas that might be derived from different perspectives. The diverse and multicultural organization, in contrast, is characterized by multiple perspectives and ways of thinking and is therefore more likely to generate new ideas and ways of doing things.[17]

FIGURE 6.5

How Diversity and Multiculturalism Promote Competitive Advantage

Many organizations today are finding that diversity and multiculturalism can be sources of competitive advantage. Various arguments have been developed to support this viewpoint. For example, an African-American sales representative for Revlon helped that firm improve its packaging and promotion for its line of darker skin-tone cosmetics.

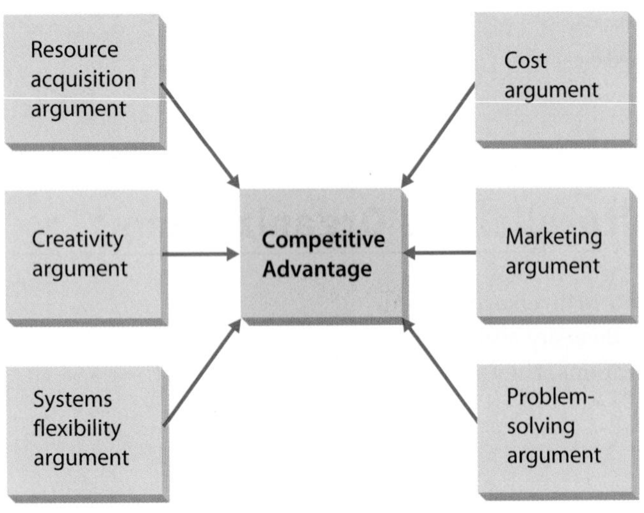

TABLE 6.1

America's Best Companies for Minorities

Rank, 2003 (2002) Company	**No. of Minorities**		**% Minorities**	
2002 Revenues (millions)	**Board of Directors**	**Top-paid 50**	**Officials and Managers**	**Workforce (Asian, Black, Hispanic, Native American)**
1 (5) **McDonald's** Oak Brook, Ill. **$15,406**	2 of 16	10	36.6%	52.6% (4.0%, 17.6%, 27.9%, 3.0%)
2 (1) **Fannie Mae** Washington, D.C. **$52,901**	5 of 17	11	32.6%	43.7% (13.6%, 25.5%, 4.2%, 0.4%)
3 (3) **Denny's** Spartanburg, S.C. **$1,128**	3 of 9	8	28.9%	46.7% (5.3%, 12.0%, 29.3%, 0.1%)
4 (11) **Union Bank of Calif.** San Francisco **$2,592**	3 of 12	2	38.9%	55.8% (25.7%, 8.3%, 21.3%, 0.5%)
5 (2) **Sempra Energy** San Diego, CA **$6,020**	4 of 14	5	28.9%	47.6% (8.6%, 10.1%, 28.2%, 0.8%)
6 (7) **Southern Calif. Edison** Rosemead, Calif. **$8,706**	2 of 11	9	28.5%	43.6% (8.5%, 8.7%, 25.5%, 0.9%)
7 (4) **SBC Communications** San Antonio **$43,138**	3 of 21	7	29.0%	37.8% (4.7%, 19.8%, 12.7%, 0.6%)
8 (9) **Freddie Mac** McLean, Va **$39,663**	3 of 18	8	28.1%	32.5% (14.4%, 14.3%, 3.4%, 0.3%)
9 (15) **PepsiCo** Purchase, N.Y. **$25,112**	4 of 14	8	17.1%	26.9% (2.3%, 13.7%, 10.6%, 0.4%)

(continued)

TABLE 6.1

America's Best Companies for Minorities (*continued*)

Rank, 2003 (2002) Company	**No. of Minorities**		**% Minorities**	
2002 Revenues (millions)	**Board of Directors**	**Top-paid 50**	**Officials and Managers**	**Workforce (Asian, Black, Hispanic, Native American)**
10 (6) **PNM Resources** Albuquerque **$1,169**	3 of 10	16	34.6%	47.9% (0.8%, 1.9%, 40.8%, 4.4%)
11 (8) **U.S. Postal Service** Washington, D.C. **$66,463**	1 of 9	18	31.3%	36.3% (7.0%, 21.2%, 7.5%, 0.6%)
12 (17) **Wyndham International** Dallas **$1,871**	2 of 19	4	30.7%	61.6% (5.0%, 21.5%, 33.8%, 1.3%)
13 (14) **Xerox** Stamford, Conn. **$15,849**	2 of 8	12	22.2%	29.8% (5.3%, 15.6%, 8.1%, 0.7%)
14 (26) **Applied Materials** Santa Clara, Calif. **$5,062**	0 of 9	14	29.9%	38.9% (24.0%, 5.2%, 9.5%, 0.3%)

Source: Adapted from *Fortune*, July 7, 2003.

Related to the creativity argument is the *problem-solving argument.* Diversity and multiculturalism are accompanied by an increased pool of information. In virtually any organization there is some information that everyone has and other information that is unique to each individual. In an organization with little diversity, the larger pool of information is common, and the smaller pool is unique. But, in a more diverse organization, the unique information is larger. Thus, because more information can be brought to bear on a problem, there is a higher probability that better solutions can be identified.[18]

Finally, the *systems flexibility argument* suggests that organizations must become more flexible as a way of managing a diverse and multicultural workforce. As a direct consequence, the overall organizational system also becomes more flexible. As we discuss in Chapters 3 and 13, organizational flexibility enables the organization to better respond to changes in its environment. Thus, by effectively managing

TECHNOLOGY toolkit

Non-Americans Online

"It gives you an incentive to use a service—if it's multilingual."

– Brigitte E. Biver, a German working for Commerzbank in the United States*

Americans were the first enthusiastic adopters of the Internet. So it is not surprising that in 1996, 80 percent of all websites were created in English. Most users, wherever they were located and whatever language they spoke, could read at least some of what they saw. But, in the last few years, the strongest online growth has occurred outside the United States. That has led to an explosion in websites that are explicitly designed for users in other cultures.

First, 50 percent of current Internet users are not fluent in English. Website designers rely on language translation tools provided by such companies as TRADOS. One TRADOS customer is Kelly Services, which provides staffing support to 200,000 customers worldwide. The company needed to translate its web content, including training materials, software documentation, and performance appraisals, from English into Spanish, French, German, Dutch, and Italian. Kelly used to perform translations with a permanent staff of ten, at a cost of $255,000 annually. With TRADOS, two employees perform the work, and expenses have dropped by half. Translation time was cut 70 percent.

Second, a mere word-for-word translation is often unsatisfactory, because users in different regions follow different conventions. Therefore, firms developing websites for overseas use must take into account variations in currencies and measurements. When a language is read from right to left or in vertical rows, so, too, are the local websites. Net icons may not be familiar to non-English speakers. Even computers are different overseas. High-speed connections are much less common outside the United States; therefore, sites that are rich in graphics may be unacceptably slow in loading.

American firms are finding that they must reach out to a multicultural customer base of overseas clients and immigrants or risk losing out to foreign competitors. eBay has twenty national sites, from Argentina to the United Kingdom. Amazon, Yahoo! and AOL have all developed international content. However, 55 percent of U.S. business websites are offered only in English. Brigitte E. Biver, a German working in the United States, prefers sites in her native language. "It gives you an incentive to use a service—if it's multilingual," she claims. On the Internet, diverse customers are speaking up, and U.S. firms had better listen.

References: "Babel.net," *BusinessWeek*, December 17, 2000, www.businessweek.com on December 17, 2002; "Kelly Services," "Language Technology for Your Business," TRADOS website, www.trades.com on December 17, 2002; Otis Port, "The Next Web," *BusinessWeek*, March 4, 2002, www.businessweek.com on December 17, 2002; Roger O. Crockett, "Surfing in Tongues," *BusinessWeek*, December 11, 2000, www.businessweek.com on December 17, 2002 (*quote).

diversity and multiculturalism within its workforce, an organization becomes better equipped to address its environment.

Diversity, Multiculturalism, and Conflict

Unfortunately, diversity and multiculturalism in an organization can also create conflict. This conflict can arise for a variety of reasons.[19] One potential avenue for conflict occurs when an individual thinks that someone has been hired, promoted, or fired because of her or his diversity status. For example, suppose that a male executive loses a promotion to a female executive. If he believes that she was promoted because the organization simply wanted to have more female managers, rather than because she was the better candidate for the job, he will likely feel resentful toward both her and the organization itself.

Another source of conflict stemming from diversity or multiculturalism occurs through misunderstood, misinterpreted, or inappropriate interactions among people of different groups.[20] For example, suppose that a male executive tells a sexually explicit joke to a new female executive. He may be intentionally trying to embarrass her, he may be clumsily trying to show her that he treats everyone the same, or he may think he is making her feel part of the team. Regardless of his intent, however, if she finds the joke offensive she will justifiably feel anger and hostility. These feelings may be directed at only the offending individual or more generally toward the entire organization if she believes that its culture facilitates such behaviors. And, of course, sexual harassment itself is both unethical and illegal.

Conflict can also arise as a result of other elements of multiculturalism. For example, when a U.S. manager publicly praises a Japanese employee for his outstanding work, the action stems from the dominant cultural belief in the United States that such recognition is important and rewarding. But, because the Japanese culture places a much higher premium on group loyalty and identity than on individual accomplishment, the employee will likely feel ashamed and embarrassed. Thus a well-intentioned action may backfire and result in unhappiness. A joint venture between IBM (a U.S. company), Siemens (a German company), and Toshiba (a Japanese company) had conflicts among team members attributed to cultural differences in work hours, working styles, and interpersonal relations.[21]

Conflict may also arise as a result of fear, distrust, or individual prejudice. Members of the dominant group in an organization may worry that newcomers from other groups pose a personal threat to their own position in the organization. For example, when U.S. firms have been taken over by Japanese firms, U.S. managers have sometimes been resentful about or hostile toward Japanese managers assigned to work with them. People may also be unwilling to accept people who are different from themselves. And personal bias and prejudices are still very real among some people today and can lead to potentially harmful conflict.

Several high-profile problems involving diversity and multiculturalism have focused attention on the potential for conflict and how important it is that managers respond appropriately when problems occur. Shoney's, Inc., a southern restaurant chain, was charged with racism throughout its managerial ranks. At Texaco, senior executives used racial slurs on a tape subsequently released to the public. A class-action lawsuit against the financial brokerage giant Smith Barney alleged widespread hostilities and discrimination toward women throughout the firm. Wal-Mart is currently under scrutiny for similar practices.[22] In each of these cases, fortunately, the organization involved has undertaken major programs designed to eliminate such problems in the future. Denny's, for example, has taken such aggressive action that it has now become recognized as one of the best companies in the United States for minorities.[23]

concept CHECK

How does diversity promote competitive advantage?	Which causes of diversity-related conflict are most likely to disappear in the future?

Managing Diversity and Multiculturalism in Organizations

Because of the tremendous potential that diversity and multiculturalism hold for competitive advantage, as well as the possible consequences of associated conflict, much attention has been focused in recent years on how individuals and organizations can better manage diversity and multiculturalism. In the sections that follow, we first discuss individual strategies for dealing with diversity and multiculturalism, and then summarize organizational approaches to managing diversity and multiculturalism.

Individual Strategies

One important element of managing diversity and multiculturalism in an organization consists of things that individuals themselves can do. The four basic attitudes that individuals can strive for are understanding, empathy, tolerance, and willingness to communicate.

Understanding The first of these is understanding the nature and meaning of diversity and multiculturalism. Some managers, for example, have taken the basic concepts of equal employment opportunity to an unnecessary extreme. They know that, by law, they cannot discriminate against people on the basis of sex, race, and so forth. Thus, in following this mandate, they come to believe that they must treat everyone the same.

But this belief can cause problems when translated into workplace behaviors among people after they have been hired, because people are not the same. Although people need to be treated fairly and equitably, managers must understand that differences among people do, in fact, exist. Thus any effort to treat everyone the same, without regard for their fundamental human differences, will only lead to problems. Managers must understand that cultural factors cause people to behave in different ways and that these differences should be accepted.

Empathy Related to understanding is empathy. People in an organization should try to understand the perspective of others. For example, suppose a woman joins a group that has traditionally comprised white men. Each man may be a little self-conscious about how to act toward the new member and may be interested in making her feel comfortable and welcome. But they may be able to do this even more effectively by empathizing with how she may feel. For example, she may feel disappointed or elated about her new assignment, she may be confident or nervous about her position in the group, or she may be experienced or inexperienced in working with male colleagues. By learning more about her feelings, the group members can further facilitate their ability to work together effectively.

Tolerance A third related individual strategy for dealing with diversity and multiculturalism is tolerance. Even though people learn to understand others, and even though they may try to empathize with others, the fact remains that they may still not accept or enjoy some aspect of their behavior. For example, one organization reported that it had experienced considerable conflict among its U.S. and Israeli employees. The Israeli employees always seemed to want to argue about every issue that arose. The U.S. managers preferred to conduct business more harmoniously and became uncomfortable with the conflict. Finally, after considerable discussion, it was learned that many of the Israeli employees simply enjoyed arguing and saw it as part of getting the work done. The firm's U.S. employees still do not enjoy the arguing, but they are more willing to tolerate it as a fundamental cultural difference between themselves and their colleagues from Israel.[24]

Willingness to Communicate A final individual approach to dealing with diversity and multiculturalism is communication. Problems often get magnified over these issues because people are afraid or otherwise unwilling to openly discuss issues that relate to diversity or multiculturalism. For example, suppose that a young employee has a habit of making jokes about the age of an older colleague. Perhaps the young colleague means no harm and is just engaging in what she sees as good-natured kidding. But the older employee may find the jokes offensive. If the two do not communicate, the jokes will continue, and the resentment will grow. Eventually, what started as a minor problem may erupt into a much bigger one.

For communication to work, it must work two ways. If a person wonders whether a certain behavior on her or his part is offensive to someone else, the curious individual should just ask. Similarly, if someone is offended by the behavior of another person, he or she should explain to the offending individual how the behavior is perceived and request that it stop. As long as such exchanges are friendly, low key, and nonthreatening, they will generally have a positive outcome. Of course, if the same message is presented in an overly combative manner or if a person continues to engage in offensive behavior after having been asked to stop, problems will only escalate. At this point, third parties within the organization may have to intervene. And, in fact, most organizations today have one or more systems in place to address questions and problems that arise as a result of diversity. We now turn our attention to various ways that organizations can better manage diversity.

Organizational Approaches

Whereas individuals are important in managing diversity and multiculturalism, the organization itself must play a fundamental role.[25] Through the organization's various policies and practices, people in the organization come to understand what behaviors are and are not appropriate. Diversity and multicultural training is an even more direct method for managing diversity. And the organization's culture is the ultimate context in which diversity and multiculturalism must be addressed.

Like many families today, Madhavi Nerurkar and her husband face many challenges in their quest to make ends meet. Just as they bought their first home and had their first child, he lost his job. His new job paid less money and also required that he travel a lot. Hence, Madhavi needed to find a job to help with finances, but also needed flexibility to pick up their son from childcare. Fortunately, her new employer, RFB&D, recognizes the value of diversity and has been more than willing to accommodate her needs.

Organizational Policies The starting point in managing diversity and multiculturalism is the policies that an organization adopts that directly or indirectly affect how people are treated. Obviously, for instance, the extent to which an organization embraces the premise of equal employment opportunity will to a large extent determine the potential diversity within an organization. But the organization that follows the law to the letter and practices only passive discrimination differs from the organization that actively seeks a diverse and varied workforce.

Another aspect of organizational policies that affects diversity and multiculturalism is how the organization addresses and responds to problems that arise from differences among people. For example, consider the example of a manager charged with sexual harassment. If the organization's policies put an excessive burden of proof on the individual being harassed and invoke only minor sanctions against the guilty party, it is sending a clear signal about the importance of such matters. But the organization that has a balanced set of policies for addressing questions like sexual harassment sends its employees a message that diversity and individual rights and privileges are important.

Indeed, perhaps the major policy through which an organization can reflect its stance on diversity and multiculturalism is its mission statement. If the organization's mission statement articulates a clear and direct commitment to differences among people, it follows that everyone who comes in contact with that mission statement will grow to understand and accept the importance of diversity and multiculturalism, at least to that particular organization.

Organizational Practices Organizations can also help manage diversity and multiculturalism through a variety of ongoing practices and procedures. Avon's creation of networks for various groups represents one example of an organizational practice that fosters diversity. In general, the idea is that, because diversity and multiculturalism are characterized by differences among people, organizations can more effectively manage that diversity by following practices and procedures that are based on flexibility rather than on rigidity.

Benefits packages, for example, can be structured to better accommodate individual situations. An employee who is part of a dual-career couple and who has no children may require relatively little insurance (perhaps because his spouse's employer provides more complete coverage) and would like to be able to schedule vacations to coincide with those of his spouse. An employee who is a single parent may need a wide variety of insurance coverage and prefer to schedule his vacation time to coincide with school holidays.

Flexible working hours are also a useful organizational practice for accommodating diversity. Differences in family arrangements, religious holidays, cultural events, and so forth may dictate that employees have some degree of flexibility in when they work. For example, a single parent may need to leave the office every day at 4:30 P.M. to pick up the children from their day-care center. An organization that truly values diversity will make every reasonable attempt to accommodate such a need.

Organizations can also facilitate diversity and multiculturalism by making sure that their important committees and executive teams are diverse. Even if diversity exists within the broader organizational context, an organization that does not reflect diversity in groups like committees and teams implies that diversity is not a fully ingrained element of its culture. In contrast, if all major groups and related work assignments reflect diversity, the message is a quite different one.

Diversity and Multicultural Training Many organizations are finding that diversity and multicultural training is an effective means for managing diversity and minimizing its associated conflict. More specifically, **diversity and multicultural training** is specifically designed to better enable members of an organization to function in a diverse and multicultural workplace.[26] This training can take a variety of forms. For example, many organizations find it useful to help people learn more about their similarities to and differences from others. Men and women can be

diversity and multicultural training Training that is specifically designed to better enable members of an organization to function in a diverse and multicultural workforce

Diversity training is one strategy for helping to manage diversity in organizations. While some experts question its effectiveness, many businesses nevertheless encourage or require their employees to participate in such training. It is especially common in settings that have recently experienced diversity problems or issues, in part perhaps because it is a tangible action that the organization can point to as part of a campaign to overcome bad press and a damaged corporate reputation that can follow a diversity-related controversy. While 3M already has an exemplary record in the area of diversity, these engineers are participating in what the company calls the "Diversity Training Advantage" to help them gain new insights into how they can more effectively work with others.

taught to work together more effectively and can gain insights into how their own behaviors affect and are interpreted by others. In one organization, a diversity training program helped male managers gain insights into how various remarks they made to one another could be interpreted by others as being sexist. In the same organization, female managers learned how to point out their discomfort with those remarks without appearing overly hostile.[27]

Similarly, white and African-American managers may need training to better understand each other. Managers at Mobil Corporation (now a part of ExxonMobil) once noticed that four black colleagues never seemed to eat lunch together. After a diversity training program, they came to realize that the black managers felt that, if they ate together, their white colleagues would be overly curious about what they might be talking about. Thus they avoided close association with one another because they feared calling attention to themselves.[28]

Some organizations even go so far as to provide language training for their employees as a vehicle for managing diversity and multiculturalism. Motorola, for example, provides English-language training for its foreign employees on assignment in the United States. At Pace Foods in San Antonio, with a total payroll of over 450 employees, staff meetings and employee handbooks are translated into Spanish for the benefit of the company's 200 or so Latino employees.

Organization Culture The ultimate test of an organization's commitment to managing diversity and multiculturalism, as discussed earlier in this chapter, is its culture.[29] Regardless of what managers say or put in writing, unless there is a basic and fundamental belief that diversity and multiculturalism are valued, it cannot ever become a truly integral part of an organization. An organization that really wants to promote diversity and multiculturalism must shape its culture so that it clearly underscores top-management commitment to and support of diversity and multiculturalism in all of its forms throughout every part of the organization. With top-management support, however, and reinforced with a clear and consistent set of organizational policies and practices, diversity and multiculturalism can become a fundamental part of an organization.[30]

concept CHECK

Name the individual strategies for managing diversity and multiculturalism in organizations.

In your opinion, which organizational approaches to managing diversity and multiculturalism are most and least likely to be effective? Why?

Toward the Multicultural Organization

Many organizations today are grappling with cultural diversity. We note back in Chapter 5 that, although many organizations are becoming increasingly global, no truly global organization exists. In similar fashion, although organizations are becoming ever

FIGURE 6.6

The Multicultural Organization

Few, if any, organizations have become truly multicultural. At the same time, more and more organizations are moving in this direction. When an organization becomes multicultural, it reflects the six basic characteristics shown here.

Source: Based on Taylor H. Cox, "The Multicultural Organization," *Academy of Management Executive*, May 1991, pp. 34–47. Reprinted with permission.

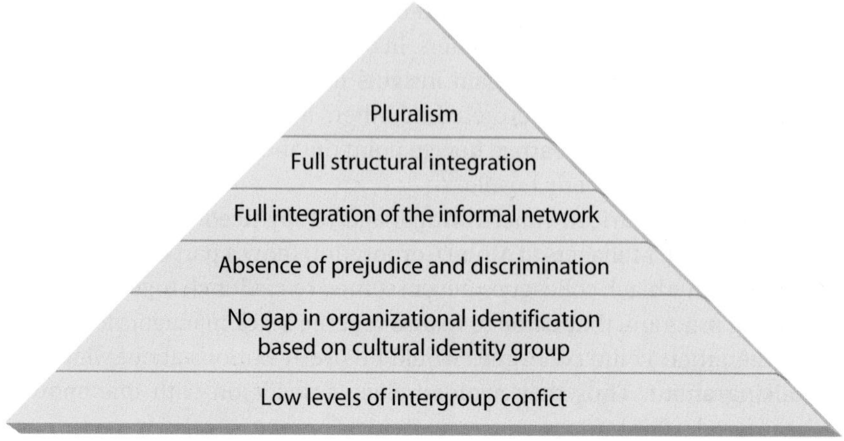

Pluralism

Full structural integration

Full integration of the informal network

Absence of prejudice and discrimination

No gap in organizational identification based on cultural identity group

Low levels of intergroup confict

multicultural organization An organization that has achieved high levels of diversity, is able to fully capitalize on the advantages of diversity, and has few diversity-related problems

more diverse, few are truly multicultural. The **multicultural organization** has achieved high levels of diversity, is able to fully capitalize on the advantages of diversity, and has few diversity-related problems. One recent article described the six basic characteristics of such an organization.[31] These characteristics are illustrated in Figure 6.6.

First, the multicultural organization is characterized by *pluralism*. This means that every group represented in an organization works to better understand every other group. Thus African-American employees try to understand white employees, and white employees try just as hard to understand their African-American colleagues. In addition, every group represented within an organization has the potential to influence the organization's culture and fundamental norms.

Second, the multicultural organization achieves *full structural integration*. Full structural integration suggests that the diversity within an organization is a complete and accurate reflection of the organization's external labor market. If around half of the labor market is female, then about half of the organization's employees are female. Moreover, this same proportion is reflected at all levels of the organization. There are no glass ceilings or other subtle forms of discrimination.

Third, the multicultural organization achieves *full integration of the informal network*. This characteristic suggests that there are no barriers to entry or participation in any organizational activity. For example, people enter and exit lunch groups, social networks, communication grapevines, and other informal aspects of organizational activity without regard to age, gender, ethnicity, or other dimension of diversity.

Fourth, the multicultural organization is characterized by an *absence of prejudice and discrimination*. No traces of bias exist, and prejudice is eliminated. Discrimination is not practiced in any shape, form, or fashion. And discrimination is nonexistent, not because it is illegal, but because of the lack of prejudice and bias. People are valued, accepted, and rewarded purely on the basis of their skills and what they contribute to the organization.

Fifth, in the multicultural organization there is *no gap in organizational identification based on cultural identity group*. In many organizations today, people tend to make presumptions about organizational roles based on group identity. For example, many people walking into an office and seeing a man and woman conversing tend to assume that the woman is the secretary and the man is the manager. No such tendencies exist in the multicultural organization. People recognize that men and women are equally likely to be managers or secretaries.

Finally, there are *low levels of intergroup conflict* in the multicultural organization. We note earlier that conflict is a likely outcome of increased diversity. The multicultural organization has evolved beyond this point to a state of virtually no conflict among people who differ. People within the organization fully understand, empathize with, have tolerance for, and openly communicate with everyone else. Values, premises, motives, attitudes, and perceptions are so well understood by everyone that any conflict that does arise is over meaningful and work-related issues as opposed to differences in age, gender, ethnicity, or other dimensions of diversity.

concept CHECK

What dimensions will reflect the multicultural organization?	*Do you think a truly multicultural business organization will ever exist? Why or why not?*

Summary of Key Points

business.college.hmco.com/students

When the people comprising an organization represent different cultures, their differences in values, beliefs, behaviors, customs, and attitudes reflect multiculturalism. Diversity exists in a community of people when its members differ from one another along one or more important dimensions.

Diversity and multiculturalism are increasing in organizations today because of changing demographics, the desire by organizations to improve their workforce, legal pressures, and increased globalization. There are several important dimensions of diversity, including age, gender, and ethnicity. The overall age of the workforce is increasing. More women are also entering the workplace, although there is still a glass ceiling in many settings. In the United States, more Latinos are also entering the workplace as the percentage of whites gradually decreases.

Diversity and multiculturalism can affect an organization in a number of different ways. For example, they can be a source of competitive advantage (cost, resource acquisition, marketing, creativity, problem-solving, and systems flexibility arguments). On the other hand, diversity and multiculturalism can also be a source of conflict in an organization.

Managing diversity and multiculturalism in organizations can be done by both individuals and the organization itself. Individual strategies include understanding, empathy, tolerance, and willingness to communicate. Major organizational approaches are through policies, practices, diversity training, and culture.

Few, if any, organizations have become truly multicultural. The major dimensions that characterize organizations as they eventually achieve this state are pluralism, full structural integration, full integration of the informal network, an absence of prejudice and discrimination, no gap in organizational identification based on cultural identity group, and low levels of intergroup conflict attributable to diversity.

Discussion Questions

Questions for Review

1. What are the dimensions of diversity?
2. Summarize the six arguments used to describe how the effective management of diversity can lead to a competitive advantage.
3. Discuss the four basic individual approaches and the four basic organizational approaches to diversity and multiculturalism.
4. What are the characteristics of a multicultural organization?

Questions for Analysis

5. In your opinion, are the "other" dimensions of diversity likely to have a greater or a lesser impact than the basic dimensions? Explain your answer.
6. The text outlines many different advantages of diversity and multiculturalism in organizations. Can you think of any disadvantages?
7. Think of a time when issues of diversity or multiculturalism created an advantage or led to positive outcomes at school or work. What actions did the participants take to lead to that positive outcome?

Questions for Application

8. Visit the registrar's office or admissions office at your college or university, or find information about admissions from your school's website. What actions, if any, is your school taking to increase diversity? If it is not taking any action, why do you think that is the case? If it is taking action, do you think the actions are likely to be effective, and why?
9. Consider the case of an employee who is part of a minority group on one dimension of diversity. What are some of the potential problems that this employee might encounter? What are some ways that this employee's supervisor can help alleviate these problems?
10. Assume that you work for a large multinational organization. You have just learned that you are being transferred overseas, to an office in which you will be the first person of your ethnicity to work there. What steps might you take before you go to minimize problems that your presence might cause?

BUILDING EFFECTIVE technical SKILLS

business.college.hmco.com/students

Exercise Overview

Technical skills are the skills necessary to accomplish or understand the specific kind of work being done in an organization. This exercise asks you to use the Internet to gather information about issues of diversity and multiculturalism, and then to consider those issues from a manager's point of view.

Exercise Background

An organization's definition and measurement of diversity are crucial to determining how diversity concerns are addressed. Assume that you are a top manager at your college or university. Your school is committed to maintaining an appropriate level of diversity within the student body. You are assigned the task of making a report to the school's policy-making board, describing the school's current level of diversity and any areas of concern.

Exercise Task

1. Use the Internet to gather information about the gender and ethnic diversity of your school's student body. Then gather information about your school's workforce—the faculty and staff. (*Hint:* Your school's web pages related to admissions and human resources might be helpful.)
2. Use the Internet to gather information about the diversity of your school's state and local communities, and about the United States as a nation. (*Hint:* The U.S. Census Bureau's web pages devoted to Census 2000 have information for country, states, and counties. See www.census.gov.)
3. Based on the information you have gathered, is your school's student body at the appropriate level of diversity? Tell why or why not.
4. What are some areas that need improvement in the diversity of your school's student body, if any?

BUILDING EFFECTIVE time-management SKILLS

Exercise Overview

Time-management skills refer to the manager's ability to prioritize work, to work efficiently, and to delegate appropriately. This exercise helps you explore your personal values and their relationship to the importance you place on various tasks.

Exercise Background

Each person is unique, based on unique characteristics, background, heritage, relationships, and experiences. Our uniqueness extends to our values, as each of us places more or less importance on different aspects of our life. For some, religion may be the primary motivator, whereas for others, a marriage or an occupation is extremely important.

Values play a key role in helping to assign priorities to tasks in daily life. In an ideal world, more time would be spent on tasks of greater importance and less time on relatively unimportant tasks. However, for many, mundane demands may take precedence. This in-class demonstration serves to clarify values and to encourage values-based time management.

Exercise Task

1. Listen as your instructor provides a demonstration to the class.
2. What are your "rocks"? What are your "pebbles"? What are your "grains of sand"?
3. Based on the above classification, what are your most important personal values?
4. Do you usually spend more time on tasks that support your most important values? Why or why not?
5. Describe some actions that you could take to ensure that more of your time is spent on tasks related to your most important values.

BUILDING EFFECTIVE decision-making SKILLS

Exercise Overview

Decision-making skills refer to the manager's ability to recognize and effectively define problems and opportunities correctly and then to select an appropriate course of action for solving problems and capitalizing on opportunities. This exercise focuses on decision making about issues related to diversity and multiculturalism.

Exercise Background

For years your firm had relatively little diversity. The thousand-member workforce was almost exclusively white and male. But in recent years you have succeeded in increasing diversity substantially. Almost one-third of your employees are now female, whereas over 40 percent are Latino or African-American.

Unfortunately, your firm has recently met with some financial setbacks. You feel that you have no choice but to lay off about three hundred employees for a period of at least six months. If everything goes well, you also expect to be able to bring them back after six months.

Exercise Task

With the background information above as context, do the following:

1. Develop a layoff plan that will not substantially reduce your firm's diversity.
2. Decide how you will communicate your decision to the workforce.
3. What obstacles do you foresee in implementing your decision?

CHAPTER CLOSING case

THE IKEA-IZATION OF AMERICA, THE AMERICANIZATION OF IKEA

"You can't take over the world, because conditions are too different, calling for different solutions. Yes for Stockholm, no for Timbuktu."

– Ruth Eaton, author of *Ideal Cities: Utopianism and the (Un)Built Environment**

In 1943 Ingvar Kamprad established a store in his hometown, the small village of Agunnaryd, Sweden. By the 1950s, IKEA, as Kamprad called the fledgling business, had the largest furniture showroom in Scandinavia and manufactured its own products. IKEA developed the idea of shipping disassembled furniture to allow the use of less-expensive flat packaging. The firm opened Europe's first warehouse store. From these innovations, the pioneering retail firm has grown to encompass 70,000 workers in 150 stores. Some 255 million worldwide shoppers visited IKEA in 2001.

The firm's products are known for their combination of Swedish-modern high style, practicality, and affordability. Sofas, for example, cost as little as $200 and are covered with washable, durable canvas. IKEA deliberately engages in social engineering, believing that better and lower-cost design can transform the lives of the average person. Peter Fiell, author of *Industrial Design A–Z*, claims that the retailer's philosophy is about "how to get the most quality to the greatest number of people for the least money." He adds, "That's the nucleus of modernism. It's inherently optimistic."

IKEA has developed a peculiarly Scandinavian culture, with emphasis on restraint and fairness, which it calls "democratic design." This slogan applies to products and also to organizational and task design. Bill Agee, an American employee who transferred to IKEA's Swedish headquarters, says, "It's a little religious or missionary in a sense, but it's who we are." Within the firm, private offices are rare, and everyone is on a first-name basis. The no-frills facilities keep the emphasis on the downscale customers, who are referred to as "people with thin wallets." Josephine Rydberg-Dumont, the firm's managing director, speaks with evangelical fervor. "We're ready for modernism now," she says. "When it first came, it was for the few. Now it's for the many."

To cope with the needs of diverse customers around the world, IKEA relies on standardization, with global production and distribution. Customers in Russia, Malaysia, and the United States buy the same linens and cupboards. Customers walk through the identical warehouses along the same predetermined pathways. IKEA encourages ongoing consumption of "throwaway" furniture, long considered a durable good. Christian Mathieu, the firm's North American marketing manager, says of the traditional attitude, "Americans change their *spouse* as often as their dining-room table, about 1.5 times in a lifetime." To change that mindset, IKEA is launching a new ad campaign called "Unböring," featuring a discarded lamp sitting out in the rain. The spokesman says, "Many of you feel bad for this lamp. That is because you are crazy." Rydberg-Dumont concurs, saying, "You value things that don't bog you down, that are easy to take care of." The message is: You can and should update your home as often as you update your wardrobe.

IKEA made some mistakes in its early globalization efforts—not surprising for a firm whose 110 million catalogues are printed in thirty-four languages. In the United States, for example, beds did not match standard sheet sizes. Another flop was the six-ounce drinking glass that was far too small for American preferences. Kent Nordin, a former IKEA manager, says, "People told us they were drinking out of our vases." Bedroom dressers contained numerous small drawers, a popular European feature, but they could not hold Americans' bulky sweaters. Storage units were not sized to hold standard coat hangers. Ultimately, top executives realized that telling American buyers to use smaller coat hangers would not work. Today, IKEA has adapted its products to local tastes. The firm is one of the top furnishings retailers in the United States, and one in ten American homes has at least one IKEA item.

In its newest venture, IKEA has expanded into designing and building entire communities of apartments furnished with IKEA products, down to the kitchen gadgets and the bath towels. They are able to provide housing that is 25 percent less expensive than comparable units. The firm's tendency toward social engineering informs every aspect of the design, from the community gardens to the cooperative governance. Many praise the developments, but some feel the concept will not work outside of Sweden. "The idea of building an ideal little street is quite laudable," says Ruth Eaton, author of *Ideal Cities: Utopianism and the (Un)Built Environment.* "But you can't put the same thing everywhere. That's where utopias go wrong. . . . You can't take over the world, because conditions are too different, calling for different solutions. Yes for Stockholm, no for Timbuktu."

The retailer may master the furniture industry, but it is not clear whether those skills will translate into a flair for suburban development. IKEA still has a long way to go before realizing its vision of complete world domination in design for the home.

Case Questions

1. Looking at IKEA and its environment, what forces are creating a need for diversity and multiculturalism at the firm?
2. What competitive advantages does IKEA enjoy as a result of its multiculturalism?
3. List two potential pitfalls or challenges, resulting from their company's multiculturalism, that IKEA managers must be aware of. Then suggest some actions that IKEA managers can take to reduce any negative impact on the firm.

Case References

Catherine Belton, "To Russia, with Love: The Multinationals' Song," *BusinessWeek*, September 16, 2002, pp. 44–46; Eryn Brown, "Putting Eames Within Reach," *Fortune*, October 30, 2002, www.fortune.com on December 16, 2002; John Leland, "A Prefab Utopia," *New York Times Magazine*, December 1, 2002, pp. 92–96; John Leland, "How the Disposable Sofa Conquered America," *New York Times Magazine*, December 1, 2002, pp. 86–96; Michael Schrage, "Whip Your Thoroughbreds," *Fortune*, October 31, 2001, www.fortune.com on December 16, 2002.

Chapter Notes

1. Brent Schlender, "Intel's $10 Billion Gamble," *Fortune*, October 27, 2002, www.fortune.com on December 11, 2002; "Intel, 1999 Edition (excerpts)," Vault website, www.vault.com on December 11, 2002; "Intel Corporation," Hoover's Online, www.hoovers.com on December 11, 2002; "Jobs at Intel," "Personal Development," Intel website, www.intel.com on December 11, 2002; Monica Mehta, "High-Tech Melting Pot," *Mother Jones*, August 4, 1998, www.motherjones.com on December 10, 2002; "Uniting Intel's Diverse Workforce," *Minority Americans in Engineering and Science National Magazine*, Spring 2001, www.maesnationalmagazine.com on December 10, 2002 (*quote).
2. Gail Robinson and Kathleen Dechant, "Building a Business Case for Diversity," *Academy of Management Executive*, August 1997, pp. 21–31. See also Orlando C. Richard, "Racial Diversity, Business Strategy, and Firm Performance: A Resource-Based View," *Academy of Management Journal*, 2000, vol. 43, no. 2, pp. 164–177.
3. "The Coming Job Bottleneck," *BusinessWeek*, March 24, 1997, pp. 184–185; Linda Thornburg, "The Age Wave Hits," *HRMagazine*, February 1995, pp. 40–46.
4. Gary Powell and D. Anthony Butterfield, "Investigating the 'Glass Ceiling' Phenomenon: An Empirical Study of Actual Promotions to Top Management," *Academy of Management Journal*, 1994, vol. 37, no. 1, pp. 68–86.
5. Karen S. Lyness and Donna E. Thompson, "Above the Glass Ceiling? A Comparison of Matched Samples of Female and Male Executives," *Journal of Applied Psychology*, 1997, vol. 82, no. 3, pp. 359–375.
6. "What Glass Ceiling?" *USA Today*, July 20, 1999, pp. 1B, 2B; see also Patricia Sellers, "True Grit—The Most Powerful Women in Business," *Fortune*, October 14, 2002, pp. 101–112.
7. *Occupational Outlook Handbook* (Washington D.C.: U.S. Bureau of Labor Statistics, 1990–1991).
8. Roy S. Johnson, "The New Black Power," *Fortune*, August 4, 1997, pp. 46–47. See also Cora Daniels, "The Most

Powerful Black Executives in America," *Fortune*, July 22, 2002, pp. 60–80.

9. "In a Factory Schedule, Where Does Religion Fit In?" *Wall Street Journal*, March 4, 1999, pp. B1, B12.
10. Jane Easter Bahls, "Make Room for Diverse Beliefs," *HRMagazine*, August 1997, pp. 89–95.
11. "Immigration Is on the Rise, Again," *USA Today*, February 28, 1997, p. 7A.
12. Based on Taylor H. Cox and Stacy Blake, "Managing Cultural Diversity: Implications for Organizational Competitiveness," *Academy of Management Executive*, August 1991, pp. 45–56. See also Jacqueline A. Gilbert and John M. Ivancevich, "Valuing Diversity: A Tale of Two Organizations," *Academy of Management Executive*, 2000, vol. 14, no. 1, pp. 93–103.
13. Michelle Neely Martinez, "Work-Life Programs Reap Business Benefits," *HRMagazine*, June 1997, pp. 110–119. See also Cox and Blake, "Managing Cultural Diversity: Implications for Organizational Competitiveness."
14. Jonathan Hickman, "America's 50 Best Companies for Minorities," *Fortune*, July 8, 2002, pp. 110–120.
15. For an example, see "A Female Executive Tells Furniture Maker What Women Want," *Wall Street Journal*, June 25, 1999, pp. A1, A11.
16. "Target Makes a Play for Minority Group Sears Has Cultivated," *Wall Street Journal*, April 12, 1999, pp. A1, A8.
17. For example, see Tony Simons, Lisa Hope Pelled, and Ken A. Smith, "Making Use of Difference: Diversity, Debate, and Decision Comprehensiveness in Top Management Teams," *Academy of Management Journal*, 2000, vol. 42, no. 6, pp. 662–673.
18. C. Marlene Fiol, "Consensus, Diversity, and Learning in Organizations," *Organization Science*, August 1994, pp. 403–415.
19. Patricia L. Nemetz and Sandra L. Christensen, "The Challenge of Cultural Diversity: Harnessing a Diversity of Views to Understand Multiculturalism," *Academy of Management Review*, 1996, vol. 21, no. 2, pp. 434–462. See also "Generational Warfare," *Forbes*, March 22, 1999, pp. 62–66.
20. Christine M. Riordan and Lynn McFarlane Shores, "Demographic Diversity and Employee Attitudes: An Empirical Examination of Relational Demography Within Work Units," *Journal of Applied Psychology*, 1997, vol. 82, no. 3, pp. 342–358.
21. "Computer Chip Project Brings Rivals Together, But the Cultures Clash," *Wall Street Journal*, May 3, 1994, pp. A1, A8.
22. Cora Daniels, "Women vs. Wal-Mart," *Fortune*, July 21, 2003, pp. 78–82; "How Shoney's, Belted by a Lawsuit, Found the Path to Diversity," *Wall Street Journal*, April 16, 1996, pp. A1, A6; Fay Rice, "Denny's Changes Its Spots," *Fortune*, May 13, 1996, pp. 133–142; "The Ugly Talk on the Texaco Tape," *BusinessWeek*, November 18, 1996, p. 58; "Smith Barney's Woman Problem," *BusinessWeek*, June 3, 1996, pp. 102–106.
23. Jonathan Hickman, "America's 50 Best Companies for Minorities," *Fortune*, July 7, 2003, pp. 103–120.
24. "Firms Address Workers' Cultural Variety," *Wall Street Journal*, February 10, 1989, p. B1.
25. Sara Rynes and Benson Rosen, "What Makes Diversity Programs Work?" *HRMagazine*, October 1994, pp. 67–75.
26. Karen Hildebrand, "Use Leadership Training to Increase Diversity," *HRMagazine*, August 1996, pp. 53–59.
27. "Learning to Accept Cultural Diversity," *Wall Street Journal*, September 12, 1990, pp. B1, B9.
28. "Firms Address Workers' Cultural Variety."
29. Anthony Carneville and Susan Stone, "Diversity—Beyond the Golden Rule," *Training and Development*, October 1994, pp. 22–27.
30. Janice R. W. Joplin and Catherine S. Daus, "Challenges of Leading a Diverse Workforce," *Academy of Management Executive*, August 1997, pp. 32–47.
31. This discussion derives heavily from Taylor H. Cox, "The Multicultural Organization," *Academy of Management Executive*, May 1991, pp. 34–47.

PART three

PLANNING AND DECISION MAKING

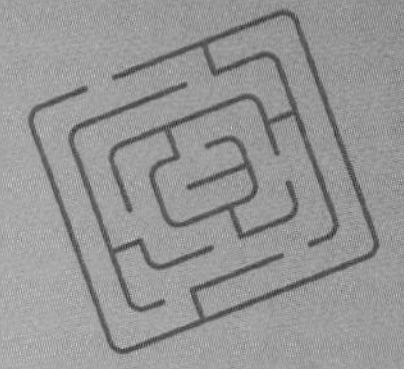

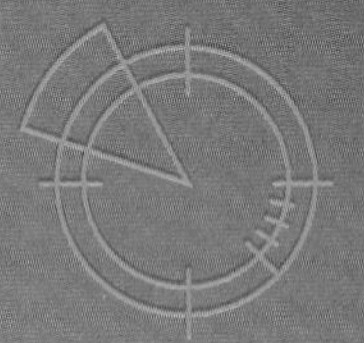

CHAPTER 7

Basic Elements of Planning and Decision Making

CHAPTER 8

Managing Strategy and Strategic Planning

CHAPTER 9

Managing Decision Making and Problem Solving

CHAPTER 10

Managing New Venture Formation and Entrepreneurship

BIRELL
ALAHRAM BEVERAGES CO.
بيريل
BIRELL
ALCOHOLIC MALT

7 Basic Elements of Planning and Decision Making

CHAPTER OUTLINE

Decision Making and the Planning Process

Organizational Goals
- Purposes of Goals
- Kinds of Goals
- Responsibilities for Setting Goals
- Managing Multiple Goals

Organizational Planning
- Kinds of Organizational Plans
- Time Frames for Planning
- Responsibilities for Planning
- Contingency Planning and Crisis Management

Tactical Planning
- Developing Tactical Plans
- Executing Tactical Plans

Operational Planning
- Single-Use Plans
- Standing Plans

Managing Goal-Setting and Planning Processes
- Barriers to Goal Setting and Planning
- Overcoming the Barriers
- Using Goals to Implement Plans

LEARNING OBJECTIVES

After studying this chapter, you should be able to:

1 ***Summarize the function of decision making and the planning process.***

OPENING INCIDENT

Fickle customers and rapid changes make planning difficult in the high-fashion end of the apparel industry. Most fashion designers—Ralph Lauren, Donna Karan, Prada, Gucci, Fendi—have adopted a design-driven business model, in which the designer dictates style to the customers. Coach, however, has taken a different approach. The company asks the customers what they want and then provides it. Coach's customer focus has created a competitive advantage for the firm, which annually sells $865 of merchandise for every square foot of store space, compared to an industry average of $200 to $300.

Coach began as a maker of indestructible, high-quality handbags, but their products were not perceived as stylish. Coach was just one among many businesses owned by Sara Lee Corporation, and the lack of focused management attention showed in slowing sales. CEO Lew Frankfort knew the company was failing, saying, "We were about to hit a wall." Frankfort knew that the company's success depended on finding the right industry niche. He wanted to attract high fashion's elite customers but remain an affordable luxury for customers who must save for a $200 bag. But how could Coach find and maintain that delicate balance?

2	3	4	5	6
Discuss the purpose of organizational goals, identify different kinds of goals, discuss who sets goals, and describe how to manage multiple goals.	***Identify different kinds of organizational plans, note the time frames for planning, discuss who plans, and describe contingency planning.***	***Discuss how tactical plans are developed and executed.***	***Describe the basic types of operational plans used by organizations.***	***Identify the major barriers to goal setting and planning, how organizations overcome those barriers, and how to use goals to implement plans.***

"To be successful you need to live your business. You have to understand it organically and thoroughly."

—Lew Frankfort, CEO, Coach

Effective planning has allowed Coach to become a major growth firm in the fashion industry.

For help, Frankfort turned to planning and forecasting. He said, "To be successful you need to live your business. You have to understand it organically and thoroughly." He introduced many new analytical tools for tracking market trends, evaluating effectiveness, and managing risk. The firm's leaders look at sales data for each store and each product type on a daily basis and, during busy seasons, several times daily. But extensive and intensive customer research remains the cornerstone of their planning. Indeed, the company spends $2 million per year on surveys. The surveys are supplemented with one-on-one interviews with customers from locations around the world, quizzing them on everything from appearance and quality to the correct length for a shoulder strap.

"The tremendous amount of testing they do differentiates them from a lot of other fashion companies," says industry analyst Robert Ohmes. Analyst Bob Drbul says, "Their execution and business planning is in the league of a Wal-Mart or a Target" (two much larger firms known for their effective business planning). New products are tested by first being shown to selected buyers in twelve worldwide markets, to gauge initial customer reaction. An initial demand forecast is then made, and six months before introduction, another twelve markets are tested. At launch time, sales are monitored closely and adjustments made quickly. For example, an unexpected spike in sales was investigated, and managers found that buying by Latino customers was on the increase. Within a week, the firm had moved up the opening date of a South Miami store and begun advertising in Spanish for the first time. Frankfort understands that, in order to be effective, plans must be translated into appropriate actions. "Not only do you need to know your business and your customers . . . you also need to be nimble to adapt," he claims.

A host of other changes has also aided Coach in its rapid rise. Frankfort hired a former Tommy Hilfiger designer, Reed Krakoff, to update the firm's classic but clunky styles. "Coach was an American icon, but something was missing," says Krakoff. "I had to take these ideas and make them fun—young in spirit." Instead of introducing new products twice a year, a common practice in the fashion industry, Coach releases new styles monthly. Customers now have a reason to visit the stores more often. Outsourcing the production function allowed the company to increase gross profit margins by 24 percent over five years. The firm has diversified into many other related lines of business, including shoes, jewelry, furniture, and more. There is even a Coach car—a co-branded Lexus with a Coach leather interior.

Women's Wear Daily, the bible of the fashion industry, named Coach the "most splurgeworthy luxury brand." Customers agree. Coach's sales grew 20 percent in 2002, and net income rose 34 percent. Investors, too, like Coach. The firm's share price has grown from less than $20 in 2002 to over $30 in 2003. Krakoff gives the credit for the firm's achievements to Frankfort's planning skills, saying, "The key to Lew's success . . . is his ability to orchestrate a decision-making process that is both inclusive and incisive."[1]

Coach's Lew Frankfort has done an outstanding job of revitalizing the firm. To jump-start his efforts, he made several critical decisions as to how the firm's performance could be improved. Among the key ingredients in his subsequent success has been the astute job he has done in planning and forecasting. In addition, embedded in his efforts has been a renewed emphasis on setting goals. These goals, in turn, have enabled the firm to boost its new product introductions, cost reductions, and revenue increases. Indeed, Coach can be held up as an example for other firms in how to improve organizational effectiveness by improving decision making and planning.

As we note in Chapter 1, planning and decision making comprise the first managerial functions that organizations must address. This chapter is the first of four that explore the planning process in detail. We begin by briefly relating decision making and planning, and then explaining the planning process that most organizations follow. We then discuss the nature of organizational goals and introduce the basic concepts of planning. Next we discuss tactical and operational planning more fully. Finally, we conclude with a discussion of how to manage the goal-setting and planning processes.

Decision Making and the Planning Process

Decision making is the cornerstone of planning. A few years ago, Procter & Gamble (P&G) set a goal of doubling its revenues over a ten-year period. The firm's top managers could have adopted an array of alternative options, including increasing revenues by only 25 percent or increasing revenues threefold. The time frame for the projected revenue growth could also have been somewhat shorter or longer than the ten-year period that was actually specified. Alternatively, the goal could have included diversifying into new markets, cutting costs, or buying competing businesses. Thus P&G's exact mix of goals and plans for growth rate and time frame reflected choices from among a variety of alternatives.

Clearly, then, decision making is the catalyst that drives the planning process. An organization's goals follow from decisions made by various managers. Likewise, deciding on the best plan for achieving particular goals also reflects a decision to adopt one course of action as opposed to others. We discuss decision making per se in Chapter 9. Our focus here is on the planning process itself. As we discuss goal setting and planning, however, keep in mind that decision making underlies every aspect of setting goals and formulating plans.[2]

The planning process itself can best be thought of as a generic activity. All organizations engage in planning activities, but no two organizations plan in exactly the same fashion. Figure 7.1 is a general representation of the planning process that many organizations attempt to follow. But, although most firms follow this general framework, each also has its own nuances and variations.[3]

As Figure 7.1 shows, all planning occurs within an environmental context. If managers do not understand this context, they are unable to develop effective plans. Thus understanding the environment is essentially the first step in planning. The four previous chapters cover many of the basic environmental issues that affect organizations and how they plan. With this understanding as a foundation, managers must then establish the organization's mission. The mission outlines the organization's purpose, premises, values, and directions. Flowing from the mission are parallel streams of goals and plans. Directly following the mission are strategic goals. These goals and the mission help determine strategic plans. Strategic goals and plans are primary inputs for developing tactical goals. Tactical goals and the original strategic plans help shape tactical plans. Tactical plans, in turn, combine with the tactical goals to shape operational goals. These goals and the appropriate tactical plans determine operational plans. Finally, goals and plans at each level can also be used as input for future activities at all levels. This chapter discusses goals and tactical and operational plans. Chapter 8 covers strategic plans.

FIGURE 7.1

The Planning Process

The planning process takes place within an environmental context. Managers must develop a complete and thorough understanding of this context to determine the organization's mission and to develop its strategic, tactical, and operational goals and plans.

concept CHECK

What is the relationship between decision making and planning?

Which do you think is easier for a top manager—making a decision or developing a plan?

Organizational Goals

Goals are critical to organizational effectiveness, and they serve a number of purposes. Organizations can also have several different kinds of goals, all of which must be appropriately managed. And a number of different kinds of managers must be involved in setting goals.

Purposes of Goals

Goals serve four important purposes.[4] First, they provide guidance and a unified direction for people in the organization. Goals can help everyone understand where the organization is going and why getting there is important.[5] Several years ago, top managers at General Electric set a goal that every business owned by the firm would be either number one or number two in its industry. This goal still helps set the tone for decisions made by GE managers as it competes with other firms like Whirlpool and Electrolux.[6] Likewise, P&G's goal of doubling revenues by the year 2006 helps everyone in the firm recognize the strong emphasis on growth and expansion that is driving the firm.

Second, goal-setting practices strongly affect other aspects of planning. Effective goal setting promotes good planning, and good planning facilitates future goal setting. For example, the ambitious revenue goal set for P&G demonstrates how setting goals and developing plans to reach them should be seen as complementary activities. The strong growth goal should encourage managers to plan for expansion by looking for new market opportunities, for example. Similarly, they must also always be alert for competitive threats and new ideas that will help facilitate future expansion.

Third, goals can serve as a source of motivation for employees of the organization. Goals that are specific and moderately difficult can motivate people to work harder, especially if attaining the goal is likely to result in rewards.[7] The Italian furniture manufacturer Industrie Natuzzi SpA uses goals to motivate its workers. Each craftsperson has a goal for how long it should take to perform her or his job, such as sewing leather sheets together to make a sofa cushion or building wooden frames for chair arms. At the completion of assigned tasks, workers enter their ID numbers and job numbers into the firm's computer system. If they get a job done faster than their goal, a bonus is automatically added to their paycheck.[8]

Finally, goals provide an effective mechanism for evaluation and control. This means that performance can be assessed in the future in terms of how successfully today's goals are accomplished. For example, suppose that officials of the United Way of America set a goal of collecting $250,000 from a particular small community. If, midway through the campaign, they have raised only $50,000, they know that they need to change or intensify their efforts. If they raise only $100,000 by the end of their drive, they will need to carefully study why they did not reach their goal and what they need to do differently next year. On the other hand, if they succeed in raising $265,000, evaluations of their efforts will take on an entirely different character.

Kinds of Goals

Organizations establish many different kinds of goals. In general, these goals vary by level, area, and time frame.[9] Figure 7.2 provides examples of each type of goal for a fast-food chain.

Level Goals are set for and by different levels within an organization. As we note earlier, the four basic levels of goals are the mission and strategic, tactical, and operational goals. An organization's **mission** is a statement of its "fundamental, unique purpose that sets a business apart from other firms of its type and identifies the scope of the business's operations in product and market terms."[10] For example, the CEO of Monsanto is attempting to reshape his firm's mission by transforming it into what he calls a "life sciences" firm.[11]

mission A statement of an organization's fundamental purpose

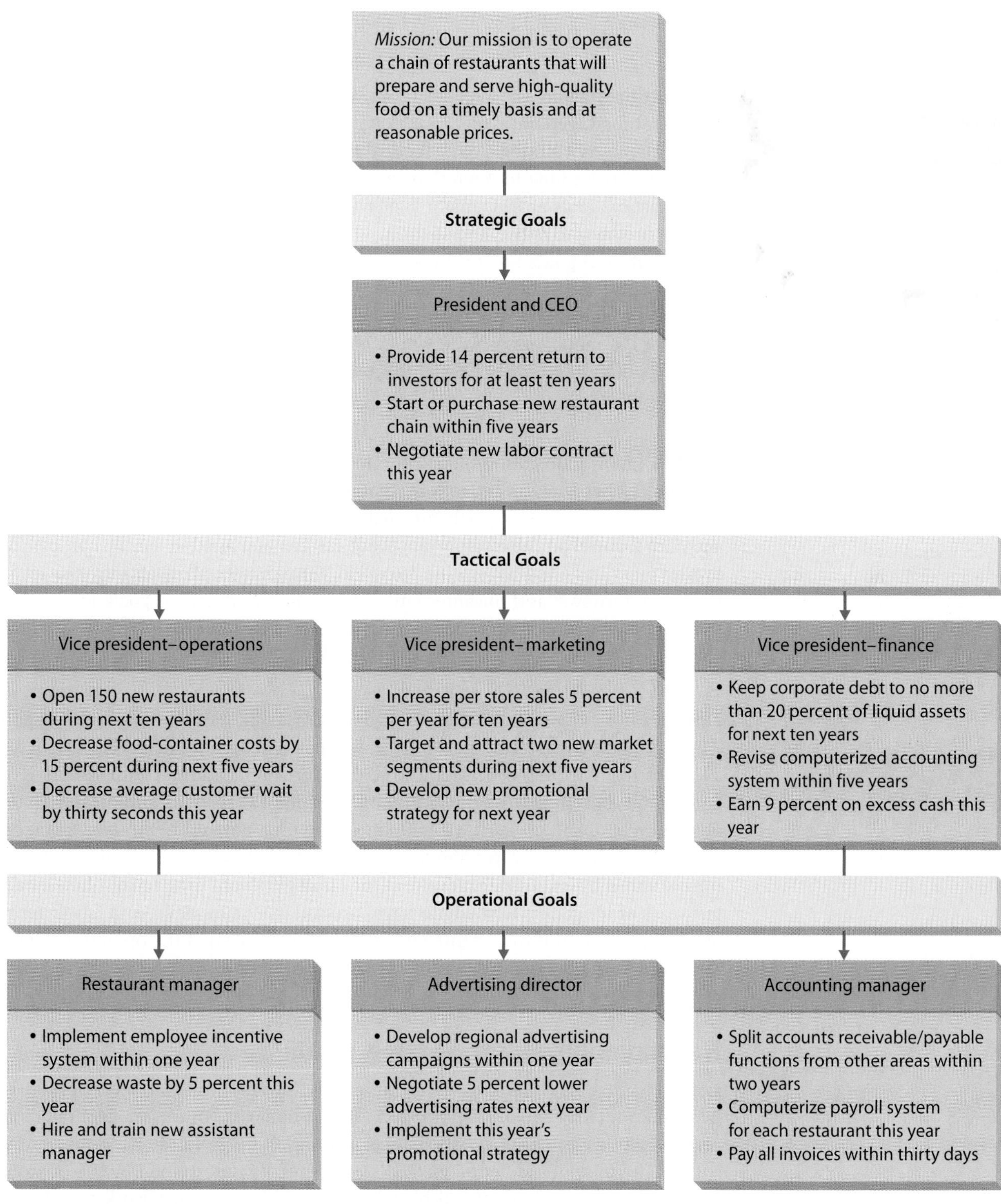

FIGURE 7.2

Kinds of Organizational Goals for a Regional Fast-Food Chain

Organizations develop many different types of goals. A regional fast-food chain, for example, might develop goals at several different levels and for several different areas.

strategic goal A goal set by and for top management of the organization

tactical goal A goal set by and for middle managers of the organization

operational goal A goal set by and for lower-level managers of the organization

Strategic goals are goals set by and for top management of the organization. They focus on broad, general issues. For example, Procter & Gamble's goal of doubling sales revenues is a strategic goal. **Tactical goals** are set by and for middle managers. Their focus is on how to operationalize actions necessary to achieve the strategic goals. Tactical goals at P&G might center on which new products to launch, which existing products to revise, and so forth.

Operational goals are set by and for lower-level managers. Their concern is with shorter-term issues associated with the tactical goals. An operational goal for P&G might be a target number of new products to launch each of the next five years. (Some managers use the words *objective* and *goal* interchangeably. When they are differentiated, however, the term *objective* is usually used instead of *operational goal.*)

Area Organizations also set goals for different areas. The restaurant chain shown in Figure 7.2 has goals for operations, marketing, and finance. Hewlett-Packard (HP) routinely sets production goals for quality, productivity, and so forth. By keeping activities focused on these important areas, HP has managed to remain competitive against organizations from around the world. Human resource goals might be set for employee turnover and absenteeism. 3M and Rubbermaid set goals for product innovation. Similarly, Bath & Body Works has a goal that 30 percent of the products sold in its retail outlets each year will be new.[12]

Time Frame Organizations also set goals across different time frames. In Figure 7.2, three goals are listed at the strategic, tactical, and operational levels. The first is a long-term goal, the second an intermediate-term goal, and the third a short-term goal. Some goals have an explicit time frame (open 150 new restaurants during the next ten years), and others have an open-ended time horizon (maintain 10 percent annual growth). Finally, we should also note that the meaning of different time frames varies by level. For example, at the strategic level, "long term" often means ten years or longer, "intermediate term" around five years or so, and "short term" around one year. But two or three years may be long term at the operational level, and short term may mean a matter of weeks or even days.

Responsibilities for Setting Goals

Who sets goals? The answer is actually quite simple: All managers should be involved in the goal-setting process. Each manager, however, generally has responsibilities for setting goals that correspond to his or her level in the organization. The mission and strategic goals are generally determined by the board of directors and top managers. Top and middle managers then work together to establish tactical goals. Finally, middle and lower-level managers are jointly responsible for operational goals. Many managers also set individual goals for themselves. These goals may involve career paths, informal work-related goals outside the normal array of official goals, or just about anything of interest or concern to the manager.

Managing Multiple Goals

Organizations set many different kinds of goals and sometimes experience conflicts or contradictions among goals. Nike had problems with inconsistent goals a few years ago. The firm was producing high-quality shoes (a manufacturing goal), but they were not particularly stylish (a marketing goal). As a result, the company lost substantial market share when Reebok International started making shoes that were both high quality and fashionable. When Nike management recognized and corrected the inconsistencies, Nike regained its industry standing.

To address such problems, managers must understand the concept of optimizing. **Optimizing** involves balancing and reconciling possible conflicts among goals. Because goals may conflict with one another, the manager must look for inconsistencies and decide whether to pursue one goal to the exclusion of another or to find a midrange target between the extremes. For example, Home Depot has achieved dramatic success in the retailing industry by offering do-it-yourselfers high-quality home improvement products at low prices and with good service. Now the firm is pursuing a goal of doubling its revenues from professional contractors. Among its plans have been to set up separate checkout areas and provide special products for contractors. The challenge, however, is to keep loyal individual customers while also satisfying professional contractors.[13] Home Depot's biggest competitor is also optimizing, but among different alternatives—trying to retain its core customer group while also appealing more to women.[14] Similarly, General Motors is currently optimizing market share, capacity, and profits by offering rebates to customers.[15] And the airlines almost always seem to face a classic optimizing question—carrying more passengers for lower prices or fewer passengers for higher prices.[16]

optimizing Balancing and reconciling possible conflicts among goals

concept CHECK

What are the four fundamental purposes of goals in an organization?	*Identify a recent situation in which you had to optimize among conflicting goals.*

Organizational Planning

Given the clear link between organizational goals and plans, we now turn our attention to various concepts and issues associated with planning itself. In particular, this section identifies kinds of plans, time frames for planning, who is responsible for planning, and contingency planning.

Kinds of Organizational Plans

Organizations establish many different kinds of plans. At a general level, these include strategic, tactical, and operational plans.

These individuals are governors of four Northwest states. They recently met to create a salmon recovery plan. Their goal is to balance fishing and economic interests in their states. The salmon recovery plan has long-term, intermediate, and short-range components and was developed in conjunction with representatives from their state planning staffs.

Strategic Plans Strategic plans are the plans developed to achieve strategic goals. More precisely, a **strategic plan** is a general plan outlining decisions of resource allocation, priorities, and action steps necessary to reach strategic goals.[17] These plans are set by the board of directors and top management, generally have an extended time horizon, and address questions of scope, resource deployment, competitive advantage, and synergy. We discuss strategic planning further in Chapter 8.

Tactical Plans A **tactical plan**, aimed at achieving tactical goals, is developed to implement specific parts of a strategic plan. Tactical plans typically involve upper and middle management and, compared with strategic plans, have a somewhat shorter time horizon and a more specific and concrete focus. Thus tactical plans are concerned more with actually getting things done than with deciding what to do. Tactical planning is covered in detail in a later section.

Operational Plans An **operational plan** focuses on carrying out tactical plans to achieve operational goals. Developed by middle and lower-level managers, operational plans have a short-term focus and are relatively narrow in scope. Each one deals with a fairly small set of activities. We also cover operational planning in more detail later.

strategic plan A general plan outlining decisions of resource allocation, priorities, and action steps necessary to reach strategic goals

tactical plan A plan aimed at achieving tactical goals and developed to implement parts of a strategic plan

operational plan Focuses on carrying out tactical plans to achieve operational goals

long-range plan A plan that covers many years, perhaps even decades; common long-range plans are for five years or more

Time Frames for Planning

As we previously note, strategic plans tend to have a long-term focus, tactical plans an intermediate-term focus, and operational plans a short-term focus. The sections that follow address these time frames in more detail. Of course, we should also remember that time frames vary widely from industry to industry.

Long-Range Plans A **long-range plan** covers many years, perhaps even decades. The founder of Matsushita Electric (maker of Panasonic and JVC electronic products), Konosuke Matsushita, once wrote a 250-year plan for his company.[18] Today, however, most managers recognize that environmental change makes it unfeasible to plan too far ahead, but large firms like General Motors and ExxonMobil still routinely develop plans for ten- to twenty-year intervals. GM executives, for example, have a pretty good idea today about new car models that they plan to introduce, for at least a decade in advance. The time span for long-range planning varies from one organization to another. For our purposes, we regard any plan that extends beyond five years as long range. Managers of organizations in complex, volatile environments face a special dilemma. These organizations probably need a longer time horizon than do organizations in less dynamic environments, yet the complexity of their environment makes long-range planning difficult. Managers at these companies therefore develop long-range plans but also must constantly monitor their environment for possible changes.

Intermediate Plans An **intermediate plan** is somewhat less tentative and subject to change than is a long-range plan. Intermediate plans usually cover periods from one to five years and are especially important for middle and first-line managers. Thus they generally parallel tactical plans. For many organizations, intermediate planning has become the central focus of planning activities. Nissan, for example, fell behind its domestic rivals Toyota and Honda in areas like profitability and productivity. To turn things around, the firm developed several plans ranging in duration from two to four years, each intended to improve some part of the company's operations. One plan (three years in duration) involved updating the manufacturing technology used in each Nissan assembly factory. Another (four years in duration) called for shifting more production to foreign plants to lower labor costs.[19] And the successful implementation of these plans has indeed helped turn things around for Nissan.

intermediate plan A plan that generally covers from one to five years

Short-Range Plans A manager also develops a **short-range plan**, which has a time frame of one year or less. Short-range plans greatly affect the manager's day-to-day activities. There are two basic kinds of short-range plans. An **action plan** operationalizes any other kind of plan. When a specific Nissan plant was ready to have its technology overhauled, its managers focused their attention on replacing the existing equipment with new equipment as quickly and as efficiently as possible, to minimize lost production time. In most cases, this was done in a matter of a few months, with actual production halted for only a few weeks. An action plan thus coordinates the actual changes at a given factory. A **reaction plan**, in turn, is a plan designed to allow the company to react to an unforeseen circumstance. At one Nissan factory, the new equipment arrived earlier than expected, and plant managers had to shut down production more quickly than expected. These managers thus had to react to events beyond their control in ways that still allowed their goals to be achieved. In fact, reacting to any form of environmental turbulence, as described in Chapter 3, is a form of reaction planning.

short-range plan A plan that generally covers a span of one year or less

action plan A plan used to operationalize any other kind of plan

reaction plan A plan developed to react to an unforeseen circumstance

Responsibilities for Planning

We earlier note briefly who is responsible for setting goals. We can now expand that initial perspective and examine more fully how different parts of the organization participate in the overall planning process. All managers engage in planning to some degree. Marketing sales managers develop plans for target markets, market penetration, and sales increases. Operations managers plan cost-cutting programs and better inventory control methods. As a general rule, however, the larger an organization becomes, the more the primary planning activities become associated with groups of managers rather than with individual managers.

Planning Staff Some large organizations maintain a professional planning staff. General Motors, Disney, Caterpillar, Raytheon, NCR, Ford, and Boeing all have planning staffs.[20] And, although the planning staff was pioneered in the United States, foreign firms like Nippon Telegraph and Telephone have also started using them. Organizations might use a planning staff for a variety of reasons. In particular, a planning staff can reduce the workload of individual managers, help coordinate the planning activities of individual managers, bring to a particular problem many different tools and techniques, take a broader view than individual managers, and go beyond pet projects and particular departments. *Technology Toolkit* describes a potentially valuable new technology that may help facilitate the work of planning staffs by making it easier for them to find the information they need to plan most effectively.

TECHNOLOGY toolkit

Grokking the Internet

"The computer world has been alphanumeric, but we perceive things visually."

— Paul Hawken, entrepreneur, author, and founder of Groxis*

Finding information on the Internet can be frustrating. Net browsers, such as Northern Lights or Google, search the entire Web and then list every "hit." This scattershot approach is both too broad and too limited. Search engines cannot prioritize data, forcing the user to plow through many documents before finding the right one. They are unable to refine a search—to look more deeply into a particular segment of the information. Also, browsers are not sophisticated enough to recognize patterns in the data and then present the results in an organized fashion. The brainchild of entrepreneur Paul Hawken, Groxis, is changing all that. Groxis CEO R. J. Pittman claims, "We don't need another search engine. What we need is a tool to make the results of the engine more useful."

Groxis is developing a data visualization tool called Grokker. (The term grok was coined by science fiction writer Robert A. Heinlein in his novel *Stranger in a Strange Land*, and it means "to understand completely.") Grokker takes the information gathered by a search engine and then groups the data into useful categories. The categories are presented as spheres, each representing a set of related data. Viewers can broaden their search as they navigate through the data by finding nearby spheres. To focus a search more narrowly, users select a sphere within a sphere. At the lowest level, single documents are displayed as circles. On screen, Grokker results resemble constellations, with each planet containing more spheres.

As an example, when the search term is "Saddam Hussein," subspheres include "The UN," "Persian Gulf War," and "Iraq's Government." This type of search mimics the way humans process and retrieve information. Memories are stored in categories and subcategories. Calling up one memory invokes a set of related memories within and across categories. "The computer world has been alphanumeric, but we perceive things visually," says Hawken.

Grokker is not the first knowledge-mapping software, but several reviewers claim it is the first that is easy to use, yet comprehensive and helpful. If Grokker becomes more widely adopted, executives may at last be able to effectively manage the tidal wave of data that has overwhelmed them.

References: Dan Gilmour, "Tools Coming for Connecting Information," *The Mercury News* (San Jose, Calif.), October 27, 2002, www.bayarea.com on December 20, 2002; David Kirkpatrick, "Making Online Searches More Useful," *Fortune*, October 29, 2002, www.fortune.com on December 20, 2002; John Markoff, "A New Company Tries to Sort the Web's Chaos," *New York Times*, October 27, 2002, p. BU4 (*quote).

Planning Task Force Organizations sometimes use a planning task force to help develop plans. Such a task force often comprises line managers with a special interest in the relevant area of planning. The task force may also have members from the planning staff if the organization has one. A planning task force is most often created when the organization wants to address a special circumstance. For example, when Electronic Data Systems (EDS) decided to expand its information management services to Europe, managers knew that the firm's normal planning approach would not suffice, and top management created a special planning task force. The task force included representatives from each of the major units within the company, the corporate planning staff, and the management team that would run the European operation. Once the plan for entering the European market was formulated and implemented, the task force was eliminated.

Board of Directors Among its other responsibilities, the board of directors establishes the corporate mission and strategy. In some companies the board takes an active role in the planning process. At CBS, for example, the board of directors has traditionally played a major role in planning. In other companies the board selects a competent chief executive and delegates planning to that individual. The *Business of Ethics* discusses recent thinking about the board's appropriate role in planning.

Chief Executive Officer The chief executive officer (CEO) is usually the president or the chair of the board of directors. The CEO is probably the single most important individual in any organization's planning process. The CEO plays a major role in the complete planning process and is responsible for implementing the strategy. The board and CEO, then, assume direct roles in planning. The other organizational players involved in the planning process have more of an advisory or consulting role.

Executive Committee The executive committee is usually composed of the top executives in the organization working together as a group. Committee members usually meet regularly to provide input to the CEO on the proposals that affect their own units and to review the various strategic plans that develop from this input. Members of the executive committee are frequently assigned to various staff committees, subcommittees, and task forces to concentrate on specific projects or problems that might confront the entire organization at some time in the future.

Line Management The final component of most organizations' planning activities is line management. Line managers are those persons with formal authority and responsibility for the management of the organization. They play an important role in an organization's planning process for two reasons. First, they are a valuable source of inside information for other managers as plans are formulated and implemented. Second, the line managers at the middle and lower levels of the organization usually must execute the plans developed by top management. Line management identifies, analyzes, and recommends program alternatives, develops budgets and submits them for approval, and finally sets the plans in motion.

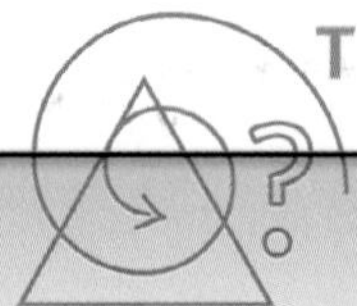

THE BUSINESS OF ethics

The Decision-making Responsibility of Corporate Boards

Boards of directors today are under pressure to become actively involved in planning and monitoring. At WorldCom, Tyco, and others, the boards were apparently unaware of the swindles taking place around them, and in some cases, supported the offenders. At Enron, for example, the board of directors several times voted to waive its policies regarding independence and arms-length transactions, allowing executives to continue their fraud unhampered. When the negligence of these boards was publicly exposed, investors cried out for reform.

The investors want boards to take a more active role in decision making and to provide more oversight. Most corporations, eager to distance themselves from scandal, are considering a transformation of their board of directors.

"People are coming to view Amazon's problems as the result of poor corporate governance. . . ."

– Pat McGurn, director of corporate programs, Institutional Shareholder Services*

The most effective boards are composed of more outsiders than insiders, who are corporate employees. This allows the directors to have independence from the powerful CEO. To enhance decision-making ability, board members should come from diverse backgrounds and have top-level management experience. Directors should own a substantial amount of the company's stock. Boards should be actively involved in decision making, such as meeting regularly, setting the overall corporate strategy, and having access to confidential information. Boards that do not meet these criteria may be too cozy with corporate executives and thus fail to vigilantly safeguard the interests of shareholders.

Many high-tech companies are defying these "rules." Boards of dot-coms contain 62 percent outsiders on average, as compared to 78 percent outsiders for the large firms of the Standard & Poor's 500. For example, the board of Amazon.com has just five members, is chaired by CEO Jeff Bezos, and lacks independence. Pat McGurn, a director at Institutional Shareholder Services, says, "People are coming to view Amazon's problems as the result of poor corporate governance rather than the effect of the economy in general. Unfortunately, the board doesn't seem to see governance as part of the solution." At Yahoo! Inc., the board has a mere six members, only one of whom is an outsider.

When the high-tech industry was flying high, the ill-structured boards went unchallenged. "It's not really until something goes wrong that people focus on [governance]," says Charles M. Elson, a professor and board expert. But in today's tougher competitive environment, newly cynical investors are demanding change.

References: Jennifer Reingold, "Dot.Com Boards Are Flouting the Rules," *BusinessWeek*, December 20, 1999, www.businessweek.com on November 18, 2002; Louis Lavelle, "The Best & Worst Boards," *BusinessWeek*, October 7, 2002, pp. 104–114; Muriel Siebert, "Mixing It Up," *Corporate Board Member*, November/December 2002, www.boardmember.com on November 18, 2002; Stefani Eads, "Why Amazon's Board Is Part of the Problem," *BusinessWeek*, April 4, 2001, www.businessweek.com on November 18, 2002 (*quote); Chamu Sundaramurthy and Marianne Lewis, "Control and Collaboration: Paradoxes of Governance," *Academy of Management Review*, 2003, Vol. 28, No. 3, pp. 397–415.

contingency planning The determination of alternative courses of action to be taken if an intended plan is unexpectedly disrupted or rendered inappropriate

Contingency Planning and Crisis Management

Another important type of planning is **contingency planning**, or the determination of alternative courses of action to be taken if an intended plan of action is unexpectedly disrupted or rendered inappropriate.[21] **Crisis management**, a related concept, is the set of procedures the organization uses in the event of a disaster or other unexpected calamity. Some elements of crisis management may be orderly and systematic, whereas others may be more ad hoc and develop as events unfold.

crisis management The set of procedures the organization uses in the event of a disaster or other unexpected calamity

An excellent recent example of widespread contingency planning occurred during the late 1990s in anticipation of what was popularly known as the "Y2K bug." Concerns about the impact of technical glitches in computers stemming from their internal clocks' changing from 1999 to 2000 resulted in contingency planning for most organizations. Many banks and hospitals, for example, had extra staff available; some organizations created backup computer systems; and some even stockpiled inventory in case they could not purchase new products or materials.[22]

The terrorist attacks on the United States on September 11, 2001, in contrast, prompted immediate crisis management responses from organizations ranging from the New York City fire and police departments to airlines to hotels to car rental firms. Literally thousands of other organizations were also affected; some responded effectively, whereas others fell into chaos. And many of those businesses still feel the effects of the event to this day.

Because of the aftermath of 9/11, more businesses than ever have developed contingency plans to deal with various potential events. Although airlines have always had contingency plans to deal with a single crash or accident, they now have more complex plans to help deal with a more far-reaching array of events. Similarly, most businesses that rely heavily on electronic communications technology have detailed plans for dealing with viruses, hackers, and other potential problems. Fortunately, most events that prompt the need for contingency plans are less dramatic than these.

The mechanics of contingency planning are shown in Figure 7.3. In relation to an organization's other plans, contingency planning comes into play at four action points.

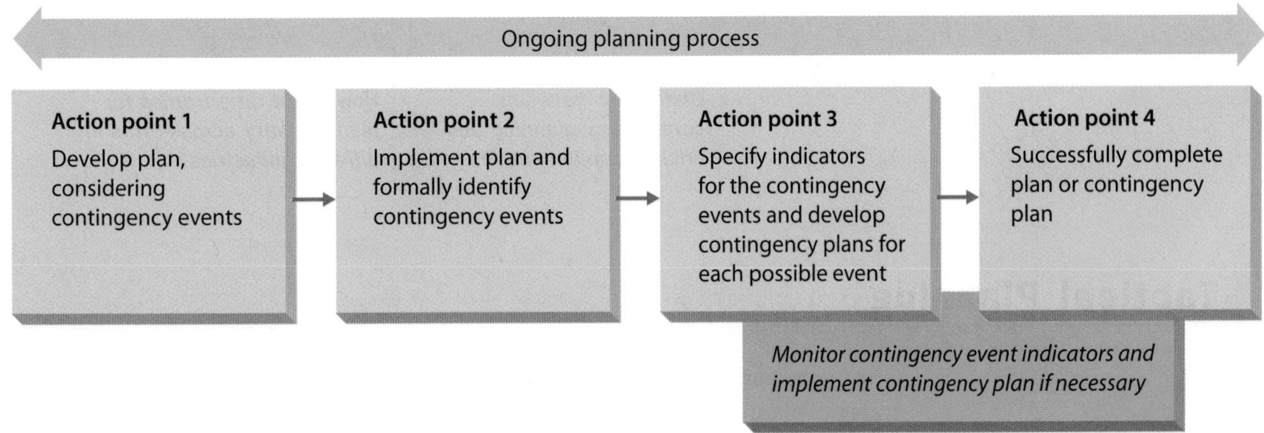

FIGURE 7.3

Contingency Planning

Most organizations develop contingency plans. These plans specify alternative courses of action to be taken if an intended plan is unexpectedly disrupted or rendered inappropriate.

At action point 1, management develops the basic plans of the organization. These may include strategic, tactical, and operational plans. As part of this development process, managers usually consider various contingency events. Some management groups even assign someone the role of devil's advocate to ask, "But what if . . . " about each course of action. A variety of contingencies is usually considered.

At action point 2, the plan that management chooses is put into effect. The most important contingency events are also defined. Only the events that are likely to occur and whose effects will have a substantial impact on the organization are used in the contingency-planning process. Next, at action point 3, the company specifies certain indicators or signs that suggest that a contingency event is about to take place. A bank might decide that a 2 percent drop in interest rates should be considered a contingency event. An indicator might be two consecutive months with a drop of .5 percent in each. As indicators of contingency events are being defined, the contingency plans themselves should also be developed. Examples of contingency plans for various situations are delaying plant construction, developing a new manufacturing process, and cutting prices.

After this stage, the managers of the organization monitor the indicators identified at action point 3. If the situation dictates, a contingency plan is implemented. Otherwise, the primary plan of action continues in force. Finally, action point 4 marks the successful completion of either the original or a contingency plan.

Contingency planning is becoming increasingly important for most organizations, especially for those operating in particularly complex or dynamic environments. Few managers have such an accurate view of the future that they can anticipate and plan for everything. Contingency planning is a useful technique for helping managers cope with uncertainty and change. Crisis management, by its very nature, however, is more difficult to anticipate. But organizations that have a strong culture, strong leadership, and a capacity to deal with the unexpected stand a better chance of successfully weathering a crisis than do other organizations.[23]

concept CHECK

Distinguish between contingency planning and crisis management.

How might time frames for planning vary across firms in different industries?

Tactical Planning

tactical plan A plan aimed at achieving tactical goals and developed to implement specific parts of a strategic plan

As we note earlier, tactical plans are developed to implement specific parts of a strategic plan. You have probably heard the saying about winning the battle but losing the war. **Tactical plans** are to battles what strategy is to a war: an organized sequence of steps designed to execute strategic plans. Strategy focuses on resources, environment, and mission, whereas tactics focus primarily on people and action.[24] Figure 7.4 identifies the major elements in developing and executing tactical plans.

Developing Tactical Plans

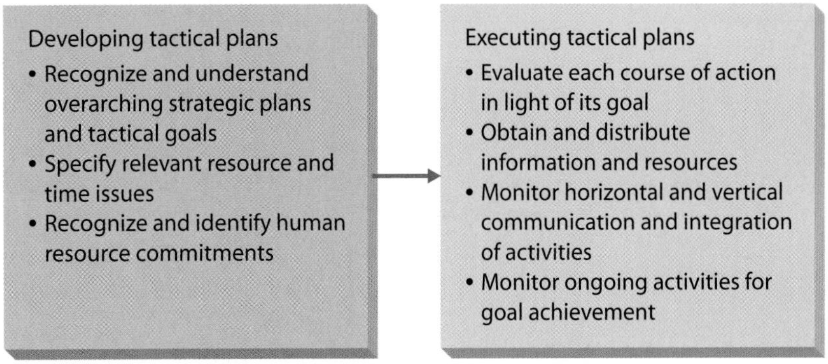

Although effective tactical planning depends on many factors, which vary from one situation to another, we can identify some basic guidelines. First, the manager needs to recognize that tactical planning must address a number of tactical goals derived from a broader strategic goal.[25] An occasional situation may call for a stand-alone tactical plan, but most of the time tactical plans flow from and must be consistent with a strategic plan.

FIGURE 7.4

Developing and Executing Tactical Plans

Tactical plans are used to accomplish specific parts of a strategic plan. Each strategic plan is generally implemented through several tactical plans. Effective tactical planning involves both development and execution.

Developing tactical plans
- Recognize and understand overarching strategic plans and tactical goals
- Specify relevant resource and time issues
- Recognize and identify human resource commitments

→

Executing tactical plans
- Evaluate each course of action in light of its goal
- Obtain and distribute information and resources
- Monitor horizontal and vertical communication and integration of activities
- Monitor ongoing activities for goal achievement

For example, top managers at Coca-Cola developed a strategic plan for cementing the firm's dominance of the soft-drink industry. As part of developing the plan, they identified a critical environmental threat—considerable unrest and uncertainty among the independent bottlers that packaged and distributed Coca-Cola's products. To simultaneously counter this threat and strengthen the company's position, Coca-Cola bought several large independent bottlers and combined them into one new organization called "Coca-Cola Enterprises." Selling half of the new company's stock reaped millions in profits while effectively keeping control of the enterprise in Coca-Cola's hands. Thus the creation of the new business was a tactical plan developed to contribute to the achievement of an overarching strategic goal.[26]

Second, although strategies are often stated in general terms, tactics must specify resources and time frames. A strategy can call for being number one in a particular market or industry, but a tactical plan must specify precisely what activities will be undertaken to achieve that goal. Consider the Coca-Cola example again. Another element of its strategic plan involves increased worldwide market share. To facilitate additional sales in Europe, managers developed tactical plans for building a new plant in the south of France to make soft-drink concentrate and for building another canning plant in Dunkirk. The firm has also invested heavily in India.[27] Building these plants represents a concrete action involving measurable resources (funds to build the plants) and a clear time horizon (a target date for completion).

Finally, tactical planning requires the use of human resources. Managers involved in tactical planning spend a great deal of time working with other people. They must be in a position to receive information from others within and outside the organization, process that information in the most effective way, and then pass it on to others who might make use of it. Coca-Cola executives have been intensively involved in planning the new plants, setting up the new bottling venture noted earlier, and exploring a joint venture with Cadbury Schweppes in the United Kingdom. Each activity has required considerable time and effort from dozens of managers. One manager, for example, crossed the Atlantic twelve times while negotiating the Cadbury deal.

Executing Tactical Plans

Regardless of how well a tactical plan is formulated, its ultimate success depends on the way it is carried out. Successful implementation, in turn, depends on the astute use of resources, effective decision making, and insightful steps to ensure that the right things are done at the right times and in the right ways. A manager can see an absolutely brilliant idea fail because of improper execution.

Proper execution depends on a number of important factors. First, the manager needs to evaluate every possible course of action in light of the goal it is intended to reach. Next, he or she needs to make sure that each decision maker has the information and resources necessary to get the job done. Vertical and horizontal communication and integration of activities must be present to minimize conflict and inconsistent activities. And, finally, the manager must monitor ongoing activities derived from the plan to make sure they are achieving the desired results. This monitoring typically takes place within the context of the organization's ongoing control systems.

For example, managers at Walt Disney Company recently developed a new strategic plan aimed at spurring growth in and profits from foreign markets. One tactical plan developed to stimulate growth involves expanding the cable Disney Channel into more and more foreign markets; another involves building the new theme park near Hong Kong that is set to open in late 2005 or early 2006. Although expanding cable television and building a new theme park are big undertakings in their own right, they are still tactical plans within the overall strategic plan focusing on international growth.[28]

concept CHECK

How are tactical plans developed?	*Which do you think is easier—developing tactical plans or implementing them? Why?*

Operational Planning

Another critical element in effective organizational planning is the development and implementation of operational plans. Operational plans are derived from tactical plans and are aimed at achieving operational goals. Thus operational plans tend to be narrowly focused, have relatively short time horizons, and involve lower-level managers. The two most basic forms of operational plans and specific types of each are summarized in Table 7.1.

Single-Use Plans

single-use plan Developed to carry out a course of action that is not likely to be repeated in the future

A **single-use plan** is developed to carry out a course of action that is not likely to be repeated in the future. As Disney proceeds with its new theme park in Hong Kong, it has developed numerous single-use plans for individual rides, attractions, and hotels. The two most common forms of single-use plans are programs and projects.

TABLE 7.1

Types of Operational Plans

Organizations develop various operational plans to help achieve operational goals. In general, there are two types of single-use plans and three types of standing plans.

Plan	Description
Single-use plan	Developed to carry out a course of action not likely to be repeated in the future
Program	Single-use plan for a large set of activities
Project	Single-use plan of less scope and complexity than a program
Standing plan	Developed for activities that recur regularly over a period of time
Policy	Standing plan specifying the organization's general response to a designated problem or situation
Standard operating procedure	Standing plan outlining steps to be followed in particular circumstances
Rules and regulations	Standing plans describing exactly how specific activities are to be carried out

Programs A **program** is a single-use plan for a large set of activities. It might consist of identifying procedures for introducing a new product line, opening a new facility, or changing the organization's mission. As part of its own strategic plans for growth, Black & Decker bought General Electric's small-appliance business. The deal involved the largest brand-name switch in history: 150 products were converted from the GE to the Black & Decker label. Each product was carefully studied, redesigned, and reintroduced with an extended warranty. A total of 140 steps were used for each product. It took three years to convert all 150 products over to Black & Decker. The total conversion of the product line was a program.

program A single-use plan for a large set of activities

project A single-use plan of less scope and complexity than a program

A program is a single-use plan for a large set of activities. Construction of the Three Gorges Dam in China certainly qualifies as a program! One of the largest construction programs ever undertaken, the Three Gorges Dam has taken years to complete, relied on the talents of hundreds of thousands of people, required millions of tons of concrete, and forced the displacement of thousands of people. Still, officials hope that the dam will help eliminate centuries old flooding problems and provide a valuable and reliable source of electricity.

Projects A **project** is similar to a program but is generally of less scope and complexity. A project may be a part of a broader program, or it may be a self-contained single-use plan. For Black & Decker, the conversion of each of the 150 products was a separate project in its own right. Each product had its own manager, its own schedule, and so forth. Projects are also used to introduce a new product within an existing product line or to add a new benefit option to an existing salary package.

Standing Plans

Whereas single-use plans are developed for nonrecurring situations, a **standing plan** is used for activities that recur regularly over a period of time. Standing plans can greatly enhance efficiency by making decision making routine. Policies, standard operating procedures, and rules and regulations are three kinds of standing plans.

Policies As a general guide for action, a policy is the most general form of standing plan. A **policy** specifies the organization's general response to a designated problem or situation. For example, McDonald's has a policy that it will not grant a franchise to an individual who already owns another fast-food restaurant. Similarly, Starbucks has a policy that it will not franchise at all, instead retaining ownership of all Starbucks coffee shops. Likewise, a university admissions office might establish a policy that admission will be granted only to applicants with a minimum SAT score of 1200 and a ranking in the top quarter of their high school class. Admissions officers may routinely deny admission to applicants who fail to reach these minimums. A policy is also likely to describe how exceptions are to be handled. The university's policy statement, for example, might create an admissions appeals committee to evaluate applicants who do not meet minimum requirements but may warrant special consideration.

Many surgeons rely heavily on standard operating procedures. For example, these doctors specialize in hip replacement surgeries. A modified industrial robot, shown above the skeleton, is used to drill a precise hole in a femur so that the implant can be fitted exactly as the doctors want it. A clearly defined set of procedures guides the team through every surgery it conducts. At the same time, however, the doctors are also prepared to deviate from established procedures as circumstances warrant.

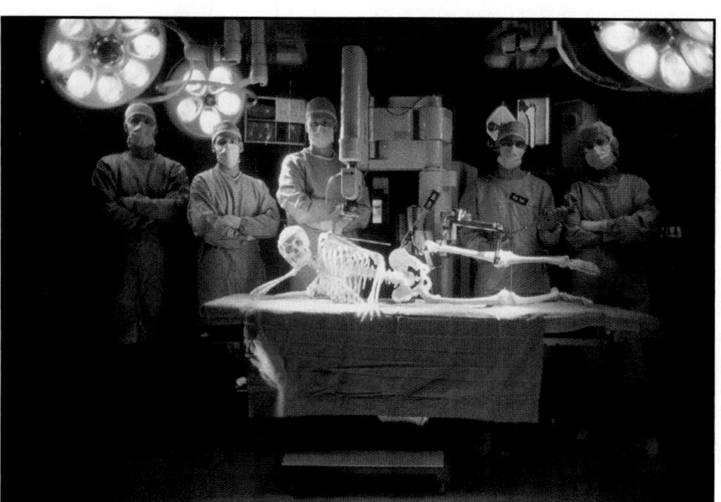

standing plan Developed for activities that recur regularly over a period of time

policy A standing plan that specifies the organization's general response to a designated problem or situation

standard operating procedure (SOP) A standing plan that outlines the steps to be followed in particular circumstances

Standard Operating Procedures Another type of standing plan is the **standard operating procedure, or SOP**. An SOP is more specific than a policy, in that it outlines the steps to be followed in particular circumstances. The admissions clerk at the university, for example, might be told that, when an application is received, he or she should (1) set up an electronic file for the applicant; (2) merge test-score records, transcripts, and letters of reference to the electronic file as they are received; and (3) forward the electronic file to the appropriate admissions director when it is complete. Gallo Vineyards in California has a 300-page manual of standard operating procedures. This planning manual is credited with making Gallo one of the most efficient wine operations in the United States. McDonald's has SOPs explaining exactly how Big Macs are to be cooked, how long they can stay in the warming rack, and so forth.

rules and regulations Describe exactly how specific activities are to be carried out

Rules and Regulations The narrowest of the standing plans, **rules and regulations**, describe exactly how specific activities are to be carried out. Rather than guiding decision making, rules and regulations actually take the place of decision making in various situations. Each McDonald's restaurant has a rule prohibiting customers from using its telephones, for example. The university admissions office might have a rule stipulating that, if an applicant's file is not complete two months

Reprinted with Special Permission of King Features Syndicate.

Standard operating procedures, rules, and regulations can all be useful methods for saving time, improving efficiency, and streamlining decision making and planning. But it is also helpful to review SOPs, rules, and regulations periodically to ensure that they remain useful. For example, as shown in this cartoon, an SOP for regularly ordering parts and supplies may become less effective if the demand for those parts and supplies changes or disappears.

before the beginning of a semester, the student cannot be admitted until the next semester. Of course, in most organizations a manager at a higher level can suspend or bend the rules. If the high school transcript of the child of a prominent university alumnus and donor arrives a few days late, the director of admissions might waive the two-month rule. Indeed, rules and regulations can become problematic if they are excessive or enforced too rigidly.

Rules and regulations and SOPs are similar in many ways. They are both relatively narrow in scope, and each can serve as a substitute for decision making. An SOP typically describes a sequence of activities, however, whereas rules and regulations focus on one activity. Recall our examples: The admissions SOP consisted of three activities, whereas the two-month rule related to only one activity. In an industrial setting, the SOP for orienting a new employee could involve enrolling the person in various benefit options, introducing him or her to coworkers and supervisors, and providing a tour of the facilities. A pertinent rule for the new employee might involve when to come to work each day.

concept CHECK

Distinguish between single-use and standing plans.	*Identify a rule or regulation that relates to you but which you think is excessive or too restrictive.*

Managing Goal-Setting and Planning Processes

Obviously, all of the elements of goal setting and planning discussed to this point involve managing these processes in some way or another. In addition, however, because major barriers sometimes impede effective goal setting and planning, knowing how to overcome some of the barriers is important.

TABLE 7.2

Barriers to Goal Setting and Planning

As part of managing the goal-setting and planning processes, managers must understand the barriers that can disrupt them. Managers must also know how to overcome the barriers.

Major barriers	Inappropriate goals Improper reward system Dynamic and complex environment Reluctance to establish goals Resistance to change Constraints
Overcoming the barriers	Understanding the purposes of goals and planning Communication and participation Consistency, revision, and updating Effective reward system

Barriers to Goal Setting and Planning

Several circumstances can serve as barriers to effective goal setting and planning; the more common ones are listed in Table 7.2.

Inappropriate Goals Inappropriate goals come in many forms. Paying a large dividend to stockholders may be inappropriate if it comes at the expense of research and development. Goals may also be inappropriate if they are unattainable. If Kmart were to set a goal of having more revenues than Wal-Mart next year, people at the company would probably be embarrassed, because achieving such a goal would be impossible. Goals may also be inappropriate if they place too much emphasis on either quantitative or qualitative measures of success. Some goals, especially those relating to financial areas, are quantifiable, objective, and verifiable. Other goals, such as employee satisfaction and development, are difficult, if not impossible, to quantify. Organizations are asking for trouble if they put too much emphasis on one type of goal to the exclusion of the other.

Improper Reward System In some settings, an improper reward system acts as a barrier to goal setting and planning. For example, people may inadvertently be rewarded for poor goal-setting behavior or go unrewarded or even be punished for proper goal-setting behavior. Suppose that a manager sets a goal of decreasing turnover next year. If turnover is decreased by even a fraction, the manager can claim success and perhaps be rewarded for the accomplishment. In contrast, a manager who attempts to decrease turnover by 5 percent but actually achieves a decrease of only 4 percent may receive a smaller reward because of her or his failure to reach the established goal. And, if an organization places too much emphasis on short-term performance and results, managers may ignore longer-term issues as they set goals and formulate plans to achieve higher profits in the short term.

Dynamic and Complex Environment The nature of an organization's environment is also a barrier to effective goal setting and planning. Rapid change, technological innovation, and intense competition can all increase the difficulty of an organization's accurately assessing future opportunities and threats. For example, when an electronics firm like IBM develops a long-range plan, it tries to take into account how much technological innovation is likely to occur during that interval. But forecasting such events is extremely difficult. During the early boom years of personal computers, data were stored primarily on floppy disks. Because these disks had a limited storage capacity, hard disks were developed. Whereas the typical floppy disk can hold hundreds of pages of information, a hard disk can store thousands of pages. Today, computers increasingly store information on optical disks that hold millions of pages. The manager attempting to set goals and plan in this rapidly changing environment faces a truly formidable task.

A dynamic and complex environment is one of the most challenging barriers to effective goal-setting and planning. Consider, for example, the situation faced by Salim Teja, co-founder and chief strategist of Accompany, a Silicon Valley-based online buying club. He took Accompany from an abstract concept to a going concern in less than three months. Teja has had to shift his firm's strategy several times, sometimes within a matter of hours, because of environmental shifts and changes. He uses e-mail to communicate these shifts to Accompany workers immediately, in part so they can better perform their jobs and in part so that they feel more invested in the outcome.

Reluctance to Establish Goals Another barrier to effective planning is some managers' reluctance to establish goals for themselves and their units of responsibility. The reason for this reluctance may be lack of confidence or fear of failure. If a manager sets a goal that is specific, concise, and time related, then whether he or she attains it is obvious. Managers who consciously or unconsciously try to avoid this degree of accountability are likely to hinder the organization's planning efforts. Pfizer, a large pharmaceutical company, ran into problems because its managers did not set goals for research and development. Consequently, the organization fell further and further behind because managers had no way of knowing how effective their R&D efforts actually were.

Resistance to Change Another barrier to goal setting and planning is resistance to change. Planning essentially involves changing something about the organization. As we see in Chapter 13, people tend to resist change. Avon Products almost drove itself into bankruptcy several years ago because it insisted on continuing a policy of large dividend payments to its stockholders. When profits started to fall, managers resisted cutting the dividends and started borrowing to pay them. The company's debt grew from $3 million to $1.1 billion in eight years. Eventually, managers were forced to confront the problem and cut dividends.

Constraints Constraints that limit what an organization can do are another major obstacle. Common constraints include a lack of resources, government restrictions, and strong competition. For example, Owens-Corning Fiberglass took on an enormous debt burden as part of its fight to avoid a takeover by Wickes Ltd. The company then had such a large debt that it was forced to cut back on capital expenditures and research and development. And those cutbacks greatly constrained what the firm could plan for the future. Time constraints are also a factor. It is easy to say, "I'm too busy to plan today; I'll do it tomorrow." Effective planning takes time, energy, and an unwavering belief in its importance.

Overcoming the Barriers

Fortunately, there are several guidelines for making goal setting and planning effective. Some of the guidelines are listed in Table 7.2.

Understand the Purposes of Goals and Planning One of the best ways to facilitate goal-setting and planning processes is to recognize their basic purposes. Managers should also recognize that there are limits to the effectiveness of setting goals and making plans. Planning is not a panacea that will solve all of an organization's problems, nor is it an ironclad set of procedures to be followed at any cost. And effective goals and planning do not necessarily ensure success; adjustments and exceptions are to be expected as time passes. For example, Coca-Cola followed a logical and rational approach to setting goals and planning a few years ago when it introduced a new formula to combat Pepsi's increasing market share. But all the plans proved to be wrong as consumers rejected the new version of Coca-Cola. Managers quickly reversed the decision and reintroduced the old formula as Coca-Cola Classic. And it has a larger market share today than before. Thus, even though careful planning resulted in a big mistake, the company came out ahead in the long run.

Communication and Participation Although goals and plans may be initiated at high levels in the organization, they must also be communicated to others in the organization. Everyone involved in the planning process should know what the overriding organizational strategy is, what the various functional strategies are, and how they are all to be integrated and coordinated. People responsible for achieving goals and implementing plans must have a voice in developing them from the outset. These individuals almost always have valuable information to contribute, and because they will be implementing the plans, their involvement is critical: People are usually more committed to plans that they have helped shape. Even when an organization is somewhat centralized or uses a planning staff, managers from a variety of levels in the organization should be involved in the planning process.

Consistency, Revision, and Updating Goals should be consistent both horizontally and vertically. Horizontal consistency means that goals should be consistent across the organization, from one department to the next. Vertical consistency means that goals should be consistent up and down the organization—strategic, tactical, and operational goals must agree with one another. Because goal setting and planning are dynamic processes, they must also be revised and updated regularly. Many organizations are seeing the need to revise and update on an increasingly frequent basis. Citicorp, for example, once used a three-year planning horizon for developing and providing new financial services. That cycle was subsequently cut to two years, and the bank now often adopts a one-year horizon.

Effective Reward Systems In general, people should be rewarded both for establishing effective goals and plans and for successfully achieving them. Because failure sometimes results from factors outside the manager's control, however, people should also be assured that failure to reach a goal will not necessarily bring punitive consequences. Frederick Smith, founder and CEO of Federal Express, has a stated goal of encouraging risk. Thus, when Federal Express lost $233 million on an unsuccessful service called ZapMail, no one was punished. Smith believed that the original idea was a good one but was unsuccessful for reasons beyond the company's control.

Using Goals to Implement Plans

Goals are often used to implement plans. Formal goal-setting programs represent one widely used method for managing the goal-setting and planning processes concurrently to ensure that both are done effectively. Some firms call this approach **management by objectives**, or **MBO**. We should also note, however, that, although many firms use this basic approach, they frequently tailor it to their own special circumstances and use a special term or name for it.[29] For example, Tenneco uses an MBO-type system but calls it the "Performance Agreement System," or PAS.

management by objectives (MBO) A formal goal-setting process involving collaboration between managers and subordinates; the extent to which goals are accomplished is a major factor in evaluating and rewarding subordinates' performance

The Nature and Purpose of Formal Goal Setting The purpose of formal goal setting is generally to give subordinates a voice in the goal-setting and planning processes and to clarify for them exactly what they are expected to accomplish in a given time span. Thus formal goal setting is often concerned with goal setting and planning for individual managers and their units or work groups.

The Formal Goal-setting Process The basic mechanics of the formal goal-setting process are shown in Figure 7.5. This process is described here from an ideal perspective. In any given organization, the steps of the process are likely to vary in importance and may even take a different sequence. As a starting point, however, most managers believe that, if a formal goal-setting program is to be successful, it must start at the top of the organization. Top managers must communicate why they have adopted the program, what they think it will do, and that they have accepted and are committed to formal goal setting. Employees must also be educated about what goal setting is and what their role in it will be. Having committed to formal goal setting, managers must implement it in a way that is consistent with overall organizational goals and plans. The idea is that goals set at the top will systematically cascade down throughout the organization.

Although establishing the organization's basic goals and plans is extremely important, collaborative goal setting and planning are the essence of formal goal setting. The collaboration involves a series of distinct steps. First, managers tell their subordinates what organizational and unit goals and plans top management has established. Then managers meet with their subordinates on a one-to-one basis to arrive at a set of goals and plans for each subordinate that both the subordinate and the manager have helped develop and to which both are committed. Next, the goals are refined to be as verifiable (quantitative) as possible and to specify a time frame for their accomplishment. They should also be written. Further, the plans developed to achieve the goals need to be as clearly stated as possible and directly relate to each goal. Managers must play the role of counselors in the goal-setting and planning meeting. For example, they must ensure that the subordinates'

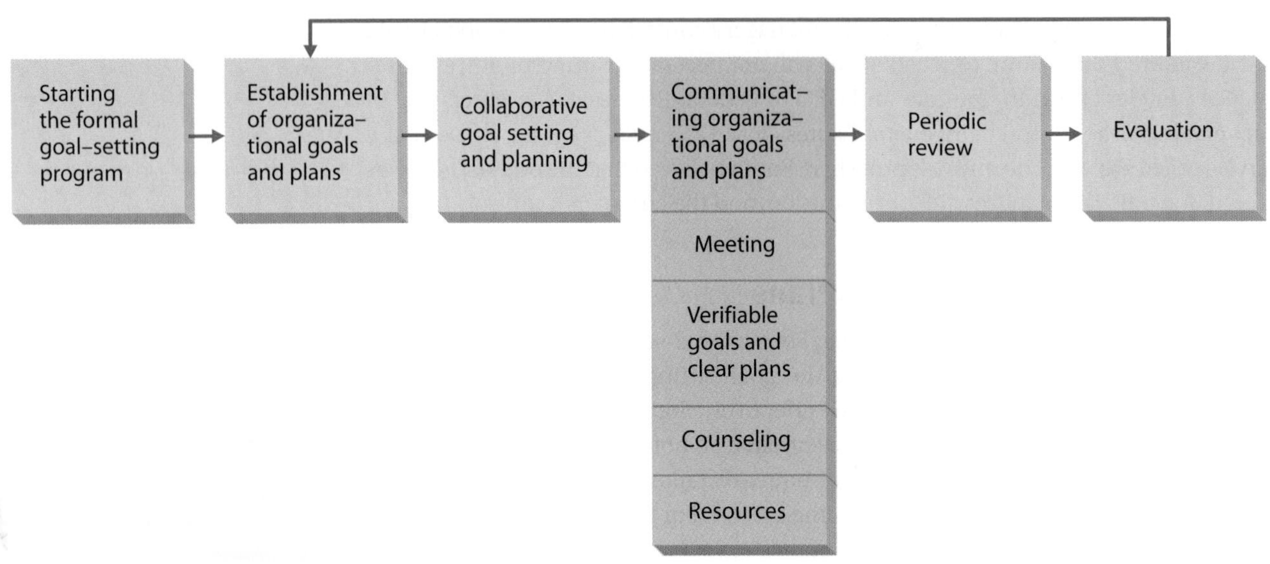

FIGURE 7.5

The Formal Goal-setting Process

Formal goal setting is an effective technique for integrating goal setting and planning. This figure portrays the general steps that most organizations use when they adopt formal goal setting. Of course, most organizations adapt this general process to fit their own unique needs and circumstances.

goals and plans are attainable and workable and that they will facilitate both the unit's and the organization's goals and plans. Finally, the meeting should spell out the resources that the subordinate will need to implement his or her plans and work effectively toward goal attainment.

Conducting periodic reviews as subordinates are working toward their goals is advisable. If the goals and plans are for a one-year period, meeting quarterly to discuss progress may be a good idea. At the end of the period, the manager meets with each subordinate again to review the degree of goal attainment. They discuss which goals were met and which were not met in the context of the original plans. The reasons for both success and failure are explored, and the employee is rewarded on the basis of goal attainment. In an ongoing goal-setting program, the evaluation meeting may also serve as the collaborative goal-setting and planning meeting for the next time period.

The Effectiveness of Formal Goal Setting A large number of organizations, including Cypress Semiconductor, Alcoa, Tenneco, DuPont, General Motors, Boeing, Caterpillar, Westinghouse Electric, and Black & Decker, all use some form of goal setting. As might be expected, goal setting has both strengths and weaknesses. A primary benefit of goal setting is improved employee motivation. By clarifying exactly what is expected, by allowing the employee a voice in determining expectations, and by basing rewards on the achievement of those expectations, organizations create a powerful motivational system for their employees.

Communication is also enhanced through the process of discussion and collaboration. And performance appraisals may be done more objectively, with less reliance on arbitrary or subjective assessment. Goal setting focuses attention on appropriate goals and plans, helps identify superior managerial talent for future promotion, and provides a systematic management philosophy that can have a positive effect on the overall organization. Goal setting also facilitates control. The periodic development and subsequent evaluation of individual goals and plans helps keep the organization on course toward its own long-run goals and plans.

On the other hand, goal setting occasionally fails because of poor implementation. Perhaps the major problem that can derail a goal-setting program is lack of top-management support. Some organizations decide to use goal setting, but then its implementation is delegated to lower management. This limits the program's effectiveness, because the goals and plans cascading throughout the organization may not actually be the goals and plans of top management and because others in the organization are not motivated to accept and become committed to them. Another problem with goal setting is that some firms overemphasize quantitative goals and plans and burden their systems with too much paperwork and record keeping. Some managers will not or cannot sit down to work out goals and plans with their subordinates. Rather, they "suggest" or even "assign" goals and plans to people. The result is resentment and a lack of commitment to the goal-setting program.[30]

concept CHECK

What are the primary barriers to goal setting and planning?

Describe how a goal-setting system such as MBO might be used in a college classroom setting.

Summary of Key Points

business.college.hmco.com/students

The planning process is the first basic managerial function that organizations must address. With an understanding of the environmental context, managers develop a number of different types of goals and plans. Decision making is the underlying framework of all planning, because every step of the planning process involves a decision.

Goals serve four basic purposes: to provide guidance and direction, to facilitate planning, to inspire motivation and commitment, and to promote evaluation and control. Kinds of goals can be differentiated by level, area, and time frame. All managers within an organization need to be involved in the goal-setting process. Managers need to pay special attention to the importance of managing multiple goals through optimizing and other approaches.

Goals are closely related to planning. The major types of plans are strategic, tactical, and operational. Plans are developed across a variety of time horizons, including long-range, intermediate, and short-range time frames. Essential people in an organization responsible for effective planning are the planning staff, planning task forces, the board of directors, the CEO, the executive committee, and line management. Contingency planning helps managers anticipate and plan for unexpected changes.

After plans have been developed, the manager must address how they will be achieved. This often involves tactical and operational plans. Tactical plans are at the middle of the organization and have an intermediate time horizon and moderate scope. Tactical plans are developed to implement specific parts of a strategic plan. They must flow from strategy, specify resource and time issues, and commit human resources. Tactical plans must be effectively executed.

Operational plans are at the lower levels of the organization, have a shorter time horizon, and are narrower in scope. Operational plans are derived from a tactical plan and are aimed at achieving one or more operational goals. Two major types of operational plans are single-use and standing plans. Single-use plans are designed to carry out a course of action that is not likely to be repeated in the future. Programs and projects are examples of single-use plans. Standing plans are designed to carry out a course of action that is likely to be repeated several times. Policies, standard operating procedures, and rules and regulations are all standing plans.

Several barriers exist to effective goal setting and planning. These include inappropriate goals, an improper reward system, a dynamic and complex environment, reluctance to establish goals, resistance to change, and various constraints. Methods for overcoming these barriers include understanding the purposes of goals and plans; communication and participation; consistency, revision, and updating; and an effective reward system. One particularly useful technique for managing goal setting and planning is formal goal setting, a process of collaborative goal setting and planning.

Discussion Questions

Questions for Review

1. Describe the nature of organizational goals. Be certain to include both the purposes and the kinds of goals.
2. Describe the scope, responsible personnel, and time frames for each kind of organizational plan. How are plans of different kinds related?
3. Explain the various types of operational plans. Give a real or hypothetical business example for each type. Do not use examples from the text.
4. List the steps in the formal goal-setting process. What are some of the advantages for companies that use this approach? What are some of the problems that may arise from use of this approach?

Questions for Analysis

5. Managers are frequently criticized for focusing too much attention on the achievement of short-term goals. In your opinion, how much attention should be given to long-term versus short-term goals? In the event of a conflict, which should be given priority? Explain your answers.
6. Read *The Business of Ethics* box, "The Decision-making Responsibility of Corporate Boards." What types of decisions require board involvement, and why? What types of decisions are not appropriate for board involvement, and why?
7. Standing plans help make an organization more effective. However, they may inhibit experimentation and organizational learning. Under what conditions, if any, should organizations ignore their own standing plans? In the area of planning, how can an organization balance the need for effectiveness against the need for creativity?

Questions for Application

8. Interview the head of the department in which your major exists. What kinds of goals exist for the department and for the members of the department? Share your findings with the rest of the class.
9. Tell about a time when an organization was not able to fully achieve all of its goals simultaneously. Why did this occur? Is complete realization of all goals impossible for an organization? Why or why not?
10. From your library or the Internet, find information about a company's mission statement and goals. List its mission and some of its strategic, tactical, and operational goals. Explain the relationship you see among the goals at different levels.

BUILDING EFFECTIVE communication and interpersonal SKILLS

Exercise Overview

Interpersonal skills refer to the manager's ability to communicate with, understand, and motivate individuals and groups. Communication skills are used both to convey information to others effectively and to receive ideas and information effectively from others. Communicating and interacting effectively with many different types of individuals are essential skills for planning. This exercise allows you to think through issues of communication and interaction as they relate to an actual planning situation.

Exercise Background

Larger and more complex organizations require greater complexity of planning in order to achieve their goals. NASA is responsible for the very complex task of managing U.S. space exploration and therefore has very complex planning needs.

In April of 1970, NASA launched the Apollo 13 manned space mission, charged with exploration of the lunar surface. On its way to the moon, the ship developed a malfunction that could have resulted in death for all the crew members. The crew members worked with scientists in Houston to develop a solution to the problem. The capsule was successful in returning to earth, and no lives were lost.

Exercise Task

1. Watch and listen to the short clip from *Apollo 13.* (This movie was made by Universal Studios in 1995 and was directed by Ron Howard. The script was based on a memoir by astronaut and mission captain Jim Lovell.) Describe the various types of planning and decision-making activities taking place at NASA during the unfolding of the disaster.
2. The biggest obstacles to effective planning in the first few minutes of this crisis were the rapid and unexpected changes occurring in a dynamic and complex environment. List elements of the situation that contributed to dynamism (elements that were rapidly changing). List elements that contributed to complexity. What kinds of actions did NASA's planning staff take to overcome obstacles presented by the dynamic and complex environment? Suggest any other useful actions the staff could have taken.
3. NASA managers and astronauts did not use a formal planning process in their approach to this situation. Why not? Is there any part of the formal planning process that could have been helpful? What does this example suggest to you about the advantages and limitations of the formal planning process?

BUILDING EFFECTIVE time-management SKILLS

Exercise Overview

Time-management skills refer to the manager's ability to prioritize work, to work efficiently, and to delegate appropriately. This exercise will help you develop your time-management skills by relating them to the process of goal optimization.

Exercise Background

All managers face myriad goals, challenges, opportunities, and demands on their time. Juggling all these requires a clear understanding of priorities, time availability, and related factors. Assume that you are planning to open your own business, a retail store in a local shopping mall. You are starting from scratch, with no prior business connections. You do, however, have a strong and impressive business plan that you know will work.

In planning your business, you know that you need to meet with the following parties:

1. The mall manager, to negotiate a lease
2. A local banker, to arrange partial financing
3. An attorney, to incorporate your business
4. An accountant, to set up a bookkeeping system
5. Suppliers, to arrange credit terms and delivery schedules
6. An advertising agency, to start promoting your business
7. A staffing agency, to hire employees
8. A design firm, to plan the physical layout of the store

Exercise Task

With the background information above as a context, do the following:

1. Develop a schedule listing the sequence in which you need to meet with the eight parties above. Your schedule should be developed to minimize backtracking (seeing one party and then having to see him or her again after seeing someone else).
2. Compare you schedule with that of a classmate and discuss differences.
3. Are there different schedules that are equally valid?

BUILDING EFFECTIVE technical SKILLS

business.college.hmco.com/students

Exercise Overview

Technical skills are the skills necessary to accomplish or understand the specific kind of work being done in an organization. By completing this exercise, you will gain an understanding of planning as it happens at different levels of the organizational hierarchy.

Exercise Background

At each organizational level, plans must reflect goals set at higher levels. Mission statements (sometimes also called "vision statements") are the highest-level goals and provide a context for planning at the strategic, tactical, and operational levels. Ideally, the entire set of mission, strategic, tactical, and operational goals should form a clear and unbroken chain from the top of the organization down to the daily task planning for every worker.

Effective mission statements share the following characteristics:

1. They should describe what is unique about the firm, something like a firm's "reason for being."

2. They should describe the firm's principal products and customers.
3. They should be motivational, exciting, inspiring, and relevant to all stakeholders.
4. They should be clear and detailed enough to serve as an effective guide to planning at lower levels. This might include establishing performance or ethical standards.

Exercise Task

1. Use the Internet to locate a mission or vision statement for a large, publicly traded corporation. (Hint: Many organizational websites include a vision or mission statement in their "About" page.)
2. Does the mission statement meet the four criteria listed above? Explain.
3. Assume that you are the firm's CEO. Give two to three examples of the types of strategic plans you could make, based on the guidance you receive from the mission statement.
4. Choose one of the strategic plans you developed in response to question 3. Assume that you are a vice president responsible for a functional area within the firm, such as marketing, production, or logistics. Then give two to three examples of the types of tactical plans you could make, based on the guidance you receive from the strategic plans.
5. Choose one of the tactical plans you developed in response to question 4. Assume that you are a supervisor responsible for overseeing the work of several functional employees within the firm. Then give two to three examples of the types of operational plans you could make, based on the guidance you receive from the tactical plans.

CHAPTER CLOSING case

CAN FORD REV UP?

"Early on, I felt like I was trying to hold up a collapsing building with an umbrella."

*– Bill Ford, CEO, Ford Motor Company**

Bill Ford, the forty-five-year-old great-grandson of Ford Motor Company founder Henry Ford, is facing the biggest challenge of his career. He became CEO of Ford in October of 2001, when the board lost confidence in Jacques Nasser and called on Bill to head the company. "Most guys who take this on had career-long ambitions and come to the job rubbing their hands together," says an executive who knows Bill well. "But this guy came with his hands over his eyes, saying, 'Why me, why me?'" Bill Ford took over a firm in a dire situation, with a critical need for careful planning and execution.

Ford, like every other auto manufacturer today, is struggling with a slowing worldwide economy. This means stagnant sales, particularly in luxury cars. Then, to combat falling sales, auto makers implemented costly rebates, no-money-down deals, free financing, and low-cost leases. The Big Three also began securitization of their loans, selling them to investors in exchange for much-needed cash. However, securitization erodes future revenues because loan payments now belong to the investor, not the firm. In addition, competitors in the auto industry have just completed a wave of international acquisitions, which ultimately could bring increased efficiency. In the short run, however, the acquisitions are proving costly and difficult to integrate.

The results have been devastating for the entire industry. Dozens of plants closed in 2002, and thousands of workers lost their jobs. No company was harder hit than Ford, whose stock price fell from $35 in mid-1999 to less than $10. Ford's financial situation was so poor that some of its bonds had been downgraded to junk status. This is part of a "financial death spiral," in which a struggling company has a harder and harder time borrowing funds.

When Bill Ford took over the ailing firm, he was well known for his twenty-three years of service to Ford, his intelligence, and his humility. But he had never held a top-level position in operations or finance, the two functions that are considered crucial in the auto industry. Even with his lack of experience, he knew that his first priority should be the creation of a sweepingly new plan for Ford. He needed to undo some of the damage done to the firm during the Nasser years, including bringing back experienced staff, cutting expenses, and improving quality. Bill also shifted the firm's R&D focus to developing cars for specific market niches, rather than the mass-volume cars of the past, such as the Taurus. Other new plans included dramatic expansion of production of profitable Jaguars, new ad campaigns, restructuring of Ford's credit division, and a tougher stance on cost cutting, especially with the United Auto Workers union.

Yet the gulf that exists between dreaming up a great strategy and effectively implementing that strategy remains wide. Although Bill is clearly more comfortable as a "big picture" planner, he has had to roll up his sleeves and tackle the firm's many fundamental problems. "It's not sexy," Bill says. "It's a lot of hard work. . . . Early on, I felt like I was trying to hold up a collapsing building with an umbrella." Bill is finding that the CEO is called on to resolve a never-ending stream of problems. "The worst part of the job is the fear of the unknown," says Bill. "Every day it's something. Every day somebody walks out on strike somewhere. The nature of the job is, you only hear problems—I guess that's what a CEO's job is—but good news is few and far between."

Some of Bill's tactics have succeeded brilliantly. He has brought together a high-powered and experienced team of executives, and they have executed several key parts of his recovery plan. However, other parts of the plan will require massive strategizing, such as the goal of closing five major plants and laying off 35,000 workers in the next five years. Bill's goal of increasing production of the Jaguar was implemented too quickly, leading to quality problems. The brand's customer satisfaction rating fell from number two to number nineteen.

Will Bill Ford be able to turn around his family firm? He certainly faces some great challenges along the way. But skeptics who doubt him should consider the case of Henry Ford II (Bill's grandfather), who took over as CEO in 1945 at the age of twenty-eight. At the time, Henry said, "I am green and reaching for answers." And then he led the company through the time of its highest growth, innovation, and profitability. If Bill Ford has inherited even just a part of the Ford family's legendary management ability, Ford Motor Company may yet weather the storm and turn up a winner.

Case Questions

1. Based on information in the case, what are some of Ford's strategic goals? What are some of Ford's tactical goals?
2. What are some of the actions that Bill Ford and other managers must take in order to ensure a successful implementation of Ford's tactical plans?
3. What barriers to planning has Bill Ford experienced? What has he done, or what should he do, in order to overcome those barriers?

Case References

Betsy Morris, "Can Ford Save Ford?" *Fortune*, November 18, 2002, pp. 52–63; Danny Hakim, "A New-Model Ford on a Risky Track," *New York Times*, September 29, 2002, pp. BU1, BU12; Janice Revell, "Ford Careens Toward the Junkyard," Fortune, October 28, 2002, www.fortune.com on November 21, 2002; Kathleen Kerwin, "Bill Ford's Long, Hard Road," *BusinessWeek*, October 7, 2002, www.businessweek.com on November 21, 2002 (*quote); Kathleen Kerwin, "Ford: Luxury Is Job One," *BusinessWeek*, November 11, 2002, pp. 116–118; "Ford's New Pick-Me-Up?" *BusinessWeek*, September 8, 2003, pp. 78–80.

Chapter Notes

1. "Teaching an Old Bag Some New Tricks," *BusinessWeek*, June 9, 2003, pp. 78–80; Julia Boorstin, "How Coach Got Hot," *Fortune*, October 28, 2002, pp. 131–134; Marilyn Much, "Consumer Research Is His Bag," *Investor's Business Daily*, December 16, 2002, http://biz.yahoo.com on December 19, 2002 (*quote); "S&P Stock Picks and Pans: Accumulate Coach," *BusinessWeek*, October 22, 2002, www.businessweek.com on December 18, 2002.
2. Patrick R. Rogers, Alex Miller, and William Q. Judge, "Using Information-Processing Theory to Understand Planning/Performance Relationships in the context of Strategy," *Strategic Management Journal*, 1999, vol. 20, pp. 567–577.
3. See Peter J. Brews and Michelle R. Hunt, "Learning to Plan and Planning to Learn: Resolving the Planning School/Learning School Debate," *Strategic Management Journal*, 1999, vol. 20, pp. 889–913.
4. Max D. Richards, *Setting Strategic Goals and Objectives*, 2nd ed. (St. Paul, Minn.: West, 1986).
5. Jim Collins, "Turning Goals into Results: The Power of Catalytic Mechanisms," *Harvard Business Review*, July–August 1999, pp. 71–81.
6. "GE, No. 2 in Appliances, Is Agitating to Grab Share from Whirlpool," *Wall Street Journal*, July 2, 1997, pp. A1, A6. See also "A Talk with Jeff Immelt," *BusinessWeek*, January 28, 2002, pp. 102–104.
7. Kenneth R. Thompson, Wayne A. Hochwarter, and Nicholas J. Mathys, "Stretch Targets: What Makes Them Effective?" *Academy of Management Executive*, August 1997, pp. 48–58.
8. "A Methodical Man," *Forbes*, August 11, 1997, pp. 70–72.
9. See Thomas Bateman, Hugh O'Neill, and Amy Kenworthy-U'Ren, "A Hierarchical Taxonomy of Top Managers' Goals," *Journal of Applied Psychology*, 2002, vol. 87, no. 6, pp. 1134–1148.
10. John A. Pearce II and Fred David, "Corporate Mission Statements: The Bottom Line," *Academy of Management Executive*, May 1987, p. 109.
11. "Monsanto Boss's Vision of 'Life Sciences' Firm Now Confronts Reality," *Wall Street Journal*, December 21, 1999, pp. A1, A10.
12. "'The McDonald's of Toiletries'," *BusinessWeek*, August 4, 1997, pp. 79–80.
13. "Home Depot: Beyond Do-It-Yourselfers," *BusinessWeek*, June 30, 1997, pp. 86–88.
14. "Lowe's Is Sprucing up Its House," *BusinessWeek*, June 3, 2002, pp. 56–58.
15. Jerry Flint, "Money Isn't Everything," *Forbes*, August 12, 2002, p. 80.
16. "Airlines Try Cutting Business Fares, Find They Don't Lose Revenue," *Wall Street Journal*, November 22, 2002, pp. A1, A6.
17. See Charles Hill and Gareth Jones, *Strategic Management*, 6th ed. (Boston: Houghton Mifflin, 2004).
18. *Hoover's Handbook of World Business 2003* (Austin, Texas: Hoover's Business Press, 2003), pp. 330–331.
19. "Nissan's Slow U-Turn," *BusinessWeek*, May 12, 1997, pp. 54–55.
20. Peter Lorange and Balaji S. Chakravarthy, *Strategic Planning Systems*, 2nd ed. (Englewood Cliffs, N.J.: Prentice-Hall, 1989).
21. K. A. Froot, D. S. Scharfstein, and J. C. Stein, "A Framework for Risk Management," *Harvard Business Review*, November–December 1994, pp. 91–102.
22. "How the Fixers Fended off Big Disasters," *Wall Street Journal*, December 23, 1999, pp. B1, B4.
23. Michael Watkins and Max Bazerman, "Predictable Surprises: The Disasters You Should Have Seen Coming," *Harvard Business Review*, March 2003, pp. 72–81.
24. James Brian Quinn, Henry Mintzberg, and Robert M. James, *The Strategy Process* (Englewood Cliffs, N.J.: Prentice-Hall, 1988).
25. Vasudevan Ramanujam and N. Venkatraman, "Planning System Characteristics and Planning Effectiveness," *Strategic Management Journal*, vol. 8, no. 2, 1987, pp. 453–468.
26. "Coca-Cola May Need to Slash Its Growth Targets," *Wall Street Journal*, January 28, 2000, p. B2. See also "Pepsi and Coke Roll out Flavors to Boost Sales," *Wall Street Journal*, May 7, 2002, pp. B1, B4.
27. "Finally, Coke Gets It Right," *BusinessWeek*, February 10, 2003, p. 47.
28. "Disney, Revisited," *USA Today*, December 14, 1999, pp. 1B, 2B.
29. Andrew Campbell, "Tailored, Not Benchmarked," *Harvard Business Review*, March–April 1999, pp. 41–48.
30. See Jack N. Kondrasuk, "Studies in MBO Effectiveness," *Academy of Management Review*, July 1981, pp. 419–430, for a review of the strengths and weaknesses of MBO.

8

Managing Strategy and Strategic Planning

CHAPTER OUTLINE

The Nature of Strategic Management
- The Components of Strategy
- Types of Strategic Alternatives
- Strategy Formulation and Implementation

Using SWOT Analysis to Formulate Strategy
- Evaluating an Organization's Strengths
- Evaluating an Organization's Weaknesses
- Evaluating an Organization's Opportunities and Threats

Formulating Business-Level Strategies
- Porter's Generic Strategies
- The Miles and Snow Typology
- Strategies Based on the Product Life Cycle

Implementing Business-Level Strategies
- Implementing Porter's Generic Strategies
- Implementing Miles and Snow's Strategies

Formulating Corporate-Level Strategies
- Single-Product Strategy
- Related Diversification
- Unrelated Diversification

Implementing Corporate-Level Strategies
- Becoming a Diversified Firm
- Managing Diversification

International and Global Strategies
- Developing International and Global Strategies
- Strategic Alternatives for International Business

LEARNING OBJECTIVES

After studying this chapter, you should be able to:

1. ***Discuss the components of strategy, types of strategic alternatives, and the distinction between strategy formulation and strategy implementation.***
2. ***Describe how to use SWOT analysis in formulating strategy.***

OPENING INCIDENT

From its founding in 1964 through the mid-1990s, Nike was one of the biggest success stories in American business. Since its earliest days, Nike has been an innovator, creating the waffle-sole shoe and the air cushion, and pioneering technical shoe design and the acceptance of sportswear as fashionable, casual street wear. The firm's growth peaked in 1997, when sales grew by 50 percent and profits topped $795 million. However, by 1999, profits had fallen to just $451 million, and the firm was clearly struggling.

Founder Phil Knight, Nike's CEO and chair, claims, "We got to be a $9 billion company with a $5 billion management." The company may be the victim of its own success. As Nike's premium products became more technologically complex and more expensive to design and manufacture, prices rose. The firm's elite shoes are priced between $150 and $300, far above the budgets of teenagers, who are the biggest consumers of active wear. Another problem was the saturated market for athletic shoes in the United States. There were few new consumers in the footwear industry, which makes up 50 percent of the firm's revenues.

To return the firm to its past splendor, Knight began a series of bold moves.

3 *Identify and describe various alternative approaches to business-level strategy formulation.*

4 *Describe how business-level strategies are implemented.*

5 *Identify and describe various alternative approaches to corporate-level strategy formulation.*

6 *Describe how corporate-level strategies are implemented.*

7 *Discuss international and global strategies.*

"Now we're a pretty well-run $10 billion company and we're ready to grow again."

—Phil Knight, Nike founder, CEO, and chair

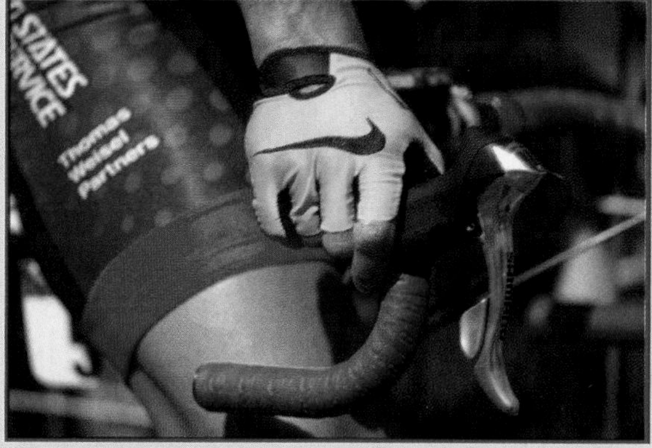

Nike is "riding high" again as it successfully extends its famous "swoosh" logo to apparel and gear for an array of sports ranging from soccer to bicycling.

In a shocking switch from its promote-from-within, athlete-dominated culture, the firm began to hire top managers from outside the sportswear industry. Donald W. Blair, formerly of PepsiCo, was hired as chief financial officer and charged with bringing fiscal discipline to the free-spending, marketing-driven company. Another outsider, Mindy Grossman, was lured away from Polo Ralph Lauren to head Nike's apparel group. Grossman's focus is on updating Nike's fashion appeal and reducing development time for new products. The firm has diversified, moving beyond its traditional strengths in running and basketball. Nike has become a leader in soccer and cycling, and is beginning to pursue the very large and lucrative golf apparel industry.

The promotion of company veterans Mark Parker and Charlie Denson to positions as copresidents has contributed to the shakeup. Parker brings extensive experience in brand management, whereas Denson's career has been built in sales. The two men together have knowledge about territories, advertising, inventory management, and other critical areas of the business. The copresidents were initially skeptical about the unorthodox arrangement but are now firm believers in its benefits. "Going into it, we both had some trepidation about learning how to dance together," says Denson. "It truly has worked out better than I thought it would." Parker agrees, saying, "We have a healthy dose of self-criticism and a desire to really understand what's going on. The fact we have brought in a number of outside management has been a real plus, too."

The changes have been pleasing to consumers, as evidenced by increasing sales, especially in the firm's apparel business. The clothing division grew to 30 percent of Nike sales in 2002. "For the first time, we're an apparel company as well as a shoe company," CEO Knight says. Investors should be happy, too, due to higher sales and rising profit margins. And the recent push to increase overseas sales could counteract flattening demand in the States, which would also benefit shareholders.

Nike seems well on its way to recovering its former glory, but two clouds remain on the horizon. First, the firm has thus far failed to effectively address accusations that it exploits Third World workers. Until the firm sheds its "sweatshop" image, some consumers will continue to boycott Nike products. Second, the rising prices of Nike products have led to conflicts with retailer Foot Locker, Nike's largest buyer. Foot Locker would prefer to see its most expensive products selling for about $100, whereas Nike thinks the market has room for products retailing for much more. In December of 2002, Nike decided to sell its elite shoes through other outlets, excluding Foot Locker from distribution of those products. Upon hearing the news, industry analysts downgraded the stocks of both Nike and Foot Locker, an indicator that the move is expected to be negative for both manufacturer and retailer.

If Nike can find a way to make peace with retailers and to respond effectively to charges of unethical labor practices, the firm may once again find itself far ahead in the race to dominate the athletic gear industry. Or, as Phil Knight puts it, "Now we're a pretty well-run $10 billion company and we're ready to grow again."[1]

The actions taken by Nike reflect one of the most critical functions that managers perform for their businesses: strategy and strategic planning. Phil Knight recognized that his firm had both significant strengths and worrisome weaknesses. He also knew that action was required to revitalize the firm. Hence, he embarked on a variety of new initiatives and made radical changes in how Nike does business. But each move he made was developed from a strategic perspective.

This chapter discusses how organizations manage strategy and strategic planning. We begin by examining the nature of strategic management, including its components and alternatives. We then describe the kinds of analysis needed for firms to formulate their strategies. Next we examine how organizations first formulate and then implement business-level strategies, followed by a parallel discussion at the corporate strategy level. We conclude with a discussion of international and global strategies.

The Nature of Strategic Management

A **strategy** is a comprehensive plan for accomplishing an organization's goals. **Strategic management**, in turn, is a way of approaching business opportunities and challenges—it is a comprehensive and ongoing management process aimed at formulating and implementing effective strategies. Finally, **effective strategies** are those that promote a superior alignment between the organization and its environment and the achievement of strategic goals.[2]

strategy A comprehensive plan for accomplishing an organization's goals

strategic management A comprehensive and ongoing management process aimed at formulating and implementing effective strategies; a way of approaching business opportunities and challenges

effective strategy A strategy that promotes a superior alignment between the organization and its environment and the achievement of strategic goals

distinctive competence An organizational strength possessed by only a small number of competing firms

scope When applied to strategy, it specifies the range of markets in which an organization will compete

resource deployment How an organization distributes its resources across the areas in which it competes

The Components of Strategy

In general, a well-conceived strategy addresses three areas: distinctive competence, scope, and resource deployment. A **distinctive competence** is something the organization does exceptionally well. (We discuss distinctive competencies more fully later.) A distinctive competence of The Limited is speed in moving inventory. It tracks consumer preferences daily with point-of-sale computers, electronically transmits orders to suppliers in Hong Kong, charters 747s to fly products to the United States, and has products in stores forty-eight hours later. Because other retailers take weeks or sometimes months to accomplish the same things, The Limited relies on this distinctive competence to remain competitive.[3]

The **scope** of a strategy specifies the range of markets in which an organization will compete. Hershey Foods has essentially restricted its scope to the confectionery business, with a few related activities in other food-processing areas. In contrast, its biggest competitor, Mars, has adopted a broader scope by competing in the pet food business and the electronics industry, among others. Some organizations, called conglomerates, compete in dozens or even hundreds of markets.

A strategy should also include an outline of the organization's projected **resource deployment**—how it will distribute its resources across the areas in which it competes. General Electric, for example, has been using profits from its highly successful U.S. operations to invest heavily in new businesses in Europe and Asia. Alternatively, the firm might have chosen to invest in different industries in its domestic market or to invest more heavily in Latin America. The choices it made as to where and how much to invest reflect issues of resource deployment.[4]

Types of Strategic Alternatives

Most businesses today also develop strategies at two distinct levels. These levels provide a rich combination of strategic alternatives for organizations. The two general levels are business-level strategies and corporate-level strategies. **Business-level strategy** is the set of strategic alternatives from which an organization chooses as it conducts business in a particular industry or market. Such alternatives help the organization focus its competitive efforts for each industry or market in a targeted and focused manner.

business-level strategy The set of strategic alternatives from which an organization chooses as it conducts business in a particular industry or market

Corporate-level strategy is the set of strategic alternatives from which an organization chooses as it manages its operations simultaneously across several industries and several markets.[5] As we discuss later, most large companies today compete in a variety of industries and markets. Thus, although they develop business-level strategies for each industry or market, they also develop an overall strategy that helps define the mix of industries and markets that are of interest to the firm.

corporate-level strategy The set of strategic alternatives from which an organization chooses as it manages its operations simultaneously across several industries and several markets

Strategy Formulation and Implementation

Drawing a distinction between strategy formulation and strategy implementation is also instructive. **Strategy formulation** is the set of processes involved in creating or determining the strategies of the organization, whereas **strategy implementation** is the methods by which strategies are operationalized or executed within the organization. The primary distinction is along the lines of content versus process: The formulation stage determines what the strategy is, and the implementation stage focuses on how the strategy is achieved.

strategy formulation The set of processes involved in creating or determining the strategies of the organization; it focuses on the content of strategies

strategy implementation The methods by which strategies are operationalized or executed within the organization; it focuses on the processes through which strategies are achieved

Sometimes the processes of formulating and implementing strategies are rational, systematic, and planned. This is often referred to as a **deliberate strategy**—a plan chosen and implemented to support specific goals.[6] Texas Instruments (TI) excels at formulating and implementing deliberate strategies. TI uses a planning process that assigns most senior managers two distinct responsibilities: an operational, short-term responsibility and a strategic, long-term responsibility. Thus one manager may be responsible for both increasing the efficiency of semiconductor operations over the next year (operational, short term) and investigating new materials for semiconductor manufacturing in the twenty-first century (strategic, long term). TI's objective is to help managers make short-term operational decisions while keeping in mind longer-term goals and objectives.

deliberate strategy A plan of action that an organization chooses and implements to support specific goals

Other times, however, organizations use an **emergent strategy**—a pattern of action that develops over time in an organization in the absence of mission and goals or despite mission and goals.[7] Implementing emergent strategies involves allocating resources even though an organization has not explicitly chosen its strategies. 3M has at times benefited from emergent strategies. The invention of invisible tape, for instance, provides a good example. Entrepreneurial engineers

emergent strategy A pattern of action that develops over time in an organization in the absence of mission and goals or despite mission and goals working independently took the invention to their boss, who concluded that it did not have major market potential because it was not part of an approved research and development plan. Only when the product was evaluated at the highest levels in the organization was it accepted and made part of 3M's product mix. Of course, 3M's Scotch tape became a major success despite the fact that it arose outside of the firm's established practices. 3M now counts on emergent strategies to help expand its numerous businesses.

concept CHECK

What are the basic components of strategy?	*Distinguish between business- and corporate-level strategy. Is one or the other more likely to be deliberate or emergent?*

Using SWOT Analysis to Formulate Strategy

SWOT An acronym that stands for strengths, weaknesses, opportunities, and threats

The starting point in formulating strategy is usually SWOT analysis. **SWOT** is an acronym that stands for strengths, weaknesses, opportunities, and threats. As shown in Figure 8.1, SWOT analysis is a careful evaluation of an organization's internal strengths and weaknesses as well as its environmental opportunities and threats. In SWOT analysis, the best strategies accomplish an organization's mission by (1)

FIGURE 8.1

SWOT Analysis

SWOT analysis is one of the most important steps in formulating strategy. Using the organization's mission as a context, managers assess internal strengths (distinctive competencies) and weaknesses as well as external opportunities and threats. The goal is then to develop good strategies that exploit opportunities and strengths, neutralize threats, and avoid weaknesses.

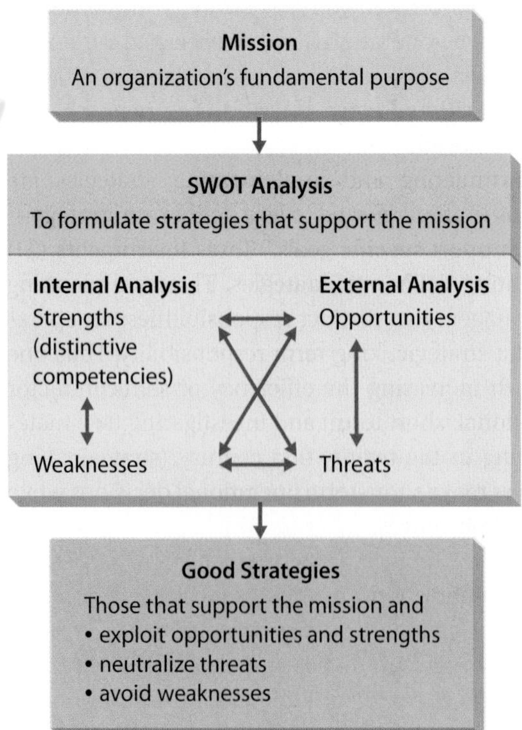

exploiting an organization's opportunities and strengths while (2) neutralizing its threats and (3) avoiding (or correcting) its weaknesses.

Evaluating an Organization's Strengths

Organizational strengths are skills and capabilities that enable an organization to conceive of and implement its strategies. Sears, for example, has a nationwide network of trained service employees who repair Sears appliances. Jane Thompson, a Sears executive, conceived of a plan to consolidate repair and home improvement services nationwide under the well-known Sears brand name and to promote them as a general repair operation for all appliances, not just those purchased from Sears. Thus the firm is capitalizing on existing capabilities and the strength of its name to launch a new operation.[8] Different strategies call on different skills and capabilities. For example, Matsushita Electric has demonstrated strengths in manufacturing and selling consumer electronics under the brand name Panasonic. Matsushita's strength in electronics does not ensure success, however, if the firm expands into insurance, swimming pool manufacturing, or retail. Different strategies like these require different organizational strengths. SWOT analysis divides organizational strengths into two categories: common strengths and distinctive competencies.

organizational strength A skill or capability that enables an organization to conceive of and implement its strategies

common strength A skill or capability held by numerous competing firms

Common Organizational Strengths

A **common strength** is an organizational capability possessed by a large number of competing firms. For example, all the major Hollywood film studios possess common strengths in lighting, sound recording, set and costume design, and makeup. *Competitive parity* exists when large numbers of competing firms are able to implement the same strategy. In this situation, organizations generally attain only average levels of performance. Thus a film company that exploits only its common strengths in choosing and implementing strategies is not likely to go beyond average performance.

Distinctive Competencies

A *distinctive competence* is a strength possessed by only a small number of competing firms. Distinctive competencies are rare among a set of competitors. George Lucas's Industrial Light & Magic (ILM), for example, has brought the cinematic art of special effects to new heights. Some of ILM's special effects can be produced by no other organization; these rare special effects are thus ILM's distinctive competencies. Organizations that exploit their distinctive competencies often obtain a *competitive advantage* and attain above-normal economic performance.[9] Indeed, a main purpose of SWOT analysis is to discover an organization's distinctive competencies so

A distinctive competence is a strength possessed by only a few firms. The owners of PlanetOut Partners, Inc., based in San Francisco, have used this organizational strength to build a profitable network of web sites targeting gay and lesbian web surfers. This strategy, in turn, has given the firm a competitive advantage that may be difficult for other firms to imitate.

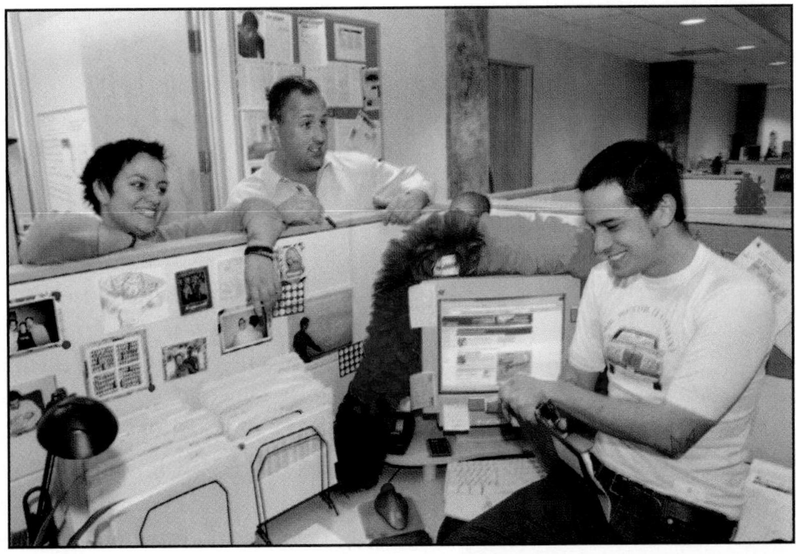

WORKING WITH diversity

Journey to Diversity

". . . a guy isn't going to miss his annual fishing week in Iceland for love or money."

– Mollie Fitzgerald, co-founder of Frontiers International Travel*

The advertisements contain tantalizing, varied details: "Golf in Scotland. 7 night small group tour, Gleneagles, day trips to castles and distilleries. Accommodation in historical properties." "Berbers of Tunisia uncovers the history and archaeology of this land. Roman mosaics, the 9th century town of Ribat, and a 4 x 4 adventure to desert oases."

For some companies, diversity is seen as an issue that affects primarily human resource practices or as a problem that must be overcome. But some firms find that diversity presents strategic opportunities. A striking example is found in the independent travel agent industry, which is struggling to survive in an increasingly wired world, with a slower economy and post-9/11 travel jitters. To cope, travel agents have turned to specialty, or niche, marketing. A quick look at InfoHub, an online guide to specialty travel for agents and consumers, lists dozens of diverse segments, ranging from language schools to honeymoons, from Biblical tours to Super Bowl travel.

Specialty marketing allows firms to charge higher prices and provides greater predictability. "We feel fortunate that we are associated with specialty interests," says Mollie Fitzgerald, co-founder of Frontiers International Travel. The firm specializes in high-end hunting and fishing retreats. "People who are skittish about travel might defer the family holiday to Europe, but a guy isn't going to miss his annual fishing week in Iceland for love or money. People who are passionate about a sport or pursuit are much more likely to travel in this environment." Specialization also allows the firms to develop expertise in meeting customers' particular needs.

Travel agents have traditionally segmented travelers by age or family status, but the new drive toward segmentation goes further. Soul Planet and Black Diamond offer tours for African-Americans to Paris and Africa. Spanish-speaking travelers use Costamar and Celestial Fantasie for advice about vacations to Latin America. A variety of agencies focus on tours for vegetarians, women, the disabled, or gays and lesbians. Or consumers can look for even more specialization. What is recommended for a single woman who is interested in cooking, music, and history? How about a female-only "hill tribes" tour of China, including the Great Wall, culinary demonstrations, concerts, and a visit to the ancient Kingdom of Women, where women were rulers and men were servants?

References: "A World of Opportunities in the Travel Industry," *BusinessWeek*, July 10, 2001, www.businessweek.com on January 6, 2003; Barry Eastbrook, "Agents' Survival Strategies," *New York Times*, November 24, 2002, p. TR6 (*quote); "Domestic Travel Market Report," Travel Industry Association of America, www.tia.org on January 6, 2003; "Frequently Asked Questions," American Society of Travel Agents website, www.astanet.com on January 6, 2003; "Info-Hub Specialty Travel Guide," www.biztravel.com on January 6, 2003.

that the organization can choose and implement strategies that exploit its unique organizational strengths. *Working with Diversity* presents an unusual take on diversity as it relates to an interesting distinctive competence.

strategic imitation The practice of duplicating another organization's distinctive competence and thereby implementing a valuable strategy

Imitation of Distinctive Competencies An organization that possesses distinctive competencies and exploits them in the strategies it chooses can expect to obtain a competitive advantage and above-normal economic performance. However, its success will lead other organizations to duplicate these advantages. **Strategic imitation** is the practice of duplicating another firm's distinctive competence and thereby implementing a valuable strategy. Although some distinctive competencies can be imitated, others cannot be. When a distinctive competence cannot be imitated, strategies that exploit these competencies generate sustained competitive advantage. A **sustained competitive advantage** is a competitive advantage that exists after all attempts at strategic imitation have ceased.[10]

A distinctive competence might not be imitated for three reasons. First, the acquisition or development of the distinctive competence may depend on unique historical circumstances that other organizations cannot replicate. Caterpillar, for example, obtained a sustained competitive advantage when the U.S. Army granted it a long-term contract during World War II. The army felt obligated to offer this contract because of the acute international construction requirements necessary to meet the army's needs. Caterpillar's current competitors, including Komatsu and John Deere & Company, cannot re-create these circumstances.

Effective business strategies generally spell out such things as distinctive competencies, resource deployment, and scope. Consider, for instance, the success currently being enjoyed by Seth Goldman, owner and "Tea-EO" of Honest Tea. The distinctive competence of Honest Tea is its brewing technology: it uses real tea leaves and spring water, and adds only a minimum amount of sweetener. It invests heavily in building strong relations with key partners such as socially conscious suppliers and retailers. And it limits operations to packaged tea beverages. Honest Tea has more than doubled its revenues each of the last three years and seems headed toward long-term "prosperi-tea."

Second, a distinctive competence might be difficult to imitate because its nature and character might not be known or understood by competing firms. Procter & Gamble, for example, considers that its sustained competitive advantage is based on its manufacturing practices. Large sections of Procter & Gamble's plants are screened off to keep this information secure. Industrial Light & Magic also refuses to disclose how it creates some of its special effects.

Finally, a distinctive competence can be difficult to imitate if it is based on complex social phenomena, like organizational teamwork or culture. Competing organizations may know, for example, that a firm's success is directly traceable to the teamwork among its managers but, because teamwork is a difficult thing to create, may not be able to imitate this distinctive competence.

Evaluating an Organization's Weaknesses

Organizational weaknesses are skills and capabilities that do not enable an organization to choose and implement strategies that support its mission. An organization has essentially two ways of addressing weaknesses. First, it may need to make investments to obtain the strengths required to implement strategies that support its mission. Second, it may need to modify its mission so that it can be accomplished with the skills and capabilities that the organization already possesses.

In practice, organizations have a difficult time focusing on weaknesses, in part because organization members are often reluctant to admit that they do not possess all the skills and capabilities needed. Evaluating weaknesses also calls into question the judgment of managers who chose the organization's mission in the first place and who failed to invest in the skills and capabilities needed to accomplish it.

Organizations that fail either to recognize or to overcome their weaknesses are likely to suffer from competitive disadvantages. An organization has a **competitive disadvantage** when it is not implementing valuable strategies that are being implemented by competing organizations. Organizations with a competitive disadvantage can expect to attain below-average levels of performance.

sustained competitive advantage A competitive advantage that exists after all attempts at strategic imitation have ceased

organizational weaknesses A skill or capability that does not enable an organization to choose and implement strategies that support its mission

competitive disadvantage A situation in which an organization is not implementing valuable strategies that are being implemented by competing organizations

Evaluating an Organization's Opportunities and Threats

organizational opportunity An area in the environment that, if exploited, may generate higher performance

organizational threat An area in the environment that increases the difficulty of an organization's achieving high performance

Whereas evaluating strengths and weaknesses focuses attention on the internal workings of an organization, evaluating opportunities and threats requires analyzing an organization's environment. **Organizational opportunities** are areas that may generate higher performance. **Organizational threats** are areas that increase the difficulty of an organization's performing at a high level. Porter's "five forces" model of the competitive environment, as discussed in Chapter 3, can be used to characterize the extent of opportunity and threat in an organization's environment.

Recall that Porter's five forces are level of competitive rivalry, power of suppliers, power of buyers, threat of substitutes, and threat of new entrants. In general, when the level of competitive rivalry, the power of suppliers and buyers, and the threat of substitutes and new entrants are all high, an industry has relatively few opportunities and numerous threats. Firms in these types of industries typically have the potential to achieve only normal economic performance. On the other hand, when the level of rivalry, the power of suppliers and buyers, and the threat of substitutes and new entrants are all low, then an industry has numerous opportunities and relatively few threats. These industries hold the potential for above-normal performance for organizations in them.[11]

concept CHECK

What do the letters S, W, O, and T represent when conducting a SWOT analysis?

Under what circumstances might a firm find it advantageous to share with others the details of one of its distinctive competencies?

Formulating Business-Level Strategies

A number of frameworks have been developed for identifying the major strategic alternatives that organizations should consider when choosing their business-level strategies. Three important classification schemes are Porter's generic strategies, the Miles and Snow typology, and strategies based on the product life cycle.

Porter's Generic Strategies

differentiation strategy A strategy in which an organization seeks to distinguish itself from competitors through the quality of its products or services

According to Michael Porter, organizations may pursue a differentiation, overall cost leadership, or focus strategy at the business level.[12] Table 8.1 summarizes each of these strategies. An organization that pursues a **differentiation strategy** seeks to distinguish itself from competitors through the quality of its products or services. Firms that successfully implement a differentiation strategy are able to charge more than competitors because customers are willing to pay more to obtain the extra value they perceive.[13] Rolex pursues a differentiation strategy. Rolex watches are handmade of precious metals like gold or platinum and stainless steel, and are subjected to strenuous tests of quality and reliability. The firm's reputation enables it to charge thousands of dollars for its watches. Coca-Cola and Pepsi are currently battling in the market for bottled water on

TABLE 8.1

Porter's Generic Strategies

Michael Porter has proposed three generic strategies. Each of these strategies—differentiation, overall cost leadership, and focus—is presumed to be widely applicable to many different competitive situations.

Strategy Type	Definition	Examples
Differentiation	Distinguish products or services	Rolex (watches) Mercedes-Benz (automobiles) Nikon (cameras) Cross (writing instruments) Hewlett-Packard (handheld calculators)
Overall cost leadership	Reduce manufacturing and other costs	Timex (watches) Hyundai (automobiles) Kodak (cameras) BIC (writing instruments) Texas Instruments (handheld calculators)
Focus	Concentrate on specific regional market, product market, or group of buyers	Tag Heuer (watches) Fiat, Alfa Romeo (automobiles) Polaroid (cameras) Waterman (writing instruments) Fisher-Price (handheld calculators)

the basis of differentiation. Coke touts its Dasani brand on the basis of its fresh taste, whereas Pepsi promotes its Aquafina brand on the basis of its purity.[14] Other firms that use differentiation strategies are Lexus, Nikon, Mont Blanc, and Ralph Lauren.

An organization implementing an **overall cost leadership strategy** attempts to gain a competitive advantage by reducing its costs below the costs of competing firms. By keeping costs low, the organization is able to sell its products at low prices and still make a profit. Timex uses an overall cost leadership strategy. For decades, this firm has specialized in manufacturing relatively simple, low-cost watches for the mass market. The price of Timex watches, starting around $39.95, is low because of the company's efficient high-volume manufacturing capacity. Poland Springs and Crystal Geyser bottled waters are promoted on the basis of their low cost. Other firms that implement overall cost leadership strategies are Hyundai, Eastman Kodak, BIC, and Old Navy.

overall cost leadership strategy A strategy in which an organization attempts to gain a competitive advantage by reducing its costs below the costs of competing firms

A firm pursuing a **focus strategy** concentrates on a specific regional market, product line, or group of buyers. This strategy may have either a differentiation focus, whereby the firm differentiates its products in the focus market, or an overall cost leadership focus, whereby the firm manufactures and sells its products at low cost in the focus market. In the watch industry, Tag Heuer follows a focus differentiation strategy by selling only rugged waterproof watches to active consumers. Fiat follows a focus cost leadership strategy by selling its automobiles only in Italy and in selected regions of Europe; Alfa Romeo uses focus differentiation to sell its high-performance cars in these same markets. Fisher-Price uses focus differentiation to sell electronic calculators with large, brightly colored buttons to the parents of preschoolers; stockbroker Edward

focus strategy A strategy in which an organization concentrates on a specific regional market, product line, or group of buyers

Jones focuses on small-town settings. General Mills is focusing new-product development on consumers who eat meals while driving—their watchword is "Can we make it 'one-handed'?" so that drivers can safely eat or drink it.[15]

The Miles and Snow Typology

A second classification of strategic options was developed by Raymond Miles and Charles Snow.[16] These authors suggested that business-level strategies generally fall into one of four categories: prospector, defender, analyzer, and reactor. Table 8.2 summarizes each of these strategies. Of course, different businesses within the same company might pursue different strategies.

prospector strategy A strategy in which the firm encourages creativity and flexibility and is often decentralized

A firm that follows a **prospector strategy** is a highly innovative firm that is constantly seeking out new markets and new opportunities and is oriented toward growth and risk taking. Over the years, 3M has prided itself on being one of the most innovative major corporations in the world. Employees at 3M are constantly encouraged to develop new products and ideas in a creative and entrepreneurial way. This focus on innovation has led 3M to develop a wide range of new products and markets, including invisible tape and antistain fabric treatments. Amazon.com is also following a prospector strategy as it constantly seeks new market opportunities for selling different kinds of products through its websites.

defender strategy A strategy in which the firm focuses on lowering costs and improving the performance of current products

Rather than seeking new growth opportunities and innovation, a company that follows a **defender strategy** concentrates on protecting its current markets, maintaining stable growth, and serving current customers, generally by lowering its costs

TABLE 8.2

The Miles and Snow Typology

The Miles and Snow typology identifies four strategic types of organizations. Three of these–the prospector, the defender, and the analyzer–can all be effective in certain circumstances. The fourth type–the reactor–represents an ineffective approach to strategy.

Strategy Type	Definition	Examples
Prospector	Is innovative and growth oriented, searches for new markets and new growth opportunities, encourages risk taking	Amazon.com 3M Rubbermaid
Defender	Protects current markets, maintains stable growth, serves current customers	BIC eBay Mrs. Fields
Analyzer	Maintains current markets and current customer satisfaction with moderate emphasis on innovation	DuPont IBM Yahoo!
Reactor	No clear strategy, reacts to changes in the environment, drifts with events	International Harvester Joseph Schlitz Brewing Co. Kmart Montgomery Ward

and improving the performance of its existing products. With the maturity of the market for writing instruments, BIC has used this approach—it has adopted a less aggressive, less entrepreneurial style of management and has chosen to defend its substantial market share in the industry. It has done this by emphasizing efficient manufacturing and customer satisfaction. Although eBay is expanding aggressively into foreign markets, the online auctioneer is still pursuing what amounts to a defender strategy, in that it is keeping its focus primarily on the auction business. Thus, while it is prospecting for new markets, it is defending its core business focus.[17]

A business that uses an **analyzer strategy**, in which it attempts to maintain its current businesses and to be somewhat innovative in new businesses, combines elements of prospectors and defenders. Most large companies use this approach because they want to both protect their base of operations and create new market opportunities. IBM uses analyzer strategies. DuPont is currently using an analyzer strategy; the firm is relying heavily on its existing chemical and fiber operations to fuel its earnings for the foreseeable future. At the same time, though, DuPont is moving systematically into new business areas such as biotech agriculture and pharmaceuticals. Yahoo! is also using this strategy by keeping its primary focus on its role as an Internet portal while simultaneously seeking to extend that portal into more and more applications.[18]

analyzer strategy A strategy in which the firm attempts to maintain its current businesses and to be somewhat innovative in new businesses

Finally, a business that follows a **reactor strategy** has no consistent strategic approach; it drifts with environmental events, reacting to but failing to anticipate or influence those events. Not surprisingly, these firms usually do not perform as well as organizations that implement other strategies. Although most organizations would deny using reactor strategies, during the 1970s International Harvester Company (IH) was clearly a reactor. At a time when IH's market for trucks, construction equipment, and agricultural equipment was booming, IH failed to keep pace with its competitors. By the time a recession cut demand for its products, it was too late for IH to respond, and the company lost millions of dollars. The firm was forced to sell off virtually all of its businesses, except its truck-manufacturing business. IH, now renamed Navistar, moved from being a dominant firm in trucking, agriculture, and construction to a medium-size truck manufacturer because it failed to anticipate changes in its environment.

reactor strategy A strategy in which a firm has no consistent approach to strategy

Strategies Based on the Product Life Cycle

The **product life cycle** is a model that shows how sales volume changes over the life of products. Understanding the four stages in the product life cycle helps managers recognize that strategies need to evolve over time. As Figure 8.2 shows, the cycle begins when a new product or technology is first introduced. In this *introduction stage,* demand may be very high and sometimes outpaces the firm's ability to supply the product. At this stage, managers need to focus their efforts on "getting product out the door" without sacrificing quality. Managing growth by hiring new employees and managing inventories and cash flow are also concerns during this stage.

product life cycle A model that portrays how sales volume for products changes over the life of products

During the *growth stage,* more firms begin producing the product, and sales continue to grow. Important management issues include ensuring quality and delivery and beginning to differentiate an organization's product from competitors' products. Entry into the industry during the growth stage may threaten an organization's competitive advantage; thus strategies to slow the entry of competitors are important.

FIGURE 8.2

The Product Life Cycle

Managers can use the framework of the product life cycle—introduction, growth, maturity, and decline—to plot strategy. For example, management may decide on a differentiation strategy for a product in the introduction stage and a prospector approach for a product in the growth stage. By understanding this cycle and where a particular product falls within it, managers can develop more effective strategies for extending product life.

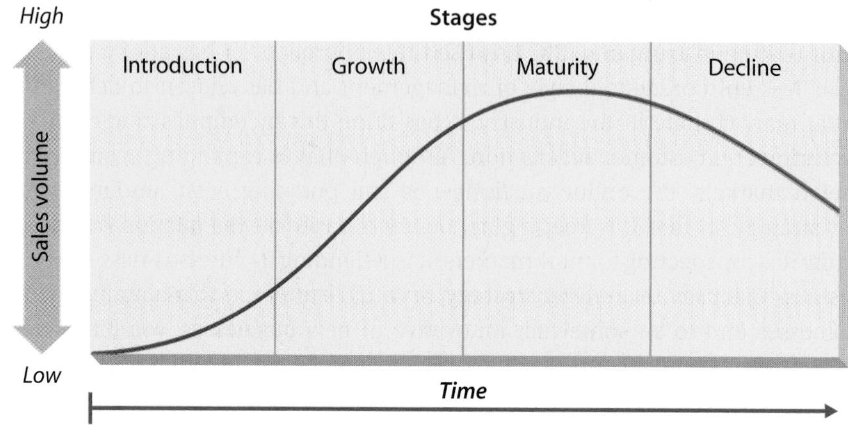

After a period of growth, products enter a third phase. During this *maturity stage,* overall demand growth for a product begins to slow down, and the number of new firms producing the product begins to decline. The number of established firms producing the product may also begin to decline. This period of maturity is essential if an organization is going to survive in the long run. Product differentiation concerns are still important during this stage, but keeping costs low and beginning the search for new products or services are also important strategic considerations.

In the *decline stage,* demand for the product or technology decreases, the number of organizations producing the product drops, and total sales drop. Demand often declines because all those who were interested in purchasing a particular product have already done so. Organizations that fail to anticipate the decline stage in earlier stages of the life cycle may go out of business. Those that differentiate their product, keep their costs low, or develop new products or services may do well during this stage.

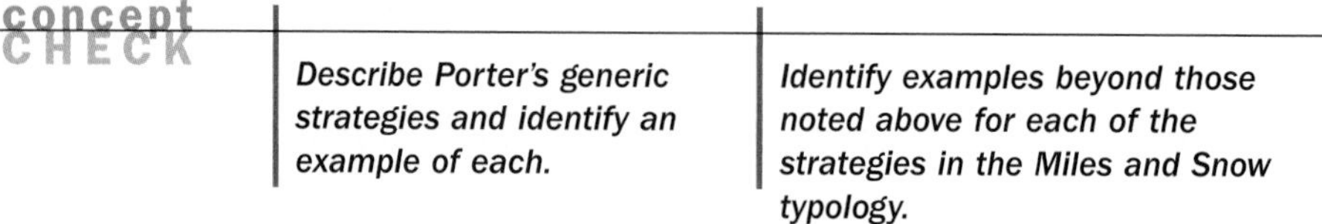

Describe Porter's generic strategies and identify an example of each.

Identify examples beyond those noted above for each of the strategies in the Miles and Snow typology.

Implementing Business-Level Strategies

As we note earlier, after business strategies are formulated, they must then be implemented. To do this effectively, managers must integrate the activities of several different functions. *Marketing* and *sales,* for example, are used to promote products or services and the overall public image of the organization (often through various types of advertising), price products or services, directly contact customers, and make sales. *Accounting* and *finance* control the flow of money both within the organization and from outside sources to the organization, and *manufacturing* creates the organization's products or services. Organizational *culture,* as discussed in Chapter 3, also helps firms implement their strategies.

Implementing business-level strategies requires the integration of several different business functions. Scholastic has been very effective in its strategy for launching its popular Harry Potter books. As most people know, each new book goes on sale at midnight—and hundreds of eager buyers are waiting in line at their nearest bookstore in what has become a party atmosphere. But to carry this off effectively, Scholastic has to use logistics (to ship the books), marketing (to maintain consumer awareness), and effective strategic alliances (with various bookstore chains and outlets).

Implementing Porter's Generic Strategies

Differentation and cost leadership can each be implemented through these basic organizational functions. (Focus is implemented through the same approaches, depending on which one it is based on.)

Differentiation Strategy In general, to support differentiation, marketing and sales must emphasize the high-quality, high-value image of the organization's products or services. Neiman Marcus, a department store for financially secure consumers, has excelled at using marketing to support its differentiation strategy. People do not go to Neiman Marcus just to buy clothes or to shop for home electronics. Instead, a trip to Neiman Marcus is advertised as a "total shopping experience." Customers who want to shop for $3,000 pet houses, $50,000 mink coats, and $7,000 exercise machines recognize that the store caters to their needs. Other organizations that have used their marketing function to implement a differentiation strategy include Chanel, Calvin Klein, and Bloomingdale's.

The function of accounting and finance in a business that is implementing a differentiation strategy is to control the flow of funds without discouraging the creativity needed to constantly develop new products and services to meet customer needs. If keeping track of and controlling the flow of money become more important than determining how money and resources are best spent to meet customer needs, then no organization, whether high-tech firm or fashion designer, will be able to implement a differentiation strategy effectively. In manufacturing, a firm implementing a differentiation strategy must emphasize quality and meeting specific customer needs, rather than simply reducing costs. Manufacturing may sometimes have to keep inventory on hand so that customers will have access to products when they want them. Manufacturing also may have to engage in costly customization to meet customer needs.

The culture of a firm implementing a differentiation strategy, like the firm's other functions, must also emphasize creativity, innovation, and response to customer needs. Lands' End's culture puts the needs of customers ahead of all other considerations. This firm, which sells men's and women's leisure clothing through a catalogue service, offers a complete guarantee on merchandise. Dissatisfied customers may return clothes for a full refund or exchange, with no questions asked. Lands' End takes orders twenty-four hours a day and will ship most orders within twenty-four hours. Items with lost buttons and broken zippers are replaced immediately. The priority given to customer needs is typical of an organization that is successfully implementing a differentiation strategy.

Overall Cost Leadership Strategy To support cost leadership, marketing and sales are likely to focus on simple product attributes and how these product attributes meet customer needs in a low-cost and effective manner. These organizations are very likely to engage in advertising. Throughout this effort, however, emphasis is on the value that an organization's products provide for the price, rather than on the special features of the product or service. Advertising for BIC pens ("Writes first time, every time"), Timex watches ("Takes a licking and keeps on ticking"), and Wal-Mart stores ("Always the low price brands you trust—always") helps these firms implement cost leadership strategies.

Proper emphasis in accounting and finance is also pivotal. Because the success of the organization depends on having costs lower than the competitors', management must take care to reduce costs wherever possible. Tight financial and accounting controls at Wal-Mart, Costco, and Wells Fargo have helped these organizations implement cost leadership strategies. Manufacturing typically helps, with large runs of highly standardized products. Products are designed both to meet customer needs and to be easily manufactured. Manufacturing emphasizes increased volume of production to reduce the per-unit costs of manufacturing. Organizations such as Toshiba (a Japanese semiconductor firm) and Texas Instruments have used this type of manufacturing to implement cost leadership strategies.

The culture of organizations implementing cost leadership strategies tends to focus on improving the efficiency of manufacturing, sales, and other business functions. Managers in these organizations are almost fanatical about keeping their costs low. Wal-Mart appeals to its customers to leave shopping carts in designated areas in its parking lots with signs that read, "Please—help us keep *your* costs low." Fujitsu Electronics, in its Tokyo manufacturing facilities, operates in plain, unpainted, cinderblock and cement facilities to keep its costs as low as possible.

Implementing Miles and Snow's Strategies

Similarly, a variety of issues must be considered when implementing any of Miles and Snow's strategic options. (Of course, no organization would purposefully choose to implement a reactor strategy.)

Prospector Strategy An organization implementing a prospector strategy is innovative, seeks new market opportunities, and takes numerous risks. To implement this strategy, organizations need to encourage creativity and flexibility. Creativity helps an organization perceive, or even create, new opportunities in its environment; flexibility enables it to change quickly to take advantage of these new opportunities. Organizations often increase creativity and flexibility by adopting a decentralized organization structure. (An organization is decentralized when major decision-making responsibility is delegated to middle- and lower-level managers.) Johnson & Johnson links decentralization with a prospector strategy. Each of the firm's different businesses is organized into a separate unit, and the managers of these units hold full decision-making responsibility and authority. Often these businesses develop new products for new markets. As the new products develop and sales grow, Johnson & Johnson reorganizes so that each new product is managed in a separate unit.

Defender Strategy An organization implementing a defender strategy attempts to protect its market from new competitors. It tends to downplay creativity and innovation in bringing out new products or services and to focus its efforts instead on lowering costs or improving the performance of current products. Often a firm implementing a prospector strategy will switch to a defender strategy. This happens when the firm successfully creates a new market or business and then attempts to protect its market from competition. A good example is Mrs. Fields. One of the first firms to introduce high-quality, high-priced cookies, Mrs. Fields sold its product in special cookie stores and grew very rapidly. This success, however, encouraged numerous other companies to enter the market. Increased competition, plus reduced demand for high-priced cookies, has threatened Mrs. Fields's market position. To maintain its profitability, the firm has slowed its growth and is now focusing on making its current operation more profitable. This behavior is consistent with the defender strategy.

A business pursuing a prospector strategy is one that constantly seeks creativity and flexibility. Corning is one such firm. For instance, this top-secret Corning facility makes calcium fluoride, an exotic product projected to be essential to next-generation chipmaking machines. While the market for this product is limited today, it is expected to be huge in the near future. By its willingness to invest today and take some risks, Corning will likely reap huge profits in the future.

Analyzer Strategy An organization implementing an analyzer strategy attempts to maintain its current business and to be somewhat innovative in new businesses. Because the analyzer strategy falls somewhere between the prospector strategy (with focus on innovation) and the defender strategy (with focus on maintaining and improving current businesses), the attributes of organizations implementing the analyzer strategy tend to be similar to both of these other types of organizations. They have tight accounting and financial controls as well as high flexibility, efficient production as well as customized products, and creativity along with low costs. Organizations maintain these multiple and contradictory processes with difficulty.

Starbucks is implementing an analyzer strategy. Although the firm is growing rapidly, its fundamental business is still coffee. At the same time, however, the firm is cautiously branching out into music and ice cream and other food products, and is experimenting with restaurants with more comprehensive menu selections. This approach is allowing Starbucks to remain focused on its core coffee business but to explore new business opportunities at the same time.

concept CHECK

Identify common implementation issues for Porter's generic strategies and Miles and Snow's strategies.

What role might organization culture play in implementing business-level strategies?

Formulating Corporate-Level Strategies

Most large organizations are engaged in several businesses, industries, and markets. Each business or set of businesses within such an organization is frequently referred to as a *strategic business unit,* or *SBU.* An organization such as General Electric operates hundreds of different businesses, making and selling products as diverse as jet engines, nuclear power plants, and light bulbs. GE organizes these businesses into approximately twenty SBUs. Even organizations that sell only one product may operate in several distinct markets.

Decisions about which businesses, industries, and markets an organization will enter, and how to manage these different businesses, are based on an organization's corporate strategy. The most important strategic issue at the corporate level concerns the extent and nature of organizational diversification. **Diversification** describes the number of different businesses that an organization is engaged in and the extent to which these businesses are related to one another. There are three types of diversification strategies: single-product strategy, related diversification, and unrelated diversification.[19]

diversification The number of different businesses that an organization is engaged in and the extent to which these businesses are related to one another

Single-Product Strategy

An organization that pursues a **single-product strategy** manufactures just one product or service and sells it in a single geographic market. The WD-40 Company, for example, manufactures only a single product, WD-40 spray lubricant, and for years sold it in just one market, North America. WD-40 has started selling its lubricant in Europe and Asia, but it continues to center all manufacturing, sales, and marketing efforts on one product.

single-product strategy A strategy in which an organization manufactures just one product or service and sells it in a single geographic market

The single-product strategy has one major strength and one major weakness. By concentrating its efforts so completely on one product and market, a firm is likely to be very successful in manufacturing and marketing the product. Because it has staked its survival on a single product, the organization works very hard to make sure that the product is a success. Of course, if the product is not accepted by the market or is replaced by a new one, the firm will suffer. This happened to slide-rule manufacturers when electronic calculators became widely available and to companies that manufactured only black-and-white televisions when low-priced color televisions were first mass-marketed. Similarly, Wrigley has long practiced what amounts to a single-product strategy with its line of chewing gums. But, because younger consumers are buying less gum than earlier generations, Wrigley is facing declining revenues and lower profits.[20]

Related Diversification

Given the disadvantage of the single-product strategy, most large businesses today operate in several different businesses, industries, or markets.[21] If the businesses are somehow linked, that organization is implementing a strategy of **related diversification**. Virtually all larger businesses in the United States use related diversification.

related diversification A strategy in which an organization operates in several businesses that are somehow linked with one another

TABLE 8.3

Bases of Relatedness in Implementing Related Diversification
Firms that implement related diversification can do so using any number of bases of relatedness. Four frequently used bases of related uses for diversification are similar technology, common distribution and marketing skills, common brand name and reputation, and common customers.

Basis of Relatedness	Examples
Similar technology	Philips, Boeing, Westinghouse, Compaq
Common distribution and marketing skills	RJR Nabisco, Philip Morris, Procter & Gamble
Common brand name and reputation	Disney, Universal
Common customers	Merck, IBM, AMF-Head

Bases of Relatedness Organizations link their different businesses, industries, or markets in different ways. Table 8.3 gives some typical bases of relatedness. In companies such as Philips, a European consumer electronics company, a similar type of electronics technology underlies all the businesses. A common technology in aircraft design links Boeing's commercial and military aircraft divisions, and a common computer design technology links Dell's various computer products and peripherals.

Organizations such as Philip Morris, RJR Nabisco, and Procter & Gamble operate multiple businesses related by a common distribution network (grocery stores) and common marketing skills (advertising). Disney and Universal rely on strong brand names and reputations to link their diverse businesses, which include movie studios and theme parks. Pharmaceutical firms such as Merck sell numerous products to a single set of customers: hospitals, doctors, patients, and drugstores. Similarly, AMF-Head sells snow skis, tennis rackets, and sportswear to active, athletic customers.

Advantages of Related Diversification Pursuing a strategy of related diversification has three primary advantages. First, it reduces an organization's dependence on any one of its business activities and thus reduces economic risk. Even if one or two of a firm's businesses lose money, the organization as a whole may still survive because the healthy businesses will generate enough cash to support the others.[22] At The Limited, sales declines at Lerners may be offset by sales increases at Express.

Second, by managing several businesses at the same time, an organization can reduce the overhead costs associated with managing any one business. In other words, if the normal administrative costs required to operate any business, such as legal services and accounting, can be spread over a large number of businesses, then the overhead costs *per business* will be lower than they would be if each business had to absorb all costs itself. Thus the overhead costs of businesses in a firm that pursues related diversification are usually lower than those of similar businesses that are not part of a larger corporation.[23]

Third, related diversification allows an organization to exploit its strengths and capabilities in more than one business. When organizations do this successfully, they capitalize on synergies, which are complementary effects that exist among their businesses. *Synergy* exists among a set of businesses when the businesses' economic value together is greater than their economic value separately. McDonald's is using synergy as it diversifies into other restaurant and food businesses. For example, its McCafe premium coffee stands in some McDonald's restaurants and investments in Donatos Pizza, Chipolte Mexican Grill, and Pret A Manger each allow the firm to create new revenue opportunities while utilizing the firm's existing strengths in food-product purchasing and distribution.[24]

Unrelated Diversification

unrelated diversification A strategy in which an organization operates multiple businesses that are not logically associated with one another

Firms that implement a strategy of **unrelated diversification** operate multiple businesses that are not logically associated with one another. At one time, for example, Quaker Oats owned clothing chains, toy companies, and a restaurant business. Unrelated diversification was a very popular strategy in the 1970s. During this time, several conglomerates like ITT and Transamerica grew by acquiring literally hundreds of other organizations and then running these numerous businesses as independent entities. Even if there are important potential synergies among their different businesses, organizations implementing a strategy of unrelated diversification do not attempt to exploit them.

In theory, unrelated diversification has two advantages. First, a business that uses this strategy should have stable performance over time. During any given period, if some businesses owned by the organization are in a cycle of decline, others may be in a cycle of growth. Unrelated diversification is also thought to have resource allocation advantages. Every year, when a corporation allocates capital, people, and other resources among its various businesses, it must evaluate information about the future of those businesses so that it can place its resources where they have the highest potential for return. Given that it owns the businesses in question and thus has full access to information about the future of those businesses, a firm implementing unrelated diversification should be able to allocate capital to maximize corporate performance.

Despite these presumed advantages, research suggests that unrelated diversification usually does not lead to high performance. First, corporate-level managers in such a company usually do not know enough about the unrelated businesses to provide helpful strategic guidance or to allocate capital appropriately. To make strategic decisions, managers must have complete and subtle understanding of a business and its environment. Because corporate managers often have difficulty fully evaluating the economic importance of investments for all the businesses under their wing, they tend to concentrate only on a business's current performance. This narrow attention at the expense of broader planning eventually hobbles the entire organization. Many of International Harvester's problems noted earlier grew from an emphasis on current performance at the expense of investments for the future success of the firm.

Second, because organizations that implement unrelated diversification fail to exploit important synergies, they are at a competitive disadvantage compared to organizations that use related diversification. Universal Studios has been at a competitive disadvantage relative to Disney because its theme parks, movie studios, and licensing divisions are less integrated and therefore achieve less synergy.

For these reasons, almost all organizations have abandoned unrelated diversification as a corporate-level strategy. Transamerica has sold off numerous businesses and now concentrates on a core set of related businesses and markets. Large corporations that have not concentrated on a core set of businesses have eventually been acquired by other companies and then broken up. Research suggests that these organizations are actually worth more when broken up into smaller pieces than when joined.[25]

concept CHECK

Distinguish between related and unrelated diversification.

The discussion above cites research that suggests that unrelated diversification is not likely to be a successful corporate strategy. If this is so, explain why General Electric remains so successful.

Implementing Corporate-Level Strategies

In implementing a diversification strategy, organizations face two important questions. First, how will the organization move from a single-product strategy to some form of diversification? Second, once the organization diversifies, how will it manage diversification effectively?

Becoming a Diversified Firm

Most organizations do not start out completely diversified. Rather, they begin operations in a single business, pursuing a particular business-level strategy. Success in this strategy then creates resources and strengths that the organization can use in related businesses.

Development of New Products Some firms diversify by developing their own new products and services within the boundaries of their traditional business operations. Honda followed this path to diversification. Relying on its traditional strength in the motorcycle market, over the years Honda learned how to make fuel-efficient, highly reliable small engines. Honda began to apply its strengths in a new business:

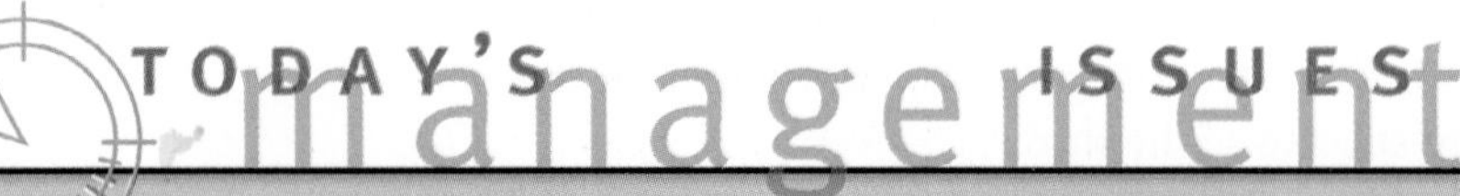

Acquisitions Hard to Swallow, Even Harder to Digest

"[The acquisition gave Dillard's] a prolonged case of indigestion."

– Robert F. Buchanan, analyst, A.G. Edwards & Sons*

Managers began a wave of merger and acquisition activity in the 1990s, to increase diversification. The upswing happened because companies were "hot," leading managers to invest in growth. High valuations made it easy to pay for mergers with stock, rather than with cash. Acquisitions presented an easy way to expand overseas. Diversification is a good thing, so when acquisition activity increased, investors applauded, right?

Wrong. The managers chose the correct strategy—diversification—but everything else was flawed—the method, the timing, the targets, and the price. Managers overestimated the ease of merging two companies and the value of anticipated synergies. In addition, most firms simply overpaid. Buyers paid, on average, a premium of 36 percent above the price of the stock acquired.

Often, firms rushed into deals quickly, with inadequate research. Dillard's purchased Mercantile for $2.9 billion, only to find that their strategies were almost impossible to integrate. "The acquisition set Dillard's back a couple of years," says analyst Robert F. Buchanan of A.G. Edwards & Sons. "It gave them a prolonged case of indigestion." The ill-advised nature of some of the deals is clear after the fact, because acquiring firms' average returns were 25 percent lower than those of comparable firms that did not acquire.

Investors punished firms that they believed had diversified inappropriately by pushing stock prices lower. A study by *BusinessWeek* of the 302 major mergers that occurred in the United States from 1995 to 2001 found that 61 percent of the buyers destroyed shareholder wealth (demonstrated by lower stock price). Deals that have yet to show positive returns include those between AOL and Time Warner, Travelers Insurance and Citicorp, Daimler-Benz and Chrysler, and Compaq and Hewlett-Packard. A few deals, such as the 1995 merger of Sandoz Pharmaceuticals and Ciba-Geigy to form Novartis, have improved performance. But good outcomes are the exception, not the rule.

Diversification remains a sound strategy, but it is clear that internal growth, although slow, may be preferable to mergers or acquisitions. Merger activity seems to follow a pattern, with surges in activity in the 1920s and the 1960s. If history repeats itself, the current wave of mergers is likely to continue for a few more years. Managers take note—there is still plenty of shareholder wealth out there to destroy.

References: Clifton Leaf, "Temptation Is All Around Us," *Fortune*, November 4, 2002, www.fortune.com on January 6, 2003; David Henry, "Mergers: Why Most Big Deals Don't Pay Off," *BusinessWeek*, October 14, 2002, pp. 60–70 (*quote p. 68); David Henry, "Addicted to Acquisitions," *BusinessWeek*, October 14, 2002, p. 68.

manufacturing small, fuel-efficient cars for the Japanese domestic market. These vehicles were first sold in the United States in the late 1960s. Honda's success in U.S. exports led the company to increase the size and improve the performance of its cars. Over the years, Honda has introduced automobiles of increasing quality, culminating in the Acura line of luxury cars. While diversifying into the market for automobiles, Honda also applied its engine-building strengths to produce a line of all-terrain vehicles, portable electric generators, and lawn mowers. In each case, Honda was able to parlay its strengths and resources into successful new businesses.

Replacement of Suppliers and Customers Firms can also become diversified by replacing their former suppliers and customers. A company that stops buying supplies (either manufactured goods or raw materials) from other companies and begins to provide its own supplies has diversified through **backward vertical integration**. Campbell Soup once bought soup cans from several different manufacturers but later began manufacturing its own cans. In fact, Campbell is currently one of the largest can-manufacturing companies in the world, although almost all the cans it makes are used in its soup operations.

An organization that stops selling to one customer and sells instead to that customer's customers has diversified through **forward vertical integration**. G.H. Bass used forward vertical integration to diversify its operations. Bass once sold its shoes and other products only to retail outlets. More recently, however, Bass opened numerous factory outlet stores, which now sell products directly to consumers. Nevertheless, Bass has not abandoned its former customers, retail outlets. Many firms are also employing forward vertical integration today, as they use the Internet to market their products and services directly to consumers.

backward vertical integration An organization's beginning the business activities formerly conducted by its suppliers

forward vertical integration An organization's beginning the business activities formerly conducted by its customers

merger The purchase of one firm by another firm of approximately the same size

acquisition The purchase of a firm by a firm that is considerably larger

Mergers and Acquisitions Another common way for businesses to diversify is through mergers and acquisitions—that is, through purchasing another organization. Such a purchase is called a **merger** when the two organizations being combined are approximately the same size. It is called an **acquisition** when one of the organizations involved is considerably larger than the other. Organizations engage in mergers and acquisitions to diversify through vertical integration by acquiring former suppliers or former customers. Mergers and acquisitions are also becoming more common in other countries, such as Germany and China.[26] Acquisitions are discussed in more detail in *Today's Management Issues.*

Most organizations use mergers and acquisitions to acquire complementary products or complementary services, which are products or services linked by a common technology and common customers. The objective of most mergers and acquisitions is the creation or exploitation of synergies.[27] Synergy can reduce the combined organizations' costs of doing business; it can increase revenues; and it may open the way to entirely new businesses for the organization to enter. For example, MGM Grand paid $4.4 billion for its largest competitor in the gambling industry, Mirage Resorts. The deal allowed MGM Grand to compete with other firms more efficiently while eliminating a major rival.[28] The cartoon illustrates another interesting perspective on mergers and acquisitions.

Mergers and acquisitions are becoming an increasingly popular way to implement corporate-level strategies. Of course, as illustrated in this cartoon, there is at least theoretically a limit to the extent to which mergers and acquisitions can occur. For example, in recent years the U.S. government has blocked the merger of Staples and Office Depot and fought the merger of America Online and Time Warner. The reasons in each case have involved concerns about reduced competition that might, in turn, lead to higher consumer prices.

"OH, WHY DOESN'T EVERYBODY JUST MERGE WITH EVERYBODY ELSE AND GET IT OVER WITH?"

Managing Diversification

However an organization implements diversification—whether through internal development, vertical integration, or mergers and acquisitions—it must monitor and manage its strategy. The two major tools for managing diversification are (1) organization structure and (2) portfolio management techniques. How organization structure can be used to manage a diversification strategy is discussed in detail in Chapter 12.[29] **Portfolio management techniques** are methods that diversified organizations use to determine which businesses to engage in and how to manage these businesses to maximize corporate performance. Two important portfolio management techniques are the BCG matrix and the GE Business Screen.

portfolio management technique A method that diversified organizations use to determine which businesses to engage in and how to manage these businesses to maximize corporate performance

BCG matrix A method of evaluating businesses relative to the growth rate of their market and the organization's share of the market

BCG Matrix The **BCG** (for Boston Consulting Group) **matrix** provides a framework for evaluating the relative performance of businesses in which a diversified organization operates. It also prescribes the preferred distribution of cash and other resources among these businesses.[30] The BCG matrix uses two factors to evaluate an organization's set of businesses: the growth rate of a particular market and the organization's share of that market. The matrix suggests that fast-growing markets in which an organization has the highest market share are more attractive business opportunities than slow-growing markets in which an organization has small market share. Dividing market growth and market share into two categories (low and high) creates the simple matrix shown in Figure 8.3.

FIGURE 8.3

The BCG Matrix

The BCG matrix helps managers develop a better understanding of how different strategic business units contribute to the overall organization. By assessing each SBU on the basis of its market growth rate and relative market share, managers can make decisions about whether to commit further financial resources to the SBU or to sell or liquidate it.

Perspectives, No. 66, "The Product Portfolio." Adapted by permission from The Boston Consulting Group, Inc., 1970.

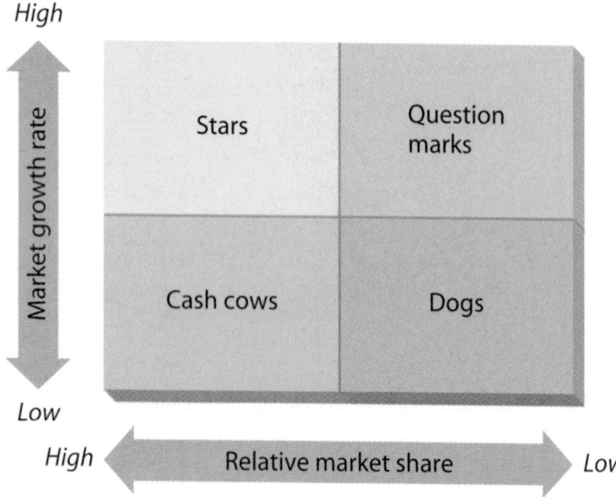

The matrix classifies the types of businesses in which a diversified organization can engage as dogs, cash cows, question marks, and stars. *Dogs* are businesses that have a very small share of a market that is not expected to grow. Because these businesses do not hold much economic promise, the BCG matrix suggests that organizations either should not invest in them or should consider selling them as soon as possible. *Cash cows* are businesses that have a large share of a market that is not expected to grow substantially. These businesses characteristically generate high profits that the organization should use to support question marks and stars. (Cash cows are "milked" for cash to support businesses in markets that have greater growth potential.) *Question marks* are businesses that have only a small share of a quickly growing market. The future performance of these businesses is uncertain. A question mark that is able to capture increasing amounts of this growing market may be very profitable. On the other hand, a question mark unable to keep up with market growth is likely to have low profits. The BCG matrix suggests that organizations should invest carefully in question marks. If their performance does not live up to expectations, question marks should be reclassified as dogs and divested. *Stars* are businesses that have the largest share of a rapidly growing market. Cash generated by cash cows should be invested in stars to ensure their preeminent position. For example, when BMW bought Rover a few years ago, experts thought its products would help the German auto maker reach new consumers. But the company was not able to capitalize on this opportunity, so it ended up selling Rover's car business to a British firm and Land Rover to Ford.[31]

GE Business Screen Because the BCG matrix is relatively narrow and overly simplistic, General Electric (GE) developed the **GE Business Screen**, a more sophisticated approach to managing diversified business units. The Business Screen is a portfolio management technique that can also be represented in the form of a matrix. Rather than focusing solely on market growth and market share, however, the GE Business Screen considers industry attractiveness and competitive position. These two factors are divided into three categories, to make the nine-cell matrix shown in Figure 8.4.[32] These cells, in turn, classify business units as winners, losers, question marks, average businesses, or profit producers.

GE Business Screen A method of evaluating businesses along two dimensions: (1) industry attractiveness and (2) competitive position; in general, the more attractive the industry and the more competitive the position, the more an organization should invest in a business

As Figure 8.4 shows, both market growth and market share appear in a broad list of factors that determine the overall attractiveness of an industry and the overall quality of a firm's competitive position. Other determinants of an industry's attractiveness (in addition to market growth) include market size, capital requirements, and competitive intensity. In general, the greater the market growth, the larger the market, the smaller the capital requirements, and the less the competitive intensity, the more attractive an industry will be. Other determinants of an organization's competitive position in an industry (besides market share) include technological know-how, product quality, service network, price competitiveness, and operating

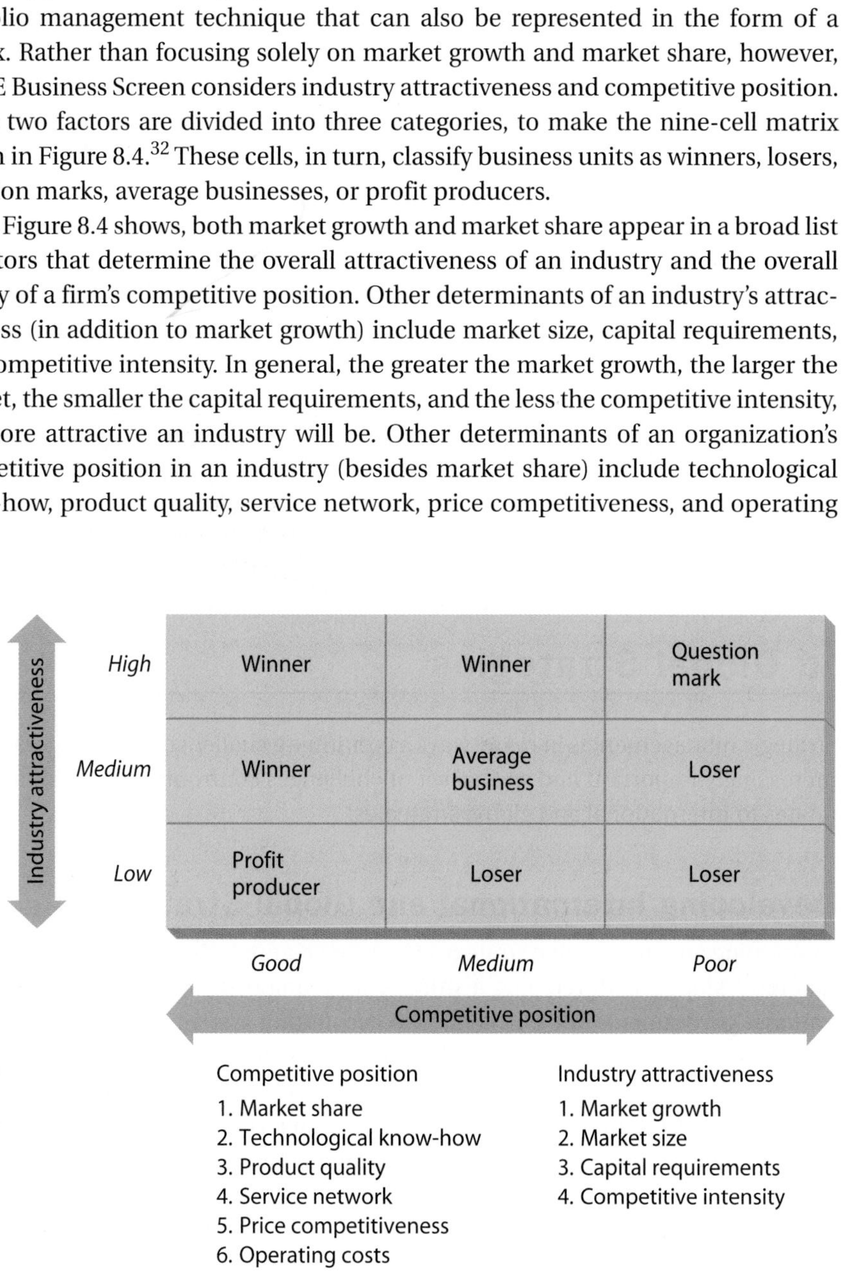

Industry attractiveness			
High	Winner	Winner	Question mark
Medium	Winner	Average business	Loser
Low	Profit producer	Loser	Loser
	Good	*Medium*	*Poor*
	Competitive position		

Competitive position
1. Market share
2. Technological know-how
3. Product quality
4. Service network
5. Price competitiveness
6. Operating costs

Industry attractiveness
1. Market growth
2. Market size
3. Capital requirements
4. Competitive intensity

FIGURE 8.4

The GE Business Screen

The GE Business Screen is a more sophisticated approach to portfolio management than the BCG matrix. As shown here, several factors combine to determine a business's competitive position and the attractiveness of its industry. These two dimensions, in turn, can be used to classify businesses as winners, question marks, average businesses, losers, or profit producers. Such a classification enables managers to allocate the organization's resources more effectively across various business opportunities.

costs. In general, businesses with large market share, technological know-how, high product quality, a quality service network, competitive prices, and low operating costs are in a favorable competitive position.

Think of the GE Business Screen as a way of applying SWOT analysis to the implementation and management of a diversification strategy. The determinants of industry attractiveness are similar to the environmental opportunities and threats in SWOT analysis, and the determinants of competitive position are similar to organizational strengths and weaknesses. By conducting this type of SWOT analysis across several businesses, a diversified organization can decide how to invest its resources to maximize corporate performance. In general, organizations should invest in winners and in question marks (where industry attractiveness and competitive position are both favorable); should maintain the market position of average businesses and profit producers (where industry attractiveness and competitive position are average); and should sell losers. For example, Unilever recently assessed its business portfolio using a similar framework and, as a result, decided to sell off several specialty chemical units that were not contributing to the firm's profitability as much as other businesses. The firm then used the revenues from these divestitures and bought more related businesses such as Ben & Jerry's Homemade and Slim-Fast.[33]

concept CHECK

Compare and contrast the BCG matrix and the GE Business Screen.

When, if ever, would it make sense for a corporation to retain ownership of a money-losing business with limited opportunities for a turnaround?

International and Global Strategies

Strategic management is in many ways a continuing challenge for managers. But an increasingly important and special set of challenges confronting today's managers relates to international and global strategies.

Developing International and Global Strategies

Developing an international strategy is far more complex than developing a domestic one.[34] Managers developing a strategy for a domestic firm must deal with one national government, one currency, one accounting system, one political system, one legal system, and usually a single language and a comparatively homogeneous culture. Conversely, managers responsible for developing a strategy for an international firm must understand and deal with multiple governments, multiple currencies, multiple accounting systems, multiple political systems, multiple legal systems, and a variety of languages and cultures.

Moreover, managers in an international business must also coordinate the implementation of their firm's strategy among business units located in different parts of the world, with different time zones, different cultural contexts, and different economic conditions, as well as monitor and control their performance. Managers usually consider these complexities acceptable tradeoffs for the additional opportunities that come with global expansion. Indeed, international businesses have the ability to exploit three sources of competitive advantage unavailable to domestic firms.

International and global strategies are becoming critical in today's business world environment. Nokia, one of the world's largest cell phone manufacturers, clearly understands this imperative. While it promotes to phones everywhere from factories to frozen ponds, the firm is also focused on the future as it keeps abreast of emerging and projected communications technologies and aggressively enters new markets whenever feasible.

Global Efficiencies International firms can improve their efficiency through several means not accessible to a domestic firm. They can capture *location efficiencies* by locating their facilities anywhere in the world that yields them the lowest production or distribution costs or that best improves the quality of service they offer their customers. Production of athletic shoes, for example, is very labor intensive, and Nike, like many of its competitors, centers its manufacturing in countries where labor costs are especially low.[35] Similarly, by building factories to serve more than one country, international firms may also lower their production costs by capturing *economies of scale.* Finally, by broadening their product lines in each of the countries they enter, international firms may enjoy *economies of scope,* lowering their production and marketing costs and enhancing their bottom line.

Multimarket Flexibility As we discuss in earlier chapters, there are wide variations in the political, economic, legal, and cultural environments of countries. Moreover, these environments are constantly changing: New laws are passed, new governments are elected, economic policies are changed, new competitors may enter (or leave) the national market, and so on. International businesses thus face the challenge of responding to these multiple diverse and changing environments. Often firms find it beneficial to empower local managers to respond quickly to such changes. However, unlike domestic firms, which operate in and respond to changes in the context of a single domestic environment, international businesses may also respond to a change in one country by implementing a change in another country. Chicken processor Tyson Foods, for example, has benefited from the increased demand by health-conscious U.S. consumers for chicken breasts. In producing more chicken breasts, Tyson also produced more chicken legs and thighs, which are considered less desirable by U.S. consumers. Tyson capitalized on its surplus by targeting the Russian market, where dark meat is preferred over light, and the Chinese market, where chicken feet are considered a tasty delicacy. Tyson exports over $250 million worth of chicken thighs and legs to Russia and China.[36]

Worldwide Learning The diverse operating environments of multinational corporations (MNCs) may also contribute to organizational learning.[37] Differences in these operating environments may cause the firm to operate differently in one country than in another. An astute firm may learn from these differences and transfer this learning to its operations in other countries.[38] For example, McDonald's U.S. managers once believed that its restaurants should be freestanding entities located in suburbs and small towns. A Japanese franchisee convinced McDonald's to allow it to open a restaurant in an inner-city office building. That restaurant's success caused McDonald's executives to rethink their store location criteria. Nontraditional locations—office buildings, Wal-Mart superstores, even airplanes—are now an important source of new growth for the firm.

Unfortunately, it is difficult to exploit these three factors simultaneously. Global efficiencies can be more easily obtained when a single unit of a firm is given worldwide responsibility for the task at hand. BMW's engineering staff at headquarters in Munich, for example, is responsible for the research and design of the company's new automobiles. By focusing its research and development (R&D) efforts at one location, BMW engineers designing new transmissions are better able to coordinate their activities with their counterparts designing new engines. However, centralizing control of its R&D operations also hinders BMW's ability to customize its product to meet the differing needs of customers in different countries. Consider the simple question of whether to include cup holders in its cars. In designing cars to be driven safely at the prevailing high speeds of Germany's autobahn, the company's engineers decided that cup holders were both irrelevant and dangerous. Driving speeds in the United States, however, are much lower, and cup holders are an important comfort feature in autos sold to U.S. consumers. Lengthy battles were fought between BMW's German engineers and its U.S. marketing managers over this seemingly trivial issue. Only in the mid-1990s did cup holders finally become a standard feature in the firm's automobiles sold in North America.

As this example illustrates, if too much power is centralized in one unit of a firm, the unit may ignore the needs of consumers in other markets. Conversely, multimarket flexibility is enhanced when a firm delegates responsibility to the managers of local subsidiaries. Vesting power in local managers allows each subsidiary to tailor its products, personnel policies, marketing techniques, and other business practices to meet the specific needs and wants of potential customers in each market the firm serves. However, this increased flexibility will reduce the firm's ability to obtain global efficiencies in such areas as production, marketing, and R&D.

Furthermore, the unbridled pursuit of global efficiencies or multimarket flexibility may stifle the firm's attempts to promote worldwide learning. Centralizing power in a single unit of the firm to capture global efficiencies may cause the unit to ignore lessons and information acquired by other units of the firm. Moreover, the other units may have little incentive or ability to acquire such information if they know that the "experts" at headquarters will ignore them. Decentralizing power in the hands of local subsidiary managers may create similar problems. A decentralized structure may make it difficult to transfer learning from one subsidiary to another. Local subsidiaries may be disposed to automatically reject outside information as not being germane to the local situation. Firms wishing to promote worldwide learning must utilize an organizational structure that promotes knowledge transfer among its subsidiaries and corporate headquarters.

The firms must also create incentive structures that motivate managers at headquarters and in subsidiaries to acquire, disseminate, and act on worldwide learning opportunities.

Consider the success of Nokia, headquartered in Helsinki, Finland, which is among the world's leaders in the cellular telephone and telecommunications industries. Nokia, like other telecommunications equipment manufacturers, was struggling to keep pace with rapid shifts in its worldwide markets. Managers in different regions had little idea what their counterparts in other markets were doing, and Nokia factories were grappling with excess inventories of some products and inventory shortages of others. In some instances, Nokia factories in one country would shut down for lack of a critical part that a Nokia factory in another country had in surplus. In response, the firm's CEO, Jorma Ollila, established what he called "commando teams" to attack these problems. The teams were charged with improving efficiency throughout the firm. Using a new worldwide information system, Nokia managers now monitor global, regional, and local sales and inventory on a real-time basis. This allows them to make internal transfers of parts and finished goods efficiently. More important, this approach has allowed Nokia to spot market trends and new product developments that arise in one region of the world and to transfer this knowledge to improve its competitiveness in other areas and product lines.[39]

Strategic Alternatives for International Business

International businesses typically adopt one of four strategic alternatives in their attempt to balance the three goals of global efficiencies, multimarket flexibility, and worldwide learning. The first of these strategic alternatives is the **home replication strategy**. In this approach, a firm utilizes the core competency or firm-specific advantage it developed at home as its main competitive weapon in the foreign markets that it enters. In other words, the firm takes what it does exceptionally well in its home market and attempts to duplicate it in foreign markets. Mercedes-Benz's home replication strategy, for example, relies on its well-known brand name and its reputation for building well-engineered, luxurious cars capable of traveling safely at very high speeds. It is this market segment that Mercedes-Benz has chosen to exploit internationally, despite the fact that only a very few countries have both the high income levels and the high speed limits appropriate for its products. But consumers in Asia, the rest of Europe, and the Americas are nevertheless attracted by the car's mystique.

home replication strategy International strategy in which a company utilizes the core competency or firm-specific advantage it developed at home as its main competitive weapon in the foreign markets that it enters

The **multidomestic strategy** is a second alternative available to international firms. A multidomestic corporation manages itself as a collection of relatively independent operating subsidiaries, each of which focuses on a specific domestic market. In addition, each of these subsidiaries is free to customize its products, its marketing campaigns, and its operating techniques to best meet the needs of its local customers. The multidomestic approach is particularly effective when there are clear differences among national markets; when economies of scale for production, distribution, and marketing are low; and when the cost of coordination between the parent corporation and its various foreign subsidiaries is high.

multidomestic strategy International strategy in which a company manages itself as a collection of relatively independent operating subsidiaries, each of which focuses on a specific domestic market

Because each subsidiary must be responsive to the local market, the parent company usually delegates considerable power and authority to managers of its subsidiaries in various host countries. International businesses operating before World War II often adopted this approach because of the difficulties in controlling distant foreign subsidiaries, given the communication and transportation technologies of that time.

global strategy International strategy in which a company views the world as a single marketplace and has as its primary goal the creation of standardized goods and services that will address the needs of customers worldwide

The **global strategy** is the third alternative philosophy available for international firms. A global corporation views the world as a single marketplace and has as its primary goal the creation of standardized goods and services that will address the needs of customers worldwide. The global strategy is almost the exact opposite of the multidomestic strategy. Whereas the multidomestic firm believes that its customers in every country are fundamentally different and must be approached from that perspective, a global corporation assumes that customers are fundamentally the same regardless of nationality. Thus the global corporation views the world market as a single entity as the corporation develops, produces, and sells its products. It tries to capture economies of scale in production and marketing by concentrating its production activities in a handful of highly efficient factories and then creating global advertising and marketing campaigns to sell the goods produced in those factories. Because the global corporation must coordinate its worldwide production and marketing strategies, it usually concentrates power and decision-making responsibility at a central headquarters.

The home replication strategy and the global strategy share an important similarity: Under either approach, a firm conducts business the same way anywhere in the world. There is also an important difference between the two approaches. A firm utilizing the home replication strategy takes its domestic way of doing business and uses that approach in foreign markets as well. In essence, a firm using this strategy believes that, if its business practices work in its domestic market, then they should also work in foreign markets. Conversely, the starting point for a firm adopting a global strategy has no such home country bias. In fact, the concept of a home market is irrelevant because the global firm thinks of its market as a global one, not one divided into domestic and foreign segments. The global firm tries to figure out the best way to serve all of its customers in the global market and then does so.

transnational strategy International strategy in which a company attempts to combine the benefits of global scale efficiencies with the benefits and advantages of local responsiveness

A fourth approach available to international firms is the **transnational strategy**. The transnational corporation attempts to combine the benefits of global scale efficiencies, such as those pursued by a global corporation, with the benefits and advantages of local responsiveness, which is the goal of a multidomestic corporation. To do so, the transnational corporation does not automatically centralize or decentralize authority. Rather, it carefully assigns responsibility for various organizational tasks to the unit of the organization best able to achieve the dual goals of efficiency and flexibility.

A transnational corporation may choose to centralize certain management functions and decision making, such as R&D and financial operations, at corporate headquarters. Other management functions, such as human resource management and marketing, may be decentralized, allowing managers of local subsidiaries to customize their business activities to better respond to the local culture and business environment. Microsoft, for example, locates most of its product development efforts in the United States, whereas responsibility for marketing is delegated to its foreign subsidiaries. Often, transnational corporations locate responsibility for one product line in one country and responsibility for a second product line in another country. To achieve an interdependent network of operations, transnational corporations focus considerable attention on integration and coordination among their various subsidiaries.

concept CHECK

What are the basic strategic options available to multinational businesses?

In what ways is international strategic planning most similar to and most different from domestic strategic planning?

Summary of Key Points

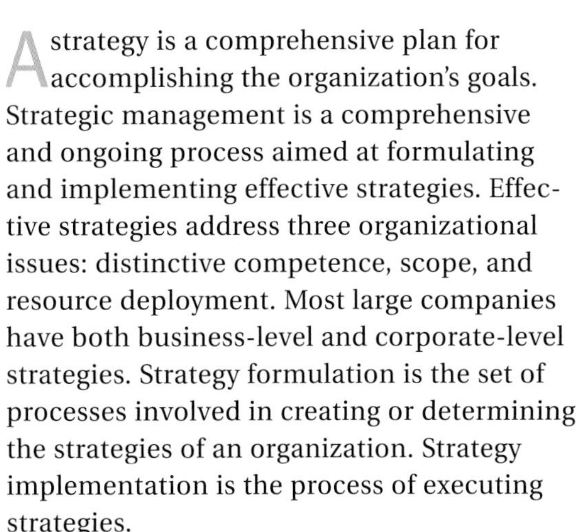

business.college.hmco.com/students

A strategy is a comprehensive plan for accomplishing the organization's goals. Strategic management is a comprehensive and ongoing process aimed at formulating and implementing effective strategies. Effective strategies address three organizational issues: distinctive competence, scope, and resource deployment. Most large companies have both business-level and corporate-level strategies. Strategy formulation is the set of processes involved in creating or determining the strategies of an organization. Strategy implementation is the process of executing strategies.

SWOT analysis considers an organization's strengths, weaknesses, opportunities, and threats. Using SWOT analysis, an organization chooses strategies that support its mission and (1) exploit its opportunities and strengths, (2) neutralize its threats, and (3) avoid its weaknesses. Common strengths cannot be ignored, but distinctive competencies hold the greatest promise for superior performance.

A business-level strategy is the plan an organization uses to conduct business in a particular industry or market. Porter suggests that businesses may formulate a differentiation strategy, an overall cost leadership strategy, or a focus strategy at this level. According to Miles and Snow, organizations may choose one of four business-level strategies: prospector, defender, analyzer, or reactor. Business-level strategies may also take into account the stages in the product life cycle.

Strategy implementation at the business level takes place in the areas of marketing, sales, accounting and finance, and manufacturing. Culture also influences strategy implementation. Implementation of Porter's generic strategies requires different emphases in each of these organizational areas. Implementation of Miles and Snow's strategies affects organization structure and practices.

A corporate-level strategy is the plan an organization uses to manage its operations across several businesses. A firm that does not diversify is implementing a single-product strategy. An organization pursues a strategy of related diversification when it operates a set of businesses that are somehow linked. Related diversification reduces the financial risk associated with any particular product, reduces the overhead costs of each business, and enables the organization to create and exploit synergy. An organization pursues a strategy of unrelated diversification when it operates a set of businesses that are not logically associated with one another.

Strategy implementation at the corporate level addresses two issues: how the organization will go about its diversification and the way an organization is managed once it has diversified. Businesses accomplish this in three ways: developing new products internally, replacing suppliers (backward vertical integration) or customers (forward vertical integration), and engaging in mergers and acquisitions. Organizations manage diversification through the organization structure that they adopt and through portfolio management techniques. The BCG matrix classifies an organization's diversified businesses as dogs, cash cows, question marks, or stars according to market share and market growth rate. The GE Business Screen classifies businesses as winners, losers, question marks, average businesses, or profit producers according to industry attractiveness and competitive position.

Although there are many similarities in developing domestic and international strategies, international firms have three additional sources of competitive advantage unavailable to domestic firms. These are global efficiencies, multimarket flexibility, and worldwide learning.

Firms participating in international business usually adopt one of four strategic alternatives: the home replication strategy, the multidomestic strategy, the global strategy, or the transnational strategy. Each of these strategies has advantages and disadvantages in terms of its ability to help firms be responsive to local circumstances and to achieve the benefits of global efficiencies.

Discussion Questions

Questions for Review

1. Define the four parts of a SWOT analysis.
2. Describe the relationship between a distinctive competency, a competitive advantage, and a sustained competitive advantage.
3. List and describe Porter's generic strategies and the Miles and Snow typology of strategies.
4. What are the characteristics of businesses in each of the four cells of the BCG matrix?

Questions for Analysis

5. Describe the process that an organization follows when using a deliberate strategy. How does this process differ when an organization implements an emergent strategy?
6. Which strategy should a firm develop first—its business-level or its corporate-level strategy? Describe the relationship between a firm's business- and corporate-level strategies.
7. Volkswagen sold its original Beetle automobile in the United States until the 1970s. The original Beetle was made of inexpensive materials, was built using an efficient mass-production technology, and offered few options. Then, in the 1990s Volkswagen introduced its new Beetle, which has a distinctive style, provides more optional features, and is priced for upscale buyers. What was Volkswagen's strategy with the original Beetle—product differentiation, low cost, or focus? Which strategy did Volkswagen implement with its new Beetle? Explain your answers.

Questions for Application

8. Assume that you are the owner and manager of a small business. Write a strategy for your business. Be sure to include each of the three primary strategic components.
9. Interview a manager and categorize the business- and corporate-level strategies of his or her organization according to Porter's generic strategies, the Miles and Snow typology, and extent of diversification.
10. Give an example of a corporation following a single-product strategy, a related diversification strategy, and an unrelated diversification strategy. What level of performance would you expect from each firm, based on its strategy? Examine the firm's profitability to see whether your expectations were accurate.

BUILDING EFFECTIVE decision-making SKILLS

business.college.hmco.com/students

Exercise Overview

Decision-making skills refer to the manager's ability to recognize and define problems and opportunities correctly and then to select an appropriate course of action to solve problems and capitalize on opportunities. As noted in the chapter, many organizations use SWOT analysis as part of the process of strategy formulation. This exercise will help you better understand how managers obtain the information they need to perform such an analysis and use it as a framework for making decisions.

Exercise Background

SWOT is an acronym for strengths, weaknesses, opportunities and threats. Good strategies are those that exploit an organization's opportunities and strengths while neutralizing threats and avoiding or correcting weaknesses.

Assume that you have just been hired to run a medium-size manufacturing company. The firm has been manufacturing electric motors, circuit breakers, and similar electronic components for industrial use. In recent years, the firm's financial performance has gradually eroded. You have been hired to turn things around.

Meetings with both current and former top managers of the firm have led you to believe that a new strategy is needed. In earlier times the firm was successful in part because its products were of top quality, which allowed the company to charge premium prices for them. Recently, however, various cost-cutting measures have resulted in a decrease in quality. Competition has also increased. As a result, your firm no longer has a reputation for top-quality products, but your manufacturing costs are still relatively high. The next thing you want to do is to conduct a SWOT analysis.

Exercise Task

With the situation described above as context, do the following:

1. List the sources you will use to obtain information about the firm's strengths, weaknesses, opportunities, and threats. If you are using the Internet, give specific websites or URLs.
2. For what types of information are data readily available on the Internet? What categories of data are difficult or impossible to find on the Internet?
3. Rate each source in terms of its probable reliability.
4. How confident should you be in making decisions based on the information obtained?

BUILDING EFFECTIVE conceptual SKILLS

Exercise Overview

Conceptual skills refer to the manager's ability to think in the abstract. Strategic management is often thought of in terms of competition. For example, metaphors involving war or sports are often invoked by strategists. However, cooperation is another viable strategic alternative to competition. Cooperation has been a popular strategy in many countries for years, and the importance of cooperative strategic alliances and joint ventures is also rising in the United States. This game will provide you with an illustration of the advantages of a cooperative strategy in comparison with a competitive strategy.

Exercise Background

Competitive and cooperative strategies are quite complex when implemented in organizations. However, a simple and clear illustration of the principles underlying competitive and cooperation can be given through the use of a game.

This game illustrates a "prisoner's dilemma" situation. The prisoner's dilemma is a classic situation used to demonstrate concepts related to game theory. In the original prisoner's dilemma, two criminals are suspected in a crime, but there is not enough evidence to convict either of them. The two criminals are separated and each is told that if he will "rat" on the other one, he will go free. Of course, if neither rats, both go free. If both rat, then both go to prison. The optimal outcome (for the prisoners!) occurs when neither rats on the other. However, in real situations, the most common outcome is just the opposite—that both "rat" and both go to jail.

The prisoner's dilemma case has been used by game theorists to describe how people make decisions about whether to act cooperatively or competitively. Although there are cases in which cooperation would be the most beneficial for both parties, human nature frequently causes the parties to choose competition instead, which often leads to the worst outcomes. In the game you are about to play, you will see how choices about competition versus cooperation affect outcomes.

Exercise Task

1. Break into small groups and play the board game according to the instructions you receive from your professor.
2. Present your group's results to the class.
3. After hearing the results from every group, be prepared to share your thoughts about the outcomes.

BUILDING EFFECTIVE diagnostic SKILLS

Exercise Overview

Diagnostic skills are the skills that enable a manager to visualize the most appropriate response to a situation. As rivalry increases in an industry, competitors develop similar capabilities, making it more difficult to achieve differentiation. In such an industry, price becomes the primary competitive weapon. (The soft-drink, fast-food, airline, and retail industries, for example, are suffering from this problem today.) This in-class demonstration will show you the difficulties of developing an effective competitive response in such a situation.

Exercise Background

Assume that you are the owner of a small business, such as a gas station or fast-food outlet, that is located directly across the street from a rival firm. Your products are not differentiated, and you cannot make them so. Customers prefer the less expensive product, and they switch based on the price difference between the products—the larger the difference, the more customers will switch. Customer switching behavior is shown in Table 8.4.

Further, the following conditions apply to both you and your competitor:

1. You both have a $1.00 cost of production per unit. This number cannot be changed.
2. At the beginning of the game, you are both charging a price of $1.10, for a per-unit profit of $.10.
3. The market consists of exactly 100 customers per period. This number cannot be changed.

Therefore, at the beginning period, you and your rival are charging the same price (0 cents difference) and thus are splitting the market 50/50, or selling 50 units per period. Both you and your rival have per-period profits of $5.00 (50 units × $.10).

For the demonstration, two teams of students, representing your firm and your rival, will separately and independently make a decision about price for the upcoming period. Price is the only variable you can control. Each team will write down its price, and then your professor will disclose the resulting market share and profits for each team. The demonstration will continue for several periods, the exact number of which is not known to the teams. The objective is to be profitable.

Exercise Task

1. Consider volunteering to be part of one of the groups involved in demonstrating this concept in front of the class.
2. Play out the scenario (participants) and observe (class).
3. Did each of the teams choose a strategy that enabled profit maximization? Were they equally profitable? Why or why not?
4. Competing firms are prohibited by law from fixing prices; that is, from jointly deciding on a price. However, price signaling, in which firms do not directly conspire but instead send subtle messages, is legal. Could the two teams in this demonstration use price signaling? What conditions are necessary to make price signaling an effective strategy?
5. What does this demonstration tell you about competitive dynamics in an industry where products are undifferentiated?

TABLE 8.4

Porter's Generic Strategies

When the price difference is . . .	The market share split is . . .
0 cents	50/50
1 cent	60/40
2 cents	70/30
3 cents	80/20
4 cents	90/10
5 cents	100/0

CHAPTER CLOSING case

Toyota Revs up U.S. Sales

"We must Americanize."

— Fujio Cho, CEO, Toyota*

Since 1903 either Chevrolet or Ford has been the best-selling car brand in the United States—that is, until 2002. In that year, Toyota Motor Corporation of Japan passed number-two Chevrolet in sales, selling 775,000 cars in the first eleven months of 2002. Ford sold just 802,000 autos during that same period. Toyota will likely pass Ford in the very near future as well.

Perhaps no one is more surprised than Toyota. The auto maker, which is known for the effectiveness of its long-term planning, had more modest goals for the U.S. market. Toyota developed a strategy in the 1990s that called for two decades of modest growth in Japan, Europe, and North America. Toyota managers saw their biggest growth opportunities in Southeast Asia. However, the economies of developing Southeast Asian countries such as Indonesia and Malaysia have slowed, as has the European economy. The Japanese market is becoming more competitive for Toyota, and the firm is losing sales to Honda and Nissan.

That leaves the American market as the firm's only chance for significant growth over the next decade. Toyota's managers intend to exploit that opportunity fully. Toyota already sells more vehicles in the States than in Japan. But, before the company can be assured of its success in the United States, says Toyota CEO Fujio Cho, "We must Americanize." One sign of its commitment is its increased hiring of local managers. According to James Press, COO of Toyota USA, "Thirty years ago, we were more dependent on Japan. Now, there's not much Japanese influence on a day-to-day basis." The firm is also using more American designers for cars to be sold in the United States. This allows the firm to compete effectively with U.S. auto makers and to stay in touch with the demands of American consumers.

In addition, Toyota relies on its U.S. factories to produce two-thirds of the cars destined for the American market. This allows the firm to reduce import taxes and to lower currency risk, by keeping revenues and expenses in U.S. dollars. Additionally, U.S. and local governments look more favorably on the firm because of the money the firm spends on salaries for its 123,000 American workers and for its facilities. Many of the facilities have provided much-needed jobs and revitalized communities in the American South and Appalachia.

However, the Toyota takeover of the U.S. market is far from assured. Some traditionalists inside Toyota do not like the new direction. They prefer that the firm stick to the "Toyota Way," which emphasizes decision making by consensus, cost cutting, quality, and customer satisfaction. Another obstacle is a lack of understanding of American preferences at the highest levels of the company. For example, U.S. designers unsuccessfully tried to persuade managers to develop a full-size pickup truck. Japanese leaders were unconvinced of the demand for such a product, until the Americans took them to a Dallas Cowboys football game. One look at the parking lot was enough to convince the Toyota executives that a full-size pickup was a winning idea.

American competitors have been slow to respond to Toyota's threat. GM's CEO, G. Richard Wagoner, Jr., claims that his firm's Japanese competitors have an unfair advantage in their home country. Wagoner says, "Once these [Japanese] manufacturers establish a foothold in the U.S., they begin to mimic our broad product lines, eventually become accepted by the public as a 'domestic' brand, and suddenly, we lose our home-field advantage." But Ford Motor CEO William C. Ford, Jr., believes that U.S. firms may use Toyota's challenge to their own advantage. "We can't handle success," Ford says. "We do our best as a company when our back is to the wall." American manufacturers are working to update styling and to improve quality and efficiency, in a direct challenge to the Japanese, who dominate in those areas.

In the meantime, however, Toyota has adjusted its strategic plans to take advantage of the current situation. Its objective is 5 percent sales growth in the United States in 2003, which would easily move it into top place in the American market. By the early 2010s, the firm aims for 15 percent of the global auto market, up from its current 10 percent. To accomplish those ambitious goals, the firm has innovative new products in development, including an emission-free car which runs on hydrogen fuel cells and a fully loaded subcompact that sells for around $10,000.

Last year, Toyota chairman Hiroshi Okuda joked that the company should move its headquarters to the United States. If Toyota can continue its performance, in just a few years that joke may become a reality.

Case Questions

1. List the threats and opportunities that Toyota is facing in its environment. Then list the strengths and weaknesses of Toyota.
2. Consider Toyota's U.S. auto business. What business-level strategy is the firm using? What factors did you rely on in reaching your decision?
3. In your opinion, is Toyota's corporate-level strategy (to focus on the U.S. market) likely to be effective over the next ten years? Why or why not?

Case References

Chester Dawson, "The Americanization of Toyota," *BusinessWeek*, April 15, 2002, pp. 52–54 (*quote p. 52); Joann Muller, "Autos: A New Industry," *BusinessWeek*, July 15, 2002, www.businessweek.com on January 7, 2003; "Toyota Aims to Boost Global Car Sales 5% Next Year," *Dow Jones Business News*, December 16, 2002, biz.yahoo.com on January 7, 2003; "Toyota Announces Best Sales Year in Its 45-Year History, Breaks Sales Record for Seventh Year in a Row," *PRNewswire*, January 3, 2003, hoovnews.hoovers.com on January 7, 2003; "Toyota Outselling Chevrolet, Closing in on Ford," *Dow Jones Business News*, December 13, 2002, biz.yahoo.com on January 7, 2003.

Chapter Notes

1. "CS First Boston Lowers Foot Locker to 'Neutral'," *BusinessWeek*, December 20, 2002, www.businessweek.com on January 4, 2003; Matthew Boyle, "How Nike Got Its Swoosh Back," *Fortune*, June 11, 2002, www.fortune.com on January 4, 2003; "Sweatshops: Finally, Airing the Dirty Linens," *BusinessWeek*, June 23, 2003, pp.100–102; Patricia O'Connell, "A Jog with Nike's New Team," *BusinessWeek*, October 28, 2002, www.businessweek.com on January 4, 2002; Stanley Holmes, "How Nike Got Its Game Back," *BusinessWeek*, November 4, 2002, pp. 129–131 (*quote p. 129).
2. For early discussions of strategic management, see Kenneth Andrews, *The Concept of Corporate Strategy*, rev. ed. (Homewood, Ill.: Dow Jones–Irwin, 1980); and Igor Ansoff, *Corporate Strategy* (New York: McGraw-Hill, 1965). For more recent perspectives, see Michael E. Porter, "What Is Strategy?" *Harvard Business Review*, November–December 1996, pp. 61–78; Kathleen M. Eisenhardt, "Strategy as Strategic Decision Making," *Sloan Management Review*, Spring 1999, pp. 65–74; Sarah Kaplan and Eric Beinhocker, "The Real Value of Strategic Planning," *Sloan Management Review*, Winter 2003, pp. 71–80.
3. *Hoover's Handbook of American Business 2003* (Austin, Texas: Hoover's Business Press, 2003), pp. 872–873.
4. Jim Rohwer, "GE Digs into Asia," *Fortune*, October 2, 2000, pp. 164–178.
5. For a discussion of the distinction between business- and corporate-level strategies, see Charles Hill and Gareth Jones, *Strategic Management: An Integrated Approach*, 6th ed. (Boston: Houghton Mifflin, 2003).
6. See Gary Hamel, "Strategy as Revolution," *Harvard Business Review*, July–August 1996, pp. 69–82.
7. See Henry Mintzberg, "Patterns in Strategy Formulation," *Management Science*, October 1978, pp. 934–948; Henry Mintzberg, "Strategy Making in Three Modes," *California Management Review*, 1973, pp. 44–53.
8. "If It's on the Fritz, Take It to Jane," *BusinessWeek*, January 27, 1997, pp. 74–75.
9. Jay Barney, "Firm Resources and Sustained Competitive Advantage," *Journal of Management*, June 1991, pp. 99–120.
10. Jay Barney, "Strategic Factor Markets," *Management Science*, December 1986, pp. 1231–1241. See also Constantinos C. Markides, "A Dynamic View of Strategy," *Sloan Management Review*, Spring 1999, pp. 55–64.
11. See Michael Porter, *Competitive Strategy* (New York: Free Press, 1980).
12. Porter, *Competitive Strategy*. See also Colin Campbell-Hunt, "What Have We Learned About Generic Competitive Strategy? A Meta-Analysis," *Strategic Management Journal*, vol. 21, 2000, pp. 127–154.
13. Ian C. MacMillan and Rita Gunther McGrath, "Discovering New Points of Differentiation," *Harvard Business Review*, July–August 1997, pp. 133–136.
14. "In a Water Fight, Coke and Pepsi Try Opposite Tacks," *Wall Street Journal*, April 18, 2002, pp. A1, A8.
15. "General Mills Intends to Reshape Doughboy in Its Own Image," *Wall Street Journal*, July 18, 2000, pp. A1, A8.
16. Raymond E. Miles and Charles C. Snow, *Organizational Strategy, Structure, and Process* (New York: McGraw-Hill, 1978).
17. "Rough Crossing for eBay," *BusinessWeek*, February 7, 2000, p. EB 48.
18. See Eric D. Beinhocker, "Robust Adaptive Strategies," *Sloan Management Review*, Spring 1999, pp. 95–105.
19. Alfred Chandler, *Strategy and Structure: Chapters in the History of the American Industrial Enterprise* (Cambridge, Mass.: MIT Press, 1962); Richard Rumelt, *Strategy, Structure, and Economic Performance* (Cambridge, Mass.: Division of Research, Graduate School of Business Administration, Harvard University, 1974); Oliver Williamson, *Markets and Hierarchies* (New York: Free Press, 1975).
20. "Not the Flavor of the Month," *BusinessWeek*, March 20, 2000, p. 128.
21. K. L. Stimpert and Irene M. Duhaime, "Seeing the Big Picture: The Influence of Industry, Diversification, and Business Strategy on Performance," *Academy of Management Journal*, vol. 40, no. 3, 1997, pp. 560–583.
22. See Chandler, *Strategy and Structure*; Yakov Amihud and Baruch Lev, "Risk Reduction as a Managerial Motive for Conglomerate Mergers," *Bell Journal of Economics*, 1981, pp. 605–617.
23. Chandler, *Strategy and Structure*; Williamson, *Markets and Hierarchies*.
24. "Did Somebody Say McBurrito?" *BusinessWeek*, April 10, 2000, pp. 166–170.
25. See Jay Barney and William G. Ouchi, *Organizational Economics* (San Francisco: Jossey-Bass, 1986), for a discussion of the limitations of unrelated diversification.
26. "Latest Merger Boom Is Happening in China, and Bears Watching," *Wall Street Journal*, July 30, 1997, pp. A1. A9; "A Breakthrough in Bavaria," *BusinessWeek*, August 4, 1997, p. 54.
27. Kathleen M. Eisenhardt and D. Charles Galunic, "Coevolving—At Last. A Way to Make Synergies Work," *Harvard Business Review*, January–February 2000, pp. 91–100.
28. "MGM Grand Pays $4.4 Billion for Mirage," *USA Today*, March 7, 2000, p. 1B.
29. See Constantinoes C. Markides and Peter J. Williamson, "Corporate Diversification and Organizational Structure: A Resource-Based View," *Academy of Management Journal*, April 1996, pp. 340–367.
30. See Barry Hedley, "A Fundamental Approach to Strategy Development," *Long Range Planning*, December 1976, pp. 2–11; Bruce Henderson, "The Experience Curve-Reviewed. IV: The Growth Share Matrix of the Product Portfolio," *Perspectives*, no. 135 (Boston: Boston Consulting Group, 1973).

31. "BMW: Unloading Rover May Not Win the Race," *BusinessWeek,* April 3, 2000, p. 59.
32. Michael G. Allen, "Diagramming G.E.'s Planning for What's WATT," in Robert J. Allio and Malcolm W. Pennington (eds.), *Corporate Planning: Techniques and Applications* (New York: AMACOM, 1979). Limits of this approach are discussed in R. A. Bettis and W. K. Hall, "The Business Portfolio Approach: Where It Falls Down in Practice," *Long Range Planning,* March 1983, pp. 95–105.
33. "Unilever to Sell Specialty-Chemical Unit to ICI of the U.K. for About $8 Billion," *Wall Street Journal,* May 7, 1997, pp. A3, A12; "For Unilever, It's Sweetness and Light," *Wall Street Journal,* April 13, 2000, pp. B1, B4.
34. Howard Thomas, Timothy Pollock, and Philip Gorman, "Global Strategic Analyses: Frameworks and Approaches," *Academy of Management Executive,* vol. 13, no. 1, 1999, pp. 70–80.
35. Kasra Ferdows, "Making the Most of Foreign Factories," *Harvard Business Review,* March–April 1997, pp. 73–88.
36. "Russia Bans U.S. Chicken Shipments, Inspiring Fears of Tough Trade Battle," *Wall Street Journal,* February 23, 1996, p. A2.
37. Anil K. Gupta and Vijay Govindarajan, "Knowledge Flows Within Multinational Corporations," *Strategic Management Journal,* vol. 21, no. 4, 2000, pp. 473–496.
38. Christopher A. Bartlett and Sumantra Ghoshal, *Transnational Management,* 2nd ed. (Chicago, Ill.: Richard D. Irwin, 1995), pp. 237–242. See also Tatiana Kostova, "Transnational Transfer of Strategic Organizational Practices: A Contextual Perspective," *Academy of Management Review,* vol. 24, no. 2, 1999, pp. 308–324.
39. "At Nokia, a Comeback—And Then Some," *BusinessWeek,* December 2, 1996, p. 106.

9 Managing Decision Making and Problem Solving

CHAPTER OUTLINE

The Nature of Decision Making
- Decision Making Defined
- Types of Decisions
- Decision-making Conditions

Rational Perspectives on Decision Making
- The Classical Model of Decision Making
- Steps in Rational Decision Making

Behavioral Aspects of Decision Making
- The Administrative Model
- Political Forces in Decision Making
- Intuition and Escalation of Commitment
- Risk Propensity and Decision Making
- Ethics and Decision Making

Group and Team Decision Making in Organizations
- Forms of Group and Team Decision Making
- Advantages of Group and Team Decision Making
- Disadvantages of Group and Team Decision Making
- Managing Group and Team Decision-making Processes

LEARNING OBJECTIVES

After studying this chapter, you should be able to:

1 ***Define decision making and discuss types of decisions and decision-making conditions.***

OPENING INCIDENT

Dr. Frank Baldino, Jr., is a risk taker. After several years working for DuPont, he left the chemical giant at age thirty-three and started his own biotech firm called Cephalon. The company, whose name derives from the Greek word for "brain," focused on neurological diseases. From that start in 1987, Cephalon has grown to employ over 1,200 workers, encompass four facilities, and generate $225 million in annual sales. Baldino still heads the firm, making him one of the longest-serving CEOs in the volatile biotechnology industry. A large portion of his success comes from his skill in navigating the difficult decisions that are common in the pharmaceutical sector.

One area of considerable risk for biotechnology firms is new-product development, because of long and uncertain lead times. Creation of the complex drug proteins used in such products may take a team of dozens of Ph.D.'s ten years or more. During that time, millions of dollars are needed for staffing, equipment, and facilities, but no revenues are generated. The development process creates products that can move on to the next stage—testing—only about half the time. The testing stage is also risky, however, because new drugs must undergo extensive analysis by the U.S. Food and Drug Administration (FDA). The testing is done

2

Discuss rational perspectives on decision making, including the steps in rational decision making.

3

Describe the behavioral aspects of decision making.

4

Discuss group and team decision making, including the advantages and disadvantages of group and team decision making and how it can be more effectively managed.

"Cephalon has taken a different path than most biotech companies."

—Cephalon's 2002 annual report

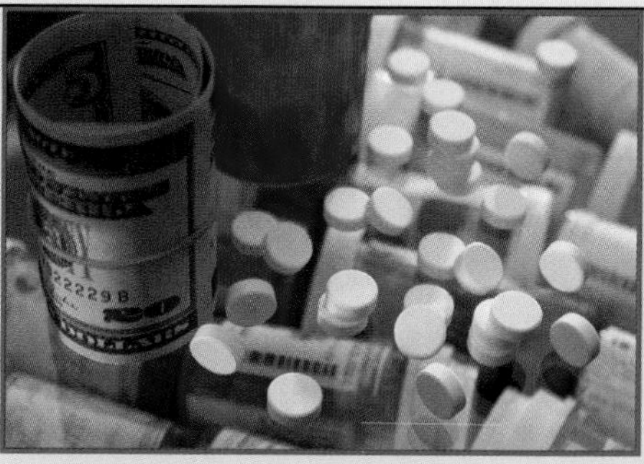

Decision-makers in the pharmaceutical industry must contend with both great opportunities and enormous risks.

in three phases that determine safety and effectiveness and continues for at least three—and sometimes up to ten—years. The FDA reports that only about 20 percent of drugs that undergo testing are ultimately approved for use.

In addition to the financial risk, drug makers face a great competitive risk. For instance, rivals may quickly create generic versions of popular new medicines. Generics can be far less expensive because the company does not have to recover high development and testing expenses. New medications can be protected by patents, which can last up to twenty years. However, the twenty-year clock starts ticking when the patent is filed, not when the drug hits the market. And companies typically file for a patent before testing, to reduce the risk of having a new drug stolen.

Dr. Baldino made choices that led to a unique strategy for his biotech firm. Cephalon's first product, a potential treatment for Lou Gehrig's disease, failed to gain FDA approval. Rather than engage in an extended regulatory battle, Baldino chose to shelve that product. His next move was unorthodox for a start-up biotech company—he looked for an existing product that could be profitably licensed. He found Provigil, a remedy for narcolepsy. Narcolepsy, which causes sudden attacks of intense sleepiness, is relatively rare; therefore, Provigil had low sales. But Baldino saw that the drug had potential for other uses. After winning FDA approval, Baldino began testing Provigil for use with other sleep disorders and even ordinary tiredness. Testing is still under way, but if Provigil is approved for conditions other than narcolepsy, it could become a blockbuster drug.

Cephalon's other drugs, including treatments for severe pain and epileptic seizures, were also developed elsewhere and licensed by the firm. Sales of each of these drugs are ten times or more their levels before licensing, due in part to Cephalon's aggressive marketing and product extension.

Baldino clearly uses a rational decision-making process at Cephalon. He did not become emotionally attached to his first, unsuccessful product but quickly abandoned it when it proved unprofitable. He chose a licensing strategy, which is not as glamorous as research but has a higher expected payoff. While other firms stubbornly continue to focus on R&D at the expense of other functions, Baldino balances research with an emphasis on marketing and sales. A look at Cephalon's website shows information related to "Current Position," "The Opportunity," and "The Goal" for each drug. This demonstrates Baldino's thorough analysis of opportunities and development of specific goals for every product. He systematically works to expand the usefulness of each drug to its fullest extent.

Thus far, Baldino's decisions have paid off. Cephalon became profitable in 1999, just three years after launching Provigil. Compare this performance with that of the other 1,200 worldwide biotech firms—only about two dozen are currently profitable. Baldino clearly intends to continue with his successful strategy. The biotech firm's 2002 annual report states, "Cephalon has taken a different path than most biotech companies.... We invested early in developing a sophisticated marketing organization and experienced specialty sales teams.... This investment enabled us to build a successful business based upon product sales, and we now let profitability fund our innovative science." And the skillful leadership and decision making will be ongoing at Cephalon. Baldino asserts, "I'll be here until either the shareholders throw me out or the company is acquired."[1]

Frank Baldino, Jr., and other managers at Cephalon make decisions every day. And apparently most of these decisions are good ones. Making effective decisions, as well as recognizing when a bad decision has been made and quickly responding to mistakes, is a key ingredient in organizational effectiveness. Indeed, some experts believe that decision making is the most basic and fundamental of all managerial activities.[2] Thus we discuss it here, in the context of the first management function, planning. Keep in mind, however, that although decision making is perhaps most closely linked to the planning function, it is also part of organizing, leading, and controlling.

We begin our discussion by exploring the nature of decision making. We then describe rational perspectives on decision making. Behavioral aspects of decision making are then introduced and described. We conclude with a discussion of group and team decision making.

The Nature of Decision Making

Managers at Ford recently made the decision to buy Land Rover from BMW for nearly $3 billion.[3] At about the same time, the general manager of the Ford dealership in Bryan, Texas, made a decision to sponsor a local youth soccer team for $200. Each of these examples reflects a decision, but the decisions differ in many ways. Thus, as a starting point in understanding decision making, we must first explore the meaning of decision making as well as types of decisions and conditions under which decisions are made.[4]

decision making The act of choosing one alternative from among a set of alternatives

Decision Making Defined

decision-making process Recognizing and defining the nature of a decision situation, identifying alternatives, choosing the "best" alternative, and putting it into practice

Decision making can refer to either a specific act or a general process. **Decision making** per se is the act of choosing one alternative from among a set of alternatives. The decision-making process, however, is much more than this. One step of the process, for example, is that the person making the decision must both recognize that a decision is necessary and identify the set of feasible alternatives before selecting one. Hence, the **decision-making process** includes recognizing and defining the nature of a decision situation, identifying alternatives, choosing the "best" alternative, and putting it into practice.[5]

The word *best*, of course, implies effectiveness. Effective decision making requires that the decision maker understand the situation driving the decision. Most people

Reprinted with permission of King Features Syndicate.

Decision making is a pervasive part of most managerial activities. Virtually everything that happens in a company involves making a decision or implementing a decision that has been made. Although some decisions are grand and significant in scope, others, like the ones shown in the center panel of this cartoon, involve more routine, day-to-day activities. And still others, illustrated in the right panel, deal with what to have for lunch or when to take a break. Regardless of their goals, however, the people making the decisions need to take them seriously and do what they believe to be best for the company.

would consider an effective decision to be one that optimizes some set of factors, such as profits, sales, employee welfare, and market share. In some situations, though, an effective decision may be one that minimizes loss, expenses, or employee turnover. It may even mean selecting the best method for going out of business, laying off employees, or terminating a strategic alliance.

We should also note that managers make decisions about both problems and opportunities. For example, making decisions about how to cut costs by 10 percent reflects a problem—an undesirable situation that requires a solution. But decisions are also necessary in situations of opportunity. Learning that the firm is earning higher-than-projected profits, for example, requires a subsequent decision. Should the extra funds be used to increase shareholder dividends, reinvest in current operations, or expand into new markets? For instance, during the crisis at Firestone, managers at Goodyear had an opportunity to significantly enlarge the firm's market share by making the right decisions. However, by most accounts, Goodyear executives made poor decisions and lost what observers saw as a golden opportunity.[6]

Of course, it may take a long time before a manager can know if the right decision was made. For example, the top management team at Eastman Kodak has made several major decisions that will affect the company for decades. Among other things, for example, it sold off several chemical- and health-related businesses, reduced the firm's debt by $7 billion in the process, launched a major new line of advanced cameras and film called Advantix, and made major new investments in emerging technology, such as digital photography. But analysts believe that the payoffs from these decisions will not be known for at least another six years.[7]

Types of Decisions

Managers must make many different types of decisions. In general, however, most decisions fall into one of two categories: programmed and nonprogrammed.[8] A **programmed decision** is one that is relatively structured or recurs with some frequency (or both). Starbucks uses programmed decisions to purchase new supplies of coffee beans, cups, and napkins, and Starbucks employees are trained in exact procedures for brewing coffee. Likewise, the Bryan Ford dealer made a decision that he will sponsor a youth soccer team each year. Thus, when the soccer club president calls, the dealer already knows what he will do. Many decisions regarding basic operating systems and procedures and standard organizational transactions are of this variety and can therefore be programmed.[9]

programmed decision A decision that is fairly structured or recurs with some frequency (or both)

Nonprogrammed decisions, on the other hand, are relatively unstructured and occur much less often. Virtually all of the decisions made at Cephalon by Frank Baldino, Jr., are nonprogrammed decisions. Likewise, Ford's decision to buy Land Rover was also a nonprogrammed decision. Managers faced with such decisions must treat each one as unique, investing enormous amounts of time, energy, and resources into exploring the situation from all perspectives. Intuition and experience are major factors in nonprogrammed decisions. Most of the decisions made by top managers involving strategy (including mergers, acquisitions, and takeovers) and organization design are nonprogrammed. So are decisions about new facilities, new products, labor contracts, and legal issues.

nonprogrammed decision A decision that is relatively unstructured and occurs much less often than a programmed decision

Decision making is the act of choosing one alternative from among a set of alternatives. Most decisions take place under conditions of certainty, risk, or uncertainty. Consider, for instance, the decision confronted by Nebraska farmer Bob Roberts during a recent drought. One option was to grow corn, which he could sell for cash. The other was to grow alfalfa to feed his cows. And clearly, each option had a degree of risk.

Decision-making Conditions

Just as there are different kinds of decisions, there are also different conditions in which decisions must be made. Managers sometimes have an almost perfect understanding of conditions surrounding a decision, but at other times they have few clues about those conditions. In general, as shown in Figure 9.1, the circumstances that exist for the decision maker are conditions of certainty, risk, or uncertainty.[10]

Decision Making Under Certainty When the decision maker knows with reasonable certainty what the alternatives are and what conditions are associated with each alternative, a **state of certainty** exists. Suppose, for example, that managers at Singapore Airlines make a decision to buy five new jumbo jets. Their next decision is from whom to buy them. Because there are only two companies in the world that make jumbo jets, Boeing and Airbus, Singapore Airlines knows its options exactly. Each has proven products and will guarantee prices and delivery dates. The airline thus knows the alternative conditions associated with each. There is little ambiguity and relatively little chance of making a bad decision.

Few organizational decisions, however, are made under conditions of true certainty. The complexity and turbulence of the contemporary business world make such situations rare. Even the airplane purchase decision we just considered has less certainty than it appears. The aircraft companies may not be able to really guarantee delivery dates, so they may write cost-increase or inflation clauses into contracts. Thus the airline may be only partially certain of the conditions surrounding each alternative.

state of certainty A condition in which the decision maker knows with reasonable certainty what the alternatives are and what conditions are associated with each alternative

state of risk A condition in which the availability of each alternative and its potential payoffs and costs are all associated with probability estimates

Decision Making Under Risk A more common decision-making condition is a state of risk. Under a **state of risk**, the availability of each alternative and its potential payoffs and costs are all associated with probability estimates. Suppose, for example, that a labor contract negotiator for a company receives a "final" offer from the union right before a strike deadline. The negotiator has two alternatives: to accept or to reject the offer. The risk centers on whether the union representatives are bluffing. If the company negotiator accepts the offer, she avoids a strike but commits to a relatively costly labor contract. If she rejects the contract, she may get a more favorable contract if the union is bluffing, but she may provoke a strike if it is not.

On the basis of past experiences, relevant information, the advice of others, and her own judgment, she may conclude that there is about a 75 percent chance that union representatives are bluffing and about a 25 percent chance that they will back up their threats. Thus she can base a calculated decision on the two alternatives (accept or reject the contract demands) and the probable consequences of each. When making decisions under a state of risk, managers must reasonably estimate the probabilities associated with each alternative. For example, if the union negotiators are committed to a strike if their demands are not met, and the company negotiator rejects their demands because she guesses they will not strike, her miscalculation will prove costly. As indicated in Figure 9.1, decision making under conditions of risk is accompanied by moderate ambiguity and chances of a bad decision.[11] Frank Baldino, Jr.'s, decision to license the rights to Provigil represents a decision made under a condition of risk. Executives at Porsche recently faced a similar dilemma—should the firm join most of the world's other auto makers and build a sports utility vehicle (and potentially earn higher revenues) or maintain its focus on high-performance sports cars? Although the additional revenue is almost certain, the true risk in the firm's ultimate decision to build its Cayenne SUV is that the brand may lose some of its cachet among its existing customers.[12]

FIGURE 9.1

Decision-making Conditions

Most major decisions in organizations today are made under a state of uncertainty. Managers making decisions in these circumstances must be sure to learn as much as possible about the situation and approach the decision from a logical and rational perspective.

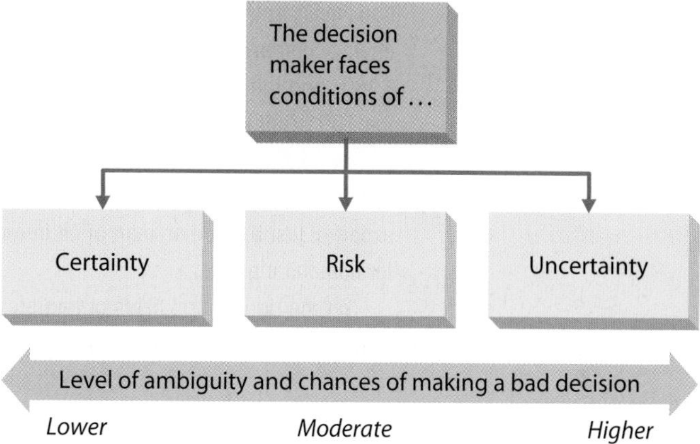

Decision Making Under Uncertainty Most of the major decision making in contemporary organizations is done under a **state of uncertainty**. The decision maker does not know all the alternatives, the risks associated with each, or the likely consequences of each alternative. This uncertainty stems from the complexity and dynamism of contemporary organizations and their environments. The emergence of the Internet as a significant force in today's competitive environment has served to increase both revenue potential and also uncertainty for most managers.

state of uncertainty A condition in which the decision maker does not know all the alternatives, the risks associated with each, or the consequences each alternative is likely to have

To make effective decisions in these circumstances, managers must acquire as much relevant information as possible and approach the situation from a logical and rational perspective. Intuition, judgment, and experience always play major roles in the decision-making process under conditions of uncertainty. Even so, uncertainty is the most ambiguous condition for managers and the one most prone to error.[13] Indeed, many of the problems associated with the downfall of Arthur Andersen resulted from the firm's apparent difficulties in responding to ambiguous and uncertain decision parameters regarding the firm's moral, ethical, and legal responsibilities.[14] And, as illustrated in *The World of Management,* conflict in the Middle East and the 2003 war between U.S.-led forces and Iraq created very high levels of uncertainty for some businesses.

concept CHECK

What are the two basic types of decisions? Provide an example of each.	*Identify examples of decisions you have recently made under each of the three general conditions.*

The Future of Multinational Energy Companies in Iraq

"Everybody is looking at what the situation in Iraq may be and how they may individually benefit from what may happen."

– Christian Lange, director of investor relations, Schlumberger*

The 2003 war between U.S.-led forces and Iraq had significant implications for multinational energy companies. After the Iraq-Iran war in the 1980s and the economic sanctions following the 1991 Gulf War, Iraq's oil fields were unproductive and its economy devastated. A United Nations-sponsored oil-for-food program allowed export of just a small amount of oil in exchange for humanitarian aid.

Yet the dormant oil fields of Iraq are the world's second-largest source of untapped reserves. Naturally, then, energy companies are interested in the possibility of reopening the Iraqi deposits. At Schlumberger, an oil services firm, the director of investor relations, Christian Lange, says, "Everybody is looking at what the situation in Iraq may be and how they may individually benefit from what may happen, and we're not unique in that regard."

Oil services companies, which maintain established fields, could be the first beneficiaries. "We expect to see oil services contracts to rehabilitate old fields," says a Deutsche Bank report, "but anticipate long-drawn-out negotiations on new fields." Repairs may cost $1.5 billion, revenues for oil services companies. Stepped-up production could take an additional investment of $38 billion by multinationals. The benefits? Access to 112 billion barrels of oil, currently selling for $30 a barrel.

Energy companies thus face a series of complex and sensitive decisions, among them whether to purchase from a country associated with concerns about human rights and terrorism, how to balance the need for resources against national security, and the appropriate extent of involvement in deciding how the profits are spent, given widespread poverty in Iraq. The decisions are complicated by the involvement of others—political factions in Iraq itself, the United Nations, the U.S. government, and the OPEC (Organization of Petroleum Exporting Countries) cartel. Rational decision making may be difficult in an environment where so many political and behavioral factors exist.

In addition, Iraq could do as Kuwait did after the Gulf War—rebuild but not allow multinationals any ownership. Thus far, Iraq has preferred to make deals with Russian and French firms. But, as the new government of Iraq begins to take shape, all bets are off, and all that oil is up for grabs.

References: "History of Iraq," World InfoZone website, www.worldinfozone.com on January 8, 2003; Neela Bannerjee, "Energy Companies Weigh Their Possible Future in Iraq," *New York Times*, October 26, 2002, p. C3 (*quote); "Oil-for-Food Distribution Plan," Office of the Iraq Programme for Food, United Nations website, www.un.org on January 8, 2003; Stanley Reed, "Energy: A Barrel of 'Ifs'," *BusinessWeek*, January 13, 2003, www.businessweek.com on January 8, 2003.

Rational Perspectives on Decision Making

Most managers like to think of themselves as rational decision makers. And, indeed, many experts argue that managers should try to be as rational as possible in making decisions.[15] This section highlights the fundamental and rational perspectives on decision making.

The Classical Model of Decision Making

The **classical decision model** is a prescriptive approach that tells managers how they should make decisions. It rests on the assumptions that managers are logical and rational and that they make decisions that are in the best interests of the organization. Figure 9.2 shows how the classical model views the decision-making process.

classical decision model A prescriptive approach to decision making that tells managers how they should make decisions; assumes that managers are logical and rational and that their decisions will be in the best interests of the organization

1. Decision makers have complete information about the decision situation and possible alternatives.
2. They can effectively eliminate uncertainty to achieve a decision condition of certainty.
3. They evaluate all aspects of the decision situation logically and rationally.

As we see later, these conditions rarely, if ever, actually exist.

Steps in Rational Decision Making

A manager who really wants to approach a decision rationally and logically should try to follow the **steps in rational decision making**, listed in Table 9.1. These steps in rational decision making help keep the decision maker focused on facts and logic and help guard against inappropriate assumptions and pitfalls.

steps in rational decision making Recognize and define the decision situation; identify appropriate alternatives; evaluate each alternative in terms of its feasibility, satisfactoriness, and consequences; select the best alternative; implement the chosen alternative; follow up and evaluate the results of the chosen alternative

Recognizing and Defining the Decision Situation The first step in rational decision making is recognizing that a decision is necessary—that is, there must be some stimulus or spark to initiate the process. For many decisions and problem situations, the stimulus may occur without any prior warning. When equipment malfunctions, the manager must decide whether to repair or replace it. Or, when a major crisis erupts, as described in Chapter 3, the manager must quickly decide how to deal with it. As we already note, the stimulus for a decision may be either positive or negative. A manager who must decide how to invest surplus funds, for example, faces a positive decision situation. A negative financial stimulus could involve having to trim budgets because of cost overruns.

Inherent in problem recognition is the need to define precisely what the problem is. The manager must develop a complete understanding of the problem, its

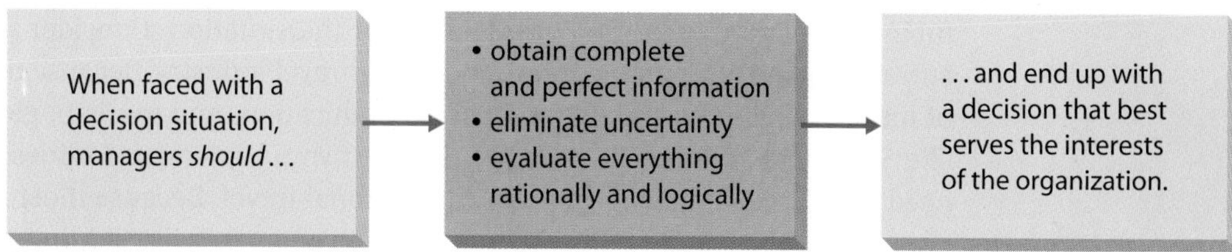

FIGURE 9.2

The Classical Model of Decision Making

The classical model of decision making assumes that managers are rational and logical. It attempts to prescribe how managers should approach decision situations.

TABLE 9.1

Steps in the Rational Decision-making Process

Although the presumptions of the classical decision model rarely exist, managers can still approach decision making with rationality. By following the steps of rational decision making, managers ensure that they are learning as much as possible about the decision situation and its alternatives.

Step	Detail	Example
1. Recognizing and defining the decision situation	Some stimulus indicates that a decision must be made. The stimulus may be positive or negative.	A plant manager sees that employee turnover has increased by 5 percent.
2. Identifying alternatives	Both obvious and creative alternatives are desired. In general, the more important the decision, the more alternatives should be generated.	The plant manager can increase wages, increase benefits, or change hiring standards.
3. Evaluating alternatives	Each alternative is evaluated to determine its feasibility, its satisfactoriness, and its consequences.	Increasing benefits may not be feasible. Increasing wages and changing hiring standards may satisfy all conditions.
4. Selecting the best alternative	Consider all situational factors and choose the alternative that best fits the manager's situation.	Changing hiring standards will take an extended period of time to cut turnover, so increase wages.
5. Implementing the chosen alternative	The chosen alternative is implemented into the organizational system.	The plant manager may need permission from corporate headquarters. The human resource department establishes a new wage structure.
6. Following up and evaluating the results	At some time in the future, the manager should ascertain the extent to which the alternative chosen in step 4 and implemented in step 5 has worked.	The plant manager notes that, six months later, turnover dropped to its previous level.

causes, and its relationship to other factors. This understanding comes from careful analysis and thoughtful consideration of the situation. Consider the situation currently being faced in the international air travel industry. Because of the growth of international travel related to business, education, and tourism, global carriers like Singapore Airlines, KLM, JAL, British Airways, American Airlines, and others need to increase their capacity for international travel. Because most major international airports are already operating at or near capacity, adding a significant number of new flights to existing schedules is not feasible. As a result, the most logical alternative is to increase capacity on existing flights. Thus Boeing and Airbus, the world's only manufacturers of large commercial aircraft, have recognized an important opportunity and have defined their decision situation as how to best respond to the need for increased global travel capacity.[16]

Identifying Alternatives Once the decision situation has been recognized and defined, the second step is to identify alternative courses of effective action. Developing both obvious, standard alternatives and creative, innovative alternatives is generally useful. In general, the more important the decision, the more attention is directed to developing alternatives. If the decision involves a multimillion-dollar relocation, a great deal of time and expertise will be devoted to identifying the best locations. J.C. Penney spent two years searching before selecting the Dallas–Fort Worth area for its new corporate headquarters. If the problem is to choose a color for the company softball team uniforms, less time and expertise will be brought to bear.

Although managers should seek creative solutions, they must also recognize that various constraints often limit their alternatives. Common constraints include legal restrictions, moral and ethical norms, authority constraints, and constraints imposed by the power and authority of the manager, available technology, economic considerations, and unofficial social norms. Boeing and Airbus identified three different alternatives to address the decision situation of increasing international airline travel capacity: They could independently develop new large planes, they could collaborate in a joint venture to create a single new large plane, or they could modify their largest existing planes to increase their capacity.

Evaluating Alternatives The third step in the decision-making process is evaluating each of the alternatives. Figure 9.3 presents a decision tree that can be used to judge different alternatives. The figure suggests that each alternative be evaluated in terms of its *feasibility,* its *satisfactoriness,* and its *consequences.* The first question to ask is whether an alternative is feasible. Is it within the realm of probability and practicality? For a small, struggling firm, an alternative requiring a huge financial outlay is probably out of the question. Other alternatives may not be feasible because of legal barriers. And limited human, material, and information resources may make other alternatives impractical.

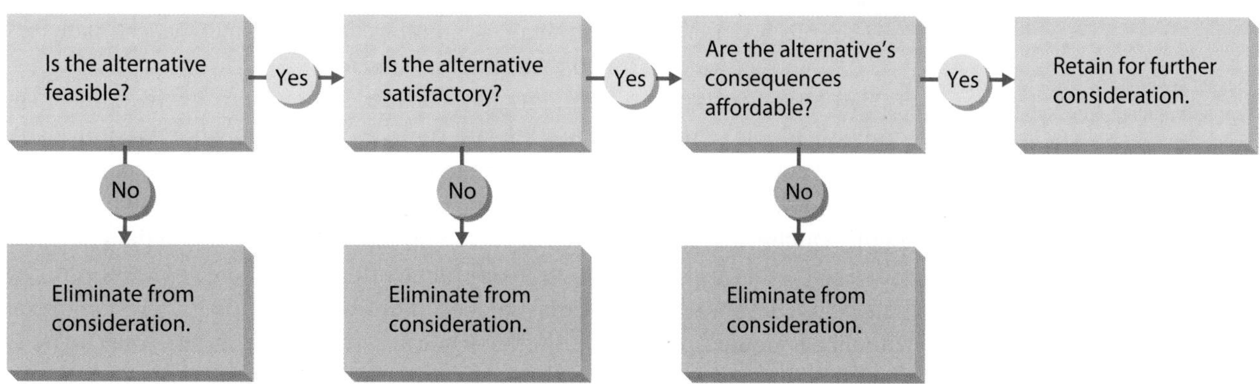

FIGURE 9.3

Evaluating Alternatives in the Decision-making Process

Managers must thoroughly evaluate all the alternatives, which increases the chances that the alternative finally chosen will be successful. Failure to evaluate an alternative's feasibility, satisfactoriness, and consequences can lead to a wrong decision.

When an alternative has passed the test of feasibility, it must next be examined to see how well it satisfies the conditions of the decision situation. For example, a manager searching for ways to double production capacity might initially consider purchasing an existing plant from another company. If more detailed analysis reveals that the new plant would increase production capacity by only 35 percent, this alternative may not be satisfactory. Finally, when an alternative has proven both feasible and satisfactory, its probable consequences must still be assessed. To what extent will a particular alternative influence other parts of the organization? What financial and nonfinancial costs will be associated with such influences? For example, a plan to boost sales by cutting prices may disrupt cash flows, require a new advertising program, and alter the behavior of sales representatives because it requires a different commission structure. The manager, then, must put "price tags" on the consequences of each alternative. Even an alternative that is both feasible and satisfactory must be eliminated if its consequences are too expensive for the total system. Airbus felt it would be at a disadvantage if it tried to simply enlarge its existing planes, because the Boeing 747 is already the largest aircraft being made and could readily be expanded to remain the largest. Boeing, meanwhile, was seriously concerned about the risk inherent in building a new and even larger plane, even if it shared the risk with Airbus as a joint venture.

Managers generally attempt to follow a logical and rational approach to making decisions. This is especially true of individuals in positions like H. Carl McCall, the sole trustee of the Common Retirement Fund for the state of New York. McCall is responsible for managing a portfolio recently valued at $122 billion. The public trust vested in his position makes it especially important that he rationally consider various investment options and then select the ones that will provide the optimal blend of risk and return for the hundreds of thousands of retired state employees who depend on the fund.

Selecting an Alternative Even though many alternatives fail to pass the triple tests of feasibility, satisfactoriness, and affordable consequences, two or more alternatives may remain. Choosing the best of these is the real crux of decision making. One approach is to choose the alternative with the optimal combination of feasibility, satisfactoriness, and affordable consequences. Even though most situations do not lend themselves to objective, mathematical analysis, the manager can often develop subjective estimates and weights for choosing an alternative.

Optimization is also a frequent goal. Because a decision is likely to affect several individuals or units, any feasible alternative will probably not maximize all of the relevant goals. Suppose that the manager of the Kansas City Royals needs to select a new outfielder for the upcoming baseball season. Bill hits .350 but has difficulty catching fly balls; Joe hits only .175 but is outstanding in the field; and Sam hits .290 and is a solid but not outstanding fielder. The manager would probably select Sam because of the optimal balance of hitting and fielding. Decision makers should also remember that finding multiple acceptable alternatives may be possible; selecting just one alternative and rejecting all the others might not be necessary. For example, the Royals' manager might decide that Sam will start each game, Bill will be retained as a pinch hitter, and Joe will be retained as a defensive substitute. In many hiring decisions, the candidates remaining after evaluation are ranked. If the top candidate rejects the offer, it may be automatically extended to the number-two candidate and, if necessary, to the remaining candidates in order.

For the reasons noted earlier, Airbus proposed a joint venture with Boeing. Boeing, meanwhile, decided that its best course of action was to modify its existing 747 to increase its capacity. As a result, Airbus then decided to proceed on its own to develop and manufacture a new jumbo jet.

Implementing the Chosen Alternative After an alternative has been selected, the manager must put it into effect. In some decision situations, implementation is fairly easy; in others, it is more difficult. In the case of an acquisition, for example, managers must decide how to integrate all the activities of the new business, including purchasing, human resource practices, and distribution, into an ongoing organizational framework. For example, when Hewlett-Packard announced its acquisition of Compaq, managers also acknowledged that it would take at least a year to integrate the two firms into a single one. Operational plans, which we discuss in Chapter 7, are useful in implementing alternatives.

Managers must also consider people's resistance to change when implementing decisions. The reasons for such resistance include insecurity, inconvenience, and fear of the unknown. When J.C. Penney decided to move its headquarters from New York to Texas, many employees resigned rather than relocate. Managers should anticipate potential resistance at various stages of the implementation process. (Resistance to change is covered in Chapter 13.) Managers should also recognize that, even when all alternatives have been evaluated as precisely as possible and the consequences of each alternative weighed, unanticipated consequences are still likely. Any number of factors—unexpected cost increases, a less-than-perfect fit with existing organizational subsystems, or unpredicted effects on cash flow or operating expenses, for example—could develop after implementation has begun. Boeing has set its engineers to work expanding the capacity of its 747 from today's 416 passengers to as many as 520 passengers by adding thirty feet to the plane's body. Airbus engineers, meanwhile, are developing design concepts for a new jumbo jet equipped with escalators and elevators, and capable of carrying 655 passengers. Airbus's development costs alone are estimated to be more than $12 billion.

Following up and Evaluating the Results The final step in the decision-making process requires that managers evaluate the effectiveness of their decision—that is, they should make sure that the chosen alternative has served its original purpose. If an implemented alternative appears not to be working, the manager can respond in several ways. Another previously identified alternative (the original second or third choice, for instance) could be adopted. Or the manager might recognize that the situation was not correctly defined to begin with and start the process all over again. Finally, the manager might decide that the original alternative is in fact appropriate but has not yet had time to work or should be implemented in a different way.

Failure to evaluate decision effectiveness may have serious consequences. The Pentagon once spent $1.8 billion and eight years developing the Sergeant York antiaircraft gun. From the beginning, tests revealed major problems with the weapon system, but not until it was in its final stages, when it was demonstrated to be completely ineffective, was the project scrapped. The examples in our Chapter Opening

Incident illustrate a much more effective approach to evaluating decision effectiveness. However, experts agree that it will be several years before the outcomes of decisions by Boeing and Airbus can be assessed.

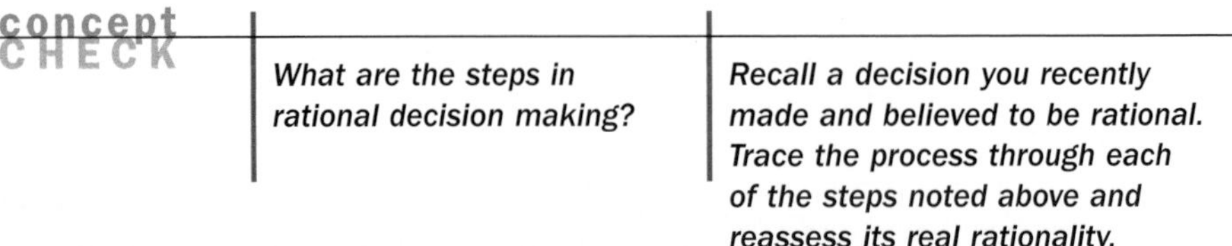

Behavioral Aspects of Decision Making

If all decision situations were approached as logically as described in the previous section, more decisions would prove to be successful. Yet decisions are often made with little consideration for logic and rationality. Some experts have estimated that U.S. companies use rational decision-making techniques less than 20 percent of the time.[17] And, even when organizations try to be logical, they sometimes fail. For example, when Starbucks opened its first coffee shops in New York, it relied on scientific marketing research, taste tests, and rational deliberation in making a decision to emphasize drip over espresso coffee. However, that decision still proved wrong, as New Yorkers strongly preferred the same espresso-style coffees that were Starbucks mainstays in the West. Hence, the firm had to hastily reconfigure its stores to better meet customer preferences.

On the other hand, sometimes when a decision is made with little regard for logic, it can still turn out to be correct.[18] An important ingredient in how these forces work is the behavioral aspect of decision making. The administrative model better reflects these subjective considerations. Other behavioral aspects include political forces, intuition and escalation of commitment, risk propensity, and ethics.

The Administrative Model

Herbert A. Simon was one of the first experts to recognize that decisions are not always made with rationality and logic.[19] Simon was subsequently awarded the Nobel Prize in economics. Rather than prescribing how decisions should be made, his view of decision making, now called the **administrative model**, describes how decisions often actually are made. As illustrated in Figure 9.4, the model holds that managers (1) have incomplete and imperfect information, (2) are constrained by bounded rationality, and (3) tend to "satisfice" when making decisions.

administrative model A decision-making model that argues that decision makers (1) have incomplete and imperfect information, (2) are constrained by bounded rationality, and (3) tend to "satisfice" when making decisions

bounded rationality A concept suggesting that decision makers are limited by their values and unconscious reflexes, skills, and habits

Bounded rationality suggests that decision makers are limited by their values and unconscious reflexes, skills, and habits. They are also limited by less-than-complete information and knowledge. Bounded rationality partially explains how U.S. auto executives allowed Japanese auto makers to get such a strong foothold in their domestic market. For years, executives at GM, Ford, and Chrysler compared their

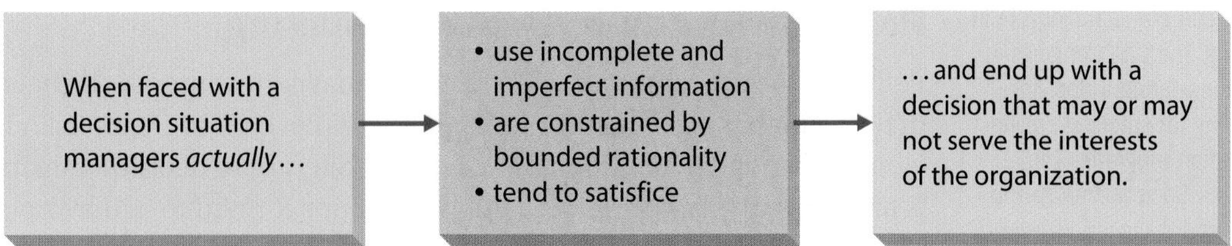

FIGURE 9.4

The Administrative Model of Decision Making

The administrative model is based on behavioral processes that affect how managers make decisions. Rather than prescribing how decisions should be made, it focuses more on describing how they are made.

companies' performance only to one another's and ignored foreign imports. The foreign "threat" was not acknowledged until the domestic auto market had been changed forever. If managers had gathered complete information from the beginning, they might have been better able to thwart foreign competitors. Essentially, then, the concept of bounded rationality suggests that, although people try to be rational decision makers, their rationality has limits.

Another important part of the administrative model is **satisficing**. This concept suggests that, rather than conducting an exhaustive search for the best possible alternative, decision makers tend to search only until they identify an alternative that meets some minimum standard of sufficiency. A manager looking for a site for a new plant, for example, may select the first site she finds that meets basic requirements for transportation, utilities, and price, even though further search might yield a better location. People satisfice for a variety of reasons. Managers may simply be unwilling to ignore their own motives (such as reluctance to spend time making a decision) and therefore not be able to continue searching after a minimally acceptable alternative is identified. The decision maker may be unable to weigh and evaluate large numbers of alternatives and criteria. Also, subjective and personal considerations often intervene in decision situations.

satisficing The tendency to search for alternatives only until one is found that meets some minimum standard of sufficiency

Because of the inherent imperfection of information, bounded rationality, and satisficing, the decisions made by a manager may or may not actually be in the best interests of the organization. A manager may choose a particular location for the new plant because it offers the lowest price and best availability of utilities and transportation. Or she may choose the location because it is located in a community where she wants to live.

In summary, then, the classical and administrative models paint quite different pictures of decision making. Which is more correct? Actually, each can be used to better understand how managers make decisions. The classical model is prescriptive: it explains how managers can at least attempt to be more rational and logical in their approach to decisions. The administrative model can be used by managers to develop a better understanding of their inherent biases and limitations.[20] In the following sections, we describe more fully other behavioral forces that can influence decisions.

Political Forces in Decision Making

Political forces are another major element that contributes to the behavioral nature of decision making. Organizational politics is covered in Chapter 17, but one major element of politics, coalitions, is especially relevant to decision making. A **coalition** is an informal alliance of individuals or groups formed to achieve a common goal. This common goal is often a preferred decision alternative. For example, coalitions of stockholders frequently band together to force a board of directors to make a certain decision.

Political forces can play a major role in decision making. The U.S. Congress was recently considering a decision regarding funding for smoking prevention and education programs. The American Cancer Society arranged to have yellow daffodils placed on every legislator's desk on the date the funding bill was coming to a vote. The purpose of the daffodils was, in part, to remind legislators that a number of public interest groups were planning to monitor the votes and publicize how each member of Congress voted.

Coalitions played a major role in the Hewlett-Packard merger with Compaq. After CEO Carly Fiorina announced the proposed deal, the foundations aligned with families of founders Hewlett and Packard came out against the merger, as did HP director Walter Hewlett (son of co-founder William Hewlett). Fiorina meanwhile worked aggressively behind the scenes to build a coalition with other directors, as well as with several major shareholders in the company. Using this coalition as a foundation, Fiorina won her victory, and the merger between the two high-technology giants became a reality.[21]

The impact of coalitions can be either positive or negative. They can help astute managers get the organization on a path toward effectiveness and profitability, or they can strangle well-conceived strategies and decisions. Managers must recognize when to use coalitions, how to assess whether coalitions are acting in the best interests of the organization, and how to constrain their dysfunctional effects.[22] *Working with Diversity* describes another venue in which coalitions are likely to play a major role in making decisions.

coalition An informal alliance of individuals or groups formed to achieve a common goal

Intuition and Escalation of Commitment

Two other important decision processes that go beyond logic and rationality are intuition and escalation of commitment to a chosen course of action.

intuition An innate belief about something, without conscious consideration

Intuition **Intuition** is an innate belief about something, without conscious consideration. Managers sometimes decide to do something because it "feels right" or they have a "hunch." This feeling is usually not arbitrary, however. Rather, it is based on years of experience and practice in making decisions in similar situations. An inner sense may help managers make an occasional decision without going through a full-blown rational sequence of steps. For example, the New York Yankees once contacted three major sneaker manufacturers—Nike, Reebok, and Adidas—and informed them that they were looking to make a sponsorship deal. While Nike and Reebok were carefully and rationally assessing the possibilities, managers at Adidas quickly realized that a partnership with the Yankees made a lot of sense for them. They responded very quickly to the idea and ended up hammering out a contract while the competitors were still analyzing details.[23] Of course, all managers, but most especially inexperienced

WORKING WITH diversity

Uneasy Partners: Rappers and the Recording Industry

"I know people probably look at me and think this is senseless. But . . . to spend [money] is still very fun for me."

– Rap artist Ja Rule, referring to his $100,000 Rolex*

Jam Master Jay of the hip-hop group Run DMC was shot to death in October 2002. Jay's murder brought attention to the often-difficult working relationships that develop between rap artists and their recording labels. Although rap's roots are in self-production, the industry has changed over the years. "When I first started working with artists like L.L. Cool J, the barrier to entry was low," says Def Jam CEO Lyor Cohen. "You could walk into a club and get the D.J. to spin your album and sell one million units. Now . . . you can't do that anymore."

Rap is big business for corporate producers, such as Vivendi Universal, which owns the Def Jam label. Hip-hop accounts for 12 percent of sales in the $13.7 billion industry. The top three highest-selling CDs of 2002 were all in the hip-hop genre. Leading music producers Vivendi, Sony, and Warner are just one business unit within a larger diversified company. Therefore, decisions must be based on objective criteria such as profitability. Conservatism rules, as the big firms profit more from a few blockbuster albums than from many smaller ones.

In contrast, many rap artists–Ja Rule, DMX, Dr. Dre, and others–see hip-hop as a culture and a way of life. They tend to make decisions based on their personal values and perceptions. Profits are for "flossing," or showing off, or for gifts to less-fortunate friends. Ja Rule says of his $100,000 Rolex watch, "I know people probably look at me and think this is senseless. But . . . to spend [money] is still very fun for me."

In the resulting conflicts about everything from musical integrity to funding for promotions, "companies make out well," says industry accountant Bert Padell. "Artists don't make out well." After expenses, fees, and taxes, a performer whose CD has $17 million in sales might wind up with as little as $70,000. To better balance the equation, rappers formed Nu America, a political action committee, in 2001. "Now that the hip-hop community has emerged as a major force in the United States," says head lobbyist Benjamin Muhammad, "it's time for us to flex some political muscle."

References: "A Powerful Few Rule the Music Industry," *New York Daily News*, December 10, 2002, hoovnews.hoovers.com on January 10, 2003; John Leland, "In Rap Industry, Rivalries as Marketing Tool," *New York Times*, November 3, 2002, pp. 1, 36 (* quote p. 36); Rod Kurtz, "Mr. Dogg Goes to Washington," *BusinessWeek*, August 10, 2001, www.businessweek.com on January 9, 2003.

ones, should be careful not to rely too heavily on intuition. If rationality and logic are continually flouted for "what feels right," the odds are that disaster will strike one day.

Escalation of Commitment Another important behavioral process that influences decision making is **escalation of commitment** to a chosen course of action. In particular, decision makers sometimes make decisions and then become so committed to the course of action suggested by that decision that they stay with it, even when it appears to have been wrong.[24] For example, when people buy stock in a company, they sometimes refuse to sell it even after repeated drops in price. They chose a course of action—buying the stock in anticipation of making a profit—and then stay with it even in the face of increasing losses. Moreover, after the value drops, they rationalize that they can't sell now because they will lose money.

escalation of commitment A decision maker's staying with a decision even when it appears to be wrong

For years Pan American World Airways ruled the skies and used its profits to diversify into real estate and other businesses. But, with the advent of deregulation, Pan Am began to struggle and lose market share to other carriers. When Pan Am managers finally realized how ineffective their airline operations had become, experts today point out that the "rational" decision would have been to sell off the remaining airline operations and concentrate on the firm's more profitable businesses. But, because they still saw the company as being first and foremost an airline, they instead began to slowly sell off the firm's profitable holdings to keep the airline flying. Eventually, the company was left with nothing but an ineffective and inefficient airline, and then had to sell off its more profitable routes before eventually being taken over by Delta. Had Pan Am managers made the more rational decision years earlier, chances are the firm could still be a profitable enterprise today, albeit one with no involvement in the airline industry.[25]

Thus decision makers must walk a fine line. On the one hand, they must guard against sticking too long with an incorrect decision. To do so can bring about financial decline. On the other hand, managers should not bail out of a seemingly incorrect decision too soon, as Adidas once did. Adidas had dominated the market for professional athletic shoes. It subsequently entered the market for amateur sports shoes and did well there also. But managers interpreted a sales slowdown as a sign that the boom in athletic shoes was over. They thought that they had made the wrong decision and ordered drastic cutbacks. The market took off again with Nike at the head of the pack, and Adidas never recovered. Fortunately, a new management team has changed the way Adidas makes decisions, and the firm is again on its way to becoming a force in the athletic shoe and apparel markets.

Risk Propensity and Decision Making

risk propensity The extent to which a decision maker is willing to gamble when making a decision

The behavioral element of **risk propensity** is the extent to which a decision maker is willing to gamble when making a decision. Some managers are cautious about every decision they make. They try to adhere to the rational model and are extremely conservative in what they do. Such managers are more likely to avoid mistakes, and they infrequently make decisions that lead to big losses. Other managers are extremely aggressive in making decisions and are willing to take risks.[26] They rely heavily on intuition, reach decisions quickly, and often risk big investments on their decisions. As in gambling, these managers are more likely than their conservative counterparts to achieve big successes with their decisions; they are also more likely to incur greater losses.[27] The organization's culture is a prime ingredient in fostering different levels of risk propensity.

Ethics and Decision Making

As we introduce in Chapter 4, individual ethics are personal beliefs about right and wrong behavior. Ethics are clearly related to decision making in a number of ways. For example, suppose that, after careful analysis, a manager realizes that her company could save money by closing her department and subcontracting with a supplier for the same services. But to recommend this course of action would result in the loss of several jobs, including her own. Her own ethical standards will clearly shape how she proceeds.[28] Indeed, each component of managerial ethics (relationships of the firm to its employees, of employees to the firm, and of the firm to other economic agents) involves a wide variety of decisions, all of which are likely to have an ethical component. A manager must remember, then, that, just as behavioral processes such as politics and risk propensity affect the decisions she makes, so, too, do her ethical beliefs.

Ethics often play a role in organizational decision making. FBI agent Coleen Rowley attracted national attention when she publicaly charged the agency with hindering efforts to investigate a suspected terrorist before the September 11, 2001 attacks. Both the circumstances underlying her charges as well as her decision to come forward with her allegations had significant ethical implications.

concept CHECK

Summarize the essential components of the administrative model of decision making.

Recall a recent decision that you observed or were involved in that had strong behavioral overtones. Describe how various behavioral elements affected the process or outcome.

Group and Team Decision Making in Organizations

In more and more organizations today, important decisions are made by groups and teams rather than by individuals. Examples include the executive committee of General Motors, product design teams at Texas Instruments, and marketing planning groups at Dell Computer. Managers can typically choose whether to have individuals or groups and teams make a particular decision. Thus knowing about forms of group and team decision making and their advantages and disadvantages is important.[29]

Forms of Group and Team Decision Making

The most common methods of group and team decision making are interacting groups, Delphi groups, and nominal groups. Increasingly, these methods of group decision making are being conducted online.[30]

interacting group or team A decision-making group or team in which members openly discuss, argue about, and agree on the best alternative

Interacting Groups and Teams **Interacting groups and teams** are the most common form of decision-making group. The format is simple—either an existing or a newly designated group or team is asked to make a decision. Existing groups or teams might be functional departments, regular work teams, or standing committees. Newly designated groups or teams can be ad hoc committees, task forces, or newly constituted work teams. The group or team members talk among themselves, argue, agree, argue some more, form internal coalitions, and so forth. Finally, after some period of

Group decision making is often used as a vehicle for making especially complex decisions under conditions of uncertainty or risk. The United Nations Security Council, for instance, is frequently called upon to make decisions regarding international disputes and related issues. At the same time, though, the group's decision-making activities often take a long time and may be fraught with disagreement and controversy.

deliberation, the group or team makes its decision. An advantage of this method is that the interaction among people often sparks new ideas and promotes understanding. A major disadvantage, though, is that political processes can play too big a role.

Delphi group A form of group decision making in which a group is used to achieve a consensus of expert opinion

Delphi Groups A **Delphi group** is sometimes used to develop a consensus of expert opinion. Developed by the Rand Corporation, the Delphi procedure solicits input from a panel of experts who contribute individually. Their opinions are combined and, in effect, averaged. Assume, for example, that the problem is to establish an expected date for a major technological breakthrough in converting coal into usable energy. The first step in using the Delphi procedure is to obtain the cooperation of a panel of experts. For this situation, experts might include various research scientists, university researchers, and executives in a relevant energy industry. At first, the experts are asked to anonymously predict a time frame for the expected breakthrough. The persons coordinating the Delphi group collect the responses, average them, and ask the experts for another prediction. In this round, the experts who provided unusual or extreme predictions may be asked to justify them. These explanations may then be relayed to the other experts. When the predictions stabilize, the average prediction is taken to represent the decision of the group of experts. The time, expense, and logistics of the Delphi technique rule out its use for routine, everyday decisions, but it has been successfully used for forecasting technological breakthroughs at Boeing, market potential for new products at General Motors, research and development patterns at Eli Lilly, and future economic conditions by the U.S. government.[31]

nominal group A structured technique used to generate creative and innovative alternatives or ideas

Nominal Groups Another useful group and team decision-making technique that is occasionally used is the **nominal group**. Unlike the Delphi method, in which group members do not see one another, nominal group members are brought together in a face-to-face setting. The members represent a group in name only, however; they do not talk to one another freely like the members of interacting groups. Nominal groups are used most often to generate creative and innovative alternatives or ideas. To begin, the manager assembles a group of knowledgeable experts and outlines the problem to them. The group members are then asked to individually write down as many alternatives as they can think of. The members then take turns stating their ideas, which are recorded on a flip chart or board at the front of the room. Discussion is limited to simple clarification. After all alternatives have been listed, more open discussion takes place. Group members then vote, usually by rank-ordering the various alternatives. The highest-ranking alternative represents the decision of the group. Of course, the manager in charge may retain the authority to accept or reject the group decision.

Advantages of Group and Team Decision Making

The advantages and disadvantages of group and team decision making relative to individual decision making are summarized in Table 9.2. One advantage is simply that more information is available in a group or team setting—as suggested by the old axiom "Two heads are better than one." A group or team represents a variety of education, experience, and perspective. Partly as a result of this increased information, groups and teams typically can identify and evaluate more alternatives than can one person.[32] The people involved in a group or team decision understand the logic and rationale behind it, are more likely to accept it, and are equipped to communicate the decision to their work group or department.[33] Finally, research evidence suggests that groups may make better decisions than individuals.[34]

Disadvantages of Group and Team Decision Making

Perhaps the biggest drawback of group and team decision making is the additional time and hence the greater expense entailed. The increased time stems from interaction and discussion among group or team members. If a given manager's

TABLE 9.2

Advantages and Disadvantages of Group and Team Decision Making

To increase the chances that a group or team decision will be successful, managers must learn how to manage the process of group and team decision making. Federal Express and IBM are increasingly using groups and teams in the decision-making process.

Advantages	Disadvantages
1. More information and knowledge are available.	1. The process takes longer than individual decision making, so it is costlier.
2. More alternatives are likely to be generated.	2. Compromise decisions resulting from indecisiveness may emerge.
3. More acceptance of the final decision is likely.	3. One person may dominate the group.
4. Enhanced communication of the decision may result.	4. Groupthink may occur.
5. Better decisions generally emerge.	

time is worth $50 an hour, and if the manager spends two hours making a decision, the decision "costs" the organization $100. For the same decision, a group of five managers might require three hours of time. At the same $50-an-hour rate, the decision "costs" the organization $750. Assuming the group or team decision is better, the additional expense may be justified, but the fact remains that group and team decision making is more costly.

Group or team decisions may also represent undesirable compromises.[35] For example, hiring a compromise top manager may be a bad decision in the long run because he or she may not be able to respond adequately to various subunits in the organization nor have everyone's complete support. Sometimes one individual dominates the group process to the point where others cannot make a full contribution. This dominance may stem from a desire for power or from a naturally dominant personality. The problem is that what appears to emerge as a group decision may actually be the decision of one person.

groupthink A situation that occurs when a group or team's desire for consensus and cohesiveness overwhelms its desire to reach the best possible decision

Finally, a group or team may succumb to a phenomenon known as "groupthink." **Groupthink** occurs when the desire for consensus and cohesiveness overwhelms the goal of reaching the best possible decision.[36] Under the influence of groupthink, the group may arrive at decisions that are not in the best interests of either the group or the organization, but rather avoid conflict among group members. One of the most clearly documented examples of groupthink involved the space shuttle *Challenger* disaster. As NASA was preparing to launch the shuttle, numerous problems and questions arose. At each step of the way, however, decision makers argued that there was no reason to delay and that everything would be fine. Shortly after its launch, the shuttle exploded, killing all seven crew members.

Managing Group and Team Decision-making Processes

Managers can do several things to help promote the effectiveness of group and team decision making. One is simply being aware of the pros and cons of having a group or team make a decision to start with. Time and cost can be managed by setting a deadline by which the decision must be made final. Dominance can be at least partially avoided if a special group is formed just to make the decision. An astute manager, for example, should know who in the organization may try to dominate and can either avoid putting that person in the group or put several strong-willed people together.

To avoid groupthink, each member of the group or team should critically evaluate all alternatives. So that members present divergent viewpoints, the leader should not make his or her own position known too early. At least one member of the group or team might be assigned the role of devil's advocate. And, after reaching a preliminary decision, the group or team should hold a follow-up meeting wherein divergent viewpoints can be raised again if any group members wish to do so.[37] Gould Paper Corporation used these methods by assigning managers to two different teams. The teams then spent an entire day in a structured debate presenting the pros and cons of each side of an issue to ensure the best possible decision. Sun Microsystems makes most of its major decisions using this same approach.

concept CHECK

Summarize the advantages and disadvantages of group decision making.	*Are some of the different types of decisions and decision-making conditions more amenable to group decision making than others? Explain how and why.*

Summary of Key Points

business.college.hmco.com/students

Decisions are an integral part of all managerial activities, but they are perhaps most central to the planning process. Decision making is the act of choosing one alternative from among a set of alternatives. The decision-making process includes recognizing and defining the nature of a decision situation, identifying alternatives, choosing the "best" alternative, and putting it into practice. Two common types of decisions are programmed and nonprogrammed. Decisions may be made under states of certainty, risk, or uncertainty.

Rational perspectives on decision making rest on the classical model. This model assumes that managers have complete information and that they will behave rationally. The primary steps in rational decision making are (1) recognizing and defining the situation, (2) identifying alternatives, (3) evaluating alternatives, (4) selecting the best alternative, (5) implementing the chosen alternative, and (6) following up and evaluating the effectiveness of the alternative after it is implemented.

Behavioral aspects of decision making rely on the administrative model. This model recognizes that managers will have incomplete information and that they will not always behave rationally. The administrative model also recognizes the concepts of bounded rationality and satisficing. Political activities by coalitions, managerial intuition, and the tendency to become increasingly committed to a chosen course of action are all important. Risk propensity is also an important behavioral perspective on decision making. Finally, ethics also affect how managers make decisions.

To help enhance decision-making effectiveness, managers often use interacting, Delphi, or nominal groups or teams. Group and team decision making in general has several advantages as well as disadvantages relative to individual decision making. Managers can adopt a number of strategies to help groups and teams make better decisions.

Discussion Questions

Questions for Review

1. Describe the difference between programmed and nonprogrammed decisions. What are the implications of these differences for decision makers?
2. Describe the behavioral nature of decision making. Be certain to provide some detail about political forces, risk propensity, ethics, and commitment in your description.

3. What is meant by the term *escalation of commitment*? In your opinion, under what conditions is escalation of commitment likely to occur?
4. Explain the differences between three common methods of group decision making—interacting groups, Delphi groups, and nominal groups.

Questions for Analysis

5. Was your decision about what college or university to attend a rational decision? Did you go through each step in rational decision making? If not, why not?
6. Most business decisions are made under conditions of either risk or uncertainty. In your opinion, is it easier to make a decision under a condition of risk or a condition of uncertainty? Why?
7. Consider the following list of business decisions. Which decisions would be handled most effectively by group or team decision making? Which would be handled most effectively by individual decision making? Explain your answers.
   - A decision about switching pencil suppliers
   - A decision about hiring a new CEO
   - A decision about firing an employee for stealing
   - A decision about calling 911 to report a fire in the warehouse
   - A decision about introducing a brand new product

Questions for Application

8. Interview a local business manager about a major decision that he or she made recently. Try to determine whether the manager used a rational decision-making process or whether behavioral elements were also present. If the process was wholly rational, why do you think there was no behavioral component? If the process contained behavioral components, why were these components present?
9. Describe a recent decision you made that relied on intuition. In your opinion, what experiences formed the source of your intuition? Did the decision lead to attainment of the desired outcomes? Did your intuition play a positive or negative role in goal attainment? Explain.
10. Interview a department head at your college or university to determine whether group or team decision making is used. If it is, how does the head attempt to overcome the disadvantages of a group decision making? Are the attempts successful? Why or why not?

BUILDING EFFECTIVE conceptual SKILLS

Exercise Overview

Conceptual skills refer to the manager's ability to think in the abstract. This exercise will aid you in understanding the effect that nonrational biases and risk propensity can have on decision making.

Exercise Background

Two psychologists, Amos Tversky and Daniel Kahneman, conducted much of the research that led to our knowledge of decision-making biases. Tversky and Kahneman found that they could understand individuals' real-life choices by presenting experimental subjects with simulated decisions in a laboratory setting. They developed a theory they called "prospect theory," which uses behavioral psychology to explain why individuals are nonrational when making economic decisions. Their work has contributed a great deal to the developing discipline of behavioral economics. In fact, Kahneman won the 2002 Nobel Prize in Economics for development of these concepts. (Tversky could not share in the award because the Nobel Prize cannot be given posthumously.)

Tversky and Kahneman's most important finding was that an individual's *perception* of gain or loss in a situation is more important than an objective measure of gain or loss. Thus individuals are nonrational; that is, they do not make decisions based purely on rational criteria. Related to this conclusion, Tversky and Kahneman found that humans think differently about gains and losses. This is called "framing." Another finding is that people allow their perceptions to be skewed positively or negatively, depending on information they receive. Later, when new information becomes available, people have a hard time letting go of their initial perceptions, even if the new information contradicts their original impression. This effect is referred to as "anchoring and adjustment."

In order to answer the questions below, you must be able to calculate an expected value. In order to calculate an expected value, multiply each possible outcome value by the probability of its occurrence, and then sum all the results. Here is a simple example: You have a 50 percent chance of earning 80 points on an exam and a 50 percent chance of earning 70 points. The expected value can be calculated as $(.5 \times 80) + (.5 \times 70)$, or a .5 chance of 80 points (equal to 40 points) plus a .5 chance of 70 points (equal to 35 points). Therefore, the expected value of your exam is 75 points.

Exercise Task

1. Answer the list of brief questions that your professor will provide to you. No answer is correct or incorrect; simply choose your most likely response. Then, when the professor asks, share your answers with the class.
2. Discuss the answers given by the class. Why do students' answers differ?
3. What have you learned about decision-making biases and risk propensity from these experiments?

BUILDING EFFECTIVE decision-making SKILLS

Exercise Overview

Decision-making skills refer to the manager's ability to recognize and define problems and opportunities correctly and then to select an appropriate course of action for solving problems and capitalizing on opportunities. This exercise will allow you to compare individual decision making with decision making conducted through use of nominal groups.

Exercise Background

Individual decision making has some advantages—for example, speed, simplicity, and lack of conflict. However, there are times when these advantages are outweighed by other considerations. Innovation, in particular, is lower when one person makes a decision alone. A group decision is preferable when innovation is required because more input from more diverse individuals can generate more varied alternative courses of action.

Nominal groups are especially well suited for fostering creativity. Nominal groups allow individuals to have freedom in listing as many creative alternatives as they can, without worrying about criticism or political pressure. Nominal groups also pool input from many individuals and allow creative responses to the pooled input. Thus nominal groups foster creativity by combining techniques for improving both individual and group innovation.

Exercise Task

1. Listen as your professor describes the problem situation to the class.
2. Write down as many creative responses to the problem as you can. Do not worry about whether the alternatives you are generating are practical or not. In fact, try to list as many different, even "far-out," responses as you can.
3. When called on by your professor, share your list with the class.
4. Ask other students questions about their suggestions only for purposes of clarification. Do not, under any circumstances, reveal whether you think any idea is "good" or "bad."
5. After all the individual ideas are listed and clarified, add to the list any other ideas you have developed.
6. Vote on the list.
7. Did the nominal group technique generate alternatives that are more creative than those you generated on your own?
8. In your opinion, is the alternative chosen by the class vote a "better" solution than those you thought of on your own? Explain your answer.
9. Give some suggestions about what types of decisions in organizations could be effectively made using nominal group decision making. When should it *not* be used?

BUILDING EFFECTIVE technical SKILLS

business.college.hmco.com/students

Exercise Overview

Technical skills are the skills necessary to accomplish or understand the specific kind of work being done in an organization. This exercise will enable you to practice technical skills using the Internet to obtain information for making a decision.

Exercise Background

Assume that you are a business owner seeking a location for a new factory. Your company makes products that are relatively "clean"—that is, they do not pollute the environment, nor will your factory produce any dangerous waste products. Thus most communities would welcome your plant.

You are seeking a place that has a stable and well-educated workforce, a good quality of life, good health care, and a good educational system. You have narrowed your choice to the towns listed below.

1. Columbia, Missouri
2. Madison, Wisconsin
3. Manhattan, Kansas
4. College Station, Texas
5. Baton Rouge, Louisiana
6. Athens, Georgia

Exercise Task

With this background information as context, do the following:

1. Use the Internet to research each of these cities.
2. Rank-order each city on the basis of the criteria noted.
3. Select the best city for your new factory.

CHAPTER CLOSING case

> *"A CEO doesn't make decisions. The job is mostly the art of balancing interests and dealing with shades of gray."*
>
> – Founder of an Internet company*

Exploding the Myth of the Superhero CEO

The modern point of view about chief executive officers casts CEOs as celebrities, even heroes. The booming economy that persisted throughout the 1990s was usually attributed to America's business leaders. But the bursting of the dot-com bubble, recent corporate scandals, and the slowing economy have revealed a new truth. CEOs are not heroes. Often, they are not smart or ethical either. Leave aside examples of blatant fraud, and there were still plenty of bad decisions made by CEOs during 2002.

Dick Brown, CEO of EDS, traveled the country reassuring investors that the technology services company had plenty of new contracts and guaranteed growth. The problem is, it was not true. One month later, Brown announced that profits for the year would fall 84 percent. At drug maker Bristol-Myers Squibb, CEO Peter Dolan entered into a $2 billion deal with ImClone to co-develop a new cancer medication. Within months, the Food and Drug Administration rejected ImClone's application. Then ImClone became involved in an insider trading scandal that implicated CEO Samuel Waksal and shareholder Martha Stewart. To top if off, Bristol came under investigation by the Securities and Exchange Commission (SEC) for misleading financial statements.

Even managers with solid reputations for competency are making poor choices. For example, Citigroup CEO Sanford Weill was often cited as an excellent manager and appeared on *BusinessWeek's* elite "Best Managers" list. However, Weill admitted putting pressure on Jack Grubman, a Citigroup stock analyst, to give favorable evaluations of investment banking clients, in return for donating $1 million to an exclusive preschool to gain admission for Grubman's toddlers. Time Warner's CEO, Gerald Levin, was praised for negotiating the successful sale of his firm to America Online. But, after SEC investigations, restatements of earnings, and $24 billion in debt, AOL Time Warner stock is worth 75 percent less than it was at the time of the merger.

Why so many bad decisions? Observers say that CEOs today are not much different from those in the past. The difference lies in the increased pressure for results. Over the last decade, powerful investors have forced CEOs to change strategy or even resign over poor financial performance. David Nadler, consultant and adviser to CEOs, claims, "There was the perception that if you [the CEO] slipped, your stock price could plunge. . . . There are tremendous temptations from the system to cut corners." Former Medtronic chairman William George agrees: "The pressure is always with you. You can't escape it, even for an hour." CEOs must deal with performance demands all by themselves. "Being a CEO is a really lonely job," says James Maxmin, former leader of several businesses. "With your subordinates and peers, you need to have a degree of detachment. There's some detachment from your board too, because they are evaluating you."

In response to pressure, CEOs are careful about what they say and how they say it. "There's a lot you can't share with anyone," says Xerox CEO Anne Mulcahy. Top executives can use "CEO-speak" to reveal or obscure information. After William B. Harrison, Jr., CEO of J.P. Morgan Chase, saw his bank's sales and stock value cut in half in 2001, he said, "No one is happy with our performance this year, but we are positioned well for a rebound in the economy." In plainer words, Harrison could be saying, "When you're at the bottom, there's nowhere to go but up."

From hedging words to bending the rules is just a short step. Stanford professor Jeffrey Pfeffer claims, "There are things that happen when you join a company that cause you to believe that the values in one's outside life aren't relevant any more on the inside." Ethical ambiguity lies everywhere for the CEO. As one Internet company founder says, "A CEO doesn't make decisions. The job is mostly the art of balancing interests and dealing with shades of gray."

At a time when tales of corporate misdeeds are everywhere, leaders may feel justified because "everyone else is doing it." Jim Collins, author of *Good to Great: Why Some Companies Make the Leap . . . and Others Don't,* asserts that most businesspeople are not evil exploiters. Rather, the current crop of CEOs contains many "conscious opportunists"—individuals who deliberately seize an opportunity to get rich quick at the expense of others. Collins believes that more regulatory oversight and enforcement can stop the worst offenders. However, his research has convinced him that greatness springs from a unique decision-making process. "[The greatest company builders] did not craft their strategies principally in reaction to the competitive landscape or in response to external conditions and shocks. . . . The fundamental drive to transform and build their companies was internal and creative. . . . In contrast, the mediocre company leaders displayed a pattern of lurching and thrashing, running about in frantic reaction to threats and opportunities."

Case Questions

1. Describe the decision-making conditions that corporate CEOs face today. What are some likely consequences of making decisions under these conditions?
2. What behavioral aspects of decision making are illustrated in this case? Does the presence of behavioral factors increase or decrease the effectiveness of decision making by CEOs? Why?
3. Over the last decade, investors and boards have played an increasingly important role in making corporate strategic decisions. Now it seems that, in the near future, regulators may also play a greater role. In what ways does increasing participation by adding more group members aid in effective decision making? In what ways does it detract from effective decision making?

Case References

Jerry Useem, "From Heroes to Goats . . . and Back Again?" *Fortune,* November 3, 2002, www.fortune.com on January 10, 2003; Keith H. Hammonds and Jim Collins, "The Secret Life of the CEO," *Fast Company,* October 2002, pp. 81–94 (*quote p. 82); "The Best (& Worst) Managers of the Year," *BusinessWeek,* January 13, 2003, pp. 58–92; Jim Collins, "The 10 Greatest CEOs of All Time," *Fortune,* July 21, 2003, pp. 54–68.

Chapter Notes

1. "2002 Annual Report," "Business Strategy," "Company Profile," "Frank Baldino, Jr., Ph.D.—Chairman & Chief Executive," "Research Strategy," Cephalon website, www.cephalon.com on January 8, 2003 (*quote from 2002 annual report); Andrew Pollack, "A Biotech Outcast Awakens," *New York Times,* October 20, 2002, pp. BU1, BU13; "Cephalon, Inc. Reports Third Quarter 2002 Financial Results," *PRNewswire,* November 6, 2002, hoovnews.hoovers.com on January 8, 2003; "Cephalon Submits Supplemental New Drug Application for Provigil," *PRNewswire,* December 23, 2002, hoovnews.hoovers.com on January 8, 2003; "Testing in Humans," U.S. Food and Drug Administration website, www.fda.gov on January 8, 2003.
2. Richard Priem, "Executive Judgment, Organizational Congruence, and Firm Performance," *Organization Science,* August 1994, pp. 421–432.
3. "Ford Grabs Big Prize as Steep Losses Force BMW to Sell Rover," *Wall Street Journal,* March 17, 2000, pp. A1, A8.
4. Paul Nutt, "The Formulation Processes and Tactics Used in Organizational Decision Making," *Organization Science,* May 1993, pp. 226–240.
5. For a recent review of decision making, see E. Frank Harrison, *The Managerial Decision Making Process,* 5th ed. (Boston: Houghton Mifflin, 1999).
6. See "How Goodyear Blew Its Chance to Capitalize on a Rival's Woes," *Wall Street Journal,* February 19, 2003, pp. A1, A10.
7. "Kodak Moment Came Early for CEO Fisher, Who Takes a Stumble," *Wall Street Journal,* July 25, 1997, pp. A1, A6.
8. George P. Huber, *Managerial Decision Making* (Glenview, Ill.: Scott, Foresman, 1980).
9. See Paul D. Collins, Lori V. Ryan, and Sharon F. Matusik, "Programmable Automation and the Locus of Decision-Making Power," *Journal of Management,* vol. 25, 1999, pp. 29–53, for an example.
10. Huber, *Managerial Decision Making.* See also David W. Miller and Martin K. Starr, *The Structure of Human Decisions* (Englewood Cliffs, N.J.: Prentice-Hall, 1976); Alvar Elbing, *Behavioral Decisions in Organizations,* 2nd ed. (Glenview, Ill: Scott, Foresman, 1978).
11. "Taking the Angst out of Taking a Gamble," *BusinessWeek,* July 14, 1997, pp. 52–53.

12. See Alex Taylor III, "Porsche's Risky Recipe," *Fortune*, February 17, 2003, pp. 90–94; "Porsche Acts to Cut Costs as Saks Falls and Euro Rises," *Financial Times*, June 19, 2003, p. 20.
13. Gerard P. Hodgkinson, Nicola J. Bown, A. John Maule, Keith W. Glaister, and Alan D. Pearman, "Breaking the Frame: An Analysis of Strategic Cognition and Decision Making Under Uncertainty," *Strategic Management Journal*, vol. 20, 1999, pp. 977–985.
14. "Andersen's Fall from Grace Is a Tale of Greed and Miscues," *Wall Street Journal*, June 7, 2002, pp. A1, A6.
15. Glen Whyte, "Decision Failures: Why They Occur and How to Prevent Them," *Academy of Management Executive*, August 1991, pp. 23–31.
16. Jerry Useem, "Boeing vs. Boeing," *Fortune*, October 2, 2000, pp. 148–160; "Airbus Prepares to 'Bet the Company' as It Builds a Huge New Jet," *Wall Street Journal*, November 3, 1999, pp. A1, A10.
17. "The Wisdom of Solomon," *Newsweek*, August 17, 1987, pp. 62–63.
18. "Making Decisions in Real Time," *Fortune*, June 26, 2000, pp. 332–334.
19. Herbert A. Simon, *Administrative Behavior* (New York: Free Press, 1945). Simon's ideas have been refined and updated in Herbert A. Simon, *Administrative Behavior*, 3rd ed. (New York: Free Press, 1976), and Herbert A. Simon, "Making Management Decisions: The Role of Intuition and Emotion," *Academy of Management Executive*, February 1987, pp. 57–63.
20. Patricia Corner, Angelo Kinicki, and Barbara Keats, "Integrating Organizational and Individual Information Processing Perspectives on Choice," *Organization Science*, August 1994, pp. 294–302.
21. See George Anders, "The Carly Chronicles," *Fast Company*, February 2003, pp. 66–73.
22. Kimberly D. Elsbach and Greg Elofson, "How the Packaging of Decision Explanations Affects Perceptions of Trustworthiness," *Academy of Management Journal*, vol. 43, 2000, pp. 80–89.
23. Charles P. Wallace, "Adidas—Back in the Game," *Fortune*, August 18, 1997, pp. 176–182.
24. Barry M. Staw and Jerry Ross, "Good Money After Bad," *Psychology Today*, February 1988, pp. 30–33; D. Ramona Bobocel and John Meyer, "Escalating Commitment to a Failing Course of Action: Separating the Roles of Choice and Justification," *Journal of Applied Psychology*, vol. 79, 1994, pp. 360–363.
25. Mark Keil and Ramiro Montealegre, "Cutting Your Losses: Extricating Your Organization When a Big Project Goes Awry," *Sloan Management Review*, Spring 2000, pp. 55–64.
26. Gerry McNamara and Philip Bromiley, "Risk and Return in Organizational Decision Making," *Academy of Management Journal*, vol. 42, 1999, pp. 330–339.
27. See Brian O'Reilly, "What It Takes to Start a Startup," *Fortune*, June 7, 1999, pp. 135–140, for an example.
28. Martha I. Finney, "The Catbert Dilemma—The Human Side of Tough Decisions," *HRMagazine*, February 1997, pp. 70–78.
29. Edwin A. Locke, David M. Schweiger, and Gary P. Latham, "Participation in Decision Making: When Should It Be Used?" *Organizational Dynamics*, Winter 1986, pp. 65–79; Nicholas Baloff and Elizabeth M. Doherty, "Potential Pitfalls in Employee Participation," *Organizational Dynamics*, Winter 1989, pp. 51–62.
30. "The Art of Brainstorming," *BusinessWeek*, August 26, 2002, pp. 168–169.
31. Andre L. Delbecq, Andrew H. Van de Ven, and David H. Gustafson, *Group Techniques for Program Planning* (Glenview, Ill.: Scott, Foresman, 1975); Michael J. Prietula and Herbert A. Simon, "The Experts in Your Midst," *Harvard Business Review*, January–February 1989, pp. 120–124.
32. Norman P. R. Maier, "Assets and Liabilities in Group Problem Solving: The Need for an Integrative Function," in J. Richard Hackman, Edward E. Lawler III, and Lyman W. Porter, eds., *Perspectives on Business in Organizations*, 2nd ed. (New York: McGraw-Hill, 1983), pp. 385–392.
33. Anthony L. Iaquinto and James W. Fredrickson, "Top Management Team Agreement About the Strategic Decision Process: A Test of Some of Its Determinants and Consequences," *Strategic Management Journal*, vol. 18, 1997, pp. 63–75.
34. Tony Simons, Lisa Hope Pelled, and Ken A. Smith, "Making Use of Difference: Diversity, Debate, and Decision Comprehensiveness in Top Management Teams," *Academy of Management Journal*, vol. 42, 1999, pp. 662–673.
35. Richard A. Cosier and Charles R. Schwenk, "Agreement and Thinking Alike: Ingredients for Poor Decisions," *Academy of Management Executive*, February 1990, pp. 69–78.
36. Irving L. Janis, *Groupthink*, 2nd ed. (Boston: Houghton Mifflin, 1982).
37. Janis, *Groupthink*.

10

Managing New Venture Formation and Entrepreneurship

CHAPTER OUTLINE

The Nature of Entrepreneurship

The Role of Entrepreneurship in Society
- Job Creation
- Innovation
- Importance to Big Business

Strategy for Entrepreneurial Organizations
- Choosing an Industry
- Emphasizing Distinctive Competencies
- Writing a Business Plan
- Entrepreneurship and International Management

Structure of Entrepreneurial Organizations
- Starting the New Business
- Financing the New Business
- Sources of Management Advice
- Franchising

The Performance of Entrepreneurial Organizations
- Trends in Small-Business Start-ups
- Reasons for Failure
- Reasons for Success

LEARNING OBJECTIVES

After studying this chapter, you should be able to:

1 ***Discuss the nature of entrepreneurship.***

OPENING INCIDENT

You are hungry. You stop for a fast-food snack. You step into a clean, attractive shop. Along one wall, sandwiches such as Smoked Salmon on Baguette and Indian Spicy Chicken Tikka. Other offerings: yogurt parfaits, freshly squeezed juices, sushi. Homemade cookies and cakes, espresso, Earl Grey tea. You choose, pay, and leave the store, all in just ninety seconds. Yes, this is not your typical "burger-in-a-box" meal. It is Pret A Manger, French for "ready to eat," the name of a British chain that is revolutionizing fast food. Or perhaps spawning a new industry. The term *fast-casual* has been coined to refer to restaurants that fall in the middle ground between traditional fast food and a full-service, sit-down, menu-and-a-waiter dining experience.

At Pret A Manger, the focus is on the food. The company was started in 1986 by two Englishmen, Sinclair Beecham and Julian Metcalfe, who were disenchanted with the unimaginative offerings at London's sandwich shops. To ensure quality, every item is made fresh every morning, at the location where it will be sold. Ingredients are top quality, such as hand-picked fresh basil and homemade mayonnaise. When Chinese crawfish were unavailable, Pret A Manger did not settle for lesser-quality

2

Describe the role of entrepreneurship in society.

3

Understand the major issues involved in choosing strategies for small firms and the role of international management in entrepreneurship.

4

Discuss the structural challenges unique to entrepreneurial firms.

5

Understand the determinants of the performance of small firms.

"We said, 'We're going to do it our way and see what happens.'"

—Andrew Rolfe, CEO, Pret A Manger

Pret a Manger, a growing "fast-casual" restaurant chain, was launched by two English entrepreneurs.

seafood. Instead, it substituted fresh Canadian shrimp. An obsession with quality has led to thirty-three revisions of the firm's brownie recipe. The wall of a Pret A Manger shop in Cambridge states, "A racehorse that runs a mile a few seconds faster is worth twice as much. That little extra proves to be the greatest value." At the end of each day, unsold food is donated to charities that feed the homeless.

Certainly another important aspect of any retail outlet's success is customer service, and Pret A Manger has adopted a unique approach. In a sharp departure from industry practice, the firm offers no training in customer service, no scripts to follow, no quotas or repetitious tasks. It simply hires enthusiastic people and then lets them do their thing. The company has been named one of the top ten best places to work in Europe, due to a friendly, casual atmosphere—and weekly "pub nights" for all employees probably helped, too. Diversity is high, with less than one-third British employees, and the workforce is also very young, as 38 percent of employees are younger than twenty-five. Every executive spends one day each quarter in stores, making sandwiches and serving coffee. Every worker is given the cell phone number of all Pret A Manger managers, including CEO Andrew Rolfe. Workers can earn Tiffany silver stars for good service and up to $1,500 for suggestions.

Pret A Manger is breaking the fast-food mold in other ways, too. Rolfe says, "We don't believe in focus groups, research, or advertising. We have a very simple principle: If it doesn't take, we stop selling it." As the chain has grown from 1 store to 130, consistency has been a key concern. The company has steadfastly refused to consider franchising and has limited growth to no more than 40 new stores annually.

The chain is expanding into the United States, but the concept may be "too British." Premade food is essential to the store's business model, because it allows customers to buy quickly, but Americans prefer a custom sandwich. Rolfe remembers seeing workers in New York look at the queue outside a deli, check the time on their watch, and then walk on. He knew then that Pret A Manger could be a success, in spite of its unorthodox approach. "Before we came, everybody we spoke to who is from New York said, 'Americans want to go to their deli and have their sandwich their way,'" Rolfe recollects. "We said, 'We're going to do it our way and see what happens.'"

In an ironic twist, McDonald's purchased 33 percent of Pret A Manger in 2001. The company is quick to distance itself from the burger maker—its website says, "McDonald's do not have any direct influence over what we sell or how we sell it." Rolfe admits that maintaining the firm's distinctiveness will be challenging. Yet he feels certain that the firm can hold onto its values and do what is right, saying, "There's no reason I would allow anything to change that."[1]

Just like Sinclair Beecham and Julian Metcalfe, thousands of people all over the world start new businesses each year. And, like Pret A Manger, some of these businesses succeed, while unfortunately, many others fail. Some of the people who fail in a new business try again, and sometimes it takes two or more failures before a successful business gets under way. Henry Ford, for example, went bankrupt twice before succeeding with Ford Motor Company.

This process of starting a new business, sometimes failing and sometimes succeeding, is part of what is called "entrepreneurship," the subject of this chapter. We begin by exploring the nature of entrepreneurship. We then examine the role of entrepreneurship in the business world and discuss strategies for entrepreneurial organizations. We then describe the structure and performance of entrepreneurial organizations.

The Nature of Entrepreneurship

entrepreneurship The process of planning, organizing, operating, and assuming the risk of a business venture

Entrepreneurship is the process of planning, organizing, operating, and assuming the risk of a business venture. An **entrepreneur**, in turn, is someone who engages in entrepreneurship. Sinclair Beecham and Julian Metcalfe, as highlighted in our

Entrepreneurship is the process of planning, organizing, operating, and assuming the risk of a business venture. Sandra and Marco Johnson became entrepreneurs when they launched Antelope Valley Medical College. The school offers vocational courses and programs that prepare students for careers as emergency medical technicians. The school also offers short courses in CPR and related medical emergency procedures. The Johnsons grossed over $1 million in 2002.

opening incident, fit this description. They put their own resources on the line and took a personal stake in the success or failure of Pret A Manger. Business owners who hire professional managers to run their businesses and then turn their attention to other interests are not true entrepreneurs. Although they are assuming the risk of the venture, they are not actively involved in organizing or operating it. Likewise, professional managers whose job is running someone else's business are not entrepreneurs, for they assume less-than-total personal risk for the success or failure of the business.

entrepreneur Someone who engages in entrepreneurship

Entrepreneurs start new businesses. We define a **small business** as one that is privately owned by one individual or a small group of individuals and has sales and assets that are not large enough to influence its environment. A small, two-person software development company with annual sales of $100,000 would clearly be a small business, whereas Microsoft Corporation is just as clearly a large business. But the boundaries are not always this clear-cut. For example, a regional retailing chain with twenty stores and annual revenues of $30 million may sound large but is really very small when compared to such giants as Wal-Mart and Sears.

small business A business that is privately owned by one individual or a small group of individuals and has sales and assets that are not large enough to influence its environment

concept CHECK

What is a small business?

How easy or difficult is it to distinguish between a small and a large business?

The Role of Entrepreneurship in Society

The history of entrepreneurship and of the development of new businesses is in many ways the history of great wealth and of great failure. Some entrepreneurs have been very successful and have accumulated vast fortunes from their entrepreneurial efforts. For example, when Microsoft Corporation first sold its stock to the public in 1986, Bill Gates, then just thirty years old, received $350 million for his share of Microsoft.[2] Today his holdings—valued at $63 billion—make him the richest person in the United States and one of the richest in the world.[3] Many more entrepreneurs, however, have lost a great deal of money. Research suggests that the majority of new businesses fail within the first few years of founding.[4] Many that last longer do so only because the entrepreneurs themselves work long hours for very little income. *Today's Management Issues* highlights another interesting slant on the role of entrepreneurship in society—specifically, when is an entrepreneurial organization a business, and when is it "something else"?

As Figure 10.1 shows, most U.S. businesses employ fewer than 100 people, and most U.S. workers are employed by small firms. For example, Figure 10.1(a) shows that 86.7 percent of all U.S. businesses employ 20 or fewer people; another 11 percent employ between 20 and 99 people. In contrast, only about one-tenth of 1 percent employs 1,000 or more workers. Figure 10.1(b) shows that 25.6 percent of all U.S. workers are employed by firms with fewer than 20 people; another 29.1 percent work in firms that employ between 20 and 99 people. The vast majority of these

Is ETS Too Entrepreneurial?

Educational Testing Service (ETS), which produces the SAT and GRE, is a nonprofit company. According to the IRS, tax-exempt organizations must be "charitable, religious, educational, scientific, or literary." The tax exemption was established to encourage organizations that provide benefits to the public, by providing a financial advantage over for-profits. But, in its entrepreneurial search for new markets and products, has ETS gone too far? Should the firm retain its nonprofit status?

"If ETS thinks of itself as a commercial enterprise, that reflects a basic misunderstanding of the difference between for-profits and not-for-profits."

— Robert Schaeffer, public education director, FairTest advocacy group*

ETS creates more than 3 million SATs each year, at $26 each. Recently, however, the firm added testing for kindergarten through twelfth grade, a rapidly growing market that accounts for 40 percent of revenues. Another 40 percent comes from overseas testing, and ETS pays no tax on those revenues either. The firm now tests teachers and other professionals, too. Altogether, the firm administers over 12 million tests annually. ETS also sells research reports about education.

These activities are appropriate for a tax-exempt organization. However, some critics wonder why a nonprofit would have revenues of $700 million and excess revenues (in other words, profits) of $34 million. And ETS paid $2 million in bonuses in 2001, on top of very high salaries. CEO Kurt Landgraf's compensation is $960,000 per year, more than all but two college presidents in the United States. "We're an organization with a very strong social mission, but we are also a very large commercial enterprise," Landgraf says in defense of his pay. "Our compensation is based on the simple principle that we have to attract people who can help us grow."

Tax lawyers say that using excess revenues to enrich executives may be improper for a nonprofit. Robert Schaeffer, director of an advocacy group, believes that nonprofits should not profit at all. "This money comes directly out of the pockets of test-takers, their parents, and taxpayers . . . people who have no choice," Schaeffer claims.

The firm created two for-profit subsidiaries, for selling technology and training. Yet the doubts remain. "If ETS thinks of itself as a commercial enterprise, that reflects a basic misunderstanding of the difference between for-profits and not-for-profits," asserts Schaeffer. ETS, in exploring new businesses and behaving like a for-profit corporation, has jeopardized its nonprofit status. Now the firm must find a way to convince an increasingly skeptical public that its purpose is charitable and thus that it deserves preferential treatment.

References: "Charities and Non-Profits," Internal Revenue Service website, www.irs.gov on January 15, 2003; "Company Capsule: Educational Testing Service," Hoover's Online, www.hoovers.com on January 15, 2003; "History," "The Mission, Vision, and Values of Educational Testing Service," "What We Do," "Who We Are," Educational Testing Service website, www.ets.org on January 15, 2003; Tamar Lewin, "Corporate Culture and Big Pay Come to Nonprofit Testing Service," *New York Times*, November 23, 2002, pp. A1, A16 (*quote p. A16).

companies are owner operated.[5] Figure 10.1(b) also shows that 12.7 percent of U.S. workers are employed by firms with 1,000 or more total employees.

On the basis of numbers alone, then, small business is a strong presence in the economy, which is true in virtually all of the world's mature economies. In Germany, for example, companies with fewer than five hundred employees produce two-thirds of the nation's gross national product, train nine of ten apprentices,

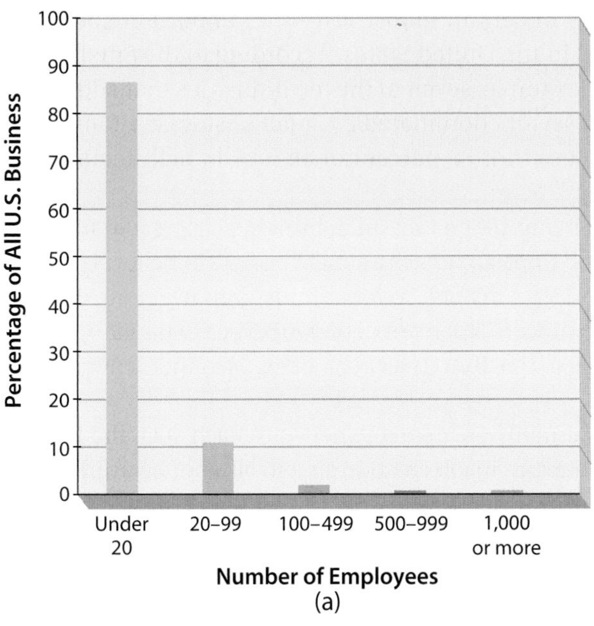

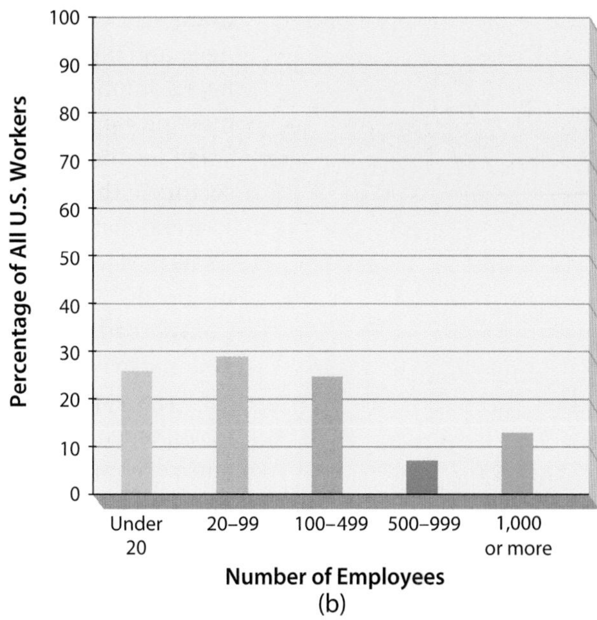

FIGURE 10.1

The Importance of Small Business in the United States

Over 86 percent of all U.S. businesses have no more than twenty employees. The total number of people employed by these small businesses is approximately one-fourth of the entire U.S. workforce. Another 29 percent work for companies with fewer than one hundred employees.

Source: U.S. Census Bureau, Statistical Abstract of the United States: 2002 (122nd Edition), Washington, D.C., 2002.

and employ four of every five workers. Small businesses also play major roles in the economies of Italy, France, and Brazil. In addition, experts agree that small businesses will be quite important in the emerging economies of countries such as Russia and Vietnam. The contribution of small business can be measured in terms of its effects on key aspects of an economic system. In the United States, these aspects include job creation, innovation, and importance to big business.

Job Creation

In the early 1980s, a widely cited study proposed that small businesses create eight of every ten new jobs in the United States. This contention touched off considerable interest in the fostering of small business as a matter of public policy. As we will see, though, relative job growth among businesses of different sizes is not easy to determine. But it is clear

New ventures are a frequent source of job creation. A small coffee cooperative in Rwanda, Africa, was started a few years ago. Today the company employs 400 people, including Olive Ahishakiye. Its gourmet coffee, sold under the label Maraba Bourbon, has become a popular item in the United Kingdom's 353 Sainsburys supermarkets.

that small business—especially in certain industries—is an important source of new (and often well-paid) jobs in the United States. According to the Small Business Administration (SBA), for example, seven of the ten industries that added the most new jobs in 1998 were in sectors dominated by small businesses. Moreover, small businesses currently account for 38 percent of all jobs in high-technology sectors of the economy.[6]

Note that new jobs are also being created by small firms specializing in international business. For example, Bob Knosp operates a small business in Bellevue, Washington, that makes computerized sign-making systems. Knosp gets over half his sales from abroad and has dedicated almost 75 percent of his workforce to handling international sales. Indeed, according to the SBA, small businesses account for 96 percent of all U.S. exporters.[7]

Although small businesses certainly create many new jobs each year, the importance of entrepreneurial big businesses in job creation should also not be overlooked. Although big businesses cut thousands of jobs in the late 1980s and early 1990s, the booming U.S. economy resulted in large-scale job creation in many larger businesses beginning in the mid-1990s. But this trend was reversed in recent years, as many larger companies began to downsize once again. Figure 10.2 details the changes in the number of jobs at sixteen large U.S. companies during the ten-year period between 1993 and 2002. As you can see, General Motors eliminated 385,000 jobs, and General Mills and Kmart eliminated over 91,000 jobs each. Wal-Mart alone, however, created 949,000 new jobs during the same period, and Albertson's an additional 149,000.

But even these data have to be interpreted with care. PepsiCo, for example, "officially" eliminated 229,000 jobs. But most of those losses came in 1997, when the firm sold its restaurant chains (KFC, Pizza Hut, and Taco Bell) to Tricon Global

FIGURE 10.2

Representative Jobs Created and Lost by Big Business, 1993–2002

All businesses create and eliminate jobs. Because of their size, the magnitude of job creation and elimination is especially pronounced in bigger businesses. This figure provides several representative examples of job creation and elimination at many big U.S. businesses during the last decade. For example, while General Motors cut 385,000 jobs, Wal-Mart created 949,000 during this period.

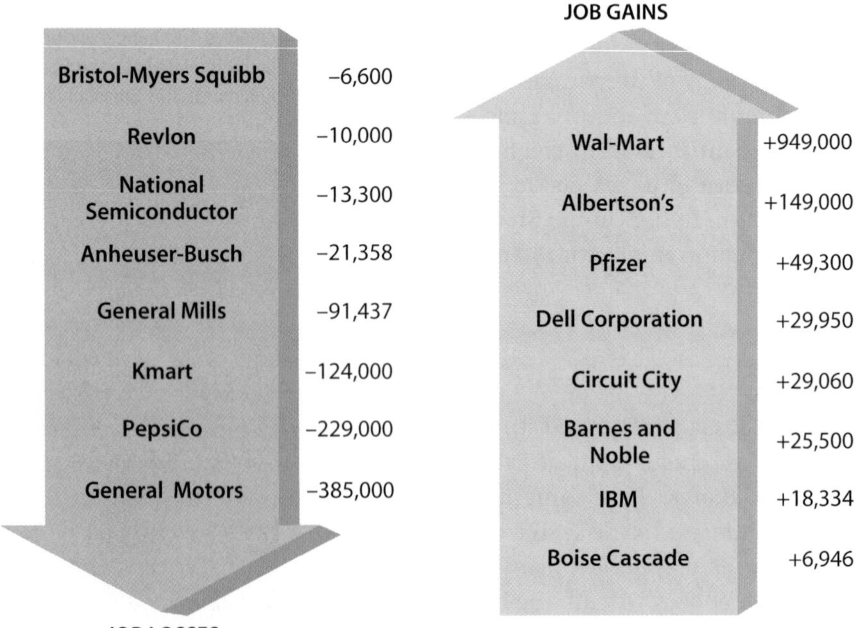

Restaurants. In reality, therefore, many of the jobs were not actually eliminated, but simply "transferred" to another employer. Likewise, although most of Wal-Mart's 949,000 new jobs were indeed "new," some came when the company acquired other businesses and were thus not net new jobs.

At least one message is clear: Entrepreneurial business success, more than business size, accounts for most new job creation. Whereas successful retailers like Wal-Mart and Albertson's have been growing and adding thousands of new jobs, struggling chains like Kmart have been eliminating thousands. At the same time, flourishing high-tech giants like Dell, Intel, and Microsoft continue to add jobs at a constant pace. It is also essential to take a long-term view when analyzing job growth. Figure 10.2, for example, shows that IBM has added 18,334 new jobs. But this ten-year increase follows on the heels of major job cuts at the firm in the preceding four years—163,381 between 1990 and 1994. Hence, most firms, especially those in complex and dynamic environments, go through periods of growth when they add new jobs but also have periods when they cut jobs.

The reality, then, is that jobs are created by entrepreneurial companies of all sizes, all of which hire workers and all of which lay them off. Although small firms often hire at a faster rate than large ones, they are also likely to eliminate jobs at a far higher rate. Small firms are also the first to hire in times of economic recovery, whereas large firms are the last. Conversely, however, big companies are also the last to lay off workers during economic downswings. In 1999, for instance, almost 35 percent of all small businesses had job openings, and almost 20 percent were planning to hire new employees. On the other hand, the SBA estimates that by 2000 large businesses employed more people than did small businesses for the first time since such statistics have been tracked.[8]

Innovation

History has shown that major innovations are as likely to come from small businesses (or individuals) as from big businesses. For example, small firms and individuals invented the personal computer and the stainless-steel razor blade, the transistor radio and the photocopying machine, the jet engine and the self-developing photograph. They also gave us the helicopter and power steering, automatic transmissions and air conditioning, cellophane, and the 19-cent ballpoint pen. Today, says the SBA, small businesses supply 55 percent of all "innovations" introduced into the American marketplace.[9]

Not surprisingly, history is repeating itself infinitely more rapidly in the age of computers and high-tech communication. For example, much of today's most innovative software is being written at new start-up companies. Yahoo! and Netscape brought the Internet into the average American living room, and online companies such as Amazon.com and eBay are using it to redefine our shopping habits. Each of these firms started out as a small business.

Of course, not all successful new start-ups are leading-edge dot-com enterprises. Drywall installer Jerry Free, for example, was frustrated by conventional methods of joining angled wallboard. In his spare time, he developed a simple handheld device that makes it easier and faster to perform this common task. He eventually licensed his invention to United States Gypsum, and it is now widely used throughout the construction industry. As for Free, the experience convinced him that "the cliché about invention being 1 percent inspiration and 99 percent perspiration is true."[10] Popular fashion designer Kate Spade has made it big by introducing a line of stylish purses and handbags sold through such exclusive retailers as Neiman Marcus. Rory Stear and Christopher Staines have succeeded with Freeplay Energy Group, a firm making environmentally friendly wind-up radios that need neither batteries nor electricity.[11] Eric Ludewig presides over fast-growing East of Chicago Pizza, a chain he founded when he was twenty-two years old and just out of college.[12]

Importance to Big Business

Most of the products made by big manufacturers are sold to consumers by small businesses. For example, the majority of dealerships selling Fords, Chevrolets, Toyotas, and Volvos are independently owned and operated. Moreover, small businesses provide big businesses with many of the services, supplies, and raw materials they need. Likewise, Microsoft relies heavily on small businesses in the course of its routine business operations. For example, the software giant outsources much of its routine code-writing functions to hundreds of sole proprietorships and other small firms. It also outsources much of its packaging, delivery, and distribution to smaller companies. Dell Computer uses this same strategy, buying most of the parts and components used in its computers from small suppliers around the world.

concept CHECK

Compare job creation success between small and large business in the United States.

Why do so many innovations seem to come from entrepreneurs and small business?

Strategy for Entrepreneurial Organizations

One of the most basic challenges facing an entrepreneurial organization is choosing a strategy. The three strategic challenges facing small firms, in turn, are choosing an industry in which to compete, emphasizing distinctive competencies, and writing a business plan.[13]

Choosing an Industry

Not surprisingly, small businesses are more common in some industries than in others. The major industry groups that include successful new ventures and small businesses are services, retailing, construction, financial and insurance, wholesaling, transportation, and manufacturing. Obviously, each group differs in its requirements for employees, money, materials, and machines. In general, the more resources an

Would-be entrepreneurs can increase their chances for success by identifying a niche or potential market that no other business is serving. Consider, for instance, the success enjoyed by Boston entrepreneur Chris Murphy. He knew that some dog owners felt that they faced the same day-care problems experienced by parents of small children. In response, he started The Common Dog, a service that picks dogs up on a school bus, takes them to a day-kennel while their owners work, and drops them off at the end of the day. The service costs the dog owners $325 a month. At the kennel, the dogs enjoy their own small swimming pool, several lounging couches, and frequent walks. They do, however, have to bring their own lunches!

industry requires, the harder it is to start a business and the less likely that the industry is dominated by small firms. Remember, too, that *small* is a relative term: The criteria (number of employees and total annual sales) differ from industry to industry and are often meaningful only when compared with businesses that are truly large. *The World of Management* discusses one interesting business start-up in Brazil and explains why an entrepreneur there chose a certain industry. Figure 10.3 shows the distribution of all U.S. businesses employing fewer than twenty people across industry groups.

Services Primarily because they require few resources, service businesses are the fastest-growing segment of small-business enterprise. In addition, no other industry group offers a higher return on time invested. Finally, services appeal to the talent for innovation typified by many small enterprises. As Figure 10.3 shows, 37.6 percent of all businesses with fewer than twenty employees are services.

Small-business services range from shoeshine parlors to car rental agencies, from marriage counseling to computer software, from accounting and

FIGURE 10.3

Small Businesses (Businesses with Fewer Than Twenty Employees) by Industry

Small businesses are especially strong in certain industries, such as retailing and services. On the other hand, there are relatively fewer small businesses in industries such as transportation and manufacturing. The differences are affected primarily by factors such as the investment costs necessary to enter markets in these industries. For example, starting a new airline would require the purchase of large passenger aircraft and airport gates, and hiring an expensive set of employees.

Source: U.S. Census Bureau, Statistical Abstract of the United States: 2002 (122nd Edition), Washington, D.C., 2002.

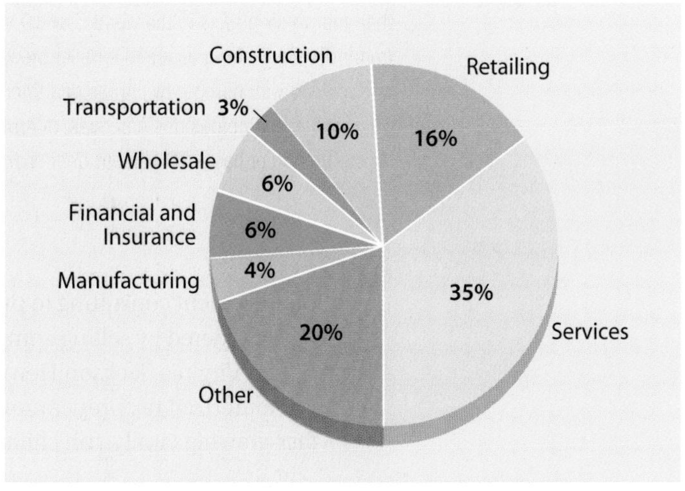

Marcel Telles—Brazilian Beer Entrepreneur

"I don't think there will be more than four to six players [in the global beer market] 5 or 10 years from now."

— Marcel Telles, CEO, Companhia de Bebidas das Américas*

Beer is popular. Global per capita consumption is 22 liters (62 cans) annually, making it the fourth highest-selling drink, behind tea, milk, and soft drinks. Europe and the United States dominate beer sales, but Asia and South America are emerging markets, poised for rapid growth. "There are only three true growth markets for beer globally—Brazil, Mexico and China," says industry analyst Marco Vera. Brazil's beer sales grew 2.5 percent in 2002, while global growth was 0.8 percent. Not surprisingly, entrepreneurial brewing companies are playing an important role in this rapidly growing industry.

In the late 1980s, Brazilian investment banker Marcel Telles was asked to turn around Brahma, Brazil's oldest and largest brewery. Telles introduced American-style business practices to the faltering firm. To increase productivity, Telles cut staff and updated the company's information and logistics systems. He implemented bonuses and a stock ownership plan, tied to profitability targets. In a society that values perquisites for senior staff, he slashed spending. "It's not a culture for everyone," Telles admits.

Telles knew the fragmented industry should consolidate, saying, "I don't think there will be more than four to six players in the world 5 or 10 years from now." So Brahma acquired smaller breweries and merged with number-two Antarctica to create Companhia de Bebidas das Américas, or AmBev. Today, the bottler has a 70 percent beer share and a 17 percent share in soft drinks, following top seller Coca-Cola. AmBev penetrated markets in Argentina and Venezuela and in 2002 entered into a joint venture covering Central America and the Caribbean. Mexico is next, where Telles plans to take on Grupo Modelo, bottler of Corona.

Will the brewing entrepreneurs maintain dominance in Brazil? As the market grows, it becomes attractive to bigger bottlers. In fact, AmBev is in a joint marketing venture with PepsiCo. And the largest global beer bottler, American-based Anheuser-Busch (A-B), is also interested in cooperation. Stephen Burrows, A-B's international CEO, says his firm's global strategic goal "is to form equity partnerships with leading brewers in high-potential-growth markets." If A-B wants to establish a presence in the Brazilian beer market, they had better hurry. AmBev is quickly becoming one of the world's largest brewers, and Telles does not plan on slowing down.

References: Alexandra Kirkman, "Thirsty," *Forbes*, October 1, 2001, pp. 74–75; "AmBev and CabCorp: Alliance Completed for Central American and Caribbean Beer Markets," *Business Wire,* October 24, 2002, hoovnews.hoovers.com on January 14, 2003; "AmBev Reports Third Quarter 2002 Results," *Business Wire*, November 11, 2002, hoovnews.hoovers.com on January 14, 2003; Bill Clifford, "AmBev, Pepsi Bottler in Beer Alliance," October 24, 2002, *CBS Market Watch*, www.marketwatch.com on January 14, 2003; Ian Katz, "Brazil's Breweries: The More Mergers the Merrier?" *BusinessWeek*, March 27, 2000, www.businessweek.com on January 14, 2003 (*quote); "The Global Beer Industry: Consolidation Continues amid Slow Growth," Beverage Marketing website, March 1, 2001, www.beveragemarketing.com on January 14, 2003.

management consulting to professional dog walking. In Dallas, for example, Jani-King has prospered by selling commercial cleaning services to local companies. In Virginia Beach, Virginia, Jackson Hewitt Tax Services has found a profitable niche in providing computerized tax preparation and electronic tax-filing services. Great Clips, Inc., is a fast-growing family-run chain of hair salons headquartered in Minneapolis.

David Flanary, Richard Sorenson, and Michael Holloway recently established an Internet-based long distance telephone service in Austin, Texas, called PointOne Telecommunications. The basic idea was hatched during a tennis match. Recalls Sorenson, "We started getting excited, volleying at the net, and then finally we put the rackets down and went to the side to talk." The firm is off to a great start. Currently, it acts as a wholesale voice carrier, but as soon as its network is completed, PointOne will start signing up its own commercial customers. Investors agree that the company will soon be a major force in telecommunications.[14]

As noted in the text, successful entrepreneurs must choose an industry, emphasize their distinctive competencies, and develop an effective business plan. Unfortunately, entrepreneurs frequently misjudge or do not effectively implement one or more of these activities. As illustrated in this cartoon, for example, providing a product that people do not really want is almost certain to result in failure. Chocolate confections, sausages, and corn-on-the-cob are often popular treats served on sticks at athletic events, fairs, festivals, and carnivals—but cucumbers, peaches, and porcupines are not as well received!

Early business failures

Retailing A retail business sells directly to consumers products manufactured by other firms. There are hundreds of different kinds of retailers, ranging from wig shops and frozen yogurt stands to automobile dealerships and department stores. Usually, however, people who start small businesses favor specialty shops—for example, big-men's clothing or gourmet coffees—which let them focus limited resources on narrow market segments. Retailing accounts for 22.7 percent of all businesses with fewer than twenty employees.

John Mackey, for example, launched Whole Foods out of his own frustration at being unable to find a full range of natural foods at other stores. He soon found, however, that he had tapped a lucrative market and started an ambitious expansion program. Today, with ninety outlets in twenty states and Washington, D.C., Whole Foods is the largest natural-foods retailer in the United States, three times larger than its biggest competitor.[15] Likewise, when Olga Tereshko found it difficult to locate just the right cloth diapers and breast-feeding supplies for her newborn son, she decided to start selling them herself. Instead of taking the conventional retailing route, however, Tereshko set up shop on the Internet. Her business, called Little Koala, has continued to expand at a rate of about 10 percent a month, and she has established a customer base of 8,000 to 9,000 loyal customers.[16]

Construction About 10 percent of businesses with fewer than twenty employees are involved in construction. Because many construction jobs are relatively small, local projects, local construction firms are often ideally suited as contractors. Many such firms are begun by skilled craftspeople who start out working for someone else and subsequently decide to work for themselves. Common examples of small construction firms include home builders, wood finishers, roofers, painters, and plumbing, electrical, and roofing contractors.

For example, Marek Brothers Construction in College Station, Texas, was started by two brothers, Pat and Joe Marek. They originally worked for other contractors but started their own partnership in 1980. Their only employee is a receptionist. They manage various construction projects, including new-home construction and remodeling, subcontracting out the actual work to other businesses or to individual craftspeople. Marek Brothers has annual gross income of about $5 million.

Finance and Insurance Financial and insurance businesses also comprise about 10 percent of all firms with fewer than twenty employees. In most cases, these businesses are either affiliates of or sell products provided by larger national firms. Although the deregulation of the banking industry has reduced the number of small local banks, other businesses in this sector are still doing quite well.

Typically, for example, local State Farm Mutual offices are small businesses. State Farm itself is a major insurance company, but its local offices are run by 16,500 independent agents. In turn, agents hire their own staff, run their own offices as independent businesses, and so forth. They sell various State Farm insurance products and earn commissions from the premiums paid by their clients. Some local savings and loan operations, mortgage companies, and pawn shops also fall into this category.

Wholesaling Small-business owners often do very well in wholesaling, too; about 8 percent of businesses with fewer than twenty employees are wholesalers. A wholesale business buys products from manufacturers or other producers and then sells them to retailers. Wholesalers usually buy goods in bulk and store them in quantity at locations that are convenient for retailers. For a given volume of business, therefore, they need fewer employees than manufacturers, retailers, or service providers.

They also serve fewer customers than other providers—usually those who repeatedly order large volumes of goods. Wholesalers in the grocery industry, for instance, buy packaged food in bulk from companies like Del Monte and Campbell and then sell it to both large grocery chains and smaller independent grocers. Luis Espinoza has found a promising niche for Inca Quality Foods, a midwestern wholesaler that imports and distributes Latino foods for consumers from Mexico, the Caribbean, and Central America. Partnered with the large grocery-store chain Kroger, Espinoza's firm continues to grow steadily.[17]

Transportation Some small firms—about 5 percent of all companies with fewer than twenty employees—do well in transportation and transportation-related businesses. Such firms include local taxi and limousine companies, charter airplane services, and tour operators. In addition, in many smaller markets, bus companies and regional airlines subcontract local equipment maintenance to small businesses.

Consider, for example, some of the transportation-related small businesses at a ski resort like Steamboat Springs, Colorado. Most visitors fly to the town of Hayden, about fifteen miles from Steamboat Springs. Although some visitors rent vehicles, many others use the services of Alpine Taxi, a small local operation, to transport them to their destinations in Steamboat Springs. While on vacation, they also rely on the local bus service, which is subcontracted by the town to another small business, to get to and from the ski slopes each day. Other small businesses offer van tours of the region, hot-air balloon rides, and helicopter lifts to remote areas for extreme skiers. Still others provide maintenance support at Hayden for Continental, American, and United aircraft that serve the area during ski season.

Manufacturing More than any other industry, manufacturing lends itself to big business—and for good reason. Because of the investment normally required in equipment, energy, and raw materials, a good deal of money is usually needed to start a manufacturing business. Automobile manufacturing, for example, calls for billions of dollars of investment and thousands of workers before the first automobile rolls off the assembly line. Obviously, such requirements shut out most individuals. Although Henry Ford began with $28,000, it has been a long time since anyone started a new U.S. car company from scratch.

Research has shown that manufacturing costs often fall as the number of units produced by an organization increases. This relationship between cost and production is called an *economy of scale*.[18] Small organizations usually cannot compete effectively on the basis of economies of scale. As depicted in Figure 10.4(a), organizations with higher levels of production have a major cost advantage over those with lower levels of production. Given the cost positions of small and large firms when there are strong economies of scale in manufacturing, it is not surprising that small manufacturing organizations generally do not do as well as large ones.

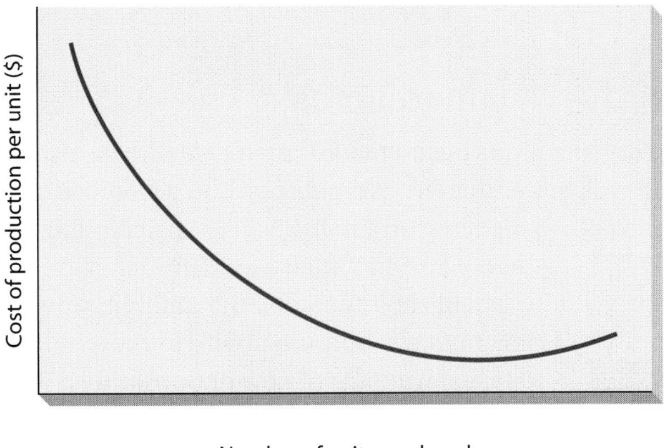

(a) Standard economies-of-scale curve

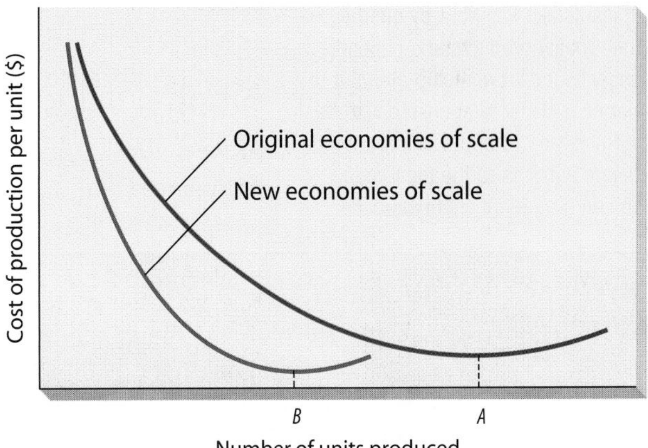

(b) Change in technology that shifts economies of scale and may make small business production possible

FIGURE 10.4

Economies of Scale in Small-Business Organizations

Small businesses sometimes find it difficult to compete in manufacturing-related industries because of the economies of scale associated with plant, equipment, and technology. As shown in (a), firms that produce a large number of units (that is, larger businesses) can do so at a lower per-unit cost. At the same time, however, new forms of technology occasionally cause the economies-of-scale curve to shift, as illustrated in (b). In this case, smaller firms may be able to compete more effectively with larger ones because of the drop in per-unit manufacturing cost.

Interestingly, when technology in an industry changes, it often shifts the economies-of-scale curve, thereby creating opportunities for smaller organizations. For example, steel manufacturing was historically dominated by a few large companies, which owned several huge facilities. With the development of mini-mill technology, however, extracting economies of scale at a much smaller level of production became possible. This type of shift is depicted in Figure 10.4(b). Point *A* in this panel is the low-cost point with the original economies of scale. Point *B* is the low-cost point with the economies of scale brought on by the new technology. Notice that the number of units needed for low costs is considerably lower for the new technology. This has allowed the entry of numerous smaller firms into the steel industry. Such entry would not have been possible with the older technology.

This is not to say that there are no small-business owners who do well in manufacturing—about 5 percent of businesses with fewer than twenty employees are involved in some aspect of manufacturing. Indeed, it is not uncommon for small manufacturers to outperform big business in such innovation-driven industries as chemistry, electronics, toys, and computer software. Some small manufacturers prosper by locating profitable niches. For example, brothers Dave and Dan Hanlon and Dave's wife Jennie recently started a new motorcycle-manufacturing business called Excelsior-Henderson. (Excelsior and Henderson are actually names of classic motorcycles from the early years of the twentieth century; the Hanlons acquired the rights to these brand names because of the images they evoke among motorcycle enthusiasts.) The Hanlons started by building 4,000 bikes in 1999 and will soon have annual production of 20,000 per year. So far, Excelsior-Henderson motorcycles have been well received (the top-end Excelsior-Henderson Super X sells for about $18,000), and many Harley-Davidson dealers have started to sell them as a means of diversifying their product line.[19]

established market A market in which several large firms compete according to relatively well-defined criteria

Emphasizing Distinctive Competencies

As we define in Chapter 8, an organization's distinctive competencies are the aspects of business that the firm performs better than its competitors. The distinctive competencies of small business usually fall into three areas: the ability to identify new niches in established markets, the ability to identify new markets, and the ability to move quickly to take advantage of new opportunities.

Identifying and capitalizing on niches can be an effective way for a new venture to take advantage of its distinctive competencies. Beverly's Pet Center in South Florida competes successfully with giants like PetsMart by offering higher quality products and superior service. Its local ownership allows it to maintain a closer relationship with its customers and to better tailor its products and services to the local market than can a national chain store.

Identifying Niches in Established Markets

An **established market** is one in which several large firms compete according to relatively well-defined criteria. For example, throughout the 1970s, several well-known computer-manufacturing companies, including IBM, Digital Equipment, and Hewlett-Packard, competed according to three product criteria: computing power, service, and price. Over the years, the computing power and quality of service delivered by these firms continued to improve, while prices (especially relative to computing power) continued to drop.

Enter Apple Computer and the personal computer. For Apple, user-friendliness, not computing power, service, or price, was to be the basis of competition. Apple targeted every manager, every student, and every home as the owner of a personal computer. Apple's major entrepreneurial act was not to invent a new technology (indeed, the first Apple computers used all standard parts taken from other computers), but to recognize a new kind of computer and a new way to compete in the computer industry.

Apple's approach to competition was to identify a new niche in an established market. A **niche** is simply a segment of a market that is not currently being exploited. In general, small entrepreneurial businesses are better at discovering these niches than are larger organizations. Large organizations usually have so many resources committed to older, established business practices that they may be unaware of new opportunities. Entrepreneurs can see these opportunities and move quickly to take advantage of them.[20]

niche A segment of a market not currently being exploited

Identifying New Markets Successful entrepreneurs also excel at discovering whole new markets. Discovery can happen in at least two ways. First, an entrepreneur can transfer a product or service that is well established in one geographic market to a second market. This is what Marcel Bich did with ballpoint pens, which occupied a well-established market in Europe before Bich introduced them to this country. Bich's company, Société Bic, eventually came to dominate the U.S. market.

Second, entrepreneurs can sometimes create entire industries. Entrepreneurial inventions of the dry paper copying process and the semiconductor have created vast new industries. Not only have the first companies into these markets been very successful (Xerox and National Semiconductor, respectively), but their entrepreneurial activity has spawned the development of hundreds of other companies and hundreds of thousands of jobs. Again, because entrepreneurs are not encumbered with a history of doing business in a particular way, they are usually better at discovering new markets than are larger, more mature organizations.

First-Mover Advantages A **first-mover advantage** is any advantage that comes to a firm because it exploits an opportunity before any other firm does. Sometimes large firms discover niches within existing markets or new markets at just about the same time small entrepreneurial firms do, but are not able to move as quickly as small companies to take advantage of these opportunities.

first-mover advantage Any advantage that comes to a firm because it exploits an opportunity before any other firm does

There are numerous reasons for this difference. For example, many large organizations make decisions slowly because each of their many layers of hierarchy has to approve an action before it can be implemented. Also, large organizations may sometimes put a great deal of their assets at risk when they take advantage of new opportunities. Every time Boeing decides to build a new model of a commercial jet, it is making a decision that could literally bankrupt the company if it does not turn out well. The size of the risk may make large organizations cautious. The dollar value of the assets at risk in a small organization, in contrast, is quite small. Managers may be willing to "bet the company" when the value of the company is only $100,000. They might be unwilling to "bet the company" when the value of the company is $1 billion.

Writing a Business Plan

business plan A document that summarizes the business strategy and structure

Once an entrepreneur has chosen an industry to compete in and determined which distinctive competencies to emphasize, these choices are usually included in a document called a business plan. In a **business plan** the entrepreneur summarizes the business strategy and how that strategy is to be implemented. The very act of preparing a business plan forces prospective entrepreneurs to crystallize their thinking about what they must do to launch their business successfully and obliges them to develop their business on paper before investing time and money in it. The idea of a business plan is not new. What is new is the growing use of specialized business plans by entrepreneurs, mostly because creditors and investors demand them for use in deciding whether to help finance a small business.

The plan should describe the match between the entrepreneur's abilities and the requirements for producing and marketing a particular product or service. It should define strategies for production and marketing, legal aspects and organization, and accounting and finance. In particular, it should answer three questions: (1) What are the entrepreneur's goals and objectives? (2) What strategies will the entrepreneur use to obtain these goals and objectives? and (3) How will the entrepreneur implement these strategies?

Business plans should also account for the sequential nature of much strategic decision making in small businesses. For example, entrepreneurs cannot forecast sales revenues without first researching markets. The sales forecast itself is one of the most important elements in the business plan. Without such forecasts, it is all but impossible to estimate intelligently the size of a plant, store, or office, or to determine how much inventory to carry or how many employees to hire.

Another important component of the overall business plan is financial planning, which translates all other activities into dollars. Generally, the financial plan is made up of a cash budget, an income statement, balance sheets, and a breakeven chart. The most important of these statements is the cash budget, because it tells entrepreneurs how much money they need before they open for business and how much money they need to keep the business operating.

Entrepreneurship and International Management

Finally, although many people associate international management with big business, many smaller companies are also finding expansion and growth opportunities in foreign countries. For example, Fuci Metals, a small but growing enterprise, buys metal from remote locations in areas such as Siberia and Africa, and then sells it to big auto makers like Ford and Toyota. Similarly, California-based Gold's Gym is expanding into foreign countries and has been especially successful in Russia.[21] And Markel Corporation, a small Philadelphia-based firm that manufactures tubing and insulated wiring, derives 40 percent of its annual revenues (currently around $26 million) from international sales.[22] Although such ventures are accompanied by considerable risks, they also give entrepreneurs new opportunities and can be a real catalyst for success.

concept CHECK

Which industries seem most and least hospitable for entrepreneurship and small business?

Identifying a distinctive competence seems like a straightforward concept, yet many entrepreneurs fail to grasp its significance. Why do you think this is the case?

Structure of Entrepreneurial Organizations

With a strategy in place and a business plan in hand, the entrepreneur can then proceed to devise a structure that turns the vision of the business plan into a reality. Many of the same concerns in structuring any business, which are described in the next five chapters of this book, are also relevant to small businesses. For example, entrepreneurs need to consider organization design and develop job descriptions, organization charts, and management control systems.

The Internet, of course, is rewriting virtually all of the rules for starting and operating a small business. Getting into business is easier and faster than ever before, there are many more potential opportunities than at any other time in history, and the ability to gather and assimilate information is at an all-time high. Even so, would-be entrepreneurs must still make the right decisions when they start. They must decide, for example, precisely how to get into business. Should they buy an existing business or build from the ground up? In addition, would-be entrepreneurs must find appropriate sources of financing and decide when and how to seek the advice of experts.

Starting the New Business

An old Chinese proverb suggests that a journey of a thousand miles begins with a single step. This is also true of a new business. The first step is the individual's commitment to becoming a business owner. Next comes choosing the goods or services to be offered—a process that means investigating one's chosen industry and market. Making this choice also requires would-be entrepreneurs to assess not only industry trends but also their own skills. Like the managers of existing businesses, new business owners must also be sure that they understand the true nature of the enterprise in which they are engaged.

Buying an Existing Business After choosing a product and making sure that the choice fits their own skills and interests, entrepreneurs must decide whether to buy an existing business or to start from scratch. Consultants often recommend the first approach. Quite simply, the odds are better: If successful, an existing business has already proved its ability to draw customers at a profit. It has also established working relationships with lenders, suppliers, and the community. Moreover, the track record of an existing business gives potential buyers a much clearer picture of what to expect than any estimate of a new business's prospects. Around 30 percent of the new businesses started in the past decade were bought from someone else. The McDonald's empire, for example, was started when Ray Kroc bought an existing hamburger business and then turned it into a global phenomenon. Likewise, Starbucks was a struggling mail-order business when Howard Schultz bought it and turned his attention to retail expansion.

Starting from Scratch Some people, however, prefer the satisfaction that comes from planting an idea, nurturing it, and making it grow into a strong and sturdy business. There are also practical reasons to start a business from scratch. A new business does not suffer the ill effects of a prior owner's errors. The start-up owner is also free to choose lenders, equipment, inventories, locations, suppliers, and workers, unbound by a predecessor's commitments and policies. Of the new businesses begun in the past decade, 64 percent were started from scratch.

Not surprisingly, though, the risks of starting a business from scratch are greater than those of buying an existing firm. Founders of new businesses can only make predictions and projections about their prospects. Success or failure thus depends heavily on identifying a genuine business opportunity—a product for which many customers will pay well but which is currently unavailable to them. To find openings, entrepreneurs must study markets and answer the following questions: (1) Who are my customers? (2) Where are they? (3) At what price will they buy my product? (4) In what quantities will they buy? (5) Who are my competitors? and (6) How will my product differ from those of my competitors?

Finding answers to these questions is a difficult task even for large, well-established firms. But where can the new business owner get the necessary information? Other sources of assistance are discussed later in this chapter, but we briefly describe three of the most accessible here. For example, the best way to gain knowledge about a market is to work in it before going into business in it. For example, if you once worked in a bookstore and now plan to open one of your own, you probably already have some idea about the kinds of books people request and buy. Second, a quick scan of the local Yellow Pages or an Internet search will reveal many potential competitors, as will advertisements in trade journals. Personal visits to these establishments and websites can give you insights into their strengths and weaknesses. And, third, studying magazines, books, and websites aimed specifically at small businesses can also be of help, as can hiring professionals to survey the market for you.

Financing the New Business

Although the choice of how to start is obviously important, it is meaningless unless a new business owner can obtain the money to set up shop. Among the more common sources for funding are family and friends, personal savings, banks and similar lending institutions, investors, and government agencies. Lending institutions are more likely to help finance the purchase of an existing business than a new business because the risks are better understood. Individuals starting up new businesses, on the other hand, are more likely to have to rely on their personal resources.

Personal Resources According to a study by the National Federation of Independent Business, an owner's personal resources, not loans, are the most important source of money. Including money borrowed from friends and relatives, personal resources account for over two-thirds of all money invested in new small businesses and one-half of that invested in the purchase of existing businesses. When Michael Dorf and his friends decided to launch a New York nightclub dubbed the Knitting Factory, he started with $30,000 of his own money. Within four months of opening, Dorf asked his father to co-sign the first of four consecutive Milwaukee bank loans (for $70,000, $200,000, $300,000, and to move to a new facility, $500,000, respectively). Dorf and his partners also engaged in creative bartering, such as putting a sound system company's logo on all its advertising in exchange for free equipment. Finally, because the Knitting Factory has become so successful, other investors are now stepping forward to provide funds—$650,000 from one investor and $4.2 million from another.[23]

Strategic Alliances Strategic alliances are also becoming a popular method for financing business growth. When Steven and Andrew Grundy decided to launch an Internet CD-exchange business called Spun.com, they had very little capital and thus made extensive use of alliances with other firms. They partnered, for example, with wholesaler Alliance Entertainment Corp. as a CD supplier. Orders to Spun.com actually go to Alliance, which ships products to customers and bills Spun.com directly. This setup has allowed Spun.com to promote a vast inventory of labels without actually having to buy inventory. All told, the firm created an alliance network that has provided the equivalent of $40 million in capital.[24]

Lenders Although banks, independent investors, and government loans all provide much smaller portions of start-up funds than the personal resources of owners, they are important in many cases. Getting money from these sources, however, requires some extra effort. Banks and private investors usually want to see formal business plans—detailed outlines of proposed businesses and markets, owners' backgrounds, and other sources of funding. Government loans have strict eligibility guidelines.

Venture Capital Companies **Venture capital companies** are groups of small investors seeking to make profits on companies with rapid growth potential. Most of these firms do not lend money: They invest it, supplying capital in return for stock. The venture capital company may also demand a representative on the board of directors. In some cases, managers may even need approval from the venture capital company before making major decisions. Of all venture capital currently committed in the United States, 29 percent comes from true venture capital firms.[25]

venture capital company A group of small investors seeking to make profits on companies with rapid growth potential.

For example, Dr. Drew Pinsky, cohost of MTV's Loveline, got venture capital funding to extend his program to the Internet from a group of investors collectively known as Garage.com. Garage.com is comprised of several individuals and other investors who specialize in financing Internet start-ups.[26] Similarly, SOFTBANK is a venture capital firm that has provided funds to over three hundred web companies, including Yahoo! and E*Trade. As founder Masayoshi Son puts it, "We're a strategic holding company, investing in companies that are very important in the digital information industry—in e-commerce, financial services, and media."

Small-Business Investment Companies Taking a more balanced approach in their choices than venture capital companies, small-business investment companies

(SBICs) seek profits by investing in companies with potential for rapid growth. Created by the Small Business Investment Act of 1958, SBICs are federally licensed to borrow money from the SBA and to invest it in or lend it to small businesses. They are themselves investments for their shareholders. Past beneficiaries of SBIC capital include Apple Computer, Intel, and Federal Express. In addition, the government has recently begun to sponsor minority enterprise small-business investment companies (MESBICs). As the name suggests, MESBICs specialize in financing businesses that are owned and operated by minorities.

SBA Financial Programs Since its founding in 1953, the SBA has offered more than twenty financing programs to small businesses that meet standards of size and independence. Eligible firms must also be unable to get private financing at reasonable terms. Because of these and other restrictions, SBA loans have never been a major source of small-business financing. In addition, budget cutbacks at the SBA have reduced the number of firms benefiting from loans. Nevertheless, several SBA programs currently offer funds to qualified applicants.

For example, under the SBA's guaranteed loans program, small businesses can borrow from commercial lenders. The SBA guarantees to repay 75 to 85 percent of the loan amount, not to exceed $750,000. Under a related program, companies engaged in international trade can borrow up to $1.25 million. Such loans may be made for as long as fifteen years. Most SBA lending activity flows through this program.

Sometimes, however, both desired bank and SBA-guaranteed loans are unavailable (perhaps because the business cannot meet stringent requirements). In such cases, the SBA may help finance the entrepreneur through its immediate participation loans program. Under this arrangement, the SBA and the bank each puts up a share of the money, with the SBA's share not to exceed $150,000. Under the local development companies (LDCs) program, the SBA works with a corporation (either for-profit or nonprofit) founded by local citizens who want to boost the local economy. The SBA can lend up to $500,000 for each small business to be helped by an LDC.

Spurred in large part by the boom in Internet businesses, both venture capital and loans are becoming easier to get. Most small businesses, for example, report that it has generally become increasingly easier to obtain loans over the last ten years. Indeed, some technology companies are being offered so much venture capital that they are turning down part of it to keep from unnecessarily diluting their ownership.

Sources of Management Advice

Financing is not the only area in which small businesses need help. Until World War II, for example, the business world involved few regulations, few taxes, few records, few big competitors, and no computers. Since then, simplicity has given way to complexity. Today, few entrepreneurs are equipped with all the business skills they need to survive. Small-business owners can no longer be their own troubleshooters, lawyers, bookkeepers, financiers, and tax experts. For these jobs, they rely on professional help. To survive and grow, however, small businesses also need advice regarding management. This advice is usually available from four sources: advisory boards, management consultants, the SBA, and a process called "networking."

Advisory Boards All companies, even those that do not legally need boards of directors, can benefit from the problem-solving abilities of advisory boards. Thus some small businesses create boards to provide advice and assistance. For example, an advisory board might help an entrepreneur determine the best way to finance a plant expansion or to start exporting products to foreign markets.

Entrepreneurs and small business owners have an array of sources to which they can turn for information and advise. The Women's Business Enterprise National Council (WBENC), for instance, provides assistance to female business owners. Julie Rodriguez owns Epic Cos., a supplier of commercial divers and utility vessels to the oil and gas industry. WBENC has enabled her to expand her business into significant new markets by providing marketing research data and new industry contacts.

Management Consultants Opinions vary widely about the value of management consultants—experts who charge fees to help managers solve problems. They often specialize in one area, such as international business, small business, or manufacturing. Thus they can bring an objective and trained outlook to problems and provide logical recommendations. They can be quite expensive, however, as some consultants charge $1,000 or more for a day of assistance.

Like other professionals, consultants should be chosen with care. They can be found through major corporations who have used their services and who can provide references and reports on their work. Not surprisingly, they are most effective when the client helps (for instance, by providing schedules and written proposals for work to be done).

The Small Business Administration Even more important than its financing role is the SBA's role in helping small-business owners improve their management skills. It is easy for entrepreneurs to spend money; SBA programs are designed to show them how to spend it wisely. The SBA offers small businesses four major management-counseling programs at virtually no cost.

A small-business owner who needs help in starting a new business can get it free through the Service Corps of Retired Executives (SCORE). All SCORE members are retired executives, and all are volunteers. Under this program, the SBA tries to match the expert to the need. For example, if a small-business owner needs help putting together a marketing plan, the SBA will send a SCORE counselor with marketing expertise.

Like SCORE, the Active Corps of Executives (ACE) program is designed to help small businesses that cannot afford consultants. The SBA recruits ACE volunteers from virtually every industry. All ACE volunteers are currently involved in successful activities, mostly as small-business owners themselves. Together, SCORE and ACE have more than 12,000 counselors working out of 350 chapters throughout the United States. They provide assistance to some 140,000 small businesses each year.

The talents and skills of students and instructors at colleges and universities are fundamental to the Small Business Institute (SBI). Under the guidance of seasoned professors of business administration, students seeking advanced degrees work closely with small-business owners to help solve specific problems, such as sagging sales or rising costs. Students earn credit toward their degree, with their grades depending on how well they handle a client's problems. Several hundred colleges and universities counsel thousands of small-business owners through this program every year.

Finally, the newest of the SBA's management counseling projects is its Small Business Development Center (SBDC) program. Begun in 1976, SBDCs are designed to consolidate information from various disciplines and institutions, including technical and professional schools. Then they make this knowledge available to new and existing small businesses. In 1995 universities in forty-five states took part in the program.

Networking More and more, small-business owners are discovering the value of networking—meeting regularly with one another to discuss common problems and opportunities and, perhaps most important, to pool resources. Businesspeople have long joined organizations such as the local chamber of commerce and the National Federation of Independent Businesses (NFIB) to make such contacts.

Today, organizations are springing up all over the United States to facilitate small-business networking. One such organization, the Council of Smaller Enterprises of Cleveland, boasts a total membership of more than 10,000 small-business owners, the largest number in the country. This organization offers its members not only networking possibilities but also educational programs and services tailored to their needs. In a typical year, its eighty-five educational programs draw more than 8,500 small-business owners.

In particular, women and minorities have found networking to be an effective problem-solving tool. The National Association of Women Business Owners (NAWBO), for example, provides a variety of networking forums. The NAWBO also has chapters in most major cities, where its members can meet regularly. Increasingly, women are relying more on other women to help locate venture capital, establish relationships with customers, and provide such essential services as accounting and legal advice. According to Patty Abramson of the Women's Growth Capital Fund, all of these tasks have traditionally been harder for women because, until now, they have never had friends in the right places. "I wouldn't say this is about discrimination," adds Abramson. "It's about not having the relationships, and business is about relationships."

Franchising

The next time you drive or walk around town, be on the alert for a McDonald's, Taco Bell, Subway, Denny's, or KFC restaurant; a 7-Eleven or Circle K convenience store; a RE/MAX or Coldwell Banker real estate office; a Super 8 or Ramada Inn motel; a Blockbuster Video store; a Sylvan Learning Center educational center; an Express Oil Change or Precision Auto Wash service center; or a Supercuts hair salon. What do these businesses have in common? In most cases, they will be franchised operations, operating under licenses issued by parent companies to local entrepreneurs who own and manage them.

franchising agreement A contract between an entrepreneur (the *franchisee*) and a parent company (the *franchiser*); the entrepreneur pays the parent company for the use of its trademarks, products, formulas, and business plans

As many would-be businesspeople have discovered **franchising agreements** are an accessible doorway to entrepreneurship. A franchise is an arrangement that permits the *franchisee* (buyer) to sell the product of the *franchiser* (seller, or parent company). Franchisees can thus benefit from the selling corporation's experience and expertise. They can also consult the franchiser for managerial and financial help.

For example, the franchiser may supply financing. It may pick the store location, negotiate the lease, design the store, and purchase necessary equipment. It may train the first set of employees and managers and provide standardized policies and procedures. Once the business is open, the franchiser may offer franchisees savings by allowing them to purchase from a central location. Marketing strategy (especially advertising) may also be handled by the franchiser. Finally, franchisees may benefit from continued management counseling. In short, franchisees receive—that is, invest in—not only their own ready-made business but also expert help in running it.

Franchises offer many advantages to both sellers and buyers. For example, franchisers benefit from the ability to grow rapidly by using the investment money provided by franchisees. This strategy has enabled giant franchisers such as McDonald's and Baskin-Robbins to mushroom into billion-dollar concerns in a brief time.

For the franchisee, the arrangement combines the incentive of owning a business with the advantage of access to big-business management skills. Unlike the person who starts from scratch, the franchisee does not have to build a business step by step. Instead, the business is established virtually overnight. Moreover, because each franchise outlet is probably a carbon copy of every other outlet, the chances of failure are reduced. McDonald's, for example, is a model of consistency—Big Macs taste the same everywhere.

Of course, owning a franchise also involves certain disadvantages. Perhaps the most significant is the start-up cost. Franchise prices vary widely. Fantastic Sams hair salon franchise fees are $30,000, but a Gingiss Formalwear franchise can run as high as $125,000. Extremely profitable or hard-to-get franchises are even more expensive. A McDonald's franchise costs at least $650,000 to $750,000, and a professional sports team can cost several hundred million dollars. Franchisees may also have continued obligations to contribute percentages of sales to the parent corporation.

Buying a franchise also entails less tangible costs. For one thing, the small-business owner sacrifices some independence. A McDonald's franchisee cannot change the way its hamburgers or milkshakes are made. Nor can franchisees create an individual identity in their community; for all practical purposes, the McDonald's owner is anonymous. In addition, many franchise agreements are difficult to terminate.

Finally, although franchises minimize risks, they do not guarantee success. Many franchisees have seen their investments—and their dreams—disappear because of poor location, rising costs, or lack of continued franchiser commitment. Moreover, figures on failure rates are artificially low because they do not include failing franchisees bought out by their franchising parent companies. An additional risk is that the chain itself could collapse. In any given year, dozens—sometimes hundreds—of franchisers close shop or stop selling franchises.

concept CHECK

What are the pros and cons of starting a new business from scratch versus buying an existing business?

Many people assume that Starbucks coffee shops are franchises, but in reality they are not. Why do you think Starbucks insists on owning all of its own retail outlets?

The Performance of Entrepreneurial Organizations

The formulation and implementation of an effective strategy plays a major role in determining the overall performance of an entrepreneurial organization. This section examines how entrepreneurial firms evolve over time and the attributes of these firms that enhance their chances of success. For every Henry Ford, Walt Disney, Mary Kay Ash, or Bill Gates—people who transformed small businesses into major corporations—there are many small-business owners and entrepreneurs who fail.

Figure 10.5 illustrates recent trends in new business start-ups and failures. As you can see, over the last ten years, new business start-ups have generally run between around 150,000 and 190,000 per year, with 155,141 new businesses being launched in 1998. Over this same period, business failures have generally run between 50,000 and 100,000, with a total of 71,857 failing in 1998. In this section, we look first at a few key trends in small-business start-ups. Then we examine some of the main reasons for success and failure in small-business undertakings.

Trends in Small-Business Start-ups

Thousands of new businesses are started in the United States every year. Several factors account for this trend, and in this section we focus on four of them.

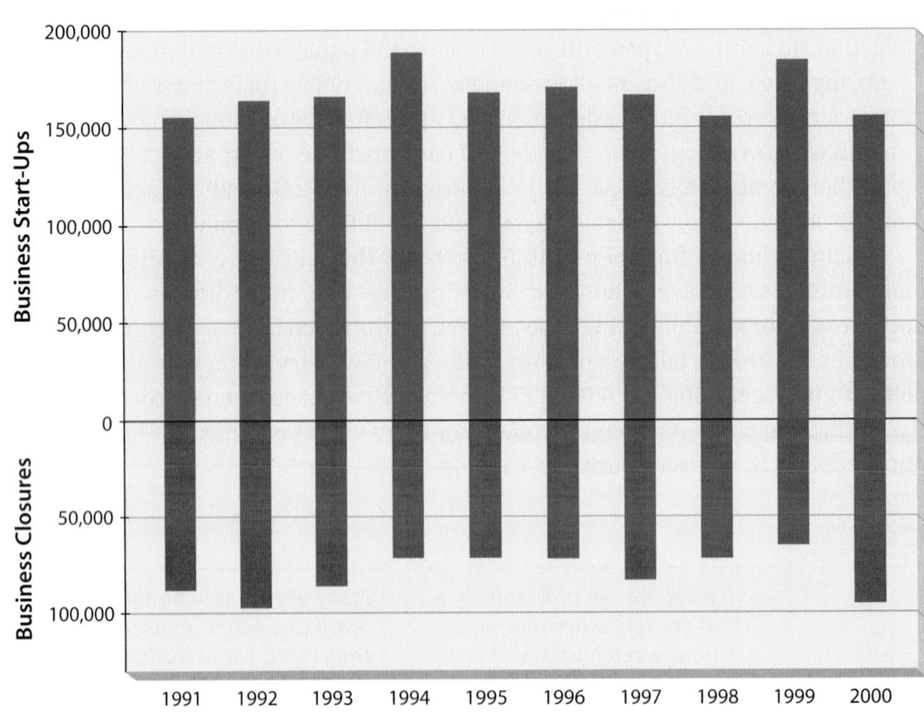

FIGURE 10.5

Business Start-up Successes and Failures

Over the most recent ten-year period for which data are available, new business start-ups numbered between 150,000 and 190,000 per year. Business failures during this same period, meanwhile, ranged from about 50,000 to nearly 100,000 per year.

Source: U.S. Census Bureau, Statistical Abstract of the United States: 2002 (122nd Edition), Washington, D.C., 2002.

Emergence of E-Commerce Clearly, one of the most significant recent trends in small-business start-ups is the rapid emergence of electronic commerce. Because the Internet has provided fundamentally new ways of doing business, savvy entrepreneurs have been able to create and expand new businesses faster and more easily than ever before. Such leading-edge firms as America Online and eBay, for example, owe their very existence to the Internet. *The Business of Ethics* describes another interesting example. At the same time, however, many would-be

THE BUSINESS OF ethics

Ethical E-mailing

"Our goal is to keep the honest people honest."

– Kumar Sreekanti, CEO, Omniva*

In each of the recent corporate scandals, e-mail constituted a key piece of evidence. At Citigroup, analyst Jack Grubman changed his stock recommendations in exchange for favors from CEO Sandy Weill and then sent an e-mail confirming the illegal arrangement. David Duncan, Arthur Andersen's head Enron auditor, deleted e-mails shortly after the start of the Justice Department's investigation. After Tim Newington, an analyst for Credit Suisse First Boston, refused to give in to pressure to change a rating, an e-mail circulated which read, in part, "Bigger issue is what to do about Newington in general. I'm not sure he's salvageable at this point." Corporations are scared about the potential liability that their employees' e-mails represent, but entrepreneurs smell an opportunity. Software development houses are designing programs to address these concerns.

Tumbleweed Communications' products encrypt e-mails, so that only the intended recipients can view them. They also search for banned words, related to dubious activities. The software is sophisticated enough to analyze the messages, so that, for example, the word *breast* is acceptable if it occurs near the word *chicken*. Questionable messages are blocked and rerouted to a supervisor for review.

Authentica's software controls the routing of e-mail messages. Rebecca Burr of chip maker Xilinx relies on Authentica to secure confidential information. "It would be my worst nightmare if the competition knew our product strategy or had our pricing books," Burr says.

Start-up Omniva—whose website appears at www.disappearing.com—uses ultra-secure 128-bit encryption, and senders specify an expiration date. After that time, the garbled messages cannot be decrypted, which is the equivalent of shredding a paper document. In addition, Omniva's software can prevent resending or printing. Users cannot delete e-mails on their own. "Our goal is to keep the honest people honest," says Omniva CEO Kumar Sreekanti. In the event of a lawsuit or investigation, administrators can hit the "red button," which ceases all deletions.

Sreekanti says, "We help organizations comply with regulations automatically so they don't have to rely on people to do it." Removing responsibility from employees has proven to be a popular strategy. Executives from Metropolitan Life, the CIA, and drug maker Eli Lilly are looking to e-mail security companies to help them avoid a David Duncan- or Jack Grubman-style fiasco.

References: Erika Brown, "To Shred and Protect," *Forbes*, November 25, 2002, pp. 114–118 (*quote p. 118); "Omniva Earns Microsoft.net Connected Logo Premium Level Status," *PRNewswire*, October 22, 2002, hoovnews.hoovers.com on January 15, 2003; "Product Overview," Omniva website, www.disappearing.com on January 15, 2003; "Solutions Overview," Tumbleweed Communications website, www.tumbleweed.com on January 15, 2003; "Tumbleweed Granted New Patent for Electronic Communication," Tumbleweed press release, November 26, 2002, biz.yahoo.com on January 15, 2003.

FIGURE 10.6

The Growth of Online Commerce

Online commerce is becoming an increasingly important part of the U.S. economy. As shown here, for example, online commerce has grown from about $2.5 trillion in 1997 to an estimated $17.4 trillion by 2001. And most indicators suggest that this trend will continue.

Source: U.S. Census Bureau, Statistical Abstract of the United States: 2002 (122nd Edition), Washington, D.C., 2002.

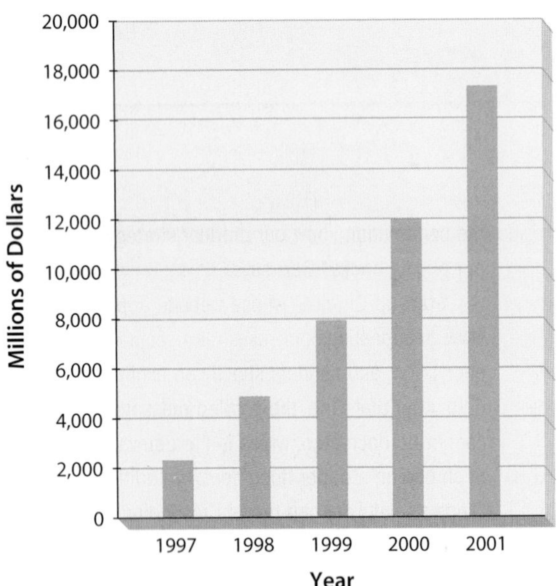

Internet entrepreneurs have gone under in the last few years, as the so-called dot-com boom quickly faded. Figure 10.6 summarizes trends in online commerce from 1997 through 2001. In addition, one recent study reported that in 1999 the Internet economy grew overall by 62 percent over the previous year and provided jobs for 2.5 million people.[27]

Indeed, it seems as if new ideas emerge virtually every day. Andrew Beebe, for example, is scoring big with Bigstep, a web business that essentially creates, hosts, and maintains websites for other small businesses. So far, Bigstep has signed up 75,000 small-business clients. Beebe actually provides his basic services for free but earns money by charging for such so-called premium services as customer billing. Karl Jacob's Keen.com is a web business that matches people looking for advice with experts who have the answers. Keen got the idea when he and his father were struggling to fix a boat motor and did not know where to turn for help. Keen.com attracted 100,000 subscribers in just three months.[28]

Crossovers from Big Business It is interesting to note that increasingly more businesses are being started by people who have opted to leave big corporations and put their experience and know-how to work for themselves. In some cases, these individuals see great new ideas they want to develop. Often, they get burned out working for a big corporation. Sometimes they have lost their job, only to discover that working for themselves was a better idea anyway.

Cisco Systems CEO John Chambers is acknowledged as one of the best entrepreneurs around. But he spent several years working first at IBM and then at Wang Laboratories before he set out on his own. Under his leadership, Cisco has become one of the largest and most important technology companies in the world. Indeed, for a few days in March 2000, Cisco had the world's highest market capitalization, and it remains one of the world's most valuable companies.[29] In a more unusual case, Gilman Louie recently left an executive position at Hasbro toy company's online group to head up a CIA-backed venture capital firm called In-Q-It. The firm's mission is to help nurture high-tech companies making products of interest to the nation's spies.[30]

Opportunities for Minorities and Women In addition to big-business expatriates, minorities and women are starting more small businesses. For example, the number of African-American-owned businesses has increased by 46 percent during the most recent five-year period for which data are available and now totals about 620,000. Chicago's Gardner family is just one of thousands of examples illustrating this trend. The Gardners are the founders of Soft Sheen Products, a firm specializing in ethnic hair products. Soft Sheen attained sales of $80 million in the year before the Gardners sold it to France's L'Oréal S.A. for more than $160 million. The emergence of such opportunities is hardly surprising, either to African-American entrepreneurs or to the corporate marketers who have taken an interest in their companies. African-American purchasing power topped $530 billion in 1999. Up from just over $300 billion in 1990, that increase of 73 percent far outstrips the 57 percent increase experienced by all Americans.[31]

Latino-owned businesses have grown at an even faster rate of 76 percent and now number about 862,000. Other ethnic groups are also making their presence felt among U.S. business owners. Business ownership among Asians and Pacific Islanders has increased 56 percent, to over 600,000. Although the number of businesses owned by American Indians and Alaska Natives is still somewhat small, at slightly over 100,000, the total nevertheless represents a five-year increase of 93 percent.[32]

The number of women entrepreneurs is also growing rapidly. Celeste Johnson, for example, left a management position at Pitney Bowes to launch Obex, Inc., which makes gardening and landscaping products from mixed recycled plastics. Katrina Garnett gave up a lucrative job at Oracle to start her own software company, Crossworlds Software. Laila Rubenstein closed her management-consulting practice to create Greeting Cards.com, Inc., an Internet-based business selling customizable electronic greetings. "Women-owned business," says Teresa Cavanaugh, director of the Women Entrepreneur's Connection at BankBoston, "is the largest emerging segment of the small-business market. Women-owned businesses are an economic force that no bank can afford to overlook."[33]

There are now 9.1 million businesses owned by women—about 40 percent of all businesses in the United States. Combined, they generate nearly $4 trillion in revenue a year—an increase of 132 percent since 1992. The number of people employed nationwide at women-owned businesses since 1992 has grown to around 27.5 million—an increase of 108 percent.[34] Figure 10.7 summarizes the

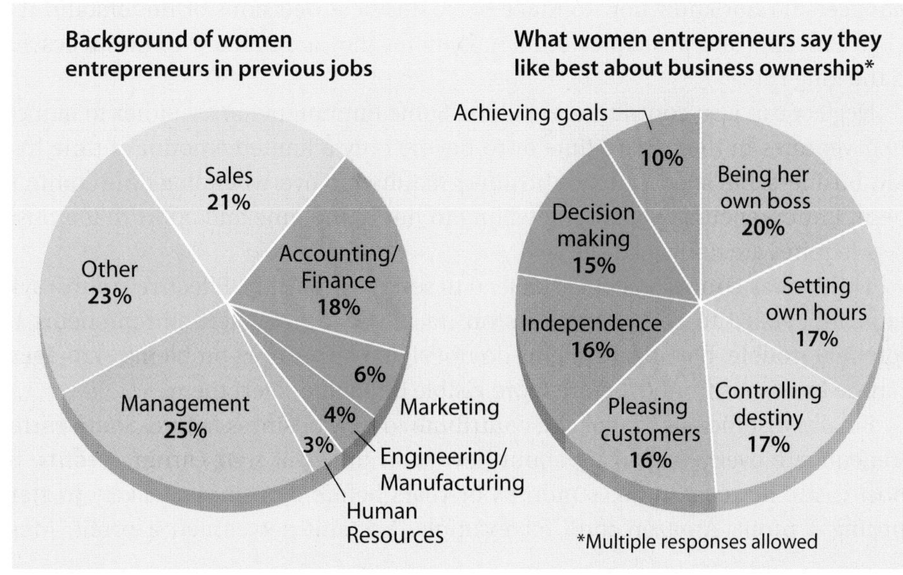

FIGURE 10.7

Where Women Entrepreneurs Come from and What They Like About Their Work

Women entrepreneurs come from all sectors of large businesses, although management and sales are especially well represented. Women entrepreneurs indicate that they really like being their own boss, setting their own hours, controlling their own destiny, and being independent.

Source: From "Women Entrepreneurs," *Wall Street Journal*, May 24, 1999. Copyright ©1999 by Dow Jones & Co., Inc. Reproduced with permission of Dow Jones & Co., Inc. via Copyright Clearance Center.

corporate backgrounds of women entrepreneurs and provides some insight into what they like about running their own businesses. Former corporate positions in general management (25 percent), sales (21 percent), and accounting and finance (18 percent) account for almost two-thirds of the women who start their own businesses. Once in charge of their own business, women also report that they like being their own boss, setting their own hours, controlling their own destiny, pleasing customers, having independence, making decisions, and achieving goals.

Better Survival Rates Finally, more people are encouraged to test their skills as entrepreneurs because the failure rate among small businesses has been declining in recent years. During the 1960s and 1970s, for example, less than half of all new start-ups survived more than eighteen months; only one in five lasted ten years. Now, however, new businesses have a better chance of surviving. Of new businesses started in the 1980s, for instance, over 77 percent remained in operation for at least three years. Today, the SBA estimates that at least 40 percent of all new businesses can expect to survive for six years. For the reasons discussed in the next section, small businesses suffer a higher mortality rate than larger concerns. Among those that manage to stay in business for six to ten years, however, the survival rate levels off.

Reasons for Failure

Unfortunately, 63 percent of all new businesses will not celebrate a sixth anniversary. Why do some succeed and others fail? Although no set pattern has been established, four general factors contribute to new business failure. One factor is managerial incompetence or inexperience. Some would-be entrepreneurs assume that they can succeed through common sense, overestimate their own managerial acumen, or think that hard work alone will lead to success. But, if managers do not know how to make basic business decisions or understand the basic concepts and principles of management, they are unlikely to be successful in the long run.

Neglect can also contribute to failure. Some entrepreneurs try either to launch their ventures in their spare time or to devote only a limited amount of time to a new business. But starting a new business requires an overwhelming time commitment. Entrepreneurs who are not willing to put in the time and effort that a business requires are unlikely to survive.

Third, weak control systems can lead to serious problems. Effective control systems are needed to keep a business on track and to help alert entrepreneurs to potential trouble. If control systems do not signal impending problems, managers may be in serious trouble before more visible difficulties alert them.

Finally, insufficient capital can contribute to new business failure. Some entrepreneurs are overly optimistic about how soon they will start earning profits. In most cases, however, it takes months or years before a business is likely to start turning a profit. Amazon.com, for example, has still not earned a profit. Most experts say that a new business should have enough capital to operate for at least six months without earning a profit; some recommend enough to last a year.[35]

Reasons for Success

Similarly, four basic factors are typically cited to explain new business success. One factor is hard work, drive, and dedication. New business owners must be committed to succeeding and be willing to put in the time and effort to make it happen. Gladys Edmunds, a single teen-age mother in Pittsburgh, washed laundry, made chicken dinners to sell to cab drivers, and sold fire extinguishers and Bibles door to door to earn money to launch her own business. Today, Edmunds Travel Consultants employs eight people and earns about $6 million in annual revenues.[36]

Careful analysis of market conditions can help new business owners assess the probable reception of their products in the marketplace. This will provide insights about market demand for proposed products and services. Whereas attempts to expand local restaurants specializing in baked potatoes, muffins, and gelato have been largely unsuccessful, hamburger and pizza chains continue to have an easier time expanding into new markets.

Managerial competence also contributes to success. Successful new business owners may acquire competence through training or experience or by using the expertise of others. Few successful entrepreneurs succeed alone or straight out of college. Most spend time working in successful companies or partner with others in order to bring more expertise to a new business.

Finally, luck also plays a role in the success of some firms. For example, after Alan McKim started Clean Harbors, an environmental cleanup firm based in New England, he struggled to keep his business afloat. Then the U.S. government committed $1.6 billion to toxic waste cleanup—McKim's specialty. He was able to get several large government contracts and put his business on solid financial footing. Had the government fund not been created at just the right time, McKim may well have failed.

concept CHECK

What are the fundamental reasons for new business failure and success?

What current trends in business start-ups can you identify?

Summary of Key Points

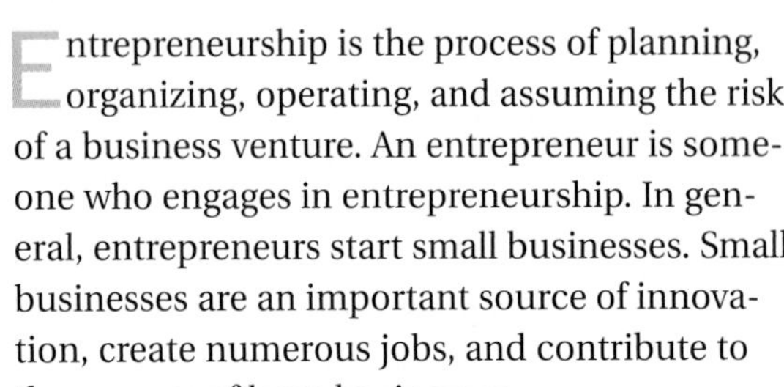

business.college.hmco.com/students

Entrepreneurship is the process of planning, organizing, operating, and assuming the risk of a business venture. An entrepreneur is someone who engages in entrepreneurship. In general, entrepreneurs start small businesses. Small businesses are an important source of innovation, create numerous jobs, and contribute to the success of large businesses.

In choosing strategies, entrepreneurs have to consider the characteristics of the industry in which they are going to conduct business. A small business must also emphasize its distinctive competencies. Small businesses generally have several distinctive competencies that they should exploit in choosing their strategy. Small businesses are usually skilled at identifying niches in established markets, identifying new markets, and acting quickly to obtain first-mover advantages. Small businesses are usually not skilled at exploiting economies of scale. Once an entrepreneur has chosen a strategy, the strategy is normally written down in a business plan. Writing a business plan forces an entrepreneur to plan thoroughly and to anticipate problems that might occur.

With a strategy and business plan in place, entrepreneurs must choose a structure to implement them. All of the structural issues summarized in the next five chapters of this book are relevant to the entrepreneur. In addition, the entrepreneur has some unique structural choices to make. For example, the entrepreneur can buy an existing business or start a new one. In determining financial structure, an entrepreneur has to decide how much personal capital to invest in an organization, how much bank and government support to obtain, and whether to encourage venture capital firms to invest. Entrepreneurs can also rely on various sources of advice.

Several interesting trends characterize new business start-ups today. There are several reasons why some new businesses fail and others succeed.

Discussion Questions

Questions for Review

1. Describe the similarities and differences between entrepreneurial firms and large firms in terms of their job creation and innovation.
2. What characteristics make an industry attractive to entrepreneurs? Based on these characteristics, which industries are most attractive to entrepreneurs?
3. Describe recent trends in new business start-ups.
4. What are the different sources of advice for entrepreneurs? What type of information would an entrepreneur be likely to get from each source? What are the drawbacks or limitations for each source?

Questions for Analysis

5. Entrepreneurs and small businesses play a variety of important roles in society. If these roles are so important, do you think that the government should do more to encourage the development of small business? Why or why not?
6. Consider the four major reasons for new business failure. What actions can entrepreneurs take to minimize or avoid each cause of failure?

7. The U.S. automotive industry is well established, with several large and many small competitors. Describe the unexploited niches in the U.S. auto industry and tell how entrepreneurs could offer products that fill those niches.

Questions for Application

8. Assume that you are opening a small business in your town. What are your financing options? Which option or options are you likely to choose, and why?
9. List five entrepreneur-owned businesses in your community. In which industry does each business compete? Based on the industry, how do you rate each business's long-term chances for success? Explain your answers.
10. Using the information about managing a small business presented in this chapter, analyze whether you would like to work in a small business—either as an employee or as a founder. Given your personality, background, and experience, does working in or starting a new business appeal to you? What are the reasons for your opinion?

BUILDING EFFECTIVE diagnostic SKILLS

Exercise Overview

Diagnostic skills are the skills that enable a manager to visualize the most appropriate response to a situation. This exercise develops your diagnostic skills by asking you to consider the factors that increase your chances of choosing an entrepreneurial career.

Exercise Background

Scholars of entrepreneurship are concerned with understanding why some individuals choose to start a new business whereas others do not. Investigators have surveyed thousands of individuals, entrepreneurs and nonentrepreneurs, in an attempt to discover factors that can distinguish between the two groups. Hundreds of studies have been conducted, each with its own unique findings, but some consensus has emerged. Based on numerous studies, entrepreneurship is more likely when an individual

- Is the parent, child, spouse, or sibling of an entrepreneur.
- Is an immigrant to the United States or the child of an immigrant.
- Is a parent.
- Is a member of the Jewish or Protestant faith.
- Holds a professional degree in a field such as medicine, law, or engineering.
- Has recently experienced a life-changing event, such as getting married, having a child, moving to a new city, or losing a job.

Exercise Task

With the background information above as context, do the following:

1. Choose one of the categories above and explain why this factor might make an individual more likely to become a business owner.
2. From the categories listed above, choose one that is true of yourself. (Choose a different category than the one you discussed in your answer to question 1.) In your opinion, does that factor make it more likely that you will become an entrepreneur? Why or why not? If none of the categories above is true of yourself, tell whether that fact makes it *less* likely that you will become an entrepreneur, and why.

BUILDING EFFECTIVE interpersonal SKILLS

Exercise Overview

Interpersonal skills refer to the manager's ability to understand and motivate individuals and groups. This exercise asks you to assess personality traits associated with entrepreneurship.

Exercise Background

Studies of successful entrepreneurs have found that they share three personality traits. That is not to say that everyone who has these three traits at a high level will become an entrepreneur. Rather, people are more likely to be successful as entrepreneurs if they have these three traits. Also, it follows that people are likely to be unsuccessful as entrepreneurs if they do not have the three traits. Finally, note that the research points out merely what is likely, not what is absolutely certain.

After you complete the questionnaire, your professor will describe and discuss the three personality traits with your class.

An interesting variation on this activity is to ask someone else to complete the questionnaire. Then you can assess the entrepreneurial aspects of his or her personality.

Exercise Task

With this background information as context, answer the following questions and record your answers. There are no right or wrong choices. Your professor will show you how to score your answers.

	Strongly Disagree	Disagree	Don't Know	Agree	Strongly Agree
1. I believe success depends on ability, not luck.					
2. I am consistent.					
3. I have little influence over things that happen to me.					
4. I have original ideas.					
5. I am stimulating.					
6. I am thorough.					
7. I often risk doing things differently.					
8. I can stand out in disagreement against a group.					
9. I prefer to work on one problem at a time.					
10. I enjoy detailed work.					
11. I prefer friends who do not "rock the boat."					
12. I will always think of something when stuck.					
13. I am methodical.					
14. I need the stimulation of frequent change.					
15. I like to vary my routines at a moment's notice.					
16. I never seek to bend or break the rules.					
17. I am predictable.					
18. When I make plans, I am sure I can achieve them.					
19. I prefer changes to occur gradually.					
20. I am more willing than other people to take risks.					

BUILDING EFFECTIVE conceptual SKILLS

business.college.hmco.com/students

Exercise Overview

Conceptual skills refer to the manager's ability to think in the abstract. This exercise will help you relate conceptual skills to entrepreneurship.

Exercise Background

Assume that you have made the decision to open a small business in the local community when you graduate (the community where you are attending college, not your home). Assume that you have funds to start a business without having to worry about finding other investors.

Without regard for market potential, profitability, or similar considerations, list five businesses that you might want to open and operate based solely on your personal interests. For example, if you enjoy bicycling, you might enjoy opening a shop that caters to cyclists.

Next, without regard for personal attractiveness, list five businesses that you might want to open and operate based solely on market opportunity. Use the Internet to help you determine which businesses might be profitable in your community, based on factors such as population, local economic conditions, local competition, franchising opportunities, and so on.

Evaluate the prospects for success for each of the ten businesses.

Exercise Task

With this background information as context, do the following:

1. Form a small group with three or four classmates and discuss your respective lists. Look for instances where the same type of business appears on either the same or alternative lists. Also look for cases where the same business appears with similar or dissimilar prospects for success.
2. How important is personal interest in small-business success?
3. How important is market potential in small-business success?

CHAPTER CLOSING case

LAUGHING ALL THE WAY TO THE BANK

> *"I cried because I did not have an office with a door, until I met a man who had no cubicle."*
>
> – Dilbert, a cartoon character created by Scott Adams*

Have you heard the one about the firm that bought laptops so employees could work while traveling—then bolted the computers to the desks for security? Yes, this is a joke, published in the business-focused *Dilbert* cartoons, drawn by unlikely entrepreneur Scott Adams. But it is also a true story. Adams has found a way to channel the absurdity, frustration, and stress of working life into a productive outlet—the creation of cartoon strips based on his real-life experiences in corporate America.

"I cried because I did not have an office with a door, until I met a man who had no cubicle." Dilbert is the hottest cartoon strip around, carried in 75 percent of U.S. daily newspapers. Scott Adams's comics have spawned 3 million copies of top-selling books, built one of the

most-visited websites, and inspired an animated television show. The "hero" of the strip is Dilbert, the prototypical white-collar office worker. Dilbert is a technology geek, and other characters include secretaries, consultants, and bosses.

Scott Adams earned a bachelor's degree in economics and worked for a bank, then obtained an M.B.A. in hopes of a promotion. "I made the observation that people who didn't have [an M.B.A.] got ahead much more slowly. I thought I was going to become a captain of industry, so I decided it would be good for my career." Adams joined Pacific Bell and began the invention of *Dilbert*. When *Dilbert*'s popularity took off and his corporate career stalled, Adams became a full-time cartoonist. He claims that the variety of jobs he has held have led to his achievements, saying, "If I could pick one thing that contributed to my success, it was that I tried many things and I didn't quit."

Most artists sell their work to syndicates, so they have little contact with the comic-reading public. Adams knew this was a faulty model for customer feedback, based on his marketing expertise. So he was one of the first to put his e-mail address on every strip, enabling readers to send him 350 to 800 comments and suggestions daily. He was also one of the first to put *Dilbert* online (at www.dilbert.com).

Another important lesson from M.B.A. school was to identify his target market. Adams claims, "I could get people to do my marketing for me through the simple trick of mentioning different occupations in the strip. . . . I'd put an accountant in a strip, and people would cut it out and send a copy to all the accountants they knew. I kept using that technique, including each of the professions, until everyone on earth had been sent a Dilbert cartoon. It was a systematic approach to building the market."

Boss: "Our policy is to employ only the best technical professionals." Dilbert: "Isn't it also our policy to base salaries on the industry average?" Boss: "Right. We like them bright but clueless." Adams used his strip to skewer the incompetence he saw in every profession. "When I originally started drawing Dilbert, I was just writing a funny little comic about a guy who had a job that was a lot like mine. People read into it that workers were brilliant and bosses were stupid. But that's only half true—what I really thought was that everyone was stupid, including me." However, customer feedback altered his original intent. Adams continues, "But it was far more commercial to go with what people wanted. . . . I just did the math: For every boss there are about ten employees. Do you want to sell a product to one boss or to ten employees? I had to go with the ten-to-one advantage."

In Adams's unique philosophy, success is more about luck than about hard work, education, or talent. Adams advises others, "The capitalist system allows nine failures for every winner, so you're either one of the many people who will fail a few times and quit, or you're one of the few people who will keep trying and win. If all the people who quit had kept going, they would have been as successful as I have been with Dilbert."

Adams has a favorite strip, in which Wally, a classic slacker and underperformer, tells the pointy-haired boss, *"Over the past year, most of my co-workers have managed expensive projects that failed. I've done nothing but drink coffee. So on an economic basis, that makes me your top performer. Watch and learn."* Advice to aspiring entrepreneurs: Watch Scott Adams and learn.

Case Questions

1. Read some *Dilbert* cartoons in a book or newspaper, or online at www.dilbert.com. What viewpoint is Adams expressing about work and careers? In your opinion, what impact did Adams's viewpoint have on his choice to leave a corporate job and become an entrepreneur?
2. What sources of information and expertise did Adams use in starting and developing his business? Did the start-up of the *Dilbert* cartoon follow the typical pattern of entrepreneurial start-ups? Why or why not?
3. Adams claims that his success is due primarily to luck and persistence. Do you agree or disagree? Do you think his advice is helpful to potential entrepreneurs? Why or why not?

Case References

Dilbert website, www.dilbert.com on January 15, 2003; Scott Adams, *The Dilbert Principle* (New York: Harpercollins, 1996); Scott Adams, *The Joy of Work* (New York: Harpercollins, 1999); "TV Newest Domain for Cultural Icon," *Scripps Howard News*, September/October 1998, www.scripps.com on January 15, 2003 (*quote).

Chapter Notes

1. Ian Parker, "An English Sandwich in New York," *The Guardian* (London), August 9, 2002, www.guardian.co.uk on January 13, 2003 (*quote); Julie Forster, "Thinking Outside the Burger Box," *BusinessWeek*, September 16, 2002, pp. 66–67; Milton Moskowitz and Robert Levering, "100 Great Companies to Work for in Europe: Pret a Manager," *Fortune*, January 22, 2002, www.fortune.com on January 13, 2003; Scott Kirshner, "Recipe for Reinvention," *Fast Company*, April 2002, pp. 38–42.
2. Bro Uttal, "Inside the Deal That Made Bill Gates $350,000,000," *Fortune*, July 21, 1986, pp. 23–33.
3. "The 400 Richest People in America," *Forbes*, October 9, 2000, p. 118.
4. Murray B. Low and Ian MacMillan, "Entrepreneurship: Past Research and Future Challenges," *Journal of Management*, June 1988, pp. 139–159.
5. U.S. Department of Commerce, *Statistical Abstract of the United States:* 2002 (Washington, D.C.: Bureau of the Census, 2002).
6. "Small Business 'Vital Statistics,'" www.sba.gov/aboutsba/ on May 24, 2000.
7. "Small Business 'Vital Statistics.'"
8. "Workforce Shifts to Big Companies," *USA Today*, March 19, 2002, p. 1B.
9. "Small Business 'Vital Statistics.'"
10. "A Five-Year Journey to a Better Mousetrap," *New York Times*, May 24, 1998, p. 8.
11. "The Top Entrepreneurs," *BusinessWeek*, January 10, 2000, pp. 80–82.
12. "New Entrepreneur, Old Economy," *Wall Street Journal*, May 22, 2000, p. R10.
13. Amar Bhide, "How Entrepreneurs Craft Strategies That Work," *Harvard Business Review*, March–April 1994, pp. 150–163.
14. "Three Men and a Baby Bell," *Forbes*, March 6, 2000, pp. 134–135.
15. *Hoover's Handbook of American Business 2003* (Austin, Texas: Hoover's Business Press, 2003), pp. 1540–1541; Wendy Zellner, "Peace, Love, and the Bottom Line," *BusinessWeek*, December 7, 1998, pp. 79–82.
16. "Giving Birth to a Web Business," *New York Times*, October 15, 1998, p. G5.
17. Nancy J. Lyons, "Moonlight over Indiana," *Inc.*, January 2000, pp. 71–74.
18. F. M. Scherer, *Industrial Market Structure and Economic Performance*, 2nd ed. (Boston: Houghton Mifflin, 1980).
19. "Three Biker-Entrepreneurs Take on Mighty Harley," *New York Times*, August 20, 1999, p. F1.
20. The importance of discovering niches is emphasized in Charles Hill and Gareth Jones, *Strategic Management: An Integrative Approach*, 6th ed. (Boston: Houghton Mifflin, 2004).
21. Gregory Patterson, "An American in . . . Siberia?" *Fortune*, August 4, 1997, p. 63; "Crazy for Crunchies," *Newsweek*, April 28, 1997, p. 49.
22. "'Ship Those Boxes; Check the Euro!'" *Wall Street Journal*, February 7, 2003, pp. C1, C7.
23. Thea Singer, "Brandapalooza," *Inc. 500*, 1999, pp. 69–72.
24. "Cheap Tricks," *Forbes*, February 21, 2000, p. 116.
25. U.S. Department of Commerce, *Statistical Abstract of the United States: 1999* (Washington, D.C.: Bureau of the Census, 1999). See also "Too Much Ventured, Nothing Gained," *Fortune*, November 25, 2002, pp. 135–144.
26. Susan Greco, "get$$$now.com," *Inc.*, September 1999, pp. 35–38.
27. "Internet Industry Surges 'Startling' 62%," *USA Today*, June 6, 2000, p. 1B.
28. "Up-and-Comers," *BusinessWeek*, May 15, 2000, pp. EB70–EB72.
29. Andy Serwer, "There's Something About Cisco," *Fortune*, May 15, 2000, pp. 114–138.
30. "High-Tech Advances Push C.I.A. into New Company," *New York Times*, September 29, 1999, p. A14.
31. "The Courtship of Black Consumers," *New York Times*, August 16, 1998, pp. D1, D5.
32. See *The Wall Street Journal Almanac* 1999, pp. 179, 182.
33. "Women Entrepreneurs Attract New Financing," *New York Times*, July 26, 1998, p. 10.
34. "Women Increase Standing as Business Owners," *USA Today*, June 29, 1999, p. 1B.
35. Norman M. Scarborough and Thomas W. Zimmerer, *Effective Small Business Management: An Entrepreneurial Approach*, 6th ed. (Upper Saddle River, NJ: Prentice Hall, 2000), pp. 412–413.
36. "Expert Entrepreneur Got Her Show on the Road at an Early Age," *USA Today*, May 24, 2000, p. 5B.

PART four

THE ORGANIZING PROCESS

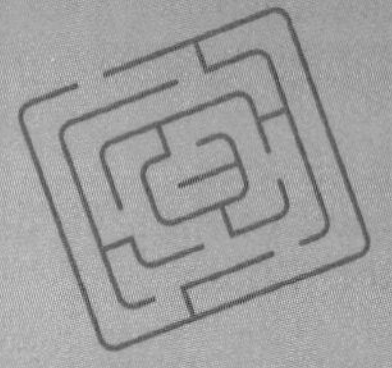

CHAPTER 11

Basic Elements of Organizing

CHAPTER 12

Managing Organization Design

CHAPTER 13

Managing Organization Change and Innovation

CHAPTER 14

Managing Human Resources in Organizations

Strathmore
EXIDE

11 Basic Elements of Organizing

CHAPTER OUTLINE

The Elements of Organizing

Designing Jobs
- Job Specialization
- Benefits and Limitations of Specialization
- Alternatives to Specialization

Grouping Jobs: Departmentalization
- Rationale for Departmentalization
- Common Bases for Departmentalization

Establishing Reporting Relationships
- Chain of Command
- Narrow Versus Wide Spans
- Tall Versus Flat Organizations
- Determining the Appropriate Span

Distributing Authority
- The Delegation Process
- Decentralization and Centralization

Coordinating Activities
- The Need for Coordination
- Structural Coordination Techniques
- Electronic Coordination

Differentiating Between Positions
- Differences Between Line and Staff
- Administrative Intensity

LEARNING OBJECTIVES

After studying this chapter, you should be able to:

1 ***Identify the basic elements of organizations.***

2 ***Describe alternative approaches to designing jobs.***

OPENING INCIDENT

Sara Lee's CEO, John H. Bryan, had a problem. During the twenty-five years of his tenure as chief executive officer, the firm had grown beyond its foundation in food products to encompass dozens of lines of business, selling insecticide, lingerie, and Coach handbags. The new businesses were acquisitions, and the original managers controlled each one like a separate company. Bryan knew that duplication was inefficient and that the firm could not afford high costs at a time when price competition was heating up. Over the next four years, Bryan sold or eliminated about one-quarter of the firm's two hundred products. He cut redundant factories and the workforce, reduced the number of products, and standardized for efficiency. Bryan called his extensive restructuring "deverticalization," because the strategy removed Sara Lee from manufacturing while strengthening marketing. In the meanwhile, however, he continued to acquire rival firms in order to grow. In spite of Bryan's efforts, Sara Lee remained expensive, unfocused, and inefficient. A Prudential analyst said about Bryan's plan, "Sometimes, the more chairs you move around, the more dust you see behind the chairs."

In 2000 C. Steven McMillan assumed the CEO position at Sara Lee, and in the words of Yogi Berra, "It was déjà vu all over again." McMillan faced the same problems

3 *Discuss the rationale and the most common bases for grouping jobs into departments.*

4 *Describe the basic elements involved in establishing reporting relationships.*

5 *Discuss how authority is distributed in organizations.*

6 *Discuss the basic coordinating activities undertaken by organizations.*

7 *Describe basic ways in which positions within an organization can be differentiated.*

"Sometimes, the more chairs you move around, the more dust you see behind the chairs."

—John M. McMillan, analyst, Prudential Securities

that Bryan faced earlier: overdiversification, duplication, and too much decentralization. One of McMillan's moves, copying rival Kraft Foods, was to merge each brand's sales force to create one customer-focused team. In meats alone, Sara Lee had ten different brands, including Ball Park, Hillshire Farms, Bryan, and Jimmy Dean. "So if you're . . . a Kroger or a Safeway, you've got to deal with 10 different organizations and multiple invoices," says McMillan. The teams reduced duplication and were more convenient for buyers—a win-win situation. National retailers, such as Wal-Mart, responded by increasing purchases of Sara Lee products. "These chains don't want regional brands because they want their stores to be laid out the same no matter where they are," says industry analyst David Adelman.

McMillan centralized decision-making power by shutting down fifty weaker regional brands and reorganizing the firm into three broad product categories: Food and Beverage, Intimates and Underwear, and Household Products. McMillan abolished several layers of the corporate hierarchy, including many of the middle managers whom the firm had gained from acquisitions. He created category managers to oversee the related lines of business. The flattening of the organizational structure led to improved accountability and control over the far-flung firm's operations.

McMillan also tried the same time-worn tactics used by his predecessor, divesting fifteen businesses, including Coach leather goods. He laid off 10 percent of his workers. In a move that has been widely questioned by industry observers, McMillan paid $2.8 billion for Earthgrains, a bread maker. Although the move increased Sara Lee's market share in baked goods, many feel that the price was too dear and the potential return too small to justify the increased complexity.

There are a few new tricks up McMillan's sleeve, however. One bold move is the development of a chain of retail stores called Inner Self. The stores use a spa-like atmosphere to sell Sara Lee's Hanes, Playtex, Bali, and Wonderbra products. Susan Nedved, head of development for Inner Self, thinks that the stores provide a more realistic and comforting environment for making underwear purchases than do some specialty outlets. "There seems to be an open void for another specialty concept that complements Victoria's Secret," Nedved says. "There was a need for shopping alternatives that really cater to the aging population."

McMillan remains confident that his strategy—more centralization, coordination, and focus—will triumph, saying, "I do believe the things we're doing will enhance the growth rate of our company."

While many people associate Sara Lee with pastries like these, the firm's organization structure must actually accommodate a wide array of products ranging from underwear to coffee to shoe polish.

Others are less optimistic. "The scary thing is, even if you fix that business, it's still apparel, and it's not really viewed as a high-value-added business," says analyst Eric K. Katzman. And, even if McMillan's strategy reduces costs and grows market share, skeptics point out that there really is no logic to support grouping together baked goods, meats, coffee, underwear, shoe polish, and household cleaners. Unless synergy among the disparate units can be found, Sara Lee seems headed for an inevitable breakup into several smaller, more focused, and more profitable companies.[1]

Sara Lee had a long and well-established way of getting things done, and this system served it well for years. But new leadership has shown some fundamental underlying flaws in how the firm has been structured and is now headed toward a better way of organizing the firm. Further, like Sara Lee, many other organizations are boldly exploring new approaches to designing work, linking jobs, and coordinating activities. And these new approaches, in turn, are fundamentally changing the way jobs, businesses, and relationships among businesses are structured.[2] As you will see in this chapter, managing the basic frameworks that organizations use to get their work done—structure—is a fundamental part of the management process.

This chapter discusses many of the critical elements of organization structure that managers can control and is the first of five devoted to organizing, the second basic managerial function identified in Chapter 1. In Part Three, we describe managerial planning—deciding what to do. Organizing, the subject of Part Four, focuses on how to do it. We first elaborate on the meaning of organization structure. Subsequent sections explore the basic elements that managers use to create an organization.

The Elements of Organizing

Imagine asking a child to build a castle with a set of building blocks. She selects a few small blocks and other, larger ones. She uses some square ones, some round ones, and some triangular ones. When she finishes, she has her own castle, unlike any other. Another child, presented with the same task, constructs a different castle. He will select different blocks, for example, and combine them in different ways. The children's activities—choosing certain combinations of blocks and then putting them together in unique ways—are in many ways analogous to the manager's job of organizing.[3]

organizing Deciding how best to group organizational activities and resources

Organizing is deciding how best to group organizational elements.[4] Just as children select different kinds of building blocks, managers can choose a variety of structural possibilities. And, just as the children can assemble the blocks in any number of ways, so, too, can managers put the organization together in many different ways. Understanding the nature of these building blocks and the different ways in which they can be configured can have a powerful impact on a firm's competitiveness.[5] In this chapter, our focus is on the building blocks themselves—**organization structure**. In Chapter 12 we focus on how the blocks can be put together—organization design.

organization structure The set of elements that can be used to configure an organization

There are six basic building blocks that managers can use in constructing an organization: designing jobs, grouping jobs, establishing reporting relationships between jobs, distributing authority among jobs, coordinating activities among jobs, and differentiating among positions. The logical starting point is the first building block—designing jobs for people within the organization.

concept CHECK

What is the meaning of organizing as a management function?

Besides building blocks, what other analogies might seem to reflect organization structure?

Designing Jobs

The first building block of organization structure is job design. **Job design** is the determination of an individual's work-related responsibilities.[6] For a machinist at Caterpillar, job design might specify what machines are to be operated, how they are to be operated, and what performance standards are expected. For a manager at Caterpillar, job design might involve defining areas of decision-making responsibility, identifying goals and expectations, and establishing appropriate indicators of success. The natural starting point for designing jobs is determining the level of desired specialization.

job design The determination of an individual's work-related responsibilities

job specialization The degree to which the overall task of the organization is broken down and divided into smaller component parts

Job Specialization

Job specialization is the degree to which the overall task of the organization is broken down and divided into smaller component parts. Job specialization evolved from the concept of *division of labor.* Adam Smith, an eighteenth-century economist, described how a pin factory used division of labor to improve productivity.[7] One man drew the wire, another straightened it, a third cut it, a fourth ground the point, and so on. Smith claimed that ten men working in this fashion were able to produce 48,000 pins in a day, whereas each man working alone could produce only 20 pins per day.

Designing jobs is a fundamental cornerstone of organizing. Most organizations today rely on a blend of job specialization and such alternatives to specialization as job enrichment and work teams. Take this Cessna factory in Independence, Kansas, for example. All of its assembly employees are expected to have a base specialization. But each is also expected to continuously learn new skills while simultaneously working as part of a team that has a lot to say about how its work gets done.

More recently, the best example of the impact of specialization is the automobile assembly line pioneered by Henry Ford and his contemporaries. Mass-production capabilities stemming from job specialization techniques have had a profound impact throughout the world. High levels of low-cost production transformed U.S. society during the last century into one of the strongest economies in the history of the world.[8]

Job specialization is a normal extension of organizational growth. For example, when Walt Disney started his company, he did everything himself—wrote cartoons, drew them, and then marketed them to theaters. As the business grew, he eventually hired others to perform many of these same functions. As growth continued, so, too, did specialization. For example, as animation artists work on Disney movies

Assembly lines represent a common form of job specialization. These women are assembling jeeps during World War II. Each one performed a single task as the vehicle moved along a conveyor belt. While today's automobile plants are much more complex and sophisticated than this one, their essential nature remains unchanged—workers perform specialized tasks as partially assembled units pass along in front of them.

today, they may specialize in drawing only a single character or doing only background scenery. And, today, the Walt Disney Company has thousands of different specialized jobs. Clearly, no one person could perform them all.

Benefits and Limitations of Specialization

Job specialization provides four benefits to organizations.[9] First, workers performing small, simple tasks will become very proficient at each task. Second, transfer time between tasks decreases. If employees perform several different tasks, some time is lost as they stop doing the first task and start doing the next. Third, the more narrowly defined a job is, the easier it is to develop specialized equipment to assist with that job. Fourth, when an employee who performs a highly specialized job is absent or resigns, the manager is able to train someone new at relatively low cost. Although specialization is generally thought of in terms of operating jobs, many organizations have extended the basic elements of specialization to managerial and professional levels as well.[10]

On the other hand, job specialization can have negative consequences. The foremost criticism is that workers who perform highly specialized jobs may become bored and dissatisfied. The job may be so specialized that it offers no challenge or stimulation. Boredom and monotony set in, absenteeism rises, and the quality of the work may suffer. Furthermore, the anticipated benefits of specialization do not always occur. For example, a study conducted at Maytag found that the time spent moving work in process from one worker to another was greater than the time needed for the same individual to change from job to job.[11] Thus, although some degree of specialization is necessary, it should not be carried to extremes because of the possible negative consequences. Managers must be sensitive to situations in which extreme specialization should be avoided. And, indeed, several alternative approaches to designing jobs have been developed in recent years.

Alternatives to Specialization

To counter the problems associated with specialization, managers have sought other approaches to job design that achieve a better balance between organizational demands for efficiency and productivity and individual needs for creativity and autonomy. Five alternative approaches are job rotation, job enlargement, job enrichment, the job characteristics approach, and work teams.[12]

job rotation An alternative to job specialization that involves systematically moving employees from one job to another

Job Rotation **Job rotation** involves systematically moving employees from one job to another. A worker in a warehouse might unload trucks on Monday, carry incoming inventory to storage on Tuesday, verify invoices on Wednesday, pull outgoing inventory from storage on Thursday, and load trucks on Friday. Thus the jobs do not change, but instead, workers move from job to job. Unfortunately, for this very reason, job rotation has not been very successful in enhancing employee motivation or satisfaction. Jobs that are amenable to rotation tend to be relatively standard and routine. Workers who are rotated to a "new" job may be more satisfied at first, but satisfaction soon wanes. Although many companies (among them American Cyanamid, Bethlehem Steel, Ford, Prudential Insurance, TRW, and Western Electric) have tried job rotation, it is most often used today as a training device to improve worker skills and flexibility.

Job Enlargement On the assumption that doing the same basic task over and over is the primary cause of worker dissatisfaction, **job enlargement** was developed to increase the total number of tasks workers perform. As a result, all workers perform a wide variety of tasks, which presumably reduces the level of job dissatisfaction. Many organizations have used job enlargement, including IBM, Detroit Edison, AT&T, the U.S. Civil Service, and Maytag. At Maytag, for example, the assembly line for producing washing-machine water pumps was systematically changed so that work that had originally been performed by six workers, who passed the work sequentially from one person to another, was performed by four workers, each of whom assembled a complete pump.[13] Unfortunately, although job enlargement does have some positive consequences, they are often offset by some disadvantages: (1) training costs usually rise, (2) unions have argued that pay should increase because the worker is doing more tasks, and (3) in many cases the work remains boring and routine even after job enlargement.

job enlargement An alternative to job specialization that involves giving the employee more tasks to perform

Job Enrichment A more comprehensive approach, **job enrichment**, assumes that increasing the range and variety of tasks is not sufficient by itself to improve employee motivation.[14] Thus job enrichment attempts to increase both the number of tasks a worker does and the control the worker has over the job. To implement job enrichment, managers remove some controls from the job, delegate more authority to employees, and structure the work in complete, natural units. These changes increase subordinates' sense of responsibility. Another part of job enrichment is to continually assign new and challenging tasks, thereby increasing employees' opportunity for growth and advancement.

job enrichment An alternative to job specialization that involves increasing both the number of tasks the worker does and the control the worker has over the job

AT&T was one of the first companies to try job enrichment. In one experiment, eight typists in a service unit prepared customer service orders. Faced with low output and high turnover, management determined that the typists felt little responsibility to clients and received little feedback. The unit was changed to create a typing team. Typists were matched with designated service representatives, the task was changed from ten specific steps to three more general steps, and job titles were upgraded. As a result, the frequency of order processing increased from 27 percent to 90 percent, the need for messenger service was eliminated, accuracy improved, and turnover became practically nil.[15] Other organizations that have tried job enrichment include Texas Instruments, IBM, and General Foods. This approach, however, also has disadvantages. For example, work systems should be analyzed before enrichment, but this seldom happens, and managers rarely ask for employee preferences when enriching jobs.

job characteristics approach An alternative to job specialization that suggests that jobs should be diagnosed and improved along five core dimensions, taking into account both the work system and employee preferences

Job Characteristics Approach The **job characteristics approach** is an alternative to job specialization that does take into account the work system and employee preferences.[16] As illustrated in Figure 11.1, the job characteristics approach suggests that jobs should be diagnosed and improved along five core dimensions:

1. *Skill variety,* the number of things a person does in a job
2. *Task identity,* the extent to which the worker does a complete or identifiable portion of the total job
3. *Task significance,* the perceived importance of the task
4. *Autonomy,* the degree of control the worker has over how the work is performed
5. *Feedback,* the extent to which the worker knows how well the job is being performed

The higher a job rates on those dimensions, the more employees will experience various psychological states. Experiencing these states, in turn, presumably leads to high motivation, high-quality performance, high satisfaction, and low absenteeism

FIGURE 11.1

The Job Characteristics Approach

The job characteristics approach to job design provides a viable alternative to job specialization. Five core job dimensions may lead to critical psychological states which, in turn, may enhance motivation, performance, and satisfaction while also reducing absenteeism and turnover.

Source: J. R. Hackman and G. R. Oldham, "Motivation Through the Design of Work: Test of a Theory," *Organizational Behavior and Human Performance*, Vol. 16 (1976), pp. 250–279. Copyright © Academic Press, Inc. Reprinted by permission of Academic Press and the authors.

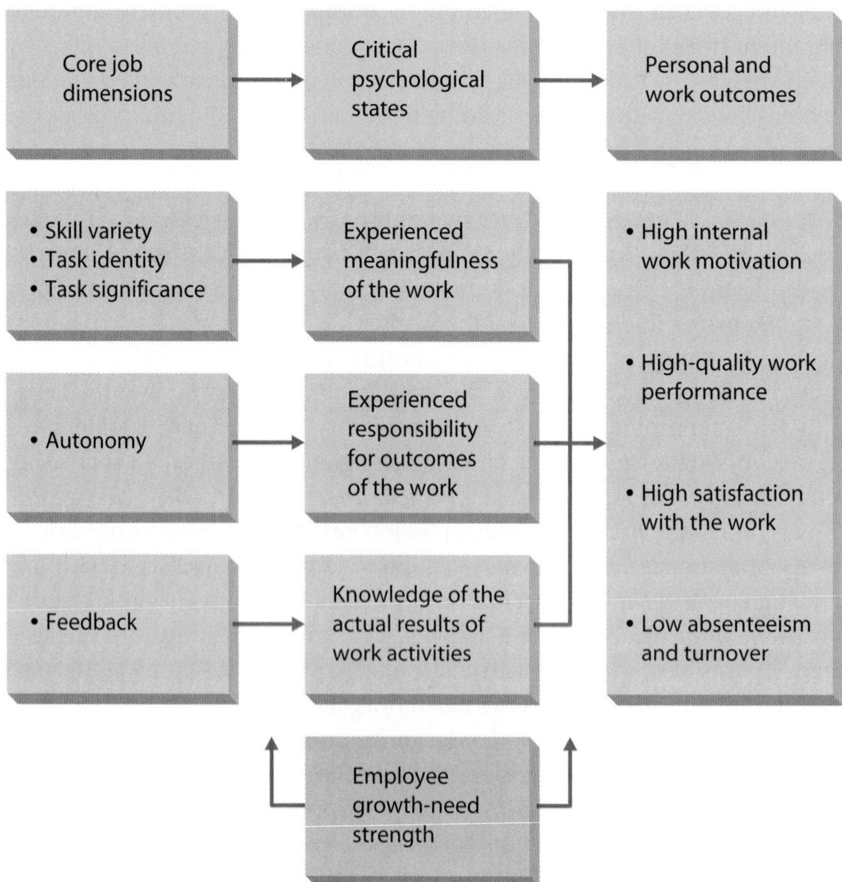

and turnover. Finally, a variable called *growth-need strength* is presumed to affect how the model works for different people. People with a strong desire to grow, develop, and expand their capabilities (indicative of high growth-need strength) are expected to respond strongly to the presence or absence of the basic job characteristics; individuals with low growth-need strength are expected not to respond as strongly or consistently.

A large number of studies have been conducted to test the usefulness of the job characteristics approach. The Southwestern Division of Prudential Insurance, for example, used this approach in its claims division. Results included moderate declines in turnover and a small but measurable improvement in work quality. Other research findings have not supported this approach as strongly. Thus, although the job characteristics approach is one of the most promising alternatives to job specialization, it is probably not the final answer.

Work Teams Another alternative to job specialization is **work teams**. Under this arrangement, a group is given responsibility for designing the work system to be used in performing an interrelated set of tasks. In the typical assembly-line system, the work flows from one worker to the next, and each worker has a specified job to perform. In a work team, however, the group itself decides how jobs will be allocated. For example, the work team assigns specific tasks to members, monitors and controls its own performance, and has autonomy over work scheduling.[17] We discuss work teams more fully in Chapter 19.

work team An alternative to job specialization that allows an entire group to design the work system it will use to perform an interrelated set of tasks

concept CHECK

What are the basic job design alternatives?

Which kind of job design best describes a job you have recently held? Do you agree or disagree with the text's assessment of that job design?

Grouping Jobs: Departmentalization

The second building block of organization structure is the grouping of jobs according to some logical arrangement. *Working with Diversity* discusses the jobs that might be more logically grouped in the long-term care industry. The process of grouping jobs is called **departmentalization**. After establishing the basic rationale for departmentalization, we identify some common bases along which departments are created.[18]

departmentalization The process of grouping jobs according to some logical arrangement

Rationale for Departmentalization

When organizations are small, the owner-manager can personally oversee everyone who works there. As an organization grows, however, personally supervising all the employees becomes more and more difficult for the owner-manager. Consequently, new managerial positions are created to supervise the work of others. Employees are not assigned to particular managers randomly. Rather, jobs are

WORKING WITH diversity

The Organization of Long-Term Care

In a traditional hospital, patients are housed in the facility. Their care is delivered by technicians and nurses, and paid for by insurance and the federal government, through Medicare and Medicaid. Hospitals are centralized, with numerous layers of management to coordinate the work of many specialists. Efficiency is important, particularly when payments are falling.

Yet this structure does not effectively meet the needs of some patients, especially the elderly and the chronically disabled. These patients often do best when cared for in their own homes, which allow more freedom and are more comfortable for long-term care. And home care can be much less expensive.

"David Jayne is a prisoner—a prisoner in his specially designed wheelchair. . . . Medicare shouldn't act as jailer too."

— Bob Dole, former senator*

The rise of the home health-care industry, fueled by an increase of baby boomers, is revolutionizing health care. One difference lies in the nature of the tasks. Home health-care nurses must be generalists, able to offer various services. Home health-care nurses are hired, trained, and compensated differently than the specialists required in traditional hospitals.

Home-based nurses also have more decision-making power, because they work more independently. Home care is coordinated by case managers, who oversee all work related to a single patient. Although case management introduces an additional hierarchical layer, the benefits in improved control and coordination make it worthwhile. The decentralization that accompanies case management also allows higher-level executives to have wider spans of control.

Congress is currently considering a Medicare reform act that would relax restrictions of payments for home care. Former senator Bob Dole favors the so-called David Jayne amendment, named for a forty-one-year-old man who suffers from paralysis caused by Lou Gehrig's disease. Dole says, "Make no mistake, David Jayne is a prisoner—a prisoner in his specially designed wheelchair. His illness has robbed him of the ability to do anything without the aid of technology. Medicare shouldn't act as jailer too."

Most families will face long-term care concerns at some time. To keep people out of institutions, cut Medicare spending, and increase customized service to patients, American Association for Homecare CEO Tom Connaughton says, "We must continue to educate the lawmakers about our issues. . . . We have to convince [them] that homecare is part of the solution."

References: "Annual Report 2001," Amedisys website, www.amedisys.com on January 20, 2003; Bob Dole, "Imprisoned by Medicare," *Washington Post*, June 27, 2002, p. A31 (*quote); J. Phillips, "Now That Congress Has Adjourned—What's in Store for 2003," American Association for Homecare website, www.aahomecare.org on January 20, 2003; Juliette Cubanski and Janet Kline, "In Pursuit of Long-Term Care: Ensuring Access, Coverage, Quality," Harvard University Bipartisan Congressional Health Policy Conference, January 17, 2002, The Commonwealth Fund website, www.cmwf.org on January 20, 2003.

grouped according to some plan. The logic embodied in such a plan is the basis for all departmentalization.[19]

Lucent Technologies, the world's largest telephone equipment maker, is organized into four basic departments. One department focuses on optical networking; one focuses on wireless communication; one is responsible for semiconductor operations; and one handles all of Lucent's e-business initiatives. The firm's managers believe that these departments help the firm remain competitive by keeping a sharp focus on these four high-growth areas.[20]

Common Bases for Departmentalization

Figure 11.2 presents a partial organizational chart for Apex Computers, a hypothetical firm that manufactures and sells computers and software. The chart shows that Apex uses each of the four most common bases for departmentalization: function, product, customer, and location.

Functional Departmentalization The most common base for departmentalization, especially among smaller organizations, is by function. **Functional departmentalization** groups together those jobs involving the same or similar activities. (The word *function* is used here to mean organizational functions such as finance and production, rather than the basic managerial functions, such as planning or controlling.) The computer department at Apex has manufacturing, finance, and marketing departments, each an organizational function.

functional departmentalization
Grouping jobs involving the same or similar activities

This approach, which is most common in smaller organizations, has three primary advantages. First, each department can be staffed by experts in that functional area. Marketing experts can be hired to run the marketing function, for example. Second, supervision is also facilitated, because an individual manager needs to be familiar with only a relatively narrow set of skills. And, third, coordinating activities inside each department is easier.

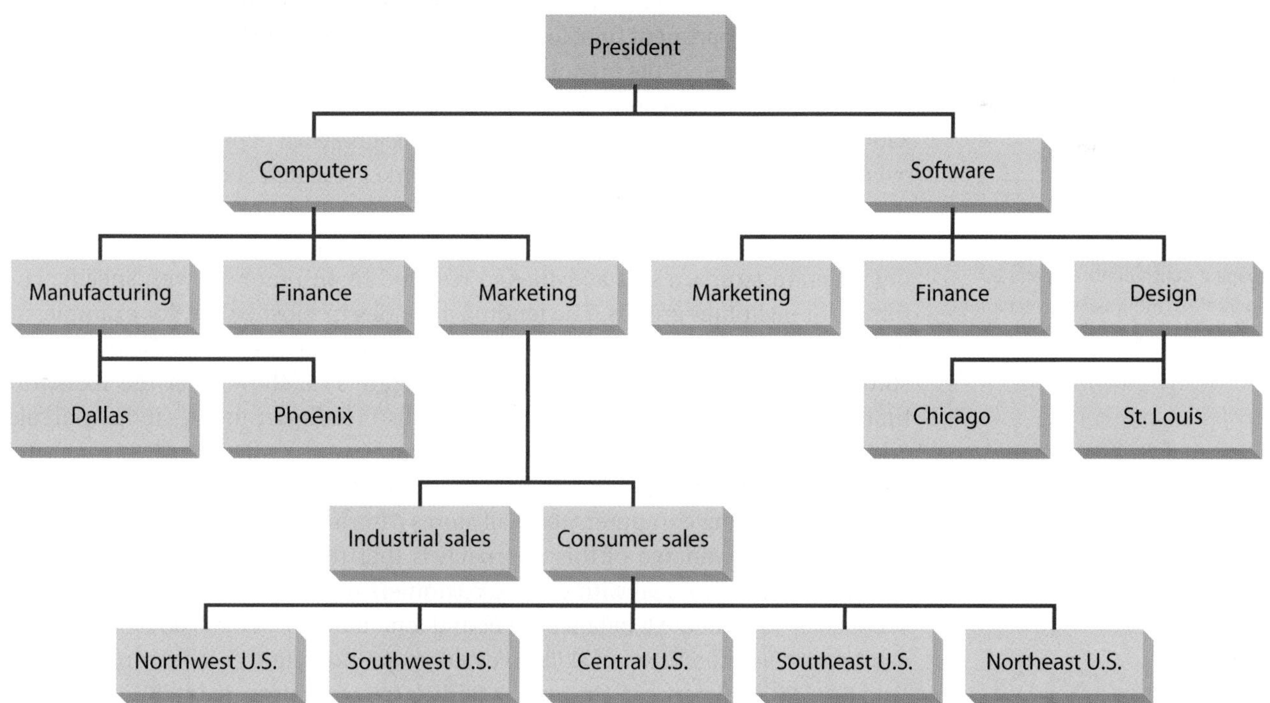

FIGURE 11.2

Bases for Departmentalization

Organizations group jobs into departments. Apex, a hypothetical organization, uses all four of the primary bases of departmentalization—function, product, customer, and location. Like Apex, most large organizations use more than one type of departmentalization.

On the other hand, as an organization begins to grow in size, several disadvantages of this approach may emerge. For one, decision making tends to become slower and more bureaucratic. Employees may also begin to concentrate too narrowly on their own unit and lose sight of the total organizational system. Finally, accountability and performance become increasingly difficult to monitor. For example, determining whether a new product fails because of production deficiencies or a poor marketing campaign may not be possible.

product departmentalization
Grouping activities around products or product groups

Product Departmentalization **Product departmentalization**, a second common approach, involves grouping and arranging activities around products or product groups. Apex Computers has two product-based departments at the highest level of the firm. One is responsible for all activities associated with Apex's personal computer business, and the other handles the software business. Most larger businesses adopt this form of departmentalization for grouping activities at the business or corporate level.

Product departmentalization has three major advantages. First, all activities associated with one product or product group can be easily integrated and coordinated. Second, the speed and effectiveness of decision making are enhanced. Third, the performance of individual products or product groups can be assessed more easily and objectively, thereby improving the accountability of departments for the results of their activities.

Product departmentalization also has two major disadvantages. For one, managers in each department may focus on their own product or product group to the exclusion of the rest of the organization. For example, a marketing manager may see her or his primary duty as helping the group rather than helping the overall organization. For another, administrative costs rise, because each department must have its own functional specialists for areas such as market research and financial analysis.

customer departmentalization
Grouping activities to respond to and interact with specific customers or customer groups

Customer Departmentalization Under **customer departmentalization**, the organization structures its activities to respond to and interact with specific customers or customer groups. The lending activities in most banks, for example, are usually tailored to meet the needs of different kinds of customers (business, consumer, mortgage, and agricultural loans). Figure 11.2 shows that the marketing branch of Apex's computer business has two distinct departments—industrial sales and consumer sales. The industrial sales department handles marketing activities aimed at business customers, whereas the consumer sales department is responsible for wholesaling computers to retail stores catering to individual purchasers.

The basic advantage of this approach is that the organization is able to use skilled specialists to deal with unique customers or customer groups. It takes one set of skills to evaluate a balance sheet and lend a business $500,000 for operating capital, and a different set of skills to evaluate an individual's creditworthiness and lend $20,000 for a new car. However, a fairly large administrative staff is required to integrate the activities of the various departments. In banks, for example, coordination is necessary to make sure that the organization does not overcommit itself in any one area and to handle collections on delinquent accounts from a diverse set of customers.

location departmentalization Grouping jobs on the basis of defined geographic sites or areas

Location Departmentalization **Location departmentalization** groups jobs on the basis of defined geographic sites or areas. The defined sites or areas may range in size from a hemisphere to only a few blocks of a large city. The manufacturing branch of Apex's computer business has two plants—one in Dallas and another in Phoenix. Similarly, the design division of its software design unit has two labs—one in Chicago and the other in St. Louis. Apex's consumer sales group has five sales territories corresponding to different regions of the United States. Transportation companies, police departments (precincts represent geographic areas of a city), and the Federal Reserve Bank all use location departmentalization.

The primary advantage of location departmentalization is that it enables the organization to respond easily to unique customer and environmental characteristics in the various regions. On the negative side, a larger administrative staff may be required if the organization must keep track of units in scattered locations.

Other Forms of Departmentalization Although most organizations are departmentalized by function, product, customer, or location, other forms are occasionally used. Some organizations group certain activities by time. One of the machine shops of Baker Hughes in Houston, for example, operates on three shifts. Each shift has a superintendent who reports to the plant manager, and each shift has its own functional departments. Time is thus the framework for many organizational activities. Other organizations that use time as a basis for grouping jobs include some hospitals and many airlines. In other situations, departmentalization by sequence is appropriate. Many college students, for instance, must register in sequence: seniors on Monday, juniors on Tuesday, and so on. Other areas that may be organized in sequence include credit departments (specific employees run credit checks according to customer name) and insurance claims divisions (by policy number).

Other Considerations Two final points about job grouping remain to be made. First, departments are often called something entirely different—*divisions, units, sections,* and *bureaus* are all common synonyms. The higher we look in an organization, the more likely we are to find departments referred to as divisions. H.J. Heinz, for example, is organized into five major divisions. Nevertheless, the underlying logic behind all the labels is the same: They represent groups of jobs that have been yoked together according to some unifying principle. Second, almost any organization is likely to employ multiple bases of departmentalization, depending on level. Although Apex Computer is a hypothetical firm that we created to explain departmentalization, it is quite similar to many real organizations in that it uses a variety of bases of departmentalization for different levels and different sets of activities.

concept CHECK

What are the common bases of departmentalization?

Identify an organization with which you have some familiarity. Based on your knowledge of the firm, describe how it is departmentalized.

Establishing Reporting Relationships

The third basic element of organizing is the establishment of reporting relationships among positions. Suppose, for example, that the owner-manager of a small business has just hired two new employees, one to handle marketing and one to handle production. Will the marketing manager report to the production manager, will the production manager report to the marketing manager, or will each report directly to the owner-manager? These questions reflect the basic issues involved in establishing reporting relationships: clarifying the chain of command and the span of management.

Chain of Command

chain of command A clear and distinct line of authority among the positions in an organization

Chain of command is an old concept, first popularized in the early years of the twentieth century. For example, early writers about the **chain of command** argued that clear and distinct lines of authority need to be established among all positions in an organization. The chain of command actually has two components. The first, called *unity of command,* suggests that each person within an organization must have a clear reporting relationship to one and only one boss (as we see in Chapter 11, newer models of organization design routinely—and successfully—violate this premise). The second, called the *scalar principle,* suggests that there must be a clear and unbroken line of authority that extends from the lowest to the highest position in the organization. The popular saying "The buck stops here" is derived from this idea—someone in the organization must ultimately be responsible for every decision.

Establishing reporting relationships is a basic element of organizing. This manager works at the Natural Foods Market in Los Angeles. She is meeting here with a group of her employees. As part of the meeting she is clarifying their areas of responsibility and ensuring that everyone knows who has authority over various activities and functions in the store.

Narrow Versus Wide Spans

span of management The number of people who report to a particular manager

Another part of establishing reporting relationships is determining how many people will report to each manager. This defines the **span of management** (sometimes called the *span of control*). For years, managers and researchers sought to determine the optimal span of management. For example, should it be relatively narrow (with few subordinates per manager) or relatively wide (with many subordinates)? One early writer, A. V. Graicunas, went so far as to quantify span of management issues.[21] Graicunas noted that a manager must deal with three kinds of interactions with and among subordinates: direct (the manager's one-to-one relationship with each subordinate), cross (among the subordinates themselves), and group (between groups of

Dilbert reprinted by permission of United Feature Syndicate, Inc.

Distributing authority is a key building block in creating an effective organization. Unfortunately, some managers prefer to avoid accountability for decisions and work to ensure that someone else can always be held responsible for mistakes and errors. This *Dilbert* cartoon, for instance, illustrates a whimsical view of a manager teaching others how to avoid accountability and pass the buck to others.

subordinates). The number of possible interactions of all types between a manager and subordinates can be determined by the following formula:

$$I = N(2^N/2 + N - 1)$$

where I is the total number of interactions with and among subordinates and N is the number of subordinates.

If a manager has only two subordinates, six potential interactions exist. If the number of subordinates increases to three, the possible interactions total eighteen. With five subordinates there are one hundred possible interactions. Although Graicunas offers no prescription for what N should be, his ideas demonstrate how complex the relationships become when more subordinates are added. The important point is that each additional subordinate adds more complexity than the previous one did. Going from nine to ten subordinates is very different from going from three to four.

Another early writer, Ralph C. Davis, described two kinds of spans: an operative span for lower-level managers and an executive span for middle and top managers. He argued that operative spans could approach thirty subordinates, whereas executive spans should be limited to between three and nine (depending on the nature of the managers' jobs, the growth rate of the company, and similar factors). Lyndall F. Urwick suggested that an executive span should never exceed six subordinates, and General Ian Hamilton reached the same conclusion.[22] Today we recognize that the span of management is a crucial factor in structuring organizations but that there are no universal, cut-and-dried prescriptions for an ideal or optimal span.[23] Later we summarize some important variables that influence the appropriate span of management in a particular situation. First, however, we describe how the span of management affects the overall structure of an organization.

Tall Versus Flat Organizations

Imagine an organization with thirty-one managers and a narrow span of management. As shown in Figure 11.3, the result is a relatively tall organization with five layers of management. With a somewhat wider span of management, however, the flat organization shown in Figure 11.3 emerges. This configuration has only three layers of management.

What difference does it make whether the organization is tall or flat? One early study at Sears, Roebuck and Company found that a flat structure led to higher levels of employee morale and productivity.[24] Researchers have also argued that a tall structure is more expensive (because of the larger number of managers involved) and that it fosters more communication problems (because of the increased number of people through whom information must pass). On the other hand, a wide span of management in a flat organization may result in a manager's having more administrative responsibility (because there are fewer managers) and more supervisory responsibility (because there are more subordinates reporting to each manager). If these additional responsibilities become excessive, the flat organization may suffer.[25]

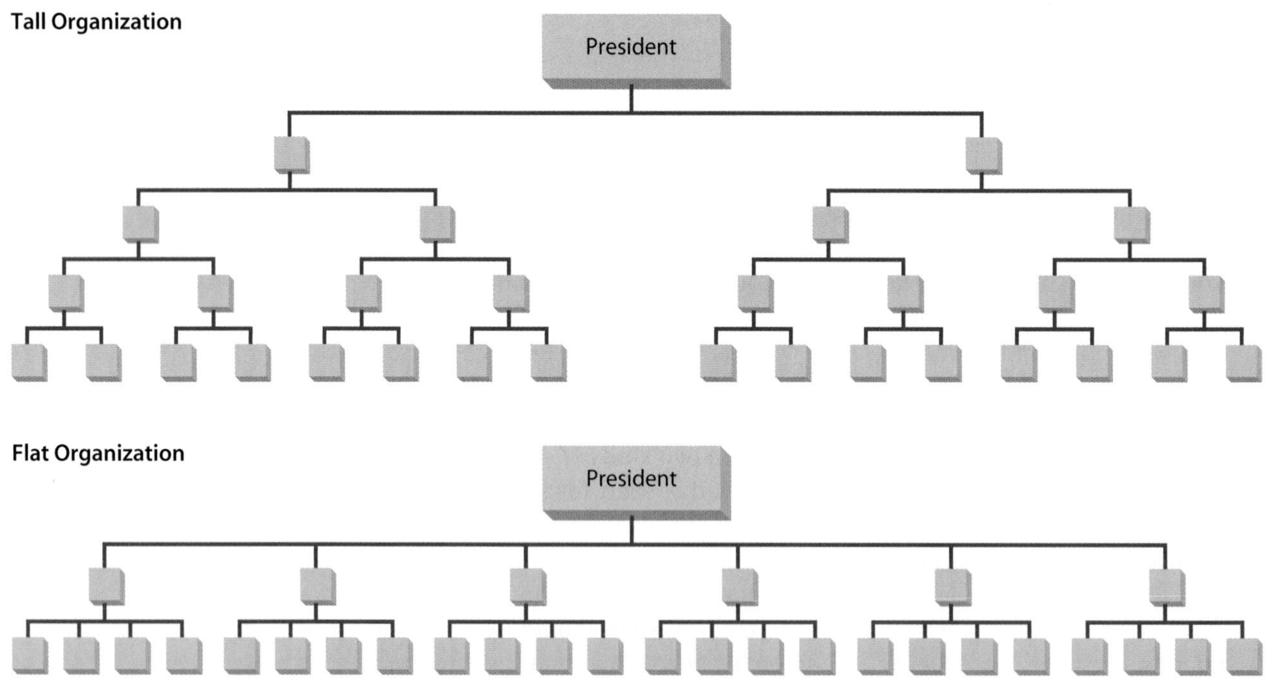

FIGURE 11.3

Tall Versus Flat Organizations

Wide spans of management result in flat organizations, which may lead to improved employee morale and productivity as well as increased managerial responsibility. Many organizations today, including IBM and General Electric, are moving toward flat structures to improve communication and flexibility.

Many experts agree that businesses can function effectively with fewer layers of organization than they currently have. The Franklin Mint, for example, reduced its number of management layers from six to four. At the same time, the CEO increased his span of management from six to twelve. In similar fashion, IBM has eliminated several layers of management. One additional reason for this trend is that improved organizational communication networks allow managers to stay in touch with a larger number of subordinates than was possible even just a few years ago.[26]

Determining the Appropriate Span

Of course, the initial question remains: How do managers determine the appropriate span for their unique situation? Although no perfect formula exists, researchers have identified a set of factors that influence the span for a particular circumstance.[27] Some of these factors are listed in Table 11.1. For example, if the manager and subordinates are competent and well trained, a wide span may be effective. Physical dispersion is also important. The more widely subordinates are scattered, the narrower the span should be. On the other hand, if all the subordinates are in one location, the span can be somewhat wider. The amount of nonsupervisory work expected of the manager is also important. Some managers, especially at the lower levels of an organization, spend most or all of their time supervising subordinates. Other managers spend a lot of time doing paperwork,

TABLE 11.1

Factors Influencing the Span of Management

Although researchers have found advantages to the flat organization (less expensive and with fewer communication problems than a tall organization, for example), a number of factors may favor a tall organization.

1. Competence of supervisor and subordinates (the greater the competence, the wider the potential span)
2. Physical dispersion of subordinates (the greater the dispersion, the narrower the potential span)
3. Extent of nonsupervisory work in manager's job (the more nonsupervisory work, the narrower the potential span)
4. Degree of required interaction (the less required interaction, the wider the potential span)
5. Extent of standardized procedures (the more procedures, the wider the potential span)
6. Similarity of tasks being supervised (the more similar the tasks, the wider the potential span)
7. Frequency of new problems (the higher the frequency, the narrower the potential span)
8. Preferences of supervisors and subordinates

planning, and engaging in other managerial activities. Thus these managers may need a narrower span.

Some job situations also require a great deal of interaction between supervisor and subordinates. In general, the more interaction that is required, the narrower the span should be. Similarly, if there is a fairly comprehensive set of standard procedures, a relatively wide span is possible. If only a few standard procedures exist, however, the supervisor usually has to play a larger role in overseeing day-to-day activities and may find a narrower span more efficient. Task similarity is also important. If most of the jobs being supervised are similar, a supervisor can handle a wider span. When each employee is performing a different task, more of the supervisor's time is spent on individual supervision. Likewise, if new problems that require supervisory assistance arise frequently, a narrower span may be called for. If new problems are relatively rare, though, a wider span can be established. Finally, the preferences of both supervisor and subordinates may affect the optimal span. Some managers prefer to spend less time actively supervising their employees, and many employees prefer to be more self-directed in their jobs. A wider span may be possible in these situations.

For example, the Case Corporation factory in Racine, Wisconsin, makes farm tractors exclusively to order in five to six weeks. Farmers can select from among a wide array of options, including engines, tires, power trains, and even a CD player. A wide assortment of machines and processes is used to construct each tractor. Although workers are highly skilled operators of their particular machines, each machine is different. In this kind of setup, the complexities of each machine and the advanced skills needed by each operator mean that one supervisor can oversee only a small number of employees.[28]

In some organizational settings, other factors may influence the optimal span of management. The relative importance of each factor also varies in different settings. It is unlikely that all eight factors will suggest the same span; some may suggest a wider span, and others may indicate a need for a narrow span. Hence, managers must assess the relative weight of each factor or set of factors when deciding the optimal span of management for their unique situation.

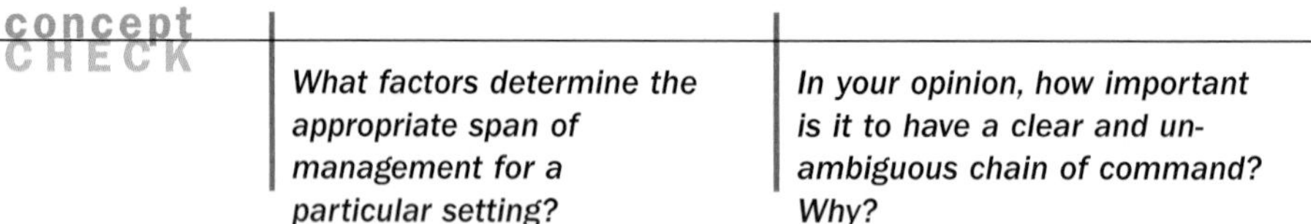

concept CHECK

What factors determine the appropriate span of management for a particular setting?

In your opinion, how important is it to have a clear and unambiguous chain of command? Why?

Distributing Authority

authority Power that has been legitimized by the organization

Another important building block in structuring organizations is the determination of how authority is to be distributed among positions. **Authority** is power that has been legitimized by the organization.[29] Distributing authority is another normal outgrowth of increasing organizational size. For example, when an owner-manager hires a sales representative to market his products, he needs to give the new employee appropriate authority to make decisions about delivery dates, discounts, and so forth. If every decision requires the approval of the owner-manager, he is no better off than he was before he hired the sales representative. The power given to the sales representative to make certain kinds of decisions, then, represents the establishment of a pattern of authority—the sales representative can make some decisions alone and others in consultation with coworkers, and the sales representative must defer some decisions to the boss. Two specific issues that managers must address when distributing authority are delegation and decentralization.[30]

Distributing authority in an organization is a vital part of the organizing function. James Parker (CEO) and Colleen Barrett (President) run Southwest Airlines. Part of their job is to make sure that the right people have the authority they need to make decisions and to get things done. For instance, they give customer service managers considerable discretion in keeping their customers happy.

The Delegation Process

Delegation is the establishment of a pattern of authority between a superior and one or more subordinates. Specifically, **delegation** is the process by which managers assign a portion of their total workload to others.[31]

delegation The process by which a manager assigns a portion of his or her total workload to others

Reasons for Delegation The primary reason for delegation is to enable the manager to get more work done. Subordinates help ease the manager's burden by doing major portions of the organization's work. In some instances, a subordinate may have more expertise in addressing a particular problem than the manager does. For example, the subordinate may have had special training in developing information systems or may be more familiar with a particular product line or geographic area. Delegation also helps develop subordinates. By participating in decision making and problem solving, subordinates learn about overall operations and improve their managerial skills.

Parts of the Delegation Process In theory, as shown in Figure 11.4, the delegation process involves three steps. First, the manager assigns responsibility or gives the subordinate a job to do. The assignment of responsibility might range from telling a subordinate to prepare a report to placing the person in charge of a task force. Along with the assignment, the individual is also given the authority to do the job. The manager may give the subordinate the power to requisition needed information from confidential files or to direct a group of other workers. Finally, the manager establishes the subordinate's accountability—that is, the subordinate accepts an obligation to carry out the task assigned by the manager. *The Business of Ethics* describes an important area of accountability in business today. Similarly, the CEO of AutoZone will sign off for the company on financial performance only when the individual manager responsible for each unit has certified his or her own results as being accurate. The firm believes that this high level of accountability will help it avoid the kind of accounting scandal that has hit many businesses in recent times.[32]

These three steps do not occur mechanically, however. Indeed, when a manager and a subordinate have developed a good working relationship, the major parts of the process may be implied rather than stated. The manager may simply mention that a particular job must be done. A perceptive subordinate may realize that the manager is actually assigning the job to her. From past experience with the boss, she may also know, without being told, that she has the necessary authority to do the job and that she is accountable to the boss for finishing the job as "agreed."

FIGURE 11.4

Steps in the Delegation Process

Good communication skills can help a manager successfully delegate responsibility to subordinates. A manager must not be reluctant to delegate, nor should he or she fear that the subordinate will do the job so well that the manager's advancement is threatened.

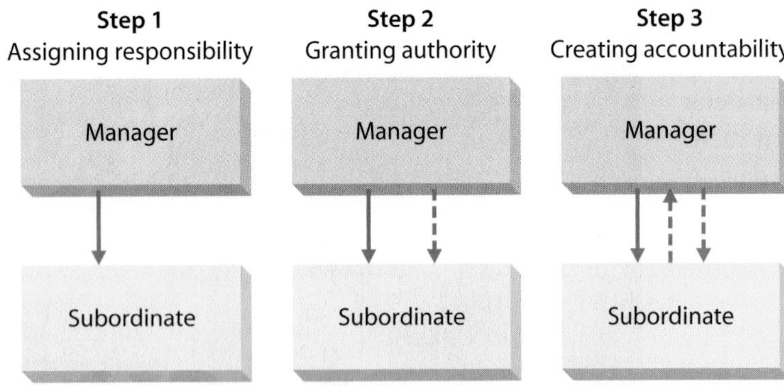

Problems in Delegation Unfortunately, problems often arise in the delegation process. For example, a manager may be reluctant to delegate. Some managers are so disorganized that they are unable to plan work in advance and, as a result, cannot delegate appropriately. Similarly, some managers may worry that subordinates will do too well and pose a threat to their own advancement. And, finally, managers may not trust the subordinate to do the job well. Similarly, some subordinates are reluctant to accept delegation. They may be afraid that failure will result in a reprimand. They may also perceive that there are no rewards for accepting

Distributing authority in an organization begins with delegation. At Yahoo!, the big Internet portal, extreme delegation is a fundamental management philosophy. When the firm hired Isabelle Bordry (left) and Clothilde de Mersan to launch and run Yahoo! France, U.S. managers were initially concerned about their ability to transfer its management style to the notoriously centralized rigid French economy. But Bordry and de Mersan have enthusiastically embraced the notion of delegation and are aggressively working to encourage their employees to make their own decisions.

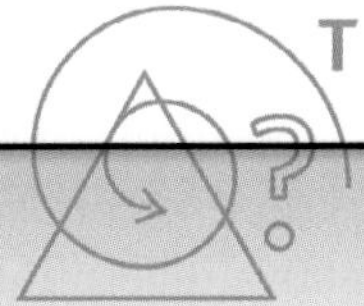

THE BUSINESS OF ethics

How to Organize an Ethical Bank

"The pendulum is shifting in favor of the investor."

– Jacob Zamansky, securities lawyer

Jack Grubman was a much-respected Wall Street investment analyst covering the telecommunications industry during the 1990s. Then that industry lost over $2 trillion in investors' equity value in a two-year period. An investigation by the Securities and Exchange Commission (SEC) showed that Grubman upgraded his recommendations on stock in AT&T and other telecom firms, due to pressure from his boss, Citigroup CEO Sanford Weill, who is a friend of AT&T CEO Michael Armstrong. AT&T is an important client for Citigroup's banking services. Today, Grubman has resigned and Citigroup is facing fraud charges.

Citigroup is not alone. The structure of investment banks has come under attack following the recent decline in the U.S. stock market and the resulting shareholder outrage and lawsuits. After the bank failures of the 1930's Great Depression, legislation prohibited banks from participating in other aspects of the financial sector, such as selling stocks. But, over the last two decades, banks have gradually crept into these activities once more.

Today, most large investment banks provide banking services, help issue corporate stock, serve as stockbrokers, sell insurance products, consult, and publish investing advice. Banks claim that these activities are independent because they take place in different departments. However, it is difficult, if not impossible, to prevent one department from influencing the behavior of another.

The scandals led to the passage of the Sarbanes-Oxley reform act, which directs the SEC to produce new rules for increasing corporate accountability. One of the SEC's proposals is a requirement that a bank not publish or sell investment advice about any firm that is a client of the bank's banking or consulting departments. Banks are protesting, claiming that the requirement would be impossible to meet in an environment where a handful of multinational banking firms service virtually every large corporation in the world.

From the bank's point of view, profitability depends on being able to offer a multitude of services to each client, and information gained in one department can be helpful to other departments. But from the stockholders' point of view, too much information in the hands of just a few people can be dangerous. And "the pendulum is shifting in favor of the investor," says securities lawyer Jacob Zamansky.

References: Amy Borrus, "How the SEC Might Lower the Boom," *BusinessWeek*, January 27, 2003, p. 39; Emily Thornton and Laura Cohn, "Creative Financing's Gaping Loopholes," *BusinessWeek*, January 8, 2003, www.businessweek.com on January 20, 2003; Gary Weiss, "Revenge of the Investor," *BusinessWeek*, December 16, 2002, pp. 116–122 (*quote p. 118); John A. Byrne, "This Corporate Reform Lacks Spine," *BusinessWeek*, January 10, 2003; "The Worst Managers: Sandy Weill," *BusinessWeek*, January 13, 2003, p. 78.

additional responsibility. Or they may simply prefer to avoid risk and therefore want their boss to take all responsibility.

Norm Brodsky, a small-business owner who built six successful companies, learned firsthand what happens when the CEO cannot effectively delegate. It took Brodsky seven years to build a messenger service into a $120 million operation—and just fourteen months to go from $120 million into bankruptcy. "Where did I go wrong?" he asks rhetorically and then provides his own answer: "The company needed management, stability, and structure, and I kept it from getting them. I was so desperate to sustain the head rush of start-up chaos that I made all the final decisions and didn't let the managers do their jobs. In the end I paid a steep price."[33]

There are no quick fixes for these problems. The basic issue is communication. Subordinates must understand their own responsibility, authority, and accountability, and the manager must come to recognize the value of effective delegation. With the passage of time, subordinates should develop to the point at which they can make substantial contributions to the organization. At the same time, managers should recognize that a subordinate's satisfactory performance is not a threat to their own career, but an accomplishment by both the subordinate who did the job and the manager who trained the subordinate and was astute enough to entrust the subordinate with the project. Ultimate responsibility for the outcome, however, continues to reside with the manager.

Decentralization and Centralization

decentralization The process of systematically delegating power and authority throughout the organization to middle and lower-level managers

centralization The process of systematically retaining power and authority in the hands of higher-level managers

Just as authority can be delegated from one individual to another, organizations also develop patterns of authority across a wide variety of positions and departments. **Decentralization** is the process of systematically delegating power and authority throughout the organization to middle and lower-level managers. It is important to remember that decentralization is actually one end of a continuum anchored at the other end by **centralization**, the process of systematically retaining power and authority in the hands of higher-level managers. Hence, a decentralized organization is one in which decision-making power and authority are delegated as far down the chain of command as possible. Conversely, in a centralized organization, decision-making power and authority are retained at the higher levels of management. When H. Ross Perot ran EDS, he practiced centralization; his successors have used decentralization. No organization is ever completely decentralized or completely centralized; some firms position themselves toward one end of the continuum, and some lean the other way.[34]

What factors determine an organization's position on the decentralization-centralization continuum? One common determinant is the organization's external environment. Usually, the greater the complexity and uncertainty of the environment, the greater is the tendency to decentralize. Another crucial factor is the history of the organization. Firms have a tendency to do what they have done in the past, so there is likely to be some relationship between what an organization did in its early history and what it chooses to do today in terms of centralization or decentralization. The nature of the decisions being made is also considered. The costlier and riskier the decisions, the more pressure there is to centralize. Organizations also consider the abilities of lower-level managers. If lower-level managers do not have the ability to make high-quality decisions, there is likely to be a high level of centralization. If lower-level managers are well qualified, top management can take advantage of their talents by decentralizing; in fact, if top management does not, talented lower-level managers may leave the organization.[35]

A manager has no clear-cut guidelines for determining whether to centralize or decentralize. Many successful organizations, such as Sears and General Electric, are quite decentralized. Equally successful firms, such as McDonald's and Wal-Mart, have remained centralized. IBM has recently undergone a transformation from using a highly centralized approach to a much more decentralized approach to managing its operations. A great deal of decision-making authority was passed from the hands of a select group of top executives down to six product and marketing groups. The reason for the move was to speed the company's ability to make decisions, introduce new products, and respond to customers. For years, most Japanese firms have been highly centralized. Recently, though, many leading Japanese firms have moved toward decentralization.

concept CHECK

What are the steps in the delegation process?

Under what circumstances would you prefer to work in a centralized organization? in a decentralized organization?

Coordinating Activities

A fifth major element of organizing is coordination. As we discuss earlier, job specialization and departmentalization involve breaking jobs down into small units and then combining those jobs into departments. Once this has been accomplished, the activities of the departments must be linked—systems must be put into place to keep the activities of each department focused on the attainment of organizational goals. This is accomplished by **coordination**—the process of linking the activities of the various departments of the organization.[36]

coordination The process of linking the activities of the various departments of the organization

The Need for Coordination

The primary reason for coordination is that departments and work groups are interdependent—they depend on one another for information and resources to perform their respective activities. The greater the interdependence between departments, the more coordination the organization requires if departments are to be able to perform effectively. There are three major forms of interdependence: pooled, sequential, and reciprocal.[37]

Pooled interdependence represents the lowest level of interdependence. Units with pooled interdependence operate with little interaction—the output of the units is pooled at the organizational level. Gap clothing stores operate with pooled interdependence. Each store is considered a "department" by the parent corporation. Each has its own operating budget, staff, and so forth. The profits or losses from each store are "added together" at the organizational level. The stores are interdependent to the extent that the final success or failure of one store affects the others, but they do not generally interact on a day-to-day basis.

pooled interdependence When units operate with little interaction; their output is simply pooled

In **sequential interdependence**, the output of one unit becomes the input for another in a sequential fashion. This creates a moderate level of interdependence. At Nissan, for example, one plant assembles engines and then ships them to a final

sequential interdependence When the output of one unit becomes the input for another in sequential fashion assembly site at another plant, where the cars are completed. The plants are interdependent in that the final assembly plant must have the engines from engine assembly before it can perform its primary function of producing finished automobiles. But the level of interdependence is generally one way—the engine plant is not necessarily dependent on the final assembly plant.

reciprocal interdependence When activities flow both ways between units

Reciprocal interdependence exists when activities flow both ways between units. This form is clearly the most complex. Within a Marriott hotel, for example, the reservations department, front-desk check-in, and housekeeping are all reciprocally interdependent. Reservations has to provide front-desk employees with information about how many guests to expect each day, and housekeeping needs to know which rooms require priority cleaning. If any of the three units does not do its job properly, all the others will be affected.

Structural Coordination Techniques

Because of the obvious coordination requirements that characterize most organizations, many techniques for achieving coordination have been developed. Some of the most useful devices for maintaining coordination among interdependent units are the managerial hierarchy, rules and procedures, liaison roles, task forces, and integrating departments.[38]

The Managerial Hierarchy Organizations that use the hierarchy to achieve coordination place one manager in charge of interdependent departments or units. In Wal-Mart distribution centers, major activities include receiving and unloading bulk shipments from railroad cars and loading other shipments onto trucks for distribution to retail outlets. The two groups (receiving and shipping) are interdependent in that they share the loading docks and some equipment. To ensure coordination and minimize conflict, one manager is in charge of the whole operation.

Rules and Procedures Routine coordination activities can be handled via rules and standard procedures. In the Wal-Mart distribution center, an outgoing truck shipment has priority over an incoming rail shipment. Thus, when trucks are to be loaded, the shipping unit is given access to all of the center's auxiliary forklifts. This priority is specifically stated in a rule. But, as useful as rules and procedures often are in routine situations, they are not particularly effective when coordination problems are complex or unusual.

Liaison Roles We introduce the liaison role of management in Chapter 1. As a device for coordination, a manager in a liaison role coordinates interdependent units by acting as a common point of contact. This individual may not have any formal authority over the groups but instead simply facilitates the flow of information between units. Two engineering groups working on component systems for a large project might interact through a liaison. The liaison maintains familiarity with each group as well as with the overall project. She can answer questions and otherwise serve to integrate the activities of all the groups.

Task Forces A task force may be created when the need for coordination is acute. When interdependence is complex and several units are involved, a single liaison person may not be sufficient. Instead, a task force might be assembled by drawing one representative from each group. The coordination function is thus spread across several individuals, each of whom has special information about one of the groups involved. When the project is completed, task force members return to their original position. For example, a college overhauling its degree requirements might establish a task force made up of representatives from each department affected by the change. Each person retains her or his regular departmental affiliation and duties but also serves on the special task force. After the new requirements are agreed on, the task force is dissolved.

Integrating Departments Integrating departments are occasionally used for coordination. These are somewhat similar to task forces but are more permanent. An integrating department generally has some permanent members as well as members who are assigned temporarily from units that are particularly in need of coordination. One study found that successful firms in the plastics industry, which is characterized by complex and dynamic environments, used integrating departments to maintain internal integration and coordination.[39] An integrating department usually has more authority than a task force and may even be given some budgetary control by the organization.

In general, the greater the degree of interdependence, the more attention the organization must devote to coordination. When interdependence is pooled or simple sequential, the managerial hierarchy or rules and procedures are often sufficient. When more complex forms of sequential or simpler forms of reciprocal interdependence exist, liaisons or task forces may be more useful. When reciprocal interdependence is complex, task forces or integrating departments are needed. Of course, the manager must also rely on her or his own experience and insights when choosing coordination techniques for the organization.

Electronic Coordination

Recent advances of electronic information technology are also providing useful mechanisms for coordination. E-mail, for example, makes it easier for people to communicate with one another. This communication, in turn, enhances coordination. Similarly, many people in organizations today use electronic scheduling, at least some of which is accessible to others. Hence, if someone needs to set up a meeting with two colleagues, he can often check their electronic schedules to determine their availability, making it easier to coordinate their activities.

Local networks, increasingly managed by hand-held electronic devices, are also making it easier to coordinate activities. Bechtel, for example, now requires its contractors, subcontractors, and suppliers to use a common web-based communication system to improve coordination among their myriad activities. The firm estimates that this improved coordination technology routinely saves it thousands of dollars on every big construction project it undertakes.

concept CHECK

What are the three kinds of interdependence that necessitate coordination?

In the future, do you think electronic coordination will eliminate the need for structural coordination?

Differentiating Between Positions

line position A position in the direct chain of command that is responsible for the achievement of an organization's goals

staff position A position intended to provide expertise, advice, and support for line positions

The last building block of organization structure is differentiating between line and staff positions in the organization. A **line position** is a position in the direct chain of command that is responsible for the achievement of an organization's goals. A **staff position** is intended to provide expertise, advice, and support for line positions. In many modern organizations these differences are beginning to disappear, and in a few the difference has been eliminated altogether. However, there are still sufficient meaningful differences to warrant discussion.

Differences Between Line and Staff

The most obvious difference between line and staff is purpose—line managers work directly toward organizational goals, whereas staff managers advise and assist. But other distinctions exist as well. One important difference is authority. Line authority is generally thought of as the formal or legitimate authority created by the organizational hierarchy. Staff authority is less concrete and may take a variety of forms. One form is the authority to advise. In this instance, the line manager can choose whether to seek or to avoid input from staff; even when advice is sought, the manager might still choose to ignore it.

Another form of staff authority is called *compulsory advice*. In this case, the line manager must listen to the advice but can choose to heed it or ignore it. For example, the pope is expected to listen to the advice of the Sacred College of Cardinals when dealing with church doctrine, but he may follow his own beliefs when making decisions. Perhaps the most important form of staff authority is called *functional authority*—formal or legitimate authority over activities related to the staff member's specialty. For example, a human resource staff manager may have functional authority when there is a question of discrimination in hiring. Conferring functional authority is probably the most effective way to use staff positions because the organization is able to take advantage of specialized expertise while also maintaining a chain of command.

Administrative Intensity

administrative intensity The degree to which managerial positions are concentrated in staff positions

Organizations sometimes attempt to balance their emphasis on line versus staff positions in terms of administrative intensity. **Administrative intensity** is the degree to which managerial positions are concentrated in staff positions. An organization with high administrative intensity is one with many staff positions relative to the number of line positions; low administrative intensity reflects relatively more line positions. Although staff positions are important in many different areas, they tend to proliferate unnecessarily. All else being equal, organizations would like to devote most of their human resource investment to line managers because, by definition, they contribute to the organization's basic goals. A surplus of staff positions represents a drain on an organization's cash and an inefficient use of resources.

Many organizations have taken steps over the past few years to reduce their administrative intensity by eliminating staff positions. CBS has cut hundreds of staff positions at its New York headquarters, and IBM has cut its corporate staff workforce from 7,000 to 2,300. Burlington Northern generates almost $7 billion in annual sales and manages a workforce of 43,000 with a corporate staff of only 77 managers.

concept CHECK

What is the basic difference between line and staff positions?

Do you think an organization can function effectively with no staff whatsoever?

Summary of Key Points

ACE self-test

business.college.hmco.com/students

Organizations are made up of a series of elements. The most common of these involve designing jobs, grouping jobs, establishing reporting relationships, distributing authority, coordinating activities, and differentiating between positions.

Job design is the determination of an individual's work-related responsibilities. The most common form is job specialization. Because of various drawbacks to job specialization, managers have experimented with job rotation, job enlargement, job enrichment, the job characteristics approach, and work teams as alternatives.

After jobs are designed, they are grouped into departments. The most common bases for departmentalization are function, product, customer, and location. Each has its own unique advantages and disadvantages. Large organizations employ multiple bases of departmentalization at different levels.

Establishing reporting relationships starts with clarifying the chain of command. The span of management partially dictates whether the organization is relatively tall or flat. In recent years there has been a trend toward flatter organizations. Several situational factors influence the ideal span.

Distributing authority starts with delegation. Delegation is the process by which the manager assigns a portion of his or her total workload to others. Systematic delegation throughout the organization is decentralization. Centralization involves keeping power and authority at the top of the organization. Several factors influence the appropriate degree of decentralization.

Coordination is the process of linking the activities of the various departments of the organization. Pooled, sequential, or reciprocal interdependence among departments is a primary reason for coordination. Managers can draw on several techniques to help achieve coordination. Electronic coordination is becoming increasingly important.

A line position is a position in the direct chain of command that is responsible for the achievement of an organization's goals. In contrast, a staff position provides expertise, advice, and support for line positions. Administrative intensity is the degree to which managerial positions are concentrated in staff positions.

Discussion Questions

Questions for Review

1. Describe the five alternatives to job specialization. What is the advantage of each, as compared to specialization?
2. What is meant by unity of command? By the scalar principle? Can an organization have one without the other? Explain.
3. Describe the organizational structure that results from each of the different bases of departmentalization. What implications does each of these structures have with regard to the distribution of authority within the organization?
4. Explain the differences between line and staff positions. What are the advantages and disadvantages of high versus low administrative intensity?

Questions for Analysis

5. Some people have claimed that the increasing technological sophistication required by many of today's corporations has led to a return to job specialization. In your opinion, what would be the consequences of a sharp increase in job specialization? Consider both positive and negative outcomes in your answer.
6. Try to develop a different way to departmentalize your college or university, a local fast-food restaurant, a manufacturing firm, or some other organization. What might be the advantages of your form of organization?
7. Consider the list of jobs below. In your opinion, what is the appropriate span of management for each? Describe the factors you considered in reaching your conclusion.
   - A physician practices medicine in a privately owned clinic, while also supervising a number of professional nurses and office staff.
   - An owner-manager of an auto body shop deals with customers and directs several experienced mechanics, and also trains and oversees the work of some unskilled laborers.
   - A manager in an international advertising agency directs a team of professionals who are located in offices around the world.

Questions for Application

8. Consider a job you have held. (Or, if you have not held a job, interview a worker.) Using the job characteristics approach, assess that job's core dimensions. Then describe how the core dimensions led to critical psychological states and, ultimately, to personal and work outcomes.

9. Use the Internet to locate organization charts for five different organizations. (Or use data from the Internet to draw the organization charts yourself.) Look for similarities and differences among them and try to account for what you find.
10. Contact two very different local organizations (retailing firm, manufacturing firm, church, civic club, and so on) and interview top managers to develop organization charts for each organization. How do you account for the similarities and differences between them?

BUILDING EFFECTIVE conceptual SKILLS

Exercise Overview

Conceptual skills refer to a person's abilities to think in the abstract. This exercise calls on your conceptual skills to address questions about appropriate span of management.

Exercise Background

Early management scholars believed that there was one optimal span of management, or that an optimal span of management could be determined by looking at just one or a very few variables. Today, however, most experts agree that the optimal span of management depends on a number of complex questions. Discovery of the optimal span of management is important in ensuring an adequate, but not stifling, level of supervision, but it can be difficult to calculate.

Exercise Task

With the background information above as context, do the following:

1. Survey ten workers and managers about the span of management used in their workplace. Notice the variation in the answers.
2. Choose one of these individuals for further investigation. Interview him or her to obtain information about the type of work he or she does, how much interaction with supervisors is required, how skilled the workers are, and other factors affecting the determination of optimal span of management. (See Table 11.1 for guidance.)
3. Does the span of management in use make sense, given the information you obtained in your answer to question 2? Why or why not?
4. If the span of management seems to be appropriate, what are some likely outcomes the organization might experience? If the span seems inappropriate, what are some likely outcomes?

BUILDING EFFECTIVE diagnostic SKILLS

Exercise Overview

Diagnostic skills are the skills that enable a manager to visualize the most appropriate response to a situation. This exercise will enable you to develop your diagnostic skills as they relate to issues of centralization and decentralization in an organization.

Exercise Background

Managers often find it necessary to change the degree of centralization or decentralization in their organization. Begin this exercise by reflecting on two very different scenarios. In scenario A, assume that you are the top manager in a large organization. The organization has a long and well-known history of being very centralized. For valid reasons beyond the scope of this exercise, assume that you have decided to make the firm much more decentralized. For scenario B, assume the exact opposite situation; that is, assume that you are the top manager of a firm that has always used decentralization but has now decided to become much more centralized.

Exercise Task

With the background information above as context, do the following:

1. List the major barriers you see to implementing decentralization in scenario A.
2. List the major barriers you see to implementing centralization in scenario B.
3. Which scenario do you think would be easiest to implement in reality? In other words, is it likely to be easier to move from centralization to decentralization, or from decentralization to centralization? Why?
4. Given a choice of starting your own career in a firm that is either highly centralized or highly decentralized, which do you think you would prefer? Why?

BUILDING EFFECTIVE technical SKILLS

business.college.hmco.com/students

Exercise Overview

Technical skills are the skills necessary to accomplish or understand the specific work being done in an organization. This exercise will allow you to develop technical skills related to departmentalization, establishment of reporting relationships, coordination, and differentiation.

Exercise Background

The task of designing organization structure, including grouping jobs, establishing span of management, and coordinating various units, is a never-ending process. Managers must continually monitor and evaluate their firms' structures and make changes when appropriate.

Assume that you are in charge of structuring a completely new organization, a large retail bookstore. Consider how you will form departments, how large a span of management each supervisor can have, and the differences between line and staff positions. Your employees include people with knowledge about management, different types of books (children's books, fiction, technical books, and so on), store design and display, advertising, accounting, law, retail sales, inventory and stocking, human resources, and computers.

Exercise Task

1. Develop an organizational structure for your store. Include details about level in the organizational hierarchy, reporting relationships, and span of management.
2. Determine which positions are line positions and which are staff positions.
3. Describe the coordination mechanisms you will use.
4. Use the Internet to investigate the elements of structure at a bookstore, such as Barnes & Noble or Borders. In what ways does your suggested structure differ from the information you find online? Why do the differences exist?

CHAPTER CLOSING case

Too Much Delegation at Nissan?

"Should I do what people think I should be doing or should I approach the problem directly?"

– Carlos Ghosn, CEO, Nissan Japan*

Delegation is a good thing. It spreads the workload, rewards subordinates with decision-making power, develops subordinates' capabilities, and allows decisions to be made by those with the most applicable experience and expertise. The limitations of delegation are often described in terms of dysfunctional fear on the part of the superior and the subordinate. However, there can be times when delegation and its companion, decentralization, do not lead to optimal choices.

Japanese firms traditionally have a team-based structure and a consensus approach to decision making. The Japanese system allows a lot of participation from employees at all levels, but it tends to result in choices "made by committee"—safe, conservative choices that are acceptable to everyone. Individuals with unusual ideas find themselves excluded from the process. High-ranking managers guide the team, but they rarely make decisions for themselves. Risk taking and innovation can be stifled in this environment. For Japanese automakers Toyota, Honda, and Nissan, the result has been high-quality, reliable vehicles, but with lackluster designs. All this changed at Nissan with the arrival of new CEO Carlos Ghosn in 1999.

Ghosn (rhymes with "cone") was appointed by Renault executives to revitalize Japan's second-largest car manufacturer—Renault owns 44 percent of Nissan. Nissan was near bankruptcy, with unappealing models, low market share, and rapidly declining profitability. "Le Cost Cutter," as Ghosn was known in France, was expected to follow the pattern of ruthless cost cutting that had led to his success at other Renault divisions. Ghosn did reduce expenses, but the bigger challenge was to restructure Nissan's way of thinking about authority and delegation.

Although many of Nissan's Japanese managers advised caution and slowness, Ghosn preferred boldness and risk taking. Ghosn explains, "The question I asked myself was: 'Should I do what people think I should be doing or should I approach the problem directly?'" Ghosn "didn't accept the old taboos about Japanese style, and he convinced people that he was the solution," says Jed Connelly, head of Nissan's U.S. sales. Ghosn laid off employees who acted as advisors but had no operational authority. He consulted his subordinates, then made decisions on his own. He hired hot designers from rival firms and gave them authority over new-product development. The results have been a slew of innovative, award-winning designs such as the Xterra and the updated, stylish new Altima.

Nowhere has the change been more evident than in the design of the 350Z. The car is a reworking of Nissan's long-neglected classic seventies muscle car, the 240Z. Nissan manager Yutaka Katayama and engineer John Yukawa wanted to revive the venerable brand but had been discouraged by previous CEOs. But "when I broached the subject of the Z, [Ghosn's] face lit up, and his eyes shone. I couldn't have been happier with his response," says Katayama. Ghosn, a 240Z fan, became involved in every detail of the 350Z's design, putting a timer on the dashboard next to the speedometer—the car can go from 0 to 60 miles per hour in under six seconds—and insisting that real sports cars have dual tailpipes. The 350Z has been a smashing success, with a design that is described as "rakish" and "tight," a powerful 287-horsepower engine, and a price that, at $26,000, is about half that of comparable sports cars. "It's not just another car in our lineup," says Ghosn. "It's really a symbol of the revival of our company."

Ghosn is far from the typical Japanese executive. Born in Brazil to a Lebanese father and a French mother, he was educated in Lebanon, then received bachelor's and master's degrees in France. "He is not Japanese, clearly," says Nissan design head Isuru Nakamura. "But he is not Brazilian or French either. He is a leader. If his personality reflected a strong nationality, he might not have been very successful." Ghosn claims a chameleonlike ability to adapt to any environment, saying, "In any country I was always different."

Under Ghosn's direction, Nissan's profits and sales are up substantially. With eight new models in 2003 and four more in 2004, Nissan has the potential to surpass Toyota, currently Japan's number-one auto maker. And the innovations continue. Along with its award-winning updates, Nissan has unveiled Micra, a new European subcompact. Another Ghosn inspiration is a car designed specifically for the Chinese market. Ghosn, too, has been winning awards. He was named "Asia's Businessman of the Year" by *Fortune* in 2002. And in 2005 Ghosn will become CEO of Nissan/Renault. Until then, he is looking for a successor to head Nissan Japan—one who will be able to carry on his tradition of personal responsibility and authority.

Case Questions

1. What are some advantages that Carlos Ghosn can expect to obtain from retaining decision-making authority at the CEO level? What are some potential pitfalls that he must be aware of?
2. Give at least three examples of decisions that can be most effectively made with a decentralized process. Give at least three examples of decisions that can be most effectively made with a centralized process. Do not use examples from the case above. Explain your choices.
3. The Japanese management system depends on high specialization. Does a high level of specialization typically lead to decentralization? Why or why not?

Case References

References: Alex Taylor III, "Asia's Businessman of the Year," *Fortune*, February 7, 2002, www.fortune.com on January 22, 2003 (*quote); Alex Taylor III, "Wheels," *Fortune Small Business*, November 1, 2002, www.fortune.com on January 22, 2003; "Carlos Ghosn," *BusinessWeek*, July 8, 2002, www.businessweek.com on January 22, 2003; Chester Dawson, "The Zen of Nissan," *BusinessWeek*, July 22, 2002, www.businessweek.com on December 17, 2002; Christine Tierney and Chester Dawson, "Negotiating Europe's Curves," *BusinessWeek*, December 16, 2002, www.businessweek.com on January 22, 2003; "Nissan Begins Making New Micra in U.K. to Boost Europe Ops," *PRNewswire*, December 2, 2002, hoovnews.hoovers.com on January 22, 2003; "Nissan Motor Co., Ltd.," Hoover's Online, www.hoovers.com on January 22, 2003.

Chapter Notes

1. "Brands," "History," "Timeline," Sara Lee website, www.saralee.com on January 19, 2003; Deborah Cohen, "Sara Lee Opens Alternative to Victoria's Secret," *Reuters*, January 3, 2003, biz.yahoo.com on January 19, 2003; Julie Forster, "Sara Lee: Changing the Recipe—Again," *BusinessWeek*, September 10, 2001, www.businessweek.com on December 18, 2002 (*quote); "Sara Lee: Looking Shapely," *BusinessWeek*, October 21, 2002, p. 52.
2. See David Lei and John Slocum, "Organization Designs to Renew Competitive Advantage," *Organizational Dynamics*, 2002, vol. 31, no. 1, pp. 1–18.
3. See Kathleen M. Eisenhardt and Shona L. Brown, "Patching—Restitching Business Portfolios in Dynamic Markets," *Harvard Business Review*, May–June 1999, pp. 106–115, for a related discussion.
4. Gareth Jones, *Organization Theory*, 4th ed. (Upper Saddle River: Prentice-Hall, 2003).
5. David A. Nadler and Michael L. Tushman, *Competing by Design: The Power of Organizational Architecture* (New York: Oxford University Press, 1997).
6. Ricky W. Griffin and Gary McMahan, "Motivation Through Job Design," in Jerald Greenberg (ed.), *Organizational Behavior: The State of the Science* (Hillsdale, N.J.: Lawrence Erlbaum Associates, 1994), pp. 23–44.
7. Adam Smith, *Wealth of Nations* (New York: Modern Library, 1937; originally published in 1776).
8. Andrea Gabor, *The Capitalist Philosophers* (New York: Times Business, 2000).
9. Ricky W. Griffin, *Task Design* (Glenview, Ill.: Scott Foresman, 1982).
10. Anne S. Miner, "Idiosyncratic Jobs in Formal Organizations," *Administrative Science Quarterly*, September 1987, pp. 327–351.
11. M. D. Kilbridge, "Reduced Costs Through Job Enlargement: A Case," *Journal of Business*, vol. 33, 1960, pp. 357–362.
12. Griffin and McMahan, "Motivation Through Job Enrichment."
13. Kilbridge, "Reduced Costs Through Job Enrichment: A Case."
14. Frederick Herzberg, *Work and the Nature of Man* (Cleveland, Ohio: World Press, 1966).
15. Robert Ford, "Job Enrichment Lessons from AT&T," *Harvard Business Review*, January–February 1973, pp. 96–106.

16. J. Richard Hackman and Greg R. Oldham, *Work Redesign* (Reading, Mass.: Addison-Wesley, 1980).
17. "Some Plants Tear out Long Assembly Lines, Switch to Craft Work," *Wall Street Journal*, October 24, 1994, pp. A1, A4.
18. See Etienne C. Wenger and William M. Snyder, "Communities of Practice: The Organizational Frontier," *Harvard Business Review*, January–February 2000, pp. 139–148, for a related discussion.
19. Richard L. Daft, *Organization Theory and Design*, 8th ed. (Cincinnati, Ohio: South-Western, 2004).
20. "Lucent to Break up into Four Divisions," Associated Press news story reported in *The Houston Chronicle*, October 27, 1999, p. B2.
21. A. V. Graicunas, "Relationships in Organizations," *Bulletin of the International Management Institute*, March 7, 1933, pp. 39–42.
22. Ralph C. Davis, *Fundamentals of Top Management* (New York: Harper & Row, 1951); Lyndall F. Urwick, *Scientific Principles and Organization* (New York: American Management Association, 1938), p. 8; Ian Hamilton, *The Soul and Body of an Army* (London: Edward Arnold, 1921), pp. 229–230.
23. David D. Van Fleet and Arthur G. Bedeian, "A History of the Span of Management," *Academy of Management Review*, 1977, pp. 356–372.
24. James C. Worthy, "Factors Influencing Employee Morale," *Harvard Business Review*, January 1950, pp. 61–73.
25. Dan R. Dalton, William D. Todor, Michael J. Spendolini, Gordon J. Fielding, and Lyman W. Porter, "Organization Structure and Performance: A Critical Review," *Academy of Management Review*, January 1980, pp. 49–64.
26. See Jerry Useem, "Welcome to the New Company Town," *Fortune*, January 10, 2000, pp. 62–70, for a related discussion.
27. David Van Fleet, "Span of Management Research and Issues," *Academy of Management Journal*, September 1983, pp. 546–552.
28. Philip Siekman, "Where 'Build to Order' Works Best," *Fortune*, April 26, 1999, pp. 160C–160V.
29. See Daft, *Organization Theory and Design*.
30. William Kahn and Kathy Kram, "Authority at Work: Internal Models and Their Organizational Consequences," *Academy of Management Review*, 1994, vol. 19, no. 1, pp. 17–50.
31. Carrie R. Leana, "Predictors and Consequences of Delegation," *Academy of Management Journal*, December 1986, pp. 754–774.
32. Jerry Useem, "In Corporate America It's Cleanup Time," *Fortune*, September 16, 2002, pp. 62–70.
33. Norm Brodsky, "Necessary Losses," *Inc.*, December 1997, p. 116–119.
34. "Remote Control," *HRMagazine*, August 1997, pp. 82–90.
35. "Toppling the Pyramids," *Canadian Business*, May 1993, pp. 61–65.
36. Kevin Crowston, "A Coordination Theory Approach to Organizational Process Design," *Organization Science*, March–April 1997, pp. 157–166.
37. James Thompson, *Organizations in Action* (New York: McGraw-Hill, 1967). For a recent discussion, see Bart Victor and Richard S. Blackburn, "Interdependence: An Alternative Conceptualization," *Academy of Management Review*, July 1987, pp. 486–498.
38. Jay R. Galbraith, *Designing Complex Organizations* (Reading, Mass.: Addison-Wesley, 1973) and *Organizational Design* (Reading, Mass.: Addison-Wesley, 1977).
39. Paul R. Lawrence and Jay W. Lorsch, "Differentiation and Integration in Complex Organizations," *Administrative Science Quarterly*, March 1967, pp. 1–47.

12

Managing Organization Design

CHAPTER OUTLINE

The Nature of Organization Design

Universal Perspectives on Organization Design
- Bureaucratic Model
- Behavioral Model

Situational Influences on Organization Design
- Core Technology
- Environment
- Organizational Size
- Organizational Life Cycle

Strategy and Organization Design
- Corporate-Level Strategy
- Business-Level Strategy
- Organizational Functions

Basic Forms of Organization Design
- Functional (U-Form) Design
- Conglomerate (H-Form) Design
- Divisional (M-Form) Design
- Matrix Design
- Hybrid Designs

Emerging Issues in Organization Design
- The Team Organization
- The Virtual Organization
- The Learning Organization
- Issues in International Organization Design

LEARNING OBJECTIVES

After studying this chapter, you should be able to:

1 ***Describe the basic nature of organization design.***

OPENING INCIDENT

It is a student's dream: attend class whenever it is convenient, receive lots of one-on-one interaction with faculty, even wear pajamas to school! It sounds like a fantasy, but it is a reality for the hundreds of thousands of students who attend online universities. With names like Apollo, UNext, and Corinthian Colleges, these are not your traditional schools, but they are some of the fastest growing. Five years ago, online universities accounted for less than 1 percent of all students, but today they have a 3 percent market share, and that number is increasing about 1 percentage point annually.

One example is Apollo, an industry pioneer, which owns the University of Phoenix Online. Apollo was founded in 1976 by entrepreneur John Sperling. At first, the college built traditional campuses, but in 1989 it developed the first accredited online university. Today, the corporation is the largest competitor in for-profit higher education and owns 180 campuses in thirty-seven states and Canada, with 57,000 students. In addition, its online school enrolls 142,000 more, from all over the world. The school offers bachelor's, master's and doctoral degrees in business, education, and nursing.

For-profit schools are managed and organized differently than traditional col-

2	3	4	5	6
Identify and explain the two basic universal perspectives on organization design.	***Identify and explain several situational influences on organization design.***	***Discuss how an organization's strategy and its design are interrelated.***	***Describe the basic forms of organization design.***	***Describe emerging issues in organization design.***

"... distance learning was like a freight train. We could get run down, get onboard, or get out of the way."

—Meyer Feldberg, Dean, Graduate School of Business, Columbia University

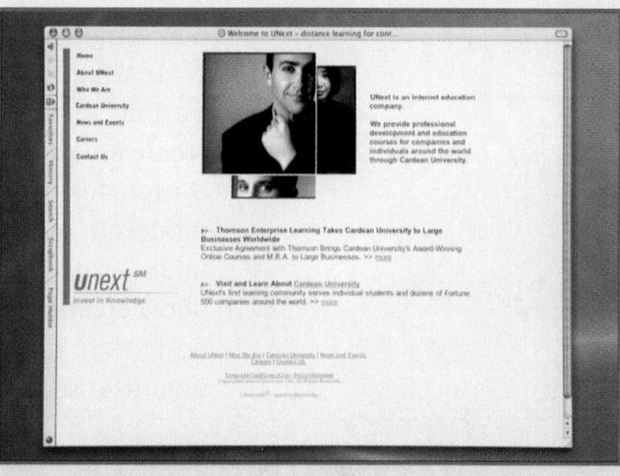

Online universities like UNext have organization designs that are much different from those of traditional colleges and universities.

leges. Learning takes place online, so the university has almost no investment in facilities such as classroom space, office buildings, libraries, or dormitories. Tenure does not exist. That gives online universities more flexibility in hiring and promotion. Also, most of the faculty members have other full-time employment, reducing salaries and benefits costs. The average price of annual tuition is about $10,000, about $500 per credit hour. With few added fees and students' living expenses already paid, the cost is less than at many traditional schools.

The philosophy at online colleges is different, too. Traditional universities are usually founded by a state government or other not-for-profit group, such as a church. Their aims are to provide a public service, develop educated citizens, and increase the intellectual capital of their community or region. On the other hand, for-profit universities are just that—developed in order to make profits. Most of them are public corporations, traded on the NASDAQ, a U.S. stock market that carries many small, new firms. They are run for the benefit of shareholders, like any other corporation.

Different goals lead for-profit universities to choose different strategies and structures. Many online colleges shun recent high school graduates and accept only older students. The University of Phoenix Online, for example, requires prospective students to be at least twenty-three years of age. Other online universities specialize in a particular discipline. UNext is focused on business training and offers primarily M.B.A. degrees, whereas California-based Concord offers graduate programs in law. Many for-profit schools have extensive corporate training programs, in addition to their academic offerings. Business's needs for training and continuing education for their employees provide a steady and reliable source of income for profit-making schools.

Online universities have become very popular with students, and Stanford Provost John Hennessy says, "We already see students opting not to go to class in order to watch the class on their computer in their dorm room." Universities are fearful of losing their monopoly on higher education, and professors are concerned about the declining emphasis on classroom skills. "The day of standing up and being a brilliant lecturer is gone," says Jerry Porras, a professor at Stanford's Graduate School of Business. "I really think that our industry as it has been in the past is dead in the future." Some professors take the threat more personally. A professor at San Jose State writes, "John Sperling [Apollo founder] represents something horrible in American education. I have an extreme loathing for him, and in a just world, he would be in jail."

To fight back, some traditional universities have started their own for-profit, online subsidiaries. New York University and the University of Maryland have both taken this approach. Another popular strategy, adopted by Stanford, Columbia, the London School of Economics, and others, is to form partnerships with for-profit firms. Columbia University dean Meyer Feldberg says, "We knew distance learning was like a freight train. We could get run down, get onboard, or get out of the way." A third technique, adopted by Brown and Cornell, for example, is the development of a nonprofit online business, such as their General Education Network.

It is not yet clear which, if any, of these structures will succeed in the long run. Online entrepreneur Peter J. Stokes, executive vice president of Eduventures, says, "Online education is a fragmented and turbulent new industry. No one knows exactly what for-profit business models will work. Everyone out there is working off their best educated guess."[1]

One of the major ingredients in managing any business is the creation of an organization design to link the various elements that comprise the organization. There is a wide array of alternatives that managers in any given organization might select for its design. Managers of both traditional and online colleges and universities are currently struggling with which alternative form of organization is right for them.

In Chapter 11, we identify the basic elements that go into creating an organization. In this chapter, we explore how those elements can be combined to create an overall design for the organization. We first discuss the nature of organization design. We then describe early approaches aimed at identifying universal models of organization design. Situational factors, such as technology, environment, size, and life cycle, are then introduced. Next we discuss the relationship between an organization's strategy and its structure. Basic forms of organization design are described next. We conclude by presenting four emerging issues in organization design.

The Nature of Organization Design

What is organization design? In Chapter 11, we note that job specialization and span of management are among the common elements of organization structure. We also describe how the appropriate degree of specialization can vary, as can the appropriate span of management. Not really addressed, however, are questions of how specialization and span might be related to each other. For example, should a high level of specialization be matched with a certain span? And will different combinations of each work best with different bases of departmentalization? These and related issues are associated with questions of organization design.[2]

organization design The overall set of structural elements and the relationships among those elements used to manage the total organization

Organization design is the overall set of structural elements and the relationships among those elements used to manage the total organization. Thus organization design is a means to implement strategies and plans to achieve organizational goals.[3] As we discuss organization design, keep in mind two important points. First, organizations are not designed and then left intact. Most organizations change almost continuously as a result of factors such as situations and people. (The processes of organization change are discussed in Chapter 13.) Second, organization design for larger organizations is extremely complex and has so many nuances and variations that descriptions of it cannot be a full and complete explanation.

concept CHECK

What is organization design?	*How does organization design relate to organization structure?*

Universal Perspectives on Organization Design

In Chapter 2, we make the distinction between contingency and universal approaches to solving management problems. Recall, for example, that universal perspectives try to identify the "one best way" to manage organizations, and contingency perspectives suggest that appropriate managerial behavior in a given situation depends on, or is contingent on, unique elements in that situation. The foundation of contemporary thinking about organization design can be traced back to two early universal perspectives: the bureaucratic model and the behavioral model.

Bureaucratic Model

bureaucracy A model of organization design based on a legitimate and formal system of authority

We also note in Chapter 2 that Max Weber, an influential German sociologist, was a pioneer of classical organization theory. At the core of Weber's writings was the bureaucratic model of organizations.[4] The Weberian perspective suggests that a **bureaucracy** is a model of organization design based on a legitimate and formal system of authority. Many people associate bureaucracy with "red tape," rigidity, and passing the buck. For example, how many times have you heard people refer disparagingly to "the federal bureaucracy"? And many U.S. managers believe that bureaucracy in the Japanese government is a major impediment to U.S. firms' ability to do business there.

Government organizations are often associated with the bureaucratic model of organization design—and sometimes for good reason! This "corridor of paper" is just one of many at the U.S. Patent and Trademark Office in Washington. Individuals and companies applying for a patent today may have to wait two years or more to get final approval. And even then the agency makes many mistakes—denying requests that should be approved or approving requests that should be denied. So far, a lack of funding has hampered efforts to modernize and computerize the agency.

Weber viewed the bureaucratic form of organization as logical, rational, and efficient. He offered the model as a framework to which all organizations should aspire—the "one best way" of doing things. According to Weber, the ideal bureaucracy exhibits five basic characteristics:

1. The organization should adopt a distinct division of labor, and each position should be filled by an expert.
2. The organization should develop a consistent set of rules to ensure that task performance is uniform.
3. The organization should establish a hierarchy of positions or offices that creates a chain of command from the top of the organization to the bottom.
4. Managers should conduct business in an impersonal way and maintain an appropriate social distance between themselves and their subordinates.
5. Employment and advancement in the organization should be based on technical expertise, and employees should be protected from arbitrary dismissal.

Perhaps the best examples of bureaucracies today are government agencies and universities. Consider, for example, the steps you must go through and the forms

Reprinted with permission of King Features Syndicate.

The bureaucratic model of organization design relies on logical, rational, and efficient rules and procedures. Many organizations attempt to standardize these rules and procedures by creating forms for people to use when initiating action or requesting approval. Unfortunately, this standardization can lead to such a proliferation of forms that people quickly come to see it all as nothing more than "red tape." This point is obviously brought home by Beetle Bailey's request for time off to visit his dentist.

you must fill out to apply for admission to college, request housing, register each semester, change majors, submit a degree plan, substitute a course, and file for graduation. Even when paper is replaced with electronic media, the steps are often the same. The reason these procedures are necessary is that universities deal with large numbers of people who must be treated equally and fairly. Hence, rules, regulations, and standard operating procedures are needed. Large labor unions are also usually organized as bureaucracies.[5]

Some bureaucracies, such as the U.S. Postal Service, are trying to portray themselves as less mechanistic and impersonal. The strategy of the Postal Service is to become more service oriented as a way to fight back against competitors like Federal Express and UPS. Similarly, as discussed in *The World of Management,* Deutsche Bank is also attempting to become less bureaucratic. The cartoon illustrates how a bureaucratic organization might attempt to alter how it operates.

A primary strength of the bureaucratic model is that several of its elements (such as reliance on rules and employment based on expertise) do, in fact, often improve efficiency. Bureaucracies also help prevent favoritism (because everyone must follow the rules) and make procedures and practices very clear to everyone. Unfortunately, however, this approach also has several disadvantages. One major disadvantage is that the bureaucratic model results in inflexibility and rigidity. Once rules are created and put in place, making exceptions or changing them is often difficult. In addition, the bureaucracy often results in the neglect of human and social processes within the organization.

Behavioral Model

behavioral model A model of organization design consistent with the human relations movement and stressing attention to developing work groups and concern with interpersonal processes

Another important universal model of organization design was the **behavioral model**, which paralleled the emergence of the human relations school of management thought. Rensis Likert, a management researcher, studied several large organizations to determine what made some more effective than others.[6] He found that the organizations in his sample that used the bureaucratic model of design tended to be less effective than those that used a more behaviorally oriented model consistent with the emerging human relations movement—in other words, organizations that paid more

THE WORLD OF management

An American Revolution at Deutsche Bank

"Young man, we've heard you're causing a lot of trouble. Well, that's exactly what we hired you for."

— A member of the Vorstand management council, Deutsche Bank, to an employee*

Deutsche Bank (DB), the world's second-largest bank, is suffering. The German economy is stagnant; sales are down. The country's rigid labor laws forbid layoffs, and generous wages are mandatory, causing high expenses. German banks, heavily invested in local businesses, are particularly vulnerable. "There is a crisis," says Dresdner Bank CEO Bernd Fahrholz, "and it is especially a banking crisis."

German banks reported average profitability of 5 percent in 2001, compared to 15 percent for all European banks. "German banks' low profitability is partly the result of their own managerial ineptitude," says industry analyst Mark Hoge. By "ineptitude," Hoge refers to the banks' adherence to traditional German management. For example, decisions are made by consensus in a council of advisors called the Vorstand. The Vorstand at DB, a force for conservatism, avoided the "reckless" risk of investing overseas. It refused to move into new services. DB's worldwide expansion shifted the bank's focus, as domestic revenues accounted for 70 percent of sales in 1995, but a mere 20 percent in 2001. Expansion led to duplication and lack of coordination, but DB's design did not keep pace.

Yet DB today is listed on the New York Stock Exchange, uses American accounting standards, and has English as its official language. There are four members in the Vorstand, including an American and a Swiss. The Vorstand gives more autonomy to regional managers. Previous CEO Rolf-Ernst Breuer resists change, but others embrace it. When employee Anshu Jain went ahead with a risky deal that was nixed by superiors, one Vorstand member said, "Young man, we've heard you're causing a lot of trouble. Well, that's exactly what we hired you for." Managers and stockholders gradually lost faith in conformist Breuer. So in 2002 Josef Ackerman, a Swiss manager, became the first foreigner to head the 132-year-old bank.

The firm is in upheaval, with Ackerman laying off workers and closing redundant operations. It is aggressively moving into new markets and products. Breuer, who is still at DB, squashes rumors that the firm may leave Germany altogether, saying, "I can deny that the headquarters . . . will be moved to a place outside the German borders." But that is beside the point. Under Ackerman's new, more global structure, Deutsche Bank's headquarters location is now irrelevant.

References: Christopher Rhoads and Marcus Walker, "Deutsche Bank Is Looking to Transform Its Management into U.S.-Style Structure," *Wall Street Journal*, January 17, 2002, p. A11; David Fairlamb, "Rough Shoals for Banks—and Germany's Economy," *BusinessWeek*, August 12, 2002, www.businessweek.com on January 23, 2003; Jack Ewing, "German Businesses Head for Lower-Cost Shores," *BusinessWeek*, December 26, 2002, biz.yahoo.com on January 23, 2003; Marcus Walker, "Deutsche Bank Finds That It Has to Cut German Roots to Grow," *Wall Street Journal*, December 14, 2002, pp. A1, A10 (*quote p. A10); Richard Tomlinson, "A Swiss Boss Cracks the Whip," *Fortune*, August 15, 2002, www.fortune.com on January 23, 2003.

attention to developing work groups and were more concerned about interpersonal processes.

Likert developed a framework that characterized organizations in terms of eight important processes: leadership, motivation, communication, interactions, decision making, goal setting, control, and performance goals. Likert believed that all organizations could be measured and categorized along a continuum associated

System 1 design Similar to the bureaucratic model

System 4 design Similar to behavioral model

with each of these dimensions. He argued that the basic bureaucratic form of organization, which he called a **System 1 design**, anchored one end of each dimension. The characteristics of the System 1 organization in Likert's framework are summarized in Table 12.1.

Also summarized in this table are characteristics of Likert's other extreme form of organization design, called **System 4 design**, which was based on the behavioral model. For example, a System 4 organization uses a wide array of motivational processes, and its interaction processes are open and extensive. Other distinctions between System 1 and System 4 organizations are equally obvious. Between the System 1 and System 4 extremes lie the System 2 and System 3 organizations. Likert argued that System 4 should be adopted by all organizations. He suggested

TABLE 12.1

System 1 and System 4 Organizations

The behavioral model identifies two extreme types of organization design called System 1 and System 4. The two designs vary in eight fundamental processes. The System 1 design is considered to be somewhat rigid and inflexible.

System 1 Organization	System 4 Organization
1. Leadership process includes no perceived confidence and trust. Subordinates do not feel free to discuss job problems with their superiors, who in turn do not solicit their ideas and opinions.	1. Leadership process includes perceived confidence and trust between superiors and subordinates in all matters. Subordinates feel free to discuss job problems with their superiors, who in turn solicit their ideas and opinions.
2. Motivational process taps only physical, security, and economic motives through the use of fear and sanctions. Unfavorable attitudes toward the organization prevail among employees.	2. Motivational process taps a full range of motives through participatory methods. Attitudes are favorable toward the organization and its goals.
3. Communication process is such that information flows downward and tends to be distorted, inaccurate, and viewed with suspicion by subordinates.	3. Communication process is such that information flows freely throughout the organization—upward, downward, and laterally. The information is accurate and undistorted.
4. Interaction process is closed and restricted. Subordinates have little effect on departmental goals, methods, and activities.	4. Interaction process is open and extensive. Both superiors and subordinates are able to affect departmental goals, methods, and activities.
5. Decision process occurs only at the top of the organization; it is relatively centralized.	5. Decision process occurs at all levels through group processes; it is relatively decentralized.
6. Goal-setting process is located at the top of the organization; discourages group participation.	6. Goal-setting process encourages group participation in setting high, realistic objectives.
7. Control process is centralized and emphasizes fixing of blame for mistakes.	7. Control process is dispersed throughout the organization and emphasizes self-control and problem solving.
8. Performance goals are low and passively sought by managers who make no commitment to developing the human resources of the organization.	8. Performance goals are high and actively sought by superiors who recognize the necessity for making a full commitment to developing, through training, the human resources of the organization.

Source: Adapted from Rensis Likert, *The Human Organization*, 1967.

that managers should emphasize supportive relationships, establish high performance goals, and practice group decision making to achieve a System 4 organization. Many organizations attempted to adopt the System 4 design during its period of peak popularity. General Motors, for instance, converted a plant in the Atlanta area from a System 2 to a System 4 organization. Over a period of three years, direct and indirect labor efficiency improved, as did tool breakage rates, scrap costs, and quality.[7]

Like the bureaucratic model, the behavioral approach has both strengths and weaknesses. Its major strength is that it emphasizes human behavior by stressing the value of an organization's employees. Likert and his associates thus paved the way for a more humanistic approach to designing organizations. Unfortunately, the behavioral approach also argues that there is one best way to design an organization—as a System 4. As we see, however, evidence is strong that there is no one best approach to organization design.[8] What works for one organization may not work for another, and what works for one organization may change as that organization's situation changes. Hence, universal models like bureaucracy and System 4 have been largely supplanted by newer models that take contingency factors into account. In the next section, we identify a number of factors that help determine the best organization design for a particular situation.

concept CHECK

Distinguish between the bureaucratic model and the behavioral model of organization design.

Why do you think managers have often been concerned with identifying the "one best way" of doing something?

Situational Influences on Organization Design

The **situational view of organization design** is based on the assumption that the optimal design for any given organization depends on a set of relevant situational factors. In other words, situational factors play a role in determining the best organization design for any particular circumstance. Four basic situational factors—technology, environment, size, and organizational life cycle—are discussed here. Another, strategy, is described in the next section.

situational view of organization design Based on the assumption that the optimal design for any given organization depends on a set of relevant situational factors

Core Technology

Technology consists of the conversion processes used to transform inputs (such as materials or information) into outputs (such as products or services). Most organizations use multiple technologies, but an organization's most important one is called its *core technology*. Although most people visualize assembly lines and

technology Conversion processes used to transform inputs into outputs

Core technology can be a major determinant of organization design. This Timken ball-bearing factory provides a good illustration. Timken, an Ohio-based company, has invested heavily in flexible manufacturing sites that allow it to quickly shift production between different product lines—this plant can do so in only 15 minutes. But in order to most effectively manage this flexible technology, Timken has also had to overhaul its entire organization design.

machinery when they think of technology, the term can also be applied to service organizations. For example, an investment firm like Vanguard uses technology to transform investment dollars into income in much the same way that Union Carbide uses natural resources to manufacture chemical products. *Technology Toolkit* discusses the role of technology at FedEx.

The link between technology and organization design was first recognized by Joan Woodward.[9] Woodward studied one hundred manufacturing firms in southern England. She collected information about such aspects as the history of each organization, its manufacturing processes, its forms and procedures, and its financial performance. Woodward expected to find a relationship between the size of an organization and its design, but no such relationship emerged. As a result, she began to seek other explanations for differences. Close scrutiny of the firms in her sample led her to recognize a potential relationship between technology and organization design. This follow up analysis led Woodward to first classify the organizations according to their technology. Three basic forms of technology were identified by Woodward:

1. *Unit or small-batch technology.* The product is custom-made to customer specifications or produced in small quantities. Organizations using this form of technology include a tailor shop like Brooks Brothers (custom suits), a printing shop like Kinko's (business cards, company stationery), and a photography studio.
2. *Large-batch or mass-production technology.* The product is manufactured in assembly-line fashion by combining component parts into another part or finished product. Examples include automobile manufacturers like Subaru, appliance makers like Whirlpool Corporation, and electronics firms like Philips.
3. *Continuous-process technology.* Raw materials are transformed to a finished product by a series of machine or process transformations. The composition of the materials themselves is changed. Examples include petroleum refineries like ExxonMobil and Shell, and chemical refineries like Dow Chemical and Hoechst AG.

These forms of technology are listed in order of their assumed levels of complexity. In other words, unit or small-batch technology is presumed to be the least complex and continuous-process technology the most complex. Woodward found that different configurations of organization design were associated with each technology.

As technology became more complex in Woodward's sample, the number of levels of management increased (that is, the organization became taller). The executive span of management also increased, as did the relative size of its staff component. The supervisory span of management, however, first increased and then decreased as technology became more complex, primarily because much of the

TECHNOLOGY toolkit

Flexible FedEx

The story has become the stuff of business legend. In the mid 1960s, undistinguished Yale student Fred Smith wrote a paper describing how the adoption of automated technology necessitated a quicker, more reliable transportation system for repair parts. As legend has it, the paper received a poor grade. But Smith himself debunks the myth, saying, "It's become a well-known story because everybody likes to flout authority. But to be honest, I don't really remember what grade I got."

Whatever grade the paper earned, the idea was a winner. Smith joined the Marines and served in Vietnam before investing his own money to start up the air transport business he called Federal Express. FedEx was revolutionary in competing with the monopolistic U.S. Post Service. In the first of what would prove to be many innovations, FedEx used a hub-and-spoke system for increased speed and efficiency. The company developed a reputation for high-quality, reliable, and fast service, albeit at a high price. The company pioneered the use of bar codes and hand-held PDAs for drivers, and online, real-time package tracking for customers.

"Companies that . . . don't take risks . . . are going to end up getting punched up by the marketplace."

– Fred Smith, founder and CEO, Federal Express*

Then, in 2000 rival UPS decided to enter the air freight segment. FedEx's very survival seemed in doubt. "The economics of airplanes are such that we couldn't just keep taking prices down," Smith says. "We finally realized that if we wanted to grow, we had to get into surface transportation." His firm acquired several key players in the ground transportation industry and renamed them to better capitalize on the FedEx brand name. Observers approve. "People say 'FedEx this' when they mean 'Get it someplace fast,'" says investor Timothy M. Ghriskey. "No one says 'UPS this.'" FedEx is unique in the industry with its system of independent, nonunion truckers.

FedEx continues to innovate, developing a proprietary pocket-size PC in conjunction with Motorola and Microsoft. FedEx is the first shipper to send package information to customers' cell phones. The firm is creating software products for small business's logistics. "Engage in constant change," is a mantra for CEO Smith, and he adds, "Companies that ... don't take risks–some of which are going to work and some of which aren't–are going to end up getting punched up by the marketplace."

References: Brian Dumaine, "How I Delivered the Goods," *Fortune Small Business*, October 2002, www.fortune.com on January 24, 2003 (*quote); Charles Haddad, "FedEx: Gaining on the Ground," *BusinessWeek*, December 16, 2002, pp. 126–128; Claudia H. Deutsch, "FedEx Has Hit the Ground Running, but Will Its Legs Tire?" *New York Times*, October 13, 2002, p. BU7; "Intuit Chooses Z-Firm Technology to Power New QuickBooks Integrated Shipping Feature," *Business Wire*, December 3, 2002, hoovnews.hoovers.com on January 24, 2003; "Motorola, FedEx Develop Wireless, Pocket PC for Couriers to Enhance Customer Service," *Business Wire*, November 26, 2002, hoovnews.hoovers.com on January 24, 2003.

work in continuous-process technologies is automated. Fewer workers are needed, but the skills necessary to do the job increase. These findings are consistent with the discussion of the span of management in Chapter 11—the more complex the job, the narrower the span should be.

At a more general level of analysis, Woodward found that the two extremes (unit or small-batch and continuous-process) tended to be very similar to Likert's System 4 organization, whereas the middle-range organizations (large-batch or mass-production) were much more like bureaucracies or System 1. The large-batch and mass-production organizations also had a higher level of specialization.[10] Finally, she found that organizational success was related to the extent to which organizations followed the typical pattern. For example, successful continuous-process organizations tended to be more like System 4 organizations, whereas less-successful firms with the same technology were less like System 4 organizations.

Thus technology clearly appears to play an important role in determining organization design. As future technologies become more diverse and complex, managers will have to be even more aware of technologies' impact on the design of organizations. For example, the increased use of robotics may necessitate alterations in organization design to better accommodate different assembly methods. Likewise, increased usage of new forms of information technology will almost certainly cause organizations to redefine the nature of work and the reporting relationships among individuals.[11]

Environment

In addition to the various relationships described in Chapter 3, environmental elements and organization design are specifically linked in a number of ways. The first widely recognized analysis of environment–organization design linkages was provided by Tom Burns and G. M. Stalker.[12] Like Woodward, Burns and Stalker worked in England. Their first step was identifying two extreme forms of organizational environment: stable (one that remains relatively constant over time) and unstable (subject to uncertainty and rapid change). Next they studied the designs of organizations in each type of environment. Not surprisingly, they found that organizations in stable environments tended to have a different kind of design than did organizations in unstable environments. The two kinds of design that emerged were called mechanistic and organic organization.

A **mechanistic organization**, quite similar to the bureaucratic or System 1 model, was most frequently found in stable environments. Free from uncertainty, organizations structured their activities in rather predictable ways by means of rules, specialized jobs, and centralized authority. Mechanistic organizations are also quite similar to bureaucracies. Although no environment is completely stable, Kmart and Wendy's use mechanistic designs. Each Kmart store, for example, has prescribed methods for store design and merchandise-ordering processes. No deviations are allowed from these methods. An **organic organization**, on the other hand, was most often found in unstable and unpredictable environments, in which constant change and uncertainty usually dictate a much higher level of fluidity and flexibility. Motorola (facing rapid technological change) and The Limited (facing constant change in consumer tastes) both use

An organization's environment can affect how it should be designed. Starbucks works to balance mechanistic and organic design characteristics as it expands into international markets. It relies on mechanistic standardization to ensure product and quality service everywhere. But it also uses organic properties to accommodate local tastes and preferences. Heavily flavored coffees such as Caramel Macchiato are popular at this Puerto Rican store, but are not as popular in Japan. The firm's operating procedures as well as its supply chain are used to help Starbucks achieve this balance.

organic designs. A manager at Motorola, for example, has considerable discretion over how work is performed and how problems can be solved.

mechanistic organization Similar to the bureaucratic or System 1 model, most frequently found in stable environments

organic organization Very flexible and informal model of organization design, most often found in unstable and unpredictable environments

These ideas were extended in the United States by Paul R. Lawrence and Jay W. Lorsch.[13] They agreed that environmental factors influence organization design but believed that this influence varies between different units of the same organization. In fact, they predicted that each organizational unit has its own unique environment and responds by developing unique attributes. Lawrence and Lorsch suggested that organizations could be characterized along two primary dimensions.

differentiation Extent to which the organization is broken down into subunits

integration Degree to which the various subunits must work together in a coordinated fashion

One of these dimensions, **differentiation**, is the extent to which the organization is broken down into subunits. A firm with many subunits is highly differentiated; one with few subunits has a low level of differentiation. The second dimension, **integration**, is the degree to which the various subunits must work together in a coordinated fashion. For example, if each unit competes in a different market and has its own production facilities, they may need little integration. Lawrence and Lorsch reasoned that the degree of differentiation and integration needed by an organization depends on the stability of the environments that its subunits face.

Organizational Size

organizational size Total number of full-time or full-time-equivalent employees

The size of an organization is yet another factor that affects its design.[14] Although several definitions of size exist, we define **organizational size** as the total number of full-time or full-time-equivalent employees. A team of researchers at the University of Aston in Birmingham, England, believed that Woodward had failed to find a size-structure relationship (which was her original expectation) because almost all of the organizations she studied were relatively small (three-fourths had fewer than 500 employees).[15] Thus they decided to undertake a study of a wider array of organizations to determine how size and technology both individually and jointly affect an organization's design.

Their primary finding was that technology did in fact influence structural variables in small firms, probably because all of their activities tend to be centered on their core technology. In large firms, however, the strong technology-design link broke down, most likely because technology is not as central to ongoing activities in large organizations. The Aston studies yielded a number of basic generalizations: When compared to small organizations, large organizations tend to be characterized by higher levels of job specialization, more standard operating procedures, more rules, more regulations, and a greater degree of decentralization. Wal-Mart is a good case in point. The firm expects to continue its dramatic growth for the foreseeable future, adding as many as 800,000 new jobs in the next few years. But, as it grows, the firm acknowledges that it will have to become more decentralized for its first-line managers to stay in tune with their customers.[16]

Organizational Life Cycle

Of course, size is not constant. As we note in Chapter 10, for example, some small businesses are formed but soon disappear. Others remain as small, independently operated enterprises as long as their owner-manager lives. A few, like Dell Computer, Liz Claiborne, and Reebok, skyrocket to become organizational giants. And occasionally large organizations reduce their size through layoffs or divestitures. For example, Navistar is today far smaller than was its previous incarnation as International Harvester Company.

organizational life cycle
Progression through which organizations evolve as they grow and mature

Although no clear pattern explains changes in size, many organizations progress through a four-stage **organizational life cycle.**[17] The first stage is the *birth* of the organization. The second stage, *youth,* is characterized by growth and the expansion of organizational resources. *Midlife* is a period of gradual growth evolving eventually into stability. Finally, *maturity* is a period of stability, perhaps eventually evolving into decline. Montgomery Ward is an example of a mature organization—it is experiencing little or no growth and appears to be falling behind the rest of the retailing industry today.

Managers must confront a number of organization design issues as the organization progresses through these stages. In general, as an organization passes from one stage to the next, it becomes bigger, more mechanistic, and more decentralized. It also becomes more specialized, devotes more attention to planning, and takes on an increasingly large staff component. Finally, coordination demands increase, formalization increases, organizational units become geographically more dispersed, and control systems become more extensive. Thus an organization's size and design are clearly linked, and this link is dynamic because of the organizational life cycle.[18]

concept CHECK

What are the most prevalent situational factors that influence organization design?

Which situational factor is the most and which is the least likely to affect a small neighborhood retailer? Why?

Strategy and Organization Design

Another important determinant of an organization's design is the strategy adopted by its top managers.[19] In general, corporate and business strategies both affect organization design. Basic organizational functions such as finance and marketing can also affect organization design in some cases.[20]

Corporate-Level Strategy

As we note in Chapter 8, an organization can adopt a variety of corporate-level strategies. Its choice will partially determine what type of design will be most effective. For example, a firm that pursues a single-product strategy likely relies on functional departmentalization and can use a mechanistic design. If either unrelated or related diversification is used to spur growth, managers need to decide how to arrange the various units within the organizational umbrella. For example, if the firm is using related diversification, there must be a high level of coordination among the various units to capitalize on the presumed synergistic opportunities inherent in this strategy. On the other hand, firms using unrelated diversification more likely rely on a strong hierarchical reporting system, so that corporate managers can better monitor the performance of individual units with the firm.

An organization that adopts the portfolio approach to implement its corporate-level strategies must also ensure that its design fits its strategy. For example, each strategic business unit may remain a relatively autonomous unit within the organization. But managers at the corporate level need to decide how much decision-making latitude to give the head of each unit (a question of decentralization), how many corporate-level executives are needed to oversee the operations of various units (a question of span of management), and what information, if any, is shared among the units (a question of coordination).[21]

Business-Level Strategy

Business-level strategies affect the design of individual businesses within the organization as well as the overall organization itself. An organization pursuing a defender strategy, for example, is likely to be somewhat tall and centralized, have narrow spans of management, and perhaps take a functional approach to departmentalization. Thus it may generally follow the bureaucratic approach to organization design.

In contrast, a prospecting type of organization is more likely to be flatter and decentralized. With wider spans of management, it tries to be very flexible and adaptable in its approach to doing business. A business that uses an analyzer strategy is likely to have an organization design somewhere between these two extremes (perhaps being a System 2 or 3 organization). Given that a reactor is essentially a strategic failure, its presumed strategy is probably not logically connected to its design.

Generic competitive strategies can also affect organization design. A firm using a differentiation strategy, for example, may structure departments around whatever it is using as a basis for differentiating its products (such as marketing in the case of image or manufacturing in the case of quality). A cost leadership strategy necessitates a strong commitment to efficiency and control. Thus such a firm is more centralized as it attempts to control costs. And a firm using a focus strategy may design itself around the direction of its focus (location departmentalization if its focus is geographic region, customer departmentalization if its focus is customer groups).

Organizational Functions

The relationship between an organization's functional strategies and its design is less obvious and may be subsumed under corporate or business-level concerns. If the firm's marketing strategy calls for aggressive marketing and promotion, separate departments may be needed for advertising, direct sales, and promotion. If its financial strategy calls for low debt, it may need only a small finance department. If production strategy calls for manufacturing in diverse locations, organization design arrangements need to account for this geographic dispersion. Human resource strategy may call for greater or lesser degrees of decentralization as a way to develop skills of new managers at lower levels in the organization. And research and development strategy may dictate various designs for managing the R&D function itself. A heavy commitment to R&D, for example, may require a separate unit with a vice president in charge. A lesser commitment to R&D may be achieved with a director and a small staff.[22]

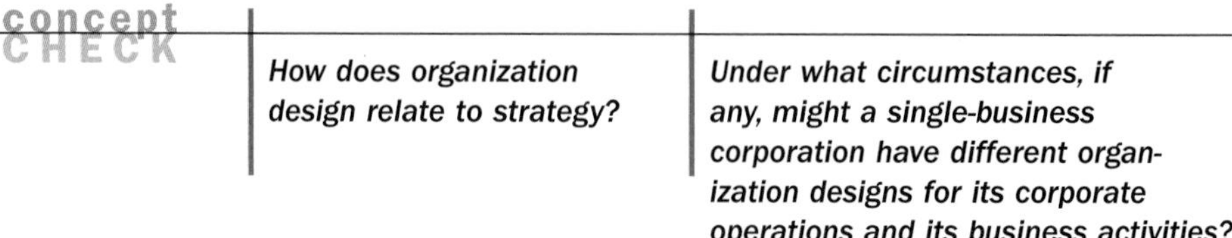

Basic Forms of Organization Design

Because technology, environment, size, life cycle, and strategy can all influence organization design, it should come as no surprise that organizations adopt many different kinds of designs. Most designs, however, fall into one of four basic categories. Others are hybrids based on two or more of the basic forms.

Functional (U-Form) Design

functional (U-form) design Based on the functional approach to departmentalization

The **functional design** is an arrangement based on the functional approach to departmentalization as detailed in Chapter 11. This design has been termed the **U form** (for unitary) by the noted economist Oliver E. Williamson.[23] Under the U-form arrangement, the members and units in the organization are grouped into functional departments such as marketing and production.

For the organization to operate efficiently in this design, there must be considerable coordination across departments. This integration and coordination are most commonly the responsibility of the CEO and members of senior management. Figure 12.1 shows the U-form design applied to the corporate level of a small manufacturing company. In a U-form organization, none of the functional areas can survive without the others. Marketing, for example, needs products from operations to sell and funds from finance to pay for advertising. The WD-40 Company, which makes a popular lubricating oil, and the McIlhenny Company, which makes TABASCO sauce, are both examples of firms that use the U-form design.

In general, this approach shares the basic advantages and disadvantages of functional departmentalization. Thus it allows the organization to staff all important positions with functional experts and facilitates coordination and integration. On the other hand, it also promotes a functional, rather than an organizational, focus and tends to promote centralization. And, as we note in Chapter 11, functionally based designs are most commonly used in small organizations because an individual CEO can easily oversee and coordinate the entire organization. As an organization grows, the CEO finds staying on top of all functional areas increasingly difficult.

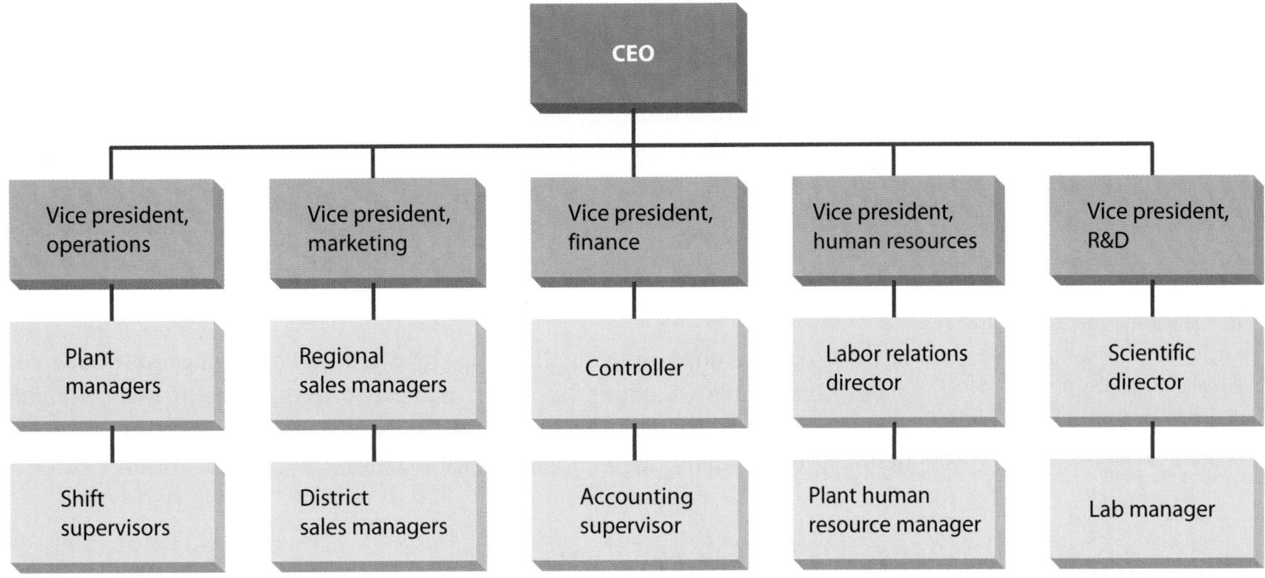

FIGURE 12.1

Functional or U-Form Design for a Small Manufacturing Company

The U-form design is based on functional departmentalization. This small manufacturing firm uses managers at the vice presidential level to coordinate activities within each functional area of the organization. Note that each functional area is dependent on the others.

Conglomerate (H-Form) Design

conglomerate (H-form) design Used by an organization made up of a set of unrelated businesses

Another common form of organization design is the **conglomerate**, or **H-form**, approach.[24] The **conglomerate design** is used by an organization made up of a set of unrelated businesses. Thus the H-form design is essentially a holding company that results from unrelated diversification. (The *H* in this term stands for holding.)

This approach is based loosely on the product form of departmentalization (see Chapter 11). Each business or set of businesses is operated by a general manager who is responsible for its profits or losses, and each general manager functions independently of the others. Samsung Electrics Co., a South Korean firm, uses the H-form design. As illustrated in Figure 12.2, Samsung consists of four business groups. Other firms that use the H-form design include General Electric (aircraft engines, appliances, broadcasting, financial services, lighting products, plastics, and other unrelated businesses) and Tenneco (pipelines, auto parts, shipbuilding, financial services, and other unrelated businesses).

In an H-form organization, a corporate staff usually evaluates the performance of each business, allocates corporate resources across companies, and shapes decisions about buying and selling businesses. The basic shortcoming of the H-form design is the complexity associated with holding diverse and unrelated businesses. Managers usually find comparing and integrating activities across a large number

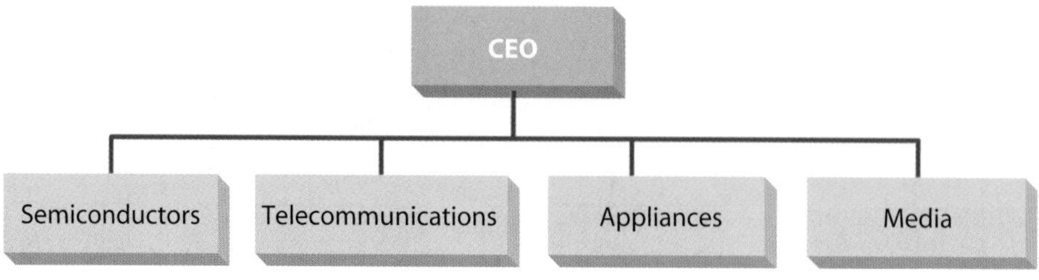

FIGURE 12.2

Conglomerate (H-Form) Design at Samsung

Samsung Electronics Co., a South Korean firm, uses the conglomerate form of organization design. This design, which results from a strategy of unrelated diversification, is a complex one to manage. Managers find that comparing and integrating activities among the dissimilar operations are difficult. Companies may abandon this design for another approach, such as the M-form design.

of diverse operations difficult. Research by Michael Porter suggests that many organizations following this approach achieve only average-to-weak financial performance.[25] Thus, although some U.S. firms are still using the H-form design, many have also abandoned it for other approaches.

Divisional (M-Form) Design

divisional (M-form) design Based on multiple businesses in related areas operating within a larger organizational framework

In the divisional design, which is becoming increasingly popular, a product form of organization is also used; in contrast to the H-form, however, the divisions are related. Thus the **divisional design, or M-form** (for multidivisional), is based on multiple businesses in related areas operating within a larger organizational framework. This design results from a strategy of related diversification.

Some activities are extremely decentralized down to the divisional level; others are centralized at the corporate level.[26] For example, as shown in Figure 12.3, The Limited uses this approach. Each of its divisions is headed by a general manager and operates with reasonable autonomy, but the divisions also coordinate their activities as is appropriate. Other firms that use this approach are the Walt Disney Company (theme parks, movies, and merchandising units, all interrelated) and Hewlett-Packard (computers, printers, scanners, electronic medical equipment, and other electronic instrumentation).

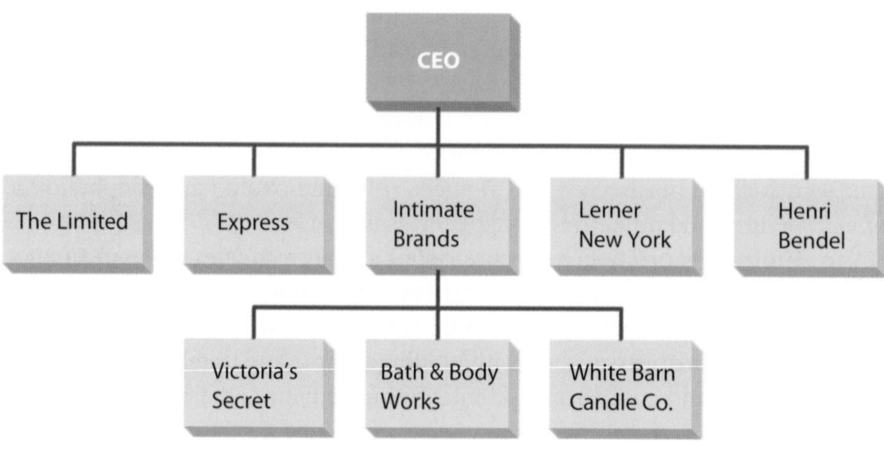

FIGURE 12.3

Multidivisional (M-Form) Design at The Limited

The Limited uses the multidivisional approach to organization design. Although each unit operates with relative autonomy, all units function in the same general market. This design resulted from a strategy of related diversification. Other firms that use M-form designs include PepsiCo and Woolworth Corporation.

The opportunities for coordination and shared resources represent one of the biggest advantages of the M-form design. The Limited's market research and purchasing departments are centralized. Thus a buyer can inspect a manufacturer's entire product line, buy some designs for The Limited chain, others for Express, and still others for Lerner New York. The M-form design's basic objective is to optimize internal competition and cooperation. Healthy competition for resources among divisions can enhance effectiveness, but cooperation should also be promoted. Research suggests that the M-form organization that can achieve and maintain this balance will outperform large U-form and all H-form organizations.[27]

Matrix Design

The **matrix design**, another common approach to organization design, is based on two overlapping bases of departmentalization.[28] The foundation of a matrix is a set of functional departments. A set of product groups, or temporary departments, is then superimposed across the functional departments. Employees in a matrix are simultaneously members of a functional department (such as engineering) and of a project team.

matrix design Based on two overlapping bases of departmentalization

Figure 12.4 shows a basic matrix design. At the top of the organization are functional units headed by vice presidents of engineering, production, finance, and marketing. Each of these managers has several subordinates. Along the side of the organization are a number of positions called *project manager*. Each project manager heads a project group composed of representatives or workers from the functional departments. Note from the figure that a matrix reflects a *multiple-command structure*—any given individual reports to both a functional superior and one or more project managers.

The project groups, or teams, are assigned to designated projects or programs. For example, the company might be developing a new product. Representatives are chosen from each functional area to work as a team on the new product. They also retain membership in the original functional group. At any given time, a person may be a member of several teams as well as a member of a functional group. Ford used this approach in creating its popular Focus automobile. It formed a group called "Team Focus" made up of designers, engineers, production specialists, marketing specialists, and other experts from different areas of the company. This group facilitated getting a very successful product to the market at least a year earlier than would have been possible using Ford's previous approaches.

Martha Stewart also uses a matrix organization for her lifestyle business. The company was first organized broadly into media and merchandising groups, each of which has specific product and product groups. Layered on top of this structure are teams of lifestyle experts organized into groups such as cooking, crafts, weddings, and so forth. Each of these groups is targeted toward specific customer needs, but they work as necessary across all of the product groups. For example, a wedding expert might contribute to an article on wedding planning for a *Martha Stewart Living* magazine, contribute a story idea for a cable television program, and supply content for a Martha Stewart website. This same individual might also help select fabrics suitable for wedding gowns for retailing.[29]

Many other organizations have also used the matrix design. Notable among them are American Cyanamid, Monsanto, NCR, Chase Manhattan Bank, Prudential, General

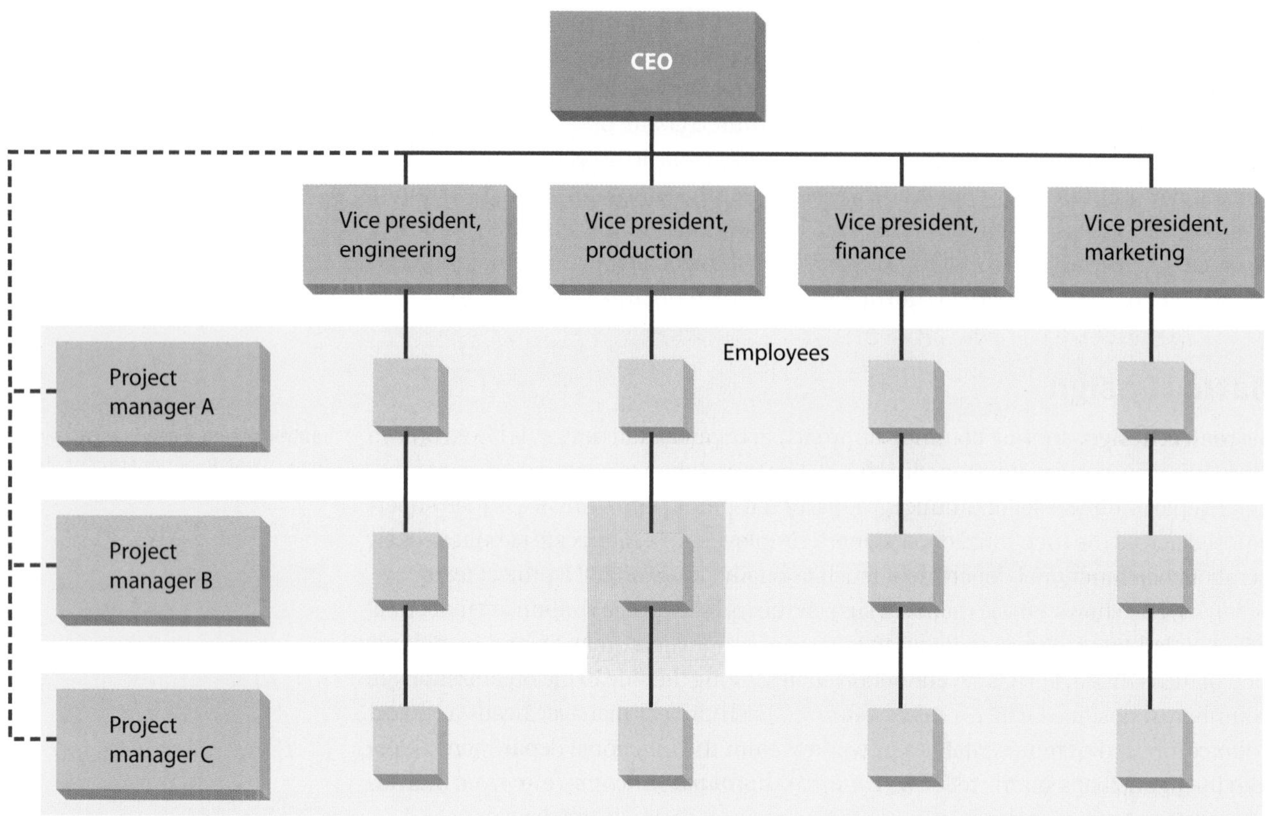

FIGURE 12.4

A Matrix Organization

A matrix organization design is created by superimposing a product form of departmentalization on an existing functional organization. Project managers coordinate teams of employees drawn from different functional departments. Thus a matrix relies on a multiple-command structure.

Motors, and several state and federal government agencies. Some organizations, however, such as Citibank and the Dutch firm Philips, adopted and then dropped the matrix design. Thus it is important to recognize that a matrix design is not always appropriate.

The matrix form of organization design is most often used in one of three situations.[30] First, a matrix may work when there is strong pressure from the environment. For example, intense external competition may dictate the sort of strong marketing thrust that is best spearheaded by a functional department, but the diversity of a company's products may argue for product departments. Second, a matrix may be appropriate when large amounts of information need to be processed. For example, creating lateral relationships by means of a matrix is one effective way to increase the organization's capacity for processing information. Third, the matrix design may work when there is pressure for shared resources. For example, a company with ten product departments may have resources for only three marketing specialists. A matrix design would allow all the departments to share the company's scarce marketing resources.

Both advantages and disadvantages are associated with the matrix design. Researchers have observed six primary advantages of matrix designs. First, they enhance flexibility because teams can be created, redefined, and dissolved as needed. Second, because they assume a major role in decision making, team members are likely to be highly motivated and committed to the organization. Third, employees in a matrix organization have considerable opportunity to learn new skills. A fourth advantage of a matrix design is that it provides an efficient way for the organization to take full advantage of its human resources. Fifth, team members retain membership in their functional unit so that they can serve as a bridge between the functional unit and the team, enhancing cooperation. Sixth, the matrix design gives top management a useful vehicle for decentralization. Once the day-to-day operations have been delegated, top management can devote more attention to areas such as long-range planning.

On the other hand, the matrix design also has some major disadvantages. Employees may be uncertain about reporting relationships, especially if they are simultaneously assigned to a functional manager and to several project managers. To complicate matters, some managers see the matrix as a form of anarchy in which they have unlimited freedom. Another set of problems is associated with the dynamics of group behavior. Groups take longer than individuals to make decisions, may be dominated by one individual, and may compromise too much. They may also get bogged down in discussion and not focus on their primary objectives. Finally, in a matrix, more time may also be required for coordinating task-related activities.[31]

Hybrid Designs

Some organizations use a design that represents a hybrid of two or more of the common forms of organization design.[32] For example, an organization may have five related divisions and one unrelated division, making its design a cross between an M-form and an H-form. Indeed, few companies use a design in its pure form; most firms have one basic organization design as a foundation for managing the business but maintain sufficient flexibility so that temporary or permanent modifications can be made for strategic purposes. Ford, for example, used the matrix approach to design the Taurus and the Mustang, but the company is basically a U-form organization showing signs of moving to an M-form design. As we note earlier, any combination of factors may dictate the appropriate form of design for any particular company.

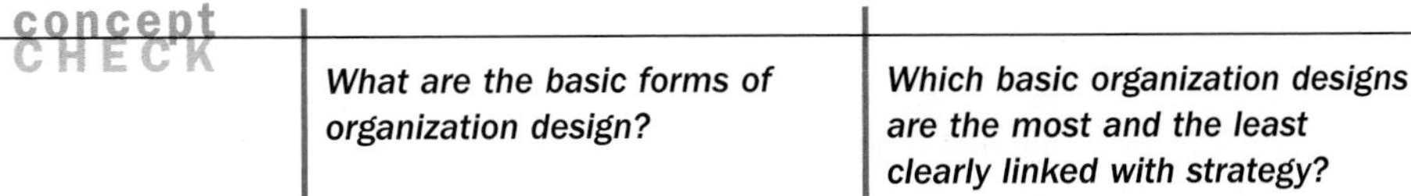

Emerging Issues in Organization Design

Finally, in today's complex and ever-changing environment, it should come as no surprise that managers continue to explore and experiment with new forms of organization design. Many organizations today are creating designs for themselves that maximize their ability to adapt to changing circumstances and to a changing environment. They try to accomplish this by not becoming too compartmentalized or too rigid. As we note earlier, bureaucratic organizations are hard to change, slow, and inflexible. To avoid these problems, then, organizations can try to be as different from bureaucracies as possible—relatively few rules, general job descriptions, and so forth. This final section highlights some of the more important emerging issues.[33]

The Team Organization

team organization An approach to organization design that relies almost exclusively on project-type teams, with little or no underlying functional hierarchy

Some organizations today are using the **team organization**, an approach to organization design that relies almost exclusively on project-type teams, with little or no underlying functional hierarchy. Within such an organization, people float from project to project as necessitated by their skills and the demands of those projects. At Cypress Semiconductor, T. J. Rodgers refuses to allow the organization to grow so large that it cannot function this way. Whenever a unit or group starts getting too large, he simply splits it into smaller units. Consequently, all units within the organization are small. This allows them to change direction, explore new ideas, and try new methods without dealing with a rigid bureaucratic organizational context. Although few organizations have actually reached this level of adaptability, Apple Computer and Xerox are among those moving toward it.[34]

virtual organization One that has little or no formal structure

The Virtual Organization

Closely related to the team organization is the virtual organization. A **virtual organization** is one that has little or no formal structure. Such an organization typically has only a handful of permanent employees and a very small staff and administrative headquarters facility. As the needs of the organization change, its managers bring in temporary workers, lease facilities, and outsource basic support services to meet the demands of each unique situation. As the situation changes, the temporary workforce changes in parallel, with some people leaving the organization and others entering. Facilities and the services subcontracted to others change as well. Thus the organization exists only in response to its needs. And, increasingly, virtual organizations are conducting most—if not all—of their business online.[35]

For example, Global Research Consortium is a virtual organization. GRC offers research and consulting services to firms doing business in Asia. As clients request various services, GRC's staff of three permanent employees subcontracts the work to an appropriate set of several dozen independent consultants and researchers with whom it has relationships. At any given time, therefore, GRC may have several projects under way and twenty or thirty people working on projects. As the projects change, so, too, does the composition of the organization.

The virtual organization represents a new and growing form of organization that allows for considerable flexibility. Consider, for instance, this teacher in an "empty" classroom. During the SARS outbreak in Southeast Asia in 2003 many schools were closed. But in some areas, like Hong Kong, teachers like Chan Cheong-chap were able to establish virtual classrooms and carry on with their lesson plans with their students via distance technology.

The Learning Organization

Another recent approach to organization design is the so-called learning organization. Organizations that adopt this approach work to integrate continuous improvement with continuous employee learning and development. Specifically, a **learning organization** is one that works to facilitate the lifelong learning and personal development of all of its employees while continually transforming itself to respond to changing demands and needs.[36]

learning organization One that works to facilitate the lifelong learning and personal development of all of its employees while continually transforming itself to respond to changing demands and needs

Although managers might approach the concept of a learning organization from a variety of perspectives, improved quality, continuous improvement, and performance measurement are frequent goals. The idea is that the most consistent and logical strategy for achieving continuous improvement is by constantly upgrading employee talent, skill, and knowledge. For example, if each employee in an organization learns one new thing each day and can translate that knowledge into work-related practice, continuous improvement will logically follow. Indeed, organizations that wholeheartedly embrace this approach believe that only through constant learning by employees can continuous improvement really occur.

In recent years, many different organizations have implemented this approach. For example, Shell Oil recently purchased an executive conference center north of its headquarters in Houston. The center boasts state-of-the-art classrooms and instructional technology, lodging facilities, a restaurant, and recreational amenities such as a golf course, swimming pool, and tennis courts. Line managers at the firm rotate through the Shell Learning Center, as the facility has been renamed, and serve as teaching faculty. Such teaching assignments last anywhere from a few days to several months. At the same time, all Shell employees routinely attend training programs, seminars, and related activities, all the while learning the latest information that they need to contribute more effectively to the firm. Recent seminar topics have ranged from time management, to implications of the Americans with Disabilities Act, to balancing work and family demands, to international trade theory.

Issues in International Organization Design

Another emerging issue in organization design is the trend toward the internationalization of business. As we discuss in Chapter 5, most businesses today interact with suppliers, customers, or competitors (or all three) from other countries. The relevant issue for organization design is how to design the firm to most effectively deal with international forces and compete in global markets. For example, consider a moderate-size company that has just decided to "go international." Should it set up an international division, retain its current structure and establish an international operating group, or make its international operations an autonomous subunit?[37]

Firms that want to expand internationally often find it necessary to alter their organization design as they grow. For example, Invacare is a growing manufacturer of wheelchairs and other equipment for disabled workers. But because of different working conditions and government regulations in different countries, Invacare has different units for designing and constructing its wheelchairs bound for such countries as Germany, England, and France.

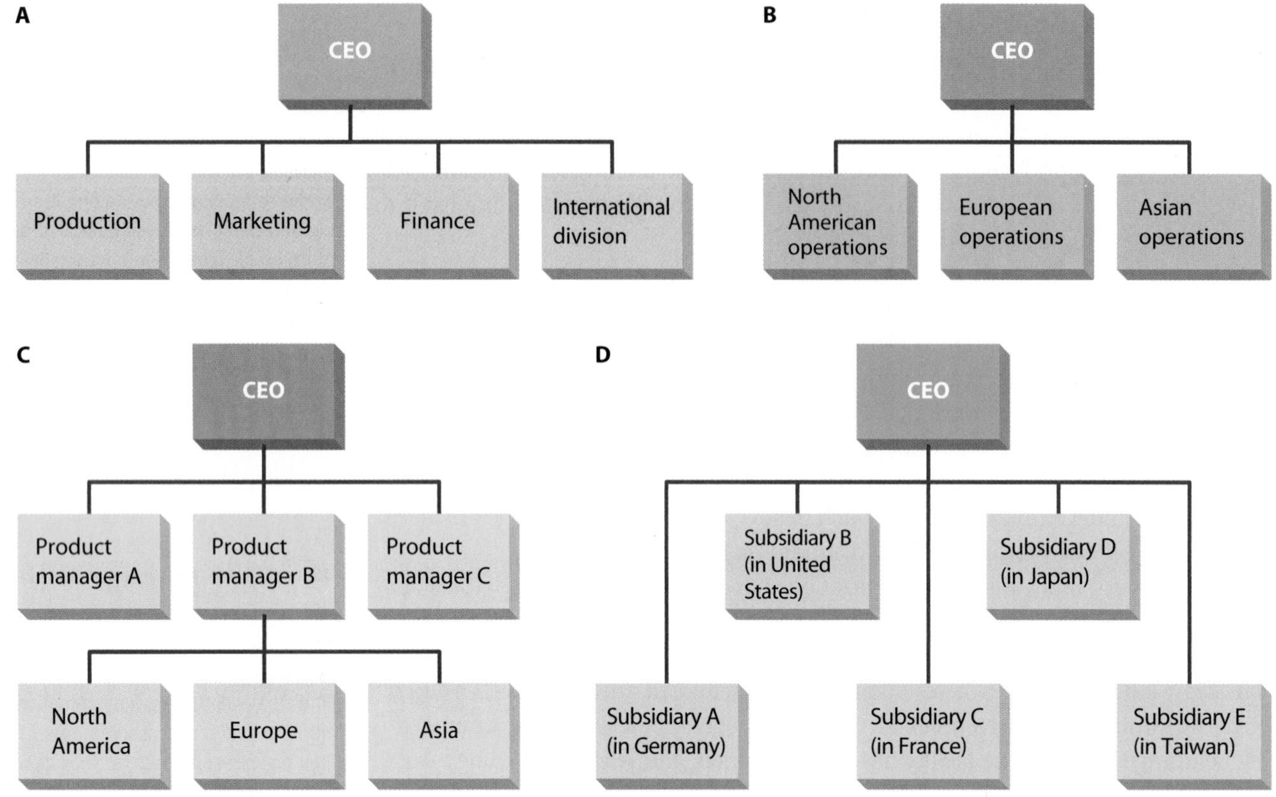

FIGURE 12.5

Common Organization Designs for International Organizations

Companies that compete in international markets must create an organization design that fits their own unique circumstances. These four general designs are representative of what many international organizations use. Each is derived from one of the basic forms of organization design.

Figure 12.5 illustrates four of the most common approaches to organization design used for international purposes. The design shown in A is the simplest, relying on a separate international division. Levi Strauss & Co. uses this approach. The design shown in B, used by Ford Motor Company, is an extension of location departmentalization to international settings. An extension of product departmentalization, with each product manager being responsible for all product-related activities regardless of location, is shown in C. Finally, the design shown in D, most typical of larger multinational corporations, is an extension of the multidivisional structure with branches located in various foreign markets. Nestlé and Unilever use this type of design.

concept CHECK

What is a team organization?	*Do you think it is possible for a one-person operation, operating as a virtual organization, to grow large enough to compete with large businesses? Why or why not?*

Summary of Key Points

ACE self-test

business.college.hmco.com/students

Organization design is the overall set of structural elements and the relationships among those elements used to manage the total organization. Two early universal models of organization design were the bureaucratic model and the behavioral model. These models attempted to prescribe how all organizations should be designed.

The situational view of organization design is based on the assumption that the optimal organization design is a function of situational factors. Four important situational factors are technology, environment, size, and organizational life cycle. Each of these factors plays a role in determining how an organization should be designed.

An organization's strategy also helps shape its design. In various ways, corporate- and business-level strategies both affect organization design. Basic organizational functions like marketing and finance also play a role in shaping design.

Many organizations today adopt one of four basic organization designs: functional (U-form), conglomerate (H-form), divisional (M-form), or matrix. Other organizations use a hybrid design derived from two or more of these basic designs.

Four emerging issues in organization design are the team organization, the virtual organization, the learning organization, and how international businesses should be designed.

Discussion Questions

Questions for Review

1. Describe the three forms of core technology. Tell about the differences in organizational structure that occur in firms with each of the three types.
2. List the changes that occur as an organization grows in size. List the changes that occur as an organization ages over time. Are the two lists the same? Explain any differences you find.
3. Describe the basic forms of organization design. What are the advantages and disadvantages of each?
4. Compare and contrast the matrix organization and the team organization, telling about any similarities and differences.

Questions for Analysis

5. The business world today is increasingly complex and variable, in virtually every country and industry. Thus organizations must become more organic. What are some of the outcomes that companies will experience as they become more organic and less mechanistic? Be sure to include both positive and negative outcomes.
6. Each of the organization designs is appropriate for some firms but not for others. Describe the characteristics that a firm using the U form should have. Then do the same for the H-form, the M-form, and the matrix design. For each item, explain the relationship between that set of characteristics and the choice of organization design.

7. What are the benefits of using the learning organization approach to design? Now consider that, in order to learn, organizations must be willing to tolerate many mistakes, because it is only through the effort of understanding mistakes that learning can occur. With this statement in mind, what are some of the potential problems with the use of the learning organization approach?

Questions for Application

8. Consider an organization (such as your workplace, a club or society, a sorority or fraternity, a church, and so on) of which you are a member. Describe some structural elements of that organization that reflect the bureaucratic model. Describe some elements that reflect the behavioral model. In your opinion, is that organization more bureaucratic or more behavioral in its structure? Why?
9. Use the Internet or library to investigate a corporation's strategy. Then use the Internet or library to obtain a description of the firm's organization design. Can you identify any links between the company's strategy and structure? Share your findings with the class.
10. What form of organization does your university or college use? What form does your city or town government use? What form do other organizations with which you are familiar use? What similarities and differences do you see? Explain your answers.

BUILDING EFFECTIVE conceptual SKILLS

business.college.hmco.com/students

Exercise Overview

Conceptual skills refer to a person's abilities to think in the abstract. Conceptual skills are developed in this exercise, as you practice analyzing organizational structures.

Exercise Background

Looking at an organization chart allows one to understand the company's structure, such as its distribution of authority, its divisions, its levels of hierarchy, its reporting relationships, and more. The reverse is also true; that is, when one understands the elements of a company's structure, an organization chart can be drawn that reflects that structure. In this exercise, you will use the Internet to research a firm's structure, then draw the appropriate organization chart.

Exercise Task

1. Alone or with a partner, use the Internet to research a publicly traded U.S. firm in which you are interested. Gather information about the firm that will help you understand its structure. For example, if you researched Ford Motor Company, you would find information about different types of vehicles, different regions where Ford products are sold, different functions that are performed at Ford, and so on. (*Hint:* The firm's annual report is usually available online and usually contains a great deal of helpful information, particularly in the section that contains an editorial message from the chairman or CEO and in the section that summarizes financial information. "Segment" data also point to divisional structure in many cases.)
2. Draw an appropriate organization structure, based on your research.
3. Share your results with another group or with the class, justifying your decisions.

BUILDING EFFECTIVE technical SKILLS

Exercise Overview

Technical skills are the skills necessary to accomplish or understand the specific work being done in an organization. This exercise asks you to develop technical skills related to understanding the impact of an organization's strategy on its structure.

Exercise Background

Assume that you are a manager of a firm that has developed a new, innovative system of personal transportation, such as the Segway HT. (If you are not familiar with the Segway, visit the website at www.segway.com and learn about the product.)

Exercise Task

Using the information about strategy given in each question below and your knowledge of the Segway product, choose the appropriate form of organization structure.

1. What would be the most appropriate organization structure if Segway's corporate-level strategy were to continue to produce a limited line of very similar products for sale in the United States?
2. What would be the most appropriate organization structure if Segway's corporate-level strategy were to continue to produce only its original product, but to sell it in Asia and Europe as well as North America?
3. What would be the most appropriate organization structure if Segway's corporate-level strategy were to move into related areas, using the innovations developed for the Segway to help design several other innovative products?
4. What would be the most appropriate organization structure if Segway's corporate-level strategy were to use its expertise in personal ground transportation to move into other areas, such as personal air or personal water transport?
5. What would be the most appropriate organization structure if Segway's corporate-level strategy were to use the funds generated by Segway sales to finance moves into several unrelated industries?
6. For each of the five strategies listed above, tell how that strategy influenced your choice of organization design.

BUILDING EFFECTIVE decision-making SKILLS

Exercise Overview

Decision-making skills refer to the manager's ability to recognize and define problems and opportunities correctly and then to select an appropriate course of action to solve problems and capitalize on opportunities. The purpose of this exercise is to give you insights into how managers must make decisions within the context of creating an organization design.

Exercise Background

Assume that you have decided to open a casual sportswear business in your local community. Your products will be athletic caps, shirts, shorts, and sweats emblazoned with the logos of your college and local high schools. You have a talented designer and have developed some ideas that will make your products unique and very popular. You have also inherited enough money to get your business up and running and to cover about one year of living expenses (in other words, you do not need to pay yourself a salary).

You intend to buy sportswear in various styles and sizes from other suppliers. Your firm will then use silkscreen processes to add the logos and other decorative touches to the products. Local clothing store owners have seen samples of your products and have indicated a keen interest in selling them. You know, however, that you will still need to service accounts and keep your customers happy.

At the present time, you are trying to determine how many people you need to get your business going and how to group them most effectively into an organization. You realize that you can start out quite small and then expand as sales warrant. However, you also worry that, if you are continually adding people and rearranging your organization, confusion and inefficiency may result.

Exercise Task

1. Under each of the scenarios below, decide how best to design your organization. Sketch a basic organization chart to show your thoughts.
   - *Scenario 1*—You will sell the products yourself, and you intend to start with a workforce of five people.
   - *Scenario 2*—You intend to oversee production yourself and to start with a workforce of nine people.
   - *Scenario 3*—You do not intend to handle any one function yourself but will instead oversee the entire operation, and you intend to start with a workforce of fifteen people.
2. Form small groups of four to five people each. Compare your various organization charts, focusing on similarities and differences.
3. Working in the same group, assume that five years have passed and that your business has been a big success. You have a large plant for making your products, and you are shipping them to fifteen states. You employ almost five hundred people. Create an organization design that you think fits this organization best.

Follow up Questions

1. How clear or ambiguous were the decisions about organization design?
2. What are your thoughts about starting out too large to maintain stability, as opposed to starting small and then growing?
3. What basic factors did you consider in choosing a design?

CHAPTER CLOSING case

Customers Say "Yum!"

> *"There's a lot to fix. This isn't something that will change overnight."*
>
> – David C. Novak, CEO and president, Yum! Brands, Inc.*

Mom likes roast chicken, Dad prefers nachos, and Junior will eat only pepperoni pizza. Now, thanks to a restructuring of Yum! Brands restaurants, everybody can eat together. Yum! developed the concept of putting more than one brand together at a single location. Co-location of multiple restaurants, called "multibranding," has proven to be immensely popular, increasing store revenues by 25 percent or more. But the tactic is just the latest in a long line of structural changes in the ever-evolving fast-food business.

Typical fast-food restaurants offer just one type of food, such as burgers or sub sandwiches. To attract customers in a slow-growing industry, fast-food chains tried to offer new products, such as the McPizza. Yet, according to David C. Novak, CEO and president of Yum!, "every time we've tried to venture into a new category, we've failed because we've lacked credibility. Nobody is waiting with bated breath for a Taco Bell burger." Another growth tactic calls for fast-food chains to add new brands. For example, McDonald's bought Boston Market, Donato's, and Chipotle Mexican Grill. Wendy's acquired Baja Fresh Mexican Grill. Every chain is also trying a third strategy—upgrading existing restaurants, with fresher ingredients, more cooked-to-order items, and upscale ambience. The new type of restaurant is called "fast-casual." "[Baby] boomers want more and will pay for it," claims Charles Rawley, Yum!'s chief development officer.

Multibranding offers a fourth option for growth. Yum! owns Pizza Hut, Taco Bell, Kentucky Fried Chicken (KFC), A&W Restaurants, and Long John Silver's. The mix of businesses increases market share, but Yum! has found a way to wring even more value from the diverse chains. The chain has nearly two thousand stores that combine two or more brands, such as KFC and Taco Bell. At a time when the fast-food industry on the whole is averaging just 2 percent annual growth in sales, Yum!'s multibranded stores can see a 25 percent increase.

Multibranding is not the first structural innovation made by fast-food firms, which have a long history of changes in structure and ownership. For example, each of Yum!'s five brands began as an independently owned, entrepreneurial start-up. Pizza Hut was begun by two brothers, college students at Wichita State University. From humble beginnings, Pizza Hut grew to become the number-one pizza restaurant in the world by selling franchises and expanding internationally. After becoming a publicly traded company in the 1960s, Pizza Hut was acquired by PepsiCo in 1977. World War II veteran Glen Bell opened the first Taco Bell in 1962. Taco Bell also developed many domestic and international franchises. When Bell was ready to retire in 1978, he sold Taco Bell to PepsiCo. Harland Sanders, founder of KFC, began offering franchises in 1952, built up the firm's international operations, and sold out in 1964. The company was owned by distiller Heublein, tobacco conglomerate R.J. Reynolds, and others before its sale to PepsiCo in 1986.

PepsiCo's purchase of Pizza Hut, Taco Bell, and KFC was designed to give the firm an edge over competitor Coca-Cola. The firm was looking to diversify beyond the stagnant soft-drink market and believed that the food industry would make a good complement for the beverage industry. Soon, however, PepsiCo realized that its competencies in marketing did not compensate for its weaknesses in customer service and food products. After years of disappointing sales and synergy that never materialized, PepsiCo spun off the three businesses into a separate firm, called Tricon Global Restaurants, in 1997.

In 2002 Tricon changed its name to Yum! Brands and purchased A&W. A&W grew from a single California root beer stand in 1919 to a nationwide chain of restaurants by the 1950s. After several changes of ownership, in 1999 the chain bought Long John Silver's (founded in 1969). Yum! is continuing with the franchising and international growth strategies. For 2003 Yum! predicts gross profit margins of well over 10 percent, with international sales accounting for 7 percent and new domestic franchises for 4 percent.

Imitation is the sincerest form of flattery, and others are copying Yum!'s multibranding structure. Allied Domecq Quick Service Restaurants has taken the multibranding concept one step further, combining Dunkin' Donuts, Togo's sandwich shops, and Baskin-Robbins. This allows a store to maintain consistent sales throughout the day, from early-morning pastries to late-night desserts.

Yum! has probably reached the logical limit of adding new brands, with the possible exception of a burger or sandwich chain, segments in which Yum! is not currently competing. Years of conducting business as usual had led to stagnation, and CEO Novak concedes, "There's a lot to fix. This isn't something that will change overnight." However, Yum!'s structure, including upgrades, multibranding, global growth, and development of fast-casual restaurants is working, for now.

Case Questions

1. Examine the development of the fast-food industry, including the impact that core technology, environment, organizational size, and organizational life cycle have had on organizational structure.
2. What seems to be Yum!'s current corporate structure?
3. Look at your answer to question 2. How has Yum!'s corporate-level strategy influenced that structure?

Case References

"About A&W," A&W Restaurants website, www.awrestaurants.com on January 24, 2003; "About KFC," Kentucky Fried Chicken website, www.kfc.com on January 26, 2003; "About Yum! Brands," Yum! Brands, Inc., website, www.yum.com on January 26, 2003; Gerry Khermouch, "Tricon's Fast-Food Smorgasbord," *BusinessWeek*, February 11, 2002, www.businessweek.com on January 16, 2003; "History," Taco Bell website, www.tacobell.com on January 24, 2003; "Long John Silver's," Long John Silver's website, www.ljsilvers.com on January 24, 2003; Melanie Wells, "Happier Meals," *Forbes*, January 8, 2003, story.news.yahoo.com on January 16, 2003 (*quote); "The Pizza Hut Story," Pizza Hut website, www.pizzahut.com on January 24, 2003.

Chapter Notes

1. Arlyn Tobias Gajilan, "An Education Revolution," *Fortune*, November 29, 2000, www.fortune.com on January 22, 2003 (*quote); James Robinson, "Online Learning: Ready or Not, Here It Comes," *Tomorrow's Professor*, February 9, 2000, learninglab.stanford.edu on January 23, 2003; Kenneth N. Gilpin, "Turning a Profit with Higher Education," *New York Times*, October 20, 2002, p. BU7; "The Nation's Leading Online University," University of Phoenix Online website, www.uoponline.com on January 22, 2003; William C. Symonds, "Giving It the Old Online Try," *BusinessWeek*, December 3, 2001, www.businessweek.com on January 22, 2003.
2. See Gareth Jones, *Organization Theory*, 4th ed. (Upper Saddle River, NJ: Prentice-Hall, 2004).
3. David Lei and John Slocum, "Organization Designs to Renew Competitive Advantage," *Organizational Dynamics*, 2002, vol. 31, no. 1, pp. 1–18.
4. Max Weber, *Theory of Social and Economic Organizations*, trans. T. Parsons (New York: Free Press, 1947).
5. Paul Jarley, Jack Fiorito, and John Thomas Delany, "A Structural Contingency Approach to Bureaucracy and Democracy in U.S. National Unions," *Academy of Management Journal*, 1997, vol. 40, no. 4, pp. 831–861.
6. Rensis Likert, *New Patterns in Management* (New York: McGraw-Hill, 1961), and *The Human Organization* (New York: McGraw-Hill, 1967).
7. William F. Dowling, "At General Motors: System 4 Builds Performance and Profits," *Organizational Dynamics*, Winter 1975, pp. 23–28.
8. Jones, *Organization Theory*. See also "The Great Transformation," *BusinessWeek*, August 28, 2000, pp. 84–99.
9. Joan Woodward, *Industrial Organization: Theory and Practice* (London: Oxford University Press, 1965).
10. Joan Woodward, *Management and Technology, Problems of Progress Industry*, no. 3 (London: Her Majesty's Stationery Office, 1958).
11. William Bridges, "The End of the Job," *Fortune*, September 19, 1994, pp. 62–74.
12. Tom Burns and G. M. Stalker, *The Management of Innovation* (London: Tavistock, 1961).
13. Paul R. Lawrence and Jay W. Lorsch, *Organization and Environment* (Homewood, Ill.: Irwin, 1967).
14. Edward E. Lawler III, "Rethinking Organization Size," *Organizational Dynamics*, Autumn 1997, pp. 24–33. See also Tom Brown, "How Big Is Too Big?" *Across the Board*, July–August 1999, pp. 14–20.

15. Derek S. Pugh and David J. Hickson, *Organization Structure in Its Context: The Aston Program I* (Lexington, Mass.: D. C. Heath, 1976).
16. "Can Wal-Mart Get Any Bigger?" *Time*, January 13, 2003, pp. 38–43.
17. Robert H. Miles and Associates, *The Organizational Life Cycle* (San Francisco: Jossey-Bass, 1980). See also "Is Your Company Too Big?" *BusinessWeek*, March 27, 1989, pp. 84–94.
18. Douglas Baker and John Cullen, "Administrative Reorganization and Configurational Context: The Contingent Effects of Age, Size, and Change in Size," *Academy of Management Journal*, 1993, vol. 36, no. 6, pp. 1251–1277. See also Kevin Crowston, "A Coordination Theory Approach to Organizational Process Design," *Organization Science*, March–April 1997, pp. 157–168.
19. See Charles W. L. Hill and Gareth Jones, *Strategic Management: An Integrated Approach*, 6th ed. (Boston: Houghton Mifflin Co., 2004).
20. See "The Corporate Ecosystem," *BusinessWeek*, August 28, 2000, pp. 166–197.
21. Richard D'Aveni and David Ravenscraft, "Economies of Integration Versus Bureaucratic Costs: Does Vertical Integration Improve Performance?" *Academy of Management Journal*, 1994, vol. 37, no. 5, pp. 1167–1206.
22. Gerardine DeSanctis, Jeffrey Glass, and Ingrid Morris Ensing, "Organizational Designs for R&D," *Academy of Management Executive*, 2002, vol. 16, no. 2, pp. 55–64.
23. Oliver E. Williamson, *Markets and Hierarchies* (New York: Free Press, 1975).
24. Williamson, *Markets and Hierarchies.*
25. Michael E. Porter, "From Competitive Advantage to Corporate Strategy," *Harvard Business Review*, May–June 1987, pp. 43–59.
26. Williamson, *Markets and Hierarchies.*
27. Jay B. Barney and William G. Ouchi (eds.), *Organizational Economics* (San Francisco: Jossey-Bass, 1986); Robert E. Hoskisson, "Multidivisional Structure and Performance: The Contingency of Diversification Strategy," *Academy of Management Journal*, December 1987, pp. 625–644. See also Bruce Lamont, Robert Williams, and James Hoffman, "Performance During 'M-Form' Reorganization and Recovery Time: The Effects of Prior Strategy and Implementation Speed," *Academy of Management Journal*, 1994, vol. 37, no. 1, pp. 153–166.
28. Stanley M. Davis and Paul R. Lawrence, *Matrix* (Reading, Mass.: Addison-Wesley, 1977).
29. "Martha, Inc.," *BusinessWeek*, January 17, 2000, pp. 63–72.
30. Davis and Lawrence, *Matrix.*
31. See Lawton Burns and Douglas Wholey, "Adoption and Abandonment of Matrix Management Programs: Effects of Organizational Characteristics and Interorganizational Networks," *Academy of Management Journal*, vol. 36, no. 1, pp. 106–138.
32. See Michael Hammer and Steven Stanton, "How Process Enterprises Really Work," *Harvard Business Review*, November–December 1999, pp. 108–118.
33. Raymond E. Miles, Charles C. Snow, John A. Mathews, Grant Miles, and Henry J. Coleman, Jr., "Organizing in the Knowledge Age: Anticipating the Cellular Form," *Academy of Management Executive*, November 1997, pp. 7–24.
34. "The Horizontal Corporation," *BusinessWeek*, December 20, 1993, pp. 76–81; Shawn Tully, "The Modular Corporation," *Fortune*, February 8, 1993, pp. 106–114.
35. "Management by Web," *BusinessWeek*, August 28, 2000, pp. 84–96.
36. Peter Senge, *The Fifth Discipline* (New York: Free Press, 1993). See also David Lei, John W. Slocum, and Robert A. Pitts, "Designing Organizations for Competitive Advantage: The Power of Unlearning and Learning," *Organizational Dynamics*, Winter 1999, pp. 24–35.
37. See William G. Egelhoff, "Strategy and Structure in Multinational Corporations: A Revision of the Stopford and Wells Model," *Strategic Management Journal*, vol. 9, 1988, pp. 1–14, for a recent discussion of these issues. See also Ricky W. Griffin and Michael Pustay, *International Business: A Managerial Perspective*, 4th ed. (Upper Saddle River, NJ: Prentice-Hall, 2004).

13

Managing Organization Change and Innovation

CHAPTER OUTLINE

The Nature of Organization Change
- Forces for Change
- Planned Versus Reactive Change

Managing Change in Organizations
- Steps in the Change Process
- Understanding Resistance to Change
- Overcoming Resistance to Change
- Participation

Areas of Organization Change
- Changing Organization Structure and Design
- Changing Technology and Operations
- Changing People, Attitudes, and Behaviors
- Changing Business Processes
- Organization Development

Organizational Innovation
- The Innovation Process
- Forms of Innovation
- The Failure to Innovate
- Promoting Innovation in Organizations

LEARNING OBJECTIVES

After studying this chapter, you should be able to:

1 ***Describe the nature of organization change, including forces for change and planned versus reactive change.***

OPENING INCIDENT

"*Conservative, wealthy, respectable but outdated suitor seeks younger, energetic, modern partner.*" A personals ad? No—this is a description of the recent "marriage" between venerable retailer Sears, Roebuck and Co., and online and catalog e-tailer Lands' End. Sears, which has struggled with stagnant sales in recent years, announced the acquisition of Lands' End in May 2002, hoping to revitalize its leadership of the fiercely competitive retailing industry.

Sears, founded in 1886, was for decades an important store for rural customers. Over the years, Sears added retail stores for city shoppers and also was at the forefront of private-label branding, creating the DieHard, Kenmore, and Craftsman brands. Today, Sears has no catalogue operations. It is also one of the last of the traditional department stores, providing everything from lawn mowers to wedding gowns to auto repair. Sears enjoys an outstanding reputation for its appliances, tools, and other "hard" goods, but its "soft" goods are seen as unstylish and poor quality. Customers seeking lower-priced clothing prefer Target, Kohl's, or Wal-Mart. Sears' major ad campaign, "Come see the softer side of Sears," and store upgrades did not increase sales of soft goods. In fact, apparel sales fell for seventeen straight months.

2

Discuss the steps in organization change and how to manage resistance to change.

3

Identify and describe major areas of organization change and discuss the assumptions, techniques, and effectiveness of organization development.

4

Describe the innovation process, forms of innovation, the failure to innovate, and how organizations can promote innovation.

"The transaction could bring a breath of fresh air to Sears' apparel operations."

—Filippe Goossens, retail industry analyst, Credit Suisse First Boston

David Dyer (right), CEO of Lands' End, shakes hands with Alan Lacy, his counterpart at Sears, as they announce that the catalog retailer has been purchased by the retailing giant.

Lands' End has some things in common with Sears. The firm began in 1963 as a mail-order-only retailer, mimicking Sears' early strategy. Tom Filline, a retired Sears executive, helped Lands' End develop its efficient mail-order operations. The firm also quickly established a reputation for selling clothing and housewares that are sturdy and reliable, echoing Sears' reputation in hard goods. Finally, Lands' End has strict quality standards and tests products at its in-house facility, a practice initiated by Sears at the turn of the century.

In three significant ways, however, Lands' End and Sears are quite different. First, Lands' End was a pioneer in online technology, creating an early online catalogue. "We were one of the first companies to recognize that selling online was not an end in itself, but another channel in a multichannel sales environment," says Lands' End spokesperson Emily C. Leuthner. Second, although Sears failed to master the apparel industry, Lands' End clearly hit on a winning formula. It offers timeless designs and high-quality materials and workmanship. It appeals to women in the thirty-five- to fifty-four-year-old category, the top spenders on apparel. Third, although Lands' End has grown, it remains a direct merchant, not opening any retail outlets. The firm runs all of its operations out of its rural Dodgeville, Wisconsin, headquarters. The enforced closeness led to the development of a unique, cohesive, and high-achieving culture, unlike Sears' bureaucratic and impersonal atmosphere. As a result, Lands' End has been named to *Fortune*'s new "Best Companies to Work For" list.

The acquisition is called "bricks and clicks," because it combines a traditional bricks-and-mortar retailer with an online e-tailer. Sears announced that it will carry Lands' End apparel in its stores, rolling out the concept in a dozen locations. Lands' End contributes its skill in selling upscale soft goods and its online expertise. "The transaction could bring a breath of fresh air to Sears' apparel operations," declares analyst Filippe Goossens. Sears brings to the table capabilities in managing stores, which can introduce Lands' End goods to a wider market.

It sounds like a marriage made in heaven, but there are some concerns. One is the two firms' different target customers. Will Lands' End's typical customers, with annual income over $100,000, shop at Sears, where typical customers earn less than $50,000? The average Lands' End item costs $27, versus $13 at Sears. Can more price conscious customers afford higher prices? Lands' End customers may switch to shopping at Sears, causing online sales to drop. The biggest challenge may be simply to blend both firms' strengths without diluting them. Analyst Kevin Murphy says, "Sears must maintain the distinctiveness of the Lands' End brand and the quality of service that Lands' End customers are used to."

Industry analyst Linda Kristiansen is optimistic, saying, "This acquisition significantly alters our previously negative view of the prospects for Sears' apparel business." Her optimism has been borne out by recent sales results. In a holiday season that showed declining sales at most stores, Sears' sales in December 2002 were 2.4 percent higher than in December 2001. Sales at stores that carried Lands' End goods grew more than those that did not. Sears CEO Alan Lacy claims, "While it is way too early to declare victory on our Lands' End strategy, it is a great beginning." Change will come slowly, but if the two firms can share their abilities, Sears can regain some of its former glory as an icon of American retailing.[1]

Managers at Sears and Lands' End have had to grapple with something all managers must eventually confront: the need for change. Sears, especially, was in dire need of an infusion of energy and opportunity, and Lands' End seems like the perfect tonic. And, for Lands' End, becoming a part of Sears introduces it to a whole new customer base and gives it the financial base to continue to grow, expand into new markets, and develop new distribution and marketing options. In short, both firms are changing in dramatic ways.

Understanding when and how to implement change is a vital part of management. This chapter describes how organizations manage change. We first examine the nature of organization change and identify the basic issues of managing change. We then identify and describe major areas of change, including business process change, a major type of change undertaken by many firms recently. We then examine organization development and conclude by discussing a related area, organizational innovation.

The Nature of Organization Change

organization change Any substantive modification to some part of the organization

Organization change is any substantive modification to some part of the organization.[2] Thus change can involve virtually any aspect of an organization: work schedules, bases for departmentalization, span of management, machinery, organization design, people themselves, and so on. It is important to keep in mind that any change in an organization may have effects extending beyond the actual area where the change is implemented. For example, when Northrop Grumman recently installed a new automated production system at one of its plants, employees were trained to operate new equipment, the compensation system was adjusted to reflect new skill levels, the span of management for supervisors was altered, and several related jobs were redesigned. Selection criteria for new employees were also changed, and a new quality control system was installed.[3] In addition, it is quite common for multiple organization change activities to be going on simultaneously.[4]

Forces for Change

Why do organizations find change necessary? The basic reason is that something relevant to the organization either has changed or is likely to change in the foreseeable future. The organization therefore may have little choice but to change as well. Indeed, a primary reason for the problems that organizations often face is failure to anticipate or respond properly to changing circumstances. The forces that compel change may be external or internal to the organization.[5]

External Forces External forces for change derive from the organization's general and task environments. For example, two energy crises, an aggressive Japanese automobile industry, floating currency exchange rates, and floating international interest rates—all manifestations of the international dimension of the general environment—profoundly influenced U.S. automobile companies. New rules of production and competition forced them to dramatically alter the way they do business. In the political area, new laws, court decisions, and regulations affect organizations. The technological dimension may yield new production techniques that the organization needs to explore. The economic dimension is affected by inflation, the cost of living, and money supplies. The sociocultural dimension, reflecting societal values, determines what kinds of products or services will be accepted in the market. *The Business of Ethics* discusses how BP changed its strategic orientation in response to external forces.

Because of its proximity to the organization, the task environment is an even more powerful force for change. Competitors influence an organization through their price structures and product lines. When Dell lowers the prices it charges for computers, Gateway may have little choice but to follow suit. Because customers determine what products can be sold at what prices, organizations must be concerned with consumer tastes and preferences. Suppliers affect organizations by raising or lowering prices or changing product lines. Regulators can have dramatic effects on an organization. For example, if OSHA rules that a particular production process is dangerous to workers, it can force a firm to close a plant until it meets higher safety standards. Unions can force change when they negotiate for higher wages or go on strike.[6]

There are a variety of forces that can create a need for change, some external and some internal. This shopper is checking out her own purchases at a Kroger supermarket. A combination of new technology (that facilities cashless transactions), customer preferences for convenience (that cause them to want to get in and out of the store quickly), and the firm's interests in lowering costs (by hiring fewer checkout operators) have together led to this increasingly popular change.

Internal Forces A variety of forces inside the organization may cause change. If top management revises the organization's strategy, organization change is likely to result. A decision by an electronics company to enter the home computer market or a decision to increase a ten-year product sales goal by 3 percent would occasion many organization changes. Other internal forces for change may be reflections of external forces. As sociocultural values shift, for example, workers' attitudes toward their job may also shift—and workers may demand a change in working hours or working conditions. In such a case, even though the force is rooted in the external environment, the organization must respond directly to the internal pressure it generates.[7]

Planned Versus Reactive Change

Some change is planned well in advance; other change comes about as a reaction to unexpected events. **Planned change** is change that is designed and implemented in an orderly and timely fashion in anticipation of future events. **Reactive change** is a piecemeal response to circumstances as they develop. Because reactive change may be hurried, the potential for poorly conceived and executed change is increased. Planned change is almost always preferable to reactive change.[8]

planned change Change that is designed and implemented in an orderly and timely fashion in anticipation of future events

reactive change A piecemeal response to circumstances as they develop

Georgia-Pacific, a large forest products business, is an excellent example of a firm that went through a planned and well-managed change process. When A. D. Correll became CEO, he quickly became alarmed at the firm's high accident rate—nine serious injuries per hundred employees each year, and twenty-six deaths during the most

THE BUSINESS of ethics

Is BP "Beyond Petroleum"?

"Bringing solar to over 160 countries. Solar, natural gas, wind, hydrogen. And, oh yes, oil."

– Billboard advertisement for British Petroleum, the number-two global oil company*

British Petroleum, the world's second-largest oil company after number-one ExxonMobil, envisions a future that may not include petroleum. CEO John Browne is preparing his company for a world dominated by alternative energy sources. British Petroleum has an 18 percent market share in solar power. Yet *Fortune* writer Cait Murphy says, "BP generates enough wind and solar power to keep a small city lit for a year. BP also produces enough oil and gas to satisfy all of America's oil needs for six months." So the question remains: Can British Petroleum change its fundamental nature and become a "green" firm—or are the changes superficial?

British Petroleum changed its name to BP, which has no negative connotations for nature lovers. Its logo is now a white, yellow, and green sunburst design. It voluntarily reduced polluting elements in its products. BP cut its own greenhouse emissions by 10 percent, eight years ahead of schedule. The firm lowered contributions to oil industry lobbyists and donates to environmental group Greenpeace instead. The company was the first to take responsibility for global warming. At a public appearance, Browne said, referring to global warming, "Companies composed of highly skilled and trained people can't live in denial of mounting evidence."

Yet the reality is that BP makes virtually all of its revenues from oil, the top contributor to global warming. BP's *Annual Report 2001* showed earnings of $15.6 billion from oil and a loss of $631 million on "Other Businesses," including solar. Yet the firm's ads state, somewhat evasively, "Bringing solar to over 160 countries. Solar, natural gas, wind, hydrogen. And, oh yes, oil." BP is seeking to open the Arctic National Wildlife Refuge, a pristine wilderness area, for oil exploration.

BP clearly appears to be a better global citizen than ExxonMobil or ChevronTexaco. These American firms are denying that global warming exists and trying to discredit scientists who disagree. Bob Malone, a BP regional president, concedes that the firm still has a long way to go, but insists that it wants to do the right thing. "The oil business has a negative reputation," Malone says. "We are trying to say that there are different kinds of oil companies."

References: Cait Murphy, "Beyond Persuasion," *Fortune*, September 5, 2002, www.fortune.com on January 28, 2003; Darcy Frey, "How Green Is BP?" *New York Times Magazine*, December 8, 2002, pp. 98–103; Heesun Wee, "Can Oil Giants and Green Energy Mix?" *BusinessWeek*, September 25, 2002, www.businessweek.com on January 28, 2003 (*quote).

recent five-year period. Although the forest products business is inherently dangerous, Correll believed that the accident rate was far too high and set out on a major change effort to improve things. He and other top managers developed a multistage change program intended to educate workers about safety, improve safety equipment in the plant, and eliminate a long-standing part of the firm's culture that made injuries almost a badge of courage. And, today, Georgia-Pacific has the best safety record in the industry, with relatively few injuries.[9]

On the other hand, Caterpillar was caught flat-footed by a worldwide recession in the construction industry, suffered enormous losses, and took several years to recover. Had managers at Caterpillar anticipated the need for change earlier, they might have been able to respond more quickly. Similarly, Kodak had to cut 10,000 jobs in reaction to sluggish sales and profits. Again, better anticipation might have forestalled those job cuts. The importance of approaching change from a planned perspective is reinforced by the frequency of organization change. Most companies or divisions of large companies implement some form of moderate change at least every year and one or more major changes every four to five years.[10] Managers who sit back and respond only when they have to are likely to spend a lot of time hastily changing and re-changing things. A more effective approach is to anticipate forces urging change and plan ahead to deal with them.[11]

concept CHECK

What are the primary forces for change? Provide several examples of each.	*Is it possible to eliminate the likelihood of reactive change altogether? Why or why not?*

Managing Change in Organizations

Organization change is a complex phenomenon. A manager cannot simply wave a wand and implement a planned change like magic. Instead, any change must be systematic and logical to have a realistic opportunity to succeed.[12] To carry this off, the manager needs to understand the steps of effective change and how to counter employee resistance to change.[13]

Steps in the Change Process

Researchers have over the years developed a number of models or frameworks outlining steps for change.[14] The Lewin model was one of the first, although a more comprehensive approach is usually more useful in today's complex business environment.

The Lewin Model Kurt Lewin, a noted organizational theorist, suggested that every change requires three steps.[15] The first step is *unfreezing*—individuals who will be affected by the impending change must be led to recognize why the change is necessary. Next, the *change itself* is implemented. Finally, *refreezing* involves reinforcing and supporting the change so that it becomes a part of the system. For example, one of the changes Caterpillar faced in response to the recession noted earlier involved a massive workforce reduction. The first step (unfreezing) was convincing the United Auto Workers to support the reduction because of its importance to long-term effectiveness. After this unfreezing was accomplished, 30,000 jobs were eliminated (implementation). Then Caterpillar worked to improve its damaged relationship with its workers (refreezing) by guaranteeing future pay hikes and promising no more cutbacks. As interesting as Lewin's model is, it unfortunately lacks operational specificity. Thus a more comprehensive perspective is often needed. *The World of Management* discusses the role of comprehensive change at the Swedish firm Ericsson.

A Reluctant Change Agent at Ericsson

"We don't have the option of doing nothing."

— Kurt Hellström, CEO, Ericsson*

To paraphrase William Shakespeare, who wrote of greatness in his play *Twelfth Night*, "Be not afraid of change: Some are born to change, some achieve change, and some have change thrust upon them." Ericsson CEO Kurt Hellström, head of the world's largest maker of wireless telecommunications networks, puts himself and Swedish firm Ericsson squarely in that last category. "I can imagine better situations to be in," Hellström says, "but the job has to be done." The telecom conglomerate is in crisis, with a total of $5 billion in losses for 2001 and 2002. The company's problems were triggered by a drastic decline in demand for telecom equipment, but that is little consolation for Hellström, who has laid off 50,000 of Ericsson's 110,000 workers.

Hellström envisions his firm shifting from the low-profit manufacturing of hardware to the more lucrative systems consulting industry. Most of Ericsson's manufacturing is moving to electronics makers in Singapore and Silicon Valley. Much of Ericsson's software R&D is now done by Wipro, based in India. Ericsson created a joint venture with rival Sony for development of mobile handsets. It even abandoned its original product.

Hellström and Chairman Michael Treschow asked for handouts to keep the firm from bankruptcy. Patriotic Swedes contributed the most, knowing that their country's economy depends heavily on giant Ericsson. "I talked to a lot of small shareholders," says Treschow. "There was a lot of emotion, a lot of national pride."

Hellström is under attack from the media and unhappy investors, but he believes that the company will be prosperous again, if it survives the present difficulties. When asked why he persists in the face of sharp criticism, Hellström replies with a self-mocking laugh, "I enjoy being beaten up." It will be very hard for Hellström to change the engineering-focused company into a service provider, according to an Ericsson engineer, who says, "They keep talking about reorganization and giving better service to customers, but we don't take it seriously." Yet Hellström continues to preach the gospel of change. "I try to tell the truth as I see it," Hellström claims. "We don't have the option of doing nothing."

References: Andy Reinhardt, "Sony Ericsson: 'In Big Bloody Trouble'?" *BusinessWeek*, November 11, 2002, p. 68; Andy Serwer, "Telcos of the Apocalypse," *Fortune*, April 22, 2002, www.fortune.com on January 28, 2003; Stanley Reed and Andy Reinhardt, "Saving Ericsson," *BusinessWeek*, November 11, 2002, pp. 64–68 (*quote p. 66).

A Comprehensive Approach to Change The comprehensive approach to change takes a systems view and delineates a series of specific steps that often leads to successful change. This expanded model is illustrated in Figure 13.1. The first step is recognizing the need for change. Reactive change might be triggered by employee complaints, declines in productivity or turnover, court injunctions, sales slumps, or labor strikes. Recognition may simply be managers' awareness that change in a certain area is inevitable. For example, managers may be aware of the general frequency of organizational change undertaken by most organizations and recognize that their organization should probably follow the same pattern. The immediate stimulus might be the result of a forecast indicating new market potential, the accumulation of a cash surplus for possible investment, or an opportunity to achieve and capitalize on a major technological breakthrough. Managers might also initiate change today because indicators suggest that it will be necessary in the near future.[16]

Managers must next set goals for the change. To increase market share, to enter new markets, to restore employee morale, to settle a strike, and to identify investment opportunities all might be goals for change. Third, managers must diagnose what brought on the need for change. Turnover, for example, might be caused by low pay, poor working conditions, poor supervisors, or employee dissatisfaction. Thus, although turnover may be the immediate stimulus for change, managers must understand its causes to make the right changes.

The next step is to select a change technique that will accomplish the intended goals. If turnover is caused by low pay, a new reward system may be needed. If the cause is poor supervision, interpersonal skills training may be called for. (Various change techniques are summarized later in this chapter.) After the appropriate technique has been chosen, its implementation must be planned. Issues to consider include the costs of the change, its effects on other areas of the organization, and the degree of employee participation appropriate for the situation. If the change is implemented as planned, the results should then be evaluated. If the change was intended to reduce turnover, managers must check turnover after the change has been in effect for a while. If turnover is still too high, other changes may be necessary.[17]

FIGURE 13.1

Steps in the Change Process

Managers must understand how and why to implement change. A manager who, when implementing change, follows a logical and orderly sequence like the one shown here is more likely to succeed than a manager whose change process is haphazard and poorly conceived.

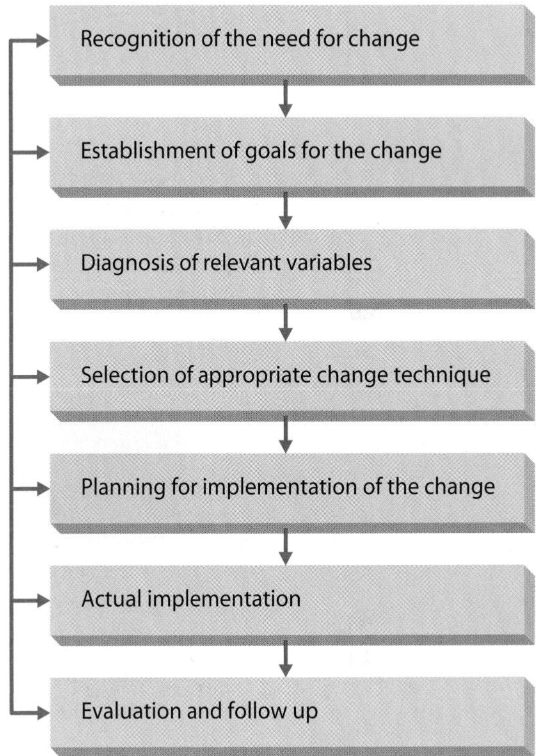

Understanding Resistance to Change

Another element in the effective management of change is understanding the resistance that often accompanies change.[18] Managers need to know why people resist change and what can be done about their resistance. When Westinghouse first provided all of its managers with personal computers, most people responded favorably. One manager, however, resisted the change to the point where he began leaving work every day at noon! It was some time before he began staying in the office all day again. This same phenomenon is illustrated in the cartoon. Such resistance is common for a variety of reasons.[19]

Uncertainty Perhaps the biggest cause of employee resistance to change is uncertainty. In the face of impending change, employees may become anxious and nervous. They may worry about their ability to meet new job demands, they may think that their job security is threatened, or they may simply dislike ambiguity. Nabisco was once the target of an extended and confusing takeover battle, and during the entire time, employees were nervous about the impending change. The *Wall Street Journal* described them this way: "Many are angry at their leaders and fearful for their jobs. They are swapping rumors and spinning scenarios for the ultimate outcome of the battle for the tobacco and food giant. Headquarters staffers in Atlanta know so little about what's happening in New York that some call their office 'the mushroom complex,' where they are kept in the dark."[20]

Change is a common event in most organizations today. And, although much of this change is necessary and beneficial, managers sometimes engage in change activities that are either unnecessary or poorly conceived. When this happens, it increases the chances that employees will resist the change—they will experience uncertainty, threatened self-interests, different perceptions, or feelings of loss. Indeed, as shown in this cartoon, change can be so poorly managed that employees sense it before it even occurs and develop resistance without even knowing the details.

Threatened Self-Interests Many impending changes threaten the self-interests of some managers within the organization. A change might diminish their power or influence within the company, so they fight it. Before deciding to merge with Lands' End, managers at Sears developed a plan calling for a new type of store. The new stores would be somewhat smaller than typical Sears stores and would not be located in large shopping malls. Instead, they would be located in smaller strip centers. They would carry clothes and other "soft goods," but not hardware, appliances, furniture, or automotive products. When executives in charge of the excluded product lines heard about the plan, they raised such strong objections that the plan was cancelled.

Different Perceptions A third reason that people resist change is due to different perceptions. A manager may make a decision and recommend a plan for change on the basis of her own assessment of a situation. Others in the organization may resist the change because they do not agree with the manager's assessment or perceive the situation differently.[21] Executives at 7-Eleven are currently battling this problem as they attempt to enact a major organizational change. The corporation wants to take its convenience stores a bit "upscale" and begin selling fancy fresh foods to go, the newest hardcover novels, some gourmet products, and higher-quality coffee. But many franchisees are balking because they see this move as taking the firm away from its core blue-collar customers.

Feelings of Loss Many changes involve altering work arrangements in ways that disrupt existing social networks. Because social relationships are important, most people resist any change that might adversely affect those relationships. Other intangibles threatened by change include power, status, security, familiarity with existing procedures, and self-confidence.

Overcoming Resistance to Change

Of course, a manager should not give up in the face of resistance to change. Although there are no surefire cures, there are several techniques that at least have the potential to overcome resistance.[22]

People in organizations often resist change for a number of different reasons. Today's breathtaking technological advancements in areas such as biotechnology and information processing seems especially troubling to some people. Harvard business professor Clayton Christensen has helped managers in many firms overcome their fear of technological change through his path-breaking work on what he calls disruptive technology. He argues, for instance, that making a change a fundamental part of an organization's culture can dramatically reduce resistance to change on the part of people who are members of that organization.

Participation

Participation is often the most effective technique for overcoming resistance to change. Employees who participate in planning and implementing a change are better able to understand the reasons for the change. Uncertainty is reduced, and self-interests and social relationships are less threatened. Having had an opportunity to express their ideas and assume the perspectives of others, employees are more likely to accept the change gracefully. A classic study of participation monitored the introduction of a change in production methods among four groups in a Virginia pajama factory.[23] The two groups that were allowed to fully participate in planning and implementing the change improved significantly in their productivity and satisfaction, relative to the two groups that did not participate. 3M Company recently attributed $10 million in cost savings to employee participation in several organization change activities.[24]

Education and Communication Educating employees about the need for and the expected results of an impending change should reduce their resistance. If open communication is established and maintained during the change process, uncertainty can be minimized. Caterpillar used these methods during many of its cutbacks to reduce resistance. First, it educated UAW representatives about the need for and potential value of the planned changes. Then management told all employees what was happening, when it would happen, and how it would affect them individually.

Facilitation Several facilitation procedures are also advisable. For instance, making only necessary changes, announcing those changes well in advance, and allowing time for people to adjust to new ways of doing things can help reduce resistance to change.[25] One manager at a Prudential regional office spent several months systematically planning a change in work procedures and job design. He then became too hurried, coming in over the weekend with a work crew and rearranging the office layout. When employees walked in on Monday morning, they were hostile, anxious, and resentful. What was a promising change became a disaster, and the manager had to scrap the entire plan.

Force-Field Analysis Although force-field analysis may sound like something out of a *Star Trek* movie, it can help overcome resistance to change. In almost any change situation, forces are acting for and against the change. To facilitate the change, managers start by listing each set of forces and then trying to tip the balance so that

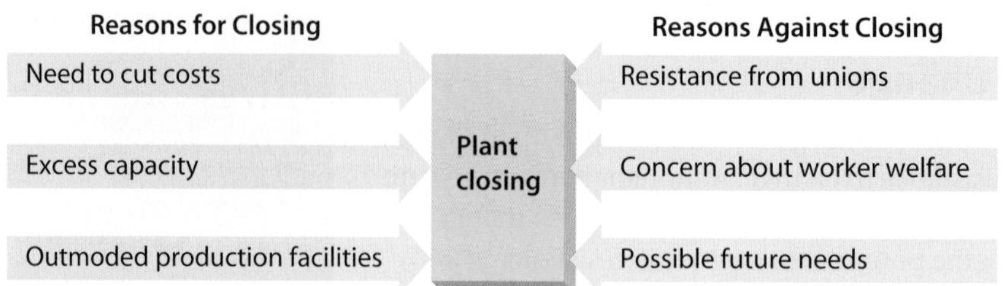

FIGURE 13.2

Force-Field Analysis for Plant Closing at General Motors

A force-field analysis can help a manager facilitate change. A manager able to identify forces acting both for and against a change can see where to focus efforts to remove barriers to change (such as offering training and relocation to displaced workers). Removing the forces against the change can at least partially overcome resistance.

the forces facilitating the change outweigh those hindering the change. It is especially important to try to remove or at least minimize some of the forces acting against the change. Suppose, for example, that General Motors is considering a plant closing as part of a change. As shown in Figure 13.2, three factors are reinforcing the change: GM needs to cut costs, it has excess capacity, and the plant has outmoded production facilities. At the same time, there is resistance from the UAW, concern for workers being put out of their jobs, and a feeling that the plant might be needed again in the future. GM might start by convincing the UAW that the closing is necessary by presenting profit and loss figures. It could then offer relocation and retraining to displaced workers. And it might shut down the plant and put it in "mothballs" so that it can be renovated later. The three major factors hindering the change are thus eliminated or reduced in importance.

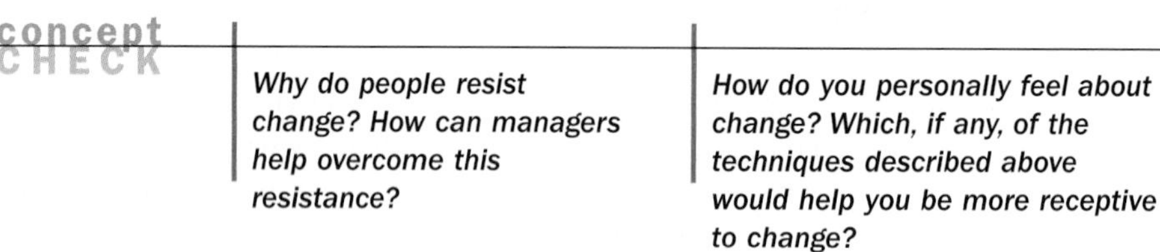

concept CHECK

Why do people resist change? How can managers help overcome this resistance?

How do you personally feel about change? Which, if any, of the techniques described above would help you be more receptive to change?

Areas of Organization Change

We note earlier that change can involve virtually any part of an organization. In general, however, most change interventions involve organization structure and design, technology and operations, or people. The most common areas of change within each of these broad categories are listed in Table 13.1. In addition, many organizations have gone through massive and comprehensive business process change programs.

TABLE 13.1

Areas of Organization Change

Organization change can affect any part, area, or component of an organization. Most change, however, fits into one of three general areas: organization structure and design, technology and operations, and people.

Organization Structure and Design	Technology and Operations	People
Job design	Information technology	Abilities and skills
Departmentalization	Equipment	Performance
Reporting relationships	Work processes	Perceptions
Authority distribution	Work sequences	Expectations
Coordination mechanisms	Control systems	Attitudes
Line-staff structure	ERP	Values
Overall design		
Culture		
Human resource management		

Changing Organization Structure and Design

Organization change might be focused on any of the basic components of organization structure or on the organization's overall design. Thus the organization might change the way it designs its jobs or its bases of departmentalization. Likewise, it might change reporting relationships or the distribution of authority. For example, we note in Chapter 11 the trend toward flatter organizations. Coordination mechanisms and line-and-staff configurations are also subject to change. On a larger scale, the organization might change its overall design. For example, a growing business could decide to drop its functional design and adopt a divisional design. Or it might transform itself into a matrix. Changes in culture usually involve the structure and design of the organization as well (recall that we discussed changing culture back in Chapter 3). Finally, the organization might change any part of its human resource management system, such as its selection criteria, its performance appraisal methods, or its compensation package.[26] Toyota has been undergoing a significant series of changes in its organization structure and design, intended to make it a flatter and more decentralized enterprise and thus more responsive to its external environment.[27]

Changing Technology and Operations

Technology is the conversion process used by an organization to transform inputs into outputs. Because of the rapid rate of all technological innovation, technological changes are becoming increasingly important to many organizations. Table 13.1 lists several areas where technological change is likely to be experienced.

Changing technology is a way of life in some parts of the world. For example, these commuters in Tokyo no longer need to purchase tickets to use the subway system. Instead, they simply flick a plastic card loaded with prepaid transfers through the turnstile ticket slot and move on. When they have used all of their transfers, they go to an automated vending machine and, using a credit card, reload their subway pass.

One important area of change today revolves around information technology. The adoption and institutionalization of information technology innovations is almost constant in most firms today. Sun Microsystems, for example, has adopted a very short-range planning cycle in order to be best prepared for environmental changes.[28] Another important form of technological change involves equipment. To keep pace with competitors, firms periodically find that replacing existing machinery and equipment with newer models is necessary.

A change in work processes or work activities may be necessary if new equipment is introduced or new products are manufactured. In manufacturing industries, the major reason for changing a work process is to accommodate a change in the materials used to produce a finished product. Consider a firm that manufactures battery-operated flashlights. For many years flashlights were made of metal, but now most are made of plastic. A firm might decide to move from metal to plastic flashlights because of consumer preferences, raw materials costs, or other reasons. Whatever the reason, the technology necessary to make flashlights from plastic differs importantly from that used to make flashlights from metal. Work process changes may occur in service organizations as well as in manufacturing firms. As traditional barbershops and beauty parlors are replaced by hair salons catering to both sexes, for example, the hybrid organizations have to develop new methods for handling appointments and setting prices.

A change in work sequence may or may not accompany a change in equipment or a change in work processes. Making a change in work sequence means altering the order or sequence of the workstations involved in a particular manufacturing process. For example, a manufacturer might have two parallel assembly lines producing two similar sets of machine parts. The lines might converge at one central quality control unit, where inspectors verify tolerances. The manager, however, might decide to change to periodic rather than final inspection. Under this arrangement, one or more inspections are established farther up the line. Work sequence changes can also be made in service organizations. The processing of insurance claims, for example, could be changed. The sequence of logging and verifying claims, requesting checks, getting countersignatures, and mailing checks could be altered in several ways, such as combining the first two steps or routing the claims through one person while another handles checks. Organizational control systems may also be targets of change.[29] For example, a firm attempting to improve the quality of its products might develop and implement a set of more rigorous and comprehensive quality-control procedures.

Finally, many businesses have been working to implement technological and operations change by installing and using complex and integrated software systems. Such systems—called *enterprise resource planning*—link virtually all facets of the business, making it easier for managers to keep abreast of related developments. **Enterprise resource planning,** or **ERP**, is a large-scale information system for integrating and synchronizing the many activities in the extended enterprise. In most cases these systems are purchased from external vendors who then tailor their products to the client's unique needs and requirements. Companywide processes—such as materials management, production planning, order management, and financial reporting—can all be managed via ERP. In effect, these are the processes that cut across product lines, departments, and geographic locations.

enterprise resource planning (ERP) A large-scale information system for integrating and synchronizing the many activities in the extended enterprise

Developing the ERP system starts by identifying the key processes that need critical attention, such as supplier relationships, materials flows, or customer order fulfillment. The system could result, for instance, in sales processes' being integrated with production planning and then integrating both of these into the firm's financial accounting system. For example, a customer in Rome can place an order that is to be produced in Ireland, schedule it to be shipped via air cargo to Rome, and then have it picked up by a truck at the airport and delivered to the customer's warehouse by a specified date. All of these activities are synchronized by activities linkages in one massive database.

The ERP integrates all activities and information flows that relate to the firm's critical processes. It also keeps updated real-time information on their current status, reports recent past transactions and upcoming planned transactions, and provides electronic notices that action is required on some items if planned schedules are to be met. It coordinates internal operations with activities by outside suppliers and notifies business partners and customers of current status and upcoming deliveries and billings. It can integrate financial flows among the firm, its suppliers, its customers, and commercial bank deposits for up-to-the-minute status reports that can be used to create real-time financial reports at a moment's notice, rather than in the traditional one-month (or longer) time span for producing a financial statement. ERP's multilanguage capabilities also allow real-time correspondence in various languages to facilitate international transactions.

Changing People, Attitudes, and Behaviors

A third area of organization change has to do with human resources. For example, an organization might decide to change the skill level of its workforce. This change might be prompted by changes in technology or by a general desire to upgrade the quality of the workforce. Thus training programs and new selection criteria might be needed. The organization might also decide to improve its workers' performance level. In this instance, a new incentive system or performance-based training might be in order. Reader's Digest has been attempting to implement significant changes in its workforce. For example, the firm has eliminated 17 percent of its employees, reduced retirement benefits, and taken away many of the "perks" (perquisites, or job benefits) that they once enjoyed. Part of the reason for the changes was to instill in the remaining employees a sense of urgency and the need to adopt a new perspective on how they do their job.[30]

Perceptions and expectations are also a common focus of organization change. Workers in an organization might believe that their wages and benefits are not as high as they should be. Management, however, might have evidence that shows the firm is paying a competitive wage and providing a superior benefit package. The change, then, would be centered on informing and educating the workforce about the comparative value of its compensation package. A common way to do this is to publish a statement that places an actual dollar value on each benefit provided and compares that amount to what other local organizations are providing their workers. Change might also be directed at employee attitudes and values. In many organizations today, managers are trying to eliminate adversarial relationships with workers and adopt a more collaborative relationship. In many ways, changing attitudes and values is perhaps the hardest thing to do.

Changing Business Processes

Many organizations today have also gone through massive and comprehensive change programs involving all aspects of organization design, technology, and people. Although various descriptions are used, the terms currently in vogue for these changes are *business process change,* or *reengineering.* Specifically, **business process change,** or **reengineering**, is the radical redesign of all aspects of a business to achieve major gains in cost, service, or time.[31] ERP, as described above, is a common platform for changing business processes. However, business process change is a more comprehensive set of changes that goes beyond software and information systems.

business process change (reengineering) The radical redesign of all aspects of a business to achieve major gains in cost, service, or time

Corning, for example, has undergone major reengineering over the last few years. Whereas the 150-year-old business once manufactured cookware and other durable consumer goods, it has transformed itself into a high-tech powerhouse making such products as the ultra-thin screens used in products like Palm Pilots and laptop computers.[32] Similarly, the dramatic overhauls of Kodak away from print film to other forms of optical imaging, of Yellow into a sophisticated freight delivery firm, and of UPS into a major international delivery giant all required business process changes throughout these organizations.

The Need for Business Process Change Why are so many organizations finding it necessary to undergo business process change? We note in Chapter 2 that all systems, including organizations, are subject to entropy—a normal process leading to system decline. An organization is behaving most typically when it maintains the status quo, does not change in synch with its environment, and starts consuming its own resources to survive. In a sense, that is what happened to Kmart. In the early and mid-1970s Kmart was in such a high-flying growth mode that it passed first J.C. Penney and then Sears to become the world's largest retailer. But then the firm's managers grew complacent and assumed that the discount retailer's prosperity would continue and that they need not worry about environmental shifts, the growth of Wal-Mart, and so forth—and entropy set in. The key is to recognize the beginning of the decline and immediately move toward changing relevant business processes. Major problems occur when managers either do not recognize the onset of entropy until it is well advanced or are complacent in taking steps to correct it.

Approaches to Business Process Change Figure 13.3 shows general steps in changing business processes, or reengineering. The first step is setting goals and developing a strategy for the changes. The organization must know in advance what new business processes are supposed to accomplish and how those accomplishments will be achieved. Next, top managers must begin and direct the reengineering effort. If a CEO simply announces that business process change is to occur but does nothing else, the program is unlikely to be successful. But, if the CEO is constantly involved in the process, underscoring its importance and taking the lead, business process change stands a much better chance of success.

Most experts also agree that successful business process change is usually accompanied by a sense of urgency. People in the organization must see the clear and present need for the changes being implemented and appreciate their importance. In addition, most successful reengineering efforts start with a new, clean slate. In other words, rather than assuming that the existing organization is a starting point and then trying to modify it, business process change usually starts by asking questions such as how customers are best served and competitors best neutralized. New approaches and systems are then created and imposed in place of existing ones.

Finally, business process change requires a careful blend of top-down and bottom-up involvement. On the one hand, strong leadership is necessary, but too much involvement by top management can make the changes seem autocratic. Similarly, employee participation is also important, but too little involvement by leaders can undermine the program's importance and create a sense that top managers do not care. Thus care must be taken to carefully balance these two countervailing forces. Our next section explores more fully one related but distinct approach called *organization development.*

FIGURE 13.3

The Reengineering Process

Reengineering is a major redesign of all areas of an organization. To be successful, reengineering requires a systematic and comprehensive assessment of the entire organization. Goals, top management support, and a sense of urgency help the organization re-create itself and blend both top-level and bottom-up perspectives.

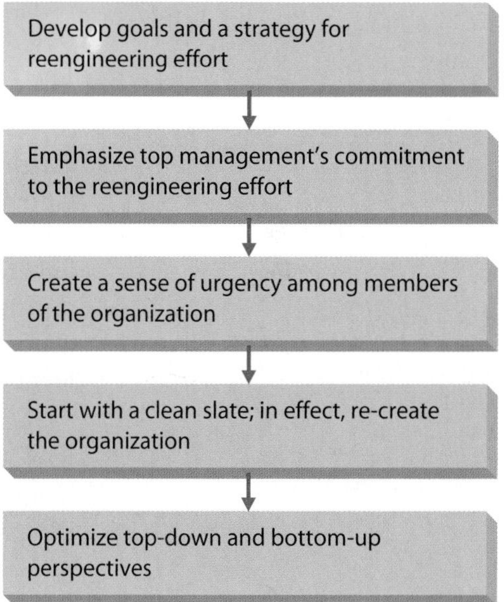

Organization Development

We note in several places the importance of people and change. Beyond those change interests discussed above, a special area of interest that focuses almost exclusively on people is organization development (OD).

OD Assumptions Organization development is concerned with changing attitudes, perceptions, behaviors, and expectations. More precisely, **organization development (OD)** is a planned effort that is organizationwide and managed from the top, intended to increase organizational effectiveness and health through planned interventions in the organization's process, using behavioral science knowledge.[33] The theory and practice of OD are based on several very important assumptions. The first is that employees have a desire to grow and develop. Another is that employees have a strong need to be accepted by others within the organization. Still another critical assumption of OD is that the total organization and the

organization development (OD) An effort that is planned, organization-wide, and managed from the top, intended to increase organizational effectiveness and health through planned interventions in the organization's process, using behavioral science knowledge way it is designed will influence the way individuals and groups within the organization behave. Thus some form of collaboration between managers and their employees is necessary to (1) take advantage of the skills and abilities of the employees and (2) eliminate aspects of the organization that retard employee growth, development, and group acceptance. Because of the intense personal nature of many OD activities, many large organizations rely on one or more OD consultants (either full-time employees assigned to this function or outside experts hired specifically for OD purposes) to implement and manage their OD program.[34]

OD Techniques Several kinds of interventions or activities are generally considered part of organization development.[35] Some OD programs may use only one or a few of these; other programs use several of them at once.

- *Diagnostic activities.* Just as a physician examines patients to diagnose their current condition, an OD diagnosis analyzes the current condition of an organization. To carry out this diagnosis, managers use questionnaires, opinion or attitude surveys, interviews, archival data, and meetings to assess various characteristics of the organization. The results of this diagnosis may generate profiles of the organization's activities, which can then be used to identify problem areas in need of correction.
- *Team building.* Team-building activities are intended to enhance the effectiveness and satisfaction of individuals who work in groups or teams and to promote overall group effectiveness. Given the widespread use of teams today, these activities have taken on increased importance. An OD consultant might interview team members to determine how they feel about the group; then an off-site meeting could be held to discuss the issues that surfaced and iron out any problem areas or member concerns. Caterpillar used team building as one method for changing the working relationships between workers and supervisors from confrontational to cooperative. An interesting new approach to team building involves having executive teams participate in group cooking classes to teach them the importance of interdependence and coordination.[36]
- *Survey feedback.* In survey feedback, each employee responds to a questionnaire intended to measure perceptions and attitudes (for example, satisfaction and supervisory style). Everyone involved, including the supervisor, receives the results of the survey. The aim of this approach is usually to change the behavior of supervisors by showing them how their subordinates view them. After the feedback has been provided, workshops may be conducted to evaluate results and suggest constructive changes.
- *Education.* Educational activities focus on classroom training. Although such activities can be used for technical or skill-related purposes, an OD educational activity typically focuses on "sensitivity skills"—that is, it teaches people to be more considerate and understanding of the people they work with. Participants often go through a series of experiential or role-playing exercises to learn better how others in the organization feel.
- *Intergroup activities.* The focus of intergroup activities is on improving the relationships between two or more groups. We note in Chapter 11 that, as

group interdependence increases, so do coordination difficulties. Intergroup OD activities are designed to promote cooperation or resolve conflicts that arose as a result of interdependence. Experiential or role-playing activities are often used to bring this about.

- *Third-party peacemaking.* Another approach to OD is through third-party peacemaking, which is most often used when substantial conflict exists within the organization. Third-party peacemaking can be appropriate on the individual, group, or organizational level. The third party, usually an OD consultant, uses a variety of mediation or negotiation techniques to resolve any problems or conflicts among individuals or groups.
- *Technostructural activities.* Technostructural activities are concerned with the design of the organization, the technology of the organization, and the interrelationship of design and technology with people on the job. A structural change such as an increase in decentralization, a job design change such as an increase in the use of automation, and a technological change involving a modification in work flow all qualify as technostructural OD activities if their objective is to improve group and interpersonal relationships within the organization.
- *Process consultation.* In process consultation, an OD consultant observes groups in the organization to develop an understanding of their communication patterns, decision-making and leadership processes, and methods of cooperation and conflict resolution. The consultant then provides feedback to the involved parties about the processes he or she has observed. The goal of this form of intervention is to improve the observed processes. A leader who is presented with feedback outlining deficiencies in his or her leadership style, for example, might be expected to change to overcome them.
- *Life and career planning.* Life and career planning helps employees formulate their personal goals and evaluate strategies for integrating their goals with the goals of the organization. Such activities might include specification of training needs and plotting a career map. General Electric has a reputation for doing an outstanding job in this area.
- *Coaching and counseling.* Coaching and counseling provide nonevaluative feedback to individuals. The purpose is to help people develop a better sense of how others see them and learn behaviors that will assist others in achieving their work-related goals. The focus is not on how the individual is performing today; instead, it is on how the person can perform better in the future.
- *Planning and goal setting.* More pragmatic than many other interventions are activities designed to help managers improve their planning and goal setting. Emphasis still falls on the individual, however, because the intent is to help individuals and groups integrate themselves into the overall planning process. The OD consultant might use the same approach as in process consultation, but the focus is more technically oriented, on the mechanics of planning and goal setting.

The Effectiveness of OD Given the diversity of activities encompassed by OD, it is not surprising that managers report mixed results from various OD interventions. Organizations that actively practice some form of OD include American Airlines,

Texas Instruments, Procter & Gamble, and BF Goodrich. Goodrich, for example, has trained sixty persons in OD processes and techniques. These trained experts have subsequently become internal OD consultants to assist other managers in applying the techniques.[37] Many other managers, in contrast, report that they have tried OD but discarded it.[38]

OD will probably remain an important part of management theory and practice. Of course, there are no sure things when dealing with social systems such as organizations, and the effectiveness of many OD techniques is difficult to evaluate. Because all organizations are open systems interacting with their environments, an improvement in an organization after an OD intervention may be attributable to the intervention, but it may also be attributable to changes in economic conditions, luck, or other factors.[39]

Identify each of the major areas of organization change and provide examples to illustrate each one.

Based on your own knowledge and experiences, which, if any, of these areas of change is likely to become more prevalent in the future? Which, if any, is likely to become less prevalent? Why?

Organizational Innovation

A final element of organization change that we address is innovation. **Innovation** is the managed effort of an organization to develop new products or services or new uses for existing products or services. Innovation is clearly important because, without new products or services, any organization will fall behind its competition.[40]

innovation The managed effort of an organization to develop new products or services or new uses for existing products or services

The Innovation Process

The organizational innovation process consists of developing, applying, launching, growing, and managing the maturity and decline of creative ideas.[41] This process is depicted in Figure 13.4.

Innovation Development Innovation development involves the evaluation, modification, and improvement of creative ideas. Innovation development can transform a product or service with only modest potential into a product or service with significant potential. Parker Brothers, for example, decided during innovation development not to market an indoor volleyball game but instead to sell separately the appealing little foam ball designed for the game. The firm will never know how well the volleyball game would have sold, but the Nerf ball and numerous related products generated millions of dollars in revenues for Parker Brothers.

Innovation Application Innovation application is the stage in which an organization takes a developed idea and uses it in the design, manufacturing, or delivery of new products, services, or processes. At this point the innovation emerges from the laboratory and is transformed into tangible goods or services. One example of innovation application is the use of radar-based focusing systems in Polaroid's instant cameras. The idea of using radio waves to discover the location, speed, and direction of moving objects was first applied extensively by Allied forces during World War II. As radar technology developed during the following years, the electrical components needed became smaller and more streamlined. Researchers at Polaroid applied this well-developed technology in a new way.[42]

Innovation is integrally related to organization change. These researchers are working on a new robotic device that can be used to map old mines and to explore underground caverns in search of mineral deposits. If this innovation can be perfected, mining companies can get certain tasks performed more efficiently and safely than is currently the case. These changes, in turn, would subsequently affect how the companies carry out various other procedures as well.

Application Launch Application launch is the stage at which an organization introduces new products or services to the marketplace. The important question is not "Does the innovation work?" but "Will customers want to purchase the innovative product and service?" History is full of creative ideas that did not generate enough interest among customers to be successful. Some notable innovation failures include Sony's seat warmer, the Edsel automobile, and Polaroid's SX-70 instant camera (which cost $3 billion to develop, but never sold more than 100,000 units in a year).[43] Thus, despite development and application, new products and services can still fail at the launch phase.

Application Growth Once an innovation has been successfully launched, it then enters the stage of application growth. This is a period of high economic performance

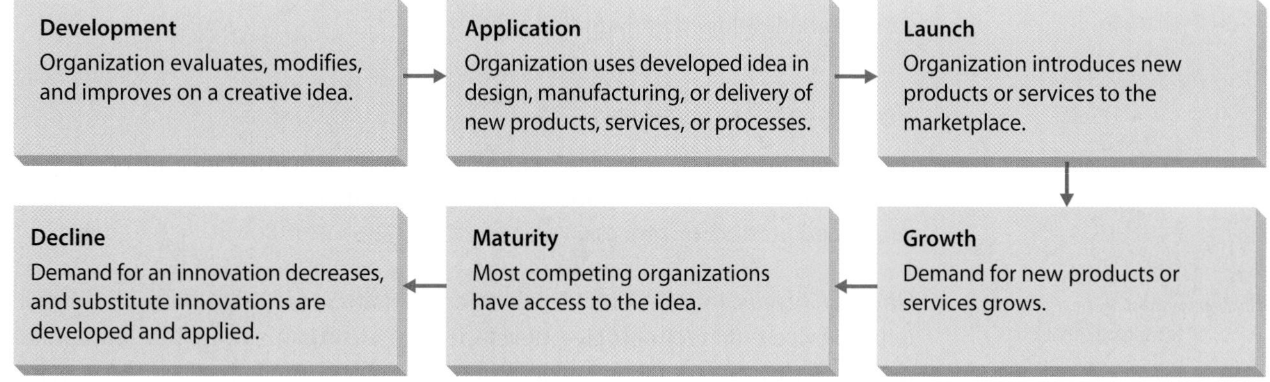

FIGURE 13.4

The Innovation Process

Organizations actively seek to manage the innovation process. These steps illustrate the general life cycle that characterizes most innovations. Of course, as with creativity, the innovation process will suffer if it is approached too mechanically and rigidly.

for an organization, because demand for the product or service is often greater than supply. Organizations that fail to anticipate this stage may unintentionally limit their growth, as Apple did by not anticipating demand for its iMac computer.[44] At the same time, overestimating demand for a new product can be just as detrimental to performance. Unsold products can sit in warehouses for years.

Innovation Maturity After a period of growing demand, an innovative product or service often enters a period of maturity. Innovation maturity is the stage at which most organizations in an industry have access to an innovation and are applying it in approximately the same way. The technological application of an innovation during this stage of the innovation process can be very sophisticated. Because most firms have access to the innovation, however, either as a result of their developing the innovation on their own or copying the innovation of others, it does not provide competitive advantage to any one of them. The time that elapses between innovation development and innovation maturity varies notably depending on the particular product or service. Whenever an innovation involves the use of complex skills (such as a complicated manufacturing process or highly sophisticated teamwork), moving from the growth phase to the maturity phase will take longer. In addition, if the skills needed to implement these innovations are rare and difficult to imitate, then strategic imitation may be delayed, and the organization may enjoy a period of sustained competitive advantage.

Innovation Decline Every successful innovation bears its own seeds of decline. Because an organization does not gain a competitive advantage from an innovation at maturity, it must encourage its creative scientists, engineers, and managers to begin looking for new innovations. This continued search for competitive advantage usually leads new products and services to move from the creative process through innovation maturity, and finally to innovation decline. Innovation decline is the stage during which demand for an innovation decreases and substitute innovations are developed and applied.

Forms of Innovation

Each creative idea that an organization develops poses a different challenge for the innovation process. Innovations can be radical or incremental, technical or managerial, and product or process.

Radical Versus Incremental Innovations **Radical innovations** are new products, services, or technologies developed by an organization that completely replace the existing products, services, or technologies in an industry.[45] **Incremental innovations** are new products or processes that modify existing ones. Firms that implement radical innovations fundamentally shift the nature of competition and the interaction of firms within their environments. Firms that implement incremental innovations alter, but do not fundamentally change, competitive interaction in an industry.

radical innovation A new product, service, or technology that completely replaces an existing one

incremental innovation A new product, service, or technology that modifies an existing one

Over the last several years, organizations have introduced many radical innovations. For example, compact disk technology has virtually replaced long-playing vinyl records in the recording industry, DVDs are replacing videocassettes, and high-definition television seems likely to replace regular television technology (both black and white and color) in the near future. Whereas radical innovations like these tend to be very visible and public, incremental innovations actually are more numerous. One example is Ford's sports utility vehicle, Explorer. Although other companies had similar products, Ford more effectively combined the styling and engineering that resulted in increased demand for all sports utility vehicles.

Technical Versus Managerial Innovations **Technical innovations** are changes in the physical appearance or performance of a product or service, or of the physical processes through which a product or service is manufactured. Many of the most important innovations over the last fifty years have been technical. For example, the serial replacement of the vacuum tube with the transistor, the transistor with the integrated circuit, and the integrated circuit with the microchip has greatly enhanced the power, ease of use, and speed of operation of a wide variety of electronic products. Not all innovations developed by organizations are technical, however. **Managerial innovations** are changes in the management process by which products and services are conceived, built, and delivered to customers. Managerial innovations do not necessarily affect the physical appearance or performance of products or services directly. In effect, business process change or reengineering, as we discuss earlier, represents a managerial innovation.

technical innovation A change in the appearance or performance of products or services, or of the physical processes through which a product or service passes

managerial innovation A change in the management process in an organization

Product Versus Process Innovations Perhaps the two most important types of technical innovations are product innovations and process innovations. **Product innovations** are changes in the physical characteristics or performance of existing products or services or the creation of brand-new products or services. **Process innovations** are changes in the way products or services are manufactured, created, or distributed. Whereas managerial innovations generally affect the broader context of development, process innovations directly affect manufacturing.

product innovation A change in the physical characteristics or performance of an existing product or service or the creation of new ones

process innovation A change in the way a product or service is manufactured, created, or distributed

The implementation of robotics, as we discuss earlier, is a process innovation. As Figure 13.5 shows, the effect of product and process innovations on economic return depends on the stage of the innovation process that a new product or service occupies. At first, during development, application, and launch, the physical attributes and capabilities of an innovation most affect organizational performance. Thus product innovations are particularly important during these beginning phases. Later, as an innovation enters the phases of growth, maturity, and decline, an organization's ability to develop process innovations, such as fine-tuning manufacturing, increasing product quality, and improving product distribution, becomes important to maintaining economic return.

Japanese organizations have often excelled at process innovation. The market for 35mm cameras was dominated by German and other European manufacturers when, in the early 1960s, Japanese organizations such as Canon and Nikon

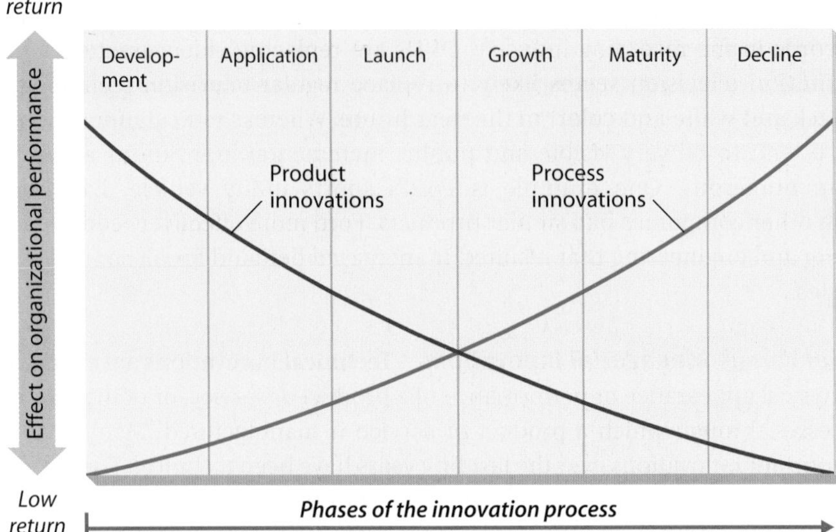

FIGURE 13.5

Effects of Product and Process Innovation on Economic Return

As the innovation process moves from development to decline, the economic return from product innovations gradually declines. In contrast, the economic return from process innovations increases during this same process.

began making cameras. Some of these early Japanese products were not very successful, but these companies continued to invest in their process technology and eventually were able to increase quality and decrease manufacturing costs.[46] Now these Japanese organizations dominate the worldwide market for 35mm cameras, and the German companies, because they were not able to maintain the same pace of process innovation, are struggling to maintain market share and profitability.

The Failure to Innovate

To remain competitive in today's economy, organizations must be innovative. And yet many organizations that should be innovative are not successful at bringing out new products or services or do so only after innovations created by others are very mature. Organizations may fail to innovate for at least three reasons.

Lack of Resources Innovation is expensive in terms of dollars, time, and energy. If a firm does not have sufficient money to fund a program of innovation or does not currently employ the kinds of employees it needs to be innovative, it may lag behind in innovation. Even highly innovative organizations cannot become involved in every new product or service its employees think up. For example, numerous other commitments in the electronic instruments and computer industry forestalled Hewlett-Packard from investing in Steve Jobs and Steve Wozniak's original idea for a personal computer. With infinite resources of money, time, and technical and managerial expertise, HP might have entered this market early. Because the firm did not have this flexibility, however, it had to make some difficult choices about which innovations to invest in.

Failure to Recognize Opportunities Because firms cannot pursue all innovations, they need to develop the capability to carefully evaluate innovations and to select the ones that hold the greatest potential. To obtain a competitive advantage, an organization usually must make investment decisions before the innovation process reaches the mature stage. The earlier the investment, however, the greater the risk. If organizations are not skilled at recognizing and evaluating opportunities, they may be overly cautious and fail to invest in innovations that later turn out to be successful for other firms.

Resistance to Change As we discuss earlier, many organizations tend to resist change. Innovation means giving up old products and old ways of doing things in favor of new products and new ways of doing things. These kinds of changes can be personally difficult for managers and other members of an organization. Thus resistance to change can slow the innovation process.

Promoting Innovation in Organizations

A wide variety of ideas for promoting innovation in organizations has been developed over the years. Three specific ways for promoting innovation are through the reward system, through the organizational culture, and through a process called *intrapreneurship.*[47] *Today's Management Issues* discusses another interesting twist on promoting innovation.

The Reward System A firm's reward system is the means by which it encourages and discourages certain behaviors by employees. Major components of the reward system include salaries, bonuses, and perquisites. Using the reward system to promote innovation is a fairly mechanical but nevertheless effective management technique. The idea is to provide financial and nonfinancial rewards to people and groups who develop innovative ideas. Once the members of an organization understand that they will be rewarded for such activities, they are more likely to work creatively. With this end in mind, Monsanto gives a $50,000 award each year to the scientist or group of scientists who develop the biggest commercial breakthrough.

It is important for organizations to reward creative behavior, but it is vital to avoid punishing creativity when it does not result in highly successful innovations. It is the nature of the creative and innovative processes that many new product ideas will simply not work out in the marketplace. Each process is fraught with too many uncertainties to generate positive results every time. An individual may have prepared herself to be creative, but an insight may not be forthcoming. Or managers may attempt to apply a developed innovation, only to recognize that it does not work. Indeed, some organizations operate according to the assumption that, if all their innovative efforts succeed, then they are probably not taking enough risks in research and development. At 3M, nearly 60 percent of the creative ideas suggested each year do not succeed in the marketplace.

Managers need to be very careful in responding to innovative failure. If innovative failure is due to incompetence, systematic errors, or managerial sloppiness, then a firm should respond appropriately, for example, by withholding raises or

Do Deviants Drive Change?

"If at first the idea is not absurd, then there is no hope for it."

— Albert Einstein, physicist, quoted on FirstMatter's website*

Futurist Watts Wacker, CEO of consulting firm FirstMatter, is the coauthor, with Ryan Mathews, of a new book that provides an alternate view of the change process in organizations. *The Deviant's Advantage: How Fringe Ideas Create Mass Markets* theorizes that many products that are taken for granted today were once considered part of the "deviant fringe." Thus, to discover the innovative products of the future, one should examine ideas that are considered deviant today. The authors' approach can be summed up in a quote from Albert Einstein: "If at first the idea is not absurd, then there is no hope for it."

Wacker and Mathews show that once-deviant products such as professional wrestling, snowboards, and rock and roll have moved into the mainstream. Deviant products follow an evolution toward acceptability, passing through phases that Wacker and Mathews identify as "Fringe," "Edge," "Cool," "The Next Big Thing," and finally, "Social Convention." Consider as an example Tim Berners-Lee's invention of the structure that became the Internet. His ideas were initially viewed as deviant, then became known to a few experts, became familiar to many "cool" computer aficionados, were referred to as "the next big thing" as they became more widely adopted, and ended by becoming commonplace.

Wacker and Mathews admit that not all deviation is good, writing, "Of course, there is positive and negative deviance—the former a force for transformation, the latter a source of unspeakable evil." Yet the authors claim that most organizations "hate [positive deviance] and work tirelessly to eliminate deviant employees." In their book, the two give examples of firms that celebrate positive deviance, including Intel. Those that resist deviants, such as Xerox, are doomed to have their best ideas stolen by competitors.

To help managers apply their inside-out thinking, Wacker and Mathews encourage development of idiosyncratic corporate cultures. The futurists suggest an "opposites analysis," in which employees visualize what would happen if everything they believe were exactly 180 degrees wrong. The authors claim, "Most of us learned to manage from the center, bringing everything into a stable environment where it can be standardized and processed. The real trick is to manage the Edge, not the center. The 'real deal' is out there somewhere, raw, messy and untamed."

References: Ryan Mathews and Watts Wacker, "Deviants, Inc." *Fast Company*, March 2002, www.fastcompany.com on January 27, 2003; "Watts Wacker, CEO, Futurist," FirstMatter LLC website, www.firstmatter.com on January 27, 2003 (*quote); "William J. Holstein, "Outside the Box? Why a Box?" *New York Times*, August 25, 2002, p. BU5; William J. Holstein, "The Fringe Is Full of Ideas," *New York Times*, August 25, 2002, p. BU5.

reducing promotion opportunities. People who act in good faith to develop an innovation that simply does not work out, however, should not be punished for failure. If they are, they will probably not be creative in the future. A punitive reward system will discourage people from taking risks and therefore reduce the organization's ability to obtain competitive advantages.

Organization Culture As we discuss in Chapter 3, an organization's culture is the set of values, beliefs, and symbols that help guide behavior. A strong, appropriately focused organizational culture can be used to support innovative activity. A well-managed culture can communicate a sense that innovation is valued and will be rewarded and that occasional failure in the pursuit of new ideas is not only acceptable but even expected. In addition to reward systems and intrapreneurial activities, firms such as 3M, Corning, Monsanto, Procter & Gamble, Texas Instruments, Johnson & Johnson, and Merck are all known to have strong, innovation-oriented cultures that value individual creativity, risk taking, and inventiveness.[48]

Intrapreneurship in Larger Organizations In recent years, many large businesses have realized that the entrepreneurial spirit that propelled their growth becomes stagnant after they transform themselves from a small but growing concern into a larger one. To help revitalize this spirit, some firms today encourage what they call "intrapreneurship." **Intrapreneurs** are similar to entrepreneurs except that they develop a new business in the context of a large organization. There are three intrapreneurial roles in large organizations.[49] To successfully use intrapreneurship to encourage creativity and innovation, the organization must find one or more individuals to perform these roles.

intrapreneurs Similar to entrepreneurs except that they develop new businesses in the context of a large organization

The *inventor* is the person who actually conceives of and develops the new idea, product, or service by means of the creative process. Because the inventor may lack the expertise or motivation to oversee the transformation of the product or service from an idea into a marketable entity, however, a second role comes into play. A *product champion* is usually a middle manager who learns about the project and becomes committed to it. He or she helps overcome organizational resistance and convinces others to take the innovation seriously. The product champion may have only limited understanding of the technological aspects of the innovation. Nevertheless, product champions are skilled at knowing how the organization works, whose support is needed to push the project forward, and where to go to secure the resources necessary for successful development. A *sponsor* is a top-level manager who approves of and supports a project. This person may fight for the budget needed to develop an idea, overcome arguments against a project, and use organizational politics to ensure the project's survival. With a sponsor in place, the inventor's idea has a much better chance of being successfully developed.

Several firms have embraced intrapreneurship as a way to encourage creativity and innovation. Colgate-Palmolive has created a separate unit, Colgate Venture Company, staffed with intrapreneurs who develop new products. General Foods developed Culinova as a unit to which employees can take their ideas for possible development. S.C. Johnson & Son established a $250,000 fund to support new product ideas, and Texas Instruments refuses to approve a new innovative project unless it has an acknowledged inventor, champion, and sponsor.

concept CHECK

Identify and describe the basic forms of innovation.

Identify several new products or variations of existing products that have been successful and several others that have been less successful.

Summary of Key Points

ACE self-test

business.college.hmco.com/students

Organization change is any substantive modification to some part of the organization. Change may be prompted by forces internal or external to the organization. In general, planned change is preferable to reactive change.

Managing the change process is very important. The Lewin model provides a general perspective on the steps involved in change, although a comprehensive model is usually more effective. People tend to resist change because of uncertainty, threatened self-interests, different perceptions, and feelings of loss. Participation, education and communication, facilitation, and force-field analysis are methods for overcoming this resistance.

Many different change techniques or interventions are used. The most common ones involve changing organizational structure and design, technology, and people. There are several specific areas of change within each of these broad categories. Business process change is a more massive and comprehensive change. Organization development is concerned with changing attitudes, perceptions, behaviors, and expectations. Its effective use relies on an important set of assumptions. There are conflicting opinions about the effectiveness of several OD techniques.

The innovation process has six steps: development, application, launch, growth, maturity, and decline. Basic categories of innovation include radical, incremental, technical, managerial, product, and process innovations. Despite the importance of innovation, many organizations fail to innovate because they lack the required creative individuals or are committed to too many other creative activities, fail to recognize opportunities, or resist the change that innovation requires. Organizations can use a variety of tools to overcome these problems, including the reward system, organizational culture, and intrapreneurship.

Discussion Questions

Questions for Review

1. What forces or kinds of events lead to organization change? Identify each force or event as a planned or a reactive change.
2. Compare planned and reactive change. What are the advantages of planned change, as compared to reactive change?
3. In a brief sentence or just a phrase, describe each of the organizational development (OD) techniques.
4. Consider the following list of products. Categorize each along all three dimensions of innovation, if possible (radical versus incremental, technical versus managerial, and product versus process). Explain your answers.
   - Teaching college courses by videotaping the instructor and sending the image over the Internet
   - The rise in popularity of virtual organizations (discussed in Chapter 12)
   - Checking the security of packages on airlines with the type of MRI scanning devices that are common in health care

- A device combining features of a cell phone and a handheld computer with Internet capability
- Robotic arms that can perform surgery that is too precise for a human surgeon's hands
- Hybrid automobiles, which run on both batteries and gasoline
- Using video games to teach soldiers how to plan and execute battles

Questions for Analysis

5. What are the symptoms that a manager should look for in determining whether an organization needs to change? What are the symptoms that indicate that an organization has been through too much change?
6. Assume that you are the manager of an organization that has a routine way of performing a task and now faces a major change in how it performs that task. Using Lewin's model, tell what steps you would take to implement the change. Using the comprehensive approach, tell what steps you would take. For each step, give specific examples of actions you would take at that step.
7. Think back to a time when a professor announced a change that you, the student, did not want to adopt. What were the reasons for your resistance to change? Was the professor able to overcome your resistance? If so, tell what he or she did. If not, tell what he or she could have done that might have been successful.

Questions for Application

8. Some people resist change, whereas others welcome it enthusiastically. To deal with the first group, one needs to overcome resistance to change; to deal with the second, one needs to overcome resistance to stability. What advice can you give a manager facing the latter situation?
9. Can a change made in one area of an organization—in technology, for instance—not lead to change in other areas? If you think that change in one area must lead to change in other areas, describe an example of an organization change to illustrate your point. If you think that change can occur in just one area without causing change in other areas, describe an example of an organization change that illustrates your point.
10. Research an innovation change that occurred in a real organization, by either interviewing an employee, reading the business press, or using the Internet. Describe the process by which the innovation was developed. Did the actual process follow the ideal process described in the chapter? Why or why not?

BUILDING EFFECTIVE time-management SKILLS

Exercise Overview

Time-management skills refer to the manager's ability to prioritize work, to work efficiently, and to delegate appropriately. This exercise demonstrates both the importance and the difficulty of change by seeking to change your use of time.

Exercise Background

Conduct the following thought experiment. What if you found out, with absolute certainty, that the world would end in one month? Some unstoppable force—say, a giant meteor—is hurtling directly toward the earth, and there is no chance of stopping or diverting it. Everyone on the planet knows the exact time of impact, which is precisely one month from today. No one will be able to survive or escape. Death will occur for everyone, instantly. Of course, this scenario is totally fictitious and unrealistic, not to mention a bit grim.

What would you do with the next month? How would you spend your time? Whom would you see? Which activities are essential? And, just as important, what would you cease doing? Whom would you stop spending time with? Which activities are just not essential? The experiment is a bit far-fetched, but attempting to answer seriously works best.

Exercise Task

With the background material above serving as context, do the following:

1. List activities, people, priorities, places, and so on that would be important to you.
2. Compare your list to your current allocation of time. Are there activities that are important to you that receive little or no time today? Are there activities that you do today that are not very important, based on your list?
3. What does the comparison suggest to you about better use of your time? What should you do more or less of?
4. Share your answers, in general terms, with a small group of classmates. Are there common themes? Do their answers suggest any new ideas to you?

Follow up Questions

Clearly, taking this exercise too far can lead to absurd results. For example, if we only had thirty days to live, few of us would visit the dentist or go on a diet. Yet those activities can have important consequences if our lives are longer, as they surely will be. Thus this exercise does not provide a prescription of how to spend every day for the rest of your life, but it can highlight those things that are truly important to us, things that tend to get overlooked in the busyness of daily tasks.

For a variation on this exercise, consider what you would do if the time remaining were one year, one week, or just one day.

For an extension of this exercise, share your list with the people in your life, especially people who appear on the list. Some interesting conversations are sure to result!

BUILDING EFFECTIVE decision-making SKILLS

business.college.hmco.com/students

Exercise Overview

Decision-making skills include the manager's ability to recognize and define problems and opportunities correctly and then to select an appropriate course of action to solve problems and capitalize on opportunities. This exercise gives you practice in making decisions related to organizational innovation.

Exercise Background

Assume that you are a manager at a venture capital firm. Your company actively seeks out promising new ideas for technological improvements and then provides financing, advice, and expertise to the start-up firms, in exchange for part ownership of the company. Your firm makes money when an idea is successfully brought to market, because the value of your company's shares increases. Your compensation and your continued employment are therefore based on choosing the right ideas and giving the inventors appropriate help.

Exercise Task

1. Use the Internet to locate information about at least five promising new technologies. (*Hint:* Visit websites of publications that report technology news, such as *TechWeb*, or visit corporate websites of innovative companies like 3M. Or use "technology venture capital" as a search term to locate firms that are investing in new technologies and then read about their clients.) Choose the new technology that interests you the most.
2. Describe the innovation's current phase of the innovation process. Explain how you arrived at your answer.
3. Tell about the kinds of advice and expertise that this idea and its inventors need in order to grow into a successful start-up.

BUILDING EFFECTIVE diagnostic SKILLS

Exercise Overview

Diagnostic skills help a manager visualize the most appropriate response to a situation. These skills are especially important during a period of organization change.

Exercise Background

Assume that you are the general manager of a hotel located on a tropical island. The hotel is situated along a beautiful stretch of beach and is one of six large resorts in the immediate area. The hotel is owned by a group of foreign investors and is one of the oldest on the island. For several years, the hotel has been operated as a franchise unit of a large international hotel chain, as are all of the others on the island.

For the last few years, the hotel's owners have been taking most of the profits for themselves and putting relatively little back into the hotel. They have also let you know that their business is not in good financial health; the money earned from your hotel is being used to offset losses they are incurring elsewhere. In contrast, most of the other hotels around have recently been refurbished, and plans have just been announced to build two new ones in the near future.

A team of executives from franchise headquarters has just visited your hotel. They expressed considerable disappointment in the property. They felt that it has not kept pace with the other resorts on the island. They also informed you that, if the property is not brought up to their standards, the franchise agreement, up for review in a year, will be revoked. You see this move as potentially disastrous because you would lose their "brand name," access to their reservation system, and so forth.

Sitting alone in your office, you have identified several alternatives that seem viable:

1. Try to convince the owners to remodel the hotel. You estimate that it will take $5 million to meet the franchisor's minimum standards and another $5 million to bring the hotel up to the standards of the top resort on the island.
2. Try to convince the franchisor to give you more time and more options for upgrading the facility.
3. Allow the franchise agreement to terminate and try to succeed as an independent hotel.
4. Assume that the hotel will fail and start looking for another job. You have a good reputation, although you might have to start at a lower level (perhaps as an assistant manager) with another firm.

Exercise Task

With the background information presented above, do the following:

1. Rank-order the four alternatives in terms of their potential success. Make assumptions as appropriate.
2. Identify other alternatives not noted above.
3. Can any alternatives be pursued simultaneously?
4. Develop an overall strategy for trying to save the hotel while also protecting your own interests.

CHAPTER CLOSING case

CHANGING CARGILL

"I am not a commodity."

— T-shirt worn by Cargill managers*

Food maker Cargill controls every step in the food production process, from farming to transport to storage to processing, yet overdiversification and lack of synergy have plagued the conglomerate for years. CEO Warren Staley is looking to change all that.

From its founding in 1865 as a grain storage business, Cargill has grown and diversified. Today, the agricultural division of Cargill is a leader in seed and fertilizer for cotton, soybeans, and other crops. They make livestock feed, operate feedlots, and research bioengineered crops. The firm controls 18 percent of the world's turkeys, 22 percent of American beef production, and 25 percent of grain exports.

Cargill used its agricultural expertise to expand into food processing. That division produces oils, flavorings, sweeteners, flours, malts, cocoas, salt, nuts, fruits, and juices, as well as prepared meats, poultry, and fish. From processing, Cargill progressed to manufacturing other commodities, such as steel, ethanol, paints, and more. Once Cargill was firmly established as a producer, it then became a merchant. Its trading unit transports products around the world, trades on worldwide commodities markets, and sells excess cargo capacity on Cargill's trains and ships.

The firm's experience in trading enabled the development of a Financial Markets group, which trades options and futures on international financial and commodities markets. The unit sells hedging and insurance products, too. Cargill's growing financial expertise led to the establishment of a venture capital group, which invests in technology companies making products related to agriculture, logistics, or financial services.

Cargill added capabilities one at a time before venturing into a new business that was logically related to previous ones. The result is a firm that allows each diverse business to run autonomously, with little oversight from corporate headquarters and little coordination between divisions. The firm has market power—Cargill is the nineteenth-largest company in the United States and has 90,000 employees in fifty-nine countries from Antigua to Zimbabwe. It is also unwieldy and unfocused.

CEO Staley has shaken up the sleeping giant, a process he calls "keeping things bubbling." He sold $2 billion in unprofitable businesses and then used that cash to consolidate in more profitable segments, through acquisitions. "To grow our opportunities we have to shrink our sandbox," Staley claims. Stunning longtime managers, he adds, "That means telling our businesses, 'We won't starve you, but we may shoot you.'" In a move that industry experts call "classic Cargill," the firm is investing most heavily in slumping markets, buying when the price is right. For example, Cargill bought a large grain seller at the bottom of a ten-year price decline.

Staley claims, "The more complex the things we do for our customers, the more they're willing to pay us." A key piece of the company's strategic change is exiting commodities, which carry low profit margins, and entering high-margin "solutions," such as processed foods. Staley passed out T-shirts to his staff that read, "I am not a commodity," as a humorous reminder of the firm's plans. Staff at Cargill are developing new and more convenient products and building closer relationships with buyers, which include brewers, restaurants, and cereal makers.

Staley has also increased Cargill's participation in joint ventures, to aid in updating the firm's products and skills. In some cases, Cargill is using joint ventures as a way to build market share or to eliminate rivals. Cargill's R&D scientists are developing innovative products, such as the processed oil that cuts fat by 48 percent which they developed for McDonald's.

Cargill managers, however, are changing slowly and reluctantly. Previously, each manager's rewards were based on the profitability of one of Cargill's ninety individual businesses. Under the new system, however, managers overseeing cocoa, sweeteners, and flavors must cooperate to provide processed chocolate to bakeries. Vice President John Geisler remembers the days when each manager defended his business "no matter what, and if that meant blood on the streets, so be it." Geisler sums up the difficulties in reducing competition between units with the quip "This is not a camel built for collaboration." Staley replaced managers who failed to implement the company's goals; some units have incurred losses of up to 70 percent.

The founding family still owns 88 percent of privately held Cargill; 12 percent is part of an employee stock ownership plan. They are confident that Staley's moves are taking their company in the right direction. With their backing, the continuation of Staley's plan is assured. But will the change be a success? Staley thinks so. Cargill's website sums up the CEO's aspirations when it says, "These changes [reflect] the more dynamic, approachable and energized company we are becoming."

Case Questions

1. What are the forces in favor of change at Cargill?
2. What are the reasons for resistance to change at Cargill? What can Cargill managers do to overcome this resistance? In your opinion, are these actions likely to be successful in overcoming resistance to change?
3. What areas of Cargill need to be changed? Based on your response, predict how easy or how hard it will be to make the required changes. Then predict some likely outcomes for Cargill if the changes do not succeed.

Case References

"Creating Distinctive Value," "Products and Businesses," "The Cargill Brand," Cargill website, www.cargill.com on January 29, 2003; "Fixing the Fat," *BusinessWeek*, September 16, 2002, www.businessweek.com on January 28, 2003; Neil Weinberg, "Going Against the Grain," *Forbes*, November 25, 2002, pp. 158–168 (*quote p. 166).

Chapter Notes

1. "Best Companies to Work For," *Fortune*, January 20, 2003, www.fortune.com on January 27, 2003; Dave Carpenter, "Sears' Earnings Rise, Helped by Lands' End," *AP Business*, January 16, 2003, hoovnews.hoovers.com on January 27, 2003; Heesun Wee, "The Solid Ground Under Lands' End," *BusinessWeek*, December 7, 2001, www.businessweek.com on January 27, 2003; Joel Grover, "Sears Boosts Brand Image with Lands' End Purchase," *Shopping Center World*, June 1, 2002, shoppingcenterworld.com on January 27, 2003 (*quote); Keith Regan, "Can Lands' End Bring Sears up to Speed Online?" *E-Commerce Times*, May 20, 2002, www.ecommercetimes.com on January 27, 2003; Robert Berner, "Sears–Lands' End: The Seams May Show," *BusinessWeek*, May 16, 2002, www.businessweek.com on January 27, 2003.
2. For an excellent review of this area, see Achilles A. Armenakis and Arthur G. Bedeian, "Organizational Change: A Review of Theory and Research in the 1990s," *Journal of Management*, 1999, vol. 25, no. 3, pp. 293–315.
3. For additional insights into how technological change affects other parts of the organization, see P. Robert Duimering, Frank Safayeni, and Lyn Purdy, "Integrated Manufacturing: Redesign the Organization Before Implementing Flexible Technology," *Sloan Management Review*, Summer 1993, pp. 47–56.
4. Joel Cutcher-Gershenfeld, Ellen Ernst Kossek, and Heidi Sandling, "Managing Concurrent Change Initiatives," *Organizational Dynamics*, Winter 1997, pp. 21–38.
5. Michael A. Hitt, "The New Frontier: Transformation of Management for the New Millennium," *Organizational Dynamics*, Winter 2000, pp. 7–15. See also Michael Beer

and Nitin Nohria, "Cracking the Code of Change," *Harvard Business Review*, May–June 2000, pp. 133–144; and Clark Gilbert, "The Disruption Opportunity," *MIT Sloan Management Review*, Summer 2003, pp. 27–32.

6. See Warren Boeker, "Strategic Change: The Influence of Managerial Characteristics and Organizational Growth," *Academy of Management Journal*, 1997, vol. 40, no. 1, pp. 152–170.
7. Alan L. Frohman, "Igniting Organizational Change from Below: The Power of Personal Initiative," *Organizational Dynamics*, Winter 1997, pp. 39–53.
8. Nandini Rajagopalan and Gretchen M. Spreitzer, "Toward a Theory of Strategic Change: A Multi-Lens Perspective and Integrative Framework," *Academy of Management Review*, 1997, vol. 22, no. 1, pp. 48–79.
9. Anne Fisher, "Danger Zone," *Fortune*, September 8, 1997, pp. 165–167.
10. John P. Kotter and Leonard A. Schlesinger, "Choosing Strategies for Change," *Harvard Business Review*, March–April 1979, p. 106.
11. Clayton M. Christensen and Michael Overdorf, "Meeting the Challenge of Disruptive Change," *Harvard Business Review*, March–April 2000, pp. 67–77.
12. "To Maintain Success, Managers Must Learn How to Direct Change," *Wall Street Journal*, August 13, 2002, p. B1.
13. See Eric Abrahamson, "Change Without Pain," *Harvard Business Review*, July–August 2000, pp. 75–85. See also Gib Akin and Ian Palmer, "Putting Metaphors to Work for Change in Organizations," *Organizational Dynamics*, Winter 2000, pp. 67–76.
14. Erik Brynjolfsson, Amy Austin Renshaw, and Marshall Van Alstyne, "The Matrix of Change," *Sloan Management Review*, Winter 1997, pp. 37–54.
15. Kurt Lewin, "Frontiers in Group Dynamics: Concept, Method, and Reality in Social Science," *Human Relations*, June 1947, pp. 5–41.
16. "Time for a Turnaround," *Fast Company*, January 2003, pp. 55–61.
17. See Connie J. G. Gersick, "Revolutionary Change Theories: A Multilevel Exploration of the Punctuated Equilibrium Paradigm," *Academy of Management Review*, January 1991, pp. 10–36.
18. See Gerald Andrews, "Mistrust, the Hidden Obstacle to Empowerment, *HRMagazine*, November 1994, pp. 66–74, for a good illustration of how resistance emerges.
19. See Clark Gilbert and Joseph Bower, "Disruptive Change," *Harvard Business Review*, May 2002, pp. 95–104.
20. "RJR Employees Fight Distraction amid Buy-out Talks," *Wall Street Journal*, November 1, 1988, p. A8.
21. Arnon E. Reichers, John P. Wanous, and James T. Austin, "Understanding and Managing Cynicism About Organizational Change," *Academy of Management Executive*, February 1997, pp. 48–59.
22. See Paul R. Lawrence, "How to Deal with Resistance to Change," *Harvard Business Review*, January–February 1969, pp. 4–12, 166–176, for a classic discussion.
23. Lester Coch and John R. P. French, Jr., "Overcoming Resistance to Change," *Human Relations*, August 1948, pp. 512–532.
24. Eric von Hippel, Stefan Thomke, and Mary Sonnack, "Creating Breakthroughs at 3M," *Harvard Business Review*, September-October 1999, pp. 47–54. See also Jerry Useem, "Tape + Light Bulbs = ?" *Fortune*, August 12, 2002, pp. 127–132.
25. Benjamin Schneider, Arthur P. Brief, and Richard A. Guzzo, "Creating a Climate and Culture for Sustainable Organizational Change," *Organizational Dynamics*, Spring 1996, pp. 7–19.
26. Paul Bate, Raza Khan, and Annie Pye, "Towards a Culturally Sensitive Approach to Organization Structuring: Where Organization Design Meets Organization Development," *Organization Science*, March–April 2000, pp. 197–211.
27. "Founding Clan Vies with Outside 'Radical' for the Soul of Toyota," *Wall Street Journal*, May 5, 2000, pp. A1, A12.
28. David Kirkpatrick, "The New Player," *Fortune*, April 17, 2000, pp. 162–168.
29. Jeffrey A. Alexander, "Adaptive Change in Corporate Control Practices," *Academy of Management Journal*, March 1991, pp. 162–193.
30. "Mr. Ryder Rewrites the Musty Old Book at Reader's Digest," *Wall Street Journal*, April 18, 2000, pp. A1, A10.
31. Thomas A. Stewart, "Reengineering—The Hot New Managing Tool," *Fortune*, August 23, 1993, pp. 41–48.
32. "Old Company Learns New Tricks," *USA Today*, April 10, 2000, pp. 1B, 2B.
33. Richard Beckhard, *Organization Development: Strategies and Models* (Reading, Mass.: Addison-Wesley, 1969), p. 9.
34. W. Warner Burke, "The New Agenda for Organization Development," *Organizational Dynamics*, Summer 1997, pp. 7–20.
35. Wendell L. French and Cecil H. Bell, Jr., *Organization Development: Behavioral Science Interventions for Organization Improvement*, 2nd ed. (Englewood Cliffs, N.J.: Prentice-Hall, 1978).
36. "Memo to the Team: This Needs Salt!" *Wall Street Journal*, April 4, 2000, pp. B1, B14.
37. Roger J. Hower, Mark G. Mindell, and Donna L. Simmons, "Introducing Innovation Through OD," *Management Review*, February 1978, pp. 52–56.
38. "Is Organization Development Catching On? A Personnel Symposium," *Personnel*, November–December 1977, pp. 10–22.
39. For a recent discussion on the effectiveness of various OD techniques in different organizations, see John M. Nicholas, "The Comparative Impact of Organization Development Interventions on Hard Criteria Measures," *Academy of Management Review*, October 1982, pp. 531–542.
40. Constantinos Markides, "Strategic Innovation," *Sloan Management Review*, Spring 1997, pp. 9–24. See also James Brian Quinn, "Outsourcing Innovation: The New Engine of Growth," *Sloan Management Review*, Summer 2000, pp. 13–21.

41. L. B. Mohr, "Determinants of Innovation in Organizations," *American Political Science Review*, 1969, pp. 111–126; G. A. Steiner, *The Creative Organization* (Chicago: University of Chicago Press, 1965); R. Duncan and A. Weiss, "Organizational Learning: Implications for Organizational Design," in B. M. Staw (ed.), *Research in Organizational Behavior*, vol. 1 (Greenwich, Conn.: JAI Press, 1979), pp. 75–123; J. E. Ettlie, "Adequacy of Stage Models for Decisions on Adoption of Innovation," *Psychological Reports*, 1980, pp. 991–995.
42. See Alan Patz, "Managing Innovation in High Technology Industries," *New Management*, September 1986, pp. 54–59.
43. "Flops," *BusinessWeek*, August 16, 1993, pp. 76–82.
44. "Apple Can't Keep up with Demand for Newest iMac," *USA Today*, August 26, 2002, p. 3B.
45. See Willow A. Sheremata, "Centrifugal and Centripetal Forces in Radical New Product Development Under Time Pressure," *Academy of Management Review*, 2000, vol. 25, no. 2, pp. 389–408. See also Richard Leifer, Gina Colarelli O'Connor, and Mark Rice, "Implementing Radical Innovation in Mature Firms: The Role of Hobs," *Academy of Management Executive*, 2001, vol. 15, no. 3, pp. 102–113.
46. See "Amid Japan's Gloom, Corporate Overhauls Offer Hints of Revival," *Wall Street Journal*, February 21, 2002, pp. A1, A11.
47. Dorothy Leonard and Jeffrey F. Rayport, "Spark Innovation Through Empathic Design," *Harvard Business Review*, November–December 1997, pp. 102–115.
48. See Steven P. Feldman, "How Organizational Culture Can Affect Innovation," *Organizational Dynamics*, Summer 1988, pp. 57–68.
49. See Gifford Pinchot III, *Intrapreneuring* (New York: Harper & Row, 1985).

14

Managing Human Resources in Organizations

CHAPTER OUTLINE

The Environmental Context of Human Resource Management
- The Strategic Importance of HRM
- The Legal Environment of HRM
- Social Change and HRM

Attracting Human Resources
- Human Resource Planning
- Recruiting Human Resources
- Selecting Human Resources

Developing Human Resources
- Training and Development
- Performance Appraisal
- Performance Feedback

Maintaining Human Resources
- Determining Compensation
- Determining Benefits
- Career Planning

Managing Labor Relations
- How Employees Form Unions
- Collective Bargaining

New Challenges in the Changing Workplace
- Managing Knowledge Workers
- Contingent and Temporary Workers

LEARNING OBJECTIVES

After studying this chapter, you should be able to:

1 ***Describe the environmental context of human resource management, including its strategic importance and its relationship with legal and social factors.***

OPENING INCIDENT

The television commercials feature a young man, fit and handsome, disguised in camouflage fatigues and face paint, crawling through the underbrush while firing a weapon. Or perhaps he is jumping out of a helicopter or skiing down a steep slope. Music video–style camera work and rock music create an impression of danger, speed, excitement. The parting shot is always the catch phrase "I'm an Army of One." You have seen the ads—now here are the changes that underlie the creation of Force XXI, the "Army of the 21st Century." The last two decades have seen profound changes in human resource management, particularly recruitment, at the U.S. Army, with its 500,000 soldiers.

In 1973 America's military switched to an all-volunteer force. This changed the focus in army enlistment, from choosing the right job and training for a group of mostly unmotivated draftees to attracting the right type of person for a soldiering career. Over the years, the army has identified a number of qualities that are desirable in a soldier: physical strength and bravery, initiative, determination, confidence, team focus, and comfort with technology. But how can the army attract men and women with these characteris-

2	3	4	5	6
Discuss how organizations attract human resources, including human resource planning, recruiting, and selecting.	**Describe how organizations develop human resources, including training and development, performance appraisal, and performance feedback.**	**Discuss how organizations maintain human resources, including the determination of compensation and benefits and career planning.**	**Discuss labor relations, including how employees form unions and the mechanics of collective bargaining.**	**Describe the issues associated with managing knowledge and contingent and temporary workers.**

"If you want to stop thinking about your future and start living it, you're ready to become an Army of One."

—U.S. Army website for recruiting, at www.goarmy.com

This Army recruiter is attempting to interest a student in a military career.

tics? One way is through the use of targeted ads, which present army life in a storybook way and appeal to their intended audience. The army has also developed an innovative program for recruiting, which it calls "PaYS," or "Partnership for Youth Success." This program allows recruits to choose a career field and then select an American organization that requires individuals with those specialized skills. After the term of enlistment is served, the trained worker is given priority for civilian jobs at that organization. Participants include the Los Angeles Police Department, Sears, PepsiCo, State Farm Insurance, and General Dynamics.

Another recruiting mechanism is the use of the army's new website, at www.goarmy.com. The site begins with "Army 101," meant to teach the basics of Army enlistment, with a focus on the benefits that recruits receive. The first text that recruits encounter at this page on the site says:

The United States Army is the most powerful ground force in the entire world. It upholds the ideals set forth in the U.S. Constitution and acts to support the interests of the United States. As a Soldier in the Army, you will gain invaluable training and job skills that will help you no matter what path you take in life. You will find ways to help pay for your college education and earn a paycheck while serving.

Discover a life filled with adventure and meet other smart, motivated people like you. Because the strength of the U.S. Army doesn't only lie in numbers, it lies in you.

If you want to stop thinking about your future and start living it, you're ready to become An Army of One.

This statement appeals to recruits' patriotism, self-interest, and thirst for adventure, which can be powerfully attractive motivators.

Also on the GoArmy site are many other useful pieces of information, presented in interesting ways. One section details the experience of six recruits through the weeks of basic training, while another lists potential job choices and even offers an interactive test to discover the best fit for each recruit. The site offers in-depth profiles of soldiers which describe their enlistment, work, and lifestyle. The information is extensive and focuses on desirable career choices in fields such as medicine, engineering, and technology.

Army recruiting is facing a host of opportunities today, such as the changing role of women in the military. Women are legally barred from working in combat-related jobs, such as infantry or armor. However, the definition of "combat-related" has narrowed, so that women today may serve as pilots or engineers, positions that were denied to them in the past. Increased freedom in specialties has coincided with an increase in female enlistees. Post 9/11, American patriotism has grown, which has increased the number and the quality of prospective recruits. Also, many young adults are having difficulty finding employment in today's slowing economy, which also increases recruits. So, the army's job is a bit easier, at least until the trend changes or the economy improves and military service once again falls out of fashion.[1]

The U.S. Army is an incredibly complex organization to manage. And, like all organizations, the army relies heavily on people to advance its mission and implement its plans. But the army also has unique advantages and disadvantages when it comes to recruiting and managing people. These vital functions are just a few of the activities necessary to successfully manage an effective workforce.

This chapter is about how organizations manage the people that comprise them. This set of processes is called "human resource management," or HRM. We start by describing the environmental context of HRM. We then discuss how organizations attract human resources. Next we describe how organizations seek to further develop the capacities of their human resources. We also examine how high-quality human resources are maintained by organizations. We conclude by discussing labor relations.

The Environmental Context of Human Resource Management

Human resource management (HRM) is the set of organizational activities directed at attracting, developing, and maintaining an effective workforce.[2] Human resource management takes place within a complex and ever-changing environmental context. Three particularly vital components of this context are HRM's strategic importance and the legal and social environments of HRM.

human resource management (HRM) The set of organizational activities directed at attracting, developing, and maintaining an effective workforce

The Strategic Importance of HRM

Human resources are critical for effective organizational functioning. HRM (or "personnel," as it is sometimes called) was once relegated to second-class status in many organizations, but its importance has grown dramatically in the last two decades. Its new importance stems from increased legal complexities, the recognition that human resources are a valuable means for improving productivity, and the awareness today of the costs associated with poor human resource management.[3]

Indeed, managers now realize that the effectiveness of their HR function has a substantial impact on the bottom-line performance of the firm. Poor human resource planning can result in spurts of hiring followed by layoffs—costly in terms of unemployment compensation payments, training expenses, and morale. Haphazard compensation systems do not attract, keep, and motivate good employees, and outmoded recruitment practices can expose the firm to expensive and embarrassing discrimination lawsuits. Consequently, the chief human resource executive of most large businesses is a vice president directly accountable to the CEO, and many firms are developing strategic HR plans and integrating those plans with other strategic planning activities.[4]

Even organizations with as few as two hundred employees usually have a human resource manager and a human resource department charged with overseeing these activities. Responsibility for HR activities, however, is shared between the HR department and line managers. The HR department may recruit and initially screen candidates, but the final selection is usually made by managers in the department where the new employee will work. Similarly, although the HR department may establish performance appraisal policies and procedures, the actual evaluation and coaching of employees is done by their immediate superiors.

The growing awareness of the strategic significance of human resource management has even led to new terminology to reflect a firm's commitment to people. **Human capital** reflects the organization's investment in attracting, retaining, and motivating an effective workforce. Hence, just as the phrase *financial capital* is an indicator of a firm's financial resources and reserves, so, too, does *human capital* serve as a tangible indicator of the value of the people who comprise an organization.[5]

human capital Reflects the organization's investment in attracting, retaining, and motivating an effective workforce

The Legal Environment of HRM

A number of laws regulate various aspects of employee-employer relations, especially in the areas of equal employment opportunity, compensation and benefits, labor relations, and occupational safety and health. Several major ones are summarized in Table 14.1.

TABLE 14.1

The Legal Environment of Human Resource Management

As much as any area of management, HRM is subject to wide-ranging laws and court decisions. These laws and decisions affect the human resource function in many areas. For example, AT&T was once fined several million dollars for violating Title VII of the Civil Rights Act of 1964.

Equal Employment Opportunity

Title VII of the Civil Rights Act of 1964 (as amended by the Equal Employment Opportunity Act of 1972). Forbids discrimination in all areas of the employment relationship.

Age Discrimination in Employment Act. Outlaws discrimination against people older than forty years.

Various executive orders, especially Executive Order 11246 in 1965. Requires employers with government contracts to engage in affirmative action.

Pregnancy Discrimination Act. Specifically outlaws discrimination on the basis of pregnancy.

Vietnam Era Veterans Readjustment Assistance Act. Extends affirmative action mandate to military veterans who served during the Vietnam War.

Americans with Disabilities Act. Specifically outlaws discrimination against disabled persons.

Civil Rights Act of 1991. Makes it easier for employees to sue an organization for discrimination but limits punitive damage awards if they win.

Compensation and Benefits

Fair Labor Standards Act. Establishes minimum wage and mandated overtime pay for work in excess of forty hours per week.

Equal Pay Act of 1963. Requires that men and women be paid the same amount for doing the same job.

Employee Retirement Income Security Act of 1974 (ERISA). Regulates how organizations manage their pension funds.

Family and Medical Leave Act of 1993. Requires employers to provide up to twelve weeks of unpaid leave for family and medical emergencies.

Labor Relations

National Labor Relations Act. Spells out procedures by which employees can establish labor unions and requires organizations to bargain collectively with legally formed unions; also known as the Wagner Act.

Labor-Management Relations Act. Limits union power and specifies management rights during a union-organizing campaign; also known as the *Taft-Hartley Act.*

Health and Safety

Occupational Safety and Health Act of 1970 (OSHA). Mandates the provision of safe working conditions.

Title VII of the Civil Rights Act of 1964 Forbids discrimination on the basis of sex, race, color, religion, or national origin in all areas of the employment relationship

adverse impact When minority group members pass a selection standard at a rate less than 80 percent of the pass rate of majority group members

Equal Employment Opportunity Commission Charged with enforcing Title VII of the Civil Rights act of 1964

Age Discrimination in Employment Act Outlaws discrimination against people older than forty years; passed in 1967, amended in 1978 and 1986

affirmative action Intentionally seeking and hiring qualified or qualifiable employees from racial, sexual, and ethnic groups that are underrepresented in the organization

Equal Employment Opportunity **Title VII of the Civil Rights Act of 1964** forbids discrimination in all areas of the employment relationship. The intent of Title VII is to ensure that employment decisions are made on the basis of an individual's qualifications rather than on the basis of personal biases. The law has reduced direct forms of discrimination (refusing to promote African-Americans into management, failing to hire men as flight attendants, refusing to hire women as construction workers) as well as indirect forms of discrimination (using employment tests that whites pass at a higher rate than African-Americans).

Employment requirements such as test scores and other qualifications are legally defined as having an **adverse impact** on minorities and women when such individuals meet or pass the requirement at a rate less than 80 percent of the rate of majority group members. Criteria that have an adverse impact on protected groups can be used only when there is solid evidence that they effectively identify individuals who are better able than others to do the job. The **Equal Employment Opportunity Commission** is charged with enforcing Title VII as well as several other employment-related laws.

The **Age Discrimination in Employment Act**, passed in 1967, amended in 1978, and amended again in 1986, is an attempt to prevent organizations from discriminating against older workers. In its current form, it outlaws discrimination against people older than forty years. Both the age discrimination act and Title VII require passive nondiscrimination, or equal employment opportunity. Employers are not required to seek out and hire minorities, but they must treat all who apply fairly.

Several executive orders, however, require that employers holding government contracts engage in **affirmative action**—intentionally seeking and hiring employees from groups that are underrepresented in the organization. These organizations must have a written affirmative action plan that spells out employment goals for underutilized groups and how those goals will be met. These employers are also required to act affirmatively in hiring Vietnam-era veterans (as a result of the Vietnam Era Veterans Readjustment Assistance Act) and qualified handicapped individuals. Finally, the Pregnancy Discrimination Act forbids discrimination against women who are pregnant.

The Americans with Disabilities Act outlaws discrimination against disabled persons. But some disabled-rights activists believe the law doesn't go far enough. These Boston protesters, for instance, want more government programs to help train and otherwise prepare disabled people for meaningful jobs.

In 1990 Congress passed the **Americans with Disabilities Act**, which forbids discrimination on the basis of disabilities and requires employers to provide reasonable accommodations for disabled employees.

More recently, the **Civil Rights Act of 1991** amended the original Civil Rights Act as well as other related laws by both making it easier to bring discrimination lawsuits (which partially explains the aforementioned backlog of cases) while simultaneously limiting the amount of punitive damages that can be awarded in those lawsuits.

Compensation and Benefits Laws also regulate compensation and benefits. The **Fair Labor Standards Act**, passed in 1938 and amended frequently since then,

Images such as this one led to some of the earliest attempts to regulate human resource management practices in the United States. These young boys were working at a cotton mill in Macon, Georgia, in 1909. Their job was to replace bobbins as they got full and to repair broken threads. Child labor, substandard wages, hazardous working conditions, and blatant discrimination led lawmakers to pass numerous statutes intended to protect workers.

sets a minimum wage and requires the payment of overtime rates for work in excess of forty hours per week. Salaried professional, executive, and administrative employees are exempt from the minimum hourly wage and overtime provisions. The **Equal Pay Act of 1963** requires that men and women be paid the same amount for doing the same job. Attempts to circumvent the law by having different job titles and pay rates for men and women who perform the same work are also illegal. Basing an employee's pay on seniority or performance is legal, however, even if it means that a man and woman are paid different amounts for doing the same job. *Today's Management Issues* explores a related controversy.

The provision of benefits is also regulated in some ways by state and federal laws. Certain benefits are mandatory—for example, worker's compensation insurance for employees who are injured on the job. Employers who provide a pension plan for their employees are regulated by the **Employee Retirement Income Security Act of 1974 (ERISA)**. The purpose of this act is to help ensure the financial security of pension funds by regulating how they can be invested. The **Family and Medical Leave Act of 1993** requires employers to provide up to twelve weeks of unpaid leave for family and medical emergencies.

Americans with Disabilities Act Prohibits discrimination against people with disabilities

Civil Rights Act of 1991 Amends the original Civil Rights Act, making it easier to bring discrimination lawsuits while also limiting punitive damages

Fair Labor Standards Act Sets a minimum wage and requires overtime pay for work in excess of forty hours per week; passed in 1938 and amended frequently since then

Equal Pay Act of 1963 Requires that men and women be paid the same amount for doing the same job

Employee Retirement Income Security Act of 1974 (ERISA) Sets standards for pension plan management and provides federal insurance if pension funds go bankrupt

Labor Relations

Union activities and management's behavior toward unions constitute another heavily regulated area. The **National Labor Relations Act** (also known as the Wagner Act), passed in 1935, sets up a procedure for employees to vote on whether to have a union. If they vote for a union, management is required to bargain collectively with the union. The **National Labor Relations Board (NLRB)** was established by the Wagner Act to enforce its provisions. Following a series of severe strikes in 1946, the **Labor-Management Relations Act** (also known as the Taft-Hartley Act) was passed in 1947 to limit union power. The law increases management's rights during an organizing campaign. The Taft-Hartley Act also contains the National Emergency Strike provision, which allows the president of the United States to prevent or end a strike that endangers national security. Taken together, these laws balance union and management power. Employees can be represented by a legally-created and -managed union, but the business can make nonemployee-related business decisions without interference.

Health and Safety

The **Occupational Safety and Health Act of 1970 (OSHA)** directly mandates the provision of safe working conditions. It requires that employers (1) provide a place of employment that is free from hazards that may cause death or serious physical harm and (2) obey the safety and health standards established by the Department of Labor. Safety standards are intended to prevent accidents, whereas occupational health standards are concerned with preventing occupational disease.

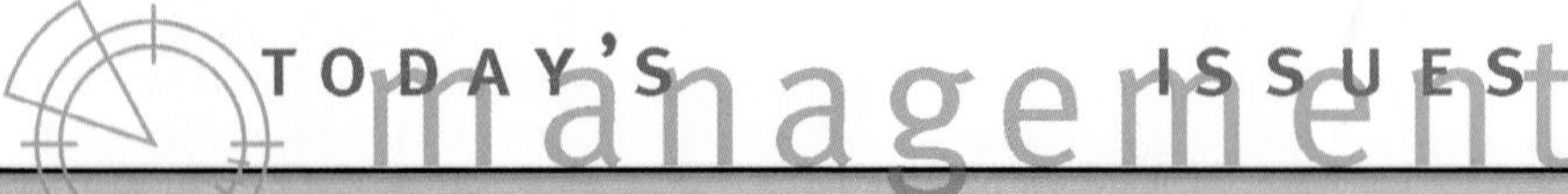

A Fair Day's Pay for a Fair Day's Work?

"[Sixty-five-hour workweeks] got to be very stressful, very tiring."

– Omar Belazi, former manager, RadioShack*

The distinction between hourly employees and salaried managers used to be clear-cut. But that was before the rise of the service economy, which led to more hard-to-categorize positions such as analyst, administrator, and engineer. The Fair Labor Standards Act of 1938 set a minimum wage and mandated overtime pay, but only for hourly workers. The law leaves a lot of room for interpretation, especially in the definition of salaried workers as those who "have management as their primary duty; who direct the work of two or more full-time employees; who have the authority to hire and fire . . . ; who regularly exercise a high degree of independent judgment in their work; and who do not devote more than 20 percent of their time to non-management functions."

Managers are rebelling. RadioShack, Starbucks, Eckerd, Pizza Hut and Wal-Mart were all taken to court by hundreds of employees who were classified as managers and denied overtime pay. The employees argued that their jobs were not inherently professional, that they had little decision-making authority, and that they performed low-level tasks. If a judge agrees, the firms could pay penalties in the millions of dollars.

In addition to the potential for lawsuits, excessive overtime leads to other risks for organizations. One is that employees will simply "burn out" and leave. Omar Belazi, former manager of a RadioShack, typically worked sixty-five-hour weeks. He says, "It got to be very stressful, very tiring. . . . They gave me all these awards, but . . . they didn't pay me." Another possibility is that overly tired workers might make mistakes, opening the firm up to lawsuits of another type. Numerous studies demonstrate that nurses working mandated overtime are twice as likely to have an accident. Two U.S. Air Force pilots mistakenly fired on American forces in Afghanistan in April of 2002. Fatigue from overtime and the pilots' subsequent use of amphetamines probably contributed to the incident.

Long hours are a given in some professions, such as law and medicine, but compensation is also high. U.S. workers already have the longest workweek in the world. At a median salary of $33,000, it is not clear how much more productivity employers can wring out of their fed-up—and tired—workforce.

References: Adam Gellar, "Workers File Suit over Long Hours," *The Eagle* (Bryan-College Station, Texas), August 3, 2002, pp. B1, B7; Arlene Weintraub, "Nursing: On the Critical List," *BusinessWeek*, June 3, 2002, www.businessweek.com on January 31, 2003; "'Friendly Fire' Pilots: Air Force Pushes 'Go Pills,'" CNN website, January 2, 2003, www.cnn.com on January 31, 2003; Michelle Conlin, "The Big Squeeze on Workers," *BusinessWeek*, May 13, 2002, www.businessweek.com on January 31, 2003; "Money Income in the United States," U.S. Census Bureau website, www.census.gov on January 31, 2003; "The Position of the Pennsylvania State Nurses Association on Mandatory Overtime," Pennsylvania State Nurses Association website, March 30, 2001, www.psna.org on January 31, 2003; "What Does the Fair Labor Standards Act Require?" U.S. Department of Labor website, www.dol.gov on January 31, 2003.

Family and Medical Leave Act of 1993 Requires employers to provide up to twelve weeks of unpaid leave for family and medical emergencies

National Labor Relations Act Passed in 1935 to set up procedures for employees to vote on whether to have a union; also known as the Wagner Act

For example, standards limit the concentration of cotton dust in the air, because this contaminant has been associated with lung disease in textile workers. The standards are enforced by OSHA inspections, which are conducted when an employee files a complaint of unsafe conditions or when a serious accident occurs. Spot inspections of plants in especially hazardous industries such as mining and chemicals are also made. Employers who fail to meet OSHA standards may be fined.

Investigators are currently looking into claims that chemical agents in the butter flavoring used in microwave popcorn are harmful to workers where such products are made. At least thirty workers at one plant in Jasper, Missouri, have contracted a rare lung disease, and some doctors believe that it resulted from conditions on their job site. Although federal health officials point out that there is no danger to those cooking or eating microwave popcorn, research is ongoing into potential hazards to those who work in the industry.[6]

National Labor Relations Board (NLRB) Established by the Wagner Act to enforce its provisions

Labor-Management Relations Act Passed in 1947 to limit union power; also known as the Taft-Hartley Act

Occupational Safety and Health Act of 1970 (OSHA) Directly mandates the provision of safe working conditions

Emerging Legal Issues Several other areas of legal concern have emerged during the past few years. One is sexual harassment. Although sexual harassment is forbidden under Title VII, it has received additional attention in the courts recently, as more and more victims have decided to publicly confront the problem. Another emerging human resource management issue is alcohol and drug abuse. Both alcoholism and drug dependence are major problems today. Recent court rulings have tended to define alcoholics and drug addicts as disabled, protecting them under the same laws that protect other handicapped people. Finally, AIDS has emerged as an important legal issue as well. AIDS victims, too, are most often protected under various laws protecting the disabled.

Social Change and HRM

Beyond the objective legal context of HRM, various social changes are also affecting how organizations interact with their employees. First, many organizations are using more and more temporary workers today. This trend, discussed more fully later, allows them to add workers as necessary without the risk that they may have to eliminate their jobs in the future.

Second, dual-career families are much more common today than just a few years ago. Organizations are finding that they must make accommodations for employees who are dual-career partners. These accommodations may include delaying transfers, offering employment to the spouses of current employees to retain them, and providing more flexible work schedules and benefits packages. A related aspect of social change and HRM, workforce diversity, was covered more fully in Chapter 6.

Employment-at-will is also becoming an important issue. Although employment-at-will has legal implications, its emergence as an issue is socially driven. **Employment-at-will** is a traditional view of the workplace that says organizations can fire an employee for any reason. Increasingly, however, people are arguing that organizations should be able to fire only people who are poor performers or who violate rules and, conversely, should not be able to fire people who report safety violations to OSHA or refuse to perform unethical activities. Several court cases in recent years have upheld this emerging view and have limited many organizations' ability to terminate employees to those cases where there is clear and just cause or there is an organization-wide cutback.

employment-at-will A traditional view of the workplace that says organizations can fire their employees for whatever reason they want; recent court judgments are limiting employment-at-will

Identify and briefly summarize the key laws that affect human resource management.

How might the importance of human capital vary across different kinds of business?

Attracting Human Resources

With an understanding of the environmental context of human resource management as a foundation, we are now ready to address its first substantive concern—attracting qualified people who are interested in employment with the organization.

Human Resource Planning

The starting point in attracting qualified human resources is planning. HR planning, in turn, involves job analysis and forecasting the demand and supply of labor.

job analysis A systematized procedure for collecting and recording information about jobs within an organization

Job Analysis **Job analysis** is a systematic analysis of jobs within an organization. A job analysis is made up of two parts. The job description lists the duties of a job, the job's working conditions, and the tools, materials, and equipment used to perform it. The job specification lists the skills, abilities, and other credentials needed to do the job. Job analysis information is used in many human resource activities. For instance, knowing about job content and job requirements is necessary to develop appropriate selection methods and job-relevant performance appraisal systems and to set equitable compensation rates.

Bertha Freeman was Detroit's first African-American female tool-and-die maker. A die is a form carved out of a block of steel to create a reverse version of, say, a car door. It's then installed in a machine that stamps out thousands of car doors. Ms. Freeman got her opportunity when General Motors first opened its apprenticeship program to women in the early 1970s. At the time, GM was doing a lot of internal recruiting; Ms. Freeman was working on one of the company's assembly lines, but was looking for better opportunities. She took the required tests and was the only woman to pass. After a rigorous four-year apprenticeship, she emerged as one of the company's top tool-and-die makers. Today she is with Focus: HOPE, a private nonprofit organization that trains mostly black inner-city kids to become precision machinists.

Forecasting Human Resource Demand and Supply After managers fully understand the jobs to be performed within the organization, they can start planning for the organization's future human resource needs. Figure 14.1 summarizes the steps most often followed. The manager starts by assessing trends in past human resources usage, future organizational plans, and general economic trends. A good sales forecast is often the foundation, especially for smaller organizations. Historical ratios can then be used to predict demand for such employees as operating employees and sales representatives. Of course, large organizations use much more complicated models to predict their future human resource needs. Wal-Mart recently completed an exhaustive planning process that projects that the firm

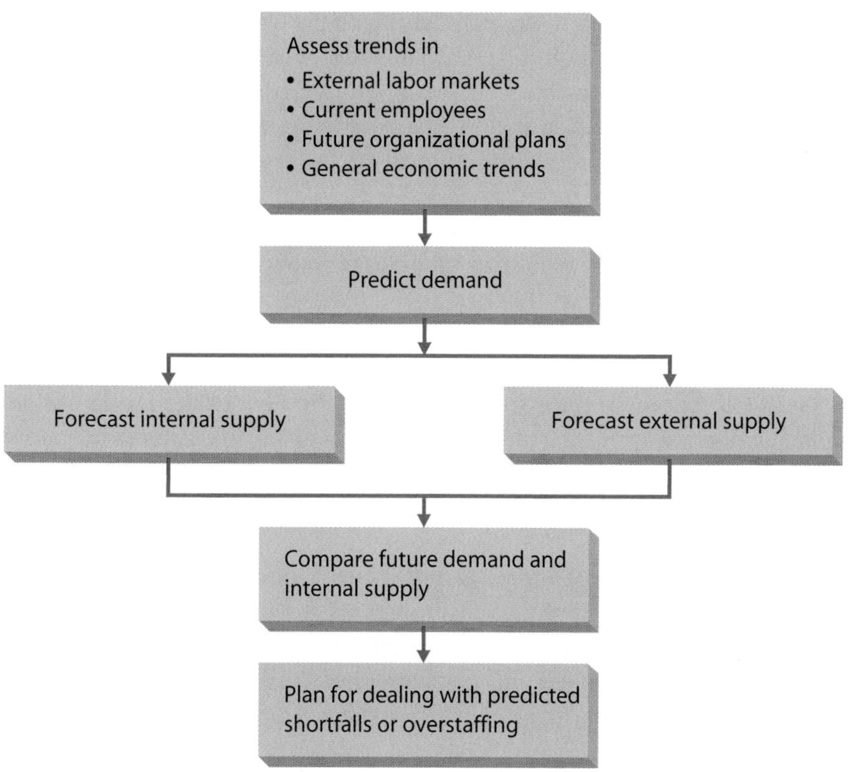

FIGURE 14.1

Human Resource Planning

Attracting human resources cannot be left to chance if an organization expects to function at peak efficiency. Human resource planning involves assessing trends, forecasting supply and demand of labor, and then developing appropriate strategies for addressing any differences.

will need to hire 1 million people over the next five years. Of this total, 800,000 are for new positions created as the firm grows, and the other 200,000 will replace current workers who leave for various reasons.[7]

Forecasting the supply of labor is really two tasks: forecasting the internal supply (the number and type of employees who will be in the firm at some future date) and forecasting the external supply (the number and type of people who will be available for hiring in the labor market at large). The simplest approach merely adjusts present staffing levels for anticipated turnover and promotions. Again, though, large organizations use extremely sophisticated models to make these forecasts. Union Oil Company of California, for example, has a complex forecasting system for keeping track of the present and future distributions of professionals and managers. The Union Oil system can spot areas where there will eventually be too many qualified professionals competing for too few promotions or, conversely, too few good people available to fill important positions.[8]

At higher levels of the organization, managers plan for specific people and positions. The technique most commonly used is the **replacement chart**, which lists each important managerial position, who occupies it, how long he or she will probably stay in it before moving on, and who (by name) is now qualified or soon will be qualified to move into the position. This technique allows ample time to plan developmental experiences for persons identified as potential successors to critical managerial jobs.[9]

replacement chart Lists each important managerial position in the organization, who occupies it, how long he or she will probably remain in the position, and who is or will be a qualified replacement

employee information system (skills inventory) Contains information on each employee's education, skills, experience, and career aspirations; usually computerized

To facilitate both planning and identifying persons for current transfer or promotion, some organizations also have an **employee information system,** or **skills inventory**. Such systems are usually computerized and contain information on each employee's education, skills, work experience, and career aspirations. Such a system can quickly locate all the employees in the organization who are qualified to fill a position requiring, for instance, a degree in chemical engineering, three years of experience in an oil refinery, and fluency in Spanish. ERP systems, as described in Chapter 13, generally include capabilities for measuring and managing the internal supply of labor in ways that best fit the needs of the organization.

Forecasting the external supply of labor is a different problem altogether. How does a manager, for example, predict how many electrical engineers will be seeking work in Georgia three years from now? To get an idea of the future availability of labor, planners must rely on information from such outside sources as state employment commissions, government reports, and figures supplied by colleges on the number of students in major fields.

Matching Human Resource Supply and Demand After comparing future demand and internal supply, managers can make plans to manage predicted shortfalls or overstaffing. If a shortfall is predicted, new employees can be hired, present employees can be retrained and transferred into the understaffed area, individuals approaching retirement can be convinced to stay on, or labor-saving or productivity-enhancing systems can be installed.

If the organization needs to hire, the external labor supply forecast helps managers plan how to recruit, based on whether the type of person needed is readily available or scarce in the labor market. As we note earlier, the trend in temporary workers also helps managers in staffing by affording them extra flexibility. If overstaffing is expected to be a problem, the main options are transferring the extra employees, not replacing individuals who quit, encouraging early retirement, and laying people off.

Recruiting Human Resources

recruiting The process of attracting individuals to apply for jobs that are open

internal recruiting Considering current employees as applicants for higher-level jobs in the organization

Once an organization has an idea of its future human resource needs, the next phase is usually recruiting new employees. **Recruiting** is the process of attracting qualified persons to apply for jobs that are open. Where do recruits come from? Some recruits are found internally; others come from outside the organization.

Internal recruiting means considering present employees as candidates for openings. Promotion from within can help build morale and keep high-quality employees from leaving the firm. In unionized firms, the procedures for notifying employees of internal job change opportunities are usually spelled out in the union contract. For higher-level positions, a skills inventory system may be used to identify internal candidates, or managers may be asked to recommend individuals who should be considered. Most businesses today routinely post job openings on their internal communication network, or intranet. One disadvantage of internal recruiting is its ripple effect. When an employee moves to a different job, someone else must be found to take his or her old job. In one organization, 454 job movements were necessary as a result of filling 195 initial openings!

External recruiting involves attracting persons outside the organization to apply for jobs. External recruiting methods include advertising, campus interviews, employment agencies or executive search firms, union hiring halls, referrals by present employees, and hiring "walk-ins" or "gate-hires" (people who show up without being solicited). Increasingly, firms are using the Internet to post job openings and to solicit applicants. Of course, a manager must select the most appropriate methods, using the state employment service to find maintenance workers but not a nuclear physicist, for example. Private employment agencies can be a good source of clerical and technical employees, and executive search firms specialize in locating top-management talent. Newspaper ads are often used because they reach a wide audience and thus allow minorities equal opportunity to find out about and apply for job openings.

external recruiting Getting people from outside the organization to apply for jobs

The organization must also keep in mind that recruiting decisions often go both ways—the organization is recruiting an employee, but the prospective employee is also selecting a job.[10] Indeed, during the late 1990s recruiters faced a difficult job, as unemployment dropped to a twenty-five-year low of 4.3 percent. As a result, recruiters at firms such as Sprint, PeopleSoft, and Cognex stressed how much "fun" it was to work for them, reinforcing this message with ice cream socials, karaoke contests, softball leagues, and free movie nights.[11]

In recent times, however, unemployment has surged, and organizations are finding it easier to recruit prospective employees. Nevertheless, even if a firm can take its pick of the best potential employees, it still should put its best foot forward, treat all applicants with dignity, and strive for a good person-job fit. *Working with Diversity* discusses this perspective in more detail. Recent estimates suggest that hiring the "wrong" operating employee—one who flops and either quits or must be fired—generally costs the organization at least $5,000 in lost productivity and training. Hiring the wrong manager can cost the organization far more.[12]

One generally successful method for facilitating a good person-job fit is the so-called **realistic job preview (RJP)**. As the term suggests, the RJP involves providing the applicant with a real picture of what performing the job that the organization is trying to fill would be like.[13] For example, it would not make sense for a firm to tell an applicant that the job is exciting and challenging when in fact it is routine and straightforward, yet some managers do this to hire the best people. The likely outcome will be a dissatisfied employee who will quickly be looking for a better job. If the company is more realistic about a job, though, the person hired will be more likely to remain in the job for a longer period of time.

realistic job preview (RJP) Provides the applicant with a real picture of what performing the job that the organization is trying to fill would be like

Selecting Human Resources

Once the recruiting process has attracted a pool of applicants, the next step is to select whom to hire. The intent of the selection process is to gather from applicants information that will predict their job success and then to hire the candidates likely to be most successful. Of course, the organization can gather information only about factors that are predictive of future performance. The process of determining the predictive value of information is called **validation**.

validation Determining the extent to which a selection device is really predictive of future job performance

Two basic approaches to validation are predictive validation and content validation. *Predictive validation* involves collecting the scores of employees or applicants

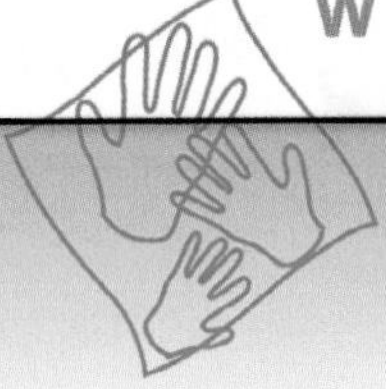

WORKING WITH diversity

A Variety of Approaches to Finding the Dream Job

"I'll get a second job before I go back,"

– Jasmin Agosto, Head Start employee and former welfare recipient*

For most of us, a dream job is a full-time, permanent, 8-to-5 position at a powerful and reputable firm, with good pay and opportunities for advancement. However, when the U.S. economy is weak and firms are faltering, for many individuals the dream job remains just that—a dream.

People who struggle to find and keep jobs are experiencing more difficulty than usual. Former welfare recipients have taken advantage of welfare-to-work programs to receive training and find employment. In New York City alone, 740,000 people have left the welfare rolls since 1996. Jasmin Agosto, a former "welfare mom," makes $16,000 for her family of three. She receives food stamps to help ease the transition but vows never to return to public assistance. "I'll get a second job before I go back," she says. "[Welfare workers] treat you like trash." Yet Agosto's success is an exception—many program participants have lost their jobs and are no longer eligible for aid.

Even those with stellar qualifications may find themselves resorting to unusual tactics. Some accept less-than-desirable working conditions. Nurse John Granucci received a promotion for taking a job on the overnight shift. He says, "It afforded me more responsibility and really opened some doors." Other workers forgo raises to prevent a layoff. Firms may offer promotion, but no salary increase. Karen Norris took a promotion at Oracle without a raise. Norris claims, "It would never enter my mind to say, 'Don't promote me [without a raise].'" Some individuals, especially those in the troubled financial, telecom, or technology sectors, take a more extreme approach. John Sawicki, with an M.B.A. and five years' banking experience, was laid off. He became an unpaid intern at a start-up firm and says, "Normally someone my age, with my qualifications, would have to be crazy to do this." Yet in the absence of a paying offer, "I'd have to be crazy *not* to take their offer."

The poor job market is a boon for employers, who are enjoying the inexpensive labor and the glut of applicants with strong credentials. But, for those individuals who are struggling to find work today, the economic rebound cannot come quickly enough.

References: David Koeppel, "On the Far Side of Day, Some Find Greater Opportunities to Shine," *New York Times*, September 1, 2002, p. MB1; Karen Alexander, "Ways to Move up When the Economy Moves Down," *New York Times*, August 18, 2002, p. BU9; Leslie Kaufman, "From Welfare to Work, and Then, to What?" *New York Times*, October 6, 2002, pp. L37, L41 (*quote p. L41); Patricia R. Olsen, "In Land of the Jobless, the Extreme Approach," *New York Times*, October 27, 2002, p. NJ1.

on the device to be validated and correlating their scores with actual job performance. A significant correlation means that the selection device is a valid predictor of job performance. *Content validation* uses logic and job analysis data to establish that the selection device measures the exact skills needed for successful job performance. The most critical part of content validation is a careful job analysis showing exactly what duties are to be performed. The test is then developed to measure the applicant's ability to perform those duties.

Application Blanks The first step in selection is usually asking the candidate to fill out an application blank. Application blanks are an efficient method of gathering information about the applicant's previous work history, educational background, and other job-related demographic data. They should not contain questions about areas not related to the job, such as gender, religion, or national origin. Application blank data are generally used informally to decide whether a candidate merits further evaluation, and interviewers use application blanks to familiarize themselves with candidates before interviewing them. Unfortunately, in recent years there has been a trend toward job applicants' either falsifying or inflating their credentials in order to stand a better chance of getting a job. Indeed, one recent survey of 2.6 million job applications found that an astounding 44 percent of them contained some false information.[14]

Tests Tests of ability, skill, aptitude, or knowledge that is relevant to the particular job are usually the best predictors of job success, although tests of general intelligence or personality are occasionally useful as well. In addition to being validated, tests should be administered and scored consistently. All candidates should be given the same directions, should be allowed the same amount of time, and should experience the same testing environment (temperature, lighting, distractions).[15]

Interviews Although a popular selection device, interviews are sometimes poor predictors of job success. For example, biases inherent in the way people perceive and judge others at a first meeting affect subsequent evaluations by the interviewer. Interview validity can be improved by training interviewers to be aware of potential biases and by increasing the structure of the interview. In a structured interview, questions are written in advance, and all interviewers follow the same question list with each candidate they interview. This procedure introduces consistency into the interview procedure and allows the organization to validate the content of the questions to be asked.[16]

For interviewing managerial or professional candidates, a somewhat less structured approach can be used. Question areas and information-gathering objectives are still planned in advance, but the specific questions vary with the candidates' backgrounds. Trammell Crow Real Estate Investors uses a novel approach in hiring managers. Each applicant is interviewed not only by two or three other managers but also by a secretary or young leasing agent. This provides information about how the prospective manager relates to nonmanagers.

Assessment Centers Assessment centers are a popular method used to select managers and are particularly good for selecting current employees for promotion. The assessment center is a content-valid simulation of major parts of the managerial job. A typical center lasts two to three days, with groups of six to twelve persons participating in a variety of managerial exercises. Centers may also include interviews, public speaking, and standardized ability tests. Candidates are assessed by several trained observers, usually managers several levels above the job for which the candidates are being considered. Assessment centers are quite valid if properly designed and are fair to members of minority groups and women.[17] For some firms, the assessment center is a permanent facility created for these activities. For other firms, the assessment activities are performed in a multipurpose location such as a conference room. AT&T pioneered the assessment center concept. For years the firm has used assessment centers to make virtually all of its selection decisions for management positions.

Other Techniques Organizations also use other selection techniques depending on the circumstances. Polygraph tests, once popular, are declining in popularity.

On the other hand, more and more organizations are requiring that applicants in whom they are interested take physical exams. Organizations are also increasingly using drug tests, especially in situations in which drug-related performance problems could create serious safety hazards. For example, applicants for jobs in a nuclear power plant would likely be tested for drug use. And some organizations today even run credit checks on prospective employees.

concept CHECK

Describe the processes of human resource planning, recruiting, and selection.	*As a potential employee, what things might a firm do in its recruiting efforts to impress you?*

Developing Human Resources

Regardless of how effective a selection system is, however, most employees need additional training if they are to grow and develop in their jobs. Evaluating their performance and providing feedback are also necessary.

training Teaching operational or technical employees how to do the job for which they were hired

development Teaching managers and professionals the skills needed for both present and future jobs

Training and Development

In HRM, **training** usually refers to teaching operational or technical employees how to do the job for which they were hired. **Development** refers to teaching managers and professionals the skills needed for both present and future jobs. Most organi-

Training and developing people is an important part of human resource management. Canon, for example, invests heavily in training its employees as part of its goal to remain a leading manufacturer of photography equipment. One of its biggest problems has been trying to balance the trend toward moving production to cheaper labor markets while maintaining high performance levels. One tactic Canon uses is to send its newly hired Malaysian workers to one of its plants in Japan for training. After these workers have gained proficiency, they are sent back to Malaysia to work in Canon's factory there.

zations provide regular training and development programs for managers and employees. For example, IBM spends more than $700 million annually on programs and has a vice president in charge of employee education. U.S. businesses spend more than $30 billion annually on training and development programs away from the workplace. And this figure does not include wages and benefits paid to employees while they are participating in such programs.

Assessing Training Needs The first step in developing a training plan is to determine what needs exist. For example, if employees do not know how to operate the machinery necessary to do their job, a training program on how to operate the machinery is clearly needed. On the other hand, when a group of office workers is performing poorly, training may not be the answer. The problem could be motivation, aging equipment, poor supervision, inefficient work design, or a deficiency of skills and knowledge. Only the last could be remedied by training. As training programs are being developed, the manager should set specific and measurable goals specifying what participants are to learn. Managers should also plan to evaluate the training program after employees complete it. The training process from start to finish is diagrammed in Figure 14.2.

Common Training Methods Many different training and development methods are available. Selection of methods depends on many considerations, but perhaps the most important is training content. When the training content is factual material (such as company rules or explanations for how to fill out forms), assigned reading, programmed learning, and lecture methods work well. When the content is interpersonal relations or group decision making, however, firms must use a method that allows interpersonal contact, such as role-playing or case discussion groups. When employees must learn a physical skill, methods allowing practice and the actual use of tools and materials are needed, as in on-the-job training or vestibule training. (Vestibule training enables participants to focus on safety, learning, and feedback rather than on productivity.)

Web-based and other electronic media–based training are also becoming popular. Such methods allow a mix of training content, are relatively easy to update and revise, let participants use a variable schedule, and lower travel costs. On the other hand, they are limited in their capacity to simulate real activities and facilitate face-to-face interaction. Xerox, Massachusetts Mutual Life Insurance, and Ford have all reported tremendous success with these methods. In addition, most training programs actually rely on a mix of methods. Boeing, for example, sends managers to an intensive two-week training seminar involving tests, simulations, role-playing exercises, and CD-ROM flight simulation exercises.[18]

Finally, some larger businesses have started creating their own self-contained training facility, often called a *corporate university.* McDonald's was among the first to start this practice with its so-called Hamburger University in Illinois. All management trainees for the firm attend training programs there to learn exactly how long to grill a burger, how to maintain good customer service, and so on. Other firms that are using this approach include Shell Oil and General Electric.

Evaluation of Training Training and development programs should always be evaluated. Typical evaluation approaches include measuring one or more relevant

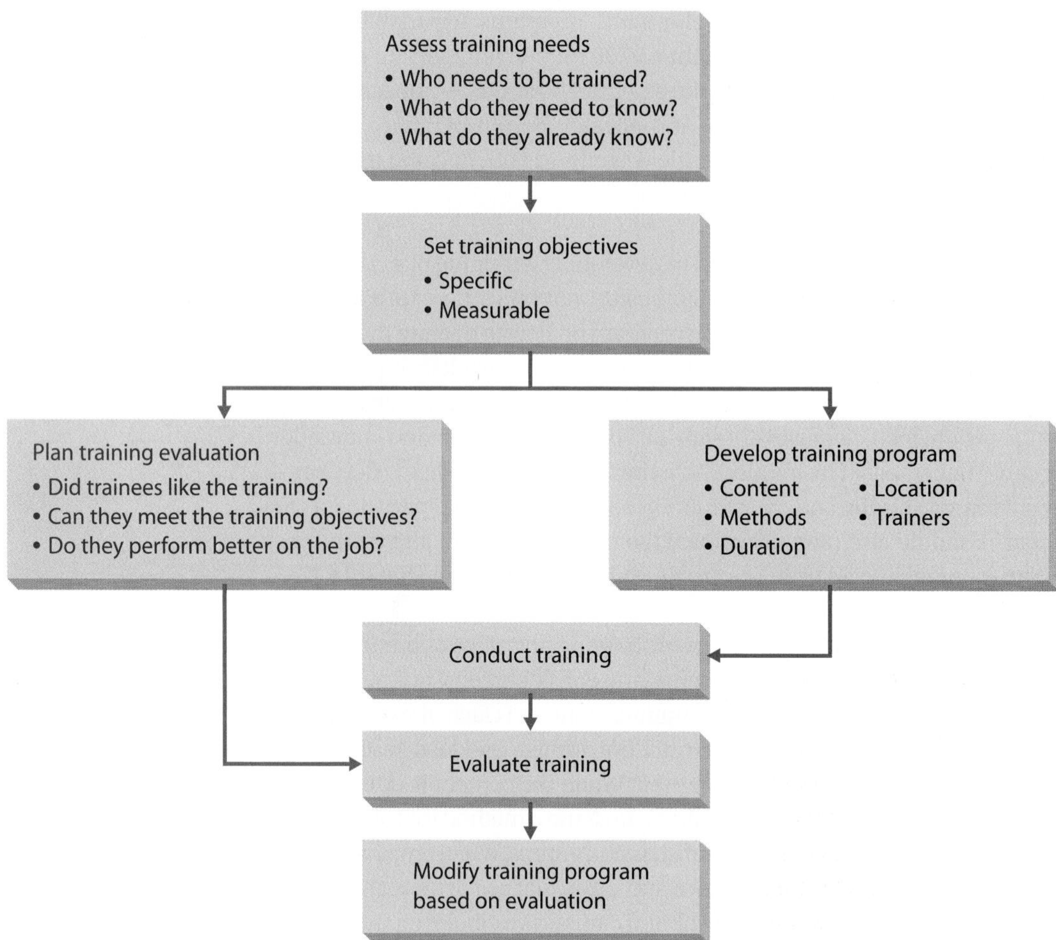

FIGURE 14.2

The Training Process

Managing the training process can go a long way toward enhancing its effectiveness. If training programs are well conceived and well executed, both the organization and its employees benefit. Following a comprehensive process helps managers meet the objectives of the training program.

criteria (such as attitudes or performance) before and after the training, and determining whether the criteria changed. Evaluation measures collected at the end of training are easy to get, but actual performance measures collected when the trainee is on the job are more important. Trainees may say that they enjoyed the training and learned a lot, but the true test is whether their job performance improves after their training.

Performance Appraisal

performance appraisal A formal assessment of how well an employee is doing his or her job

Once employees are trained and settled into their jobs, one of management's next concerns is performance appraisal. **Performance appraisal** is a formal assessment of how well employees are doing their job. Employees' performance should be evaluated regularly for many reasons. One reason is that performance appraisal may be necessary for validating selection devices or assessing the impact of training programs. A second reason is administrative—to aid in making decisions about pay raises, promotions, and training. Still another reason is to provide feedback to employees to help them improve their present performance and plan future careers.

Because performance evaluations often help determine wages and promotions, they must be fair and nondiscriminatory. In the case of appraisals, content validation is used to show that the appraisal system accurately measures performance on important job elements and does not measure traits or behavior that are irrelevant to job performance.

Common Appraisal Methods Two basic categories of appraisal methods commonly used in organizations are objective methods and judgmental methods. Objective measures of performance include actual output (that is, number of units produced), scrap rate, dollar volume of sales, and number of claims processed. Objective performance measures may be contaminated by "opportunity bias" if some persons have a better chance to perform than others. For example, a sales representative selling snow blowers in Michigan has a greater opportunity than does a colleague selling the same product in Arkansas. Fortunately, adjusting raw performance figures for the effect of opportunity bias and thereby arriving at figures that accurately represent each individual's performance is often possible.

Another type of objective measure, the special performance test, is a method in which each employee is assessed under standardized conditions. This kind of appraisal also eliminates opportunity bias. For example, Verizon Southwest has a series of prerecorded calls that operators in a test booth answer. The operators are graded on speed, accuracy, and courtesy in handling the calls. Performance tests measure ability but do not measure the extent to which one is motivated to use that ability on a daily basis. (A high-ability person may be a lazy performer except when being tested.) Special performance tests must therefore be supplemented by other appraisal methods to provide a complete picture of performance.

Judgmental methods, including ranking and rating techniques, are the most common way to measure performance. Ranking compares employees directly with one another and orders them from best to worst. Ranking has a number of drawbacks. Ranking is difficult for large groups, because the persons in the middle of the distribution may be hard to distinguish from one another accurately. Comparisons of people in different work groups are also difficult. For example, an employee ranked third in a strong group may be more valuable than an employee ranked first in a weak group. Another criticism of ranking is that the manager must rank people on the basis of overall performance, although each person likely has both strengths and weaknesses. Furthermore, rankings do not provide useful information for feedback. To be told that one is ranked third is not nearly as helpful as to be told that the quality of one's work is outstanding, its quantity is satisfactory, one's punctuality could use improvement, or one's paperwork is seriously deficient.

FIGURE 14.3

Graphic Rating Scales for a Bank Teller

Graphic rating scales are very common methods for evaluating employee performance. The manager who is doing the rating circles the point on each scale that best reflects her or his assessment of the employee on that scale. Graphic rating scales are widely used for many different kinds of jobs.

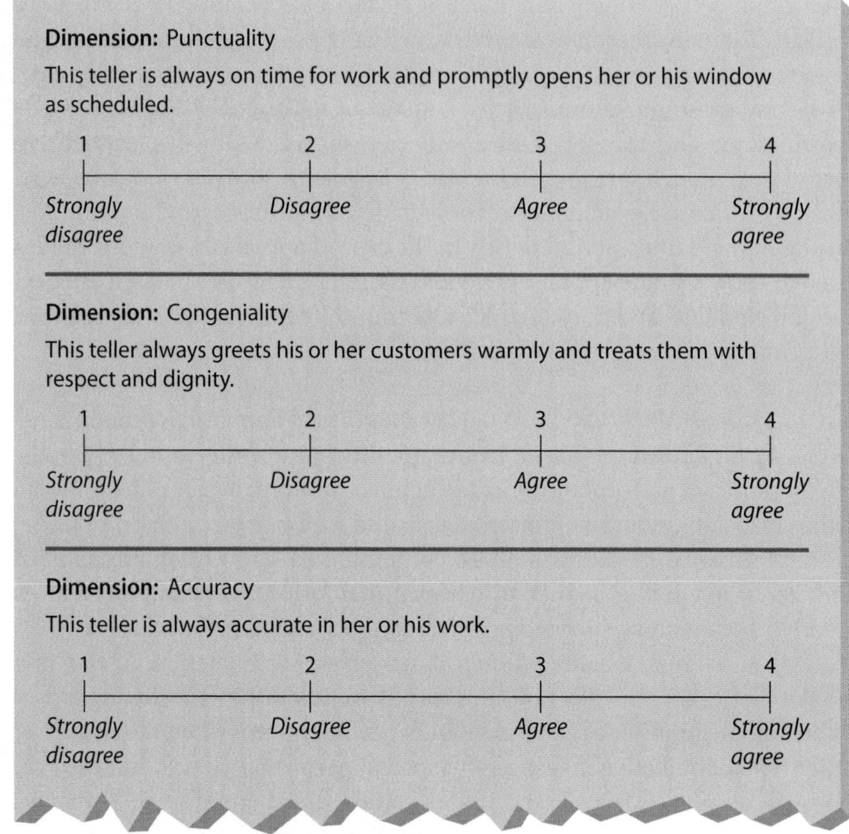

Rating differs from ranking in that it compares each employee with a fixed standard rather than comparison with other employees. A rating scale provides the standard. Figure 14.3 gives examples of three graphic rating scales for a bank teller. Each consists of a performance dimension to be rated (punctuality, congeniality, and accuracy) followed by a scale on which to make the rating. In constructing graphic rating scales, performance dimensions that are relevant to job performance must be selected. In particular, they should focus on job behaviors and results rather than on personality traits or attitudes.

Behaviorally Anchored Rating Scale (BARS) A sophisticated rating method in which supervisors construct a rating scale associated with behavioral anchors

The **Behaviorally Anchored Rating Scale (BARS)** is a sophisticated and useful rating method. Supervisors construct rating scales with associated behavioral anchors. They first identify relevant performance dimensions and then generate anchors—specific, observable behaviors typical of each performance level. Figure 14.4 shows an example of a behaviorally anchored rating scale for the dimension "Inventory control."

The other scales in this set, developed for the job of department manager in a chain of specialty stores, include "Handling customer complaints," "Planning special promotions," "Following company procedures," "Supervising sales personnel," and "Diagnosing and solving special problems." BARS can be effective because they require that management take proper care in constructing the scales and they pro-

Job: Specialty store manager
Dimension: Inventory control

7 Always orders in the right quantities and at the right time

6 Almost always orders at the right time but occasionally orders too much or too little of a particular item

5 Usually orders at the right time and almost always in the right quantities

4 Often orders in the right quantities and at the right time

3 Occasionally orders at the right time but usually not in the right quantities

2 Occasionally orders in the right quantities but usually not at the right time

1 Never orders in the right quantities or at the right time

FIGURE 14.4

Behaviorally Anchored Rating Scale

Behaviorally anchored rating scales help overcome some of the limitations of standard rating scales. Each point on the scale is accompanied by a behavioral anchor–a summary of an employee behavior that fits that spot on the scale.

vide useful anchors for supervisors to use in evaluating people. They are costly, however, because outside expertise is usually needed and because scales must be developed for each job within the organization.

Errors in Performance Appraisal Errors or biases can occur in any kind of rating or ranking system. One common problem is *recency error*—the tendency to base judgments on the subordinate's most recent performance because it is most easily recalled. Often a rating or ranking is intended to evaluate performance over an entire time period, such as six months or a year, so the recency error does introduce error into the judgment. Other errors include overuse of one part of the scale—being too lenient, being too severe, or giving everyone a rating of "average."

Halo error is allowing the assessment of an employee on one dimension to "spread" to ratings of that employee on other dimensions. For instance, if an employee is outstanding on quality of output, a rater might tend to give her or him higher marks than deserved on other dimensions. Errors can also occur because of race, sex, or age discrimination, intentionally or unintentionally. The best way to offset these errors is to ensure that a valid rating system is developed at the outset and then to train managers in how to use it.

A recent innovation in performance appraisal used in many organizations today is called **360-degree feedback**, in which managers are evaluated by everyone around them—their boss, their peers, and their subordinates. Such a complete and thorough approach provides people with a far richer array of information about their performance than does a conventional appraisal given just by the boss. Of course, such a system also takes considerable time and must be handled so as not to breed fear and mistrust in the workplace.[19]

360-degree feedback A performance appraisal system in which managers are evaluated by everyone around them—their boss, their peers, and their subordinates

Reprinted with permission of King Features Syndicate.

Providing performance feedback is a difficult process for many managers. For example, they may have a hard time giving negative feedback or simply feel uncomfortable with the process. And, in some cases, as illustrated here, a manager may feel that it is only his or her opinion that counts. The employee, of course, is likely to figure out what is going on, and thus the information value of the performance feedback process can be completely lost.

Performance Feedback

The last step in most performance appraisal systems is giving feedback to subordinates about their performance. This is usually done in a private meeting between the person being evaluated and his or her boss. The discussion should generally be focused on the facts—the assessed level of performance, how and why that assessment was made, and how it can be improved in the future. Feedback interviews are not easy to conduct. Many managers are uncomfortable with the task, especially if feedback is negative and subordinates are disappointed by what they hear. These points are amplified in the cartoon. Properly training managers, however, can help them conduct more effective feedback interviews.[20]

Some firms use a very aggressive approach to terminating people who do not meet expectations. General Electric actually implemented a system whereby each year the bottom 10 percent of its workforce is terminated and replaced with new employees. Company executives claim that this approach, although stressful for all employees, helps it to continuously upgrade its workforce. Other firms have started using this same approach. However, both Ford and Goodyear recently agreed to abandon similar approaches in response to age discrimination lawsuits.[21]

concept CHECK

What are the most common methods for training employees and assessing their performance?

What kind of performance appraisal techniques or methods would you prefer to use as a manager? As someone being evaluated? Why?

Maintaining Human Resources

After organizations have attracted and developed an effective workforce, they must also make every effort to maintain that workforce. To do so requires effective compensation and benefits as well as career planning.

Determining Compensation

Compensation is the financial remuneration given by the organization to its employees in exchange for their work. There are three basic forms of compensation. *Wages* are the hourly compensation paid to operating employees. The minimum hourly wage paid in the United States today is $5.15. *Salary* refers to compensation paid for total contributions, as opposed to pay based on hours worked. For example, managers earn an annual salary, usually paid monthly. They receive the salary regardless of the number of hours they work. Some firms have started paying all their employees a salary instead of hourly wages. For example, all employees at Chaparral Steel earn a salary, starting at $30,000 a year for entry-level operating employees. Finally, *incentives* represent special compensation opportunities that are usually tied to performance. Sales commissions and bonuses are among the most common incentives.

compensation The financial remuneration given by the organization to its employees in exchange for their work

Compensation is an important and complex part of the organization-employee relationship. Basic compensation is necessary to provide employees with the means to maintain a reasonable standard of living. Beyond this, however, compensation also provides a tangible measure of the value of the individual to the organization. If employees do not earn enough to meet their basic economic goals, they will seek employment elsewhere. Likewise, if they believe that their contributions are undervalued by the organization, they may leave or exhibit poor work habits, low morale, and little commitment to the organization. Thus designing an effective compensation system is clearly in the organization's best interests.[22]

A good compensation system can help attract qualified applicants, retain present employees, and stimulate high performance at a cost reasonable for one's industry and geographic area. To set up a successful system, management must make decisions about wage levels, the wage structure, and the individual wage determination system.

Wage-Level Decision The wage-level decision is a management policy decision about whether the firm wants to pay above, at, or below the going rate for labor in the industry or the geographic area. Most firms choose to pay near the average, although those that cannot afford more pay below average. Large, successful firms may like to cultivate the image of being "wage leaders" by intentionally paying more than average and thus attracting and keeping high-quality employees. IBM, for example, pays top dollar to get the new employees it wants. McDonald's, on the other hand, often pays close to the minimum wage. The level of unemployment in the labor force also affects wage levels. Pay declines when labor is plentiful and increases when labor is scarce.

Once managers make the wage-level decision, they need information to help set actual wage rates. Managers need to know what the maximum, minimum, and average wages are for particular jobs in the appropriate labor market. This information is collected by means of a wage survey. Area wage surveys can be conducted by individual firms or by local HR or business associations. Professional and industry associations often conduct surveys and make the results available to employers.

job evaluation An attempt to assess the worth of each job relative to other jobs

Wage Structure Decision Wage structures are usually set up through a procedure called **job evaluation**—an attempt to assess the worth of each job relative to other jobs. At Ben & Jerry's Homemade, company policy once dictated that the highest-paid employee in the firm could not make more than seven times what the lowest-paid employee earned. But this policy had to be modified when the company found that it was simply unable to hire a new CEO without paying more than this amount. The simplest method for creating a wage structure is to rank jobs from those that should be paid the most (for example, the president) to those that should be paid the least (for example, a mail clerk or a janitor).

In a smaller firm with few jobs (like Ben & Jerry's, for example), this method is quick and practical, but larger firms with many job titles require more sophisticated methods. The next step is setting actual wage rates on the basis of a combination of survey data and the wage structure that results from job evaluation. Jobs of equal value are often grouped into wage grades for ease of administration.

Individual Wage Decisions After wage-level and wage structure decisions are made, the individual wage decision must be addressed. This decision concerns how much to pay each employee in a particular job. Although the easiest decision is to pay a single rate for each job, more typically a range of pay rates is associated with each job. For example, the pay range for an individual job might be $5.85 to $6.39 per hour, with different employees earning different rates within the range.

A system is then needed for setting individual rates. This may be done on the basis of seniority (enter the job at $6.85, for example, and increase 10 cents per hour every six months on the job), initial qualifications (inexperienced people start at $6.85; more experienced people start at a higher rate), or merit (raises above the entering rate are given for good performance). Combinations of these bases may also be used.

The Internet is also playing a key role in compensation patterns today, because both job seekers and current employees can more easily get a sense of what their true market value is. If they can document the claim that their value is higher than what their current employer now pays or is offering, they are in a position to demand a higher salary. Consider the case of one compensation executive who met recently with a subordinate to discuss her raise. He was surprised when she produced data from five different websites backing up her claim for a bigger raise than he had intended to offer.[23]

Determining Benefits

benefits Things of value other than compensation that an organization provides to its workers

Benefits are things of value other than compensation that the organization provides to its workers. The average company spends an amount equal to more than one-third of its cash payroll on employee benefits. Thus an average employee who is paid $18,000 per year averages about $6,588 more per year in benefits.

Benefits come in several forms. Pay for time not worked includes sick leave, vacation, holidays, and unemployment compensation. Insurance benefits often include life and health insurance for employees and their dependents. Workers' compensation is a legally required insurance benefit that provides medical care and disability income for employees injured on the job. Social security is a government pension plan to which both employers and employees contribute. Many employers also provide a private pension plan to which they and their employees contribute. Employee service benefits include such extras as tuition reimbursement and recreational opportunities.

Compensation and benefits often play key roles in helping organizations retain their most valuable employees. Gerry Harkins and Brack Maggard own Southern Pan Services Co., a concrete-formwork construction company. They recently created a stock ownership plan that allows them to sell stock in their business to their employees. Harkins and Maggard believe that this will motivate people to work toward the best interests of the firm and to stay in their present jobs rather than looking for work elsewhere.

Some organizations have instituted "cafeteria benefit plans," whereby basic coverage is provided for all employees but employees are then allowed to choose which additional benefits they want (up to a cost limit based on salary). An employee with five children might choose medical and dental coverage for dependents, a single employee might prefer more vacation time, and an older employee might elect increased pension benefits. Flexible systems are expected to encourage people to stay in the organization and even help the company attract new employees.[24]

In recent years, companies have also started offering more innovative benefits as a way of accommodating different needs. On-site childcare, mortgage assistance, and paid leave programs are interesting new benefits that some firms offer.[25] A good benefits plan may encourage people to join and stay with an organization, but it seldom stimulates high performance, because benefits are tied more to membership in the organization than to performance. To manage their benefits programs effectively, companies should shop carefully, avoid redundant coverage, and provide only those benefits that employees want. Benefits programs should also be explained to employees in clear and straightforward language, so that they can use the benefits appropriately and appreciate what the company is providing. Finally, as a result of economic pressures, some firms have started to reduce employee benefits in the last few years. For example, in 2002 17% of employees in the United States with employer healthcare coverage saw their benefits cut. Some employers have also reduced their contributions to employee retirement plans and/or cut the amount of annual leave they offer to employees.[26]

Career Planning

A final aspect of maintaining human resources is career planning. Few people work in the same job their entire career. Some people change jobs within one organization, others change organizations, and many do both. When these movements are haphazard and poorly conceived, both the individual and the organization suffer. Thus planning career progressions in advance is in everyone's best interests. Of course, planning a thirty-year career for a newcomer just joining the organization is difficult. But planning can help map out what areas the individual is most interested in and help the person see what opportunities are available within the organization.[27]

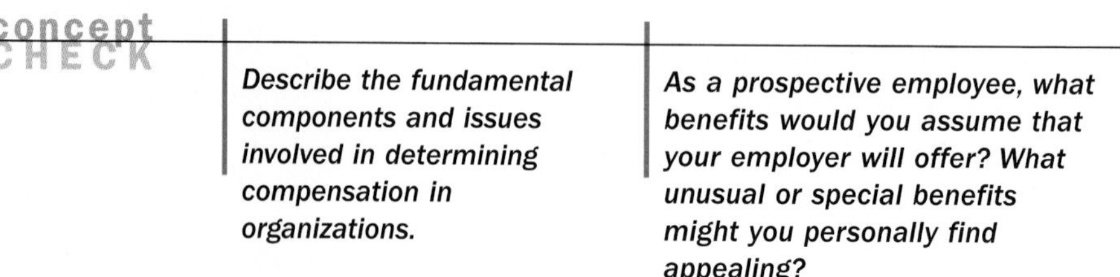

Managing Labor Relations

Labor relations is the process of dealing with employees who are represented by a union.[28] Managing labor relations is an important part of HRM. However, most large firms have separate labor relations specialists to handle these activities apart from other human resource functions.

labor relations The process of dealing with employees who are represented by a union

How Employees Form Unions

For employees to form a new local union, several things must occur. First, employees must become interested in having a union. Nonemployees who are professional organizers employed by a national union (such as the Teamsters or United Auto Workers) may generate interest by making speeches and distributing literature outside the workplace. Inside, employees who want a union try to convince other workers of the benefits of a union.

The second step is to collect employees' signatures on authorization cards. These cards state that the signer wishes to vote to determine whether the union will represent him or her. To show the National Labor Relations Board (NLRB) that interest is sufficient to justify holding an election, 30 percent of the employees in the potential bargaining unit must sign these cards. Before an election can be held, however, the bargaining unit must be defined. The bargaining unit consists of all employees who will be eligible to vote in the election and to join and be represented by the union if one is formed.

The election is supervised by an NLRB representative (or, if both parties agree, the American Arbitration Association—a professional association of arbitrators) and is conducted by secret ballot. If a simple majority of those voting (not of all those eligible to vote) votes for the union, then the union becomes certified as the official representative of the bargaining unit.[29] The new union then organizes itself by officially signing up members and electing officers; it will soon be ready to negotiate the first contract. The union-organizing process is diagrammed in Figure 14.5. If workers become disgruntled with their union or if management presents strong evidence that the union is not representing workers appropriately, the NLRB can arrange a decertification election. The results of such an election determine whether the union remains certified.

Organizations usually prefer that employees not be unionized because unions limit management's freedom in many areas. Management may thus wage its own campaign to convince employees to vote against the union. "Unfair labor practices" are often committed at this point. For instance, it is an unfair labor practice for management to promise to give employees a raise (or any other benefit) if the union is defeated. Experts agree that the best way to avoid unionization is to practice good employee relations all the time—not just when threatened by a union election. Providing absolutely fair treatment with clear standards in the areas of pay, promotion, layoffs, and discipline; having a complaint or appeal system for persons who feel unfairly treated; and avoiding any kind of favoritism will help

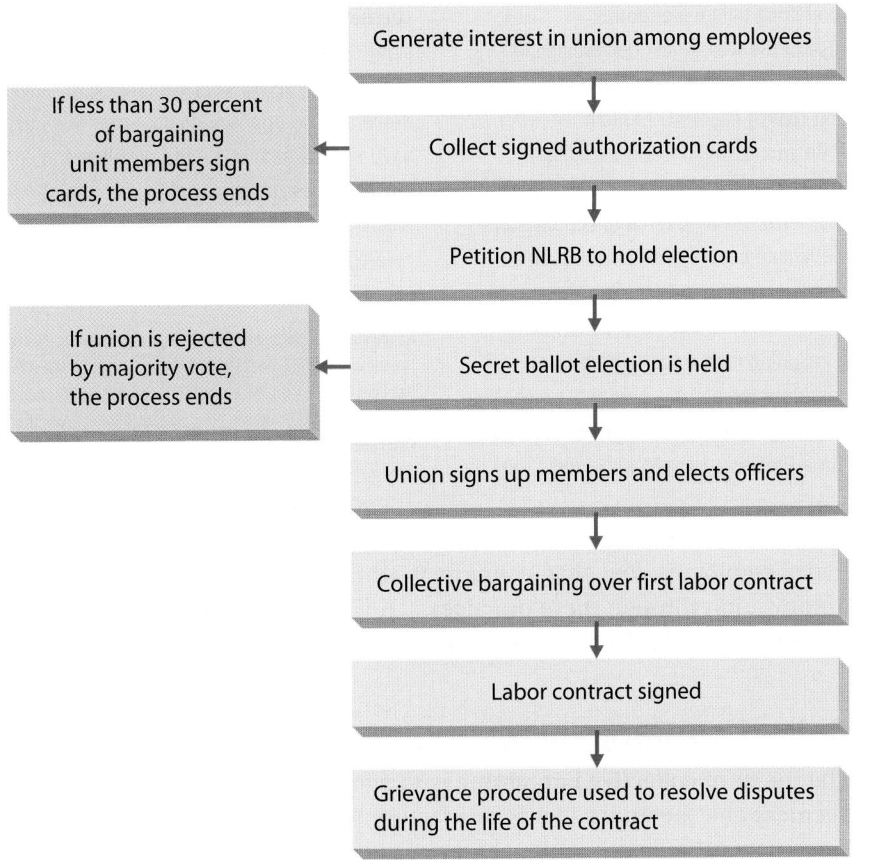

FIGURE 14.5

The Union-organizing Process

If employees of an organization want to form a union, the law prescribes a specific set of procedures that both employees and the organization must follow. Assuming that these procedures are followed and the union is approved, the organization must engage in collective bargaining with the new union.

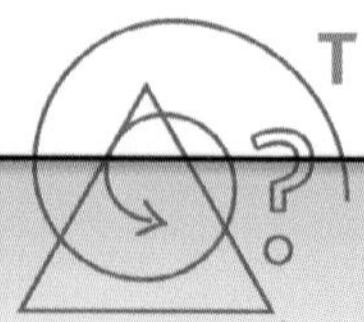

THE BUSINESS OF ethics

An Ethical Stand-off for Unions and Corporations

"The question should be, 'Why shouldn't blue-collar workers be able to share in the benefits of increased productivity?'"

– Steve Stallone, spokesman, International Longshore and Warehouse Union*

In an ethical stand-off, which would win, corporations or labor unions? It might be a draw. United Airlines is near bankruptcy. Its most expensive input is unionized labor, so United wants wage concessions. Although United pilots make the most money, they initially refused to accept a pay freeze. Contrast United with Sam's Clubs (owned by Wal-Mart). The retailing giant, with labor costs 20 percent lower than unionized competitors, opposes organized labor. Las Vegas employees say the firm fired and harassed pro-union leaders, for example, by positioning surveillance cameras to continuously monitor suspected union supporters. Thus do unions and corporations maintain a shifting balance of power.

The case of the West Coast dockworkers is illustrative. The International Longshore and Warehouse Union (ILWU) has 45,000 members, with 10,500 in California, Oregon, and Washington. Members' average pay and benefits are $100,000 annually. The ILWU has a powerful effect on—some would say absolute control over—issues such as pay and working conditions. These few thousand workers handle more than $300 billion in cargo each year, including most imports from Asia. "[West Coast dockworkers] are one of the highest paid blue-collar groups because of their strategic location," says Professor Howard Kimeldorf. "They have enormous clout because they have the power to stop all those goods." Professor David J. Olson agrees, noting, "[The workers] see themselves as lord of the docks." Shipping companies sought automated equipment to make loading more efficient, but the dockworkers refused, in fear of losing their jobs. In retaliation, the ports closed, stranding dozens of ships.

Unions and corporations will continue their battle for the moral "high ground." *Forbes* writer Dan Seligman shows a promanagement bias, calling labor's position "incredible," "grotesque," "hilarious," and "false." United's chief financial officer, Jake Brace, also favors management, although he stresses the need for cooperation. "[Wage concession] discussions need to be brought to a quick resolution to achieve our common goal," says Brace. On the opposing team, Steve Stallone, an ILWU spokesman, says, "The question shouldn't be, 'Why does this group of [dockworkers] earn so much?' The question should be, 'Why shouldn't blue-collar workers be able to share in the benefits of increased productivity?'"

References: Dan Seligman, "Labor's Lingering Monopoly," *Forbes*, November 11, 2002, pp. 112–114; Edward Wong, "UAL and Unions Set Goal for Cost Cuts," *New York Times*, October 19, 2002, p. C3; Steven Greenhouse, "A Union Wins the Global Game," *New York Times*, October 6, 2002, pp. WK1, WK3 (*quote p. WK3); Wendy Zellner, "How Wal-Mart Keeps Unions at Bay," *BusinessWeek*, pp. 94–96.

make employees feel that a union is unnecessary. Wal-Mart strives to avoid unionization through these practices.[30] A variety of related issues are covered in *The Business of Ethics.*

Collective Bargaining

collective bargaining The process of agreeing on a satisfactory labor contract between management and a union

The intent of **collective bargaining** is to agree on a labor contract between management and the union that is satisfactory to both parties. The contract contains agreements about such issues as wages, hours, conditions of employment promotion, layoffs, discipline, benefits, methods of allocating overtime, vacations, rest periods, and the grievance procedure. The process of bargaining may go on for weeks, months, or longer, with representatives of management and the union meeting to make proposals and counterproposals. The resulting agreement must be ratified by the union membership. If it is not approved, the union may strike to put pressure on management, or it may choose not to strike and simply continue negotiating until a more acceptable agreement is reached.

The **grievance procedure** is the means by which the contract is enforced. Most of what is in a contract concerns how management will treat employees. When employees feel that they have not been treated fairly under the contract, they file a grievance to correct the problem. The first step in a grievance procedure is for the aggrieved employee to discuss the alleged contract violation with her immediate superior. Often the grievance is resolved at this stage. If the employee still believes that she is being mistreated, however, the grievance can be appealed to the next level. A union official can help an aggrieved employee present her case. If the manager's decision is also unsatisfactory to the employee, additional appeals to successively higher levels are made until, finally, all in-company steps are exhausted. The final step is to submit the grievance to binding arbitration. An arbitrator is a labor law expert who is paid jointly by the union and management. The arbitrator studies the contract, hears both sides of the case, and renders a decision that both parties must obey. The grievance system for resolving disputes about contract enforcement prevents any need to strike during the term of the contract.

grievance procedure The means by which a labor contract is enforced

concept CHECK

What are the basic steps employees follow to form a union?

In your personal opinion, do unions serve a useful purpose today? Why or why not?

New Challenges in the Changing Workplace

As we have seen throughout this chapter, human resource managers face several ongoing challenges in their efforts to keep their organization staffed with an effective workforce. To complicate matters, new challenges arise as the economic and social environments of business change. We conclude this chapter with a look at two of the most important human resource management issues facing business today.

Managing Knowledge Workers

Employees traditionally added value to organizations because of what they did or because of their experience. In the "information age," however, many employees add value because of what they know.[31]

The Nature of Knowledge Work These employees are usually called **knowledge workers**, and the skill with which they are managed is a major factor in determining which firms will be successful in the future. Knowledge workers, including computer

knowledge workers Workers whose contributions to an organization are based on what they know scientists, engineers, and physical scientists, provide special challenges for the HR manager. They tend to work in high-technology firms and are usually experts in some abstract knowledge base. They often like to work independently and tend to identify more strongly with their profession than with any organization—even to the extent of defining performance in terms recognized by other members of their profession.

As the importance of information-driven jobs grows, the need for knowledge workers continues to grow as well. But these employees require extensive and highly specialized training, and not every organization is willing to make the human capital investments necessary to take advantage of these jobs. In fact, even after knowledge workers are on the job, retraining and training updates are critical to prevent their skills from becoming obsolete. It has been suggested, for example, that the "half-life" of a technical education in engineering is about three years. The failure to update such skills will not only result in the loss of competitive advantage but also increase the likelihood that the knowledge worker will go to another firm that is more committed to updating them.

Knowledge Worker Management and Labor Markets Even though overall demand for labor has slowed in recent years due to the economic downturn, the demand for knowledge workers remains strong. As a result, organizations that need these workers must introduce regular market adjustments (upward) in order to pay them enough to keep them. This is especially critical in areas in which demand is growing, as even entry-level salaries for these employees are high. Once an employee accepts a job with a firm, the employer faces yet another dilemma. Once hired, workers are more subject to the company's internal labor market, which is not likely to be growing as quickly as the external market for knowledge workers as a whole. Consequently, the longer an employee remains with a firm, the further behind the market his or her pay falls—unless, of course, it is regularly adjusted (upward).

Not surprisingly, the growing demand for these workers has inspired some fairly extreme measures for attracting them in the first place.[32] High starting salaries and sign-on bonuses are common. BP Exploration was recently paying starting petroleum engineers with undersea platform-drilling knowledge—not experience, just knowledge—salaries in the six figures, plus sign-on bonuses of over $50,000 and immediate profit sharing. Even with these incentives, HR managers complain that, in the Gulf Coast region, they cannot retain specialists because young engineers soon leave to accept sign-on bonuses with competitors. Laments one HR executive, "We wind up six months after we hire an engineer having to fight off offers for that same engineer for more money."[33]

Contingent and Temporary Workers

A final contemporary HR issue of note involves the use of contingent or temporary workers. Indeed, recent years have seen an explosion in the use of such workers by organizations. The FBI, for example, routinely employs a cadre of retired agents in various temporary jobs.[34]

Trends in Contingent and Temporary Employment In recent years, the number of contingent workers in the workforce has increased dramatically. A contingent worker is a person who works for an organization on something other than a permanent or full-time basis. Categories of contingent workers include independent contractors, on-call workers, temporary employees (usually hired through outside agencies), and contract and leased employees. Another category is part-time workers. The financial services giant Citigroup, for example, makes extensive use of part-time sales agents to pursue new clients. About 10 percent of the U.S. workforce currently uses one of these alternative forms of employment relationships. Experts suggest, however, that this percentage is increasing at a consistent pace.

Managing Contingent and Temporary Workers Given the widespread use of contingent and temporary workers, HR managers must understand how to use such employees most effectively. In other words, they need to understand how to manage contingent and temporary workers.

One key is careful planning. Even though one of the presumed benefits of using contingent workers is flexibility, it is still important to integrate such workers in a coordinated fashion. Rather than having to call in workers sporadically and with no prior notice, organizations try to bring in specified numbers of workers for well-defined periods of time. The ability to do so comes from careful planning.

A second key is understanding contingent workers and acknowledging both their advantages and their disadvantages. In other words, the organization must recognize what it can and cannot achieve from the use of contingent and temporary workers. Expecting too much from such workers, for example, is a mistake that managers should avoid.

Third, managers must carefully assess the real cost of using contingent workers. We noted above, for example, that many firms adopt this course of action to save labor costs. The organization should be able to document precisely its labor-cost savings. How much would it be paying people in wages and benefits if they were on permanent staff? How does this cost compare with the amount spent on contingent workers? This difference, however, could be misleading. We also noted, for instance, that contingent workers might be less effective performers than permanent and full-time employees. Comparing employee for employee on a direct-cost basis, therefore, is not necessarily valid. Organizations must learn to adjust the direct differences in labor costs to account for differences in productivity and performance.

Finally, managers must fully understand their own strategies and decide in advance how they intend to manage temporary workers, specifically focusing on how to integrate them into the organization. On a very simplistic level, for example, an organization with a large contingent workforce must make some decisions about the treatment of contingent workers relative to the treatment of permanent, full-time workers. Should contingent workers be invited to the company holiday party? Should they have the same access to such employee benefits as counseling services and childcare? There are no right or wrong answers to such questions.

Managers must understand that they need to develop a strategy for integrating contingent workers according to some sound logic and then follow that strategy consistently over time.[35]

concept CHECK

What are the fundamental issues and considerations regarding the use of contingent and temporary employees?	*Have trends in employment for knowledge workers changed since the publication of this book?*

Summary of Key Points

ACE self-test

business.college.hmco.com/students

Human resource management is concerned with attracting, developing, and maintaining the human resources an organization needs. Its environmental context consists of its strategic importance and the legal and social environments that affect human resource management.

Attracting human resources is an important part of the HRM function. Human resource planning starts with job analysis and then focuses on forecasting the organization's future need for employees, forecasting the availability of employees both within and outside the organization, and planning programs to ensure that the proper number and type of employees will be available when needed. Recruitment and selection are the processes by which job applicants are attracted, assessed, and hired. Methods for selecting applicants include application blanks, tests, interviews, and assessment centers. Any method used for selection should be properly validated.

Organizations must also work to develop their human resources. Training and development enable employees to perform their present job effectively and to prepare for future jobs. Performance appraisals are important for validating selection devices, assessing the impact of training programs, deciding pay raises and promotions, and determining training needs. Both objective and judgmental methods of appraisal can be applied, and a good system usually includes several methods. The validity of appraisal information is always a concern, because it is difficult to accurately evaluate the many aspects of a person's job performance.

Maintaining human resources is also important. Compensation rates must be fair compared with rates for other jobs within the organization and with rates for the same or similar jobs in other organizations in the labor market. Properly designed incentive or merit pay systems can encourage high performance, and a good benefits program can help attract and retain employees. Career planning is also a major aspect of human resource management.

If a majority of a company's nonmanagement employees so desire, they have the right to be represented by a union. Management must engage in collective bargaining with the union in an effort to agree on a contract. While the contract is in effect, the grievance system is used to settle disputes with management.

Two important new challenges in the workplace include the management of knowledge workers and issues associated with the use of contingent and temporary workers.

Discussion Questions

Questions for Review

1. Describe the steps in the process of human resource planning. Explain the relationships between the steps.
2. Describe the common selection methods. Which method or methods are the best predictors of future job performance? Which are the worst? Why?
3. Compare training and development, noting any similarities and differences. What are some commonly used training methods?
4. Define wages and benefits. List different benefits that organizations can offer. What are the three decisions that managers must make to determine compensation and benefits? Explain each decision.

Questions for Analysis

5. The Family and Medical Leave Act of 1993 is seen as providing much-needed flexibility and security for families and workers. Others think that it places an unnecessary burden on business. Yet another opinion is that the act hurts women, who are more likely to ask for leave, and shuffles them off to a low-paid "mommy track" career path. In your opinion, what are the likely consequences of the act? You can adopt one of the viewpoints expressed above or develop another. Explain your answer.
6. How do you know a selection device is valid? What are the possible consequences of using invalid selection methods? How can an organization ensure that its selection methods are valid?
7. In a right-to-work state, workers are permitted to decide for themselves whether or not to join a union. In other states, workers may be required to join a union in order to obtain certain types of employment. If you live in a right-to-work state, do you agree that the choice to join a union should be made by each individual worker? If you do not live in a right-to-work state, do you agree that individuals should be required to join a union? Finally, if the choice were yours to make, would you join a union? Explain your answers. (*Hint:* Right-to-work states are generally in the South, Midwest, and parts of the West. If you do not know whether you live in a right-to-work state, visit the National Right to Work Legal Defense Foundation website, at www.nrtw.org/rtws.htm.)

Questions for Application

8. Choose three occupations that interest you. (The Labor Department's website has a full list, if you need help choosing.) Then access the Department of Labor, Bureau of Labor Statistics, online *Occupational Outlook Handbook*, at www.bls.gov/oco. What are the job prospects like in each of these fields? Based on what you read at the website, do you think you would enjoy any of these occupations? Why or why not?
9. Consider a job that you have held or with which you are familiar. Describe how you think an organization could best provide a realistic job preview for that position. What types of information and experiences should be conveyed to applicants? What techniques should be used to convey the information and experiences?
10. Contact a local organization to determine how that organization evaluates the performance of employees in complex jobs such as middle- or higher-level manager, scientist, lawyer, or market researcher. What problems with performance appraisal can you note?

BUILDING EFFECTIVE decision-making SKILLS

business.college.hmco.com/students

Exercise Overview

Decision-making skills include the manager's ability to recognize and define problems and opportunities correctly and then to select an appropriate course of action to solve problems and capitalize on opportunities. This exercise gives you practice in making career choices.

Exercise Background

Job seekers must understand a variety of information about their own abilities, preferences, and so on, in order to make appropriate career choices. The problem is particularly acute for recent college graduates, who are often preparing to enter a career field that is largely unknown to them. Fortunately, a variety of sources of information can help. The Bureau of Labor Statistics maintains data about occupations, employment prospects, compensation, working conditions, and many other issues of interest to job seekers. The information is available by industry, occupation, employer type, and region.

Exercise Task

1. Access a summary of the Department of Labor's *National Compensation Survey,* at stats.bls.gov/ncs/ocs/sp/ncbl0449.pdf. (Or search for the survey's title, if the page has moved.) Find the detailed data related to the occupation that you think is your most likely career choice upon graduation. Then locate detailed data about two other occupations that you might consider—one with a higher salary than your most likely choice and one with a lower salary.
2. Record the hourly salary data for each of your three choices. Use the hourly salary to calculate an expected annual income. (*Hint:* Full-time jobs require about 2,000 hours annually.)
3. Based purely on salary information, which occupation would be the "best" for you?
4. Now access job descriptions for various occupations, at www.bls.gov/oco. Read the description for each of your three choices.
5. Based purely on job characteristics, which occupation would be the "best" for you?
6. Is there a conflict between your answers to questions 3 and 5? If so, how do you plan to resolve it?
7. Are there any job characteristics that you desire strongly enough to sacrifice pay in order to have them? What are they? What are the limits, if any, on your willingness to sacrifice pay?

BUILDING EFFECTIVE communication SKILLS

Exercise Overview

Communication skills refer to the manager's ability both to convey ideas and information effectively to others and to receive ideas and information effectively from others. This exercise provides you with practice in presenting yourself in the best possible light to others.

Exercise Background

One of the first tasks that you will be called upon to do in your job search is to introduce yourself to company recruiters at a job fair, career day, informational meeting, or interview. This exercise gives you a quick, two-minute self-introduction tool for making a quick but memorable impression on anyone who might help you in your career advancement. It can be used to make a professional impression on anyone, not just potential employers.

The hour or so that you take to write this introduction and practice using it can be the difference between getting and not getting the job or interview you want. The most commonly asked question is "Tell me about yourself." If you can answer this briefly, by saying something distinctive and memorable, you rise above the crowd.

The two-minute self-introduction should

- Be brief, so the listener will not get bored.
- Highlight what makes you unique.
- Reveal information not necessarily found in your résumé.
- Explain your interest in the firm.
- Show how your goals and background can benefit the firm.
- Encourage the listener to want to know more.
- Highlight aspects the listener is interested in.
- Sell you—especially your skills, knowledge, and ability.
- Be truthful but positive.
- Be adapted to fit the listener and his or her firm.
- Tell an interesting story, in a conversational way.
- Not mention dates or years, because they are too hard to remember.
- Not include anything that is potentially biasing.

Exercise Task

1. Write a two-minute self-introduction following the format below. Make minor adjustments, if necessary, to accommodate your unique history.
   - *Early Life—15 seconds.* Who are you? Where do you come from? What are your roots? "How" did you grow up? Include any unique or memorable fact or early experience or interest that connects to the desired job, even by inference.
   - *Education—15 seconds.* Degrees, honors, awards? Major? Significant leadership, interests, or community activity while in school?
   - *Work Life—45 seconds.* What are your work habits? Accomplishments—not duties? How did interests lead you in this direction? Projects you were enthusiastic about or proudest moment? What have you learned that is relevant to the listener? If you do not have enough work experience, spend more time talking about your education.
   - *Sales Pitch—45 seconds.* What do you have to offer? Key skills you have gained, from school, work, leadership or relationships? How do you want to use your key skills? How do your key skills fit the job or firm? End with "I want to work for (I am considering) your company because . . . ." Do not forget to thank them for the opportunity to talk with them!
2. Practice speaking your introduction aloud, with a firm handshake and a smile, until you can say everything in two minutes. One approach is to start alone or in front of a mirror, then work up to saying it to friends.
3. Practice your two-minute self-introduction in class, using classmates as stand-ins for interviewers. Or take turns presenting in front of the class, with the professor or another student as a partner. Share constructive comments with one another.

BUILDING EFFECTIVE technical SKILLS

Exercise Overview

Technical skills refer to the manager's abilities to accomplish or understand work done in an organization. Many managers must have technical skills to be able to hire appropriate people to work in the organization. This exercise will help you use technical skills as part of the selection process.

Exercise Background

Variation One. If you currently work or have worked in the past, select two jobs with which you have some familiarity. Select one job that is relatively low in skill level, responsibility, required education, and pay, and one job that is relatively high in the same categories. It will make the exercise more useful to you if you use real jobs that you can relate to at a personal level.

Variation Two. If you have never worked or are not personally familiar with an array of jobs, assume that you are a manager of a small manufacturing facility. You need to hire individuals to fill two jobs. One job is for the position of plant custodian. This individual will sweep floors, clean bathrooms, empty trash cans, and so forth. The other person will be an office manager. This individual will supervise a staff of three clerks and secretaries, administer the plant payroll, and coordinate the administrative operations of the plant.

Exercise Task

With the information above as background, do the following:

1. Identify the most basic skills that you think are necessary for someone to perform each job effectively.
2. Identify the general indicators or predictors of whether or not a given individual can perform each job.
3. Develop a brief set of interview questions that you might use to determine whether or not an applicant has the qualifications to perform each job.
4. How important is it that a manager hiring employees to perform a job have the technical skills to do that job him- or herself?

CHAPTER CLOSING case

The Retirement That Isn't

He had hoped for time to relax, travel, and enjoy hobbies, but the economic slump forced him back to work. In spite of his industry experience, Joseph Turner failed to get a single interview and went to work for himself, doing odd jobs for his neighbors at about half his former pay. Is Turner a dot-com tycoon gone bust, a twenty-something millionaire whose high-tech start-up failed? No. He is a fifty-six-year-old senior manager who retired from Nortel in 2001, then saw the value of his 401(k) retirement account lose two-thirds of its value in just one year.

Unfortunately, Joseph Turner is not alone. Labor force participation of senior citizens is up 32 percent since 1990. That is the good news, but the bad news is that many people are returning to work because their retirement benefits do not cover their living expenses. Millions of retirees are covered by company-funded pension plans, which have experienced a decline in value of 19 percent in the last two years. Meanwhile, obligations grew 49 percent, due to an increasing number of retirees, including those who accepted offers of early retirement. The worsening economy, low profits, and bankruptcies have caused many companies to reduce or even eliminate postretirement benefits. Retirees are discovering, to their surprise, that "promised" benefits cannot be legally enforced, if the fine print of the contract gives the firm the right to modify the program. The federal government guarantees pensions for some employers, but well under half of Americans are covered by this insurance, putting millions at risk. "These people were promised a secure retirement, and now they're not getting it," says retiree advocate James Leas.

Even worse off are the 20 million retirees who depend on their own investments, such as savings or 401(k) accounts, which have cumulatively lost $678 billion in value since 2000. Ironically, the higher an individual's salary during his or her career, the more likely that person will depend heavily on investments. "It's the higher-income retirees who are out seeking jobs," reports economics professor William Rodgers.

Many retirees have opted to return to work, but "they're apprehensive about having to compete for positions with younger workers who may be more technologically advanced," says counselor Dr. Michael Nuccitelli. Retirees often take technology classes or begin exercise regimens to increase their knowledge and stamina. Others simply find it humiliating to accept an entry-level job and the paycheck that goes along with it.

Some firms are happy to employ seniors, finding them more reliable, more experienced, and even more honest than younger employees.

> *"These people were promised a secure retirement, and now they're not getting it."*
>
> — James Leas, former IBM engineer and retiree advocate*

Shel Hart, a staffing expert, thinks older workers have an advantage in the stagnant economy. "Companies are tied at the purse strings, and they can't afford to take risks," says Hart. "They need a quick return on investment. They need people with expertise." Bill Coleman, a compensation consultant, agrees. "Position yourself as a bargain," Coleman tells retirees. "Tout the fact that you have 40 years' experience. . . . Don't say, 'I'm old.' By doing that, you're admitting to a defect that's probably not even there."

Yet recruiter Jeff Kaye claims, "In many fields, retirees are considered washed up." This is particularly true in fields that require technical knowledge. Author Barbara M. Morris concurs, saying, "Those who return after retiring have lost a lot of their skills. Their thinking slows, their response time is slower, and they just can't grasp the technological changes." Kaye goes on to say, "The people who used to work in the [telecommunications and technology] fields aren't even getting in to see recruiters. They're getting jobs ripping tickets at movie theaters or punching the clock at Wal-Mart."

Age discrimination may be part of the problem, but employers are also wary of investing in someone whose sole reason for working is financial. "Nobody wants to hire somebody who they think is just temporary," says Professor Dennis A. Ahlburg. His advice to older job seekers: "Don't say you're out of money. Say that you were bored in retirement and you want to be an active part of the labor force."

Some retirees are filing lawsuits against their former employers, who are cutting retirement benefits while realizing high profits. Nynex retiree C. William Jones asserts, "[Companies] are now starting to view retirees as a cost center, and they're cutting their losses." Others are willing to return to work, but the barriers, especially the psychological ones, can be formidable. Norman Doroson, a pharmacist who returned to work after four years of retirement, sighs and says, "Most days at work, I just sit here thinking, 'I would rather be at home.' That's a little bit depressing."

Case Questions

1. What are the benefits that firms can obtain by hiring older workers? What are the potential problems that might be experienced by the organization and by the older workers themselves?
2. How would the hiring of retirees affect a company's human resource management? Consider the impact on recruiting and selecting, training, and compensation.
3. One expert recommends that retirees be treated as contingent or temporary workers. What would be the advantages and disadvantages of this approach for the organization, as compared to full-time, permanent employment? What would be the advantages and disadvantages of this approach from the older worker's point of view?

Case References

"Can Retiree Health Benefits Provided by Your Employer Be Cut?" U.S. Department of Labor website, www.dol.gov on January 30, 2003; David Henry and Michael Arndt, "Where's My Pension?" *BusinessWeek*, December 2, 2002, pp. 96–97; Melinda Ligos, "As Portfolios Shrink, Retirees Warily Seek Work," *New York Times*, September 8, 2002, p. BU10; Michelle Conlin, "Grandpa? He's Busy at the Office," *BusinessWeek*, January 3, 2003, www.businessweek.com on January 30, 2003; Michelle Conlin, "Revenge of the Retirees," *BusinessWeek*, November 18, 2002, p. 125 (*quote).

Chapter Notes

1. "Army 101," "Basic Training," "Jobs," "Soldier Profiles," U.S. Army website, www.goarmy.com on January 30, 2003 (*quote); "Background of Selective Service," U.S. Selective Service System website, www.sss.gov on January 30, 2003; "Officer Evaluation Report," U.S. Army Personnel Command website, www.perscom.army.mil on January 30, 2003.
2. For a complete review of human resource management, see Angelo S. DeNisi and Ricky W. Griffin, *Human Resource Management*, 2nd ed. (Boston: Houghton Mifflin, 2005).
3. Patrick Wright and Gary McMahan, "Strategic Human Resources Management: A Review of the Literature," *Journal of Management*, June 1992, pp. 280–319.
4. Augustine Lado and Mary Wilson, "Human Resource Systems and Sustained Competitive Advantage: A Competency-based Perspective," *Academy of Management Review*, 1994, vol. 19, no. 4, pp. 699–727.
5. David Lepak and Scott Snell, "Examining the Human Resource Architecture: The Relationships Among Human Capital, Employment, and Human Resource Configurations," *Journal of Management*, 2002, vol. 28, no. 4, pp. 517–543.
6. "Is Butter Flavoring Ruining Popcorn Workers' Lungs?" *USA Today*, June 20, 2002, pp. 1A, 8A.
7. "While Hiring at Most Firms Chills, Wal-Mart's Heats Up," *USA Today*, August 26, 2002, p. 1B.
8. "The New Workforce," *BusinessWeek*, March 20, 2000, pp. 64–70.
9. John Beeson, "Succession Planning," *Across the Board*, February 2000, pp. 38–41.
10. Robert Gatewood, Mary Gowan, and Gary Lautenschlager, "Corporate Image, Recruitment Image, and Initial Job Choice Decisions," *Academy of Management Journal*, 1993, vol. 36, no. 2, pp. 414–427.
11. "Firms Cook up New Ways to Keep Workers," *USA Today*, January 18, 2000, p. 1B.
12. Claudio Fernandez-Araoz, "Hiring Without Firing," *Harvard Business Review*, July–August 1999, pp. 109–118.
13. James A. Breaugh and Mary Starke, "Research on Employee Recruiting: So Many Studies, So Many Remaining Questions," *Journal of Management*, 2000, vol. 26, no. 3, pp. 405–434.
14. "Pumping up Your Past," *Time*, June 10, 2002, p. 96.
15. Frank L. Schmidt and John E. Hunter, "Employment Testing: Old Theories and New Research Findings," *American Psychologist*, October 1981, 1128–1137.

16. Robert Liden, Christopher Martin, and Charles Parsons, "Interviewer and Applicant Behaviors in Employment Interviews," *Academy of Management Journal*, 1993, vol. 36, no. 2, pp. 372–386.
17. Paul R. Sackett, "Assessment Centers and Content Validity: Some Neglected Issues," *Personnel Psychology*, vol. 40, 1987, pp. 13–25.
18. "'Boeing U': Flying by the Book," *USA Today*, October 6, 1997, pp. 1B, 2B. See also "Is Your Airline Pilot Ready for Surprises?" *Time*, October 14, 2002, p. 72.
19. See Angelo S. DeNisi and Avraham N. Kluger, "Feedback Effectiveness: Can 360-Degree Appraisals Be Improved?" *Academy of Management Executive*, 2000, vol. 14, no. 1, pp. 129–139.
20. Barry R. Nathan, Allan Mohrman, and John Milliman, "Interpersonal Relations as a Context for the Effects of Appraisal Interviews on Performance and Satisfaction: A Longitudinal Study," *Academy of Management Journal*, June 1991, pp. 352–369.
21. "Goodyear to Stop Labeling 10% of Its Workers as Worst," *USA Today*, September 12, 2002, p. 1B.
22. Jaclyn Fierman, "The Perilous New World of Fair Pay," *Fortune*, June 13, 1994, pp. 57–64.
23. Stephanie Armour, "Show Me the Money, More Workers Say," *USA Today*, June 6, 2000, p. 1B.
24. "To Each According to His Needs: Flexible Benefits Plans Gain Favor," *Wall Street Journal*, September 16, 1986, p. 29.
25. "The Future Look of Employee Benefits," *Wall Street Journal*, September 7, 1988, p. 21.
26. See "Companies Chisel Away at Workers' Benefits," *USA Today*, November 18, 2002, pp. 1B, 2B.
27. See Sherry E. Sullivan, "The Changing Nature of Careers: A Review and Research Agenda," *Journal of Management*, 1999, vol. 25, no. 3, pp. 457–484.
28. Barbara Presley Nobel, "Reinventing Labor," *Harvard Business Review*, July–August 1993, pp. 115–125.
29. John A. Fossum, "Labor Relations: Research and Practice in Transition," *Journal of Management*, Summer 1987, pp. 281–300.
30. "How Wal-Mart Keeps Unions at Bay," *BusinessWeek*, October 28, 2002, pp. 94–96.
31. Max Boisot, *Knowledge Assets* (Oxford, U.K.: Oxford University Press, 1998).
32. Thomas Stewart, "In Search of Elusive Tech Workers," *Fortune*, February 16, 1998, pp. 171–172.
33. "Need for Computer Experts Is Making Recruiters Frantic," *New York Times*, December 18, 1999, p. C1.
34. "FBI Taps Retiree Experience for Temporary Jobs," *USA Today*, October 3, 2002, p. 1A.
35. "When Is a Temp Not a Temp?" *BusinessWeek*, December 7, 1998, pp. 90–92.

PART five

The Leading Process

CHAPTER 15

Basic Elements of Individual Behavior in Organizations

CHAPTER 16

Managing Employee Motivation and Performance

CHAPTER 17

Managing Leadership and Influence Processes

CHAPTER 18

Managing Interpersonal Relations and Communication

CHAPTER 19

Managing Work Groups and Teams

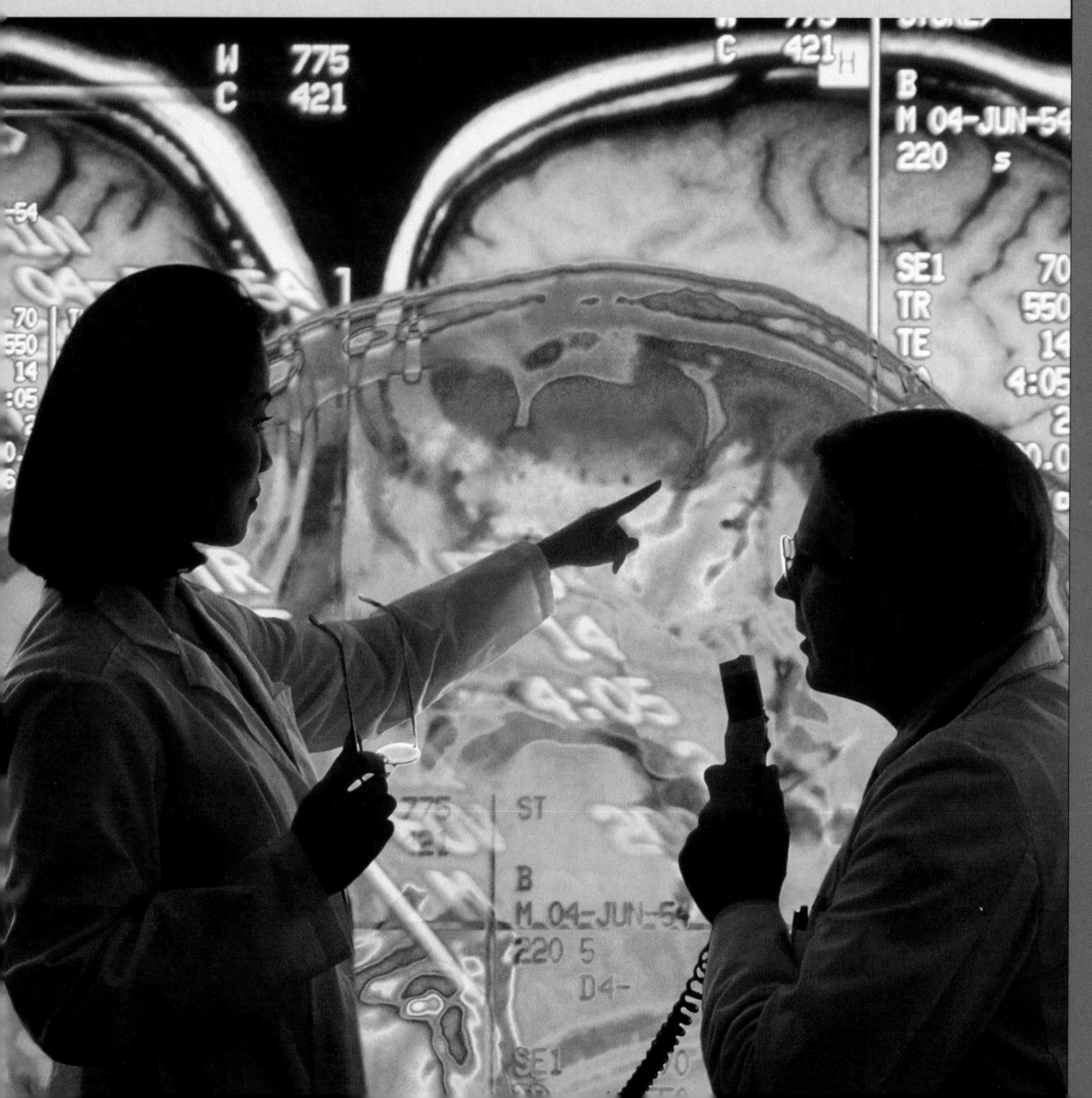
W 775
C 421
B
M 04-JUN-54
220 s
SE1 70
TR 550
TE 14
4:05
ST
B
M 04-JUN-54
220 5
D4-
SE1

15

Basic Elements of Individual Behavior in Organizations

CHAPTER OUTLINE

Understanding Individuals in Organizations
- The Psychological Contract
- The Person-Job Fit
- The Nature of Individual Differences

Personality and Individual Behavior
- The "Big Five" Personality Traits
- The Myers-Briggs Framework
- Other Personality Traits at Work
- Emotional Intelligence

Attitudes and Individual Behavior
- Work-related Attitudes
- Affect and Mood in Organizations

Perception and Individual Behavior
- Basic Perceptual Processes
- Perception and Attribution

Stress and Individual Behavior
- Causes and Consequences of Stress
- Managing Stress

Creativity in Organizations
- The Creative Individual
- The Creative Process
- Enhancing Creativity in Organizations

Types of Workplace Behavior
- Performance Behaviors
- Withdrawal Behaviors
- Organizational Citizenship
- Dysfunctional Behaviors

LEARNING OBJECTIVES

After studying this chapter, you should be able to:

1 ***Explain the nature of the individual-organization relationship.***

2 ***Define personality and describe personality attributes that affect behavior in organizations.***

OPENING INCIDENT

You can love your job, but will it love you back? Psychologists and other experts who study job-related mental health report a disturbing trend—more and more workers say that they prefer long hours. Many employees routinely put in twelve-hour days or work from home every weekend. It is an ironic twist in a society where "formerly, personal success was evinced by the ability to not work, to be a part of a leisure class, to be idle," says psychotherapist and author Ilene Philipson. "Today, we measure our success by how *much* we work," she adds.

Philipson's book *Married to the Job: Why We Live to Work and What We Can Do About It* contains numerous examples. One high-performing manager fell out of favor after asking for a raise. The lack of praise caused deep depression and anxiety attacks. Philipson says that this client is typical of the career-obsessed worker: "What they have done is to transfer all of their unmet emotional needs to the workplace." Many of these employees believe that work is the most important thing in their life, to which Philipson responds, "Your boss is not your friend. Your colleagues are not your family. Workplaces are intensely political environments. If you bring your heart and soul there, you're likely setting yourself up for feeling betrayed."

3	4	5	6	7
Discuss individual attitudes in organizations and how they affect behavior.	***Describe basic perceptual processes and the role of attributions in organizations.***	***Discuss the causes and consequences of stress and describe how it can be managed.***	***Describe creativity and its role in organizations.***	***Explain how workplace behaviors can directly or indirectly influence organizational effectiveness.***

"... formerly, personal success was evinced by the ability to not work.... Today, we measure our success by how much we work."

— Ilene Philipson, psychotherapist and author of Married to the Job

In today's busy work environment some people, like this office manager, even eat lunch at their desk.

Benjamin Hunnicutt, a professor, claims, "Work has become how we define ourselves. It is now answering the traditional religious questions: Who am I? How do I find meaning and purpose? Work is no longer just about economics; it's about identity." Most of Philipson's patients have few social relationships outside of work. Many use work to help them through tough times. Yet the praise they receive at work is powerfully addictive, and that can also be dangerous. Yolanda Perry-Pastor, a patient of Philipson's, kept assuming more job duties until she suffered a nervous breakdown. She says, "I've been through a lot in my life," referring to domestic abuse and single parenthood. "But that was nothing compared with this."

Another contributing factor is companies that "ensnare" workers by offering a homelike environment, providing personal services, or just encouraging workers to consider their coworkers family. For example, Houston-based BMC Software offers hammocks, a gym, sports leagues, a movie theater, live piano music, free gourmet meals, massages, banking, hairdressing, oil changes and car washes, childcare, eldercare, pet care, medical exams, and even bedrooms for those who cannot make it home. BMC's chief of human resources claims, "I know this is hard to believe, but ... [it] gives you a balanced life without having to leave." Psychologist Maynard Brusman disagrees: "The workplace has become [workers'] community. They come to me anxious, and they don't know why. They've become caught up in the culture. The question is, 'Is that healthy?' From what I've seen, it isn't."

Workers who are obsessed with their career find that work consumes all their passion and time, leaving nothing for other relationships. Perry-Pastor says of her two children during the time she was overworking, "They were never allowed to be sick. ... I would pay for baby sitters, lessons, tutors, whatever they needed. I thought they were taken care of." Work relationships become more rewarding than relationships at home. Sociologist Arlie Hochschild theorizes that dual-income couples work long hours to escape their hectic home lives. "At home, you don't always get a pat on the back," says Karin Hanson, formerly of Microsoft. "In your office, you can hear, 'Hey, good work.'" Some managers may believe that an all-consuming interest in work is acceptable and even desirable, but the quality and quantity of work drops, and the incidence of absence, turnover, accidents, and workplace violence increases with stress. Many workers drop out of the workforce entirely—a loss for families and for society.

Philipson claims that career-obsessed individuals are not weak or insecure. "These people are in the same boat with all of the rest of us who work longer hours, take fewer vacations, and wake up and go to sleep thinking about work," she asserts. So how can one avoid becoming overinvolved in work? The psychotherapists recommend that you start by defining yourself and your worth in nonwork terms. Look to religion, family, or community for praise and comfort. Develop compelling interests and strong friendships outside of work. Take "real" nights, weekends, vacations—no work allowed. Focus less on praise, which can put you under someone else's control, and more on developing your own sense of self-worth. And, oh yes, miss work every now and then. Play hooky. Take an occasional day off and just relax.[1]

People and the organizations where they work are continually defining and redefining their relationship in much the same way as the relationship between people evolves and changes over time. Of course, in order to do so, they must assess how well their respective needs and capabilities match the other's. As evidenced in the opening vignette, some people even risk developing an unhealthy attachment to or dependence on their work. Of course, many other people develop and maintain a healthy and productive relationship with their employer. A variety of different and unique characteristics that reside in each and every employee affect how they feel about the organization, how they will alter their future attitudes about the firm, and how they perform their job. These characteristics reflect the basic elements of individual behavior in organizations.

This chapter describes several of these basic elements and is the first of several chapters designed to develop a more complete perspective on the leading function of management. In the next section we investigate the psychological nature of individuals in organizations. The following section introduces the concept of personality and discusses several important personality attributes that can influence behavior in organizations. We then examine individual attitudes and their role in organizations. The role of stress in the workplace is then discussed, followed by a discussion of individual creativity. Finally, we describe a number of basic individual behaviors that are important to organizations.

Understanding Individuals in Organizations

As a starting point in understanding human behavior in the workplace, we must consider the basic nature of the relationship between individuals and organizations. We must also gain an appreciation of the nature of individual differences.

The Psychological Contract

Most people have a basic understanding of a contract. Whenever we buy a car or sell a house, for example, both buyer and seller sign a contract that specifies the terms of the agreement. A psychological contract is similar in some ways to a standard legal contract but is less formal and well defined. In particular, a **psychological contract** is the overall set of expectations held by an individual with respect to what he or she will contribute to the organization and what the organization will provide in return.[2] Thus a psychological contract is not written on paper, nor are all of its terms explicitly negotiated.

psychological contract The overall set of expectations held by an individual with respect to what he or she will contribute to the organization and what the organization will provide in return

contributions What the individual provides to the organization

The essential nature of a psychological contract is illustrated in Figure 15.1. The individual makes a variety of **contributions** to the organization—effort, skills, ability, time, loyalty, and so forth. These contributions presumably satisfy various needs and requirements of the organization. In other words, because the organization may have hired the person because of her skills, it is reasonable for the organization to expect that she will subsequently display those skills in the performance of her job.

inducements What the organization provides to the individual

In return for these contributions, the organization provides **inducements** to the individual. Some inducements, like pay and career opportunities, are tangible rewards. Others, like job security and status, are more intangible. Just as the contributions available from the individual must satisfy the needs of the organization, the inducements offered by the organization must serve the needs of the individual. Thus, if a person accepts employment with an organization because he thinks he will earn an attractive salary and have an opportunity to advance, he will subsequently expect that those rewards will actually be forthcoming.

If both the individual and the organization perceive that the psychological contract is fair and equitable, they will be satisfied with the relationship and will likely continue it. On the other hand, if either party sees an imbalance or inequity in the contract, it may initiate a change. For example, the individual may request a pay raise or promotion, decrease her contributed effort, or look for a better job elsewhere. The organization can also initiate change by requesting that the individual improve his skills through training, transfer the person to another job, or terminate the person's employment altogether.

A basic challenge faced by the organization, then, is to manage psychological contracts. The organization must ensure that it is getting value from its employees. At the same time, it must be sure that it is providing employees with appropriate inducements. If the organization is underpaying its employees for their contributions, for example, they may perform poorly or leave for better jobs elsewhere. On the other hand, if they are being overpaid relative to their contributions, the organization is incurring unnecessary costs.[3] *Today's Management Issues* discusses some recent issues regarding the balance between inducements and contributions.

The Person-Job Fit

One specific aspect of managing psychological contracts is managing the person-job fit. **Person-job fit** is the extent to which the contributions made by the individual match the inducements offered by the organization. In theory, each employee has a specific set of needs that he wants fulfilled and a set of job-related behaviors and abilities to contribute. Thus, if the

FIGURE 15.1

The Psychological Contract

Psychological contracts are the basic assumptions that individuals have about their relationships with their organization. Such contracts are defined in terms of contributions by the individual relative to inducements from the organization.

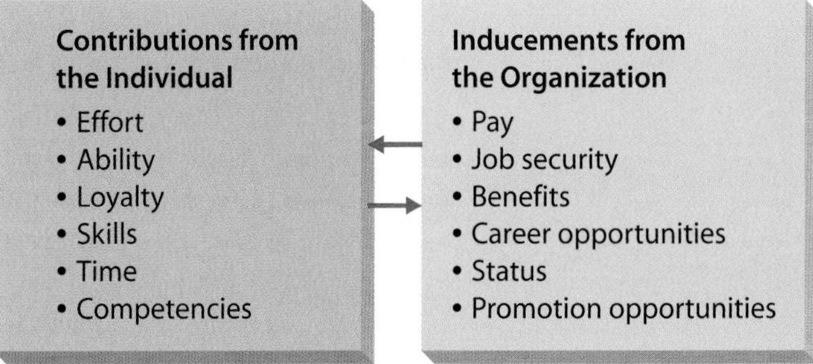

Person-job fit is an important element in individual behavior in organizations. While the personal factors that contribute to this fit are often internal qualities like personality and motivation, they may also be physical in nature. For instance, all else equal, relatively shorter persons perform better as jockeys. Similarly, relatively taller persons are more likely to excel in basketball. Physical strength, dexterity, and coordination are other physical factors that may affect person-job fit in a variety of settings.

Up—and Down—the Economic Roller-Coaster

"In boom times, some of the wealthier local economies tend to price themselves out of the market."

– Mark Zandi, economist*

Decatur, Alabama, is a sleepy southern town, population 54,000. Most adults in the blue-collar town do not have a college degree, and $30,000 is a good annual wage. "The image of this area was,'We weren't educated; we didn't have skills,'" says resident Mike Blizzard. In 1992 McDonald's, for example, paid minimum wage, and security guards earned $6 per hour. Local unemployment topped 8 percent, compared to the nation's 5.5 percent. But in 1995 the U.S. economy soared high. Prosperity finally hit Decatur, and when it did, the sleepy town woke up.

A new steel mill employed 325. Boeing opened a factory and announced plans to hire 2,000 workers. Business boomed. Real estate prices jumped, and big-name retailers entered the market. New restaurants and hotels opened. Wages reached up to $50,000, so local employers had to give raises. Unemployment fell to 4.1 percent by 1998, and median income jumped to $40,000, an increase of 23 percent. Waitress Genise McCarley switched to an upscale steakhouse that paid twice as much. "That was the greatest thing that ever happened to me," McCarley says. Decatur, like other less-desirable locations, became more attractive during the expansion, thanks to a nonunion labor pool and inexpensive land and taxes. "In boom times, some of the wealthier local economies tend to price themselves out of the market," says economist Mark Zandi.

But, in the wink of an eye, the boom was over. By 2000 Trico had declared bankruptcy, closing its factory, and Boeing capped employment at 550. The bad news rippled through the local economy. Workers again took on second jobs to make ends meet. Median income fell to $35,000, and unemployment went up to 6.4 percent.

An expanding economy provides a boost to everyone. As the popular adage has it, "A rising tide lifts all boats." Between 1996 and 2000, average income in the bottom 40 percent of U.S. families grew at the national average of 2.7 percent. However, in 2001 those families' average income fell 2.6 percent, double the national rate. Decatur's story graphically illustrates the delicate balance between individual contributions and organizational inducements, particularly in economically vulnerable locations. One could coin a new saying: "A falling tide sinks poor boats more than rich boats."

References: Bob Davis, "Boom Came Late, Left All Too Soon in Decatur, Alabama," *Wall Street Journal*, November 14, 2002, pp. A1, A10 (*quote p. A10); Justin Fox, "This Tunnel Has an End," *Fortune*, January 6, 2003, www.fortune.com on February 3, 2003; William Symonds, "The Economy Is Still in Limbo," *BusinessWeek*, February 10, 2003, www.businessweek.com on February 3, 2003.

person-job fit The extent to which the contributions made by the individual match the inducements offered by the organization

organization can take perfect advantage of those behaviors and abilities and exactly fulfill his needs, it will have achieved a perfect person-job fit.

Of course, such a precise level of person-job fit is seldom achieved. There are several reasons for this. For one thing, organizational selection procedures are imperfect. Organizations can make approximations of employee skill levels when making hiring decisions and can improve them through training. But even simple performance dimensions are hard to measure objectively and validly. The cartoon provides a humorous example of poor "person"-job fit.

Another reason for imprecise person-job fits is that both people and organizations change. An individual who finds a new job stimulating and exciting may find the same job boring and monotonous after a few years of performing it. And, when the organization adopts new technology, it has changed the skills it needs from its employees. Still another reason for imprecision in the person-job fit is that each individual is unique. Measuring skills and performance is difficult enough. Assessing needs, attitudes, and personality is far more complex. Each of these individual differences serves to make matching individuals with jobs a difficult and complex process.

"I'M PUTTING YOU ON THE CHINA SHOP ACCOUNT. DO YOU THINK YOU CAN HANDLE IT?"

P. C. Vey

Person-job fit is a very important construct in organizations. A good person-job fit benefits both the employee and the organization. But a poor person-job fit can result in a dissatisfied and low-performing employee. In the example portrayed here, for example, the manager is literally picking a bull to work in a china shop. And the result is likely to be chaos!

The Nature of Individual Differences

Individual differences are personal attributes that vary from one person to another. Individual differences may be physical, psychological, or emotional. Taken together, all of the individual differences that characterize any specific person serve to make that individual unique from everyone else. Much of the remainder of this chapter is devoted to individual differences. Before proceeding, however, we must also note the importance of the situation in assessing the behavior of individuals.

Are specific differences that characterize a given individual good or bad? Do they contribute to or detract from performance? The answer, of course, is that it depends on the circumstances. One person may be very dissatisfied, withdrawn, and negative in one job setting, but very satisfied, outgoing, and positive in another. Working conditions, coworkers, and leadership are all important ingredients.

Thus, whenever an organization attempts to assess or account for individual differences among its employees, it must also be sure to consider the situation in which behavior occurs. Individuals who are satisfied or productive workers in one context may prove to be dissatisfied or unproductive workers in another context. Attempting to consider both individual differences and contributions in relation to inducements and contexts, then, is a major challenge for organizations as they attempt to establish effective psychological contracts with their employees and achieve optimal fits between people and jobs.

individual differences Personal attributes that vary from one person to another

concept CHECK

What is a psychological contract, and what are its fundamental components?

Describe different jobs that would result in both a very good and a very bad person-job fit for you personally.

Personality and Individual Behavior

Personality traits represent some of the most fundamental sets of individual differences in organizations. **Personality** is the relatively stable set of psychological attributes that distinguish one person from another.[4] Managers should strive to

personality The relatively permanent set of psychological and behavioral attributes that distinguish one person from another understand basic personality attributes and the ways they can affect people's behavior in organizational situations, not to mention their perceptions of and attitudes toward the organization. *The World of Management* describes a startling example of personality-related issues in the context of an unusual Japanese organization.

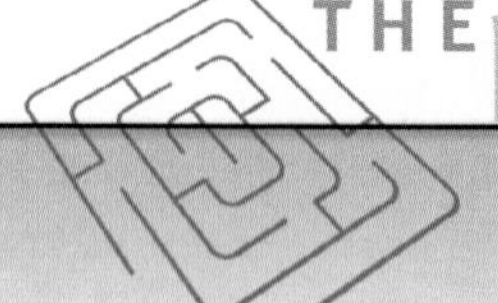

THE WORLD OF management

American-Style Management Comes to Global-Dining

"There is no question that the Japanese personnel system is at a crossroads."

— Iwao Nakatani, director, Sony*

Hayato Miyauchi stood in front of eighteen coworkers, asking for higher pay. His colleagues criticized his personality and performance while Miyauchi slouched in embarrassment. The group then voted against the raise. This evaluation procedure, tough even by American standards, is shocking in conflict-averse Japan. Global-Dining, a restaurant corporation founded by Kozo Hasegawa, has adopted a U.S.-style pay-for-performance system. Sounding like an American CEO, Hasegawa asserts, "Just as sharks need to keep swimming to stay alive, we only want people who are constantly craving challenges."

Traditional Japanese management is consensual, and arguments are rare. Pay is based on seniority; lifelong employment is the norm. In contrast, American workplaces are characterized by disagreement, frank discussions, performance-based compensation, and competition for advancement. By switching to Americanized methods, Global-Dining challenges strongly held Japanese values. Differences include team versus individual reward systems, a firm's loyalty to its workers, and managers' responsibility for their subordinates' poor performance.

Global-Dining's system sets clearly defined goals, then rewards high performers generously. One twenty-seven-year-old manager made $150,000—more than most senior executives in Japan. But poor performers receive no bonus, lose pay, are demoted, and may be fired. Employees watch each other constantly and report to management. Every employee's pay is posted publicly. *Wall Street Journal* writer Yumiko Ono says, "It's U.S.-style performance-based pay on steroids."

Global-Dining's style can be inflexible, for example, penalizing workers for poor performance due to other factors. Koki Ohta, a fourteen-year veteran, was blamed by Hasegawa for the failure of a new restaurant concept. Surprisingly for the obedient and respectful Japanese, other managers protested and insisted on a vote. One manager said, "I'm afraid that good people might quit." But Hasegawa defended his plan, replying, "This is designed to light a fire under all of you." In spite of the managers' support, Ohta left Global-Dining, saying, "You can't always measure everything by numbers. . . . I don't think that was really fair."

Yet, for the most part, the pay-for-performance system is working. Global-Dining represents the leading edge of change in tradition-bound Japan. "There is no question that the Japanese personnel system is at a crossroads," says Iwao Nakatani, a director at Sony. Nakatani claims that, if Japanese companies do not update their methods, "they're not going to survive in this age of global competition."

References: Bill Hersey, "Party Line," *Tokyo Weekender*, May 26, 2000, www.weekender.co.jp on February 3, 2003; "Company Profile," "Employment Information," Global-Dining website, www.global-dining.com on February 3, 2003; Miki Fujii, "Restaurant Chain Caters Foreign Customers' Needs," *The Daily Yomiuri* (Osaka, Japan), 2000, www.yomiuri.co.jp on February 3, 2003; Yumiko Ono, "A Restaurant Chain in Japan Chops up the Social Contract," *Wall Street Journal*, January 17, 2001, pp. A1, A19 (*quote p. A1).

The "Big Five" Personality Traits

Psychologists have identified literally thousands of personality traits and dimensions that differentiate one person from another. But, in recent years, researchers have identified five fundamental personality traits that are especially relevant to organizations. Because these five traits are so important and because they are currently the subject of so much attention, they are now commonly referred to as the **"Big Five" personality traits.**[5] Figure 15.2 illustrates the Big Five traits.

"Big Five" personality traits A popular personality framework based on five key traits

agreeableness A person's ability to get along with others

Agreeableness refers to a person's ability to get along with others. Agreeableness causes some people to be gentle, cooperative, forgiving, understanding, and good-natured in their dealings with others. But it results in others' being irritable, short-tempered, uncooperative, and generally antagonistic toward other people. Although research has not yet fully investigated the effects of agreeableness, it would seem likely that highly agreeable people will be better able to develop good working relationships with coworkers, subordinates, and higher-level managers, whereas less agreeable people will not have particularly good working relationships. This same pattern might also extend to relationships with customers, suppliers, and other key organizational constituents.

conscientiousness The number of goals on which a person focuses

Conscientiousness refers to the number of goals on which a person focuses. People who focus on relatively few goals at one time are likely to be organized, systematic, careful, thorough, responsible, and self-disciplined as they work to pursue those goals. Others, however, tend to take on a wider array of goals and, as a result, are more disorganized, careless, and irresponsible, as well as less thorough and self-disciplined. Research has found that more conscientious people tend to be higher performers than less conscientious people across a variety of different jobs. This pattern seems logical, of course, because more conscientious people will take their job seriously and will approach the performance of their job in a highly responsible fashion.

negative emotionality Extent to which a person is poised, calm, resilient, and secure

The third of the Big Five personality dimensions is **negative emotionality**. People with less negative emotionality will be relatively poised, calm, resilient, and secure.

Agreeableness

High agreeableness — *Low agreeableness*

Conscientiousness

High conscientiousness — *Low conscientiousness*

Negative Emotionality

Less negative emotionality — *More negative emotionality*

Extraversion

More extraversion — *More introversion*

Openness

More openness — *Less openness*

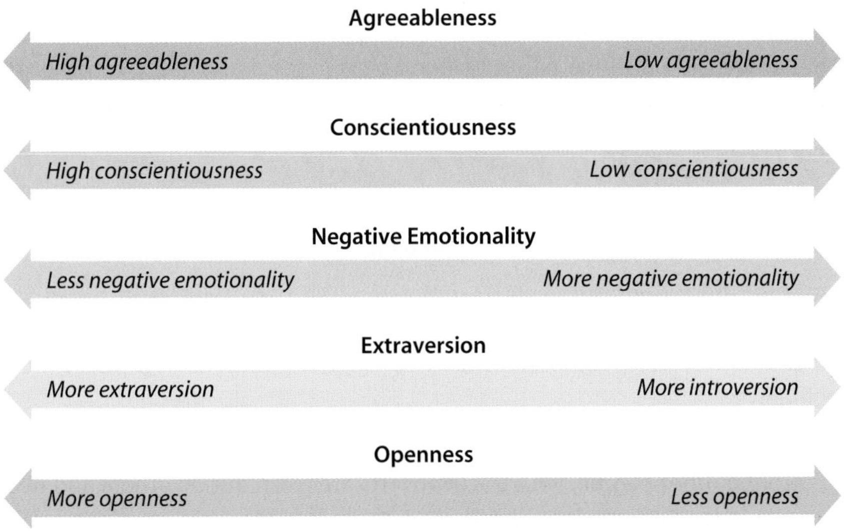

FIGURE 15.2

The "Big Five" Model of Personality

The "Big Five" personality model represents an increasingly accepted framework for understanding personality traits in organizational settings. In general, experts tend to agree that personality traits toward the left end of each dimension, as illustrated in this figure, are more positive in organizational settings, whereas traits closer to the right are less positive.

But people with more negative emotionality will be more excitable, insecure, reactive, and subject to extreme mood swings. People with less negative emotionality might be expected to better handle job stress, pressure, and tension. Their stability might also lead them to be seen as more reliable than their less stable counterparts.

extraversion A person's comfort level with relationships

Extraversion refers to a person's comfort level with relationships. People who are called "extraverts" are sociable, talkative, assertive, and open to establishing new relationships. But introverts are much less sociable, talkative, and assertive, and less open to establishing new relationships. Research suggests that extraverts tend to be higher overall job performers than introverts and that they are also more likely to be attracted to jobs based on personal relationships, such as sales and marketing positions.

openness A person's rigidity of beliefs and range of interests

Finally, **openness** refers to a person's rigidity of beliefs and range of interests. People with high levels of openness are willing to listen to new ideas and to change their own ideas, beliefs, and attitudes as a result of new information. They also tend to have broad interests and to be curious, imaginative, and creative. On the other hand, people with low levels of openness tend to be less receptive to new ideas and less willing to change their mind. Further, they tend to have fewer and narrower interests and to be less curious and creative. People with more openness might be expected to be better performers, owing to their flexibility and the likelihood that they will be better accepted by others in the organization. Openness may also encompass an individual's willingness to accept change. For example, people with high levels of openness may be more receptive to change, whereas people with low levels of openness may be more likely to resist change.

The Big Five framework continues to attract the attention of both researchers and managers. The potential value of this framework is that it encompasses an integrated set of traits that appear to be valid predictors of certain behaviors in certain situations. Thus managers who can develop both an understanding of the framework and the ability to assess these traits in their employees will be in a good position to understand how and why employees behave as they do.[6] On the other hand, managers must also be careful not to overestimate their ability to assess the Big Five traits in others. Even assessment using the most rigorous and valid measures, for instance, is still likely to be somewhat imprecise. Another limitation of the Big Five framework is that it is based primarily on research conducted in the United States. Thus there are unanswered questions as to its generalizability to other cultures. And, even within the United States, a variety of other factors and traits are also likely to affect behavior in organizations.

The Myers-Briggs Framework

Another interesting approach to understanding personalities in organizations is the Myers-Briggs framework. This framework, based on the classic work of Carl Jung, differentiates people in terms of four general dimensions. These are defined as follows:

- *Extraversion (E) Versus Introversion (I).* Extraverts get their energy from being around other people, whereas introverts are worn out by others and need solitude to recharge their energy.

- *Sensing (S) Versus Intuition (N).* The sensing type prefers concrete things, whereas intuitives prefer abstract concepts.
- *Thinking (T) Versus Feeling (F).* Thinking individuals base their decisions more on logic and reason, whereas feeling individuals base their decisions more on feelings and emotions.
- *Judging (J) Versus Perceiving (P).* People who are the judging type enjoy completion or being finished, whereas perceiving types enjoy the process and open-ended situations.

To use this framework, people complete a questionnaire designed to measure their personality on each dimension. Higher or lower scores in each of the dimensions are used to classify people into one of sixteen different personality categories.

The Myers-Briggs Type Indicator (MBTI) is one popular questionnaire that some organizations use to assess personality types. Indeed, it is among the most popular selection instruments used today, with as many as 2 million people taking it each year. Research suggests that the MBTI is a useful method for determining communication styles and interaction preferences. In terms of personality attributes, however, questions exist about both the validity and the reliability of the MBTI.

locus of control The degree to which an individual believes that his or her behavior has a direct impact on the consequences of that behavior

self-efficacy An individual's beliefs about her or his capabilities to perform a task

Other Personality Traits at Work

Besides the Big Five and the Myers-Briggs framework, there are several other personality traits that influence behavior in organizations. Among the most important are locus of control, self-efficacy, authoritarianism, Machiavellianism, self-esteem, and risk propensity.

Locus of control is the extent to which people believe that their behavior has a real effect on what happens to them.[7]

Some people, for example, believe that, if they work hard, they will succeed. They also may believe that people who fail do so because they lack ability or motivation. People who believe that individuals are in control of their lives are said to have an *internal locus of control.* Other people think that fate, chance, luck, or other people's behavior determines what happens to them. For example, an employee who fails to get a promotion may attribute that failure to a politically motivated boss or just bad luck, rather than to her or his own lack of skills or poor performance record. People who think that forces beyond their control dictate what happens to them are said to have an *external locus of control.*

Self-efficacy is a related but subtly different personality characteristic. Self-efficacy is a person's beliefs about his or her capabilities to perform a task.[8] People with high self-efficacy believe that they can perform well on a specific task, whereas people with low self-efficacy tend to doubt their ability to perform a specific task. Although self-assessments of ability contribute to self-efficacy, so, too, does the individual's personality. Some people simply have more self-confidence than do others. This belief in their ability to perform a task effectively results in their being more self-assured and more able to focus their attention on performance.

Locus of control is the degree to which an individual believes that behavior has a direct impact on the consequences of that behavior. Most professional athletes, for instance, are very self-confident and assume that they can defeat their opponent. Venus Williams, for instance, shown here winning the Wimbledon title, expects to win every time she steps on the tennis court. Thus, she clearly has an internal locus of control.

authoritarianism The extent to which an individual believes that power and status differences are appropriate within hierarchical social systems like organizations

Another important personality characteristic is **authoritarianism**, the extent to which an individual believes that power and status differences are appropriate within hierarchical social systems like organizations.[9] For example, a person who is highly authoritarian may accept directives or orders from someone with more authority purely because the other person is "the boss." On the other hand, although a person who is not highly authoritarian may still carry out appropriate and reasonable directives from the boss, he or she is also more likely to question things, express disagreement with the boss, and even refuse to carry out orders if they are for some reason objectionable. A highly authoritarian manager may be autocratic and demanding, and highly authoritarian subordinates will be more likely to accept this behavior from their leader. On the other hand, a less authoritarian manager may allow subordinates a bigger role in making decisions, and less authoritarian subordinates will respond positively to this behavior.

Machiavellianism Behavior directed at gaining power and controlling the behavior of others

Machiavellianism is another important personality trait. This concept is named after Niccolo Machiavelli, a sixteenth-century Italian political philosopher. In his book entitled *The Prince*, Machiavelli explained how the nobility could more easily gain and use power. *Machiavellianism* is now used to describe behavior directed at gaining power and controlling the behavior of others. Research suggests that Machiavellianism is a personality trait that varies from person to person. More Machiavellian individuals tend to be rational and nonemotional, may be willing to lie to attain their personal goals, may put little weight on loyalty and friendship, and may enjoy manipulating others' behavior. Less Machiavellian individuals are more emotional, less willing to lie to succeed, value loyalty and friendship highly, and get little personal pleasure from manipulating others. By all accounts, Dennis Kozlowski, the indicted former CEO of Tyco International, had a high degree of Machiavellianism. He apparently came to believe that his position of power in the company gave him the right to do just about anything he wanted with company resources.[10]

self-esteem The extent to which a person believes that he or she is a worthwhile and deserving individual

Self-esteem is the extent to which a person believes that she is a worthwhile and deserving individual.[11] A person with high self-esteem is more likely to seek high-status jobs, be more confident in her ability to achieve higher levels of performance, and derive greater intrinsic satisfaction from her accomplishments. In contrast, a person with less self-esteem may be more content to remain in a lower-level job, be less confident of his ability, and focus more on extrinsic rewards. Among the major personality dimensions, self-esteem is the one that has been most widely studied in other countries. Although more research is clearly needed, the published evidence does suggest that self-esteem as a personality trait does indeed exist in a variety of countries and that its role in organizations is reasonably important across different cultures.[12]

risk propensity The degree to which an individual is willing to take chances and make risky decisions

Risk propensity is the degree to which an individual is willing to take chances and make risky decisions. A manager with a high risk propensity, for example, might be expected to experiment with new ideas and gamble on new products. She might also lead the organization in new and different directions. This manager might also be a catalyst for innovation. On the other hand, the same individual might also jeopardize the continued well-being of the organization if the risky decisions prove to be bad ones. A manager with low risk propensity might lead to a stagnant and overly conservative organization or help the organization successfully weather turbulent and unpredictable times by maintaining stability and calm. Thus the potential consequences of risk propensity to an organization are heavily dependent on that organization's environment.

Emotional Intelligence

The concept of emotional intelligence has been identified in recent years and provides some interesting insights into personality. **Emotional intelligence,** or **EQ**, refers to the extent to which people are self-aware, can manage their emotions, can motivate themselves, express empathy for others, and possess social skills.[13] These various dimensions can be described as follows:

emotional intelligence (EQ) The extent to which people are self-aware, can manage their emotions, can motivate themselves, express empathy for others, and possess social skills

- *Self-Awareness.* This is the basis for the other components. It refers to a person's capacity for being aware of how they are feeling. In general, more self-awareness allows people to more effectively guide their own life and behaviors.
- *Managing Emotions.* This refers to a person's capacities to balance anxiety, fear, and anger so that they do not overly interfere with getting things accomplished.
- *Motivating Oneself.* This dimension refers to a person's ability to remain optimistic and to continue striving in the face of setbacks, barriers, and failure.
- *Empathy.* Empathy refers to a person's ability to understand how others are feeling, even without being explicitly told.
- *Social Skill.* This refers to a person's ability to get along with others and to establish positive relationships.

Preliminary research suggests that people with high EQs may perform better than others, especially in jobs that require a high degree of interpersonal interaction and that involve influencing or directing the work of others. Moreover, EQ appears to be something that is not biologically based but can be developed.[14]

concept CHECK

What is personality? Identify several basic personality dimensions.

Describe your own personality in terms of the various personality dimensions discussed in this section. For instance, do you think you have an internal or an external locus of control?

Attitudes and Individual Behavior

Another important element of individual behavior in organizations is attitudes. **Attitudes** are complexes of beliefs and feelings that people have about specific ideas, situations, or other people. Attitudes are important because they are the mechanism through which most people express their feelings. An employee's statement that he feels underpaid by the organization reflects his feelings about his pay.

attitudes Complexes of beliefs and feelings that people have about specific ideas, situations, or other people

Similarly, when a manager says that she likes the new advertising campaign, she is expressing her feelings about the organization's marketing efforts.

Attitudes have three components. The *affective component* of an attitude reflects feelings and emotions an individual has toward a situation. The *cognitive component* of an attitude is derived from knowledge an individual has about a situation. It is important to note that cognition is subject to individual perceptions (something we discuss more fully later). Thus one person might "know" that a certain political candidate is better than another, whereas someone else might "know" just the opposite. Finally, the *intentional component* of an attitude reflects how an individual expects to behave toward or in the situation.

To illustrate these three components, consider the case of a manager who places an order for some supplies for his organization from a new office supply firm. Suppose many of the items he orders are out of stock, others are overpriced, and still others arrive damaged. When he calls someone at the supply firm for assistance, he is treated rudely and gets disconnected before his claim is resolved. When asked how he feels about the new office supply firm, he might respond, "I don't like that company [affective component]. They are the worst office supply firm I've ever dealt with [cognitive component]. I'll never do business with them again [intentional component]."

cognitive dissonance Caused when an individual has conflicting attitudes

People try to maintain consistency among the three components of their attitudes as well as among all their attitudes. However, circumstances sometimes arise that lead to conflicts. The conflict individuals may experience among their own attitudes is called **cognitive dissonance.**[15] Say, for example, that an individual who has vowed never to work for a big, impersonal corporation intends instead to open her own business and be her own boss. Unfortunately, a series of financial setbacks leads her to have no choice but to take a job with a large company and work for someone else. Thus cognitive dissonance occurs: The affective and cognitive components of the individual's attitude conflict with intended behavior. In order to reduce cognitive dissonance, which is usually an uncomfortable experience for most people, the individual might tell herself that the situation is only temporary and that she can go back out on her own in the near future. Or she might revise her cognitions and decide that working for a large company is more pleasant than she had expected.

Work-related Attitudes

People in organizations form attitudes about many different things. For example, employees are likely to have attitudes about their salary, promotion possibilities, their boss, employee benefits, the food in the company cafeteria, and the color of the company softball team uniforms. Of course, some of these attitudes are more important than others. Especially important attitudes are job satisfaction or dissatisfaction and organizational commitment.[16]

job satisfaction or **dissatisfaction** An attitude that reflects the extent to which an individual is gratified by or fulfilled in his or her work

Job Satisfaction or Dissatisfaction **Job satisfaction** or **dissatisfaction** is an attitude that reflects the extent to which an individual is gratified by or fulfilled in his or her work. Extensive research conducted on job satisfaction has indicated that personal factors, such as an individual's needs and aspirations, determine this attitude, along with group and organizational factors, such as relationships with coworkers and supervisors, and working conditions, work policies, and compensation.[17]

A satisfied employee also tends to be absent less often, to make positive contributions, and to stay with the organization.[18] In contrast, a dissatisfied employee may be absent more often, may experience stress that disrupts coworkers, and may be continually looking for another job. Contrary to what many managers believe, however, high levels of job satisfaction do not necessarily lead to higher levels of performance. One survey has also indicated that, contrary to popular opinion, Japanese workers are less satisfied with their jobs than their counterparts in the United States.[19]

Organizational Commitment **Organizational commitment** is an attitude that reflects an individual's identification with and attachment to the organization itself. A person with a high level of commitment is likely to see herself as a true member of the organization (for example, referring to the organization in personal terms like "We make high-quality products"), to overlook minor sources of dissatisfaction with the organization, and to see herself remaining a member of the organization. In contrast, a person with less organizational commitment is more likely to see himself as an outsider (for example, referring to the organization in less personal terms like "They don't pay their employees very well"), to express more dissatisfaction about things, and to not see himself as a long-term member of the organization. Research suggests that Japanese workers may be more committed to their organizations than are American workers.[20]

organizational commitment An attitude that reflects an individual's identification with and attachment to the organization itself

Research also suggests that commitment strengthens with an individual's age, years with the organization, sense of job security, and participation in decision making.[21] Employees who feel committed to an organization have highly reliable habits, plan a long tenure with the organization, and muster more effort in performance. Although there are few definitive things that organizations can do to create or promote commitment, there are a few specific guidelines available. For one thing, if the organization treats its employees fairly and provides reasonable rewards and job security, those employees will more likely be satisfied and committed. Allowing employees to have a say in how things are done can also promote all three attitudes.

Affect and Mood in Organizations

Researchers have recently started to focus renewed interest on the affective component of attitudes. Recall from our discussion above that the affective component of an attitude reflects our feelings and emotions. Although managers once believed that emotion and feelings varied among people from day to day, research now suggests that, although some short-term fluctuation does indeed occur, there are also underlying stable predispositions toward fairly constant and predictable moods and emotional states.[22]

Some people, for example, tend to have a higher degree of **positive affectivity**. This means that they are relatively upbeat and optimistic, have an overall sense of well-being, and usually see things in a positive light. Thus they always seem to be in a good mood. Other people, those with more **negative affectivity**, are just the opposite. They are generally downbeat and pessimistic, and they usually see things in a negative way. They seem to be in a bad mood most of the time.

positive affectivity A tendency to be relatively upbeat and optimistic, have an overall sense of well-being, see things in a positive light, and seem to be in a good mood

negative affectivity A tendency to be generally downbeat and pessimistic, see things in a negative way, and seem to be in a bad mood

Of course, as noted above, there can be short-term variations among even the most extreme types. People with a lot of positive affectivity, for example, may still be in a bad mood if they have just received some bad news—being passed over for a promotion, getting extremely negative performance feedback, or being laid off or fired, for instance. Similarly, those with negative affectivity may still be in a good mood—at least for a short time—if they have just been promoted, received very positive performance feedback, or had other good things befall them. After the initial impact of these events wears off, however, those with positive affectivity will generally return to their normal positive mood, whereas those with negative affectivity will gravitate back to their normal bad mood.

concept CHECK

Identify and describe the three components of an attitude.

Using a job you have either held in the past or currently hold, describe the level of job satisfaction or dissatisfaction and organizational commitment you felt or feel. Describe what caused those attitudes and how they affected your behavior.

Perception and Individual Behavior

As noted earlier, an important element of an attitude is the individual's perception of the object about which the attitude is formed. Because perception plays a role in a variety of other workplace behaviors, managers need to have a general understanding of basic perceptual processes.[23] The role of attributions is also important.

Basic Perceptual Processes

perception The set of processes by which an individual becomes aware of and interprets information about the environment

Perception is the set of processes by which an individual becomes aware of and interprets information about the environment. As shown in Figure 15.3, basic perceptual

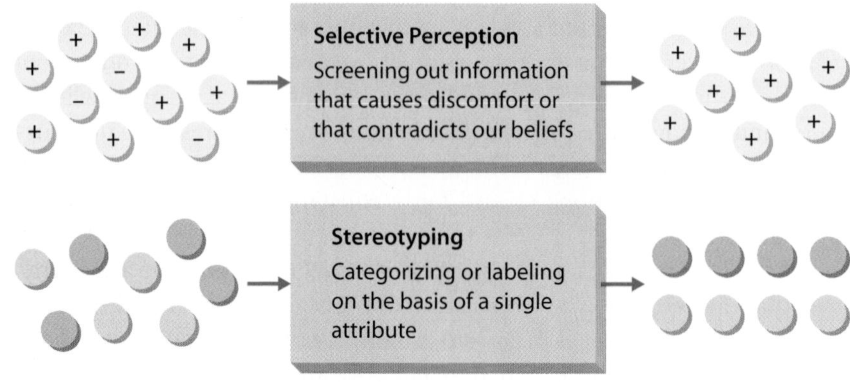

FIGURE 15.3

Perceptual Processes

Two of the most basic perceptual processes are selective perception and stereotyping. As shown here, selective perception occurs when we screen out information (represented by the - symbols) that causes us discomfort or that contradicts our beliefs. Stereotyping occurs when we categorize or label people on the basis of a single attribute, illustrated here by color.

processes that are particularly relevant to organizations are selective perception and stereotyping. *The Business of Ethics* also provides a clear illustration of how different people can perceive things in very different ways.

selective perception The process of screening out information that we are uncomfortable with or that contradicts our beliefs

Selective Perception **Selective perception** is the process of screening out information that we are uncomfortable with or that contradicts our beliefs. For example, suppose a manager is exceptionally fond of a particular worker. The manager has a very positive attitude about the worker and thinks he is a top performer. One day the manager notices that the worker seems to be goofing off. Selective perception

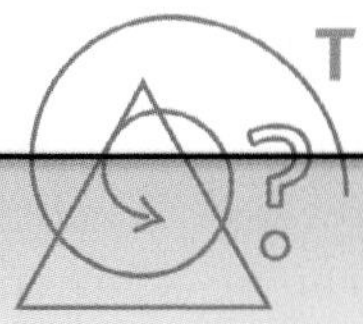

THE BUSINESS OF ethics

No Longer "The Sweetest Place on Earth"

"Hershey Trust Is an Oxymoron."

– Seen on a protest sign, by residents protesting the sale of Hershey*

Milton Hershey built more than a giant chocolate maker; he built a community. The townspeople of Hershey, Pennsylvania, have felt a sense of entitlement since Hershey's earliest days. Skeptics claim that the entitlement is false because modern firms operate differently—lifetime employment, extravagant benefits, and even the concept of a company town are outdated. Yet, in a classic David-and-Goliath story, the community recently rose up against the powerful Hershey Trust, and the little guy won.

In central Pennsylvania in 1902, Hershey desired an idyllic company town. He built comfortable housing, a park, a community center, a junior college, and an amusement park. His town was a model of early urban planning, with green space and a public trolley. Hershey added an orphanage that equaled the best private prep schools. Jobs were lifelong, too. During the depression, not one Hershey worker lost a job.

After Milton Hershey's death in 1945, the Hershey Trust carried on, until the 1960s. Over the next three decades, facilities were demolished. The company diversified, adding outsiders to the board. In 1994 then-CEO Ken Wolfe trimmed four hundred jobs. "I changed the culture," Wolfe says. "No longer was everybody guaranteed a job." Internal squabbles showed that the bonds among school, company, and community were unraveling. In July of 2002, the trust insisted on selling Hershey in order to diversify its portfolio. Residents and workers signed petitions and held protest rallies. One sign read, "Hershey Trust Is an Oxymoron."

Gum manufacturer Wrigley offered $12.5 billion for the company. However, after three months' consideration, Hershey management caved in to pressure from locals and refused the offer. Residents celebrated the preservation of not only 3,000 jobs, but also their way of life. Community leader Bruce McKinney exulted, "Hershey is a quilt, made up of many patches of beautiful texture and fabric, woven very tightly together. We weren't going to stand by and let someone tear apart the quilt."

Former CEO Dick Zimmerman was not so pleased. "We're really involved in a lose-lose situation," Zimmerman said. "The relationship among all the entities has been changed dramatically. There will always be antagonism." Hershey, PA, doesn't seem to be living up to its nickname—"the sweetest place on earth"—any more.

References: "Hershey Cancels Plan to be Sold," *BusinessWeek*, September 18, 2002, www.businessweek.com on January 23, 2003; John Helyar, "The Hershey Kiss-Off," *Fortune*, December 18, 2002, www.fortune.com on February 2, 2003; John Helyar, "Sweet Surrender," *Fortune*, October 1, 2002, www.fortune.com on February 2, 2003 (*quote).

may cause the manager to quickly forget what he observed. Similarly, suppose a manager has formed a very negative image of a particular worker. She thinks this worker is a poor performer and never does a good job. When she happens to observe an example of high performance from the worker, she, too, may not remember it for very long. In one sense, selective perception is beneficial because it allows us to disregard minor bits of information. Of course, this holds true only if our basic perception is accurate. If selective perception causes us to ignore important information, however, it can become quite detrimental.

stereotyping The process of categorizing or labeling people on the basis of a single attribute

Stereotyping **Stereotyping** is the process of categorizing or labeling people on the basis of a single attribute. Common attributes from which people often stereotype are race and sex. Of course, stereotypes along these lines are inaccurate and can be harmful. For example, suppose a manager forms the stereotype that women can perform only certain tasks and that men are best suited for other tasks. To the extent that this affects the manager's hiring practices, the manager is (1) costing the organization valuable talent for both sets of jobs, (2) violating federal law, and (3) behaving unethically. On the other hand, certain forms of stereotyping can be useful and efficient. Suppose, for example, that a manager believes that communication skills are important for a particular job and that speech communication majors tend to have exceptionally good communication skills. As a result, whenever he interviews candidates for jobs, he pays especially close attention to speech communication majors. To the extent that communication skills truly predict job performance and that majoring in speech communication does indeed provide those skills, this form of stereotyping can be beneficial.

Perception and Attribution

attribution The process of observing behavior and attributing causes to it

Perception is also closely linked with another process called "attribution." **Attribution** is a mechanism through which we observe behavior and then attribute causes to it.[24] The behavior that is observed may be our own or that of others. For example, suppose someone realizes one day that she is working fewer hours than before, that she talks less about her work, and that she calls in sick more frequently. She might conclude from this that she must have become disenchanted with her job and subsequently decide to quit. Thus she observed her own behavior, attributed a cause to it, and developed what she thought was a consistent response.

More common is attributing cause to the behavior of others. For example, if the manager of the individual described above has observed the same behavior, he might form exactly the same attribution. On the other hand, he might instead decide that she has a serious illness, that he is driving her too hard, that she is experiencing too much stress, that she has a drug problem, or that she is having family problems.

The basic framework around which we form attributions is *consensus* (the extent to which other people in the same situation behave the same way), *consistency* (the extent to which the same person behaves in the same way at different times), and *distinctiveness* (the extent to which the same person behaves in the same way in other situations). For example, suppose a manager observes that an employee is late for a meeting. The manager might further realize that he is the only one who is late (low consensus), recall that he is often late for other meetings (high consistency), and subsequently realize that the same employee is sometimes late for work and returning from lunch (low distinctiveness). This pattern of attributions might cause the manager to decide that the individual's behavior is something that should be changed. As a result, the manager might meet with the subordinate and establish some punitive consequences for future tardiness.

concept CHECK

Define perception and discuss two fundamental perceptual processes.

Recall a vivid example of behavior exhibited by someone and then describe that behavior from an attributional perspective.

Stress and Individual Behavior

stress An individual's response to a strong stimulus, which is called a **stressor**

General Adaptation Syndrome (GAS) General cycle of the stress process

Another important element of behavior in organizations is stress. **Stress** is an individual's response to a strong stimulus.[25] This stimulus is called a **stressor**. Stress generally follows a cycle referred to as the **General Adaptation Syndrome**, or GAS,[26] shown in Figure 15.4. According to this view, when an individual first encounters a stressor, the GAS is initiated, and the first stage, alarm, is activated. He may feel panic, wonder how to cope, and feel helpless. For example, suppose a manager is told to prepare a detailed evaluation of a plan by his firm to buy one of its competitors. His first reaction may be, "How will I ever get this done by tomorrow?"

If the stressor is too intense, the individual may feel unable to cope and never really try to respond to its demands. In most cases, however, after a short period of alarm, the individual gathers some strength and starts to resist the negative effects of the stressor. For example, the manager with the evaluation to write may calm down, call home to say he is working late, roll up his sleeves, order out for coffee, and get to work. Thus, at stage 2 of the GAS, the person is resisting the effects of the stressor.

A variety of techniques and methods have been proposed as ways people can better manage the stress in their lives. Both meditation and yoga, as practiced by these individuals, are increasingly popular methods that many people seem to find helpful.

In many cases, the resistance phase may end the GAS. If the manager is able to complete the evaluation earlier than expected, he may drop it in his briefcase, smile to himself, and head home tired but satisfied. On the other hand, prolonged exposure to a stressor without resolution may bring on stage 3 of the GAS—exhaustion. At this stage, the individual literally gives up and can no longer resist the stressor. The manager, for example, might fall asleep at his desk at 3:00 A.M. and never finish the evaluation.

FIGURE 15.4

The General Adaptation Syndrome

The general adaptation syndrome represents the normal process by which we react to stressful events. At stage 1—alarm—we feel panic and alarm, and our level of resistance to stress drops. Stage 2—resistance—represents our efforts to confront and control the stressful circumstance. If we fail, we may eventually reach stage 3—exhaustion—and just give up or quit.

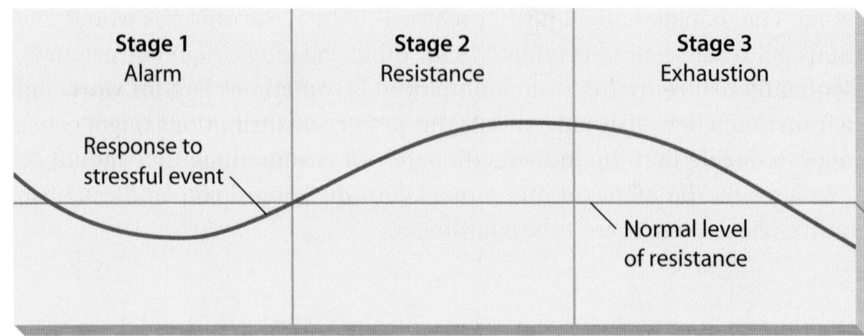

We should note that stress is not all bad. In the absence of stress, we may experience lethargy and stagnation. An optimal level of stress, on the other hand, can result in motivation and excitement. Too much stress, however, can have negative consequences. It is also important to understand that stress can be caused by "good" as well as "bad" things. Excessive pressure, unreasonable demands on our time, and bad news can all cause stress. But even receiving a bonus and then having to decide what to do with the money can be stressful. So, too, can receiving a promotion, gaining recognition, and similar good things.

Type A Individuals who are extremely competitive, very devoted to work, and have a strong sense of time urgency

Type B Individuals who are less competitive, less devoted to work, and have a weaker sense of time urgency

One important line of thinking about stress focuses on **Type A** and **Type B** personalities.[27] Type A individuals are extremely competitive, very devoted to work, and have a strong sense of time urgency. They are likely to be aggressive, impatient, and very work oriented. They have a lot of drive and want to accomplish as much as possible as quickly as possible. Type B individuals are less competitive, less devoted to work, and have a weaker sense of time urgency. Such individuals are less likely to experience conflict with other people and more likely to have a balanced, relaxed approach to life. They are able to work at a constant pace without time urgency. Type B people are not necessarily more or less successful than are Type A people. But they are less likely to experience stress.

Causes and Consequences of Stress

Stress is obviously not a simple phenomenon. As listed in Figure 15.5, several different things can cause stress. Note that this list includes only work-related conditions. We should keep in mind that stress can also be the result of personal circumstances.[28]

Causes of Stress Work-related stressors fall into one of four categories—task, physical, role, and interpersonal demands. *Task demands* are associated with the task itself. Some occupations are inherently more stressful than others. Having to make fast decisions, decisions with less than complete information, or decisions that have relatively serious consequences are some of the things that can make some jobs stressful. The jobs of surgeon, airline pilot, and stockbroker are relatively more stressful than the jobs of general practitioner, baggage handler, and office receptionist. Although a general practitioner makes important decisions, he is also likely to have time to make a considered diagnosis and fully explore a number of

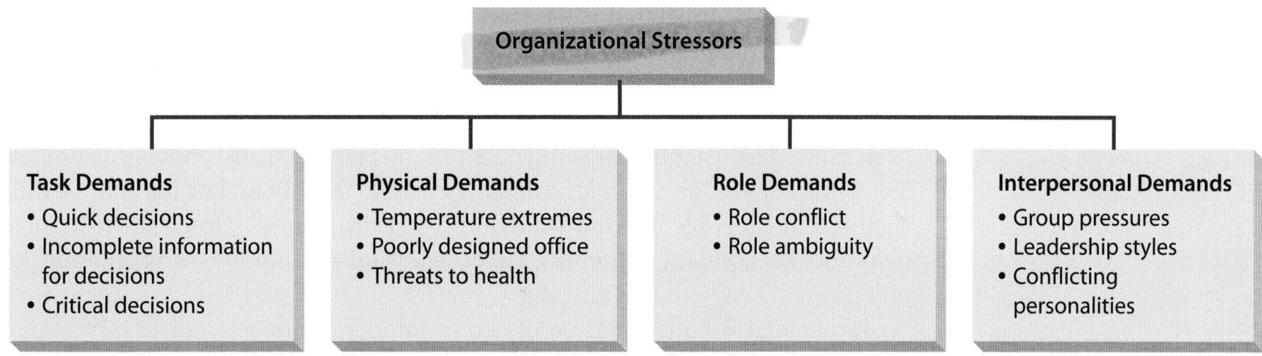

FIGURE 15.5

Causes of Work Stress

There are several causes of work stress in organizations. Four general sets of organizational stressors are task demands, physical demands, role demands, and interpersonal demands.

different treatments. But, during surgery, the surgeon must make decisions quickly while realizing that the wrong one may endanger her patient's life.

Physical demands are stressors associated with the job setting. Working outdoors in extremely hot or cold temperatures, or even in an improperly heated or cooled office, can lead to stress. A poorly designed office, which makes it difficult for people to have privacy or promotes too little social interaction, can result in stress, as can poor lighting and inadequate work surfaces. Even more severe are actual threats to health. Examples include jobs like coal mining, poultry processing, and toxic waste handling.

Role demands can also cause stress. (Roles are discussed more fully in Chapter 18). A role is a set of expected behaviors associated with a position in a group or organization. Stress can result from either role conflict or role ambiguity which people can experience in groups. For example, an employee who is feeling pressure from her boss to work longer hours or to travel more, while also being asked by her family for more time at home, will almost certainly experience stress as a result of role conflict.[29] Similarly, a new employee experiencing role ambiguity because of poor orientation and training practices by the organization will also suffer from stress.

Interpersonal demands are stressors associated with relationships that confront people in organizations. For example, group pressures regarding restriction of output and norm conformity can lead to stress. Leadership styles may also cause stress. An employee who feels a strong need to participate in decision making may feel stress if his boss refuses to allow participation. And individuals with conflicting personalities may experience stress if required to work too closely together. For example, a person with an internal locus of

Stress can be caused by a number of different things. Cameron Eyhorn has had his work hours reduced, lowering his weekly pay substantially. To better prepare for future advancement, he is currently enrolled in an evening vocational certificate program. Having less money, facing the pressures of school, and helping with his family have clearly raised the level of stress he is experiencing.

control might be frustrated when working with someone who prefers to wait and just let things happen.

Consequences of Stress As noted earlier, the results of stress may be positive or negative. The negative consequences may be behavioral, psychological, or medical. Behaviorally, for example, stress may lead to detrimental or harmful actions, such as smoking, alcoholism, overeating, and drug abuse. Other stress-induced behaviors are accident proneness, violence toward self or others, and appetite disorders.

Psychological consequences of stress interfere with an individual's mental health and well-being. These outcomes include sleep disturbances, depression, family problems, and sexual dysfunction. Managers are especially prone to sleep disturbances when they experience stress at work.[30] Medical consequences of stress affect an individual's physiological well-being. Heart disease and stroke have been linked to stress, as have headaches, backaches, ulcers and related disorders, and skin conditions such as acne and hives.

Individual stress also has direct consequences for businesses. For an operating employee, stress may translate into poor-quality work and lower productivity. For a manager, it may mean faulty decision making and disruptions in working relationships. Withdrawal behaviors can also result from stress. People who are having difficulties with stress in their job are more likely to call in sick or to leave the organization. More subtle forms of withdrawal may also occur. A manager may start missing deadlines, for example, or taking longer lunch breaks. Employees may also withdraw by developing feelings of indifference. The irritation displayed by people under great stress can make them difficult to get along with. Job satisfaction, morale, and commitment can all suffer as a result of excessive levels of stress. So, too, can motivation to perform.

burnout A feeling of exhaustion that may develop when someone experiences too much stress for an extended period of time

Another consequence of stress is **burnout**—a feeling of exhaustion that may develop when someone experiences too much stress for an extended period of time. Burnout results in constant fatigue, frustration, and helplessness. Increased rigidity follows, as do a loss of self-confidence and psychological withdrawal. The individual dreads going to work, often puts in longer hours but get less accomplished than before, and exhibits mental and physical exhaustion. Because of the damaging effects of burnout, some firms are taking steps to help avoid it. For example, British Airways provides all of its employees with training designed to help them recognize the symptoms of burnout and develop strategies for avoiding it.

Managing Stress

Given the potential consequences of stress, it follows that both people and organizations should be concerned about how to limit its more damaging effects. Numerous ideas and approaches have been developed to help manage stress. Some are strategies for individuals; others are strategies for organizations.[31]

One way people manage stress is through exercise. People who exercise regularly feel less tension and stress, are more self-confident, and feel more optimistic. Their better physical condition also makes them less susceptible to many common illnesses. People who do not exercise regularly, on the other hand, tend to feel more stress and are more likely to be depressed. They are also more likely to have heart attacks. And, because of their physical condition, they are more likely to contract illnesses.

Another method people use to manage stress is relaxation. Relaxation allows individuals to adapt to, and therefore better deal with, their stress. Relaxation comes in many forms, such as taking regular vacations. A recent study found that people's attitudes toward a variety of workplace characteristics improved significantly following a vacation. People can also learn to relax while on the job. For example, some experts recommend that people take regular rest breaks during their normal workday.

People can also use time management to control stress. The idea behind time management is that many daily pressures can be reduced or eliminated if individuals do a better job of managing time. One approach to time management is to make a list every morning of the things to be done that day. The items on the list are then grouped into three categories: critical activities that must be performed, important activities that should be performed, and optional or trivial things that can be delegated or postponed. The individual performs the items on the list in their order of importance.

Finally, people can manage stress through support groups. A support group can be as simple as a group of family members or friends to enjoy leisure time with. Going out after work with a couple of coworkers to a basketball game or a movie, for example, can help relieve stress built up during the day. Family and friends can help people cope with stress on an ongoing basis and during times of crisis. For example, an employee who has just learned that she did not get the promotion she has been working toward for months may find it helpful to have a good friend to lean on, talk to, or yell at. People also may make use of more elaborate and formal support groups. Community centers or churches, for example, may sponsor support groups for people who have recently gone through a divorce, the death of a loved one, or some other tragedy.

Organizations are also beginning to realize that they should be involved in helping employees cope with stress. One argument for this is that, because the business is at least partially responsible for stress, it should also help relieve it. Another is that stress-related insurance claims by employees can cost the organization considerable sums of money. Still another is that workers experiencing lower levels of detrimental stress will be able to function more effectively. AT&T has initiated a series of seminars and workshops to help its employees cope with the stress they face in their job. The firm was prompted to develop these seminars for all three of the reasons noted above.

A wellness stress program is a special part of the organization specifically created to help deal with stress. Organizations have adopted stress-management programs, health promotion programs, and other kinds of programs for this purpose. The AT&T seminar program noted earlier is similar to this idea, but true wellness programs are ongoing activities that have a number of different components. They commonly include exercise-related activities as well as classroom instruction programs dealing with smoking cessation, weight reduction, and general stress management.

Some companies are developing their own programs or using existing programs of this type. Johns Manville, for example, has a gym at its corporate headquarters. Other firms negotiate discounted health club membership rates with local establishments. For the instructional part of the program, the organization can again either sponsor its own training or perhaps jointly sponsor seminars with a local YMCA, civic organization, or church. Organization-based fitness programs facilitate employee exercise, a very positive consideration, but such programs are also quite costly. Still, more and more companies are developing fitness programs for employees.

concept CHECK

Define stress and list its primary causes and consequences.	*Are you more of a Type A or a Type B person? How do you feel about this?*

Creativity in Organizations

creativity The ability of an individual to generate new ideas or to conceive of new perspectives on existing ideas

Creativity is yet another important component of individual behavior in organizations. **Creativity** is the ability of an individual to generate new ideas or to conceive of new perspectives on existing ideas. What makes a person creative? How do people become creative? How does the creative process work? Although psychologists have not yet discovered complete answers to these questions, examining a few general patterns can help us understand the sources of individual creativity within organizations.[32]

The Creative Individual

Numerous researchers have focused their efforts on attempting to describe the common attributes of creative individuals. These attributes generally fall into three categories: background experiences, personal traits, and cognitive abilities.

Background Experiences and Creativity Researchers have observed that many creative individuals were raised in an environment in which creativity was nurtured. Mozart was raised in a family of musicians and began composing and performing music at age six. Pierre and Marie Curie, great scientists in their own right, also raised a daughter, Irene, who won the Nobel Prize in chemistry. Thomas Edison's creativity was nurtured by his mother. However, people with background experiences very different from theirs have also been creative. Frederick Douglass was born into slavery in Tuckahoe, Maryland, and had very limited opportunities for education. Nonetheless, his powerful oratory and creative thinking helped lead to the Emancipation Proclamation, which outlawed slavery in the United States.

Personal Traits and Creativity Certain personal traits have also been linked to creativity in individuals. The traits shared by most creative people are openness, an attraction to complexity, high levels of energy, independence and autonomy, strong self-confidence, and a strong belief that one is, in fact, creative. Individuals who possess these traits are more likely to be creative than are those who do not have them.

Cognitive Abilities and Creativity Cognitive abilities are an individual's power to think intelligently and to analyze situations and data effectively. Intelligence may be a precondition for individual creativity—although most creative people are highly intelligent, not all intelligent people are necessarily creative. Creativity is also linked with the ability to think divergently and convergently. *Divergent thinking* is a skill that allows people to see differences among situations, phenomena, or events. *Convergent thinking* is a skill that allows people to see similarities among situations, phenomena, or events. Creative people are generally very skilled at both divergent and convergent thinking.

Interestingly, Japanese managers have come to question their own creative ability. The concern is that their emphasis on group harmony may have stifled individual initiative and hampered the development of individual creativity. As a result, many Japanese firms, including Omron Corporation, Fuji Photo, and Shimizu Corporation, have launched employee training programs intended to boost the creativity of their employees.[33]

Some organizations actively seek ways to enhance creativity among their employees. For instance, at Electronic Arts, a videogame developer, creativity is a critical element in the firm's success. To help people both counteract the stress from their hectic worklife and provide a place for calm mental relaxation, Electronic Arts provides a most unusual amenity—a maze. Game developers can walk in the maze whenever they feel that their creative juices need a boost.

The Creative Process

Although creative people often report that ideas seem to come to them "in a flash," individual creative activity actually tends to progress through a series of stages. Not all creative activity has to follow these four stages, but much of it does.

Preparation The creative process normally begins with a period of *preparation.* To make a creative contribution to business management or business services, individuals must usually receive formal training and education in business. Formal education and training are usually the most efficient ways of becoming familiar with this vast amount of research and knowledge. This is one reason for the strong demand for undergraduate and master's level business education. Formal business education can be an effective way for an individual to get "up to speed" and begin making creative contributions quickly. Experiences that managers have on the job after their formal training has finished can also contribute to the creative process. In an important sense, the education and training of creative people never really ends. It continues as long as they remain interested in the world and curious about the way things work. Bruce Roth earned a Ph.D. in chemistry and then spent years working in the pharmaceutical industry learning more and more about chemical compounds and how they work in human beings.

Incubation The second phase of the creative process is *incubation*—a period of less intense conscious concentration during which the knowledge and ideas acquired during preparation mature and develop. A curious aspect of incubation is that it is often helped along by pauses in concentrated rational thought. Some creative people rely on physical activity such as jogging or swimming to provide a break from thinking. Others may read or listen to music. Sometimes sleep may even supply the needed pause. Bruce Roth eventually joined Warner-Lambert, an up-and-coming drug company, to help develop medication to lower cholesterol. In his spare time, Roth read mystery novels and hiked in the mountains. He later acknowledged that this was when he did his best thinking.

Insight Usually occurring after preparation and incubation, *insight* is a spontaneous breakthrough in which the creative person achieves a new understanding of some problem or situation. Insight represents a coming together of all the scattered thoughts and ideas that were maturing during incubation. It may occur suddenly or develop slowly over time. Insight can be triggered by some external event, such as a new experience or an encounter with new data, which forces the individual to think about old issues and problems in new ways, or it can be a completely internal event in which patterns of thought finally coalesce in ways that generate new understanding. One day Bruce Roth was reviewing some data from some earlier studies that had found the new drug under development to be no more effective than other drugs already available. But this time he saw some statistical relationships that had not been identified previously. He knew then that he had a major breakthrough on his hands.

Verification Once an insight has occurred, *verification* determines the validity or truthfulness of the insight. For many creative ideas, verification includes scientific experiments to determine whether or not the insight actually leads to the results expected. Verification may also include the development of a product or service prototype. A prototype is one product or a very small number of products built just to see if the ideas behind this new product actually work. Product prototypes are rarely sold to the public but are very valuable in verifying the insights developed in the creative process. Once the new product or service is developed, verification in the marketplace is the ultimate test of the creative idea behind it. Bruce Roth and his colleagues set to work testing the new drug compound and eventually won FDA approval. The drug, named Lipitor, is already the largest-selling pharmaceutical in history. And Pfizer, the firm that bought Warner-Lambert in a hostile takeover, is expected to soon earn more than $10 billion a year on the drug.[34]

Enhancing Creativity in Organizations

Managers who wish to enhance and promote creativity in their organization can do so in a variety of ways.[35] One important method for enhancing creativity is to make it a part of the organization's culture, often through explicit goals. Firms that truly want to stress creativity, like 3M and Rubbermaid, for example, state goals that some percentage of future revenues are to be gained from new products. This clearly communicates that creativity and innovation are valued.

Another important part of enhancing creativity is to reward creative successes, while being careful not to punish creative failures. Many ideas that seem worthwhile on paper fail to pan out in reality. If the first person to come up with an idea that fails is fired or otherwise punished, others in the organization will become more cautious in their own work. And, as a result, fewer creative ideas will emerge.

concept CHECK

Define creativity and describe its likely causes.

Think of an important idea you recently had and try to explain how you derived it, based on the creative process discussed in this section.

Types of Workplace Behavior

Now that we have looked closely at how individual differences can influence behavior in organizations, let's turn our attention to what we mean by workplace behavior. **Workplace behavior** is a pattern of action by the members of an organization that directly or indirectly influences organizational effectiveness. Important workplace behaviors include performance and productivity, absenteeism and turnover, and organizational citizenship. Unfortunately, a variety of dysfunctional behaviors can also occur in organizational settings.

workplace behavior A pattern of action by the members of an organization that directly or indirectly influences organizational effectiveness

Performance Behaviors

Performance behaviors are the total set of work-related behaviors that the organization expects the individual to display. Thus they derive from the psychological contract. For some jobs, performance behaviors can be narrowly defined and easily measured. For example, an assembly-line worker who sits by a moving conveyor and attaches parts to a product as it passes by has relatively few performance behaviors. He or she is expected to remain at the workstation and correctly attach the parts. Performance can often be assessed quantitatively by counting the percentage of parts correctly attached.

performance behaviors The total set of work-related behaviors that the organization expects the individual to display

For many other jobs, however, performance behaviors are more diverse and much more difficult to assess. For example, consider the case of a research and development scientist at Merck. The scientist works in a lab trying to find new scientific breakthroughs that have commercial potential. The scientist must apply knowledge learned in graduate school with experience gained from previous research. Intuition and creativity are also important elements. And the desired breakthrough may take months or even years to accomplish. As we discussed in Chapter 14, organizations rely on a number of different methods for evaluating performance. The key, of course, is to match the evaluation mechanism with the job being performed.

Withdrawal Behaviors

Another important type of work-related behavior is that which results in withdrawal—absenteeism and turnover. **Absenteeism** occurs when an individual does not show up for work. The cause may be legitimate (illness, jury duty, death in the family, and so

absenteeism When an individual does not show up for work forth) or feigned (reported as legitimate but actually just an excuse to stay home). When an employee is absent, her or his work does not get done at all, or a substitute must be hired to do it. In either case, the quantity or quality of actual output is likely to suffer. Obviously, some absenteeism is expected. The key concern of organizations is to minimize feigned absenteeism and to reduce legitimate absences as much as possible. High absenteeism may be a symptom of other problems as well, such as job dissatisfaction and low morale.

turnover When people quit their job

Turnover occurs when people quit their job. An organization usually incurs costs in replacing individuals who have quit, but if turnover involves especially productive people, it is even more costly. Turnover seems to result from a number of factors, including aspects of the job, the organization, the individual, the labor market, and family influences. In general, a poor person-job fit is also a likely cause of turnover. The current labor shortage is also resulting in higher turnover in many companies due to the abundance of more attractive alternative jobs that are available to highly qualified individuals.[36]

Efforts to directly manage turnover are frequently fraught with difficulty, even in organizations that concentrate on rewarding good performers. Of course, some turnover is inevitable, and in some cases it may even be desirable. For example, if the organization is trying to cut costs by reducing its staff, having people voluntarily choose to leave is preferable to having to terminate them. And, if the people who choose to leave are low performers or express high levels of job dissatisfaction, the organization may also benefit from turnover.

Organizational Citizenship

organizational citizenship The behavior of individuals that makes a positive overall contribution to the organization

Organizational citizenship is the behavior of individuals that makes a positive overall contribution to the organization.[37] Consider, for example, an employee who does work that is acceptable in terms of both quantity and quality. However, she refuses to work overtime, will not help newcomers learn the ropes, and is generally unwilling to make any contribution to the organization beyond the strict performance of her job. Although this person may be seen as a good performer, she is not likely to be seen as a good organizational citizen.

Another employee may exhibit a comparable level of performance. In addition, however, he will always work late when the boss asks him to, take time to help newcomers learn their way around, and is perceived as being helpful and committed to the organization's success. Although his level of performance may be seen as equal to that of the first worker, he is also likely to be seen as a better organizational citizen.

The determinant of organizational citizenship behaviors is likely to be a complex mosaic of individual, social, and organizational variables. For example, the personality, attitudes, and needs of the individual will have to be consistent with citizenship behaviors. Similarly, the social context in which the individual works, or work group, will need to facilitate and promote such behaviors (we discuss group dynamics in Chapter 18). And the organization itself, especially its culture, must be capable of promoting, recognizing, and rewarding these types of behaviors if they are to be maintained. Although the study of organizational citizenship is still in its infancy, preliminary research suggests that it may play a powerful role in organizational effectiveness.[38]

Dysfunctional Behaviors

Some work-related behaviors are dysfunctional in nature. **Dysfunctional behaviors** are those that detract from, rather than contribute to, organizational performance. Two of the more common ones, absenteeism and turnover, are discussed above. But other forms of dysfunctional behavior may be even more costly for an organization. Theft and sabotage, for example, result in direct financial costs for an organization. Sexual and racial harassment also cost an organization, both indirectly (by lowering morale, producing fear, and driving off valuable employees) and directly (through financial liability if the organization responds inappropriately). So, too, can politicized behavior, intentionally misleading others in the organization, spreading malicious rumors, and similar activities. Workplace violence is also a growing concern in many organizations. Violence by disgruntled workers or former workers results in dozens of deaths and injuries each year.[39]

dysfunctional behaviors Those that detract from, rather than contribute to, organizational performance

Distinguish between performance behaviors, withdrawal behaviors, organizational citizenship, and dysfunctional behaviors.

Have you ever called in sick for work when you were well, or missed class using sickness as a false excuse? Can such actions be justified?

Summary of Key Points

ACE self-test

business.college.hmco.com/students

Understanding individuals in organizations is an important consideration for all managers. A basic framework that can be used to facilitate this understanding is the psychological contract—the set of expectations held by people with respect to what they will contribute to the organization and what they expect to get in return. Organizations strive to achieve an optimal person-job fit, but this process is complicated by the existence of individual differences.

Personality is the relatively stable set of psychological and behavioral attributes that distinguish one person from another. The "Big Five" personality traits are agreeableness, conscientiousness, negative emotionality, extraversion, and openness. The Myers-Briggs framework can also be a useful mechanism for understanding personality. Other important traits are locus of control, self-efficacy, authoritarianism, Machiavellianism, self-esteem, and risk propensity. Emotional intelligence, a fairly new concept, may provide additional insights into personality.

Attitudes are based on emotion, knowledge, and intended behavior. Whereas personality is relatively stable, some attitudes can be formed and changed easily. Others are more constant. Job satisfaction or dissatisfaction and organizational commitment are important work-related attitudes.

Perception is the set of processes by which an individual becomes aware of and interprets information about the environment. Basic perceptual processes include selective perception and stereotyping. Perception and attribution are also closely related.

Stress is an individual's response to a strong stimulus. The General Adaptation Syndrome outlines the basic stress process. Stress can be caused by task, physical, role, and interpersonal demands.

Consequences of stress include organizational and individual outcomes, as well as burnout. Several things can be done to manage stress.

Creativity is the capacity to generate new ideas. Creative people tend to have certain profiles of background experiences, personal traits, and cognitive abilities. The creative process itself includes preparation, incubation, insight, and verification.

Workplace behavior is a pattern of action by the members of an organization that directly or indirectly influences organizational effectiveness. Performance behaviors are the set of work-related behaviors that the organization expects the individual to display in order to fulfill the psychological contract. Basic withdrawal behaviors are absenteeism and turnover. Organizational citizenship refers to behavior that makes a positive overall contribution to the organization. Dysfunctional behaviors can be very harmful to an organization.

Discussion Questions

Questions for Review

1. What is a psychological contract? List the things that might be included in individual contributions. List the things that might be included in organizational inducements.
2. Describe the three components of attitudes and tell how the components are related. What is cognitive dissonance? How do individuals resolve cognitive dissonance?
3. Identify and discuss the steps in the creative process. What can an organization do to increase employees' creativity?
4. Identify and describe several important workplace behaviors.

Questions for Analysis

5. Organizations are increasing their use of personality tests to screen job applicants. What are the advantages and disadvantages of this approach? What can managers do to avoid some of the potential pitfalls?
6. As a manager, how can you tell that an employee is experiencing job satisfaction? How can you tell that employees are highly committed to the organization? If a worker is not satisfied, what can a manager do to improve satisfaction? What can a manager do to improve organizational commitment?
7. Managers cannot pay equal attention to every piece of information, so selective perception is a fact of life. How does selective perception help managers? How does it create difficulties for them? How can a manager increase their "good" selective perception and decrease the "bad"?

Questions for Application

8. Write the psychological contract you have in this class. In other words, what do you contribute, and what inducements are available? Ask your professor to tell the class about the psychological contract that he or she intended to establish with the students in your class. How does the professor's intended contract compare with the one you wrote? If there are differences, why do you think the differences exist? Share your ideas with the class.
9. Assume that you are going to hire three new employees for the department store you manage. One will sell shoes, one will manage the toy department, and one will work in the stockroom. Identify the basic characteristics you want in each of the people, to achieve a good person-job fit.
10. Describe a time when someone displayed each one of the Big Five personality traits at

either a very high or a very low level. For example, tell about someone who appeared to be highly agreeable or highly disagreeable. Then tell about the outcomes that person experienced as a result of displaying that particular personality trait. Do the outcomes seem logical; that is, do positive personality traits usually lead to good outcomes and negative traits to bad ones? Explain your answer.

BUILDING EFFECTIVE interpersonal SKILLS

business.college.hmco.com/students

Exercise Overview

Interpersonal skills refer to the ability to communicate with, understand, and motivate individuals and groups. This exercise shows you a widely used tool for personality assessment. It shows how an understanding of personality can aid in developing effective interpersonal relationships within organizations.

Exercise Background

There are many different ways of viewing personality, but one that is widely used is called the Myers-Briggs Type Indicator. According to Isabel Myers, each individual's personality type varies in four dimensions:

1. *Extraversion (E) Versus Introversion (I).* Extraverts get their energy from being around other people, whereas introverts are worn out by others and need solitude to recharge their energy.
2. *Sensing (S) Versus Intuition (N).* The sensing type prefers concrete things, whereas the intuitivist prefers abstract concepts.
3. *Thinking (T) Versus Feeling (F).* Thinking individuals base their decisions more on logic and reason, whereas feeling individuals base their decisions more on feelings and emotions.
4. *Judging (J) Versus Perceiving (P).* People who are the judging type enjoy completion or being finished, whereas perceiving types enjoy the process and open-ended situations.

Based on answers to a survey, individuals are classified into sixteen personality types—all the possible combinations of the four dimensions above. The resulting personality type is then expressed as a four-character code, such as ESTP or INFJ, for example. These four-character codes can then be used to describe an individual's preferred way of interacting with others.

Exercise Task

1. Use an online Meyers-Briggs assessment form to determine your own personality type. One place to find the form online is www.keirsey.com/scripts/newkts.cgi. This website also contains additional information about personality type. (*Note:* You do *not* need to pay fees or agree to receive emails in order to take the Temperament Sorter.)
2. When you have determined the four-letter code for your personality type, obtain a handout from your professor. The handout will show how your personality type affects your preferred style of working and your leadership style.
3. Conclude by addressing the following questions:
   - How easy is it to measure personality?
   - Do you feel that the online test accurately assessed your personality?
   - Why or why not? Share your assessment results and your answers with the class.

BUILDING EFFECTIVE conceptual SKILLS

Exercise Overview

Conceptual skills refer to a manager's ability to think in the abstract. This exercise provides practice in understanding differing perceptions, which can be an important source of organizational conflict and misunderstanding.

Exercise Background

Everyone has had the experience of witnessing an event with another person, sharing perceptions about the event at a later time, and finding that each person's perceptions are widely different, even though they observed exactly the same event. Differing perceptions can occur due to selective perception, stereotyping, and attribution. This exercise provides a common set of information to every student in the class and then explores their perceptions and attributions related to that information.

Exercise Task

Read or listen to the story that your professor will supply in class. Then answer the following questions:

1. Whose fault was the tragedy? Try to single out one individual. If you *must* spread the blame, pick no more than two individuals and apportion the blame to each. For example, are both equally responsible, or is one more responsible than the other?
2. List your reasons for choosing that person or persons.
3. Share your choice and reasons with the class. Listen to the choices and reasons of the other students.
4. After hearing everyone's choices and reasons, what was the outcome? Did you change your mind? Did you come to understand the positions of those who disagreed with you? Did you become emotionally involved in the discussion?
5. Looking back on the entire experience, did you learn anything about the processes of perception and attribution and their impact on people within organizations? What are the lessons for managers in this exercise?

BUILDING EFFECTIVE time-management SKILLS

Exercise Overview

Time-management skills help people prioritize work, work more efficiently, and delegate appropriately. Poor time-management skills, in turn, may result in stress. This exercise will help you relate time-management skills to stress reduction.

Exercise Background

List several of the major events or expectations that cause stress for you. Stressors might involve school (hard classes, too many exams), work (financial pressures, demanding work schedule), or personal circumstances (friends, romance, family). Try to be as specific as possible. Also try to identify at least ten different stressors.

Exercise Task

Using the list that you developed, do each of the following:

1. Evaluate the extent to which poor time-management skills on your part play a role

in how each stressor affects you. For example, do exams cause stress because you delay studying?
2. Develop a strategy for using time more efficiently in relation to each stressor that relates to time.
3. Note interrelationships among different kinds of stressors and time. For example, financial pressures may cause you to work, but work may interfere with school. Can any of these interrelationships be managed more effectively vis-à-vis time?
4. How do you manage the stress in your life? Is it possible to manage stress in a more time-effective manner?

CHAPTER CLOSING case

Too Much Character Building?

> *"Stress is like a violin string. If there's no tension, there's no music. But if the string is too tight, it will break."*
>
> – Dr. Allen Elkin of the Stress Management and Counseling Center*

There is good stress and there is bad stress. Dr. Allen Elkin, stress expert, says, "Stress is like a violin string. If there's no tension, there's no music. But if the string is too tight, it will break." Good stress helps us to do our best work, motivates us to complete projects on time, inspires creativity as we attempt to resolve the conflicting tensions we feel. Bad stress, on the other hand, makes our personality characteristics more pronounced. If you are naturally shy, you become reclusive. If you are naturally irritable, you become explosively angry. Bad stress leads to negative physical outcomes, from headaches to heart attacks; negative psychological outcomes such as depression, indecision, and forgetfulness; and negative social outcomes—anger, impatience, rudeness. "Don't let anyone tell you [stress] is just in your head," says professor Jim Quick. "It is in your body too."

The bad news, according to stress experts, is that Americans are experiencing the highest levels of stress ever. Author and stress expert Dr. Stephen Schoonover says, "People are absolutely nuts, stressed off the map. I've never seen it this bad." Stress experts, including physicians, psychiatrists, professors, and career counselors, back up their opinion with some scary statistics. Half of American workers report that stress is their major problem—double the rate ten years ago. The number of people missing work due to stress has tripled in the last four years. And 42 percent of employees think that their coworkers are suffering from dangerously high stress and need professional help to manage it.

What is causing this national epidemic of stress? Sally Helgesen, author of *Thriving in 24/7*, blames technology. The rise of the knowledge-based economy means that work is more competitive and unstable, so workers experience more chaos, rivalry, and conflict. Helgesen also sees technology, such as pagers, as "intrusive," because it allows workers to work all the time. Workers cannot, and cannot afford to, "turn their job off." Other suspected culprits include fear of terrorism, declining profitability, and recent corporate scandals. One president of a financial services firm became paralyzed by indecision every time he read about executive misdeeds at other companies.

Everyone experiences stress. The traditional view holds that middle managers have the most, because they are squeezed between their superiors and their subordinates. However, experts see a rise among top executives, perhaps due to the increased financial and ethical pressure on business leaders today. CEOs complain that they do not have as much autonomy; others whine that no one takes them seriously because scandals have destroyed their credibility. The stress of success also hits CEOs hard, because high achievers may be expected to keep up that level of performance forever.

Stress is tougher on top-level executives, because overcoming adversity is a hallmark trait of a successful leader. The myth of executive stress says that managers who cannot manage their own stress cannot possibly handle the pressure of managing a corporation. Therefore, many managers hide their stress, which results in . . . more stress! CEO Alexandra Lebenthal admits, "Fortunately or unfortunately, stress is part of our character building. But there is a moment when you think, I don't need any more character building. What I need is a vacation." Executives would rather admit to depression or alcoholism than own up to an inability to manage stress.

On the positive side, the experts also have plenty of ideas for coping with stress. Clearly, for stress that may result in harm to the employee or others, a professional counselor is required. There are even in-patient stress-management programs. However, for moderate stress, a stress-management workshop, such as those offered by the American Management Association, would be helpful. Other suggestions include the mundanely practical, such as turning off your pager during dinner. More complex solutions include setting up a napping area at your workplace or visiting an Indian ashram to learn yoga and deep-breathing techniques.

However, the suggestions that are the most difficult to implement—those that involve radical life changes—are also the most likely to lead to success. Experts recommend that managers rethink and revolutionize their life strategies. Suggestions include volunteering in order to feel a connection with others, developing exciting and active hobbies outside of work, and budgeting large blocks of time for important relationships with family and friends. In other words, do what Helgesen calls "making a living *and* making a life." These answers may sound obvious and simplistic, but to those with stress-impaired reason and emotion, following these proposals could be literally a life saver.

Case Questions

1. Consider the causes of stress experienced by CEOs, according to the four types of demands listed in your text. What demands are made on CEOs? How do these demands affect them and their performance?
2. The case suggests a number of actions that managers can take to cope with stress. What can organizations do to help their employees cope with stress? In your opinion, should companies take these steps? Why or why not?
3. Some firms are subjecting prospective employees to "stress tests," to assess the job candidate's ability to cope with stress. Based on what you have read in the case, what positive and negative consequences will come to firms that try to hire people who can cope with a lot of stress?

Case References

Anni Layne Rodgers, "Surviving la Vida Loca," *Fast Company*, September 2001, www.fastcompany.com on February 3, 2003; Diane Brady, "Rethinking the Rat Race," *BusinessWeek*, August 26, 2002, www.businessweek.com on February 3, 2003; Mark Albion, "The Beauty of Burnout," *Fast Company*, May 2001, www.fastcompany.com on February 3, 2003; Michael Lewis, "The Last Taboo," *Fortune*, October 28, 2002, pp. 137–144 (*quote p. 144).

Chapter Notes

1. Andrea Sachs, "Wedded to Work," *Time*, September 2002, p. A21; Ilene Philipson, "Work Is Life," PsychotherapistResources.com website, November 2001, www.psychotherapistresources.com on February 1, 2003 (*quote); Jerry Useem, "Welcome to the New Company Town," *Fortune*, January 10, 2000, www.fortune.com on February 1, 2003; Pamela Kruger, "Betrayed by Work," *Fast Company*, November 1999, www.fastcompany.com on February 1, 2003.
2. Lynn McGarlane Shore and Lois Tetrick, "The Psychological Contract as an Explanatory Framework in the Employment Relationship," in C. L. Cooper and D. M. Rousseau (eds.), *Trends in Organizational Behavior* (London: John Wiley & Sons Ltd., 1994).
3. Elizabeth Wolfe Morrison and Sandra L. Robinson, "When Employees Feel Betrayed: A Model of How Psychological Contract Violation Develops," *Academy of Management Review*, January 1997, pp. 226–256.
4. Lawrence Pervin, "Personality" in Mark Rosenzweig and Lyman Porter, eds., *Annual Review of Psychology*, vol. 36 (Palo Alto, Calif.: Annual Reviews, 1985), pp. 83–114; S. R. Maddi, *Personality Theories: A Comparative Analysis*, 4th ed. (Homewood, Ill.: Dorsey, 1980).
5. L. R. Goldberg, "An Alternative 'Description of Personality': The Big Five Factor Structure," *Journal of Personality and Social Psychology*, vol. 59, 1990, pp. 1216–1229.
6. Michael K. Mount, Murray R. Barrick, and J. Perkins Strauss, "Validity of Observer Ratings of the Big Five

Personality Factors," *Journal of Applied Psychology,* vol. 79, no. 2, 1994, pp. 272–280; Timothy A. Judge, Joseph J. Martocchio, and Carl J. Thoreson, "Five-Factor Model of Personality and Employee Absence," *Journal of Applied Psychology,* vol. 82, no. 5, 1997, pp. 745–755.

7. J. B. Rotter, "Generalized Expectancies for Internal vs. External Control of Reinforcement," *Psychological Monographs,* vol. 80, 1966, pp. 1–28. See also Simon S. K. Lam and John Schaubroeck, "The Role of Locus of Control in Reactions to Being Promoted and to Being Passed Over: A Quasi Experiment," *Academy of Management Journal,* 2000, vol. 43, no. 1, pp. 66–78.
8. Marilyn E. Gist and Terence R. Mitchell, "Self-Efficacy: A Theoretical Analysis of Its Determinants and Malleability," *Academy of Management Review,* April 1992, pp. 183–211.
9. T. W. Adorno, E. Frenkel-Brunswick, D. J. Levinson, and R. N. Sanford, *The Authoritarian Personality* (New York: Harper & Row, 1950).
10. "The Rise and Fall of Dennis Kozlowski," *BusinessWeek,* December 23, 2002, pp. 64–77.
11. Jon L. Pierce, Donald G. Gardner, and Larry L. Cummings, "Organization-based Self-Esteem: Construct Definition, Measurement, and Validation," *Academy of Management Journal,* vol. 32, 1989, pp. 622–648.
12. Michael Harris Bond and Peter B. Smith, "Cross-Cultural Social and Organizational Psychology," in Janet Spence, ed., *Annual Review of Psychology,* vol. 47 (Palo Alto, Calif.: Annual Reviews, 1996), pp. 205–235.
13. See Daniel Goleman, *Emotional Intelligence: Why It Can Matter More Than IQ* (New York: Bantam Books, 1995).
14. Daniel Goleman, "Leadership That Gets Results," *Harvard Business Review,* March–April 2000, pp. 78–90.
15. Leon Festinger, *A Theory of Cognitive Dissonance* (Palo Alto, Calif.: Stanford University Press, 1957).
16. See John J. Clancy, "Is Loyalty Really Dead?" *Across the Board,* June 1999, pp. 15–19.
17. Patricia C. Smith, L. M. Kendall, and Charles Hulin, *The Measurement of Satisfaction in Work and Behavior* (Chicago: Rand-McNally, 1969).
18. "Companies Are Finding Real Payoffs in Aiding Employee Satisfaction," *Wall Street Journal,* October 11, 2000, p. B1.
19. James R. Lincoln, "Employee Work Attitudes and Management Practice in the U.S. and Japan: Evidence from a Large Comparative Study," *California Management Review,* Fall 1989, pp. 89–106.
20. Ibid.
21. Richard M. Steers, "Antecedents and Outcomes of Organizational Commitment," *Administrative Science Quarterly,* vol. 22, 1977, pp. 46–56.
22. For research work in this area, see Jennifer M. George and Gareth R. Jones, "The Experience of Mood and Turnover Intentions: Interactive Effects of Value Attainment, Job Satisfaction, and Positive Mood," *Journal of Applied Psychology,* vol. 81, no. 3, 1996, pp. 318–325; Larry J. Williams, Mark B. Gavin, and Margaret Williams, "Measurement and Nonmeasurement Processes with Negative Affectivity and Employee Attitudes," *Journal of Applied Psychology,* vol. 81, no. 1, 1996, pp. 88–101.
23. Kathleen Sutcliffe, "What Executives Notice: Accurate Perceptions in Top Management Teams," *Academy of Management Journal,* 1994, vol. 37, no. 5, pp. 1360–1378.
24. See H. H. Kelley, *Attribution in Social Interaction* (Morristown, N.J.: General Learning Press, 1971), for a classic treatment of attribution.
25. For a recent overview of the stress literature, see Frank Landy, James Campbell Quick, and Stanislav Kasl, "Work, Stress, and Well-Being," *International Journal of Stress Management,* 1994, vol. 1, no. 1, pp. 33–73.
26. Hans Selye, *The Stress of Life* (New York: McGraw-Hill, 1976).
27. M. Friedman and R. H. Rosenman, *Type A Behavior and Your Heart* (New York: Alfred A. Knopf, 1974).
28. "Work & Family," *BusinessWeek,* June 28, 1993, pp. 80–88.
29. Richard S. DeFrank, Robert Konopaske, and John M. Ivancevich, "Executive Travel Stress: Perils of the Road Warrior," *Academy of Management Executive,* 2000, vol. 14, no. 2, pp. 58–67.
30. "Breaking Point," *Newsweek,* March 6, 1995, pp. 56–62. See also "Rising Job Stress Could Affect Bottom Line," *USA Today,* July 28, 2003, p. 18.
31. John M. Kelly, "Get a Grip on Stress," *HRMagazine,* February 1997, pp. 51–58.
32. See Richard W. Woodman, John E. Sawyer, and Ricky W. Griffin, "Toward a Theory of Organizational Creativity," *Academy of Management Review,* April 1993, pp. 293–321.
33. Emily Thornton, "Japan's Struggle to be Creative," *Fortune,* April 19, 1993, pp. 129–134.
34. John Simons, "The $10 Billion Pill," *Fortune,* January 20, 2003, pp. 58–68.
35. Christina E. Shalley, Lucy L. Gilson, and Terry C. Blum, "Matching Creativity Requirements and the Work Environment: Effects on Satisfaction and Intentions to Leave," *Academy of Management Journal,* 2000, vol. 43, no. 2, pp. 215–223. See also Filiz Tabak, "Employee Creative Performance: What Makes It Happen?" *Academy of Management Executive,* vol. 11, no. 1, 1997, pp. 119–122.
36. "That's It, I'm Outa Here," *BusinessWeek,* October 3, 2000, pp. 96–98.
37. See Philip M. Podsakoff, Scott B. MacKenzie, Julie Beth Paine, and Daniel G. G. Bacharah, "Organizational Citizenship Behaviors: A Critical Review of the Theoretical and Empirical Literature and Suggestions for Future Research," *Journal of Management,* 2000, vol. 26, no. 3, pp. 513–563 for recent findings regarding this behavior.
38. Dennis W. Organ "Personality and Organizational Citizenship Behavior," *Journal of Management,* 1994, vol. 20, no. 2, pp. 465–478; Mary Konovsky and S. Douglas Pugh, "Citizenship Behavior and Social Exchange," *Academy of Management Journal,* 1994, vol. 37, no. 3, pp. 656–669; and Jacqueline A-M. Coyle-Shapiro, "A Psychological Contract Perspective on Organizational Citizenship," *Journal of Organizational Behavior,* 2002, vol. 23, pp. 927–946.
39. See Anne O'Leary-Kelly, Ricky W. Griffin, and David J. Glew, "Organization-motivated Aggression: A Research Framework," *Academy of Management Review,* January 1996, pp. 225–253.

16 Managing Employee Motivation and Performance

CHAPTER OUTLINE

The Nature of Motivation
- The Importance of Employee Motivation in the Workplace
- Historical Perspectives on Motivation

Content Perspectives on Motivation
- The Needs Hierarchy Approach
- The Two-Factor Theory
- Individual Human Needs
- Implications of the Content Perspectives

Process Perspectives on Motivation
- Expectancy Theory
- Equity Theory
- Goal-setting Theory
- Implications of the Process Perspectives

Reinforcement Perspectives on Motivation
- Kinds of Reinforcement in Organizations
- Providing Reinforcement in Organizations
- Implications of the Reinforcement Perspectives

Popular Motivational Strategies
- Empowerment and Participation
- Alternative Forms of Work Arrangements

Using Reward Systems to Motivate Performance
- Merit Reward Systems
- Incentive Reward Systems
- Team and Group Incentive Reward Systems
- Executive Compensation
- New Approaches to Performance-based Rewards

LEARNING OBJECTIVES

After studying this chapter, you should be able to:

1 ***Characterize the nature of motivation, including its importance and basic historical perspectives.***

OPENING INCIDENT

Pleasant Rowland was looking for a Christmas gift for her two nieces. It was 1985, and Cabbage Patch dolls were the "hot" toy that year, but Rowland felt that her nieces, ages eight and ten, were too grown up for baby dolls. Yet Barbie did not appeal to her midwestern morals. When she could not find a gift to capture her nieces' imagination, Rowland was inspired to build a better doll for "tweens"—preteen girls who are no longer little children but are not yet teenagers. The result was the American Girl collection of dolls, a $700 million toy empire.

Rowland's extraordinary success was motivated by a number of factors. Her deep-seated convictions played a big part. She wanted to present role models for young girls that were not too "babyish" but also were not too mature. She was looking for an image that was wholesome *and* empowering. "Here I was, in a generation of women at the forefront of redefining women's roles, and yet our daughters were playing with dolls that celebrated being a teen queen or a mommy. I knew I couldn't be the only woman in America who was unhappy with those choices," says Rowland. She adds,

2	3	4	5	6
Identify and describe the major content perspectives on motivation.	***Identify and describe the major process perspectives on motivation.***	***Describe reinforcement perspectives on motivation.***	***Identify and describe popular motivational strategies.***	***Describe the role of organizational reward systems in motivation.***

"For all the money the company made subsequently, none of it was as fun or rewarding as that first million dollars."

— Pleasant Rowland, founder and former CEO, Pleasant Company

The creator of the American Girl doll was motivated to find an alternative to Barbie.

"Mothers yearned for a product that would both capture their child's interest and allow little girls to be little girls for a little longer."

Rowland was enthused by a visit to Williamsburg, Virginia, where she was excited by tales of colonial America. She says, "I remember . . . reflecting on what a poor job schools do of teaching history, and how sad it was that more kids couldn't visit this fabulous classroom of living history." The two ideas—teaching history and better toys for preteens—collided, and as Rowland says, "the concept literally exploded in my brain. Once the idea had formed, I could think of nothing else. In one weekend I wrote out the concept in great detail." Her concept was a series of books about girls growing up in different places and times in American history. The books are accompanied by dolls, accessories, and toys.

Development of the American Girl concept allowed Rowland to build on her background in education and writing. Rowland began her career in the 1960s as an elementary school teacher, but she was dismayed by the poor quality of classroom materials. She became a very successful writer of books for children. Business advisors told her that there was no profit in selling educational toys or dolls. Yet Rowland was confident that the dolls would sell.

In the first four months, Pleasant Company sold $1.7 million of dolls and books. Office workers had to help with the sewing. The small, decrepit warehouse was unreliably heated, so workers wore mittens. Rowland thrived on the chaos, saying, "For all the money the company made subsequently, none of it was as fun or rewarding as that first million dollars." However, money was never the most important motivator for Rowland. She was already a millionaire from her book royalties and worked more for love than for money. When Rowland was diagnosed with cancer in 1989, work became her source of strength. "I never missed a day of work, and work is probably what saved me. I loved what I was doing."

In 1995 Rowland sold Pleasant Company to Mattel for $700 million. "Finally my vision was complete, my original business plan had been executed, and I was tired. It was time to sell the company," says Rowland. She was criticized by some for selling out to the company whose Barbie products stimulated her quest for a better concept. But Rowland saw Mattel's former CEO, Jill Barad, as a kindred spirit—a tough, ambitious, smart, and passionate businesswoman. Did Rowland regret the sale? Not at all. "As I walked out the door, I stopped and looked around at all I had built, expecting to be overwhelmed by sadness or loss. But no emotion came. . . . It was then that I realized that I had never felt I 'owned' American Girl. I had been its steward, and I had given it my best during the prime of my career. It was time for someone else to take care of it."[1]

Several different factors have contributed to the remarkable success enjoyed by Pleasant Rowland. But a fundamental ingredient was the drive and motivation that led her to pursue her goals. If a business could attract an entire workforce of Pleasant Rowlands, it would be hard pressed not to succeed. Although such a motivated workforce is perhaps unrealistic, virtually any organization is capable of developing and maintaining a reasonably motivated workforce. The trick is figuring out how to create a system in which employees can receive rewards that they genuinely want by performing in ways that fit the organization's goals and objectives.

In most settings, people can choose how hard they work and how much effort they expend. Thus managers need to understand how and why employees make different choices regarding their own performance. The key ingredient behind this choice is motivation, the subject of this chapter. We first examine the nature of employee motivation and then explore the major perspectives on motivation. Newly emerging approaches are then discussed. We conclude with a description of rewards and their role in motivation.

The Nature of Motivation

Motivation is the set of forces that cause people to behave in certain ways.[2] On any given day, an employee may choose to work as hard as possible at a job, work just hard enough to avoid a reprimand, or do as little as possible. The goal for the manager is to maximize the likelihood of the first behavior and minimize the likelihood of the last. This goal becomes all the more important when we understand how important motivation is in the workplace.

motivation The set of forces that cause people to behave in certain ways

The Importance of Employee Motivation in the Workplace

Individual performance is generally determined by three things: motivation (the desire to do the job), ability (the capability to do the job), and the work environment (the resources needed to do the job). If an employee lacks ability, the manager can provide training or replace the worker. If there is a resource problem, the manager can correct it. But, if motivation is the problem, the task for the manager is more challenging.[3] Individual behavior is a complex phenomenon, and the manager may be hard pressed to figure out the precise nature of the problem and how to solve it. Thus motivation is important because of its significance as a determinant of performance and because of its intangible character.[4]

The motivation framework in Figure 16.1 is a good starting point for understanding how motivated behavior occurs. The motivation process begins with a need deficiency. For example, when a worker feels that she is underpaid, she experiences a need for more income. In response, the worker searches for ways to satisfy the need, such as working harder to try to earn a raise or seeking a new job. Next she chooses an option to pursue. After carrying out the chosen option—working harder and putting in more hours for a reasonable period of time, for example—she then evaluates her success. If her hard work resulted in a pay raise, she probably feels good about things and will continue to work hard. But, if no raise has been provided, she is likely to try another option.

Motivation is both an incredibly important and extremely complex phenomenon. Take Hank Schmelzer for example. After several years as a successful CEO, Schmelzer decided that he wanted to do something different—and more meaningful. He eventually took the job as president of the Maine Community Foundation. While he gave up both prestige and a huge salary to take the job, he says he is content and at peace for the first time in years.

Historical Perspectives on Motivation

To appreciate what we know about employee motivation, it is helpful to review earlier approaches. The traditional, human relations, and human resource approaches have each shed partial light on motivation.[5]

The Traditional Approach The traditional approach is best represented by the work of Frederick W. Taylor.[6] As noted in Chapter 2, Taylor advocated an incentive pay system. He believed that managers knew more about the jobs being performed than did workers, and he assumed that economic gain was the primary thing that motivated everyone. Other assumptions of the traditional approach were that work is inherently unpleasant for most people and that the money they earn is more important to employees than the nature of the job they are performing. Hence, people could be expected to perform any kind of job if they were paid enough. Although the role of money as a motivating factor cannot be dismissed, proponents of the traditional approach took too narrow a view of the role of monetary compensation and failed to consider other motivational factors.

The Human Relations Approach The human relations approach was also summarized in Chapter 2.[7] The human relationists emphasized the role of social processes in the workplace. Their basic assumptions were that employees want to

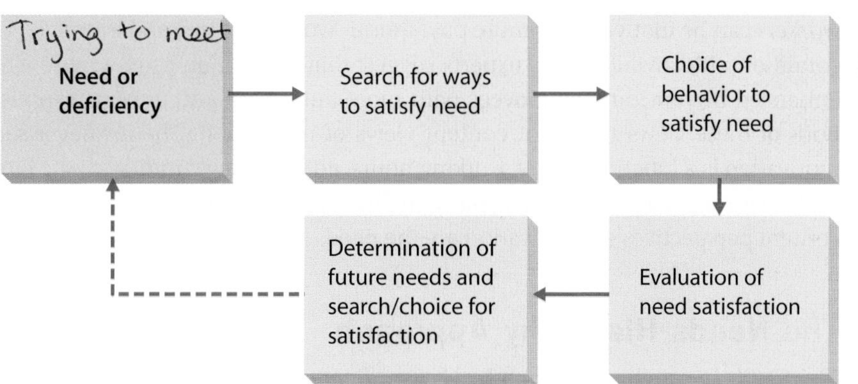

FIGURE 16.1

The Motivation Framework
The motivation process progresses through a series of discrete steps. Content, process, and reinforcement perspectives on motivation address different parts of this process.

feel useful and important, that employees have strong social needs, and that these needs are more important than money in motivating them. Advocates of the human relations approach advised managers to make workers feel important and allow them a modicum of self-direction and self-control in carrying out routine activities. The illusion of involvement and importance was expected to satisfy workers' basic social needs and result in higher motivation to perform. For example, a manager might allow a work group to participate in making a decision, even though he or she had already determined what the decision would be. The symbolic gesture of seeming to allow participation was expected to enhance motivation, even though no real participation took place.

The Human Resource Approach The human resource approach to motivation carries the concepts of needs and motivation one step farther. Whereas the human relationists believed that the illusion of contribution and participation would enhance motivation, the human resource view assumes that the contributions themselves are valuable to both individuals and organizations. It assumes that people want to contribute and are able to make genuine contributions. Management's task, then, is to encourage participation and to create a work environment that makes full use of the human resources available. This philosophy guides most contemporary thinking about employee motivation. At Ford, Westinghouse, Texas Instruments, and Hewlett-Packard, for example, work teams are being called upon to solve a variety of problems and to make substantive contributions to the organization.

concept CHECK

Summarize historical perspectives on employee motivation.	*Use Figure 16.1 to trace through a motivational cycle you have recently experienced.*

Content Perspectives on Motivation

content perspectives Approach to motivation that tries to answer the question: What factor or factors motivate people?

Content perspectives on motivation deal with the first part of the motivation process—needs and need deficiencies. More specially, **content perspectives** address the question: What factors in the workplace motivate people? Labor leaders often argue that workers can be motivated by more pay, shorter working hours, and improved working conditions. Meanwhile, some experts suggest that motivation can be more effectively enhanced by providing employees with more autonomy and greater responsibility.[8] Both of these views represent content views of motivation. The former asserts that motivation is a function of pay, working hours, and working conditions; the latter suggests that autonomy and responsibility are the causes of motivation. Two widely known content perspectives on motivation are the needs hierarchy and the two-factor theory.

The Needs Hierarchy Approach

The needs hierarchy approach has been advanced by many theorists. Needs hierarchies assume that people have different needs that can be arranged in a hierarchy of importance. The two best known are Maslow's hierarchy of needs and the ERG theory.

Maslow's Hierarchy of Needs Abraham Maslow, a human relationist, argued that people are motivated to satisfy five need levels.[9] **Maslow's hierarchy of needs** is shown in Figure 16.2. At the bottom of the hierarchy are the *physiological needs*—things like food, sex, and air, which represent basic issues of survival and biological function. In organizations, these needs are generally satisfied by adequate wages and the work environment itself, which provides restrooms, adequate lighting, comfortable temperatures, and ventilation. *Today's Management Issues* discusses the role of these needs in motivating today's low-paid workers.

Maslow's hierarchy of needs Suggests that people must satisfy five groups of needs in order—physiological, security, belongingness, esteem, and self-actualization

Next are the *security needs* for a secure physical and emotional environment. Examples include the desire for housing and clothing and the need to be free from worry about money and job security. These needs can be satisfied in the workplace by job continuity (no layoffs), a grievance system (to protect against arbitrary supervisory actions), and an adequate insurance and retirement benefit package (for security against illness and provision of income in later life). Even today, however, depressed industries and economic decline can put people out of work and restore the primacy of security needs.

Belongingness needs relate to social processes. They include the need for love and affection and the need to be accepted by one's peers. These needs are satisfied for most people by family and community relationships outside of work and by friendships on the job. A manager can help satisfy these needs by allowing social interaction and by making employees feel like part of a team or work group.

Esteem needs actually comprise two different sets of needs: the need for a positive self-image and self-respect, and the need for recognition and respect from others. A manager can help address these needs by providing a variety of extrinsic symbols of accomplishment, such as job titles, nice offices, and similar rewards as appropriate. At a more intrinsic level, the manager can provide challenging job assignments and opportunities for the employee to feel a sense of accomplishment.

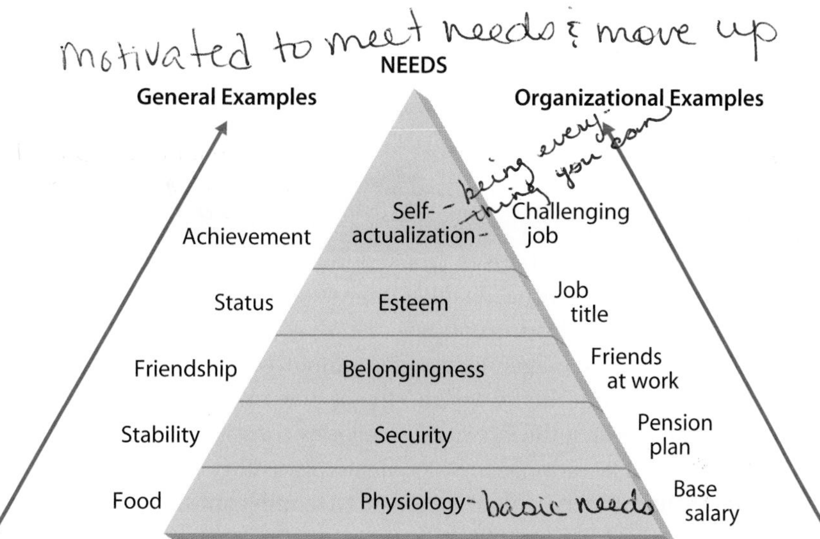

FIGURE 16.2

Maslow's Hierarchy of Needs

Maslow's hierarchy suggests that human needs can be classified into five categories and that these categories can be arranged in a hierarchy of importance. A manager should understand that an employee may not be satisfied with only a salary and benefits; he or she may also need challenging job opportunities to experience self-growth and satisfaction.

Source: Adapted from Abraham H. Maslow, "A Theory of Human Motivation," *Psychology Review*, 1943, vol. 50, pp. 370–396.

TODAY'S management ISSUES

Does It Pay to Work?

"... people working at low-wage jobs have more income [today]. Whether they are better off in a broader sense is in dispute."

– Mark Levitan, Community Service Society of New York*

Money is an important component of motivation. It is a generic reward because it can fulfill any need. Those who earn more obtain higher status. They can spend more time developing relationships and meeting higher-level needs. Money is the easiest reward to measure and to compare. Yet, for workers in low-paid jobs, the money they earn is not sufficient to meet their lowest-level needs. What is a living wage? And what can companies do to improve the motivation of workers at or below that level?

Clearly, a living wage depends on more than gross pay. Taxes, government benefits, and cost of living must be considered, too. The minimum wage is $5.15 per hour—that amounts to $10,300 for full-time work. At that rate, workers qualify for welfare, Medicaid, subsidized daycare, and other aid. But workers who make 1.5 times that receive $7.73, or about $15,500 per year. As their income goes up, their government benefits are cut and their taxes rise. As a result, a raise from $5.15 to $8.50 per hour provides only 20 percent more take-home pay.

Take-home pay for those making $7.73 is about $13,000 after taxes. In low-income areas, this wage could provide a barely adequate standard of living. But, in expensive areas, $13,000 hardly covers the cost of housing. In addition, many workers earning $15,000 or less are the sole support for a family that includes children. For example, 40 percent of the unmarried mothers in New York City earn less than $14,000, the federal poverty line for a family of three. A second wage earner in the family does not help much, because child care and other expenses eat up more than half of the additional income, and the higher household earnings further reduce government benefits. "There is no doubt that people working at low-wage jobs have more income [today]," says analyst Mark Levitan. "Whether they are better off in a broader sense is in dispute."

Businesses that employ low-wage workers may find that their employees prefer untaxed benefits over taxed pay. And why should workers show up for work at all, when staying home pays as much? Employers will have to offer more than money. Training, education, and opportunities for promotion are better answers.

References: Cait Murphy, "Money Talks: Wage War," *Fortune Small Business*, July 1, 2002, www.fortune.com on January 30, 2003; Daniel Akst, "Low-Paid Workers Bear a Hidden Burden," *New York Times*, September 1, 2002, p. BU4; Leslie Eaton, "For Unmarried Mothers, a City of Jobs," *New York Times*, September 8, 2002, p. NJ1 (*quote).

At the top of the hierarchy are the *self-actualization needs*. These involve realizing one's potential for continued growth and individual development. The self-actualization needs are perhaps the most difficult for a manager to address. In fact, it can be argued that these needs must be met entirely from within the individual. But a manager can help by promoting a culture wherein self-actualization is possible. For instance, a manager could give employees a chance to participate in making decisions about their work and the opportunity to learn new things.

Maslow suggests that the five need categories constitute a hierarchy. An individual is motivated first and foremost to satisfy physiological needs. As long as they remain unsatisfied, the individual is motivated to fulfill only them. When satisfaction of physiological needs is achieved, they cease to act as primary motivational factors, and the individual moves "up" the hierarchy and becomes concerned with security needs. This process continues until the individual reaches the self-actualization level. Maslow's concept of the need hierarchy has a certain intuitive logic and has been accepted by many managers. But research has revealed certain shortcomings and defects in the theory. Some research has found that five levels of need are not always present and that the order of the levels is not always the same, as postulated by Maslow.[10] In addition, people from different cultures are likely to have different need categories and hierarchies.

The ERG Theory In response to these and similar criticisms, an alternative hierarchy of needs, called the **ERG theory of motivation** was developed.[11] This theory collapses the need hierarchy developed by Maslow into three levels. *Existence needs* correspond to the physiological and security needs. *Relatedness needs* focus on how people relate to their social environment. In Maslow's hierarchy, these would encompass both the need to belong and the need to earn the esteem of others. *Growth needs,* the highest level in this schema, include the needs for self-esteem and self-actualization.

ERG theory of motivation Suggests that people's needs are grouped into three possibly overlapping categories—existence, relatedness, and growth

Although the ERG theory assumes that motivated behavior follows a hierarchy in somewhat the same fashion as suggested by Maslow, there are two important differences. First, the ERG theory suggests that more than one level of need can cause motivation at the same time. For example, it suggests that people can be motivated by a desire for money (existence), friendship (relatedness), and the opportunity to learn new skills (growth) all at once. Second, the ERG theory has what has been called a *frustration-regression* element. Thus, if needs remain unsatisfied, the individual will become frustrated, regress to a lower level, and begin to pursue those things again. For example, a worker previously motivated by money (existence needs) may have just been awarded a pay raise sufficient to satisfy those needs. Suppose that he then attempts to establish more friendships to satisfy relatedness needs. If for some reason he finds that it is impossible to become better friends with others in the workplace, he eventually gets frustrated and regresses to being motivated to earn even more money.

The Two-Factor Theory

Another popular content perspective is the **two-factor theory of motivation.**[12] Frederick Herzberg developed his theory by interviewing two hundred accountants and engineers. He asked them to recall occasions when they had been satisfied and motivated and occasions when they had been dissatisfied and unmotivated. Surprisingly, he found that different sets of factors were associated with satisfaction and with dissatisfaction—that is, a person might identify "low pay" as causing dissatisfaction but would not necessarily mention "high pay" as a cause of satisfaction. Instead, different factors—such as recognition or accomplishment—were cited as causing satisfaction and motivation.

two-factor theory of motivation Suggests that people's satisfaction and dissatisfaction are influenced by two independent sets of factors—motivation factors and hygiene factors

This finding led Herzberg to conclude that the traditional view of job satisfaction was incomplete. That view assumed that satisfaction and dissatisfaction are at

Motivation Factors
- Achievement
- Recognition
- The work itself
- Responsibility
- Advancement and growth

Hygiene Factors
- Supervisors
- Working conditions
- Interpersonal relations
- Pay and security
- Company policies and administration

Satisfaction ⟷ *No satisfaction*

Dissatisfaction ⟷ *No dissatisfaction*

FIGURE 16.3

The Two-Factor Theory of Motivation

The two-factor theory suggests that job satisfaction has two dimensions. A manager who tries to motivate an employee using only hygiene factors, such as pay and good working conditions, will likely not succeed. To motivate employees and produce a high level of satisfaction, managers must also offer factors such as responsibility and the opportunity for advancement (motivation factors).

opposite ends of a single continuum. People might be satisfied, dissatisfied, or somewhere in between. But Herzberg's interviews had identified two different dimensions altogether: one ranging from satisfaction to no satisfaction and the other ranging from dissatisfaction to no dissatisfaction. This perspective, along with several examples of factors that affect each continuum, is shown in Figure 16.3. Note that the factors influencing the satisfaction continuum—called *motivation factors*—are related specifically to the work content. The factors presumed to cause dissatisfaction—called *hygiene factors*—are related to the work environment.

Based on these findings, Herzberg argued that there are two stages in the process of motivating employees. First, managers must ensure that the hygiene factors are not deficient. Pay and security must be appropriate, working conditions must be safe, technical supervision must be acceptable, and so on. By providing hygiene factors at an appropriate level, managers do not stimulate motivation but merely ensure that employees are "not dissatisfied." Employees whom managers attempt to "satisfy" through hygiene factors alone will usually do just enough to get by. Thus managers should proceed to stage two—giving employees the opportunity to experience motivation factors such as achievement and recognition. The result is predicted to be a high level of satisfaction and motivation. Herzberg also went a step further than most other theorists and described exactly how to use the two-factor theory in the workplace. Specifically, he recommended job enrichment, as discussed in Chapter 11. He argued that jobs should be redesigned to provide higher levels of the motivation factors.

Although widely accepted by many managers, Herzberg's two-factor theory is not without its critics. One criticism is that the findings in Herzberg's initial interviews are subject to different explanations. Another charge is that his sample was not representative of the general population and that subsequent research often failed to uphold the theory.[13] At the present time, Herzberg's theory is not held in high esteem by researchers in the field. The theory has had a major impact on managers, however, and has played a key role in increasing their awareness of motivation and its importance in the workplace.

Individual Human Needs

In addition to these theories, research has focused on specific individual human needs that are important in organizations. The three most important individual needs are achievement, affiliation, and power.[14]

need for achievement The desire to accomplish a goal or task more effectively than in the past

need for affiliation The desire for human companionship and acceptance

need for power The desire to be influential in a group and to control one's environment

The **need for achievement**, the best known of the three, is the desire to accomplish a goal or task more effectively than in the past. People with a high need for achievement have a desire to assume personal responsibility, a tendency to set moderately difficult goals, a desire for specific and immediate feedback, and a preoccupation with their task. David C. McClelland, the psychologist who first identified this need, argues that only about 10 percent of the U.S. population has a high need for achievement. In contrast, almost one quarter of the workers in Japan have a high need for achievement.

The **need for affiliation** is less well understood. Like Maslow's belongingness need, the need for affiliation is a desire for human companionship and acceptance. People with a strong need for affiliation are likely to prefer (and perform better in) a job that entails a lot of social interaction and offers opportunities to make friends. The need for power has also received considerable attention as an important ingredient in managerial success.

The **need for power** is the desire to be influential in a group and to control one's environment. Research has shown that people with a strong need for power are likely to be superior performers, have good attendance records, and occupy supervisory positions. One study found that managers as a group tend to have a stronger power motive than the general population and that successful managers tend to have stronger power motives than less successful managers.[15] Dennis Kozlowski, disgraced former CEO of Tyco International, clearly had a strong need for power. This was reflected in the way he routinely took control over resources and used them for his own personal gain. Indeed, the things he bought with company money were probably intended to convey to the world the extent of his power.[16]

The need for affiliation compels people to seek out human companionship and acceptance. Working mothers sometimes find that they do not fit in well with either working career women without children or with stay-at-home moms. This sense of isolation sometimes leads them to form their own support groups with other working moms. This group, for instance, is a working mothers club founded by Linda Tulloch in Greenwich, Connecticut.

Implications of the Content Perspectives

Managers should remember that Maslow's needs hierarchy, the ERG theory, the two-factor theory, and the needs for achievement, affiliation, and power all provide useful insights into factors that cause motivation. What they do not do is shed much light on the process of motivation. They do not explain why people might be motivated by one factor rather than by another at a given level or how people might go about trying to satisfy the different needs. These questions involve behaviors or actions, goals, and feelings of satisfaction—concepts that are addressed by various process perspectives on motivation.

concept CHECK

Summarize the needs hierarchy approaches to employee motivation.	How would you assess yourself regarding the needs for achievement, affiliation, and power?

Process Perspectives on Motivation

process perspectives Approaches to motivation that focus on why people choose certain behavioral options to fulfill their needs and how they evaluate their satisfaction after they have attained these goals

expectancy theory Suggests that motivation depends on two things—how much we want something and how likely we think we are to get it

Process perspectives are concerned with how motivation occurs. Rather than attempting to identify motivational stimuli, **process perspectives** focus on why people choose certain behavioral options to satisfy their needs and how they evaluate their satisfaction after they have attained these goals. Three useful process perspectives on motivation are the expectancy, equity, and goal-setting theories.

Expectancy Theory

Expectancy theory suggests that motivation depends on two things—how much we want something and how likely we think we are to get it.[17] Assume that you are approaching graduation and looking for a job. You see in the want ads that General Motors is seeking a new vice president with a starting salary of $500,000 per year. Even though you might want the job, you will not apply because you realize that you have little chance of getting it. The next ad you see is for someone to scrape bubble gum from underneath theater seats for a starting salary of $6 an hour. Even though you could probably get this job, you do not apply because you do not want it. Then you see an ad for a management trainee at a big company, with a starting salary of $40,000. You will probably apply for this job because you want it and because you think you have a reasonable chance of getting it.

Expectancy theory rests on four basic assumptions. First, it assumes that behavior is determined by a combination of forces in the individual and in the environment. Second, it assumes that people make decisions about their own behavior in organizations. Third, it assumes that different people have different types of needs, desires, and goals. Fourth, it assumes that people make choices from among alternative plans of behavior, based on their perceptions of the extent to which a given behavior will lead to desired outcomes.

Figure 16.4 summarizes the basic expectancy model. The model suggests that motivation leads to effort and that effort, combined with employee ability and environmental factors, results in performance. Performance, in turn, leads to various outcomes, each of which has an associated value, called its *valence*. The most important parts of the expectancy model cannot be shown in the figure, however. These are the individual's expectation that effort will lead to high performance, that performance will lead to outcomes, and that each outcome will have some kind of value.

Equity comparisons are common in organizations as individuals evaluate their contributions and rewards relative to those of others. For professional athletes like Nomar Garciaparra, shortstop of the Boston Red Sox, these comparisons are relatively easy—he can readily check out what Derek Jeter or Alex Rodriguez is making just by reading the sports section. But in every organization people make similar comparisons all the time—sometimes based on accurate information and sometimes on false perceptions.

Effort-to-Performance Expectancy The **effort-to-performance expectancy** is the individual's perception of the probability that effort will lead to high performance. When the individual believes that effort will lead directly to high performance, expectancy will be quite strong (close to 1.00). When the individual believes that effort and performance are unrelated, the effort-to-performance expectancy is very weak (close to 0). The belief that effort is somewhat but not strongly related to performance carries with it a moderate expectancy (somewhere between 0 and 1.00).

Performance-to-Outcome Expectancy The **performance-to-outcome expectancy** is the individual's perception that performance will lead to a specific outcome. For example, if the individual believes that high performance *will* result in a pay raise, the performance-to-outcome expectancy is high (approaching 1.00). The individual who believes that high performance *may* lead to a pay raise has a moderate expectancy (between 1.00 and 0). The individual who believes that performance has no relationship to rewards has a low performance-to-outcome expectancy (close to 0).

Outcomes and Valences Expectancy theory recognizes that an individual's behavior results in a variety of **outcomes**, or consequences, in an organizational setting. A high performer, for example, may get bigger pay raises, faster promotions, and more praise from the boss. On the other hand, she may also be subject to more stress and incur resentment from coworkers. Each of these outcomes also has an associated value, or **valence**—an index of how much an individual values a particular outcome. If the individual wants the outcome, its valence is positive; if the individual does not want the outcome, its valence is negative; and if the individual is indifferent to the outcome, its valence is zero.

effort-to-performance expectancy The individual's perception of the probability that effort will lead to high performance

performance-to-outcome expectancy The individual's perception that performance will lead to a specific outcome

outcomes Consequences of behaviors in an organizational setting, usually rewards

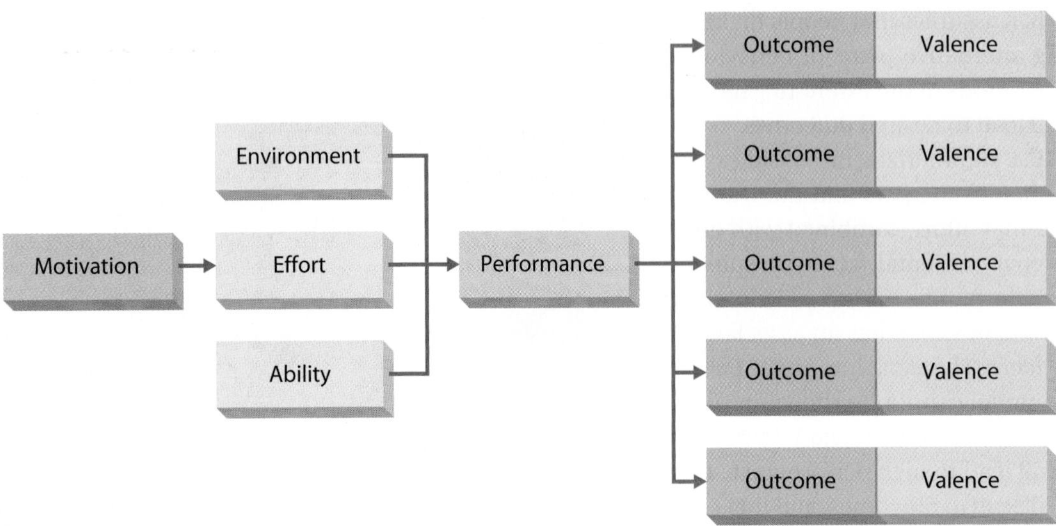

FIGURE 16.4

The Expectancy Model of Motivation

The expectancy model of motivation is a complex but relatively accurate portrayal of how motivation occurs. According to this model, a manager must understand what employees want (such as pay, promotions, or status) to begin to motivate them.

valence An index of how much an individual desires a particular outcome; the attractiveness of the outcome to the individual

It is this part of expectancy theory that goes beyond the content perspectives on motivation. Different people have different needs, and they will try to satisfy these needs in different ways. For an employee who has a high need for achievement and a low need for affiliation, the pay raise and promotions cited above as outcomes of high performance might have positive valences, the praise and resentment zero valences, and the stress a negative valence. For a different employee, with a low need for achievement and a high need for affiliation, the pay raise, promotions, and praise might all have positive valences, whereas both resentment and stress could have negative valences.

For motivated behavior to occur, three conditions must be met. First, the effort-to-performance must be greater than 0 (the individual must believe that, if effort is expended, high performance will result). The performance-to-outcome expectancy must also be greater than 0 (the individual must believe that, if high performance is achieved, certain outcomes will follow). And the sum of the valences for the outcomes must be greater than 0. (One or more outcomes may have negative valences if they are more than offset by the positive valences of other outcomes. For example, the attractiveness of a pay raise, a promotion, and praise from the boss may outweigh the unattractiveness of more stress and resentment from coworkers.) Expectancy theory suggests that, when these conditions are met, the individual is motivated to expend effort.

Starbucks credits its unique stock ownership program with maintaining a dedicated and motivated workforce. Based on the fundamental concepts of expectancy theory, Starbucks employees earn stock as a function of their seniority and performance. Thus their hard work helps them earn shares of ownership in the company.[18]

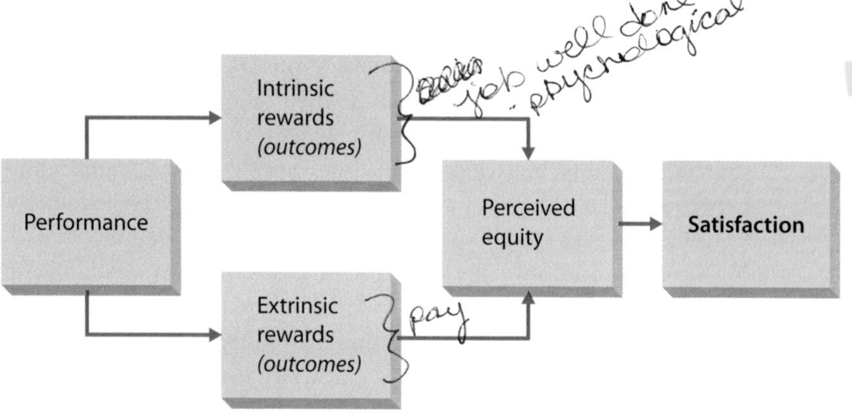

Source: Edward E. Lawler III and Lyman W. Porter, "The Effect of Performance On Job Satisfaction," *Industrial Relations*, October 1967, p. 23. Used with permission of the University of California.

FIGURE 16.5

The Porter-Lawler Extension of Expectancy Theory

The Porter-Lawler extension of expectancy theory suggests that, if performance results in equitable rewards, people will be more satisfied. Thus performance can lead to satisfaction. Managers must therefore be sure that any system of motivation includes rewards that are fair, or equitable, for all.

The Porter-Lawler Extension An interesting extension of expectancy theory has been proposed by Porter and Lawler.[19] Recall from Chapter 2 that the human relationists assumed that employee satisfaction causes good performance. We also noted that research has not supported such a relationship. Porter and Lawler suggested that there may indeed be a relationship between satisfaction and performance but that it goes in the opposite direction—that is, high performance may lead to high satisfaction. Figure 16.5 summarizes Porter and Lawler's logic. Performance results in rewards for an individual. Some of these are extrinsic (such as pay and promotions); others are intrinsic (such as self-esteem and accomplishment). The individual evaluates the equity, or fairness, of the rewards relative to the effort expended and the level of performance attained. If the rewards are perceived to be equitable, the individual is satisfied.

Equity Theory

After needs have stimulated the motivation process and the individual has chosen an action that is expected to satisfy those needs, the individual assesses the fairness, or equity, of the resultant outcome. **Equity theory** contends that people are motivated to seek social equity in the rewards they receive for performance.[20] Equity is an individual's belief that the treatment he or she is receiving is fair relative to the treatment received by others. According to equity theory, outcomes from a job include pay, recognition, promotions, social relationships, and intrinsic rewards. To get these rewards, the individual makes inputs to the job, such as time, experience, effort, education, and loyalty. The theory suggests that people view their outcomes and inputs as a ratio and then compare it to someone else's ratio. This other "person" may be someone in the work group or some sort of group average or composite. The process of comparison looks like this:

equity theory Suggests that people are motivated to seek social equity in the rewards they receive for performance

$$\frac{\text{Outcomes (self)}}{\text{Inputs (self)}} = \frac{\text{Outcomes (other)}}{\text{Inputs (other)}}$$

Both the formulation of the ratios and comparisons between them are very subjective and based on individual perceptions. As a result of comparisons, three conditions may result: The individual may feel equitably rewarded, underrewarded, or overrewarded. A feeling of equity will result when the two ratios are equal. This may occur even though the other person's outcomes are greater than the individual's own outcomes—provided that the other's inputs are also proportionately greater. Suppose that Mark has a high school education and earns $30,000. He may still feel equitably treated relative to Susan, who earns $35,000, because she has a college degree.

People who feel underrewarded try to reduce the inequity. Such an individual might decrease her inputs by exerting less effort, increase her outcomes by asking for a raise, distort the original ratios by rationalizing, try to get the other person to change her or his outcomes or inputs, leave the situation, or change the object of comparison. An individual may also feel overrewarded relative to another person. This is not likely to be terribly disturbing to most people, but research suggests that some people who experience inequity under these conditions are somewhat motivated to reduce it. Under such a circumstance, the person might increase his inputs by exerting more effort, reduce his outcomes by producing fewer units (if paid on a per-unit basis), distort the original ratios by rationalizing, or try to reduce the inputs or increase the outcomes of the other person. *Working with Diversity* illustrates several interesting perspectives on equity among athletes.

Goal-setting Theory

The goal-setting theory of motivation assumes that behavior is a result of conscious goals and intentions.[21] Therefore, by setting goals for people in the organization, a manager should be able to influence their behavior. Given this premise, the challenge is to develop a thorough understanding of the processes by which people set goals and then work to reach them. In the original version of goal-setting theory, two specific goal characteristics—goal difficulty and goal specificity—were expected to shape performance.

Goal Difficulty *Goal difficulty* is the extent to which a goal is challenging and requires effort. If people work to achieve goals, it is reasonable to assume that they will work harder to achieve more difficult goals. But a goal must not be so difficult that it is unattainable. If a new manager asks her sales force to increase sales by 300 percent, the group may become disillusioned. A more realistic but still difficult goal—perhaps a 30 percent increase—would be a better incentive. A substantial body of research supports the importance of goal difficulty. In one study, for example, managers at Weyerhauser set difficult goals for truck drivers hauling loads of timber from cutting sites to wood yards. Over a nine-month period, the drivers increased the quantity of wood they delivered by an amount that would have required $250,000 worth of new trucks at the previous per-truck average load.[22]

Goal Specificity *Goal specificity* is the clarity and precision of the goal. A goal of "increasing productivity" is not very specific; a goal of "increasing productivity by 3 percent in the next six months" is quite specific. Some goals, such as those involving costs, output, profitability, and growth, are readily amenable to specificity. Other goals, however, such as improving employee job satisfaction, morale, company image and

WORKING WITH diversity

Female Athletes Say "Show Me the Money"

". . . I don't think they'd ever put a male athlete on the cover of anything if he'd never won anything."

– Sue Bird, guard, Seattle Storm WNBA team*

Athletes want to be "like Mike"—that is, like his product endorsements. Michael Jordan has more celebrity endorsements than any other professional athlete, with a value estimated at $17 million annually. Dozens of male athletes earn millions, and a growing number of female athletes are starting to achieve that level of recognition. Athletes claim that their love of the game and their will to compete are the primary motivating factors. But, as women are finding out, money can be nice, too.

Sheryl Swoopes broke Bill Walton's record for the most points ever scored in a Division I NCAA championship game; she was named WNBA Most Valuable Player. Yet, when Nike named a shoe Air Swoopes, she was speechless. "I cried. I bawled," Swoopes says. "I thought they were joking. . . . I thought I was dreaming." Swoopes loaned her name to Kellogg's and the Discover Card, netting $1.2 million, more than any other female in a team sport.

Individual sports give higher name recognition, so players can command more. Thirty-year-old Picabo Street, winner of an Olympic gold medal for downhill skiing in 1998, earns $1.5 million from Charles Schwab, Sprint, and Allstate. The youngest woman ever to qualify at the Indianapolis 500, Sarah Fisher, has deals with Aventis Pharmaceuticals and Dial soap. Swiss watchmaker TAG Heuer recently signed Fisher, which "helps establish her as a legitimate player in the field of marketable sports stars," according to a company press release.

Conventional marketing wisdom holds that buyers are attracted to celebrities who are like themselves. But marketers also know that young men buy products endorsed by attractive young women. Russian-born tennis player Anna Kournikova makes $10 million annually from endorsements, although she has never won a tournament. Sue Bird, a top WNBA rookie, is sympathetic but says, "I think [Anna's] taking advantage of what's in front of her. We live in a man's world, so that's what's going to make money these days. . . . But at the same time, I don't think they'd ever put a male athlete on the cover of anything if he'd never won anything."

References: "Advantage Lycos," Terra Lycos press release, March 19, 2001, www.terralycos.com on February 5, 2003; "Breaking All Kinds of Barriers," *New York Times*, September 15, 2002, p. BU2; Chris Isidore, "Anna Can Keep Winning off the Court," *CNN/Money*, July 8, 2002, money.cnn.com on February 5, 2003; David Dukevich, "Going for Endorsement Gold," *Forbes*, February 11, 2002, www.forbes.com on February 5, 2003; Erin Davies, "Heir Jordan," *Texas Monthly Biz*, June 1999, www.texasmonthly.com on February 5, 2003; "This Is What I Think," WNBA website, July 30, 2002, www.nba.com on February 5, 2003 (*quote).

reputation, ethics, and socially responsible behavior, may be much harder to state in specific terms. Like difficulty, specificity has been shown to be consistently related to performance. The study of timber truck drivers mentioned above, for example, also examined goal specificity. The initial loads the truck drivers were carrying were found to be 60 percent of the maximum weight each truck could haul. The managers set a new goal for drivers of 94 percent, which the drivers were soon able to reach. Thus the goal was both specific and difficult.

Because the theory attracted so much widespread interest and research support from researchers and managers alike, an expanded model of the goal-setting process

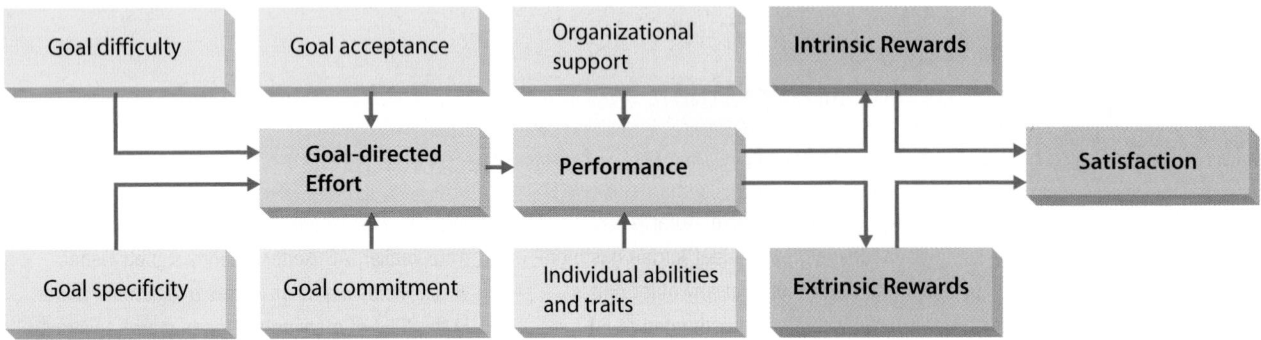

FIGURE 16.6

The Expanded Goal-setting Theory of Motivation

One of the most important emerging theories of motivation is goal-setting theory. This theory suggests that goal difficulty, specificity, acceptance, and commitment combine to determine an individual's goal-directed effort. This effort, when complemented by appropriate organizational support and individual abilities and traits, results in performance. Finally, performance is seen as leading to intrinsic and extrinsic rewards that, in turn, result in employee satisfaction.

Source: Reprinted from *Organizational Dynamics*, Autumn 1979, Gary P. Latham and Edwin A. Locke, "A Motivational Technique That Works," p. 79, copyright © 1979 with permission from Elsevier Science.

was eventually proposed. The expanded model, shown in Figure 16.6, attempts to capture more fully the complexities of goal setting in organizations.

The expanded theory argues that goal-directed effort is a function of four goal attributes: difficulty and specificity, as already discussed, and acceptance and commitment. *Goal acceptance* is the extent to which a person accepts a goal as his or her own. *Goal commitment* is the extent to which she or he is personally interested in reaching the goal. The manager who vows to take whatever steps are necessary to cut costs by 10 percent has made a commitment to achieve the goal. Factors that can foster goal acceptance and commitment include participating in the goal-setting process, making goals challenging but realistic, and believing that goal achievement will lead to valued rewards.

The interaction of goal-directed effort, organizational support, and individual abilities and traits determines actual performance. Organizational support is whatever the organization does to help or hinder performance. Positive support might mean making available adequate personnel and a sufficient supply of raw materials; negative support might mean failing to fix damaged equipment. Individual abilities and traits are the skills and other personal characteristics necessary for doing a job. As a result of performance, a person receives various intrinsic and extrinsic rewards, which in turn influence satisfaction. Note that the latter stages of this model are quite similar to the Porter and Lawler expectancy model discussed earlier.

Implications of the Process Perspectives

Expectancy theory can be useful for managers who are trying to improve the motivation of their subordinates. A series of steps can be followed to implement the basic ideas of the theory. First, figure out the outcomes each employee is likely to want. Second, decide what kinds and levels of performance are needed to meet organizational goals. Then make sure that the desired levels of performance are attainable. Also make sure that desired outcomes and desired performance are linked. Next, analyze the complete situation for conflicting expectancies and ensure that the rewards are large enough. Finally, make sure the total system is equitable (fair to all). The single most important idea for managers to remember from equity theory is that, if rewards are to motivate employees, they must be perceived as being equitable and fair. A second implication is that managers need to consider the nature of the "other" to whom the employee is comparing herself or himself. Goal-setting theory can be used to implement both expectancy and equity theory concepts.

concept CHECK

Describe the basic motivational process that employees go through as reflected in expectancy theory.

Recall a situation in which you experienced inequity. Analyze the situation in terms of equity theory. Was your feeling of inequity justified?

Reinforcement Perspectives on Motivation

A third element of the motivational process addresses why some behaviors are maintained over time and why other behaviors change. As we have seen, content perspectives deal with needs, whereas process perspectives explain why people choose various behaviors to satisfy needs and how they evaluate the equity of the rewards they get for those behaviors. Reinforcement perspectives explain the role of those rewards as they cause behavior to change or remain the same over time. Specifically, **reinforcement theory** argues that behavior that results in rewarding consequences is likely to be repeated, whereas behavior that results in punishing consequences is less likely to be repeated.[23]

reinforcement theory Approach to motivation that argues that behavior that results in rewarding consequences is likely to be repeated, whereas behavior that results in punishing consequences is less likely to be repeated

Kinds of Reinforcement in Organizations

There are four basic kinds of reinforcement that can result from behavior—positive reinforcement, avoidance, punishment, and extinction.[24] These are summarized in Table 16.1. Two kinds of reinforcement strengthen or maintain behavior, whereas the other two weaken or decrease behavior.

Positive reinforcement, a method of strengthening behavior, is a reward or a positive outcome after a desired behavior is performed. When a manager observes an employee doing an especially good job and offers praise, the praise serves to positively reinforce the behavior of good work. Other positive reinforcers in organizations include pay raises, promotions, and awards. Employees who work at General Electric's customer service center receive clothing, sporting goods, and even trips to

positive reinforcement A method of strengthening behavior with rewards or positive outcomes after a desired behavior is performed

Table 16.1

Elements of Reinforcement Theory

A manager who wants the best chance of reinforcing a behavior would likely offer the employee a positive reinforcement after a variable number of behaviors (variable-ratio reinforcement). For example, the manager could praise the employee after the third credit card application was received. Additional praise might be offered after the next five applications, then again after the next three, the next seven, the next four, and so on.

Arrangement of the Reinforcement Contingencies	
1. *Positive Reinforcement.* Strengthens behavior by providing a desirable consequence.	3. *Punishment.* Weakens behavior by providing an undesirable consequence.
2. *Avoidance.* Strengthens behavior by allowing escape from an undesirable consequence.	4. *Extinction.* Weakens behavior by ignoring it.
Schedules for Applying Reinforcement	
1. *Fixed-Interval.* Reinforcement is applied at fixed time intervals, regardless of behavior.	1. *Fixed-Ratio.* Reinforcement is applied after a fixed number of behaviors, regardless of time.
2. *Variable-Interval.* Reinforcement is applied at variable time intervals.	2. *Variable-Ratio.* Reinforcement is applied after a variable number of behaviors.

avoidance Used to strengthen behavior by avoiding unpleasant consequences that would result if the behavior were not performed

punishment Used to weaken undesired behaviors by using negative outcomes or unpleasant consequences when the behavior is performed

extinction Used to weaken undesired behaviors by simply ignoring or not reinforcing them

Disney World as rewards for outstanding performance. The other method of strengthening desired behavior is through **avoidance**. An employee may come to work on time to avoid a reprimand. In this instance, the employee is motivated to perform the behavior of punctuality to avoid an unpleasant consequence that is likely to follow tardiness.

Punishment is used by some managers to weaken undesired behaviors. When an employee is loafing, coming to work late, doing poor work, or interfering with the work of others, the manager might resort to reprimands, discipline, or fines. The logic is that the unpleasant consequence will reduce the likelihood that the employee will choose that particular behavior again. Given the counterproductive side effects of punishment (such as resentment and hostility), it is often advisable to use the other kinds of reinforcement if at all possible. **Extinction** can also be used to weaken behavior, especially behavior that has previously been rewarded. When an employee tells an off-color joke and the boss laughs, the laughter reinforces the behavior and the employee may continue to tell off-color jokes. By simply ignoring this behavior and not reinforcing it, the boss can cause the behavior to subside and eventually become "extinct."

Providing Reinforcement in Organizations

fixed-interval schedule Provides reinforcement at fixed intervals of time, such as regular weekly paychecks

Not only is the kind of reinforcement important, but so is when or how often it occurs. Various strategies are possible for providing reinforcement. These are also listed in Table 16.1. The **fixed-interval schedule** provides reinforcement at fixed intervals of time, regardless of behavior. A good example of this schedule is the weekly or monthly paycheck. This method provides the least incentive for good work, because employees know they will be paid regularly regardless of their effort. A **variable-interval schedule** also uses time as the basis for reinforcement, but the time interval varies from one reinforcement to the next. This schedule is appropriate for praise or other rewards based on visits or inspections. When employees do not know when the boss is going to drop by, they tend to maintain a reasonably high level of effort all the time.

variable-interval schedule Provides reinforcement at varying intervals of time, such as occasional visits by the supervisor

A **fixed-ratio schedule** gives reinforcement after a fixed number of behaviors, regardless of the time that elapses between behaviors. This results in an even higher level of effort. For example, when Sears is recruiting new credit card customers, salespersons get a small bonus for every fifth application returned from their department. Under this arrangement, motivation will be high because each application gets the person closer to the next bonus. The **variable-ratio schedule**, the most powerful schedule in terms of maintaining desired behaviors, varies the number of behaviors needed for each reinforcement. A supervisor who praises an employee for her second order, the seventh order after that, the ninth after that, then the fifth, and then the third is using a variable-ratio schedule. The employee is motivated to increase the frequency of the desired behavior because each performance increases the probability of receiving a reward. Of course, a variable-ratio schedule is difficult (if not impossible) to use for formal rewards such as pay because it would be too complicated to keep track of who was rewarded when.

fixed-ratio schedule Provides reinforcement after a fixed number of behaviors regardless of the time interval involved, such as a bonus for every fifth sale

variable-ratio schedule Provide reinforcement after varying numbers of behaviors are performed, such as the use of complements by a supervisor on an irregular basis

Managers wanting to explicitly use reinforcement theory to motivate their employees generally do so with a technique called **behavior modification,** or **OB Mod.**[25] An OB Mod program starts by specifying behaviors that are to be increased (such as producing more units) or decreased (such as coming to work late). These target behaviors are then tied to specific forms or kinds of reinforcement. Although many organizations (such as Procter & Gamble and Ford) have used OB Mod, the best-known application was at Emery Air Freight. Management felt that the containers used to consolidate small shipments into fewer, larger shipments were not being packed efficiently. Through a system of self-monitored feedback and rewards, Emery increased container usage from 45 percent to 95 percent and saved over $3 million during the first three years of the program.[26]

behavior modification (OB Mod) Method for applying the basic elements of reinforcement theory in an organizational setting

Implications of the Reinforcement Perspectives

Reinforcement in organizations can be a powerful force for maintaining employee motivation. Of course, for reinforcement to be truly effective, managers need to use it in a manner consistent with the various types and schedules of reinforcement discussed above. In addition, managers must understand that they may be inadvertently motivating undesired or dysfunctional behaviors. For instance, if an employee routinely comes to work late but experiences no consequences, both that worker and others will see that it is all right to be late for work.

concept CHECK

What are the basic kinds and schedules of reinforcement available to managers in organizations?

Describe a time when each of the different kinds of reinforcement affected your behavior.

Popular Motivational Strategies

Although the various theories discussed thus far provide a solid explanation for motivation, managers must use various techniques and strategies to actually apply them. Among the most popular motivational strategies today are empowerment and participation and alternative forms of work arrangements. Various forms of performance-based reward systems, discussed in the next section, also reflect efforts to boost motivation and performance.

Empowerment and Participation

empowerment The process of enabling workers to set their own work goals, make decisions, and solve problems within their sphere of responsibility and authority

participation The process of giving employees a voice in making decisions about their own work

Empowerment and participation represent important methods that managers can use to enhance employee motivation. **Empowerment** is the process of enabling workers to set their own work goals, make decisions, and solve problems within their sphere of responsibility and authority. **Participation** is the process of giving employees a voice in making decisions about their own work. Thus empowerment is a somewhat broader concept which promotes participation in a wide variety of areas, including but not limited to work itself, work context, and work environment.[27]

The role of participation and empowerment in motivation can be expressed in terms of both content perspectives and expectancy theory. Employees who participate in decision making may be more committed to executing decisions properly. Furthermore, the successful process of making a decision, executing it, and then seeing the positive consequences can help satisfy one's need for achievement, provide recognition and responsibility, and enhance self-esteem. Simply being asked to participate in organizational decision making also may enhance an employee's self-esteem. In addition, participation should help clarify expectancies; that is, by participating in decision making, employees may better understand the linkage between their performance and the rewards they want most.

Areas of Participation At one level, employees can participate in addressing questions and making decisions about their own job. Instead of just telling them how to do their job, for example, managers can ask employees to make their own decisions about how to do it. Based on their own expertise and experience with their tasks, workers might be able to improve their own productivity. In many situations, they might also be well qualified to make decisions about what materials to use, what tools to use, and so forth.

It might also be helpful to let workers make decisions about administrative matters, such as work schedules. If jobs are relatively independent of one another, employees might decide when to change shifts, take breaks, go to lunch, and so forth. A work group or team might also be able to schedule vacations and days off for all of its members. Furthermore, employees are getting increasing opportunities to participate in broader issues of product quality. Such participation has become a hallmark of successful Japanese and other international firms, and many U.S. companies have followed suit.

Techniques and Issues in Empowerment In recent years, many organizations have actively sought ways to extend participation beyond the traditional areas. Simple techniques, such as suggestion boxes and question-and-answer meetings, allow a certain degree of participation, for example. The basic motive has been to better capitalize on the assets and capabilities inherent in all employees. Thus many managers today prefer the term *empowerment* to *participation* because of its more comprehensive character.

One method used to empower workers is the use of work teams. Such teams are collections of employees empowered to plan, organize, direct, and control their own work. Their supervisor, rather than being a traditional "boss," plays more the role of a coach. The other method for empowerment is to change the team's overall method of organizing. The basic pattern is for an organization to eliminate layers from its hierarchy, thereby become much more decentralized. Power, responsibility, and authority are delegated as far down the organization as possible, placing the control over work squarely in the hands of those who actually do it.[28]

Regardless of the specific technique or method used, however, empowerment will enhance organizational effectiveness only if certain conditions exist. First of all, the organization must be sincere in its efforts to spread power and autonomy to lower levels of the organization. Token efforts to promote participation in only a few areas are not likely to succeed. Second, the organization must be committed to maintaining participation and empowerment. Workers will be resentful if they are given more control, only to later have it reduced or taken away altogether. Third, workers must truly believe that they and their managers are working together in their joint best interests. In some factory settings, for instance, high-performing workers routinely conceal the secrets of their high output. They fear that, if management learns those secrets, it will use them to ratchet up performance expectations.[29]

In addition, the organization must be systematic and patient in its efforts to empower workers. Turning over too much control too quickly can spell disaster. And, finally, the organization must be prepared to increase its commitment to training. Employees given more freedom in how they work will quite likely need additional training to help them exercise that freedom most effectively.[30] Indeed, *The Business of Ethics* vividly shows what can happen when workers are empowered, but not in ways that serve the interests of the organization.

Alternative Forms of Work Arrangements

Many organizations today are also experimenting with a variety of alternative work arrangements. These alternative arrangements are generally intended to enhance employee motivation and performance by providing employees with greater flexibility in how and when they work. Among the more popular alternative work arrangements are variable work schedules, flexible work schedules, job sharing, and telecommuting.[31]

Variable Work Schedules Although there are many exceptions, of course, the traditional work schedule starts at 8:00 or 9:00 in the morning and ends at 5:00 in the evening, five days a week (and, of course, many managers work many additional hours outside of these times). Unfortunately, this schedule makes it difficult to attend to routine personal business—going to the bank, seeing a doctor or dentist for a routine checkup, having a parent-teacher conference, getting an automobile serviced, and so forth. At a surface level, then, employees locked into this sort of arrangement may find it necessary to take a sick day or a vacation day to handle these activities. At a more

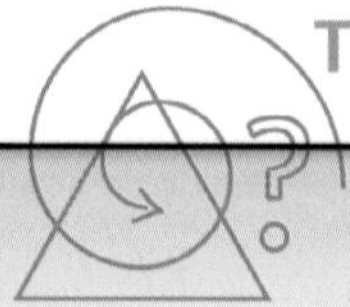

THE BUSINESS OF ethics

"Us Versus Them" at United Airlines

"[United CEO] Goodwin backed up a Brink's truck to the dock and dumped out the cash."

– Patrick Palazzolo, United pilot*

If companies are like families, then United Airlines is a sprawling, squabbling, dysfunctional family, similar to that on *The Sopranos*. The sibling rivalry pits United management against three labor unions representing pilots, mechanics, and flight attendants. Both sides accuse the other of lying, greed, and hostility. Meanwhile, United is spiraling downward toward failure and bankruptcy. If improvements are not made soon, the world's second-largest airline may cease to exist.

After decades of labor troubles, by 1995 United seemed to be on the right path. Employees gave up $4.8 billion in raises and benefits in exchange for an employee stock ownership plan. The plan gave employees 55 percent of the stock and put workers on the board of directors. "There were extremely high hopes that [then-CEO] Gerald Greenwald could change the culture that had been calcified here over the years, the 'us versus them' mentality," says pilot Patrick Palazzolo. Greenwald intended to motivate workers by giving them a personal stake, but it backfired when he failed to replace the middle managers who workers felt had created the problem in the first place.

Two years later, angry pilots went on a work slowdown that held the company hostage for weeks and cost United $700 million. To appease them, then-CEO James F. Goodwin granted a hefty pay increase. Even the pilots felt that the increase–30 percent on an average salary of $150,000–was overly generous. Palazzolo says, "Goodwin backed up a Brink's truck to the dock and dumped out the cash." Machinists, at two-thirds lower pay, were infuriated by the raises, as were flight attendants, who earned between $23,000 and $50,000. To top it off, the value of United shares dropped sharply, falling from a peak of nearly $100 in 1998 to about $1 in January 2003. At those prices, the stock ownership plan was not adding much to motivation.

Is there anything that new CEO Glenn F. Tilton can do to motivate United's workers? *BusinessWeek* writer Michael Arndt suggests imitating rival Continental, which survived near-bankruptcy and motivated workers by instituting a pay-for-performance plan. The system rewarded workers for achieving standards in every area, such as on-time arrivals and accurate ticketing. It may be a long, tough struggle, but if Continental can do it, so can United.

References: Edward Wong, "United Air's Family Is Anything But," *New York Times*, October 6, 2002, pp. BU1, BU11 (*quote p. BU11); John Helyar, "United We Fall," *Fortune*, February 3, 2002, www.fortune.com on February 5, 2003; Michael Arndt, "How to Keep United Flying," *BusinessWeek*, December 23, 2002, www.businessweek.com on February 5, 2003; Shawn Tully, "Why United's Crisis Is Good for Flying," *Fortune*, September 2, 2002, www.fortune.com on February 5, 2003.

unconscious level, some people may also feel so powerless and constrained by their job schedule as to feel increased resentment and frustration.

compressed work schedule Working a full forty-hour week in fewer than the traditional five days

To help counter these problems, some businesses have adopted a **compressed work schedule**, working a full forty-hour week in fewer than the traditional five days.[32] One approach involves working ten hours a day for four days, leaving an extra day off. Another alternative is for employees to work slightly less than ten hours a day, but to complete the forty hours by lunchtime on Friday. And a few firms have tried having employees work twelve hours a day for three days, followed by four days off. Organizations that have used these forms of compressed workweeks include John Hancock, BP Amoco, and Philip Morris. One problem with this schedule is that, when employees put in too much time in a single day, they tend to get tired and perform at a lower level later in the day.

A schedule that some organizations today are beginning to use is what they call a "nine-eighty" schedule. Under this arrangement, an employee works a traditional schedule one week and a compressed schedule the next, getting every other Friday off. In other words, they work eighty hours (the equivalent of two weeks of full-time work) in nine days. By alternating the regular and compressed schedules across half of its workforce, the organization can be fully staffed at all times, while still giving employees two full days off each month. Shell Oil and BP Amoco Chemicals are two of the firms that currently use this schedule.

Flexible Work Schedules Another promising alternative work arrangement is **flexible work schedules**, sometimes called **flextime**. Flextime gives employees more personal control over the times they work. The workday is broken down into two categories: flexible time and core time. All employees must be at their workstation during core time, but they can choose their own schedules during flexible time. Thus one employee may choose to start work early in the morning and leave in midafternoon, another to start in the late morning and work until late afternoon, and still another to start early in the morning, take a long lunch break, and work until late afternoon. Organizations that have used the flexible work schedule method for arranging work include Hewlett-Packard, Compaq Computer, Microsoft, and Texas Instruments.

flexible work schedules(flextime) Allowing employees to select, within broad parameters, the hours they work

job sharing When two part-time employees share one full-time job

telecommuting Allowing employees to spend part of their time working offsite, usually at home

Job Sharing Yet another potentially useful alternative work arrangement is job sharing. In **job sharing**, two part-time employees share one full-time job. One person may perform the job from 8:00 A.M. to noon and the other from 1:00 P.M. to 5:00 P.M. Job sharing may be desirable for people who want to work only part time or when job markets are tight. For its part, the organization can accommodate the preferences of a broader range of employees and may benefit from the talents of more people.

Flexible work schedules can be a powerful motivational strategy. Consider, for example, Tina Willford and her employer, First Tennessee Bank. The bank allows Willford to leave work early each day so that she can spend time with her young children. She makes up the time after her children are in bed. First Tennessee considers Willford to be a rising star and is interested in doing whatever it can to both motivate her and keep her satisfied.

Telecommuting A relatively new approach to alternative work arrangements is **telecommuting**—allowing employees to spend part of their time working offsite, usually at home. By using e-mail, the Internet, and other forms of information technology, many employees can maintain close contact with their organization and still get just as much work done at home as if they were in their office. The increased power and sophistication of modern communication technology is making telecommuting easier and easier.

concept CHECK

Summarize the basic concepts underlying employee empowerment and participation.	*What work schedule would be most attractive to you? least attractive?*

Using Reward Systems to Motivate Performance

Aside from these types of motivational strategies, an organization's reward system is its most basic tool for managing employee motivation. An organizational **reward system** is the formal and informal mechanisms by which employee performance is defined, evaluated, and rewarded. Rewards that are tied specifically to performance, of course, have the greatest impact on enhancing both motivation and actual performance.

Managers sometimes resort to unusual rewards as a way to retain valuable employees. Mercer Management, a consulting firm, was having trouble holding on to its best consultants, who were beginning to feel a bit restless. Mercer found that some of them were leaving to help implement strategies they had developed for Mercer clients. So, the firm now allows its consultants to take a leave of absence of up to one year to work for other companies. Mercer consultant Gregg Dixon, for example, helped Binney & Smith develop a new strategy for its popular Crayola crayons. He then went to work for Binney & Smith to help implement the strategy. After he has finished, he will return to his old job at Mercer Management.

Performance-based rewards play a number of roles and address a variety of purposes in organizations. The major purposes involve the relationship of rewards to motivation and to performance. Specifically, organizations want employees to perform at relatively high levels and need to make it worth their effort to do so. When rewards are associated with higher levels of performance, employees will presumably be motivated to work harder in order to achieve those awards. At that point, their own self-interests coincide with the organization's interests. Performance-based rewards are also relevant regarding other employee behaviors. Unfortunately, current economic conditions have forced many companies to reduce the rewards they provide to their employees or to lengthen the period of time between rewards. In 2002, for instance, Ford deferred merit raises for its 50,000 salaried workers by six months, from spring until August 1.[33]

Merit Reward Systems

Merit reward systems are one of the most fundamental forms of performance-based rewards. **Merit pay** generally refers to pay awarded to employees on the basis of the relative value of their contributions to the organization. Employees who make greater contributions are given higher pay than those who make lesser contributions. **Merit pay plans**, then, are compensation plans that formally base at least some meaningful portion of compensation on merit.

The most general form of merit pay plan is to provide annual salary increases to individuals in the organization based on their relative merit. Merit, in turn, is usually determined or defined based on the individual's performance and overall contributions to the organization. For example, an organization using such a traditional merit pay plan might instruct its supervisors to give all their employees an average pay raise of, say, 4 percent. But the individual supervisor is further instructed to differentiate among high, average, and low performers. Under a simple system, for example, a manager might give the top 25 percent of her employees a 6 percent pay raise, the middle 50 percent a 4 percent or average pay raise, and the bottom 25 percent a 2 percent pay raise.

Incentive Reward Systems

Incentive reward systems are among the oldest forms of performance-based rewards. For example, some companies were using individual piece-rate incentive plans over a hundred years ago.[34] Under a **piece-rate incentive plan**, the organization pays an employee a certain amount of money for every unit she or he produces. For example, an employee might be paid one dollar for every dozen units of products that are successfully completed. But such simplistic systems fail to account for such facts as minimum wage levels and rely very heavily on the assumptions that performance is totally under an individual's control and that the individual employee does a single task continuously throughout his or her work time. Thus most organizations today that try to use incentive compensation systems use more sophisticated methodologies.

"I think I should warn you that the flip side of our generous bonus-incentive program is capital punishment."

Organizations provide rewards and incentives that can serve as positive reinforcement for desired behavior. Similarly, most also have various forms of punishment that can be used to weaken or eliminate undesired behaviors. Although not as extreme as the humorous example shown here, positive reinforcement and punishment that are clearly linked to desired and undesired behaviors, respectively, can play a major role in boosting employee performance and organizational effectiveness.

Incentive Pay Plans Generally speaking, *individual incentive plans* reward individual performance on a real-time basis. In other words, rather than increasing a person's base salary at the end of the year, an individual instead receives some level of salary increase or financial reward in conjunction with demonstrated outstanding performance in close proximity to when that performance occurred. Individual incentive systems are most likely to be used in cases in which performance can be objectively assessed in terms of number of units of output or similar measures, rather than on a subjective assessment of performance by a superior.

Some variations on a piece-rate system are still fairly popular. Although many of these still resemble the early plans in most ways, a well-known piece-rate system at Lincoln Electric illustrates how an organization can adapt the traditional model to achieve better results. For years, Lincoln's employees were paid individual incentive payments based on their performance. However, the amount of money shared (or the incentive pool) was based on the company's profitability. There was also a well-organized system whereby employees could make suggestions for increasing productivity. There was motivation to do this because the employees received one-third of the profits (another third went to the stockholders, and the last share was retained for improvements and seed money). Thus the pool for incentive payments was determined by profitability, and an employee's share of this pool was a function of his or her base pay and rated performance based on the piece-rate system. Lincoln Electric was most famous, however, because of the stories (which were apparently typical) of production workers' receiving a year-end bonus payment that equaled

reward system The formal and informal mechanisms by which employee performance is defined, evaluated, and rewarded

merit pay Pay awarded to employees on the basis of the relative value of their contributions to the organization

merit pay plan Compensation plan that formally bases at least some meaningful portion of compensation on merit

piece-rate incentive plan Reward system wherein the organization pays an employee a certain amount of money for every unit she or he produces their yearly base pay.[35] In recent years, Lincoln has partially abandoned its famous system for business reasons, but it still serves as a benchmark for other companies seeking innovative piece-rate pay systems.

Perhaps the most common form of individual incentive is *sales commissions* that are paid to people engaged in sales work. For example, sales representatives for consumer products firms and retail sales agents may be compensated under this type of commission system. In general, the person might receive a percentage of the total volume of attained sales as her or his commission for a period of time. Some sales jobs are based entirely on commission, whereas others use a combination of base minimum salary with additional commission as an incentive. Notice that these plans put a considerable amount of the salespersons' earnings "at risk." In other words, although organizations often have drawing accounts to allow the salesperson to live during lean periods (the person then "owes" this money back to the organization), if he or she does not perform well, he or she will not be paid much. The portion of salary based on commission is simply not guaranteed and is paid only if sales reach some target level.

Other Forms of Incentive Occasionally organizations may also use other forms of incentives to motivate people. For example, a nonmonetary incentive, such as additional time off or a special perk, might be a useful incentive. For example, a company might establish a sales contest in which the sales group that attains the highest level of sales increase over a specified period of time will receive an extra week of paid vacation, perhaps even at an arranged place, such as a tropical resort or a ski lodge.[36]

A major advantage of incentives relative to merit systems is that incentives are typically a one-shot reward and do not accumulate by becoming part of the individual's base salary. Stated differently, an individual whose outstanding performance entitles him or her to a financial incentive gets the incentive only one time, based on that level of performance. If the individual's performance begins to erode in the future, then the individual may receive a lesser incentive or perhaps no incentive in the future. As a consequence, his or her base salary remains the same or is perhaps increased at a relatively moderate pace; he or she receives one-time incentive rewards as recognition for exemplary performance. Furthermore, because these plans, by their very nature, focus on one-time events, it is much easier for the organization to change the focus of the incentive plan. At a simple level, for example, an organization can set up an incentive plan for selling one product during one quarter, but then shift the incentive to a different product the next quarter, as the situation requires. Automobile companies like Ford and GM routinely do this by reducing sales incentives for models that are selling very well and increasing sales incentives for models that are selling below expectations or are about to be discontinued.

Team and Group Incentive Reward Systems

The merit compensation and incentive compensation systems described in the preceding sections deal primarily with performance-based reward arrangements for individuals. There also exists a different set of performance-based reward programs that are targeted for teams and groups. These programs are particularly important for managers to understand today, given the widespread trends toward team and group-based methods of work and organizations.[37]

Common Team and Group Reward Systems There are two commonly used types of team and group reward systems. One type used in many organizations is an approach called gainsharing. **Gainsharing programs** are designed to share the cost savings from productivity improvements with employees. The underlying assumption of gainsharing is that employees and the employer have the same goals and thus should appropriately share in incremental economic gains.[38]

gainsharing programs Designed to share the cost savings from productivity improvements with employees

In general, organizations that use gainsharing start by measuring team- or group-level productivity. It is important that this measure be valid and reliable and that it truly reflect current levels of performance by the team or group. The team or work group itself is then given the charge of attempting to lower costs and otherwise improve productivity through any measures that its members develop and its manager approves. Resulting cost savings or productivity gains that the team or group is able to achieve are then quantified and translated into dollar values. A predetermined formula is then used to allocate these dollar savings between the employer and the employees themselves. A typical formula for distributing gainsharing savings is to provide 25 percent to the employees and 75 percent to the company.

One specific type of gainsharing plan is an approach called the Scanlon plan. This approach was developed by Joseph Scanlon in 1927. The **Scanlon plan** has the same basic strategy as gainsharing plans, in that teams or groups of employees are encouraged to suggest strategies for reducing costs. However, the distribution of these gains is usually tilted much more heavily toward employees, with employees usually receiving between two-thirds and three-fourths of the total cost savings that the plan achieves. Furthermore, the distribution of cost savings resulting from the plan is given not just to the team or group that suggested and developed the ideas, but across the entire organization.

Scanlon plan Similar to gainsharing, but the distribution of gains is tilted much more heavily toward employees

Other Types of Team and Group Rewards Although gainsharing and Scanlon-type plans are among the most popular group incentive reward systems, there are other systems that are also used by some organizations. Some companies, for example, have begun to use true incentives at the team or group level. Just as with individual incentives, team or group incentives tie rewards directly to performance increases. And, like individual incentives, team or group incentives are paid as they are earned rather than being added to employees' base salary. The incentives are distributed at the team or group level, however, rather than at the individual level. In some cases, the distribution may be based on the existing salary of each employee, with incentive bonuses' being given on a proportionate basis. In other settings, each member of the team or group receives the same incentive pay.

Some companies also use nonmonetary rewards at the team or group level—most commonly in the form of prizes and awards. For example, a company might designate the particular team in a plant or subunit of the company that achieves the highest level of productivity increase, the highest level of reported customer satisfaction, or a similar index of performance. The reward itself might take the form of additional time off, as described earlier in this chapter, or a tangible award, such as a trophy or plaque. In any event, the idea is that the reward is at the team level and serves as recognition of exemplary performance by the entire team.

There are also other kinds of team or group level incentives that go beyond the contributions of a specific work group. These are generally organizationwide kinds of incentives. One long-standing method for this approach is *profit sharing.* In a profit-sharing approach, at the end of the year some portion of the company's profits is paid into a profit-sharing pool that is then distributed to all employees. Either this amount is distributed at that time, or it is put into an escrow account and payment is deferred until the employee retires.

The basic rationale behind profit-sharing systems is that everyone in the organization can expect to benefit when the company does well. But, on the other side of the coin, during bad economic times, when the company is perhaps achieving low or perhaps no profits, then no profit sharing is paid out. This sometimes results in negative reactions from employees, who have perhaps come to feel that profit sharing is really a part of their annual compensation.

Employee stock ownership plans (ESOPs) also represent a group-level reward system that some companies use. Under the employee stock ownership plan, employees are gradually given a major stake in ownership of a corporation. The typical form of this plan involves the company's taking out a loan, which is then used to buy a portion of its own stock in the open market. Over time, company profits are then used to pay off this loan. Employees, in turn, receive a claim on ownership of some portion of the stock held by the company, based on their seniority and perhaps on their performance. Eventually, each individual becomes an owner of the company.

Executive Compensation

The top-level executives of most companies have separate compensation programs and plans. These are intended to reward these executives for their performance and for the performance of the organization.

Standard Forms of Executive Compensation Most senior executives receive their compensation in two forms. One form is a *base salary.* As with the base salary of any staff member or professional member of an organization, the base salary of an executive is a guaranteed amount of money that the individual will be paid. For example, in 2001 Coca-Cola paid its chairman and CEO, Douglas Daft, $4.2 million in base salary.[39]

Above and beyond this base salary, however, most executives also receive one or more forms of incentive pay. The traditional method of incentive pay for executives is in the form of bonuses. Bonuses, in turn, are usually determined by the performance of the organization. Thus, at the end of the year, some portion of a corporation's profits may be diverted into a bonus pool. Senior executives then receive a bonus expressed as a percentage of this bonus pool. The chief executive officer and president are obviously likely to get a larger percentage bonus than a vice president.

The exact distribution of the bonus pool is usually specified ahead of time in the individual's employment contract. Some organizations intentionally leave the distribution unspecified, so that the board of directors has the flexibility to give larger rewards to those individuals deemed to be most deserving. Douglas Daft received a $1 million bonus in 2001.

Special Forms of Executive Compensation Beyond base salary and bonuses, many executives receive other kinds of compensation as well. A form of executive compensation that has received a lot of attention in recent years has been various kinds of stock options. A **stock option plan** is established to give senior managers the option to buy company stock in the future at a predetermined fixed price. The basic idea underlying stock option plans is that, if the executives contribute to higher levels of organizational performance, then the company stock should increase in value. Then the executive will be able to purchase the stock at the predetermined price, which theoretically should be lower than its future market price. The difference then becomes profit for the individual. Coca-Cola's Douglas Daft received various stock options potentially worth as much as $49.9 million.

stock option plan Established to give senior managers the option to buy company stock in the future at a predetermined fixed price

Stock options continue to grow in popularity as a means of compensating top managers. Options are seen as a means of aligning the interests of the manager with those of the stockholders, and given that they do not cost the organization much (other than some possible dilution of stock values), they will probably be even more popular in the future. In fact, a recent study by KPMG Peat Marwick indicates that, for senior management whose salary exceeds $250,000, stock options represent the largest share of the salary mix (relative to salary and other incentives). Furthermore, when we consider all of top management (annual salary over $750,000), stock options comprise a full 60 percent of their total compensation. And the Peat Marwick report indicates that, even among exempt employees at the $35,000-a-year level, stock options represent 13 percent of total compensation.

But events in recent years have raised serious questions about the use of stock options as incentives for executives. For example, several executives at Enron allegedly withheld critical financial information from the markets, cashed in their stock options (while Enron stock was trading at $80 a share), and then watched as the financial information was made public and the stock fell to less than $1 a share. Of course, these actions (if proven) are illegal, but they raise questions in the public's mind about the role of stock options and about the way organizations treat stock options from an accounting perspective. Most organizations have *not* treated stock options as liabilities, even though, when exercised, they are exactly that. There is concern that, by not carrying stock options as liabilities, the managers are overstating the value of the company, which, of course, can help raise the stock price. Finally, when stock markets generally fell during the middle of 2002, many executives found that their options were worthless, as the price of the stock fell below the option price. When stock options go "under water" in this way, they have no value to anyone.

Aside from stock option plans, other kinds of executive compensation are also used by some companies. Among the more popular are such perquisites as memberships in private clubs, access to company recreational facilities, and similar considerations. Some organizations also make available to senior executives low- or no-interest loans. These are often given to new executives whom the company is hiring from other companies and serve as an incentive for the individual to leave his or her current job in order to join a new organization.

Criticisms of Executive Compensation In recent years, executive compensation has come under fire for a variety of reasons. One major reason is that the levels of executive compensation attained by some managers seem simply too large for the average shareholder to understand. It is not uncommon, for instance, for a senior executive of a major corporation to earn total income from his or her job in a given year of well in excess of $1 million. Sometimes the income of chief executive officers can be substantially more than this. Coca-Cola's Douglas Daft earned a total of $55 million in 2001 from all sources combined. Thus, just as the typical person has difficulty comprehending the astronomical salaries paid to some movie stars and sports stars, so, too, would the average person be aghast at the astronomical salaries paid to some senior executives.

Compounding the problem created by perceptions of executive compensation is the fact that there often seems to be little or no relationship between the performance of the organization and the compensation paid to its senior executives.[40] Certainly, if an organization is performing at an especially high level and its stock price is increasing consistently, then most observers would agree that the senior executives responsible for this growth should be entitled to attractive rewards.[41] However, it is more difficult to understand a case in which executives are paid huge salaries and other forms of rewards when their company is performing at only a marginal level, yet this is fairly common today. For example, in 2002 Oracle's CEO, Lawrence Ellison, pocketed over $700 million from the sale of previously granted stock options, while the value of Oracle stock was dropping by 57 percent.

Finally, we should note that the gap between the earnings of the CEO and the earnings of a typical employee is enormous. First of all, the size of the gap has been increasing in the United States. In 1980 the typical CEO earned forty-two times the earnings of an ordinary worker, but by 1990 this ratio had increased to eighty-five times the earnings of an ordinary worker. In Japan, on the other hand, the relationship in 1990 was that a typical CEO made less than twenty times the earnings of an ordinary worker.[42]

New Approaches to Performance-based Rewards

Some organizations have started to recognize that they can leverage the value of the incentives that they offer to their employees and to groups in their organization by allowing those individuals and groups to have a say in how rewards are distributed. For example, at the extreme, a company could go so far as to grant salary increase budgets to work groups and then allow the members of those groups themselves to determine how the rewards are going to be allocated among the various members of the group. This strategy would appear to hold considerable promise if everyone understands the performance arrangements that exist in the work group and everyone is committed to being fair and equitable. Unfortunately, it can also create problems if people in a group feel that rewards are not being distributed fairly.[43]

Organizations are also getting increasingly innovative in their incentive programs. For example, some now offer stock options to all their employees, rather than just to top executives. In addition, some firms are looking into ways to purely individualize reward systems. For instance, a firm might offer one employee a paid three-month sabbatical every two years in exchange for a 20 percent reduction in salary. Another employee in the same firm might be offered a 10 percent salary increase in exchange for a 5 percent reduction in company contributions to the person's retirement account. Corning, General Electric, and Microsoft are among the firms closely studying this option.[44]

Regardless of the method used, however, it is also important that managers in an organization effectively communicate what rewards are being distributed and the basis for that distribution. In other words, if incentives are being distributed on the basis of perceived individual contributions to the organization, then members of the organization should be informed of that fact. This will presumably better enable them to understand the basis on which pay increases and other incentives and performance-based rewards have been distributed.

concept CHECK

Summarize the essential elements of merit and incentive reward systems.	What are your personal opinions regarding executive compensation?

Summary of Key Points

business.college.hmco.com/students

Motivation is the set of forces that cause people to behave in certain ways. Motivation is an important consideration for managers because it, along with ability and environmental factors, determines individual performance. Thinking about motivation has evolved from the traditional view through the human relations approach to the human resource view.

Content perspectives on motivation are concerned with what factor or factors cause motivation. Popular content theories include Maslow's needs hierarchy, the ERG theory, and Herzberg's two-factor theory. Other important needs are the needs for achievement, affiliation, and power.

Process perspectives on motivation deal with how motivation occurs. Expectancy theory suggests that people are motivated to perform if they believe that their effort will result in high performance, that this performance will lead to rewards, and that the positive aspects of the outcomes outweigh the negative aspects. Equity theory is based on the premise that people are motivated to achieve and maintain social equity. Attribution theory is a new process theory.

The reinforcement perspective focuses on how motivation is maintained. Its basic assumption is that behavior that results in rewarding consequences is likely to be repeated, whereas behavior resulting in negative consequences is less likely to be repeated. Reinforcement contingencies can be arranged in the form of positive reinforcement, avoidance, punishment, and extinction, and they can be provided on fixed-interval, variable-interval, fixed-ratio, or variable-ratio schedules.

Managers use a variety of motivational strategies derived from the various theories of motivation. Common strategies include empowerment and participation and alternative forms of work arrangements, such as variable work schedules, flexible work schedules, and telecommuting.

Reward systems also play a key role in motivating employee performance. Popular methods include merit reward systems, incentive reward systems, and team and group incentive reward systems. Executive compensation is also intended to serve as motivation for senior managers but has currently come under close scrutiny and criticism.

Discussion Questions

Questions for Review

1. Each historical perspective on motivation built on the earlier perspectives and differed from them in some ways. Describe the similarities and differences between the traditional approach and the human relations approach. Then describe the similarities and differences between the human relations approach and the human resource approach.
2. Compare and contrast content, process, and reinforcement perspectives on motivation.
3. Explain how goal-setting theory works. How is goal setting different from merely asking a worker to "do your best"?
4. Describe some new forms of working arrangements. How do these alternative arrangements increase motivation?

Questions for Analysis

5. Choose one theory from the content perspectives and one from the process perspectives. Describe actions that a manager might take to increase worker motivation under each of the theories. What differences do you see between the theories in terms of their implications for managers?
6. Can factors from both the content and the process perspectives be acting on a worker at the same time? Explain why or why not. Whether you answered yes or no to the previous question, explain the implications for managers.
7. How do rewards increase motivation? What would happen if an organization gave too few rewards? What would happen if it gave too many?

Questions for Application

8. Think about the worst job you have held. What approach to motivation was used in that organization? Now think about the best job you have held. What approach to motivation was used there? Can you base any conclusions on this limited information? If so, what are they?
9. Interview both a manager and a worker (or administrator and faculty member) from a local organization. What views of or approaches to motivation seem to be in use in that organization? Do the manager's views differ from the worker's? If so, how do you explain the differing perceptions?
10. Consider a class you have taken. Using just that one class, offer examples of times when the professor used positive reinforcement, avoidance, punishment, and extinction to manage students' behavior.

BUILDING EFFECTIVE interpersonal and communication SKILLS

Exercise Overview

Interpersonal skills refer to the manager's ability to understand and motivate individuals and groups, and communication skills refer to the ability to effectively send and receive information. This exercise shows in a very explicit way how essential understanding and communicating are for motivating workers.

Exercise Background

One implication of reinforcement theory is that both positive reinforcement (reward) and punishment can be effective in altering employee behavior. However, the use of punishment may also cause resentment on the worker's part, which can reduce the effectiveness of punishment over the long term. Therefore, positive reinforcement is more effective over time.

Exercise Task

Your professor will ask for volunteers to perform a demonstration in front of the class. Consider volunteering or observe the demonstration. Then answer the following questions:

1. Based on what you saw, which is more effective: positive reinforcement or punishment?
2. How did positive reinforcement and punishment affect the "employee" in the demonstration? How did it affect the "boss"?
3. What do you think are the likely long-term consequences of positive reinforcement and punishment?

BUILDING EFFECTIVE decision-making SKILLS

Exercise Overview

Decision-making skills include the manager's ability to recognize and define situations correctly and to select courses of action. This exercise allows you to build decision-making skills, while using goal-setting theory to help you plan your career.

Exercise Background

Lee Iacocca started his career at Ford in 1946, in an entry-level engineering job. By 1960 he was a vice president and in charge of the group that designed the Mustang. By 1970 he was a president of the firm. After being fired from Ford in 1978, he became a president at Chrysler and rose to the CEO spot, retiring in 1992. What is really remarkable in Iacocca's rise to power is that he had it all planned out, even before he completed college.

As legend has it, Iacocca wrote out a list, while he was still an undergraduate, of all the positions he would like to hold throughout his career. The first item on his list was "Engineer at an auto maker." He then wrote down all the career steps he planned to make, ending with CEO. He also wrote down a timetable for his promotions. He put the list on a three-by-five-inch card, which he folded and stowed in his wallet. The story tells us that Iacocca took out that card frequently to look at it and that, each time he did so, he gained fresh confidence and drive. Apparently he reached the pinnacle several years earlier than he anticipated, but he followed the career path faithfully. Iacocca used goal-setting theory to motivate himself to reach his ultimate career aspirations, and you can do the same.

Exercise Task

1. Consider what position you would like to hold at the peak of your career. It may be CEO, or it may be owner of a chain of stores, or partner in a law or accounting firm, or president of a university. It may be something less lofty. Whatever it is, write it down.
2. Choose a career path that will lead you toward that goal. It may help to work "backwards"; that is, to start with your final positions and work backwards in time, back to an entry-level position. If you do not know the career path that will lead to your ultimate goal, do some research. You can talk to someone in that career field, ask a professor in that subject, or get online. For example, the AICPA has a section titled "Career Resources," which includes information about career paths and position descriptions for accounting.
3. Write down each step in your path on a card or a sheet of paper.
4. If you were to carry this paper with you and refer to it often, do you think it would help you achieve your ultimate goals? Why or why not?

BUILDING EFFECTIVE conceptual and diagnostic SKILLS

business.college.hmco.com/students

Exercise Overview

Conceptual skills refer to a manager's ability to think in the abstract, and diagnostic skills focus on responses to situations. These skills must be used together to relate motivation theory to your individual needs and your future career choices.

Exercise Background

First, you will develop a list of things you want from life and categorize them according to one of the theories in the chapter. Then you will find out about motivating factors that are present in a career of your choice. Finally, you will reconcile how your needs can be met at the career you choose.

Exercise Task

1. Prepare a list of approximately fifteen things you want from an entry-level job, the job you will seek following graduation. These can be very specific (such as a new car) or very general (such as a feeling of accomplishment).
2. Choose the content theory that best fits your set of needs. Classify each item from your wish list in terms of the need or needs it might satisfy.
3. Use the Internet to research your entry-level job. (*Hint:* One good source is the *Occupational Outlook Handbook*, on the Bureau of Labor Statistics website, at www.bls.gov.) Investigate any items that relate to the needs you specified in response to question 1 above, such as compensation, benefits, working conditions, and so on.
4. Did the theoretical framework provide help in classifying your individual needs? Explain. As a result, do you now place more or less trust in the need theories as viable management tools?
5. In what ways does your chosen entry-level job fulfill your needs? In what ways does it fail to do so? If it does satisfy your needs, will you be motivated? If it does not satisfy your needs, will you be unmotivated, or will you find another way to address any discrepancies (such as working a second job)? Explain.

CHAPTER CLOSING case

YOU'VE GOT TO LOVE THIS JOB

"I enjoy what I do. I'm living a dream. It was a round peg in a round hole."

– Pat Connors, recreational site manager, Agilent*

During the high-technology boom of the late 1990s, companies were not able to attract and retain enough qualified workers. To encourage job applicants, start-ups awarded catchy job titles. Amy Berkus, a marketing coordinator, changed her job title to "Marketing Mechanic." Berkus says, "Everyone was creating new titles in Internet-speak. We wanted titles that conveyed team spirit and a fun atmosphere. . . . It just fit the time." Other hip names included "VP of Buzz," "Chief People Officer," "Guru of Fun," "Gladiator," and "Chief Evangelist." The titles encouraged creativity, getting employees to think differently about their job. They also demonstrated that the firm was hip. "It was a matter of doing away with everything that seemed to reek of the old," says Professor Donna Hoffman. "The feeling was,'We're going to make new rules. We need new titles.'" Yet, as executive recruiter Marc Lewis explains, "As the market has cooled, the interest in creative and unusual job titles has diminished."

Companies are now attempting to create an image of legitimacy, respectability, and honesty. "I think the traditional titles ["customer care manager," "production supervisor"] lend themselves more to the image of a stable company that is driving toward profitability," says Berkus. Does a return to boring job titles mean that companies have abandoned the task of encouraging employee creativity? No. Innovation is just as important during tough times as during boom times. However, the method is different. Today, firms that want to encourage and reward creativity are not merely updating the "window dressing," they are changing the job itself.

Firms are finding that creating positions based on an employee's interests can be more effective than trying to fit unique individuals into predetermined slots. Often, a customized job is a reward for high performance. Steve Gluckman is a bicycle designer for REI, a supplier of outdoor gear. Gluckman worked his way up from service manager to designer over thirteen years. An avid cyclist, he says, "Some people sing. Some people paint. I ride my bike. Like a ballet dancer, like a gymnast, like a skateboarder, I express myself in my job." Starbucks' coffee education manager, Aileen Carrell, travels around the world educating employees about coffee. "I was hired as temporary Christmas help in 1990, and I fell madly in love with the fact that coffees came from the most amazing places, like Sulawesi." After working as a store manager for several years, Carrell moved into her exciting and challenging position.

Sometimes individuals are so motivated by an activity that they look around for an employer who will allow them to do what they love. Holly Brewster Jones was an independent artist for years but wanted more job security. She says, "I applied for a graphic design job at SAS Institute, which I really wasn't qualified for. They called me about a week later for the artist-in-residence job." She paints about sixty works a year for display in the company's campus-like headquarters. "I'll paint until I retire, probably," asserts Jones. "And even then I'll still be an artist."

When high-performing workers define their dream jobs, they can come up with offbeat ideas that take the company in new and interesting directions. At financial services firm Citigroup, Sandra Feagan Stern has carved out a unique niche: ranching. Stern is a private banker, serving clients who invest $3 million or more. The combination of her extensive knowledge of ranching and her financial savvy makes Stern the perfect person to recommend and manage investments in thoroughbreds and second homes.

Pat Connors found his dream job—managing Agilent's corporate retreat in the Pennsylvania Poconos. He previously worked on the firm's manufacturing line but wanted a change. "I'm a naturalist at heart," says Connors. "I enjoy what I do.

I'm living a dream." Connors finds the work itself rewarding, because it utilizes his talents and skills. "It was a round peg in a round hole," he claims.

As these examples show, if companies want to motivate workers, maybe they should focus less on offering incentives to individuals who are doing tasks they find unexciting and uninspiring. Instead, firms could ask employees to tell them how to make their job more motivating. Employees are the experts in what motivates them. Perhaps they are also the most effective job designers.

Case Questions

1. For each of the employees mentioned in the case, determine which needs they are working to fulfill, using Maslow's hierarchy. Explain how you arrived at your answers.
2. Tell whether the workers described in the case are high or low on satisfaction and dissatisfaction, according to Herzberg's theory. Do the examples tend to support Herzberg's claim that satisfaction and dissatisfaction are based on two independent sets of factors?
3. Allowing employees control over their job design is empowering. What are some benefits that firms might expect from empowering their employees? What are some problem areas that firms might encounter as they empower their employees? In the case, are there any examples of the benefits or problems associated with empowerment? If so, describe them.

Case References

Eric Wahlgren, "Online Extra: Goodbye, 'Guru of Fun,'" *BusinessWeek*, August 27, 2001, www.businessweek.com on February 6, 2003; Lee Clifford, "Citigroup Bets (on) the Ranch," *Fortune*, January 8, 2002, www.fortune.com on February 6, 2003; "You Get Paid to Do What?" *Fortune*, January 20, 2003, www.fortune.com on January 13, 2003 (*quote).

Chapter Notes

1. "Company Profile," "Welcome to Pleasant Company," American Girl website, www.americangirl.com on February 5, 2003; Heesun Wee, "Barbie Is Turning Heads on Wall Street Again," *BusinessWeek*, February 9, 2001, www.businessweek.com on February 5, 2003; Julie Sloane, "How We Got Started: Pleasant Rowland," *Fortune Small Business*, October 1, 2002, www.fortune.com on January 27, 2003 (*quote); "Our Toys: American Girl," Mattel website, www.mattel.com on February 5, 2003; Pleasant Rowland, "A New Twist on Timeless Toys," *Fortune Small Business*, October 1, 2002, www.fortune.com on January 27, 2003.
2. Richard M. Steers, Gregory A. Bigley, and Lyman W. Porter, *Motivation and Leadership at Work*, 6th ed. (New York: McGraw-Hill, 1996). See also Maureen L. Ambrose and Carol T. Kulik, "Old Friends, New Faces: Motivation Research in the 1990s," *Journal of Management*, 1999, vol. 25, no. 3, pp. 231–292.
3. See Nigel Nicholson, "How to Motivate Your Problem People," *Harvard Business Review*, January 2003, pp. 57–67.
4. See Jeffrey Pfeffer, *The Human Equation* (Cambridge, Mass.: Harvard Business School Press, 1998).
5. See Craig Pinder, *Work Motivation in Organizational Behavior* (Upper Saddle River, New Jersey: Prentice-Hall, 1998).
6. Frederick W. Taylor, *Principles of Scientific Management* (New York: Harper and Brothers, 1911).
7. Elton Mayo, *The Social Problems of an Industrial Civilization* (Cambridge, Mass.: Harvard University Press, 1945); Fritz J. Rothlisberger and W. J. Dickson, *Management and the Worker* (Cambridge, Mass.: Harvard University Press, 1939).
8. See Eryn Brown, "So Rich So Young—But Are They Really Happy?" *Fortune*, September 18, 2000, pp. 99–110, for a recent discussion of these questions.
9. Abraham H. Maslow, "A Theory of Human Motivation," *Psychological Review*, vol. 50, 1943, pp. 370–396; Abraham H. Maslow, *Motivation and Personality* (New York: Harper & Row, 1954). Maslow's most recent work is Abraham H. Maslow and Richard Lowry, *Toward a Psychology of Being* (New York: Wiley, 1999).
10. For a review, see Pinder, *Work Motivation in Organizational Behavior.*
11. Clayton P. Alderfer, *Existence, Relatedness, and Growth* (New York: Free Press, 1972).
12. Frederick Herzberg, Bernard Mausner, and Barbara Snyderman, *The Motivation to Work* (New York: Wiley, 1959); Frederick Herzberg, "One More Time: How Do You Motivate Employees?" *Harvard Business Review*, January–February 1987, pp. 109–120 (reprinted in *Harvard Business Review*, January 2003, pp. 87–98).
13. Robert J. House and Lawrence A. Wigdor, "Herzberg's Dual-Factor Theory of Job Satisfaction and Motivation: A Review of the Evidence and a Criticism," *Personnel Psychology*, Winter 1967, pp. 369–389; Victor H. Vroom, *Work and Motivation* (New York: Wiley, 1964). See also Pinder, *Work Motivation.*
14. David C. McClelland, *The Achieving Society* (Princeton, N.J.: Van Nostrand, 1961); David C. McClelland, *Power: The Inner Experience* (New York: Irvington, 1975).

15. David McClelland and David H. Burnham, "Power Is the Great Motivator," *Harvard Business Review*, March–April 1976, pp. 100–110 (reprinted in *Harvard Business Review*, January 2003, pp. 117–127).
16. See "The Rise and Fall of Dennis Kozlowski," *BusinessWeek*, December 23, 2002, pp. 64–77.
17. Victor H. Vroom, *Work and Motivation* (New York: Wiley, 1964).
18. "Starbucks' Secret Weapon," *Fortune*, September 29, 1997, p. 268.
19. Lyman W. Porter and Edward E. Lawler III, *Managerial Attitudes and Performance* (Homewood, Ill.: Dorsey Press, 1968).
20. J. Stacy Adams, "Towards an Understanding of Inequity," *Journal of Abnormal and Social Psychology*, November 1963, pp. 422–436.
21. See Edwin A. Locke, "Toward a Theory of Task Performance and Incentives," *Organizational Behavior and Human Performance*, vol. 3, 1968, pp. 157–189.
22. Gary P. Latham and J. J. Baldes, "The Practical Significance of Locke's Theory of Goal Setting," *Journal of Applied Psychology*, vol. 60, 1975, pp. 187–191.
23. B. F. Skinner, *Beyond Freedom and Dignity* (New York: Knopf, 1971).
24. Fred Luthans and Robert Kreitner, *Organizational Behavior Modification and Beyond: An Operant and Social Learning Approach* (Glenview, Ill.: Scott, Foresman, 1985).
25. Ibid.; W. Clay Hamner and Ellen P. Hamner, "Behavior Modification on the Bottom Line," *Organizational Dynamics*, Spring 1976, pp. 2–21.
26. "At Emery Air Freight: Positive Reinforcement Boosts Performance," *Organizational Dynamics*, Winter 1973, pp. 41–50; for a recent update, see Alexander D. Stajkovic and Fred Luthans, "A Meta-Analysis of the Effects of Organizational Behavior Modification on Task Performance, 1975–95," *Academy of Management Journal*, vol. 40, no. 5, 1997, pp. 1122–1149.
27. David J. Glew, Anne M. O'Leary-Kelly, Ricky W. Griffin, and David D. Van Fleet, "Participation in Organizations: A Preview of the Issues and Proposed Framework for Future Analysis," *Journal of Management*, 1995, vol. 21, no. 3, pp. 395–421.
28. Robert E. Quinn and Gretchen M. Spreitzer, "The Road to Empowerment: Seven Questions Every Leader Should Consider," *Organizational Dynamics*, Autumn 1997, pp. 37–47.
29. "On Factory Floors, Top Workers Hide Secrets to Success," *Wall Street Journal*, July 1, 2002, pp. A1, A10.
30. Russ Forrester, "Empowerment: Rejuvenating a Potent Idea," *Academy of Management Executive*, 2000, vol. 14, no. 3, pp. 67–77.
31. Baxter W. Graham, "The Business Argument for Flexibility, *HRMagazine*, May 1996, pp. 104–110.
32. A. R. Cohen and H. Gadon, *Alternative Work Schedules: Integrating Individual and Organizational Needs* (Reading, Mass.: Addison Wesley, 1978).
33. "Companies Stretch Time Between Pay Raises," *USA Today*, August 30, 2002, p. 1B.
34. Daniel Wren, *The Evolution of Management Theory*, 4th ed. (New York: Wiley, 1994).
35. C. Wiley, "Incentive Plan Pushes Production," *Personnel Journal*, August 1993, p. 91.
36. "When Money Isn't Enough," *Forbes*, November 18, 1996, pp. 164–169.
37. Jacquelyn DeMatteo, Lillian Eby, and Eric Sundstrom, "Team-Based Rewards: Current Empirical Evidence and Directions for Future Research," in L. L. Cummings and Barry Staw (eds.), *Research in Organizational Behavior*, vol. 20 (Greenwich, Conn.: JAI Press, 1998), pp. 141–183.
38. Theresa M. Welbourne and Luis R. Gomez-Mejia, "Gainsharing: A Critical Review and a Future Research Agenda," *Journal of Management*, 1995, vol. 21, no. 3, pp. 559–609.
39. "Executive Pay," *BusinessWeek*, April 15, 2002, pp. 80–100.
40. Harry Barkema and Luis Gomez-Mejia, "Managerial Compensation and Firm Performance: A General Research Framework," *Academy of Management Journal*, 1998, vol. 41, no. 2, pp. 135–145.
41. Rajiv D. Banker, Seok-Young Lee, Gordon Potter, and Dhinu Srinivasan, "Contextual Analysis of Performance Impacts of Outcome-Based Incentive Compensation," *Academy of Management Journal*, 1996, vol. 39, no. 4, pp. 920–948.
42. M. Blair, "CEO Pay: Why Such a Contentious Issue?" *The Brookings Review*, Winter 1994, pp. 23–27.
43. Steve Kerr, "The Best-Laid Incentive Plans," *Harvard Business Review*, January 2003, pp. 27–40.
44. "Now It's Getting Personal," *BusinessWeek*, December 16, 2002, pp. 90–92.

17

Managing Leadership and Influence Processes

CHAPTER OUTLINE

The Nature of Leadership
- The Meaning of Leadership
- Leadership and Management
- Leadership and Power

Generic Approaches to Leadership
- Leadership Traits
- Leadership Behaviors

Situational Approaches to Leadership
- LPC Theory
- Path-Goal Theory
- Vroom's Decision Tree Approach
- The Leader-Member Exchange Approach

Related Approaches to Leadership
- Substitutes for Leadership
- Charismatic Leadership
- Transformational Leadership

Emerging Approaches to Leadership
- Strategic Leadership
- Cross-Cultural Leadership
- Ethical Leadership

Political Behavior in Organizations
- Common Political Behaviors
- Impression Management
- Managing Political Behavior

LEARNING OBJECTIVES

After studying this chapter, you should be able to:

1 ***Describe the nature of leadership and relate leadership to management.***

OPENING INCIDENT

Shareholders, employees, and charitable organizations appreciated the money HealthSouth made—and the generosity with which chairman, CEO, and founder Richard M. Scrushy spent it. On the other hand, stock analysts, reporters, and government regulators found him "brash" and "abrasive." Scrushy seemed to be one of those people whom others either love or hate. Recently, however, Scrushy's fan club was dwindling because HealthSouth had lost money, share value had declined, and the firm was facing lawsuits. Was Scrushy's leadership failing due to unsympathetic outsiders, as he would have had the public believe? Or were HealthSouth's problems merely the logical consequences of Scrushy's brand of autocratic leadership?

Scrushy trained as a respiratory therapist before working at hospital corporation Lifemark. There he rose to oversee a division with $100 million in sales. His ex-wife, Karon Brooks, says that Scrushy "was always driven to be very successful." In 1986 he founded a rehabilitative services firm, which he called HealthSouth. Today, HealthSouth is the largest health-care firm in the country, treating 120,000 patients daily at one of its 2,000 rehabilitation, outpatient surgery, and diagnostic facilities.

Scrushy's personality and methods came under closer scrutiny as his company grew. He tended to be arrogant, even for a CEO. For example, Health-

2	3	4	5	6
Discuss and evaluate the two generic approaches to leadership.	***Identify and describe the major situational approaches to leadership.***	***Identify and describe three related approaches to leadership.***	***Describe three emerging approaches to leadership.***	***Discuss political behavior in organizations and how it can be managed.***

"[Richard is] flamboyant and somewhat of an autocrat. It's easy to make him the next Martha Stewart."

—Janis L. Jones, former HealthSouth director

Richard Scrushy walks to federal court to face charges brought by the U.S. Justice Department.

South's website calls its corporate officers "the top commanders of one of the nation's leading healthcare providers," and Scrushy himself claimed, "We know this business better than anybody in the world." One government official, on a first meeting with Scrushy, was greeted with, "I hear you never had a real job." About stock advisors, Scrushy complained, "I'm running a business and all they do is read and analyze this." Such sentiments and the way they were expressed, did not endear Scrushy to opinion makers.

Scrushy's extravagant lifestyle also invited criticism. He lives in a mansion in Birmingham, Alabama, where HealthSouth is headquartered. He also has three other luxury homes, along with a seaplane and a 92-foot yacht. In response to claims that he is ostentatious, Scrushy protests, "I'm not bigger than life. I don't even own a Ferrari. I don't even own a Bentley." However, Scrushy's compensation in 2001 was $10.5 million, ten times the average for health-care CEOs.

Questionable decisions were also part of Scrushy's leadership. He billed Medicare for equipment that HealthSouth bought from a firm owned by his parents. (The firm paid $7.9 million in 2001 to settle Medicare's claim.) HealthSouth sold property that cost $1.9 million to Scrushy for $640,000 just two years later. The company also sold $58 million in property to a real estate firm owned by Scrushy, then leased it back. Scrushy denied any impropriety, stating, "Everything was disclosed. Everybody knew exactly what was going on all the time."

That was probably true and was certainly part of the problem. HealthSouth's board of directors contained few outside members. (In January 2003, the firm announced that it would seek more outside members.) Many of HealthSouth's numerous acquisitions were of companies owned by Scrushy and members of the board. In fact, Scrushy and the directors had interlocking board membership and investments in several firms. HealthSouth made loans worth $36 million to board members and Scrushy.

In August 2002, Scrushy announced that HealthSouth would face higher-than-expected losses, due to changes in Medicare. In the month before the announcement, board members and Scrushy made significant stock sales, which led to an insider trading investigation by the FBI. Immediately afterwards, Scrushy resigned as CEO but remained active. Board members reviewed Scrushy's actions and cleared him of any wrongdoing. In January 2003, Scrushy reassumed the CEO position. A judge ruled that the board was not sufficiently independent and called for an objective performance audit.

Scrushy refused to provide reasonable justification for his actions. At a recent interview, he brushed off inquiries, saying, "I have answered these questions a thousand times." He claimed that analysts were vindictive because of their failures. "The first thing [the analysts] are going to do is slam the management," argued Scrushy.

Former HealthSouth director Janis L. Jones defended Scrushy: "Richard's flamboyant and somewhat of an autocrat. It's easy to make him the next Martha Stewart." For his part, Scrushy showed no qualms about continuing to lead the healthcare giant. Yet Kevin R. McCloskey, a portfolio manager, spoke for many investors when he asserted, "Their credibility as a management team is zero. It's been shot."[1] Unfortunately, Scrushy's problems are far from over—he is currently under investigation by the U.S. Justice Department.

Richard Scrushy illustrates what some people would call the best and the worst things about leadership. On the one hand, he took bold risks early in his career, founded a small firm that grew to become an industry giant, and created tremendous wealth for shareholders and the charities he supported. But, on the other hand, he also exhibited questionable behaviors, made controversial decisions, and alienated key people. But, love him or hate him, just about everyone agrees that Scrushy exemplifies strong leadership.

This chapter examines people like Richard Scrushy more carefully by focusing on leadership and its role in management. We characterize the nature of leadership and trace through the three major approaches to studying leadership—traits, behaviors, and situations. After examining other perspectives on leadership, we conclude by describing another approach to influencing others—political behavior in organizations.

The Nature of Leadership

In Chapter 16, we described various models and perspectives on employee motivation. From the manager's standpoint, trying to motivate people is an attempt to influence their behavior. In many ways, leadership, too, is an attempt to influence the behavior of others. In this section, we first define leadership, then differentiate it from management, and conclude by relating it to power.

leadership As a process, the use of noncoercive influence to shape the group's or organization's goals, motivate behavior toward the achievement of those goals, and help define group or organizational culture; as a property, the set of characteristics attributed to individuals who are perceived to be leaders

The Meaning of Leadership

Leadership is both a process and a property.[2] As a process—focusing on what leaders actually do—leadership is the use of noncoercive influence to shape the group or organization's goals, motivate behavior toward the achievement of those goals,

Leadership is a critical ingredient to the success of an organization. Carly Fiorina, CEO of Hewlett-Packard, clearly demonstrated both her leadership skills and her understanding of power and politics in organizations when she spearheaded her firm's acquisition of Compaq against the wishes of several major shareholders. Ms. Fiorina believed that the merger was necessary in order for the firm to regain its competitiveness in the computer industry. While some skeptics doubted her ability to complete the deal, she carried the day and, so far at least, seems to have made all the right moves.

and help define group or organizational culture.[3] As a property, leadership is the set of characteristics attributed to individuals who are perceived to be leaders. Thus **leaders** are people who can influence the behaviors of others without having to rely on force or people whom others accept as leaders.

leaders People who can influence the behaviors of others without having to rely on force; those accepted by others as leaders

Leadership and Management

From these definitions, it should be clear that leadership and management are related, but they are not the same. A person can be a manager, a leader, both, or neither.[4] Some of the basic distinctions between the two are summarized in Table 17.1. At the left side of the table are four elements that differentiate leadership from management. The two columns show how each element differs when considered from a management and from a leadership point of view. For example, when executing plans, managers focus on monitoring results, comparing them with goals, and correcting deviations. In contrast, the leader focuses on energizing people to overcome bureaucratic hurdles to reach goals.

TABLE 17.1

Distinctions Between Management and Leadership

Management and leadership are related, but distinct, constructs. Managers and leaders differ in how they create an agenda, develop a rationale for achieving the agenda, and execute plans, and in the types of outcomes they achieve.

Activity	Management	Leadership
Creating an agenda	*Planning and Budgeting*. Establishing detailed steps and timetables for achieving needed results; allocating the resources necessary to make those needed results happen	*Establishing Direction*. Developing a vision of the future, often the distant future, and strategies for producing the changes needed to achieve that vision
Developing a human network for achieving the agenda	*Organizing and Staffing*. Establishing some structure for accomplishing plan requirements, staffing that structure with individuals, delegating responsibility and authority for carrying out the plan, providing policies and procedures to help guide people, and creating methods or systems to monitor implementation	*Aligning People*. Communicating the direction by words and deeds to everyone whose cooperation may be needed to influence the creation of teams and coalitions that understand the visions and strategies and accept their validity
Executing plans	*Controlling and Problem Solving*. Monitoring results versus planning in some detail, identifying deviations, and then planning and organizing to solve these problems	*Motivating and Inspiring*. Energizing people to overcome major political, bureaucratic, and resource barriers by satisfying very basic, but often unfulfilled, human needs
Outcomes	Produces a degree of predictability and order and has the potential to produce consistently major results expected by various stakeholders (for example, for customers, always being on time; for stockholders, being on budget)	Produces change, often to a dramatic degree, and has the potential to produce extremely useful change (for example, new products that customers want, new approaches to labor relations that help make a firm more competitive)

Source: Reprinted with permission of The Free Press, a division of Simon & Schuster Adult Publishing Group, from *A Force for Change: How Leadership Differs from Management* by John P. Kotter. Copyright © 1990 by John P. Kotter, Inc.

Organizations need both management and leadership if they are to be effective. Leadership is necessary to create change, and management is necessary to achieve orderly results. Management in conjunction with leadership can produce orderly change, and leadership in conjunction with management can keep the organization properly aligned with its environment. Indeed, perhaps part of the reason why executive compensation has soared in recent years is the belief that management and leadership skills reflect a critical but rare combination that can lead to organizational success. *Today's Management Issues* discusses this perspective in more detail.

TODAY'S management ISSUES

Should We Stop the CEO Compensation Madness?

"I've generally worried [CEOs] weren't getting paid enough. But now even I'm troubled."

– Michael Jensen, Harvard professor*

Many people think CEOs are paid simply too much. Too much in relation to workers' pay, too much for struggling companies to afford, too much compared to the value they provide. Charles Elson, a corporate governance expert, says compensation is "outrageous in many cases and unrelated to services rendered." Harvard professor Michael Jensen adds, "I've generally worried [CEOs] weren't getting paid enough. But now even I'm troubled." Overpaying CEOs is not a minor embarrassment—it can lead to unmotivated workers and disenchanted investors.

CEO pay includes salary, bonuses, stock options, benefits, and perquisites. Steve Jobs of Apple was the highest-paid executive in the world in 2000, receiving $381 million, including a $90 million jet. Former Citicorp CEO John Reed made $1.2 million in 1990; his successor, Sandy Weill, made $151 million in 2000. GE's Jack Welch saw his compensation rise from $5 million to $125 million in a decade. Michael Eisner of Disney earned $29 million the same year profits fell 30 percent. Compare that to a professional baseball player earning $1.9 million, the president of Princeton University earning $413,000, or the president of the United States earning $200,000. Median household income was $42,000.

How did CEO pay get so high? It is a circular process. A poorly performing but highly paid CEO is fired. The new CEO argues that he deserves more than his predecessor. Compensation committees note that average CEO pay is increasing. When the new CEO is replaced, the pay is even higher.

One well-paid CEO describes how he dominates his board: "Since I know more than they do about this subject . . . it's like shooting fish in a barrel." Do external consultants provide some objectivity? Not at all, this CEO replies. "It is unusual to find a consultant who does not end up, at the least, being a prostitute," he says. "The consultants are hired by management."

CEOs claim that they should make more than athletes and movie stars, ignoring the fact that athletes and movie stars, unlike CEOs, are judged in a competitive open market. Pay for performance sounds great in good times, but less so in tough times. "Incentive compensation works fine as long as the people who are incenting have the guts to follow what they say they're going to do—but usually they don't," says one CEO.

References: Carol J. Loomis, "This Stuff Is Wrong," *Fortune*, June 11, 2001, www.fortune.com on February 9, 2003; Daniel Altman, "How to Tie Pay to Goals, Instead of the Stock Price," *New York Times*, September 8, 2002, p. BU4; David Cay Johnston, "Designers of Executive Salary Plans Fear More Abuses," *New York Times*, October 5, 2002, p. C2; Geoffrey Colvin, "The Great CEO Pay Heist," *Fortune*, June 25, 2001, www.fortune.com on December 2, 2002 (*quote).

Leadership and Power

To fully understand leadership, it is necessary to understand power. **Power** is the ability to affect the behavior of others. One can have power without actually using it. For example, a football coach has the power to bench a player who is not performing up to par. The coach seldom has to use this power, because players recognize that the power exists and work hard to keep their starting positions. In organizational settings, there are usually five kinds of power: legitimate, reward, coercive, referent, and expert power.[5]

power The ability to affect the behavior of others

Legitimate Power **Legitimate power** is power granted through the organizational hierarchy; it is the power defined by the organization to be accorded to people occupying a particular position. A manager can assign tasks to a subordinate, and a subordinate who refuses to do them can be reprimanded or even fired. Such outcomes stem from the manager's legitimate power as defined and vested in her or him by the organization. Legitimate power, then, is authority. All managers have legitimate power over their subordinates. The mere possession of legitimate power, however, does not by itself make someone a leader. Some subordinates follow only orders that are strictly within the letter of organizational rules and policies. If asked to do something not in their job description, they refuse or do a poor job. The manager of such employees is exercising authority but not leadership.

legitimate power Power granted through the organizational hierarchy; the power defined by the organization to be accorded to people occupying particular positions

Reward Power **Reward power** is the power to give or withhold rewards. Rewards that a manager may control include salary increases, bonuses, promotion recommendations, praise, recognition, and interesting job assignments. In general, the greater the number of rewards a manager controls and the more important the rewards are to subordinates, the greater is the manager's reward power. If the subordinate sees as valuable only the formal organizational rewards provided by the manager, then he or she is not a leader. If the subordinate also wants and appreciates the manager's informal rewards, such as praise, gratitude, and recognition, however, then the manager is also exercising leadership.

reward power The power to give or withhold rewards, such as salary increases, bonuses, promotions, praise, recognition, and interesting job assignments

Coercive Power **Coercive power** is the power to force compliance by means of psychological, emotional, or physical threat. In the past, physical coercion in organizations was relatively common. In most organizations today, however, coercion is limited to verbal reprimands, written reprimands, disciplinary layoffs, fines, demotion, and termination. Some managers occasionally go so far as to use verbal abuse, humiliation, and psychological coercion in an attempt to manipulate subordinates. (Of course, most people would agree that these are not appropriate managerial behaviors.) James Dutt, former CEO of Beatrice Company, once told a subordinate that, if his wife and family got in the way of his working a twenty-four-hour day seven days a week, he should get rid of them.[6] The more punitive the elements under a manager's control and the more important they are to subordinates, the more coercive power the manager possesses. On the other hand, the more a manager uses coercive power, the more likely he is to provoke resentment and hostility and the less likely he is to be seen as a leader.[7]

coercive power The power to force compliance by means of psychological, emotional, or physical threat

Referent power accrues to someone based on identification, imitation, loyalty, or charisma. Michele Kwan, the most decorated American figure skater in history, seems to have virtually unlimited referent power. Children everywhere, for example, love to watch her skate and many aspire to follow in her footsteps. She is now using her power to help promote the Children's Miracle Network, an organization that raises money for 170 children's hospitals in North America.

referent power The personal power that accrues to someone based on identification, imitation, loyalty, or charisma

expert power The personal power that accrues to someone based on the information or expertise that they possess

Referent Power Compared with legitimate, reward, and coercive power, which are relatively concrete and grounded in objective facets of organizational life, **referent power** is abstract. It is based on identification, imitation, loyalty, or charisma. Followers may react favorably because they identify in some way with a leader, who may be like them in personality, background, or attitudes. In other situations, followers might choose to imitate a leader with referent power by wearing the same kind of clothes, working the same hours, or espousing the same management philosophy. Referent power may also take the form of charisma, an intangible attribute of the leader that inspires loyalty and enthusiasm. Thus a manager might have referent power, but it is more likely to be associated with leadership.

Expert Power **Expert power** is derived from information or expertise. A manager who knows how to interact with an eccentric but important customer, a scientist who is capable of achieving an important technical breakthrough that no other company has dreamed of, and a secretary who knows how to unravel bureaucratic red tape all have expert power over anyone who needs that information. The more important the information and the fewer the people who have access to it, the greater is the degree of expert power possessed by any one individual. In general, people who are both leaders and managers tend to have a lot of expert power.

Using Power How does a manager or leader use power? Several methods have been identified.[8] One method is the *legitimate request,* which is based on legitimate power. The manager requests that the subordinate comply because the subordinate recognizes that the organization has given the manager the right to make the request. Most day-to-day interactions between manager and subordinate are of this type. Another use of power is *instrumental compliance,* which is based on the reinforcement theory of motivation. In this form of exchange, a subordinate complies in order to get the reward the manager controls. Suppose that a manager asks a subordinate to do something outside the range of the subordinate's normal duties, such as working extra hours on the weekend, terminating a relationship with a long-standing buyer, or delivering bad news. The subordinate complies and, as a direct result, reaps praise and a bonus from the manager. The next time the subordinate is asked to perform a similar activity, that subordinate will recognize that compliance will be instrumental in her getting more rewards. Hence the basis of instrumental compliance is clarifying important performance-reward contingencies.

A manager is using *coercion* when she suggests or implies that the subordinate will be punished, fired, or reprimanded if he does not do something. *Rational persuasion* occurs when the manager can convince the subordinate that compliance is in the subordinate's best interests. For example, a manager might argue that the subordinate should accept a transfer because it would be good for the subordinate's career. In some ways, rational persuasion is like reward power, except that the manager does not really control the reward.

Still another way a manager can use power is through *personal identification.* A manager who recognizes that she has referent power over a subordinate can shape the behavior of that subordinate by engaging in desired behaviors: The manager consciously becomes a model for the subordinate and exploits personal identification. Sometimes a manager can induce a subordinate to do something consistent with a set of higher ideals or values through *inspirational appeal.* For example, a plea for loyalty represents an inspirational appeal. Referent power plays a role in determining the extent to which an inspirational appeal is successful, because its effectiveness depends at least in part on the persuasive abilities of the leader.

A dubious method of using power is through *information distortion.* The manager withholds or distorts information to influence subordinates' behavior. For example, if a manager has agreed to allow everyone to participate in choosing a new group member but subsequently finds one individual whom she really prefers, she might withhold some of the credentials of other qualified applicants so that the desired member is selected. This use of power is dangerous. It may be unethical, and if subordinates find out that the manager has deliberately misled them, they will lose their confidence and trust in that manager's leadership.[9]

concept CHECK

Summarize the key differences between leadership and management.

Identify an example you have experienced or observed to illustrate each of the five types of power discussed in this section.

Generic Approaches to Leadership

Early approaches to the study of leadership adopted what might be called a "universal" or "generic" perspective. Specifically, they assumed that there was one set of answers to the leadership puzzle. One generic approach focused on leadership traits, and the other looked at leadership behavior.

Leadership Traits

The first organized approach to studying leadership analyzed the personal, psychological, and physical traits of strong leaders. The trait approach assumed that some basic trait or set of traits existed that differentiated leaders from nonleaders. If those traits could be defined, potential leaders could be identified. Researchers thought that leadership traits might include intelligence, assertiveness, above-average height, good vocabulary, attractiveness, self-confidence, and similar attributes.[10]

During the first half of the twentieth century, hundreds of studies were conducted in an attempt to identify important leadership traits. For the most part, the results of the studies were disappointing. For every set of leaders who possessed a common trait, a long list of exceptions was also found, and the list of suggested traits soon grew so long that it had little practical value. Alternative explanations usually existed even for relationships between traits and leadership that initially appeared valid. For example, it was observed that many leaders have good communication skills and are assertive. Rather than those traits' being the cause of leadership, however, successful leaders may begin to display those traits after they have achieved a leadership position.

Although most researchers gave up trying to identify traits as predictors of leadership ability, many people still explicitly or implicitly adopt a trait orientation.[11] For example, politicians are all too often elected on the basis of personal appearance, speaking ability, or an aura of self-confidence. In addition, traits like honesty and integrity may very well be fundamental leadership traits that do serve an important purpose.

Leadership Behaviors

Spurred on by their lack of success in identifying useful leadership traits, researchers soon began to investigate other variables, especially the behaviors or actions of leaders. The new hypothesis was that effective leaders somehow behaved differently than less-effective leaders. Thus the goal was to develop a fuller understanding of leadership behaviors.

Michigan Studies Researchers at the University of Michigan, led by Rensis Likert, began studying leadership in the late 1940s.[12] Based on extensive interviews with both leaders (managers) and followers (subordinates), this research identified two basic forms of leader behavior: job centered and employee centered. Managers using **job-centered leader behavior** pay close attention to subordinates' work, explain work procedures, and are keenly interested in performance. Managers using **employee-centered leader behavior** are interested in developing a cohesive work group and ensuring that employees are satisfied with their job. Their primary concern is the welfare of subordinates.

job-centered leader behavior The behavior of leaders who pay close attention to the job and work procedures involved with that job

employee-centered leader behavior The behavior of leaders who develop cohesive work groups and ensure employee satisfaction

The two styles of leader behavior were presumed to be at the ends of a single continuum. Although this suggests that leaders may be extremely job centered, extremely employee centered, or somewhere in between, Likert studied only the two end styles for contrast. He argued that employee-centered leader behavior generally tends to be more effective. We should also note the similarities between Likert's leadership research and his Systems 1 through 4 organization designs (discussed in Chapter 12). Job-centered leader behavior is consistent with the System 1 design (rigid and bureaucratic), whereas employee-centered leader behavior is consistent with the System 4 design (organic and flexible). When Likert advocates moving organizations from System 1 to System 4, he is also advocating a transition from job-centered to employee-centered leader behavior.

Ohio State Studies At about the same time that Likert was beginning his leadership studies at the University of Michigan, a group of researchers at Ohio State University also began studying leadership.[13] The extensive questionnaire surveys conducted during the Ohio State studies also suggested that there are two basic leader behaviors or styles: initiating-structure behavior and consideration behavior. When using **initiating-structure behavior**, the leader clearly defines the leader-subordinate role so that everyone knows what is expected, establishes formal lines of communication, and determines how tasks will be performed. Leaders using **consideration behavior** show concern for subordinates and attempt to establish a warm, friendly, and supportive climate. The behaviors identified at Ohio State are similar to those described at Michigan, but there are important differences. One major difference is that the Ohio State researchers did not interpret leader behavior as being one-dimensional; each behavior was assumed to be independent of the other. Presumably, then, a leader could exhibit varying levels of initiating structure and at the same time varying levels of consideration.

initiating-structure behavior The behavior of leaders who define the leader-subordinate role so that everyone knows what is expected, establish formal lines of communication, and determine how tasks will be performed

consideration behavior The behavior of leaders who show concern for subordinates and attempt to establish a warm, friendly, and supportive climate

At first, the Ohio State researchers thought that leaders who exhibit high levels of both behaviors would tend to be more effective than other leaders. A study at International Harvester (now Navistar International), however, suggested a more complicated pattern.[14] The researchers found that employees of supervisors who ranked high on initiating structure were high performers but expressed low levels of satisfaction and had a higher absence rate. Conversely, employees of supervisors who ranked high on consideration had low performance ratings but high levels of satisfaction and few absences from work. Later research isolated other variables that make consistent prediction difficult and determined that situational influences also occurred. (This body of research is discussed in the section on situational approaches to leadership.)

Managerial Grid Yet another behavioral approach to leadership is the Managerial Grid.[15] The Managerial Grid provides a means for evaluating leadership styles and then training managers to move toward an ideal style of behavior. The Managerial Grid is shown in Figure 17.1. The horizontal axis represents **concern for production** (similar to job-centered and initiating-structure behaviors), and the vertical axis represents **concern for people** (similar to employee-centered and consideration behaviors). Note the five extremes of managerial behavior: the 1,1 manager (impoverished management), who exhibits minimal concern for both production and people; the 9,1 manager (authority-compliance), who is highly concerned about production but exhibits little concern for people; the 1,9 manager (country club management), who has exactly opposite concerns from the 9,1 manager; the 5,5 manager (middle-of-the-road management), who maintains adequate concern for both people and production; and the 9,9 manager (team management), who exhibits maximum concern for both people and production.

concern for production The part of the Managerial Grid that deals with the job and task aspects of leader behavior

concern for people The part of the Managerial Grid that deals with the human aspects of leader behavior

According to this approach, the ideal style of managerial behavior is 9,9. There is a six-phase program to assist managers in achieving this style of behavior. A.G. Edwards, Westinghouse, the FAA, Equicor, and other companies have used the

FIGURE 17.1

The Leading Grid

The Leadership Grid® is a method of evaluating leadership styles. The overall objective of an organization using the Grid® is to train its managers using organization development techniques so that they are simultaneously more concerned for both people and production (9,9 style on the Grid®).

Source: The Leadership Grid Figure for *Leadership Dilemmas—Grid Solutions* by Robert R. Blake and Anne Adams McCanse. (Formerly the Managerial Grid by Robert R. Blake and Jane S. Mouton.) Houston: Gulf Publishing Company, p. 29. Copyright © 1997 by Grid International, Inc. Reproduced by permission of the owners.

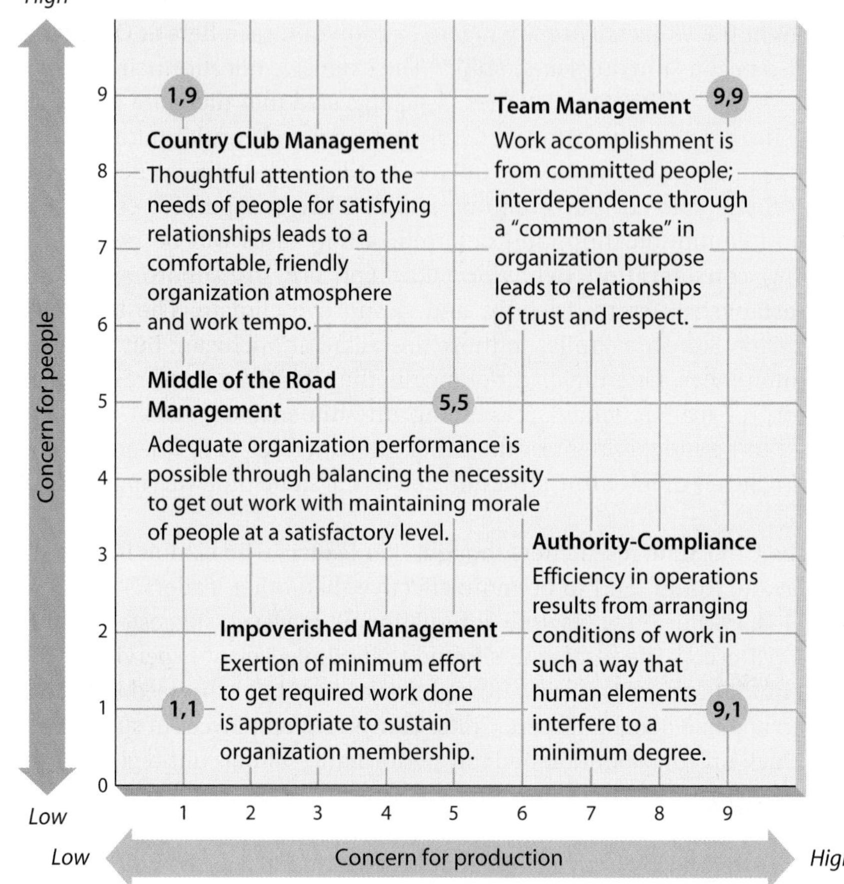

Managerial Grid with reasonable success. However, there is little published scientific evidence regarding its true effectiveness.

The leader-behavior theories have played an important role in the development of contemporary thinking about leadership. In particular, they urge us not to be preoccupied with what leaders are (the trait approach) but to concentrate on what leaders do (their behaviors). Unfortunately, these theories also make universal generic prescriptions about what constitutes effective leadership. When we are dealing with complex social systems composed of complex individuals, however, few if any relationships are consistently predictable, and certainly no formulas for success are infallible. Yet the behavior theorists tried to identify consistent relationships between leader behaviors and employee responses in the hope of finding a dependable prescription for effective leadership. As we might expect, they often failed. Other approaches to understanding leadership were therefore needed. The catalyst for these new approaches was the realization that, although interpersonal and task-oriented dimensions might be useful for describing the behavior of leaders, they were not useful for predicting or prescribing it. The next step in the evolution of leadership theory was the creation of situational models.

concept CHECK

Describe the basic types of leader behavior identified in the generic approaches to leadership.

Setting aside the validity of the concept, what traits would you see as being most important for effective leadership?

Situational Approaches to Leadership

Situational models assume that appropriate leader behavior varies from one situation to another. The goal of a situational theory, then, is to identify key situational factors and to specify how they interact to determine appropriate leader behavior. Before discussing the major situational theories, we should first discuss an important early model that laid the foundation for subsequent developments. In a 1958 study of the decision-making process, Robert Tannenbaum and Warren H. Schmidt proposed a continuum of leadership behavior. Their model is much like the original Michigan framework.[16] Besides purely job-centered behavior (or "boss-centered" behavior, as they termed it) and employee-centered ("subordinate-centered") behavior, however, they identified several intermediate behaviors that a manager might consider. These are shown on the leadership continuum in Figure 17.2.

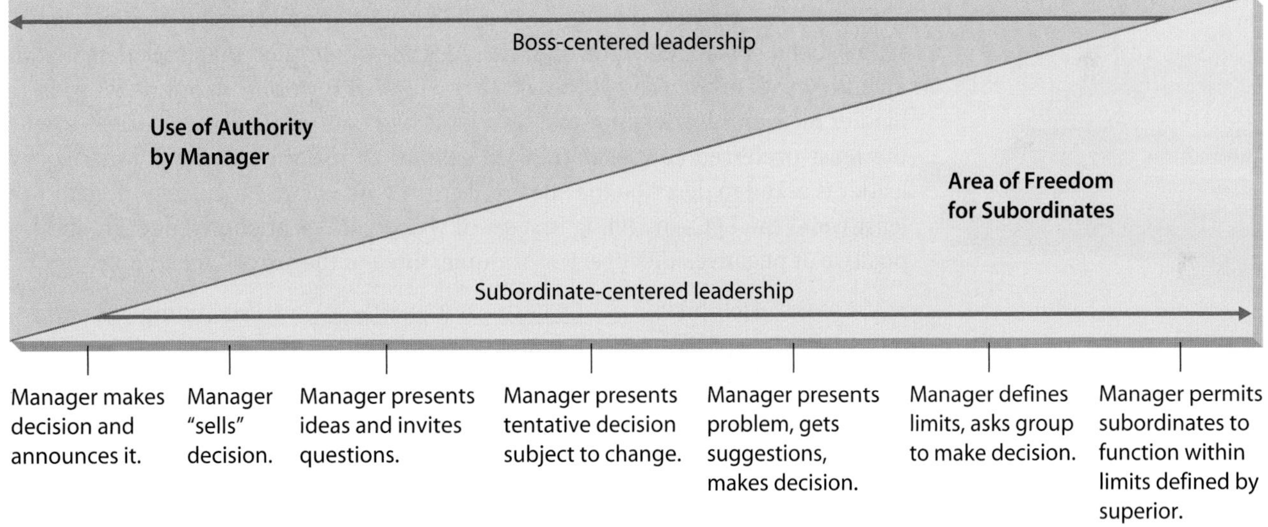

FIGURE 17.2

Tannenbaum and Schmidt's Leadership Continuum

The Tannenbaum and Schmidt leadership continuum was an important precursor to modern situational approaches to leadership. The continuum identifies seven levels of leadership, which range between the extremes of boss-centered and subordinate-centered leadership.

Source: Reprinted by permission of the *Harvard Business Review*. An exhibit from "How to Choose a Leadership Pattern" by Robert Tannenbaum and Warren Schmidt (May–June 1973).

This continuum of behavior moves from one extreme, of having the manager make the decision alone, to the other extreme, of having the employees make the decision with minimal guidance. Each point on the continuum is influenced by characteristics of the manager, the subordinates, and the situation. Managerial characteristics include the manager's value system, confidence in subordinates, personal inclinations, and feelings of security. Subordinate characteristics include the subordinates' need for independence, readiness to assume responsibility, tolerance for ambiguity, interest in the problem, understanding of goals, knowledge, experience, and expectations. Situational characteristics that affect decision making include the type of organization, group effectiveness, the problem itself, and time pressures. Although this framework pointed out the importance of situational factors, it was only speculative. It remained for others to develop more comprehensive and integrated theories. In the following sections, we describe four of the most important and widely accepted situational theories of leadership: the LPC theory, the path-goal theory, Vroom's decision tree approach, and the leader-member exchange approach.

LPC Theory

LPC theory A theory of leadership that suggests that the appropriate style of leadership varies with situational favorableness

The **LPC theory**, developed by Fred Fiedler, was the first truly situational theory of leadership.[17] As we will discuss later, LPC stands for least-preferred coworker. Beginning with a combined trait and behavioral approach, Fiedler identified two styles of leadership: task oriented (analogous to job-centered and initiating-structure behavior) and relationship oriented (similar to employee-centered and consideration behavior). He went beyond the earlier behavioral approaches by arguing that the style of behavior is a reflection of the leader's personality and that most personalities fall into one of his two categories—task oriented or relationship oriented by nature. Fiedler measures leadership style by means of a controversial questionnaire called the **least-preferred coworker (LPC) measure**. To use the measure, a manager or leader is asked to describe the specific person with whom he or she is able to work least well—the LPC—by filling in a set of sixteen scales anchored at each end by a positive or negative adjective. For example, three of the sixteen scales are:

least-preferred coworker (LPC) measure The measuring scale that asks leaders to describe the person with whom he or she is able to work least well

Helpful	___	___	___	___	___	___	___	___	Frustrating
	8	7	6	5	4	3	2	1	
Tense	___	___	___	___	___	___	___	___	Relaxed
	1	2	3	4	5	6	7	8	
Boring	___	___	___	___	___	___	___	___	Interesting
	1	2	3	4	5	6	7	8	

The leader's LPC score is then calculated by adding up the numbers below the line checked on each scale. Note in these three examples that the higher numbers are associated with positive qualities (helpful, relaxed, and interesting), whereas the negative qualities (frustrating, tense, and boring) have low point values. A high total score is assumed to reflect a relationship orientation and a low score a task orientation on the part of the leader. The LPC measure is controversial because researchers disagree about its validity. Some question exactly what an LPC measure reflects and whether the score is an index of behavior, personality, or some other factor.[18]

Favorableness of the Situation The underlying assumption of situational models of leadership is that appropriate leader behavior varies from one situation to another. According to Fiedler, the key situational factor is the favorableness of the situation from the leader's point of view. This factor is determined by leader-member relations, task structure, and position power. *Leader-member relations* refer to the nature of the relationship between the leader and the work group. If the leader and the group have a high degree of mutual trust, respect, and confidence, and if they like one another, relations are assumed to be good. If there is little trust, respect, or confidence, and if they do not like one another, relations are poor. Naturally, good relations are more favorable.

Task structure is the degree to which the group's task is well defined. The task is structured when it is routine, easily understood, and unambiguous, and when the group has standard procedures and precedents to rely on. An unstructured task is nonroutine, ambiguous, and complex, with no standard procedures or precedents. You can see that high structure is more favorable for the leader, whereas low structure is less favorable. For example, if the task is unstructured, the group will not know what to do, and the leader will have to play a major role in guiding and directing its activities. If the task is structured, the leader will not have to get so involved and can devote time to nonsupervisory activities.

Position power is the power vested in the leader's position. If the leader has the power to assign work and to reward and punish employees, position power is assumed to be strong. But, if the leader must get job assignments approved by someone else and does not administer rewards and punishment, position power is weak, and it is more difficult to accomplish goals. From the leader's point of view, strong position power is clearly preferable to weak position power. However, position power is not as important as task structure and leader-member relations.

Favorableness and Leader Style Fiedler and his associates conducted numerous studies linking the favorableness of various situations to leader style and the effectiveness of the group.[19] The results of these studies—and the overall framework of the theory—are shown in Figure 17.3. To interpret the model, look first at the situational factors at the top of the figure. Good or bad leader-member relations, high or low task structure, and strong or weak leader position power can be combined to yield six unique situations. For example, good leader-member relations, high task structure, and strong leader position power (at the far left) are presumed to define the most favorable situation; bad leader-member relations, low task structure, and weak leader power (at the far right) are the least favorable. The other combinations reflect intermediate levels of favorableness.

Below each set of situations are shown the degree of favorableness and the form of leader behavior found to be most strongly associated with effective group performance for those situations. When the situation is most and least favorable, Fiedler found that a task-oriented leader is most effective. When the situation is only moderately favorable, however, a relationship-oriented leader is predicted to be most effective.

Flexibility of Leader Style Fiedler argued that, for any given individual, leader style is essentially fixed and cannot be changed; leaders cannot change their behavior

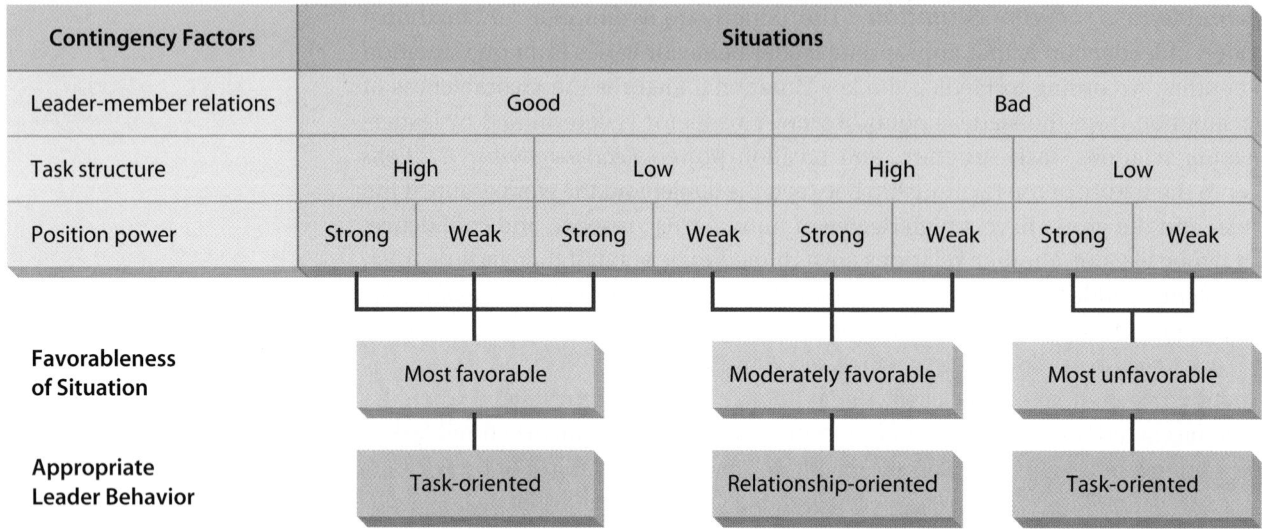

FIGURE 17.3

The Least-preferred Coworker Theory of Leadership

Fiedler's LPC theory of leadership suggests that appropriate leader behavior varies as a function of the favorableness of the situation. Favorableness, in turn, is defined by task structure, leader-member relations, and the leader's position power. According to the LPC theory, the most and least favorable situations call for task-oriented leadership, whereas moderately favorable situations suggest the need for relationship-oriented leadership.

to fit a particular situation because it is linked to their particular personality traits. Thus, when a leader's style and the situation do not match, Fiedler argued that the situation should be changed to fit the leader's style. When leader-member relations are good, task structure low, and position power weak, the leader style that is most likely to be effective is relationship oriented. If the leader is task oriented, a mismatch exists. According to Fiedler, the leader can make the elements of the situation more congruent by structuring the task (by developing guidelines and procedures, for instance) and increasing power (by requesting additional authority or by other means).

Fiedler's contingency theory has been attacked on the grounds that it is not always supported by research, that his findings are subject to other interpretations, that the LPC measure lacks validity, and that his assumptions about the inflexibility of leader behavior are unrealistic.[20] However, Fiedler's theory was one of the first to adopt a situational perspective on leadership. It has helped many managers recognize the important situational factors they must contend with, and it has fostered additional thinking about the situational nature of leadership. Moreover, in recent years Fiedler has attempted to address some of the concerns about his theory by revising it and adding such additional elements as cognitive resources.

path-goal theory A theory of leadership suggesting that the primary functions of a leader are to make valued or desired rewards available in the workplace and to clarify for the subordinate the kinds of behavior that will lead to those rewards

Path-Goal Theory

The **path-goal theory** of leadership—associated most closely with Martin Evans and Robert House—is a direct extension of the expectancy theory of motivation discussed in Chapter 14.[21] Recall that the primary components of expectancy theory included the likelihood of attaining various outcomes and the value associated with those outcomes. The path-goal theory of leadership suggests that the primary functions of a leader are to make valued or desired rewards available in the workplace and to clarify for the subordinate the kinds of behavior that will lead to goal accomplishment and valued rewards—that is, the leader should clarify the paths to goal attainment.

The path-goal theory is an important situational model of leadership. Mari Matsunaga is a good example of a leader who has successfully used the path-goal theory. She designed I-mode, an astonishingly successful mobile-phone Internet service provided by NTT and which is today among the world's largest mobile-phone companies. Ms. Matsunaga found it necessary to adopt a variety of leadership styles as she dealt with old-line technical engineers, modern consumers, and government bureaucrats, and she had to constantly account for a variety of environmental characteristics as she developed her new enterprise.

Leader Behavior The most fully developed version of path-goal theory identifies four kinds of leader behavior. *Directive leader behavior* lets subordinates know what is expected of them, gives guidance and direction, and schedules work. *Supportive leader behavior* is being friendly and approachable, showing concern for subordinate welfare, and treating members as equals. *Participative leader behavior* includes consulting with subordinates, soliciting suggestions, and allowing participation in decision making. *Achievement-oriented leader* behavior means setting challenging goals, expecting subordinates to perform at high levels, encouraging subordinates, and showing confidence in subordinates' abilities.

In contrast to Fiedler's theory, path-goal theory assumes that leaders can change their style or behavior to meet the demands of a particular situation. For example, when encountering a new group of subordinates and a new project, the leader may be directive in establishing work procedures and in outlining what needs to be done. Next, the leader may adopt supportive behavior to foster group cohesiveness and a positive climate. As the group becomes familiar with the task and as new problems are encountered, the leader may exhibit participative behavior to enhance group members' motivation. Finally, achievement-oriented behavior may be used to encourage continued high performance.

Situational Factors Like other situational theories of leadership, path-goal theory suggests that appropriate leader style depends on situational factors. Path-goal theory focuses on the situational factors of the personal characteristics of subordinates and environmental characteristics of the workplace.

Important personal characteristics include the subordinates' perception of their own ability and their locus of control. If people perceive that they are lacking in ability, they may prefer directive leadership to help them understand path-goal relationships better. If they perceive themselves to have a lot of ability, however, employees may resent directive leadership. Locus of control is a personality trait. People who have an internal locus of control believe that what happens to them is a function of their own efforts and behavior. Those who have an external locus of control assume that fate, luck, or "the system" determines what happens to them. A person with an internal locus of control may prefer participative leadership, whereas a person with an external locus of control may prefer directive leadership.

Most effective leaders demonstrate sincere interest in the personal welfare of their followers. This interest can extend to concern about their family and personal life as well. When the interest is real, employees may feel more valued and appreciated by their leader and develop stronger job satisfaction and dedication. But, if the leader's interest is superficial and is an obvious ploy to show interest, employees will likely see what is going on and come to resent and lose respect for the leader.

DILBERT reprinted by permission of United Feature Syndicate, Inc.

Managers can do little or nothing to influence the personal characteristics of subordinates, but they can shape the environment to take advantage of these personal characteristics by, for example, providing rewards and structuring tasks.

Environmental characteristics include factors outside the subordinates' control. Task structure is one such factor. When structure is high, directive leadership is less effective than when structure is low. Subordinates do not usually need their boss to continually tell them how to do an extremely routine job. The formal authority system is another important environmental characteristic. Again, the higher the degree of formality, the less directive is the leader behavior that will be accepted by subordinates. The nature of the work group also affects appropriate leader behavior. When the work group provides the employee with social support and satisfaction, supportive leader behavior is less critical. When social support and satisfaction cannot be derived from the group, the worker may look to the leader for this support.

The basic path-goal framework as illustrated in Figure 17.4 shows that different leader behaviors affect subordinates' motivation to perform. Personal and environmental characteristics are seen as defining which behaviors lead to which outcomes. The path-goal theory of leadership is a dynamic and incomplete model. The original intent was to state the theory in general terms so that future research could explore a variety of interrelationships and modify the theory. Research that has been done suggests that the path-goal theory is a reasonably good description of the leadership process and that future investigations along these lines should enable us to discover more about the link between leadership and motivation.[22]

Vroom's decision tree approach Predicts what kinds of situations call for different degrees of group participation

Vroom's Decision Tree Approach

The third major contemporary approach to leadership is **Vroom's decision tree approach**. The earliest version of this model was proposed by Victor Vroom and

FIGURE 17.4

The Path-Goal Framework

The path-goal theory of leadership suggests that managers can use four types of leader behavior to clarify subordinates' paths to goal attainment. Personal characteristics of the subordinate and environmental characteristics within the organization both must be taken into account when determining which style of leadership will work best for a particular situation.

Philip Yetton and later revised and expanded by Vroom and Arthur Jago.[23] Most recently, Vroom has developed yet another refinement of the original model.[24] Like the path-goal theory, this approach attempts to prescribe a leadership style appropriate to a given situation. It also assumes that the same leader may display different leadership styles. But Vroom's approach concerns itself with only a single aspect of leader behavior: subordinate participation in decision making.

Basic Premises Vroom's decision tree approach assumes that the degree to which subordinates should be encouraged to participate in decision making depends on the characteristics of the situation. In other words, no one decision-making process is best for all situations. After evaluating a variety of problem attributes (characteristics of the problem or decision), the leader determines an appropriate decision style that specifies the amount of subordinate participation.

Vroom's current formulation suggests that managers use one of two different decision trees.[25] To do so, the manager first assesses the situation in terms of several factors. This assessment involves determining whether the given factor is high or low for the decision that is to be made. For instance, the first factor is decision significance. If the decision is extremely important and may have a major impact on the organization (such as choosing a location for a new plant), its significance is high. But, if the decision is routine and its consequences are not terribly important (selecting a color for the firm's softball team uniforms), its significance is low. This assessment guides the manager through the paths of the decision tree to a recommended course of action. One decision tree is to be used when the manager is interested primarily in making the decision as quickly as possible; the other is to be used when time is less critical and the manager is interested in helping subordinates to improve and develop their own decision-making skills.

The two decision trees are shown in Figures 17.5 and 17.6. The problem attributes (situational factors) are arranged along the top of the decision tree. To use the model, the decision maker starts at the left side of the diagram and assesses the first problem attribute (decision significance). The answer determines the path to the second node on the decision tree, where the next attribute (importance of commitment) is assessed. This process continues until a terminal node is reached. In this way, the manager identifies an effective decision-making style for the situation.

FIGURE 17.5

Vroom's Time-driven Decision Tree

This matrix is recommended for situations where time is of the highest importance in making a decision. The matrix operates like a funnel. You start at the left with a specific decision problem in mind. The column headings denote situational factors that may or may not be present in that problem. You progress by selecting high or low (H or L) for each relevant situational factor. Proceed down the funnel, judging only those situational factors for which a judgment is called, until you reach the recommended process.

Source: Adapted and reprinted by permission from *Leadership and Decision-Makings*, by Victor H. Vroom and Philip W. Yetton, by permission of the University of Pittsburgh Press. Copyright © 1973 by University of Pittsburgh Press.

PROBLEM STATEMENT	Decision Significance	Importance of Commitment	Leader Expertise	Likelihood of Commitment	Group Support	Group Expertise	Team Competence	
	H	H	H	H	—	—	—	Decide
				L	H	H	H	Delegate
							L	Consult (group)
						L	—	
					L	—	—	
			L	H	H	H	H	Facilitate
							L	Consult (individually)
						L	—	
					L	—	—	
				L	H	H	H	Facilitate
							L	Consult (group)
						L	—	
					L	—	—	
		L	H	—	—	—	—	Decide
			L	—	H	H	H	Facilitate
							L	Consult (individually)
						L	—	
					L	—	—	
	L	H	—	H	—	—	—	Decide
				L	—	—	H	Delegate
							L	Facilitate
		L	—	—	—	—	—	Decide

Decision-Making Styles The various decision styles reflected at the ends of the tree branches represent different levels of subordinate participation that the manager should attempt to adopt in a given situation. The five styles are defined as follows:

- *Decide.* The manager makes the decision alone and then announces or "sells" it to the group.
- *Consult (individually).* The manager presents the program to group members individually, obtains their suggestions, and then makes the decision.
- *Consult (group).* The manager presents the problem to group members at a meeting, gets their suggestions, and then makes the decision.
- *Facilitate.* The manager presents the problem to the group at a meeting, defines the problem and its boundaries, and then facilitates group member discussion as they make the decision.
- *Delegate.* The manager allows the group to define for itself the exact nature and parameters of the problem and then to develop a solution.

PROBLEM STATEMENT	Decision Significance	Importance of Commitment	Leader Expertise	Likelihood of Commitment	Group Support	Group Expertise	Team Competence	
	H	H	—	H	H	H	H	**Decide**
							L	**Facilitate**
						L	—	**Consult (group)**
					L	—	—	
				L	H	H	H	**Delegate**
							L	**Facilitate**
						L	—	
					L	—	—	**Consult (group)**
		L	—	—	H	H	H	**Delegate**
							L	**Facilitate**
						L	—	**Consult (group)**
					L	—	—	
	L	H	—	H	—	—	—	**Decide**
				L	—	—	—	**Delegate**
		L	—	—	—	—	—	**Decide**

FIGURE 17.6

Vroom's Development-driven Decision Tree

This matrix is to be used when the leader is more interested in developing employees than in making the decision as quickly as possible. Just as with the time-driven tree shown in Figure 17.5, the leader assesses up to seven situational factors. These factors, in turn, funnel the leader to a recommended process for making the decision.

Source: Adapted and reprinted by permission from *Leadership and Decision-Makings*, by Victor H. Vroom and Philip W. Yetton, by permission of the University of Pittsburgh Press. Copyright © 1973 by University of Pittsburgh Press.

Vroom's decision tree approach represents a very focused but quite complex perspective on leadership. To compensate for this difficulty, Vroom has developed elaborate expert system software to help managers assess a situation accurately and quickly and then to make an appropriate decision regarding employee participation.[26] Many firms, including Halliburton Company, Litton Industries, and Borland International, have provided their managers with training in how to use the various versions of this model.

Evaluation and Implications Because Vroom's current approach is relatively new, it has not been fully scientifically tested. The original model and its subsequent refinement, however, attracted a great deal of attention and generally was supported by research.[27] For example, there is some support for the idea that individuals who make decisions consistent with the predictions of the model are more effective than those who make decisions inconsistent with it. The model therefore appears to be a tool that managers can apply with some confidence in deciding how much subordinates should participate in the decision-making process.

The Leader-Member Exchange Approach

Because leadership is such an important area, managers and researchers continue to study it. As a result, new ideas, theories, and perspectives are continuously being developed. The **leader-member exchange (LMX) model** of leadership, conceived by George Graen and Fred Dansereau, stresses the importance of variable relationships

leader-member exchange (LMX) model Stresses that leaders have different kinds of relationships with different subordinates

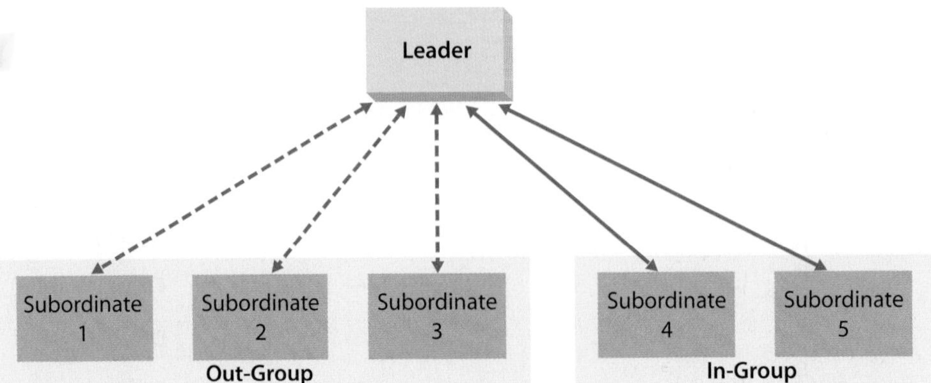

FIGURE 17.7

The Leader-Member Exchange (LMX) Model

The LMX model suggests that leaders form unique independent relationships with each of their subordinates. As illustrated here, a key factor in the nature of this relationship is whether the individual subordinate is in the leader's out-group or in-group.

between supervisors and each of their subordinates.[28] Each superior-subordinate pair is referred to as a "vertical dyad." The model differs from earlier approaches in that it focuses on the differential relationship leaders often establish with different subordinates. Figure 17.7 shows the basic concepts of the leader-member exchange theory.

The model suggests that supervisors establish a special relationship with a small number of trusted subordinates, referred to as "the in-group." The in-group usually receives special duties requiring responsibility and autonomy; they may also receive special privileges. Subordinates who are not a part of this group are called "the out-group," and they receive less of the supervisor's time and attention. Note in the figure that the leader has a dyadic, or one-to-one, relationship with each of the five subordinates.

Early in his or her interaction with a given subordinate, the supervisor initiates either an in-group or an out-group relationship. It is not clear how a leader selects members of the in-group, but the decision may be based on personal compatibility and subordinates' competence. Research has confirmed the existence of in-groups and out-groups. In addition, studies generally have found that in-group members have a higher level of performance and satisfaction than do out-group members.[29]

concept CHECK

Summarize the essential elements of each of the situational approaches to leadership.

Which situational approach do you think is most useful and which the least useful for managers in organizations?

Related Approaches to Leadership

Because of its importance to organizational effectiveness, leadership continues to be the focus of a great deal of research and theory building. New approaches that have attracted much attention are the concepts of substitutes for leadership and transformational leadership.

Substitutes for Leadership

The concept of **substitutes for leadership** was developed because existing leadership models and theories do not account for situations in which leadership is not needed.[30] They simply try to specify what kind of leader behavior is appropriate. The substitutes concept, however, identifies situations in which leader behaviors are neutralized or replaced by characteristics of the subordinate, the task, and the organization. For example, when a patient is delivered to a hospital emergency room, the professionals on duty do not wait to be told what to do by a leader. Nurses, doctors, and attendants all go into action without waiting for directive or supportive leader behavior from the emergency room supervisor.

substitutes for leadership A concept that identifies situations in which leader behaviors are neutralized or replaced by characteristics of subordinates, the task, and the organization

Characteristics of the subordinate that may serve to neutralize leader behavior include ability, experience, need for independence, professional orientation, and indifference toward organizational rewards. For example, employees with a high level of ability and experience may not need to be told what to do. Similarly, a subordinate's strong need for independence may render leader behavior ineffective. Task characteristics that may substitute for leadership include routineness, the availability of feedback, and intrinsic satisfaction. When the job is routine and simple, the subordinate may not need direction. When the task is challenging and intrinsically satisfying, the subordinate may not need or want social support from a leader.

charismatic leadership Assumes that charisma is an individual characteristic of the leader

charisma A form of interpersonal attraction that inspires support and acceptance

Organizational characteristics that may substitute for leadership include formalization, group cohesion, inflexibility, and a rigid reward structure. Leadership may not be necessary when policies and practices are formal and inflexible, for example. Similarly, a rigid reward system may rob the leader of reward power and thereby decrease the importance of the role. Preliminary research has provided support for the concept of substitutes for leadership.[31]

Charismatic Leadership

The concept of **charismatic leadership**, like trait theories, assumes that charisma is an individual characteristic of the leader. **Charisma** is a form of interpersonal attraction that inspires support and acceptance. All else being equal, then, someone with charisma is more likely to be able to influence others than is someone without charisma. For example, a highly charismatic supervisor will be more successful in influencing subordinate behavior than a supervisor who lacks charisma. Thus influence is again a fundamental element of this perspective.

Robert House first proposed a theory of charismatic leadership in 1977, based on research findings from a variety of social science disciplines.[32] His theory suggests that charismatic leaders are

Phil Jackson is considered to be one of the top coaches in the National Basketball Association, having won world championships first with the Chicago Bulls and more recently with the Los Angeles Lakers. One key to his success is his personal charisma. Jackson is able to simultaneously command both the respect and the affection of his players. This rare combination allows him to channel and direct the energies of players toward the singular goal of winning basketball games, putting aside personal goals and petty differences of opinion.

likely to have a lot of self-confidence, a firm conviction in their beliefs and ideals, and a strong need to influence people. They also tend to communicate high expectations about follower performance and express confidence in followers. Donald Trump is an excellent example of a charismatic leader. Even though he has made his share of mistakes and generally is perceived as only an "average" manager, many people view him as larger than life.[33]

There are three elements of charismatic leadership in organizations that most experts acknowledge today.[34] First, the leader needs to be able to envision the future, set high expectations, and model behaviors consistent with meeting those expectations. Next, the charismatic leader must be able to energize others through a demonstration of personal excitement, personal confidence, and patterns of success. And, finally, the charismatic leader enables others by supporting them, empathizing with them, and expressing confidence in them.

Charismatic leadership ideas are quite popular among managers today and are the subject of numerous books and articles. Unfortunately, few studies have attempted to specifically test the meaning and impact of charismatic leadership. There are also lingering ethical issues about charismatic leadership, however, that trouble some people. For instance, President Bill Clinton was a charismatic leader. But some of his critics argued that this very charisma caused his supporters to overlook his flaws and to minimize some of his indiscretions.

Transformational Leadership

transformational leadership Leadership that goes beyond ordinary expectations by transmitting a sense of mission, stimulating learning experiences, and inspiring new ways of thinking

Another new perspective on leadership has been called by a number of labels: charismatic leadership, inspirational leadership, symbolic leadership, and transformational leadership. We use the term **transformational leadership** and define it as leadership that goes beyond ordinary expectations by transmitting a sense of mission, stimulating learning experiences, and inspiring new ways of thinking.[35] Because of rapid change and turbulent environments, transformational leaders are increasingly being seen as vital to the success of business.

A recent article in the popular press identified seven keys to successful leadership: trusting one's subordinates, developing a vision, keeping cool, encouraging risk, being an expert, inviting dissent, and simplifying things.[36] Although this list was the result of a simplistic survey of the leadership literature, it is nevertheless consistent with the premises underlying transformational leadership. So, too, are recent examples cited as effective leadership. Take the case of 3M. The firm's new CEO is working to make the firm more efficient and profitable while simultaneously keeping its leadership role in new product innovation. He has also changed the reward system, overhauled procedures, and restructured the entire firm. And so far, at least, analysts have applauded these changes.[37] *Working with Diversity* presents another interesting example.

concept CHECK

What are leadership substitutes? What specific substitutes might work in a classroom setting?

Identify a person you would consider to be a charismatic leader and describe why the person fits the definition.

WORKING WITH diversity

The Dragon Lady of TruServ

"... it doesn't matter what the gender of the [CEO] is, as long as they can be successful."

– Pamela Forbes Lieberman, CEO, TruServ*

When subordinates referred to Pamela Forbes Lieberman as a "dragon lady," she did not get mad. She hung a painting of a dragon in her office. In 2001 Lieberman assumed the top spot in the TruServ hardware cooperative, becoming the first woman to head the firm. Her no-nonsense style helped her overcome the "good ol' boy" attitude at TruServ. "In a turnaround situation, it doesn't matter what the gender of the person is, as long as they can be successful," Lieberman claims.

Forty-eight-year-old Lieberman joined TruServ as CFO in February of 2001. Prior to that, she earned an MBA from Northwestern, worked for Pricewaterhouse for thirteen years, and held management positions in distribution and manufacturing firms. TruServ board members quickly realized the depth of her experience and ability, and she was promoted to COO in July 2001 and to CEO in November.

TruServ was on the verge of bankruptcy, with spiraling debt, top-heavy and outdated management, poorly performing locations, and too much inventory. The Securities and Exchange Commission was investigating TruServ for sloppy record keeping. Lieberman was assured by former CEO Donald Hoye that the firm could cover its debt obligations, but after taking the job she learned they had already missed scheduled payments.

Lieberman began a turnaround that included divestiture of the company's unprofitable Canadian stores. She slashed expenses. Lieberman says, "I don't think [the firm] really understood the changes in the economy, as well as members' buying patterns, and they didn't cut costs fast enough." She earned a reputation as a stern taskmaster, saying, "If [employees] succeed, then they will be rewarded, but if they don't, then we're going to have to look for new people sitting in their chairs." Her frankness helped to rebuild TruServ's reputation.

So far, the restructuring is working. Debt and inventory are down, as is payroll expense. TruServ met SEC filing requirements in August 2002. However, the co-op's membership has fallen from more than 8,000 in 1998 to 6,700 today, and Lieberman expects more stores to leave. She is visiting owners to persuade them to be patient. She tells them, "There is nothing so broken here it can't be fixed."

References: "Hardlines Buying Groups Analysis: TruServ Corp.," *Home Channel News*, www.homechannelnews.com on February 9, 2003; Ian Mount and Brian Caulfield, "The Missing Link: What You Need to Know About Supply-Chain Technology," *Business 2.0*, May 2001, www.business2.com on February 9, 2003; Jo Napolitano, "No, She Doesn't Breathe Fire," *New York Times*, September 1, 2002, p. BU2 (*quote); "Pamela Forbes Lieberman Elected CEO of TruServ Corporation," "TruServ Names New CEO," "TruServ Names New Chief Financial Officer," TruServ press releases, www.truserv.com on February 9, 2003.

Emerging Approaches to Leadership

Recently, three potentially very important new approaches to leadership have emerged. One is called "strategic leadership"; the others deal with cross-cultural leadership and ethical leadership.

strategic leadership The capability to understand the complexities of both the organization and its environment and to lead change in the organization in order to achieve and maintain a superior alignment between the organization and its environment

Strategic Leadership

Strategic leadership is a new concept that explicitly relates leadership to the role of top management. We will define **strategic leadership** as the capability to understand the complexities of both the organization and its environment and to lead change in the organization in order to achieve and maintain a superior alignment between the organization and its environment. This definition reflects an integration of the leadership concepts covered in this chapter with our discussion of strategic management in Chapter 8.

To be effective in this role, a manager needs to have a thorough and complete understanding of the organization—its history, its culture, its strengths, and its weaknesses. In addition, the leader needs a firm grasp of the organization's environment. This understanding must encompass current conditions and circumstances as well as significant trends and issues on the horizon. The strategic leader also needs to recognize how the firm is currently aligned with its environment—where it relates effectively and where it relates less effectively with that environment. Finally, looking at environmental trends and issues, the strategic leader works to improve both the current alignment and the future alignment.

Andrea Jung (CEO of Avon Products), Fujio Cho (CEO of Toyota), Michael Dell (founder and CEO of Dell Computer), and A.G. Lafley (CEO of Procter & Gamble) have all been recognized as strong strategic leaders. Reflecting on his dramatic turnaround at Procter & Gamble, for instance, Lafley commented, "I have made a lot of symbolic, very physical changes so people understand we are in the business of leading change." On the other hand, Sandy Weill (CEO of Citigroup), Dick Brown (CEO of Electronic Data Systems), and Peter Dolan (CEO of Bristol-Myers Squibb) have been cited as less effective strategic leaders. Dolan, for instance, took over in May 2001 and managed to cut the Bristol-Myers Squibb stock price in half in less than two years.[38]

Cross-Cultural Leadership

Another new approach to leadership is based on cross-cultural issues. In this context, culture is used as a broad concept to encompass both international differences and diversity-based differences within one culture. For instance, when a Japanese firm sends an executive to head the firm's operations in the United States, that person will need to become acclimated to the cultural differences that exist between the two countries and to change his or her leadership style accordingly. As noted in Chapter 5, Japan is generally characterized by collectivism, whereas the United States is based more on individualism. The Japanese executive, then, will find it necessary to recognize the importance of individual contributions and rewards, as well as the differences in individual and group roles, that exist in Japanese and U.S. businesses.

Similarly, cross-cultural factors play a growing role in organizations as their workforce becomes more and more diverse. Most leadership research, for instance, has been conducted on samples or case studies involving white male leaders (until several years ago most business leaders were white males). But, as more females, African-Americans, and Latinos achieve leadership positions, it may be necessary to reassess how applicable current theories and models of leadership are when applied to an increasingly diverse pool of leaders.

Ethical Leadership

Most people have long assumed that top managers are ethical people. But, in the wake of recent corporate scandals, faith in top managers has been shaken. To

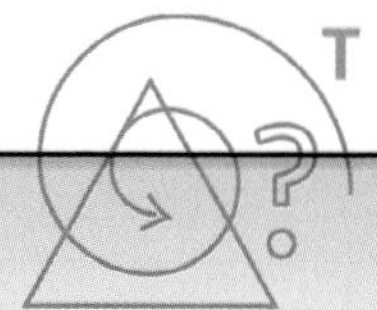

THE BUSINESS OF ethics

"Mamas, Don't Let Your Babies Grow up to Be CEOs"

"I know you're trying to drive the stock price down, and you've done a pretty good job of it."

– Ken Lay, former CEO, Enron, to a stock analyst*

CEOs used to be our heroes. In the heady business expansion of the 1990s, corporate leaders became the new celebrities, wealthy and powerful, and able to create wealth for others. Jack Welch, former CEO of GE, was revered for his management wisdom, as were Disney's Michael Eisner, Jacques Nasser of Ford, and others. But, as a result of recent corporate scandals, CEOs have fallen from grace. Today they are on the receiving end of unkind jokes and shareholder lawsuits. Here are some of their tactics.

Stonewalling Jeffrey Skilling, former CEO of Enron, testified to Congress that people "have a right to know what happened. I have not exercised my rights to refuse to answer a single question." Skilling then answered, "I do not recall," twenty-six times. When Martha Stewart was asked by a guest on her television show about her possible use of insider information, she responded, "I want to focus on my salad."

Lying Clerical staff members at Enron were asked to impersonate energy traders during a visit from Wall Street analysts. WorldCom improperly accounted for $3.8 billion in expenses, and Qwest did the same for $1 billion in revenues.

Blaming Enron's former CEO, Ken Lay, answering an analyst's question about trouble at the firm, replied, "I know you're trying to drive the stock price down, and you've done a pretty good job of it." Qwest CEO Joseph Nacchio responded to rumors of reporting problems by saying, "Analysts who believe [the rumors] need to go back to school and learn accounting. My job isn't to educate the analysts. . . . Morgan Stanley analysts maybe aren't the sharpest knives in the drawer either."

Countersuing When all else fails, CEOs respond with counter-lawsuits, such as Leo Hindery's claim against Global Crossing. The ex-CEO is suing the now-bankrupt firm for over $100,000 a month in promised benefits. Meanwhile, the firm owes $12.4 billion to creditors.

The government has adopted or is considering numerous regulatory changes to reform some of the worst problems. But no reform can guard against wily and dogged crooks, just as no security system can stop a determined burglar. The dilemma remains: Who will be our heroes now that CEOs have lost our faith? Here is at least one vote for whistle blowers.

References: Jerry Useem, "From Heroes to Goats . . . and Back Again?" *Fortune*, November 18, 2002, www.fortune.com on December 2, 2002; Joseph Nocera, "Of Fame and Fortune," *Fortune*, November 18, 2002, www.fortune.com on December 2, 2002; Joseph Nocera, "System Failure," *Fortune*, June 9, 2002, www.fortune.com on January 10, 2003; Tim Carvell, "Let Us Now Braise Famous Men," *Fortune*, November 18, 2002, pp. 135–140 (*quote p. 136).

illustrate this point, see *The Business of Ethics.* Perhaps now more than ever, high standards of ethical conduct are being held up as a prerequisite for effective leadership. More specifically, top managers are being called upon to maintain high ethical standards for their own conduct, to exhibit ethical behavior unfailingly, and to hold others in their organization to the same standards.

The behaviors of top leaders are being scrutinized more than ever, and those responsible for hiring new leaders for a business are looking more and more closely at the background of those being considered. And the emerging pressures for stronger corporate governance models are likely to further increase commitment to selecting only those individuals with high ethical standards and to hold them more accountable than in the past for both their actions and the consequences of those actions.[39]

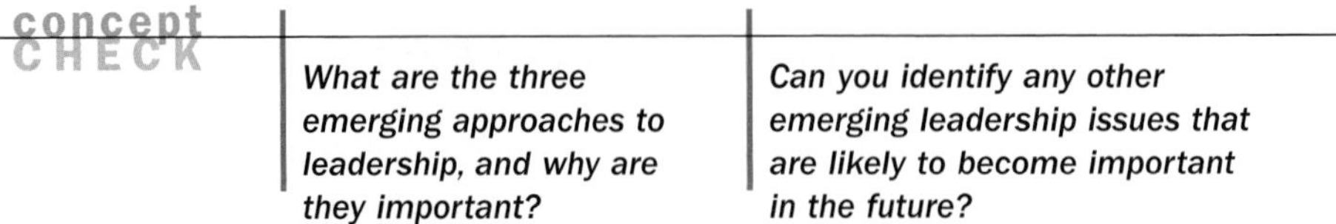

Political Behavior in Organizations

political behavior The activities carried out for the specific purpose of acquiring, developing, and using power and other resources to obtain one's preferred outcomes

Another common influence on behavior is politics and political behavior. **Political behavior** describes activities carried out for the specific purpose of acquiring, developing, and using power and other resources to obtain one's preferred outcomes.[40] Political behavior may be undertaken by managers dealing with their subordinates, subordinates dealing with their managers, and managers and subordinates dealing with others at the same level. In other words, it may be directed upward, downward, or laterally. Decisions ranging from where to locate a manufacturing plant to where to put the company coffee maker are subject to political action. In any situation, individuals may engage in political behavior to further their own ends, to protect themselves from others, to further goals they sincerely believe to be in the organization's best interests, or simply to acquire and exercise power. And power may be sought by individuals, by groups of individuals, or by groups of groups.[41]

Although political behavior is difficult to study because of its sensitive nature, one early survey found that many managers believed that politics influenced salary and hiring decisions in their firm. Many also believed that the incidence of political behavior was greater at the upper levels of their organization and lesser at the lower levels. More than half of the respondents felt that organizational politics was bad, unfair, unhealthy, and irrational, but most suggested that successful executives have to be good politicians and be political to get ahead.[42]

Common Political Behaviors

Research has identified four basic forms of political behavior widely practiced in organizations.[43] One form is *inducement,* which occurs when a manager offers to give something to someone else in return for that individual's support. For example, a product manager might suggest to another product manager that she will put in a good word with his boss if he supports a new marketing plan that she has developed. By most accounts, former WorldCom CEO Bernard Ebbers made frequent use of this tactic to retain his leadership position in the company. For example, he allowed board members to use the corporate jet whenever they wanted and invested heavily in their pet projects.

A second tactic is *persuasion,* which relies on both emotion and logic. An operations manager wanting to construct a new plant on a certain site might persuade others to support his goal on grounds that are objective and logical (is less expensive; taxes are lower) as well as subjective and personal. Bernard Ebbers also used this approach. For instance, when one board member attempted to remove him from his position, he worked behind the scenes to persuade the majority of board members to allow him to stay on.

A third political behavior involves the *creation of an obligation*. For example, one manager might support a recommendation made by another manager for a new advertising campaign. Although he might really have no opinion on the new campaign, he might think that, by going along, he is incurring a debt from the other manager and will be able to "call in" that debt when he wants to get something done and needs additional support. Bernard Ebbers loaned WorldCom board members money, for example, but then forgave the loans in exchange for their continued support.

Coercion is the use of force to get one's way. For example, a manager may threaten to withhold support, rewards, or other resources as a way to influence someone else. This, too, was a common tactic used by Bernard Ebbers. He reportedly belittled any board member who dared question him, for example. In the words of one former director, "Ebbers treated you like a prince—as long as you never forgot who was king."[44]

Impression Management

Impression management is a subtle form of political behavior which deserves special mention. **Impression management** is a direct and intentional effort by someone to enhance his or her image in the eyes of others. People engage in impression management for a variety of reasons. For one thing, they may do so in order to further their own career. By making themselves look good, they think they are more likely to receive rewards, to be given attractive job assignments, and to receive promotions. They may also engage in impression management in order to boost their self-esteem. When people have a solid image in an organization, others make them aware of it through compliments, respect, and so forth. Still another reason people use impression management is in an effort to acquire more power and hence more control.

impression management A direct and intentional effort by someone to enhance his or her image in the eyes of others

People attempt to manage how others perceive them through a variety of mechanisms. Appearance is one of the first things people think of. Hence, a person motivated by impression management will pay close attention to choice of attire, selection of language, and use of manners and body posture. People interested in impression management are also likely to jockey for association only with successful projects. By being assigned to high-profile projects led by highly successful managers, a person can begin to link his or her own name with such projects in the minds of others.

Sometimes people too strongly motivated by impression management become obsessed with it and may resort to dishonest or unethical means. For example, some people have been known to take credit for others' work in an effort to make themselves look better. People have also been known to exaggerate or even falsify their personal accomplishments in an effort to build an enhanced image.[45]

Managing Political Behavior

By its very nature, political behavior is tricky to approach in a rational and systematic way. But managers can handle political behavior so that it does not do excessive damage.[46] First, managers should be aware that, even if their actions are not politically motivated, others may assume that they are. Second, by providing subordinates with autonomy, responsibility, challenge, and feedback, managers reduce the likelihood of political behavior by subordinates. Third, managers should avoid using power if they want to avoid charges of political motivation. Fourth, managers should get disagreements out in the open so that subordinates will have less opportunity for political behavior through using conflict for their own purposes. Finally, managers should avoid covert activities. Behind-the-scenes activities give the impression of political intent, even if none really exists.[47] Other guidelines include clearly communicating the bases and processes for performance evaluation, tying rewards directly to performance, and minimizing competition among managers for resources.[48]

Of course, these guidelines are much easier to list than they are to implement. The well-informed manager should not assume that political behavior does not exist or, worse yet, attempt to eliminate it by issuing orders or commands. Instead, the manager must recognize that political behavior exists in virtually all organizations and that it cannot be ignored or stamped out. It can, however, be managed in such a way that it will seldom inflict serious damage on the organization. It may even play a useful role in some situations.[49] For example, a manager may be able to use his or her political influence to stimulate a greater sense of social responsibility or to heighten awareness of the ethical implications of a decision.

concept CHECK

What are the most common forms of political behavior in organizations?

Have you ever intentionally used impression management? When might impression management be an acceptable behavior, and when might it be an unacceptable behavior?

Summary of Key Points

ACE self-test

business.college.hmco.com/students

As a process, leadership is the use of noncoercive influence to shape the group's or organization's goals, motivate behavior toward the achievement of those goals, and help define group or organization culture. As a property, leadership is the set of characteristics attributed to those who are perceived to be leaders. Leadership and management are often related but are also different. Managers and leaders use legitimate, reward, coercive, referent, and expert power.

The trait approach to leadership assumed that some basic trait or set of traits differentiated leaders from nonleaders. The leadership behavior approach to leadership assumed that the behavior of effective leaders was somehow different from the behavior of nonleaders. Research at the University of Michigan and Ohio State University identified two basic forms of leadership behavior—one concentrating on work and performance and the other concentrating on employee welfare and support. The Managerial Grid attempts to train managers to exhibit high levels of both forms of behavior.

Situational approaches to leadership recognize that appropriate forms of leadership behavior are not universally applicable and attempt to specify situations in which various behaviors are appropriate. The LPC theory suggests that a leader's behaviors should be either task oriented or relationship oriented, depending on the favorableness of the situation. The path-goal theory suggests that directive, supportive, participative, or achievement-oriented leader behaviors may be appropriate, depending on the personal characteristics of subordinates and the environment. Vroom's decision tree approach maintains that leaders should vary the extent to which they allow subordinates to participate in making decisions as a function of problem attributes. The leader-member exchange model focuses on individual relationships between leaders and followers and on in-group versus out-group considerations.

Related leadership perspectives are the concept of substitutes for leadership, charismatic leadership, and the role of transformational leadership in organizations. Emerging approaches include strategic, cross-cultural, and ethical leadership.

Political behavior is another influence process frequently used in organizations. Impression management, one especially important form of political behavior, is a direct and intentional effort by someone to enhance his or her image in the eyes of others. Managers can take steps to limit the effects of political behavior.

Discussion Questions

Questions for Review

1. What activities do managers perform? What activities do leaders perform? Do organizations need both managers and leaders? Why or why not?
2. What are the situational approaches to leadership? Briefly describe each and compare and contrast their findings.
3. Describe the subordinate's characteristics, leader behaviors, and environmental characteristics used in path-goal theory. How do these factors combine to influence motivation?
4. In your own words, define political behavior. Describe four political tactics and give an example of each.

Questions for Analysis

5. Even though the trait approach to leadership has no empirical support, it is still widely used. In your opinion, why is this so? In what ways is the use of the trait approach helpful to those who use it? In what ways is it harmful to those who use it?
6. The behavioral theories of leadership claim that an individual's leadership style is fixed. Do you agree or disagree? Give examples to support your position. The behavioral theories also claim that the ideal style is the same in every situation. Do you agree or disagree? Again, give examples.
7. A few universities are experimenting with alternative approaches, such as allowing students to design their own majors, develop a curriculum for that major, choose professors and design courses, or self-direct and self-evaluate their studies. These are examples of substitutes for leadership. Do you think this will lead to better outcomes for students than a traditional approach? Would you personally like to have that type of alternative approach at your school? Explain your answers.

Questions for Application

8. Consider the following list of leadership situations. For each situation, describe in detail the kinds of power the leader has. If the leader were the same but the situation changed—for example, if you thought of the president as the head of his family rather than of the military—would your answers change? Why?

- The president of the United States is commander-in-chief of the U.S. military.
- An airline pilot is in charge of a particular flight.
- Fans look up to a movie star.
- Your teacher is the head of your class.

9. Think about a decision that would affect you as a student. Use Vroom's decision tree approach to decide whether the administrator making that decision should involve students in the decision. Which parts of the model seem most important in making that decision? Why?
10. Describe a time when you or someone you know was part of an in-group or an out-group. What was the relationship between each of the groups and the leader? What was the relationship between the members of the two different groups? What was the outcome of the situation for the leader? for the members of the two groups? for the organization?

BUILDING EFFECTIVE diagnostic SKILLS

Exercise Overview

Diagnostic skills help a manager visualize appropriate responses to a situation. One situation managers often face is how to use different types of power to most effectively respond to different situations.

Exercise Background

In 1599 Shakespeare's *Henry V* was performed for the first time. The play's themes of war, leadership, brotherhood, and treachery are just as relevant today. *Henry V* also contains a speech, the "St. Crispin's Day speech," that is widely considered to be the most inspiring speech ever written.

To set the scene: In 1415 England, under Henry's leadership, has attacked France to regain control of some disputed lands, which are currently held by France. (England's claim is legitimate, in Shakespeare's play, and the war is therefore "just.") England's 6,000 soldiers won several key battles, moving from the coast into the interior of France. The English are sick, cold, hungry, and dispirited. They arrive at the French town of Agincourt and face an army of 25,000 soldiers who are well rested and much better equipped, with horses and armor. Through a mixture of courage, strategy, and plain luck, the English are victorious, losing only 200 men, as they inflict over 5,000 casualties on the French. The French crown prince is injured, their commanding general is killed, and they surrender to the English.

This short scene occurs just before the start of the battle of Agincourt. Henry's officers are worried about their chances of victory, and Henry motivates them to plunge into battle and do their best. If you find it hard to understand Shakespeare's English, your professor has a transcript of the scene.

Exercise Task

View the short excerpt from Henry V that your professor will show in class. (The film was made in 1989 and was directed by and stars Kenneth Branagh.) In addition, read the transcript of Henry's monologue. Then answer the following questions:

1. What types of power is Henry using in this speech? Give specific examples of each type.
2. Henry had a rebellious and wayward youth before becoming king. Does his past tend to increase or decrease his referent power, in your opinion? Why?
3. In Shakespeare's play, Henry's speech inspired his soldiers to an almost impossible victory. Is this speech inspiring to you? Why or why not?

BUILDING EFFECTIVE decision-making SKILLS

Exercise Overview

Vroom's decision tree approach to leadership is an effective method for determining how much participation a manager might allow his or her subordinates in making a decision. This exercise will enable you to refine your decision-making skills by applying Vroom's approach to a hypothetical situation.

Exercise Background

Assume that you are the branch manager of the West Coast region of the United States for an international manufacturing and sales company. The company is making a major effort to control costs and boost efficiency. As part of this effort, the firm recently installed a networked computer system linking sales representatives, customer service employees, and other sales support staff. The goal of this network was to increase sales while simultaneously cutting sales expenses.

Unfortunately, just the opposite has resulted—sales are down slightly, but expenses are increasing. You have looked into this problem and believe that the computer hardware that people are using is fine. You also believe, however, that the software used to run the system is flawed: It is too hard to use and provides less than complete information.

Your employees disagree with your assessment, however. They believe that the entire system is fine. They attribute the problems to poor training in using the system and a lack of incentive for using it to solve many problems that they already know how to handle using other methods. Some of them also think that their colleagues are just resisting change.

Your boss has just called and instructed you to "solve the problem." She indicated that she has complete faith in your ability to do so, that decisions about how to proceed will be left to you, and that she wants a report suggesting a course of action in five days.

Exercise Task

Using the information presented above, do the following:

1. Using your own personal preferences and intuition, describe how you think you would proceed.
2. Now use Vroom's approach to determine a course of action.
3. Compare and contrast your initial approach and the actions suggested by Vroom's approach.

BUILDING EFFECTIVE conceptual SKILLS

business.college.hmco.com/students

Exercise Overview

Conceptual skills refer to the manager's ability to think in the abstract. This exercise allows you to analyze one practical approach to assessing leadership skills and to relate practice to theory.

Exercise Background

Current publications contain an abundance of practical advice on leadership. (On the top ten business best-sellers' list in early 2003 were *Good to Great*, by Jim Collins; *First, Break All the Rules*, by Marcus Buckingham; and *Execution: The Discipline of Getting Things Done*, by Larry Bossidy.) Some of these books, such as *Jack: Straight from the Gut*, by former General Electric CEO Jack Welch, are written by managers with years of experience. Others are written by consultants, professors, or reporters. But many—in fact, most—of these books do not have a strong theoretical foundation, nor are their suggestions supported by scientific evidence.

Many of these books contain ideas that may nevertheless be of use to managers. However, learning how to analyze publications in the popular press and to investigate them carefully is an important skill for today's managers. This exercise gives you practice in doing just that.

Exercise Task

1. Visit *Fortune* magazine's website, at www.fortune.com/fortune/quizzes/careers/boss_quiz.html. Complete the leadership assessment quiz that was written by management guru Stephen Covey. Then look at Covey's scoring and comments.
2. Look carefully at each of the questions and the suggested answers. Do you see any correlation between the questions and the theoretical models presented to you in this chapter? Which model or models do you think Covey is using? What led you to that conclusion?
3. Use the Internet to discover something about Stephen Covey's background, training, and experiences. Does the information you found give you any clues about Covey's attitudes and beliefs about leadership? Do you see any connection between Covey's attitudes and the items on the quiz? Explain.
4. Based on what you found, how confident are you that the quiz is an accurate measure of leadership ability? Explain.

CHAPTER CLOSING case

THE "NEW AND IMPROVED" PROCTER & GAMBLE

"I have made a lot of symbolic, very physical changes so people understand we are in the business of change."

— A. G. Lafley, CEO, Procter & Gamble*

Low-key, bespectacled Alan G. Lafley is the unlikely looking yet successful CEO of Procter & Gamble (P&G), the largest household products company in the world and the maker of megabrands such as Tide, Crest, Charmin, Downy, Pampers, Folgers, Bounty, and Pringles. "If there were 15 people sitting around the conference table, it wouldn't be obvious that he was the CEO," says analyst Ann Gillin-Lefever. Johnathan Rodgers, a P&G board member, says, "He doesn't have that superstar CEO personality." *Fortune* writer Katrina Booker calls Lafley "the un-CEO." But quiet and unassuming Lafley has succeeded in turning around the once-ailing manufacturer when other, more flamboyant leaders have failed. His victory demonstrates the power of a back-to-basics strategy and straightforward leadership.

Procter & Gamble was troubled before Lafley took the reins in 2000. After phenomenal growth through the 1980s, P&G was struggling to expand when sales already topped $40 billion. In the 1990s, for the first time, P&G did not meet its target of doubling sales growth each decade.

The firm had three different CEOs during the 1990s, and the most recent, Durk Jager, served just seventeen months. Jager's aggressive reorganization plan called for focusing attention on new products, rather than best-sellers, but the innovations, such as Olay cosmetics, bombed. Jager moved 110,000 workers into new jobs. P&G began putting American brand names on its global products, but shoppers in Germany and Hong Kong did not recognize "Pantene" and "Dawn." Jager sought to acquire drug makers Warner-Lambert and American Home Products but dropped the idea due to pressure from investors.

Under Jager's strategy, P&G missed earnings targets and lost $70 billion in market value. An aggressive personality did not endear Jager to P&G employees either. "I was lost," says Chris Start, a P&G vice president. "It was like no one knew how to get anything done anymore." After Jager, there was little confidence in Lafley, and P&G stock fell $4 when Lafley's promotion was announced.

Lafley worked at P&G for twenty-five years before becoming CEO. He knew that the firm could do a better job of selling its winners. Lafley gave the managers of P&G's top ten brands more resources. Lafley claims, "The trick was to find the few things that were really going to sell, and sell as many of them as you could." He adds, "The essence of our strategy is incredibly simple, but I believe the simplicity is its power. . . . It's Sesame Street–simple, but it works." For example, hair-care managers reinvented top-selling Pantene. Rather than group products by hair type—oily, fine, normal—new groups focused on the look the customer wanted—curls, volumizing. Sales of Pantene grew 8 percent.

Rather than insisting that new products be developed internally, Lafley acquired small, idea-driven firms. Lafley states that 50 percent of innovation should come through acquisitions. He says, "That means we would double the productivity of our current investment in R&D." Lafley is demanding better marketability of new products, telling researchers, "Innovation is in the consumer's eyes. . . . It isn't a great innovation until she loves it and purchases it."

Lafley is shaking up the firm's staid culture in other ways, too. "I have made a lot of symbolic, very physical changes so people understand we are in the business of change," he says. At the company's historic Cincinnati headquarters, product managers are leaving their executive suites to move closer to their employees. Wood paneling and oil paintings are coming down, so that top managers can work as a team in one open, modern space. The rest of the penthouse floor is now a learning center, where top executives deliver some of the training. Lafley asked for the changes because, as he says, "I really believe knowledge is power, and translating knowledge into action in the marketplace is one of the things that distinguishes leadership." Communication between managers, workers, board members, and even competitors has opened up. "You can tell him bad news or things you'd be afraid to tell other bosses," says vice president Start. Lafley rewards managers for financial results and is harsh on poor performers—half of the top team is new.

With a series of small changes, Lafley had a powerful impact on P&G's performance. Earnings beat expectations, and stock price rose 70 percent. Profits are up 49 percent over the previous year. Lafley continues to emphasize the basics. "Nearly two billion times a day, P&G products are put to the test when consumers use [them]," Lafley reminds his employees. "When we get this right . . . then we begin to earn the trust on which great brands are built." Under Lafley's leadership, P&G is again earning consumers' trust—and their dollars.

Case Questions

1. In what ways is Procter & Gamble's CEO A. G. Lafley acting as a leader? In what ways is he acting like a manager?
2. Does Lafley show job-centered leader behavior, employee-centered leader behavior, or some combination of the two? Explain your answer.
3. Using one or more of the leadership theories presented in the chapter, explain why Lafley is a more effective leader than his predecessor, Durk Jager.

Case References

A. G. Lafley, "Letter to Shareholders," *Procter & Gamble: 2002 Annual Report,* www.pg.com on February 10, 2003; Daniel Eisenberg, "A Healthy Gamble," *Time,* September 16, 2002, pp. 46–48; Katrina Booker, "The Un-CEO," *Fortune,* September 16, 2002, pp. 88–96; Robert Berner, "Procter & Gamble's Renovator-in-Chief," *BusinessWeek,* December 11, 2002, www.businessweek.com on February 9, 2003; Robert Berner, "Why P&G's Smile Is so Bright," *BusinessWeek Small Biz,* www.businessweek.com on February 10, 2003; "The Best and Worst Managers: A. G. Lafley, Procter & Gamble," *BusinessWeek* January 13, 2003, p. 67 (*quote);.

Chapter Notes

1. "FBI Confirms Probe of HealthSouth," *Associated Press*, February 6, 2003, hoovnews.hoovers.com on February 8, 2003; "HealthSouth Announced Realignment of Executive Management Responsibilities," HealthSouth press release, January 6, 2003, hoovnews.hoovers.com on February 8, 2003; "HealthSouth Corporation," www.hoovers.com on February 8, 2003; "Judge: HealthSouth Can't Review CEO," *Associated Press*, January 21, 2003, hoovnews.hoovers.com on February 8, 2003; Ralph King, "Insider Loans: Everyone Was Doing It," *Business 2.0*, November 2002, www.business2.com on February 8, 2003; Reed Abelson and Milt Freudenheim, "Will an Imperial Boss Bend with the Times?" *New York Times*, October 6, 2002, pp. BU1, BU10 (*p. BU10).
2. See Ronald A. Heifetz and Donald L. Laurie, "The Work of Leadership," *Harvard Business Review*, January–February 1997, pp. 124–134. See also Arthur G. Jago, "Leadership: Perspectives in Theory and Research," *Management Science*, March 1982, pp. 315–336, and "The New Leadership," *BusinessWeek*, August 28, 2000, pp. 100–187.
3. Gary A. Yukl, *Leadership in Organizations*, 3rd ed. (Englewood Cliffs, N.J.: Prentice-Hall, 1994), p. 5. See also Gregory G. Dess and Joseph C. Pickens, "Changing Roles: Leadership in the 21st Century," *Organizational Dynamics*, Winter 2000, pp. 18–28.
4. John P. Kotter, "What Leaders Really Do," *Harvard Business Review*, May–June 1990, pp. 103–111 (reprinted in *Harvard Business Review*, December 2001, pp. 85–93). See also Daniel Goleman, "Leadership That Gets Results," *Harvard Business Review*, March–April 2000, pp. 78–88; and Keith Grints, *The Arts of Leadership* (Oxford, U.K.: Oxford University Press, 2000).
5. John R. P. French and Bertram Raven, "The Bases of Social Power," in Dorwin Cartwright, ed., *Studies in Social Power* (Ann Arbor, Mich.: University of Michigan Press, 1959), pp. 150–167.
6. Hugh D. Menzies, "The Ten Toughest Bosses," *Fortune*, April 21, 1980, pp. 62–73.
7. Bennett J. Tepper, "Consequences of Abusive Supervision," *Academy of Management Journal*, 2000, vol. 43, no. 2, pp. 178–190.
8. Thomas A. Stewart, "Get with the New Power Game," *Fortune*, January 13, 1997, pp. 58–62.
9. For more information on the bases and uses of power, see Philip M. Podsakoff and Chester A. Schriesheim, "Field Studies of French and Raven's Bases of Power: Critique, Reanalysis, and Suggestions for Future Research," *Psychological Bulletin*, vol. 97, 1985, pp. 387–411; Robert C. Benfari, Harry E. Wilkinson, and Charles D. Orth, "The Effective Use of Power," *Business Horizons*, May–June 1986, pp. 12–16; and Yukl, *Leadership in Organizations.*
10. Bernard M. Bass, *Bass & Stogdill's Handbook of Leadership*, 3rd ed. (Riverside, N.J.: Free Press, 1990).
11. Shelley A. Kirkpatrick and Edwin A. Locke, "Leadership: Do Traits Matter?" *Academy of Management Executive*, May 1991, pp. 48–60. See also Robert J. Sternberg, "Managerial Intelligence: Why IQ Isn't Enough," *Journal of Management*, vol. 23, no. 3, 1997, pp. 475–493.
12. Rensis Likert, *New Patterns of Management* (New York: McGraw-Hill, 1961); Rensis Likert, *The Human Organization* (New York: McGraw-Hill, 1967).
13. The Ohio State studies stimulated many articles, monographs, and books. A good overall reference is Ralph M. Stogdill and A. E. Coons, eds., *Leader Behavior: Its Description and Measurement* (Columbus, Ohio: Bureau of Business Research, Ohio State University, 1957).
14. Edwin A. Fleishman, E. F. Harris, and H. E. Burt, *Leadership and Supervision in Industry* (Columbus, Ohio: Bureau of Business Research, Ohio State University, 1955).
15. Robert R. Blake and Jane S. Mouton, *The Managerial Grid* (Houston: Gulf Publishing, 1964); Robert R. Blake and Jane S. Mouton, *The Versatile Manager: A Grid Profile* (Homewood, Ill.: Dow Jones-Irwin, 1981).
16. Robert Tannenbaum and Warren H. Schmidt, "How to Choose a Leadership Pattern," *Harvard Business Review*, March–April 1958, pp. 95–101.
17. Fred E. Fiedler, *A Theory of Leadership Effectiveness* (New York: McGraw-Hill, 1967).
18. Chester A. Schriesheim, Bennett J. Tepper, and Linda A. Tetrault, "Least Preferred Co-Worker Score, Situational Control, and Leadership Effectiveness: A Meta-Analysis of Contingency Model Performance Predictions," *Journal of Applied Psychology*, 1994, vol. 79, no. 4, pp. 561–573.
19. Fiedler, *A Theory of Leadership Effectiveness*; Fred E. Fiedler and M. M. Chemers, *Leadership and Effective Management* (Glenview, Ill.: Scott, Foresman, 1974).
20. For recent reviews and updates, see Lawrence H. Peters, Darrell D. Hartke, and John T. Pohlmann, "Fiedler's Contingency Theory of Leadership: An Application of the Meta-Analysis Procedures of Schmidt and Hunter," *Psychological Bulletin*, vol. 97, pp. 274–285; and Fred E. Fiedler, "When to Lead, When to Stand Back," *Psychology Today*, September 1987, pp. 26–27.
21. Martin G. Evans, "The Effects of Supervisory Behavior on the Path-Goal Relationship," *Organizational Behavior and Human Performance*, May 1970, pp. 277–298; Robert J. House and Terence R. Mitchell, "Path-Goal Theory of Leadership," *Journal of Contemporary Business*, Autumn 1974, pp. 81–98. See also Yukl, *Leadership in Organizations.*
22. For a recent review, see J. C. Wofford and Laurie Z. Liska, "Path-Goal Theories of Leadership: A Meta-Analysis," *Journal of Management*, 1993, vol. 19, no. 4, pp. 857–876.
23. See Victor H. Vroom and Philip H. Yetton, *Leadership and Decision Making* (Pittsburgh: University of Pittsburgh Press, 1973); and Victor H. Vroom and Arthur G. Jago, *The New Leadership* (Englewood Cliffs, N.J.: Prentice-Hall, 1988).
24. Victor Vroom, "Leadership and the Decision-Making Process," *Organizational Dynamics*, 2000, vol. 28, no. 4, pp. 82–94.
25. Vroom and Jago, *The New Leadership.*
26. Ibid.

27. See Madeline E. Heilman, Harvey A. Hornstein, Jack H. Cage, and Judith K. Herschlag, "Reaction to Prescribed Leader Behavior as a Function of Role Perspective: The Case of the Vroom-Yetton Model," *Journal of Applied Psychology*, February 1984, pp. 50–60; R. H. George Field, "A Test of the Vroom-Yetton Normative Model of Leadership," *Journal of Applied Psychology*, February 1982, pp. 523–532.
28. George Graen and J. F. Cashman, "A Role-Making Model of Leadership in Formal Organizations: A Developmental Approach," in J. G. Hunt and L. L. Larson (eds.), *Leadership Frontiers* (Kent, Ohio: Kent State University Press, 1975), pp. 143–165; Fred Dansereau, George Graen, and W. J. Haga, "A Vertical Dyad Linkage Approach to Leadership Within Formal Organizations: A Longitudinal Investigation of the Role-Making Process," *Organizational Behavior and Human Performance*, vol. 15, 1975, pp. 46–78.
29. See Kathryn Sherony and Stephen Green, "Coworker Exchange: Relationships Between Coworkers, Leader-Member Exchange, and Work Attitudes," *Journal of Applied Psychology*, 2002, vol. 87. no. 3, pp. 542–548.
30. Steven Kerr and John M. Jermier, "Substitutes for Leadership: Their Meaning and Measurement," *Organizational Behavior and Human Performance*, December 1978, pp. 375–403.
31. See Charles C. Manz and Henry P. Sims, Jr., "Leading Workers to Lead Themselves: The External Leadership of Self-managing Work Teams," *Administrative Science Quarterly*, March 1987, pp. 106–129. See also "Living Without a Leader," *Fortune*, March 20, 2000, pp. 218–219.
32. See Robert J. House, "A 1976 Theory of Charismatic Leadership," in J. G. Hunt and L. L. Larson, eds., *Leadership: The Cutting Edge* (Carbondale, Ill.: Southern Illinois University Press, 1977), pp. 189–207. See also Jay A. Conger and Rabindra N. Kanungo, "Toward a Behavioral Theory of Charismatic Leadership in Organizational Settings," *Academy of Management Review*, October 1987, pp. 637–647.
33. Stratford P. Sherman, "Donald Trump Just Won't Die," *Fortune*, August 13, 1990, pp. 75–79.
34. David A. Nadler and Michael L. Tushman, "Beyond the Charismatic Leader: Leadership and Organizational Change," *California Management Review*, Winter 1990, pp. 77–97.
35. James MacGregor Burns, *Leadership* (New York: Harper & Row, 1978). See also Rajnandini Pillai, Chester A. Schriesheim, and Eric J. Williams, "Fairness Perceptions and Trust as Mediators for Transformational and Transactional Leadership: A Two-Sample Study," *Journal of Management*, 1999, vol. 25, no. 6, pp. 897–933.
36. Labich, "The Seven Keys to Business Leadership."
37. Jerry Useem, "Tape + Light Bulbs = ?" *Fortune*, August 12, 2002, pp. 127–132.
38. "The Best (& Worst) Managers of the Year," *BusinessWeek*, January 13, 2003, pp. 58–92.
39. See Kurt Dirks and Donald Ferrin, "Trust in Leadership," *Journal of Applied Psychology*, 2002, vol. 87, no. 4, pp. 611–628.
40. Jeffrey Pfeffer, *Power in Organizations* (Marshfield, Mass.: Pitman Publishing, 1981), p. 7.
41. Timothy Judge and Robert Bretz, "Political Influence Behavior and Career Success," *Journal of Management*, 1994, vol. 20, no. 1, pp. 43–65.
42. Victor Murray and Jeffrey Gandz, "Games Executives Play: Politics at Work," *Business Horizons*, December 1980, pp. 11–23; Jeffrey Gandz and Victor Murray, "The Experience of Workplace Politics," *Academy of Management Journal*, June 1980, pp. 237–251.
43. Don R. Beeman and Thomas W. Sharkey, "The Use and Abuse of Corporate Power," *Business Horizons*, March–April 1987, pp. 26–30.
44. "How Ebbers Kept the Board in His Pocket," *BusinessWeek*, October 14, 2002, pp. 138–139.
45. See William L. Gardner, "Lessons in Organizational Dramaturgy: The Art of Impression Management," *Organizational Dynamics*, Summer 1992, pp. 51–63; Elizabeth Wolf Morrison and Robert J. Bies, "Impression Management in the Feedback-Seeking Process: A Literature Review and Research Agenda," *Academy of Management Review*, July 1991, pp. 522–541.
46. See Chad Higgins, Timothy Judge, and Gerald Ferris, "Influence Tactics and Work Outcomes: A Meta-Analysis," *Journal of Organizational Behavior*, 2003, vol. 24, pp. 89–106.
47. Murray and Gandz, "Games Executives Play."
48. Beeman and Sharkey, "The Use and Abuse of Corporate Power."
49. Stefanie Ann Lenway and Kathleen Rehbein, "Leaders, Followers, and Free Riders: An Empirical Test of Variation in Corporate Political Involvement," *Academy of Management Journal*, December 1991, pp. 893–905.

18

Managing Interpersonal Relations and Communication

CHAPTER OUTLINE

The Interpersonal Nature of Organizations

Interpersonal Dynamics

Outcomes of Interpersonal Behaviors

Communication and the Manager's Job

A Definition of Communication

The Role of Communication in Management

The Communication Process

Forms of Communication in Organizations

Interpersonal Communication

Communication in Networks and Work Teams

Organizational Communication

Electronic Communication

Informal Communication in Organizations

The Grapevine

Management by Wandering Around

Nonverbal Communication

Managing Organizational Communication

Barriers to Communication

Improving Communication Effectiveness

LEARNING OBJECTIVES

After studying this chapter, you should be able to:

1 ***Describe the interpersonal nature of organizations.***

OPENING INCIDENT

The last twenty years have given us an explosion of new communication technology. Cell phones, videoconferencing, chat rooms, e-bulletin boards, and instant messaging have revolutionized the way we communicate at home and at work. Out of all these innovations, e-mail has had perhaps the most powerful impact on interpersonal communication. Although that impact has been largely positive, it has also created a host of unique dangers for organizations.

E-mail seems like a dream come true for managers, allowing rapid, inexpensive communication to almost anywhere. E-mail can substitute for written communications, which are slow over distances; for phone calls, which are not possible in some areas; and for face-to-face meetings, which are expensive for far-flung attendees. Some of the immediacy of a conversation can be maintained, while also enabling the participants to keep a written record. Through features such as mailing lists and auto reply, e-mail can broadcast to a large group simultaneously or tell senders that the receiver is unavailable.

Yet e-mail presents several problems. For one thing, it encourages poor communication skills. Conversations send a great deal of information about context—such as tone of voice and body language—along with the message

2	3	4	5
Describe the role and importance of communication in the manager's job.	***Identify the basic forms of communication in organizations.***	***Discuss informal communication, including its various forms and types.***	***Describe how the communication process can be managed to recognize and overcome barriers.***

"E-mail is as private as sending a message on a postcard."

—Common saying among computer experts

New technology like this Nokia device makes communication easier—and more complex—than ever before.

content. But e-mail provides no context. Traditional written communication also provides no context but takes time to prepare, allowing the sender to reflect carefully before transmission. E-mail, on the other hand, is quick and easy. Thus it combines the worst of verbal and written communications by allowing the sender to convey a thoughtless message that does not contain context clues. When intentional, these messages are called "flames," but offensive and confusing messages are often sent by accident, too.

The Direct Marketing Association has released a list of guidelines for eliminating unsolicited junk e-mail, called "spam," but few companies have adopted the guidelines. Spam can cost an organization thousands of dollars each year in lost productivity and increased resource demand, simply through the time employees take to delete such e-mails.

Critics also worry that e-mail is making workplace relationships more impersonal. Fewer direct interactions between employees can lessen organizational commitment, reduce teamwork, and block creativity.

E-mail, unlike mail or phone conversations, is not protected by any privacy laws. Corporate monitoring of employee e-mail is very common. A Pillsbury employee, for example, lost a privacy suit against his employer. The judges wrote, "We do not find a reasonable expectation of privacy in e-mail communications . . . notwithstanding any assurances that such communications would not be intercepted by management . . . the company's interest in preventing inappropriate and unprofessional comments or even illegal activity over its e-mail system outweighs any privacy interest the employee may have." In other words, it is perfectly legal for an employer to monitor employees' e-mail, even if it promises not to.

Liability issues related to e-mail have become problematic also. Recently, many analysts have been sued by disgruntled investors. The investors obtained e-mails that show the analysts' deliberate attempts to mislead. E-mails between two analysts covering AOL said, "I will NOT lower [earnings estimates] on AOL, even though they can't make them." William F. Galvin, the Secretary of Massachusetts, who is investigating the analysts, claims, "It seems to me this is really a smoking gun. These analysts knew they were misleading investors and yet they gave bad advice."

E-mail messages are sent over the Internet or through a firm's internal network, which allows individuals to intercept or view messages not intended for them. One expert says, "Email is as private as sending a message on a postcard." Confidential information is easy to steal from an e-mail. In a recent case at the *New York Times*, hacker Adrian Lamo obtained illegal access to reporters' online address books. Lamo discovered private home phone numbers and addresses for *Times* contributors including commentator Rush Limbaugh, Robert Redford, and former president Jimmy Carter.

Of course, one does not have to be a computer expert to steal e-mails. When criminals wanted personal information contained in e-mails at the TriWest Healthcare Alliance, they simply stole the hard drives right out of the computer cases![1]

E-mail has become a ubiquitous part of the manager's job. And new technology that provides quick and easy wireless access to the Internet from virtually anywhere promises to further revolutionize electronic communication. But communication has always been a vital part of managerial work. Indeed, managers around the world agree that communication is one of their most important tasks. It is important for them to communicate with others in order to convey their vision and goals for the organization. And it is important for others to communicate with them so that they will better understand what is going on in their environment and how they and their organization can become more effective.

This chapter is the first of two that focuses on interpersonal processes in organizations. We first establish the interpersonal nature of organizations and then discuss communication, one of the most basic forms of interaction among people. We begin by examining communication in the context of the manager's job. We then identify and discuss forms of interpersonal, group, and organizational communication. After discussing informal means of communication, we describe how organizational communication can be effectively managed. In our next chapter, we discuss other elements of interpersonal relations: group and team processes and conflict.

The Interpersonal Nature of Organizations

In Chapter 1, we noted how much of a manager's job involves scheduled and unscheduled meetings, telephone calls, e-mail, and related activities. Indeed, a great deal of what all managers do involves interacting with other people, both directly and indirectly and both inside and outside of the organization. The schedule that follows is a typical day for the president of a Houston-based company, part of a larger firm headquartered in California. He kept a log of his activities for several different days so that you could better appreciate the nature of managerial work.

7:45–8:15 A.M. Arrive at work; review hardcopy mail sorted by assistant.

8:15–8:30 A.M. Scan the *Wall Street Journal*; read and respond to e-mail.

8:30–9:00 A.M. Meet with labor officials and plant manager to resolve minor labor disputes.

9:00–9:30 A.M. Review internal report; read and respond to new e-mail.

9:30–10:00 A.M. Meet with two marketing executives to review advertising campaign; instruct them to fax approvals to advertising agency.

10:00–11:30 A.M. Meet with company executive committee to discuss strategy, budgetary issues, and competition (this committee meets weekly).

11:30–12:00 noon Send several e-mails; read and respond to new e-mail.

12:00–1:15 P.M. Lunch with the financial vice president and two executives from another subsidiary of the parent corporation. Primary topic of discussion is the Houston Rockets basketball team. Place three calls from cellular phone en route to lunch and receive one call en route back to office.

1:15–1:45 P.M. Meet with human resource director and assistant about a recent OSHA inspection; establish a task force to investigate the problems identified and to suggest solutions.

1:45–2:00 P.M. Read and respond to new e-mail.
2:00–2:30 P.M. Conference call with four other company presidents.
2:30–3:00 P.M. Meet with financial vice president about a confidential issue that came up at lunch (unscheduled).
3:00–3:30 P.M. Work alone in office; read and respond to new e-mail; send several e-mails.
3:30–4:15 P.M. Meet with a group of sales representatives and the company purchasing agent.
4:15–5:30 P.M. Work alone in office.
5:30–7:00 P.M. Play racquetball at nearby athletic club with marketing vice president.
9:00–9:30 P.M. Read and respond to e-mail from home; send e-mail to assistant about an emergency meeting to be scheduled for the next day.

By their very nature organizations include many different patterns and types of interpersonal relationships. These people, for instance, are all authors affiliated wity the University of New Mexico. They regularly interact with one another at work and occasionally outside of work as well, such as at this recent dinner. Their interactions are usually positive and help them maintain a strong social support network as they go about their work.

How did this manager spend his time? He spent most of it working, communicating, and interacting with other people. And this compressed daily schedule does not include several other brief telephone calls, brief conversations with his assistant, and brief conversations with other managers. Clearly, interpersonal relations, communication, and group processes are a pervasive part of all organizations and a vital part of all managerial activities.[2]

Interpersonal Dynamics

The nature of interpersonal relations in an organization is as varied as the individual members themselves. At one extreme, interpersonal relations can be personal and positive. This occurs when the two parties know each other, have mutual respect and affection, and enjoy interacting. Two managers who have known each other for years, play golf together on weekends, and are close personal friends will likely interact at work in a positive fashion. At the other extreme, interpersonal dynamics can be personal but negative. This is most likely when the parties dislike each other, do not have mutual respect, and do not enjoy interacting. Suppose a manager has fought openly for years to block the promotion of another manager within the organization. Over the objections of the first manager, however, the other manager eventually gets promoted to the same rank. When the two of them must interact, it will most likely be in a negative manner.

Most interactions fall between these extremes, as members of the organization interact in a professional way focused primarily on goal accomplishment. The interaction deals with the job at hand, is relatively formal and structured, and is task directed. Two managers may respect each other's work and recognize the professional competence that each brings to the job. However, they may also have few common interests and little to talk about besides the job they are doing. These different types of interactions may occur between individuals, between groups, or between individuals and groups, and they can change over time. The two managers in the second scenario, for example, might decide to bury the hatchet and adopt a detached, professional manner. The two managers in the third example could find more common ground than they anticipated and evolve to a personal and positive interaction.

Outcomes of Interpersonal Behaviors

A variety of things can happen as a result of interpersonal behaviors. Recall from Chapter 16, for example, that numerous perspectives on motivation suggest that people have social needs. Interpersonal relations in organizations can be a primary source of need satisfaction for many people. For a person with a strong need for affiliation, high-quality interpersonal relations can be an important positive element in the workplace. However, when this same person is confronted with poor-quality working relationships, the effect can be just as great in the other direction.

Interpersonal relations also serve as a solid basis for social support. Suppose that an employee receives a poor performance evaluation or is denied a promotion. Others in the organization can lend support because they share a common frame of reference—an understanding of the causes and consequences of what happened. Good interpersonal relations throughout an organization can also be a source of synergy. People who support one another and who work well together can accomplish much more than people who do not support one another and who do not work well together. Another outcome, implied earlier, is conflict—people may leave an interpersonal exchange feeling angry or hostile. But a common thread is woven through all of these outcomes—communication between people in the organization.[3]

concept CHECK

What kinds of interpersonal interactions can be identified in organizational settings?

How much of your daily life involves interacting with other people?

Communication and the Manager's Job

As evidenced by the daily log presented earlier, a typical day for a manager includes doing desk work, attending scheduled meetings, placing and receiving telephone calls, reading and answering correspondence (both print and electronic), attending unscheduled meetings, and making tours.[4] Most of these activities involve communication. In fact, managers usually spend over half their time on some form of communication. Communication always involves two or more people, so other behavioral processes, such as motivation, leadership, and group and team interactions, all come into play. Top executives must handle communication effectively if they are to be true leaders.

A Definition of Communication

Imagine three managers working in an office building. The first is all alone but is nevertheless yelling for a subordinate to come help. No one appears, but he continues to yell. The second is talking on the telephone to a subordinate, but static on the line causes the subordinate to misunderstand some important numbers being provided by the manager. As a result, the subordinate sends 1,500 crates of eggs to 150 Fifth Street, when he should have sent 150 crates of eggs to 1500 Fifteenth Street. The third manager is talking in her office with a subordinate who clearly hears and understands what is being said. Each of these managers is attempting to communicate, but with different results.

Communication is the process of transmitting information from one person to another. Did any of our three managers communicate? The last did, and the first did not. How about the second? In fact, she did communicate. She transmitted information, and information was received. The problem was that the message transmitted and the message received were not the same. The words spoken by the manager were distorted by static and noise. **Effective communication**, then, is the process of sending a message in such a way that the message received is as close in meaning as possible to the message intended. Although the second manager engaged in communication, it was not effective.

communication The process of transmitting information from one person to another

effective communication The process of sending a message in such a way that the message received is as close in meaning as possible to the message intended

Our definition of effective communication is based on the ideas of meaning and consistency of meaning. Meaning is the idea that the individual who initiates the communication exchange wishes to convey. In effective communication, the meaning is transmitted in such a way that the receiving person understands it. For example, consider these messages:

1. The high today will be only 40 degrees.
2. It will be cold today.
3. Ceteris paribus
4. Xn1gp bo5cz4ik ab19

You probably understand the meaning of the first statement. The second statement may seem clear at first, but it is somewhat less clear than the first statement, because cold is a relative condition and the word can mean different things to different people. Fewer still understand the third statement, because it is written in Latin. None of you understands the last statement, because it is written in a secret code that your author developed as a child.

The Role of Communication in Management

We noted earlier the variety of activities that fill a manager's day. Meetings, telephone calls, and correspondence are all a necessary part of every manager's job—and all clearly involve communication. On a typical Monday, Gordon Bethune, CEO of Continental Airlines, attended five scheduled meetings and two unscheduled meetings; had fifteen telephone conversations; received and/or sent over one hundred e-mails and twenty-nine letters, memos, and reports; and dictated ten letters.

To better understand the linkages between communication and management, recall the variety of roles that managers must fill. Each of the ten basic managerial roles discussed in Chapter 1 (see Table 1.2) would be impossible to fill without communication.[5] Interpersonal roles involve interacting with supervisors, subordinates, peers, and others outside the organization. Decisional roles require managers to seek out information to use in making decisions and then communicate those decisions to others. Informational roles focus specifically on acquiring and disseminating information.

Communication also relates directly to the basic management functions of planning, organizing, leading, and controlling. Environmental scanning, integrating planning-time horizons, and decision making, for example, all necessitate communication. Delegation, coordination, and organization change and development also entail communication. Developing reward systems and interacting with subordinates as a part of the leading function would be impossible without some form of communication. And communication is essential to establishing standards, monitoring performance, and taking corrective actions as a part of control. Clearly, then, communication is a pervasive part of virtually all managerial activities.[6]

The Communication Process

Figure 18.1 illustrates how communication generally takes place between people. The process of communication begins when one person (the sender) wants to

FIGURE 18.1

The Communication Process

As the figure shows, noise can disrupt the communication process at any step. Managers must therefore understand that a conversation in the next office, a fax machine out of paper, and the receiver's worries may all thwart the manager's best attempts to communicate.

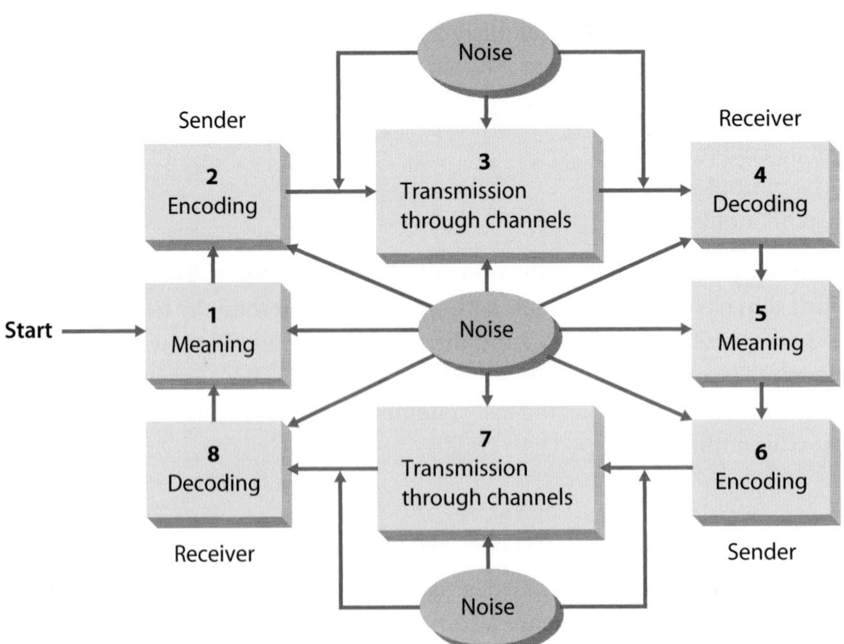

The numbers indicate the sequence in which steps take place.

transmit a fact, idea, opinion, or other information to someone else (the receiver). This fact, idea, or opinion has meaning to the sender, whether it be simple and concrete or complex and abstract. For example, Linda Porter, a marketing representative at Canon, recently landed a new account and wanted to tell her boss about it. This fact and her motivation to tell her boss represented meaning.

The next step is to encode the meaning into a form appropriate to the situation. The encoding might take the form of words, facial expressions, gestures, or even artistic expressions and physical actions. For example, the Canon representative might have said, "I just landed the Acme account," "We just got some good news from Acme," "I just spoiled Xerox's day," "Acme just made the right decision," or any number of other things. She actually chose the second message. Clearly, the encoding process is influenced by the content of the message, the familiarity of sender and receiver, and other situational factors.

After the message has been encoded, it is transmitted through the appropriate channel or medium. The channel by which this encoded message is being transmitted to you is the printed page. Common channels in organizations include meetings, e-mail, memos, letters, reports, and telephone calls. Linda Porter might have written her boss a note, sent him an e-mail, called him on the telephone, or dropped by his office to convey the news. Because both she and her boss were out of the office when she got the news, she called and left a message for him on his voicemail.

After the message is received, it is decoded back into a form that has meaning for the receiver. As noted earlier, the consistency of this meaning can vary dramatically. Upon hearing about the Acme deal, the sales manager at Canon might have thought, "This'll mean a big promotion for both of us," "This is great news for the company," or "She's blowing her own horn too much again." His actual feelings were closest to the second statement. In many cases, the meaning prompts a response, and the cycle is continued when a new message is sent by the same steps back to the original sender. The manager might have called the sales representative to offer congratulations, written her a personal note of praise, offered praise in an e-mail, or sent a formal letter of acknowledgment. Linda's boss wrote her a personal note.

"Noise" may disrupt communication anywhere along the way. Noise can be the sound of someone coughing, a truck driving by, or two people talking close at hand. It can also include disruptions such as a letter lost in the mail, a dead telephone line, an interrupted cell phone call, an e-mail misrouted or infected with a virus, or one of the participants in a conversation being called away before the communication process is completed. If the note written by Linda's boss had gotten lost, she might have felt unappreciated. As it was, his actions positively reinforced not only her efforts at Acme but also her effort to keep him informed.

concept CHECK

Distinguish between communication and effective communication.	***Recall a recent communication exchange in which you participated and analyze it in terms of the model in Figure 18.1.***

Forms of Communication in Organizations

Managers need to understand several kinds of communication that are common in organizations today. These include interpersonal communication, communication in networks and teams, organizational communication, and electronic communication.

Interpersonal Communication

Interpersonal communication generally takes one of two forms: oral and written. As we will see, each has clear strengths and weaknesses. *Working with Diversity* also underscores some of the language issues associated with interpersonal communication.

WORKING WITH diversity

The Language of Diversity

"You can no longer say . . . 'This is a great African-American. . . . '"

— Julie M. Browning, dean of undergraduate enrollment, Rice University*

The U.S. Supreme Court recently ruled that race can be used as an admission criterion to colleges and universities. But, whether or not a university considers race, fear of appearing preferential or prejudiced toward any group is changing the way that universities' admissions personnel talk about applicants. Affirmative action categories require complex semantic distinctions. For example, should a student with a heritage that blends white and African-American be called a "minority"? What about a student with one-quarter Native American ancestry? What about one-sixteenth? Is it fair to categorize a first-generation Vietnamese student in the same "Asian" group as a third-generation Japanese?

If a school is not using affirmative action, new communication dilemmas arise. Julie M. Browning, dean of undergraduate enrollment at Houston's Rice University, claims, "You can no longer say to the committee, 'This is a great African-American from New York.' You have to drop a lot of language associated with affirmative action." At universities around the country, admissions staffers instead might praise a student's "desire to represent his or her heritage." Minority students might be referred to as an "overcome," as in "I really like this 'overcome' applicant." Other catch phrases include "first-generation college" or "good community spokesperson."

Some universities try to avoid language altogether and rely instead on nonverbal signals. In one system, minority students get color-coded folders. Other schools look for cues such as an "ethnic" name or participation in a race-related activity—for example, a Latino student association. Many admissions workers are familiar with the ethnic composition of local schools and communities, so they can make fairly accurate guesses about race.

Colleges and universities are not likely to give up in their quest for a diverse student body. But they may have to learn to talk about race—or rather *not* talk about race—a little differently.

References: Adam Liptak, "Diversity's Precarious Moorings," *New York Times*, December 8, 2002, p. WK3; Jacques Sternberg, "Not All of Them Are Pre-Med," *New York Times*, February 2, 2003, p. WK3; Jacques Sternberg, "The New Calculus of Diversity on Campus," *New York Times*, February 2, 2003, p. WK3; Jacques Sternberg, "Using Synonyms for Race, College Strives for Diversity," *New York Times*, December 8, 2002, pp. L1, L45 (*quote p. L45).

oral communication Face-to-face conversation, group discussions, telephone calls, and other circumstances in which the spoken word is used to transmit meaning

written communication Memos, letters, reports, notes, and other circumstances in which the written word is used to transmit meaning

Oral Communication **Oral communication** takes place in conversations, group discussions, telephone calls, and other situations in which the spoken word is used to express meaning. One study (conducted before the advent of e-mail) demonstrated the importance of oral communication by finding that most managers spent between 50 and 90 percent of their time talking to people.[7] Oral communication is so prevalent for several reasons. The primary advantage of oral communication is that it promotes prompt feedback and interchange in the form of verbal questions or agreement, facial expressions, and gestures. Oral communication is also easy (all the sender needs to do is talk), and it can be done with little preparation (though careful preparation is advisable in certain situations). The sender does not need pencil and paper, typewriter, or other equipment. In another survey, 55 percent of the executives sampled felt that their own written communication skills were fair or poor, so they chose oral communication to avoid embarrassment![8]

People communicate with one another in a variety of ways and in many different settings. Consider this team of Netscape employees. They are using oral communication as they talk while they eat lunch. They are also using written communication from the papers stacked on the table and electronic communication in the form of e-mail. Moreover, they are using nonverbal communication with their body language and facial expressions.

However, oral communication also has drawbacks. It may suffer from problems of inaccuracy if the speaker chooses the wrong words to convey meaning or leaves out pertinent details, if noise disrupts the process, or if the receiver forgets part of the message.[9] In a two-way discussion, there is seldom time for a thoughtful, considered response or for introducing many new facts, and there is no permanent record of what has been said. In addition, although most managers are comfortable talking to people individually or in small groups, fewer enjoy speaking to larger audiences.[10]

Written Communication "Putting it in writing" in a letter, report, memorandum, handwritten note, or e-mail can solve many of the problems inherent in oral communication. Nevertheless, and perhaps surprisingly, **written communication** is not as common as one might imagine, nor is it a mode of communication much respected by managers. One sample of managers indicated that only 13 percent of the printed mail they received was of immediate use to them.[11] Over 80 percent of the managers who responded to another survey indicated that the written communication they received was of fair or poor quality.[12]

The biggest single drawback of traditional forms of written communication is that they inhibit feedback and interchange. When one manager sends another manager a letter, it must be written or dictated, typed, mailed, received, routed, opened, and read. If there is a misunderstanding, it may take several days for it to be recognized, let alone rectified. Although the use of e-mail is, of course, much faster, both sender and receiver must still have access to a computer, and the receiver must open and read the message in order for it to actually be received. A phone call could settle the whole matter in just a few minutes. Thus written communication often inhibits feedback and interchange and is usually more difficult and time consuming than oral communication.

Of course, written communication offers some advantages. It is often quite accurate and provides a permanent record of the exchange. The sender can take the

People in organizations rely on a variety of forms of communication. Joe Lowe, for instance, is South Dakota's State Wildland Coordinator. He is shown here briefing both firefighting experts and the media on how he will be coordinating efforts to control a major wildfire. Lowe is presenting the major points in the plan orally, but also distributes more detailed written instructions. Hence, he is combining different approaches to take advantage of the strengths of each.

time to collect and assimilate the information and can draft and revise it before it is transmitted. The receiver can take the time to read it carefully and can refer to it repeatedly, as needed. For these reasons, written communication is generally preferable when important details are involved. At times it is important to one or both parties to have a written record available as evidence of exactly what took place. Julie Regan, founder of Toucan-Do, an importing company based in Honolulu, relies heavily on formal business letters in establishing contacts and buying merchandise from vendors in Southeast Asia. She believes that such letters give her an opportunity to carefully think through what she wants to say, tailor her message to each individual, and avoid later misunderstandings.

Choosing the Right Form Which form of interpersonal communication should the manager use? The best medium will be determined by the situation. Oral communication or e-mail is often preferred when the message is personal, nonroutine, and brief. More formal written communication is usually best when the message is more impersonal, routine, and longer. And, given the prominent role that e-mails have played in several recent court cases, managers should always use discretion when sending messages electronically.[13] For example, private e-mails made public during legal proceedings have played major roles in litigation involving Enron, Tyco, and WorldCom.[14]

The manager can also combine media to capitalize on the advantages of each. For example, a quick telephone call to set up a meeting is easy and gets an immediate response. Following up the call with a reminder e-mail or handwritten note helps ensure that the recipient will remember the meeting, and it provides a record of the meeting's having been called. Electronic communication, discussed more fully later, blurs the differences between oral and written communication and can help each be more effective.

Communication in Networks and Work Teams

communication network The pattern through which the members of a group communicate

Although communication among team members in an organization is clearly interpersonal in nature, substantial research also focuses specifically on how people in networks and work teams communicate with one another. A **communication network** is the pattern through which the members of a group or team communicate. Researchers studying group dynamics have discovered several typical networks in groups and teams consisting of three, four, and five members. Representative networks among members of five-member teams are shown in Figure 18.2.[15]

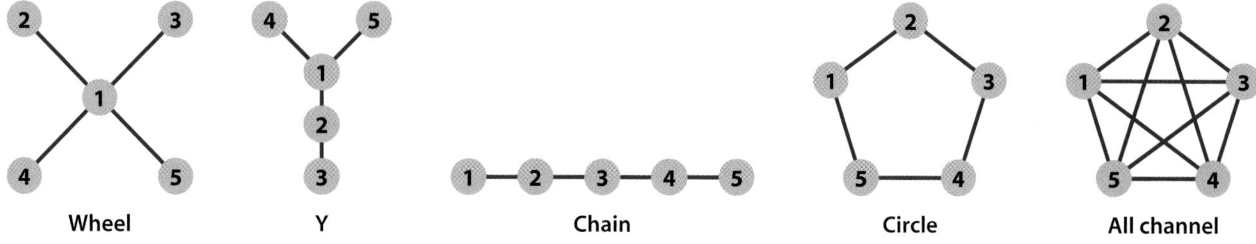

FIGURE 18.2

Types of Communication Networks

Research on communication networks has identified five basic networks for five-person groups. These networks vary in terms of information flow, position of the leader, and effectiveness for different types of tasks. Managers might strive to create centralized networks when group tasks are simple and routine. Alternatively, managers can foster decentralized groups when group tasks are complex and nonroutine.

In the wheel pattern, all communication flows through one central person, who is probably the group's leader. In a sense, the wheel is the most centralized network, because one person receives and disseminates all information. The Y pattern is slightly less centralized—two people are close to the center. The chain offers a more even flow of information among members, although two people (the ones at each end) interact with only one other person. This path is closed in the circle pattern. Finally, the all-channel network, the most decentralized, allows a free flow of information among all group members. Everyone participates equally, and the group's leader, if there is one, is not likely to have excessive power.

Research conducted on networks suggests some interesting connections between the type of network and group performance. For example, when the group's task is relatively simple and routine, centralized networks tend to perform with greatest efficiency and accuracy. The dominant leader facilitates performance by coordinating the flow of information. When a group of accounting clerks is logging incoming invoices and distributing them for payment, for example, one centralized leader can coordinate things efficiently. When the task is complex and nonroutine, such as making a major decision about organizational strategy, decentralized networks tend to be most effective, because open channels of communication permit more interaction and a more efficient sharing of relevant information. Managers should recognize the effects of communication networks on group and organizational performance and should try to structure networks appropriately.

Organizational Communication

Still other forms of communication in organizations are those that flow among and between organizational units or groups. Each of these involves oral or written communication, but each also extends to broad patterns of communication across the organization.[16] As shown in Figure 18.3, two of these forms of communication follow vertical and horizontal linkages in the organization.

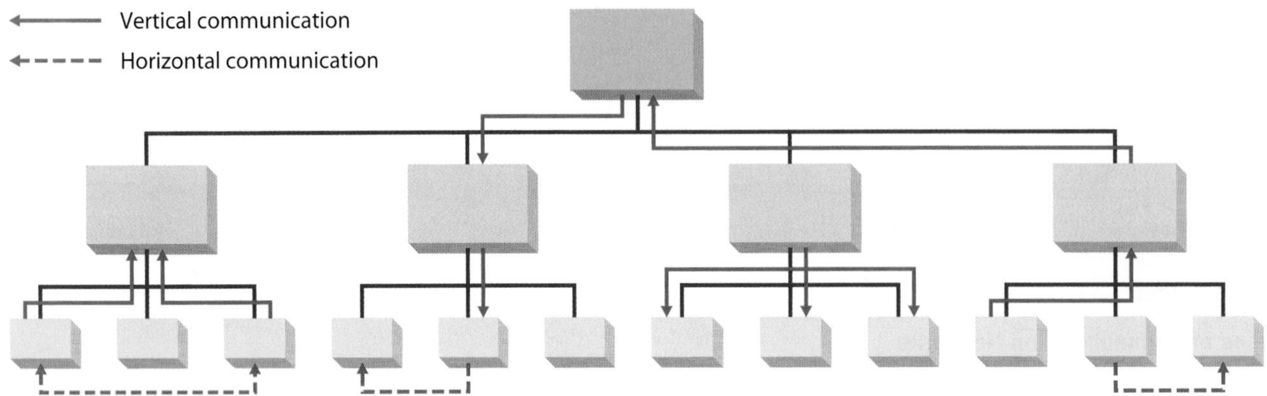

FIGURE 18.3

Formal Communication in Organizations

Formal communication in organizations follows official reporting relationships or prescribed channels. For example, vertical communication, shown here with the solid lines, flows between levels in the organization and involves subordinates and their managers. Horizontal communication, shown with dashed lines, flows between people at the same level and is usually used to facilitate coordination.

vertical communication
Communication that flows up and down the organization, usually along formal reporting lines; takes place between managers and their superiors and subordinates and may involve several different levels of the organization

Vertical Communication **Vertical communication** is communication that flows up and down the organization, usually along formal reporting lines—that is, it is the communication that takes place between managers and their superiors and subordinates. Vertical communication may involve only two people, or it may flow through several different organizational levels. A common perspective on vertical communication that exists in some organizations is illustrated in the cartoon.

Upward communication consists of messages from subordinates to superiors. This flow is usually from subordinates to their direct superior, then to that person's direct superior, and so on up the hierarchy. Occasionally, a message might bypass a particular superior. The typical content of upward communication is requests, information that the lower-level manager thinks is of importance to the higher-level manager, responses to requests from the higher-level manager, suggestions, complaints, and financial information. Research has shown that upward communication is more subject to distortion than is downward communication. Subordinates are likely to withhold or distort information that makes them look bad. The greater

Vertical communication is communication that flows up and down the organizational hierarchy, usually along formal reporting channels involving supervisors and subordinates. In some organizational settings, generally those characterized by trust and openness, anyone can feel free to talk to others several levels higher or lower in the organization. But, in other cases, like the one shown here, individuals who bypass the formal chain of command can create serious problems for themselves. This result usually relates to a feeling of insecurity or strong needs for power and control on the part of those who may feel bypassed.

DILBERT reprinted by permission of United Feature Syndicate, Inc.

the degree of difference in status between superior and subordinate and the greater the degree of distrust, the more likely the subordinate is to suppress or distort information.[17] For example, subordinates might choose to withhold information about problems from their boss if they think the news will make him angry and if they think they can solve the problem themselves without his ever knowing about it.

Downward communication occurs when information flows down the hierarchy from superiors to subordinates. The typical content of these messages is directives on how something is to be done, the assignment of new responsibilities, performance feedback, and general information that the higher-level manager thinks will be of value to the lower-level manager. Vertical communication can and usually should be two-way in nature. In other words, give-and-take communication with active feedback is generally likely to be more effective than one-way communication.[18] *The World of Management* illustrates one manager's commitment to face-to-face communication with his subordinates, even when they work halfway around the world.

Horizontal Communication Whereas vertical communication involves a superior and a subordinate, **horizontal communication** involves colleagues and peers at the same level of the organization. For example, an operations manager might communicate to a marketing manager that inventory levels are running low and that projected delivery dates should be extended by two weeks. Horizontal communication probably occurs more among managers than among nonmanagers.

horizontal communication
Communication that flows laterally within the organization; involves colleagues and peers at the same level of the organization and may involve individuals from several different organizational units

This type of communication serves a number of purposes.[19] It facilitates coordination among interdependent units. For example, a manager at Motorola was once researching the strategies of Japanese semiconductor firms in Europe. He found a great deal of information that was relevant to his assignment. He also uncovered some additional information that was potentially important to another department, so he passed it along to a colleague in that department, who used it to improve his own operations. Horizontal communication can also be used for joint problem solving, as when two plant managers at Northrop Grumman got together to work out a new method to improve productivity. Finally, horizontal communication plays a major role in work teams with members drawn from several departments.

Electronic Communication

Finally, as already noted, electronic communication has taken on much greater importance for managers in recent times. Both formal information systems and personal information technology have reshaped how managers communicate with one another.

Formal Information Systems Most larger businesses manage at least a portion of their organizational communication through information systems. Some firms go so far as to create a position for a chief information officer, or CIO. General Mills, Xerox, and Burlington Industries have all created such a position. The CIO is responsible for determining the information-processing needs and requirements of the organization and then putting in place systems that facilitate smooth and efficient organizational communication.

THE WORLD OF management

"There's No Substitute for Being There"

"The complexities [of cross-cultural communication] aren't going away."

– Robert Bishop, CEO, Silicon Graphics*

Silicon Graphics (SGI) develops networks for sharing and managing data on multiple computers, software for presenting complex data in graphic form, and high-performance computing. In other words, the company is in the business of organizing, storing, analyzing, and presenting information—the business of helping client firms communicate. SGI is headquartered in Silicon Valley and has manufacturing facilities near Minneapolis, but the multinational firm also coordinates sixty worldwide sales and distribution offices. So, in addition to helping others communicate, Silicon Graphics needs employees who can communicate with diverse coworkers and with customers from around the globe. From that perspective, CEO Robert Bishop is an apt choice to lead SGI. Bishop, born in Australia, educated in the United States, and married to a Japanese wife, has extensive global experience. He has worked in Asia, Europe, and the Americas and has taught at universities from Switzerland to Malaysia.

Bishop's approach begins with personal contact. He takes two trips around the world each year, meeting face to face with SGI workers. "The complexities [of cross-cultural communication] aren't going away," Bishop claims. "There's no substitute for being there." Wherever he goes, he immerses himself in the daily life of ordinary people, visiting shipping docks and working-class neighborhoods. "Understanding the underside of society in the struggle between rich and poor helps me develop empathy for the people of a country," Bishop asserts.

Bishop's people skills develop with each new position. Bishop tells the story of a midlevel Algerian manager who was inexplicably holding up progress on a project. Bishop realized the man lacked technical knowledge and was fearful of making a wrong decision. Presenting a simplified version of the sales pitch persuaded him. Bishop states, "You learn to psychoanalyze people to get under the surface of what they're saying."

Bishop uses lessons he has learned at his far-flung assignments to teach SGI managers better communication skills. From the Germans Bishop learned to share corporate information with workers at all levels of the company. While in Japan, Bishop learned decisiveness and persistence.

Robert Bishop's international background has led him to what he calls the core principle of his career: "No country has a monopoly on good ideas."

References: "Company Fact Sheet," "Executive Biographies: Robert Bishop," "France "Locations," "SGI Decision Support Center," Silicon Graphics website, www.sgi.com on February 11, 2003; Jonathan B. Levine, "Fending off Babel in a Global Village," *New York Times*, September 15, 2002, p. BU12 (*quote); "SGI Addresses Diverse Needs of User Community with Launch of Worldwide User Group," *PR Newswire*, January 22, 2003, hoovnews.hoovers.com on February 11, 2003.

Part of the CIO's efforts also involves the creation of one or more formal information systems linking all relevant managers, departments, and facilities in the organization. Most enterprise resource-planning systems play this role very effectively. In the absence of such a system, a marketing manager, for example, may need to call a warehouse manager to find out how much of a particular product is in stock before promising shipping dates to a customer. An effective formal information system allows the marketing manager to get the information more quickly, and probably more accurately, by plugging directly into a computerized information system. Because of the increased emphasis on and importance of these kinds of information systems, we cover them in detail in Chapter 22.

Personal Electronic Technology In recent years, the nature of organizational communication has changed dramatically, mainly because of breakthroughs in personal electronic communication technology, and the future promises even more change. Electronic typewriters and photocopying machines were early breakthroughs. The photocopier, for example, makes it possible for a manager to have a typed report distributed to large numbers of other people in an extremely short time. Personal computers have accelerated the process even more. E-mail networks, the Internet, and corporate intranets are carrying communication technology even further.

It is also becoming common to have teleconferences in which managers stay at their own location (such as offices in different cities) but are seen on television or computer monitors as they "meet." A manager in New York can keyboard a letter or memorandum at her personal computer, point and click with a mouse, and have it delivered to hundreds or even thousands of colleagues around the world in a matter of seconds. Highly detailed information can be retrieved with ease from large electronic databanks. This has given rise to a new version of an old work arrangement—cottage industry. In cottage industry, people work at home (in their "cottage") and periodically bring the products of their labors in to the company. "Telecommuting" is the label given to a new electronic cottage industry. In telecommuting, people work at home on their computer and transmit their work to the company via telephone line or cable modem.

Cellular telephones and facsimile machines have made it even easier for managers to communicate with one another. Many now use cell phones to make calls while commuting to and from work, and carry them in their briefcase so that they can receive calls while at lunch. Facsimile machines make it easy for people to use written communication media and get rapid feedback. And new personal computing devices, such as Palm Pilots, are further revolutionizing how people communicate with one another.

Psychologists, however, are beginning to associate some problems with these communication advances. For one thing, managers who are seldom in their "real" office are likely to fall behind in their field and to be victimized by organizational politics because they are not present to keep in touch with what is going on and to protect themselves. They drop out of the organizational grapevine and miss out on much of the informal communication that takes place. Moreover, the use of electronic communication at the expense of face-to-face meetings and conversations makes it hard to build a strong culture, develop solid working relationships, and create a mutually supportive atmosphere of trust and cooperativeness.[20] Finally, electronic communication is also opening up new avenues for dysfunctional employee behavior, such as the passing of lewd or offensive materials to others. For example, the *New York Times* recently fired almost 10 percent of its workers at one of its branch offices for sending inappropriate e-mails at work.[21]

concept CHECK

What are the primary forms of communication that are used by managers in organizations today?

What kinds of electronic communication have you used in the last twenty-four hours?

Informal Communication in Organizations

The forms of organizational communication discussed in the previous section all represent planned and relatively formal communication mechanisms. However, in many cases some of the communication that takes place in an organization transcends these formal channels and instead follows any of several informal methods. Figure 18.4 illustrates numerous examples of informal communication. Common forms of informal communication in organizations include the grapevine, management by wandering around, and nonverbal communication.

The Grapevine

grapevine An informal communication network among people in an organization

The **grapevine** is an informal communication network that can permeate an entire organization. Grapevines are found in all organizations except the very smallest, but they do not always follow the same patterns as, nor do they necessarily coincide with, formal channels of authority and communication. Research has identified several kinds of grapevines.[22] The two most common are illustrated in Figure 18.5. The gossip chain occurs when one person spreads the message to many other

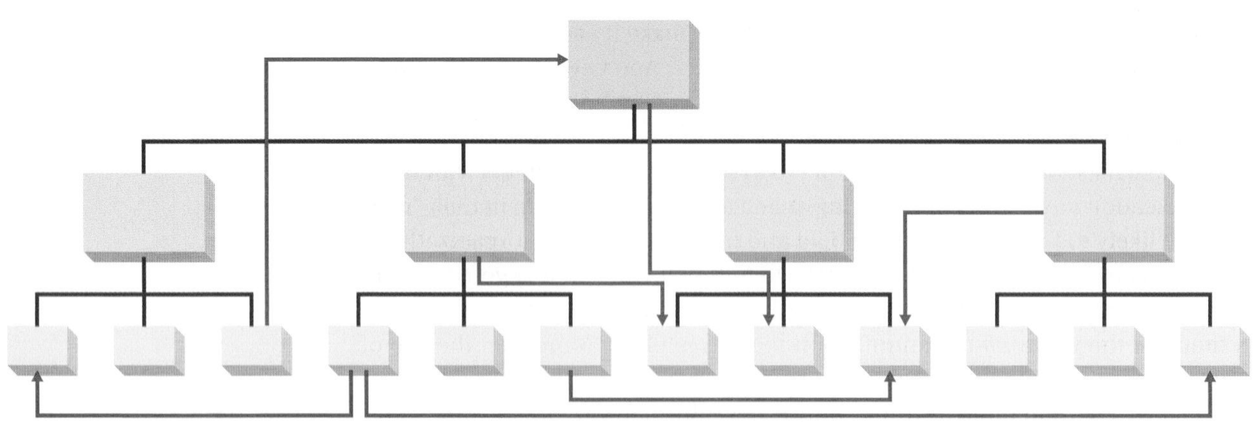

FIGURE 18.4

Informal Communication in Organizations

Informal communication in organizations may or may not follow official reporting relationships or prescribed channels. It may cross different levels and different departments or work units, and may or may not have anything to do with official organizational business.

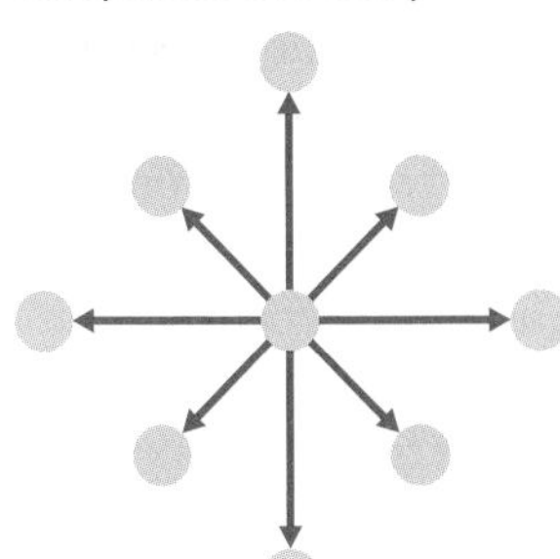

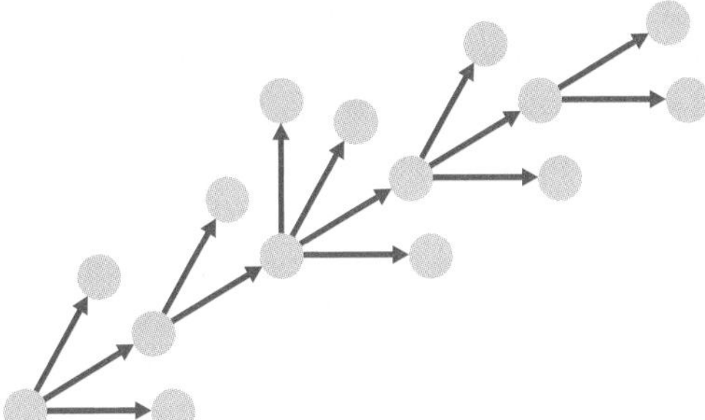

FIGURE 18.5

Common Grapevine Chains Found in Organizations

The two most common grapevine chains in organizations are the gossip chain (in which one person communicates messages to many others) and the cluster chain (in which many people pass messages to a few others).

Source: From Keith Davis and John W. Newstrom, *Human Behavior at Work: Organizational Behavior,* Eighth Edition, 1989. Copyright © 1989 The McGraw-Hill Companies, Inc. Reprinted with permission.

people. Each one, in turn, may either keep the information confidential or pass it on to others. The gossip chain is likely to carry personal information. The other common grapevine is the cluster chain, in which one person passes the information to a selected few individuals. Some of the receivers pass the information to a few other individuals; the rest keep it to themselves.

There is some disagreement about how accurate the information carried by the grapevine is, but research is increasingly finding it to be fairly accurate, especially when the information is based on fact rather than speculation. One study found that the grapevine may be between 75 percent and 95 percent accurate.[23] That same study also found that informal communication is increasing in many organizations for two basic reasons. One contributing factor is the recent increase in merger, acquisition, and takeover activity. Because such activity can greatly affect the people within an organization, it follows that they may spend more time talking about it.[24] The second contributing factor is that, as more and more corporations move facilities from inner cities to suburbs, employees tend to talk less and less to others outside the organization and more and more to one another.

Attempts to eliminate the grapevine are fruitless, but fortunately the manager does have some control over it. By maintaining open channels of communication and responding vigorously to inaccurate information, the manager can minimize the damage the grapevine can do. The grapevine can actually be an asset. By learning who the key people in the grapevine are, for example, the manager can partially control the information they receive and use the grapevine to sound out employee reactions to new ideas, such as a change in human resource policies or benefit packages. The manager can also get valuable information from the grapevine and use it to improve decision making.[25]

Management by Wandering Around

Another increasingly popular form of informal communication is called, interestingly enough, **management by wandering around.**[26] The basic idea is that some managers keep in touch with what is going on by wandering around and talking with people—immediate subordinates, subordinates far down the organizational

management by wandering around
An approach to communication that involves the manager's literally wandering around and having spontaneous conversations with others

hierarchy, delivery people, customers, or anyone else who is involved with the company in some way. Bill Marriott, for example, frequently visits the kitchens, loading docks, and custodial work areas whenever he tours a Marriott hotel. He claims that, by talking with employees throughout the hotel, he gets new ideas and has a better feel for the entire company. And, when Gordon Bethune travels on Continental Airlines, he makes a point of talking to flight attendants and other passengers to gain continuous insights into how the business can be run more effectively.

A related form of organizational communication that really has no specific term is the informal interchange that takes place outside the normal work setting. Employees attending the company picnic, playing on the company softball team, or taking fishing trips together will almost always spend part of their time talking about work. For example, Texas Instruments engineers at TI's Lewisville, Texas, facility often frequent a local bar in town after work. On any given evening, they talk about the Dallas Cowboys, the newest government contract received by the company, the weather, their boss, the company's stock price, local politics, and problems at work. There is no set agenda, and the key topics of discussion vary from group to group and from day to day. Still, the social gatherings serve an important role. They promote a strong culture and enhance understanding of how the organization works.

Nonverbal Communication

nonverbal communication Any communication exchange that does not use words or uses words to carry more meaning than the strict definition of the words themselves

Nonverbal communication is a communication exchange that does not use words or uses words to carry more meaning than the strict definition of the words themselves. Nonverbal communication is a powerful but little-understood form of communication in organizations. It often relies on facial expressions, body movements, physical contact, and gestures. One study found that as much as 55 percent of the content of a message is transmitted by facial expressions and body posture and that another 38 percent derives from inflection and tone. Words themselves account for only 7 percent of the content of the message.[27]

Research has identified three kinds of nonverbal communication practiced by managers—images, settings, and body language.[28] In this context, images are the kinds of words people elect to use. "Damn the torpedoes, full speed ahead" and "Even though there are some potential hazards, we should proceed with this course of action" may convey the same meaning. Yet the person who uses the first expression may be perceived as a maverick, a courageous hero, an individualist, or a reckless and foolhardy adventurer. The person who uses the second might be described as aggressive, forceful, diligent, or narrow minded and resistant to change. In short, our choice of words conveys much more than just the strict meaning of the words themselves.

The setting for communication also plays a major role in nonverbal communication. Boundaries, familiarity, the home turf, and other elements of the setting are all important. Much has been written about the symbols of power in organizations. The size and location of an office, the kinds of furniture in the office, and the accessibility of the person in the office all communicate useful information. For example, H. Ross Perot positions his desk so that it is always between him and a visitor.

This keeps him in charge. When he wants a less formal dialogue, he moves around to the front of the desk and sits beside his visitor. Michael Dell of Dell Computer has his desk facing a side window so that, when he turns around to greet a visitor, there is never anything between them.

A third form of nonverbal communication is body language.[29] The distance we stand from someone as we speak has meaning. In the United States, standing very close to someone you are talking to generally signals either familiarity or aggression. The English and Germans stand farther apart than Americans when talking, whereas the Arabs, Japanese, and Mexicans stand closer together.[30] Eye contact is another effective means of nonverbal communication. For example, prolonged eye contact might suggest either hostility or romantic interest. Other kinds of body language include body and hand movement, pauses in speech, and mode of dress.

The manager should be aware of the importance of nonverbal communication and recognize its potential impact. Giving an employee good news about a reward with the wrong nonverbal cues can destroy the reinforcement value of the reward. Likewise, reprimanding an employee but providing inconsistent nonverbal cues can limit the effectiveness of the sanctions. The tone of the message, where and how the message is delivered, facial expressions, and gestures can all amplify or weaken the message or change the message altogether.

concept CHECK

What are the three fundamental kinds of informal communication that occur in an organization?

Spend thirty minutes observing other people and note the various kinds of nonverbal communication they exhibit.

Managing Organizational Communication

In view of the importance and pervasiveness of communication in organizations, it is vital for managers to understand how to manage the communication process.[31] Managers should understand how to maximize the potential benefits of communication and minimize the potential problems. We begin our discussion of communication management by considering the factors that might disrupt effective communication and how to deal with them.

Barriers to Communication

Several factors may disrupt the communication process or serve as barriers to effective communication.[32] As shown in Table 18.1, these may be divided into two classes: individual barriers and organizational barriers.

Individual Barriers Several individual barriers may disrupt effective communication. One common problem is conflicting or inconsistent signals. A manager is sending conflicting signals when she says on Monday that things should be done

Many managers would like to improve communication effectiveness in their organizations. While there are several basic things that can be done, they sometimes seek out unusual and creative methods as well. Ellen Moore, for instance, is a professional ethnographer—someone who studies cultures and societies through first-hand observation. Moore works as a communications consultant to several businesses. She spends time watching how people interact and communicate with each other and then offers suggestions for making those processes more effective.

one way, but then prescribes an entirely different procedure on Wednesday. Inconsistent signals are being sent by a manager who says that he has an "open door" policy and wants his subordinates to drop by, but keeps his door closed and becomes irritated whenever someone stops in.

Another barrier is lack of credibility. Credibility problems arise when the sender is not considered a reliable source of information. He may not be trusted or may not be perceived as knowledgeable about the subject at hand. When a politician is caught withholding information or when a manager makes a series of bad decisions, the extent to which he or she will be listened to and believed thereafter diminishes. In extreme cases, people may talk about something they obviously know little or nothing about.

Some people are simply reluctant to initiate a communication exchange. This reluctance may occur for a variety of reasons. A manager may be reluctant to tell subordinates about an impending budget cut because he knows they will be unhappy about it. Likewise, a subordinate may be reluctant to transmit information upward for fear of reprisal or because it is felt that such an effort would be futile.

Poor listening habits can be a major barrier to effective communication. Some people are simply poor listeners. When someone is talking to them, they may be daydreaming, looking around, reading, or listening to another conversation. Because they are not concentrating on what is being said, they may not comprehend part or all of the message. They may even think that they really are paying attention, only to realize later that they cannot remember parts of the conversation.

TABLE 18.1

Barriers to Effective Communication

Numerous barriers can disrupt effective communication. Some of these barriers involve individual characteristics and processes. Others are functions of the organizational context in which communication is taking place.

Individual Barriers	Organizational Barriers
Conflicting or inconsistent signals	Semantics
Credibility about the subject	Status or power differences
Reluctance to communicate	Different perceptions
Poor listening skills	Noise
Predispositions about the subject	Overload
	Language differences

Receivers may also bring certain predispositions to the communication process. They may already have their mind made up, firmly set in a certain way. For example, a manager may have heard that his new boss is unpleasant and hard to work with. When she calls him in for an introductory meeting, he may go into that meeting predisposed to dislike her and discount what she has to say.

Organizational Barriers Other barriers to effective communication involve the organizational context in which the communication occurs. Semantics problems arise when words have different meanings for different people. Words and phrases such as *profit, increased output, and return on investment* may have positive meanings for managers but less positive meanings for labor.

Communication problems may also arise when people of different power or status try to communicate with each other. The company president may discount a suggestion from an operating employee, thinking, "How can someone at that level help me run my business?" Or, when the president goes out to inspect a new plant, workers may be reluctant to offer suggestions because of their lower status. The marketing vice president may have more power than the human resource vice president and consequently may not pay much attention to a staffing report submitted by the human resource department.

If people perceive a situation differently, they may have difficulty communicating with one another. When two managers observe that a third manager has not spent much time in her office lately, one may believe that she has been to several important meetings, and the other may think she is "hiding out." If they

Numerous barriers can disrupt effective communication. These men are surfing the Internet in Beijing in the People's Republic of China. While the Internet is growing in popularity in the PRC, the government is also aggressively seeking to keep web users from viewing what it deems to be undesirable content. As an example, the PRC recently blocked access to search engines such as Google and instead diverted users to a less effective—but more "acceptable"—Chinese site.

need to talk about her in some official capacity, problems may arise because one has a positive impression and the other a negative impression.

Environmental factors may also disrupt effective communication. As mentioned earlier, noise may affect communication in many ways. Similarly, overload may be a problem when the receiver is being sent more information than he or she can effectively handle. As e-mail becomes increasingly common, many managers report getting so many messages each day as to sometimes feel overwhelmed.[33] And, when the manager gives a subordinate many jobs on which to work and at the same time the subordinate is being told by family and friends to do other things, overload may result and communication effectiveness diminishes.

Finally, as businesses become more and more global, different languages can create problems. To counter this problem, some firms are adopting an "official language." For example, when the German chemical firm Hoechst merged with the French firm Rhone-Poulenc, the new company adopted English as its official language. Indeed, English is increasingly becoming the standard business language around the world.[34]

Improving Communication Effectiveness

Considering how many factors can disrupt communication, it is fortunate that managers can resort to several techniques for improving communication effectiveness.[35] As shown in Table 18.2, these techniques include both individual and organizational skills.

Individual Skills The single most important individual skill for improving communication effectiveness is being a good listener.[36] Being a good listener requires that the individual be prepared to listen, not interrupt the speaker, concentrate on both the words and the meaning being conveyed, be patient, and ask questions as appropriate.[37] So important are good listening skills that companies like Delta, IBM,

TABLE 18.2

Overcoming Barriers to Communication

Because communication is so important, managers have developed several methods of overcoming barriers to effective communication. Some of these methods involve individual skills, whereas others are based on organizational skills.

Individual Skills	Organizational Skills
Develop good listening skills	Follow up
Encourage two-way communication	Regulate information flows
Be aware of language and meaning	Understand the richness of media
Maintain credibility	
Be sensitive to receiver's perspective	
Be sensitive to sender's perspective	

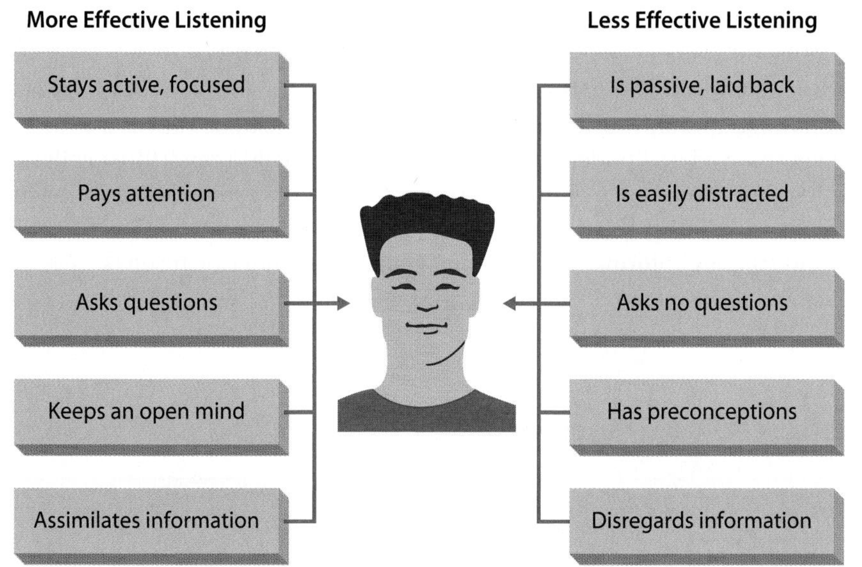

FIGURE 18.6

More and Less Effective Listening Skills

Effective listening skills are a vital part of communication in organizations. There are several barriers that can contribute to poor listening skills by individuals in organizations. Fortunately, there are also several practices for improving listening skills.

and Boeing conduct programs to train their managers to be better listeners. Figure 18.6 illustrates the characteristics of poor listeners versus good listeners.

In addition to being a good listener, several other individual skills can promote effective communication. Feedback, one of the most important, is facilitated by two-way communication. Two-way communication allows the receiver to ask questions, request clarification, and express opinions that let the sender know whether he or she has been understood. In general, the more complicated the message, the more useful two-way communication is. In addition, the sender should be aware of the meanings that different receivers might attach to various words. For example, when addressing stockholders, a manager might use the word *profits* often. When addressing labor leaders, however, she may choose to use *profits* less often.

Furthermore, the sender should try to maintain credibility. This can be accomplished by not pretending to be an expert when one is not, by "doing one's homework" and checking facts, and by otherwise being as accurate and honest as possible. The sender should also try to be sensitive to the receiver's perspective. A manager who must tell a subordinate that she has not been recommended for a promotion should recognize that the subordinate will be frustrated and unhappy. The content of the message and its method of delivery should be chosen accordingly. The manager should be primed to accept a reasonable degree of hostility and bitterness without getting angry in return.[38]

Finally, the receiver should also try to be sensitive to the sender's point of view. Suppose that a manager has just received some bad news—for example, that his position is being eliminated next year. Others should understand that he may be disappointed, angry, or even depressed for a while. Thus they might make a special effort not to take too much offense if he snaps at them, and they might look for signals that he needs someone to talk to. *Today's Management Issues* illustrates how difficult it is for some people to simply say, "I'm sorry."

Organizational Skills Three useful organizational skills can also enhance communication effectiveness for both the sender and the receiver—following up, regulating information flow, and understanding the richness of different media. Following up simply involves checking at a later time to be sure that a message has been received and understood. After a manager mails a report to a colleague, she might call a few days later to make sure the report has arrived. If it has, the manager might ask whether the colleague has any questions about it.

Regulating information flow means that the sender or receiver takes steps to ensure that overload does not occur. For the sender, this could mean not passing

TODAY'S management ISSUES

Heartfelt Apologies

Corporate managers have a lot to apologize for. Accounting scandals, insider trading, fraud, unsafe products, environmental disasters, discrimination, and invasion of privacy have made headlines in recent months. Why, then, do executives find it so hard to say, "I'm sorry"?

Blame it on the lawyers. Corporate leaders are afraid to express remorse for fear of looking guilty in court. "The first reaction in many companies . . . is to hunker down and fight," says lawyer Philip K. Howard. "A lot of times, that just gets them into a bigger mess." Managers in denial include Martha Stewart, who calls insider-trading charges "ridiculous," and former Enron CEO Jeffrey Skilling, who claims he is "immensely proud" of what he accomplished there.

"I'm not sure if [Jim Koch, founder of Boston Brewing] is sorry he did what he did or if he's just sorry he got caught."

— Jim McGettrick, owner of the Beachcomber bar in Quincy, Massachusetts*

Thirty-seven percent of malpractice patients say they would not have sued if the doctor had apologized. One Veteran's Administration hospital always apologizes for errors, without regard for legal consequences. That hospital has the lowest malpractice claims of any VA facility. An America West vice president went on the *Today* show to apologize to a customer who was thrown off a flight for making a joke. The passenger publicly forgave the airline.

Yet, even when managers apologize, they must do so correctly. Merrill Lynch issued an apology for e-mails that showed company analysts misleading their clients. But the apology only expressed regret for the e-mails themselves, not for the fraudulent behavior that the e-mails exposed. Jim Koch, founder of Boston Brewing, sponsored a distasteful public relations stunt involving Saint Patrick's Cathedral, the site of funerals for many of the firefighters who perished on September 11. Offended bar owners forced Koch to confess. However, the apology was two weeks late, and Koch failed to accept responsibility. Bar owner Jim McGettrick says, "I'm not sure if he's sorry he did what he did or if he's just sorry he got caught."

BusinessWeek writer Mike France recommends that, first, managers apologize quickly. Second, they should apologize bravely, speaking in plain English instead of legalese. Third, they should apologize clearly. They need to acknowledge the law that was violated, admit its importance, and accept the consequences. Fourth, managers must apologize authoritatively, accepting responsibility at the highest level of the organization.

References: "Grubman Hit with $15 Million Fine," *CNN/Money*, December 20, 2002, www.cnn.com on February 12, 2003; Joshua Hyatt, "What Was He Drinking?" *Fortune Small Business*, November 1, 2002, www.fortune.com on November 24, 2002 (*quote); Mike France, "The Mea Culpa Defense," *BusinessWeek*, August 26, 2002, pp. 76–78.

too much information through the system at one time. For the receiver, it might mean calling attention to the fact that he is being asked to do too many things at once. Many managers limit the influx of information by periodically weeding out the list of journals and routine reports they receive, or they train their assistant to screen phone calls and visitors. Indeed, some executives now get so much e-mail that they have it routed to an assistant. That person reviews the e-mail, discards those that are not useful (such as "spam"), responds to those that are routine, and passes on to the executive only those that require her or his personal attention.

Both parties should also understand the richness associated with different media. When a manager is going to lay off a subordinate temporarily, the message should be delivered in person. A face-to-face channel of communication gives the manager an opportunity to explain the situation and answer questions. When the purpose of the message is to grant a pay increase, written communication may be appropriate, because it can be more objective and precise. The manager could then follow up the written notice with personal congratulations.

concept CHECK

What are the primary barriers to communication in organizations, and how can they most effectively be overcome?

Think of two recent situations in which you encountered a barrier to communication. How was it—or how might it have been—overcome?

Summary of Key Points

business.college.hmco.com/students

Communication is the process of transmitting information from one person to another. Effective communication is the process of sending a message in such a way that the message received is as close in meaning as possible to the message intended.

Communication is a pervasive and important part of the manager's world. The communication process consists of a sender's encoding meaning and transmitting it to one or more receivers, who receive the message and decode it into meaning. In two-way communication, the process continues with the roles reversed. Noise can disrupt any part of the overall process.

Several forms of organizational communication exist. Interpersonal communication focuses on communication among a small number of people. Two important forms of interpersonal communication, oral and written, both offer unique advantages and disadvantages. Thus the manager should weigh the pros and cons of each when choosing a medium for communication.

Communication networks are recurring patterns of communication among members of a group or work team. Vertical communication between superiors and subordinates may flow upward or downward. Horizontal communication involves peers and colleagues at the same level in the organization. Organizations also use information systems to manage communication. Electronic communication is having a profound effect on managerial and organizational communication.

There is also a great deal of informal communication in organizations. The grapevine is the informal communication network among people in an organization. Management by wandering around is also a popular informal method of communication. Nonverbal communication includes facial expressions, body movement, physical contact, gestures, and inflection and tone.

Managing the communication process necessitates recognizing the barriers to effective communication and understanding how to overcome them. Barriers can be identified at both the individual and the organizational level. Likewise, both individual and organizational skills can be used to overcome these barriers.

Discussion Questions

Questions for Review

1. Describe the difference between communication and effective communication. How can a sender verify that a communication was effective? How can a receiver verify that a communication was effective?
2. Which form of interpersonal communication is best for long-term retention? Why? Which form is best for getting across subtle nuances of meaning? Why?
3. What are the similarities and differences of oral and written communication? What kinds of situations call for the use of oral methods? What situations call for written communication?
4. Describe the individual and organizational barriers to effective communication. For each barrier, describe one action that a manager could take to reduce the problems caused by that barrier.

Questions for Analysis

5. "Personal friendships have no place at work." Do you agree or disagree with this statement, and why?
6. At what points in the communication process can problems occur? Give examples of how noise can interfere with the communication process. What can managers do to reduce problems and noise?
7. How are electronic communication devices (cell phones, e-mail, and websites) likely to affect the communication process in the future? Describe both the advantages and the disadvantages of these three devices over traditional communication methods, such as face-to-face conversations, written notes, and phone calls.

Questions for Application

8. What forms of communication have you experienced today? What form of communication is involved in a face-to-face conversation with a friend? a telephone call from a customer? a traffic light or crossing signal? a picture of a cigarette in a circle with a slash across it? an area around machinery defined by a yellow line painted on the floor?
9. Keep track of your own activities over the course of a few hours of leisure time to determine what forms of communication you encounter. Which forms were most common? If you had been tracking your communications while at work, how would the list be different? Explain why the differences occur.
10. For each of the following situations, tell which form of communication you would use. Then ask the same question of someone who has been in the workforce for at least ten years. For any differences that occur, ask the worker to explain why his or her choice is better than yours. Do you agree with his or her assessment? Why or why not?

- Describing complex changes in how health-care benefits are calculated and
- Administered to every employee of a large firm
- Asking your boss a quick question about how she wants something done
- Telling customers that a new two-for-one promotion is available at your store
- Reprimanding an employee for excessive absences on the job
- Reminding workers that no smoking is allowed in your facility

BUILDING EFFECTIVE technical SKILLS

business.college.hmco.com/students

Exercise Overview

Technical skills are the skills necessary to perform the work of the organization. This exercise will help you develop and apply technical skills involving the Internet and its potential for gathering information relevant to making important decisions.

Exercise Background

Assume that you are a manager for a large national retailer. You have been assigned the responsibility for identifying potential locations for the construction of a warehouse and distribution center. The idea behind such a center is that the firm can use its enormous purchasing power to buy many products in bulk quantities at relatively low prices. Individual stores can then order the specific quantities they need from the warehouse.

The location will need an abundance of land. The warehouse itself, for example, will occupy more than four square acres of land. In addition, it must be close to railroads and major highways, because shipments will be arriving by both rail and truck, although outbound shipments will be exclusively by truck. Other important variables are that land prices and the cost of living should be relatively low and weather conditions should be mild (to minimize disruptions to shipments).

The firm's general experience is that small to midsize communities work best. Moreover, warehouses are already in place in the western and eastern parts of the United States, so this new one will most likely be in the central or south-central area. Your boss has asked you to identify three or four possible sites.

Exercise Task

With the information above as a framework, do the following:

1. Use the Internet to identify as many as ten possible locations.
2. Using additional information from the Internet, narrow the set of possible locations to three or four.
3. Again using the Internet, find out as much as possible about the potential locations.

BUILDING EFFECTIVE interpersonal SKILLS

Exercise Overview

A manager's interpersonal skills include his or her abilities to understand and to motivate individuals and groups. This in-class demonstration gives you practice in understanding the nonverbal and verbal behavior of a pair of individuals.

Exercise Background

Nonverbal communication conveys more than half of the information in any face-to-face exchange, and body language is a significant part of our nonverbal behavior. Consider, for example, the impact of a yawn or a frown or a shaking fist. At the same time, however, nonverbal communication is often neglected by managers. The result can be confusing and misleading signals.

In this exercise, you will examine interactions between two people without sound, with only visual clues to meaning. Then you will examine those same interactions with both visual and verbal clues.

Exercise Task

1. Observe the silent video segments that your professor shows to the class. For each segment, describe the nature of the relationship and interaction between the two individuals. What nonverbal clues did you use in reaching your conclusions?
2. Next, observe the same video segments, but this time with audio included. Describe the interaction again, along with any verbal clues you used.
3. How accurate were your assessments when you had only visual information? Explain why you were or were not accurate.
4. What does this exercise show you about the nature of nonverbal communication? What advice would you now give managers about their nonverbal communication?

BUILDING EFFECTIVE communication SKILLS

business.college.hmco.com/students

Exercise Overview

This exercise gives you practice in using e-mail to effectively convey and receive ideas and information.

Exercise Background

E-mail accounts for an increasing percentage of managers' communication time. According to Andy Grove, chairman of the board and former CEO of Intel, e-mail takes time, but he says, "It also replaces time. I mean, I used to spend probably an hour-and-a-half to two hours a day reading paper mail—and that has almost disappeared." Grove's e-mail use may be on the low side. One study of high-tech managers showed that, on average, they spent two hours per day reading, sending, or gathering data for e-mail. Given the growing importance and prevalence of e-mail, it is important for managers to understand how to use it effectively.

Exercise Task

1. Visit the website of author Virginia Shea's book *Netiquette,* at www.albion.com/netiquette/. The site provides key excerpts from her book. Go to the page "The Core Rules of Netiquette," which gives a useful brief summary of the full text. Read the sections "Introduction" and "Rule 1: Remember the Human."
2. Write an e-mail message to a hypothetical firm, describing your dissatisfaction with a product or service they sold to you. Bring the printout of the message to class.
3. Exchange e-mail messages with a classmate. Read each other's messages and give feedback. Evaluate the clarity and tone of each message. Is the message polite yet firm? Does it clearly indicate the problem? Does it suggest a solution? If you were the employee who received this message, what would be your reaction? Share your feedback with your classmate.

CHAPTER CLOSING case

Communicating the Truth about Smoking

> *"'Please don't smoke; it's not good for your health' doesn't work for kids."*
>
> – Colleen Stevens, spokeswoman, California Department of Health*

A young man stands near a pile of body bags outside the high-rise headquarters of Philip Morris. He shouts up: "We're gonna leave these here, so you can see what 1,200 people actually look like!" The body bags represent the 1,200 daily deaths in the United States attributable to tobacco products. The American Legacy Foundation developed the innovative television advertisements to inform and warn teens about the dangers of smoking. So far, the commercials have been remarkably effective.

In 1998 Big Tobacco agreed to pay $206 billion. $300 million of that, each year, was earmarked for smoking education and prevention, especially among youth. The nonprofit American Legacy Foundation (ALF) was established to administer those programs.

Dozens of crawling baby dolls cover an urban sidewalk. Passersby are bemused. One doll falls face up, allowing viewers to read its T-shirt: "How do infants avoid secondhand smoke? 'At some point, they learn to crawl.'—Tobacco executive" ALF developed the unique "truth" ads to raise awareness of the dangers of smoking. The commercials feature diverse teens taking direct action against tobacco companies. The style is edgy and confrontational. Market researcher Peter Zollo calls the ads "the 'un-marketing' of high-risk youth behaviors." He explains why the commercials have been so effective with teenagers: "The truth campaign creates a brand with which [teens] want to affiliate. Truth understands teenagers' emotional needs to rebel, defy authority, and assert their independence. So instead of rebelling by smoking, truth encourages teens to rebel by confronting and rejecting the tobacco industry."

The messages appeal to young people's distrust of big business and their desire for nonconformity. Zollo claims, "We've found that humor also goes a long way in gaining teens' acceptance and establishing credibility." High schooler Katie Hardison agrees. "They're not saying we're smarter than you; we know what you should do," says Hardison. "They never say don't smoke." In fact, the ads show a teen saying, "If I want to smoke that's my own decision," and another ad claims, "We totally respect people's freedom of choice—different strokes for different folks."

Philip Morris's own ad campaign features the tag line "Think. Don't Smoke." Teenagers rate those ads as far less effective. The Philip Morris ads "imply that people who smoke are stupid. They imply that people who smoke can simply choose to quit," Hardison states. ALF contends that the ads present smoking as a behavior that is reserved for adults, which makes smoking appear forbidden and therefore more desirable. Surveys show that teens who view the Philip Morris ads are more likely to smoke. "What we learned very early on is that 'Please don't smoke; it's not good for your health' doesn't work for kids," says Colleen Stevens of the California Department of Health.

A young woman pushes a baby carriage on a busy city sidewalk. She abruptly runs away, abandoning the carriage near the curb. Bewildered pedestrians approach. Inside, they see a baby doll, and a sign proclaims, "Every year, smoking leaves about 13,000 kids motherless." ALF not only produces commercials, it creates print ads for publications geared to teens. A truth tour visits beaches and concerts with thirteen vans full of DJs, video monitors, and game consoles. The tour was seen by 4.3 million people in 2002. Its website, www.thetruth.com, attracts over 8,000 visitors daily. ALF sponsors a nationally syndicated hip-hop radio show called TRUTH-FM. The nonprofit provides $10 million each year to fund grassroots, youth-led antismoking activities. ALF's research division conducts surveys to evaluate the organization's effectiveness.

Thus far, performance has been high. ALF CEO Cheryl G. Healton claims that, after one year of the truth campaign, "75 percent of all 12 to 17 year olds . . . could accurately describe at least one of the truth ads. Nearly 90 percent of these . . . said the ad they saw was convincing." Even more encouraging, truth ads were judged most effective by those at the highest risk—young people who are already smoking or are considering smoking.

Tobacco firm Lorillard is suing ALF. In its claim, Lorillard states, "ALF's 'truth' campaign is not about conveying the truth. . . . The message of the 'truth' campaign is that the [tobacco] manufacturers and their executives are dishonest, deceitful, callous, malicious, or otherwise unscrupulous." ALF replies that tobacco companies are upset precisely because ALF has been so effective. CEO Healton cites the drop in smoking among college students, from 31 percent in 1999 to 26 percent in 2001. *A young woman holds an electronic display, showing the digit 8. The view is grainy, off-center, unsteady. The text reads, "Every 8 seconds, big tobacco loses another customer." Pause. "They die."*

Case Questions

1. Describe the steps in the communication process that occur as ALF attempts to educate teens about smoking. Use specific examples from the case.
2. Show how ALF is using oral, written, electronic, and nonverbal communication.
3. In your opinion, why is ALF successful when other organizations sending the same basic message are not? Is there anything ALF could do to increase its effectiveness?

Case References

Alina Tugend, "Cigarette Makers Take Anti-Smoking Ads Personally," *New York Times*, October 27, 2002, p. BU4 (*quote); "American Legacy Foundation," "Applied Research and Evaluation," "Fact Sheet on College Students and Smoking," "First Look Report 9," "Lorillard Tobacco Company," "Remarks as Prepared for Delivery by Peter Zollo," American Legacy Foundation website, www.americanlegacy.org on February 16, 2003; Cara B. DiPasquale, "Anti-Tobacco Group Blasts Philip Morris Ads," *Ad Age*, May 29, 2002, www.adage.com on February 16, 2003; Wendy McElroy, "Paying for the Rope That Hangs Them," September 25, 2000, Wendy McElroy's website, www.zetetics.com on February 16, 2003.

Chapter Notes

1. Doug Sample, "TriWest Answers Questions on Stolen Computer Info, Increased Security," *Defense Link*, www.defenselink.mil on February 11, 2003; Gretchen Morgenson, "Analyze This: What Those Analysts Said in Private," *New York Times*, September 15, 2002, p. BU2; Heidi L. McNeil and Robert M. Kort, "Discovery of E-Mail and Other Computerized Information," Scottsdale Law website, www.scottsdalelaw.com on October 29, 2002; Joseph Nchor, "Self-Policing of Email Marketing Industry May Work," *Email Today*, www.emailtoday.com on February 10, 2003; Kevin Poulsen, "New York Times Internal Network Hacked," *BusinessWeek*, February 27, 2002, www.businessweek.com on February 10, 2003; Michelle Delio, "The Internet: It's Full of Holes," *Wired News*, February 6, 2001, www.wired.com on February 11, 2003 (*quote).
2. See John J. Gabarro, "The Development of Working Relationships," in Jay W. Lorsch, ed., *Handbook of Organizational Behavior* (Englewood Cliffs, N.J.: Prentice-Hall, 1987), pp. 172–189. See also "Team Efforts, Technology, Add New Reasons to Meet," *USA Today*, December 8, 1997, pp. 1A, 2A.
3. See C. Gopinath and Thomas E. Becker, "Communication, Procedural Justice, and Employee Attitudes: Relationships Under Conditions of Divestiture," *Journal of Management*, 2000, vol. 26, no. 1, pp. 63–83.
4. Henry Mintzberg, *The Nature of Managerial Work* (New York: Harper & Row, 1973).
5. Ibid.
6. See Batia M. Wiesenfeld, Sumita, and Raghu Garud, "Communication Patterns as Determinants of Organizational Identification in a Virtual Organization," *Organization Science*, 1999, vol. 10, no. 6, pp. 777–790.
7. Mintzberg, *The Nature of Managerial Work.*
8. Reid Buckley, "When You Have to Put It to Them," *Across the Board*, October 1999, pp. 44–48.
9. "'Did I Just Say That?!' How to Recover from Foot-in-Mouth," *Wall Street Journal*, June 19, 2002, p. B1.
10. "Executives Who Dread Public Speaking Learn to Keep Their Cool in the Spotlight," *Wall Street Journal*, May 4, 1990, pp. B1, B6.
11. Mintzberg, *The Nature of Managerial Work.*
12. Buckley, "When You Have to Put It to Them."
13. See "Watch What You Put in That Office Email," *BusinessWeek*, September 30, 2002, pp. 114–115.
14. Nicholas Varchaver, "The Perils of E-mail," *Fortune*, February 17, 2003, pp. 96–102; "How a String of E-Mail Came to Haunt CSFB and Star Banker," *Wall Street Journal*, February 28, 2003, pp. A1, A6.
15. A. Vavelas, "Communication Patterns in Task-oriented Groups," *Journal of the Accoustical Society of America*, vol. 22, 1950, pp. 725–730; Jerry Wofford, Edwin Gerloff, and Robert Cummins, *Organizational Communication* (New York: McGraw-Hill, 1977).

16. Nelson Phillips and John Brown, "Analyzing Communications in and Around Organizations: A Critical Hermeneutic Approach," *Academy of Management Journal,* 1993, vol. 36, no. 6, pp. 1547–1576.
17. Walter Kiechel III, "Breaking Bad News to the Boss," *Fortune,* April 9, 1990, pp. 111–112.
18. Mary Young and James Post, "How Leading Companies Communicate with Employees," *Organizational Dynamics,* Summer 1993, pp. 31–43.
19. For one example, see Kimberly D. Elsbach and Greg Elofson, "How the Packaging of Decision Explanations Affects Perceptions of Trustworthiness," *Academy of Management Journal,* 2000, vol. 43, no. 1, pp. 80–89.
20. Walter Kiechel III, "Hold for the Communicaholic Manager," *Fortune,* January 2, 1989, pp. 107–108.
21. "Those Bawdy E-Mails Were Good for a Laugh—Until the Ax Fell," *Wall Street Journal,* February 4, 2000, pp. A1, A8.
22. Keith Davis, "Management Communication and the Grapevine," *Harvard Business Review,* September–October 1953, pp. 43–49.
23. "Spread the Word: Gossip Is Good," *Wall Street Journal,* October 4, 1988, p. B1.
24. See David M. Schweiger and Angelo S. DeNisi, "Communication with Employees Following a Merger: A Longitudinal Field Experiment," *Academy of Management Journal,* March 1991, pp. 110–135.
25. Nancy B. Kurland and Lisa Hope Pelled, "Passing the Word: Toward a Model of Gossip and Power in the Workplace," *Academy of Management Review,* 2000, vol. 25, no. 2, pp. 428–438.
26. See Tom Peters and Nancy Austin, *A Passion for Excellence* (New York: Random House, 1985).
27. Albert Mehrabian, *Non-verbal Communication* (Chicago: Aldine, 1972).
28. Michael B. McCaskey, "The Hidden Messages Managers Send," *Harvard Business Review,* November–December 1979, pp. 135–148.
29. David Givens, "What Body Language Can Tell You That Words Cannot," *U.S. News & World Report,* November 19, 1984, p. 100.
30. Edward J. Hall, *The Hidden Dimension* (New York: Doubleday, 1966).
31. For a detailed discussion of improving communication effectiveness, see Courtland L. Bovee, John V. Thill, and Barbara E. Schatzman *Business Communication Today,* 7th ed. (Upper Saddle River, N.J.: Prentice Hall, 2003).
32. See Otis W. Baskin and Craig E. Aronoff, *Interpersonal Communication in Organizations* (Glenview, Ill.: Scott, Foresman, 1980).
33. See "You Have (Too Much) E-Mail," *USA Today,* March 12, 1999, p. 3B.
34. Justin Fox, "The Triumph of English," *Fortune,* September 18, 2000, pp. 209–212.
35. Joseph Allen and Bennett P. Lientz, *Effective Business Communication* (Santa Monica, Calif.: Goodyear, 1979).
36. See "Making Silence Your Ally," *Across the Board,* October 1999, p. 11.
37. Boyd A. Vander Houwen, "Less Talking, More Listening," *HRMagazine,* April 1997, pp. 53–58.
38. For a discussion of these and related issues, see Eric M. Eisenberg and Marsha G. Witten, "Reconsidering Openness in Organizational Communication," *Academy of Management Review,* July 1987, pp. 418–426.

19

Managing Work Groups and Teams

CHAPTER OUTLINE

Groups and Teams in Organizations
- Types of Groups and Teams
- Why People Join Groups and Teams
- Stages of Group and Team Development

Characteristics of Groups and Teams
- Role Structures
- Behavioral Norms
- Cohesiveness
- Formal and Informal Leadership

Interpersonal and Intergroup Conflict
- The Nature of Conflict
- Causes of Conflict

Managing Conflict in Organizations
- Stimulating Conflict
- Controlling Conflict
- Resolving and Eliminating Conflict

LEARNING OBJECTIVES

After studying this chapter, you should be able to:

1 ***Define and identify types of groups and teams in organizations, discuss reasons why people join groups and teams, and list the stages of group and team development.***

OPENING INCIDENT

Dr. Peter B. Corr, newly named head of research at drug maker Pfizer, has a lot of experience working with and integrating teams. In 2000 Corr was the head of the research team at Warner-Lambert when his firm was acquired by Pfizer. He was the only top executive from Warner-Lambert to remain and was "recognized for forming a successful partnership with John Niblack [Pfizer's research leader]," says health-care industry expert Viren Mehta. Corr's ability to form a sound working relationship with Niblack helped bring about the peaceful integration of research personnel from both companies and led to Corr's assumption of the leadership role after Niblack's retirement. Without that integration, the acquisition would likely have failed to achieve its potential.

Then, in 2003, Corr was called upon to oversee another acquisition, this time as Pfizer purchased Pharmacia. And Corr was again instrumental in achieving a smooth integration between the two research teams. Critics assert that prior mergers in the pharmaceutical industry

2

Identify and discuss four essential characteristics of groups and teams.

3

Discuss interpersonal and intergroup conflict in organizations.

4

Describe how organizations manage conflict.

"We don't want to spend years on something that will have no impact on patient care."

—Dr. Peter B. Corr, senior vice president for science and technology, Pfizer

Teamwork has become an integral part of the culture at Pfizer.

have not lived up to their promise, proving that bigger is not better when it comes to research teams. Industry consultant Ashish Singh states, "It is quite clear that greater scale in research and development does not mean greater productivity." Corr disagrees. He feels that more researchers will not necessarily come up with more innovations, but they will increase the chances of successful commercialization. "You need the power of scale to exploit the science," he says.

Corr believes that an integrated and focused research team can help Pfizer achieve his three goals. First, Corr is increasing team autonomy in order to boost innovation and attract creative staff. At the same time, he calls for more knowledge sharing and cooperation between units. In February 2003, Pfizer won an Arbor Award for its human resources. The award stated, "Pfizer integrated operations from New Jersey and other cities into a single location resulting in a new collaborative culture that has increased Pfizer's productivity and ability to bring life-saving drugs to patients faster." To soothe researchers who resist the changes, Corr visits each research site. "It is important that [the researchers] see you and realize that you're just like them," says Corr, a cardiologist. "I'm not bigger than life."

Second, Pfizer is working to reduce the number of projects that fail in the later, more expensive development phases. Third, Corr is building close ties with marketing staff, who can help researchers identify drugs that are needed by consumers. "We don't want to spend years on something that will have no impact on patient care," says Corr.

Pfizer's teamwork extends to the establishment of partnerships with smaller drug makers to perform cooperative research. These joint ventures help Pfizer fill in weak areas in its product line, such as oncology and ophthalmology. Thanks in part to its joint venture partners, Pfizer has six new drugs scheduled for introduction in 2003, compared to four at close rival Eli Lilly.

Pfizer had 2002 annual sales of \$32.4 billion, an increase of 12 percent over 2001. (After the Pharmacia acquisition and integration are completed, sales are expected to reach \$48 billion annually. The annual research budget would be \$7 billion.) The increase occurred in a year in which the pharmaceutical industry as a whole grew by a mere 1 percent. Pfizer spends more on research than any of its rivals, so the collaboration and innovation are likely to continue in the future. CEO Hank McKinnell claims, "To be successful in this industry, you have to be able to discover drugs. That's why we're spending \$100 million a week on R&D."[1]

Peter Corr clearly recognizes the importance of teamwork in organizations. He knows that, if groups and teams are poorly managed, they can wreak havoc in a business. But, if they and the organization are on the same page, then great things can result. Beyond simply understanding the power of teams, however, Corr also has demonstrated the ability to successfully merge groups from different organizations into new and even more effective teams.

This chapter is about processes that lead to and follow from activities like those at Pfizer. In our last chapter we established the interpersonal nature of organizations. We extend that discussion here by first introducing basic concepts of group and team dynamics. Subsequent sections explain the characteristics of groups and teams in organizations. We then describe interpersonal and intergroup conflict. Finally, we conclude with a discussion of how conflict can be managed.

Groups and Teams in Organizations

group Consists of two or more people who interact regularly to accomplish a common purpose or goal

Groups are a ubiquitous part of organizational life. They are the basis for much of the work that gets done, and they evolve both inside and outside the normal structural boundaries of the organization. We will define a **group** as two or more people who interact regularly to accomplish a common purpose or goal.[2] The purpose of a group or team may range from preparing a new advertising campaign, to informally sharing information, to making important decisions, to fulfilling social needs.

A task group is one that is created by the organization to accomplish a relatively narrow range of purposes within a stated or implied time horizon. In the aftermath of the crash of the space shuttle Columbia, numerous task groups were assembled to collect debris, analyze information, and attempt to determine what went wrong. This team, for instance, is working on debris from the wreckage in a hangar at Cape Canaveral. By attempting to reconstruct sections of the shuttle, the team hopes to develop new methods for avoiding future disasters.

Types of Groups and Teams

In general, three basic kinds of groups are found in organizations—functional groups, task groups and teams, and informal or interest groups.[3] These are illustrated in Figure 19.1.

Functional Groups A **functional group** is a permanent group created by the organization to accomplish a number of organizational purposes with an unspecified time horizon. The advertising department at Target, the management department at the University of North Texas, and the nursing staff at the Mayo Clinic are functional groups. The advertising department at Target, for example, seeks to plan effective advertising campaigns, increase sales, run in-store promotions, and develop a unique identity for the company. It is assumed that the functional group will remain in existence after it attains its current objectives—those objectives will be replaced by new ones.

functional group A permanent group created by the organization to accomplish a number of organizational purposes with an unspecified time horizon

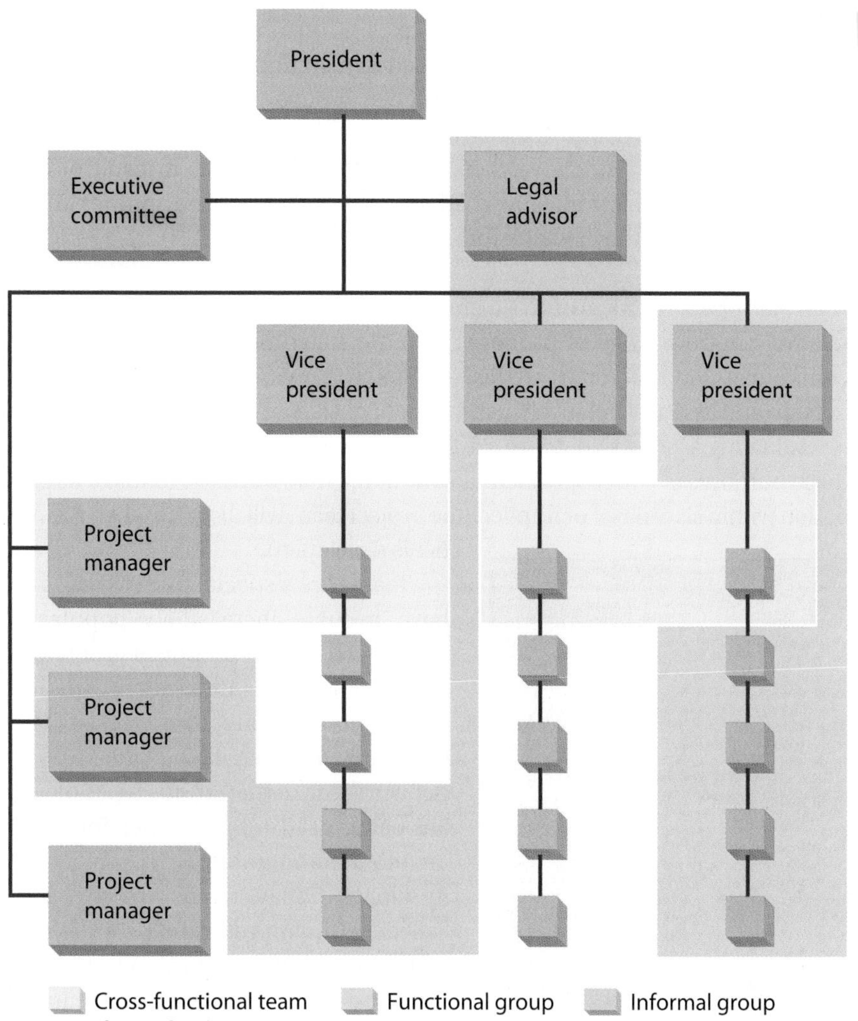

FIGURE 19.1

Types of Groups in Organizations

Every organization has many different types of groups. In this hypothetical organization, a functional group is shown within the purple area, a cross-functional team within the yellow area, and an informal group within the green area.

informal or interest group Created by its members for purposes that may or may not be relevant to those of the organization

Informal or Interest Groups An **informal or interest group** is created by its own members for purposes that may or may not be relevant to organizational goals. It also has an unspecified time horizon. A group of employees who lunch together every day may be discussing how to improve productivity, how to embezzle money, or local politics and sports. As long as the group members enjoy eating together, they will probably continue to do so. When lunches cease to be pleasant, they will seek other company or a different activity.

Informal groups can be a powerful force that managers cannot ignore.[4] One writer described how a group of employees at a furniture factory subverted their boss's efforts to increase production. They tacitly agreed to produce a reasonable amount of work but not to work too hard. One man kept a stockpile of completed work hidden as a backup in case he got too far behind. In another example, auto workers described how they left out gaskets and seals and put soft-drink bottles inside doors.[5] Of course, informal groups can also be a positive force, as demonstrated recently when Continental Airlines employees worked together to buy a new motorcycle for Gordon Bethune, the company's CEO, to show their support and gratitude for his excellent leadership.

task group A group created by the organization to accomplish a relatively narrow range of purposes within a stated or implied time horizon

team A group of workers that functions as a unit, often with little or no supervision, to carry out work-related tasks, functions, and activities

In recent years the Internet has served as a platform for the emergence of more and different kinds of informal or interest groups. Just as one example, Yahoo! includes a wide array of interest groups that bring together people with common interests. And increasingly workers who lose their jobs as a result of layoffs are banding together electronically to offer moral support to one another and to facilitate networking as they all look for new jobs.[6]

Task Groups A **task group** is a group created by the organization to accomplish a relatively narrow range of purposes within a stated or implied time horizon. Most committees and task forces are task groups. The organization specifies group membership and assigns a relatively narrow set of goals, such as developing a new product or evaluating a proposed grievance procedure. The time horizon for accomplishing these purposes is either specified (a committee may be asked to make a recommendation within sixty days) or implied (the project team will disband when the new product is developed).

Task groups are created by the organization to accomplish a relatively narrow range of purposes within a stated or implied time horizon. Take this group of software engineers, for example. They work for Trilogy Software, a high-tech firm based in Austin, Texas. The group is working on the development of a new software application program. Once the program is finished, the task group members will return to their previous responsibilities.

Teams are a special form of task group that have become increasingly popular.[7] In the sense used here, a **team** is a group of workers that functions as a unit, often with little or no supervision, to carry out work-related tasks, functions, and activities. Table 19.1 lists and defines some of the various types of teams that are being used today. Earlier forms of teams included autonomous work groups and quality circles. Today, teams are also sometimes called "self-managed teams," "cross-functional teams," or "high-performance teams." Many firms today are routinely using teams to carry out most of their daily operations.[8]

TABLE 19.1

Types of Teams

Type	Description
Problem-solving Team	Most popular type of team; comprises knowledge workers who gather to solve a specific problem and then disband
Management Team	Consists mainly of managers from various functions like sales and production; coordinates work among other teams
Work Team	An increasingly popular type of team; work teams are responsible for the daily work of the organization; when empowered, they are self-managed teams
Virtual Team	A new type of work team that interacts by computer; members enter and leave the network as needed and may take turns serving as leader
Quality Circle	Declining in popularity, quality circles, comprising workers and supervisors, meet intermittently to discuss workplace problems.

Organizations create teams for a variety of reasons. For one thing, they give more responsibility for task performance to the workers who are actually performing the tasks. They also empower workers by giving them greater authority and decision-making freedom. In addition, they allow the organization to capitalize on the knowledge and motivation of their workers. Finally, they enable the organization to shed its bureaucracy and to promote flexibility and responsiveness. Ford used teams to design its new Thunderbird and Focus models. Similarly, General Motors used a team to develop its new model of the Chevrolet Blazer.

When an organization decides to use teams, it is essentially implementing a major form of organization change, as discussed in Chapter 13. Thus it is important to follow a logical and systematic approach to planning and implementing teams in an existing organization design. It is also important to recognize that resistance may be encountered. This resistance is most likely from first-line managers who will be giving up much of their authority to the team. Many organizations find that they must change the whole management philosophy of such managers away from being a supervisor to being a coach or facilitator.[9]

After teams are in place, managers should continue to monitor their contributions and how effectively they are functioning. In the best circumstances, teams will become very cohesive groups with high performance norms. To achieve this state, the manager can use any or all of the techniques described later in this chapter for enhancing cohesiveness. If implemented properly, and with the support of the workers themselves, performance norms will likely be relatively high. In other words, if the change is properly implemented, the team participants will understand the value and potential of teams and the rewards they may expect to get as a result of their contributions. On the other hand, poorly designed and implemented teams will do a less effective job and may detract from organizational effectiveness.[10] *Technology Toolkit* highlights a new kind of team that is emerging in some organizations—the virtual team.

TECHNOLOGY toolkit

The Reality of Virtual Teams

"Is it more important for people to spend long hours at work or to know how to use their time effectively?"

– Cynthia Froggatt, author of Work Naked: Eight Essential Principles for Peak Performance in the Virtual Workplace*

Management gurus have talked about a virtual workplace for over a decade. They are finally right—the tools to create an efficient and reliable virtual workplace are here.

Surgeon Laura Esserman envisions an online network that pulls together information about diagnosis and treatment for cancer patients. The patient can seek a "virtual second opinion." "Very often doctors recommend a particular treatment because they're more familiar with it," Esserman says. Information also helps the physicians seek expert help from others. "A medical opinion is really just one physician's synthesis of the information," says Esserman, and adds that more information is equivalent to consulting multiple experts.

Banks hold meetings about loan deals on secure websites. Jeff McLane, a manager at Fleet Securities, remembers the laborious process of preparing and mailing written documents. By posting directly to the Web, "you've eliminated the entire printing process," Lane states. And web management tools enable the bankers to control who sees what information and to receive notice when material is viewed. "You can see who looked at which document," Lane claims. "I can call up John Smith and say, 'You downloaded the book this morning. Do you have questions . . .?'"

Virtual teams save travel money and time by meeting online, but in some cases, they can accomplish things that are not possible in a "real" meeting. Product developers at Texas Instruments pulled together participants from around the world for a virtual meeting. Afterwards, they realized that the virtual attendees made more comments and asked more questions than they would expect at a face-to-face encounter. Evan Miller, team manager, explains, "So many of our international partners are not comfortable with English. On a conference call, or even in person, accents can be tricky. . . . We found that many people could type English better than they could speak it. It made everything so much smoother."

Now if only corporate attitudes would catch up with the technology. Cynthia Froggatt, author of *Work Naked*, says that companies need to allow employees the freedom to choose where and how they work. Froggatt responds to skeptics with a question: "Is it more important for people to spend long hours at work or to know how to use their time effectively?"

References: Alison Overholt, "Virtually There?" *Fast Company*, March 2002, pp. 108–114; "Cool Friends: Cynthia Froggatt," Tom Peters website, www.tompeters.com on February 12, 2003; Cynthia Froggatt, "Are You Holding Your Business Back?" *Fortune Small Business*, February 12, 2003, www.fortune.com on February 12, 2003 (*quote).

Why People Join Groups and Teams

People join groups and teams for a variety of reasons. They join functional groups simply by virtue of joining organizations. People accept employment to earn money or to practice their chosen profession. Once inside the organization, they are assigned to jobs and roles and thus become members of functional groups. People in existing functional groups are told, are asked, or volunteer to serve on committees, task forces, and teams. People join informal or interest groups for a variety of reasons, most of them quite complex.[11] Indeed, the need to be a team player has grown so strong today that many organizations will actively resist hiring someone who does not want to work with others.[12]

Interpersonal Attraction One reason why people choose to form informal or interest groups is that they are attracted to one another. Many different factors contribute to interpersonal attraction. When people see a lot of each other, pure proximity increases the likelihood that interpersonal attraction will develop. Attraction is increased when people have similar attitudes, personalities, or economic standings.

People join groups for a variety of reasons. These women actually reflect two different reasons for joining a group. First, they individually joined the Delta Sigma Theta sorority for a variety of reasons, including interpersonal attraction, group activities, need satisfaction, and other reasons. Second, they then joined a larger group walking in support of breast cancer survivors because they support its goal.

Group Activities Individuals may also be motivated to join a group because the activities of the group appeal to them. Jogging, playing bridge, bowling, discussing poetry, playing war games, and flying model airplanes are all activities that some people enjoy. Many of them are more enjoyable to participate in as a member of a group, and most require more than one person. Many large firms like Shell Oil and Apple Computer have a football, softball, or bowling league. A person may join a bowling team, not because of any noticeable attraction to other group members, but simply because being a member of the group allows that person to participate in a pleasant activity. Of course, if the group's level of interpersonal attraction is very low, a person may choose to forgo the activity rather than join the group.

Group Goals The goals of a group may also motivate people to join. The Sierra Club, which is dedicated to environmental conservation, is a good example of this kind of interest group. Various fund-raising groups are another illustration. Members may or may not be personally attracted to the other fundraisers, and they probably do not enjoy the activity of knocking on doors asking for money, but they join the group because they subscribe to its goal. Workers join unions like the United Auto Workers because they support its goals.

Need Satisfaction Still another reason for joining a group is to satisfy the need for affiliation. New residents in a community may join the Newcomers Club partially as a way to meet new people and partially just to be around other people. Likewise, newly divorced people often join support groups as a way to have companionship.

Instrumental Benefits A final reason why people join groups is that membership is sometimes seen as instrumental in providing other benefits to the individual. For example, it is fairly common for college students entering their senior year to join several professional clubs or associations, because listing such memberships on a résumé is thought to enhance the chances of getting a good job. Similarly, a manager might join a certain racquet club not because she is attracted to its members (although she might be) and not because of the opportunity to play

FIGURE 19.2

Stages of Group Development

As groups mature, they tend to evolve through four distinct stages of development. Managers must understand that group members need time to become acquainted, accept one another, develop a group structure, and become comfortable with their role in the group before they can begin to work directly to accomplish goals.

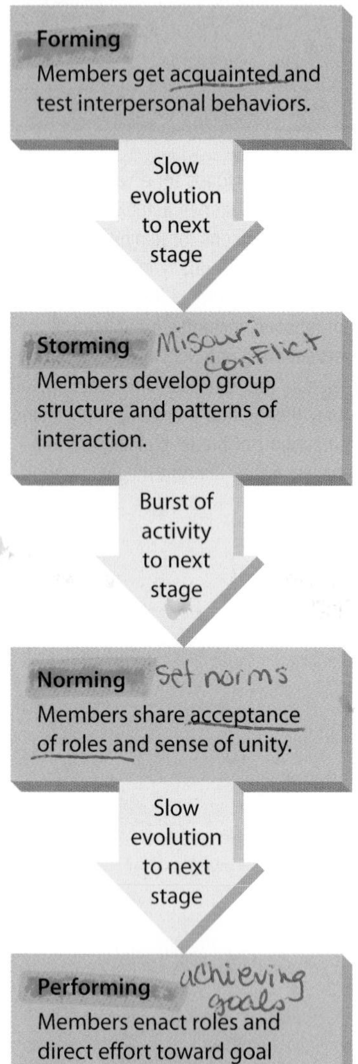

tennis (although she may enjoy it). The club's goals are not relevant, and her affiliation needs may be satisfied in other ways. However, she may feel that being a member of this club will lead to important and useful business contacts. The racquet club membership is instrumental in establishing those contacts. Membership in civic groups such as the Junior League and Rotary may be solicited for similar reasons.

Stages of Group and Team Development

Imagine the differences between a collection of five people who have just been brought together to form a group or team and a group or team that has functioned like a well-oiled machine for years. Members of a new group or team are unfamiliar with how they will function together and are tentative in their interactions. In a group or team with considerable experience, members are familiar with one another's strengths and weaknesses and are more secure in their role in the group. The former group or team is generally considered to be immature; the latter, mature. To progress from the immature phase to the mature phase, a group or team must go through certain stages of development, as shown in Figure 19.2.[13]

The first stage of development is called *forming*. The members of the group or team get acquainted and begin to test which interpersonal behaviors are acceptable and which are unacceptable to the other members. The members are very dependent on others at this point to provide cues about what is acceptable. The basic ground rules for the group or team are established, and a tentative group structure may emerge. At Reebok, for example, a merchandising team was created to handle its sportswear business. The team leader and his members were barely acquainted and had to spend a few weeks getting to know one another.

The second stage of development, often slow to emerge, is *storming*. During this stage, there may be a general lack of unity and uneven interaction patterns. At the same time, some members of the group or team may begin to exert themselves to become recognized as the group leader or at least to play a major role in shaping the group's agenda. In Reebok's team, some members advocated a rapid expansion into the marketplace; others argued for a slower entry. The first faction won, with disastrous results. Because of the rush, product quality was poor and deliveries were late. As a result, the team leader was fired and a new manager placed in charge.

The third stage of development, called *norming*, usually begins with a burst of activity. During this stage, each person begins to recognize and accept her or his role and to understand the roles of others. Members also begin to accept one another and to develop a sense of unity. There may also be temporary regressions to the previous stage. For example, the group or team might begin to accept one particular member as the leader. If this person later violates important norms or otherwise jeopardizes his or her claim to leadership, conflict might reemerge as the group rejects this leader and searches for another. Reebok's new leader transferred several people away from the team and set up a new system and structure for managing things. The remaining employees accepted his new approach and settled into doing their job.

Performing, the final stage of group or team development, is again slow to develop. The team really begins to focus on the problem at hand. The members enact the roles they have accepted, interaction occurs, and the efforts of the group are directed toward goal attainment. The basic structure of the group or team is no longer an issue but has become a mechanism for accomplishing the purpose of the group. Reebok's sportswear business is now growing consistently and has successfully avoided the problems that plagued it at first.

concept CHECK

What are the basic types of groups and teams in organizations?	*Identify four groups that you belong to and describe why you joined each one.*

Characteristics of Groups and Teams

As groups and teams mature and pass through the four basic stages of development, they begin to take on four important characteristics—a role structure, norms, cohesiveness, and informal leadership.[14]

Role Structures

Each individual in a team has a part, or **role**, to play in helping the group reach its goals. Some people are leaders, some do the work, some interface with other teams, and so on. Indeed, a person may take on a *task specialist role* (concentrating on getting the group's task accomplished) or a *socioemotional role* (providing social and emotional support to others on the team). A few people, usually the leaders, perform both roles; a few others may do neither. The group's **role structure** is the set of defined roles and interrelationships among those roles that the group or team members define and accept. Each of us belongs to many groups and therefore plays multiple roles—in work groups, classes, families, and social organizations.[15]

roles The parts individuals play in groups in helping the group reach its goals

role structure The set of defined roles and interrelationships among those roles that the group members define and accept

Role structures emerge as a result of role episodes, as shown in Figure 19.3. The process begins with the expected role—what other members of the team expect the

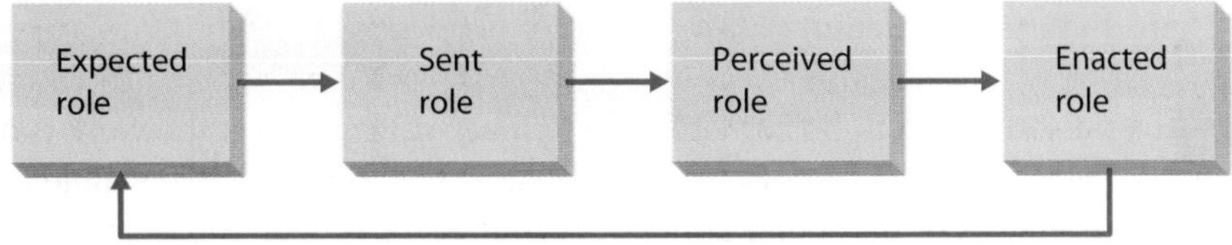

FIGURE 19.3

The Development of a Role

Roles and role structures within a group generally evolve through a series of role episodes. The first two stages of role development are group processes, as the group members let individuals know what is expected of them. The other two parts are individual processes, as the new group members perceive and enact their roles.

individual to do. The expected role gets translated into the sent role—the messages and cues that team members use to communicate the expected role to the individual. The perceived role is what the individual perceives the sent role to mean. Finally, the enacted role is what the individual actually does in the role. The enacted role, in turn, influences future expectations of the team. Of course, role episodes seldom unfold this easily. When major disruptions occur, individuals may experience role ambiguity, conflict, or overload.[16]

role ambiguity Arises when the sent role is unclear and the individual does not know what is expected of him or her

Role Ambiguity **Role ambiguity** arises when the sent role is unclear. If your instructor tells you to write a term paper but refuses to provide more information, you will probably experience role ambiguity. You do not know what the topic is, how long the paper should be, what format to use, or when the paper is due. In work settings, role ambiguity can stem from poor job descriptions, vague instructions from a supervisor, or unclear cues from coworkers. The result is likely to be a subordinate who does not know what to do. Role ambiguity can be a significant problem for both the individual who must contend with it and the organization that expects the employee to perform.

role conflict Occurs when the messages and cues composing the sent role are clear but contradictory or mutually exclusive

Role Conflict **Role conflict** occurs when the messages and cues composing the sent role are clear but contradictory or mutually exclusive.[17] One common form is *interrole conflict*—conflict between roles. For example, if a person's boss says that one must work overtime and on weekends to get ahead, and the same person's spouse says that more time is needed at home with the family, conflict may result. In a matrix organization, interrole conflict often arises between the roles one plays in different teams as well as between team roles and one's permanent role in a functional group.

Intrarole conflict may occur when the person gets conflicting demands from different sources within the context of the same role. A manager's boss may tell her that she needs to put more pressure on subordinates to follow new work rules. At the same time, her subordinates may indicate that they expect her to get the rules changed. Thus the cues are in conflict, and the manager may be unsure about which course to follow. *Intrasender conflict* occurs when a single source sends clear but contradictory messages. This might arise if the boss says one morning that there can be no more overtime for the next month but after lunch tells someone to work late that same evening. *Person-role conflict* results from a discrepancy between the role requirements and the individual's personal values, attitudes, and needs. If a person is told to do something unethical or illegal, or if the work is distasteful (for example, firing a close friend), person-role conflict is likely. Role conflict of all varieties is of particular concern to managers. Research has shown that conflict may occur in a variety of situations and lead to a variety of adverse consequences, including stress, poor performance, and rapid turnover.

role overload Occurs when expectations for the role exceed the individual's capabilities to perform

Role Overload A final consequence of a weak role structure is **role overload**, which occurs when expectations for the role exceed the individual's capabilities. When a manager gives an employee several major assignments at once, while increasing the person's regular workload, the employee will probably experience role overload. Role overload may also result when an individual takes on too many roles at one time. For example, a person trying to work extra hard at work, run for election to the school board, serve on a committee in church, coach Little League baseball, maintain an active exercise program, and be a contributing member to her or his family will probably encounter role overload.

In a functional group or team, the manager can take steps to avoid role ambiguity, conflict, and overload. Having clear and reasonable expectations and sending clear and straightforward cues go a long way toward eliminating role ambiguity. Consistent expectations that take into account the employee's other roles and personal value system may minimize role conflict. Role overload can be avoided simply by recognizing the individual's capabilities and limits. In friendship and interest groups, role structures are likely to be less formal; hence, the possibility of role ambiguity, conflict, or overload may not be so great. However, if one or more of these problems does occur, they may be difficult to handle. Because roles in friendship and interest groups are less likely to be partially defined by a formal authority structure or written job descriptions, the individual cannot turn to those sources to clarify a role.

Behavioral Norms

norms Standards of behavior that the group accepts for and expects of its members

Norms are standards of behavior that the group or team accepts for and expects of its members. Most committees, for example, develop norms governing their discussions. A person who talks too much is perceived as doing so to make a good impression or to get his or her own way. Other members may not talk much to this person, may not sit nearby, may glare at the person, and may otherwise "punish" the individual for violating the norm. Norms, then, define the boundaries between acceptable and unacceptable behavior.[18] Some groups develop norms that limit the upper bounds of behavior to "make life easier" for the group. In general, these norms are counterproductive—do not make more than two comments in a committee discussion or do not produce any more than you have to. Other groups may develop norms that limit the lower bounds of behavior. These norms tend to reflect motivation, commitment, and high performance—do not come to meetings unless you have read the reports to be discussed or produce as much as you can. Managers can sometimes use norms for the betterment of the organization. For example, Kodak has successfully used group norms to reduce injuries in some of its plants.[19]

Norm Generalization The norms of one group cannot always be generalized to another group. Some academic departments, for example, have a norm that suggests that faculty members dress up on teaching days. People who fail to observe this norm are "punished" by sarcastic remarks or even formal reprimands. In other departments, the norm may be casual clothes, and the person unfortunate enough to wear dress clothes may be punished just as vehemently. Even within the same work area, similar groups or teams can develop different norms. One team may strive always to produce above its assigned quota; another may maintain productivity just below its quota. The norm of one team may be to be friendly and cordial to its supervisor; that of another team may be to remain aloof and distant. Some differences are due primarily to the composition of the teams.

Norm Variation In some cases, there can also be norm variation within a group or team. A common norm is that the least senior member of a group is expected to perform unpleasant or trivial tasks for the rest of the group. These tasks might be to wait on customers who are known to be small tippers (in a restaurant), to deal with complaining customers (in a department store), or to handle the low-commission line of merchandise (in a sales department). Another example is when certain individuals, especially informal leaders, may violate some norms. If the team is going to meet at 8:00 A.M., anyone arriving late will be chastised for holding things up. Occasionally, however, the informal leader may arrive a few minutes late. As long as this does not happen too often, the group will probably not do anything about it.

Norm Conformity Four sets of factors contribute to norm conformity. First, factors associated with the group are important. For example, some groups or teams may exert more pressure for conformity than others. Second, the initial stimulus that prompts behavior can affect conformity. The more ambiguous the stimulus (for example, news that the team is going to be transferred to a new unit), the more pressure there is to conform. Third, individual traits determine the individual's propensity to conform (for example, more intelligent people are often less susceptible to pressure to conform). Finally, situational factors, such as team size and unanimity, influence conformity. As an individual learns the group's norms, he can do several different things. The most obvious is to adopt the norms. For example, the new male professor who notices that all the other men in the department dress up to teach can also start wearing a suit. A variation is to try to obey the "spirit" of the norm while retaining individuality. The professor may recognize that the norm is actually to wear a tie; thus he might succeed by wearing a tie with his sport shirt, jeans, and sneakers.

The individual may also ignore the norm. When a person does not conform, several things can happen. At first the group may increase its communication with the deviant individual to try to bring her back in line. If this does not work, communication may decline. Over time, the group may begin to exclude the individual from its activities and, in effect, ostracize the person. Finally, we need to briefly consider another aspect of norm conformity—socialization. **Socialization** is generalized norm conformity that occurs as a person makes the transition from being an outsider to being an insider. A newcomer to an organization, for example, gradually begins to learn about such norms as dress, working hours, and interpersonal relations. As the newcomer adopts these norms, she is being socialized into the organizational

Cohesiveness is the extent to which members are loyal and committed to the group. Factors such as agreement on goals, intergroup competition, and favorable evaluation (i.e., success) can increase cohesiveness. The members of this group, for instance, likely agreed on their goal (beating their adversaries), competed with that group of adversaries on the field of battle, and were ultimately successful. Consequently, the group is now more cohesive than ever before!

"Two, four, six, eight, who do we appreciate ..."

culture. Some organizations, like Texas Instruments, work to actively manage the socialization process; others leave it to happenstance.

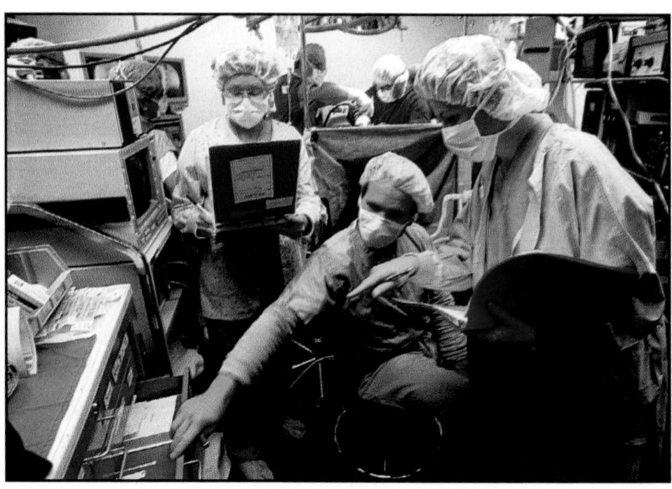

Cohesive teams can be highly effective contributors to the success of any organization. This team, for example, consists of doctors and nurses working together to lower costs at Methodist Healthcare System in San Antonio. The team members share the same performance norms, and their close personal relationships have led the team to become more cohesive as they find new answers and help reach their goal. To date, the overall cost reduction program to which they belong has yielded savings of over $60 million.

socialization Generalized norm conformity that occurs as a person makes the transition from being an outsider to being an insider in the organization

cohesiveness The extent to which members are loyal and committed to the group; the degree of mutual attractiveness within the group

Cohesiveness

A third important team characteristic is cohesiveness. **Cohesiveness** is the extent to which members are loyal and committed to the group. In a highly cohesive team, the members work well together, support and trust one another, and are generally effective at achieving their chosen goal.[20] In contrast, a team that lacks cohesiveness is not very coordinated, its members do not necessarily support one another fully, and it may have a difficult time reaching goals. Of particular interest are the factors that increase and reduce cohesiveness and the consequences of team cohesiveness. These are listed in Table 19.2.

Factors That Increase Cohesiveness Five factors can increase the level of cohesiveness in a group or team. One of the strongest is intergroup competition. When two or more groups are in direct competition (for example, three sales groups competing for top sales honors or two football teams competing for a conference championship), each group is likely to become more cohesive. Second, just as personal attraction plays a role in causing a group to form, so, too, does attraction seem to enhance cohesiveness. Third, favorable evaluation of the entire group by outsiders can increase cohesiveness. Thus a group's winning a sales contest or a conference title, or receiving recognition and praise from a superior, will tend to increase cohesiveness.

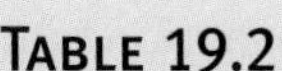

TABLE 19.2

Factors That Influence Group Cohesiveness

Several different factors can influence the cohesiveness of a group. For example, a manager can establish intergroup competition, assign compatible members to the group, create opportunities for success, establish acceptable goals, and foster interaction to increase cohesiveness. Other factors can be used to decrease cohesiveness.

Factors That Increase Cohesiveness	Factors That Reduce Cohesiveness
Intergroup competition	Group size
Personal attraction	Disagreement on goals
Favorable evaluation	Intragroup competition
Agreement on goals	Domination
Interaction	Unpleasant experiences

Similarly, if all the members of the group or team agree on their goals, cohesiveness is likely to increase.[21] And the more frequently members of the group interact with one another, the more likely the group is to become cohesive. A manager who wants to foster a high level of cohesiveness in a team might do well to establish some form of intergroup competition, assign members to the group who are likely to be attracted to one another, provide opportunities for success, establish goals that all members are likely to accept, and allow ample opportunities for interaction.

Factors That Reduce Cohesiveness There are also five factors that are known to reduce team cohesiveness. First of all, cohesiveness tends to decline as a group increases in size. Second, when members of a team disagree on what the goals of the group should be, cohesiveness may decrease. For example, when some members believe the group should maximize output and others think output should be restricted, cohesiveness declines. Third, intragroup competition reduces cohesiveness. When members are competing among themselves, they focus more on their own actions and behaviors than on those of the group.

Fourth, domination by one or more persons in the group or team may cause overall cohesiveness to decline. Other members may feel that they are not being given an opportunity to interact and contribute, and they may become less attracted to the group as a consequence. Finally, unpleasant experiences that result from group membership may reduce cohesiveness. A sales group that comes in last in a sales contest, an athletic team that sustains a long losing streak, and a work group reprimanded for poor-quality work may all become less cohesive as a result of their unpleasant experience.

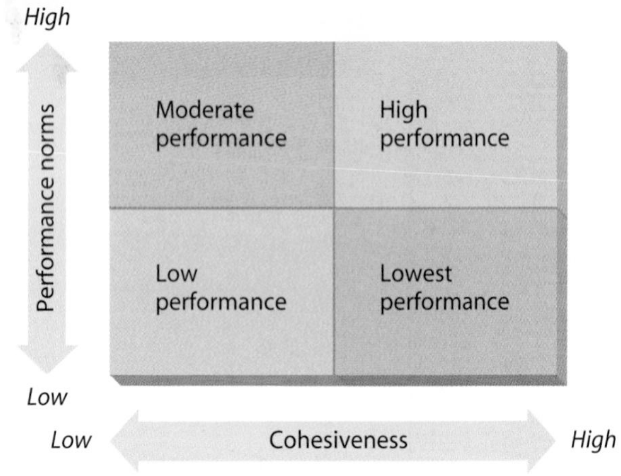

Consequences of Cohesiveness In general, as teams become more cohesive, their members tend to interact more frequently, conform more to norms, and become more satisfied with the team. Cohesiveness may also influence team performance. However, performance is also influenced by the team's performance norms. Figure 19.4 shows how cohesiveness and performance norms interact to help shape team performance.

When both cohesiveness and performance norms are high, high performance should result, because the team wants to perform at a high level (norms) and its members are working together toward that end (cohesiveness). When norms are high and cohesiveness is low, performance will be moderate. Although the team wants to perform at a high level, its members are not necessarily working well together. When norms are low, performance will be low, regardless of whether group cohesiveness is high or low. The least desirable situation occurs when low performance norms are combined with high cohesiveness. In this case, all team members embrace the standard of restricting performance (owing to the low performance norm), and the group is united in its efforts to maintain that standard (owing to the

FIGURE 19.4

The Interaction Between Cohesiveness and Performance Norms

Group cohesiveness and performance norms interact to determine group performance. From the manager's perspective, high cohesiveness combined with high performance norms is the best situation, and high cohesiveness with low performance norms is the worst situation. Managers who can influence the level of cohesiveness and performance norms can greatly improve the effectiveness of a work group.

Performance norms / Cohesiveness	Low	High
High	Moderate performance	High performance
Low	Low performance	Lowest performance

high cohesiveness). If cohesiveness were low, the manager might be able to raise performance norms by establishing high goals and rewarding goal attainment or by bringing in new group members who are high performers. But a highly cohesive group is likely to resist these interventions.[22]

Formal and Informal Leadership

Most functional groups and teams have a formal leader—that is, one appointed by the organization or chosen or elected by the members of the group. Because friendship and interest groups are formed by the members themselves, however, any formal leader must be elected or designated by the members. Although some groups do designate such a leader (a softball team may elect a captain, for example), many do not. Moreover, even when a formal leader is designated, the group or team may also look to others for leadership. An **informal leader** is a person who engages in leadership activities but whose right to do so has not been formally recognized. The formal and the informal leader in any group or team may be the same person, or they may be different people. We noted earlier the distinction between the task specialist and socioemotional roles within groups. An informal leader is likely to be a person capable of carrying out both roles effectively. If the formal leader can fulfill one role but not the other, an informal leader often emerges to supplement the formal leader's functions. If the formal leader can fill neither role, one or more informal leaders may emerge to carry out both sets of functions.

informal leader A person who engages in leadership activities but whose right to do so has not been formally recognized by the organization or group

Is informal leadership desirable? In many cases informal leaders are quite powerful because they draw from referent or expert power. When they are working in the best interests of the organization, they can be a tremendous asset. Notable athletes like Brett Favre and Mia Hamm are classic examples of informal leaders. However, when informal leaders work counter to the goals of the organization, they can cause significant difficulties. Such leaders may lower performance norms, instigate walkouts or wildcat strikes, or otherwise disrupt the organization.

concept CHECK

Identify and describe the fundamental characteristics of groups and teams.	*Assume you were assigned to manage a highly cohesive group with low performance norms. What would you do to try to change things?*

Interpersonal and Intergroup Conflict

Of course, when people work together in an organization, things do not always go smoothly. Indeed, conflict is an inevitable element of interpersonal relationships in organizations. *The World of Management* provides a vivid example. In this section, we will look at how conflict affects overall performance. We also explore the causes of conflict between individuals, between groups, and between an organization and its environment.

THE WORLD OF management

Transatlantic Teamwork at Citigroup

"Highly competitive and individualistically driven executives . . . reach the top, only to find that globalization . . . [requires] a more team-oriented approach to succeed."

— Elisabeth Marx, author of Breaking Through Culture Shock*

Citigroup managers in the firm's London and New York offices seemed to have all the attributes of success: technical skills, self-sufficiency, ambition, competitive spirit, and results orientation. Yet Terry Lockhart, Citigroup's senior vice president for organizational effectiveness, sensed trouble. Relations between the two branches were strained, and managers could not resolve the conflicts. Personal criticism and hostility were displayed openly. New York managers complained that their British counterparts were too bureaucratic and indecisive, while Londoners accused the Americans of carelessly "shooting from the hip" on important issues. "There was a cross-cultural divide between London and New York," claims Lockhart.

The tension was "distracting the team from concentrating on the competition and developing new clients and more innovative products," says Lockhart. So he called in psychologist and consultant Elisabeth Marx, who is an expert on organizational culture. At first, managers resisted her help. "[Intervention] was a counter-intuitive approach for them. The culture of financial services is not characterized by a deep psychological interest in, or affinity for, softer issues," Marx says. Yet "the buy-in for them was money," she adds. "If they could improve their performance, they could improve their pay."

Marx conducted surveys and observations and interviewed managers before providing feedback to leaders on both sides of the Atlantic. Her conclusion? That Citigroup needed to work on teamwork skills. "Highly competitive and individualistically driven executives . . . reach the top, only to find that the globalization and complexity of today's business require a more team-oriented approach to succeed." Marx asked Citigroup employees to describe their ideal teammate. She heard answers ranging from good listening skills to flexibility to sensitivity on cross-cultural issues. Marx then helped managers create a plan for developing those qualities in themselves and their workers. The plan calls for public commitments to change, training, and coaching from peers.

After Marx's intervention, employee morale improved. Although 36 percent of employees had said that the lack of teamwork was their least favorite thing about their job, only 23 percent say that now. Revenues increased 64 percent over the previous year. And that is something that the numbers-oriented, performance-driven Citigroup managers can cheer about.

References: Alison Maitland, "Bridging the Culture Gap," *Financial Times* (London), January 28, 2002, p. 8 (*quote); Elisabeth Marx, *Breaking Through Culture Shock: What You Need to Succeed in International Business* (London: Nicholas Brealey Intercultural, June 2001); Elisabeth Marx, "Viewpoint Elisabeth Marx," *Financial Times* (London), January 8, 2003, reprinted on the Independent Director website, www.independentdirector.co.uk on February 12, 2003.

The Nature of Conflict

conflict A disagreement among two or more individuals or groups

Conflict is a disagreement among two or more individuals, groups, or organizations. This disagreement may be relatively superficial or very strong. It may be short-lived or exist for months or even years, and it may be work related or personal. Conflict may manifest itself in a variety of ways. People may compete with one another, glare at one another, shout, or withdraw. Groups may band together to protect popular members or oust unpopular members. Organizations may seek legal remedies.

Most people assume that conflict is something to be avoided because it connotes antagonism, hostility, unpleasantness, and dissension. Indeed, managers and management theorists have traditionally viewed conflict as a problem to be avoided.[23] In recent years, however, we have come to recognize that, although conflict can be a major problem, certain kinds of conflict may also be beneficial.[24] For example, when two members of a site selection committee disagree over the best location for a new plant, each may be forced to more thoroughly study and defend his or her preferred alternative. As a result of more systematic analysis and discussion, the committee may make a better decision and be better prepared to justify it to others than if everyone had agreed from the outset and accepted an alternative that was perhaps less well analyzed.

As long as conflict is being handled in a cordial and constructive manner, it is probably serving a useful purpose in the organization. On the other hand, when working relationships are being disrupted and the conflict has reached destructive levels, it has likely become dysfunctional and needs to be addressed.[25] We discuss ways of dealing with such conflict later in this chapter.

Figure 19.5 depicts the general relationship between conflict and performance for a group or organization. If there is absolutely no conflict in the group or organization, its members may become complacent and apathetic. As a result, group or organizational performance and innovation may begin to suffer. A moderate level of conflict among group or organizational members, on the other hand, can spark motivation, creativity, innovation, and initiative, and raise performance. Too much conflict, though, can produce such undesirable results as hostility and lack of cooperation, which lower performance. The key for managers is to find and maintain the optimal amount of conflict that fosters performance. Of course, what constitutes optimal conflict varies with both the situation and the people involved.[26]

FIGURE 19.5

The Nature of Organizational Conflict

Either too much or too little conflict can be dysfunctional for an organization. In either case, performance may be low. However, an optimal level of conflict that sparks motivation, creativity, innovation, and initiative can result in higher levels of performance. T. J. Rodgers, CEO of Cypress Semiconductor, maintains a moderate level of conflict in his organization as a way of keeping people energized and motivated.

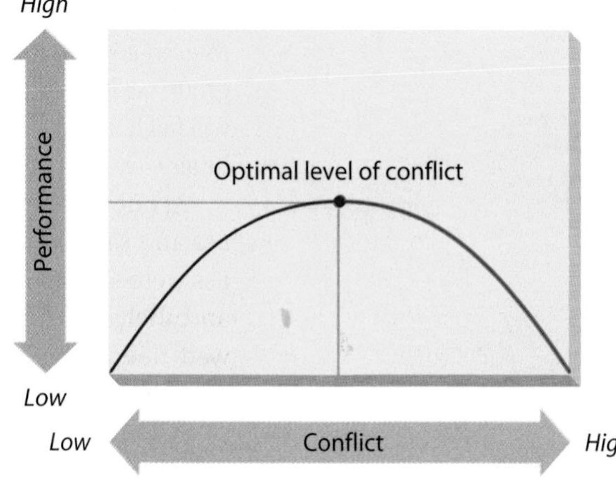

Causes of Conflict

Conflict may arise in both interpersonal and intergroup relationships. Occasionally conflict between individuals and groups may be caused by particular organizational strategies and practices. A third arena for conflict is between an organization and its environment.

Interpersonal Conflict Conflict between two or more individuals is almost certain to occur in any organization, given the great variety in perceptions, goals, attitudes, and so forth among its members. William Gates, founder and CEO of Microsoft, and Kazuhiko Nishi, a former business associate from Japan, ended a long-term business relationship because of interpersonal conflict. Nishi accused Gates of becoming too political, while Gates charged that Nishi became too unpredictable and erratic in his behavior.[27]

A frequent source of interpersonal conflict in organizations is what many people call a "personality clash"—when two people distrust each other's motives, dislike each other, or for some other reason simply cannot get along.[28] Conflict may also arise between people who have different beliefs or perceptions about some aspect of their work or their organization. For example, one manager might want the organization to require that all employees use Microsoft Office software, to promote standardization. Another manager might believe that a variety of software packages should be allowed, in order to recognize individuality. Similarly, a male manager may disagree with his female colleague over whether the organization is guilty of discriminating against women in promotion decisions. Defense Secretary Donald Rumsfeld frequently has conflicts with others because of his abrasive and confrontational style.[29]

Conflict can also result from excess competitiveness among individuals. Two people vying for the same job, for example, may resort to political behavior in an effort to gain an advantage. If either competitor sees the other's behavior as inappropriate, accusations are likely to result. Even after the "winner" of the job is determined, such conflict may continue to undermine interpersonal relationships, especially if the reasons given in selecting one candidate are ambiguous or open to alternative explanations. Robert Allen resigned as CEO of Delta Airlines a few years ago because he disagreed with other key executives over how best to reduce the carrier's costs. After he began looking for a replacement for one of his rivals without the approval of the firm's board of directors, the resultant conflict and controversy left him no choice but to leave.[30]

Intergroup Conflict Conflict between two or more organizational groups is also quite common. For example, the members of a firm's marketing group may disagree with the production group over product quality and delivery schedules. Two sales groups may disagree over how to meet sales goals, and two groups of managers may have different ideas about how best to allocate organizational resources.

Many intergroup conflicts arise more from organizational causes than from interpersonal causes. In Chapter 11, we described three forms of group interdependence—pooled, sequential, and reciprocal. Just as increased interdependence makes coordination more difficult, it also increases the potential for conflict. For example, recall that, in sequential interdependence, work is passed from one unit to another. Intergroup conflict may arise if the first group turns out too much work (the second group will fall behind), too little work (the second group will not meet its own goals), or poor-quality work.

At one J.C. Penney department store, conflict arose between stockroom employees and sales associates. The sales associates claimed that the stockroom employees were slow in delivering merchandise to the sales floor so that it could be priced and shelved. The stockroom employees, in turn, claimed that the sales associates were not giving them enough lead time to get the merchandise delivered and failed to understand that they had additional duties besides carrying merchandise to the sales floor.

Just like people, different departments often have different goals. Further, these goals may often be incompatible. A marketing goal of maximizing sales, achieved partially by offering many products in a wide variety of sizes, shapes, colors, and models, probably conflicts with a production goal of minimizing costs, achieved partially by long production runs of a few items. Reebok recently confronted this very situation. One group of managers wanted to introduce a new sportswear line as quickly as possible, but other managers wanted to expand more deliberately and cautiously. Because the two groups were not able to reconcile their differences effectively, conflict between the two factions led to quality problems and delivery delays that plagued the firm for months.

Competition for scarce resources can also lead to intergroup conflict. Most organizations—especially universities, hospitals, government agencies, and businesses in depressed industries—have limited resources. In one New England town, for example, the public works department and the library battled over funds from a federal construction grant. The Buick, Pontiac, and Chevrolet divisions of General Motors have frequently fought over the right to manufacture various new products developed by the company.

Conflict Between Organization and Environment Conflict that arises between one organization and another is called *interorganizational conflict.* A moderate amount of interorganizational conflict resulting from business competition is, of course, expected, but sometimes conflict becomes more extreme. For example, the owners of Jordache Enterprises, Inc., and Guess?, Inc., battled in court for years over ownership of the Guess? label, allegations of design theft, and several other issues.[31] Similarly, General Motors and Volkswagen went to court to resolve a bitter conflict that spanned more than four years. It all started when a key GM executive, Jose Ignacio Lopez de Arriortua, left for a position at Volkswagen. GM claimed that he took with him key secrets that could benefit its German competitor. After the messy departure, dozens of charges and counter-charges were made by the two firms, and only a court settlement was able to put the conflict to an end.[32]

Conflict can also arise between an organization and other elements of its environment. For example, an organization may conflict with a consumer group over claims it makes about its products. McDonald's faced this problem a few years ago when it published nutritional information about its products that omitted details about fat content. A manufacturer might conflict with a governmental agency such as OSHA. For example, the firm's management may believe it is in compliance with OSHA regulations, whereas officials from the agency itself feel that the firm is not in compliance. Or a firm might conflict with a supplier over the quality of raw materials. The firm may think the supplier is providing inferior materials, while the supplier thinks the materials are adequate. Finally, individual managers may obviously have disagreements with groups of workers. For example, a manager may think her workers are doing poor-quality work and that they are unmotivated. The workers, on the other hand, may believe they are doing a good job and that the manager is doing a poor job of leading them.

concept CHECK

Define conflict and identify its primary causes.	Try to think of a time when you were involved in conflict that had a positive outcome.

Managing Conflict in Organizations

How do managers cope with all this potential conflict? Fortunately, as Table 19.3 shows, there are ways to stimulate conflict for constructive ends, to control conflict before it gets out of hand, and to resolve it if it does. Below we look at ways of managing conflict.[33]

Stimulating Conflict

In some situations, an organization may stimulate conflict by placing individual employees or groups in competitive situations. Managers can establish sales contests, incentive plans, bonuses, or other competitive stimuli to spark competition. As long as the ground rules are equitable and all participants perceive the contest as fair, the conflict created by the competition is likely to be constructive because each participant will work hard to win (thereby enhancing some aspect of organizational performance).

Another useful method for stimulating conflict is to bring in one or more outsiders who will shake things up and present a new perspective on organizational

TABLE 19.3

Methods for Managing Conflict

Conflict is a powerful force in organizations and has both negative and positive consequences. Thus managers can draw on several different techniques to stimulate, control, or resolve and eliminate conflict, depending on their unique circumstances.

Stimulating Conflict
- Increase competition among individuals and teams.
- Hire outsiders to shake things up.
- Change established procedures.

Controlling Conflict
- Expand resource base.
- Enhance coordination of interdependence.
- Set superordinate goals.
- Match personalities and work habits of employees.

Resolving and Eliminating Conflict
- Avoid conflict.
- Convince conflicting parties to compromise.
- Bring conflicting parties together to confront and negotiate conflict.

practices. Outsiders may be new employees, current employees assigned to an existing work group, or consultants or advisors hired on a temporary basis. Of course, this action can also provoke resentment from insiders who feel they were qualified for the position. The Beecham Group, a British company, once hired an executive from the United States for its CEO position, expressly to change how the company did business. His arrival brought with it new ways of doing things and a new enthusiasm for competitiveness. Unfortunately, some valued employees also chose to leave Beecham because they resented some of the changes that were made.

Changing established procedures, especially procedures that have outlived their usefulness, can also stimulate conflict. Such actions cause people to reassess how they perform their job and whether they perform it correctly. For example, one university president announced that all vacant staff positions could be filled only after written justification had received his approval. Conflict arose between the president and the department heads, who felt they were having to do more paperwork than was necessary. Most requests were approved, but because department heads now had to think through their staffing needs, a few unnecessary positions were appropriately eliminated.

Controlling Conflict

One method of controlling conflict is to expand the resource base. Suppose a top manager receives two budget requests for $100,000 each. If she has only $180,000 to distribute, the stage is set for conflict because each group will feel its proposal is worth funding and will be unhappy if it is not fully funded. If both proposals are indeed worthwhile, it may be possible for her to come up with the extra $20,000 from some other source and thereby avoid difficulty.

As noted earlier, pooled, sequential, and reciprocal interdependence can all result in conflict. If managers use an appropriate technique for enhancing coordination, they can reduce the probability that conflict will arise. Techniques for coordination (described in Chapter 11) include making use of the managerial hierarchy, relying on rules and procedures, enlisting liaison people, forming task forces, and integrating departments. At the J.C. Penney store mentioned earlier, the conflict was addressed by providing salespeople with clearer forms on which to specify the merchandise they needed and in what sequence. If one coordination technique does not have the desired effect, a manager might shift to another one.

Competing goals can also be a source of conflict among individuals and groups. Managers can sometimes focus employee attention on higher-level, or superordinate, goals as a way of eliminating lower-level conflict. When labor unions like the United Auto Workers make wage concessions to ensure survival of the automobile industry, they are responding to a superordinate goal. Their immediate goal may be higher wages for members, but they realize that, without the automobile industry, their members would not even have jobs.

Finally, managers should try to match the personalities and work habits of employees so as to avoid conflict between individuals. For instance, two valuable subordinates, one a chain smoker and the other a vehement antismoker, should probably not be required to work together in an enclosed space. If conflict does arise between incompatible individuals, a manager might seek an equitable transfer for one or both of them to other units.

Resolving and Eliminating Conflict

Despite everyone's best intentions, conflict will sometimes flare up. If it is disrupting the workplace, creating too much hostility and tension, or otherwise harming the organization, attempts must be made to resolve it. Some managers who are uncomfortable dealing with conflict choose to avoid the conflict and hope it will go away. Avoidance may sometimes be effective in the short run for some kinds of interpersonal disagreements, but it does little to resolve long-run or chronic conflict. Even more unadvisable, though, is "smoothing"—minimizing the conflict and telling everyone that things will "get better." Often the conflict will only worsen as people continue to brood over it.

Compromise is striking a middle-range position between two extremes. This approach can work if it is used with care, but in most compromise situations someone wins and someone loses. Budget problems are one of the few areas amenable to compromise, because of their objective nature. Assume, for example, that additional resources are not available to the manager mentioned earlier. She has $180,000 to divide, and each of two groups claims to need $100,000. If the manager believes that both projects warrant funding, she can allocate $90,000 to each. The fact that the two groups have at least been treated equally may minimize the potential conflict.

The confrontational approach to conflict resolution—also called *interpersonal problem solving*—consists of bringing the parties together to confront the conflict. The parties discuss the nature of their conflict and attempt to reach an agreement or a solution. Confrontation requires a reasonable degree of maturity on the part of the participants, and the manager must structure the situation carefully. If handled well, this approach can be an effective means of resolving conflict. In recent years, many organizations have experimented with a technique called *alternative dispute resolution*, using a team of employees to arbitrate conflict in this way.[34]

Regardless of the approach, organizations and their managers must realize that conflict must be addressed if it is to serve constructive purposes and be prevented from bringing about destructive consequences. Conflict is inevitable in organizations, but its effects can be constrained with proper attention. For example, Union Carbide sent two hundred of its managers to a three-day workshop on conflict management. The managers engaged in a variety of exercises and discussions to learn with whom they were most likely to come in conflict and how they should try to resolve it. As a result, managers at the firm later reported that hostility and resentment in the organization had been greatly diminished and that people in the firm reported more pleasant working relationships.[35]

concept CHECK

What techniques are available to managers to stimulate, control, and resolve conflict?	*What are the primary risks involved if a manager decides to stimulate conflict?*

Summary of Key Points

business.college.hmco.com/students

A group is two or more people who interact regularly to accomplish a common purpose or goal. General kinds of groups in organizations are functional groups, task groups and teams, and informal or interest groups. A team is a group of workers that functions as a unit, often with little or no supervision, to carry out organizational functions.

People join functional groups and teams to pursue a career. Their reasons for joining informal or interest groups include interpersonal attraction, group activities, group goals, need satisfaction, and potential instrumental benefits. The stages of team development include testing and dependence, intragroup conflict and hostility, development of group cohesion, and focusing on the problem at hand.

Four important characteristics of teams are role structures, behavioral norms, cohesiveness, and informal leadership. Role structures define task and socioemotional specialists and may be disrupted by role ambiguity, role conflict, or role overload. Norms are standards of behavior for group members. Cohesiveness is the extent to which members are loyal and committed to the team and to one another. Several factors can increase or reduce team cohesiveness. The relationship between performance norms and cohesiveness is especially important. Informal leaders are those leaders whom the group members themselves choose to follow.

Conflict is a disagreement between two or more people, groups, or organizations. Too little or too much conflict may hurt performance, but an optimal level of conflict may improve performance. Interpersonal and intergroup conflict in organizations may be caused by personality differences or by particular organizational strategies and practices.

Organizations may encounter conflict with one another and with various elements of the environment. Three methods of managing conflict are to stimulate it, control it, or resolve and eliminate it.

Discussion Questions

Questions for Review

1. What is a group? Describe the several different types of groups and indicate the similarities and differences between them. What is the difference between a group and a team?
2. What are the stages of group development? Do all teams develop through all the stages discussed in this chapter? Why or why not? How might the management of a mature team differ from the management of teams that are not yet mature?
3. Describe the development of a role within a group. Tell how each role leads to the next.
4. Describe the causes of conflict in organizations. What can a manager do to control conflict? to resolve and eliminate conflict?

Questions for Analysis

5. Individuals join groups for a variety of reasons. Most groups contain members who joined for different reasons. What is likely to be the result when members join a group for different reasons? What can a group

leader do to reduce the negative impact of a conflict in reasons for joining the group?

6. Consider the case of a developed group, where all members have been socialized. What are the benefits to the individuals of norm conformity? What are the benefits of not conforming to the group's norms? What are the benefits to an organization of conformity? What are the benefits to an organization of nonconformity?
7. Do you think teams are a valuable new management technique that will endure, or are they just a fad that will be replaced with something else in the near future?

Questions for Application

8. Think of several groups of which you have been a member. Why did you join each? Did each group progress through the stages of development discussed in this chapter? If not, why do you think it did not?
9. Describe the behavioral norms that are in effect in your management class. To what extent are the norms generalized; in other words, how severely are students "punished" for not observing norms? To what extent is there norm variation; that is, are some students able to "get away" with violating norms to which others must conform?
10. Describe a case of interpersonal conflict that you have observed in an organization. Describe a case of intergroup conflict that you have observed. (If you have not observed any, interview a worker or manager to obtain examples.) In each case, was the conflict beneficial or harmful to the organization, and why?

BUILDING EFFECTIVE decision-making SKILLS

Exercise Overview

Decision-making skills include the manager's ability to recognize and define situations correctly and to select courses of action. This exercise uses a military problem-solving case to build your skills in team decision making.

Exercise Background

The case that is summarized below was written by a British army officer, Major General Ernest Swinton, following the end of the Boer War. Prior to the Boer War, British officers were noblemen, not professional soldiers. They had little or no practical experience in leadership or soldiering skills. The results were disastrous and led to the deaths of many British soldiers and officers. This case was a first step in training officers through the use of realistic simulations and is still in use at U.S. Army training centers, such as the Command and General Staff College in Fort Leavenworth, Kansas. You will use this case to set up a simulated decision-making situation, then work with a group to suggest solutions.

The Defense of Duffer's Drift

Dutch settlers (Boers) first arrived in South Africa in the 1600s. Following the British seizure of the Cape of Good Hope at the southern tip of South Africa during the Napoleonic Wars of the early 1800s, Boer farmers went north into the interior, where they settled the Transvaal. Disputes continued between the British and the Boers, and war broke out in 1899. Boer guerillas besieged British towns, and the British responded by bringing in more than

300,000 troops. The British finally prevailed through confining parts of the Boer population to concentration camps and destroying their farms.

You are the leaders of a company of British soldiers. Your group consists of several lieutenants, who are in charge of platoons of twenty men. Your company has just arrived at a river near a ford (a "drift"), where the banks are flat, making an easy crossing for troops and wagons. This ford is important because it is the only place where wheeled traffic can pass this part of the river. Your orders are to hold the ford at all costs. The British are in the south and do not want any Boer enemies to cross from the north to the south side of the river.

When you were dropped off, you were told you would be reinforced in three to four days. You may possibly be attacked before that time, but no enemy is known to be within a hundred miles. If the enemy comes this way, they will very badly want to use the ford because they will have cannons on horse-drawn carriages. These cannons have an effective range of 3,000 meters or more. The enemy is also armed with rifles similar to yours.

You take stock of your resources. Your troops are good soldiers and have been trained to do anything you require. You have rifles with an effective range of 500 meters, but they can suppress the enemy (keep his head down) for up to 1,000 meters. You do not have cannons. You are well supplied with ammunition and food rations, including whiskey and tobacco. You have a number of picks, shovels, and sandbags.

You begin to look around you, observing your environment. The river is currently just a trickle of water. The banks are very steep, too steep for wagons to cross anywhere except at the ford. At the top of the banks are dense bushes, forming a screen impenetrable to sight. The banks have a number of ravines and are very rough where the earth has been eaten away by the river.

About 1,200 meters to the northeast there is a small rocky hill covered with bushes and boulders. It is steep on the south but gently falling to the north. On the south side of this hill is a farmhouse, run by a "cooperative" Boer farmer and his wife and grown children. They have written passes that state they are loyal to Great Britain. They assure you that there are no Boer guerrillas anywhere within miles. They ask your permission to sell milk, eggs, and butter to your soldiers. Because your soldiers have not had such luxuries in a while, you give the Boer farmers permission to enter your camp.

About 1,000 meters south of the drift is another larger hill, also covered with bushes and boulders. On top of this hill is a native village, consisting of a few grass and mud huts surrounded by a stockade fence. The village is occupied by about twenty natives from a tribe that has remained neutral in the fighting between the British and the Boers.

Other than the river and two hills, the ground around the ford is a flat, grassy plain. The dirt is hard packed and brown. However, when the dirt is freshly turned over, it is a much brighter red color.

You decide to set your camp on a spot just south of the drift. At this point, the river surrounds you on three sides, forming a natural horseshoe-shaped obstacle. It is close to the drift, which you think is necessary to properly guard it. You consider splitting up your forces to cover more area, but decide to keep them concentrated in one position to mass their fire on the drift. Accordingly, you tell all of your soldiers to aim at the drift to prevent anyone from crossing it.

You have come to the conclusion that, as the enemy are not within a hundred miles, there will be no need to improve the defenses of your camp until the following day. The men are tired after their long walk, and there is just enough time left in the day for them to arrange all the stores and tools, pitch their tents, and get their tea before dark.

You order two guard posts to be set up outside the main camp, one on the drift and one farther down the river, to the east. As it will be a cold night, you allow the guard posts to have fires to keep the men warm. This also serves notice to anyone approaching that this is a British sentry on full alert and ready to challenge anyone trying to enter camp.

Satisfied that you have done everything you need to do for the evening, you go to sleep. You wake up in the morning to a hoarse cry of "Halt! Who goes . . ." cut short by the unmistakable pop of a Mauser rifle. You and your men react as quickly as possible as the enemy starts firing at you in earnest. Unfortunately, you cannot see where the enemy is. They, however, seem to know exactly how your camp is set up. Your men have nothing to hide behind but the canvas of their tents and are being wounded and killed at a terrible rate. With nothing left to do, you decide to hoist the white flag and surrender.

Exercise Task

Swinton, the author of this case, called it "Duffer's Drift," because a "duffer" was someone who sat around on his duff—in other words, a nineteenth-century equivalent of a slacker. Clearly, the duffer in this case (you) has made one or more errors, leading to your ignominious defeat. With the information above as background, jot down some answers to the following questions.

1. What problems existed with your initial approach to the defense of Duffer's Drift? In particular, consider how the enemy knew where you were, how they were able to surprise you, and how they were able to inflict casualties on you so quickly.
2. What limitations and constraints are hindering you? What resources and other opportunities may be helpful to you?
3. What things should you have done differently to avoid the disastrous outcome? More than one suggestion is possible.

Next, meet in a small group of three to five students. Share your answers and try to synthesize your suggestions into one final solution. Finally, share your group's final solution with the class. Are there any solutions the class can agree on? Your professor also has some solution ideas. At the end of the discussion, consider how your answers evolved, from individual to group to large class. Did the answers identify more problems? Did they identify more limitations and more opportunities? Did the class come up with a solution that is more likely to be effective than your individual solution? Explain your answers.

BUILDING EFFECTIVE conceptual SKILLS

business.college.hmco.com/students

Exercise Overview

Groups and teams are becoming ever more important in organizations. This exercise will allow you to practice your conceptual skills as they apply to work teams in organizations.

Exercise Background

Several highly effective groups exist outside the boundaries of typical business organizations. For example, a basketball team, a military squadron, a government policy group such as the president's Cabinet, a student committee, and the leadership of a church or religious organization are all teams.

Exercise Task

1. Use the Internet to identify an example of a real team. Choose one that (a) is not part of a normal for-profit business and (b) you can argue is highly effective.
2. Determine the reasons for the team's effectiveness. (*Hint:* You might look for websites sponsored by that group, look at online news sources for current articles, or enter the group's name as a search term in a search engine.) Consider team characteristics and activities, such as role structures, norms, cohesiveness, and conflict management.
3. What can a manager learn from this particular team? How can this team's success factors be used in a business setting?

BUILDING EFFECTIVE communication SKILLS

Exercise Overview

Communication skills are essential to effective teamwork, because teams depend on members' ability to accurately send and receive information. This game demonstrates how good communication skills can lead to improved teamwork and team performance.

Exercise Background

This game is played three times. The first time, you act alone. The second time, you work in small groups, sharing information. The third time, you again work in a small group, but you also have the benefit of some suggestions for performance improvement. Typically, students find that performance improves over the three turns. Creativity is enhanced when information is shared.

Exercise Task

1. Play the "Name Game" that your professor will describe to you. The first time, work out your answers individually. Report your individual score to the class.
2. The second time you play, join a small group of three to five students. Work out your answers together, writing them on a single answer sheet. Allow each group member to look at the sheet. If you can do so without being overheard by other groups, whisper your answers to your group members. Report your group score to the class.
3. Then ask the highest-performing individuals and groups to share their methods with everyone. Your professor may also have some suggestions. Make sure that you understand at least two strategies for improving your score.
4. Play the game for a third time, working together in the same small group in which you participated before. Report your group scores to the class.
5. Did the average group scores improve on the average individual scores? Why or why not?
6. Did the average group scores rise after discussing methods for improvement? Why or why not?
7. What does this game teach you about teamwork and effectiveness? Share your thoughts with the class.

CHAPTER CLOSING case

No Teamwork at Disney?

> *"[I am] an isolated and brilliant ruler who lacks introspection."*
>
> – Michael Eisner, CEO of Disney*

"Michael Eisner is more than the CEO of Walt Disney Co. He is a star," says *Fortune* writer Marc Gunther. Before joining Disney, Eisner had a string of triumphs at ABC and Paramount. Under his leadership, Disney prospered; Eisner was admired. No one disputed his brilliance, but Eisner has a difficult time working with others. Since 2000 Disney has been in financial decline, and lack of teamwork is one contributing factor.

Over two decades, Disney's animation studios exploded with innovation, creating *The Lion King, Beauty and the Beast,* and more. Eisner exploited a movie hit in every channel—theme park rides, merchandise, TV, and Broadway shows. Eisner's Disney became a powerful force in every medium, from radio to the Internet, through aggressive acquisitions. Eisner expanded Disney's appeal beyond families, with Miramax films for grownups and resorts appealing to young adults and senior citizens. Eisner founded the Disney Cruise Line and Disney-owned housing developments.

However, critics describe Eisner as "arrogant," "egotistical," and "a control freak." In his 1998 autobiography, *Work in Progress,* Eisner admits that he is "an isolated and brilliant ruler who lacks introspection." Marc Gunther writes, "When things go wrong, he tends to distance himself and blame others; when things go well, he takes the credit." These traits discourage the trust and camaraderie needed for effective teamwork and alienate coworkers.

Eisner's poor teamwork skills have alienated former supporters. He had the support of powerful board members, including Disney nephew Roy E. Disney and Disney family friend Stanley P. Gold. For years, Roy Disney and Gold backed Eisner's bold moves and defended controversial decisions. But, in August 2002, Disney announced that earnings would be lower than expected. Stock price fell to an eight-year low, and the Disney family holdings dropped 65 percent. The relationship between Eisner and the Disney family is faltering. Gold says, "The family owes a great debt of gratitude to Michael for what he has done. But my goal is to try to get the Disney Company to perform at a level of efficiency it hasn't seen for a number of years, given its fine assets."

Eisner and Disney are also battling over Winnie the Pooh. The bear was created by author A. A. Milne in 1926. Today, Milne's heirs are fighting Disney over royalties from Pooh products. Disney already paid $352 million, but claims may reach $1 billion. Disney deliberately destroyed documents that might have settled the issue and may lose rights to the popular Pooh characters.

As Disney grows, so does its need for capable executives. Yet Eisner is paranoid about losing his success, making him uncomfortable with talented subordinates. His poor people skills have caused the defection of several top managers. "People get tired of being second-guessed and beaten down," says a former Disney employee. Jeffrey Katzenberg left Disney to found DreamWorks, the makers of *Shrek* and *Chicken Run.* Disney's "brain drain" also led to the resignation of theme park chairman Paul Pressler, who became CEO of Gap.

Eisner is also fighting publicly with Pixar, maker of *Toy Story, A Bug's Life, Monsters, Inc* and *Finding Nemo.* Pixar is headed by Steve Jobs, also the CEO of Apple. Both Eisner and Jobs are known for their pride and stubbornness, and their feud is escalating. A twelve-year deal between the companies called for the production of five films. In 2001 Jobs claimed that a third *Toy Story* film would count against the limit; Eisner said a sequel did not count. (The project is now shelved.) In testimony before Congress, Eisner accused Apple of aiding Internet piracy. Jobs retaliated by making a mouse the star of Pixar's next film, in a clear jab at Disney. The agreement will expire in 2005, and Jobs is looking for a new partner. Jobs wants a bigger share of profits—

Pixar earned $235 million for *Monsters*, Inc., but could have earned $500 million alone. Disney cannot afford to lose Pixar, yet dueling egos may prevent a relationship that could be profitable for both companies.

Eisner is ignoring critics. "I spend my life being Odysseus," he says. "I tie myself to the mast and I don't listen to the Sirens . . . [who] say that your testosterone level is gone because you haven't made an acquisition in the last ten minutes." The analogy is appropriate—Eisner sees himself as a mythic hero, battered by uncontrollable forces but triumphing in the end through individual effort and strength of will. Yet Eisner's self-perception is the heart of the problem. Can any man, even a great one, manage a sprawling multinational firm alone? Eisner may think so, but his followers are dwindling.

Case Questions

1. Describe the level of cohesiveness in Disney's corporate management. What are some likely consequences of this level of cohesiveness?
2. What types of conflict do you see at Disney? Give one example from the case for each type. Do you think there is too much, not enough, or about the correct amount of conflict at Disney? Why?
3. In your opinion, what could Michael Eisner do to improve teamwork at Disney? If he took your advice, what outcomes could he expect? If he does not improve teamwork, what outcomes can he expect? Consider outcomes from the point of view of Eisner, Disney employees, stockholders, and customers.

Case References

Bridget Byrne, "Bio Rats out Head Mouse Eisner," *E! Online News*, May 17, 2000, 222.eonline.com on February 13, 2003 (*quote); Laura M. Holson, "As Disney Loses Steam, Insider Loses Patience," *New York Times*, August 18, 2002, pp. BU1, BU11; Marc Gunther, "Has Eisner Lost the Disney Magic?" *Fortune*, December 23, 2001, www.fortune.com on February 13, 2003; Marc Gunther, "The Directors," *Fortune*, September 29, 2002, www.fortune.com on February 13, 2003; Ronald Grover, "Is Steve Jobs About to Move His Cheese?" *BusinessWeek*, February 10, 2003, www.businessweek.com on February 13, 2003; Ronald Glover, "The Miserable Lives of Media Moguls," *BusinessWeek*, January 27, 2003, www.businessweek.com on February 13, 2003; Ronald Grover, "Why Is Christopher Robin Sobbing?" *BusinessWeek*, September 16, 2002, p. 51.

Chapter Notes

1. David Shook, "The Rx for Growth: 'Discover Drugs,'" *BusinessWeek*, January 24, 2003, www.businessweek.com on February 12, 2003; David Shook, "Two Pep Pills in Big Pharma," *BusinessWeek*, January 24, 2003, www.businessweek.com on February 12, 2003; "Drugmaker Pfizer Undergoes Change, Expansion," *The Day* (New London, Conn.), January 29, 2003, www.theday.com on February 12, 2003; Melody Petersen, "Revving up the Labs at Pfizer," *New York Times*, September 8, 2002, p. BU2 (*quote); "Pfizer, GM and UAW/BCBSM Capture Top Honors at 7th Annual Arbor Awards," *PR Newswire*, February 4, 2003, hoovnews.hoovers.com on February 12, 2003.
2. See Gregory Moorhead and Ricky W. Griffin, *Organizational Behavior*, 7th ed. (Boston: Houghton Mifflin, 2004), for a review of definitions of groups.
3. Dorwin Cartwright and Alvin Zander, eds., *Group Dynamics: Research and Theory*, 3rd ed. (New York: Harper & Row, 1968).
4. Rob Cross, Nitin Nohria, and Andrew Parker, "Six Myths About Informal Networks—And How to Overcome Them," *Sloan Management Review*, Spring 2002, pp. 67–77.
5. Robert Schrank, *Ten Thousand Working Days* (Cambridge, Mass.: MIT Press, 1978); Bill Watson, "Counter Planning on the Shop Floor," in Peter Frost, Vance Mitchell, and Walter Nord, eds., *Organizational Reality*, 2nd ed. (Glenview, Ill.: Scott, Foresman, 1982), pp. 286–294.
6. "After Layoffs, More Workers Band Together," *Wall Street Journal*, February 26, 2002, p. B1.
7. Bradley L. Kirkman and Benson Rosen, "Powering up Teams," *Organizational Dynamics*, Winter 2000, pp. 48–58.
8. Brian Dumaine, "Payoff from the New Management," *Fortune*, December 13, 1993, pp. 103–110.
9. "Why Teams Fail," *USA Today*, February 25, 1997, pp. 1B, 2B.
10. Brian Dumaine, "The Trouble with Teams," *Fortune*, September 5, 1994, pp. 86–92. See also Susan G. Cohen and Diane E. Bailey, "What Makes Teams Work: Group Effectiveness Research from the Shop Floor to the Executive Suite," *Journal of Management*, 1997, vol. 23, no. 3, pp. 239–290.
11. Marvin E. Shaw, *Group Dynamics-The Psychology of Small Group Behavior*, 4th ed. (New York: McGraw-Hill, 1985).
12. "How to Avoid Hiring the Prima Donnas Who Hate Teamwork," *Wall Street Journal*, February 15, 2000, p. B1.
13. See Connie Gersick, "Marking Time: Predictable Transitions in Task Groups," *Academy of Management Journal*, June 1989, pp. 274–309. See also Avan R. Jassawalla and Hemant C. Sashittal, "Building Collaborative Cross-Functional New Product Teams," *Academy of Management Review*, 1999, vol. 13, no. 3, pp. 50–60.
14. See Michael Campion, Gina Medsker, and A.Catherine Higgs, "Relations Between Work Group Characteristics and Effectiveness: Implications for Designing Effective Work Groups," *Personnel Psychology*, Winter 1993, pp. 823–850, for a review of other team characteristics.
15. David Katz and Robert L. Kahn, *The Social Psychology of Organizations*, 2nd ed. (New York: Wiley, 1978), pp. 187–221. See also Greg L. Stewart and Murray R. Barrick, "Team Structure and Performance: Assessing the Mediating Role of Intrateam Process and the Moderating Role of Task Type," *Academy of Management Journal*, 2000, vol. 43, no. 2, pp. 135–148, and Michael G. Pratt and Peter O. Foreman, "Classifying Managerial Responses to Multiple Organizational Identities," *Academy of Management Review*, 2000, vol. 25, no. 1, pp. 18–42.
16. See Travis C. Tubre and Judith M. Collins, "Jackson and Schuler (1985) Revisited: A Meta-Analysis of the Relationships Between Role Ambiguity, Role Conflict, and Job Performance," *Journal of Management*, 2000, vol. 26, no. 1, pp. 155–169.
17. Robert L. Kahn, D. M. Wolfe, R. P. Quinn, J. D. Snoek, and R. A. Rosenthal, *Organizational Stress: Studies in Role Conflict and Role Ambiguity* (New York: Wiley, 1964).
18. Daniel C. Feldman, "The Development and Enforcement of Group Norms," *Academy of Management Review*, January 1984, pp. 47–53.
19. "Companies Turn to Peer Pressure to Cut Injuries as Psychologists Join the Battle," *Wall Street Journal*, March 29, 1991, pp. B1, B3.
20. James Wallace Bishop and K. Dow Scott, "How Commitment Affects Team Performance," *HRMagazine*, February 1997, pp. 107–115.
21. Anne O'Leary-Kelly, Joseph Martocchio, and Dwight Frink, "A Review of the Influence of Group Goals on Group Performance," *Academy of Management Journal*, 1994, vol. 37, no. 5, pp. 1285–1301.
22. Philip M. Podsakoff, Michael Ahearne, and Scott B. MacKenzie, "Organizational Citizenship Behavior and the Quantity and Quality of Work Group Performance, *Journal of Applied Psychology*, vol. 82, no. 2, 1997, pp. 262–270.
23. Suzy Wetlaufer, "Common Sense and Conflict," *Harvard Business Review*, January–February 2000, pp. 115–125.
24. Kathleen M. Eisenhardt, Jean L. Kahwajy, and L. J. Bourgeois III, "How Management Teams Can Have a Good Fight," *Harvard Business Review*, July–August 1997, pp. 77–89.
25. Thomas Bergmann and Roger Volkema, "Issues, Behavioral Responses and Consequences in Interpersonal Conflicts," *Journal of Organizational Behavior*, 1994, vol. 15, pp. 467–471.
26. Robin Pinkley and Gregory Northcraft, "Conflict Frames of Reference: Implications for Dispute Processes and Outcomes," *Academy of Management Journal*, 1994, vol. 37, no. 1, pp. 193–205.
27. "How 2 Computer Nuts Transformed Industry Before Messy Breakup," *Wall Street Journal*, August 27, 1996, pp. A1, A10.
28. Bruce Barry and Greg L. Stewart, "Composition, Process, and Performance in Self-Managed Groups: The Role of Personality," *Journal of Applied Psychology*, vol. 82, no. 1, 1997, pp. 62–78.

29. "Rumsfeld's Abrasive Style Sparks Conflict with Military Command," *USA Today*, December 10, 2002, pp. 1A, 2A.
30. "Delta CEO Resigns After Clashes with Board," *USA Today*, May 13, 1997, p. B1.
31. "A 'Blood War' in the Jeans Trade," *BusinessWeek*, November 13, 1999, pp. 74–81.
32. Peter Elkind, "Blood Feud," *Fortune*, April 14, 1997, pp. 90–102.
33. See Patrick Nugent, "Managing Conflict: Third-Party Interventions for Managers," *Academy of Management Executive*, 2002, vol. 16, no. 1, pp. 139–148.
34. "Solving Conflicts in the Workplace Without Making Losers," *Wall Street Journal*, May 27, 1997, p. B1.
35. "Teaching Business How to Cope with Workplace Conflicts," *BusinessWeek*, February 18, 1990, pp. 136, 139.

PART SIX

THE CONTROLLING PROCESS

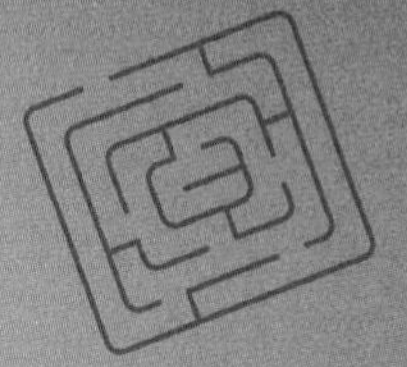

CHAPTER 20

Basic Elements of Control

CHAPTER 21

Managing Operations, Quality, and Productivity

CHAPTER 22

Managing Information and Information Technology

20 Basic Elements of Control

LEARNING OBJECTIVES

After studying this chapter, you should be able to:

1 *Explain the purpose of control, identify different types of control, and describe the steps in the control process.*

CHAPTER OUTLINE

The Nature of Control
- The Purpose of Control
- Types of Control
- Steps in the Control Process

Operations Control
- Preliminary Control
- Screening Control
- Postaction Control

Financial Control
- Budgetary Control
- Other Tools for Financial Control

Structural Control
- Bureaucratic Control
- Decentralized Control

Strategic Control
- Integrating Strategy and Control
- International Strategic Control

Managing Control in Organizations
- Characteristics of Effective Control
- Resistance to Control
- Overcoming Resistance to Control

OPENING INCIDENT

The airline industry is one of the most challenging industries for managers. Skills in scheduling, purchasing, customer service, and mechanical maintenance are required. Teams of diverse individuals, from pilots to baggage handlers, must be coordinated. Fixed costs for planes and equipment are high and revenues uncertain. Competition is intense, with fierce price wars. In this hostile environment, few companies survive—both United and US Airways declared bankruptcy recently. Of the twenty-seven carriers that have gone public since 1980, only eight survive today. How, then, has JetBlue, founded in 2000, become one of the most profitable airlines in the United States?

First and foremost, credit CEO David Neeleman's planning skills. Neeleman founded Morris Air, a discount carrier based in Salt Lake City. In 1993 Southwest Airlines bought Morris Air for $128 million. Neeleman worked briefly at Southwest and then was fired. He planned to beat rival Southwest at its own game. He consulted—and in some cases hired—experienced managers from competitors. He copied elements of Southwest's discount strategy, such as point-to-point scheduling, reliance on a

2	3	4	5	6
Identify and explain the three forms of operations control.	***Describe budgets and other tools for financial control.***	***Identify and distinguish between two opposing forms of structural control.***	***Discuss the relationship between strategy and control, including international strategic control.***	***Identify characteristics of effective control, why people resist control, and how managers can overcome this resistance.***

"It's easy for JetBlue to be golden with 30 airplanes, but it doesn't mean it can manage 100."

—A. K. Darby, president, Aviation Information Resources, Inc.

JetBlue has become the darling of the airline industry.

single type of aircraft, and use of nonunion employees. Then he added some extras: reserved seats, upscale snacks, leather seats, seat-back televisions with twenty-four channels of DirecTV. "JetBlue is not merely a clone of Southwest Airlines; it is the new gold standard among low-cost carriers," claims industry consultant James Craun.

Neeleman, with his extensive industry expertise, focused most of his attention on the few significant factors that could make or break his company. By hiring younger, less experienced workers and giving them stock options in lieu of high wages, JetBlue kept labor expenses down to 25 percent of revenues, compared to Southwest's 33 percent and Delta's 44 percent. JetBlue also fills up its planes and gets more flying hours out of each aircraft. Maintenance costs are low because the planes are all brand new. Even the luxurious leather seats were chosen for their cost-effectiveness—they are easier to clean. On-time arrival is critical for customer service, so Neeleman's pager beeps any time a flight is more than one minute late. He even wears his pager to bed.

Neeleman's dedication to monitoring the airline's performance is matched by his passion for feedback. He jumps on a plane once a week or so, serving drinks and loading baggage. Along the way, he smiles politely at praise but asks passengers to tell him more about their complaints. No concern is too small or too large, from a desire for better biscotti to a request for flights to Chicago. Customers' suggestions are taken seriously. A frequent flyer program, a service desired by travelers, was added in July 2002. Neeleman gives employees the autonomy to make customer service decisions immediately. "Employees at other airlines get so caught up in procedure—rules, rules, rules—that they often forget there is a paying customer there," Neeleman asserts. JetBlue passengers, for example, receive discount coupons and free accommodations if their flight is diverted, compensation that rival airlines do not always provide.

JetBlue's success is clear. But the real question is: Can that success be sustained? Expansion is the trap that ensnared the now-failed airline ventures. "It's easy for JetBlue to be golden with 30 airplanes, but it doesn't mean it can manage 100," says expert A. K. Darby. As increasing size leads to increasing complexity, Neeleman will have to guard against inefficiencies and too much bureaucracy. Costs will surely rise, as planes age and low-paid workers demand raises. Unionization will probably occur, further increasing labor costs. "In a lot of places now, there's no low-fare nonstop service," claims Neeleman. "That creates some opportunities for us." Yet JetBlue will have a harder and harder time finding opportunities as it grows. Funds for expansion are cheap right now, because JetBlue raised start-up capital from outside investors. But the firm will have to borrow to buy more planes, and that will increase debt expense.

The CEO welcomes the challenge. "I can't believe how quickly we got out of the gate and how profitable we became," says Neeleman. "Now I don't think there's a limit to how big JetBlue can get." Under Neeleman's guidance, the sky may indeed be the limit for JetBlue.[1]

David Neeleman has almost single-handedly made JetBlue one of the twenty-first century's first success stories. One key to his accomplishments has been a well-constructed business model detailing how he wanted his business to be managed. Another key has been effective control systems that serve their intended purpose. In a nutshell, effective control helps managers like David Neeleman decide where they want their business to go, point it in that direction, and create systems to keep it on track. Ineffective control, on the other hand, can result in a lack of focus, weak direction, and poor overall performance.

As we discuss in Chapter 1, control is one of the four basic managerial functions that provide the organizing framework for this book. This is the first of three chapters devoted to this important area. In the first section of the chapter we explain the purpose of control. We then look at types of control and the steps in the control process. The rest of the chapter examines the four levels of control that most organizations must employ in order to remain effective: operations, financial, structural, and strategic control. We conclude by discussing the characteristics of effective control, noting why some people resist control and describing what organizations can do to overcome this resistance. The remaining two chapters in this part focus on managing operations and managing information.

The Nature of Control

control The regulation of organizational activities in such a way as to facilitate goal attainment

Control is the regulation of organizational activities so that some targeted element of performance remains within acceptable limits. Without this regulation, organizations have no indication of how well they are performing in relation to their goals. Control, like a ship's rudder, keeps the organization moving in the

Control helps organizations cope with change and complexity. Public schools, for instance, face growing problems concerning safety and the legal rights of individuals to pick up children from school. This New Jersey elementary school is implementing an iris recognition system to better control access to its campus and facilities. The iris-scanning technology will be used for employees, parents, and guardians as a way to better protect the students at the school.

proper direction. At any point in time, it compares where the organization is in terms of performance (financial, productive, or otherwise) to where it is supposed to be. Like a rudder, control provides an organization with a mechanism for adjusting its course if performance falls outside of acceptable boundaries. For example, FedEx has a performance goal of delivering 99.5 percent of its packages on time. If on-time deliveries fall to 98 percent, control systems will signal the problem to managers, so that they can make necessary adjustments in operations to regain the target level of performance. An organization without effective control procedures is not likely to reach its goals—or, if it does reach them, to know that it has!

The Purpose of Control

As Figure 20.1 illustrates, control provides an organization with ways to adapt to environmental change, to limit the accumulation of error, to cope with organizational complexity, and to minimize costs. These four functions of control are worth a closer look. Indeed, the situation described in *Today's Management Issues* clearly demonstrates why control is so important.

Adapting to Environmental Change In today's complex and turbulent business environment, all organizations must contend with change.[2] If managers could establish goals and achieve them instantaneously, control would not be needed. But, between the time a goal is established and the time it is reached, many things can happen in the organization and its environment to disrupt movement toward the goal—or even to change the goal itself. A properly designed control system can help managers anticipate, monitor, and respond to changing circumstances.[3] In contrast, an improperly designed system can result in organizational performance that falls far below acceptable levels.

For example, Michigan-based Metalloy, a forty-six-year-old, family-run metal-casting company, signed a contract to make engine-seal castings for NOK, a big Japanese auto parts maker. Metalloy was satisfied when its first 5,000-unit production run yielded 4,985 acceptable castings and only 15 defective ones. NOK, however, was quite unhappy with this performance and insisted that Metalloy raise its

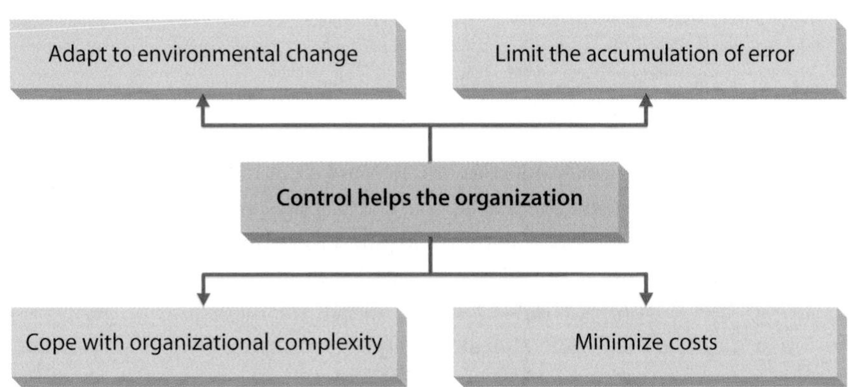

FIGURE 20.1

The Purpose of Control

Control is one of the four basic management functions in organizations. The control function, in turn, has four basic purposes. Properly designed control systems can fulfill each of these purposes.

"The Most Inefficient Organization in the Federal Government"

". . . producing results seems to be an alien concept [at the Department of Energy]."

– Anonymous official at the Office of Management and Budget*

The project is mind-boggling. The U.S government began producing radioactive materials for use in nuclear weapons in the 1940s. Today, many of those weapons programs are obsolete, and the United States is now faced with cleaning up thousands of tons of deadly waste at six hundred contaminated sites. This task is important and sensitive, yet Congress calls the Department of Energy, who oversees the cleanup, "one of the most inefficient organizations in the federal government." The problem? A failure to control the project.

Project manager Jessie Roberson admits, "I have been embarrassed by our lack of progress." Her embarrassment springs from the $60 billion cost of the project thus far and its striking lack of results. The cleanup at a South Carolina site should have taken three years and cost $32 million. Fourteen years and $500 million later, the unfinished project was abandoned. At Savannah River, cleanup was expected to be complete by 1999 but now has a completion date of 2038.

The DOE employs 100,000 contract workers but just recently began oversight by DOE managers. Supervisors admit that they award contracts without ever examining the site, leading to the type of underestimation that occurred at Savannah River. There, contractors estimated that one phase would generate five boxes of waste; it ended up filling hundreds. Once the work is under way, DOE managers rarely visit the site. Each site is operated autonomously, and innovations made in one location are not shared.

Unfavorable audits state, "producing results seems to be an alien concept [at the DOE]" and "[there is] no indication of improved performance." Roberson says that the criticism, perversely, reduces her staff's willingness to change. In response to perceived attacks, workers defensively "stand firm and explain the problems away. And with that posture, the problems don't get better over time."

Energy Secretary Spencer Abraham vows that "we will no longer give contractors a license for unending cleanup and open-ended budgets." But the DOE's own report comes to a different conclusion: "The cost of the program will . . . increase and increase . . . the ultimate . . . goal will never be met." For the taxpayers and citizens of the United States, that answer is simply unacceptable. DOE will have to learn to do better.

References: "DOE, States and Regulators Agree to Accelerate Cleanup," *EM Progress Newsletter*, Department of Energy website, Summer 2002, www.em.doe.gov on February 14, 2003; "Inside Savannah River," Savannah River Operations Office website, sro.srs.gov on February 14, 2003; James Malone, "Paducah Plan Cleanup Costs Escalate," *The Courier-Journal* (Louisville, Kentucky), November 21, 2000, www.courier-journal.com on February 14, 2003; Joel Brinkley, "Energy Dept. Contractors Due for More Scrutiny," *New York Times*, November 24, 2002, p. L28 (*quote); "Savannah River Site Environment Management Plan," Department of Energy website, August 7, 2002, www.em.doe.gov on February 14, 2003.

standards. In short, global quality standards are such that customers demand near-perfection from their suppliers. A properly designed control system can help managers like those at Metalloy stay better attuned to rising standards.

Limiting the Accumulation of Error Small mistakes and errors do not often seriously damage the financial health of an organization. Over time, however, small errors may accumulate and become very serious. For example, Whistler Corporation, a large radar detector manufacturer, was once faced with such rapidly escalating demand that it essentially stopped worrying about quality. The defect rate rose from 4 percent to 9 percent to 15 percent and eventually reached 25 percent. One day, a manager realized that 100 of the firm's 250 employees were spending all their time fixing defective units and that $2 million worth of inventory was awaiting repair. Had the company adequately controlled quality as it responded to increased demand, the problem would never have reached such proportions. Similarly, Fleetwood Enterprises, a large manufacturer of recreational vehicles, has suffered because its managers did not adequately address several small accounting and production problems years ago. As these small problems grew into large ones, the firm has struggled with how to correct them.[4]

Coping with Organizational Complexity When a firm purchases only one raw material, produces one product, has a simple organization design, and enjoys constant demand for its product, its managers can maintain control with a very basic and simple system. But a business that produces many products from myriad raw materials and has a large market area, a complicated organization design, and many competitors needs a sophisticated system in order to maintain adequate control. When large firms merge, the short-term results are often disappointing. The typical reason for this is that the new enterprise is so large and complex that the existing control systems are simply inadequate. Daimler-Benz and Chrysler faced just this problem when they merged to create DaimlerChrysler.

Minimizing Costs When it is practiced effectively, control can also help reduce costs and boost output. For example, Georgia-Pacific Corporation, a large wood products company, learned of a new technology that could be used to make thinner blades for its saws. The firm's control system was used to calculate the amount of wood that could be saved from each cut made by the thinner blades relative to the costs used to replace the existing blades. The results have been impressive—the wood that is saved by the new blades each year fills eight hundred rail cars. As Georgia-Pacific discovered, effective control systems can eliminate waste, lower labor costs, and improve output per unit of input. In their bids to further reduce costs, businesses are cutting back on everything from health insurance coverage to overnight shipping to business lunches for clients.[5]

Types of Control

The examples of control given thus far have illustrated the regulation of several organizational activities, from producing quality products to coordinating complex organizations. Organizations practice control in a number of different areas and at different levels, and the responsibility for managing control is widespread.

Areas of Control Control can focus on any area of an organization. Most organizations define areas of control in terms of the four basic types of resources they use: physical, human, information, and financial.[6] Control of physical resources includes inventory management (stocking neither too few nor too many units in inventory), quality control (maintaining appropriate levels of output quality), and equipment control (supplying the necessary facilities and machinery). Control of human resources includes selection and placement, training and development, performance appraisal, and compensation. Control of information resources includes sales and marketing forecasting, environmental analysis, public relations, production scheduling, and economic forecasting. Financial control involves managing the organization's debt so that it does not become excessive, ensuring that the firm always has enough cash on hand to meet its obligations but does not have excess cash in a checking account, and ensuring that receivables are collected and bills are paid on a timely basis.

operations control Focuses on the processes the organization uses to transform resources into products or services

financial control Concerned with the organization's financial resources

structural control Concerned with how the elements of the organization's structure are serving their intended purpose

strategic control Focuses on how effectively the organization's strategies are succeeding in helping the organization meet its goals

In many ways, the control of financial resources is the most important area, because financial resources are related to the control of all the other resources in an organization. Too much inventory leads to storage costs; poor selection of personnel leads to termination and rehiring expenses; inaccurate sales forecasts lead to disruptions in cash flows and other financial effects. Financial issues tend to pervade most control-related activities.

The crisis in the U.S. airline industry precipitated by the terrorist attacks on September 11, an economic downturn that reduced business travel, and rising fuel costs can be fundamentally traced back to financial issues. Essentially, airline revenues dropped while their costs increased. Because of high labor costs and other expenses, the airlines have faced major problems in making appropriate adjustments.[7] In 2002, for instance, United Airlines spent over half of its revenues on labor; in contrast, JetBlue spent only 25 percent of its revenues on labor.[8]

FIGURE 20.2

Levels of Control

Managers use control at several different levels. The most basic levels of control in organizations are strategic, structural, operations, and financial control. Each level must be managed properly if control is to be most effective.

Levels of Control Just as control can be broken down by area, Figure 20.2 shows that it can also be broken down by level within the organizational system. **Operations control** focuses on the processes the organization uses to transform resources into products or services.[9] Quality control is one type of operations control. **Financial control** is concerned with the organization's financial resources. Monitoring receivables to make sure customers are paying their bills on time is an example of financial control. **Structural control** is concerned with how the elements of the organization's structure are serving their intended purpose. Monitoring the administrative ratio to make sure staff expenses do not become excessive is an example of structural control. Finally, **strategic control** focuses on how effectively the organization's corporate, business, and functional strategies are succeeding in helping the organization meet its goals. For example, if a corporation has been unsuccessful in implementing its strategy of related diversification, its managers need to identify the reasons and either change the strategy or renew their efforts to implement it. We discuss these four levels of control more fully later in this chapter.

Responsibilities for Control Traditionally, managers have been responsible for overseeing the wide array of control systems and concerns in organizations. They decide which types of control the organization will use, and they implement control systems and take actions based on the information provided by control systems. Thus ultimate responsibility for control rests with all managers throughout an organization.

Most larger organizations also have one or more specialized managerial positions called *controller*. A **controller** is responsible for helping line managers with their control activities, for coordinating the organization's overall control system, and for gathering and assimilating relevant information. Many businesses that use an H-form or M-form organization design have several controllers: one for the corporation and one for each division. The job of controller is especially important in organizations where control systems are complex.[10]

controller A position in organizations that helps line managers with their control activities

In addition, many organizations are also beginning to use operating employees to help maintain effective control. Indeed, employee participation is often used as a vehicle for allowing operating employees an opportunity to help facilitate organizational effectiveness. For example, Whistler Corporation increased employee participation in an effort to turn its quality problems around. As a starting point, the quality control unit, formerly responsible for checking product quality at the end of the assembly process, was eliminated. Next, all operating employees were encouraged to check their own work and told that they would be responsible for correcting their own errors. As a result, Whistler has eliminated its quality problems and is now highly profitable once again.

Steps in the Control Process

Regardless of the type or levels of control systems an organization needs, there are four fundamental steps in any control process.[11] These are illustrated in Figure 20.3.

Establishing Standards The first step in the control process is establishing standards. A **control standard** is a target against which subsequent performance will be

control standard A target against which subsequent performance will be compared

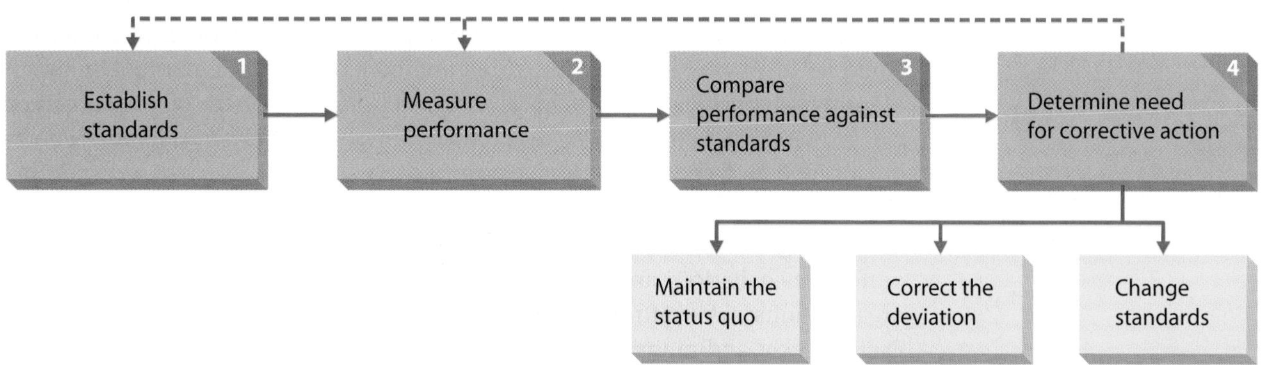

FIGURE 20.3

Steps in the Control Process

Having an effective control system can help ensure that an organization achieves its goals. Implementing a control system, however, is a systematic process that generally proceeds through four interrelated steps.

Establishing standards, measuring performance, and correcting deviations are parts of the control process. In the European Union, all eggs must now be electronically marked for identification. This marking system provides information about the environment in which the chicken was raised, the country where the eggs were produced, and the specific producer who brought the eggs to market. This information, in turn, will be useful to monitor quality and to aid in eliminating any public health hazards that might arise.

compared.[12] Employees at a Taco Bell fast-food restaurant, for example, work toward the following service standards:

1. A minimum of 95 percent of all customers will be greeted within three minutes of their arrival.
2. Preheated tortilla chips will not sit in the warmer more than thirty minutes before they are served to customers or discarded.
3. Empty tables will be cleaned within five minutes after being vacated.

Standards established for control purposes should be expressed in measurable terms. Note that standard 1 above has a time limit of three minutes and an objective target of 95 percent of all customers. In standard 3, the objective target of "all" empty tables is implied.

Control standards should also be consistent with the organization's goals. Taco Bell has organizational goals involving customer service, food quality, and restaurant cleanliness. A control standard for a retailer like Home Depot should be consistent with its goal of increasing its annual sales volume by 25 percent within five years. A hospital trying to shorten the average hospital stay for a patient will have control standards that reflect current averages. A university reaffirming its commitment to academics might adopt a standard of graduating 80 percent of its student athletes within five years of their enrollment. Control standards can be as narrow or as broad as the level of activity to which they apply and must follow logically from organizational goals and objectives.

A final aspect of establishing standards is to identify performance indicators. Performance indicators are measures of performance that provide information that is directly relevant to what is being controlled. For example, suppose an organization is following a tight schedule in building a new plant. Relevant performance indicators could be buying a site, selecting a building contractor, and ordering equipment. Monthly sales increases are not, however, directly relevant. On the other hand, if control is being focused on revenue, monthly sales increases are relevant, whereas buying land for a new plant is less relevant.

Measuring Performance The second step in the control process is measuring performance. Performance measurement is a constant, ongoing activity for most organizations. For control to be effective, performance measures must be valid. Daily, weekly, and monthly sales figures measure sales performance, and production performance may be expressed in terms of unit cost, product quality, or volume produced. Employees' performance is often measured in terms of quality or quantity of output, but for many jobs measuring performance is not so straightforward.

A research and development scientist at Merck, for example, may spend years working on a single project before achieving a breakthrough. A manager who takes over a business on the brink of failure may need months or even years to turn things around. Valid performance measurement, however difficult to obtain, is nevertheless vital in maintaining effective control, and performance indicators usually can be developed. The scientist's progress, for example, may be partially assessed by peer review, and the manager's success may be evaluated by her ability to convince creditors that she will eventually be able to restore profitability.

Comparing Performance Against Standards The third step in the control process is comparing measured performance against established standards. Performance may be higher than, lower than, or identical to the standard. In some cases comparison is easy. The goal of each product manager at General Electric is to make the product either number one or number two (on the basis of total sales) in its market. Because this standard is clear and total sales are easy to calculate, it is relatively simple to determine whether this standard has been met. Sometimes, however, comparisons are less clear-cut. If performance is lower than expected, the question is how much deviation from standards to allow before taking remedial action. For example, is increasing sales by 7.9 percent when the standard was 8 percent close enough?

The timetable for comparing performance to standards depends on a variety of factors, including the importance and complexity of what is being controlled. For longer-run and higher-level standards, annual comparisons may be appropriate. In other circumstances, more frequent comparisons are necessary. For example, a business with a severe cash shortage may need to monitor its on-hand cash reserves daily.

Considering Corrective Action The final step in the control process is determining the need for corrective action. Decisions regarding corrective action draw heavily on a manager's analytic and diagnostic skills. After comparing performance against control standards, one of three actions is appropriate: maintain the status quo (do nothing), correct the deviation, or change the standards. Maintaining the status quo is preferable when performance essentially matches the standards, but it is more likely that some action will be needed to correct a deviation from the standards.

Sometimes, performance that is higher than expected may also cause problems for organizations. For example, when DaimlerChrysler first introduced its PT Cruiser, demand was so strong that there were waiting lists, and many customers were willing to pay more than the suggested retail price to obtain a car. The company was reluctant to increase production, primarily because it knew demand would eventually drop. At the same time, however, it did not want to alienate potential customers. Consequently, the firm decided to simply reduce its advertising. This curtailed demand a bit and limited customer frustration.

Changing an established standard usually is necessary if it was set too high or too low at the outset. This is apparent if large numbers of employees routinely beat the standard by a wide margin or if no employees ever meet the standard. Also, standards that seemed perfectly appropriate when they were established may need to be adjusted because circumstances have since changed.

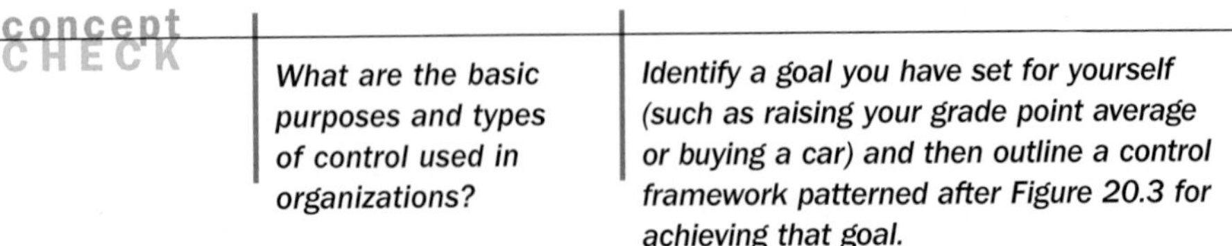

What are the basic purposes and types of control used in organizations?

Identify a goal you have set for yourself (such as raising your grade point average or buying a car) and then outline a control framework patterned after Figure 20.3 for achieving that goal.

Operations Control

operations control Focuses on the processes the organization uses to transform resources into products or services

One of the four levels of control practiced by most organizations, **operations control**, is concerned with the processes the organization uses to transform resources into products or services. As Figure 20.4 shows, the three forms of operations control—preliminary, screening, and postaction—occur at different points in relation to the transformation processes used by the organization.

Preliminary Control

preliminary control Attempts to monitor the quality or quantity of financial, physical, human, and information resources before they actually become part of the system

Preliminary control concentrates on the resources—financial, material, human, and information—the organization brings in from the environment. Preliminary control attempts to monitor the quality or quantity of these resources before they enter the organization. Firms like PepsiCo and General Mills hire only college graduates for their management training program, and even then only after applicants satisfy several interviewers and selection criteria. In this way, they control the quality of the human resources entering the organization. When Sears orders merchandise to be manufactured under its own brand name, it specifies rigid standards of quality, thereby controlling physical inputs. Organizations also control financial and information resources. For example, privately held companies like UPS and Mars limit the extent to which outsiders can buy their stock, and television networks verify the accuracy of news stories before they are broadcast.

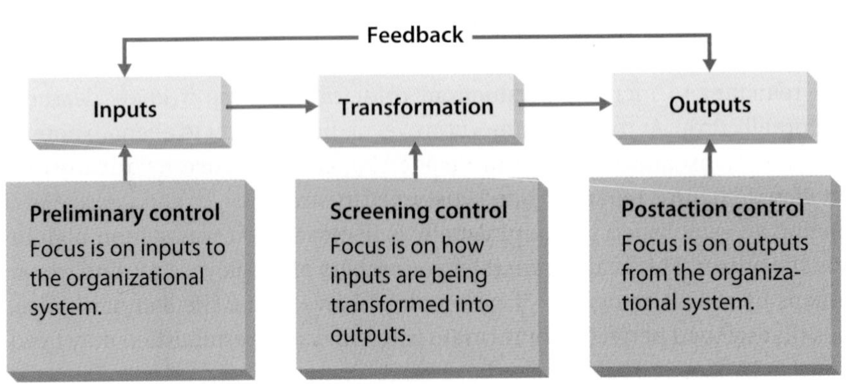

FIGURE 20.4

Forms of Operations Control

Most organizations develop multiple control systems that incorporate all three basic forms of control. For example, the publishing company that produced this book screens inputs by hiring only qualified employees, typesetters, and printers (preliminary control). In addition, quality is checked during the transformation process, such as after the manuscript is typeset (screening control), and the outputs—printed and bound books—are checked before they are shipped from the bindery (postaction control).

Screening Control

Screening control focuses on meeting standards for product or service quality or quantity during the actual transformation process itself. Screening control relies heavily on feedback processes. For example, in a Dell Computer assembly factory, computer system components are checked periodically as each unit is being assembled. This is done to ensure that all the components that have been assembled up to that point are working properly. The periodic quality checks provide feedback to workers so that they know what, if any, corrective actions to take. Because they are useful in identifying the cause of problems, screening controls tend to be used more often than other forms of control.

More and more companies are adopting screening controls because they are an effective way to promote employee participation and catch problems early in the overall transformation process. For example, Corning adopted screening controls for use in manufacturing television glass. In the past, finished television screens were inspected only after they were finished. Unfortunately, over 4 percent of them were later returned by customers because of defects. Now the glass screens are inspected at each step in the production process, rather than at the end, and the return rate from customers has dropped to .03 percent.

Final inspections are a common part of postaction control systems. Maria Martinez, for example, is shown here inspecting batches of Chiquita brand bananas that have been grown on a plantation in Panama and are being prepared for export. She carefully assesses their weight, size, and appearance to ensure that they meet the company's standards.

Postaction Control

Postaction control focuses on the outputs of the organization after the transformation process is complete. Corning's old system was postaction control—final inspection after the product was completed. Although Corning abandoned its postaction control system, this still may be an effective method of control, primarily if a product can be manufactured in only one or two steps or if the service is fairly simple and routine. Although postaction control alone may not be as effective as preliminary or screening control, it can provide management with information for future planning. For example, if a quality check of finished goods indicates an unacceptably high defect rate, the production manager knows that he or she must identify the causes and take steps to eliminate them. Postaction control also provides a basis for rewarding employees. Recognizing that an employee has exceeded personal sales goals by a wide margin, for example, may alert the manager that a bonus or promotion is in order.

Most organizations use more than one form of operations control. For example, Honda's preliminary control includes hiring only qualified employees and specifying strict quality standards when ordering parts from other manufacturers. Honda uses numerous screening controls in checking the quality of components during assembly of cars. A final inspection and test drive as each car rolls off the assembly line is part of the company's postaction control.[13] Indeed, most successful organizations employ a wide variety of techniques to facilitate operations control.

screening control Relies heavily on feedback processes during the transformation process

postaction control Monitors the outputs or results of the organization after the transformation process is complete

Postaction control focuses on the outputs of an organization after the transformation process is complete. These Ford inspectors, for example, are taking a close look at a freshly minted Mustang that has just rolled off the assembly line. While the car received numerous screening control inspections as it was being built, this final inspection is one last step intended to ensure that no major defects or other problems have been missed.

concept CHECK

Distinguish between preliminary, screening, and postaction control.

Describe how a college or university is likely to use each type of operations control to monitor student progress.

Financial Control

Financial control Concerned with the organization's financial resources

Financial control is the control of financial resources as they flow into the organization (revenues, shareholder investments), are held by the organization (working capital, retained earnings), and flow out of the organization (pay, expenses). Businesses must manage their finances so that revenues are sufficient to cover costs and still return a profit to the firm's owners. Not-for-profit organizations such as universities have the same concerns: Their revenues (from tax dollars or tuition) must cover operating expenses and overhead. Dickson Poon is a Chinese investor who has profited by relying heavily on financial control. He buys distressed upscale retailers like Britain's Harvey Nichols and the United States' Barneys, imposes strict financial controls to correct problems, and begins generating hefty profits. A complete discussion of financial management is beyond the scope of this book, but we will examine the control provided by budgets and other financial control tools.

Budgetary Control

Financial audits are becoming increasingly important tools in financial control. These Procter & Gamble employees, for instance, lost much of their retirement investment through poor financial management on the part of an A.G. Edwards stockbroker. As a result, the investment firm has strengthened its financial control system and is conducting both more frequent and more thorough audits.

A **budget** is a plan expressed in numerical terms.[14] Organizations establish budgets for work groups, departments, divisions, and the whole organization. The usual time period for a budget is one year, although breakdowns of budgets by the quarter or month are also common. Budgets are generally expressed in financial terms, but they may occasionally be expressed in units of output, time, or other quantifiable factors. When Disney launches the production of a new animated cartoon feature, it creates a budget for how much the movie should cost. Several years ago, when movies like *The Lion King* were raking in hundreds of millions of dollars, Disney executives did not require the animation division to adhere too closely to those budgets. But, on the heels of several animated flops, such as *Atlantis: The Lost Empire* and *Treasure Planet*, the company has taken a much harder line on budget overruns.[15]

Because of their quantitative nature, budgets provide yardsticks for measuring performance and facilitate comparisons across departments, between levels in the organization, and from one time period to another. Budgets serve four primary purposes. They help managers coordinate resources and projects (because they use a common denominator, usually dollars). They help define the established standards for control. They provide guidelines about the organization's resources and expectations. Finally, budgets enable the organization to evaluate the performance of managers and organizational units.

Types of Budgets Most organizations develop and make use of three different kinds of budgets—financial, operating, and nonmonetary. Table 20.1 summarizes the characteristics of each of these.

budget A plan expressed in numerical terms

A *financial budget* indicates where the organization expects to get its cash for the coming time period and how it plans to use it. Because financial resources are critically important, the organization needs to know where those resources will be coming from and how they are to be used. The financial budget provides answers to both these questions. Usual sources of cash include sales revenue, short- and long-term loans, the sale of assets, and the issuance of new stock.

For years Exxon was very conservative in its capital budgeting. As a result, the firm amassed a huge financial reserve but was being overtaken in sales by Royal Dutch/Shell. But executives at Exxon were then able to use their reserves to help finance the firm's merger with Mobil, creating ExxonMobil, and to regain the number-one sales position. And, since that time, the firm has become more aggressive in capital budgeting in order to stay ahead of its European rival.

TABLE 20.1

Developing Budgets in Organizations

Organizations use various types of budgets to help manage their control function. The three major categories of budgets are financial, operating, and nonmonetary. There are several different types of budgets in each category. To be most effective, each budget must be carefully matched with the specific function being controlled.

Types of Budget	What Budget Shows
Financial Budget	*Sources and Uses of Cash*
Cash-flow or cash budget	All sources of cash income and cash expenditures in monthly, weekly, or daily periods
Capital expenditures budget	Costs of major assets such as a new plant, machinery, or land
Balance sheet budget	Forecast of the organization's assets and liabilities in the event all other budgets are met
Operating Budget	*Planned Operations in Financial Terms*
Sales or revenue budget	Income the organization expects to receive from normal operations
Expense budget	Anticipated expenses for the organization during the coming time period
Profit budget	Anticipated differences between sales or revenues and expenses
Nonmonetary Budget	*Planned Operations in Nonfinancial Terms*
Labor budget	Hours of direct labor available for use
Space budget	Square feet or meters of space available for various functions
Production budget	Number of units to be produced during the coming time period

An *operating budget* is concerned with planned operations within the organization. It outlines what quantities of products or services the organization intends to create and what resources will be used to create them. IBM creates an operating budget that specifies how many of each model of its personal computer will be produced each quarter.

A *nonmonetary budget* is simply a budget expressed in nonfinancial terms, such as units of output, hours of direct labor, machine hours, or square-foot allocations. Nonmonetary budgets are most commonly used by managers at the lower levels of an organization. For example, a plant manager can schedule work more effectively knowing that he or she has 8,000 labor hours to allocate in a week, rather than trying to determine how to best spend $86,451 in wages in a week.

Developing Budgets Traditionally, budgets were developed by top management and the controller and then imposed on lower-level managers. Although some organizations still follow this pattern, many contemporary organizations now allow all managers to participate in the budget process. As a starting point, top management generally issues a call for budget requests, accompanied by an indication of overall patterns the budgets may take. For example, if sales are expected to drop in the next year, managers may be told up front to prepare for cuts in operating budgets.

As Figure 20.5 shows, the heads of each operating unit typically submit budget requests to the head of their division. An operating unit head might be a department manager in a manufacturing or wholesaling firm or a program director in a social service agency. The division heads might include plant managers, regional sales managers, or college deans. The division head integrates and consolidates the budget requests from operating unit heads into one overall division budget request. A great deal of interaction among managers usually takes place at this stage, as the division head coordinates the budgetary needs of the various departments.

Division budget requests are then forwarded to a budget committee. The budget committee is usually composed of top managers. The committee reviews budget requests from several divisions, and once again, duplications and inconsistencies are corrected. Finally, the budget committee, the controller, and the CEO review and agree on the overall budget for the organization, as well as specific budgets for each operating unit. These decisions are then communicated back to each manager.

FIGURE 20.5

Developing Budgets in Organizations

Most organizations use the same basic process to develop budgets. Operating units are requested to submit their budget requests to divisions. These divisions, in turn, compile unit budgets and submit their own budgets to the organization. An organizational budget is then compiled for approval by the budget committee, controller, and CEO.

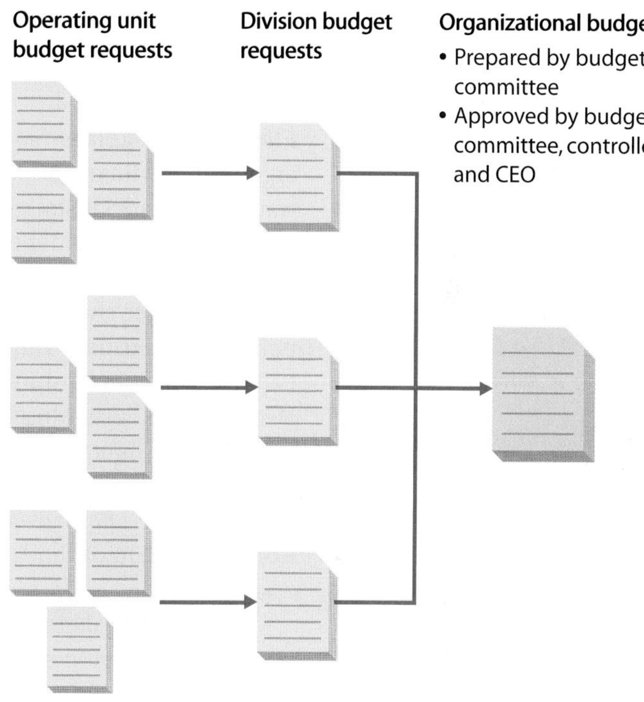

Strengths and Weaknesses of Budgeting Budgets offer a number of advantages, but they also have weaknesses. On the plus side, budgets facilitate effective control. Placing dollar values on operations enables managers to monitor operations better and pinpoint problem areas. Budgets also facilitate coordination and communication between departments because they express diverse activities in a common denominator (dollars). Budgets help maintain records of organizational performance and are a logical complement to planning. In other words, as managers develop plans, they should simultaneously consider control measures to accompany them. Organizations can use budgets to link plans and control by first developing budgets as part of the plan and then using those budgets as part of control.

On the other hand, some managers apply budgets too rigidly. Budgets are intended to serve as frameworks, but managers sometimes fail to recognize that changing circumstances may warrant budget adjustments. The process of developing budgets can also be very time consuming. Finally, budgets may limit innovation and change. When all available funds are allocated to specific operating budgets, it may be impossible to procure additional funds to take advantage of an unexpected opportunity. Indeed, for these very reasons, some organizations are working to scale back their budgeting system. Although most organizations are likely to continue to use budgets, the goal is to make them less confining and rigid.

Other Tools for Financial Control

Although budgets are the most common means of financial control, other useful tools are financial statements, ratio analysis, and financial audits.

financial statement A profile of some aspect of an organization's financial circumstances

Financial Statements A **financial statement** is a profile of some aspect of an organization's financial circumstances. There are commonly accepted and required ways that financial statements must be prepared and presented.[16] The two most basic financial statements prepared and used by virtually all organizations are a balance sheet and an income statement.

balance sheet List of assets and liabilities of an organization at a specific point in time

The **balance sheet** lists the assets and liabilities of the organization at a specific point in time, usually the last day of an organization's fiscal year. For example, the balance sheet may summarize the financial condition of an organization on December 31, 2004. Most balance sheets are divided into current assets (assets that are relatively liquid, or easily convertible into cash), fixed assets (assets that are longer term in nature and less liquid), current liabilities (debts and other obligations that must be paid in the near future), long-term liabilities (payable over an extended period of time), and stockholders' equity (the owners' claim against the assets).

income statement A summary of financial performance over a period of time

Whereas the balance sheet reflects a snapshot profile of an organization's financial position at a single point in time, the **income statement** summarizes financial performance over a period of time, usually one year. For example, the income statement might be for the period January 1, 2004, through December 31, 2004. The income statement summarizes the firm's revenues less its expenses to report net income (profit or loss) for the period. Information from the balance sheet and income statement is used in computing important financial ratios.

ratio analysis The calculation of one or more financial ratios to assess some aspect of the organization's financial health

Ratio Analysis Financial ratios compare different elements of a balance sheet or income statement to one another. **Ratio analysis** is the calculation of one or more financial ratios to assess some aspect of the financial health of an organization. Organizations use a variety of different financial ratios as part of financial control. For example, *liquidity ratios* indicate how liquid (easily converted into cash) an organization's assets are. *Debt ratios* reflect ability to meet long-term financial obligations. *Return ratios* show managers and investors how much return the organization is generating relative to its assets. *Coverage ratios* help estimate the organization's ability to cover interest expenses on borrowed capital. *Operating ratios* indicate the effectiveness of specific functional areas rather than of the total organization. The Walt Disney Company relies heavily on financial ratios to keep its financial operations on track.[17]

Financial Audits **Audits** are independent appraisals of an organization's accounting, financial, and operational systems. The two major types of financial audit are the external audit and the internal audit.

audit An independent appraisal of an organization's accounting, financial, and operational systems

External audits are financial appraisals conducted by experts who are not employees of the organization.[18] External audits are typically concerned with determining that the organization's accounting procedures and financial statements are compiled in an objective and verifiable fashion. The organization contracts with certified public accountants (CPAs) for this service. The CPAs' main objective is to verify for stockholders, the IRS, and other interested parties that the methods by which the organization's financial managers and accountants prepare documents and reports are legal and proper. External audits are so important that publicly held corporations are required by law to have external audits regularly, as assurance to investors that the financial reports are reliable.

Unfortunately, flaws in the auditing process played a major role in the downfall of Enron and several other major firms. The problem can be traced back partially to auditing groups' facing problems with conflicts of interest and eventually losing their objectivity. For instance, Enron was such an important client for its auditing firm, Arthur Andersen, that the auditors started letting the firm take liberties with its accounting systems for fear that, if they were too strict, Enron might take its business to another auditing firm. In the aftermath of the resulting scandal, Arthur Andersen was forced to close its doors, Enron is a shell of its former self, indictments continue to be handed down, and the entire future of the accounting profession has been called into question.[19]

Some organizations are also starting to employ external auditors to review other aspects of their financial operations. For example, there are now auditing firms that specialize in checking corporate legal bills. An auditor for the Fireman's Fund Insurance Company uncovered several thousands of dollars in legal fee errors. Other auditors are beginning to specialize in real estate, employee benefits, and pension plan investments.

Whereas external audits are conducted by external accountants, an *internal audit* is handled by employees of the organization. Its objective is the same as that of an external audit—to verify the accuracy of financial and accounting procedures used by the organization. Internal audits also examine the efficiency and appropriateness of financial and accounting procedures. Because the staff members who conduct them are a permanent part of the organization, internal audits tend to be more expensive than external audits. But employees, who are more familiar with the organization's practices, may also point out significant aspects of the accounting system besides its technical correctness. Large organizations like Halliburton and Ford have an internal auditing staff that spends all its time conducting audits of different divisions and functional areas of the organization. Smaller organizations may assign accountants to an internal audit group on a temporary or rotating basis.

The findings of an internal auditor led to the recent financial scandal at WorldCom. The firm's new CEO asked an internal auditor to spot-check various records related to capital expenditures. She subsequently discovered that the firm's chief financial officer was misapplying major expenses: Instead of treating them as current expenses, he was treating them as capital expenditures. This treatment, in turn, made the firm look much more profitable than it really was. The CFO was fired, but it will take WorldCom a long time to sort out the $3.8 billion it has so far found to have been handled improperly.[20]

concept CHECK

What are the basic kinds of budgets used in most organizations?

Given that financial control relies so heavily on numbers, how can problems like those at Enron occur?

Structural Control

Organizations can create designs for themselves that result in very different approaches to control. Two major forms of structural control, bureaucratic control and decentralized control, represent opposite ends of a continuum, as shown in Figure 20.6.[21] The six dimensions shown in the figure represent perspectives adopted by the two extreme types of structural control. In other words, they have different

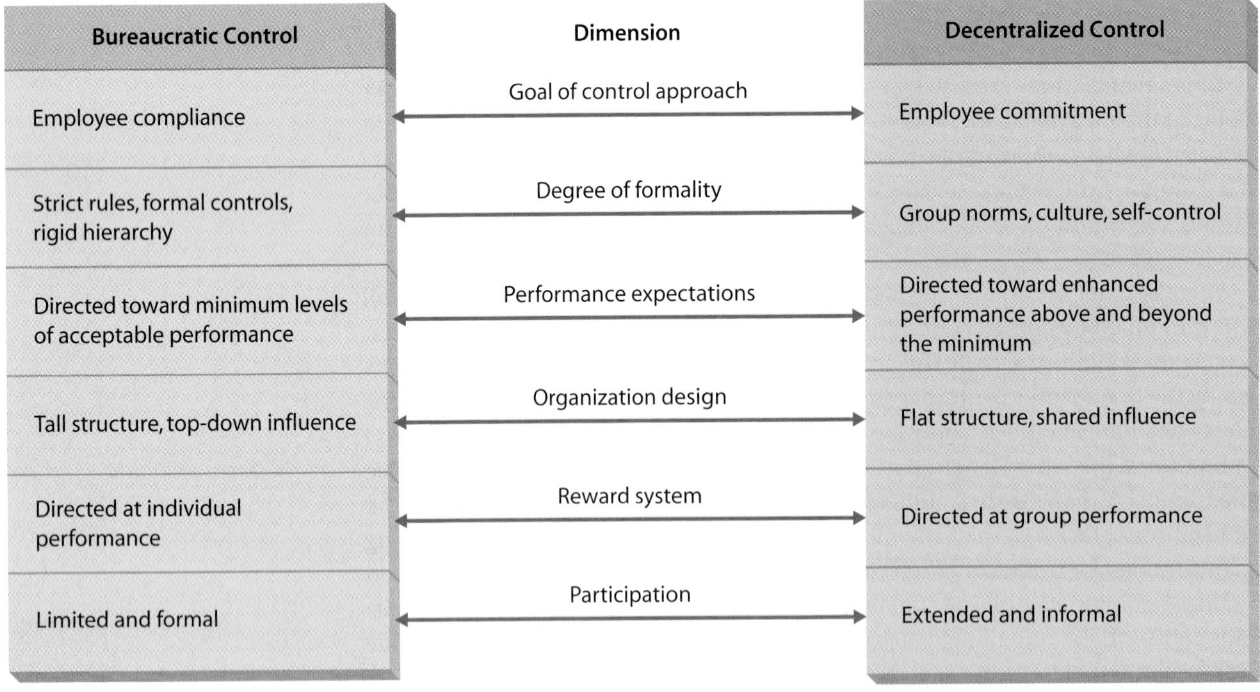

FIGURE 20.6

Organizational Control

Organizational control generally falls somewhere between the two extremes of bureaucratic and decentralized control. NBC television uses bureaucratic control, whereas Levi Strauss uses decentralized control.

goals, degrees of formality, performance expectations, organization designs, reward systems, and levels of participation. Although a few organizations fall precisely at one extreme or the other, most tend toward one end but may have specific characteristics of either.

Bureaucratic Control

Bureaucratic control is an approach to organization design characterized by formal and mechanistic structural arrangements. As the term suggests, it follows the bureaucratic model. The goal of bureaucratic control is employee compliance. Organizations that use it rely on strict rules and a rigid hierarchy, insist that employees meet minimally acceptable levels of performance, and often have a tall structure. They focus their rewards on individual performance and allow only limited and formal employee participation.

bureaucratic control A form of organizational control characterized by formal and mechanistic structural arrangements

NBC television applies structural controls that reflect many elements of bureaucracy. The organization relies on numerous rules to regulate employee travel, expense accounts, and other expenses. A new performance appraisal system precisely specifies minimally acceptable levels of performance for everyone. The organization's structure is considerably taller than those of the other major networks, and rewards are based on individual contributions. Perhaps most significantly, many NBC employees have argued that they have too small a voice in how the organization is managed.

In another example, a large oil company recently made the decision to allow employees to wear casual attire to work. But a committee then spent weeks developing a twenty-page set of guidelines on what was and was not acceptable. For example, denim pants are not allowed. Similarly, athletic shoes may be worn as long as they are not white. And all shirts must have a collar. Nordstrom, the department store chain, is also moving toward bureaucratic control as it works to centralize all of its purchasing in an effort to lower costs.[22] Similarly, Home Depot is moving more toward bureaucratic control in order to cut its costs and more effectively compete with its hard-charging rival, Lowe's.[23]

Decentralized Control

Decentralized control, in contrast, is an approach to organizational control characterized by informal and organic structural arrangements. As Figure 20.6 shows, its goal is employee commitment to the organization. Accordingly, it relies heavily on group norms and a strong corporate culture, and gives employees the responsibility for controlling themselves. Employees are encouraged to perform beyond minimally acceptable levels. Organizations using this approach are usually relatively flat. They direct rewards at group performance and favor widespread employee participation.

decentralized control An approach to organizational control based on informal and organic structural arrangements

Levi Strauss practices decentralized control. The firm's managers use groups as the basis for work and have created a culture wherein group norms help facilitate high performance. Rewards are subsequently provided to the higher-performing groups and teams. The company's culture also reinforces contributions to the overall team effort, and employees have a strong sense of loyalty to the organization. Levi's has a flat structure, and power is widely shared. Employee participation is encouraged in all areas of operation. Another company that uses this approach is Southwest Airlines. When Southwest made the decision to "go casual," the firm resisted the temptation to develop dress guidelines. Instead, managers decided to allow employees to exercise discretion over their attire and to deal with clearly inappropriate situations on a case-by-case basis.

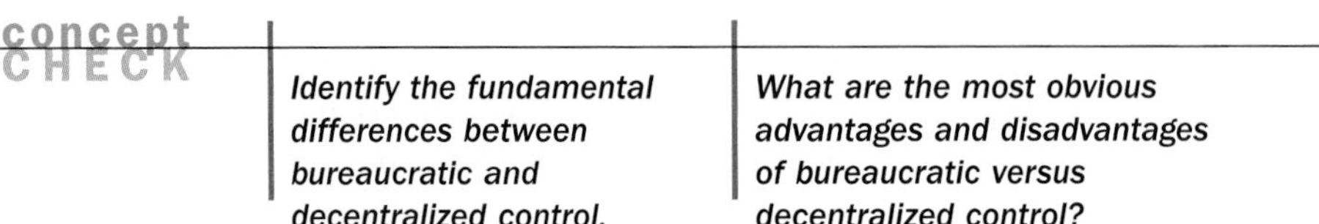

Strategic Control

Given the obvious importance of an organization's strategy, it is also important that the organization assess how effective that strategy is in helping the organization meet its goals.[24] To do this requires that the organization integrate its strategy and control systems. This is especially true for the global organization. *The World of Management* presents a vivid example of what can happen when strategic controls are ignored.

Integrating Strategy and Control

strategic control Control aimed at ensuring that the organization is maintaining an effective alignment with its environment and moving toward achieving its strategic goals

Strategic control generally focuses on five aspects of organizations—structure, leadership, technology, human resources, and information and operational control systems. For example, an organization should periodically examine its structure to determine whether or not it is facilitating the attainment of the strategic goals being sought. Suppose a firm using a functional (U-form) design has an established goal of achieving a 20 percent sales growth rate per year. However, performance indicators show that it is currently growing at a rate of only 10 percent per year. Detailed analysis might reveal that the current structure is inhibiting growth in some way (for example, by slowing decision making and inhibiting innovation) and that a divisional (M-form) design is more likely to bring about the desired growth (by speeding decision making and promoting innovation).

In this way, strategic control focuses on the extent to which implemented strategy achieves the organization's strategic goals. If, as outlined above, one or more avenues of implementation are inhibiting the attainment of goals, that avenue should be changed. Consequently, the firm might find it necessary to alter its structure, replace key leaders, adopt new technology, modify its human resources, or change its information and operational control systems. For example, IKEA, the Swedish furniture manufacturer, experienced disappointing performance from its internationalization strategy. As a result, the company changed how it manages its international operations and has begun enjoying much better results.

THE WORLD OF management

Is Vivendi "the Enron of France"?

"I've got the unpleasant feeling of being in a car whose driver is accelerating in the turns and I'm in the death seat."

– Guillaume Hannezo, former chief financial officer, Vivendi*

At what point should investors be informed that a corporation is out of control? When the CEO first suspects? When auditors provide tangible proof? When financial statements are issued? Or only after months of investigation and dispute? Clearly, the most ethical response lies somewhere in the middle, not at either extreme. Nonetheless, Jean-Marie Messier, CEO of Vivendi, kept everyone in the dark about the French conglomerate's finances until the firm reached the brink of bankruptcy.

In 1996 Messier began transforming the utility into an entertainment giant through acquisitions. Analysts and investors expressed few concerns. Yet, underneath the surface, a storm was brewing.

The crisis began when debt grew from $3 billion to $21 billion by June 2002. As Vivendi struggled to pay the interest, the acquisition spree continued. Messier's questionable stock transactions risked billions of dollars. He borrowed billions to conceal the firm's negative cash flow. And he did it all against the advice of his staff and without the knowledge of the board. In fact, Messier repeatedly assured directors that "Vivendi is in better-than-good health." Some of Vivendi's directors say that board meetings led by Messier, conducted in English and full of complex financial information, were intended to confuse and deceive. Others blame chief financial officer Guillaume Hannezo, a notoriously disorganized manager whose finance department employed just twelve staff members.

Hannezo had the role of "being Dr. No, limiting company spending as much as possible," says a former Vivendi manager. In 2001 Hannezo wrote to Messier, "I've got the unpleasant feeling of being in a car whose driver is accelerating in the turns and I'm in the death seat." By March 2002, Hannezo sent a desperate e-mail: "Our jobs, our reputations are at stake. . . . The problem isn't our businesses; it's us, or more exactly, it's you." Messier continued to stonewall.

Messier was eventually forced to resign and is under investigation for fraud. Vivendi reversed its strategic course, selling off assets to pay down debt and make the company simpler—and easier to control. Lack of oversight, too much authority in the hands of one individual, and a lust for power allowed Vivendi to spiral out of control and may yet cause the firm's demise.

References: Janet Guyon, "Getting Messier by the Minute," *Fortune*, May 28, 2002, www.fortune.com on February 15, 2003; Janet Guyon, "Reviving Vivendi," *Fortune*, July 8, 2002, www.fortune.com on February 15, 2003; John Carreyrou and Martin Peers, "How Messier Kept Cash Crisis at Vivendi Hidden for Months," *Wall Street Journal*, October 31, 2002, pp. A1, A15 (*quote p. A15); Ron Glover, "The Dark Horse in the Vivendi Race," *BusinessWeek*, February 10, 2003, www.businessweek.com on February 15, 2003.

International Strategic Control

Because of both their relatively large size and the increased complexity associated with international business, global organizations must take an especially pronounced strategic view of their control systems. One very basic question that has to be addressed is whether to manage control from a centralized or a decentralized perspective.[25] Under a centralized system, each organizational unit around the world is responsible for frequently reporting the results of its performance to headquarters.

Managers from the home office often visit foreign branches to observe first-hand how the units are functioning.

BP, Unilever, Procter & Gamble, and Sony all use this approach. They believe centralized control is effective because it allows the home office to keep better informed of the performance of foreign units and to maintain more control over how decisions are made. For example, BP discovered that its Australian subsidiary was not billing its customers for charges as quickly as were its competitors. By shortening the billing cycle, BP now receives customer payments five days faster than before. Managers believe that they discovered this oversight only because of a centralized financial control system.

Organizations that use a decentralized control system require foreign branches to report less frequently and in less detail. For example, each unit may submit summary performance statements on a quarterly basis and provide full statements only once a year. Similarly, visits from the home office are less frequent and less concerned with monitoring and assessing performance. IBM, Ford, and Shell all use this approach. Because Ford practices decentralized control of its design function, European designers have developed several innovative automobile design features. Managers believe that, if they had been more centralized, designers would not have had the freedom to develop their new ideas.

concept CHECK

How are strategy and control most commonly integrated?

In what ways are domestic and international control issues similar, and in what ways do they differ?

Managing Control in Organizations

Effective control, whether at the operations, financial, structural, or strategic level, successfully regulates and monitors organizational activities. To use the control process, managers must recognize the characteristics of effective control and understand how to identify and overcome occasional resistance to control.[26]

Characteristics of Effective Control

Control systems tend to be most effective when they are integrated with planning and when they are flexible, accurate, timely, and objective.

Integration with Planning Control should be linked with planning. The more explicit and precise this linkage, the more effective the control system is. The best way to integrate planning and control is to account for control as plans develop. In other words, as goals are set during the planning process, attention should be paid to developing standards that will reflect how well the plan is realized. Managers at Champion Spark Plug Company decided to broaden their product line to include a full range of automotive accessories—a total of twenty-one new products. As part of this plan, managers decided in advance what level of sales they wanted to realize from each product for each of the next five years. They established these sales goals as standards against which actual sales would be compared. Thus, by accounting for their control system as they developed their plan, managers at Champion did an excellent job of integrating planning and control.

Flexiblity The control system itself must be flexible enough to accommodate change. Consider, for example, an organization whose diverse product line requires seventy-five different raw materials. The company's inventory control system must be able to manage and monitor current levels of inventory for all seventy-five materials. When a change in product line changes the number of raw materials needed, or when the required quantities of the existing materials change, the control system should be flexible enough to handle the revised requirements. The alternative—designing and implementing a new control system—is an avoidable expense. Champion's control system included a mechanism that automatically shipped products to major customers to keep their inventory at predetermined levels. The firm had to adjust this system when one of its biggest customers decided not to stock the full line of Champion products. Because its control system was flexible, though, modifying it for the customer was relatively simple.

Accuracy Managers make a surprisingly large number of decisions based on inaccurate information. Field representatives may hedge their sales estimates to make themselves look better. Production managers may hide costs to meet their targets. Human resource managers may overestimate their minority recruiting prospects to meet affirmative action goals. In each case, the information that other managers receive is inaccurate, and the results of inaccurate information may be quite dramatic. If sales projections are inflated, a manager might cut advertising (thinking it is no longer needed) or increase advertising (to further build momentum). Similarly, a production manager unaware of hidden costs may quote a sales price much lower than desirable. Or a human resources manager may speak out publicly on the effectiveness of the company's minority recruiting, only to find out later that these prospects have been overestimated. In each case, the result of inaccurate information is inappropriate managerial action.

Timeliness Timeliness does not necessarily mean quickness. Rather, it describes a control system that provides information as often as is necessary. Because Champion has a wealth of historical data on its sparkplug sales, it does not need information on sparkplugs as frequently as it needs sales feedback for its newer products. Retail organizations usually need sales results daily, so that they can manage cash flow and adjust advertising and promotion. In contrast, they may require information about physical inventory only quarterly or annually. In general, the more uncertain and unstable the circumstances, the more frequently measurement is needed.

Objectivity The control system should provide information that is as objective as possible. To appreciate this, imagine the task of a manager responsible for control of his organization's human resources. He asks two plant managers to submit reports. One manager notes that morale at his plant is "okay," that grievances are "about where they should be," and that turnover is "under control." The other reports that absenteeism at her plant is running at 4 percent, that sixteen grievances have been filed this year (compared with twenty-four last year), and that turnover is 12 percent. The second report will almost always be more useful than the first. Of course, managers also need to look beyond the numbers when assessing performance. For example, a plant manager may be boosting productivity and profit margins by putting too much pressure on workers and using poor-quality materials. As a result, impressive short-run gains may be overshadowed by longer-run increases in employee turnover and customer complaints.

Resistance to Control

Managers may sometimes make the mistake of assuming that the value of an effective control system is self-evident to employees. This is not always so, however. Many employees resist control, especially if they feel overcontrolled, if they think control is inappropriately focused or rewards inefficiency, or if they are uncomfortable with accountability.

Overcontrol Occasionally, organizations try to control too many things. This becomes especially problematic when the control directly affects employee behavior. An organization that instructs its employees when to come to work, where to park, when to have morning coffee, and when to leave for the day exerts considerable control over people's daily activities. Yet many organizations attempt to control not only these but other aspects of work behavior as well. Of particular relevance in recent years is some companies' effort to control their employees' access to private e-mail and the Internet during work hours. Some companies have no policies governing these activities, some attempt to limit it, and some attempt to forbid it altogether.[27]

Troubles arise when employees perceive these attempts to limit their behavior as being unreasonable. A company that tells its employees how to dress, how to arrange their desk, and how to wear their hair may meet with more resistance. Employees at DaimlerChrysler used to complain because, if they drove a non-DaimlerChrysler vehicle, they were forced to park in a distant parking lot. People felt that these efforts to control their personal behavior (what kind of car to drive) were excessive. Managers eventually removed these controls and now allow open parking. Some employees at Abercrombie & Fitch argue that the firm is guilty of overcontrol because of its strict dress and grooming requirements—for example, no necklaces or facial hair for men and only natural nail polish and earrings no larger than a dime for women. Likewise, Enterprise Rent-A-Car has a set of thirty dress-code rules for women and twenty-six rules for men. The firm was recently sued by one former employee who was fired because of the color of her hair.[28]

Inappropriate Focus The control system may be too narrow, or it may focus too much on quantifiable variables and leave no room for analysis or interpretation. A sales standard that encourages high-pressure tactics to maximize short-run sales may do so at the expense of goodwill from long-term customers. Such a standard is too narrow. A university reward system that encourages faculty members to publish large numbers of articles but fails to consider the quality of the work is also inappropriately focused. Employees resist the intent of the control system by focusing their efforts only at the performance indicators being used. The cartoon features another example of inappropriately focused control.

Rewards for Inefficiency Imagine two operating departments that are approaching the end of the fiscal year. Department 1 expects to have $25,000 of its budget left over; department 2 is already $10,000 in the red. As a result, department 1 is likely to have its budget cut for the next year ("They had money left, so they obviously got too much to begin with"), and department 2 is likely to get a budget increase ("They obviously haven't been getting enough money"). Thus department 1 is punished for being efficient, and department 2 is rewarded for being inefficient. (No wonder departments commonly hasten to deplete their budgets as the end of the year approaches!) As with inappropriate focus, people resist the intent of this control and behave in ways that run counter to the organization's intent.

"You've got to really wonder just how many more cut-backs this department can absorb!"

Bradford Veley

In recent years, many organizations have sought ways to lower their costs through cost-cutting programs. They have reduced their workforce, eliminated perquisites, and outsourced services that independent contractors can do for a lower price. But some experts worry that many organizations have cut too much, increasing pressure and stress on the employees who are left. Although it is doubtful that any organization has gone to the lengths illustrated in this cartoon, many employees nevertheless are feeling the consequences of these cutbacks.

Too Much Accountability Effective controls allow managers to determine whether or not employees successfully discharge their responsibilities. If standards are properly set and performance accurately measured, managers know when problems arise and which departments and individuals are responsible. People who do not want to be answerable for their mistakes or who do not want to work as hard as their boss might like therefore resist control. For example, American Express has a system that provides daily information on how many calls each of its customer service representatives handles. If one representative has typically worked at a slower pace and handled fewer calls than other representatives, that individual's deficient performance can now more easily be pinpointed.

Overcoming Resistance to Control

Perhaps the best way to overcome resistance to control is to create effective control to begin with. If control systems are properly integrated with organizational planning and if the controls are flexible, accurate, timely, and objective, the organization will be less likely to overcontrol, to focus on inappropriate standards, or to reward inefficiency. Two other ways to overcome resistance are encouraging employee participation and developing verification procedures.

Encourage Employee Participation Chapter 12 notes that participation can help overcome resistance to change. By the same token, when employees are involved with planning and implementing the control system, they are less likely to resist it. For instance, employee participation in planning, decision making, and quality control at the Chevrolet Gear and Axle plant in Detroit has resulted in increased employee concern for quality and a greater commitment to meeting standards.

Develop Verification Procedures Multiple standards and information systems provide checks and balances in control and allow the organization to verify the accuracy of performance indicators. Suppose a production manager argues that she failed to meet a certain cost standard because of increased prices of raw materials. A properly designed inventory control system will either support or contradict her explanation. Suppose that an employee who was fired for excessive absences argues that he was not absent "for a long time." An effective human resource control system should have records that support the termination. Resistance to control declines because these verification procedures protect both employees and management. If the production manager's claim about the rising cost of raw materials is supported by the inventory control records, she will not be held solely accountable for failing to meet the cost standard, and some action will probably be taken to lower the cost of raw materials.

concept CHECK

What are the essential characteristics of effective control?

Recall an incident in which you resisted control. What was done, or what might have been done better, to help overcome your resistance?

Summary of Key Points

ACE self-test

business.college.hmco.com/students

Control is the regulation of organizational activities so that some targeted element of performance remains within acceptable limits. Control provides ways to adapt to environmental change, to limit the accumulation of errors, to cope with organizational complexity, and to minimize costs. Control can focus on financial, physical, information, and human resources and includes operations, financial, structural, and strategic levels. Control is the function of managers, the controller, and, increasingly, of operating employees.

Steps in the control process are (1) establish standards of expected performance, (2) measure actual performance, (3) compare performance to the standards, and (4) evaluate the comparison and take appropriate action.

Operations control focuses on the processes the organization uses to transform resources into products or services. Preliminary control is concerned with the resources that serve as inputs to the system. Screening control is concerned with the transformation processes used by the organization. Postaction control is concerned with the outputs of the organization. Most organizations need multiple control systems because no one system alone can provide adequate control.

Financial control focuses on controlling the organization's financial resources. The foundation of financial control is budgets, plans expressed in numerical terms. Most organizations rely on financial, operating, and nonmonetary budgets. Financial statements, various kinds of ratios, and external and internal audits are also important tools organizations use as part of financial control.

Structural control addresses how well an organization's structural elements serve their intended purpose. Two basic forms of structural control are bureaucratic and decentralized control. Bureaucratic control is relatively formal and mechanistic, whereas decentralized control is informal and organic. Most organizations use a form of organizational control somewhere between these two extremes.

Strategic control focuses on how effectively the organization's strategies are succeeding in helping the organization meet its goals. The integration of strategy and control is generally achieved through organization structure, leadership, technology, human resources, and information and operational control systems. International strategic control is also important for multinational organizations. The foundation of international strategic control is whether to practice centralized or decentralized control.

One way to increase the effectiveness of control is to fully integrate planning and control. The control system should also be flexible, accurate, timely, and as objective as possible. Employees may resist organizational controls because of overcontrol, inappropriate focus, rewards for inefficiency, and a desire to avoid accountability. Managers can overcome this resistance by improving the effectiveness of controls and by allowing employee participation and developing verification procedures.

Discussion Questions

Questions for Review

1. What is the purpose of organizational control? Why is it important?
2. What are the different levels of control? What are the relationships between the different levels?
3. Describe how a budget is created in most organizations. How does a budget help a manager with financial control?
4. Describe the differences between bureaucratic and decentralized control. What are the advantages and disadvantages of each?

Questions for Analysis

5. How can a manager determine whether his or her firm needs improvement in control? If improvement is needed, how can the manager tell what type of control needs improvement (operations, financial, structural, or strategic)? Describe some steps a manager can take to improve each of these types of control.
6. One company uses strict performance standards. Another has standards that are more flexible. What are the advantages and disadvantages of each system?
7. Are the differences in bureaucratic control and decentralized control related to differences in organization structure? If so, how? If not, why not? (The terms do sound similar to those used to discuss the organizing process.)

Questions for Application

8. Many organizations today are involving lower-level employees in control. Give at least two examples of specific actions that a lower-level worker could do to help his or

her organization better adapt to environmental change. Then do the same for limiting the accumulation of error, coping with organizational complexity, and minimizing costs.

9. Describe ways that the top management team, midlevel managers, and operating employees can participate in each step of the control process. Do all participate equally in each step, or are some steps better suited for personnel at one level? Explain your answer.
10. Interview a worker to determine which areas and levels of control exist for him or her on the job. Does the worker resist efforts at control? Why or why not?

BUILDING EFFECTIVE time-management SKILLS

Exercise Overview

Time-management skills—a manager's ability to prioritize work, to work efficiently, and to delegate appropriately—play a major role in the control function; that is, a manager can use time-management skills to control his or her own work more effectively. This exercise will help demonstrate the relationship between time-management skills and control.

Exercise Background

You are a middle manager in a small manufacturing plant. Today is Monday, and you have just returned from a week of vacation. The first thing you discover is that your assistant will not be in today. His aunt died, and he is out of town at the funeral. He did, however, leave you the following note:

> Dear Boss:
>
> Sorry about not being here today. I will be back tomorrow. In the meantime, here are some things you need to know:
>
> 1. Ms. Glinski [your boss] wants to see you today at 4:00.
> 2. The shop steward wants to see you as soon as possible about a labor problem.
> 3. Mr. Bateman [one of your big customers] has a complaint about a recent shipment.
> 4. Ms. Ferris [one of your major suppliers] wants to discuss a change in delivery schedules.
> 5. Mr. Prescott from the Chamber of Commerce wants you to attend a breakfast meeting on Wednesday to discuss our expansion plans.
> 6. The legal office wants to discuss our upcoming OSHA inspection.
> 7. Human resources wants to know when you can interview someone for the new supervisor's position.
> 8. Jack Williams, the machinist you fired last month, has been hanging around the parking lot, and his presence is making some employees uncomfortable.

Exercise Task

With the information above as context, do the following:

1. Prioritize the work that needs to be done by sorting the information above into three categories: very timely, moderately timely, and less timely.
2. Are importance and timeliness the same thing?
3. What additional information must you acquire before you can begin to prioritize this work?
4. How would your approach differ if your secretary were in today?

BUILDING EFFECTIVE decision-making and diagnostic SKILLS

business.college.hmco.com/students

Exercise Overview

Decision-making skills refer to the manager's ability to recognize and respond to problems and opportunities, whereas diagnostic skills focus on the visualization of appropriate responses. This exercise asks you to examine one component of an organization's control system, to diagnose any weaknesses in the system, and to develop a plan for strengthening control in that part of the system.

Exercise Background

Organizations use a wide variety of methods for control. One control system is the corporate board of directors. This group of individuals is often chosen by the firm's CEO or by other directors. Boards of directors are especially important in strategic control. They have the responsibility of ensuring that the corporation is achieving its strategic goals while acting ethically, to oversee the performance of the CEO and other members of the top-management team, and to look out for the interests of shareholders. Yet the recent corporate scandals at Enron, WorldCom, and other firms have shown that some boards provide inadequate control.

The U.S. Securities and Exchange Commission (SEC) has put forth proposals for a number of reforms that it hopes will enhance the control power of boards. Some of its recommendations focus on board composition. If boards do not contain the right number and kind of directors, the SEC claims, they are less likely to be effective. The SEC recommends that firms

- Keep the size of the board to one dozen or fewer directors, so that each has a more personal stake in the process.
- Choose outside directors for the most part, to increase their objectivity. (Outside directors are not employees of the firm, not related to any employees, and not involved in significant business dealings with the CEO or the firm.)
- Require directors to hold significant amounts of company stock, to align their interests more closely with those of stockholders.
- Choose several experts in corporate accounting or finance, especially on the audit and compensation committees.
- Ensure that directors do not serve on more than three boards altogether, to ensure that they have sufficient time for this board.

Exercise Task

Choose an organization that interests you. Use the Internet to research its board of directors. (*Hint:* Company websites contain much of this information. Also search the Web for biographies of each individual director.)

1. Use information from the Internet to provide answers to each of the items listed above (board size, outside directors, stock ownership, financial expertise, and board service). Answer as many of the questions as you can for each board member.
2. In which of the five areas is your firm's board of directors acceptable? In which of the five areas is your firm's board not acceptable?
3. What are some likely consequences for organizational control? Consider both positive and negative consequences.
4. What can your organization do to increase the effectiveness of its board?

BUILDING EFFECTIVE technical SKILLS

Exercise Overview

Technical skills are the skills necessary to accomplish or understand the specific kind of work being done in an organization. This exercise gives you practice in technical skills related to building a budget and evaluating the effectiveness of a budget.

Exercise Background

Although corporate budgets are much more complicated, the steps in creating a personal budget and creating a corporate budget are much the same. Both begin with estimations of inflow and outflow. Then both compare actual results with estimated results. And both end with the development of a plan for corrective action.

Exercise Task

1. Prepare your estimated expenditures and income for one month. This is a budgeted amount, not the amount you actually spent. Instead, it should represent a typical month or a reasonable minimum. For example, is $200 a reasonable amount to spend on groceries? Estimate your necessary monthly expenses for tuition, rent, car payments, childcare, food, utilities, and so on. Then estimate your income from all sources, such as wages, allowance, loans, and funds borrowed on credit cards. Calculate the totals.
2. Write down all of your actual expenses over the last month. Then write down all your actual income. If you do not have exact figures, estimate as closely as you can. Calculate the totals.
3. Compare your estimates to your actual expenses and actual income. Are there any discrepancies? What caused the discrepancies, if any?
4. Did you expect to have a surplus or a deficit for the month? Did you actually have a deficit or a surplus? What are your plans for making up any deficit or managing any surplus?
5. Do you regularly use a personal budget? Is a personal budget likely to be helpful? Why or why not?

CHAPTER CLOSING case

WAKE UP, "ZOMBIES"!

If the U.S. economy is "sluggish," then the Japanese economy must be described as "comatose." The world's second-largest economy is suffering from a host of problems: Banks are overloaded with bad loans, the Tokyo real estate market bubble has burst, and stock prices have lost much of their value. In addition, the government props up failing businesses through low-cost or no-cost loans, which only increases distrust of the system. "This kind of intervention can work in the short term. But from a long-term point of view it has terrible implications: Investors understand that the market is artificial, and accordingly they pull back," states analyst Jean-Marie Eveillard.

Yet many of the problems plaguing Japanese corporations today are not related to economic or political woes, but rather to poor management. "90 percent of the Japanese economy is made up of domestic companies that are low-tech and low-productivity," claims consultant Masao Hirano. However, a few pioneering firms are starting to demonstrate that "by becoming better focused, [Japanese companies] can survive and even prosper," says analyst Satoru Oyama.

Cosmetics maker Shiseido held too much inventory and had overly high expenses, leading to a $550 million loss over two years. But, rather than call for a government bailout, Shiseido executives focused on fundamental improvements. Better technology allowed them to control and forecast inventory more effectively. They cut costs throughout the corporation and curtailed their product line. After Shiseido returned to profitability, chief logistics officer Seiji Nishimori boasted, "We're showing other Japanese companies that it's possible to reverse a slide."

Canon, the world's leading maker of copiers and laser printers, has also taken a disciplined approach to performance improvement. CEO Fujio Mitarai replaced every manufacturing line at the firm's twenty-nine Japanese factories with small, self-directed teams of half a dozen workers that do the work previously done by thirty laborers. The teams discovered more efficient inventory management techniques, and Canon was able to close twenty of its thirty-four parts warehouses. "Manufacturing is where most of the costs lie," Mitarai claims. Canon earnings improved by 53 percent, enabling Mitarai to conclude, "We're much more profitable today because of these changes."

The success of notable high performers such as multinational Toyota has caused Japanese firms to realize the benefits of global cost competitiveness. High-tech companies are abandoning manufacturing and switching attention to R&D to counteract an influx of inexpensive electronics from China, Taiwan, and Korea. For example, NEC has moved

> *"We're showing other Japanese companies that it's possible to reverse a slide."*
>
> – Seiji Nishimori, chief logistics officer, Shiseido*

out of the unprofitable semiconductor chip–making business and focused on more lucrative cell phones and software. Sharp, too, has given up on low-margin PC monitors and refocused its operations on innovative products such as liquid crystal displays for PDAs. Sony is working on revolutionary new computer chips while reducing its investment in consumer electronics.

All three companies say they now listen to their consumers more closely. "We were proud of our great technology, and [we] just pumped out products without thinking of our customers' needs," says NEC director Kaoru Tosaka. "Now, we're emphasizing efficiency, profits, and clients."

These companies are an exception in Japan, where so-called zombie firms are bailed out over and over again by a government that fears unemployment and chaos if businesses fail. But the zombies need to hear the lessons these stellar firms have learned. Watch inventory. Cut costs where possible. Use information technology more effectively. Simplify product lines. Experiment with new ways of organizing. Shut down money-losing businesses. Choose areas where the firm can add value. Listen to customer feedback. If the zombies could adopt these suggestions, the Japanese—and the rest of the world—would surely benefit.

Case Questions

1. Use the case to find at least one example of each purpose of control—adapting to environmental change, limiting the accumulation of error, coping with organizational complexity, and minimizing costs. What are the consequences for firms that do not achieve these purposes?
2. List every improvement that is mentioned in the case above—for example, closing warehouses or adopting customers' suggestions. For each item, tell whether it represents preliminary, screening, or postaction control. Then tell whether it represents operations, financial, structural, or strategic control.
3. Japanese firms are likely to encounter a great deal of resistance to change as they attempt to improve their control. What advice would you give to managers whose workers are resisting efforts to improve control?

Case References

Clay Chandler, "Japan's Horror Show," *Fortune*, November 10, 2002, www.fortune.com on February 15, 2003; Irene M. Kunii, "Quick Studies," *BusinessWeek*, November 18, 2002, pp. 48–49 (*quote p. 48); Justin Lahart, "Bank of Japan to Buy Stocks," *CNN/Money*, September 18, 2002, www.cnnmoney.com on February 15, 2003.

Chapter Notes

1. Julia Boorstin, "JetBlue's IPO Takes Off," *Fortune*, April 29, 2002, www.fortune.com on February 14, 2003; Melanie Wells, "Lord of the Skies," *Forbes*, October 14, 2002, pp. 130–138 (*quote p. 138); Paul C. Judge, "How Will Your Company Adapt?" *Fast Company*, November 2001, www.fastcompany.com on February 14, 2003; Robert Barker, "Is JetBlue Flying Too High?" *BusinessWeek*, April 29, 2002, www.businessweek.com on February 14, 2003.
2. Thomas A. Stewart, "Welcome to the Revolution," *Fortune*, December 13, 1993, pp. 66–77.
3. William Taylor, "Control in an Age of Chaos," *Harvard Business Review*, November–December 1994, pp. 64–70.
4. "Fleetwood: Not a Happy Camper Company," *BusinessWeek*, October 9, 2000, pp. 88–90.
5. "An Apple a Day," *BusinessWeek*, October 14, 2002, pp. 122–125; "More Business People Say: Let's Not Do Lunch," *USA Today*, December 24, 2002, p. 1B; David Stires, "The Breaking Point," *Fortune*, March 3, 2003, pp. 107–114.
6. Mark Kroll, Peter Wright, Leslie Toombs, and Hadley Leavell, "Form of Control: A Critical Determinant of Acquisition Performance and CEO Rewards," *Strategic Management Journal*, vol. 18, no. 2, 1997, pp. 85–96.
7. "It's Showtime for the Airlines," *BusinessWeek*, September 2, 2002, pp. 36–37.
8. "United's Bid to Cut Labor Costs Could Force Rivals to Follow," *Wall Street Journal*, February 25, 2003, pp. A1, A6.
9. Sim Sitkin, Kathleen Sutcliffe, and Roger Schroeder, "Distinguishing Control from Learning in Total Quality Management: A Contingency Perspective," *Academy of Management Review*, 1994, vol. 19, no. 3, pp. 537–564.
10. Robert Lusch and Michael Harvey, "The Case for an Off-Balance-Sheet Controller," *Sloan Management Review*, Winter 1994, pp. 101–110.
11. Edward E. Lawler III and John G. Rhode, *Information and Control in Organizations* (Pacific Palisades, Calif.: Goodyear, 1976).
12. Charles W. L. Hill, "Establishing a Standard: Competitive Strategy and Technological Standards in Winner-Take-All Industries," *Academy of Management Executive*, vol. 11, no. 2, 1997, pp. 7–16.
13. "An Efficiency Guru Refits Honda to Fight Auto Giants," *Wall Street Journal*, September 15, 1999, p. B1.
14. See Belverd E. Needles, Jr., Henry R. Anderson, and James C. Caldwell, *Principles of Accounting*, 2002e (Boston: Houghton Mifflin, 2002).
15. "At Disney, String of Weak Cartoons Leads to Cost Cuts," *Wall Street Journal*, June 18, 2002, pp. A1, A6.
16. Needles, Anderson, and Caldwell, *Principles of Accounting*.
17. "Mickey Mouse, CPA," *Forbes*, March 10, 1997, pp. 42–43.
18. Needles, Anderson, and Caldwell, *Principles of Accounting*.
19. Jeremy Kahn, "Do Accountants Have a Future?" *Fortune*, March 3, 2003, pp. 115–117.
20. "Inside WorldCom's Unearthing of a Vast Accounting Scandal," *Wall Street Journal*, June 27, 2002, pp. A1, A12.
21. William G. Ouchi, "The Transmission of Control Through Organizational Hierarchy," *Academy of Management Journal*, June 1978, pp. 173–192; Richard E. Walton, "From Control to Commitment in the Workplace," *Harvard Business Review*, March–April 1985, pp. 76–84.
22. "Nordstrom Cleans out Its Closets," *BusinessWeek*, May 22, 2000, pp. 105–108.
23. Patricia Sellers, "Something to Prove," *Fortune*, June 24, 2002, pp. 88–98.
24. Peter Lorange, Michael F. Scott Morton, and Sumantra Ghoshal, *Strategic Control* (St. Paul, Minn: West, 1986).

See also Joseph C. Picken and Gregory G. Dess, "Out of (Strategic) Control," *Organizational Dynamics*, Summer 1997, pp. 35–45.

25. See Hans Mjoen and Stephen Tallman, "Control and Performance in International Joint Ventures," *Organization Science*, May–June 1997, pp. 257–265.
26. See Diana Robertson and Erin Anderson, "Control System and Task Environment Effects on Ethical Judgment: An Exploratory Study of Industrial Salespeople," *Organization Science*, November 1993, pp. 617–629, for a recent study of effective control.
27. "Workers, Surf at Your Own Risk," *BusinessWeek*, June 12, 2000, pp. 105–106.
28. "Enterprise Takes Idea of Dressed for Success to a New Extreme," *Wall Street Journal*, November 20, 2002, p. B1.

21

Managing Operations, Quality, and Productivity

CHAPTER OUTLINE

The Nature of Operations Management
The Importance of Operations
Manufacturing and Production Operations
Service Operations
The Role of Operations in Organizational Strategy

Designing Operations Systems
Determining Product-Service Mix
Capacity Decisions
Facilities Decisions

Organizational Technologies
Manufacturing Technology
Service Technology

Implementing Operations Systems Through Supply Chain Management
Operations Management as Control
Purchasing Management
Inventory Management

Managing Total Quality
The Meaning of Quality
The Importance of Quality
Total Quality Management
TQM Tools and Techniques

Managing Productivity
The Meaning of Productivity
The Importance of Productivity
Productivity Trends
Improving Productivity

LEARNING OBJECTIVES

After studying this chapter, you should be able to:

1 ***Describe and explain the nature of operations management.***

OPENING INCIDENT

In 1965, when color televisions were rare and slide rules prevailed, engineer Gordon Moore predicted, "Integrated circuits will lead to such wonders as home computers, automatic controls for automobiles, and personal portable communications equipment." Moore also noted that the number of transistors (roughly equivalent to processing capacity) on a semiconductor chip was doubling each year. This statement was interpreted by others to mean that capacity *must* double yearly, and it became known as "Moore's Law." (Today, the doubling time is about twenty-one months.) Moore went on to found Intel, the semiconductor chip maker that successfully applied his law to its design and manufacturing operations.

Moore never intended for his observation to become a "law," however. But Intel CEO Craig Barrett uses it to goad his employees to higher performance. "Every time we don't live up to Moore's Law, somebody else does," Barrett tells his researchers. "We don't adhere to Moore's Law for the hell of it," Barrett adds. "We dangle Moore's Law in front of the new young minds . . . and say,'Hey, your predecessors were smart enough to figure this out for the past 20 or 30 years—why the hell aren't you?'" Senior vice president of technology and manufacturing Sunlin Chou thinks that the

2	3	4	5	6
Identify and discuss the components involved in designing effective operations systems.	***Discuss organizational technologies and their role in operations management.***	***Identify and discuss the components involved in implementing operations systems through supply chain management.***	***Explain the meaning and importance of managing quality and total quality management.***	***Explain the meaning and importance of managing productivity, productivity trends, and ways to improve productivity.***

"The point is to move the whole product line ... to a more competitive performance position . . . rather than lower the price to be competitive."

—Gordon Moore, founder of Intel and creator of Moore's Law

Intel uses a variety of operations management techniques to stay at the forefront of its industry.

law is "a self-fulfilling prophecy." He states, "In the end, Moore's Law is a philosophy as well as a strategy. It gives us the confidence to believe in the future."

Intel's faith in Moore's Law has led it to take risks in the development of innovative new products. The firm is currently building its largest-ever fabrication plant, a $2.5 billion facility to produce the new Itanium chips, and three more just like it are planned. Former CEO Andy Grove claims that "capacity is strategy." Worldwide, Intel sells 81 percent of PC microprocessors, trouncing number-two Advanced Micro Devices (AMD). Intel's advantage lies in its superior design—its Pentium 4 processor has speeds of up to 3 gigahertz, whereas AMD's best efforts still fall short of 2. Barrett believes that Intel can build enough capacity to drive rivals out of the industry. Some, like analyst Jonathon Joseph, worry that Intel may be overbuilding. "Intel has a phobia about capacity," Joseph claims. "They're very concerned that they'll miss the next upturn [in demand for chips]. . . . They aimed forward to hit the duck, and the duck isn't there." Intel plans to shut down older plants as it opens new ones to keep capacity at a sustainable level.

The state-of-the-art factory employs flexible manufacturing to ensure that the plant can produce the next generation of chips. Intel's three planned facilities will "copy exactly" the design of the first, a cornerstone of the chip maker's innovation strategy. Chou explains, "Once we come up with a manufacturing process, we don't let the chip design team tinker with it." The copy-exactly technique ensures that new facilities become productive immediately and that they do not introduce any new errors into the exacting process of chip fabrication. Moore emphasizes the importance of "copy exactly," saying, "it takes a couple of years out of the life span of a generation of products. That in turn allows us to set a faster pace of innovation for our competitors to keep up with."

Another key piece of Intel's operations strategy is constant innovation, even if that means cannibalizing sales of older products. The new Itanium, for example, will replace the Pentium. During the transition, Pentium chips will be cheaper, but once the Itanium facility is operational, Intel will cease manufacture of Pentiums. Moore says, "The point is to move the whole product line, not just a single part, to a more competitive performance position . . . rather than lower the price to be competitive."

Even as the first factory is nearing completion, Chou and his R&D team have begun work on the next-generation processor, which they hope to produce starting in late 2004. The manufacturer is also bringing the efficiencies of Moore's Law to the manufacture of communications chips. These chips are currently made in small batches to meet each assembler's unique requirements. Intel wants to place standardized wireless and computing technology on the same chip. The semiconductors could create a national wireless communications network that would provide wireless connectivity to any device, anywhere in the United States.

It is a foregone conclusion that Intel will dominate chip design and manufacture for the foreseeable future. However, the ailing economy means that businesses and households have less to spend on the latest and greatest technology. Intel has mastered the art of high-tech manufacturing. Can it master the marketing challenges that it now faces? [1]

Managers at Intel have made innovation a hallmark of their company's operations. This innovation, in turn, has allowed them to charge premium prices and earn superior profits. But, to be successful with this strategy, the firm must also maintain its position as industry leader. And Intel seems to be doing just that by relying heavily on operations management as a centerpiece of its overall strategy.

In this chapter we explore operations management, quality, and productivity. We first introduce operations management and discuss its role in general management and organizational strategy. The next three sections discuss the design of operations systems, organizational technologies, and implementing operations systems. We then introduce and discuss various issues in managing for quality and total quality. Finally, we discuss productivity, which is closely related to quality.

The Nature of Operations Management

operations management The total set of managerial activities used by an organization to transform resource inputs into products, services, or both

Operations management is at the core of what organizations do as they add value and create products and services. But what exactly are operations? And how are they managed? **Operations management** is the set of managerial activities used by an organization to transform resource inputs into products and services. When Dell Computer buys electronic components, assembles them into PCs, and then ships them to customers, it is engaging in operations management. When a Pizza Hut employee orders food and paper products and then combines dough, cheese, and tomato paste to create a pizza, he or she is engaging in operations management.

Manufacturing and production are frequently key components of a company's quality management efforts. IGT Corporation makes electronic slot machines that are sold to casinos and other gambling operations around the world. Because of the stringent government regulations that affect this industry, and the potential costs that errors might create, it is extremely important that all machines be of the highest quality. Thus this inspector is closely examining a transparent cover sheet that will announce whether or not the player has struck it rich!

The Importance of Operations

Operations is an important functional concern for organizations, because efficient and effective management of operations goes a long way toward ensuring competitiveness and overall organizational performance, as well as quality and productivity. Inefficient or ineffective operations management, on the other hand, will almost inevitably lead to poorer performance and lower levels of both quality and productivity.

In an economic sense, operations management creates value and utility of one type or another, depending on the nature of the firm's products or services. If the product is a physical good, such as a Harley-Davidson motorcycle, operations creates value and provides form utility by combining many dissimilar inputs (sheet metal, rubber, paint, combustion engines, and human skills) to make something (a motorcycle) that is more valuable than the actual cost of the inputs used to create it. The inputs are converted from their incoming form into a new physical form. This conversion is typical of manufacturing operations and essentially reflects the organization's technology.

In contrast, the operations activities of American Airlines create value and provide time and place utility through its services. The airline transports passengers and freight according to agreed-upon departure and arrival places and times. Other service operations, such as a Coors beer distributorship or a Gap retail store, create value and provide place and possession utility by bringing together the customer and products made by others. Although the organizations in these examples produce different kinds of products or services, their operations processes share many important features.[2]

Manufacturing and Production Operations

Because manufacturing once dominated U.S. industry, the entire area of operations management used to be called "production management." **Manufacturing** is a form of business that combines and transforms resources into tangible outcomes that are then sold to others. The Goodyear Tire & Rubber Company is a manufacturer because it combines rubber and chemical compounds and uses blending equipment and molding machines to create tires. Broyhill is a manufacturer because it buys wood and metal components, pads, and fabric and then combines them into furniture.

manufacturing A form of business that combines and transforms resource inputs into tangible outcomes

During the 1970s, manufacturing entered a long period of decline in the United States, primarily because of foreign competition. U.S. firms had grown lax and sluggish, and new foreign competitors came onto the scene with better equipment and much higher levels of efficiency. For example, steel companies in the Far East were able to produce high-quality steel for much lower prices than were U.S. companies like Bethlehem Steel and U.S. Steel (now USX Corporation). Faced with a battle for survival, many companies underwent a long and difficult period of change by eliminating waste and transforming themselves into leaner and more efficient and responsive entities. They reduced their workforce dramatically, closed antiquated or unnecessary plants, and modernized their remaining plants. In the last decade, their efforts have started to pay dividends, as U.S. business has regained its competitive position in many different industries. Although manufacturers from other parts of the world are still formidable competitors, and U.S. firms may never again be competitive in some markets, the overall picture is much better than it was just a few years ago. And prospects continue to look bright.[3]

Service operations continue to grow in importance. Peapod, for example, is a growing online grocery buying service. Customers complete an online shopping list, the next day a Peapod employee delivers it—for the price of the groceries plus a service charge of around $10. The service appeals to busy working consumers who gladly pay the extra charge to avoid having to do their own shopping. Online grocery shopping is expected to reach an annual volume of over $3 billion by 2005.

Service Operations

During the decline of the manufacturing sector, a tremendous growth in the service sector kept the U.S. economy from declining at the same rate. A **service organization** is one that transforms resources into an intangible output and creates time or place utility for its customers. For example, Merrill Lynch makes stock transactions for its customers, Avis leases cars to its customers, and your local hairdresser cuts your hair. In 1947 the service sector was responsible for less than half of the U.S. gross national product (GNP). By 1975, however, this figure reached 65 percent, and by 1999 it was over 75 percent. The service sector has been responsible for almost 90 percent of all new jobs created in the United States during the 1990s. Managers have come to see that many of the tools, techniques, and methods that are used in a factory are also useful to a service firm. For example, managers of automobile plants and hair salons both have to decide how to design their facility, identify the best location for it, determine optimal capacity, make decisions about inventory storage, set procedures for purchasing raw materials, and set standards for productivity and quality.

The Role of Operations in Organizational Strategy

service organization An organization that transforms resources into services

It should be clear by this point that operations management is very important to organizations. Beyond its direct impact on such factors as competitiveness, quality, and productivity, it also directly influences the organization's overall level of effectiveness. For example, the deceptively simple strategic decision of whether to stress high quality regardless of cost, lowest possible cost regardless of quality, or some combination of the two has numerous important implications. A highest-possible-quality strategy will dictate state-of-the-art technology and rigorous control of product design and materials specifications. A combination strategy might call for lower-grade technology and less concern about product design and materials specifications. Just as strategy affects operations management, so, too, does operations management affect strategy. Suppose that a firm decides to upgrade the quality of its products or services. The organization's ability to implement the decision is dependent in part on current production capabilities and other resources. If existing technology will not permit higher-quality work, and if the organization lacks the resources to replace its technology, increasing quality to the desired new standards will be difficult.

concept CHECK

Distinguish between manufacturing and production operations and service operations.

Why do you think the manufacturing sector of the U.S. economy has declined while the service sector has grown?

Designing Operations Systems

The problems, challenges, and opportunities faced by operations managers revolve around the acquisition and utilization of resources for conversion. Their goals include both efficiency and effectiveness. A number of issues and decisions must be addressed as operations systems are designed. The most basic ones are product-service mix, capacity, and facilities.

product-service mix How many and what kinds of products or services (or both) to offer

capacity The amount of products, services, or both that can be produced by an organization

Determining Product-Service Mix

A natural starting point in designing operations systems is determining the **product-service mix**. This decision flows from corporate, business, and marketing strategies. Managers have to make a number of decisions about their products and services, starting with how many and what kinds to offer.[4] Procter & Gamble, for example, makes regular, tartar-control, gel, and various other formulas of Crest toothpaste and packages them in several different sizes of tubes, pumps, and other dispensers. Similarly, workers at Subway sandwich shops can combine different breads, vegetables, meats, and condiments to create hundreds of different kinds of sandwiches. Decisions also have to be made regarding the level of quality desired, the optimal cost of each product or service, and exactly how each is to be designed. GE, for example, recently reduced the number of parts in its industrial circuit breakers from 28,000 to 1,275. This whole process was achieved by carefully analyzing product design and production methods.

Facilities decisions can play a key role in the effectiveness of a firm's operations management systems. This company, Camden International, imports cocoa beans from West Africa. By placing its warehouse near ship terminals and efficiently designing the facility, a forklift operator can quickly move a load of beans from the dock receiving area into temporary storage inside the warehouse—or even move it directly through the facility and load it onto a truck.

Capacity Decisions

The **capacity** decision involves choosing the amount of products, services, or both that can be produced by the organization. Determining whether to build a factory capable of making 5,000 or 8,000 units per day is a capacity decision. So, too, is deciding whether to build a restaurant with 100 or 150 seats, or a bank with five or ten teller stations. The capacity decision is truly a high-risk one because of the uncertainties of future product demand and the large monetary stakes involved. An organization that builds capacity exceeding its needs may commit resources (capital investment) that will never be recovered. Alternatively, an organization can build a facility with a smaller capacity than expected demand. Doing so may result in lost market opportunities, but it may also free capital resources for use elsewhere in the organization.

A major consideration in determining capacity is demand. A company operating with fairly constant monthly demand might build a plant capable of producing an amount each month roughly equivalent to its demand. But, if its market is characterized by seasonal fluctuations, building a smaller plant to meet normal demand and then adding extra shifts staffed with temporary workers or paying permanent workers extra to work more hours during peak periods might be the most effective choice. Likewise, a restaurant that needs 150 seats for Saturday night but never needs more than 100 at any other time during the week would probably be foolish to expand to 150 seats. During the rest of the week, it must still pay to light, heat, cool, and clean the excess capacity.

Facilities Decisions

facilities The physical locations where products or services are created, stored, and distributed

Facilities are the physical locations where products or services are created, stored, and distributed. Major decisions pertain to facilities location and facilities layout.

location The physical positioning or geographic site of facilities

Location **Location** is the physical positioning or geographic site of facilities and must be determined by the needs and requirements of the organization. A company that relies heavily on railroads for transportation needs to be located close to rail facilities. GE decided that it did not need six plants to make circuit breakers, so it invested heavily in automating one plant and closed the other five. Different organizations in the same industry may have different facilities requirements. Benetton uses only one distribution center for the entire world, whereas Wal-Mart has several distribution centers in the United States alone. A retail business must choose its location very carefully to be convenient for consumers.

layout The physical configuration of facilities, the arrangement of equipment within facilities, or both

product layout A physical configuration of facilities arranged around the product; used when large quantities of a single product are needed

process layout A physical configuration of facilities arranged around the process; used in facilities that create or process a variety of products

Layout The choice of physical configuration, or the **layout**, of facilities is closely related to other operations decisions. The three entirely different layout alternatives shown in Figure 21.1 help demonstrate the importance of the layout decision. A **product layout** is appropriate when large quantities of a single product are needed. It makes sense to custom-design a straight-line flow of work for a product when a specific task is performed at each workstation as each unit flows past. Most assembly lines use this format. For example, Dell's personal computer factories use a product layout.

Process layouts are used in operations settings that create or process a variety of products. Auto repair shops and health-care clinics are good examples. Each car and each person is a separate "product." The needs of each incoming job are diagnosed as it enters the operations system, and the job is routed through the unique sequence of workstations needed to create the desired finished product. In a process layout, each type of conversion task is centralized in a single workstation or department. All welding is done in one designated shop location, and any car that requires welding is moved to that area. This setup is in contrast to the product layout, in which several different workstations may perform welding operations if the conversion task sequence so dictates. Similarly, in a hospital, all X-rays are

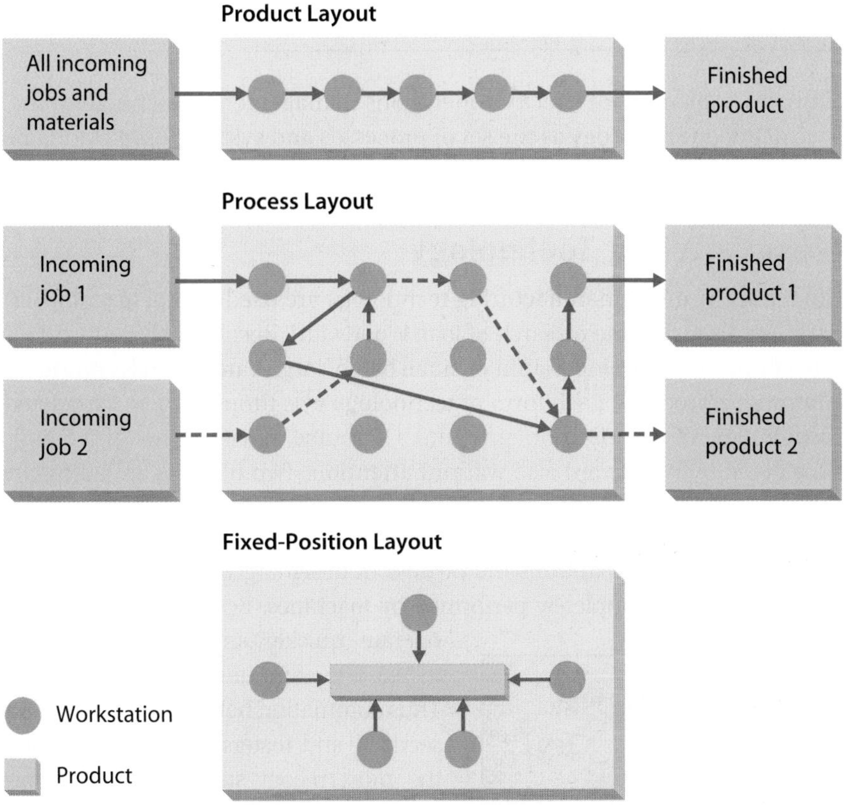

FIGURE 21.1

Approaches to Facilities Layout

When a manufacturer produces large quantities of a product (such as cars or computers), it may arrange its facilities in an assembly line (product layout). In a process layout, the work (such as patients in a hospital or custom pieces of furniture) moves through various workstations. Locomotives and bridges are both manufactured in a fixed-position layout.

done in one location, all surgeries in another, and all physical therapy in yet another. Patients are moved from location to location to get the services they need.

The **fixed-position layout** is used when the organization is creating a few very large and complex products. Aircraft manufacturers like Boeing and shipbuilders like Newport News use this method. An assembly line capable of moving a 747 would require an enormous plant, so instead the airplane itself remains stationary, and people and machines move around it as it is assembled.

fixed-position layout A physical configuration of facilities arranged around a single work area; used for the manufacture of large and complex products such as airplanes

The cellular layout is a relatively new approach to facilities design. **Cellular layouts** are used when families of products can follow similar flow paths. A clothing manufacturer, for example, might create a cell, or designated area, dedicated to making a family of pockets, such as pockets for shirts, coats, blouses, and slacks. Although each kind of pocket is unique, the same basic equipment and methods are used to make all of them. Hence, all pockets might be made in the same area and then delivered directly to different product layout assembly areas where the shirts, coats, blouses, and slacks are actually being assembled.

cellular layout A physical configuration of facilities used when families of products can follow similar flow paths

concept CHECK

What are the three basic components in designing operations systems? Identify the basic decisions that relate to each.

Think of three local restaurants or other establishments that you have visited recently. Characterize the three components of the operations systems used by each.

Organizational Technologies

One central element of effective operations management is technology. In Chapter 3 we defined **technology** as the set of processes and systems used by organizations to convert resources into products or services.

Manufacturing Technology

technology The set of processes and systems used by organizations to convert resources into products or services

Numerous forms of manufacturing technology are used in organizations. In Chapter 11 we discussed the research of Joan Woodward. Recall that Woodward identified three forms of technology—unit or small batch, large batch or mass production, and continuous process.[5] Each form of technology was thought to be associated with a specific type of organization structure. Of course, newer forms of technology not considered by Woodward also warrant attention. Two of these are automation and computer-assisted manufacturing.

automation The process of designing work so that it can be completely or almost completely performed by machines

Automation **Automation** is the process of designing work so that it can be completely or almost completely performed by machines. Because automated machines operate quickly and make few errors, they increase the amount of work that can be done. Thus automation helps to improve products and services, and fosters innovation. Automation is the most recent step in the development of machines and machine-controlling devices. Machine-controlling devices have been around since the 1700s. James Watt, a Scottish engineer, invented a mechanical speed control to regulate the speed of steam engines in 1787. The Jacquard loom, developed by a French inventor, was controlled by paper cards with holes punched in them. Early accounting and computing equipment was controlled by similar punched cards.

Manufacturing technology continues to become increasingly sophisticated. Take this DaimlerChrysler automobile factory in Indiana, for instance. The machinist is using traditional assembly-line technology and equipment to perform a basic job. In addition, though, the PC monitor is also providing the machinist with information about how well the job is being performed. This allows the machinist to do both faster and higher-quality work.

Automation relies on feedback, information, sensors, and a control mechanism. Feedback is the flow of information from the machine back to the sensor. Sensors are the parts of the system that gather information and compare it to preset standards. The control mechanism is the device that sends instructions to the automatic machine. Early automatic machines were primitive, and the use of automation was relatively slow to develop. These elements are illustrated by the example in Figure 21.2. A thermostat has sensors that monitor air temperature and compare it to a preset low value. If the air temperature falls below the preset value, the thermostat sends an electrical signal to the furnace, turning it on. The furnace heats the air. When the sensors detect that the air temperature has reached a value higher than the low preset value, the thermostat stops the furnace. The last step (shutting off the furnace) is known as *feedback*, a critical component of any automated operation.

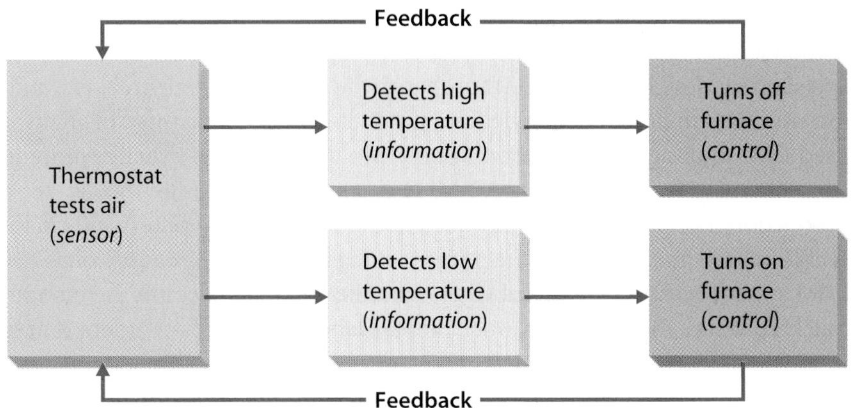

FIGURE 21.2

A Simple Automatic Control Mechanism

All automation includes feedback, information, sensors, and a control mechanism. A simple thermostat is an example of automation. Another example is Benetton's distribution center in Italy. Orders are received, items pulled from stock and packaged for shipment, and invoices prepared and transmitted, with no human intervention.

The big move to automate factories began during World War II. The shortage of skilled workers and the development of high-speed computers combined to bring about a tremendous interest in automation. Programmable automation (the use of computers to control machines) was introduced during this era, far outstripping conventional automation (the use of mechanical or electromechanical devices to control machines). The automobile industry began to use automatic machines for a variety of jobs. In fact, the term automation came into use in the 1950s in the automobile industry. The chemical and oil-refining industries also began to use computers to regulate production. During the 1990s, automation became a major element in the manufacture of computers and computer components, such as electronic chips and circuits. It is this computerized, or programmable, automation that presents the greatest opportunities and challenges for management today.

The impact of automation on people in the workplace is complex. In the short term, people whose jobs are automated may find themselves without a job. In the long term, however, more jobs are created than are lost. Nevertheless, not all companies are able to help displaced workers find new jobs, so the human costs are sometimes high. In the coal industry, for instance, automation has been used primarily in mining. The output per miner has risen dramatically from the 1950s on. The demand for coal, however, has decreased, and productivity gains resulting from automation have lessened the need for miners. Consequently, many workers have lost their jobs, and the industry has not been able to absorb them. In contrast, in the electronics industry, the rising demand for products has led to increasing employment opportunities despite the use of automation.[6]

Computer-assisted Manufacturing Current extensions of automation generally revolve around computer-assisted manufacturing. **Computer-assisted manufacturing** is technology that relies on computers to design or manufacture products. One type of computer-assisted manufacturing is *computer-aided design (CAD)*—the use of computers to design parts and complete products and to simulate performance so

computer-assisted manufacturing A technology that relies on computers to design or manufacture products that prototypes need not be constructed. Boeing uses CAD technology to study hydraulic tubing in its commercial aircraft. Japan's automotive industry uses it to speed up car design. GE used CAD to change the design of circuit breakers, and Benetton uses CAD to design new styles and products. Oneida Ltd., the table flatware firm, used CAD to design a new spoon in only two days.[7] CAD is usually combined with *computer-aided manufacturing (CAM)* to ensure that the design moves smoothly to production. The production computer shares the design computer's information and is able to have machines with the proper settings ready when production is needed. A CAM system is especially useful when reorders come in, because the computer can quickly produce the desired product, prepare labels and copies of orders, and send the product out to where it is wanted.

Closely aligned with this approach is *computer-integrated manufacturing (CIM)*. In CIM, CAD and CAM are linked together, and computer networks automatically adjust machine placements and settings to enhance both the complexity and the flexibility of scheduling. In settings that use these technologies, all manufacturing activities are controlled by the computer network. Because the network can access the company's other information systems, CIM is both a powerful and a complex management control tool.

Flexible manufacturing systems (FMS) usually have robotic work units or workstations, assembly lines, and robotic carts or some other form of computer-controlled transport system to move material as needed from one part of the system to another. FMS like the one at IBM's manufacturing facility in Lexington, Kentucky, rely on computers to coordinate and integrate automated production and materials-handling facilities. And Ford Motor Company recently used FMS to transform an English factory producing Ford Escorts into a Jaguar plant making its new Jaguar X-TYPE luxury cars. Using traditional methods, the plant would have been closed, its workers laid off, and the facility virtually rebuilt from the ground up. But, by using FMS, Ford was able to keep the plant open and running continuously while new equipment was being installed and its workers were being retrained in small groups.[8]

These systems are not without disadvantages, however. For example, because they represent fundamental change, they also generate resistance. Additionally, because of their tremendous complexity, CAD systems are not always reliable. CIM systems are so expensive that they raise the breakeven point for firms using them. This means that the firm must operate at high levels of production and sales to be able to afford the systems.

robot Any artificial device that is able to perform functions ordinarily thought to be appropriate for human beings

Robotics Another trend in manufacturing technology is computerized robotics. A **robot** is any artificial device that is able to perform functions ordinarily thought to be appropriate for human beings. Robotics refers to the science and technology of the construction, maintenance, and use of robots. The use of industrial robots has steadily increased since 1980 and is expected to continue to increase slowly as more companies recognize the benefits that accrue to users of industrial robots.[9]

Welding was one of the first applications for robots, and it continues to be the area for most applications. In second place and close behind is materials handling. Other applications include machine loading and unloading, painting and finishing, assembly, casting, and such machining applications as cutting, grinding, polishing, drilling, sanding, buffing, and deburring. DaimlerChrysler, for instance, recently replaced about two hundred welders with fifty robots on an assembly line and increased productivity about 20 percent. The use of robots in inspection work is increasing. They can check for cracks and holes, and they can be equipped with vision systems to perform visual inspections.

Robots are also beginning to move from the factory floor to all manner of other applications. The Dallas police used a robot to apprehend a suspect who had barricaded himself in an apartment building. The robot smashed a window and reached with its mechanical arm into the building. The suspect panicked and ran outside. At the Long Beach Memorial Hospital in California, brain surgeons are assisted by a robot arm that drills into the patient's skull with excellent precision. Some newer applications involve remote work. For example, the use of robot submersibles controlled from the surface can help divers in remote locations. Surveillance robots fitted with microwave sensors can do things that a human guard cannot do, such as "seeing" through nonmetallic walls and in the dark. In other applications, automated farming (called "agrimation") uses robot harvesters to pick fruit from a variety of trees.

Robots are also used by small manufacturers. One robot slices carpeting to fit the inside of custom vans in an upholstery shop. Another stretches balloons flat so that they can be spray-painted with slogans at a novelties company. At a jewelry company, a robot holds class rings while they are engraved by a laser. These robots are lighter, faster, stronger, and more intelligent than those used in heavy manufacturing and are the types that more and more organizations will be using in the future.

Service Technology

Service technology is also changing rapidly. And it, too, is moving more and more toward automated systems and procedures. In banking, for example, new technological breakthroughs led to automated teller machines and made it much easier to move funds between accounts or between different banks. Many people now have their paycheck deposited directly into a checking account from which many of their bills are then automatically paid. And credit card transactions by Visa customers are recorded and billed electronically.

Hotels use increasingly sophisticated technology to accept and record room reservations. Universities use new technologies to electronically store and provide access to books, scientific journals, government reports, and articles. Hospitals and other healthcare organizations use new forms of service technology to manage patient records, dispatch ambulances, and monitor vital signs. Restaurants use technology to record and fill customer orders, order food and supplies, and prepare food. Given the increased role that service organizations are playing in today's economy, even more technological innovations are certain to be developed in the years to come.[10]

Identify and describe three relatively new manufacturing technologies.

Identify as many examples as you can of how service technology at your college or university has changed in recent times.

Implementing Operations Systems Through Supply Chain Management

After operations systems have been properly designed and technologies developed, they must then be put into use by the organization. Their basic functional purpose is to control transformation processes to ensure that relevant goals are achieved in such areas as quality and costs. Operations management has a number of special purposes within this control framework, including purchasing and inventory management. Indeed, this area of management has become so important in recent years that a new term—*supply chain management*—has been coined. Specifically, **supply chain management** can be defined as the process of managing operations control, resource acquisition and purchasing, and inventory so as to improve overall efficiency and effectiveness.[11]

supply chain management The process of managing operations control, resource acquisition, and inventory so as to improve overall efficiency and effectiveness

Operations Management as Control

One way of using operations management as control is to coordinate it with other functions. Monsanto Company, for example, established a consumer products division that produces and distributes fertilizers and lawn chemicals. To facilitate control, the operations function was organized as an autonomous profit center. Monsanto finds this effective because its manufacturing division is given the authority to determine not only the costs of creating the product but also the product price and the marketing program.

In terms of overall organizational control, a division like the one used by Monsanto should be held accountable only for the activities over which it has decision-making authority. It would be inappropriate, of course, to make operations accountable for profitability in an organization that stresses sales and market share over quality and productivity. Misplaced accountability results in ineffective organizational control, to say nothing of hostility and conflict. Depending on the strategic role of operations, then, operations managers are accountable for different kinds of results. For example, in an organization using bureaucratic control, accountability will be spelled out in rules and regulations. In a decentralized system, it is likely to be understood and accepted by everyone.

Within operations, managerial control ensures that resources and activities achieve primary goals such as a high percentage of on-time deliveries, low unit-production cost, or high product reliability. Any control system should focus on the elements that are most crucial to goal attainment. For example, firms in which product quality is a major concern (as it is at Rolex) might adopt a screening control system to monitor the product as it is being created. If quantity is a higher priority (as it is at Timex), a postaction system might be used to identify defects at the end of the system without disrupting the manufacturing process itself.

Purchasing Management

purchasing management Buying materials and resources needed to produce products and services

Purchasing management is concerned with buying the materials and resources needed to create products and services. In many ways, purchasing is at the very heart of effective supply chain management. The purchasing manager for a retailer like Sears, Roebuck is responsible for buying the merchandise the store will sell. The purchasing manager for a manufacturer buys raw materials, parts, and machines needed by the organization. Large companies like GE, IBM, and Siemens have large purchasing departments.[12] The manager responsible for purchasing must balance a number of constraints. Buying too much ties up capital and increases storage costs. Buying too little might lead to shortages and high reordering costs. The manager must also make sure that the quality of what is purchased meets the organization's needs, that the supplier is reliable, and that the best financial terms are negotiated.

Many firms have recently changed their approach to purchasing as a means to lower costs and improve quality and productivity. In particular, rather than relying on hundreds or even thousands of suppliers, many companies are reducing their number of suppliers and negotiating special production-delivery arrangements.[13] For example, the Honda plant in Marysville, Ohio, found a local business owner looking for a new opportunity. They negotiated an agreement whereby he would start a new company to mount car stereo speakers into plastic moldings. He delivers finished goods to the plant three times a day, and Honda buys all he can manufacture. Thus he has a stable sales base, Honda has a local and reliable supplier, and both companies benefit.

Inventory Management

Inventory control, also called *materials control,* is essential for effective operations management. The four basic kinds of inventories are *raw materials, work-in-process, finished-goods,* and *in-transit* inventories. As shown in Table 21.1, the sources of control over these inventories are as different as their purposes. Work-in-process inventories, for example, are made up of partially completed products that need further processing; they are controlled by the shop-floor system. In contrast, the quantities and costs of finished-goods inventories are under the control of the overall production

inventory control Managing the organization's raw materials, work in process, finished goods, and products in transit

TABLE 21.1

Inventory Types, Purposes, and Sources of Control

JIT is a recent breakthrough in inventory management. With JIT inventory systems, materials arrive just as they are needed. JIT therefore helps an organization control its raw materials inventory by reducing the amount of space it must devote to storage.

Type	Purpose	Source of Control
Raw materials	Provide the materials needed to make the product.	Purchasing models and systems
Work in process	Enable overall production to be divided into stages of manageable size.	Shop-floor control systems
Finished goods	Provide ready supply of products on customer demand and enable long, efficient production runs.	High-level production scheduling systems in conjunction with marketing
In transit (pipeline)	Distribute products to customers.	Transportation and distribution control systems

scheduling system, which is determined by high-level planning decisions. In-transit inventories are controlled by the transportation and distribution systems.

Like most other areas of operations management, inventory management changed notably in recent years. One particularly important breakthrough is the **just-in-time (JIT) method**. First popularized by the Japanese, the JIT system reduces the organization's investment in storage space for raw materials and in the materials themselves. Historically, manufacturers built large storage areas and filled them with materials, parts, and supplies that would be needed days, weeks, and even months in the future. A manager using the JIT approach orders materials and parts more often and in smaller quantities, thereby reducing investment in both storage space and actual inventory. The ideal arrangement is for materials to arrive just as they are needed—or just in time.[14]

just-in-time (JIT) method An inventory system that has necessary materials arriving as soon as they are needed (just in time) so that the production process is not interrupted

Recall our example about the small firm that assembles stereo speakers for Honda and delivers them three times a day, making it unnecessary for Honda to carry large quantities of the speakers in inventory. In an even more striking example, Johnson Controls makes automobile seats for DaimlerChrysler and ships them by small truckloads to a DaimlerChrysler plant seventy-five miles away. Each shipment is scheduled to arrive two hours before it is needed. Clearly, the JIT approach requires high levels of coordination and cooperation between the company and its suppliers. If shipments arrive too early, DaimlerChrysler has no place to store them. If they arrive too late, the entire assembly line may have to be shut down, resulting in enormous expense. When properly designed and used, the JIT method controls inventory very effectively.

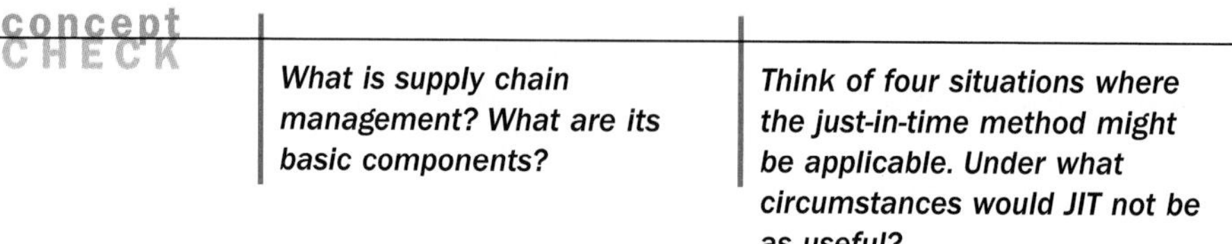

Managing Total Quality

Quality and productivity have become major determinants of business success or failure today and are central issues in managing organizations.[15] But, as we will see, achieving higher levels of quality is not an easy accomplishment. Simply ordering that quality be improved is about as effective as waving a magic wand.[16] The catalyst for its emergence as a mainstream management concern was foreign business, especially Japanese. And nowhere was it more visible than in the auto industry. During the energy crisis in the late 1970s, many people bought Toyotas, Hondas, and Nissans because they were more fuel-efficient than U.S. cars. Consumers soon found, however, that not only were the Japanese cars more fuel-efficient, they were also of higher quality than U.S. cars. Parts fit together better, the trim work was neater, and the cars were more reliable. Thus, after the energy crisis subsided, Japanese cars remained formidable competitors because of their reputation for quality.

The Meaning of Quality

The American Society for Quality Control defines **quality** as the totality of features and characteristics of a product or service that bear on its ability to satisfy stated or implied needs.[17] Quality has several different attributes. Table 21.2 lists eight basic dimensions that determine the quality of a particular product or service. For example, a product that has durability and is reliable is of higher quality than a product with less durability and reliability.

quality The totality of features and characteristics of a product or service that bear on its ability to satisfy stated or implied needs

Quality is also relative. For example, a Lincoln is a higher-grade car than a Ford Taurus, which, in turn, is a higher-grade car than a Ford Focus. The difference in quality stems from differences in design and other features. The Focus, however, is considered a high-quality car relative to its engineering specifications and price. Likewise, the Taurus and Lincoln may also be high-quality cars, given their standards and prices. Thus quality is both an absolute and a relative concept.

Quality is relevant for both products and services. Although its importance for products like cars and computers was perhaps recognized first, service firms ranging from airlines to restaurants have also come to see that quality is a vitally important determinant of their success or failure. Service quality, as we will discuss later in this chapter, has thus also become a major competitive issue in U.S. industry today.[18]

The Importance of Quality

To help underscore the importance of quality, the U.S. government created the **Malcolm Baldrige Award**, named after the former secretary of commerce who

Malcolm Baldrige Award Named after a former secretary of commerce, this prestigious award is given to firms that achieve major quality improvements

TABLE 21.2

Eight Dimensions of Quality

These eight dimensions generally capture the meaning of quality, which is a critically important ingredient to organizational success today. Understanding the basic meaning of quality is a good first step to managing it more effectively.

1. *Performance*. A product's primary operating characteristic; examples are automobile acceleration and a television's picture clarity
2. *Features*. Supplements to a product's basic functioning characteristics, such as power windows on a car
3. *Reliability*. A probability of not malfunctioning during a specified period
4. *Conformance*. The degree to which a product's design and operating characteristics meet established standards
5. *Durability*. A measure of product life
6. *Serviceability*. The speed and ease of repair
7. *Aesthetics*. How a product looks, feels, tastes, and smells
8. *Perceived quality*. As seen by a customer

Source: Reprinted by permission of *Harvard Business Review*. Exhibit from "Competing on the Eight Dimensions of Quality," by David A. Garvin, November/December 1987.

championed quality in U.S. industry. The award, administered by an agency of the Commerce Department, is given annually to firms that achieve major improvements in the quality of their products or services. In other words, the award is based on changes in quality, as opposed to absolute quality. In addition, numerous other quality awards have been created. For example, the Rochester Institute of Technology and *USA Today* award their Quality Cup award not to entire organizations but to individual teams of workers within organizations. Quality is also an important concern for individual managers and organizations for three very specific reasons: competition, productivity, and costs.[19]

Competition Quality has become one of the most competitive points in business today. Ford, DaimlerChrysler, General Motors, and Toyota, for example, each argues that its cars and trucks are higher in quality than the cars and trucks of the others. And American, United, and Continental Airlines each claims that it provides the best and most reliable service. Indeed, it seems that virtually every U.S. business has adopted quality as a major point of competition. Thus a business that fails to keep pace may find itself falling behind not only foreign competition but also other U.S. firms.[20]

Productivity Managers have also come to recognize that quality and productivity are related. In the past, many managers thought that they could increase output (productivity) only by decreasing quality. Managers today have learned the hard way that such an assumption is almost always wrong. If a firm installs a meaningful quality enhancement program, three things are likely to result. First, the number of defects is likely to decrease, causing fewer returns from customers. Second, because the number of defects goes down, resources (materials and people) dedicated to reworking flawed output will be decreased. Third, because making employees responsible for quality reduces the need for quality inspectors, the organization is able to produce more units with fewer resources.

Costs Improved quality also lowers costs. Poor quality results in higher returns from customers, high warranty costs, and lawsuits from customers injured by faulty products. Future sales are lost because of disgruntled customers. An organization with quality problems often has to increase inspection expenses just to catch defective products. We noted in Chapter 20, for example, how at one point Whistler Corporation was using 40 percent of its workforce just to fix poorly assembled radar detectors made by the other 60 percent.[21]

Total Quality Management

total quality management (TQM) (quality assurance) A strategic commitment by top management to change its whole approach to business in order to make quality a guiding factor in everything it does

Once an organization makes a decision to enhance the quality of its products and services, it must then decide how to implement this decision. The most pervasive approach to managing quality has been called **total quality management,** or **TQM (sometimes called quality assurance)**—a real and meaningful effort by an organi-

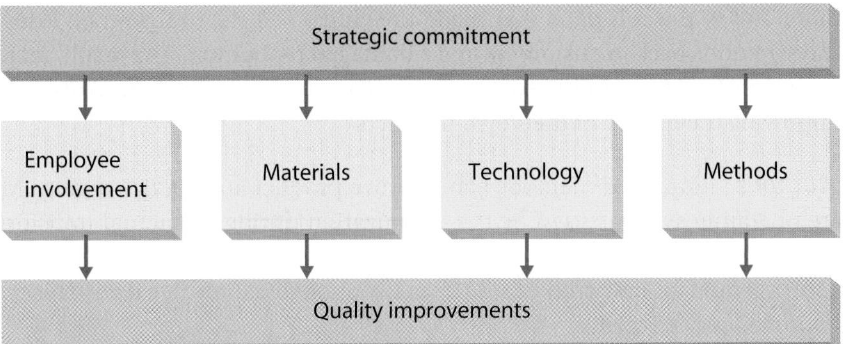

FIGURE 21.3

Total Quality Management

Quality is one of the most important issues facing organizations today. Total quality management, or TQM, is a comprehensive effort to enhance an organization's product or service quality. TQM involves the five basic dimensions shown here. Each is important and must be addressed effectively if the organization expects to truly increase quality.

zation to change its whole approach to business in order to make quality a guiding factor in everything the organization does.[22] Figure 21.3 highlights the major ingredients in TQM.

Strategic Commitment The starting point for TQM is a strategic commitment by top management. Such commitment is important for several reasons. First, the organizational culture must change to recognize that quality is not just an ideal but an objective goal that must be pursued.[23] Second, a decision to pursue the goal of quality carries with it some real costs—for expenditures such as new equipment and facilities. Thus, without a commitment from top management, quality improvement will prove to be just a slogan or gimmick, with little or no real change.

Employee Involvement Employee involvement is another critical ingredient in TQM. Virtually all successful quality enhancement programs involve making the person responsible for doing the job responsible for making sure it is done right.[24] By definition, then, employee involvement is a critical component in improving quality. Work teams, discussed in Chapter 19, are common vehicles for increasing employee involvement.

Technology New forms of technology are also useful in TQM programs. Automation and robots, for example, can often make products with higher precision and better consistency than can people. Investing in higher-grade machines capable of doing jobs more precisely and reliably often improves quality. For example, Nokia has achieved notable improvements in product quality by replacing many of its machines with new equipment. Similarly, most U.S. auto and electronics firms make regular investments in new technology to help boost quality.

Materials Another important part of TQM is improving the quality of the materials that organizations use. Suppose that a company that assembles stereos buys chips and circuits from another company. If the chips have a high failure rate, consumers will return defective stereos to the company whose nameplate appears on

value-added analysis The comprehensive evaluation of all work activities, materials flows, and paperwork to determine the value that they add for customers

benchmarking The process of learning how other firms do things in an exceptionally high quality manner

them, not to the company that made the chips. The stereo firm then loses in two ways: refunds back to customers and a damaged reputation. As a result, many firms have increased the quality requirements they impose on their suppliers as a way of improving the quality of their own products.

Methods Improved methods can improve product and service quality. Methods are operating systems used by the organization during the actual transformation process. American Express Company, for example, has found ways to cut its approval time for new credit cards from twenty-two to only five days. This results in improved service quality.

TQM Tools and Techniques

Beyond the strategic context of quality, managers can also rely on several specific tools and techniques for improving quality. Among the most popular today are value-added analysis, benchmarking, outsourcing, reducing cycle times, ISO 9000:2000 and ISO 14000, and statistical quality control. Another, Six Sigma, is discussed in *Technology Toolkit.*

Value-Added Analysis **Value-added analysis** is the comprehensive evaluation of all work activities, materials flows, and paperwork to determine the value that they add for customers. Such an analysis often reveals wasteful or unnecessary activities that can be eliminated without jeopardizing customer service. For example, during a value-added analysis, Hewlett-Packard determined that its contracts were unnecessarily long, confusing, and hard to understand. The firm subsequently cut its standard contract form down from twenty to two pages and experienced an 18 percent increase in its computer sales.

Effective total quality management requires major commitments from an organization. Thorough and rigorous quality checks and inspections are often a fundamental part of quality management. But managers who pay only lip service to inspections, like the managers illustrated here checking water quality, should not be surprised later when they discover major quality problems throughout their organization. Only by using objective and rigorous statistical quality control measures can the firm be assured of high-quality products and services.

Benchmarking **Benchmarking** is the process of learning how other firms do things in an exceptionally high quality manner. Some approaches to benchmarking are simple and straightforward. For example, Xerox routinely buys copiers made by other firms and takes them apart to see how they work. This enables the firm to stay abreast of improvements and changes its competitors are using. When Ford was planning the newest version of the Taurus, it identified the four hundred features customers identified as being most important to them. It then found the competing cars that did the best job on each feature. Ford's goal was to equal or surpass each of its competitors on those four hundred features. Other benchmarking strategies are more indirect. For example,

TECHNOLOGY toolkit

Is an Ounce of Prevention Really Worth a Pound of Cure?

Six Sigma is a popular and effective quality control tactic. It works by reducing service errors or manufacturing defects. Yet skeptics are proposing a different solution: Use those errors to increase customer satisfaction.

Six Sigma was developed in the 1980s for Motorola. The tool can be used by manufacturing or service organizations. The Six Sigma method tries to eliminate mistakes. Although firms rarely obtain Six Sigma quality, it does provide a challenging target.

"Sigma" refers to a standard deviation, so a "Six Sigma" defect rate is 6 standard deviations above the mean rate; 1 sigma quality would produce 690,000 errors per million items. Three sigmas is challenging–66,000 errors per million. Six Sigma is obtained when a firm produces a mere 3.4 mistakes per million.

Implementing Six Sigma requires making corrections until errors virtually disappear. At GE, the technique has saved the firm $8 billion in three years. GE is now teaching its customers, including Wal-Mart and Dell, about the approach. Quality consultant Gregory H. Watson claims, "Six Sigma might be the maturation of everything we've learned over the last 100 years about quality."

Or not. Customers are pleased by error-free services or products, but they give higher satisfaction ratings to firms that respond well after a mistake. "A customer whose complaint is satisfied will actually use more of your service or product than she did before the unhappy service incident," says consultant Peggy Morrow. Quality control at some firms now focuses on "recovery management." One hotel chain is even identifying a list of "harmless" mistakes that it can deliberately commit, to create an opportunity to make it up to disgruntled customers. Morrow recommends that every firm have a low-cost, token gesture of apology, such as a first-class upgrade for a delayed flight. Managers should listen sympathetically and offer the apology quickly and cheerfully.

"After all," as *Fortune* writer Michael Schrage claims, "it's customer perception–not Deming-trained statisticians–that ultimately determines product and service quality. Fixing your mistakes may prove a better business investment than preventing them." If that is the case, we can reverse the Ben Franklin saying. According to Schrage, it should now say, "An ounce of recovery can be worth a pound of prevention."

"A customer whose complaint is satisfied will actually use more of your service or product than she did before the unhappy service incident."

– Peggy Morrow, customer service consultant*

References: Michael Arndt, "Quality Isn't Just for Widgets," *BusinessWeek*, July 22, 2002, www.businessweek.com on December 9, 2002; Michael Arndt, "Where Precision Is Life or Death," *BusinessWeek*, July 22, 2002, www.businessweek.com on December 9, 2002; Michael Schrage, "Make No Mistake?" *Fortune*, December 11, 2001, www.fortune.com on February 17, 2003; Peggy Morrow, "Recovering from Service Mistakes," *Inc.*, May 13, 2002, www.inc.com on February 17, 2003 (*quote); "Table: The Nuts and Bolts of Six Sigma," *BusinessWeek*, July 22, 2002, www.businessweek.com on December 9, 2002.

many firms study how L.L. Bean manages its mail-order business, how Disney recruits and trains employees, and how FedEx tracks packages for applications they can employ in their own businesses.[25]

Outsourcing Another innovation for improving quality is outsourcing. **Outsourcing** is the process of subcontracting services and operations to other firms that can perform them cheaper or better. If a business performs each and every one of its own administrative and business services and operations, it is almost certain to be

outsourcing Subcontracting services and operations to other firms that can perform them cheaper or better

Outsourcing involves subcontracting services and operations to other firms. While Sears does some of its own manufacturing, it outsources a portion of it as well. These workers, for instance, are employed by Pentair, a Mississippi firm. While they work for Pentair, they are making power tools to be sold under the Craftsman label at Sears.

doing at least some of them in an inefficient or low-quality manner. If those areas can be identified and outsourced, the firm will save money and realize a higher-quality service or operation.[26] For example, until recently Eastman Kodak handled all of its own computing operations. Now, however, those operations are subcontracted to IBM, which handles all of Kodak's computing. The result is higher-quality computing systems and operations at Kodak for less money than it was spending before.

Reducing Cycle Time Another popular TQM technique is reducing cycle time. **Cycle time** is the time needed by the organization to develop, make, and distribute products or services.[27] If a business can reduce its cycle time, quality will often improve. A good illustration of the power of cycle time reduction comes from General Electric. At one point the firm needed six plants and three weeks to produce and deliver custom-made industrial circuit breaker boxes. By analyzing and reducing cycle time, the same product can now be delivered in three days, and only a single plant is involved. Table 21.3 identifies a number of basic suggestions that have helped companies reduce the cycle time of their operations. For example, GE found it better to start from scratch with a remodeled plant. GE also wiped out the need for approvals by eliminating most managerial positions and set up teams as a basis for organizing work. Stressing the importance of the schedule helped Motorola build a new plant and start production of a new product in only eighteen months.

cycle time The time needed by the organization to accomplish activities such as developing, making, and distributing products or services

ISO 9000:2000 A set of quality standards created by the International Organization for Standardization and revised in 2000

ISO 14000 A set of standards for environmental performance

ISO 9000:2000 and ISO 14000 Still another useful technique for improving quality is ISO 9000. **ISO 9000:2000** refers to a set of quality standards created by the International Organization for Standardization; the standards were revised and updated in 2000. These standards cover such areas as product testing, employee training, record keeping, supplier relations, and repair polices and procedures. Firms that want to meet these standards apply for certification and are audited by a firm chosen by the organization's domestic affiliate (in the United States, this is the American National Standards Institute). These auditors review every aspect of the firm's business operations in relation to the standards. Many firms report that merely preparing for an ISO 9000 audit has been helpful. Many firms today, including General Electric, DuPont, Eastman Kodak, British Telecom, and Philips Electronics are urging—or in some cases requiring—that their suppliers achieve ISO 9000 certification.[28] All told, more than 140 countries have adopted ISO 9000 as a national standard, and more than 400,000 certificates of compliance have been issued. **ISO 14000** is an extension of the same concept to environmental performance. Specifically, ISO 14000 requires that firms document how they are using raw materials more efficiently, managing pollution, and reducing their impact on the environment.

TABLE 21.3

Guidelines for Increasing the Speed of Operations

Many organizations today are using speed for competitive advantage. Listed in the table are six common guidelines that organizations follow when they want to shorten the time they need to get things accomplished. Although not every manager can do each of these things, most managers can do at least some of them.

1. Start from scratch. It is usually easier than trying to do what the organization does now faster.
2. Minimize the number of approvals needed to do something. The fewer people who have to approve something, the faster approval will get done.
3. Use work teams as a basis for organization. Teamwork and cooperation work better than individual effort and conflict.
4. Develop and adhere to a schedule. A properly designed schedule can greatly increase speed.
5. Do not ignore distribution. Making something faster is only part of the battle.
6. Integrate speed into the organization's culture. If everyone understands the importance of speed, things will naturally get done quicker.

Source: From *Fortune*, February 13, 1989.

Statistical Quality Control A final quality control technique is **statistical quality control (SQC)**. As the term suggests, SQC is concerned primarily with managing quality.[29] Moreover, it is a set of specific statistical techniques that can be used to monitor quality. *Acceptance sampling* involves sampling finished goods to ensure that quality standards have been met. Acceptance sampling is effective only when the correct percentage of products that should be tested (for example, 2, 5, or 25 percent) is determined. This decision is especially important when the test renders the product useless. Flash cubes, wine, and collapsible steering wheels, for example, are consumed or destroyed during testing. Another SQC method is *in-process sampling*. In-process sampling involves evaluating products during production so that needed changes can be made. The painting department of a furniture company might periodically check the tint of the paint it is using. The company can then adjust the color as necessary to conform to customer standards. The advantage of in-process sampling is that it allows problems to be detected before they accumulate.

statistical quality control (SQC) A set of specific statistical techniques that can be used to monitor quality; includes acceptance sampling and in-process sampling

concept CHECK

What are the basic components of total quality management, and what are the common tools used to manage quality?

Identify and describe three product families that illustrate the concept of absolute versus relative quality.

Managing Productivity

Although the current focus on quality by American companies is a relatively recent phenomenon, managers have been aware of the importance of productivity for several years. The stimulus for this attention was a recognition that the gap between productivity in the United States and productivity in other industrialized countries was narrowing. This section describes the meaning of productivity and underscores its importance. After summarizing recent productivity trends, we suggest ways that organizations can increase their productivity.

The Meaning of Productivity

productivity An economic measure of efficiency that summarizes what is produced relative to resources used to produce it

In a general sense, **productivity** is an economic measure of efficiency that summarizes the value of outputs relative to the value of the inputs used to create them.[30] Productivity can be and often is assessed at different levels of analysis and in different forms.

Levels of Productivity By level of productivity we mean the units of analysis used to calculate or define productivity. For example, *aggregate productivity* is the total level of productivity achieved by a country. *Industry productivity* is the total productivity achieved by all the firms in a particular industry. *Company productivity,* just as the term suggests, is the level of productivity achieved by an individual company. *Unit and individual productivity* refer to the productivity achieved by a unit or department within an organization and the level of productivity attained by a single person.

Forms of Productivity There are many different forms of productivity. *Total factor productivity* is defined by the following formula:

$$\text{Productivity} = \frac{\text{Outputs}}{\text{Inputs}}$$

Total factor productivity is an overall indicator of how well an organization uses all of its resources, such as labor, capital, materials, and energy, to create all of its products and services. The biggest problem with total factor productivity is that all the ingredients must be expressed in the same terms—dollars (it is difficult to add hours of labor to number of units of a raw material in a meaningful way). Total factor productivity also gives little insight into how things can be changed to improve productivity. Consequently, most organizations find it more useful to calculate a partial productivity ratio. Such a ratio uses only one category of resource. For example, labor productivity could be calculated by this simple formula:

$$\text{Labor Productivity} = \frac{\text{Outputs}}{\text{Direct Labor}}$$

This method has two advantages. First, it is not necessary to transform the units of input into some other unit. Second, this method provides managers with specific insights into how changing different resource inputs affects productivity. Suppose that an organization can manufacture 100 units of a particular product with 20 hours of direct labor. The organization's labor productivity index is 100/20, or 5 (5 units per labor hour). Now suppose that worker efficiency is increased (through one of the ways to be discussed later in this chapter) so that the same 20 hours of labor result in the manufacture of 120 units of the product. The labor productivity index increases to 120/20, or 6 (6 units per labor hour), and the firm can see the direct results of a specific managerial action.

The Importance of Productivity

Managers consider it important that their firm maintains high levels of productivity for a variety of reasons. Firm productivity is a primary determinant of an organization's level of profitability and, ultimately, of its ability to survive. If one organization is more productive than another, it will have more products to sell at lower prices and have more profits to reinvest in other areas. Productivity also partially determines people's standard of living within a particular country. At an economic level, businesses consume resources and produce goods and services. The goods and services created within a country can be used by that country's own citizens or exported for sale in other countries. The more goods and services the businesses within a country can produce, the more goods and services the country's citizens will have. Even goods that are exported result in financial resources' flowing back into the home country. Thus the citizens of a highly productive country are likely to have a notably higher standard of living than are the citizens of a country with low productivity.

Productivity Trends

The United States has one of the highest levels of productivity in the world. For instance, in the time it takes a U.S. worker to produce $100 worth of goods, Japanese workers produce about $68 worth. But, as discussed in *The World of Management,* this may (or may not) be as good as it sounds. Sparked by gains made in other countries, however, U.S. business has begun to focus more attention on productivity.[31] Indeed, this was a primary factor in the decisions made by U.S. businesses to retrench, retool, and become more competitive in the world marketplace. For example, General Electric's dishwasher plant in Louisville has cut its inventory requirements by 50 percent, reduced labor costs from 15 percent to only 10 percent of total manufacturing costs, and cut product development time in half. As a result of these kinds of efforts, productivity trends have now leveled out, and U.S. workers are generally maintaining their lead in most industries.[32]

One important factor that has hurt U.S. productivity indices has been the tremendous growth of the service sector in the United States. Although this sector grew, its productivity levels did not. One part of this problem relates to measurement. For example, it is fairly easy to calculate the number of tons of steel produced at a steel mill and divide it by the number of labor hours used; it is more difficult to determine the output of an attorney or a certified public accountant. Still, virtually everyone agrees that improving service sector productivity is the next major hurdle facing U.S. business.[33]

Figure 21.4 illustrates manufacturing productivity growth since 1970 in terms of annual average percentage of increase. As you can see, that growth slowed during the 1970s but began to rise again in the late 1980s. Some experts believe that productivity in both the United States and abroad will continue to improve at even more impressive rates. Their confidence rests on the technology's potential ability to improve operations.

THE WORLD OF management

Pity the Rich, Overworked Americans

When multinational firms discuss cross-cultural barriers frankly, the difference between the work habits of Americans and those of their overseas counterparts are typically mentioned. Studies show that U.S. workers work longer hours than do Europeans. In addition, Americans' work hours are increasing, while Europeans' are declining. Yet there is no consensus about why the differences exist.

The economic indicators paint a mixed picture. The United States is far more productive than any country in Europe, per person. The closest countries are Ireland and Denmark, where each person's share of gross domestic product (GDP) is 81 percent of the average American's share. The least productive is Portugal, whose rate is 49 percent. But, when measuring productivity as GDP per hour worked, Belgium, France, and the Netherlands all top the United States, and Ireland, Austria, Denmark, and Germany come very close.

"Europeans want to enjoy some of their wealth in the form of greater leisure."

– Martin Wolf, economist and author for London's Financial Times*

Part of the difference in the two measures is the unemployment rate—6 percent in the United States in December 2002; 7.8 percent for the European Union. The difference is also demographic, because a young population has fewer citizens of working age.

Some experts claim that the most important cause is culture. They note, for example, that Mediterranean countries are among the least productive. Economist Martin Wolf writes, "I find the U.S. addiction to ceaseless work appalling. . . . Europeans want to enjoy some of their wealth in the form of greater leisure." Worker surveys show that most Europeans would prefer to reduce their work hours, whereas Americans would like to increase theirs.

Economists Linda A. Bell and Richard B. Freeman suggest another reason—differing career expectations in the United States and Europe. Bell and Freeman believe that workers in the United States see more upside potential to hard work, in the form of pay raises and promotions, than do European workers. On average, Bell and Freeman find that increases in working time raise future earnings. Also, Americans have less job security and fewer jobless benefits than do Europeans, so fear of losing their job motivates them to work longer and harder.

Are Americans better off, or are Europeans? It depends on one's preference—the chance to work hard and earn more, or the opportunity for leisure.

References: Gene Koretz, "Why Americans Work So Hard," *BusinessWeek*, June 6, 2001, www.businessweek.com on February 17, 2003; Martin Wolf, "Hard Work Versus Joie de Vivre," *Financial Times* (London), February 20, 2002, p. 15 (*quote); Polly LaBarre, "How to Lead a Rich Life," *Fast Company*, March 2003, www.fastcompany.com on February 17, 2003; "Unemployment Rates in Nine Countries," Bureau of Labor Statistics website, www.bls.gov on February 17, 2003.

Improving Productivity

How does a business or industry improve its productivity? Numerous specific suggestions made by experts generally fall into two broad categories: improving operations and increasing employee involvement.

Improving Operations One way that firms can improve operations is by spending more on research and development. R&D spending helps identify new products, new uses for existing products, and new methods for making products. Each of these contributes to productivity. For example, Bausch & Lomb almost missed the boat on extended-wear contact lenses because the company had neglected R&D. When it became apparent that its major competitors were almost a year ahead of Bausch & Lomb in developing the new lenses, management made R&D a top-priority concern. As a result, the company made several scientific breakthroughs, shortened the time needed to introduce new products, and greatly enhanced both total sales and profits—and all with a smaller workforce than the company used to employ. Even though other countries are greatly increasing their R&D spending, the United States continues to be the world leader in this area.

Another way firms can boost productivity through operations is by reassessing and revamping their transformation facilities. We noted earlier how one of GE's modernized plants does a better job than six antiquated ones. Just building a new factory is no guarantee of success, but IBM, Ford, Caterpillar, and many other businesses have achieved dramatic productivity gains by revamping their production facilities. Facilities refinements are not limited to manufacturers. Most McDonald's restaurants now have drive-through windows, and many have moved soft-drink dispensers out to the restaurant floor so that customers can get their own drinks. Each of these moves is an attempt to increase the speed with which customers can be served, and thus to increase productivity.

FIGURE 21.4

Manufacturing and Service Productivity Growth Trends

Both manufacturing productivity and service productivity in the United States continue to grow, although manufacturing productivity is growing at a faster pace. Total productivity, therefore, also continues to grow.

Source: U.S. Bureau of Labor Statistics.

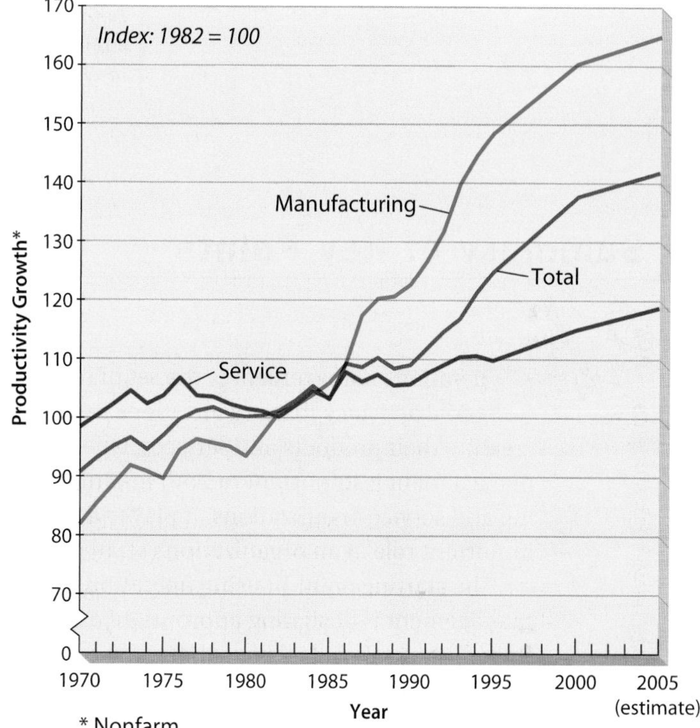

Increasing Employee Involvement The other major thrust in productivity enhancement has been toward employee involvement. We noted earlier that participation can enhance quality. So, too, can it boost productivity. Examples of this involvement are an individual worker's being given a bigger voice in how she does her job, a formal agreement of cooperation between management and labor, and total involvement throughout the organization. GE eliminated most of the supervisors at its one new circuit breaker plant and put control in the hands of workers.

Another method popular in the United States is increasing the flexibility of an organization's workforce by training employees to perform a number of different jobs. Such cross-training allows the firm to function with fewer workers because workers can be transferred easily to areas where they are most needed. For example, at one Motorola plant, 397 of 400 employees have learned at least two skills under a similar program.

Rewards are essential to making employee involvement work. Firms must reward people for learning new skills and using them proficiently. At Motorola, for example, workers who master a new skill are assigned for five days to a job requiring them to use that skill. If they perform with no defects, they are moved to a higher pay grade, and then they move back and forth between jobs as they are needed. If there is a performance problem, they receive more training and practice. This approach is fairly new, but preliminary indicators suggest that it can increase productivity significantly. Many unions resist such programs because they threaten job security and reduce a person's identification with one skill or craft.

concept CHECK

Define productivity and identify the different levels at which it can be assessed.	*Will improving productivity always be worth the time and money that might be required? Why or why not?*

Summary of Key Points

ACE self-test

business.college.hmco.com/students

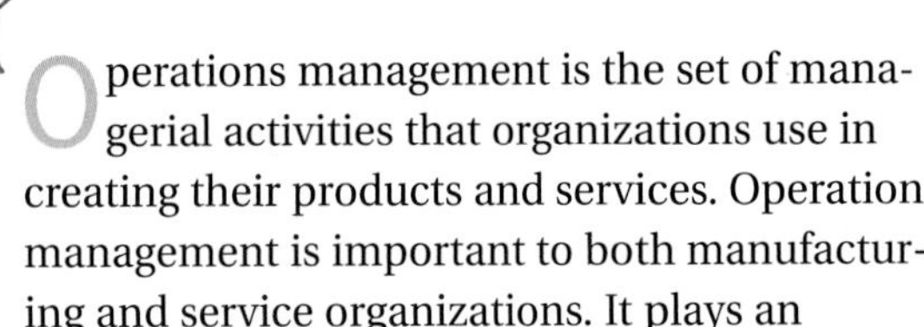

Operations management is the set of managerial activities that organizations use in creating their products and services. Operations management is important to both manufacturing and service organizations. It plays an important role in an organization's strategy.

The starting point in using operations management is designing appropriate operations systems. Key decisions that must be made as part of operations systems design relate to product and service mix, capacity, and facilities.

Technology also plays an important role in quality. Automation is especially important today. Numerous computer-aided manufacturing techniques are widely practiced. Robotics is also a growing area. Technology is as relevant to service organizations as to manufacturing organizations.

After an operations system has been designed and put in place, it must then be implemented. Major areas of interest during the use of operations systems are purchasing and inventory management. Supply chain management is a comprehensive view of managing all of these activities in a more efficient manner.

Quality is a major consideration for all managers today. Quality is important because it affects competition, productivity, and costs. Total quality management is a comprehensive, organizationwide effort to enhance quality through a variety of avenues.

Productivity is also a major concern to managers. Productivity is a measure of how efficiently an organization is using its resources to create products or services. The United States is a world leader in individual productivity, but firms still work to achieve productivity gains.

Discussion Questions

Questions for Review

1. What is the relationship of operations management to overall organizational strategy? Where do productivity and quality fit into that relationship?

2. Describe three basic decisions that must be addressed in the design of operations systems. For each decision, what information do managers need to make that decision?
3. What are some approaches to facilities layout? How do they differ from one another? How are they similar?
4. What is total quality management? What are the major characteristics of TQM?

Questions for Analysis

5. Is operations management linked most closely to corporate-level, business-level, or functional strategies? Why or in what way?
6. "Automation is bad for the economy, because machines will eventually replace almost all human workers, creating high unemployment and poverty." Do you agree or disagree? Explain your answer.
7. Some quality gurus claim that high-quality products or services are those that are error free. Others claim that high quality exists when customers' needs are satisfied. Still others claim that high-quality products or services must be innovative. Do you subscribe to one of these views? If not, how would you define quality? Explain how the choice of a quality definition affects managers' behavior.

Questions for Application

8. How can a service organization use techniques from operations management? Give specific examples from your college or university (a provider of educational services).
9. Think of a firm that, in your opinion, provides a high-quality service or product. What attributes of the product or service give you the perception of high quality? Do you think that everyone would agree with your judgment? Why or why not?
10. What advice would you give to the manager of a small local service business, such as a pizza parlor or dry cleaner, about improvements in quality and productivity? Would your advice differ if the small business were a manufacturing company—for example, a T-shirt printing firm? Describe any differences you would expect to see.

BUILDING EFFECTIVE communication SKILLS

Exercise Overview

Communication skills refer to a manager's ability to convey ideas and information to others and to receive ideas and information from others. This exercise develops your communication skills in addressing issues of quality.

Exercise Background

Assume that you are a customer service manager of a large auto parts distributor. The general manager of a large auto dealer, one of your best customers, wrote the following letter. It will be your task to write a letter in response.

> Dear Customer Service Manager:
>
> On the first of last month, ABC Autos submitted a purchase order to your firm. Attached to this letter is a copy of the order. Unfortunately, the parts shipment that we received from you did not contain every item on the order. Further, that fact was not noted on the packing slip that accompanied your shipment, and

ABC was charged for the full amount of the order. To resolve the problem, please send the missing items immediately. If you are unable to do so by the end of the week, please cancel the remaining items and refund the overpayment. In the future, if you ship a partial order, please notify us at that time and do not bill for items not shipped.

I look forward to your reply and a resolution to my problem.

Sincerely,

A. N. Owner, ABC Autos

Attachment: Purchase Order 00001

Exercise Task

1. Write an answer to the above letter, assuming that you now have the parts available.
2. How would your answer differ if ABC Autos were not a valued customer?
3. How would your answer differ if you found out that the parts were in the original shipment but had been stolen by one of your delivery personnel?
4. How would your answer differ if you found out that the owner of ABC Autos made a mistake and the order was filled correctly by your workers?
5. Based on your answers to the questions above, what are the important components of responding effectively to a customer's quality complaint—the tone of the letter, expressing an apology, suggesting a solution, and so on. Explain how you used these components in your response.

BUILDING EFFECTIVE diagnostic SKILLS

Exercise Overview

As noted in the chapter, the quality of a product or service is relative to price and expectations. A manager's diagnostic skills—the ability to visualize responses to a situation—can be useful in helping to position quality relative to price and expectations.

Exercise Background

Think of a recent occasion when you purchased a tangible product—for example, clothing, electronic equipment, luggage, or professional supplies—which you subsequently came to feel was of especially high quality. Now recall another product that you evaluated as having appropriate or adequate quality, and a third that you felt had low or poor quality. Next, recall parallel experiences involving purchases of services. Examples might include an airline, train, or bus trip; a meal in a restaurant; a haircut; or an oil change for your car.

Finally, recall three experiences in which both products and services were involved. Examples might include having questions answered by someone about a product you were buying or returning a defective or broken product for a refund or warranty repair. Try to recall instances in which there was an apparent disparity between product and service quality (for instance, a poor-quality product accompanied by outstanding service or a high-quality product accompanied by mediocre service).

Exercise Task

Using the nine examples identified above, do the following:

1. Assess the extent to which the quality you associated with each was a function of price and your expectations.
2. Could the quality of each be improved without greatly affecting price? If so, how?
3. Can high-quality service offset only adequate or even poor product quality? Can outstanding product quality offset only adequate or even poor-quality service?

BUILDING EFFECTIVE conceptual SKILLS

business.college.hmco.com/students

Exercise Overview

A manager's conceptual skills are his or her ability to think in the abstract. This exercise asks you to investigate the relationship between quality and financial performance.

Exercise Background

Is there a relationship between quality and performance? Among those who believe that the relationship exists, some think that high-quality products lead to high earnings, whereas others believe that only firms with high performance can afford to have high quality. A third group believes that there is no relationship.

Exercise Task

1. Find a list of recent winners of the Malcolm Baldrige Award for quality. Choose three firms from the list and investigate the recent financial performance of their parent company, using earnings per share (EPS) as the measure of performance.
2. Do the winners have high performance—for example, did their EPS rise?
3. If any of the winners show high performance, did the high performance come before or after the award (or both before and after)?
4. What do the answers to these questions tell you about the relationship between high performance and quality?

CHAPTER CLOSING case

AMERICA'S (CIVILIAN) MILITARY

"... using a contractor ... saves you from having to use troops, so troops can focus on war fighting."

— Colonel Thomas W. Sweeney, U.S. Army*

In February 2003 headlines proclaimed that the U.S. military was deploying thousands of soldiers and sailors to the Middle East in preparation for war. The largest and most powerful military force in the world placed 156,000 troops within striking distance of Iraq. Over 40,000 Australian and British personnel reinforced the American troops. But, behind the headlines, thousands of civilian employees and hundreds of contractors were providing support to the war effort.

The U.S. military, by law, is structured into two separate commands: the operational and the administrative. The two separate commands increase wartime efficiency by relieving combat commanders of responsibility for administrative matters. Although only military personnel can fulfill operational tasks, civilians may serve in the administrative chain of command. The military relies on civilian support because of the complexity of modern war-fighting operations. Armies simply cannot produce and maintain all of the necessary equipment and skills.

Costs are a factor, too. America's military capabilities are limited by the resources of its Department of Defense (DoD). In 2002 the federal budget gave $309 billion to national defense. This amount may seem astronomical, but military spending in the United States represents about 4 percent of its gross domestic product. Finally, the use of civilians is a matter of efficiency. During peacetime, the size of the military can decline, but when conflicts loom, the forces must be rapidly expanded. Use of independent contractors allows the military to grow without long-term obligations, much as corporations might employ "temps."

One important role for civilians lies in the research and manufacturing capability of defense-related industries. The primary suppliers for the U.S. military are American defense-sector firms such as Northrop Grumman, Boeing, Lockheed Martin, General Dynamics, and Raytheon. For example, the U.S. Navy needs aircraft carriers, but it does not need to build them for itself. The navy can hire a corporation to design and make its ships. The U.S. military purchases items ranging from uniforms to radios to weapons to satellites.

The U.S. military also calls upon civilian employees of the Department of Defense. Altogether, there are 800,000 DoD civilians, as compared to 1.5 million active-duty personnel and 900,000 reserve members. Edwin Dorn, undersecretary of defense, says, "DoD's civilian employees are partners in our national defense. They [perform jobs and] sometimes go into harm's way to support our military forces." Civilian workers can fill hundreds of support positions: engineer, firefighter, nurse, photographer, janitor, musician, accountant, chaplain, computer programmer, construction worker, cook, dentist, mechanic, lawyer, scientist, secretary, barber, welder, or truck driver.

In November 2001 Secretary of the Army Thomas E. White announced a reorganization that would include reducing the number of civilians employed by the army. Any function that was "not inherently governmental" should be outsourced. The army would save money by choosing the company that submitted the lowest bid for that job. "The Army must focus its energies and talents on our core competencies and seek to obtain other needed products or services from the private sector where it makes sense," White claimed. "Moreover, the Army must quickly free up resources for the global war on terrorism." In practice, however, there are questions about the plan. Would civilians be willing to deploy? Would civilians risk their lives, guard military secrets, or understand the needs of soldiers? Are low bidders likely to be conscientious—a real concern when lives are at stake?

The most controversial of the Pentagon's schemes to supplement its forces is the use of private military contractors, or "soldiers for hire." The U.S. government hires contractors to serve as military advisors in places like Nigeria and Colombia, where it would be politically impractical to send American troops. The administration has used contractors to avoid congressional or U.N. limits on the use of force. Yet, when the employees fight alongside American soldiers and sailors, they are not obliged to take orders or follow military codes of conduct. Their sole responsibility is to their employer, not to their country. At times, catastrophe has resulted. Local forces in Croatia, trained by U.S.-backed contractors, committed ethnic cleansing, killing hundreds of noncombatants.

Colonel Thomas W. Sweeney claims, "The main reason for using a contractor is that it saves you from having to use troops, so troops can focus on war fighting. It's cheaper." But Representative Jan Schakowsky, a Democrat from Illinois, disagrees. "Are we outsourcing in order to avoid public scrutiny, controversy or embarrassment? . . . American taxpayers already pay $300 billion a year to fund the world's most powerful military. Why should they have to pay a second time in order to privatize our operations?"

Case Questions

1. National defense is a service, not a tangible good. Therefore, what techniques and technologies can the military use to improve its operations? Based on what you read in the case or what you know from personal experience, is it in fact using those techniques and technologies? If so, describe them. If not, tell why not.
2. What other organizations, besides the military, might find that outsourcing could potentially hurt productivity and quality? Why does this occur?
3. In your opinion, is the U.S. military forced to make a tradeoff between productivity and quality in its use of civilians? Or is the military capable of increasing both productivity and quality simultaneously through the use of civilians? Explain.

Case References

"Department of Defense Budget for FY 2001," February 7, 2000, *Defense Link*, www.defenselink.mil on February 18, 2003; Gary Sheftick, "Army Realigns Headquarters, Centralizes Base Operations," *Army Link*, December 18, 2001, www.dtic.mil on February 18, 2003; Gerry J. Gilmore, "DoD Civilians: Partners in America's Defense," *Defense Link*, May 1996, www.defenselink.mil on February 18, 2003; Leslie Wayne, "America's For-Profit Secret Army," *New York Times*, October 13, 2002, pp. BU1, BU10, BU11 (*quote p. BU10); "Military Expenditures—Percent of GDP," *The World Factbook 2002*, CIA website, www.cia.gov on February 18, 2003; "More Than 150,000 U.S. Troops in Place," CNN, February 13, 2003, www.cnn.com on February 18, 2003; Stanley Holmes, "A Call to Arms Awakens Defense," *BusinessWeek*, October 1, 2001, www.businessweek.com on February 18, 2003.

Chapter Notes

1. Brent Schlender, "How Intel Took Moore's Law from Idea to Ideology," *Fortune*, October 27, 2002, www.fortune.com on February 17, 2003 (*quote); Brent Schlender, "Intel's $10 Billion Gamble," *Fortune*, November 11, 2002, pp. 90–102; Cliff Edwards, "A Weaker David to Intel's Goliath," *BusinessWeek*, October 21, 2002, p. 48; John Markoff and Steve Lohr, "Intel's Huge Bet Turns Iffy," *New York Times*, September 29, 2002, pp. BU1, BU12, BU13.
2. Paul M. Swamidass, "Empirical Science: New Frontier in Operations Management Research," *Academy of Management Review*, October 1991, pp. 793–814.
3. See Anil Khurana, "Managing Complex Production Processes," *Sloan Management Review*, Winter 1999, pp. 85–98.
4. For an example, see Robin Cooper and Regine Slagmulder, "Develop Profitable New Products with Target Costing," *Sloan Management Review*, Summer 1999, pp. 23–34.
5. Joan Woodward, *Industrial Organization: Theory and Practice* (London: Oxford University Press, 1965).
6. See "Tight Labor? Tech to the Rescue," *BusinessWeek*, March 20, 2000, pp. 36–37.
7. "Computers Speed the Design of More Workaday Products," *Wall Street Journal*, January 18, 1985, p. 25.
8. "New Plant Gets Jaguar in Gear," *USA Today*, November 27, 2000, p. 4B.
9. "Thinking Machines," *BusinessWeek*, August 7, 2000, pp. 78–86.
10. James Brian Quinn and Martin Neil Baily, "Information Technology: Increasing Productivity in Services," *Academy of Management Executive*, 1994, vol. 8, no. 3, pp. 28–37.
11. See Charles J. Corbett, Joseph D. Blackburn, and Luk N. Van Wassenhove, "Partnerships to Improve Supply Chains," *Sloan Management Review*, Summer 1999, pp. 71–82, and Jeffrey K. Liker and Yen-Chun Wu, "Japanese Automakers, U.S. Suppliers, and Supply-Chain Superiority," *Sloan Management Review*, Fall 2000, pp. 81–93.
12. See "Siemens Climbs Back," *BusinessWeek*, June 5, 2000, pp. 79–82.
13. See M. Bensaou, "Portfolios of Buyer-Supplier Relationships," *Sloan Management Review*, Summer 1999, pp. 35–44.
14. "Just-in-Time Manufacturing Is Working Overtime," *BusinessWeek*, November 8, 1999, pp. 36–37.
15. "Quality—How to Make It Pay," *BusinessWeek*, August 8, 1994, pp. 54–59.
16. Rhonda Reger, Loren Gustafson, Samuel DeMarie, and John Mullane, "Reframing the Organization: Why Implementing Total Quality Is Easier Said Than Done," *Academy of Management Review*, 1994, vol. 19, no. 3, pp. 565–584.
17. Ross Johnson and William O. Winchell, *Management and Quality* (Milwaukee: American Society for Quality Control, 1989). See also Carol Reeves and David Bednar, "Defining Quality: Alternatives and Implications," *Academy of Management Review*, 1994, vol. 19, no. 3, pp. 419–445, and C. K. Prahalad and M. S. Krishnan, "The New Meaning of Quality in the Information Age," *Harvard Business Review*, September–October 1999, pp. 109–120.
18. "Quality Isn't Just for Widgets," *BusinessWeek*, July 22, 2002, pp. 72–73.
19. W. Edwards Deming, *Out of the Crisis* (Cambridge, Mass.: MIT Press, 1986).
20. David Waldman, "The Contributions of Total Quality Management to a Theory of Work Performance," *Academy of Management Review*, 1994, vol. 19, no. 3, pp. 510–536.
21. Joel Dreyfuss, "Victories in the Quality Crusade," *Fortune*, October 10, 1988, pp. 80–88.
22. Thomas Y. Choi and Orlando C. Behling, "Top Managers and TQM Success: One More Look After All These Years," *Academy of Management Executive*, vol. 11, no. 1, 1997, pp. 37–48.
23. James Dean and David Bowen, "Management Theory and Total Quality: Improving Research and Practice Through Theory Development," *Academy of Management Review*, 1994, vol. 19, no. 3, pp. 392–418.
24. Edward E. Lawler, "Total Quality Management and Employee Involvement: Are They Compatible?" *Academy of Management Executive*, 1994, vol. 8, no. 1, pp. 68–79.
25. Jeremy Main, "How to Steal the Best Ideas Around," *Fortune*, October 19, 1992, pp. 102–106.
26. See James Brian Quinn, "Strategic Outsourcing: Leveraging Knowledge Capabilities," *Sloan Management Review*, Summer 1999, pp. 8–22.
27. Thomas Robertson, "How to Reduce Market Penetration Cycle Times," *Sloan Management Review*, Fall 1993, pp. 87–96.
28. Ronald Henkoff, "The Hot New Seal of Quality," *Fortune*, June 28, 1993, pp. 116–120. See also Mustafa V. Uzumeri, "ISO 9000 and Other Metastandards: Principles for Management Practice?" *Academy of Management Executive*, vol. 11, no. 1, 1997, pp. 21–28.
29. Paula C. Morrow, "The Measurement of TQM Principles and Work-related Outcomes," *Journal of Organizational Behavior*, July 1997, pp. 363–376.
30. John W. Kendrick, *Understanding Productivity: An Introduction to the Dynamics of Productivity Change* (Baltimore: Johns Hopkins, 1977).
31. "Study: USA Losing Competitive Edge," *USA Today*, April 25, 1997, p. 9D.
32. "Why the Productivity Revolution Will Spread," *BusinessWeek*, February 14, 2000, pp. 112–118. See also "Productivity Grows in Spite of Recession," *USA Today*, July 29, 2002, pp. 1B, 2B, and "Productivity's Second Wind," *BusinessWeek*, February 17, 2003, pp. 36–37.
33. Michael van Biema and Bruce Greenwald, "Managing Our Way to Higher Service-Sector Productivity," *Harvard Business Review*, July–August 1997, pp. 87–98.

22

Managing Information and Information Technology

CHAPTER OUTLINE

Information and the Manager
- The Role of Information in the Manager's Job
- Characteristics of Useful Information
- Information Management as Control
- Building Blocks of Information Technology

Types of Information Systems
- User Groups and System Requirements
- Major Systems by Level
- The Internet

Managing Information Systems
- Creating Information Systems
- Integrating Information Systems
- Using Information Systems
- Managing Information Security
- Understanding Information System Limitations

The Impact of Information Systems on Organizations
- Leaner Organizations
- More Flexible Operations
- Increased Collaboration
- More Flexible Work Sites
- Improved Management Processes
- Changed Employee Behaviors

LEARNING OBJECTIVES

After studying this chapter, you should be able to:

1 ***Describe the role and importance of information in the manager's job and identify the basic building blocks of information technology.***

OPENING INCIDENT

Just as managers are becoming used to the changes that e-mail brought, they are being asked to embrace another new communications technology: instant messaging. Although instant messaging (IM) is better known as a tool for personal communications, it is catching on at work, too. One estimate claims that 65 million businesspeople are using IM today, and 207 million will do so by 2006.

Instant messaging brings the benefits of e-mail, including the ability to communicate quickly. In fact, IM goes further than e-mail in this regard because it enables real-time online conversations. Communications exchanges can happen more rapidly in IM than in e-mail, avoiding the problems caused when e-mail messages cross at the same time. "Chat is the Internet version of an intercom. You can summon a person quickly," claims manager Gregg Gallagher.

Another benefit of instant messaging is the perception it creates of being present in a face-to-face conversation, unlike e-mail, which is perceived as similar to writing a note. IM is ideal for applications like customer help lines, because shoppers who get immediate answers to their questions are more likely to complete a purchase.

2

Discuss the basic factors that determine an organization's information technology needs and describe the basic types of information systems used by organizations.

3

Discuss how information systems can be managed.

4

Describe how information systems affect organizations.

"Isn't e-mail fast enough?"

*—Erica Adams, partner, The Blueshirt Group**

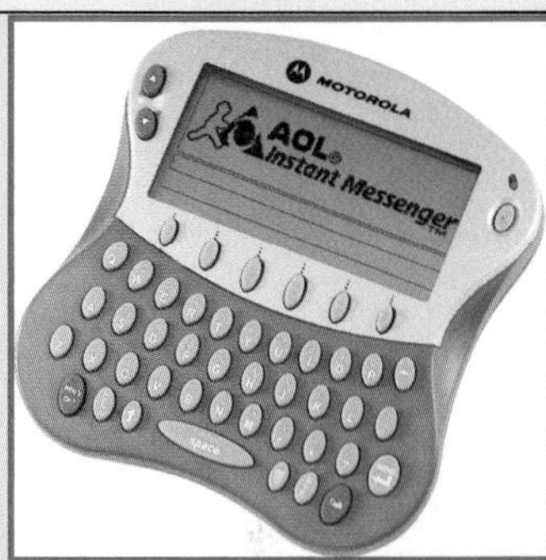

One of Motorola's newest products offers instant messaging through AOL.

Some large corporations are building their own IM system, rather than relying on such widely used products as AOL, Microsoft, or Yahoo! One reason is security. "Companies don't feel comfortable sending messages out through their firewalls to a server that somebody else has control over," says Sun engineer John Tang, who develops Awarenex IM software. Jennifer Bélissent, a Sun product manager, adds, "There is a risk of exposing your networks to viruses and spam." Yes, that is right. That plague of e-mail, the unwanted mass mailings called "spam," has also invaded instant messaging.

Proprietary systems can offer features not available on public networks, such as "presence detection." This allows users to see the status of their colleagues, whether they are on the phone, online, or out of the office, for example. A "polling" feature asks for answers from a group of respondents. Hubbub, a wireless IM system for computers and PDAs, is programmed to play a distinct sound or tune as each user logs on and off, so that everyone can hear others' "presence." Ellen Isaacs, who helped design Hubbub, claims, "The sound ends up fading into the background. So you hear people's tunes coming and going just as you would hear co-workers walk by your office."

On the downside, many users report that it is irritating to have tones or pop-up windows disturb their concentration. Executive Tom Mallon calls it "a screaming post-it." Erica Abrams, a partner in an investor relations firm, tried IM but quit using it. "It bothered me too much," Abrams claims. "My clients are satisfied with my services already. I'm not sure I need to be more responsive than that. Isn't e-mail fast enough?"

Supervisors worry that employees find it too easy to socialize with IM, leading to lower productivity. Certainly some employees are exchanging messages during dull meetings, which managers tend to frown on. Labor economist David Autor says, "My strong suspicion is that there are no further productivity gains to immediate communication that haven't already been realized by e-mail."

Tom Austin, a technology consultant, believes that instant messaging's biggest threat to productivity is the distraction it affords. Workers may be tempted to do too much multitasking, leading to mistakes. Austin claims that using instant messaging while working is equivalent to talking on a cell phone while driving. "It can create an accident," he says. "You're not fully engaged."

Yet instant messaging is so popular that companies are finding that they must offer it or risk having sensitive company information spread across public chat forums. To more effectively manage IM, firms are employing the same kinds of security measures they use for e-mail, such as encryption and archiving. One feature of Awarenex is a virtual "good-bye wave," which discreetly lets the receiver know that the sender is ready to end the conversation. A short message appears, followed by a string of disappearing dots. According to Awarenex developer Tang, "That gives a signal that the person wants to end the conversation, but it leaves a window for you to ask one last question or make one final remark."

The software has become such a good substitute for real face-to-face conversations that, at some companies, employees will send instant messages to coworkers in the same room or across the hall. One manager—who lives in a large house—claims he even uses it to call his teenagers to supper.[1]

As the opening vignette clearly demonstrates, information and communications technology continues to evolve at an almost breathtaking pace. And, indeed, today's businesses rely on information management in ways that could not have been foreseen as recently as just a decade ago. Managers now turn to digital technology as an integral part of organizational resources and as a means of conducting everyday business. Every major firm's business activities—such as designing services, ensuring product delivery and cash flow, evaluating employees, and creating advertising—are linked to information systems. Effective information management requires a commitment of resources to establish, maintain, and upgrade as new technologies emerge.

This chapter is about advances made by organizations doing this. We describe the role and importance of information to managers, the characteristics of useful information, and information management as control, and we identify the basic building blocks of information systems. We discuss the general and specific determinants of information technology needs. We then discuss the primary types of information technology used in organizations and describe how this technology is managed.

Information and the Manager

Information has always been an integral part of every manager's job. Its importance, however, and therefore the need to manage it, continue to grow at a rapid clip. To appreciate this trend, we need to understand the role of information in the

Organizations rely on information that needs to be accurate, timely, complete, and relevant. Consider, for example, Sameday.com, an Internet firm based in Southern California. Sameday.com handles inventory and delivery for a roster of web businesses in the Los Angeles area. The firm prides itself on getting shipments to customers as close to "now" as possible. But in order to do this, these Sameday.com drivers must have information that tells them exactly what needs to be delivered, where, when, and in what sequence.

manager's job, characteristics of useful information, and the nature of information management as control.

The Role of Information in the Manager's Job

In Chapters 1 and 18 we highlighted the role of communication in the manager's job. Given that information is a vital part of communication, it follows that management and information are closely related. Indeed, it is possible to conceptualize management itself as a series of steps involving the reception, processing, and dissemination of information. As illustrated in Figure 22.1, the manager is constantly bombarded with data and information (the difference between the two is noted later).

Suppose that Bob Henderson is an operations manager for a large manufacturing firm. During the course of a normal day, Bob receives many different pieces of information from formal and informal conversations and meetings, telephone calls, personal observation, e-mails, letters, reports, memos, the Internet, and trade publications. He gets a report from a subordinate that explains exactly how to solve a pressing problem, so he calls the subordinate and tells him to put the solution into effect immediately. He scans a copy of a report prepared for another manager, sees that it has no relevance to him, and discards it. He sees a *Wall Street Journal* article that he knows Sara Ferris in marketing should see, so he passes it on to her. He gets an electronic summary of yesterday's production report, but because he knows he will not need to analyze it for another week, he stores it. He observes a worker doing a job incorrectly and realizes that the incorrect method is associated with a mysterious quality problem that someone told him about last week.

A key part of information-processing activity is differentiating between data and information. **Data** are raw figures and facts reflecting a single aspect of reality. The facts that a plant has 35 machines, that each machine is capable of producing 1,000 units of output per day, that current and projected future demand for the

data Raw figures and facts reflecting a single aspect of reality

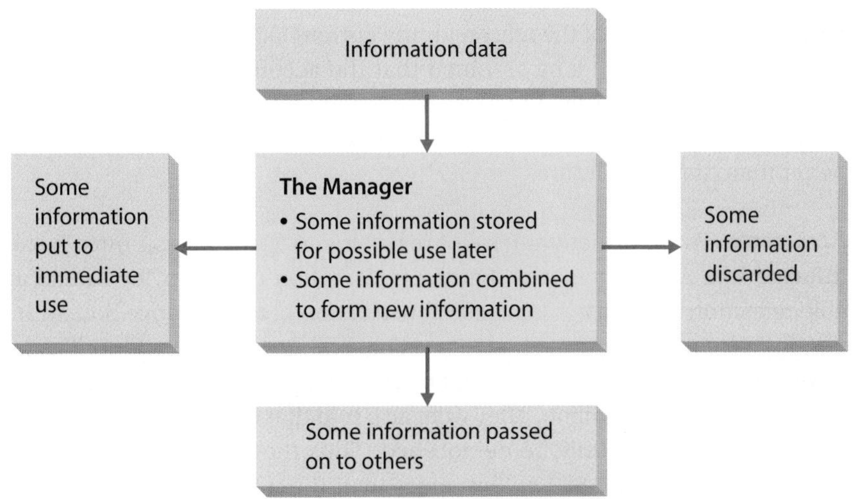

FIGURE 22.1

Managers as Information Processors

Managers who receive information and data must decide what to do with it. Some is stored for possible later use, and other information is combined to form new information. Subsequently, some is used immediately, some is passed on to others, and some is discarded.

Managers at Ben & Jerry's rely heavily on information to make sure that they have the right flavors of ice cream in the right locations at the right time. But to be of value, of course, the information has to be accurate, timely, complete, and relevant. After all, if a customer wants to buy a carton of Cherry Garcia at their local market today, its in Ben & Jerry's best interests that the store has an ample supply!

units is 30,000 per day, and that workers sufficiently skilled to run the machines make $20 an hour are data.

Information is data presented in a way or form that has meaning.[2] Thus combining and summarizing the four pieces of data given above provides information: The plant has excess capacity and is therefore incurring unnecessary costs. Information has meaning to a manager and provides a basis for action. The plant manager might use the information and decide to sell four machines (perhaps keeping one as a backup) and transfer five operators to other jobs.

A related term is **information technology,** or **IT**. Information technology refers to the resources used by an organization to manage information that it needs in order to carry out its mission. IT may consist of computers, computer networks, telephones, fax machines, and other pieces of hardware. In addition, IT involves software that facilitates the system's ability to manage information in a way that is useful for managers.[3]

The grocery industry uses data, information, and information technology to automate inventory and checkout facilities. The average Kroger store, for example, carries over 21,000 items. Computerized scanning machines at the checkout counters can provide daily sales figures for any product. These numbers alone are data and have little meaning in their pure form. But information is created from these data by another computerized system. Using this IT system, managers can identify how any given product or product line is selling in any number of stores over any meaningful period of time.

information Data presented in a way or form that has meaning

information technology (IT) Refers to the resources used by an organization to manage information that it needs in order to carry out its mission

Characteristics of Useful Information

What factors differentiate between information that is useful and information that is not useful? In general, information is useful if it is accurate, timely, complete, and relevant. Indeed, part of the reason for the current lack of confidence in business is that stakeholders have long assumed that the accounting information that businesses provided was "true." But myriad scandals and controversies have shown that accounting procedures and reporting formats can vary to make things look much better than they actually are.[4]

accurate information Provides a valid and reliable reflection of reality

Accurate For information to be of real value to a manager, it must be **accurate information**. Accuracy means that the information must provide a valid and reliable reflection of reality. A Japanese construction company once bought information from a consulting firm about a possible building site in London. The Japanese were told that the land, which would be sold in a sealed-bid auction, would attract bids of close to $250 million. They were also told that the land currently held an old building that could easily be demolished. Thus the Japanese bid $255 million—which ended up being $90 million more than the next-highest bid. And, to make matters worse, a few days later the British government declared the building historic, preempting any thought of demolition. Clearly, the Japanese acted on information that was less than accurate.

Breakthroughs in information technology continue to come at a breakneck pace. At Peribit, for example, Amit Singh continues to look for ways to move more data over corporate networks faster and at lower cost. His technology allows networks to compress repetitive information, thus reducing bandwidth requirements. In just over a year, Peribit has snagged such major clients as ChevronTexaco and Network Appliance.

Timely Information also needs to be timely. Timeliness does not necessarily mean speediness; it means only that information needs to be available in time for appropriate managerial action. What constitutes timeliness is a function of the situation facing the manager. When Marriott was gathering information for a new hotel project, managers allowed themselves a six-month period for data collection. They felt this would give them an opportunity to do a good job of getting the information they needed while not delaying things too much. In contrast, Marriott's computerized reservation and accounting system can provide a manager today with last night's occupancy level at any Marriott facility.[5]

Complete Information must tell a complete story for it to be useful to a manager. If it is less than **complete information**, the manager is likely to get an inaccurate or distorted picture of reality. For example, managers at Kroger used to think that house-brand products were more profitable than national brands because they yielded higher unit profits. On the basis of this information, they gave house brands a great deal of shelf space and centered promotional activities around them. As Kroger's managers became more sophisticated in understanding their information, however, they realized that national brands were actually more profitable over time because they sold many more units than house brands during any given period of time. Hence, although a store might sell 10 cans of Kroger coffee in a day, with a profit of 50 cents per can (total profit of $5), it would also sell 15 cans of Maxwell House with a profit of 40 cents per can (total profit of $6) and 10 vacuum bags of Starbucks coffee with a profit of $1 per bag (total profit of $10). With this more complete picture, managers could do a better job of selecting the right mix of Kroger, Maxwell House, and Starbucks coffee to display and promote.

complete information Provides the manager with all the information he or she needs

Relevant Finally, information must be relevant if it is to be useful to managers. **Relevant information**, like **timely information**, is defined according to the needs and circumstances of a particular manager. Operations managers need information on costs and productivity; human resource managers need information on hiring needs and turnover rates; and marketing managers need information on sales projections and advertising rates. As Wal-Mart contemplates countries as possible expansion opportunities, it gathers information about local regulations, customs, and so forth. But the information about any given country is not really relevant until the decision is made to enter that market.

relevant information Information that is useful to managers in their particular circumstances for their particular needs

timely information Available in time for appropriate managerial action

Information Management as Control

The manager also needs to appreciate the role of information in control—indeed, to see information management as a vital part of the control process in the organization.[6] As already noted, managers receive much more data and information than they need or can use. Accordingly, deciding how to handle each piece of data and information involves a form of control.[7] *The World of Management* illustrates this point with its description of how Blockbuster uses information to control its international operations.

The control perspective on information management is illustrated in Figure 22.2. Information enters, is used by, and leaves the organization. For example,

THE WORLD OF management

Blockbuster Controls Its European Operations

Blockbuster is the number-one video chain, with more than 8,000 locations around the world. Three million customers visit its outlets every day. The company has 2,600 international stores. In the United Kingdom, for example, Blockbuster has 700 stores and is the largest rental firm. Its widespread operations and the size and complexity of the firm have created a need for sophisticated information systems.

Blockbuster controls its European operations from a regional headquarters in Uxbridge, U.K. Each country is led by a country manager, who supervises multiple district managers. The district managers oversee a dozen or so stores. At each level of the firm, there is a need for information about sales, inventory, cash flow, and pricing. Under Blockbuster's old system, district managers phoned each store with a five-minute daily report. They would write down the information, calculate totals, type a paper report, and send it by overnight mail to country headquarters. Managers at the country level repeated the process for reports to the European regional office. In addition, each store manager sent a written copy of each transaction every day. The process could take fifty or more person-hours daily. Even worse, the final reports took seventy-two hours to create. That meant that top-level managers never had real-time information to use in decision making.

"Guessing the demand for a film . . . is easy enough when you only have a few stores. But when you're bulk purchasing across an entire continent, . . . the logistics . . . are very different. . . ."

– XcelleNet report on Blockbuster*

Blockbuster managers needed to get tighter control of costs and more timely information. They turned to XcelleNet, a maker of software products that gather information from bar-code scanners at retail outlets, store it in databases, and then automatically transmit it to centralized computers for analysis. The fifty-person-hour process now takes no time, and the reports can be generated in an hour. The user-friendly system requires only one technician and needs no help desk at all.

The cost and time savings were certainly appreciated at Blockbuster. But, more importantly, XcelleNet understood how better information could help Blockbuster master its strategic challenges. XcelleNet reports state, "Guessing the demand for a film . . . is easy enough when you only have a few stores. But when you're bulk purchasing across an entire continent, with all the inherent tastes and cultural variations it entails, the logistics of Blockbuster Entertainment are very different from the problems faced by the store manager in the '80s."

References: "About Us," Blockbuster website, www.blockbuster.com on February 19, 2003; "Case Studies: Blockbuster Entertainment," XcelleNet website (*quote), www.xcellenet.com on December 10, 2002; "Provider Summary: XcelleNet, Inc.," KnowledgeStorm, *Fast Company website*, partners.knowledgestorm.com on February 19, 2003.

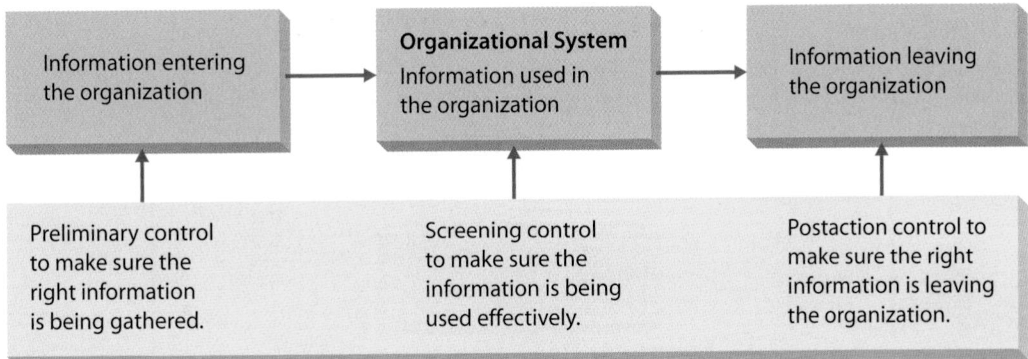

FIGURE 22.2

Information Management as Control

Information management can be part of the control system via preliminary, screening, and postaction control mechanisms. Because information from the environment is just as much a resource as raw materials or finances, it must be monitored and managed to promote its efficient and effective utilization.

Marriott took great pains to make sure it got all the information it needed to plan for and enter the economy lodging business. Once this preliminary information was gathered, it was necessary to make sure that the information was made available in the proper form to everyone who needed it. In general, the effort to ensure that information is accurate, timely, complete, and relevant is a form of screening control. Finally, Marriott wanted to make sure that its competitors did not learn about its plans until the last possible minute. It also wanted to time and orchestrate news releases, public announcements, and advertising for maximum benefit. These efforts thus served a postaction control function.

Building Blocks of Information Technology

Information technology is generally of two types—manual or computer based. All information technology, and the systems that it defines, has five basic parts. Figure 22.3 diagrams these parts for a computer-based information technology system. The *input medium* is the device that is used to add data and information into the system. For example, the optical scanner at Kroger enters point-of-sale information. Likewise, someone can enter data through a keyboard, with a mouse, using a bar code reader, or from other computers or the Internet.

The data that are entered into the system typically flow first to a processor. The *processor* is the part of the system that is capable of organizing, manipulating, sorting, or performing calculations or other transformations with the data. Most systems also have one or more *storage devices*—places where data can be stored for later use. Floppy disks, hard drives, CD-ROMs, and optical disks are common forms of storage devices. As data are transformed into usable information, the resultant information must be communicated to the appropriate person by means of an *output medium*. Common ways to display output are through video displays, printers, and fax machines, as well as through transmission to other computers or web pages.

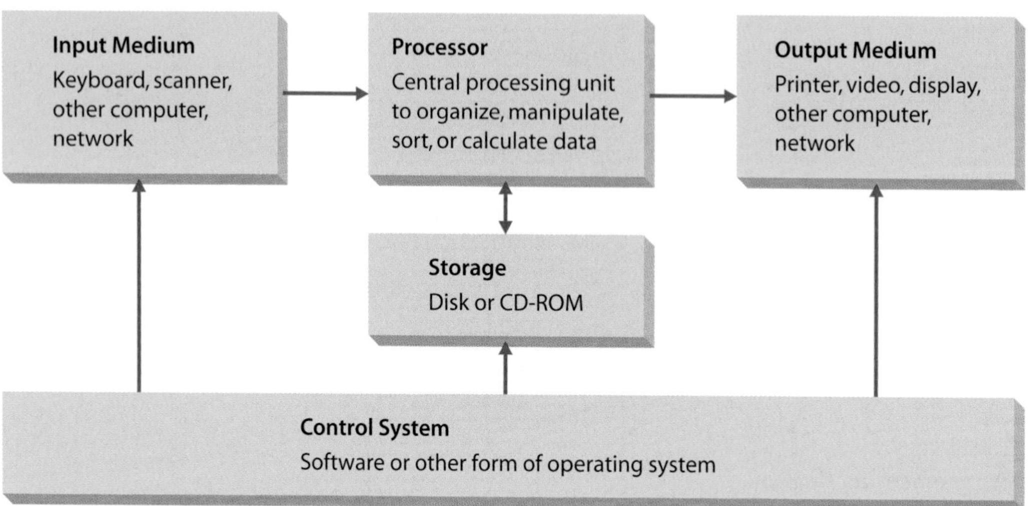

FIGURE 22.3

Building Blocks of a Computer-based Information System

Computer-based information systems generally have five basic components—an input medium, a processor, an output medium, a storage device, and a control system. Noncomputer-based systems use parallel components for the same basic purposes.

Finally, the entire information technology system is operated by a *control system*—most often software of one form or another. Simple systems in smaller organizations can use off-the-shelf software. Microsoft Windows and DOS are general operating systems that control more specialized types of software. Microsoft Word and WordPerfect are popular systems for word processing. Lotus 123 and Excel are popular spreadsheet programs, and dBase and Access are frequently used for database management. Of course, elaborate systems of the type used by large businesses require a special, customized operating system. When organizations start to link computers together in a network, the operating system must be even more complex. Enterprise resource planning networks are also increasingly being used for this purpose.

As we note earlier, information technology systems need not be computerized. Many small organizations still function quite well with a manual system using paper documents, routing slips, paper clips, file folders, file cabinets, and a single personal computer. Increasingly, however, even small businesses are abandoning their manual systems for computerized ones. As hardware prices continue to drop and software becomes more and more powerful, computerized information systems will likely be within the reach of any business that wants to have one.

concept CHECK

What are the characteristics of useful information?	*Identify examples of both data and information that you have seen or heard in the last twenty-four hours.*

Types of Information Systems

In a sense, the phrase *information system* may be a misnomer. It suggests that there is one system, but in fact a firm's employees will have different interests, job responsibilities, and decision-making requirements. One information system cannot accommodate such a variety of information requirements. Instead, "the information system" is a complex of several information systems that share information while serving different levels of the organization, different departments, or different operations.

User Groups and System Requirements

To understand the different kinds of information systems that organizations use, it is instructive to first consider user groups and system requirements. This perspective is illustrated in Figure 22.4. In general, there are four user groups, each with different system requirements: first-line, middle, and top managers, and knowledge workers. Knowledge workers represent a special user category. **Knowledge workers** are specialists, usually professionally trained and certified—engineers, scientists, information technology specialists, psychologists—who rely on information technology to design new products or create new business processes.

knowledge workers Specialists, usually professionally trained and certified—engineers, scientists, information technology specialists, psychologists—who rely on information technology to design new products or create new business processes

Managers at Different Levels Because they work on different kinds of problems, first-line, middle, and top managers, as well as knowledge workers, have different information needs. First-line (or operational) managers, for example, need information to oversee the day-to-day details of their department or projects. Middle managers need summaries and analyses for setting intermediate and long-range goals for the department or projects under their supervision. Top management analyzes broader trends in the economy, the business environment, and overall company performance, in order to conduct long-range planning for the entire organization. Finally, knowledge workers need special information for conducting technical projects.

Regardless of their business or industry, managers are always on the alert for new ways to use information. This dairy farmer, for instance, relies on an information system to help him assess the best times of the day to collect milk from each of his cows. This system has resulted in increased output from his farm and higher profits for his dairy business.

Consider the various information needs for a flooring manufacturer. Sales managers (first-line managers) supervise salespeople, assign territories to the sales force, and handle customer service and delivery problems. They need current information on the sales and delivery of products: lists of incoming customer orders and daily delivery schedules to customers in their territory. Regional managers (middle managers) set sales quotas for each sales manager, prepare budgets, and plan staffing needs for the upcoming year. They need information on monthly sales by product

FIGURE 22.4

Determinants of an Organization's Information-processing Needs

Information-processing needs are determined by user groups and system requirements, as well as by such specific managerial factors as area and level in the organization.

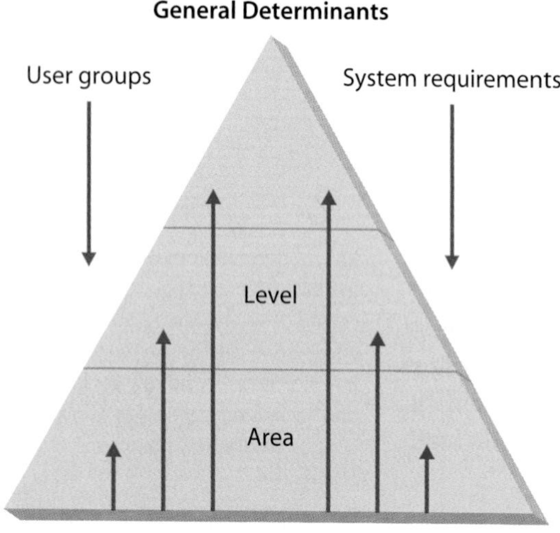

and region. Top managers need both external and internal information. Internally, they use sales data summarized by product, customer type, and geographic region, along with comparisons to previous years. Equally important is external information on consumer behavior patterns, the competition's performance, and economic forecasts. Finally, knowledge workers developing new flooring materials need information on the chemical properties of adhesives and compression strengths for floor structures.

Functional Areas and Business Processes Each business function—marketing, human resources, accounting, operations, finance—has its own information requirements. In addition, many businesses are organized according to various business processes, and these process groups also need special information. Each of these user groups and departments, then, is represented by an information system. When organizations add to these systems the types of systems needed by the four levels of users discussed above, the total number of information systems and applications increases significantly. Top-level finance managers, for example, are concerned with long-range planning for capital expenditures for future facilities and equipment, as well as with determining sources of capital funds.

In contrast, a business process group will include users—both managers and employees—drawn from all organizational levels. The supply chain management group, for instance, may be in the process of trimming down the number of suppliers. The information system supporting this project would contain information ranging across different organizational functions and management levels. The group will need information and expert knowledge on marketing, warehousing and distribution, production, communications technology, purchasing, suppliers, and finance. It will also need different perspectives on operational, technical, and managerial issues: determining technical requirements for new suppliers, specifying task responsibilities for participating firms, and determining future financial requirements.

Major Systems by Level

In this section, we discuss different kinds of systems that provide applications at some organizational levels but not at others. For any routine, repetitive, highly structured decision, a specialized application will suffice. System requirements for knowledge workers, however, will probably vary because knowledge workers often face a variety of specialized problems. Applications of information systems for middle or top-level management decisions must also be flexible, though for different reasons. In particular, they will use a broader range of information collected from a variety of sources, both external and internal.

transaction-processing system (TPS) Application of information processing for basic day-to-day business transactions

Transaction-processing Systems **Transaction-processing systems (TPS)** are applications of information processing for basic day-to-day business transactions.

Customer order taking by online retailers, approval of claims at insurance companies, receipt and confirmation of reservations by airlines, payroll processing and bill payment at almost every company—all are routine business processes. Typically, the TPS for first-level (operational) activities is well defined, with predetermined data requirements, and follows the same steps to complete all transactions in the system.

Information has become a major component in the work of all managers and in the activities of all organizations. Indeed, new and exciting methods and sources for gathering and analyzing information are appearing almost daily. Of course, as shown in this cartoon, managers must ensure that they are getting the information they truly need and that it is of sufficient quality to meet their needs. Flawed or old information may do more harm than no information at all!

Systems for Knowledge Workers and Office Applications Systems for knowledge workers and office applications support the activities of both knowledge workers and employees in clerical positions. They provide assistance for data processing and other office activities, including the creation of communications documents. Like other departments, the IS department includes both knowledge workers and data workers.

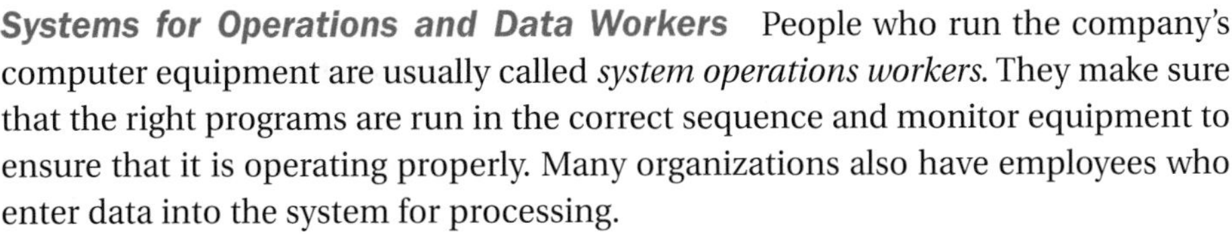

Systems for Operations and Data Workers People who run the company's computer equipment are usually called *system operations workers.* They make sure that the right programs are run in the correct sequence and monitor equipment to ensure that it is operating properly. Many organizations also have employees who enter data into the system for processing.

Knowledge-Level and Office Systems Needless to say, the explosion of new support systems—word processing, document imaging, desktop publishing, computer-aided design, simulation modeling—has increased the productivity of both knowledge and office workers. Desktop publishing combines graphics and word-processing text to publish professional-quality print and web documents. Document-imaging systems can scan paper documents and images, convert them into digital form for storage on disks, retrieve them, and transmit them electronically to workstations throughout the network.

management information system (MIS) Supports an organization's managers by providing daily reports, schedules, plans, and budgets

Management Information Systems **Management information systems (MIS)** support an organization's managers by providing daily reports, schedules, plans, and budgets. A simple MIS is shown in Figure 22.5. Each manager's information activities vary according to his or her functional area (say, accounting or marketing) and management level. Whereas midlevel managers focus mostly on internal activities and information, higher-level managers are also engaged in external activities. Middle managers, the largest MIS user group, need networked information to plan such upcoming activities as personnel training, materials movements, and cash flows. They also need to know the current status of the jobs and projects being carried out in their department: What stage is it at now? When will it be finished? Is there an opening so we can start the next job? Many of a firm's management information

FIGURE 22.5

A Basic Management Information System

A basic management information system relies on an integrated database. Managers in various functional areas can access the database and get the information they need to make decisions. For example, operations managers can access the system to determine sales forecasts by marketing managers, and financial managers can check human resource files to identify possible candidates for promotion into the finance department.

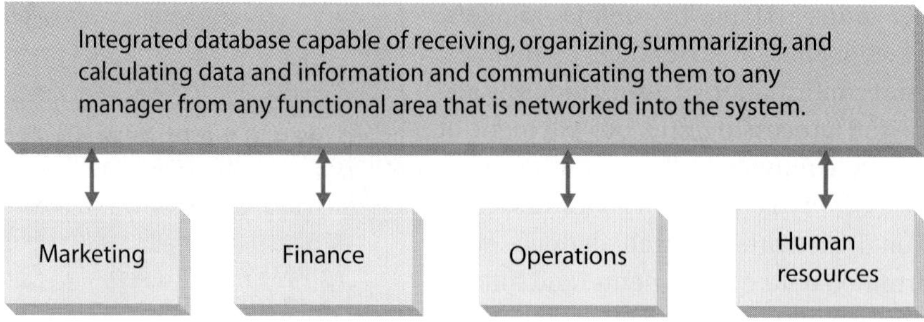

systems—cash flow, sales, production scheduling, shipping—are indispensable in helping managers find answers to such questions.

decision support system (DSS) An interactive system that locates and presents information needed to support the decision-making process

Decision Support Systems Middle and top-level managers receive decision-making assistance from a **decision support system (DSS)**: an interactive system that locates and presents information needed to support the decision-making process. Whereas some DSSs are devoted to specific problems, others serve more general purposes, allowing managers to analyze different types of problems. Thus a firm that often faces decisions on plant capacity, for example, may have a capacity DSS: The manager inputs data on anticipated levels of sales, working capital, and customer delivery requirements. Then the DSS's built-in transaction processors manipulate the data and make recommendations on the best levels of plant capacity for each future time period. In contrast, a general-purpose system, such as a marketing DSS, might respond to a variety of marketing-related problems. It may be programmed to handle "what if" questions, such as "When is the best time to introduce a new product if my main competitor introduces one in three months, our new product has an eighteen-month expected life, demand is seasonal with a peak in autumn, and my goal is to gain the largest possible market share?" The DSS can assist in decisions for which predetermined solutions are unknown by using sophisticated modeling tools and data analysis.

executive support system (ESS) A quick-reference, easy-access application of information systems specially designed for instant access by upper-level managers

Executive Support Systems An **executive support system (ESS)** is a quick-reference, easy-access application of information systems specially designed for instant access by upper-level managers. ESSs are designed to assist with executive-level decisions and problems, ranging from "What lines of business should we be in five years from now?" to "Based on forecasted developments in electronic technologies, to what extent should our firm be globalized in five years? in ten years?" The ESS also uses a wide range of both internal information and external sources, such as industry reports, global economic forecasts, and reports on competitors' capabilities. Because senior-level managers do not usually possess advanced computer skills, they prefer systems that are easily accessible and adaptable. Accordingly, ESSs are not designed to address only specific, predetermined problems. Instead, they allow the user some flexibility in attacking a variety of problem situations. They are easily accessible by means of simple keyboard strokes or even voice commands.

Artificial Intelligence and Expert Systems **Artificial intelligence (AI)** can be defined as the construction of computer systems, both hardware and software, to imitate human behavior—in other words, systems that perform physical tasks, use thought processes, and learn. In developing AI systems, knowledge workers—business specialists, modelers, information technology experts—try to design computer-based systems capable of reasoning, so that computers, instead of people, can perform certain business activities.

artificial intelligence (AI) The construction of computer systems, both hardware and software, to imitate human behavior; that is, to perform physical tasks, use thought processes, and learn

One example is a credit evaluation system that decides which loan applicants are creditworthy and which ones risky and then composes acceptance and rejection letters accordingly. Another example is an applicant selection system that receives interviewees' job applications, screens them, then decides which applicants are best matched with each of several job openings. There are also AI systems that possess sensory capabilities, such as lasers that "see," "hear," and "feel." In addition, as machines become more sophisticated in processing natural language, humans can give instructions and ask questions merely by speaking to a computer.

A special form of AI program, the *expert system,* is designed to imitate the thought processes of human experts in a particular field. Expert systems incorporate the rules that an expert applies to specific types of problems, such as the judgments a physician makes in diagnosing illnesses. In effect, expert systems supply everyday users with "instant expertise." General Electric's Socrates Quick Quote, for example, imitates the decisions of a real estate expert and then places a package of recommendations about real estate transactions at the fingertips of real estate dealers on GE's private computer network. A system called MOCA (for Maintenance Operations Center Advisor), by imitating the thought processes of a maintenance manager, schedules routine maintenance for American Airlines' entire fleet. *Technology Toolkit* provides another example of artificial intelligence applications.

The Internet

Although not everyone would automatically think of it this way, the Internet is also an information system, one that is becoming more and more important to business every day. The **Internet** (or **"the Net,"** for short)—the largest public data communications network—is a gigantic network of networks serving millions of computers; offering information on business, science, and government; and providing communications flows among more than 170,000 separate networks around the world. Originally commissioned by the Pentagon as a communications tool for use during wartime, the Internet allows personal computers in virtually any location to be linked together. The Net has gained in popularity because it is an efficient tool for information retrieval which makes available an immense wealth of academic, technical, and business information.

Internet (the Net) A gigantic network of networks serving millions of computers; offering information on business, science, and government; and providing communications flows among more than 170,000 separate networks around the world

Because it can transmit information quickly and at low cost—lower than long distance phone service, postal delivery, and overnight delivery—the Net has also become the most important e-mail system in the world. For thousands of businesses, therefore, the Net has joined—and is even replacing—the telephone, fax machine, and express mail as a standard means of communication. Although individuals cannot connect directly to the Internet, for a small monthly usage fee they

TECHNOLOGY toolkit

"Meet My New Partner—A Computer"

"Things that a human can do intuitively we're getting the computer to do, too."

— Dr. Hsinchun Chen, director, Artificial Intelligence Laboratory at the University of Arizona and developer of COPLINK*

In Fall 2002 a pair of gunmen terrified residents of Washington, D.C., shooting eighteen randomly chosen victims. Baffled police found no clues, no reliable eyewitnesses, no informants. They were stumped. The city was paralyzed with fear. Local police and the FBI came under intense pressure to solve the crimes. Ultimately, old-fashioned police work found the culprits. But they might have been identified much earlier if a new "electronic cop" had been fully implemented.

COPLINK is Internet-based artificial intelligence software designed to analyze large data sets. It combines information across jurisdictions and then uses expert systems logic to find associations. Sergeant Jenny Schroeder of the Tucson Police Department is testing the system. "COPLINK takes legacy data, puts it into a warehouse, and uses a Web-based interface to make the information available." After amassing information, COPLINK "uses a data-mining tool that points out the relationships between objects, whether those objects are people, vehicles, organizations, locations, weapons, or crimes," says professor Hsinchun Chen, COPLINK developer. He adds, "It's the Google for law enforcement. Things that a human can do intuitively we're getting the computer to do, too." COPLINK became feasible only recently, with the development of security and artificial intelligence software.

The Washington snipers, John Muhammad and Lee Malvo, left evidence in Washington, Louisiana, Alabama, Georgia, Virginia, Maryland, and the District of Columbia. Changes in jurisdiction led to delays in sharing data. For example, the Montgomery police did not send a fingerprint to the FBI for twenty-seven days, not realizing its significance. By the time Malvo's fingerprint was identified, police had the two snipers in custody.

Today, COPLINK is implemented in half a dozen cities. With nationwide usage, investigators speculate that the crime would have been solved more quickly. One reason for the hesitation in adopting COPLINK is expense. Installation of the system can cost hundreds of thousands of dollars. Another reason is lack of trust in technology. Technology expert James X. Dempsey claims that human detectives will never be fully replaced by computers. He says, "There seems to be a classic case of believing that technology can solve every problem, and I'm very skeptical that it can."

References: "Antigua: Muhammad Smuggled Malvo to U.S.," *CNN*, November 10, 2002, www.cnn.com on February 19, 2003; "Coplink: Database Detective," *TechBeat*, National Law Enforcement and Corrections Technology Center website, www.nlectc.org on February 19, 2003; David M. Halbfinger, "Sniper Clue Sat for Weeks in Crime Lab in Alabama," *New York Times*, October 26, 2002, p. A14; Mindy Sink, "An Electronic Cop That Plays Hunches," *New York Times*, November 2, 2002, pp. B1, B11 (*quote p. B1); William Matthews, "Sniper Leaves a Mark," *Federal Computer Week*, October 29, 2002, www.fcw.com on February 19, 2003.

Internet service provider (ISP) A commercial firm that maintains a permanent connection to the Net and sells temporary connections to subscribers

can subscribe to the Net via an **Internet service provider (ISP)**, such as Prodigy, America Online, or Earthlink. An ISP is a commercial firm that maintains a permanent connection to the Net and sells temporary connections to subscribers.[8]

The Internet's popularity continues to grow for both business and personal applications. In 2000 more than 302 million Net users were active on links connecting more than 180 countries. In the United States alone, more than 50 million users were on the Net every day. Its power to change the way business is conducted has been amply demonstrated in both large and small firms as their members use the Net to communicate both within and across organizational boundaries, to buy and sell products and services, and to glean information from myriad sources around the world.

The Net has also benefited small companies, especially as a means of expanding market research and improving customer service, as well as serving as a source of information. In San Leandro, California, for example, TriNet Employer Group subscribes to Ernst & Young's online consulting program, Ernie. For $3,500 a year, TriNet controller Lyle DeWitt sends questions from his computer and gets an answer from an Ernst & Young expert within forty-eight hours. Aiming for small clients who cannot afford big-name consulting advice, Ernie answers questions on health insurance, benefit plans, immigration issues, and payroll taxes.

The World Wide Web Thanks to the **World Wide Web (WWW,** or simply **"the Web")**, the Internet is easy to use and allows users around the world to communicate electronically with little effort. The World Wide Web is a system with universally accepted standards for storing, retrieving, formatting, and displaying information.[9] It provides the common language that enables us to "surf" the Net and makes the Internet available to a general audience, rather than only to technical users like computer programmers. To access a website, for example, the user must specify the *Uniform Resource Locator (URL)* that points to the resource's unique address on the Web.

World Wide Web (WWW) A system with universally accepted standards for storing, retrieving, formatting, and displaying information

Servers and Browsers Each website opens with a *home page*—a screen display that welcomes the visitor with a greeting that may include graphics, sound, and visual enhancements introducing the user to the site. Additional pages give details on the sponsor's products and explain how to contact help in using the site. Often, they furnish URLs for related websites, to which the user can link by simply pointing and clicking. The person who is responsible for maintaining an organization's website is usually called the *webmaster*. Large websites use dedicated workstations—large computers—known as *web servers*, which are customized for managing, maintaining, and supporting websites.

With hundreds of thousands of new web pages appearing each day, cyberspace is now serving up billions of pages of publicly accessible information. Sorting through this maze would be frustrating and inefficient without access to a **web browser**—the software that enables the user to access information on the Web. A browser runs on the user's PC and supports the graphics and linking capabilities needed to navigate the Web. Netscape Navigator has enjoyed as much as an 80 percent market share, although its dominance is being challenged by other browsers, including its own Netscape Communicator and Microsoft's Internet Explorer.

web browser The software that enables the user to access information on the Web

Directories and Search Engines The web browser offers additional tools—website directories and search engines—for navigating on the Web. Among the most successful cyberspace enterprises are companies like Yahoo! which maintain free directories of web content. When Yahoo! is notified about new websites, it classifies them in its directory. The user enters one or two key words (say, "compact disk"), and the directory responds by retrieving from the directory a list of websites with titles containing those words.

In contrast to a directory, a search engine will search cyberspace's millions of web pages without preclassifying them into a directory. It searches for web pages that contain the same words as the user's search terms. Then it displays addresses for those that come closest to matching, then the next closest, and so on. A search engine, such as AltaVista, Radar, or Google, may respond to more than 10 million inquiries per day. It is thus no surprise that both directories and search engines are packed with paid ads.[10] At the beginning of 2003, Yahoo! was the leader in *portal sites*—sites used by Net surfers as primary home pages—although Lycos was closing fast in the race for most users.

intranet A communications network similar to the Internet but operating within the boundaries of a single organization

Intranets The success of the Internet has led some companies to extend the Net's technology internally, using it for internal websites containing information about the firm. These private networks, or **intranets**, are accessible only to employees via entry through electronic firewalls. Firewalls, discussed later, are used to limit access to an intranet. At Compaq Computer, the intranet allows employees to shuffle their retirement savings among various investment funds. Ford's intranet connects 120,000 workstations in Asia, Europe, and the United States to thousands of Ford websites containing private information on Ford activities in production, engineering, distribution, and marketing. Sharing such information has helped reduce the lead time for getting models into production from thirty-six to twenty-four months. Ford's latest project in improving customer service through internal information sharing is called *manufacturing on demand.* Now, for example, the Mustang that required fifty days' delivery time in 1996 is available in less than two weeks. The savings to Ford, of course, will be billions of dollars in inventory and fixed costs.[11]

extranet A communications network that allows selected outsiders limited access to an organization's internal information system, or intranet

Extranets Sometimes firms allow outsiders access to their intranets. These so-called **extranets** allow outsiders limited access to a firm's intranet. The most common application allows buyers to enter the seller's system to see which products are available for sale and delivery, thus providing product availability information quickly to outside buyers. Industrial suppliers, too, are often linked into their customers' intranets so that they can see planned production schedules and make supplies ready as needed for customers' upcoming operations.

concept CHECK

Identify the various different levels of information systems that exist today.

Identify examples of how you use the Internet for informational purposes.

Managing Information Systems

At this point, the value and importance of information systems should be apparent. There are still important questions to be answered, however. How are such systems developed, and how are they used on a day-to-day basis? This section provides insights into these issues and related areas.

Creating Information Systems

The basic steps involved in creating an information system are outlined in Figure 22.6. The first step is to determine the information needs of the organization and to establish goals for what is to be achieved with the proposed system. It is absolutely imperative that the project have full support and an appropriate financial commitment from top management if it is to be successful. Once the decision has been made to develop and install an information system, a task force is usually constituted to oversee everything. Target users, as discussed earlier, must be well represented on such a task force.

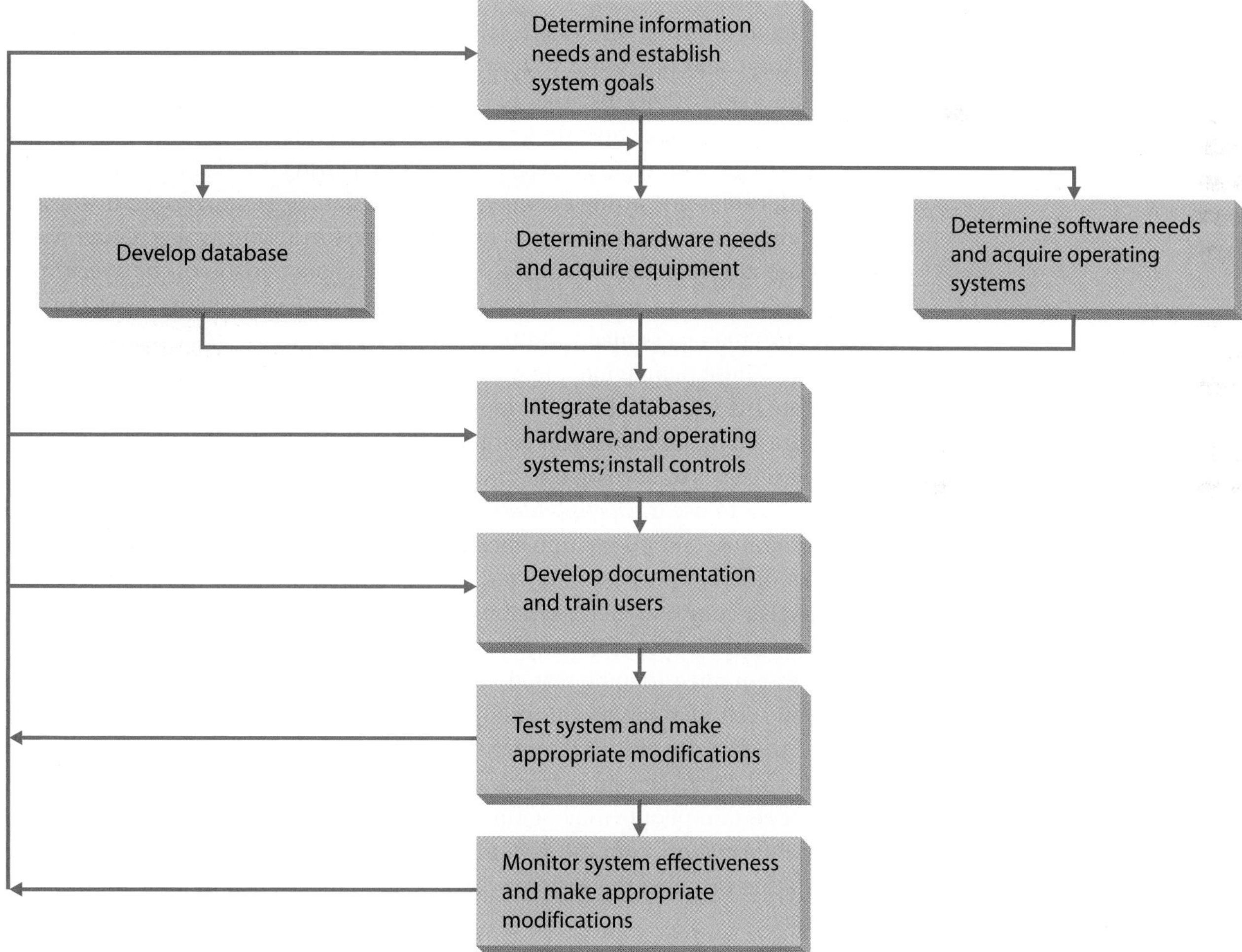

FIGURE 22.6

Establishing an Information System

Establishing an information system is a complex procedure. Managers must realize, however, that the organization's information management needs will change over time, and some steps of the process may have to be repeated in the future.

Next, three tasks can be done simultaneously. One task is to develop a database. Most organizations already possess the information they need for an information system, but it is often not in the correct form. The Pentagon has spent large sums of money to transform all of its paper records into computer records. Many other branches of the government are also working hard to computerize their data.[12]

While the database is being assembled, the organization also needs to determine its hardware needs and acquire the appropriate equipment. Some systems rely solely on one large mainframe computer; others are increasingly using personal computers. Equipment is usually obtained from large manufacturers like IBM, Compaq, Sun, and Dell. Finally, software needs must also be determined and an appropriate operating system obtained. Again, off-the-shelf packages will sometimes work, although most companies find it necessary to do some customization to suit their needs.[13]

The actual information system is created by integrating the databases, hardware, software, and operating system. Obviously, the mechanics of doing this are beyond the scope of this discussion. However, the company usually has to rely on the expertise of outside consulting firms, along with the vendors who provided the other parts of the system, to get it all put together. During this phase, the equipment is installed, cables are strung between units, the data are entered into the system, the operating system is installed and tested, and so forth. During this phase, system controls are also installed. A control is simply a characteristic of the system that limits certain forms of access or limits what a person can do with the system. For example, top managers may want to limit access to certain sensitive data to a few key people. These people may be given private codes that must be entered before the data are made available. It is important to make sure that data cannot be accidentally erased by someone who just happens to press the wrong key.

The next step is to develop documentation of how the system works and to train people in how to use it. *Documentation* refers to manuals, computerized help programs, diagrams, and instruction sheets. Essentially, it tells people how to use the system for different purposes. Beyond pure documentation, however, training sessions are also common. Such sessions allow people to practice using the system under the watchful eyes of experts.

The system must then be tested and appropriate modifications made. Regardless of how well planned an information system is, there will almost certainly be glitches. For example, the system may be unable to generate a report that needs to be made available to certain managers. Or the report may not be in the appropriate format. Or certain people may be unable to access data that they need in order to get other information from the system. In most cases, the consultants or the internal group that installed the system will be able to make such modifications as the need arises.

The organization must recognize that information management needs will change over time. Hence, even though the glitches get straightened out and the information system is put into normal operation, modifications may still be needed in the future. For example, after Black & Decker acquired General Electric's small-appliance business, it had to overhaul its own information system to accommodate all the new information associated with its new business. Information management is a continuous process. Even if an effective information system can be created and put into use, there is still a good chance that it will occasionally need to be modified to fit changing circumstances.

Integrating Information Systems

In very large and complex organizations, information systems must also be integrated. This integration may involve linkages between different information systems within the same organization or between different organizations altogether. Within an organization, for example, it is probably necessary for the marketing system and the operations system to be able to communicate with each other.

Linking systems together is not as easy. Consider, for example, the complexities involved when Hewlett-Packard acquired Compaq Computer. Each firm had its own complex and integrated information network. But, because each firm's network relied on different technologies, hardware, and operating systems, integrating the two firms has been a costly and complex undertaking. Similarly, suppose a firm installs one system in one of its divisions, using Dell equipment and Microsoft software, and then installs a different system in another division, using Hewlett-Packard equipment and Lotus software. Just as with Hewlett-Packard and Compaq, if and when the firm decides to tie its two distinct systems together, it may face considerable difficulties.

There are two ways to overcome this problem. One is to develop everything at once. Unfortunately, doing so is expensive, and sometimes managers simply cannot anticipate today exactly what their needs will be tomorrow. The other method is to adopt a standard type of system at the beginning, so that subsequent additions fit properly.[14] Even then, however, breakthroughs in information system technology may still make it necessary to change approaches in midstream.

Using Information Systems

The real test of the value of an information system is how it can be used. Ideally, an information system should be simple to use and nontechnical—that is, one should not have to be a computer expert to use the system. In theory, a manager should be able to access a modern information system by turning on a computer and clicking an icon with a mouse. The manager should also be able to enter appropriate new data or request that certain kinds of information be provided. The requested information might first be displayed on a computer screen or monitor. After the manager is satisfied, the information can then be printed out in paper form on a standard printer, or the manager can store the information back in the system for possible future use or for use by others.

One implication relates to the span of management and the number of levels of an organization. Innovations in information technology enable a manager to stay in touch with an increasingly large number of managers and subordinates. T. J. Rodgers, CEO of Cypress Semiconductor, uses the firm's information system to check on the progress of each of his employees every week. Using this and related approaches, spans of management are likely to widen and organizational levels to decrease. And some organizations are using their information-processing capabilities to network with other companies. Pacific Intermountain Express, a large western trucking company, gives customers access to its own computer network so they can check on the status of their shipments.

Travelers Insurance has made effective use of its information system by hiring a team of trained nurses to review health insurance claims. The nurses tap into the company's regular information system and analyze the medical diagnoses provided with each claim. They can use this information to determine whether a second opinion is warranted before a particular surgical procedure is approved. They enter their decision directly into the system. When the claim form is printed out, it contains a provision that spells out whether the claimant must seek a second opinion before proceeding with a particular treatment.

Managing Information Security

An increasingly common concern for businesses today is security. Security measures for protection against intrusion are a constant challenge. To gain entry into most systems, users have protected passwords that guard against unauthorized access, but many firms rely on additional protective software as a safeguard. To protect against intrusions by unauthorized outsiders, companies use security devices, called *electronic firewalls,* in their systems. **Firewalls** are software and hardware systems that allow employees access to both the Internet and the company's internal computer network while barring entry by outsiders.

firewall Software and hardware system that allows employees access to both the Internet and the company's internal computer network while barring access by outsiders

Security for electronic communications is an additional concern. Electronic transmissions can be intercepted, altered, and read by intruders. To prevent unauthorized access, many firms rely on *encryption:* use of a secret numeric code to scramble the characters in the message, so that the message is not understandable during transmission. Only personnel with the deciphering codes can read them. Protection for preserving data files and databases is not foolproof and typically involves making backup copies to be stored outside the computer system, usually in a safe. Damaged system files can thus be replaced by backups.

Finally, the most important security factor is the people in the system. At most firms, personnel are trained in the responsibilities of computer use and warned of the penalties for violating system security. For example, each time the computer boots up, a notice displays the warning that software and data are protected and spells out penalties for unauthorized use.

Understanding Information System Limitations

It is also necessary to recognize the limits of information systems. Several of these are listed in Table 22.1. First of all, as already noted, information systems are expensive and difficult to develop and implement. Thus organizations may try to cut corners too much or install a system in such a piecemeal fashion that its effectiveness suffers.

TABLE 22.1

Limitations of Information Systems

Although information systems play a vital role in modern organizations, they are not without their limitations. In particular, information systems have six basic limitations. For example, one major limitation of installing an information system is cost. For a large company, an information system might cost several million dollars.

1. Information systems are expensive and difficult to develop and implement.
2. Information systems are not suitable for all tasks or problems.
3. Managers sometimes rely too much on information systems.
4. Information provided to managers may not be as accurate, timely, complete, or relevant as it first appears to be.
5. Managers may have unrealistic expectations of what information systems can do.
6. The information system may be subject to sabotage, computer viruses, or downtime.

Information systems simply are not suitable for some tasks or problems. Complex problems requiring human judgment must still be addressed by humans. Information systems are often a useful tool for managers, but they can seldom actually replace managers. Managers also may come to rely too much on information systems. As a consequence, the manager may lose touch with the real-world problems he or she needs to be concerned about. Similarly, access to unlimited information can result in overload, rendering managers less effective than they would be with reduced access to information.[15]

Information may not be as accurate, timely, complete, or relevant as it appears. There is a strong tendency for people to think that, because a computer performed the calculations, the answer must be correct—especially if the answer is calculated to several decimal places. But the fact of the matter is that, if the initial information was flawed, all resultant computations using it are likely to be flawed as well.

Managers sometimes have unrealistic expectations about what information systems can accomplish. They may believe that the first stage of implementation will result in a full-blown Orwellian communications network that a child could use. When the manager comes to see the flaws and limitations of the system, she or he may become disappointed and as a result not use the system effectively. Finally, the information system may be subject to sabotage, computer viruses, or downtime. Disgruntled employees have been known to enter false data deliberately. And a company that relies too much on a computerized information system may find itself totally paralyzed in the event of a simple power outage or a crippling computer virus.

concept CHECK

Describe how information systems are created.

Identify personal examples of information system limitations that you have encountered or experienced.

The Impact of Information Systems on Organizations

Information systems are clearly an important part of most modern organizations. Their effects are felt in a variety of ways. Indeed, the rapid growth of information technologies has changed the very structure of business organizations.

Leaner Organizations

Information networks are leading to leaner companies with fewer employees and simpler structures. Because today's networked firm can maintain information linkages among both employees and customers, more work can be accomplished with fewer people. Bank customers, for example, can dial into a twenty-four-hour information system and find out their current balances from a digital voice. In the industrial sector, assembly workers at an IBM plant used to receive instructions from supervisors or special staff. Now instructions are delivered electronically to their workstation.

Widespread reductions in middle-management positions and the shrinkage of layers in organizational structure are possible because information networks now provide direct communications between top managers and workers at lower levels. The operating managers who formerly communicated company policies, procedures, or work instructions to lower-level employees are being replaced by electronic information networks.

More Flexible Operations

Electronic networks allow businesses to offer customers greater variety and faster delivery cycles. Recovery after heart surgery, for example, is expedited by custom-tailored rehabilitation programs designed with integrated information systems. Each personalized program integrates the patient's history with information from physicians and rehabilitation specialists and then matches the patient with an electronically monitored exercise regimen. Products such as cellular phones, PCs, and audio systems can be custom-ordered, too, with your choice of features and options and next-day delivery. The underlying principle is called *mass customization.* Although companies produce in large volumes, each unit features the unique variations and options that the customer prefers.

Flexible production and fast delivery depend on an integrated network to coordinate all of the transactions, activities, and process flows necessary to make quick adjustments in the production process. The ability to organize and store massive volumes of information is crucial, as are the electronic linkages between customers, manufacturer, materials suppliers, and shippers.

Increased Collaboration

Collaboration, not only among internal units but with outside firms as well, is on the rise because networked systems make it cheaper and easier to contact everyone, whether other employees or outside organizations.[16] Aided by intranets, more companies are learning that complex problems can be solved better by means of collaboration, either in formal teams or through spontaneous interaction. In the new, networked organization, decisions that were once the domain of individuals are now shared, as both people and departments have become more interdependent. The design of new products, for example, was once an engineering responsibility. Now, in contrast, it can be a shared responsibility because so much information is accessible for evaluation from various perspectives. Marketing, finance, production, engineering, and purchasing can now share their different stores of information and determine a best overall design.

Naturally, networked systems are also helpful in business-to-business (often referred to as "B2B") relationships. Increasingly, organizational buyers and suppliers are becoming so closely networked that they sometimes seem to be working for one organization. In the financial services industry, for example, institutional investors are networked with investment bankers, thus allowing efficient buying and selling of initial stock offerings. In manufacturing, Ford's parts suppliers are linked to Ford's extranet. Because they know Ford's current production schedules and upcoming requirements, they can move materials into Ford plants more quickly and more accurately.

A step toward even greater collaboration between companies—the so-called virtual company—has become possible through networking. As we saw in Chapter 12, a virtual company can be a temporary team assembled by a single organization. But a virtual company can also be created when several firms join forces. Each contributes different skills and resources that collectively result in a competitive business that would not be feasible for any of the collaborators acting alone. A company with marketing and promotional skills, for example, may team up with firms that are experts in warehousing and distribution, engineering, and production. Networking allows collaborators to exchange ideas, plan daily activities, share customer information, and otherwise coordinate their efforts, even if their respective facilities are far apart.

Breakthoughs in information technology will continue to impact organizations in myriad ways. This Siemens engineer demonstrates one of the newest breakthroughs on the horizon—a virtual keyboard. A mini projector is used to create keys and a mousepad—all the user has to do is touch the worksurface and the keystroke is entered into a computer or other device. Such breakthroughs may be especially significant for use in so-called "clean" work environments such as medical labs and high-tech research facilities.

More Flexible Work Sites

Geographic separation of the workplace from the company headquarters is more common than ever because of networked organizations. Employees no longer work only at the office or the factory, nor are all of a company's operations performed at one location. The sales manager for an advertising agency may visit the company office in New York once every two weeks, preferring instead to work over the firm's electronic network from her home office in Florida. A medical researcher for the Cleveland Clinic may work at a home office networked into the clinic's system.[17]

A company's activities may also be geographically scattered but highly coordinated thanks to a networked system. Many e-businesses, for example, conduct no activities at one centralized location. When you order products from an Internet storefront—say, a chair, a sofa, a table, and two lamps—the chair may come from a cooperating warehouse in Philadelphia and the lamps from a manufacturer in California, while the sofa and table may be shipped directly from two manufacturers in North Carolina. All these activities are launched instantaneously by the customer's order and coordinated through the network, just as if all of them were being processed at one location.[18]

Improved Management Processes

Networked systems have changed the very nature of the management process. The activities, methods, and procedures of today's manager differ significantly from those that were common just a few years ago. Once, for example, upper-level managers did not concern themselves with all the detailed information that filtered upward in the workplace. Why? Because it was expensive to gather, slow in coming, and quickly out of date. Workplace management was delegated to middle and first-line managers.

With networked systems, however, instantaneous information is accessible in a convenient, usable format. Consequently, more and more upper managers use it routinely for planning, leading, directing, and controlling operations. Today, a top manager can find out the current status of any customer order, inspect productivity statistics for each workstation, and analyze the delivery performance of any driver and vehicle. More importantly, managers can better coordinate company-wide performance. They can identify departments that are working well together and those that are creating bottlenecks. Hershey's networked system, for example, includes SAP, an enterprise resource-planning model that identifies the current status of any order and traces its progress from order entry through customer delivery and receipt of payment. Progress and delays at intermediate stages—materials ordering, inventory availability, production scheduling, packaging, warehousing, distribution—can be checked continuously to determine which operations should be more closely coordinated with others to improve overall performance.

Changed Employee Behaviors

Information systems also directly affect the behaviors of people in organizations. Some of these effects are positive; others can be negative. On the plus side, information systems usually improve individual efficiency. Some people also enjoy their work more because they have fun using the new technology. Through computerized bulletin boards and e-mail, groups can form across organizational boundaries.

On the negative side, information systems can lead to isolation, as people have everything they need to do their job without interacting with others. Managers can work at home easily, with the possible side effects of being unavailable to others who need them or being removed from key parts of the social system. Computerized working arrangements also tend to be much less personal than other methods. For example, a computer-transmitted "pat on the back" will likely mean less than a real one. Researchers are just beginning to determine how individual behaviors and attitudes are affected by information systems.[19]

concept CHECK

What are the primary impacts of information systems on organizations?	*What are the primary ways in which information systems affect you personally?*

Summary of Key Points

business.college.hmco.com/students

Information is a vital part of every manager's job. For information to be useful, it must be accurate, timely, complete, and accurate. Information technology is best conceived of as part of the control process. Information technology systems contain five basic components. These are an input medium, a processor, an output medium, a storage device, and a control system. Although the form will vary, both manual and computerized information systems have these components.

An organization's information technology needs are determined by several factors—most notably, user groups and systems requirements. There are several basic levels of information systems, including transaction-processing systems, systems for various types of workers, basic management information systems, decision support systems, and executive support systems, as well as artificial intelligence and expert systems. Each provides certain types of information and is most valuable for specific types of managers. Each should also be matched to the needs of user groups.

Managing information systems involves five basic elements. The first is deciding how to create information systems. Of course, this step actually involves a wide array of specific activities and steps. The systems must then be integrated. Managers must also be able to use them. Information security is also an important consideration in managing information systems. Finally, managers should be aware of the limitations of information systems.

Information systems have an impact on organizations in a variety of ways. Major influences include leaner organizations, more flexible operations, increased collaboration, more flexible work sites, improved management processes, and changed employee behaviors.

Discussion Questions

Questions for Review

1. What are the differences between data and information? Give three examples of data and then show how those data can be turned into information.
2. Who uses information systems in organizations? What types of functions do the systems perform for each type of user?
3. Describe each of the levels of major information technology systems. Give an

example of each, other than the examples in the text.

4. What are some of the positive impacts that information technology can have on organizations? What are some of the negative impacts?

Questions for Analysis

5. Very often, managers making decisions in real organizations have to work with information that does not perfectly meet all four criteria for useful information. In that case, should the manager use the imperfect information or not? What can the manager do to increase the usefulness of imperfect information?
6. At higher organizational levels, the information technology tools used become more sophisticated. Yet, in many organizations, higher-level managers are the least sophisticated and experienced with hands-on use of information technology. How can unsophisticated users effectively employ a sophisticated IT tool? What are some of the potential problems they should be aware of?
7. It has been said that the information revolution is like the Industrial Revolution in terms of the magnitude of its impact on organizations and society. What leads to such a view? Why might that view be an overstatement?

Questions for Application

8. Interview a business manager about the use of information in his or her organization. How is the information managed? Is a computer system used? How well is the information system integrated with other aspects of organizational control?
9. Visit a local organization, such as a university administration office, a restaurant, or a supermarket. Stand in its facility and look around you. How many different information systems can you spot? Do not look just for "computers"; also look for less-obvious examples, such as the digital thermostat on the wall or the electronic cash register. What type of information system is each?
10. A knowledge worker can be defined as "someone who creates, transforms, or repackages information." Choose a knowledge worker occupation that interests you. Use the Internet to investigate the job qualifications for that occupation. What skills, knowledge, and experience are needed? How do the qualifications for knowledge workers differ from the qualifications of white collar workers?

BUILDING EFFECTIVE technical SKILLS

business.college.hmco.com/students

Exercise Overview

Technical skills are the skills necessary to accomplish or understand the specific kind of work being done in an organization. This exercise asks you to consider the potential benefits and costs of automating a manual process.

Exercise Background

So many innovative information technology products, both hardware and software, are available to businesses today. Yet many firms continue to use manual processes for much of the work they do. Are these businesses unaware of or indifferent to the benefits that technology could bring them? Is the technology just too expensive? Or might there be sound reasons, other than budgetary ones, to limit the use of information technology?

Exercise Task

1. Observe a business that is using a manual process—for example, a hospital that maintains patient records on paper, a receptionist who answers calls and routes them to the appropriate person, or a library that loans books.
2. Use the Internet to find an example of a company that is using information technology to perform that process. (*Hint:* Look for organizations of the same type, such as another hospital. Or look at the websites of companies that provide software or hardware. Many of them will have a section about their clients, called "Case Studies" or "Success Stories.")
3. Investigate and then describe how the business you observed could use information technology.
4. Describe the benefits that you would expect the business to obtain if it automated that process. Then describe the costs, limitations, or potential problems you would expect.
5. Should the business automate? Why or why not?

BUILDING EFFECTIVE interpersonal SKILLS

Exercise Overview

Interpersonal skills refer to the ability to communicate with, understand, and motivate individuals and groups. Information technology has obvious links with interpersonal skills.

Exercise Background

Your company is at the forefront of modern information technology. All of your managers have voice-mail and e-mail, all are networked, and many have started working at home. They point out that they are more productive at home and do not really need to come in to the office every day to get their work done. And, indeed, productivity is booming.

But a situation recently arose that has caused you some concern. Specifically, you have two employees who have worked for you for almost six months and who communicate with one another on a regular basis but have not met face to face. Because you have always thought of your company as a warm and friendly place to work, you are alarmed that you may be losing those characteristics.

Exercise Task

With the background information above as context, decide whether or not face-to-face communication is important today. Then do one of the following:

1. If you think face-to-face communication *is* important, develop a plan for enhancing interpersonal relations among your employees without losing the competitive advantage you have gained from information technology.
2. If you think face-to-face communication is *not* important, develop a rationale that you might use to placate or comfort an employee who complains about the lack of interpersonal relations.

BUILDING EFFECTIVE time-management SKILLS

Exercise Overview

Time-management skills refer to the manager's ability to prioritize work, to work efficiently, and to delegate appropriately. This exercise analyzes the ways in which your use of information technology influences your time management.

Exercise Background

One of the biggest implied advantages of modern information technology is time management. Modern technology is supposed to make us more productive and more efficient and to make it easier to communicate with one another. At the same time, most people acknowledge that information technology can also get out of hand.

Think back to your use of information technology over the last week. Consider cell phones, e-mail, the Internet, instant messaging, handheld devices such as Palm Pilots, and so on. Think about ways that each of these forms can both save and waste time.

Exercise Task

With the background information above as context, do the following:

1. List every form of technology that you used. Note how frequently you used it and for how long. (Alternatively, keep track of your use over the upcoming week. Then continue with the exercise.)
2. Which did you use most often? least often? Which did you use for the longest total time? for the shortest total time? Which performed critically important functions for you? less important functions? Explain your answers.
3. For each device, list alternative, less technologically sophisticated ways of achieving that same function—for example, use of a pay phone instead of a cell phone.
4. For each type of technology, decide whether that device was a time saver, performing functions more efficiently than the alternatives. Which were time wasters?
5. What ideas does a review of your answers give you about more time-efficient use of technology?

CHAPTER CLOSING case

THE RIGHT WAY TO DELIVER GROCERIES

> *"I'm not a corporate CEO. I'm not a dot-commer. I'm just a %#&@ lunatic who knows about food."*
>
> – Joe Fedele, CEO, FreshDirect*

Webvan had a bright idea—sell food on the Internet for home delivery—but in 2001 it went spectacularly bankrupt, to the tune of $1 billion. Many similar businesses also failed. But don't give up on that terrific concept just yet. A new firm, FreshDirect, is building a successful online grocery business by downplaying "online" and emphasizing "grocery." Its motto? "It's all about the food."

A few online grocery companies have achieved modest success by partnering with traditional groceries. At these firms, a "personal shopper" pushes a cart around the store, and the bags are then delivered. This inefficient method requires the store to charge a 35 percent markup. FreshDirect is using a unique, low-cost business model. For a start, CEO Joe Fedele is a grocery expert who has already founded one thriving grocery store. Fedele likes to say, "This is a company based on food people, not dot-com people."

At FreshDirect, most food is purchased directly from suppliers, rather than from intermediaries. This cuts costs by 25 percent and increases freshness. (FreshDirect is capitalizing on changing consumer tastes. In 1970 30 percent of food dollars were spent on fresh—not packaged—food. Today, 70 percent are.) The firm does not own a store. Instead, it built a state-of-the-art 300,000-square-foot warehouse on Long Island, near Manhattan. FreshDirect offers baked goods, prepared meals, fresh pasta, deli salads, and more, all prepared by chefs trained at top restaurants. The company delivers only to twenty-two zip codes in Manhattan, Queens, and Long Island. FreshDirect also delivers to "depots" set up at large corporations, so that employees can have groceries delivered to their work site at the end of the day. The delivery charge is a flat $3.95, the minimum order is $40.00, and there is no tipping. Deliveries are scheduled only in the evening and weekend hours, when Manhattan traffic is lighter. These strategic decisions allow FreshDirect to offer unique and tempting goods, for a lower price than the corner market and with the convenience of home delivery.

Although Fedele cares more about the food, the company's web pages must be simple and appealing. The site, www.freshdirect.com, is attractive, uncluttered, and easy to navigate. You can change your view—with or without pictures, with large pictures or thumbnails. Signup takes just minutes. Categories, subcategories, and a search feature make it easy to find a product. You can also see items sorted by brand or price. Expert recommendations and lists of top sellers are there, too. A helpful grocer points out foods that go together, so you will not forget jelly when buying peanut butter. And, if you do not know what kind of cheese you want, a brief description accompanies every category. Still not sure? A table shows each cheese by taste, and the categories vary. For example, cheddars are rated on sharpness, hardness, and age, and mozzarellas are categorized by pliability and intensity. Every product shows its USDA nutritional labeling and complete information on ingredients.

Information technology is integrated throughout the facility, with nine climate-controlled rooms providing the optimal conditions for everything from avocados to smoked salmon. Equipment is linked to controls in a central room, where alarms sound if a conveyor belt stops or a freezer warms up. The entire plant is automatically hosed down nightly with antiseptic foam and then sprayed with an antibacterial coating, to ensure food safety.

FreshDirect borrowed FedEx's ideas about logistics. Customers have bar codes, and so do boxes. At any given moment, your order can be pinpointed within twenty feet. Delivery personnel use the bar codes to access address information.

In its most ambitious move yet, FreshDirect has asked each of its chefs to develop recipes that are then programmed into artificial intelligence software. If an ingredient's bar code, the reading on an electronic scale, or the computer-controlled oven setting are not correct, the equipment shuts down, and the work cannot proceed. This ensures that hourly workers follow the recipe exactly. FreshDirect can control and standardize quality while using less expensive workers.

Some users report problems—overripe grapes, mixed-up deliveries. Some people worry about the lack of contact, because they want to sniff the melons or squeeze the bread. A few bemoan the impersonal nature of our society. But most shoppers seem to find online grocery shopping a liberating experience. One reports his satisfaction with FreshDirect and then adds sarcastically, "Yes, fewer visits to [traditional grocer] Key Food will be tragic." FreshDirect CEO Fedele sums up his winning philosophy: "I'm not a corporate CEO. I'm not a dot-commer. I'm just a %#&@ lunatic who knows about food."

Case Questions

1. Describe the different types of information systems in use at FreshDirect. What type is each?
2. What advantages does FreshDirect get from its use of information technology? What are some potential problems?
3. Would FreshDirect CEO Joe Fedele agree that, for an online retailer, technology is the most important contributor to success? Why or why not? Do you think his opinion is correct? Why or why not?

Case References

"About Us," "Michael Stark: Kitchen," FreshDirect website, www.freshdirect.com on February 19, 2003; David Kirkpatrick, "The Online Grocer Version 2.0," *Fortune*, November 25, 2002, www.fortune.com on December 2, 2002; Florence Fabricant, "Fresh Groceries Right off the Assembly Line," *New York Times*, November 6, 2002, www.nytimes.com on February 19, 2003; Jane Black, "Online at the Grocer's: Can FreshDirect.com Deliver?" *New York*, October 14, 2002, www.newyorkmetro.com on February 19, 2003 (*quote); Jane Black, "Can FreshDirect Bring Home the Bacon?" *BusinessWeek Online*, September 24, 2002, www.businessweek.com on February 19, 2003.

Chapter Notes

1. Alex Salkever, "Toward a More Secure 2003," *BusinessWeek*, December 31, 2002, www.businessweek.com on February 18, 2003; Francis deSouza, "Get the Message—Instantly," *Fast Company*, www.fastcompany.com on February 18, 2003; Heath Row, "It's Real Time to Talk," *Fast Company*, June 1998, www.fastcompany.com on February 18, 2003; Yudhijit Bhattacharjee, "A Swarm of Little Notes," *Time*, September 2002, pp. A4–A8 (*quote p. A6).
2. See Michael H. Zack, "Managing Codified Knowledge," *Sloan Management Review*, Summer 1999, pp. 45–58.
3. Donald A. Marchand, William J. Kettinger, and John D. Rollins, "Information Orientation: People, Technology, and the Bottom Line," *Sloan Management Review*, Summer 2000, pp. 69–79.
4. Justin Fox, "Inside the New Earnings Game," *Fortune*, March 3, 2003, pp. 97–103.
5. Edward W. Desmond, "How Your Data May Soon Seek You Out," *Fortune*, September 1997, pp. 149–154.
6. William J. Burns, Jr., and F. Warren McFarlin, "Information Technology Puts Power in Control Systems," *Harvard Business Review*, September–October 1987, pp. 89–94.
7. N. Venkatraman, "IT-Enabled Business Transformation: From Automation to Business Scope Redefinition," *Sloan Management Review*, Winter 1994, pp. 73–84.
8. Kenneth C. Laudon and Jane P. Laudon, *Essentials of Management Information Systems*, 3rd ed. (Upper Saddle River, NJ: Prentice Hall, 1999), p. 267.
9. Laudon and Laudon, *Essentials of Management Information Systems*, p. 270.
10. See "The Killer Ad Machine," *Forbes*, December 11, 2000, pp. 168–178.
11. Mary Cronin, "Ford's Intranet Success," *Fortune*, March 30, 1998, p. 158.
12. "The Messy Business of Culling Company Files," *Wall Street Journal*, May 22, 1997, pp. B1, B2.
13. "Software That Plows Through Possibilities," *BusinessWeek*, August 7, 2000, p. 84.
14. See "Do One Thing, and Do It Well," *BusinessWeek*, June 19, 2000, pp. 94–100.
15. For example, see "Swamped Workers Switch to 'Unlisted' E-Mails," *USA Today*, September 7, 1999, p. 1A. See also Nicholas Varchaver, "The Perils of E-Mail," *Fortune*, February 17, 2003, pp. 96–103.
16. Robert Kraut, Charles Steinfield, Alice P. Chan, Brian Butler, and Anne Hoag, "Coordination and Virtualization: The Role of Electronic Networks and Personal Relationships," *Organization Science*, vol. 10, no. 6, 1999, pp. 722–740.
17. See Mahmoud M. Watad and Frank J. DiSanzo, "The Synergism of Telecommuting and Office Automation," *Sloan Management Review*, Winter 2000, pp. 85–96.
18. Manju K. Ahuja and Kathleen M. Carley, "Network Structure in Virtual Organizations," *Organization Science*, vol. 10, no. 6, 1999, pp. 741–757.
19. "Worksite Face-off: Techie vs. User," *USA Today*, June 17, 1997, pp. B1, B2.

Appendix

Tools for Planning and Decision Making

APPENDIX OUTLINE

Forecasting
- Sales and Revenue Forecasting
- Technological Forecasting
- Other Types of Forecasting
- Forecasting Techniques

Other Planning Techniques
- Linear Programming
- Breakeven Analysis
- Simulations
- PERT

Decision-Making Tools
- Payoff Matrices
- Decision Trees
- Other Techniques

Strengths and Weaknesses of Planning Tools
- Weaknesses and Problems
- Strengths and Advantages

This appendix discusses a number of the basic tools and techniques that managers can use to enhance the efficiency and effectiveness of planning and decision making. We first describe forecasting, an extremely important tool, and then discuss several other planning techniques. Next we discuss several tools that relate more to decision making. We conclude by assessing the strengths and weaknesses of the various tools and techniques.

Forecasting

To plan, managers must make assumptions about future events. But unlike Harry Potter and his friends, planners cannot simply look into a crystal ball or wave a wand. Instead, they must develop forecasts of probable future circumstances. **Forecasting** is the process of developing assumptions or premises about the future that managers can use in planning or decision making.

forecasting The process of developing assumptions or premises about the future that managers can use in planning or decision making

Sales and Revenue Forecasting

As the term implies, **sales forecasting** is concerned with predicting future sales. Because monetary resources (derived mainly from sales) are necessary to finance both current and future operations, knowledge of future sales is of vital importance. Sales forecasting is something that every business, from Exxon Mobil to a neighborhood pizza parlor, must do. Consider, for example, the following questions that a manager might need to answer:

sales forecasting The prediction of future sales

1. How much of each of our products should we produce next week? next month? next year?
2. How much money will we have available to spend on research and development and on new-product test marketing?
3. When and to what degree will we need to expand our existing production facilities?
4. How should we respond to union demands for a 5 percent pay increase?
5. If we borrow money for expansion, when can we pay it back?

None of these questions can be answered adequately without some notion of what future revenues are likely to be. Thus, sales forecasting is generally one of the first steps in planning.

Unfortunately, the term *sales forecasting* suggests that this form of forecasting is appropriate only for organizations that have something to sell. But other kinds of organizations also depend on financial resources, and so they also must forecast. The University of South Carolina, for example, must forecast future state aid before planning course offerings, staff size, and so on. Hospitals must forecast their future income from patient fees, insurance payments, and other sources to assess their ability to expand. Although we will continue to use the conventional term, keep in mind that what is really at issue is **revenue forecasting**.

revenue forecasting The prediction of future revenues from all sources

Several sources of information are used to develop a sales forecast. Previous sales figures and any obvious trends, such as the company's growth or stability, usually serve as the base. General economic indicators, technological improvements, new marketing strategies, and the competition's behavior all may be added together to ensure an accurate forecast. Once projected, the sales (or revenues) forecast becomes a guiding framework for various other activities. Raw-material expenditures, advertising budgets, sales-commission structures, and similar operating costs are all based on projected sales figures.

Organizations often forecast sales across several time horizons. The longer-run forecasts may then be updated and refined as various shorter-run cycles are completed. For obvious reasons, a forecast should be as accurate as possible, and the accuracy of sales forecasting tends to increase as organizations learn from their previous forecasting experience. But the more uncertain and complex future conditions are likely to be, the more difficult it is to develop accurate forecasts. To offset these problems partially, forecasts are more useful to managers if they are expressed as a range rather than as an absolute index or number. If projected sales increases are expected to be in the range of 10 to 12 percent, a manager can consider all the implications for the entire range. A 10 percent increase could dictate one set of activities; a 12 percent increase could call for a different set of activities.

Technological Forecasting

technological forecasting The prediction of what future technologies are likely to emerge and when they are likely to be economically feasible

Technological forecasting is another type of forecasting used by many organizations. It focuses on predicting what future technologies are likely to emerge and when they are likely to be economically feasible. In an era when technological breakthrough and innovation have become the rule rather than the exception, it is important that managers be able to anticipate new developments. If a manager invests heavily in existing technology (such as production processes, equipment, and computer systems) and the technology becomes obsolete in the near future, the company has wasted its resources.

The most striking technological innovations in recent years have been in electronics, especially semiconductors. Personal computers, electronic games, and sophisticated communications equipment such as cell phones with wireless Internet capabilities are all evidence of the electronics explosion. Given the increasing importance of technology and the rapid pace of technological innovation, it follows that managers will grow increasingly concerned with technological forecasting in the years to come.

Other Types of Forecasting

Other types of forecasting are also important to many organizations. Resource forecasting projects the organization's future needs for and the availability of human resources, raw materials, and other resources. General economic conditions are the subject of economic forecasts. For example, some organizations undertake population or market-size forecasting. Some organizations also attempt to forecast future government fiscal policy and various government regulations that might be put into practice. Indeed, almost any component in an organization's environment may be an appropriate area for forecasting.

Forecasting Techniques

To carry out the various kinds of forecasting we have identified, managers use several different techniques.[1] Time-series analysis and causal modeling are two common quantitative techniques.

Time-Series Analysis The underlying assumption of **time-series analysis** is that the past is a good predictor of the future. This technique is most useful when the manager has a lot of historical data available and when stable trends and patterns are apparent. In a time-series analysis, the variable under consideration (such as sales or enrollment) is plotted across time, and a "best-fit" line is identified.[2] Figure A.1 shows how a time-series analysis might look. The dots represent the number of units sold for each year from 1997 through 2005. The best-fit line has also been drawn in. It is the line around which the dots cluster with the least variability. A manager who wants to know what sales to expect in 2006 simply extends the line. In this case the projection would be around eighty-two hundred units.

time-series analysis A forecasting technique that extends past information into the future through the calculation of a best-fit line

Real time-series analysis involves much more than simply plotting sales data and then using a ruler and a pencil to draw and extend the line. Sophisticated mathematical procedures, among other things, are necessary to account for seasonal and cyclical fluctuations and to identify the true best-fit line. In real situations, data seldom follow the neat pattern found in Figure A.1. Indeed, the data points may be so widely dispersed that they mask meaningful trends from all but painstaking, computer-assisted inspection.

Causal Modeling Another useful forecasting technique is **causal modeling**. Actually, the term *causal modeling* represents a group of several techniques.

causal modeling A group of different techniques that determine casual relationships between different variables

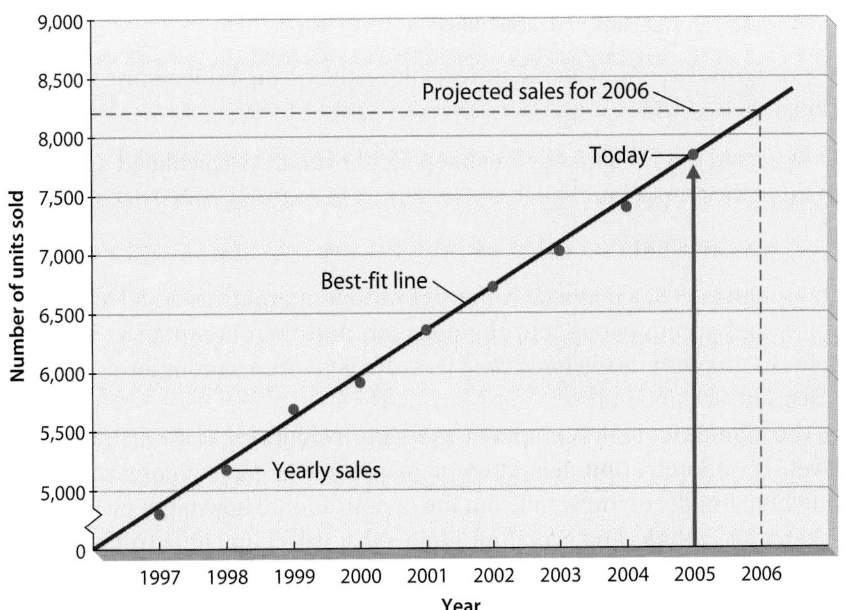

FIGURE A.1

An Example of Time-Series Analysis

Because time-series analysis assumes that the past is a good predictor of the future, it is most useful when historical data are available, trends are stable, and patterns are apparent. For example, it can be used for projecting estimated sales for products like shampoo, pens, and automobile tires. (Of course, few time-series analyses yield such clear results because there is almost always considerably more fluctuation in data from year to year.)

TABLE A.1

Summary of Causal Modeling Forecasting Techniques

Managers use several different types of causal models in planning and decision making. Three popular models are regression models, econometric models, and economic indicators.

Regression models	Used to predict one variable (called the dependent variable) on the basis of known or assumed other variables (called independent variables). For example, we might predict future sales based on the values of price, advertising, and economic levels.
Econometric models	Make use of several multiple-regression equations to consider the impact of major economic shifts. For example, we might want to predict what impact the migration toward the Sun Belt might have on our organization.
Economic indicators	Various population statistics, indexes, or parameters that predict organizationally relevant variables such as discretionary income. Examples include cost-of-living index, inflation rate, and level of unemployment.

regression model An equation that uses one set of variables to predict another variable

Table A.1 summarizes three of the most useful approaches. **Regression models** are equations created to predict a variable (such as sales volume) that depends on several other variables (such as price and advertising). The variable being predicted is called the *dependent variable*; the variables used to make the prediction are called *independent variables*. A typical regression equation used by a small business might take this form:

$$y = ax_1 + bx_2 + cx_3 + d$$

where

y = the dependent variable (sales in this case)

x_1, x_2, and x_3 = independent variables (advertising budget, price, and commissions)

a, b, and c = weights for the independent variables calculated during development of the regression model

d = a constant

To use the model, a manager can insert various alternatives for advertising budget, price, and commissions into the equation and then compute y. The calculated value of y represents the forecasted level of sales, given various levels of advertising, price, and commissions.[3]

econometric model A causal model that predicts major economic shifts and the potential impact of those shifts on the organization

Econometric models employ regression techniques at a much more complex level. **Econometric models** attempt to predict major economic shifts and the potential impact of those shifts on the organization. They might be used to predict various age, ethnic, and economic groups that will characterize different regions of the United States in the year 2025 and also to predict the kinds of products and services these groups may want. A complete econometric model may consist of hundreds or even thousands of equations. Computers are almost always necessary to apply them. Given the complexities involved in developing econometric models, many firms that decide to use them rely on outside consultants specializing in this approach.

Economic indicators, another form of causal model, are population statistics or indexes that reflect the economic well-being of a population. Examples of widely used economic indicators include the current rates of national productivity, inflation, and unemployment. In using such indicators, the manager draws on past experiences that have revealed a relationship between a certain indicator and some facet of the company's operations. Pitney Bowes Data Documents Division, for example, can predict future sales of its business forms largely on the basis of current GNP estimates and other economic growth indexes.

Economic indicators A key population statistic or index that reflects the economic well-being of a population

Qualitative Forecasting Techniques Organizations also use several qualitative techniques to develop their forecasts. A **qualitative forecasting technique** relies more on individual or group judgment or opinion rather than on sophisticated mathematical analyses. The Delphi procedure, described in Chapter 9 as a mechanism for managing group decision-making activities, can also be used to develop forecasts. A variation of it—the *jury-of-expert-opinion* approach—involves using the basic Delphi process with members of top management. In this instance, top management serves as a collection of experts asked to make a prediction about something—competitive behavior, trends in product demand, and so forth. Either a pure Delphi or a jury-of-expert-opinion approach might be useful in technological forecasting.

qualitative forecasting technique One of several techniques that rely on individual or group judgment rather than on mathematical analyses

The *sales-force-composition* method of sales forecasting is a pooling of the predictions and opinions of experienced salespeople. Because of their experience, these individuals are often able to forecast quite accurately what various customers will do. Management combines these forecasts and interprets the data to create plans. Textbook publishers use this procedure to project how many copies of a new title they might sell.

The *customer evaluation* technique goes beyond an organization's sales force and collects data from customers of the organization. The customers provide estimates of their own future needs for the goods and services that the organization supplies. Managers must combine, interpret, and act on this information. This approach, however, has two major limitations. Customers may be less interested in taking time to develop accurate predictions than members of the organization itself, and the method makes no provision for including any new customers that the organization may acquire. Wal-Mart helps its suppliers use this approach by providing them with detailed projections regarding what it intends to buy several months in advance.

Selecting an appropriate forecasting technique can be as important as applying it correctly. Some techniques are appropriate only for specific circumstances. For example, the sales-force-composition technique is good only for sales forecasting. Other techniques, like the Delphi method, are useful in a variety of situations. Some techniques, such as the econometric models, require extensive use of computers, whereas others, such as customer evaluation models, can be used with little mathematical expertise. For the most part, selection of a particular technique depends on the nature of the problem, the experience and preferences of the manager, and available resources.[4]

Other Planning Techniques

Of course, planning involves more than just forecasting. Other tools and techniques that are useful for planning purposes include linear programming, breakeven analysis, and simulations.

Linear Programming

linear programming A planning technique that determines the optimal combination of resources and activities

Linear programming is one of the most widely used quantitative tools for planning. **Linear programming** is a procedure for calculating the optimal combination of resources and activities. It is appropriate when there is some objective to be met (such as a sales quota or a certain production level) within a set of constraints (such as a limited advertising budget or limited production capabilities).

To illustrate how linear programming can be used, assume that a small electronics company produces two basic products—a high-quality cable television tuner and a high-quality receiver for picking up television audio and playing it through a stereo amplifier. Both products go through the same two departments, first production and then inspection and testing. Each product has a known profit margin and a high level of demand. The production manager's job is to produce the optimal combination of tuners (T) and receivers (R) that maximizes profits and uses the time in production (PR) and in inspection and testing (IT) most efficiently. Table A.2 gives the information needed for the use of linear programming to solve this problem.

TABLE A.2

Production Data for Tuners and Receivers

Linear programming can be used to determine the optimal number of tuners and receivers an organization might make. Essential information needed to perform this analysis includes the number of hours each product spends in each department, the production capacity for each department, and the profit margin for each product.

	Number of Hours Required per Unit		Production Capacity for Day (in Hours)
Department	**Tuners (T)**	**Receivers (R)**	
Production (PR)	10	6	150
Inspection and testing (IT)	4	4	80
Profit margin	$30	$20	

The *objective function* is an equation that represents what we want to achieve. In technical terms, it is a mathematical representation of the desirability of the consequences of a particular decision. In our example, the objective function can be represented as follows:

$$\text{Maximize profit} = \$30X_T + \$20X_R$$

where

$$R = \text{the number of receivers to be produced}$$

$$T = \text{the number of tuners to be produced}$$

The \$30 and \$20 figures are the respective profit margins of the tuner and receiver, as noted in Table A.2. The objective, then, is to maximize profits.

However, this objective must be accomplished within a specific set of constraints. In our example, the constraints are the time required to produce each product in each department and the total amount of time available. These data are also found in Table A.2 and can be used to construct the relevant constraint equations:

$$10T + 6R \leq 150$$

$$4T + 4R \leq 80$$

(that is, we cannot use more capacity than is available), and of course,

$$T \geq 0$$

$$R \geq 0$$

The set of equations consisting of the objective function and constraints can be solved graphically. To start, we assume that production of each product is maximized when production of the other is at zero. The resultant solutions are then plotted on a coordinate axis. In the PR department, if $T = 0$ then:

$$10T + 6R \leq 150$$

$$10(0) + 6R \leq 150$$

$$R \leq 25$$

In the same department, if $R = 0$ then:

$$10T + 6R \leq 150$$

$$10T + 6(0) \leq 150$$

$$T \leq 15$$

Similarly, in the IT department, if no tuners are produced,

$$4T + 4R \leq 80$$

$$4(0) + 4R \leq 80$$

$$R \leq 20$$

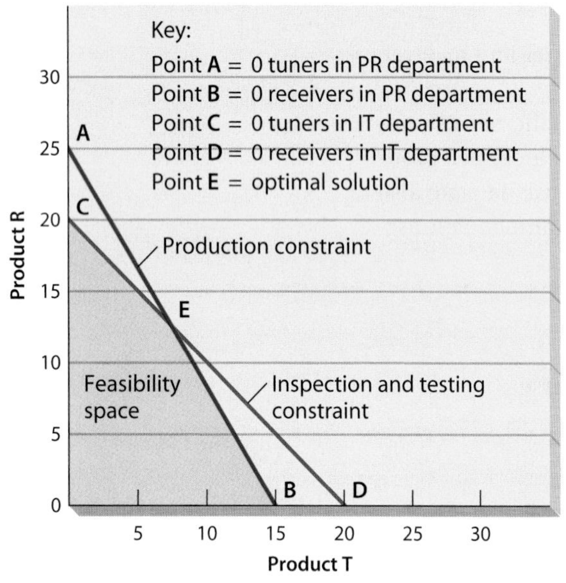

FIGURE A.2

The Graphical Solution of a Linear Programming Problem

Finding the graphical solution to a linear programming problem is useful when only two alternatives are being considered. When problems are more complex, computers that can execute hundreds of equations and variables are necessary. Virtually all large firms, such as General Motors, Chevron Texaco, and Sears, use linear programming.

and, if no receivers are produced,

$$4T + 4R \leq 80$$

$$4T + 4(0) \leq 80$$

$$T \leq 20$$

The four resulting inequalities are graphed in Figure A.2. The shaded region represents the feasibility space, or production combinations that do not exceed the capacity of either department. The optimal number of products will be defined at one of the four corners of the shaded area—that is, the firm should produce twenty receivers only (point C), fifteen tuners only (point B), thirteen receivers and seven tuners (point E), or no products at all. With the constraint that production of both tuners and receivers must be greater than zero, it follows that point E is the optimal solution. That combination requires 148 hours in PR and 80 hours in IT and yields \$470 in profit. (Note that if only receivers were produced, the profit would be \$400; producing only tuners would mean \$450 in profit.)

Unfortunately, only two alternatives can be handled by the graphical method, and our example was extremely simple. When there are other alternatives, a complex algebraic method must be employed. Real-world problems may require several hundred equations and variables. Clearly, computers are necessary to execute such sophisticated analyses. Linear programming is a powerful technique, playing a key role in both planning and decision making. It can be used to schedule production, select an optimal portfolio of investments, allocate sales representatives to territories, or produce an item at some minimum cost.

Breakeven Analysis

Linear programming is called a *normative procedure* because it prescribes the optimal solution to a problem. Breakeven analysis is a *descriptive procedure* because it simply describes relationships among variables; then it is up to the manager to make decisions. We can define **breakeven analysis** as a procedure for identifying the point at which revenues start covering their associated costs. It might be used to analyze the effects on profits of different price and output combinations or various levels of output.

breakeven analysis A procedure for identifying the point at which revenues start covering their associated costs

Figure A.3 represents the key cost variables in breakeven analysis. Creating most products or services includes three types of costs: fixed costs, variable costs, and total costs. *Fixed costs* are costs that are incurred regardless of what volume of output is being generated. They include rent or mortgage payments on the building, managerial salaries, and depreciation of plant and equipment. *Variable costs* vary with the number of units produced, such as the cost of raw materials and direct labor used to make each unit. *Total costs* are fixed costs plus variable costs. Note that because of fixed costs, the line for total costs never begins at zero.

Other important factors in breakeven analysis are revenue and profit. Revenue, the total dollar amount of sales, is computed by multiplying the number of units sold by the sales price of each unit. *Profit* is then determined by subtracting total costs from total revenues. When revenues and total costs are plotted on the same axes, the breakeven graph shown in Figure A.4 emerges. The point at which the lines representing total costs and total revenues cross is the breakeven point. If the company represented in Figure A.4 sells more units than are represented by point A, it will realize a profit; selling below that level will result in a loss.

Mathematically, the breakeven point (expressed as units of production or volume) is shown by the formula

$$BP = \frac{TFC}{P - VC}$$

where

BP = breakeven point

TFC = total fixed costs

P = price per unit

VC = variable cost per units

FIGURE A.3

An Example of Cost Factors for Breakeven Analysis

To determine the breakeven point for profit on sales for a product or service, the manager must first determine both fixed and variable costs. These costs are then combined to show total costs.

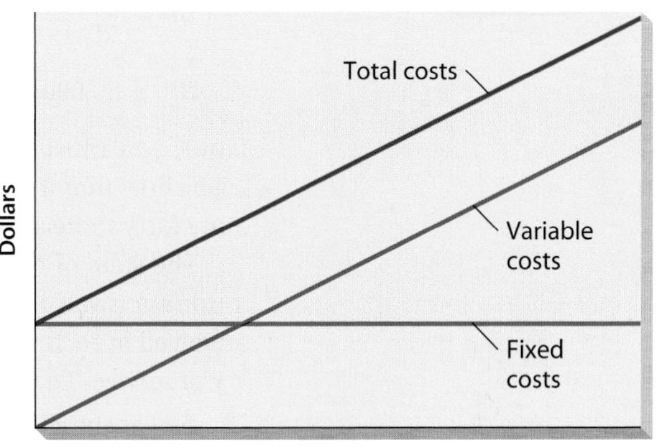

Assume that you are considering the production of a new garden hoe with an ergonomically-curved handle. You have determined that an acceptable selling price will be $20. You have also determined that the variable costs per hoe will be $15, and you have total fixed costs of $400,000 per year. The question is, How

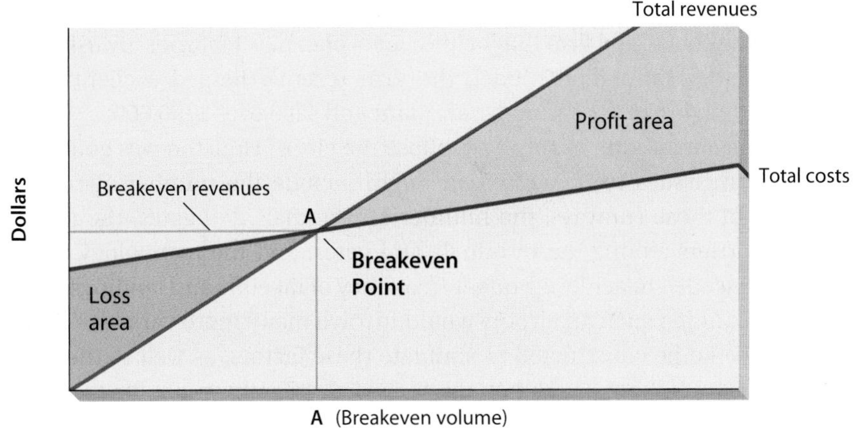

FIGURE A.4

Breakeven Analysis

After total costs are determined and graphed, the manager then graphs the total revenues that will be earned on different levels of sales. The regions defined by the intersection of the two graphs show loss and profit areas. The intersection itself shows the breakeven point—the level of sales at which all costs are covered but no profits are earned.

many hoes must you sell each year to break even? Using the breakeven model, you find that

$$BP = \frac{TFC}{P - VC}$$

$$BP = \frac{400{,}000}{20 - 15}$$

$$BP = 80{,}000 \text{ units}$$

Thus, you must sell eighty thousand hoes to break even. Further analysis would also show that if you could raise your price to $25 per hoe, you would need to sell only forty thousand to break even, and so on.

The state of New York used a breakeven analysis to evaluate seven variations of prior approvals for its Medicaid service. Comparisons were conducted of the costs involved in each variation against savings gained from efficiency and improved quality of service. The state found that only three of the variations were cost effective.[5]

Breakeven analysis is a popular and important planning technique, but it also has noteworthy weaknesses. It considers revenues only up to the breakeven point, and it makes no allowance for the time value of money. For example, because the funds used to cover fixed and variable costs could be used for other purposes (such as investment), the organization is losing interest income by tying up its money prior to reaching the breakeven point. Thus, managers often use break-even analysis as only the first step in planning. After the preliminary analysis has been completed, more sophisticated techniques (such as rate-of-return analysis or discounted-present-value analysis) are used. Those techniques can help the manager decide whether to proceed or to divert resources into other areas.

Simulations

organizational simulation A model of a real-world situation that can be manipulated to discover how it functions

Another useful planning device is simulation. The word *simulate* means to copy or to represent. An **organizational simulation** is a model of a real-world situation that can be manipulated to discover how it functions. Simulation is a descriptive, rather than a prescriptive, technique. Northern Research & Engineering Corporation is an engineering consulting firm that helps clients plan new factories. By using a sophisticated factory simulation model, the firm recently helped a client cut several machines and operations from a new plant and save over $750,000.

To consider another example, suppose the city of Houston was going to build a new airport. Issues to be addressed might include the number of runways, the direction of those runways, the number of terminals and gates, the allocation of various carriers among the terminals and gates, and the technology and human resources needed to achieve a target frequency of takeoffs and landings. (Of course, actually planning such an airport would involve many more variables than these.) A model could be constructed to simulate these factors, as well as their interrelationships. The planner could then insert several different values for each factor and observe the probable results.

Simulation problems are in some ways similar to those addressed by linear programming, but simulation is more useful in very complex situations characterized by diverse constraints and opportunities. The development of sophisticated simulation models may require the expertise of outside specialists or consultants, and the complexity of simulation almost always necessitates the use of a computer. For these reasons, simulation is most likely to be used as a technique for planning in large organizations that have the required resources.

PERT

A final planning tool that we will discuss is PERT. **PERT**, an acronym for Program Evaluation and Review Technique, was developed by the U.S. Navy to help coordinate the activities of three thousand contractors during the development of the Polaris nuclear submarine, and it was credited with saving two years of work on the project. It has subsequently been used by most large companies in different ways. The purpose of PERT is to develop a network of activities and their interrelationships and thus highlight critical time intervals that affect the overall project. PERT follows six basic steps:

PERT A planning tool that uses a network to plan projects involving numerous activities and their interrelationships

1. Identify the activities to be performed and the events that will mark their completion.
2. Develop a network showing the relationships among the activities and events.
3. Calculate the time needed for each event and the time necessary to get from each event to the next.
4. Identify within the network the longest path that leads to completion of the project. This path is called the critical path.
5. Refine the network.
6. Use the network to control the project.

Suppose that a marketing manager wants to use PERT to plan the test marketing and nationwide introduction of a new product. Table A.3 identifies the basic steps involved in carrying out this project. The activities are then arranged in a network like the one shown in Figure A.5. In the figure, each completed event is represented by a number in a circle. The activities are indicated by letters on the lines connecting the events. Notice that some activities are performed independently of one another and that others must be performed in sequence. For example, test production (activity a) and test site location (activity c) can be done at the same time, but test site location has to be done before actual testing (activities f and g) can be done.

The time needed to get from one activity to another is then determined. The normal way to calculate the time between each activity is to average the most optimistic, most pessimistic, and most likely times, with the most likely time weighted by 4. Time is usually calculated with the following formula:

$$\text{Expected time} = \frac{a + 4b + c}{6}$$

Where

a = optimistic time

b = most likely time

c = pessimistic time

TABLE A.3

Activities and Events for Introducing a New Product

PERT is used to plan schedules for projects, and it is particularly useful when many activities with critical time intervals must be coordinated. Besides launching a new product, PERT is useful for projects like constructing a new factory or building, remodeling an office, or opening a new store.

Activities	Events
	1 Origin of project.
a Produce limited quantity for test marketing.	2 Completion of production for test marketing.
b Design preliminary package.	3 Completion of design for preliminary package.
c Locate test market.	4 Test market located.
d Obtain local merchant cooperation.	5 Local merchant cooperation obtained.
e Ship product to selected retail outlets.	6 Product for test marketing shipped to retail outlets.
f Monitor sales and customer reactions.	7 Sales and customer reactions monitored.
g Survey customers in test-market area.	8 Customers in test-market area surveyed.
h Make needed product changes.	9 Product changes made.
i Make needed package changes.	10 Package changes made.
j Mass-produce the product.	11 Product mass-produced.
k Begin national advertising.	12 National advertising carried out.
l Begin national distribution.	13 National distribution completed.

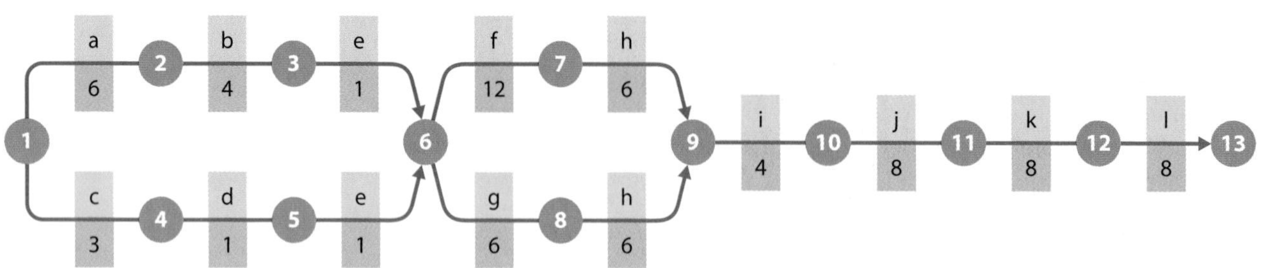

The blue numbers and letters correspond to the numbers and letters used in Table A.3.

The orange numbers refer to the expected number of weeks for each activity.

FIGURE A.5

A PERT Network for Introducing a New Product

The expected number of weeks for each activity in our example is shown in parentheses along each path in Figure A.5. The **critical path**—or the longest path through the PERT network—is then identified. This path is considered critical because it shows the shortest time in which the project can be completed. In our example, the critical path is 1-2-3-6-7-9-10-11-12-13, totaling fifty-seven weeks. PERT thus tells the manager that the project will take fifty-seven weeks to complete.

critical path The longest path through a PERT network

The first network may be refined. If fifty-seven weeks to completion is too long a time, the manager might decide to begin preliminary package design before the test products are finished. Or the manager might decide that ten weeks rather than twelve is a sufficient time period to monitor sales. The idea is that if the critical path can be shortened, so too can the overall duration of the project. The PERT network serves as an ongoing framework for both planning and control throughout the project. For example, the manager can use it to monitor where the project is relative to where it needs to be. Thus, if an activity on the critical path takes longer than planned, the manager needs to make up the time elsewhere or live with the fact that the entire project will be late.

Decision-Making Tools

Managers can also use a number of tools that relate more specifically to decision making than to planning. Two commonly used decision-making tools are payoff matrices and decision trees.

Payoff Matrices

A **payoff matrix** specifies the probable value of different alternatives, depending on different possible outcomes associated with each. The use of a payoff matrix requires that several alternatives be available, that several different events could occur, and that the consequences depend on which alternative is selected and on which event or set of events occurs. An important concept in understanding the payoff matrix, then, is probability. A **probability** is the likelihood, expressed as a percentage, that a particular event will or will not occur. If we believe that a particular event will occur seventy-five times out of one hundred, we can say that the probability of its occurring is 75 percent, or .75. Probabilities range in value from 0 (no chance of occurrence) to 1.00 (certain occurrence—also referred to as 100 percent). In the business world, there are few probabilities of either 0 or 1.00. Most probabilities that managers use are based on subjective judgment, intuition, and historical data.

payoff matrix A decision-making tool that specifies the probable value of different alternatives, depending on different possible outcomes associated with each

probability The likelihood, expressed as a percentage, that a particular event will or will not occur

The **expected value** of an alternative course of action is the sum of all possible values of outcomes from that action multiplied by their respective probabilities. Suppose, for example, that a venture capitalist is considering investing in a new company. If he believes there is a .40 probability of making $100,000, a .30 probability of

expected value When applied to alternative courses of action, the sum of all possible values of outcomes from that action multiplied by their respective probabilities making \$30,000, and a .30 probability of losing \$20,000, the expected value *(EV)* of this alternative is

$$EV = .40(100{,}000) + .30(30{,}000) + .30(-20{,}000)$$

$$EV = 40{,}000 + 9{,}000 - 6{,}000$$

$$EV = \$43{,}000$$

The investor can then weigh the expected value of this investment against the expected values of other available alternatives. The highest *EV* signals the investment that should most likely be selected.

For example, suppose another venture capitalist wants to invest \$20,000 in a new business. She has identified three possible alternatives: a leisure products company, an energy enhancement company, and a food-producing company. Because the expected value of each alternative depends on short-run changes in the economy, especially inflation, she decides to develop a payoff matrix. She estimates that the probability of high inflation is .30 and the probability of low inflation is .70. She then estimates the probable returns for each investment in the event of both high and low inflation. Figure A.6 shows what the payoff matrix might look like (a minus sign indicates a loss). The expected value of investing in the leisure products company is

$$EV = .30(-10{,}000) + .70(50{,}000)$$

$$EV = -3{,}000 + 35{,}000$$

$$EV = \$32{,}000$$

Similarly, the expected value of investing in the energy enhancement company is

$$EV = .30(90{,}000) + .70(-15{,}000)$$

$$EV = 27{,}000 + (-10{,}500)$$

$$EV = \$16{,}500$$

FIGURE A.6

An Example of a Payoff Matrix

A payoff matrix helps the manager determine the expected value of different alternatives. A payoff matrix is effective only if the manager ensures that probability estimates are as accurate as possible.

		High inflation (*probability of .30*)	Low inflation (*probability of .70*)
Investment alternative **1**	Leisure products company	–\$10,000	+\$50,000
Investment alternative **2**	Energy enhancement company	+\$90,000	–\$15,000
Investment alternative **3**	Food-processing company	+\$30,000	+\$25,000

And, finally, the expected value of investing in the food-processing company is

$$EV = .30(30{,}000) + .70(25{,}000)$$

$$EV = 9{,}000 + 17{,}500$$

$$EV = \$26{,}500$$

Investing in the leisure products company, then, has the highest expected value.

Other potential uses for payoff matrices include determining optimal order quantities, deciding whether to repair or replace broken machinery, and deciding which of several new products to introduce. Of course, the real key to using payoff matrices effectively is making accurate estimates of the relevant probabilities.

Decision Trees

decision tree A planning tool that extends the concept of a payoff matrix through a sequence of decisions

Decision trees are like payoff matrices because they enhance a manager's ability to evaluate alternatives by making use of expected values. However, they are most appropriate when there are several decisions to be made in sequence.

Figure A.7 illustrates a hypothetical decision tree. The small firm represented wants to begin exporting its products to a foreign market, but limited capacity restricts it to only one market at first. Managers feel that either France or China would be the best place to start. Whichever alternative is selected, sales for the product in that country may turn out to be high or low. In France, there is a .80 chance of high sales and a .20 chance of low sales. The anticipated payoffs in these situations are predicted to be \$20 million and \$3 million, respectively. In China, the probabilities of high versus low sales are .60 and .40, respectively, and the associated payoffs are presumed to be \$25 million and \$6 million. As shown in Figure A.7, the expected value of shipping to France is \$16,600,000, whereas the expected value of shipping to China is \$17,400,000.

The astute reader will note that this part of the decision could have been set up as a payoff matrix. However, the value of decision trees is that we can extend the model to include subsequent decisions. Assume, for example, that the company begins shipping to China. If high sales do in fact materialize, the company will soon reach another decision situation. It might use the extra revenues to (1) increase shipments to China, (2) build a plant close to China and thus cut shipping costs, or (3) begin shipping to France. Various outcomes are possible for each decision, and each outcome will also have both a probability and an anticipated payoff. It is therefore possible to compute expected values back through several tiers of decisions all the way to the initial one. As it is with payoff matrices, determining probabilities accurately is the crucial element in the process. Properly used, however, decision trees can provide managers with a useful road map through complex decision situations.

Other Techniques

In addition to payoff matrices and decision trees, several other quantitative methods are also available to facilitate decision making.

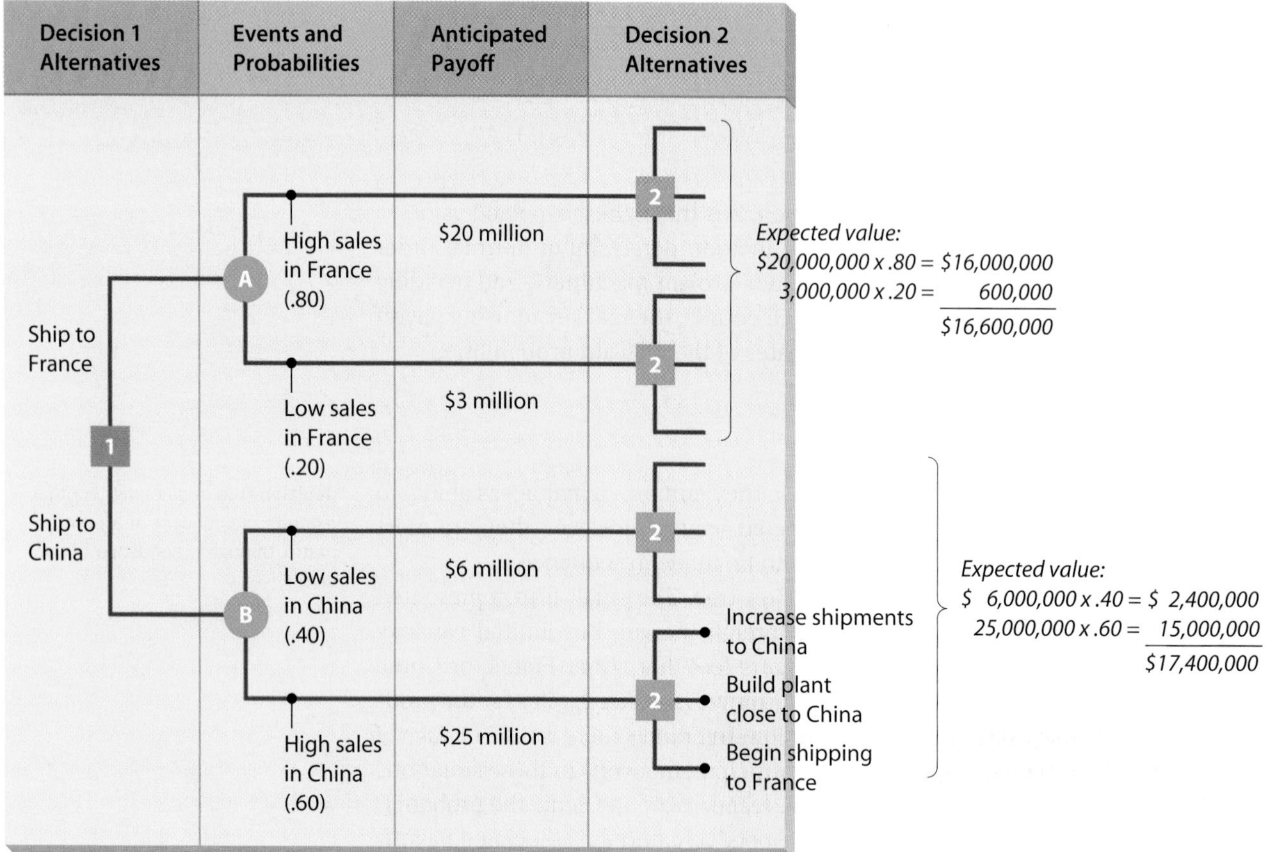

FIGURE A.7

An Example of a Decision Tree

A decision tree extends the basic concepts of a payoff matrix through multiple decisions. This tree shows the possible outcomes of two levels of decisions. The first decision is whether to expand to China or to France. The second decision, assuming that the company expands to China, is whether to increase shipments to China, build a plant close to China, or initiate shipping to France.

inventory model A technique that helps managers decide how much inventory to maintain

Inventory Models **Inventory models** are techniques that help the manager decide how much inventory to maintain. Target Stores uses inventory models to help determine how much merchandise to order, when to order it, and so forth. Inventory consists of both raw materials (inputs) and finished goods (outputs). Polaroid, for example, maintains a supply of the chemicals that it uses to make film, the cartons it packs film in, and packaged film ready to be shipped. For finished goods, both extremes are bad: excess inventory ties up capital, whereas a small inventory may result in shortages and customer dissatisfaction. The same holds for raw materials: too much inventory ties up capital, but if a company runs out of resources, work stoppages may occur. Finally, because the process of placing an order for raw materials and supplies has associated costs (such as clerical time, shipping expenses, and higher unit costs for small quantities), it is important to minimize the frequency of ordering. Inventory models help the manager make decisions that optimize the size of inventory. New innovations in inventory management such as **just-in-time,** or **JIT**, rely heavily on decision-making models. A JIT system involves scheduling materials to arrive in small batches as they are needed, thereby eliminating the need for a big reserve inventory, warehouse space, and so forth.[6]

just-in-time (JIT) An inventory management technique in which materials are scheduled to arrive in small batches as they are needed, eliminating the need for resources such as big reserves and warehouse space

queuing model A model used to optimize waiting lines in organizations

Queuing Models **Queuing models** are intended to help organizations manage waiting lines. We are all familiar with such situations: shoppers waiting to pay for groceries at Kroger, drivers waiting to buy gas at an Exxon station, travelers calling American Airlines for reservations, and customers waiting for a teller at Citibank. Take the Kroger example. If a store manager has only one check-out stand in operation, the store's cost for check-out personnel is very low; however, many customers are upset by the long line that frequently develops. To solve the problem, the store manager could decide to keep twenty check-out stands open at all times. Customers would like the short waiting period, but personnel costs would be very high. A queuing model would be appropriate in this case to help the manager determine the optimal number of check-out stands: the number that would balance personnel costs and customer waiting time. Target Stores uses queuing models to determine how many check-out lanes to put in its retail stores.

Distribution Models A decision facing many marketing managers relates to the distribution of the organization's products. Specifically, the manager must decide where the products should go and how to transport them. Railroads, trucking, and air freight have associated shipping costs, and each mode of transportation follows different schedules and routes. The problem is to identify the combination of routes that optimize distribution effectiveness and distribution costs. **Distribution models** help managers determine this optimal pattern of distribution.

distribution model A model used to determine the optimal pattern of distribution across different carriers and routes

game theory A planning tool used to predict how competitors will react to various activities that an organization might undertake

Game Theory **Game theory** was originally developed to predict the effect of one company's decisions on competitors. Models developed from game theory are intended to predict how a competitor will react to various activities that an organization might undertake, such as price changes, promotional changes, and the introduction of new products. If Wells Fargo Bank were considering raising its prime lending rate by 1 percent, it might use a game theory model to predict whether Citicorp would follow suit. If the model revealed that Citicorp would do so, Wells Fargo would probably proceed; otherwise, it would probably maintain the current interest rates. Unfortunately, game theory is not yet as useful as it was originally expected to be. The complexities of the real world combined with the limitation of the technique itself restrict its applicability. Game theory, however, does provide a useful conceptual framework for analyzing competitive behavior, and its usefulness may be improved in the future.

Artificial Intelligence A fairly new addition to the manager's quantitative tool kit is **artificial intelligence (AI)**. The most useful form of AI is the expert system.[7] An expert system is essentially a computer program that attempts to duplicate the thought processes of experienced decision makers. For example, Hewlett-Packard

artificial intelligence (AI) A computer program that attempts to duplicate the thought processes of experienced decision makers has developed an expert system that checks sales orders for new computer systems and then designs preliminary layouts for those new systems. HP can now ship the computer to a customer in components for final assembly on site. This approach has enabled the company to cut back on its own final-assembly facilities.

Strengths and Weaknesses of Planning Tools

Like all issues confronting management, planning tools of the type described here have several strengths and weaknesses.

Weaknesses and Problems

One weakness of the planning and decision-making tools discussed in this appendix is that they may not always adequately reflect reality. Even with the most sophisticated and powerful computer-assisted technique, reality must often be simplified. Many problems are also not amenable to quantitative analysis because important elements of them are intangible or nonquantifiable. Employee morale or satisfaction, for example, is often a major factor in managerial decisions.

The use of these tools and techniques may also be quite costly. For example, only larger companies can afford to develop their own econometric models. Even though the computer explosion has increased the availability of quantitative aids, some expense is still involved and it will take time for many of these techniques to become widely used. Resistance to change also limits the use of planning tools in some settings. If a manager for a retail chain has always based decisions for new locations on personal visits, observations, and intuition, she or he may be less than eager to begin using a computer-based model for evaluating and selecting sites. Finally, problems may arise when managers have to rely on technical specialists to use sophisticated models. Experts trained in the use of complex mathematical procedures may not understand or appreciate other aspects of management.

Strengths and Advantages

On the plus side, planning and decision-making tools offer many advantages. For situations that are amenable to quantification, they can bring sophisticated mathematical processes to bear on planning and decision making. Properly designed models and formulas also help decision makers "see reason." For example, a manager might not be inclined to introduce a new product line simply because she or he doesn't think it will be profitable. After seeing a forecast predicting first-year sales of one hundred thousand units coupled with a breakeven analysis showing profitability after only twenty thousand, however, the manager will probably change her or his mind. Thus, rational planning tools and techniques force the manager to look beyond personal prejudices and predispositions. Finally, the computer explosion is rapidly making sophisticated planning techniques available in a wider range of settings than ever before.

The crucial point to remember is that planning tools and techniques are a means to an end, not an end in themselves. Just as a carpenter uses a hand saw in some situations and an electric saw in others, a manager must recognize that a particular model may be useful in some situations but not in others that may call for a different approach. Knowing the difference is one mark of a good manager.

Summary of Key Points

business.college.hmco.com/students

Managers often use various tools and techniques as they develop plans and make decisions. Forecasting is one widely used method. Forecasting is the process of developing assumptions or premises about the future. Sales or revenue forecasting is especially important. Many organizations also rely heavily on technological forecasting. Time-series analysis and causal modeling are important forecasting techniques. Qualitative techniques are also widely used.

Managers also use other planning tools and techniques in different circumstances. Linear programming helps optimize resources and activities. Breakeven analysis helps identify how many products or services must be sold to cover costs. Simulations model reality. PERT helps plan how much time a project will require.

Other tools and techniques are useful for decision making. Constructing a payoff matrix, for example, helps a manager assess the expected value of different alternatives. Decision trees are used to extend expected values across multiple decisions. Other popular decision-making tools and techniques include inventory models, queuing models, distribution models, game theory, and artificial intelligence.

Various strengths and weaknesses are associated with each of these tools and techniques, as well as with their use by a manager. The key to success is knowing when each should and should not be used and knowing how to use and interpret the results that each provides.

Chapter Notes

1. For a classic review, see John C. Chambers, S. K. Mullick, and D. Smith, "How to Choose the Right Forecasting Technique," *Harvard Business Review*, July–August 1971, pp. 45–74.
2. Charles Ostrom, *Time-Series Analysis: Regression Techniques* (Beverly Hills, Calif.: Sage Publications, 1980).
3. Fred Kerlinger and Elazar Pedhazur, *Multiple Regression in Behavioral Research* (New York: Holt, 1973).
4. Chambers, Mullick, and Smith, "How to Choose the Right Forecasting Technique"; see also J. Scott Armstrong, *Long-Range Forecasting: From Crystal Ball to Computers* (New York: Wiley, 1978).
5. Edward Hannan, Linda Ryan, and Richard Van Orden, "A Cost-Benefit Analysis of Prior Approvals for Medicaid Services in New York State," *Socio-Economic Planning Sciences*, 1984, Vol. 18, pp. 1–14.
6. Ramon L. Alonso and Cline W. Fraser, "JIT Hits Home: A Case Study in Reducing Management Delays," *Sloan Management Review*, Summer 1991, pp. 59–68.
7. Beau Sheil, "Thinking about Artificial Intelligence," *Harvard Business Review*, July–August 1987, pp. 91–97; and Dorothy Leonard-Barton and John J. Sviokla, "Putting Expert Systems to Work," *Harvard Business Review*, March–April 1988, pp. 91–98.

Photo Credits

Part One: pp. 2–3: Michael Rosenfeld/Getty Images; *Chapter 1*: p. 5: Bill Greenblatt/CORBIS Sygma; p. 7: AP/Wide World Photos; p. 13: AP/Wide World Photos; p. 19: Pablo Bartholomew/Netphotograph.com; p. 20: Jean-François Campos/Agence VU; p. 28: Mike Simons/Getty Images. *Chapter 2*: p. 39: Mark Richards/PhotoEdit, Inc.; p. 40: © Sue Van Etten Lawson; p. 41: Bettmann/CORBIS; p. 48: Permission of AT&T Archives; p. 55: Bob Rives; p. 59: AP/Wide World Photos. *Part Two*: pp. 70–71: AP/Wide World Photos; *Chapter 3*: p. 73: AP/Wide World Photos; p. 76: Radhika Chalasani/SIPA Press; p. 80: Munshi Ahmed; p. 85: Michael Newman/PhotoEdit, Inc.; p. 89: Paula Bronstein/Getty Images. *Chapter 4*: p. 107: PhotoDisc/Getty Images; p. 108: Brian Coats; p. 121: Dilip Mehta/Contact Press Images; p. 122: Douglas McFadd/Getty Images. *Chapter 5*: p. 141: Reuters/NewMedia Inc./CORBIS; p. 145: Bonnie Kamin/PhotoEdit, Inc.; p. 157: AFP/CORBIS; p. 158: AP/Wide World Photos; p. 166: Jerome Ming/CORBIS SABA. *Chapter 6*: p. 175: AFP/CORBIS; p. 177: Adam Friedberg; p. 181: AP/Wide World Photos; p 191: Scott Jones; p. 192: AP/Wide World Photos. *Part Three*: pp. 202–203: AP/Wide World Photos; *Chapter 7*: p. 205: James Leynse/CORBIS SABA; p. 212: AP/Wide World Photos; p. 221: AP/Wide World Photos; p. 222: George Steinmetz; p. 225: Gerry Gropp. *Chapter 8*: p. 237: Tim De Waele & Vincent Kalut/CORBIS TempSport; p. 241: AP/Wide World Photos; p. 243: Evan Kafka; p. 249: Michael Newman/PhotoEdit Inc.; p. 251: Steven Ahlgren; p. 261: Paul Schirnhofer/Contact Press Images. *Chapter 9*: p. 275: RF/CORBIS; p. 278: Steve Liss/Getty Images; p. 284: Karen Keuhn; p. 288: AP/Wide World Photos; p. 291 (top): Mark Wilson/Getty Images; p. 291 (bottom): Reuters NewMedia Inc./CORBIS. *Chapter 10*: p. 303: John Li/Getty Images; p. 304: Sammy Davis; p. 307: AP/Wide World Photos; p. 311: Globe Photos/David L. Ryan; p. 316: David Friedman; p. 323: David G. Spielman. *Part Four*: pp. 338–339: CORBIS/Stock Market; *Chapter 11*: p. 341: Bill Aron/PhotoEdit, Inc.; p. 343: Eli Reichman for Time; p. 344: AP/Wide World Photos; p. 352: Bill Aron/PhotoEdit, Inc.; p. 357 (top): Chris Covatta; p. 357 (bottom): Luc Choquer/METIS Images. *Chapter 12*: p. 373: David Young-Wolff/PhotoEdit, Inc.; p. 375: Charlie Archambault for U. S. News & World Report; p. 380: Kelly Culpepper Photography; p. 382: AP/Wide World Photos; p. 392: AP/Wide World Photos; p. 393: Scott Goldsmith. *Chapter 13*: p. 403: Henry A. Koshollek/Capital Times/CORBIS Sygma; p. 405: Dennis MacDonald/PhotoEdit, Inc.; p. 411: Dana Smith/Black Star; p. 414: AP/Wide World Photos; p. 421: AP/Wide World Photos. *Chapter 14*: p. 437: Amy Etra/PhotoEdit, Inc.; p. 440: AP/Wide World Photos; p. 441: CORBIS; p. 444: Erin Patrice O'Brien; p. 450: Greg Girard/Contact Press Images; p. 459: Ann States. *Part Five*: pp. 474–475: CORBIS/StockMarket; *Chapter 15*: p. 477: Larry Kolvoord/The Image Works; p. 479: AP/Wide World Photos; p. 485: Dylan Martinez/Getty Images; p. 493: Jeff Greenberg/The Image Works;

p. 495: Eli Reichman; p. 499: Michael Lewis. *Chapter 16*: p. 511: Monika Graff/The Image Works; p. 513: Jose Azel/AURORA; p. 519: Andreanna Lynn Seymore Photography; p. 521: AP/Wide World Photos; p. 533: Kenneth Jarecke/Contact Press Images; p. 534: Pham. *Chapter 17*: p. 549: AP/Wide World Photos; p. 550: Justin Sulivan/Getty Images; p. 554: AP/Wide World Photos; p. 563: Makoto Ishida; p. 569: Todd Warshaw/ICON Sports Media, Inc. *Chapter 18*: p. 585: David McNew/Getty Images; p. 587: AP/Wide World Photos; p. 592: Olivier Laude; p. 593: AP/Wide World Photos; p. 604 (top): David Deal; p. 604 (bottom): AP/Wide World Photos. *Chapter 19*: p. 617: Scott Olson/Getty; p. 618: AP/Wide World Photos; p. 620: Phillippe Diederich; p. 623: J. D. Pooley/Getty Images; p. 629: Will Panich Photography. *Part Six*: p. 648–649: CORBIS/StockMarket; *Chapter 20*: p. 651: James Leynse/CORBIS Sygma; p. 652: William Thomas Cain/Getty Images; p. 658: AP/Wide World Photos; p. 661: AP/Wide World Photos; p. 662: Todd Buchanan; p. 663: Ann States. *Chapter 21*: p. 685: Christopher J. Morris/CORBIS; p. 686: Mark Richards/PhotoEdit, Inc.; p. 688: Tim Boyle/Getty Images; p. 689: AP/Wide World Photos; p. 692: Louis Psihoyos; p. 704: Berndt Auers. *Chapter 22*: p. 717: AP/Wide World Photos; p. 718: Emily Mott; p. 720: PAXTON; p. 721: Elena Dorfman; p. 725: AP/Wide World Photos; p. 739: AP/Wide World Photos.

Name Index

Abelson, Reed, 582n1
Abraham, Spencer, 654
Abrahamson, Eric, 434n13
Abramson, Patty, 324
Ackerman, Josef, 377
Adams, Erica, 717
Adams, J. Stacy, 547n20
Adams, Marilyn, 137
Adams, Scott, 60, 335–336
Adelman, David, 341
Adorno, T. W., 509n9
Agee, Bill, 199
Agosto, Jasmin, 448
Ahearne, Michael, 646n22
Ahishakiye, Olive, 307
Ahlburg, Dennis A., 471
Ahuja, Manju K., 747n18
Akin, Gib, 434n13
Akst, Daniel, 516
Albion, Mark, 508
Alderfer, Clayton P., 546n11
Alexander, Jeffrey A., 424n29
Alexander, Karen, 448
Alexander the Great, 42
Aley, James, 17
Alfarabi, 42
Allen, Joseph, 615n35
Allen, Michael G., 273n32
Allen, Robert, 634
Allio, Robert J., 273n32
Altman, Daniel, 552
Ambrose, Maureen L., 546n2
Amihud, Yakov, 272n22
Amlong, William, 137
Anders, George, 301n21
Anderson, Erin, 683n26
Anderson, Henry R., 682n14, 682n16
Anderson, Jerry W., Jr., 138n22
Andrews, Gerald, 434n18
Andrews, Kenneth, 272n2
Ansoff, Igor, 272n2
Aragon-Correa, J. Alberto, 138n17
Armenakis, Achilles A., 433n2
Armour, Stephanie, 472n23
Armstrong, Michael, 359
Arndt, Michael, 472, 532, 703
Aronoff, Craig E., 615n32
Ash, Mary Kay, 326
Ashmos, Donde P., 69n27
Atkinson, Anthony A., 105n32
Austin, James T., 424n21
Austin, Nancy, 615n26
Austin, Tom, 717
Autor, David, 717
Avila, John, 181

Babbage, Charles, 42, 43, 69n10
Bacharah, G. G., 509n37
Bahls, Jane Easter, 200n10
Bailey, Diane E., 646n10
Baily, Martin Neil, 715n10
Baker, Douglas, 401n18
Baker, Stephen, 172n1
Baldes, J. J., 547n22
Baldino, Frank, Jr., 274–275, 277, 279
Baloff, Nicholas, 301n29
Banker, Rajiv D., 547n41
Bannerjee, Neela, 280
Barad, Jill, 511
Barkema, Harry, 547n40
Barker, Robert, 682n1
Barnard, Chester, 46, 69n17
Barney, Jay B., 105n4, 105n17, 272n9, 272n10, 272n25, 401n27
Barrett, Colleen, 35, 36, 357
Barrett, Craig, 684
Barrick, Murray R., 508n6, 646n15
Barrionuevo, Alexei, 87
Barry, Bruce, 646n28
Barry, Dave, 37n14
Barry, Norman, 138n2
Bartholomew, Brad, 35
Bartlett, Christopher A., 37n4, 172n6, 273n38
Baskin, Otis W., 615n32
Bass, Bernard M., 582n10
Bass, R. E., 69n27
Bate, Paul, 424n26
Bateman, Thomas, 235n9
Bates, Courtney, 73
Baum, Joel A. C., 105n23
Bazerman, Max H., 138n31, 235n23
Becker, Thomas E., 614n3
Beckhard, Richard, 424n33
Bedeian, Arthur G., 371n23, 433n2
Beebe, Andrew, 328
Beecham, Sinclair, 302
Beeman, Don R., 583n43, 583n48
Beer, Michael, 433n5
Beeson, John, 472n9
Begley, Thomas, 172n3
Behling, Orlando C., 715n22
Beinhocker, Eric D., 104n3, 272n2, 272n18
Bélissent, Jennifer, 717
Belkin, Lisa, 182
Bell, Cecil H., Jr., 424n35
Bell, Charlie, 11
Belton, Catherine, 200
Benfari, Robert C., 582n9
Bensaou, M., 715n13
Bergmann, Thomas, 646n25
Berkus, Amy, 545
Berner, Robert, 433n1, 582
Berners-Lee, Tim, 426
Bernstein, Aaron, 180
Berra, Yogi, 340
Bethune, Gordon, 16, 35, 589, 602, 620
Bettis, R. A., 273n32
Bezos, Jeff, 22, 216
Bhattacharjee, Yudhijit, 747n1
Bhide, Amar, 337n13
Bich, Marcel, 317
Bies, Robert J., 583n45
Bilefsky, Dan, 172n1
Bird, Sue, 525
Bishop, James Wallace, 646n20
Bishop, Robert, 598
Biver, Brigitte, 187
Black, Jane, 746
Blackburn, Joseph D., 715n11
Blackburn, Richard S., 371n37
Blair, Donald W., 237
Blair, M., 547n42
Blake, Robert R., 582n15
Blake, Stacy, 200n12, 200n13
Blizzard, Mike, 480
Bloom, Richard, 68n1
Bluedorn, Allen C., 105n21
Blum, Terry C., 509n35
Bobocel, D. Ramona, 301n24
Boeker, Warren, 434n6
Boisot, Max, 473n31
Bond, Michael Harris, 509n12
Booker, Katrina, 581, 582
Boorstin, Julia, 234n1, 682n1
Bordry, Isabelle, 357
Borrus, Amy, 359
Bourgeois, L. J., III, 646n24
Bove, Courtland L., 615n31
Bowen, David, 715n23
Bower, Joseph, 434n19
Boyd, David, 172n3
Boyd, Michael, 35
Brace, Jake, 462
Brady, Diane, 104, 508
Brantley, Cheryl, 13
Breaugh, James A., 472n13
Breen, Edward D., 15
Brennan, Terry, 182

Bretz, Robert, 583n41
Brews, Peter J., 235n3
Bridges, William, 400n11
Brief, Arthur P., 424n25
Brinkley, Joel, 654
Bristow, Nigel J., 68n4
Brodsky, Norm, 359, 371n33
Bromiley, Philip, 301n26
Brooks, Carl, 84
Brooks, Karon, 548
Brown, Dick, 299, 572
Brown, Erika, 327
Brown, Eryn, 37n1, 200, 546n8
Brown, John, 615n16
Brown, Nicola J., 301n13
Brown, Shona L., 370n3
Browne, John, 406
Browning, Lynnley, 114
Bruer, Rolf-Ernst, 377
Brusman, Maynard, 477
Bryan, John H., 340
Brynjolfsson, Erik, 434n14
Buchanan, Robert F., 256
Buckley, Reid, 614n8, 614n12
Burke, W. Warner, 424n34
Burnham, David H., 547n15
Burns, James MacGregor, 583n35
Burns, Lawton, 401n31
Burns, Tom, 382, 400n12
Burns, William J., Jr., 747n6
Burr, Rebecca, 327
Burrows, Stephen, 312
Burt, H. E., 582n14
Bush, George W., 6, 157
Butler, Brian, 747n16
Butler, Timothy, 37n19
Butterfield, D. Anthony, 200n4
Byrd, Robert, 158
Byrne, Bridget, 645
Byrne, John A., 87, 359
Byrnes, Nanette, 38, 68n1, 138n1

Caddell, Lynn, 68
Cage, Jack H., 583n27
Caldwell, James C., 682n14, 682n16
Campbell, Andrew, 235n29
Campion, Michael, 646n14
Cannella, Albert, 138n13
Carley, Kathleen M., 747n18
Carnegie, Andrew, 41
Carneville, Anthony, 201n29
Carpenter, Dave, 433n1
Carrell, Aileen, 545
Carreyrou, John, 671
Carroll, Stephen J., 37n14
Carson, Katerina, 73
Cartwright, Dorwin, 646n3
Carvell, Tim, 573
Cashman, J. F., 583n28
Castagnier, Jennifer, 28
Cates, Jon, 73
Caulfield, Brian, 571
Cavanagh, Gerald F., 116, 138n11
Cavanaugh, Teresa, 329
Chakravarthy, Balaji S., 105n27, 235n20
Challenger, John, 180
Chambers, John, 328
Chan, Alice P., 747n16
Chandler, Alfred, 272n19, 272n22, 272n23
Chandler, Clay, 682
Chao, Elaine L., 180
Chemers, M. M., 582n19
Chen, Christine Y., 138n20
Chen, Hsinchun, 730
Cheong-chap, Chan, 392
Cho, Fujio, 270, 572
Choi, Thomas Y., 715n22
Chou, Sunlin, 684, 685
Christensen, Clayton M., 411, 434n11
Christensen, Sandra L., 37n26, 200n19
Churchill, Winston, 42
Clancy, John J., 509n16
Clement, Ken, 11
Clifford, Bill, 312
Clifford, Lee, 546
Clinton, Bill, 570
Coch, Lester, 424n23
Cohen, A. R., 547n32
Cohen, Deborah, 370n1
Cohen, Lyor, 289
Cohen, Susan G., 646n10
Cohn, Laura, 359
Colby, Laura, 160
Coleman, Bill, 471
Coleman, Henry J., Jr., 401n33
Collins, Jim, 37n6, 39, 60, 138n1, 235n5, 300
Collins, Judith M., 646n16
Collins, Paul D., 300n9
Colvin, Geoffrey, 15, 37n27, 131, 552
Conger, Jay A., 583n32
Conlin, Michelle, 37n1, 442, 472
Connaughton, Tom, 348
Connelly, Jed, 369
Connor, Michael, 137
Connors, Pat, 545
Coons, A. E., 582n13
Cooper, C. L., 508n2
Cooper, Cynthia, 131
Cooper, Robin, 715n4
Corbett, Charles J., 715n11
Cordle, Vaughn, 35
Corner, Patricia, 301n20
Corr, Peter B., 616
Correll, A. D., 405, 406
Coubrough, J. A., 69n15
Covey, Stephen, 60
Cox, Taylor H., 200n12, 200n13, 201n31
Coy, Peter, 36
Coyle-Shapiro, Jacqueline A-M., 509n38
Cramton, Catherine Durnell, 37n14
Crockett, Roger O., 187
Cronan, Tim, 131
Cronin, Mary, 747n11
Cross, Rob, 646n4
Crowston, Kevin, 371n36, 401n18
Cubanski, Juliette, 348
Cullen, John, 401n18
Cullen, Lisa Takeguchi, 50
Cummings, Larry L., 509n11, 547n37
Cummins, Robert, 614n15
Curie, Irene, 498
Curie, Marie, 498
Curie, Pierre, 498
Cutcher-Gershenfeld, Joel, 433n4

Daft, Douglas, 538, 539, 540
Daft, Richard L., 371n19, 371n29
Daily, Catherine, 138n13
Dalton, Dan R., 138n13, 371n25
Dalziel, Thomas, 105n11
Daniels, Cora, 104n1, 200n8, 200n22
Dansereau, Fred, 567, 583n28
Darby, A. K., 651
Daus, Catherine S., 201n30
D'Aveni, Richard, 401n21
David, Fred, 235n10
David, Grainger, 11
Davies, Erin, 525
Davis, Bob, 480
Davis, James H., 37n17
Davis, Keith, 615n22
Davis, Luke, 20
Davis, Ralph C., 353, 371n22
Davis, Stanley M., 401n28, 401n30
Dawson, Chester, 104n1, 271, 370
Deal, Terrence E., 105n15
Dean, James, 715n23
Dechant, Kathleen, 200n2
DeFrank, Richard S., 509n29
De Geus, Arie, 104n2
Delany, John Thomas, 400n5
de la Torre, Gustavo, 175
Delbecq, Andre L., 301n31
Delio, Michelle, 614n1
Dell, Michael, 25, 26, 572
Dellinger, Walter, 95
DeMarie, Samuel, 715n16
DeMatteo, Jacquelyn, 547n37
de Mersan, Clothilde, 357
Deming, W. Edwards, 715n19
Dempsey, James X., 730
DeNisi, Angelo S., 472n2, 472n19, 615n24
Denson, Charlie, 237
DeSanctis, Gerardine, 401n22
Desmond, Edward W., 747n5
DeSouza, Francis, 747n1
Dess, Gregory G., 582n3, 683n243
"Destroyer, The," 106
Deutsch, Claudia H., 381
Dibachi, Farzad, 119
Dickson, J., 69n21
Dickson, W. J., 546n7
Digh, Patricia, 138n7
Dill, William, 138n10
Dirks, Kurt, 583n39
DiSanzo, Frank J., 747n17
Disney, Walt, 87, 88, 326, 343

Dixon, Gregg, 534
DMX, 289
Doherty, Elizabeth M., 301n29
Dolan, Peter, 299, 572
Dole, Bob, 348
Donaldson, Lex, 37n17
Donaldson, Thomas, 138n3, 138n14
Donnelly, Sally B., 36
Dorf, Michael, 321
Doroson, Norman, 471
Douglas, Scott, 139n33
Douglass, Frederick, 492
Dowling, William F., 400n7
Drbl, Bob, 205
Dre, Dr., 289
Dreher, Bill, 39
Dreyfuss, Joel, 715n21
Drucker, Peter, 68n3
Dublon, Dina, 182
Duhaime, Irene M., 272n21
Duimering, P. Robert, 433n3
Dukevich, David, 525
Dumaine, Brian, 381, 646n10
Duncan, David, 327
Duncan, R., 435n41
Dunfee, Thomas W., 138n3
Dunlap, Al, 106
Dunn, Debra, 17
Dunning, John H., 172n6
Dutt, James, 553
Dyer, David, 403

Eads, Stefani, 216
Eastbrook, Barry, 242
Eaton, Leslie, 516
Eaton, Ruth, 198, 199
Ebbers, Bernard, 106, 117
Eby, Lillian, 547n37
Edison, Thomas, 104, 492
Edmonds, Doug, 119
Edmunds, Gladys, 331
Edwards, Cliff, 715n1
Egelhoff, William G., 401n37
Einstein, Albert, 426
Eisenberg, Daniel, 582
Eisenberg, Eric M., 615n38
Eisenhardt, Kathleen M., 69n29, 272n2, 272n27, 370n3, 646n24
Eisner, Michael, 106, 118, 552, 573, 644–645
Elkin, Allen, 507
Elkind, Peter, 647n32
Ellison, Lawrence, 540
Ellwood, T., 180
Elofson, Greg, 301n22, 615n19
Elsbach, Kimberly D., 615n19
Elsbach, Kimberly E., 301n22
Elson, Charles M., 216, 552
Emerson, Harrington, 44
Ensing, Ingrid Morris, 401n22
Espinoza, Luis, 314
Esserman, Laura, 622
Ettlie, J. E., 435n41
Evans, Martin G., 562, 583n21
Eveillard, Jean-Marie, 681
Ewing, Jack, 377
Eyhorn, Cameron, 495

Fabricant, Florence, 746
Fahrholz, Bernd, 377
Fairlamb, David, 377
Fastow, Andrew, 87
Favre, Brett, 631
Fayol, Henri, 46, 69n15
Fedele, Joe, 745–746
Feldberg, Meyer, 373
Feldman, Daniel C., 646n18
Feldman, Steven P., 435n48
Fendi, 204
Ferdows, Kasra, 273n35
Ferguson, Marilyn, 6
Fernandez-Araoz, Claudio, 472n12
Ferrin, Donald, 583n39
Ferris, Gerald, 583n46
Festinger, Leon, 509n15
Fiedler, Fred E., 560, 582n17, 582n19, 582n20
Field, R. H. George, 583n27
Fielding, Gordon J., 371n25
Fields, Debbie, 6
Fiell, Peter, 198
Fierman, Jaclyn, 472n22
Filline, Tom, 403
Finney, Martha I., 68n6, 301n28
Fiol, C. Marlene, 200n18
Fiorina, Carly, 6, 10, 12, 16, 17, 25, 88, 182, 288, 550
Fiorito, Jack, 400n5
Fisher, Anne, 434n9
Fisher, Sarah, 525
Fitzgerald, Mollie, 242
Flanary, David, 313
Fleishman, Edwin A., 582n14
Flint, Jerry, 235n15
Follett, Mary Parker, 49
Fondas, Nanette, 69n7
Ford, Bill, 233–234
Ford, Henry, 233, 304, 326, 343
Ford, Henry, II, 234
Ford, Robert, 370n15
Ford, William C., Jr., 270
Foreman, Peter O., 646n15
Forrester, Russ, 547n30
Forster, Julie, 11, 337n1, 370n1
Fossum, John A., 473n29
Fox, Justin, 104, 480, 615n34, 747n4
France, Mike, 608
Frankfort, Lew, 204–205, 206
Fredrickson, James W., 301n33
Free, Jerry, 309, 310
Freeman, Bertha, 444
Freeman, Chris, 61
Freeman, R. Edward, 138n14
French, John R. P., 582n5
French, John R. P., Jr., 424n23
French, Wendell L., 424n35
Frenkel-Brunswick, E., 509n9
Freudenheim, Milt, 582n1
Frey, Darcy, 406
Friedman, M., 509n27
Friedman, Milton, 123
Frink, Dwight, 646n21
Froggatt, Cynthia, 622
Frohman, Alan L., 434n7
Froot, K. A., 235n21
Frost, Peter, 646n5
Fujii, Miki, 482

Gabarro, John J., 614n2
Gabor, Andrea, 370n8
Gadon, H., 547n32
Gajilan, Arlyn Tobias, 400n1
Galbraith, Jay R., 371n38
Gallagher, Greg, 716
Galpin, Timothy, 105n20
Galunic, D. Charles, 69n29, 272n27
Gandz, Jeffrey, 583n42, 583n47
Gantt, Henry, 44, 45, 52
Garciaparra, Nomar, 521
Gardner, Donald G., 509n11
Gardner, William L., 583n45
Gardner family, 328
Garnett, Katrina, 329
Garud, Raghu, 614n6
Garud, Sumita, 614n6
Garvin, David A., 699
Gates, Bill, 305, 326, 633
Gatewood, Robert, 472n10
Gavin, Mark B., 509n22
Geisler, John, 433
Gellar, Adam, 442
George, Jennifer M., 509n22
George, William, 299
Georgopoules, B. S., 105n30
Gerloff, Edwin, 614n15
Gersick, Connie J. G., 434n17, 646n13
Ghoshal, Sumantra, 172n6, 273n38, 682n24
Ghosn, Carlos, 369–370
Ghospal, Sumantsa, 37n4
Ghriskey, Timothy M., 381
Gilbert, Clark, 434n5, 434n19
Gilbert, Jacqueline, 200n12
Gilbreth, Frank, 44, 45
Gilbreth, Lillian, 44, 45
Gilligan, Carol, 131
Gillin-Lefever, Ann, 580
Gilmore, Gerry J., 714
Gilmour, Dan, 214
Gilpin, Kenneth N., 400n1
Gilson, Lucy L., 509n35
Gist, Marilyn E., 509n8
Givens, David, 615n29
Glaister, Keith W., 301n13
Glass, Jeffrey, 401n22
Glew, David J., 509n39, 547n27
Glover, Ronald, 645, 671
Gluckman, Steve, 545
Gold, Stanley P., 644

Goldberg, Beverly, 104n2
Goldberg, L. R., 508n5
Goldman, Seth, 243
Goleman, Daniel, 509n14, 582n4
Gomez-Mejia, Luis R., 547n38, 547n40
Gonzalez, Jairo, 112
Goodwin, James F., 532
Goossens, Filippe, 403
Gopinath, C., 614n3
Gorman, Philip, 273n34
Govindarajan, Vijay, 273n37
Gowan, Mary, 472n10
Graen, George, 567, 583n28
Graham, Baxter W., 547n31
Graicunas, A. V., 352, 353, 371n21
Grant, Linda, 138n18
Granucci, John, 448
Green, Stephen, 583n29
Greenberg, Jerald, 370n6
Greenhouse, Steven, 462
Greenwald, Bruce, 715n33
Greenwald, Gerald, 532
Grego, Susan, 337n26
Griffin, Ricky W., 69n25, 105n7, 172n2, 173n19, 173n21, 173n29, 370n6, 370n9, 370n12, 401n37, 472n2, 509n32, 509n39, 547n27, 646n2
Grints, Keith, 582n4
Grossman, Mindy, 237
Grove, Andy, 685
Grover, Joel, 433n1
Grover, Ronald, 645
Grubman, Jack, 299, 327, 359
Grundy, Andrew, 321
Grundy, Steven, 321
Gucci, 204
Gundlach, Michael, 139n33
Gunn, Eileen P., 173n22
Gunther, Marc, 644, 645
Gupta, Anil K., 273n37
Gupta, Sanjeev, 19
Gustafson, David H., 301n31
Gustafson, Loren, 715n16
Guyon, Janet, 160, 671
Guzzo, Richard A., 424n25

Hackman, J. Richard, 301n32, 371n16
Haddad, Charles, 381
Haga, W. J., 583n28
Hagedoorn, John, 105n10
Hakim, Danny, 234
Halbfinger, David M., 730
Hall, Edward J., 615n30
Hall, W. K., 273n32
Hamel, Gary, 37n18, 60, 272n6
Hamilton, Ian, 353, 371n22
Hamilton, Joan O'C., 61
Hamm, Mia, 631
Hammer, Michael, 401n32
Hammonds, Keith, 300
Hamner, Ellen P., 547n25
Hamner, W. Clay, 547n25
Hanlon, Dan, 316
Hanlon, Dave, 316
Hanlon, Jennie, 316
Hannezo, Guillaume, 671
Hanson, Karin, 477
Hardison, Katie, 613
Harkins, Gerry, 459
Harris, E. F., 582n14
Harrison, E. Frank, 300n5
Harrison, Jeffrey S., 138n14
Harrison, William B., Jr., 299
Hart, Shel, 471
Hartke, Darrell D., 582n20
Harvey, Michael, 682n10
Hasegawa, Kozo, 482
Hawken, Paul, 214
Healton, Cheryl G., 613
Hedley, Barry, 272n30
Heifetz, Ronald A., 582n2
Heilman, Madeline E., 583n27
Heinlein, Robert A., 214
Helgesen, Sally, 507
Heller, Richard, 37n1
Helliker, Kevin, 104n1
Hellström, Kurt, 408
Helyar, John, 491, 532
Hempel, C. G., 69n27
Henderson, Bruce, 272n30
Henkoff, Ronald, 715n28
Hennessy, John, 373
Henry, David, 256, 472
Herbert, Bob, 95
Hernandez, Jason, 14
Herschlag, Judith K., 583n27
Hersey, Bill, 482
Hershey, Milton, 491
Herzberg, Frederick, 370n14, 517, 518, 546n12
Hester, Tracy, 55
Hewlett, Bill, 88
Hewlett, Walter, 288
Hewlett, William, 288
Hickman, Jonathan, 200n14, 201n23
Hickson, David J., 401n15
Higgins, Chad, 583n46
Higgs, A. Catherine, 646n14
Hildebrand, Karen, 201n26
Hill, Charles W. L., 235n17, 272n5, 337n20, 401n19, 682n12
Hillman, Amy, 105n11
Hindery, Leo, 573
Hippel, Eric von, 424n24
Hirano, Masao, 681
Hitt, Michael A., 37n16, 433n5
Hoag, Anne, 747n16
Hochschild, Arlie, 477
Hochwarter, Wayne A., 235n7
Hodgkinson, Gerard P., 301n13
Hof, Robert D., 61
Hoffman, Donna, 545
Hoffman, James, 401n27
Hofstede, Geert, 161, 173n33, 173n35
Hoge, Mark, 377
Holloway, Michael, 313
Holmes, Stanley, 104n1, 272n1, 714
Holson, Laura M., 645
Holstein, William J., 426
Homer, 42
Hornstein, Harvey A., 583n27
Hoskisson, Robert E., 401n27
Hough, Jill, 69n14
House, Robert J., 546n13, 562, 569, 583n21, 583n32
Howard, Philip K., 608
Hower, Roger J., 424n37
Hoye, Donald, 571
Huber, George P., 69n27, 300n8, 300n10
Hulin, Charles, 509n17
Hunnicutt, Benjamin, 477
Hunt, J. G., 583n28, 583n32
Hunt, Michelle R., 235n3
Hunt-Campbell, Colin, 272n12
Hunter, John E., 472n15
Hyatt, Joshua, 608

Iacocca, Lee, 60
Iaquinto, Anthony L., 301n33
Immelt, Jeff, 104
Inch, John, 104
Irwin, Richard D., 273n38
Isaacs, Ellen, 717
Isidore, Chris, 525
Ivancevich, John M., 200n12, 509n29

Jackson, Phil, 569
Jacob, Karl, 328
Jager, Durk, 581
Jago, Arthur G., 565, 582n2, 583n23, 583n25, 583n26
Jain, Anshu, 377
James, Lawrence, 68n2
Janis, Irving L., 301n36, 301n37
Jarley, Paul, 400n5
Jassawalla, Avan R., 646n13
Jay, Jam Master, 289
Jayne, David, 348
Jenkins, Daryl, 35
Jensen, Michael, 552
Jermier, John M., 583n30
Jeter, Derek, 521
Jobs, Steve, 424, 552, 644
John Paul II (Pope), 6
Johnson, Celeste, 329
Johnson, Marco, 304
Johnson, Ross, 715n17
Johnson, Roy S., 200n8
Johnson, Sandra, 304
Johnston, David Cay, 552
Jonas, H., 69n27
Jones, C. William, 471
Jones, Edward, 245, 246
Jones, Gareth, 105n28, 105n31, 235n17, 272n5, 337n20, 370n4, 400n2, 400n8, 401n19, 509n22

Jones, Holly Brewster, 545
Jones, Janis L., 549
Joplin, Janice R. W., 201n30
Jordan, Michael, 525
Jorgenson, Dale W., 180
Joseph, Jonathon, 685
Judge, Paul C., 682n1
Judge, Timothy A., 509n6, 583n41, 583n46
Judge, William Q., 234n2
Jung, Andrea, 572

Kahan, William, 371n30
Kahn, Jeremy, 138n6, 682n19
Kahn, Robert L., 646n15, 646n17
Kahwajy, Jean L., 646n24
Kamprad, Ingvar, 198
Kanigel, Robert, 69n14
Kantrow, Alan M., 69n8
Kanungo, Rabindra N., 583n32
Kaplan, Sarah, 272n2
Karan, Donna, 204
Karsky, Marc, 95
Kasl, Stanislav, 509n25
Kast, Fremont E., 69n27, 69n30
Katayama, Yutaka, 369
Katz, David, 646n15
Katz, Ian, 312
Katz, Robert L., 37n10
Katzenburg, Jeffrey, 644
Katzman, Eric K., 341
Kaufman, Leslie, 448
Kaye, Jeff, 471
Keats, Barbara, 301n20
Keil, Mark, 301n25
Kelleher, Herb, 25, 35
Kelley, H. H., 509n24
Kelly, John M., 509n31
Kendall, L. M., 509n17
Kendrick, John W., 715n30
Kennedy, Allan A., 105n15
Kenworthy-U'Ren, Amy, 235n9
Kerr, Steve, 547n43
Kerr, Steven, 583n30
Kerstetter, Jim, 119
Kerwin, Kathleen, 234
Kettinger, William J., 747n3
Khan, Raza, 424n26
Khermouch, Gerry, 400
Khurana, Anil, 7151n3
Khurana, Rakesh, 37n24
Kiechel, Walter, III, 37n20, 615n17, 615n20
Kilbridge, M. D., 370n11, 370n13
Kilts, Jim, 107
Kimeldorf, Howard, 462
King, Ralph, 582n1
Kinicki, Angelo, 301n20
Kirkman, Alexanadra, 312
Kirkman, Bradley L., 646n7
Kirkpatrick, David, 214, 424n28, 746
Kirkpatrick, Shelley A., 582n11
Kirshner, Scott, 337n1
Kline, Janet, 348
Kluger, Avraham N., 472n19
Knight, Phil, 6, 236–237
Koch, Jim, 608
Koeppel, David, 448
Kondrasuk, Jack N., 235n30
Konopaske, Robert, 509n29
Konovsky, Mary, 509n38
Korn, Helaine J., 105n23
Kort, Robert M., 614n1
Kossek, Ellen Ernst, 433n4
Kostova, Tatiana, 273n38
Kotter, John P., 37n8, 60, 434n10, 582n4
Kournikova, Anna, 525
Kozlowski, Dennis, 15, 106, 117, 486, 519
Krakoff, Reed, 205
Kram, Kathy, 371n30
Kramwe, Mark, 138n30
Kranhold, Kathryn, 87
Kraut, Robert, 747n16
Kreie, Jennifer, 131
Kreitner, Robert, 547n24
Krishnan, M. S., 715n17
Kristiansen, Linda, 403
Kristie, James, 84
Kroc, Ray, 83, 320
Kroll, Mark, 682n6
Kruger, Pamela, 508n1
Kuhlmann, Ron, 35
Kulik, Carol T., 546n2
Kunii, Irene M., 682
Kurland, Nancy B., 615n25
Kurtz, Rod, 289
Kwan, Michele, 554

Labich, Kenneth, 583n36
Lachman, Ran, 37n25
Lacy, Alan, 403
Lado, Augustine, 472n4
Lafley, A. G. (Alan), 21, 572, 580–581, 582
Lahart, Justin, 682
Lam, Simon S. K., 509n7
Lamont, Bruce, 401n27
Landgraf, Kurt, 306
Landy, Frank, 509n25
Lane, Vicki R., 105n8
Lange, Christian, 280
Langlois, Rick, 137
Larson, Gary, 628
Larson, L. L., 583n28, 583n32
Latham, Gary P., 301n29, 547n22
Laudon, Jane P., 747n8, 747n9
Laudon, Kenneth C., 747n8, 747n9
Lauren, Ralph, 204
Laurie, Donald L., 582n2
Lautenschlager, Gary, 472n10
Lavelle, Louis, 15, 216
Lawler, Edward E., 715n24
Lawler, Edward E., III, 301n32, 400n14, 547n19, 682n11
Lawrence, Paul R., 371n39, 383, 400n13, 401n28, 401n30, 424n22
Lay, Kenneth, 87, 106, 117, 573
Leaf, Clifton, 256
Leana, Carrie R., 371n31
Leas, James, 471
Leavell, Hadley, 682n6
LeBarre, Polly, 17
Lebenthal, Alexandra, 508
Lee, Seok-Young, 547n41
Lei, David, 370n2, 400n3, 401n36
Leifer, Richard, 435n45
Leland, John, 200, 289
Lenway, Stefanie Ann, 583n49
Leonard, Dorothy, 435n47
Lepak, David, 472n5
Lepore, Dawn, 182
Leung, Shirley, 11, 104n1
Leuthner, Emily C., 403
Lev, Baruch, 272n22
Levering, Robert, 337n1
Levin, Gerald, 299
Levine, Jonathan B., 598
Levinson, D. J., 509n9
Levitan, Mark, 516
Lewin, Kurt, 407, 434n15
Lewin, Tamar, 306
Lewis, Marc, 545
Lewis, Michael, 508
Liden, Robert, 472n16
Lieberman, Pamela Forbes, 571
Lientz, Bennett P., 615n35
Ligos, Melinda, 472
Liker, Jeffrey K., 715n11
Likert, Rensis, 56, 376–378, 379, 400n6, 582n12
Lincoln, James R., 509n19, 509n20
Lindsay, Greg, 138n20
Liske, Laurie Z., 583n22
Locke, Edwin A., 301n29, 547n21, 582n11
Lockhart, Terry, 632
Lohr, Steve, 715n1
Loomis, Carol J., 105n18, 552
Lopez de Arriortua, Jose Ignacio, 635
Lorange, Peter, 235n20, 682n24
Lorsch, Jay W., 371n39, 383, 400n13, 614n2
Louie, Gilman, 328
Low, Murray B., 337n4
Lowe, Joe, 593
Lowe, Richard, 119
Lowry, Richard, 546n9
Lucas, Brittany, 87
Ludewig, Eric, 310
Lusch, Robert, 682n10
Luthans, Fred, 37n2, 547n24, 547n26
Lyness, Karen S., 200n5
Lyons, Nancy J., 337n17

Machiavelli, Niccolo, 42, 486
MacKenzie, Scott B., 646n22
Mackey, John, 313
MacMillan, Ian C., 272n13, 337n4
Maggard, Brack, 459
Maier, Norman P. R., 301n32
Main, Jeremy, 173n15, 725n25

Maitland, Alison, 632
Mallon, Tom, 717
Malone, Bob, 406
Malone, James, 654
Malvo, Lee, 730
Manz, Charles C., 583n31
Marchand, Donald A., 747n3
Marek, Joe, 313
Marek, Pat, 313
Markides, Constantinos, 272n10, 272n29, 434n40
Markoff, John, 214, 715n1
Marriott, J. W. (Bill), 4–5, 6, 9, 25, 602
Martin, Christopher, 472n16
Martinez, Maria, 661
Martinez, Michelle Neely, 200n13
Martinko, Mark, 139n33
Martocchio, Joseph J., 509n6, 646n21
Marx, Elisabeth, 632
Maslow, Abraham H., 49, 50, 69n22, 546n9
Mathews, John A., 401n33
Mathews, Ryan, 426
Mathieu, Christian, 199
Mathys, Nicholas J., 235n7
Matsunaga, Mari, 563
Matthews, William, 730
Matusik, Sharon F., 300n9
Maule, A. John, 301n13
Mausner, Bernard, 546n12
Maxim, James, 299
Maxwell, Wayne, 15
Mayo, Elton, 48, 50, 56, 69n21, 546n7
McAllister, Bill, 137
McCall, H. Carl, 284
McCarley, Genise, 480
McCaskey, Michael B., 615n28
McClelland, David C., 519, 546n14, 547n15
McCloskey, Kevin R., 549
McFarlin, F. Warren, 747n6
McGettrick, Jim, 608
McGrath, Rita Gunther, 272n13
McGregor, Douglas, 49, 50, 69n23
McGuire, Jean B., 138n22
McGurn, Pat, 216
McKay, John, 38
McKenzie, Scott B., 509n37
McKim, Alan, 331
McKinnell, Hank, 617
McKinney, Bruce, 491
McLane, Jeff, 622
McMahan, Gary, 370n6, 370n12, 472n3
McMillan, Steven, 340
McNamara, Gerry, 301n26
McNeil, Heidi L., 614n1
Medsker, Gina, 646n14
Mehrabian, Albert, 615n27
Mehta, Monica, 200n1
Mehta, Viren, 616
Menzies, Hugh D., 582n6
Messick, David M., 138n31
Messier, Jean-Marie, 671
Messmer, Harold, 107
Metcalfe, Julian, 302
Meyer, John, 301n24
Miceli, Marcia P., 139n33
Miles, Grant, 401n33
Miles, Raymond E., 246, 272n16, 401n33
Miles, Robert H., 401n17
Miller, David W., 300n10
Miller, Evan, 622
Milliman, John, 472n20
Milne, A. A., 644
Mindell, Mark G., 424n37
Miner, Anne S., 370n10
Mintzberg, Henry, 18, 19, 37n9, 235n24, 272n7, 614n4, 614n5, 614n7, 614n11
Mitarai, Fujio, 681
Mitchell, Terence R., 68n2, 509n8, 583n21
Mitchell, Vance, 646n5
Miyauchi, Hayato, 482
Mjoen, Hans, 173n16, 683n25
Moberg, Dennis J., 116
Mohr, L. B., 435n41
Mohrman, Allan, 472n20
Montealegre, Ramiro, 301n25
Moore, Ellen, 604
Moore, Gordon, 684
Moorhead, Gregory, 69n25, 646n2
Morgenson, Gretchen, 614n1
Morris, Barbara M., 471
Morris, Betsy, 182, 234
Morrison, Elizabeth Wolfe, 508n3, 583n45
Morrissey, Peter, 7
Morrow, Paula C., 715n29
Morrow, Peggy, 703
Morton, Michael F. Scott, 682n24
Moskowitz, Milton, 337n1
Mount, Ian, 571
Mount, Michael K., 508n6
Mouton, Jane S., 582n15
Mozart, 498
Much, Marilyn, 234n1
Muhammad, Benjamin, 289
Muhammad, John, 730
Mulcahy, Anne, 182, 299
Mullane, John, 715n16
Mullaney, Timothy J., 61
Muller, Joann, 271
Munsterberg, Hugo, 48, 50, 69n19
Murphy, Cait, 406, 516
Murphy, Chris, 311
Murphy, Kevin, 403
Murray, Victor, 583n42, 583n47

Nacchio, Joseph, 573
Nadler, David A., 299, 370n5, 583n34
Nakamura, Isuru, 369
Nakatani, Iwao, 482
Napolitano, Jo, 571
Nasser, Jacques, 233, 573
Nathan, Barry R., 472n20
Nchor, Joseph, 614n1
Near, Janet P., 139n33
Nedved, Susan, 341
Needles, Belverd E., Jr., 682n14, 682n16
Neeleman, David, 650
Nemetz, Patricia L., 37n26, 200n19
Nerurkar, Madhavi, 191
Neubauer, Joseph, 107, 117
Neubert, Ralph L., 138n22
Newington, Tim, 327
Niblack, John, 616
Nicholas, John M., 424n39
Nicholson, Nigel, 546n3
Nishi, Kazuhiko, 633
Nishimori, Seiji, 681
Nobel, Barbara Presley, 473n28
Nocera, Joseph, 573
Nohria, Nitin, 434n5, 646n4
Nord, Walter, 646n5
Nordin, Ken, 199
Norris, Karen, 448
Northcraft, Gregory, 646n26
Nuccitelli, Michael, 471
Nugent, Patrick, 647n33
Nusbaum, Marci Alboher, 182
Nutt, Paul, 300n4

O'Connell, Patricia, 272n1
O'Connor, Gina Colarelli, 435n45
Oesterreicher, James E., 180
Ohmae, Kenichi, 173n14
Ohmes, Robert, 205
Ohta, Koki, 482
Okuda, Hiroshi, 271
Oldham, Greg R., 371n16
O'Leary, Michael, 36
O'Leary-Kelly, Anne M., 509n39, 547n27, 646n21
Ollila, Jorma, 263
Olsen, Patricia R., 448
Olson, David J., 462
O'Neal, Stanley, 16
O'Neill, Hugh, 235n9
Ono, Yumiko, 482
O'Reilly, Brian, 301n27
Organ, Dennis W., 509n38
Orth, Charles D., 582n9
Osborn, Richard N., 105n10
Osmond, Charles P., 37n28
Ouchi, William G., 60, 105n4, 272n25, 401n27, 682n21
Overdorf, Michael, 434n11
Overholt, Allison, 622
Owen, Robert, 42
Oyama, Satoru, 681

Packard, David, 88
Padell, Bert, 289
Paine, Julie Beth, 509n37
Paine, Lynn Sharp, 138n28
Palazzolo, Patrick, 532
Palmer, Ian, 434n13

Palmeri, Christopher, 37n1
Parker, Andrew, 646n4
Parker, Ian, 337n1
Parker, James, 357
Parker, Jim, 35
Parker, Mark, 237
Parloff, Roger, 95
Parsons, Charles, 472n16
Parsons, T., 69n16
Passariello, Christina W., 104n1
Patterson, Gregory, 337n21
Patz, Alan, 435n42
Pearce, Craig L., 37n28
Pearce, John A., II, 235n10
Pearman, Alan D., 301n13
Peers, Martin, 671
Pelled, Lisa Hope, 200n17, 301n34, 615n25
Penney, James Cash, 87
Pennington, Malcolm W., 273n32
Perot, H. Ross, 87, 602
Perroni, Amedeo G., 69n13
Perry, James L., 37n25
Perry-Pastor, Yolanda, 477
Pervin, Lawrence, 508n4
Peter, Thomas, 60
Peters, Lawrence H., 582n20
Peters, Tom, 60, 615n26, 622
Pfeffer, Jeffrey, 299, 546n4, 583n40
Philipson, Ilene, 476, 477
Phillips, J., 348
Phillips, Nelson, 615n16
Pickens, Joseph C., 582n3, 683n24
Pierce, Jon L., 509n11
Pillai, Rajnandini, 583n35
Pinchot, Gifford, III, 435n49
Pinder, Craig, 546n5, 546n10
Pinkley, Robin, 646n26
Pinsky, Drew, 321
Pittman, R. J., 214
Pitts, Robert A., 401n36
Plato, 42
Podsakoff, Philip M., 509n37, 582n9, 646n22
Pohlmann, John T., 582n20
Pollock, Timothy, 273n34
Poon, Dickson, 662
Porras, Jerry, 373
Port, Otis, 187
Porter, Linda, 591
Porter, Lyman W., 301n32, 371n25, 508n4, 546n2, 547n19
Porter, Michael E., 60, 90, 91, 105n23, 138n30, 244, 272n2, 272n11, 272n12, 387, 401n25
Post, James, 615n18
Potter, Gordon, 547n41
Poulsen, Kevin, 614n1
Powell, Gary, 200n4
Prada, 204
Prahalad, C. K., 37n18, 715n17
Prakash, Assem, 138n15
Pratt, Michael G., 646n115
Prentice, Robert, 114
Press, James, 270
Pressler, Paul, 107, 644
Preston, Lee E., 138n14
Priem, Richard, 300n2
Prietula, Michael J., 301n31
Pugh, Derek S., 401n15
Pugh, S. Douglas, 509n38
Pukanecz, Todd, 119
Purdy, Lyn, 433n3
Pustay, Michael, 105n7, 172n2, 173n19, 173n21, 173n29, 401n37
Pye, Annie, 424n26

Quick, James Campbell, 507, 509n25
Quinn, James Brian, 235n24, 424n40, 715n10, 715n26
Quinn, R. P., 646n17
Quinn, Robert E., 547n28

Raber, Roger, 84
Raghavan, Anita, 87
Rainey, Hal G., 37n25
Rajagopalan, Nandini, 434n8
Ramanujam, Vasudevan, 235n25
Raven, Bertram, 582n5
Ravenscraft, David, 401n21
Rayport, Jeffrey F., 435n47
Reed, John, 552
Reed, Stanley, 160, 280, 408
Regan, Julie, 593
Regan, Keith, 433n1
Reger, Rhonda, 715n16
Rehbein, Kathleen, 583n49
Reichers, Arnon E., 434n21
Reingold, Jennifer, 216
Reinhardt, Andy, 408
Reinhardt, Forest L., 138n15
Renshaw, Amy Austin, 434n14
Revell, Janice, 234
Rhoads, Christopher, 377
Rhode, John G., 682n11
Rice, Fay, 200n22
Rice, Mark, 435n45
Richard, Orlando C., 200n2
Richards, Max D., 235n4
Rigas, John, 106
Riordan, Christine M., 200n20
Roberson, Jessie, 654
Roberts, Bob, 278
Robertson, Diana, 683n26
Robertson, Thomas, 715n27
Robinson, Gail, 200n2
Robinson, James, 400n1
Robinson, Sandra L., 508n3
Rockefeller, John D., 41
Rodgers, Anni Layne, 508
Rodgers, Johnathan, 580
Rodgers, T. J., 392, 735
Rodgers, William, 471
Rodriguez, Alex, 521
Rodriguez, Julie, 323
Roethlisberg, Fritz J., 69n21
Rogers, Patrick R., 234n2
Rohwer, Jim, 272n4
Rolfe, Andrew, 303
Rollins, John D., 747n3
Rosen, Benson, 201n25, 646n7
Rosenman, R. H., 509n27
Rosenthal, R. A., 646n17
Rosenzweig, James E., 69n27, 69n30
Rosenzweig, Mark, 508n4
Ross, Ian M., 41
Ross, Jerry, 301n24
Roth, Bruce, 500
Rothlisberger, Fritz J., 546n7
Rotter, J. B., 509n7
Rousseau, D. M., 508n2
Rowland, Pleasant, 510–511
Rowley, Coleen, 291
Rubenstein, Laila, 329
Rubin, Harriet, 69n7
Rule, Ja, 289
Rumelt, Richard, 272n19
Rumsfeld, Donald, 634
Ryan, Lori V., 300n9
Rydberg-Dumont, Josephine, 199
Rynes, Sara L., 69n24, 201n25

Sachs, Andrea, 508n1
Sackett, Paul R., 472n17
Safayeni, Frank, 433n3
Salkever, Alex, 747n1
Sample, Doug, 614n1
Sandling, Heidi, 433n4
Sanford, R. N., 509n9
Sasaki, Mikio, 6
Sashittal, Hemant C., 646n13
Sawicki, John, 448
Sawyer, John E., 509n32
Scanlon, Joseph, 537
Scarborough, Norman M., 337n35
Scardino, Albert, 160
Scardino, Marjorie, 160
Schaeffer, Robert, 306
Scharfstein, D. S., 235n21
Schatzman, Barbara E., 615n31
Schaubroeck, John, 509n7
Scherer, F. M., 337n18
Schlender, Brent, 200n1, 715n1
Schlesinger, Leonard A., 434n10
Schmelzer, Hank, 513
Schmidt, Frank L., 472n15
Schmidt, Jeff, 73
Schmidt, Warren H., 559, 582n16
Schmitt, Richard B., 114
Schneeweis, Thomas, 138n22
Schneider, Benjamin, 424n25
Schoonover, Stephen, 507
Schoorman, F. David, 37n17
Schrage, Michael, 200, 703
Schrank, Robert, 646n5

Schriesheim, Chester A., 582n9, 582n18, 583n35
Schroeder, Jenny, 730
Schroeder, Roger, 682n9
Schultz, Howard, 13, 21, 25, 320
Schultz, Susan, 84
Schulz, Howard, 104n1
Schulze, Horst, 20
Schweiger, David M., 301n29, 615n24
Scott, K. Dow, 646n20
Scott, Susanne G., 105n8
Scrushy, Richard M., 548, 549, 550
Seashore, S., 105n29
Seligman, Dan, 462
Sellers, Patricia, 37n5, 138n1, 200n6, 682n23
Selye, Hans, 509n26
Senge, Peter, 60, 401n36
Serwer, Andy, 337n29, 408
Shalley, Christina E., 509n35
Sharkey, Thomas W., 583n43, 583n48
Sharma, Sanjay, 138n17
Shatteen, Westina Matthews, 84
Shaw, Marvin E., 646n11
Sheftick, Gary, 714
Sheremata, Willow A., 435n45
Sherman, Mike, 6
Sherman, Stratford P., 173n37, 583n33
Sherony, Kathryn, 583n29
Shook, David, 646n1
Shore, Lynn McGarlane, 508n2
Shores, Lynn McFarlane, 200n20
Siebert, Muriel, 216
Siekman, Philip, 371n28
Sifonis, John G., 104n2
Simmons, Donna L., 424n37
Simon, Herbert A., 286, 301n19, 301n31
Simons, John, 509n34
Simons, Tony, 200n17, 301n34
Sims, Henry P., Jr., 583n31
Sinegal, James, 38–39, 41, 107, 117
Singer, Andrew, 138n24
Singer, Thea, 337n23
Singh, Amit, 721
Singh, Ashish, 617
Sink, Mindy, 730
Sitkin, Sim, 682n9
Skilling, Jeffrey, 87, 106, 114, 573, 608
Skinner, B. F., 547n23
Slagmulder, Regine, 715n4
Slaman, Norma, 73
Slocum, John W., 370n2, 400n3, 401n36
Smith, Adam, 343, 370n7
Smith, Fred, 381
Smith, Frederick, 227
Smith, Geri, 172
Smith, Ken A., 200n17, 301n34
Smith, Page, 68n5
Smith, Patricia C., 509n17
Smith, Peter B., 509n12
Snell, Scott, 472n5
Snoek, J. D., 646n17
Snow, Charles C., 246, 272n16, 401n33
Snyder, William M., 371n18
Snyderman, Barbara, 546n12
Socrates, 42
Son, Masayoshi, 321
Sonnack, Mary, 424n24
Sorenson, Richard, 313
Spade, Kate, 310
Spence, Janet, 509n12
Spendolini, Michael J., 371n25
Sperling, John, 372
Spreitzer, Gretchen M., 434n8, 548m29
Sreekanti, Kumar, 327
Srinivasan, Dhinu, 547n41
Staines, Christopher, 310
Stajkovic, Alexander D., 547n26
Staley, Warren, 432–433
Stalker, G. M., 382, 400n12
Stallone, Steve, 462
Stanton, Steven, 401n32
Starke, Mary, 472n13
Starr, Martin K., 300n10
Start, Chris, 581
Staw, Barry M., 301n24, 547n37
Stear, Rory, 310
Steers, Richard M., 509n21, 546n2
Stein, J. C., 235n21
Steiner, G. A., 435n41
Steinfield, Charles, 747n16
Stern, Sandra Feagan, 545
Sternberg, Robert J., 582n11
Stevens, Anne, 182
Stevens, Bill, 182
Stevens, Colleen, 613
Stevenson, Dennis, 160
Stewart, Greg L., 646n15, 646n28
Stewart, Martha, 299, 389, 573, 608
Stewart, Rosemary, 37n7
Stewart, Thomas A., 424n31, 473n32, 582n8, 682n2
Stimpert, K. L., 272n21
Stires, David, 682n5
Stogdill, Ralph M., 582n13
Stoka, Ann Marie, 69n13
Stokes, Peter J., 373
Stone, Susan, 201n29
Strauss, Gary, 84
Strauss, J. Perkins, 508n6
Stroup, Margaret A., 138n22
Sullivan, Sherry E., 472n27
Sundaramurthy, Chamu, 216
Sundgren, Alison, 138n22
Sundstrom, Eric, 547n37
Sutcliffe, Kathleen, 509n23, 682n9
Swamidass, Paul M., 715n2
Swoopes, Sheryl, 525
Swygert, Patrick, 84
Symonds, William C., 15, 400n1, 480

Tabak, Filiz, 509n35
Tallman, Stephen, 173n16, 683n25
Tam, Pui-Wang, 17
Tang, John, 717
Tannenbaum, A. S., 105n30
Tannenbaum, Robert, 559, 582n16
Taylor, Alex, III, 301n12, 370
Taylor, Frederick W., 41, 44, 45, 52, 69n12, 513, 546n6
Taylor, William, 682n3
Teja, Salim, 225
Telles, Maracel, 312
Tepper, Bennett J., 582n7, 582n18
Tereshko, Olga, 313
Tetrault, Linda A., 582n18
Tetrick, Lois, 508n2
Thill, John V., 615n31
Thomas, Howard, 273n34
Thomke, Stefan, 424n24
Thompson, Donna E., 200n5
Thompson, James D., 89, 90, 105n22, 371n37
Thompson, Jane, 241
Thompson, Kenneth R., 235n7
Thoreson, Carl J., 509n6
Thornburg, Linda, 200n3
Thornton, Emily, 359, 509n33
Tierney, Christine, 370
Tilton, Glenn F., 532
Todor, William D., 371n25
Toffler, Barbara Ley, 114
Tomlinson, Richard 377
Toombs, Leslie, 682n6
Tosaka, Kaoru, 681
Trank, Christine Quinn, 69n24
Trapani, Frances, 5
Treschow, Michael, 408
Trump, Donald, 13, 60, 570
Tsao, Amy, 11, 36, 172
Tubre, Travis C., 646n16
Tully, Shawn, 401n34, 532
Turner, Joseph, 470–471
Tushman, Michael L., 370n5, 583n34

Urwick, Lyndall F., 46, 353, 371n22
Useem, Jerry, 15, 138n1, 300, 301n16, 371n26, 371n32, 508n1, 573, 583n37
Uttal, Bro, 337n2
Uzumeri, Mustafa V., 715n28

Van Alstyne, Marshall, 434n14
Van Biema, Michael, 715n33
Vanderbilt, Cornelius, 41
Vander Houwen, Boyd A., 615n37
Van de Ven, Andrew H., 301n31
Van Fleet, David D., 371n23, 371n27, 547n27
Van Wassenhove, Luk N., 715n11
Varchaver, Nicholas, 15, 614n14, 747n15
Vavelas, A., 614n15
Velasquez, Manuel, 116
Venkatraman, N., 235n25, 747n7
Victor, Bart, 371n37
Volkema, Roger, 646n25
von Bertalanffy, Ludwig, 69n27
Vroom, Victor H., 546n13, 547n17, 564, 565, 566, 583n23, 583n24, 583n25, 583n26

Wacker, Watts, 426
Wager, Deidra, 13
Wagner, Jenny, 15
Wagoner, G. Richard, Jr., 270
Wahlgren, Eric, 546
Waksal, Samuel, 299
Waldman, David, 715n20
Waldroop, James, 37n19
Walker, Marcus, 377
Wallace, Charles P., 301n23
Wallner, George, 112
Walton, Bill, 525
Walton, Richard E., 682n21
Walton, Sam, 87
Wanous, John P., 424n21
Warner, Melanie, 104
Watad, Mahmoud M., 747n17
Waterhouse, John H., 105n32
Waterman, Robert, 60
Watkins, Michael, 235n23
Watkins, Sherron, 131
Watson, Bill, 646n5
Watson, Gregory H., 703
Watt, James, 692
Wayne, Leslie, 714
Weber, Max, 46, 69n16, 400n4
Wee, Heesun, 406, 433n1
Weill, Sanford, 106, 299, 327, 359, 552, 572
Weinberg, Neil, 433
Weintraub, Arlene, 442
Weiss, A., 435n41
Weiss, Gary, 359
Welbourne, Theresa M., 547n38
Welch, Jack, 60, 103, 106, 552, 573
Welch, James, 67
Wells, Melanie, 400, 682n1
Wells, Robert B., 105n32
Wenger, Etienne C., 371n18
Werhane, Patricia H., 138n8
Wetlaufer, Suzy, 646n23
Wexner, Leslie, 56
Wheat, Alynda, 37n1
White, Margaret, 69n14
Wholey, Douglas, 401n31
Whyte, Glen, 301n15
Wiesenfeld, Batia M., 614n6
Wigdor, Lawrence A., 546n13
Wiley, C., 547n35
Wilkins, Alan L., 68n4
Wilkinson, Harry E., 582n9
Willford, Tina, 533
Williams, Eric J., 583n35
Williams, Larry J., 509n22
Williams, Margaret, 509n22
Williams, Robert, 401n27
Williams, Venus, 485
Williamson, Oliver E., 272n19, 386, 401n23, 401n24, 401n26
Williamson, Peter J., 272n29
Wilson, Mary, 472n4
Wilson, Sir David, 6
Winchell, William O., 715n17
Witten, Marsha G., 615n38
Wofford, Jerry C., 583n22, 614n15
Wolfe, D. M., 646n17
Wolfe, Ken, 491
Wong, Edward, 462, 532
Woodman, Richard W., 509n32
Woodward, Joan, 380, 400n9, 400n10, 692, 715n5
Worthy, James C., 371n24
Wozniak, Steve, 424
Wrege, Charles D., 69n13
Wren, Daniel, 68n5, 69n9, 69n11, 69n20, 69n26, 547n34
Wright, Patrick, 472n3
Wright, Peter, 682n6
Wu, Yen-Chun, 715n11

Yamashita, Keith, 17
Yetton, Philip, 565, 566
Yetton, Philip H., 583n23
Young, May, 615n18
Yuchtman, E., 105n29
Yukawa, John, 369
Yukl, Gary A., 582n3, 582n9, 583n21

Zack, Michael H., 747n2
Zamansky, Jacob, 359
Zander, Alvin, 646n3
Zandi, Mark, 480
Zell, Doug, 73
Zellner, Wendy, 36, 87, 337n15, 462
Zesinger, Sue, 105n16
Zimmerer, Thomas W., 337n35
Zimmerman, Dick, 491
Zollars, Bill, 67–68
Zollo, Peter, 613

Organization and Product Index

A. G. Edwards, 256, 557, 663
ABC, 103, 644
Academy Awards Center, 85
Access, 724
Accompany, 225
Acme, 591
Active Corps of Executives (ACE), 323
Acura, 256
Adelphia, 106
Adidas, 79, 288, 290
Advanced Micro Devices (AMD), 685
Advantix, 277
Agilent, 545
Ahold, 172
Airbus, 91, 140, 278, 282–285
Albertson's, 79, 171, 308 fig. 10.2
Alcoa, 129, 228
Alfa Romeo, 245, 245 table 8.1
Alliance Entertainment Corp., 321
Allianz, 165 table 5.2
Allied Domecq Quick Service Restaurants, 400
Allkauf, 82
Allstate, 525
Alpine Taxi, 314
AltaVista, 732
Altima, 369
Altria Group, 165 table 5.2
Amazon.com, 22, 90, 118, 187, 216, 246, 309
AmBev, 312
America Online, 730
  See also AOL
America West, 608
America West Airlines, 68
American Airlines, 142, 282, 315
  MOCA system and, 729
  operations management and, 687
  organization development by, 420
American Arbitration Association, 460
American Association for Homecare, 348
American Cancer Society, 288
American Cyanamid, 345, 389
American Express, 91, 142, 675, 702
American Girl doll collection, 510–511
American Home Products, 581
American International Group, 165 table 5.2
American Legacy Foundation, 613–614
American Management Association, 508
American National Standards Institute, 704
American Society for Quality Control, 699
Amerisourcebergen, 98 table 3.1, 165 table 5.2
AMF-Head, 253
Anheuser-Busch, 308 fig. 10.2, 312
Antelope Valley Medical College, 304
AOL, 56, 187, 256, 257, 299, 327, 717
AOL/Time Warner, 165 table 5.2, 256, 299
Apollo, 372, 373
Apple Computer, 27, 317, 322, 392, 422
  executive compensation and, 552
  group activities and, 623
  organization conflict, 644
Applied Mateials, 186 table 6.1
Aquafina, 245
Aramark, 107, 117
Arbor Award, 617
Arch Deluxe (sandwich), 80
Arthur Andersen, 124, 125, 126, 279, 327, 667
Artificial Intelligence Laboratory at the University of Arizona, 730
ASDA, 171
Ashland Oil, 122
Assicurazioni Generali, 165 table 5.2
Associated Press, 16
Astra USA, 124
Atlantis: The Lost Empire, 663
AT&T, 165 table 5.2, 345, 359, 497
AT&T Bell Laboratories, 41
Authentica, 327
AutoZone, 358
Aventis Pharmaceuticals, 525
Aviation Information Resources, Inc., 651
Avis, 688
Aviva, 165 table 5.2
Avon, 184
  international revenues, 144
  organizational practices for diversity, 191
  resistance to change, 225
  strategic leader of, 572
Awarenex, 717
A & W Restaurants, 399
Axa, 165 table 5.2

Baja Fresh Mexican Grill, 399
Baker Hughes, 351
Bali, 341
Ball Corporation, 90
Ball Park, 341
Bang & Olufsen, 145
Bank of America Corp., 86, 165 table 5.2
Barbie doll, 510
Barnes & Noble, 308 fig. 10.2
Barneys, 662
Baskin-Robbins, 400
Bass beer, 141
Bath & Body Works, 388
Bausch & Lomb, 708, 709
Baylor University, 160
Beachcomber, The, 608
Beatrice Company, 553
Beauty and the Beast, 644
Beck's beer, 141
Benetton, 694
Ben & Jerry's Homemade, 124, 260, 458, 720
Berkshire Hathaway, 98 table 3.1, 165 table 5.2
Best Buy, 171
Bethlehem Steel, 44, 45, 345, 687
Beverly's Pet Center, 316
BF Goodrich, 420
Bic, 245, 245 table 8.1, 246 table 8.2, 247, 250
Big Mac, 325
Bigstep, 328
Binney & Smith, 534
Black & Decker, 41, 228, 734
Black Diamond, 242
Blockbuster Video, 324, 722
Bloomingdale's, 249
BMC Software, 477
BMW, 165 table 5.2, 259, 262, 276
BNP Paribas, 165 table 5.2
Boeing, 26, 35, 76, 78, 91
  CAD technology and, 694
  decision making and, 282–285
  employment cap by, 480
  ethics training at, 113
  first-mover advantage by, 317
  fixed-position layout and, 691
  global environment, 142
  goal setting and, 228
  international competition, 140
  jumbo jets, 278
  listening skills training program and, 607
  planning staff of, 213, 214
  ranked world's largest MNCs, 165 table 5.2
  related diversification of, 253
  supplier for military, 714
  training programs and, 451
Boeing 777, 91
Boise Cascade, 308 fig. 10.2
Borland International, 567
Boston Brewing, 608
Boston Market, 399
Boston Red Sox, 521
Bounty, 580
BP, 25, 165 table 5.2, 672
BP Amoco, 131, 532, 533
BP Exploration, 464
Brahma, 312
Bristol-Myers Squibb, 299, 308 fig. 10.2, 572
British Airways, 282
British Museum, 6
British Telecom, 704
Broadway Cafe, 73

Brooks Brothers, 380
Brown University, 373
Broyhill, 687
Bryan, 341
Bryan (Texas) Ford, 276, 277
Bug's Life, A, 644
Buick, 635
Bulgari Hotels, 5
Burger King, 79
Burlington Industries, 597
Business Engine, 119

Cabbage Patch doll, 510
Cadbury Schweppes, 219
California Department of Health, 613
California Supreme Court, 95
Calvin Klein, 249
Calvin Klein jeans, 38
Cambridge University, 160
Camden International, 689
Campbell Soup, 94, 257, 314
Canon, 423, 424, 450, 591, 681
Caramel Macchiato (coffee), 382
Cardinal Health, 165 table 5.2
Cargill, 432–433
Caribbean Common Market, 159
Carnation Company, 164
Carnival Cruise Lines, 79
Carrefour, 165 table 5.2, 172
Casa de Avila, 181
Case Corporation, 356
Caterpillar, 26, 142, 228, 343
  competitive advantage of, 243
  Lewin Model and, 407
  organization change and, 411
  planning staff of, 213, 214
  productivity and, 709
  reactive change in, 406, 407
  team building by, 418
Cayenne SUV, 279
CBS, 25
Celebrity Cruise Lines, 94
Celestial Fantasie, 242
Center for the Study of Responsive Law (Nader), 82
Century 21 Real Estate, 25
Cephalon, 274–275, 277
Cereal Partners Worldwide (CPW), 146
  See also General Mills; Nestlé
Cessna, 343
Champion Spark Plug Company, 672, 673
Chanel, 249
Chaparral Steel, 457
Charles Schwab, 182, 525
Charles Wells Brewery, 146
Charmin, 580
Chase Manhattan Bank, 389
Chemical Bank, 113
Cherry Garcia, 720
Chevrolet, 142, 161, 270, 310, 635
Chevrolet Blazer, 621
Chevrolet Gear and Axle, 676
Chevron, 123, 142
ChevronTexaco, 165 table 5.2, 721
Chicken Run, 644
Children's Miracle Network, 554
China National Petroleum, 165 table 5.2
Chipotle Mexican Grill, 83, 254, 399
  See also McDonald's
Chiquita, 661
Chrysler, 93, 256, 286, 287, 655
CIA, 327, 328
Ciba-Geigy, 256
Circle K, 324
Circuit City, 308 fig. 10.2
Cisco Systems, 328
Citibank, 390
Citicorp, 25, 226, 256, 552
Citigroup, 106, 165 table 5.2, 299, 327, 359, 545
  less effective strategic leader of, 572
  teamwork and, 632
Citizens Bank of New England, 52
Clean Harbors, 331
Cleveland Clinic, 739
Club Med, 79
Coach, 204–205, 206, 340, 341
Coca-Cola, 19, 26, 80, 91
  base salary and, 538
  as Brazilian business competitor, 312
  differentiation strategy of, 244, 245
  executive compensation and, 539, 540
  goal setting and, 226
  international competition, 140
  PepsiCo competitor, 399
  strategical/tactical planning of, 219
Coldwell Banker, 324
Colgate-Palmolive, 427
Colgate Venture Company, 427
Collin Street Bakery, 164, 166
Columbia University, 114, 373
Commerzbank, 187
Common Dog, The, 311
Common Retirement Fund, 284
Companhia de Bebias das Américas, 312
Compaq Computer, 10, 12, 56, 90, 256
  acquisition of, 285
  coalition against merger with, 288
  flexible work schedule and, 533
  information system equipment and, 734
  integrating systems and, 735
  intranets and, 732
Concord, 373
ConocoPhillips, 165 table 5.2
Consolidated Edison of New York, 25
Consolidated Freightways, 25, 53
Consumers Union, 82
Container Store, The, 108
Continental Airlines, 16, 35, 62, 88, 95, 315, 589
  informal groups and, 620
  management by wandering around and, 602
Coors, 687
COPLINK, 730
Corinthian Colleges, 372
Cornell University, 373
Corning, 251, 416, 661
Corona, 312
Costamar, 242
Costco, 38–39, 41, 107, 117, 165 table 5.2, 250
Council of Better Business Bureaus, 82
Council of Smaller Enterprises of Cleveland, 324
Court Classic shoes, 39
Craftsman, 402
Crayola, 534
Credit Agricole, 165 table 5.2
Credit Suisse, 165 table 5.2
Credit Suisse First Boston, 327, 403
Crest, 580, 689
Cross pens, 245 table 8.1
Crossworlds Software, 329
Cruise vacations, 39
Crystal Geyser, 245
Cypress Semiconductor, 228, 392, 633, 735

Dai-Ichi Mutual Life Insurance, 165 table 5.2
Daimler-Benz, 92, 93, 256, 655
DaimlerChrysler, 41, 52, 53, 90, 91, 93
  global environment, 142
  international competition, 140
  inventory management and, 698
  manufacturing technology and, 692
  organizational complexity and, 655
  performance and, 659
  ranked world's largest MNCs, 165 table 5.2
  robots and, 695
Dairy Queen, 79
Dallas Cowboys, 270, 602
Dallas Police Department, 695
Dasani, 245
Dawn, 581
Dayton Hudson Corporation, 129, 309
dBase, 724
Def Jam, 289
Dell Computer, 25, 98 table 3.1, 120
  external forces and, 405
  global environment, 142
  group decision making by, 292
  importance of small businesses and, 310
  information system equipment and, 734
  integrating systems and, 735
  jobs created by, 308 fig. 10.2, 309
  operations management and, 686
  organizational life cycle of, 383
  product layout and, 690
  related diversification of, 253
  screening control and, 661
  Six Sigma and, 703
  strategic leader of, 572
Del Monte, 314
Delta Air Lines, 25, 85, 91, 290
  conflict at, 634
  labor expenses and, 651
  listening skills training program and, 607
Delta Sigma Theta sorority, 623
Denny's, 185 table 6.1, 188, 324
Department of Defense, 158
Department of Labor, 127

Detroit Edison, 52, 345
Deutsche Bank, 165 table 5.2, 171, 280, 376, 377
Deutsche Post, 165 table 5.2
Deutsche Telekom, 165 table 5.2
Dial, 525
DieHard, 402
Digital Equipment, 316
Dillard's, 256
Direct Marketing Association, 585
DirecTV, 651
Discover Card, 525
Disney
  benchmarking and, 703
  board independence, 118
  budgets and, 663
  competitive advantage of, 255
  corporate culture, 88
  ethical leadership and, 573
  executive compensation and, 552
  financial ratios and, 666
  Finding Nemo, 56
  importance of archives, 42
  joint ventures, 81
  managerial ethics, 106
  planning staff of, 213, 214
  relatedness and, 253
Disney Channel, 220
Disney Cruise Line, 644
Disney World, 56, 79, 528
Dom Perignon champagne, 39
Donatos Pizza, 83, 254, 399
  See also McDonald's
Donnelly Corporation, 81
DOS, 724
DoubleClick, 118
Dow Chemical Company, 16, 380
Downy, 580
Dreamworks, 644
Dresdner Bank, 377
Dunkin' Donuts, 400
DuPont, 52, 228, 246 table 8.2, 247, 274, 704
Durham Athletic Club, 55
DVD players, 91, 94
DVDs, 423

Earthgrains, 341
Earthlink, 730
Eastman Kodak. *See* Kodak
East of Chicago Pizza, 310
eBay, 90, 118, 187, 247, 309
  defender strategy by, 246 table 8.2
  email and, 327
Economist, The, 160
Edmunds Travel Consultants, 331
EDS, 299, 360, 572
Edsel, 421
Educational Testing Service (ETS), 306
Eduventures, 373
Electricite de France, 165 table 5.2
Electrolux, 208
Electronic Arts, 499
Eli Lilly, 17, 327
Emery Air Freight, 529
ENI, 165 table 5.2
Enron, 103, 106, 111, 117
  auditing process and, 667
  barriers to effective communication and, 608
  corporate board and, 216
  electronic communication and, 593
  ethical leadership and, 573
  integrity assessment of M.B.A. applicants, 114
  obstructionist stance and, 124, 125, 126
  whistle blowers, 131
Enterprise Resource Planning, 93
Environmental Protection Agency (EPA), 26, 81, 94, 127, 137
E.ON, 165 table 5.2
Equal Employment Opportunity Commission (EEOC), 81, 82, 127
Equicor, 557
Ericsson, 407, 408
Ernst & Young, 731
Esso, 161
Ethics Officer Association, 114
E*Trade, 321
European Union (EU), 658
Excel, 724
Excelsior-Henderson motorcycles, 316
Excelsior-Henderson Super X, 316
Executive Leadership Council, 84
Express, 388, 389
Express Oil Change, 324
Exxon, 663
ExxonMobil, 25, 26, 85, 122, 124, 380, 663
  charitable causes and, 125
  international revenues, 144
  long range plans, 212
  ranked world's largest MNCs, 165 table 5.2

FAA, 557
Fannie Mae, 165 table 5.2, 177, 185 table 6.1
Fantastic Sam's, 325
FBI, 464, 730
Federal Express, 126, 128, 227, 322, 376, 380, 381
Federal Paper Board, 90
Federal Reserve Bank, 351
Federal Trade Commission (FTC), 26, 127
FedEx, 98 table 3.1, 653
  benchmarking and, 703
  logistics and, 745
  See also Federal Express
Fed Expac, 128
Ferrari, 145
Fiat, 26, 41, 165 table 5.2, 245, 245 table 8.1
Financial Times, 160, 708
Finding Nemo, 644
Fireman's Fund Insurance Company, 667
First Interstate, 88
FirstMatter, 426
First Tennessee Bank, 533
Fisher-Price calculators, 245, 245 table 8.1
Fleet Securities, 622
Fleetwood Enterprises, 655
Focus, 389, 621
Focus: HOPE, 444
Food and Drug Administration (FDA), 500
Folgers, 580
Foot Locker, 237
Ford Escort, 694
Ford Focus, 699
Ford Motor Company, 16, 26, 42, 60, 79, 81, 85
  age discrimination and, 456
  benchmarking and, 702
  bounded rationality and, 286, 287
  competitive advantage of, 270
  decentralized control and, 672
  decision making by, 276
  entrepreneurship, 304
  environmentally sensitive and, 121
  ethical leadership and, 573
  exporting by, 145
  extranet and, 739
  FMS and, 694
  Ford Focus, 143
  global environment, 142
  goals and planning, 233–234
  incentive plans and, 536
  as independently owned business, 310
  internal audit and, 667
  international management and, 318
  international organization design and, 394
  intranets and, 732
  job rotation and, 345
  Land Rover purchase by, 259
  low threat of new entrants, 91
  matrix design, 389
  media-based training by, 451
  merit pay and, 534
  moving Lincoln Mercury division, 86
  multinational business of, 143
  planning staff of, 213, 214
  productivity and, 709
  ranked world's largest MNCs, 165 table 5.2
  stability and complexity of, 90
  teams and, 621
  women executives and, 182
Ford Taurus, 699
Forest Laboratories, 98 table 3.1
Fortis, 165 table 5.2
France Telecom, 165 table 5.2
Franklin Mint, The, 355
Freddie Mac, 165 table 5.2, 185 table 6.1
Freeplay Energy Group, 310
FreshDirect, 745–746
Frontiers International Travel, 242
Fuci Metals, 318
Fuji, 91, 146
Fuji Bank, 25
Fuji Photo, 499
Fujitsu, 165 table 5.2
Fujitsu Electronics, 250

G. H. Bass, 257
Gallo Vineyards, 223

Gap, 107, 361, 644, 687
Garage.com, 321
Garden District Gift Shop, 6
Gateway, 405
Gator, 119
Gatorade, 39
General Dynamics, 714
General Education Network, 373
General Electric, 26, 48, 52, 60, 78, 98 table 3.1
  CAD technology and, 694
  (case study), 103
  corporate university and, 451
  cycle time and, 704
  decentralized, 360
  employee involvement and, 709
  flat structure management of, 354
  GE Business Screen developed by, 259, 260
  global environment, 142
  information management and, 734, 735
  ISO 9000 certification and, 704
  location of facilities and, 690
  managerial ethics, 106
  operations management and, 689
  organizational goals by, 207, 208
  organizing by managers, 166
  positive reinforcement by, 527
  productivity and, 707, 709
  purchasing management and, 697
  ranked world's largest MNCs, 165 table 5.2
  resource deployment by, 238, 239
  Six Sigma and, 703
  and social responsibility, 123
  Socrates Quick Quote, 729
  standards and, 659
  strategic business units and, 252
  workforce termination method and, 456
General Electric Capital, 103
General Foods, 345, 427
General Instrument Corporation, 53
General Mills, 25, 113
  chief information officer and, 597
  jobs eliminated by, 308 fig. 10.2
  preliminary control and, 660
  strategies by, 246
General Motors, 26, 53, 72, 85, 270
  apprenticeship program and, 444
  bounded rationality and, 286, 287
  competition conflict, 635
  goal setting and, 228
  group decision making by, 291
  incentive plans and, 536
  international competition, 140
  jobs eliminated by, 308 fig. 10.2
  long range plans, 212
  matrix design, 390
  Nova, 161
  optimizing by, 211
  organization culture of, 88
  planning staff of, 213, 214
  ranked world's largest MNCs, 165 table 5.2
  stability and complexity of, 90
  use of System 4 organization, 379
Georgia-Pacific, 405, 406, 655
Gillette, 107
Gingiss Formalwear, 325
Girl Scouts of America, 26, 125
Global Crossing, 573
Global-Dining, 482
Global Research Consortium (GRC), 392
Gold's Gym, 164, 318
Goodyear Tire & Rubber Company, 277, 456, 687
Google, 604, 730, 732
Gould Paper Corporation, 294
Great Clips, Inc., 312
Green Bay Packers, 6
Greeting Cards.com, Inc., 329
Groxis, 214
Grupo Modelo, 312
GTE Southwest, Inc., 453
Guess?, Inc., 635

H. J. Heinz, 351
Halliburton, 567, 667
Hallmark Cards, 88
Hanes, 341
Harley-Davidson, 316
Harley-Davidson motorcycle, 687
Harry Potter books, 249
Harvard University, 35, 74, 87, 90, 107, 131
Harvey Nichols, 662
Hasbro, 328
Heineken, 140, 141, 142
Heinz, 80
Henri Bendel, 388
Hershey Foods, 238
Hershey Trust, 491
Heublein, 399
Hewlett-Packard
  Carly Fiorina, 182
  coalition at, 288
  code of ethics, 113
  and Compaq, 256
  corporate culture of, 88
  differentiation strategy by, 245 table 8.1
  division (M-form) organization design, 388
  established market by, 316
  failure to innovate by, 424
  flexible work schedule and, 533
  impact of manager on, 6, 10, 12
  implementing alternative decisions by, 285
  integrating systems and, 735
  manager examples, 25
  merger with Compaq, 56
  organization culture, 86
  printer software, 19
  ranked world's largest MNCs, 165 table 5.2
  reaction to Stone Yamashita, 17
  suppliers and, 80
  value-added analysis and, 702
  values of, 87
Hillshire Farms, 341
Hilton Hotels, 4
Hitachi, 165 table 5.2
HMOs (health maintenance organizations), 26
Hoechst AG, 121, 143, 144, 380, 606
Home Depot, 53, 165 table 5.2, 211
  bureaucratic control and, 669
  control standards and, 658
Honda, 42, 81
  competitive advantage by, 270
  delegation limitations by, 369
  diversification by, 255, 256
  intermediate plan, 213
  inventory management and, 698
  local suppliers and, 164
  operations control and, 661
  purchasing management and, 697
  quotas and, 158
  ranked world's largest MNCs, 165 table 5.2
Honda motorcycle, 142
Honda of America, 85
Honest Tea, 243
Howard University, 84
HSBC Holdings, 165 table 5.2
Hubbub, 717
Hyatt Corporation, 121
Hypercom, 112, 130
Hypovereinsbank, 165 table 5.2
Hyundai, 78, 165 table 5.2, 245, 245 table 8.1

IBM, 60, 90, 118, 122, 188, 225, 247
  analyzer strategy by, 246 table 8.2
  charitable causes and, 125
  decentralized, 361
  decentralized control and, 672
  employee education, 451
  established market by, 316
  flat structure management of, 354
  FMS and, 694
  information system equipment and, 734
  job enlargement and, 345
  job enrichment and, 345
  jobs created by, 308 fig. 10.2
  John Chambers at, 328
  listening skills training program and, 607
  management levels eliminated at, 355
  productivity and, 709
  purchasing management and, 697
  ranked world's largest MNCs, 165 table 5.2
  staff workforce cuts by, 365
  as "wage leader," 457
IGT Corporation, 686
IKEA, 198, 670
iMac, 422
ImClone, 299
I-mode, 563
Imperial Oil, 161
Inca Quality Foods, 314
Indiana Heart Hospital, 28
Industrial Light & Magic (ILM), 241, 243
Industrie Natuzzi SpA, 208
ING Group, 165 table 5.2
Inner Self, 341
In-Q-It, 328
Institutional Shareholder Services, 216
Intel, 90, 176, 309, 322, 684, 685

Intelligentsia Coffee Roasters, 73
Interbrew, 140, 142
International Harvester (IH), 246 table 8.2, 247, 255, 384, 557
International Longshore and Warehouse Union (ILWU), 462
International Olympic Committee, 26
Internet, 39, 91, 426
- compensation patterns and the, 458
- information system, 729
- People's Republic of China, 604
- piracy of, 644

Interspar, 171
Interstate Commerce Commission, 45
Intimate Brands, 388
Invacare, 393
Iowa State University, 6, 7
IRS, 667
Islip Airport, 35
Itanium, 685
Itochu, 165 table 5.2
It's A Grind, 72, 73
ITT, 254

J. C. Penney, 87, 283, 285, 416
- controlling conflict, 634, 637

J. D. Power, 62
J. P. Morgan Chase, 165 table 5.2, 182, 299
Jackson Hewitt Tax Services, 312
Jacquard loom, 692
Jaguar, 694
Jaguar X-Type, 694
JAL, 282
Jani-King, 312
JetBlue, 35, 650
Jimmy Dean, 341
John Deere & Company, 243
John Hancock, 532
Johns Manville, 498
Johnson Controls, 698
Johnson & Johnson, 98 table 3.1, 113, 120, 130
- prospector strategy and, 250

Jordache Enterprises, Inc., 635
Joseph Schlitz Brewing Co., 246 table 8.2
Junior League, 624
JVC, 212

Kamprad, 198
Kansas City Royals, 284
Katerina's, 73
Kawasaki motorcycle, 142
Keen.com, 328
Kellogg's, 525
Kelly Services, 25, 187
Kenmore, 402
Kennedy Airport, 35
Kentucky Fried Chicken (KFC), 309, 324, 399
KinderCare Learning Center, 25
Kinko's, 380
Kirin Brewery, 146

KLM Royal Dutch Airlines, 91, 282
Kmart, 56, 86, 88
- business process change and, 416
- jobs eliminated by, 308 fig. 10.2, 309
- mechanistic designs by, 383

Knitting Factory, 321
Kodak, 91, 142, 146, 245, 245 table 8.1, 406
- decision making by, 277
- group norms and, 627
- ISO 9000 certification and, 704
- outsourcing, 704
- reengineering by, 416

Kohl's, 402
Komatsu, 243
Konosuke Matsushita, 212
Kraft Foods, 341
Kroger, 41, 79, 165 table 5.2, 314, 341, 405, 720, 721, 723

L. L. Bean, 120, 703
LaGuardia Airport, 35
Land Rover, 259, 276
Lands' End, 120, 249, 402–403, 410
Latin American Integration Association, 159
LatteLand, 73
League of Women Voters, 82
Lee, 90
Lerner New York, 253, 388, 389
Levi's 550 jeans, 39
Levi Strauss, 25, 41, 90
- decentralized control and, 669, 670
- international organization design and, 394

Levi Strauss jeans, 142
Lexus, 245
Limited, The, 56, 238, 253
- multidivision (M-form) organization design, 388, 389
- organic designs by, 383, 384

Lincoln, 699
Lincoln Electric, 535, 536
Lincoln Mercury, 86
Lion King, The, 644, 663
Lipitor, 500
Little Koala, 313
Little League Baseball, 26, 125
Litton Industries, 567
Liz Claiborne, 383
Lloyd's of London, 42
Lockheed Martin, 714
London School of Economics, 373
Long Beach Memorial Hospital, 695
Long John Silver's, 399
L'Oréal S. A., 328
Lorillard, 614
Los Angeles Lakers, 569
Los Angeles Police Department, 437
Lotus 123, 724
Loveline, 321
Lowe's, 98 table 3.1, 669
Lucent Technologies, 348
Lycos, 732

Maine Community Foundation, 513
Malcolm Baldridge Award, 699
Maraba Bourbon, 307
Marek Brothers Construction, 313, 314
Market Coffee Company, 73
Market Corporation, 318
Marriott, 4–5, 362, 602, 721, 723
Mars, 85, 238, 660
Mars candy, 142
Marubeni, 165 table 5.2
Massachusetts Mutual Life Insurance, 451
Massey Ferguson, 26
Matsushita, 165 table 5.2
Matsushita Electric, 212, 241
Mattel, 55, 510
Maxwell House, 721
Mayo Clinic, 619
Maytag, 345
Mazda, 145
McDonald's
- America's Best Companies for Minorities, 185 table 6.1
- and Cargill, 433
- centralized, 360
- conflict between environment and, 635
- corporate training, 24
- European and Asian expansions, 10
- existing business bought by, 320
- franchise advantages for, 325
- franchised operations of, 324
- franchise limitation policy, 222
- general environment, 76, 77 fig. 3.2
- global environment, 142
- Hamburger University, 451
- impact of cultures and international businesses, 78, 79
- location efficiencies and, 262
- McCafe coffee, 254
- minimum wage and, 457, 480
- organization change due to customers, 80
- owner of, 83
- productivity and, 709
- retirees as employees, 27
- Ronald McDonald House program, 125, 126
- rules and regulations at, 223
- standard operating procedures and, 223
- structural changes in, 399
- synergy and, 254
- task environment, 79 fig. 3.3
- in theme parks, 81

McIlhenny Company, 386
McKesson, 165 table 5.2
McKinsey & Company, 87
McPizza, 399
Medicare, 130
Medtronic, 299
Mercantile, 256
Mercedes-Benz, 145, 157, 245 table 8.1, 263
Mercer Management, 534
Merck, 17, 165 table 5.2, 253, 501, 659
Merrill Lynch, 16, 84, 104, 608, 688
Metalloy, 653

Methodist Healthcare System, 629
Metro, 165 table 5.2
Metropolitan Life Insurance, 25, 327
MGM Grand, 257
Micra, 370
Microsoft, 19, 78, 86, 98 table 3.1, 305, 310
conflict at, 633
and FedEx, 381
flexible work schedule and, 533
IM system and, 717
individual behavior and, 477
integrating systems and, 735
jobs created by, 309
Microsoft Office software, 634
Microsoft's Internet Explorer, 731
Microsoft Windows, 724
Microsoft Word, 724
Midvale Steel Company, 44, 45
MilkyWay candy bars, 85
Minnesota Mining and Manufacturing Company, *See* 3M Company
Mirage Resorts, 257
Miramax, 644
Mitsubishi, 6, 94, 129, 165 table 5.2
Mitsui, 165 table 5.2
Mobil, 663
Molson, 146
Monsanto, 17, 25, 41, 121, 208, 389
operations management and, 696
reward system and, 425
Monsters, Inc., 644, 645
Mont Blanc, 245
Montgomery Police Department, 730
Montgomery Ward, 246 table 8.2, 384
Morgan Stanley, 573
Morris Air, 650
Morrissey and Co., 7
Mothers Against Drunk Drivers (MADD), 82
Motorola, 16, 81
employee involvement and, 709, 710
and FedEx, 381
horizontal communication and, 597
IM system and, 717
organic designs by, 383, 384
Six Sigma and, 703
Mrs. Fields, 6, 246 table 8.2, 251
MTV, 321
Munich Re Group, 165 table 5.2
Mustang, 391, 662, 732

Nabisco, 409
NASA, 12, 17, 294
NASDAQ, 373
National Association of Women Business Owners, 324
National Basketball Association, 569
National Federation of Independent Businesses (NFIB), 320, 324
National Labor Relations Board, 127, 460
National Organization for Women (NOW), 82
National Rifle Association (NRA), 82, 127
National Science Foundation, 26
National Semiconductor, 308 fig. 10.2, 317
Natural Foods Market, 352
Navistar International, 247, 384
See also International Harvester (IH)
NBC, 669
NCAA, 525
NCR, 213, 389
NEC, 165 table 5.2, 681
Neiman Marcus, 249, 310
Nerf ball, 420
Nestlé, 26, 78, 157
and Carnation Company, 164
international organization design and, 394
ranked world's largest MNCs, 165 table 5.2
Netscape, 309, 592
Netscape Communicator, 731
Netscape Navigator, 731
Network Appliance, 721
Newbreak Coffee, 73
Newcomers Club, 623
New Jersey Bell Telephone Company, 46
New Mexico State University, 131
Newport News, 691
New York City, 7
New York Stock Exchange, 377
New York Times, 585
New York Times Company, The, 25
New York University, 373
New York Yankes, 288
Nike, 6, 39, 79, 95, 211, 236–237
Air Swoopes, 525
decision making and, 290
decision making by, 288
low labor costs and, 261
Nikon, 245, 245 table 8.1, 423, 424
Niku Corporation, 119
Nippon Life Insurance, 165 table 5.2
Nippon Telegraph & Telephone, 165 table 5.2, 213
Nissan, 81, 165 table 5.2, 213, 361
competitive advantage by, 270
delegation of authority by, 369–370
Nissan/Renault, 370
Nissho Iwai, 165 table 5.2
Nobel Prize, 286, 498
NOK, 653
Nokia, 261, 263
Nordstrom, 669
Nortel, 470
Northrop Grumman, 404, 597, 714
Northwest, 91
Norwegian Cruise Lines, 137
Nova, 161
Novartis, 256
NTT, 563
Nu America, 289
NutraSweet, 91
Nynex, 471
Obex, Inc., 329
Office Depot, 257
Office of Management and Budget, 654
Olay, 581
Old Navy, 245
Omniva, 327
Omron Corporation, 499
Oneida Ltd., 694
Online investment services, 39
OPEC (Organization of Petroleum Exporting Countries), 280
Oracle, 329, 448, 540
Ortho McNeil Pharmaceutical, 184
OSHA, 405, 635
Owens-Corning Fiberglass, 225
Oxford University, 160

Pacific Bell, 336
Pacific Gas & Electric, 25
Pacific Intermountain Express, 736
Palm Pilots, 416
Pampers, 580
Pan American World Airways, 290
Panasonic, 212, 241
Pantene, 581
Paramount, 644
Parker Brothers, 420
Password Tracker, 119
Peace Corps, 79
Peapod, 688
Pearson PLC, 160, 388
Pemex, 165 table 5.2
Penguin Publishing, 160
Pentagon, 285, 729
Pentium 4, 685
Pepsi, 226, 244, 245
PepsiCo, 91, 140, 185 table 6.1, 237
jobs eliminated by, 308 fig. 10.2
joint venture with, 312
multidivision (M-form) organization design, 388
preliminary control and, 660
purchase of Pizza Hut, 399
specialized skilled jobs, 437
Pepsi drink, 142
Peribit, 721
Perulac, 157
PetsMart, 171, 316
Peugeot, 165 table 5.2
Pfizer, 225, 308 fig. 10.2, 500, 616, 617
Pharmacia, 616, 617
Philip Morris, 16, 125, 253, 532, 613
Philips Electronics, 253, 380, 390, 704
Pillsbury, 585
Pitney Bowes, 329
Pixar, 644, 645
Pizza Hut, 145, 309, 399
operations management and, 686
PlanetOut Partners, Inc., 241
Playtex, 341
Pleasant Company, 510

PNM Resources, 186 table 6.1
PointOne Telecommunications, 313
Poland Springs, 245
Polaroid, 245 table 8.1, 421
Polaroid SX-70, 421
Polo Ralph Lauren, 237
Pontiac, 635
Porsche, 279
Post-it notes, 20
Precision Auto Wash, 324
Prentice Hall, 160
Pret A Manger, 254, 302–303
  See also McDonald's
Princeton University, 552
Pringles, 580
Procter & Gamble, 21, 24, 25, 86, 98 table 3.1, 121
  centralized control and, 672
  decision making goals and, 206
  financial control and, 663
  goals of, 208
  leadership and, 580–581
  OB Mod and, 529
  organization development by, 420
  product-service mix and, 689
  ranked world's largest MNCs, 165 table 5.2
  related diversification and, 253
  strategic leader of, 572
  sustained competitive advantage by, 243
Prodigy, 730
Progressive, 98 table 3.1
Promodes, 172
Provigil, 275, 279
Prudential, 389, 411
Prudential Insurance, 17, 25, 345
Prudential Securities, 340, 341
PT Cruiser, 91, 659
Public Broadcasting System (PBS), 26

Quaker Oats, 254
Quarter Pounder (hamburger), 80
Qwest, 573

R. J. Reynolds, 399
Radar, 732
Radar detectors, 62
Ralph Lauren, 245
Ramada Inn, 324
Rand Corporation, 292
Raytheon, 213, 714
Reader's Digest, 415
Reebok International, 79, 211, 383, 624, 625, 635
  decision making by, 288
REI, 545
RE/Max, 324
Renault, 369
Revlon, 184, 308 fig. 10.2
RFB & D, 191
Rhone-Poulenc, 606
Ritz-Carlton, 20
RJR Nabisco, 253
Robert Half International, 107
Rockwell International, 17
Rolex, 244, 245 table 8.1, 289, 696
Roman Catholic Church, 6, 26
Ronald McDonald House, 125
Rotary International Club, 624
Rover, 259
Royal Ahold, 165 table 5.2
Royal Caribbean Cruise Lines, 94, 136
Royal Dutch/Shell, 6, 7, 26, 165 table 5.2, 663
Rubbermaid, 53, 246, 500
RWE, 165 table 5.2
Ryanair, 36

S. C. Johnson & Co., 427
Safeway, 25, 79, 341
Sainsbury supermarkets, 307
Saint Patrick's Cathedral, 608
Salvation Army, 76
Sameday.com, 718
Sam's Club, 171, 462
Samsung Electronics, 165 table 5.2, 166
Sandoz Pharmaceuticals, 256
Sanyo, 145
Sara Lee, 204, 340–341
SAS Institute, 121, 545
SBC Communications, 165 table 5.2, 185 table 6.1
Schlumberger, 280
Scholastic, 249
Schwinn bicycles, 79
Sears, 25, 72, 94, 125
  building Latino customers, 184
  business size of, 305
  decentralized, 360
  flat *vs.* tall organizational structure, 354
  growth of, 416
  input control and, 660
  international business of, 143
  organizational strengths used by, 241
  organization change, 402–403
  outsourcing and, 704
  purchasing management and, 697
  ranked world's largest MNCs, 165 table 5.2
  reinforcement theory and, 529
  resistance to change and, 410
  specialized skilled jobs, 437
Seattle Coffee Company, 94
Securities and Exchange Commission (SEC), 81, 127, 299, 359, 571
Seiko, 41
Sempra Energy, 185 table 6.1
Sergeant York anti-aircraft gun, 285
Service Corps of Retired Executives (SCORE), 323
Sesame Street, 581
7-Eleven, 324, 410
Sharp, 681
Shell Oil, 24, 25, 41, 42, 60, 88, 380
  corporate university and, 451
  decentralized control and, 672
  group activities and, 623
  Learning Center, 393
  learning organization and, 393
  natural environment and, 121
  "nine-eighty" schedule and, 533
Sheraton Hotels, 4
Shimizu Corporation, 499
Shiseido, 681
Shoney's, Inc., 188
Shrek, 644
Siemens, 78, 165 table 5.2, 188, 697, 739
Sierra Club, 82, 623
Silicon Graphics (SGI), 598
Simonds Rolling Machine Company, 44, 45
Singapore Airlines, 278, 282
Sinopec, 165 table 5.2
Slim-Fast, 260
Small Business Administration (SBA), 308, 309, 323, 330
Small Business Institute (SBI), 323
Smith Barney, 188
SmithKline, 130
Snickers candy bars, 85
Société Bic, 317
Softbank, 321
Soft Sheen, 328
Sony, 78, 90, 94, 129, 408
  centralized control and, 672
  decision making and, 289
  exporting by, 145
  innovative product of, 421
  organization control and, 681
  personnel system, 482
  ranked world's largest MNCs, 165 table 5.2
Soriana, 172
Soul Planet, 242
Southern California Edison, 185 table 6.1
Southern Pan Services Co., 459
Southwest Airlines, 16, 25, 86, 98 table 3.1, 357, 650
  case study, 35
  employee participation and, 670
  social responsibility and, 121
Sprint, 525
Spun.com, 321
St. Jude Medical, 98 table 3.1
Standard Oil Company, 72
Standard & Poor's, 216
Stanford University, 299, 373
Staples, 257
Starbucks
  analyzer strategy and, 251
  art of management, 23
  behavioral aspect decisions by, 286
  complete information and, 721
  educating employees at, 545
  example of admired companies, 98 table 3.1
  failure of original owners, 21
  first-line managers, 15
  franchise policy, 222
  goal of, 6
  industry success story, 11
  international market expansions, 93

as mail-order business, 320
manager examples, 25
marketing managers, 16
motivation and, 522
operating procedures used by, 382
organizations environment, 72–73
programmed decisions by, 277
regional managers, 14
scope of management, 25
top manager, 13
Starwood Hotels, 4
State Farm Insurance, 25, 165 table 5.2, 437
State Farm Mutual, 314
Stella Artois beer, 141
Stone Yamashita, 17
Stress Management and Counseling Center, 507
Studebaker, 56
Subaru, 380
Subway, 79, 90, 324, 689
Suez, 165 table 5.2
Sumitomo, 165 table 5.2, 188
Sumitomo Life Insurance, 165 table 5.2
Sun, 717, 734
Sunbeam, 106
Sun Microsystems, 294, 414
Supercuts, 324
Super 8 motel, 324
Susan's Corner Grocery Store, 7
Suzuki motorcycle, 142
Sylvan Learning Center, 324

TABASCO sauce, 386
Taco Bell, 90, 309, 324, 399, 658
TAG Heuer, 245, 245 table 8.1, 525
Taliban, 89
Target, 25, 41, 80, 125, 165 table 5.2, 402, 619
building Latino customers, 184
business planning, 205
Taurus, 234, 391, 702
Teamsters, 460
Tenneco, 25, 227, 228
Tesco, 165 table 5.2
Texaco, 188
Texas Instruments, 41, 86, 113, 239, 245 table 8.1, 250, 291, 345, 420
flexible work schedule and, 533
informal interchange and, 602
socialization process and, 629
virtual team meetings and, 622
The Sopranos, 532
Three Gorges Dam, 221
3M Company
creativity and, 500
Diversity Training Advantage, 192
emergent strategy by, 239, 240
leadership and, 570
organization change and, 411
Post-it notes, 19, 20
prospector strategy by, 246
reward system and, 425
social responsibility and, 121
350Z, 369
Thunderbird, 621
Tide, 580
Tiffany jewelry, 39
Time Warner, 56, 256, 257, 299
See also AOL
Timex, 245 table 8.1, 250, 696
Timken, 380
Today Show, 608
Togo's, 400
Tokyo Electric Power, 165 table 5.2
Tommy Hilfiger, 205
Torrington, 158
Toshiba, 165 table 5.2, 188, 250
Total, 165 table 5.2
Toucan-Do, 539
Toyota Motor Corp.
competitive advantage/disadvantage of, 270–271 (case study)
delegation limitations by, 369
efficiency and effectiveness of, 7, 8, 25
global cost competitiveness, 681
as independently owned business, 310
intermediate plan, 213
international management and, 318
local suppliers and, 164
low threat of new entrants, 91
ranked world's largest MNCs, 165 table 5.2
strategic leader of, 572
Toyota USA, 270
Toys "R" Us, 125, 171
Toy Story, 644
TRADOS, 187
Transamerica, 254, 255
Travelers Insurance, 256, 736
Travel Industry Association of America, 242
Treasure Planet, 663
Trico, 480
Tricon Global Restaurants, 309, 399
Trilogy Software, 620
TriNet Employer Group, 731
Tri-West Healthcare Alliance, 585
TruServ, 571
TRUTH-FM, 613
TRW, 345
Tucson Police Department, 730
Tumbleweed Communications, 327
240Z, 369
Tyburn Convent, 20
Tyco, 15, 106, 117, 165 table 5.2, 486
corporate board and, 216
Tyco International, 519
electronic communication and, 593
Tyson Foods, 261

U. S. Army, 6, 243, 436–438, 713
U. S. Bureau of Labor Statistics, 180
U. S. Census Bureau, 328
U. S. Chamber of Commerce, 94
U. S. Civil Service, 345
U. S. Coast Guard, 136
U. S. Congress, 288
U. S. Department of Defense, 713
U. S. Department of Energy, 654
U. S. Department of Labor, 180, 441
U. S. Food and Drug Administration (FDA), 81, 127, 274, 275, 299
U. S. Justice Department, 327
U. S. Navy, 714
U. S. Patent and Trademark Office, 375
U. S. Postal Service, 26, 165 table 5.2, 186 table 6.1, 376
U. S. President, 552
U. S. Steel, 687
UBS, 165 table 5.2
UNext, 372, 373
Unilever, 25, 42, 165 table 5.2, 260
centralized control and, 672
international organization design and, 394
Union Bank of California, 185 table 6.1
Union Carbide, 19, 380, 638
Union Oil Company of California, 445
United Airlines, 35, 53, 315, 650
labor expenses, 656
motivation and, 532
unionized labor and, 462
United Auto Workers (UAW), 234, 407, 411, 460, 623, 637
United Health Group, 98 table 3.1
United Nations, 280
United Nations Security Council, 291
United States Gypsum, 310
United Way, 6, 26, 208
Universal Studios, 253, 255
University of Arkansas, 131
University of Aston, 383
University of Maryland, 373
University of Missouri, 74
University of New Mexico, 587
University of North Texas, 619
University of Phoenix Online, 372, 373
University of Texas, 114
Unocal Corporation, 144
UPS, 376, 416, 660
US Airways, 650
USX Corporation, 687

Vanguard, 380
VCRs, 91
Verizon Communications, 165 table 5.2
Veterans Administration, 608
Victoria's Secret, 341, 388
Visa, 91
Vivendi, 671
Vivendi Universal, 165 table 5.2, 289
Vodafone, 165 table 5.2
Volkswagen, 81, 145, 158, 165 table 5.2, 635
Volvo, 310
Vorstand, 377

W. R. Hambrecht & Company, 39
W. T. Grant, 246 table 8.2
Wall Street, 38
Wal-Mart, 39, 72, 81, 82, 85, 98 table 3.1

Wal-Mart(*Continued*)
  advertising by, 250
  business planning, 205
  business size of, 305
  centralized, 360
  coordination activities by, 362
  cost leadership strategies by, 250
  discrimination and, 188
  expansion by, 309
  forecasting labor supply, 444, 445
  globalization and, 171–172 (case study)
  growth of, 416
  jobs created by, 308 fig. 10.2
  labor union avoidance by, 461, 462
  location efficiencies and, 262
  lower priced clothing of, 402
  ranked world's largest MNCs, 165 table 5.2
  relevant information and, 721
  retirees and, 471
  same store layouts at, 341
  Six Sigma and, 703
Walt Disney Company
  division (M-form) organization design, 388
  incentives from France to, 157
  organization conflict, 644–645
  strategic/tactical plans of, 220
  use of synergy, 55
  See also Disney
Walt Disney World, *See* Disney World
Wang Laboratories, 328
Warner Books, 104
Warner-Lambert, 500, 581, 616, 617
Washington Redskins, 119
Waterford crystal, 39
Waterman, 245 table 8.1
WD-40 Company, 252, 386
Webvan, 745
Wellpoint Health Networks, 98 table 3.1
Wells Fargo Bank, 25, 42, 250
Wendy's, 79, 383, 399
Wertkauf, 171
Western Electric, 48, 345
Westinghouse Electric, 228, 409, 557
Westin Hotels, 4
Wharton, 15, 114
Whirlpool, 113, 208, 380
Whistler Corporation, 62, 655, 657
White Barn Candle Co., 388
Whole Foods, 313
Wichita State University, 399
Wickes Ltd., 225
Wimbledon, 485
Winnie the Pooh, 644
Wipro, 408
WNBA, 525
Women Entrepreneur's Connection (BankBoston), 329
Women's Business Enterprise National Council (WBENC), 323
Women's Growth Capital Fund, 324
Wonderbra, 341
Woolco, 171
Woolworth Corporation, 388
WordPerfect, 724
Work in Progress, 644
WorldCom, 106, 114, 117, 131
  corporate board and, 216
  electronic communication and, 593
  ethical leadership and, 573
  internal audit and, 667, 668
World Trade Center, 4
Wrangler, 90
Wrigley, 252, 491
Wyndham International, 186 table 6.1

XcelleNet, 722
Xerox, 25, 91, 113, 182, 186 table 6.1, 299, 317
  benchmarking and, 702
  chief information officer and, 597
  encoded communication, 591
  media-based training by, 451
  resisting deviants, 426
  team organization, 392
Xilinx, 327
Xterra, 369

Yahoo!, 118, 187, 216, 309
  analyzer strategy by, 246 table 8.2
  free directories and, 731
  funded by venture capital company, 321
  IM system and, 717
  interest groups and, 620
  management philosophy of, 357
  portal sites and, 732
Yamaha motorcycle, 79, 142
Yellow, 416
Yellow Freight System (case study), 67–68
Yum! Brands, 399

ZapMail, 227
Zurich Financial Services, 165 table 5.2

Subject Index

Absenteeism, as withdrawal behavior, 501
Acceptance sampling, in statistical quality control, 705
Accommodative stance, social responsibility and, 125
Accountability, control and, 675
Accounting
  business strategies and, 248
  differentiation strategy and, 249
Accuracy, control and, 673
Accurate information, 720, 721
Achievement-oriented leader, 563
Acquisitions, 94, 233, 257
Action plan, 213
Administrative intensity, 364, 365
Administrative management, 45
Administrative managers, 16
Administrative model, in decision making, 286, 287 fig. 9.4
Adverse impact, equal employment opportunity and, 440
Advisory boards, for small businesses, 323
Aesthetics, of quality, 699
Affective component, of attitudes, 488
Affirmative action, 440
African Americans, *see* Ethnicity
Age Discrimination in Employment Act, 440
Age distributions, in workforce, 179
Aggregate productivity, 706
Aggressive goal behavior, in goal orientation, 162 fig. 5.4, 163
Agreeableness, as personality trait, 483
Aligning people, as leadership action, 551
All channel pattern, in communication networks, 595
Alternative dispute resolution, conflict and, 638
Alternative work arrangements, motivation and, 531–533
Amazon River Basin, 121
Americans with Disabilities Act, 182, 440
  training programs and, 393
  violation of rights, 82
  workforce diversity, 28
America's Best Companies for Minorities, 185–186 table 6.1
Analyzer strategy, in Miles and Snow typology, 246 table 8.2, 247
Angola, 156
Application, stage of innovation process, 420, 421
Areas of management, 16
Artificial intelligence (AI), 729
Asians, in workforce, 181
Attitudes
  affective component and, 489
  affective component of, 488
  cognitive component of, 488
  cognitive dissonance and, 488
  definition of, 487
  intentional component of, 488
  job satisfaction/dissatisfaction and, 488, 489
  managers and, 489
  organizational commitment and, 489
  work-related, 488, 489
Attribution, perception and, 492, 493
Audits, 667, 668
Australia, 152
Authoritarianism, as personality trait, 486
Authority
  centralization/decentralization of, 360, 361
  definition of, 356
  delegation of, 356–360
  leadership compared to, 553
  line position in, 364
  staff position in, 364
Authority-Compliance, *see* Leadership
Automation
  organizational technology and, 692
  total quality management and, 701
Avoidance, in reinforcement theory of motivation, 528

Baby boom generation, 179
Babylonians, management by, 43 fig. 2.1
Background experiences, creativity and, 498
Backward vertical integration, 257
Balance sheet, 666
Base salary, executive compensation and, 538, 539
B2B, *see* Business–to–business (B2B)
BCG matrix
  definition of, 258
  market growth/market share as, 258 fig. 8.3
  types of businesses of, 258
Beetle Bailey, 222, 376
Behaviorally Anchored Rating Scale (BARS), 454, 455 fig. 14.4
Behavioral management perspective
  contributions and limitations of, 51 table 2.3
  definition of, 48
  early psychologist influence on, 48
  employee morale improved by, 41
  general summary of, 51 table 2.3
  Hawthorne studies and, 48, 49
  human relations movement, 49, 50, 513
  influences on, 49
  within model of management timeline, 58, 59 fig. 2.5
  motivating performance, 57
  organizational behavior and, 51
Behavioral model
  Likert and, 376–378, 379
  in organization design, 376–378, 379
Behavior modification (OB Mod), 529
Belongingness needs, in Maslow's hierarchy of needs, 515
Benchmarking, 702
Benefits, 458, 459
  See also Compensation
"Big Five" personality traits, 483, 484
"Big picture," 21
Birth stage, of organizational life cycle, 384
Board of directors
  decision-making responsibility of, 216
  definition of, 83
  and diversity, 84
  and ethics, 117, 118
  organization's mission and strategic goals, 210
  planning and, 215
Body language, as nonverbal communication, 602, 603
Bonuses, as executive incentive pay, 538
"Boss-centered" behavior, *see* Leadership
Boston Consulting Group, *see* BCG matrix
Boundary spanner, 92
Bounded rationality, decision making and, 286, 287
Brazil
  emerging economic community, 158
  market potential of, 152
  quotas and, 158
  rain forest, 156
Bricklayers, 45
Budgets
  balance sheet, 664 table 20.1
  capital expenditures, 664 table 20.1
  cash-flow, 664 table 20.1
  definition of, 663
  development of, 664 table 20.1
  division budget requests and, 665 fig. 20.5
  expense, 664 table 20.1
  financial, 663
  information systems and, 733
  labor, 664 table 20.1
  managers and, 664–666
  nonmonetary, 664 table 20.1
  operating, 664
  planned financial operations and, 664 table 20.1

Budgets (*Continued*)
planned nonfinancial operations and, 664 table 20.1
production, 664 table 20.1
profit, 664 table 20.1
sales/revenue, 664 table 20.1
sources/uses of cash and, 664 table 20.1
space, 664 table 20.1
strengths of, 665
weaknesses of, 665, 666
Bureaucracy
groups/teams and, 621
See also Bureaucratic model
Bureaucratic control, 669
Bureaucratic model, organization by Weber, 46, 375, 376
Bureaus, *see* Departmentalization
Burnout, stress and, 496
Business-level strategy, *see* Strategy
Business of Ethics, The
corporate culture, 87
emailing, 327
ethics training, 114
globalization and labor force, 148
leadership, 573
motivation, 532
organization change, 406
organization structure, 359
perception, 491
unethical CEOs, 14–15
unions and organizations, 462
Business plan, 318
Business process change (reengineering), 416, 417 fig. 13.3
Business-to-business (B2B)
efficiency as goal, 47
networked systems and, 739
Business Week, 11, 15, 17
Business Week's Best Performing Companies (2003), 98 table 3.1
Buyers, power of, 91, 244
"Buy national" laws, 157, 158
Buzzards Bay, 122
Byrd Amendment, 158

Cafeteria benefit plans, 459
Cape Cod, 122
Career planning, 459, 460
Caribbean Common Market, 159
Caring, ethical decision-making and, 116 fig. 4.2
Case studies
competitive advantages/disadvantages, 270–271
decision making, 299–300
diversity/multiculturalism, 198–199
effective communication, 613–614
efficiency and effectiveness, 35–36
entrepreneurs, 335–336
globalization, 171–172
goals and planning, 233–234
information technology/systems, 745–746
leadership, 580–581
motivation, 545–546
organization challenges, 67–68
organization change, 432–433
organization conflict, 644–645
organization environment, 103–104
organization structure, 399–400
outsourcing, 713–714
poor management, 681
retirees, 470–471
social responsibility, 136–137
workplace stress, 507–508
Cash cows (businesses), in BCG matrix, 258
Cellular layout, of facilities, 691
Chain of command, in organization structure, 352
Chain pattern, in communication networks, 595
Challenger disaster, 294
Change, *see* Organization change
Charisma, 569
Charismatic leadership, 569, 570
Chief Executive Officer, planning and, 215
China
cultural differences and, 159
market potential of, 152
Chinese, management by, 43 fig. 2.1
Circle pattern, in communication networks, 595
Civil Rights Act of 1964, 178
Civil Rights Act of 1991, 440
Classical management perspective
administrative management viewpoint, 44, 45, 46
contributions and limitations of, 46, 47 table 2.1
definition of, 43, 44
methods of, 57
within model of management timeline, 58, 59 fig. 2.5
scientific management viewpoint, 44, 45
Closed system, 54
Cluster chain, in grapevine network, 601
Coaching and counseling, in organization development (OD), 419
Coalition, in decision making, 288
Code of ethics, 130
definition of, 113
See also Ethics
Coercion, method for using power, 554
Coercive power, 553
Cognitive abilities, creativity and, 499
Cognitive component, of attitudes, 488
Cognitive dissonance, attitudes and, 488
Cohesiveness
in groups/teams, 629–630, 631
performance norms and, 630, 630 fig. 19.4, 631
See also Groups/teams
Collaboration, information systems and, 738, 739
Collective bargaining, 462
Collectivism, in social orientation, 161, 162 fig. 5.4
Columbia, 618
Common strength, *see* SWOT analysis
Commonwealth of Independent States, 153
Communication
advantages/disadvantages of written, 593
definition of, 589
for diversity/multiculturalism, 190
effective, 589
encoding/decoding in, 590, 591
horizontal, 597
incident on, 584–585
interpersonal, 592–593, 594
management role in, 589, 590
managers and, 586, 595
manager's job and, 588, 589
networks, 594, 595
organizational, 595, 596 fig. 18.3, 597
organizational informal, 600–602, 603
overcoming resistance to organization change by, 411
process of, 590 fig. 18.1, 591
telecommuting and, 533
types of networks of, 595 fig. 18.2
vertical, 596, 597
See also Electronic communication; Informal Communication
Communication networks, 594, 595
Communication skills
definition of, 21
e-mail and, 584
Companies
business mission, 123
management training programs, 24, 25
See also Organization(s)
Company productivity, 706
Compensation
definition of, 457
individual wage decisions and, 458
wage-level decision and, 457
wage structure decision and, 458
Competition
conflict stimulus, 634
defender strategy, 246, 247
for organization resources, 635
portfolio management and, 259
Competitive advantage
diversity/multiculturalism and, 184
increasing operations speed and, 705 table 21.3
innovation and, 422, 425
international business and, 260–262, 263
knowledge workers and, 464
sustained, 243
SWOT analysis and, 241, 242
Toyota case study, 270–271
Competitive disadvantage, 243
See also Competitive advantage; Strategy
Competitive parity, 241
Competitive rivalry, 91, 244
Competitor(s)
definition of, 79
ethical treatment of, 113
in organization environment, 90, 91
organizations influencing, 94

Complete information, 721
Comprehensive approach, to organization change, 408, 409
Compressed work schedule, motivation and, 532, 533
Compulsory advice, in staff authority, 364
Computer-aided design (CAD), 693
Computer-aided manufacturing (CAM), 694
Computer-assisted manufacturing, in organizational technology, 693
Computer-integrated manufacturing (CIM), 694
Computer programmers, *see* Knowledge workers
Conceptual skills, 21
Concern for people, as behavioral approach to leadership, 557
Concern for production, as behavioral approach to leadership, 557
Confidentiality, and ethics, 109, 110
Conflict
  avoidance of, 633
  benefits of, 633
  causes of, 633–635
  compromise and, 638
  confrontation approach and, 638
  controlling, 637, 638
  definition of, 632
  diversity/multiculturalism and, 187–188
  intergroup, 634, 635
  interorganizational, 635
  interpersonal, 633, 634
  managers and, 636–638
  managing, 636–638
  methods for managing, 636 table 19.3
  between organization and environment, 635
  performance and, 633
  personality differences and, 634
  relationship of performance and, 633 fig. 19.5
  resolving/eliminating, 638
  stimulating, 636, 637
Conflicts of interest, and ethics, 109, 110
Conformance, of quality, 699
Conglomerate (H-form) organization design, 387, 388 fig. 12.2
Conscientiousness, as personality trait, 483
Consensus, attributions and, 492
Consideration behavior, of leadership, 557
Consistency, attributions and, 492
Consult (group) style, in Vroom's decision tree approach, 566
Consult (individually) style, in Vroom's decision tree approach, 566
Consumer(s), international strategy and, 260–262, 263
Contemporary applied perspective
  impact of authors on, 60
  within model of management timeline, 58, 59 fig. 2.5
Contemporary management
  issues and challenges, 58–62
  workforce challenges, 67, 68
Contemporary management theory, 51
Content perspectives, on motivation, 514–519, 520
Content validation, human resource selection and, 447, 448
Contingency perspective
  within model of management timeline, 58, 59 fig. 2.5
  situational management, 57
Contingency planning, 216–218, 217 fig. 7.3
Continuous-process technology, 380
Contributions, in psychological contract, 478
Control
  accountability and, 675
  accuracy and, 673
  areas of, 655, 656
  change and, 653, 654
  costs minimization and, 655
  definition of, 652
  effective, 672–673, 674
  employee participation and, 676
  error limits and, 654, 655
  financial, 656, 662–667, 668
  flexibility and, 673
  inappropriate focus and, 674, 675
  incident on, 650–651
  information management as, 723 fig. 22.2
  ISO 14000 and, 704
  levels of, 656, 656 fig. 20.2, 657
  management of, 672–675, 676
  managers and, 673, 674
  objectivity and, 673, 674
  operations control, 656, 660–661, 662
  organizational complexity and, 655
  overcoming resistance to, 675
  overcontrol and, 674
  planning and, 672
  process of, 657 fig. 20.2
  purpose of, 653–654, 653 fig. 20.1, 655
  resistance to, 674–675, 676
  responsibilities for, 656, 657
  rewards for inefficiency and, 675
  strategic, 656, 670–671, 672
  structural, 656, 668–669, 670
  timeliness and, 673
  verification procedures and, 676
Controller
  budget developed by, 664
  definition of, 657
Controlling
  definition of, 12
  in a global economy, 167
  managerial activities, 8
Controlling and problem solving, as management action, 551
Control process
  comparison between performance and standards, 659
  corrective action determination and, 659
  performance measuring in, 658
  standards in, 657, 658
  steps in, 657 fig. 20.2
Control standard, 657, 658
Control system, in information technology system, 724
Convergent thinking, creativity and, 499
Coordination
  definition of, 361
  need for, 361, 362
  techniques for achieving, 362, 363
Core technology, in organization design, 379–381, 382
Corporate culture, 39
  See also Organization culture
Corporate governance, and ethics, 117, 118
Corporate-level strategy, *see* Strategy
Corporate social audit, 131, 132
Corporate university, 451
Corporations, *see* Organization(s)
Corrective action, determination in control process, 659
Cost argument, for diversity/multiculturalism, 184
Cottage industry, 599
  See also Telecommuting
Country Club Management, *see* Leadership
Coverage ratios, in ratio analysis, 666
Creation of an obligation, as political behavior, 574, 575
Creativity
  background experiences and, 498
  cognitive abilities and, 499
  definition of, 498
  divergent/convergent thinking and, 499
  enhancing in organizations, 500, 501
  incubation stage of, 499, 500
  insight stage of, 500
  personal traits and, 498, 499
  preparation stage of, 499
  process of, 499, 500
  verification stage of, 500
Creativity argument, for diversity/multiculturalism, 184
Crisis management, 216, 217
  See also Planning
Cross-cultural leadership, 572
Cross-functional teams, 620
Cultures
  absence of organization identification based on, 194, 195
  behavioral differences, 161–163, 162 fig. 5.4
  ethical business practices by international, 111
  international management and, 159–163
  leadership and, 572
  motivational needs and, 517
  multimarket flexibility in, 261
  and organizations, 77, 78
  transnational strategy and, 264, 265
  varied behavioral processes, 60, 61
  See also Organization culture
Customer departmentalization, 350
Customer(s)
  definition of, 80
  departmentalization, 350
  ethical treatment of, 113

Customer(s) (*Continued*)
extranets and, 732
needs and business strategies, 249
organization's social responsibility and, 120
satisfaction, 67, 68
service, 36, 303
Cycle time, total quality management (TQM) and, 704

Dagwood, 112, 276
Data, compared with information, 719, 720
Database, information system(s) and, 734
Debt ratios, in ratio analysis, 666
Decentralized control, 669, 670
Decide style, in Vroom's decision tree approach, 566
Decisional roles of managers
definition of, 18 table 1.2
types of, 19, 20
Decision making
administrative model of, 286, 287 fig. 9.4
alternatives in, 283–284, 285
behavioral aspects of, 286–290, 291
certainty/uncertainty state and, 278–279
classical model of, 281 fig. 9.2
commitment to, 288–289, 290
conditions and levels for, 278 fig. 9.1
conditions surrounding, 278–279
creating information systems and, 733
decision support system (DSS) and, 728
definition of, 10, 276
delegation of authority in, 358
effective, 276, 277, 279
ethics and, 116 fig. 4.2, 290, 291
evaluating alternatives in, 283 fig. 9.3
evaluating results of, 285, 286
executive support systems (ESS) and, 728
in global economy, 166
group/team, 291–294
implementing alternative, 285
incident on, 204–205
incident on risk taking in, 274–275
intuition and, 279, 288, 289, 290
managerial activities, 8
managerial process, 205
optimization, 284, 285
and planning process, 206, 207
political forces in, 288
process of, 276
programmed/nonprogrammed, 277
rational perspectives on, 280–285, 286
rational steps in, 281, 282 table 9.1
responsibility of corporate boards for, 216
risk propensity and, 290
risk state and, 278, 279
styles of, 566, 567
types of, 277
use of grapevine network in, 601
Vroom's decision tree approach to, 564–567
Decision-making skills
corrective action in control process and, 659
definition of, 21
Decision-making tools, and quantitative management, 53, 54
Decision support system (DSS), 728
Decline stage
of innovation process, 422
in product life cycle, 248, 248 fig. 8.2
Defender strategy, in Miles and Snow typology, 246, 247
Defensive stance, social responsibility and, 125
Delegate style, in Vroom's decision tree approach, 566
Delegation
of authority, 357–360, 361
by centralization/decentralization, 360, 361
process of, 357–359, 360
process steps of, 358 fig. 11.4
Deliberate strategy, *see* Strategy
Delphi groups, for group/team decision making, 292
Demand, capacity decisions and, 690
Departmentalization
bases for, 349 fig. 11.2
customer, 350
definition of, 347
functional, 349–351, 386, 387, 389
labels, 351
location, 351
managers and, 350
multiple bases of, 351
product, 350, 387, 388 fig. 12.2, 389
rationale for, 347–348
by sequence, 351
by time, 351
Development
stage of innovation process, 420
See also Training
Diagnostic activities, in organization development, 418
Diagnostic skills, 21
Differentiation
in organization design, 383
Differentiation strategy, in Porter's generic strategies, 244, 245 table 8.1, 249
Dilbert, 60, 161, 335–336, 353, 410, 564
Direct influence, 94
Direct investment, 147
Directive leader behavior, 563
Directories and search engines
World Wide Web (WWW) and, 731
Directors & Boards, 84
Discrimination
conflict stimulus, 634
as dysfunctional employee behavior, 503
equal employment opportunity and, 440
in multicultural organization, absence of prejudice and, 194
in the workforce, 181, 182
Disseminator, managerial role, 10, 18 table 1.2
Distinctive competence
definition of, 238
imitation of, 242, 243
SWOT analysis and, 241
Distinctiveness, attributions and, 492
Disturbance handler, managerial role, 18 table 1.2, 20
Divergent thinking, creativity and, 499
Diversification
by acquisition, 257
BCG matrix for, 258, 258 fig. 8.3, 259
definition of, 252
GE Business Screen for, 259 fig. 8.4
managing, 258–259, 260
by merger, 257
related and unrelated, 252, 253–255, 253 table 8.3
Today's Management Issues, 256
Diversity
contemporary challenge, 60
corporate boards, 84
definition of, 27
of employees, 84, 85
organizations commitment to, 175
See also Diversity/multiculturalism
Diversity/multiculturalism
age distributions and, 179, 179 fig. 6.2
aging population and, 179 fig. 6.3
communication for, 190
competitive advantage and, 184, 184 fig. 6.5
conflict and, 187–188
definition of, 176
dimensions of, 179–182, 183
effects of, 183–186
empathy for, 189, 190
entrepreneurship and, 303
ethnicity and, 181, 182
gender and, 181
handicapped/physically challenged and, 182
immigration and, 183
incident on organization(s) and, 174–175
individual strategies for, 189, 190
international businesses and, 183
language barriers and, 159
multicultural organization and, 193–194, 195
online multilingual services and, 187
organizational approaches for, 190–192, 193
organizational managing of, 189–192, 193
organization culture and, 193
problem-solving argument for, 186
reasons for increases in, 178, 178 fig. 6.1
religious beliefs and, 182
systems flexibility argument for, 186, 187
tolerance for, 189
training for, 192, 193
trends in, 177–178
understanding for, 189
Diversity/multiculturalism, leadership and, 572
Divisional (M-form) organization design, 388
Division of labor, 343
Divisions, *see* Departmentalization
Documentation, information system(s) and, 734
Dogs (businesses), in BCG matrix, 258
Domestic business, 143
Domination, in noncohesive groups, 629, 630
Downward communication, 597

Durability, of quality, 699
Dysfunctional behaviors, 503, 599

E-commerce
ethical treatment by, 111
Internet storefront, 740
search engines and, 732
trends in, 327, 328 fig. 10.6
virtual organization and, 392
Economic agents, ethical treatment of, 111
Economic communities, 158
See also European Union (EU)
Economic dimension
definition of, 76
of general environment, 75 fig. 3.1, 76
See also International management
Economic return, effect of innovation process on, 424 fig. 13.5
Economies of scale
global efficiencies and, 261
in manufacturing, 315, 315 fig. 10.4, 316
multidomestic approach and, 263
Economies of scope, 261
Economy, contemporary challenge, 60
Education
importance of, 24
in management, 20–24
in organization development, 418
overcoming resistance to organization change by, 411
Effective
definition of, 7, 8
See also Management
Effective communication
conflicting/inconsistent signals and, 603, 604
credibility and, 604, 607
definition of, 589
environmental factors and, 606
feedback and, 607
following-up and, 608
improving individual skills and, 606–607
improving organizational skills and, 608, 609
individual barriers to, 603–604, 605 table 18.1
language differences and, 606
listening skills and, 605, 606, 607 fig. 18.6
managers and, 604, 606–609
noise and, 606
organizational barriers to, 605, 606
overcoming barriers to, 606–608, 606 table 18.2, 609
overload and, 606
perceptions and, 605, 606
perspective and, 607
point of view and, 607
power and, 605
predisposition and, 605
regulating information flow and, 609
reluctance to communicate and, 604, 605
semantics and, 605
two-way communication and, 607
understanding richness of different media and, 609
vocabulary meanings and, 607
Effectiveness, *see* Organization(s), *see* Organizational effectiveness
Effective strategy, *see* Strategy
Efficiency and effectiveness
core to, 97
enhancement of, 45
methods of, 57
Southwest Airlines case, 35–36
Toyota Motor Company, 7, 8
Efficient, 7, 8
Effort-to-performance expectancy, 521
Egyptians, management by, 43 fig. 2.1
Electronic communication
email, 584, 589, 599
email overload and, 606
encoding/decoding in, 590, 591
formal information systems and, 597–598, 599
information system security and, 736
managers and, 597, 598, 599
organizational disadvantages of, 599
personal electronic technology, 599
Electronic firewalls, 736
Electronic information, *see* Technology
Emancipation Proclamation, 498
Emergent strategy, *see* Strategy
Emotional intelligence (EQ), as personality trait, 487
Empathy
for diversity/multiculturalism, 189, 190
as personality dimension, 487
Employee-centered leader behavior, 556
Employee information system (skills inventory), 446
Employee involvement
productivity and, 709, 710
total quality management and, 701
Employee participation
bureaucratic control and, 669
control and, 676
motivation and, 530, 531
Employee privacy
ethical treatment of, 109
management challenge, 60
Employee Retirement Income Security Act of 1974 (ERISA), 441
Employee(s)
advantage of diversity in, 178
behavioral change of, 67
behavioral processes and, 52
behavior and information systems and, 740, 741
boundary spanner, 92
bureaucratic control and, 669
CEO earnings gap and, 540
code of ethics, 130
compensation and benefits and, 457–458, 459
corporate culture and, 87
corporate environment effect on, 87
customer satisfaction by, 67
diversity and multiculturalism of, 174–175, 190
elderly, 27
empowerment of, 530
enthusiastic and young, 303
ethical treatment of organization by, 109, 110, 111
flexible work sites and, 739
influences on, 49
information systems and, 740, 741
information system training sessions, 734
internal environment element, 84, 85
internal recruiting and, 446
job rotation by, 344, 345
job specialization limitations/benefits by, 344
and labor unions, 85
legal environment and, 439–443
management treatment of, 108, 109
Multicultural Education Program and, 175
opportunities for growth/advancement by, 345
organizational size of, 383
organization development of, 417–419, 420
part-time, 27
performance appraisals and, 452–455
regulation violations of, 95
reporting relationships and, 352–355, 356, 391
resistance to organization change and, 410
rewarding behavior of, 88
reward systems and, 534–540, 541
studies of productivity of, 48, 49
temporary workers, 84, 85, 392, 443
termination of, 456
understanding diversity/multiculturalism and, 189
use of scientific management for, 44, 45, 48, 49
Employee stock ownership plans (ESOPs), 538
Employment-at-will, 443
Employment practices
hiring standards, 82
and regulatory agencies, 81, 82
Empowerment
conditions of organizational effectiveness and, 531
decentralization and, 531
motivation and, 530
techniques in, 530, 531
Encryption, information system security and, 736
Enterprise resource planning (ERP), 54, 414, 724
Entrants, threat of new, 91, 244
Entrepreneur(s)
definition of, 305
"Generation X-ers," 28
managerial role, 18 table 1.2, 19, 20
Entrepreneurship
business plan for, 318
crossover from big business to, 328
definition of, 304, 305
distinctive competencies of, 316–317

Entrepreneurship (*Continued*)
economic system and, 306, 307
existing business bought by, 319, 320
failure of, 330, 331
financial planning in, 318
first-mover advantages of, 317
franchising and, 324–325
incident on, 302–303
industry choice for, 310–316
innovation by, 309, 310
international management and, 318
job creation by, 307–308, 309
management advice sources for, 322–323, 324
managers and, 330
minorities and women, 328–329, 329 fig. 10.7, 330
new business financing for, 320
new business starts by, 319
new markets identified by, 317
niches in established markets and, 316, 317
organization structure for, 319–325
role in society of, 305–309, 310
sales forecast in, 318
starting from scratch for, 320
strategy for, 310–318
success of, 330
See also New business; Small business
Entropy, 56, 416
Environmental change
long range plans and, 212
reaction plan and, 213
Environmental scanning, observation and reading in, 92
Environment(s)
as a barrier to goals, 225
basic perspectives affecting organizations by, 89–91, 92
change and complexity in, 89, 90 fig. 3.4
crisis, 92
dimensions of, 89
direct influence, 94
entropy in, 416
ethical behavior in organization, 112, 113
five competitive forces in, 90, 91, 244
formal authority system of, 564
incident on organizational change, 72–73
innovation and, 422
methods used to adapt to, 92–94, 93 fig. 3.5, 95
models of organizational effectiveness in, 96, 97 fig. 3.6
monitoring feedback, 56
organizational flexibility and, 184 fig. 6.5, 186, 187
organization design and, 382, 383
organization flexibility, 94
and planning process, 207 fig. 7.1
resources from, 6
risk propensity and, 486, 487
stable and simple, 90
systems perspective and, 54, 55
transnational strategy and, 264, 265
turbulence in, 92
uncertainty in, 89, 90
uncertainty levels in, 90 fig. 3.4
See also External environment; Internal environment; International management; Organization(s)
Equal employment opportunity, 440
Equal Employment Opportunity Commission, 440
Equal Pay Act of 1963, 441
Equity theory, of motivation, 523, 524
ERG theory, of motivation, 517
Established market, entrepreneurs identifying niches in, 316, 317
Establishing direction, as leadership action, 551
Esteem needs, in Maslow's hierarchy of needs, 515
Ethical behavior
definition of, 108, 109
See also Ethics
Ethical compliance, 129
Ethical leadership, 572, 573
Ethics
applicable steps for judging, 113–114
areas of managerial concern, 110 fig. 4.1
business conduct standards, 78
and decision-making, 116 fig. 4.2
decision making and, 290, 291
definition of, 108
determinant factors of individual's, 109
diversity/multiculturalism conflict and, 187, 188
and Enron, 87
and General Electric, 103–104
and information technology, 118–119
and leadership, 117, 572–573, 574
management challenge, 61
managing behavioral, 113–115
in organization culture, 87
social responsibility and, 129, 130
Ethics Project, The, 114
Ethnicity
America's best companies for minorities, 185–186 table 6.1
definition of, 181
distribution trends of, 183 fig. 6.4
diversity and immigration, 175
employee qualifications and, 178
ethical treatment of minorities, 109
leadership and, 572
minorities in management, 84
in the workplace, 27
See also Diversity/multiculturalism; Workforce
Europe, mature market system, 151
European Union (EU)
definition of, 151
global economy and, 152
history of, 151, 152
Evaluation, favorable, in group cohesiveness, 629
Excellence perspective, within model of management timeline, 58, 59 fig. 2.5
Executive committee, planning and, 215
Executive support systems (ESS), 728
Existence needs, in ERG theory of motivation, 517
Expanded goal-setting theory of motivation, 526 fig. 16.6
Expectancy theory, of motivation, 520–521, 522
Expense accounts, and ethics, 115
Experiences, unpleasant, in noncohesive groups, 629, 630
Expert power, 554
Expert systems, 729
Exporting business, 145
Export restraint agreements, 158
External audits, 667
External environment
definition of, 74
general environments, 74–78, 75 fig. 3.1, 79
task environment, 74, 75 fig. 3.1, 79–82
External locus of control, 485, 563
External recruiting, 447
Extinction, in reinforcement theory of motivation, 528
Extranets, 732
Extraversion, as personality trait, 484
Extroversion vs. Introversion, 484
Exxon Valdez, 82, 122

Facilitate style, in Vroom's decision tree approach, 566
Facilitation, procedures in organization change, 411
Facilities, in operations systems, 690
Fair Labor Standards Act, 440, 441
Family and Medical Leave Act of 1993, 441, 443
Far Side, The, 628
Fast Company, 17
Favorable evaluation, in group cohesiveness, 629
Favors, organizational/governmental influence by, 128
Features, of quality, 699
Feedback, 54, 55, 56
in automated operations, 692
operations control and, 660–661
Figurehead, managerial role, 18 table 1.2, 19
Finance
business strategies and, 248
differentiation strategy and, 249
Financial budgets, 663
Financial capital, 439
Financial control
audits for, 663
balance sheet for, 666
definition of, 656, 662
financial audits and, 667, 668
financial statements for, 666
income statement for, 666
ratio analysis for, 666
See also Budgets
Financial managers, 16
Financial statements, 666

Finished-goods inventory, 697
Firewalls, information system(s) and, 736
First-line managers
 definition of, 15, 16
 ethical training sessions by, 113
 information systems and, 725, 726
 intermediate plan and, 213
 management training programs for, 24
 resistance to groups/teams, 621
 as teaching faculty, 393
 technical skills for, 20
First-mover advantage, 317
Five competitive forces, 91
Fixed-interval schedule, of reinforcement, 528
Fixed-position layout, of facilities, 691
Fixed-ratio schedule, of reinforcement, 529
Flexibility, control and, 673
Flexible manufacturing systems (FMS), 694
Flexible work schedules (flextime), motivation and, 533
Flextime, 533
Focus, control and inappropriate, 674, 675
Focus strategy, in Porter's generic strategies, 245
Force-field analysis, overcoming resistance to change by, 411, 412, 412 fig. 13.2
Forming stage, of group development, 624
Fortune, 11, 15, 17
Fortune's Most Admired Companies (2003), 98 table 3.1
Forward vertical integration, 257
Franchising agreements, 324–325
"Free riding," 628
Front line managers, planning and, 215
Frustration-regression element, in ERG theory of motivation, 517
Full integration of the informal network, in multicultural organization, 194
Full structural integration, in multicultural organization, 194
Functional authority, in staff authority, 364
Functional departmentalization, 349
Functional group, 619
Functional (U-form) organization design, 386, 387 fig. 12.1

Gainsharing programs, 537
Gantt chart, 45
GATT, 153, 154
GE Business Screen, in BCG matrix, 259, 259 fig. 8.4
Gender, diversity/multiculturalism and, 181, 182
General Agreement on Tariffs and Trade (GATT), *see* GATT
General environment
 definition of, 75
 economic dimension of, 76
 international dimension of, 78, 79
 of McDonald's, 76, 77 fig. 3.2
 political-legal dimension of, 78
 sociocultural dimension of, 77, 78
 technological dimension of, 76, 77
"General X-ers," 28
Glass ceiling, 181, 182
Global business, 143
Global economy
 competing in, 164–166
 controlling in a, 167
 decision-making in a, 167
 GATT and, 153
 high-potential-high-growth economies, 152, 153
 leading in a, 167
 management challenges in, 166–167
 market economies and systems of, 150–153, 151 fig. 5.2, 154
 medium-size organizations and, 164
 multinational corporations and, 164, 165 table 5.2
 oil-exporting regions of, 153
 organizing in a, 167
 planning in a, 167
 small organizations and, 164, 166
 structure of, 150–153, 154
 WTO and, 154
 See also International business
Global efficiencies, 262
Globalization
 contemporary challenge, 60
 factor in multiculturalism, 178
 See also Global economy; International business
Global strategy, 264
Goal acceptance, in expanded goal-setting theory of motivation, 526
Goal approach, organizational effectiveness by, 96
Goal commitment, in expanded goal-setting theory of motivation, 526
Goal difficulty, in goal-setting theory of motivation, 524
Goal orientation, 162 fig. 5.4, 163
Goals
 agreement for group cohesiveness, 629
 areas of, 210
 barriers to implementing, 223–225, 224 table 7.2, 226
 communication and, 224 table 7.2, 226
 conflict of organization, 635
 consistency, revision, and updating, 224 table 7.2, 226
 constraints and, 225, 226
 developing strategic/tactical plans, 219
 disageement in noncohesive groups, 629, 630
 environment and, 225
 formal process of setting, 228 fig. 7.5
 inappropriate, 224
 kinds of, 208, 209 fig. 7.2, 210
 level of, 208
 management by objectives (MBO), 227–228, 229
 managing multiple, 211
 operational, 210
 optimizing, 211
 organizational effectiveness and, 207–211, 212
 participation and, 224 table 7.2, 226
 purposes of, 207, 208, 224 table 7.2, 226
 for reengineering, 417
 reluctance to establish, 225
 resistance to change and, 225
 responsibilities for setting, 210
 reward systems and, 224, 224 table 7.2, 226, 227
 strategic, 210
 strategic management and, 238–239, 240
 tactical, 210
 time frames of, 210
Goal-setting theory, of motivation, 524–525, 526 fig. 16.6
Goal specificity, in goal-setting theory of motivation, 524, 525
Gossip chain, in grapevine network, 601
Government
 business influence and, 126 fig. 4.6
 impact on business, 78
 regulations by, 127
 social responsibility and, 126–127, 128
 stability, 156, 157
Government organizations (agencies)
 as bureaucratic model, 375
 management of, 26
Grapevine, 600, 601
Graphic rating scales, in performance appraisals, 454 fig. 14.3
Greeks, management by, 43 fig. 2.1
Grievance procedure, 463
Group
 definition of, 618
 See also Groups/teams
Group size, in noncohesive groups, 629, 630
Groups/teams
 activities and, 623
 avoidance of roles in, 627
 careers and, 620, 623, 624
 characteristics of, 625–630, 631
 cohesiveness in, 629–630, 629 table 19.1, 631
 conflict in, 631–638
 decentralized control and, 669
 developmental stages of, 624, 624 fig. 19.2, 625
 formal leader of, 631
 forming stage of, 624
 functional, 619
 goals and, 623
 implementation of, 621
 incident on, 616–617
 informal leader of, 631
 informal or interest, 620
 instrumental benefits and, 623, 624
 interpersonal attraction and, 623
 managers and, 621, 624, 627, 630
 need satisfaction and, 623
 norming stage of, 624
 norms of behaviors in, 627–628
 performance norms and, 621
 performing stage of, 624, 625
 reasons for joining, 622–623, 624
 reasons for organizational, 621

Groups/teams (*Continued*)
resistance to, 621
role ambiguity in, 626
role conflict in, 626
role development of, 625 fig. 19.3
role overload in, 626, 627
role structures in, 625
socialization and, 628
storming stage of, 624
task, 620
types of, 619–621, 619 fig. 19.1, 621 table 19.1
virtual, 622
Group/team decision making
advantages of, 293
Delphi groups for, 292
disadvantages of, 293 table 9.2, 294
interacting groups for, 291
managers and, 294
nominal groups for, 291
uncertainty conditions for, 291
Groupthink
in group/team decision making, 294
Growth needs, in ERG theory of motivation, 517
Growth stage
of innovation process, 421, 422
in product life cycle, 247, 248 fig. 8.2

Halo error, in performance appraisal, 455
Health-care facilities, management of, 26
High-performance teams, 620
Hispanics, *see* Ethnicity
Home page
of web site, 731
Home replication strategy, 263, 264
Honesty, and ethics, 110
Hong Kong, 152
Horizontal communication, 597
Hostile takeover, 94, 107
Human capital, 439
Human relations approach, to motivation, 513, 514
Human relations movement
definition of, 49, 50
Theory Y, 49 table 2.2
Human resource approach, to motivation, 514
Human resource management (HRM)
AIDS and, 443
alcohol and drug abuse and, 443
applications and, 447, 448, 449
assessment centers and, 440
benefits and, 439 table 14.1, 440, 441, 458, 459
career planning and, 459, 460
compensation and, 439 table 14.1, 440, 441, 457
contingent workers and, 464, 465
definition of, 438
dual-career families and, 443
employment-at-will and, 443
equal employment opportunity and, 439 table 14.1, 440
forecasting labor demand and supply, 444–445, 446
health and safety and, 439 table 14.1, 441, 442
incident on, 436–437
interviews by, 440
job analysis and, 444
knowledge workers and, 463, 464
labor relations and, 439 table 14.1, 460–462, 463
legal environment of, 439–443, 439 table 14.1
managers and, 445, 446, 449, 450, 455, 456, 464
performance appraisal, 452–455
planning, 444–445, 445 fig. 14.1, 446
recruiting, 446, 447
replacement chart and, 445
retirees and, 470–471
selection and validation process, 447–450
sexual harassment and, 443, 503
social change and, 443
strategic importance of, 438, 439
temporary workers and, 465
tests by, 449, 450
training and development, 450–456
Human resource managers, 16, 129
Human resources, employment practices, 82
Hybrid organization design, 391
Hygiene factors, in two-factor theory of motivation, 518

Images, as nonverbal communication, 602
Importing business, 145
Impoverished Management, *see* Leadership
Impression management, 575
Incentive pay plans, 535
Incentives
compensation and, 457
international trade and, 157
See also International business
Incremental innovation, 422
Incubation stage, of creativity, 499, 500
Individual behavior in organizations
attitudes and, 487–489, 490
creativity and, 498–500, 501
incident on, 476–477
individual differences and, 481
perception and, 490–492, 493
personality and, 481–486, 487
person-job fit and, 479–480, 481
psychological contract and, 478, 479, 479 fig. 15.1
stress and, 493–497, 498
workplace and, 501–503, 504
Individual differences, behavior in organizations and, 481
Individual incentive plans, 535
Individualism, in social orientation, 161, 162 fig. 5.4
Individual wage decisions, compensation and, 458
Indonesia, 152
Inducements
as political behavior, 574
in psychological contract, 478
Industrial psychology, 45
Industry productivity, 706
Inefficiency, resistance to control and, 675
Influence, government/organization relationship by, 126–127, 126 fig. 4.6, 128
Informal communication
factors for increase in grapevine, 601
grapevine, 600, 601
informal interchange outside work setting, 602
management by wandering around, 601, 602
managers and, 603
nonverbal communication, 602
in organizations, 600 fig. 18.4, 601 fig. 18.5
Informal interchange outside work setting, 602
Informal leader, 631
Informal or interest groups, 620
Information
accurate, 720, 721
characteristics of useful, 720–721
complete, 721
data compared to, 719, 720
managers and, 718, 720, 721, 722
relevant, 721
timely, 721
Informational roles of managers
definition of, 18 table 1.2, 19
as processors, 719 fig. 22.1
types of, 19
Information distortion, method for using power, 555
Information management
control perspective on, 723 fig. 22.2
method used to adapt to environments, 92, 93
Information systems (IS)
applicant selection system and, 729
artificial intelligence (AI), 729
components of, 724 fig. 22.3
creating, 733–734, 735
credit evaluation system and, 729
database and, 734
decision support system (DSS), 728
desktop publishing and, 727
documentation and, 734
document-imaging systems and, 727
employee training sessions and, 734
enterprise resource planning (ERP) and, 414
executive support systems (ESS), 728
expert systems, 729
firewalls and, 736
functional areas and business processes, 726
hardware/software needs of, 734
instant messaging (IM), 716–717
integration of, 734, 735
Internet, 729–731, 732
knowledge-level and office systems, 727
knowledge workers and, 725, 726

knowledge workers and office applications, 727
limitations of, 736–737, 737 table 22.1
Maintenance Operations Center Advisor (MOCA), 729
management information systems (MIS), 727, 728, 728 fig. 22.5
managers and, 725, 726, 735, 737
managing, 732–737
modifications and, 734
need determinants of, 726 fig. 22.4
networking and, 739
office support systems and, 727
for operations and data workers, 727
organizational impact of, 738–740, 741
organizations with, 93
security and, 736
steps for establishing, 733 fig. 22.6
system controls and, 734
system operations workers, 727
transaction-processing system (TPS), 726, 727
types of, 725–731, 732
user groups, system requirements and, 725, 726
using, 735, 736
virtual company and, 739
viruses and, 737

Information technology (IT)
chief information officer, 597, 598
definition of, 720
and ethics, 118–119
incident on, 716–717
online education, 451
organization change with, 414
types of, 723–724

Infrastructure, 156

In-group, leader and, 568

Initiating-structure behavior, of leadership, 557

Innovation
acquisition and, 581
benefits and, 459
budgets and, 665, 666
definition of, 420
effects on economic return, 424 fig. 13.5
failure to initiate, 424, 425
forms of, 422–423, 424
incremental, 422, 423
information systems and, 735, 736
managerial, 423
organizational culture and, 426, 427
in performance appraisal, 455
process, 423, 424
process of, 420–421, 421 fig. 13.4, 422
product, 423, 424
promoting, 425–427
radical, 422
resistance to change, 425
reward system and, 425, 426
technical, 423

In-process sampling, in statistical quality control, 705

Input medium, in information technology system, 723

Inputs
definition of, 54
equity theory and, 523
operations control and, 660
product development by, 184

In Search of Excellence (Peters and Waterman), 60

Insight stage, of creativity, 500

Inspirational appeal, method for using power, 555

Instant messaging (IM), 716–717

Instrumental compliance, method for using power, 554

Integrating framework, 56, 58 fig. 2.4

Integration
backward vertical, 257
for coordination, 363
forward vertical, 257
in multicultural organization, 194
in organization design, 383

Integration departments, for coordination, 363

Intentional component, of attitudes, 488

Interacting groups, for group/team decision making, 291

Interaction, in group cohesiveness, 629

Interest group
definition of, 81
influence of, 82

Intergroup activities, in organization development, 418, 419

Intergroup competition, in group cohesiveness, 629

Intermediate plan, 213

Internal audit, 667, 668

Internal consultants, 17

Internal environment
board of directors, 83
definition of, 74
employees element of, 84, 85
organization culture element, 86–88, 89
owners, 83
physical environment element, 85

Internal locus of control, 485, 563

Internal processes approach, organizational effectiveness by, 96

Internal recruiting, 446

International business
advantages/disadvantages of, 145, 149 table 5.1
challenges of, 141
competitive advantage and, 260–262, 263
controls on international trade, 157, 158
definition of, 143
direct investment by, 147, 148, 149 table 5.1
domestic business vs., 143
franchising of, 145
GATT, 153, 154
global environment, 142–143, 144
importing/exporting, 145, 149 table 5.1
incident on competitive rivalry in, 140–141
joint ventures and, 145, 146, 149 table 5.1
levels of activity, 143 fig. 5.1
licensing of, 145, 146, 149 table 5.1
multiculturalism and, 183
multinational, 143
oil-exporting regions of, 153
organization design and, 393, 394 fig. 12.5
small business in, 308
strategic alliances, 146, 149 table 5.1
strategic alternatives for, 263–264, 265
strategies for, 145–148, 149 table 5.1
trends in, 144
types of, 145
violence in countries, 153
WTO, 154
See also Global economy

International dimension
definition of, 78
of general environment, 75 fig. 3.1
See also International management

International management
centralized and decentralized, 264, 265, 671, 672
challenges of, 141, 153–156
controls for international trade, 157, 158
cultural behavioral differences and, 161–163, 162 fig. 5.4
cultural environment and, 155 fig. 5.3, 159–163, 265
direct investment by, 147, 148
domestic management vs., 149
economic communities and, 158
economic environment, 155, 155 fig. 5.3, 156
entrepreneurship and, 318
environmental challenges of, 154–163
ethical business practices by, 111
global economy of, 148–153, 154
globalization process of, 145–154
government stability and, 156, 157
impact of foreign business, 78, 79
incentives for international trade and, 157
infrastructure and, 156
language barriers and, 159
mistakes of, 142, 143
MNCs and, 147, 148, 149
natural resources and, 155, 156
political/legal environment, 155 fig. 5.3, 156–158, 159
values, symbols, beliefs, and language, 159–160, 161

International organizations, and strategic partners (allies), 81

International strategy
alternatives for, 263–264, 265
developing, 260–264, 265
by global efficiencies, 261
global strategy for, 264
home replication strategy for, 263
multidomestic strategy for, 263
multimarket flexibility and, 261, 263
transnational strategy for, 264
worldwide learning and, 261–262, 263

International trade
controls on, 157, 158
economic communities and, 158, 159
global competition in, 144
importing/exporting, 145
incentives for, 157
product restrictions, 145, 158
Internet (Net)
benefits of, 730, 731
business communication and, 729
business strategy and, 60
chat and, 716
compensation patterns and, 458
competitive advantage web sites on the, 241
as competitive environment force, 279
cyberspace, 731, 732
definition of, 729
e-commerce and, 61
extranets and, 732
firewalls and, 732
information retrieval and, 729
interest group platform and, 620
internet service provider (ISP) and, 730
intranets, 732, 738, 739
multilingual web sites, 187
origin of, 729
personal use at work, 110
portal sites, 732
privacy guidelines and, 118
search engines of the, 214
small business and, 319
storefront and, 740
World Wide Web (WWW), 731
See also World Wide Web (WWW)
Internet service provider (ISP), 76, 730
Interorganizational conflict, 635
Interpersonal attraction, groups/teams and, 623
Interpersonal conflict, 633, 634
Interpersonal demands, as work-related stressor, 495
Interpersonal dynamics, 587, 588
Interpersonal problem solving, conflict and, 638
Interpersonal relations
of organizations, 586–588
social support and, 588
See also Communication
Interpersonal roles of managers
definition of, 18 table 1.2, 19
types of, 19
Interpersonal skills, 21
Interrole conflict, in groups/teams, 626
Intragroup competition, in noncohesive groups, 629, 630
Intranets, 732
In-transit inventory, 697
Intrapreneurs, 427
Intrapreneurship, innovation and, 425
Intrarole conflict, in groups/teams, 626
Intrasender conflict, in groups/teams, 626
Introduction stage, in product life cycle, 247, 248 fig. 8.2
Intuition, in decision making, 288, 289
Inventor, as intrapreneur, 427
Inventory
control, 697
management, 697
total quality management and, 701
types, purposes, and sources of control, 697 table 21.1
Iran, 153, 156
Iraq, 153, 156, 280
ISO 9000:2000, 704
ISO 14000, 704
Israel, 190

Japan, 152, 155, 156
cultural differences and, 159
workforce and age distribution, 179 fig. 6.3
Job analysis, 444
Job-centered leader behavior, 556
Job characteristics approach, to job design, 346, 347
Job design
definition of, 343
job characteristics approach and, 346, 346 fig. 11.1, 347
job enlargement and, 345
job enrichment and, 345, 346
job rotation and, 344, 345
job specialization and, 343, 344
managers and, 343
work teams and, 347
Job enlargement, 345
Job enrichment, 345, 346
Job evaluation, 458
Job rotation, 344, 345
Job satisfaction/dissatisfaction, work-related attitudes and, 488, 489
Job sharing, 533
Job specialization, 45, 343
Joint venture(s)
definition of, 146
diversity/multiculturalism conflict and, 188
Judging vs. Perceiving, 485
Judgmental methods, performance appraisal by, 453
Justice, ethical decision-making and, 116 fig. 4.2
Just-in-time (JIT) method, inventory management and, 698

Key words, search engines and, 731
Knowledge-level and office systems, for information systems (IS), 727
Knowledge workers
definition of, 463
demand for, 464
information systems and, 725, 726
and office applications, and information systems (IS), 727
training and, 464
Kuwait, 153, 156
Labor, Department of, 441
Labor-Management Relations Act, 441, 443
Labor relations
collective bargaining and, 462, 463
definition of, 460
grievance procedure and, 463
managers and, 463
Labor unions
as bureaucracies, 376
competing goals, 637
formation of, 460–461, 462
internal recruiting and, 446
organization process of, 461 fig. 14.5
power limitations of, 441
Large-batch (mass-production) technology, 380
Latin American Integration Association, 159
Latinos, *see* Ethnicity
Launch stage, of innovation process, 421
Layout, of facilities, 690
Leader, managerial role, 18 table 1.2, 19
Leader-member exchange (LMX) model, of leadership, 567, 568 fig. 17.7
Leader-member relations, in LPC theory of leadership, 561
Leaders, 551
Leadership
charismatic, 569, 570
cross-cultural, 572
definition of, 550
employee-centered leader behavior and, 556
ethical, 572, 573
favorableness, flexibility and style of, 561, 562
formal/informal group, 631
generic behavioral approaches to, 555–558
incident on, 548–549
job-centered leader behavior and, 556, 559
leader-member exchange (LMX) model of, 567, 568 fig. 17.7
Leadership Grid, 558 fig. 17.1
Least-preferred Coworker Theory of, 562 fig. 17.3
LPC theory of, 560–561, 562
management and, 551–554, 555
management compared to, 551 table 17.1
Managerial Grid, 557, 558
managers and, 553, 564
Michigan studies of, 556
Ohio State studies, 557
path-goal framework of, 565 fig. 17.4
path-goal theory of, 562–563, 564
political behavior and, 574–576
power and, 553–554, 555
situational approaches to, 559–567, 568
strategic, 571, 572
substitutes for, 568, 569
Tannenbaum and Schmidt's continuum, 559 fig. 17.2
traits of, 555, 556
transformational, 570
Vroom's decision tree approach to, 564–566, 567 fig. 17.6

Leading
definition of, 12
in a global economy, 166, 167
managerial activities, 8
Learning organization, 393
Least-preferred coworker (LPC) measure, 560
Legal compliance, 129
Legitimate power, 553
Legitimate request, method for using power, 554
Lenders, financing new business and, 321
Levels of management
and areas of management, 14 fig. 1.3
definition of, 13
increasing with technology complexity, 380, 381
Lewin model, of organization change, 407
Liaison
managerial role, 18 table 1.2, 19
roles in coordination, 362
Libya, 153
Licensing, 145
See also International business
Life and career planning, in organization development (OD), 419
Linear programming, and operation management, 53
Line position, 364
Liquidity ratios, in ratio analysis, 666
Lobbying
definition of, 127
direct influence, 94, 128
Location, of facilities, 690
Location departmentalization, 351
Location efficiencies, 261
Locus of control, as personality trait, 485, 563
Long-range plan, 212
Loss, feelings of, resistance to organization change and, 410
LPC theory, of leadership, 560–561, 562

Machiavellianism, as personality and, 486
Maintenance Operations Center Advisor (MOCA), 729
Malaysia, 152
Malcolm Baldridge Award, 699
Management
activities of, 8 fig. 1.1, 10–12
areas of, 16–17
art of, 23
characteristics of, 8–12, 27–29
contemporary issues and challenges of, 58–62
definition of, 7, 8
of diversity, 27
effective, 25
effective and efficient, 57 fig. 2.4
environmental change and complexity of, 89
fundamental skills of, 20–22
globalization vs. regionalism, 149, 150
government organizations, 26
health-care facilities, 26
incident on fundamentals for success, 38–39
incident on managers and, 4–5
levels of, 13–15, 16
networked systems and, 738–740, 741
operative and executive span for, 353
in organizations, 7, 8 fig. 1.1
process of, 9 fig. 1.2
science of, 23
scope of, 25–26, 27
similarities /differences in process of, 9
sources of skills in, 23 fig. 1.4
as tall vs. flat, 354, 354 fig. 11.3, 355
titles of, 13
Management and labor, relationship between, 43
Management by objectives (MBO), 227
Management by wandering around, communication approach by, 601, 602
Management consultants, 45
for small businesses, 323
Management history
in antiquity, 43 fig. 2.1
antiquity and, 42
importance of, 41, 42
mathematics in, 43
pioneers, 42, 43
See also Management theories
Management information systems (MIS), 727, 728
Management perspectives
application of (case study), 57, 58
historical development of, 58, 59 fig. 2.5
integrating framework of, 57 fig. 2.4
See also Management theories
Management process
core of, 46
functions in the, 9–12
Management science, 52, 53
Management team, 621 table 19.1
Management theories
application of, 57, 58
impact of authors on, 60
importance of, 41
originator of, 43
See also Behavioral management perspective; Classical management perspective; Quantitative management perspective
Managerial ethics
definition of, 109, 110 fig. 4.1, 111
incident on, 106–107
relationships of, 110 fig. 4.1, 111
Managerial hierarchy
controlling conflict by, 637
structural coordination technique and, 362
Managerial innovation, 423
Managerial roles
activities of, 18 table 1.2
categories of, 18 table 1.2
concept of, 18
Managerial skills
communication, 20, 21
conceptual, 20, 21
decision-making, 20, 21, 22
diagnostic, 20, 21
interpersonal, 20, 21
sources of, 23 fig. 1.4
technical, 20
time-management, 20, 22
Manager(s)
activities of, 8 fig. 1.1, 9 fig. 1.2
administrative, 16
attitudes and, 489
categories of, 18 table 1.2
centralization/decentralization authority by, 360, 361
classification of businesses by, 259 fig. 8.4
compensation and benefits and, 457–458, 459
controller, 657
controlling conflict, 637, 638
corporate universities, 24
defensive stance and, 125
definition of, 8
distributing authority by, 356, 357
diversity/multiculturalism conflict and, 188
education, 23, 23 fig. 1.4, 24
effectiveness achieved by, 97
environment created by, 28
ethics and, 109, 110 fig. 4.1, 111, 113–115
experience, 23 fig. 1.4, 24, 25
financial, 16
forecasting trends, 444
functions of, 7, 9
globalization vs. regionalism, 149, 150
goal setting responsibilities by, 210
human resource, 16
implementation of business strategies by, 248–251
information and, 718–724, 727
innovative failure, 425, 426
international expertise of, 25
international vs. domestic, 149
"keeping cost low" by, 250
levels of, 13–15, 16
marketing, 16, 213
matrix organization design and, 390 fig. 12.4
MNCs and, 164
motivating employees, 28
online educational development, 24
operations, 16, 213
organizational change, 28
organizational goals and, 207–211, 212
organization change and, 416, 417
organization culture concerns by, 88, 89
organization design and, 384, 388 fig. 12.2, 389
organization development and, 417–419, 420
organization environment, 91, 572
organization's mission by, 207
organizing in a global economy, 166
performance appraisals and, 452–455
planning function of, 206
political behavior and, 574–576

Manager(s) (*Continued*)
public relations, 16
research and development (R & D), 16, 17
resistance to organization change and, 410
responsibility of middle, 14, 15, 210
responsibility of top, 13, 14, 129, 210
reward system(s) for motivation and, 534–540, 541
roles of, 18–19, 18 table 1.2, 20
skills for success, 18–22
technology impact on, 29
understanding diversity/multiculturalism by, 189
use of resources, 6
Vroom's decision tree approach and, 567
See also International management
Managing emotions, as personality dimension, 487
Manufacturing
business strategy and, 249
operations management and, 687, 688
Manufacturing on demand, intranets and, 732
Maquiladoras, 147
Marketing
business strategies and, 248
departmentalization and, 350
differentiation strategy and, 249
Marketing argument, for diversity/multiculturalism, 184
Marketing managers, 16
Market systems
continents of the, 151 fig. 5.2
countries of the, 152, 153
definition of, 150
Maslow's hierarchy of needs, 49, 515–516, 515 fig. 16.2, 517
Mass customization principle, information systems and, 738
Materials control, 697
See also Inventory
Mathematical models, 52, 54
Matrix organization design, 389–390, 391
Maturity stage
of innovation process, 422
of organizational life cycle, 384
in product life cycle, 248, 248 fig. 8.2
MBA degree, 23
Mechanistic organization design, 94, 382
Medium-size organizations, 164
Mergers
diversification by, 257
strategic approach by, 93
Merit pay, 535
Merit pay plans, 534, 535
Mexico
maquiladoras and, 147
quotas and, 158
workforce in, 148
MFN (most favored national), 154
Michigan studies, of leadership, 556
Middle East, global economy and the, 153
Middle managers
decision support system (DSS) and, 728
information systems and, 725, 726
intermediate plan and, 213
as MIS user group, 727
organization levels and, 14, 15
product champions as, 427
responsibilities of, 210
Middle of the Road Management, *see* Leadership
Midlife stage, of organizational life cycle, 384
Miles and Snow typology
analyzer strategy and, 246 table 8.2, 247, 251
business-level strategy of, 246, 246 table 8.2, 247
defender strategy and, 246, 247, 251
implementing, 250–251
prospector strategy and, 246, 250, 251
reactor strategy and, 246 table 8.2, 247
Minorities, *see* Ethnicity
Minority enterprise small-business investment companies (MESBICs), 322
Mission, 208
MNCs, *see* Multinational corporations (MNCs)
Monitor, managerial role, 18 table 1.2, 19
Monongahela River, 122
Motivating and inspiring, as leadership action, 551
Motivating oneself, as personality dimension, 487
Motivation
content perspectives on, 514–519, 520
definition of, 512
employee participation and, 530, 531
empowerment and, 530
equity theory of, 523, 524
ERG theory of, 517
expectancy model of, 522 fig. 16.4
expectancy theory of, 520–521, 522
framework for, 512, 513 fig. 16.1
goal-setting theory of, 524
groups/teams and, 621
human relations approach to, 513, 514
human resource approach to, 514
incident on, 510–511
managers and, 514, 516, 526, 527, 529
Maslow's hierarchy of needs, 515–516, 515 fig. 16.2, 517
needs hierarchy approach to, 514, 515
process perspectives on, 520–526, 527
reinforcement theory of, 527, 528 table 16.1
reward systems and, 534–540, 541
strategies for, 530–533
traditional approach to, 513
two-factor theory of, 517–518, 518 fig. 16.3, 519
Motivation factors, in two-factor theory of motivation, 518
Multiculturalism, training programs, 175
Multicultural organization, 193–194, 194 fig. 6.6, 195
Multidivisional (M-form) organization design, 388 fig. 12.3
Multidomestic strategy, 263
Multimarket flexibility, 261, 262
Multinational business, 143
Multinational corporations (MNCs)
definition of, 143
global approach and, 147
in Iraq/Kuwait, 280
organization size and, 164, 165 table 5.2
Myers-Briggs framework
Myers-Briggs Type Indicator (MBTI), 485
personality dimensions in, 484, 485

NAFTA, *see* North American Free Trade Agreement (NAFTA)
National Emergency Strike, 441
Nationalized, 157
National Labor Relations Act of 1935, 85, 441, 443
National Labor Relations Board (NLRB), 441, 443
Natural environment, 156
pollution, 136–137
social responsibility and, 121, 122
Need(s)
for achievement, 519
for affiliation, 519
for power, 519, 520
Needs hierarchy approach, to motivation, 514, 515
Negative affectivity, 489, 490
Negative emotionality, as personality trait, 483, 484
Negotiator, managerial role, 18 table 1.2, 20
Net, the, *see* Internet (Net)
Networked systems
B2B relationships and, 739
collaboration and, 738, 739
flexible work sites and, 739, 740
management process and, 740
virtual company and, 739
Networking, as small business management source, 324
New business
buying existing business for, 319
E-commerce and, 327, 329
failure of, 330, 331
financing of, 320–322
franchising and, 324–325
managers and, 330
minorities and women in, 328–329, 330
starting of, 320
success of, 326–330, 326 fig. 10.5, 331
trends of, 326–329, 330
See also Entrepreneurship
Newsweek, 16
New York Times bestseller list, 60
Niches, entrepreneurial businesses locating, 316, 317
"Nine-eighty," alternative work schedule and, 533
Noise, 590, 591, 606
Nominal groups, for group/team decision making, 291

Non-national company, 144
Nonverbal communication, 592
Norm conformity, of behaviors in groups/teams, 628
Norm generalization, of behaviors in groups/teams, 627–628
Norming stage, of group development, 624
Norms
  of behaviors in groups/teams, 627
  See also Groups/teams
Norm variation, of behaviors in groups/teams, 628
North American Free Trade Agreement (NAFTA)
  definition of, 151
  economic community formation from, 158
Not-for-profit organizations, intangible goals, 26

Objective methods, performance appraisal by, 453
Objectivity, control and, 673, 674
Obstructionist stance, social responsibility and, 124, 125
Occupational Safety and Health Act of 1970 (OSHA), 441, 442, 443
Oil-producing regions, 153, 156
Online privacy, 118, 585
"Open door policy," 604
Openness, as personality trait, 484
Open systems
  definition of, 54
  organization-environment relationships in, 89–91, 92
Operating employees, 24
  effective control and, 657
Operating ratios, in ratio analysis, 666
Operational planning, 220–222, 223
Operational plan(s), 212, 221 table 7.1
Operations and data workers, information systems (IS) and, 727
Operations control
  definition of, 656, 660
  forms of, 660 fig. 20.4
  postaction control in, 661
  preliminary control in, 660
  screening control in, 661
Operations management
  definition of, 53, 686
  facilities layout approach to, 691 fig. 21.2
  importance of, 687
  incident on, 684–685
  managers and, 688
  manufacturing and, 687, 688
  organizational strategy and, 688
  productivity and, 705–709, 710
  quantitative management perspective and, 41
  service operations and, 688
  techniques of, 53
  technologies and, 692–695
  total quality and, 698–704, 705
Operations managers, 16
Operations systems
  capacity decisions and, 689, 690
  facilities and, 690–691
  information systems and, 738
  managers and, 698
  product-service mix and, 689
  supply chain management and, 696–697, 798
Opportunities, innovation and, 425
Opportunity bias, objective performance method and, 453
Oral communication, 592
Organic organization design, 94, 382, 383
Organization
  distributing authority for effective, 353
  hybrid, 391
Organization(s)
  annual reports, 132
  bankruptcy, 56
  bases of relatedness and diversification in, 253 table 8.3
  becoming diversified, 255–260
  companies business mission, 123
  competitive position of, 258–259, 260
  complexity and control, 655
  conflict between environment and, 635
  contemporary life in, 60
  corporate-level strategies, 252–253, 254
  cost advantage of, 315
  culture, 130
  customer needs and, 81, 249
  definition of, 6
  design, 94
  diversity/multiculturalism and, 177
  diversity/multiculturalism conflict in, 187–188
  effective functioning of, 438
  employees treatment of, 109, 110, 111
  enhancing creativity in, 500, 501
  entropy in, 56
  environmental context, 207 fig. 7.1
  environments, 74–99
  equity comparisons, 521
  ethical leadership, 117
  ethics officer and, 114
  ethics within, 111, 112, 113
  evaluating market growth/share of, 258
  firewalls and, 732
  flexibility and, 184 fig. 6.5, 186, 187
  flexibility in, 94
  foreign manufacturing by domestic, 145, 146
  franchise advantages for, 325
  free speech of, 95
  general social welfare and, 122
  global competition by, 144
  goals achieved by, 7, 8
  groups and teams in, 618–624, 625
  implementing business strategies in, 248–251
  incentive programs in, 541
  industry attractiveness of, 258–259, 260
  influencing government, 127, 128
  information systems, 93
  information systems and, 738–740, 741
  information theft, 119, 503
  interdependence in, 56, 57
  intergroup conflict, 634, 635
  interpersonal relations of, 586–588
  intranets/extranets and, 732
  job specializations in, 343, 344
  labor unions and, 461
  leadership and, 572
  levels of management, 13–15, 16
  management by objectives, 227–229
  management change in, 28
  management training programs, 24
  managing conflict in, 636–638
  managing diversity/multiculturalism in, 189–192, 193
  medium size, 164
  mergers, 56, 88, 257
  mergers and acquisitions, 257
  mission of, 207
  models of effectiveness, 96, 97 fig. 3.6
  multiculturalism and, 174–175
  multiple control systems and, 660
  non-for-profit, intangible goals of, 26
  older workers and, 179, 180
  operations control in, 660–661, 662
  political behavior in, 574–575
  relationship of government and, 126–127, 128
  social responsibility and, 95, 120–125, 126
  stockholders, 83
  SWOT analysis and, 240–243, 244
  synergy, 56
  systems perspective of, 54, 55 fig. 2.3
  telecommuting and, 533
  titles of management, 13
  turbulence, 92
  use of environmental resources, 6, 7
  webmaster and, 731
  workforce demographics of, 178
  See also Entrepreneurship; Small business
Organizational behavior
  definition of, 51
  status quo and, 416
  use of contemporary ideas, 57
Organizational citizenship, 502
Organizational commitment, attitudes and, 489
Organizational communication, managing, 603–608, 609
Organizational culture
  business strategies and, 249
  customers needs met by, 249
  improving efficiency by strategies, 250
  See also Environment(s)
Organizational effectiveness
  empowerment and, 531
  examples of, 98 table 3.1
  models of, 96, 97
  reward systems and, 541
Organizational goals, *see* Goals
Organizational innovation, *see* Innovation
Organizational life cycle, 383, 384
Organizational opportunity, *see* SWOT analysis

Organizational policies, for diversity/multiculturalism, 191
Organizational practices, for diversity/multiculturalism, 191, 192
Organizational stakeholder(s)
  definition of, 120
  elements of, 120 fig. 4.3
Organizational strengths, *see* SWOT analysis
Organizational technology
  automation and, 692, 693 fig. 21.2
  computer-assisted manufacturing and, 693, 694
  definition of, 692
  manufacturing and, 692–694, 695
  robotics and, 694, 695
  service technology and, 695
Organizational threat, *see* SWOT analysis
Organizational weaknesses, *see* SWOT analysis
Organization change
  areas of, 412–419, 413 table 13.1, 420
  attitudes in, 415, 416
  by business process change (reengineering), 416, 417 fig. 13.3
  communication and, 411
  comprehensive approach to, 408, 409
  controls systems and, 414
  definition of, 404
  education, 411
  expectations of, 416
  external forces for, 404, 405
  force-field analysis, 411, 412 fig. 13.2
  in human resources, 415, 416
  incident on innovation and, 402–403
  innovation and, 420–427
  internal forces for, 405
  Lewin model of, 407
  loss, feelings of, and, 410
  managers and, 409
  managers in, 17, 416
  managing, 407–411, 412
  in operations, 414, 415
  in organization design, 413
  organization development for, 417–419, 420
  in organization structure, 413
  participation for, 411
  perceptions of, 410, 416
  planned, 405, 406
  reactive, 405–406, 407
  self-interests and, 410
  steps in the process of, 409 fig. 13.1
  technology and, 413, 414
  uncertainty and, 409
  values and, 415, 416
  workforce changes and, 415
  See also Environmental change
Organization change, resistance to
  managers and, 410
  overcoming, 411, 412
  reasons for, 409–410
Organization culture
  crisis management and, 218
  definition of, 86
  determinants of, 86–87, 88, 178
  diversity/multiculturalism and, 176, 193
  importance of, 86
  innovation and, 426, 427
  internal environment element, 86–88, 89
  managing of, 88, 89
  merger problems, 88
  risk propensity and, 290
Organization design
  Aston studies and, 383
  behavioral model of, 376
  bureaucratic control and, 669
  bureaucratic model of, 375
  conglomerate (H-form), 387, 388 fig. 12.2
  controller and, 657
  definition of, 374
  environment and, 382, 383
  functional strategies and, 385, 386
  functional (U-form), 386, 387 fig. 12.1
  international business and, 393, 394 fig. 12.5
  learning organization and, 393
  managers and, 384, 388 fig. 12.2, 389
  matrix, 389–391, 390 fig. 12.4
  mechanistic, 382
  nonprogrammed decision in, 277
  organic, 382
  reengineering and, 417
  situational influences on, 379–383, 384
  size of, 383
  strategy and, 384–385, 386
  System 1 design of, 378, 556
  System 4 design of, 378, 556
  team organization and, 392
  technology in, 379–381, 382
  types of, 378 table 12.1
  universal perspectives on, 375–378, 379
  virtual organization and, 392
Organization development (OD)
  assumptions of, 417, 418
  definition of, 417
  effectiveness of, 419, 420
  techniques of, 418, 419
Organization environment, *see* Environment(s), *see* Organization(s)
Organization-environment relationships
  basic perspectives of, 89–91, 92
  kinds of, 382, 383
Organization structure
  authority distribution in, 356–360, 361
  coordination of, 361–363
  definition of, 342
  departmentalization of, 347–351
  differentiating positions in, 364, 365
  elements of an, 342–364, 365
  incident on online education, 372–373
  incident on reasons for, 340–341
  information systems and, 738
  job design and, 343–346, 347
  managers and, 352–356, 357
  reporting relationships in, 352–355, 356, 391
  span of management in, 352–353, 380, 381
  as tall vs. flat, 354, 354 fig. 11.3, 355
Organizing
  basic elements of, 10, 11
  definition of, 11, 342
  managerial activities, 8
  obstacles to, 10
Organizing and staffing, as management action, 551
Outcomes expectancy, 521
Out-group, leader and, 568
Output medium, in information technology system, 723
Outputs
  definition of, 54
  operations control and, 660
Outsourcing, for total quality management (TQM), 703, 704
Overall cost leadership strategy, in Porter's generic strategies, 245, 245 table 8.1, 250
Overcontrol, 674
Owners
  definition of, 83
  social responsibility and, 123
Ownership, 155

PAC, *see* Political Action Committees (PACs)
Pacific Asia, mature market system and, 151 fig. 5.2., 152
Participation
  areas of, 530
  motivation and employee, 530
  overcoming resistance to organization change, 411
  See also Employee involvement
Participative leader behavior, 563
Partnership (alliance), 94
Passive goal behavior, in goal orientation, 162 fig. 5.4, 163
Path-goal theory, of leadership, 562–563, 564
People's Republic of China, *see* China
Perception
  attribution and, 492, 493
  basic processes of, 490 fig. 15.3
  definition of, 490
  managers and, 492, 493
  of quality, 699
  resistance to organization change and, 410
  selective, 491, 492
  stereotyping, 492
Performance
  comparison to standards and, 659
  of quality, 699
Performance appraisal
  definition of, 452, 453
  errors in, 453, 455
  feedback in, 453, 456
  methods for, 453–454, 455
  ranking techniques in, 453
  rating scale techniques in, 453, 454 fig. 14.3, 455
  termination and, 456
Performance behaviors, 501

Performance measuring, in control process, 658, 659
Performance-to-outcome expectancy, 521
Performing stage, of group development, 624, 625
Personal attraction, in group cohesiveness, 629
Personal contacts, organizational influence on government by, 127
Personal identification, method for using power, 555
Personality
agreeableness and, 483
assessment of, 485
authoritarianism and, 486
"big five" model of, 483 fig. 15.2
"big five" traits, 483, 484
conscientiousness and, 483
definition of, 481
emotional intelligence (EQ) and, 487
extraversion and, 484
locus of control and, 485, 563
Machiavellianism and, 486
managers and, 484, 486
Myers-Briggs framework, 484, 485
negative emotionality and, 483, 484
openness and, 484
risk propensity and, 486, 487
self-efficacy and, 485
self-esteem and, 486
Personality clash, 634
Personal traits, creativity and, 498, 499
Person-job fit, 479–480, 481
Personnel management, 45
Person-role conflict, in groups/teams, 626
Persuasion, as political behavior, 574, 575
Peru, 156, 157
Philanthropic giving, 129
Philippines, 152
Physical demands, as work-related stressor, 495
Physical work environment, element of internal environment, 85
Physiological needs, in Maslow's hierarchy of needs, 515
Piece-rate incentive plan, 535
Planned change, 405
Planning
action, 213
barriers to implementation of, 223–225, 224 table 7.2, 226
board of directors and, 215
CEO and, 215
communication and, 224 table 7.2, 226
consistency, revision, and updating, 224 table 7.2, 226
contingency, 216, 217, 217 fig. 7.3
control and, 672
crisis management and, 216, 217
decision-making and, 206, 207
definition of, 10
executive committee and, 215
in global economy, 166
intermediate, 213
kinds of organizational, 211, 212
line management and, 215
long-range, 212, 213
managerial activities, 8
managerial function, 205
operational, 207 fig 7.1, 212, 220–222, 223
participation and, 224 table 7.2, 226
purposes of, 224 table 7.2, 226
reaction, 213
responsibilities for, 213–215, 216
reward systems and, 224, 224 table 7.2, 226, 227
short-range, 213
single use, 220, 221 table 7.1
staff for, 213, 214
standing, 221 table 7.1, 222–223
strategic, 207 fig 7.1, 212
tactical, 207 fig 7.1, 212, 218–219, 220
task force of, 215, 733
time frames for, 212, 213
Planning and budgeting, as management action, 551
Planning and controlling, quantitative management and, 53, 54
Planning and goal setting, in organization development (OD), 419
Planning process, framework for, 206, 207 fig. 7.1
Plant managers, 14
Pluralism, in multicultural organization, 194
Policies, as standing plans, 222
Political action committees (PACs), 126, 128
Political behavior
managing of, 575, 576
in organization(s), 574–575
Political-legal dimension
definition of, 78
of general environment, 75 fig. 3.1
importance of, 78
of international environment, 155 fig. 5.3, 156, 157–158, 159
See also International management
Pooled interdependence, 361
Portal sites, 732
Porter-Lawler extension of expectancy theory, of motivation, 523, 523 fig. 16.5
Porter's generic strategies
classification schemes of, 243–244, 245, 245 table 8.1
differentiation, 244, 245 table 8.1, 249
focus strategy in, 245, 245 table 8.1, 246
implementing, 249, 250
Portfolio management technique, 258
Position power, in LPC theory of leadership, 561
Positive affectivity, 489, 490
Positive reinforcement
employee performance and, 535
in reinforcement theory of motivation, 527
Postaction control, 661, 662
Power
coercive, 553
definition of, 553
expert, 554
legitimate, 553
managers and, 553–554, 555
methods of using, 554, 555
referent, 554
reward, 553
Power orientation, 162
Power respect, in power orientation, 161–163, 162 fig. 5.4
Power tolerance, in power orientation, 162 fig. 5.4, 163
Predictive validation, human resource selection and, 447, 448
Pregnancy Discrimination Act, 440
Preliminary control, 660
Preparation stage, of creativity, 499
Privacy, *see* Employee privacy, *see* Online privacy
Proactive stance, social responsibility and, 125
Problem-solving argument, for diversity/multiculturalism, 184 fig. 6.5, 186
Problem-solving team, 621 table 19.1
Process consultation, in organization development (OD), 419
Process innovation, 423, 424
Process layouts, of facilities, 690, 691
Processor, in information technology system, 723
Process perspectives, on motivation, 520–526, 527
Producing change, as leadership action, 551
Producing predictability and order, as management action, 551
Product champion, as intrapreneur, 427
Product departmentalization, 350
Product innovation, 423, 424
Productivity
business problem, 44
definition of, 706
employee involvement and, 709, 710
forms of, 706, 707
growth trends of, 709 fig. 21.4
importance of, 707
improving, 708–710
innovation and, 581
levels of, 706
operation improvement and, 708, 709
quality in, 62
research and development for, 708, 709
revamping transformation facilities and, 709
reward systems and assessment of, 537
scientific management and, 57
service sector, 707
technology and, 707
total factor, 706
trends of, 707
workforce flexibility and, 709
Product layout, of facilities, 690
Product life cycle, stages in the, 247, 248, 248 fig. 8.2
Products, threat of substitute, 91, 244
Product-service mix, operations systems and, 689

Profit sharing, 538
Profit-sharing plans, 43
Programs, as single-use plan, 221
Projects, as single-use plan, 221
Prospector strategy, in Miles and Snow typology, 246
Psychological contract, 478, 479
Public administration, 26
Public relations managers, 16
Punishment
employee performance and, 535
in reinforcement theory of motivation, 528
Purchasing management, 696, 697

Qatar, 153
Quality, 699
competition and, 700
costs and, 700
definition of, 699
dimensions of, 699 table 21.2
importance of, 699, 700
Malcolm Baldridge Award and, 699, 700
management challenge, 62
productivity and, 700
Six Sigma, 703
See also Total quality management (TQM)
Quality assurance, *see* Total quality management (TQM)
Quality circle, 621 table 19.1
Quantitative management perspective
contributions and limitations of, 53 table 2.4
definition of, 52
general summary of, 53 table 2.4
management science, 52, 53
within model of management timeline, 58, 59 fig. 2.5
operations management, 52, 53
planning and controlling, 53, 54
techniques of, 41, 57
Question marks (businesses), in BCG matrix, 258
Quotas, 157, 158

Radical innovation, 422
Rain forest, 156
Ratio analysis, 666
Rational persuasion, method for using power, 554
Raw materials inventory, 697
Reaction plan, 213
Reactive change, 405
Reactor strategy, in Miles and Snow typology, 246 table 8.2, 247
Realistic job preview (RJP), 447
Reciprocal interdependence, 362
Recruiting process, 446
Reengineering, 416
Referent power, 554
Refreezing, in Lewin model of change, 407
Regency error, in performance appraisal, 455
Regulations
direct/indirect, 127
managing social responsibility and, 129
and rules in organizations, 376
Regulators
definition of, 81
elements of, 81, 82
organizations influencing, 94
Regulatory agency, 81
Reinforcement theory, of motivation, 527, 528 table 16.1
Related diversification, 252, 253, 253 table 8.3
Relatedness needs, in ERG theory of motivation, 517
Relevant information, 721
Reliability, of quality, 699
Replacement chart, for human resource management, 445
Reporting relationships, in organization structure, 352–355, 356
Research and development (R & D) managers, 16, 17
Resistance to change, *see* Innovation, *see* Organization change, resistance to
Resource acquisition argument, for diversity/multiculturalism, 184
Resource handler, managerial role, 18 table 1.2, 20
Resources
control and financial, 656
controlling conflict by, 637
control of information, 656
examples used by organizations, 6, 7 table 1.1
financial, 6
human, 6
information, 6
innovation and lack of, 424
organization's environmental, 660
physical, 6
Return ratios, in ratio analysis, 666
Reward power, 553
Reward system(s)
advantages of incentives, 536
definition of, 534, 535
employee involvement and productivity and, 709
employee stock ownership plans (ESOPs), 538
executive compensation and, 538–539, 540
executive incentive pay, 538
gainsharing programs and, 537
incentive system, 535, 536
innovation and, 425, 426
managers and, 541
merit pay plans, 534
motivation and, 534–540, 541
nonmonetary, 537, 538
performance and, 537
performance-based, 540, 541
perks for, 539, 540
profit sharing as, 535, 536, 538
special perks and, 536
stock option plans for, 539, 540
team/group incentive, 536–537, 538
Rights, ethical decision-making and, 116 fig. 4.2
Risk propensity
decision making and, 290
as personality trait, 486, 487
Robotics, 694, 695
Robot(s), 694, 701
Role ambiguity, in groups/teams, 626
Role conflict, in groups/teams, 626
Role demands, as work-related stressor, 495
Role overload, in groups/teams, 626
Roles, in groups/teams, 625
Role structure, in groups/teams, 625, 626
Roman Empire, communication and control management in, 42
Romans, management by, 43 fig. 2.1
Rules
and procedures for coordination, 362
and regulations in organizations, 376
Rules and regulations, as standing plans, 223

Salary, 457
Sales
business strategies and, 248
differentiation strategy and, 249
Sales commission, 536
Sarbanes-Oxley Act of 2002, 117, 359
Satisficing, decision making and, 287
Saudi Arabia, 153, 156, 159
Scalar principle, 352
Scanlon plan, reward systems and, 537
Scientific management
assembly lines, 41
definition of, 44, 45
development of, 44, 45
labor against, 45
pay system, 44
productivity and, 57
steps in, 44 fig. 2.2
Theory X, 49 table 2.2
Scope, of strategy, 238
Screening control, 661
Sections, *see* Departmentalization
Security needs, in Maslow's hierarchy of needs, 515
Selective perception, 491, 492
Self-actualization needs, in Maslow's hierarchy of needs, 516, 517
Self-awareness, as personality dimension, 487
Self-efficacy, as personality trait, 485
Self-esteem, as personality trait, 486
Self-interests, resistance to organization change and, 410
Self-managed teams, 620
Sensing vs. Intuition, 485
September 11, 2001
crisis management and, 217
tourism/business travel and, 4–5, 92, 656
Sequential interdependence, 361, 362
Servers and browsers, for World Wide Web (WWW), 731

Serviceability, of quality, 699
Service economy, 62
Service organization, 688
Service technology, organizational technology and, 695
Settings, as nonverbal communication, 602, 603
Short-range plan, 213
Singapore, 152
Single-product strategy, 252
Single-use plan, 220, 221 table 7.1
Six Sigma, 703
Small business
  construction as, 313, 314
  definition of, 305
  E-commerce and, 327, 329
  economies of scale in, 315 fig. 10.4
  finance and insurance as, 314
  importance of, 307 fig. 10.1
  importance to big business, 210
  by industry, 311 fig. 10.3
  job creation by, 307–308, 309
  management advice sources for, 322–323, 324
  manufacturing as, 315
  minorities and women in, 328–329, 330
  retailing as, 313
  services as, 311–312, 313
  success of, 330
  transportation as, 314, 315
  wholesaling as, 313, 314
  See also Entrepreneurship; New business
Small Business Administration (SBA)
  financial programs for new business, 322
  management advice from, 323, 324
Small Business Investment Act of 1958, 322
Small-business investment companies (SBICs)
  for financing new business, 321, 322
Small organizations, 164, 166
Socialization, groups/teams and, 628
Social orientation, 162
Social responsibility
  accommodative stance and, 125
  approaches to organizational, 124–125, 124 fig. 4.5, 126
  approach to (case study), 136–137
  arguments against, 123 fig. 4.4, 124
  arguments for, 122, 123 fig. 4.4
  corporate social audit, 131, 132
  defensive stance and, 125
  definition of, 120
  ethical compliance and, 129
  evaluating, 130
  general social welfare and, 122
  government and, 126–127, 128
  leadership and, 130
  legal compliance and, 129
  management challenge, 61
  managing, 128–131
  natural environment and, 121, 136–137
  obstructionist stance and, 124
  organization culture and, 130
  philanthropic giving and, 129
  proactive stance and, 125
  and stakeholders, 120, 121
  whistle-blowing and, 130
  See also Ethics
Social skill, as personality dimension, 487
Social welfare, organizations and, 122, 125
Sociocultural dimension
  definition of, 77
  of general environment, 75
Socioemotional role, 625
Soldiering, 44
SOP, *see* Standard operating procedure(s) (SOP)
South Korea, 152
"Spam," 585
Span of control, *see* Span of management
Span of management
  definition of, 352
  determining appropriate, 355, 356
  factors influencing, 355 table 11.1
  information systems and, 735, 736
  managers and, 352–355, 356
  narrow vs. wide spans, 352–353
  tall vs. flat, 354 fig. 11.3
Special performance test, objective performance method and, 453
Spokesperson, managerial role, 18 table 1.2, 19
Sponsor, as intrapreneur, 427
Staff position, 364
Stakeholder, organizational, *see* Organization(s)
Standard operating procedure(s) (SOP), 5, 94, 222, 223, 277, 376
Standing plan(s), 221 table 7.1, 222
Stars (businesses), in BCG matrix, 258
Statistical quality control, 705
Stereotyping, 492
Stock option plan, 539
Storage devices, in information technology system, 723
Storming stage, of group development, 624
Strategic alliances
  advantages/disadvantages of, 146
  definition of, 146
  diversity/multiculturalism and, 178
  for financing new business, 321
Strategic business unit (SBU), 252
Strategic constituencies approach, organizational effectiveness by, 96
Strategic control
  definition of, 656, 670
  integrating strategy and control in, 670
  international, 671, 672
Strategic imitation, 242, 243
Strategic leadership, 571, 572
Strategic management
  definition of, 238
  incident on, 236–237
  leadership and, 571, 572
Strategic partners (allies) dimension
  definition of, 81
  joint ventures and, 81, 145, 149 table 5.1
Strategic plan, 212
Strategic response, 93
Strategy
  business-level, 239, 244–251, 384, 385
  business plan as, 318
  components of, 238, 239
  corporate-level, 239, 252–259, 260, 384, 385
  definition of, 238
  deliberate, 239
  distinctive competence and, 238
  effective, 238, 248
  emergent, 239, 240
  formulation of, 239
  implementation of, 239
  international (*see* International strategy)
  levels of, 239, 240
  Miles and Snow typology, 246, 246 table 8.2, 247
  new product development and, 255, 256, 263, 274, 275
  nonprogrammed decisions in, 277
  product life cycle used in, 247, 248
  for reengineering, 417
  related and unrelated diversification as, 253–255
  resource deployment of a, 238, 239
  scope and, 238
  strategic control with control and, 670–671, 672
  with SWOT, 240, 241
Stress
  burnout and, 496
  causes of, 494–495
  consequence of, 496
  definition of, 493
  exercise and, 496, 497
  General Adaptation Syndrome (GAS), 493, 494 fig. 15.4
  management of, 496–497, 498
  managers and, 496
  organization concerns of, 497
  relaxation and, 497
  support groups for management of, 497
  time management and, 497
  Type A, 493
  Type B, 493
  wellness programs for, 497
  well programs for, 498
  work-related causes of, 495 fig. 15.5
  work-related stressors, 494–495
Stressor, 493, 494–495
Structural control
  bureaucratic control and, 668 fig. 20.6, 669
  clan control and, 668 fig. 20.6
  decentralized control and, 669, 670
  definition of, 656
  dimensions of, 668 fig. 20.6
  dress policy and, 669
  organizational control and, 668 fig. 20.6
  perspectives of, 668 fig. 20.6
"Subordinate-centered" behavior, *see* Leadership
Subordinate participation, *see* Employee(s), *see* Leadership

Substitutes for leadership, 568, 569
Subsystems, 55
Sumerians, management by, 43 fig. 2.1
Suppliers
  access to company's training program, 81
  definition of, 80, 81
  direct influence of, 94
  ethical treatment of, 113
  in organization environment, 90, 91
  power of, 91, 244
Supply chain management
  definition of, 696
  inventory management and, 697
  operations control management and, 696
  purchasing management and, 696, 697
  quantitative management perspective and, 54
Supportive leader behavior, 563
Survey feedback
  in organization development, 418
  wages and, 458
SWOT analysis
  common strengths and, 240, 241
  distinctive competencies and, 241, 242, 243
  of formulating strategies, 240 fig. 8.1
  GE Business Screen applied by, 260
  opportunities/threats evaluated by, 244
  organizational strengths evaluated by, 240–243
  organizational weaknesses evaluated by, 243
Synergy, 55, 56
Syria, 153
System, 54
System 1 design, 378
System 4 design, 378
System operations workers, for information systems (IS), 727
Systems flexibility argument, for diversity/multiculturalism, 184 fig. 6.5, 186
Systems perspective, 54, 55 fig. 2.3
  entropy, 56
  environmental influences in, 57
  interdependence influences in, 55, 57
  within model of management timeline, 58, 59 fig. 2.5
Systems resource approach, organizational effectiveness by, 96

Tactical plan, 212
Tactical planning, 218–219, 219 fig. 7.4, 220
Taft-Hartley Act, *see* Labor-Management Relations Act
Taiwan, 152
Tannenbaum and Schmidt's leadership continuum, 559 fig. 17.2, 560
Task demands, as work-related stressor, 494
Task environment
  competitors dimension, 79, 80
  customers dimension, 80
  definition of, 76
  of external environment, 75 fig. 3.1
  of McDonald's, 79 fig. 3.3
  regulators dimension, 81
  strategic partners (allies) dimension, 81
  suppliers dimension, 80, 81
Task forces
  in coordination, 363
  information systems and, 733
Task groups, 620
Task specialist role, 625
Task structure, in LPC theory of leadership, 561, 564
Team
  definition of, 620
  See also Groups/teams
Team-building, in organization development, 418
Team/group reward systems, 536–537, 538
Team Management, *see* Leadership
Team organization, organization design and, 392
Technical innovation, 423
Technical skills, 20
Technological dimension
  of general environment, 75
  Internet Service Provider, 76
  use of high and low, 17
  use of Internet and business software systems, 77
Technology
  contemporary challenge, 60
  contingency planning and, 217
  continuous-process, 380
  core, 379–381, 382
  E-business, 61
  electronic coordination, 363
  e-mail and, 584–585
  and ethics, 118–119
  and information theft, 119
  innovations for customers, 68
  international operations and, 174–175
  large-batch (mass-production), 380
  online education, 372–373, 451
  unit (small-batch), 380
Technology Toolkit, 17, 60, 61, 118, 119
  Grokker, 214
  information technology systems, 730
  quality control, 703
  virtual teams, 622
Technostructural activities, in organization development (OD), 419
Telecommuting, 533
Thailand, 152
Theory, 41
Theory of competition, 41
Theory X, 49, 49 table 2.2, 50
Theory Y, 49, 49 table 2.2, 50
Theory Z, within model of management timeline, 58, 59 fig. 2.5
Theory Z (Ouchi), 60
Thinking vs. Feeling, 485
Third-party peacemaking, in organization development (OD), 419
360-degree feedback, in performance appraisal, 455
Timeliness, control and, 673
Timely information, 721
Time-management skills, 22
Time off, misuse of, 110
Time orientation, 162 fig. 5.4, 163
Title VII, Civil Rights Act of 1964, 440
Today's Management Issues, 50, 51, 95
  diversification, 256
  effective communication, 608
  executive compensation, 552
  for-profit and not-for-profit enterprises, 306
  individual behavior in organizations, 480
  labor shortage, 180
  motivation, 516
  organization control, 654
  overworked management, 442
Tolerance, diversity/multiculturalism and, 189
Top managers
  budgets and, 664
  decision support system (DSS) and, 728
  information system control and, 734
  information systems and, 725, 726
  legal compliance and, 129
  nonprogrammed decisions by, 277
  organization levels and, 13, 14
  sponsors as, 427
  strategic planning and, 237
  tactical goals, 210
Total factor productivity, 706
Total quality management (TQM)
  benchmarking for, 702
  cycle time and, 704
  definition of, 700
  dimensions of, 701 fig. 21.2
  employee involvement in, 701
  ISO 9000:2000 and, 704
  ISO 14000 and, 704
  materials and, 701, 702
  methods and, 702
  origins of, 698
  outsourcing for, 703, 704
  speed and, 705 table 21.3
  statistical quality control for, 705
  strategic commitment in, 701
  technology and, 701
Tourism and business travel
  decision making for, 92
  impact of September 11, 2001, 4–5
Traditional approach, to motivation, 513
Training
  conflict management, 638
  definition of, 450
  evaluation of, 451, 452
  methods for, 451
  needs assessment, 451
  online education, 451
  process of, 452 fig. 14.2
Traits, *see* Personality
Transaction-processing system (TPS), 726, 727

Transformation
operations control and, 660
processes, 54
Transformational leadership, 570
Transnational strategy, 264
Turnover, as withdrawal behavior, 502
Two-factory theory, of motivation, 517–518, 518 fig. 16.3, 519
Type A personality, 493
Type B, 493

U. S. Constitution, 95
U-form organization design, 386
Uncertainty, resistance to organization change and, 409
Uncertainty acceptance, in uncertainty orientation, 162 fig. 5.4, 163
Uncertainty avoidance, in uncertainty orientation, 162 fig. 5.4, 163
Uncertainty orientation, 163
Understanding, diversity/multiculturalism and, 189
Unethical behavior
definition of, 108, 109
See also Ethics
Unfair labor practices, 461
Unfreezing, in Lewin model of change, 407
Uniform Resource Locator (URL), 731
Unions, *see* Labor unions
Unit and individual productivity, 706
United Arab Emirates, 153
Units, *see* Departmentalization
Unit (small-batch) technology, 380
Unity of command, 352
Unrelated diversification, 254, 255
Upward communication, 596
User groups, for system requirements, 725, 726
Utility, ethical decision-making and, 116 fig. 4.2

Valence, in expectancy theory of motivation, 521, 522
Validation process, 447, 448
Value-added analysis, in total quality management, 702
Variable-interval schedule, of reinforcement, 529
Variable-ratio schedule, of reinforcement, 529
Variable work schedules, motivation and, 531
Venetians, management by, 43 fig. 2.1
Venture capital companies, financing new business and, 321
Verification procedures, control and, 676
Verification stage, of creativity, 500
Vertical communication, 596, 597
Vestibule training, 451
Vietnam, 152
Vietnam Era Veterans Readjustment Assistance Act, 440
Virtual company, information systems (IS) and, 739
Virtual groups/teams, 622
Virtual organization
e-commerce and, 392
organization design and, 392
Virtual teams, 621 table 19.1, 622
Vroom's decision tree approach to leadership, 564–566, 567
Vroom's time-driven decision tree, 566 fig. 17.5, 567 fig. 17.6

Wage-level decision, compensation and, 457
Wages
definition of, 457
ethical treatment through, 109
gender and, 181
knowledge workers and, 464
legal environment and, 440, 441
performance appraisal and, 453
piecework pay system, 44, 45, 48, 49
survey, 458
See also Reward system(s)
Wage structure decision, compensation and, 458
Wagner Act, *see* National Labor Relations Act
Wall Street Journal, 11, 17
Warehouse retailing industry, 41
Web, the (WWW), *see* Internet (Net)
Web browser, 731
Webmaster, 731
Web servers, 731
Web sites
Ad Age, 614
American Association for Homecare, 348
American Girl, 546–1
American Legacy Foundation, 614
BBC News, 172n1
Beverage Marketing, 312
Business Journal, 68n1
Business Week, 17
California First Amendment Coalition, 95
Cargill, 433
CBS Market Watch, 312
CBS News, 50
The Center for Ethics and Business, 131
Cephalon, 300n1
CNN Money, 50
Commonwealth Fund, 348
Corporate Board Member, 216
Costco, 68n1
The Courier-Journal, 654
Daily Yomiuri, 482
Defense Link, 614n1
definition of, 731
Dilbert, 336
E-Commerce Times, 433n1
Email Today, 614n1
EM Progress Newsletter, 654
Fast Company, 17
FirstMatter, 426
Food and Drug Administration, 300n1
Forbes, 37n1
Fortune, 15
Global-Dining, 482
The Globe and Mail, 68n1
The Guardian, 337n1
Heineken, 172n1
Home Channel News, 571
Hoover's, 68n1
Intel, 200n1
Interbrew, 172n1
Internal Revenue Service, 306
Internet Tips, 119
The Juneau Empire, 137
Kentucky Fried Chicken, 400
KIP Business Report, 84
Long John Silver's, 400
Mattel, 546n1
The Mercury News, 214
Minority Americans in Engineering and Science National Magazine, 200n1
Mother Jones, 200n1
Oceana, 137
Omniva, 327
Pennsylvania State Nurses Association, 442
Pizza Hut, 400
Psychotherapist Resources, 508n1
Reuters, 137
Savannah River Operations Office, 654
Scottdale Law, 614n1
Scripps Howard News, 336
Shopping Center World, 433n1
Silicon Graphics (SGI), 598
Small Business Administration (SBA), 337n6
Taco Bell, 400
Terra Lycos, 525
Texas Monthly, 525
Time, 50
Tokyo Weekender, 482
TruServ, 571
Tumbleweed Communications, 327
U. S. Army, 437
U. S. Census Bureau, 442
U. S. Department of Labor, 442
U. S. Selective Service System, 472n1
United Nations, 280
U.S. Army Personnel Command, 472n1
Vault, 200n1
Virginia Polytechnic Institute, 119
Wal-Mart, 172
Wired News, 614n1
WNBA, 525
World InfoZone, 280
A & W Restaurants, 400
Yahoo! News, 50
Yum! Brands, Inc., 400
Wheel pattern, in communication networks, 595
Whistle blowing, 130, 131
Withdrawal behaviors, 501, 502
Women's Wear Daily, 205
Workers, *see* Employee(s)
Workforce
age distribution and, 179 fig. 6.2
changing nature of, 27, 84, 85
created and eliminated by big business, 308 fig. 10.2

Workforce (*Continued*)
  and diversity, 27, 84
  diversity/multiculturalism trends and the, 178 fig. 6.1
  efficient output based on scientific management, 44
  ethical decisions by the, 131
  ethnicity in the, 181–183
  exploitation of, 237
  H-1B temporary visa, 175
  human capital in, 439
  labor unions and, 461
  of maquiladoras, 147
  in Mexico, 148
  organizational change by, 67
  recruiting impact on, 446
  represented by labor unions, 85
  retirees, 27
  telecommuting, 60
  two-class, 85
  women in the, 5, 131, 177, 178, 344
  young, 303
  See also Diversity/multiculturalism; Employee(s)
Working Mother, 5
Working with Diversity
  cultural differences, 160
  effect of job market, 448
  job specialization, 348
  language and affirmative action, 594
  leadership, 571
  motivation, 525
  organizational strengths, 242
  whistleblowers, 130
Work-in-process inventory, 697
Workplace
  automation and, 693
  behavior, 501–503, 504
  violence, 92, 503
Work processes, change in, 414
Work sequence, change in, 414
Work teams
  as alternative to job specialization, 347
  empowerment of, 531
  as type of teams, 621 table 19.1
World of Management, The
  cross-cultural communication, 598
  decision making, 280
  entrepreneurship, 312
  information systems, 722
  organization control, 671
  pay-for-performance system, 482
  productivity, 707
World Trade Organization (WTO), *see* WTO
Worldwide learning, 261–262, 263
World Wide Web (WWW)
  directories and search engines for, 731, 732
  servers and browsers for, 731
  surf, 731
  Uniform Resource Locator (URL), 731
  web sites, 731
  See also Internet (Net)
Written communication, 592, 593
WTO, 154

Youth stage, of organizational life cycle, 384
Y pattern, in communication networks, 595
"Yuppies" (Young Urban Professionals), 28

Zombie firms, 681

For Students

Student Website. The student site at *http://college.hmco.com/business/students* provides additional information, study aids, activities, and resources that help reinforce the concepts presented in the text. Features include ACE self-testing, management-skills assessments, ready notes, interactive flashcards to study key terms, term paper help, related web resources, learning objectives, outlines, and company links. In addition, the site will feature links to important job and career sites.

HM eStudy CD-ROM. Free with a new textbook, this CD has been carefully tailored to supplement and enhance the content of the text and to help students succeed. Included on the CD are ACE Self-Tests, selected videos, and Knowledgebank. Chapter outlines, company web links, a glossary, learning objectives, ready notes, self-assessment exercises, and chapter summaries are designed and presented to students as an interactive study guide.

Manager: A Simulation. This business simulation, developed by the successful team of Jerald R. Smith and Peggy Golden, allows student players to make business decisions through simulated real-world experiences.

Study Guide. The *Study Guide* has been revised to optimize student comprehension of definitions, concepts, and relationships presented in the text. Each chapter contains an expanded chapter outline to facilitate note taking, multiple-choice and true/false questions, and targeted questions that ask students to integrate material from lectures and the text. Annotated answers appear at the end of the *Study Guide.*

Exercises in Management. This student manual provides experiential exercises for every chapter. The overall purpose of each exercise is given, along with the time required for each step, the materials needed, the procedure to be followed, and questions for discussion.

The Ultimate Job Hunter's Guidebook, Third Edition. This practical, how-to handbook by Susan Greene and Melanie Martel is a concise manual containing abundant examples, practical advice, and exercises related to each of the job hunter's major tasks.